# SIMESTER AND SULLIVAN'S CRIMINAL LAW

# Simester and Sullivan's Criminal Law

## Theory and Doctrine

Ninth Edition

J J Child

A P Simester

J Stanton-Ife

F Stark

and

G J Virgo

• HART •

OXFORD • LONDON • NEW YORK • NEW DELHI • SYDNEY

HART PUBLISHING
Bloomsbury Publishing Plc
Kemp House, Chawley Park, Cumnor Hill, Oxford, OX2 9PH, UK
1385 Broadway, New York, NY 10018, USA
Bloomsbury Publishing Ireland Limited, 29 Earlsfort Terrace, Dublin 2, D02 AY28, Ireland

HART PUBLISHING, the Hart/Stag logo, BLOOMSBURY and the Diana logo are trademarks of Bloomsbury Publishing Plc

1st edition, 2000; 2nd edition, 2003; 3rd edition, 2007; 4th edition, 2010; 5th edition, 2013; 6th edition, 2016; 7th edition, 2019; 8th edition, 2022.

This edition first published in Great Britain 2026

1



A catalogue record for this book is available from the British Library.

Library of Congress Control Number: 2026946956

ISBN: PB: 978-1-50999-485-4
HB: 978-1-50999-890-6
ePDF: 978-1-50999-487-8
ePub: 978-1-50999-486-1

Typeset by Amnet, Chennai, India
Printed and bound in Great Britain

For product safety related questions contact productsafety@bloomsbury.com

# PREFACE

This new edition incorporates some important changes in the substantive criminal law. In keeping with its practice in recent years, the Supreme Court has not considered many substantive criminal law appeals. Nonetheless, it has made significant decisions on the scope of strict liability (discussed in Chapter 6) and in the realm of dishonesty (Chapter 13).

By contrast, the Court of Appeal Criminal Division has been very busy. *Inter alia*, it has addressed the specific defences to criminal damage (see Chapter 14) and the status of digital assets as "property" that can be stolen (Chapter 13). As may be expected, not every decision has been warmly received. For instance, there are decisions that undermine the initial expectation that the Supreme Court had, in *Jogee*, brought to an end the excesses of the joint enterprise doctrine. Contrariwise, the Court of Appeal has ensured that "parasitic accessorial liability" lives on to some considerable extent, in the form of the so-called doctrine of "overwhelming supervening acts". There has also been a resurgence of *Gnango*-like cases. Those developments are covered in Chapter 7.

Consent to sexual activity (Chapter 12) continues to be an exceptionally difficult area of English criminal law. It is impossible to reconcile all of the many decisions on this topic. A review by the Supreme Court of this area is overdue: the same can be said of the law on consent in the context of non-fatal offences against the person, something that the Law Commission will be looking at in its fourteenth programme.

Parliament has also been busy, at least in certain areas such as corporate criminal liability for the actions of "senior managers" (see Chapter 8). The Law Commission, too, has launched projects on a range of significant criminal law matters, and some of its early work on these projects is discussed at various points in the text.

For this edition, we have added some new sections, including non-fatal strangulation in chapter 11, and added references to a wealth of secondary literature produced on substantive criminal law, and its theoretical underpinnings, since the last edition. Those writings are enormously helpful in making this a book about theory as well as doctrine. Their authors are owed our thanks.

Finally, there is a change of personnel to report. After retiring from his chair at Cambridge in 2013, and from teaching altogether in 2020, John Spencer has now stepped down from *Simester and Sullivan* too. John became an academic more than five decades ago: he has been an enormously influential figure in the development of the law, not least through his devotion to education at Selwyn and, latterly, Murray Edwards College.[1] *Simester and Sullivan* is a book about doctrine as well as theory and there is no better doctrinal writer than John. His clear and richly informed prose will be greatly missed.

[1] For a fascinating profile, see https://www.squire.law.cam.ac.uk/eminent-scholars-archiveprofessor-john-rason-spencer/extended-biography-professor-john-rason-spencer.

John Stanton-Ife has taken over first-authorship responsibilities for the property offence chapters. We count ourselves most fortunate to have John on board for this edition, and look forward to his contributions across the years to come.

JJC
APS
FS
GJV
May 2026

# CONTENTS

# EXPANDED TABLE OF CONTENTS

# ABBREVIATIONS

The following abbreviations for standard textbooks and statutory materials are used in the text and footnotes.

| | |
|---|---|
| *Archbold* (2026) | M. Lucraft (ed.), *Archbold: Criminal Pleading, Evidence and Practice* (London: Sweet and Maxwell, 2025) |
| ECHR | European Convention on Human Rights |
| ECtHR | European Court of Human Rights |
| *Hart and Honoré* | H.L.A. Hart and A.M. Honoré, *Causation in the Law* (Oxford: Oxford University Press, 2nd ed., 1985) |
| HRA 1998 | Human Rights Act 1998 |
| Model Penal Code | American Law Institute, *Model Penal Code* (Philadelphia: American Law Institute, Revised ed., 1985). |
| OAPA 1861 | Offences Against the Person Act 1861 |
| Simester, *Fundamentals* | A.P. Simester, *Fundamentals of Criminal Law: Responsibility, Culpability, and Wrongdoing* (Oxford: Oxford University Press, 2021) |
| *Smith, Hogan, and Ormerod* | D. Ormerod, K. Laird, and M. Gibson, *Smith, Hogan, and Ormerod's Criminal Law* (Oxford: Oxford University Press, 17th ed., 2024) |
| *Williams, CLGP* | G. Williams, Criminal Law: The General Part (London: Stevens, 2nd ed., 1961) |
| *Williams, TBCL* | G. Williams, Textbook of Criminal Law (London: Stevens, 2nd ed., 1983) |

# TABLE OF CASES

**A**

## C

**D**

## E



## F

## H

## K

## P

## Q



## R

## S

## T

## X



## Y

## Z

# TABLE OF LEGISLATION

## STATUTES

# TABLE OF INTERNATIONAL INSTRUMENTS

## NEW ZEALAND



## NORWAY



## UNITED STATES

# 1

# CRIMINAL LAW: DEFINITION AND AMBIT

This chapter introduces some of the theory that surrounds the criminal law: it explains why the criminal law matters, and highlights various issues it raises. The chapter begins by considering the defining features of the criminal law, those which distinguish it from other varieties of law. Secondly, the nature of criminal law is investigated—what does it mean to declare someone a criminal? Finally, we draw out the implications of our exploration for the basic structure of a criminal offence. The discussion in this chapter will lead on, in Chapter 2, to a discussion of the constitutional and Rule of Law principles that constrain the enactment and interpretation of criminal law; and later, in Chapter 16, to consideration of what sorts of actions properly attract criminal prohibitions.

## § 1.1 A search for definition

Like other types of law, the criminal law is a means by which the state participates in the ordering of its citizens' lives. Yet throughout the world, every society with a formal legal system distinguishes between criminal and civil law.[1] This raises a question about the scope of criminal law: what marks a law out as criminal rather than civil? One way of approaching that question is to look for a definition of the criminal law. Broadly speaking, a crime is an event that is prohibited by law, one which can be followed by a prosecution in criminal proceedings and, thereafter, by punishment on conviction:[2]

> "A crime must be defined by reference to the *legal* consequences of the act. We must distinguish, primarily, not between crimes and civil wrongs but between criminal and civil proceedings. A crime then becomes an act that is capable of being followed by criminal proceedings, having one of the types of outcome (punishment etc.) known to follow these proceedings."

Criminal law, in turn, is the variety of law that prohibits such crimes.

But to define criminal law only in these procedural terms fails to shed any light on a more fundamental question: why does the distinction between criminal and other law matter? It is true that criminal prosecutions follow a different legal procedure from their civil counterparts. But if that is the sole difference, and there is no underlying reason for separating the two, drawing the distinction would be pointless.[3] We need to identify the distinguishing features that also justify treating crimes as a separate body of law.

[1] Robinson, "The Criminal–Civil Distinction and the Utility of Desert" (1996) 76 *Boston ULR* 201, 201–2.

[2] Williams, "The Definition of Crime" (1955) 8 *CLP* 107, 123.

[3] Moreover there would be a problem explaining why the distinction is maintained in those countries which do not observe the procedural safeguards normally found in criminal law. See Robinson, "The Criminal–Civil Distinction and the Utility of Desert" (1996) 76 *Boston ULR* 201, 203.

### *(i) The seriousness of the prohibited event?*

One suggestion might be that the harm proscribed by criminal law is greater in degree than that in the civil law, or is somehow public rather than private in nature. For example, across most if not all cultures, the criminal law contains provisions proscribing serious forms of violence and dishonesty. However, while it is true that prevention of harm is central to the criminal law, the distinctiveness of criminal wrongs cannot be captured by reference simply to the moral gravity of the wrongdoing and the importance of the interest being violated. For one thing, most harms are both public and private. The major oil spillage in Sydney harbour that gave rise to the *Wagon Mound* tort cases affected more than one person,[4] while by contrast an ordinary assault typically involves a single victim. Similarly, consider the situation where V Ltd has placed a large order for the supply of raw materials from D plc. D is aware that, without the supplies, V would be unable to fulfil its own contracts and would suffer considerable losses. If, despite this, D fails to deliver, it commits no offence. Compare this case with the situation where a company fails to send its annual return to the Registrar of Companies within the time limits prescribed by the Companies Act 2006: the latter is a criminal offence.[5] It seems, therefore, that the types of events prohibited by criminal laws are not inherently distinguishable from those regulated by other sorts of law. Indeed, the same conduct can sometimes lead to both criminal and civil liability. If D takes V's car without V's consent, for example, she may be prosecuted for theft. She can also be sued in tort for conversion.

That said, there is intuitive appeal in the idea that criminal wrongs are typically more serious than their civil counterparts; sufficiently serious that, whether or not they also give rise to civil causes of action, the state feels constrained to step in and regulate them directly. There is a meaningful sense in which the wrongs with which the criminal law is concerned are *public*. This public aspect of criminal law can be seen in the rule that a victim who forgives his attacker may discontinue his civil suit for damages, but cannot stop the prosecution of that attacker. Criminal offences are not merely a private matter. They are public wrongs, at least in the sense that the public as a whole has an interest in their prevention and prosecution.[6] Thus, according to Allen, behaviour is criminalised "because it consists in wrongdoing which directly and in serious degree threatens the security or well-being of society, and because it is not safe to leave it redressable only by compensation of the party injured".[7] Allen's remark is a useful pointer to why assaults are crimes, while breaches of contract are not. Assault involves an interference with fundamental rights of the victim,

[4] *Overseas Tankship (UK) Ltd v Morts Dock Engineering* [1961] AC 388 (PC); *Overseas Tankship (UK) Ltd v Miller Steamship Co Pty* [1967] AC 617 (PC). Cp. public nuisance cases: *Halsey v Esso Petroleum* [1961] 1 WLR 683 (DC).

[5] *Per* s. 451.

[6] Some claim that there is another, more important sense in which being a "public wrong" is a criterion of criminalisation. See, e.g., Duff, "Towards a Modest Legal Moralism" (2014) 8 *Crim Law and Philosophy* 217; Duff, *The Realm of Criminal Law* (2018). Contrast Edwards and Simester, "What's Public About Crime?" (2017) 37 *OJLS* 105; for a reply, see Duff and Marshall, "Crimes, Public Wrongs, and Civil Order" (2019) 13 *Crim Law and Philosophy* 27. We cannot pursue that debate here.

[7] *Legal Duties and Other Essays in Jurisprudence* (1931) 233–4. Compare Coffee: "Characteristically, tort law prices, while criminal law prohibits". On this view, the criminal law should be invoked when the "price" of an action, that the defendant would have to pay in tortious damages, is insufficiently prohibitive. Coffee, "Does 'Unlawful' Mean 'Criminal'?: Reflections on the Disappearing Tort/Crime Distinction in American Law" (1991) 71 *Boston ULR* 193, 194.

rights which the state is perceived to have a duty to protect. By contrast, individuals are normally able to protect themselves against breach of contract through mechanisms such as insurance, and can satisfactorily undo any damage suffered with the aid of the civil law.

Another possible basis for differentiating civil from criminal law is that criminal acts are those acts which are intrinsically morally wrong. (Such acts are sometimes called *mala in se*.) To some extent this is true of the more serious, stigmatic offences—assault, murder, and so forth.[8] But much of the modern criminal law involves prohibitions which constrain conduct which may be wrong only in the technical sense of breaching the terms of the prohibition (*mala prohibita*). Prohibitions of that kind are often in the public interest. For example, driving on the roads is safer overall because of speed limits. Yet there is little intrinsic moral difference, for instance, between driving safely at 70 miles per hour on the motorway and driving safely at 75; but the latter is an offence.[9] And conversely, lying may be immoral, but it is not *per se* a criminal act.

More generally, the sheer variety of conduct that has been designated a criminal wrong defies reduction to any "essential" minimum. One finds no unifying thread to the subject matter of the multifarious crimes known to England and Wales.[10] The criminal law has been used—indeed, overused—as a regulatory device, and consequently extends to conduct that can lack any inherent moral turpitude, such as failing to notify the licensing authority of a change of address for one's driving licence.[11] In this jurisdiction, the fact that some particular action is criminal may reflect only a decision on the part of a regulatory body that the public interest requires resort to public means of suppression, and that the matter cannot be left to private redress or bargaining. Amongst the available public means of suppression, the criminal law is the most commonly employed coercive mechanism.

There are, in short, limits to the extent to which we can safely elaborate upon our initial definition by reference to the things that criminal law prohibits. In part, this reflects the fact that criminal law engages with political and societal pressures which find expression in the form and content of the law. In Chapter 16, once we have discussed the major interpersonal and property offences, we shall consider some of the reasons for the state to criminalise such actions and not to criminalise others. But it should always be borne in mind that, in practice, criminal laws are characteristically deployed to control behaviour and events because there is perceived to be a societal, and political, interest in doing so.

### *(ii) Punishment?*

A second element of the preliminary definition given in § 1.1 was punishment.[12] Perhaps the main distinction between criminal and civil law is that the criminal law licenses punishment whereas redress for civil law wrongs is predominantly in the form of monetary compensation?

[8] Gross, *A Theory of Criminal Justice* (1979) 13.

[9] A great deal of modern, statutory criminal law proscribes conduct that is not intrinsically problematic but which is suppressed for anticipatory or pre-emptive reasons. For a discussion and defence of such offences see Horder, "Harmless Wrongdoing and the Anticipatory Perspective on Criminalisation" in Sullivan and Dennis (eds.), *Seeking Security* (2012) 79; a more critical discussion of such offences in the same volume is Simester, "Prophylactic Crimes", *ibid*., 60. See also Chapter 16 below.

[10] See Ashworth, "Is the Criminal Law a Lost Cause?" (2000) 116 *LQR* 225.

[11] Road Traffic Act 1988, s. 99(4)–(5).

[12] See generally the essays in Ryberg (ed.), *The Oxford Handbook on the Philosophy of Punishment* (2024).

Punishment is an important facet of the criminal process. Indeed, it is an indispensable feature of criminal prohibitions. Parliament does not say, "Do not assault other people, *please*". Rather, the law declares, "Do not assault other people, *or else …*". Of course, civil laws also specify sanctions. As Posner points out, however, the nature of the civil sanction differs from that found in criminal law. A defendant who is convicted of a crime will normally be imprisoned or fined. By contrast, someone who loses a civil action faces perhaps an injunction, an order for specific performance, or a requirement to pay damages.

Posner argues that this difference reflects a crucial distinction between the functions of criminal and civil laws. In his opinion, the criminal law exists to impose punishments such as imprisonment in situations where tortious remedies are an insufficient deterrent.[13] But Posner's explanation is doubtful. Both criminal and tortious remedies can operate as deterrents. Each is likely to be regarded as unwelcome by a defendant, and indeed civil damages awards that compensate to the extent of the harm done often far exceed criminal fines in magnitude.

On the other hand, it is instructive to consider the reasons *apart from deterrence* which underlie the imposition of sanctions in these cases. In particular, whether or not they have deterrent effects, civil remedies are not normally regarded as punitive. Punishment involves more than simply imposing something unwelcome upon a defendant. A *punitive* sanction imposes hardship *because the recipient deserves it*.[14] Damages in a contract dispute, for instance, are a sanction; but ordinarily they are imposed whether or not deserved by the defendant. It is not necessary to show that a defendant is at fault when he breaches his contractual obligations.

Punishment, by contrast, is imposed with censure as an integral aspect. It responds to the fact that the defendant has culpably done something wrong.[15] Indeed, the level of sentence is one way in which a court signals the wrongfulness of the defendant's actions.[16] Of course, there are also punitive damages in the law of tort. Nonetheless, in England and Wales at least, damages for tort losses are normally compensatory, not punitive, and are understood as such. That is why one may usually insure against contractual or tortious damages, but not against criminal fines.[17]

Punishment, then, is one function of the criminal law. But punishment is not what is unique about crime. Indeed, punishment is not even a specifically legal phenomenon, let alone specifically the province of criminal law. We do not require a criminal conviction before punishing children for misbehaviour, or issuing a football player with a red card,[18] and, as noted, it is sometimes possible to obtain exemplary (or "punitive") damages in civil

[13] Posner, "An Economic Theory of the Criminal Law" (1985) 85 *Columbia LR* 1193.

[14] Which is not to say that all defendants actually convicted of a criminal offence deserve punishment, particularly in the case of strict liability offences (below, § 1.2(ii)(c); Chapter 6). But it is to suggest that there is something morally problematic about imposing punitive sanctions upon defendants who do not deserve it.

[15] For discussion, see von Hirsch, *Censure and Sanctions* (1993).

[16] Cp. *Martineau* (1990) 79 CR (3d) 129, 138 (Lamer CJ): it is a "fundamental principle of a morally based system of law that those causing harm intentionally be punished more severely than those causing harm unintentionally".

[17] *Askey v Golden Wine Co Ltd* [1948] 2 All ER 35 (KB). Compare too *Clunis v Camden and Islington Health Authority* [1998] QB 978 (QB).

[18] At the same time, criminal punishment is a distinctive variety of punishment in as much as its imposition is the responsibility of the community as a whole: Lamond, "What is a Crime" (2007) 27 *OJLS* 609, 614ff.

cases. One may be fined or even imprisoned for a civil contempt of court.[19] Conversely, neither is a conviction always accompanied by punitive sanctions. Sometimes offenders are discharged without receiving any sentence for their wrongdoing. Offenders may also be subject to confiscation orders,[20] or indeed to life sentences or extended sentences of imprisonment for purposes of public safety rather than punishment.[21] This suggests that while punishment is an important facet of the criminal law, it is not its most distinctive feature.[22]

### *(iii) Convictions*

In addition to prohibition and punishment, a third aspect of the criminal process is the conviction itself—the type of verdict that the court makes. Convictions are the most distinctive aspect of criminal law. In particular, while it also licenses the imposition of punishment, a criminal conviction (at least for stigmatic offences) is regarded as a penalty *in its own right*, both by legal officials, such as judges, and by the public. This is because a conviction has the effect of labelling the accused as a criminal.[23] A conviction makes a public, condemnatory statement about the defendant: that she is blameworthy for doing the prohibited action. It is, literally, a pronouncement that she is "guilty".[24] By contrast, civil judgments seem merely to pin the salient breach upon a defendant, without necessarily saying anything about her culpability. Thus, as we have noted, a claimant can sue for breach of contract without having to show any fault by the defendant. The adverse civil verdict is made for the claimant's benefit and entails no formal public censure.[25] An adverse criminal verdict, on the other hand, is a pronouncement made on behalf of society and is a form of community condemnation.

This public pronouncement of community condemnation is not mentioned in the definition of criminal law that we proposed earlier. Rather, it is something that accompanies the procedural differences. Thus the essential distinction between criminal and civil law lies not so much in the operation as in the social significance of the criminal law—in the way criminal laws and convictions are understood. The criminal law has a communicative function which the civil law does not, and its judgments against the accused have a symbolic significance that civil judgments lack. They are a form of condemnation: a declaration that the accused culpably did wrong.[26] Public recognition of this fact can be seen

[19] On civil penalties more generally, see White, "Civil Penalties: Oxymoron, Chimera and Stealth Sanction" (2010) 126 *LQR* 593.

[20] Proceeds of Crime Act 2002. See Ulph, "Confiscation Orders, Human Rights, and Penal Measures" (2010) 126 *LQR* 251; Alldridge, "The Limits of Confiscation" [2011] *Crim LR* 827. The proportionality constraints on confiscation orders appear to be outer bounds rather than core determinants: *Waya* [2012] UKSC 51, [2013] 1 AC 294. For example, in *Varma* [2012] UKSC 42, [2013] 1 AC 463, the Supreme Court upheld the imposition of confiscation orders even in the context of a conditional discharge.

[21] Sentencing Act 2020, part 10, ch. 6.

[22] For a telling critique of attempts to justify the criminal law in terms of punishment, see Edwards, "Criminalization without Punishment" (2017) 23 *Legal Theory* 69.

[23] Chalmers and Leverick, "Fair Labelling in Criminal Law" (2008) 71 *MLR* 217. See below, § 2.4.

[24] For extensive discussion of the communicative function of the criminal law, see Duff, *Punishment, Communication and Community* (2001). Note that, for the purposes of this book, we treat "culpable" and "blameworthy" as synonymous.

[25] As noted above, § 1.1(i), tort law allows the possibility of punitive damages for culpable conduct, but such awards are rare in this jurisdiction.

[26] Sometimes, this can result in the state's *mis*speaking. See below, § 1.2(ii)(a), (c).

in the relevance of the criminal law to applications for a visa, or for admission to practise as a lawyer, in which applicants are required to disclose any previous convictions. Or consider the difference between publicly denouncing someone as a "convicted criminal" and calling her a "tortfeasor".[27] The law exists in society, not in the abstract. Correspondingly, the law's labelling of a defendant as "criminal" imports all the resonance and social meaning of that term. Having a criminal record marks a person out in society. It can have substantial adverse consequences in its own right, over and above any punitive sentence: including deprivation of civil rights, loss of public benefits, and disqualifications from employment and licence-holding.[28]

## § 1.2 Ambit

Three salient functions of criminal law emerge from the discussion so far. The first might be called *criminalisation*: the law sets out for citizens those things which must not be done.[29] The second thing the law does is *convict* persons who are proved to have transgressed its prohibitions. Finally, it authorises the *punishment* of those whom it convicts; and, more generally, the criminal law offers the prospect of punishment to reinforce its function of criminalisation.

The criminal law, then, is a powerful and condemnatory response by the state to wrongdoing. It is also a bluntly coercive system, directed at controlling the behaviour of citizens. Criminalisation involves rules backed up by threats. In a sense, criminal law is the means by which the state forces citizens into complying with its injunctions.

*When* should the criminal law be invoked? No one, including the state, should coerce others without good reason. The constriction of people's conduct calls for justification, especially when it is accompanied by censorious and punitive treatment of those who do not comply. Unless there are compelling reasons, the criminal law should not be deployed to regulate people's conduct.

Nonetheless, sometimes the use of the criminal law *is* justified. Imagine the following scenario:

> One fine September morning, Jim is discovered dead in his home. His skull has been crushed by a blow inflicted with a heavy object. The police are called. Upon further investigation, they establish that he was murdered by his daughter, Alice, who killed him in order to receive her inheritance under his will.

Intuitively, most persons would regard this as a classic example of criminal wrongdoing. The reasons are twofold. First, what Alice has done is precisely the sort of activity that the state should prohibit. Murder is both harmful and wrong, and people ought to be protected against it. Secondly, Alice is clearly blameworthy, and deserving of censure for her actions.

[27] The former is certainly defamatory. Cp. *Carver v Pierce*, an action for slander based on the words, "Thou art a thief, for thou hast stollen my dung" (1648) Sty 66, 82 ER 534.

[28] See, e.g., Hoskins, "Collateral Restrictions" in Flanders and Hoskins (eds.), *The New Philosophy of Criminal Law* (2016) 249; Hoskins, "Ex-Offender Restrictions" (2014) 31 *J Applied Philosophy* 33; Hoskins, *Beyond Punishment?* (2019); Chin, "Race, the War on Drugs, and the Collateral Consequences of Criminal Conviction" (2002) 6 *J Gender, Race & Justice* 255.

[29] Or allowed to subsist: below, § 4.1(ii).

She is precisely the sort of person who deserves the condemnation of a criminal conviction, as well as the punishment that a conviction exposes her to.

Alice's behaviour is a central case for the application of criminal law. However, not every case is as clear as hers. Suppose the following alternatives:

> Case I: Jim is discovered dead in his home. This time, the police establish that he died instantly after being struck by a vase. The vase was accidentally dislodged from the bookshelf by Barbara.
>
> Case II: During an argument, Clare insults Jim. Jim is deeply hurt by Clare's words.

It is much less obvious that the criminal law should intervene in these situations. In case I, Barbara has caused Jim's death, but there is no suggestion that she is to blame. Given this, it is inappropriate—indeed, wrong—to apply to her the sanctions of public condemnation and punishment. In case II, Clare has wronged Jim, and deserves censure. But not by the criminal law. Unlike murder, this is not the sort of behaviour that ordinarily should be prohibited by the Draconian technique of criminalisation. Censure, most notably by Jim, should be remaindered to the private sphere.

Cases I and II raise some difficult questions concerning the appropriate ambit of the criminal law. In questioning when application of criminal law is legitimate, it is important to note that there are two dimensions to its operation: *ex ante* and *ex post*. *Ex ante*, the law marks out actions that are prohibited, and warns citizens not to do those actions lest they be punished. *Ex post*, it censures (convicts) and punishes (sentences) persons who transgress its prohibitions. In the following pages, we investigate these two roles separately, and discuss some of the issues affecting when they should be invoked.

### *(i) Criminalisation* **ex ante**

Why should some behaviour be criminalised, while other behaviour is permitted? The answer to that question is complex and somewhat fragmented. Prima facie, a legislature has the power to proscribe almost any sort of conduct.[30] Earlier, we pointed out that there is no obvious distinction between actions which are criminal and those which generate civil liability (§ 1.1(i)). When the legislature marks some action as criminal, however, it condemns it and rules it out as an acceptable option for citizens.[31] A responsible legislature ought to take such drastic measures only if there are compelling reasons to do so.

There are a number of reasons not to resort too readily to the criminal law. The most important of them is concern for individual *autonomy*. The need for tolerance, which underpins any liberal society, is grounded in autonomy. Prohibiting whatever is "wrongful" is likely to intrude much too far upon the liberties of citizens. This is not only to say that, in a liberal society, freedom of choice is to be fostered. It is also to claim that if the law is to respect the right of citizens to control their own lives, it should not deprive them of that control without good reason.

[30] The Human Rights Act 1998 requires a Minister to make a statement in Parliament to the effect that a Bill's provisions are compatible with the ECHR (s. 19). This inhibits the passing of legislation which contravenes ECHR rights. In formal terms, however, the Act leaves parliamentary sovereignty intact. See below, § 2.5.

[31] Cp. Corda, "The Transformational Function of the Criminal Law: In Search of Operational Boundaries" (2020) 23 *New Crim LR* 584.

The criminal law stands in the way of free choice. It coerces people by threatening them with criminal liability unless they comply with its prohibitions. In so doing, it circumscribes their capacities to live their own lives in a manner they themselves endorse. By restricting the ways in which people may shape their lives, the law has the potential to prevent them from pursuing the goals and aspirations that matter to them.[32] Indirectly, the criminal law imposes the legislature's view and, on occasion, even a judge's view,[33] of an acceptable life.

Of course, if one considers each crime separately, most criminal prohibitions are unlikely to interfere with someone's freedom in any substantial, pervasive, or long-term sense. Outlawing arson still leaves us with a wide range of alternative activities. But the point about autonomy is more general than that. The effect of criminalisation must be assessed cumulatively, not in isolation. There are already thousands of things the state forbids. Respect for autonomy requires us to have good reason before further extending the reach of the criminal law.

None of this is to say that people ought to be allowed to disregard the interests of others, or that there is anything wrong with many of the criminal prohibitions we presently have. But it helps to explain why the legislature (and the courts) should beware of allowing the criminal law to interfere more than the minimum necessary—a prima facie reason against the use of criminal sanctions. Bearing this in mind, once we have discussed various specific offences, we will return to this issue in Chapter 16 and ask, what *should* the state prohibit through the criminal law? What sorts of considerations should responsible legislators (and judges) take into account when deciding whether to create (or interpret expansively) a criminal offence?

### *(ii)* Ex post: *censure*

The search for definition in § 1.1 fastened upon the pronouncement of guilt through conviction as the distinguishing mark of criminal law. This pronouncement connotes culpability on the part of the criminal. It is a connotation that can sometimes be at variance with the facts, as when a blameless defendant is found guilty of a strict liability offence. When a court finds an accused guilty of committing a crime, and purports to punish her through sentencing, there is a public implication that she is blameworthy. Of course, there are offences of a minor character (e.g. related to parking infringements) where this element of reproof may be relatively trivial—such offences are often characterised as not being "truly" criminal in nature. Paradigmatically, though, censure is inherent in criminal convictions: so too, therefore, is blameworthiness.

#### *(a) The need for mens rea*

An institution that condemns and punishes people must take care to do so accurately. If a person is not to blame when, for example, somebody else is harmed, the censure of the criminal law is not appropriate—and if it is inflicted upon her, the public will tend to think that is because she is to blame.

The grounds for wanting to avoid mislabelling defendants are twofold. First, it is unfair and unjust to stigmatise someone as a criminal when they do not deserve condemnation.

[32] Raz, *The Morality of Freedom* (1986) 382.

[33] For a notorious example, see *Shaw v DPP* [1962] AC 220; below, § 16.3.

Secondly, if the criminal law is seen regularly to make mistakes, it will lose its moral credibility. This, Robinson points out, will diminish its effectiveness as a tool of social control:[34]

> "The criminal law can also be more directly effective in increasing compliance with its commands. If it earns a reputation as a reliable statement of what the community perceives as condemnable and not condemnable, people are more likely to defer to its commands as morally authoritative. . . . A distribution of liability that the community perceives as doing justice enhances the criminal law's moral credibility; a distribution of liability that deviates from community perceptions of justice undermines it."

For these reasons, the criminal law ought not to convict people unless they are culpable for doing a prohibited wrong.[35] Therefore, in so far as possible, criminal offences should be structured so that there can be no conviction without proof of elements that establish blameworthiness.

Suppose the following example:

> Pam has killed Alex. Pam is a doctor, and Alex was one of her patients. Pam gave him a painkiller, to which he had an allergic reaction and died. Causing another's death is generally regarded as a very undesirable thing, and is at the heart of the crimes of murder and manslaughter. The police investigate. They establish that Pam's actions caused Alex's death, and conclude that she has committed a homicide.

On these facts alone, is Pam therefore bad, or blameworthy? Should we convict her of murder? Of manslaughter? The answer, to all of these questions, is no, or at least not without more information. Alex may have been the one patient in a million who was unknowably allergic to the painkiller and died as a consequence. It is important not to kill people, but it does not follow from the fact that killing is undesirable, and normally prohibited, that someone should automatically be convicted or punished for causing another's death. More should be required.

In the criminal law, this principle is embedded in the maxim, *actus non facit reum nisi mens sit rea*:[36] an act does not make a man guilty unless his mind is (also) guilty.[37] There must be *mens rea*. The action must be done intentionally or recklessly, or wilfully or knowingly, or negligently, or with some other mental state because of which we can say that the defendant is culpable. In Kenny's words, "no external conduct, however serious or even fatal its consequences may have been, is ever punished unless it is produced by some form of *mens rea*".[38]

[34] "The Criminal–Civil Distinction and the Utility of Desert" (1996) 76 *Boston ULR* 201, 212–13. Robinson's point is made about criminalisation, but applies in this context also.

[35] For an interesting debate which touches on this proposition, see Reiman and van den Haag, "On the Common Saying that it is Better that Ten Guilty Persons Escape than that One Innocent Suffer: Pro and Con" in Paul, Miller, and Paul (eds.), *Crime, Culpability, and Remedy* (1990) 226.

[36] Coke, *Third Institute* (1641) 6, 107; an adaptation of the rubric, *reum non facit nisi mens rea*, found in the context of perjury in *Leges Henrici Primi* c. 5, § 28.

[37] A translation typically ascribed to Lord Hailsham in *Haughton v Smith* [1975] AC 476, 491.

[38] *Outlines of Criminal Law* (2nd ed., 1904) 39. This proposition is subject to qualification in respect of strict liability and, arguably, constructive liability (below, § 1.2(ii)(c) and Chapter 6). Note that the present claim is only that mens rea is *necessary* for culpability. Unfortunately, liability for an offence requiring mens rea is sometimes incurred notwithstanding the absence of culpability: *Yip Chiu-Cheung v R.* [1995] 1 AC 111 (PC), following *dicta* in *Kingston* [1995] 2 AC 355, 364–6. These cases are, however, somewhat unusual: where mens rea is present but culpability is absent, this is usually recognised by the availability of defences. See below, § 1.2(ii)(d); Fletcher, *Rethinking Criminal Law* (1978) 511f, 799f.

*(b) Theories of culpability*

The argument for having a mens rea element in criminal offences assumes that, in the absence of a defence (to which we come later in § 1.2(ii)(d)), proof of mens rea establishes culpability. However, to what extent this is true is debated by criminal theorists.[39] Academics disagree about when and why we may legitimately blame someone for her actions. There are many different culpability theories, which cannot all be sketched here. Broadly speaking, however, such theories lie on a spectrum whereby they are more, or less, "subjective" or "objective".[40]

One familiar theory, which is reflected in the law regarding serious crimes, offers a more subjective analysis: that culpability depends upon morally defective choices. We blame someone for choosing to do a wrong action—for instance, for choosing to set fire to the house, or at least to risk setting fire to the house. Conversely, blame is not warranted unless someone *advertently* does something bad.

The upshot of this approach is that the *actus non facit reum nisi mens sit rea* maxim transforms into a requirement that we should not convict without D's being aware of the wrong-making features of D's conduct. As will be seen in the chapter on mens rea, this would include such mental states as intention and (advertent) recklessness. If Pam gave Alex the painkiller in order to kill him, we can blame her for causing his death because she intended to do so. Conversely, on the subjective account, Pam should not be held culpable for dosing Alex if she is unaware that the medicine will kill him. Failing to take account of the risk of death is not something for which she can be blamed.[41]

Some other accounts are more objective in nature. They tend to ground blame primarily in faulty *conduct* rather than choices, arguing that an action attracts blame if it inflicts harm when a reasonable person would not have acted that way. Under an objective analysis, awareness of wrongdoing need not be essential to blameworthiness. If homicide is undesirable, then Pam has a reason not to do it whether or not she foresees the risk of killing Alex. Homicide does not become acceptable just because it is done inadvertently. Since it involves harm, not only does Pam have a moral (and, in this case, legal) duty not to do it, but she also has a duty to *take care* so that she does not do it inadvertently either. On this account, Pam may legitimately be convicted of a crime if she is unreasonably careless about the risk of killing Alex.

The objective view works best when explaining why someone may be blamed for negligence, and in giving substance to the idea of the "reasonable person". The "reasonable person" is archetypally a decent person, whose behaviour sets a standard for evaluating the conduct of our fellow citizens. In turn, if the defendant has failed to behave like a reasonable

[39] See, e.g., Bayles, "Character, Purpose and Criminal Responsibility" (1982) 1 *Law and Philosophy* 5; Duff, "Choice, Character and Criminal Liability" (1993) 12 *Law and Philosophy* 345; Hart, "Negligence, Mens Rea, and Criminal Responsibility" in *Punishment and Responsibility* (1968) 136; Sullivan, "Making Excuses" in Simester and Smith (eds.), *Harm and Culpability* (1996) 131; Alexander and Ferzan, *Crime and Culpability* (2009); Moore, *Placing Blame* (1997); Moore and Hurd, "Punishing the Awkward, the Stupid, the Weak, and the Selfish: the Culpability of Negligence" (2011) 5 *Crim Law and Philosophy* 147; Simester, *Fundamentals* (2021); Sarch, "Too Objective for Culpability?" (2024) 18 *Crim Law and Philosophy* 19.

[40] As will be noted in the text below, we do not mean to suggest that the possible theories must be exclusively *either* subjective or objective. For instance, a "character" account of criminal responsibility is neither purely subjective nor objective. For an example of such an account, see Tadros, *Criminal Responsibility* (2005).

[41] For an extended argument that culpability is a function of the act of choosing rather than the material consequences that may arise from choices, see Alexander and Ferzan, *Crime and Culpability* (2009) esp. chaps. 2, 3, and 5.

person, we may (on the objective view) infer culpability, since her conduct has fallen short of what we are entitled to expect of each other.

These subjective and objective approaches are relatively extreme alternatives, and middle ground is available. In the criminal law, inadvertent negligence *is* normally thought to be a standard of culpability, but foresight of wrongdoing generally involves *greater* blame. As we shall see in Chapter 5, adjudicating between the two approaches has not always been easy, particularly in the debate over subjective or objective interpretations of "recklessness", which is the minimum fault requirement for many stigmatic criminal offences. Suppose that David causes a fire in a house and is charged with reckless arson. In the common law, "recklessness" has for the most part been interpreted to require some degree of actual foresight of the relevant risk. So, for David to be guilty he must have actually foreseen the risk of setting fire to the house when he did the act that caused it. Were he to lack such foresight, and be merely negligent (even grossly so), he would have to be acquitted. Where that view is taken, the subjectivist account of culpability holds sway. On the other hand, for two decades prior to 2003 the law in England regarding this offence was objective:[42] David could have been convicted of reckless arson even though he did not notice the risk, at least if the risk was an obvious one.

If culpability is a prerequisite of criminal liability, then it is easy to see why foresight-based mental states are so often required before a defendant can be convicted for his actions. Much more difficult are statutes that define an action to be an offence when it is done negligently. Indeed, subjectivists often argue that people should never be convicted on the basis of negligence.[43] We disagree, and it seems to us that one may fairly be blamed for an unreasonable failure to take care; albeit no doubt the criminalisation of such cases ought to be sparing. But whether one adopts a subjective or objective stance, and whatever one's views regarding the culpability of negligence, one thing is clear: without at least some form of fault element, a defendant should not be convicted of a crime. In relation to the very serious criminal offences discussed in this book, this proposition is generally reflected in English criminal law. In the absence of at least recklessness about the harm (or, in some cases, of negligence), a defendant must generally be acquitted of any serious criminal offence. Indeed, some crimes require that the defendant *intended* the relevant wrongdoing.

It would be misleading, however, to suggest that crimes requiring proof of culpability regarding the prohibited conduct are numerically dominant. The vast majority of criminal offences utilise strict liability, and dispense with proof of culpability with regard to one or more aspects of the offence.

### *(c) Strict liability offences*

There are many crimes for which the prosecution need not prove fault regarding each and every aspect of the prohibited conduct. Indeed, in some offences, the prosecution need not prove any fault at all. In these offences, the defendant's liability is said to be "strict", and the *actus non fit reum* maxim is said not to apply. For example, under the Environmental Permitting (England and Wales) Regulations 2016 a defendant may be convicted for discharging polluting matter into controlled waters if the prosecution establishes that

[42] *Caldwell* [1982] AC 341. The decision in *Caldwell* was eventually reversed by *G* [2003] UKHL 50, [2004] 1 AC 1034, which restored the law to a subjective test. See below, § 5.2.

[43] Below, § 5.5(iv).

she caused the pollutant to be discharged.[44] There is no need to prove that the defendant's involvement was a culpable one. Even if the defendant took reasonable care to prevent the discharge, she will be held criminally liable.

We deal with strict liability offences more fully in Chapter 6. For now, two observations may be made. The first is that, as we shall see, the courts in some common-law jurisdictions have moved to interpret "strict" liability as a formal *presumption*—where culpability on the part of the defendant is presumed, but may be rebutted. If D can prove that the harm was not at all his fault, he will be acquitted. Thus the essential difference, in other countries, between offences of strict liability and those of negligence is the burden of proof. Arguably, for some minor offences it may be appropriate for that burden to rest upon the defendant rather than the prosecution; and it is to be regretted that English courts have rejected this possibility, which would substantially have ameliorated the harshness of strict liability in this jurisdiction.[45]

Strict liability offences also tend to be regulatory, which raises a second point. Strict liability offences tend not to involve the same level of public censure as serious crimes. A parking offence, for example, comprises an altogether different order of wrongdoing from murder. This is not to deny that traffic offences and their like are part of the criminal law, although perhaps they should not be.[46] But most people distinguish in ordinary life between minor, regulatory-type offences and "true" crimes, and the element of public condemnation is and should be conveyed only by a conviction of the latter type. The difference in social significance is illustrated by the question we mentioned earlier, commonly found in visa and employment applications, about an applicant's criminal record. It is not a request that is intended to elicit disclosure of minor infractions such as parking infringements. To the extent that English law restricts strict liability to minor, regulatory offences (and it does not do so invariably[47]), its use is therefore somewhat less objectionable.

### *(d) Allowing defences*

The medical homicide example (§ 1.2(ii)(a)), in which Pam kills Alex, illustrates one way in which the defendant may be absolved of blame when a prohibited consequence occurs. Her answer is that, although she killed Alex, it was an accident. She neither intended his death, nor was she negligent in bringing it about: she lacked mens rea. Sometimes,

44 Regulations 12(1), 38(1). Cp. *Alphacell Ltd v Woodward* [1972] AC 824, considering the predecessor offence under s. 85 of the Water Resources Act 1991.

45 Neither has Parliament responded to the Law Commission's proposal that a due diligence defence be provided for strict liability offences: LCCP No. 195, *Criminal Liability in Regulatory Contexts* (2010) para. 6.95.

46 According to Robinson, "[s]erious deterrent sanctions can and ought to be imposed [for regulatory violations] but they can as easily and effectively be imposed under an administrative system distinct from criminal law that carries a noncriminal label, such as 'violation'": "The Criminal–Civil Distinction and the Utility of Desert" (1996) 76 *Boston ULR* 201, 214. Cp. Mann's proposal for a separate system of justice to deal with such minor crimes, in "Punitive Civil Sanctions: The Middle Ground Between Criminal and Civil Law" (1992) 101 *Yale LJ* 1795. No such distinction exists in English law: cf. Reid, "Strict Liability: Some Principles for Parliament" (2008) *Stat LR* 173. Notably, however, Part 3 of the Regulatory Enforcement and Sanctions Act 2008 empowers ministers to make orders that authorise regulatory bodies to impose civil fines in lieu of criminal prosecutions: a bypass mechanism that allows for practical "civilisation" of many regulatory crimes. For an illuminating contrast with France and Germany, see Spencer and Pedain, "Approaches to Strict and Constructive Liability in Continental Criminal Law" in Simester (ed.), *Appraising Strict Liability* (2005) 237.

47 See, e.g., the child sex offences proscribed by ss. 5–8 of the Sexual Offences Act 2003; below, § 12.11.

however, a person may not be culpable even though she harms another person deliberately. For example:

> Ian is an authorised firearms officer. He is called to the scene of a bank robbery. John, who is one of the robbers, comes out of the bank and runs toward Ian, pointing a gun. In order to protect himself, Ian shoots and injures John.

Ian satisfies both the actus reus and the mens rea of a crime. Ian cannot claim that he shot John by accident. Nevertheless, Ian is not to blame. His action, we would say, is *justified*, and he does not deserve to be convicted of any crime.

In order to deal with this sort of case, the law recognises a number of general justificatory defences, under which the defendant may acknowledge that he did an otherwise prohibited act and yet escape conviction. Examples of these justificatory defences are self-defence, prevention of crime, and defence of property. In effect such defences allege that, although D's conduct was harmful and normally unlawful, his conduct was nevertheless appropriate in the circumstances.[48] They claim that the defendant's conduct was the right (or at least an acceptable) thing to do, and so was not deserving of censure. As such, justifications are generalised: they involve judgements about the situation which apply to all the participants; so, e.g., John is not entitled to resist Ian's justified use of defensive force.

There are other predicaments where inflicting harm can be defensible on a more restricted basis. In these cases, a person may choose to do something that is unjustified, but we may nevertheless think her insufficiently blameworthy to warrant the censure of the criminal law. For example:

> Susan is arrested after taking part in the bombing of a Government building. She drove the car in which the bombers, a gang of terrorists, had made their escape. After her arrest, it is discovered that she did so only because the terrorists had threatened to kill her otherwise.

In this type of case, Susan's conduct may not be justified, and other people would be entitled to try to stop her. Nevertheless, her culpability is lessened by the fact that she was coerced. Thus she has an *excuse*. The rationale for allowing excusatory defences is that advanced by H.L.A. Hart: "unless a man has the capacity and a fair opportunity or chance to alter his behaviour to the law its penalties ought not to be applied to him".[49] Susan's wrongdoing was deliberate, but understandable. By admitting duress as a defence,[50] the criminal law acknowledges that Susan did not have a genuine and fair opportunity to choose not to break the law. She does not warrant the penalties of the criminal law, because she is below the threshold of blameworthiness that is appropriately required for criminal liability.

### *(e) Accountability*

We have argued above that the criminal law should convict only people who are culpable when a prohibited event occurs, and that events should be prohibited only when they are

[48] Indeed, one may say of such cases that no prohibited harm occurred. Thus A.T.H. Smith remarks, "[w]here the defendant's conduct can fairly be described as coming within the terms of the proscribed activity, an offence has, prima facie, been committed: liability will ensue unless he advances some explanation of his conduct which shows that it was justified, in which case there is no actus reus": "On Actus Reus and Mens Rea" in Glazebrook (ed.), *Reshaping the Criminal Law* (1978) 95, 97.

[49] "Punishment and the Elimination of Responsibility" in *Punishment and Responsibility* (1968) 158, 181.

[50] Subject to restrictions: below, Chapter 20.

sufficiently harmful to override considerations such as the need to preserve the autonomy of citizens. There is, however, a further requirement to be met before the criminal law may convict someone of a crime: accountability. Recall the example with which we began this discussion:

> One fine September morning, Jim is discovered dead in his home. His skull has been crushed by a blow inflicted with a heavy object. The police are called. Upon investigation, they establish that he was murdered by his daughter, Alice, who killed him in order to receive her inheritance under his will.

This, as we said earlier, is a plain case of criminal behaviour. But it is not just the fact that Alice is culpable which licenses her conviction. Suppose that Jim's brother, David, had suspected Alice might try to murder Jim and had done nothing to warn him? David may be blameworthy, but ought we to prosecute him? Certainly not for homicide, at any rate. The difference between David and Alice is that only Alice is legally accountable, or *responsible*, for Jim's death. Only Alice has performed an action that caused Jim's death. Because he is not legally responsible, there is simply no point in prosecuting David, however much we may disapprove of his conduct.[51]

Although a great range of differing conduct can be subjected to criminal sanction, the process of finding guilt and pronouncing a conviction entails certain limits on criminalisation. The finding of guilt on which the conviction is based assumes a degree of accountability for something done or omitted to be done. Unless one subscribes to some extreme version of Calvinism or other doctrine of the damned, guilt is not a state of being, a natural property. Guilt can be generated only in respect of something additional to what the defendant is; something for which he is accountable. Otherwise, the "presumption of innocence" is meaningless. Consider, for example, a nation-state where the government is following a policy of expelling all citizens who are not members of the dominant ethnic group. Acting through civil law process, such a state could pass legislation confiscating the property of minority citizens and impose various forms of disability in terms of profession, marriage, etc., in ways all too familiar. But it would be incoherent for the state to make it a crime simply to be a member of a minority racial grouping; there would be nothing on which the conviction could be based.[52]

The constraint may be ineffective in practice. Where the political environment is so extreme that a state is willing to create an offence simply of being a member of less favoured groups, it is likely the judges of that state would be unreceptive to the argument sketched here. But in countries with a judiciary prepared to judge in good faith, the need for accountability—for something additional to one's state of being—should properly limit the scope of criminalisation. This should have been recognised in the notorious case of *Larsonneur*,[53] a decision castigated by Jerome Hall as the "acme of strict injustice!"[54] On what can be ascertained from the available law reports, D, in circumstances wholly beyond her control, was brought from Eire into police custody in the United Kingdom. Once here, she was charged

[51] Or, as Lord Esher MR put it, "[a] man is entitled to be as negligent as he pleases towards the whole world if he owes no duty to them": *Le Lievre v Gould* [1893] 1 QB 491, 497.

[52] See further Sullivan, "Conduct and Proof of Conduct: Two Necessary Conditions for the Imposition of Criminal Liability" in Kaikobad and Bohlander (eds.), *International Law and Power* (2009) 235.

[53] (1934) 24 Cr App R 74. The case is discussed further below, § 4.1(ii)(a).

[54] *General Principles of Criminal Law* (2nd ed., 1960) 329 n. 14.

with being an alien (she was French) who was in the United Kingdom without permission to land. With an excessively literal interpretation of the legislation in question, the Divisional Court upheld Larsonneur's conviction. Lord Hewart ruled that the circumstances of her entry and continuing confinement were "perfectly immaterial".[55] It was enough, said the Court, that she was an alien who was present in the United Kingdom without permission. In substance then, she was convicted on the basis of her *status*, and not because of her conduct. But that, in our submission, is not enough.

Even at the level of principle, the objection to such a crime is narrow. It would be perfectly coherent, however unconscionable, for the nation-state described above to make it a crime for members of a minority group to give birth to children. Neither does the argument rule out other status and "situational" offences, such as being an illegal immigrant or a parent of a child of compulsory school age who is not regularly attending school. If it can be shown that there were acts or omissions for which D is responsible and by which D could have avoided the proscribed status, then the accountability requirement is satisfied. Translated into criminal law doctrine, this condition is embodied in a requirement of *voluntariness*, which is discussed in § 4.3. Where one's status is involuntary, it cannot legitimately be a criminal offence simply to be what one *is*. The criminal law is concerned with the acts, omissions and, on occasion, the acquired status of human beings. It takes human beings as its starting point and then asks what they are accountable *for*.

In addition to the requirement of voluntariness, the need for accountability can raise other difficult issues. Suppose a further variation on the death of Jim:

> Case III: Jim is discovered dead in his home. The police establish that he died after being struck by a vase which fell accidentally from the bookshelf. However, his daughter, Edith, had observed the scene and deliberately failed to summon an ambulance in time to save him.

This is very similar to Alice's case, except for one aspect: our complaint here is not about what Edith did, but about what she *failed* or *omitted* to do. (Another way of expressing the difference might be to say that, unlike Alice, Edith did not *cause* Jim's death.[56]) Because Edith's conduct was an omission, criminal liability does not necessarily follow.

The issues of omission and causation will be discussed in more detail in Chapter 4, but it is important to note that these, too, are crucial matters affecting the range and intrusiveness of the criminal law. Prohibiting an omission is not like prohibiting an action. When the law prevents Ian from (say) punching Bob, it leaves him with plenty of options and rules out only one. Ian is free to choose what to do or not do instead. By contrast, when the law proscribes an omission, it tells him exactly what to do. If Jim is dying, Edith *must* rescue him—she is not free to choose what to do or not do instead. One option is *required*, and all the other options are ruled out. Thus liability for omissions is much more likely to impinge upon individual autonomy and freedom of action.

In a liberal community, the concern with autonomy is fundamental.[57] If the law is to acknowledge and respect individuals as independent members of society, it must judge them according to their own actions, and not those of others. The process of shaping and controlling a person's life should be left to that person, and would be undermined were

[55] (1934) 24 Cr App R 74, 78.
[56] Cp. Moore, *Act and Crime* (1993) 267–78. But the law may disagree: see below, § 4.2(iv)(a).
[57] Above, § 1.2(i).

citizens constantly forced to assume responsibility for events they do not bring about.[58] For this reason, it is a guiding principle of the law that defendants are liable according to what *they* do, not what others do and they might prevent;[59] correspondingly, they should be left free to live their own lives and pursue their own goals without having legal duties to act or intervene constantly thrust upon them, unanticipated, unpredictable, and unwanted, because of the actions of others. This is why there is no general duty to prevent crime,[60] and why principles of accountability are so important.[61]

Implicit in this reasoning, however, is that omissions are special not because they deny culpability, but because of the implications that prohibiting omissions has for individual freedom. As such, they are not ruled out *tout court*. In practice, a criminal law duty to intervene is imposed, if at all, only when the defendant has a special connection to the harm—for example, when the defendant is the victim's parent.[62] But even that need not be true. Sometimes an altruistic reason for a stranger to get involved may justify the extension of responsibility. Suppose that Jane, a passer-by, sees a child drowning in a paddling pool. She can rescue the child at no risk to herself. In this situation, for Jane not to intervene would be monstrous. Although English criminal law does not at the moment criminalise such cases, it might justifiably do so, depending upon such factors as the seriousness of the impending harm and the degrees of risk and inconvenience involved in averting it. In many other jurisdictions, it is a crime not to rescue someone in peril when doing so involves no personal danger.[63]

Similarly, the criminal law need not always require D's behaviour to *cause* a specified consequence. For example, the law of secondary liability recognises the responsibility of those who do not themselves perpetrate a crime, but are nevertheless parties to its commission.[64] Suppose, for example, that David plans to kill Tony. Knowing this, Rebecca lends David her gun. Rebecca is a participant in Tony's murder, and his death may be attributed to her as a secondary party. The point here is that Rebecca does not cause Tony's death.[65] (David would have killed him anyway, using someone else's gun.) But she is not like a mere bystander, who can claim that David's action has nothing to do with her; that it is none of her business. Instead, she has involved herself in the murder, *making* it her business. Thus, although it is David who kills Tony, Rebecca shares in the responsibility for his death.

[58] Thus *Hart and Honoré* lxxx–xi: "respect for ourselves and others as distinct persons would be much weakened, if not dissolved, if we could not think of ourselves as the separate authors of the changes we make in the world". See further below, § 4.1(i).

[59] To a degree, criminal liability as an accomplice to another's crime may be seen as a qualification to this principle. However, proof of complicity by D in P's crime requires proof of an actus reus and mens rea personal to D: see below, Chapter 7. There is also some limited use of vicarious criminal liability, discussed below, Chapter 8.

[60] *Coney* (1882) 8 QBD 534, 557–8.

[61] There is a pragmatic side to accountability. If a swimmer drowns, the law cannot afford to prosecute every person on the beach. More generally, the state could not possibly contemplate prosecuting everyone who might have prevented it each time a prohibited harm occurs. So the general principle against liability for omissions has a realistic air about it as well as a philosophical justification.

[62] See below, § 4.1(i)(b). There can also be something to be said for offences, separate from homicide, of failing to take reasonable steps to safeguard the lives of others. For instance, members of households must take reasonable steps to safeguard (*inter alia*) the lives of children or vulnerable adults who reside in the household: Domestic Violence, Crime and Victims Act 2004, s. 5.

[63] See Ashworth, "The Scope of Criminal Liability for Omissions" (1989) 105 *LQR* 424.

[64] Below, Chapter 7.

[65] See, e.g., *Hart and Honoré* 51ff, 363ff; J.C. Smith, "Aid, Abet, Counsel, or Procure" in Glazebrook (ed.), *Reshaping the Criminal Law* (1978) 120, 131–4.

Like liability for omissions, secondary liability involves an extension of the criminal law beyond the core cases of wrongdoing. As such, it involves a greater intrusion upon people's freedom of action: not only may D not strike V, she may not do anything to help someone else strike V either, a much greater limitation upon what she is left free to do. This raises difficult questions of policy: if Rebecca is a shopkeeper, should she refuse to sell matches to David if she suspects or believes he has an illicit purpose? Secondary liability can force individuals to monitor the actions of others, and squarely raises issues of autonomy once more.[66] It is a hard question how far such extensions of responsibility should go, since, like vicarious liability,[67] they can have the effect of imposing liability largely on the basis of the defendant's status rather than his behaviour. Yet, once again, accountability which takes this form is not ruled out *tout court*.

## § 1.3 The structure of a criminal offence

Let us recap with an eye to basic legal doctrine. The discussion in this chapter has practical implications for criminal offences. We have characterised the criminal law as a system of prohibition and censure. Correspondingly, the main elements of crimes are twofold, action (or omission) and culpability. The first of these is primarily an external element:[68] an event or conduct which causes the harm that the law is designed to prevent. For example, the external element in murder is the killing of one human being by another.[69] This external element is known as the *actus reus* of the offence. It sets out the physical thing that must happen before the criminal law can be invoked, and will be discussed in detail in Chapter 4.

Generally, the actus reus is not enough by itself to constitute an offence. In § 1.2(ii)(a) we discussed the example of Pam, a doctor, who killed Alex by injecting him with a painkiller to which he was allergic. Pam has done the actus reus of a murder. But if Alex's allergy was unknowable, then Pam is not to blame, and should not be convicted. Alex's death is simply a tragic accident. The need for culpability in an offence gives us the second element, which is known as *mens rea*. This is what might be termed the "mental" element—the so-called "guilty mind", such as the intention, knowledge, or recklessness, of the defendant with respect to the actus reus. Mens rea is the subject of Chapter 5.

Like the actus reus, the mens rea varies for each offence. In some crimes, intention or recklessness will be required before D can be convicted, while in others negligence or some other fault element may suffice. An example will help to illustrate. Imagine that Tom has

[66] Particularly in cases of complicit liability for omissions, which may arise when the secondary party has some form of control over the wrongdoer. See for example *Du Cros v Lambourne* [1907] 1 KB 40, in which the passenger in a car was convicted of being a party to dangerous driving, on the basis that he owned the car and failed to exercise his right of control over the driver's actions. The case is further discussed below, § 7.4(iii).

[67] The doctrine of vicarious liability provides a second route with which a causal requirement may be bypassed. However, vicarious liability is normally to be avoided in criminal law, since it arises out of a more general relationship between the defendant and the actual perpetrator of a wrong, and so is not specific to the wrongful action; consequently the defendant risks being convicted of a crime for which he is not morally responsible. As a rule, "*Qui peccat per alium peccat per se* is not a maxim of criminal law": *Tesco Supermarkets Ltd v Nattrass* [1972] AC 153, 199 (Lord Diplock). See further below, § 8.1.

[68] Although it may not be entirely external. Sometimes actions acquire a harmful or criminal character only when done with a particular mental state. For illustrative discussion of this point, see Horder, "Crimes of Ulterior Intent" in Simester and Smith (eds.), *Harm and Culpability* (1996) 153; see also below, § 5.3.

[69] Below, Chapter 10.

been charged with an offence against section 15(1) of the Forgery and Counterfeiting Act 1981. He recently purchased a toaster from the local shop, paying for it in £10 notes. However, it later turns out that the notes are not genuine, as both Tom and the shopkeeper had thought, but very high-quality forgeries. The relevant section provides as follows:

> 15. Offences of passing etc. counterfeit notes and coins.
>
> (1) It is an offence for a person—
>
> (a) to pass or tender as genuine any thing which is, and which he knows or believes to be, a counterfeit of a currency note or of a protected coin ….

In this crime, the actus reus is passing or tendering as genuine money which is in fact counterfeit. The mens rea of the crime is knowing or believing that the money is counterfeit. On the facts given, Tom will not be guilty of passing counterfeit notes since he lacks the mens rea required for an offence against section 15(1).

Sometimes the mens rea can be present without the actus reus. Suppose instead that Tom found the notes on the street and believed that they were counterfeit, but that they were actually genuine. In this case Tom does not commit the offence of passing forged notes, because the actus reus is missing.[70]

### *(i) Defences: a separate element*

The examples above illustrate that both specified parts of the offence, the actus reus and the mens rea, must be proved before there is any question of D's being guilty of a crime. Even if both parts are proved, however, there might still be a defence available, and so we have a third basic element of every crime: the absence of a valid defence.

Suppose, for example, that Tom had indeed known the notes were counterfeit, but had been forced to make the purchase because he had been accosted outside the store by two men who had supplied the notes and "asked" him to buy the toaster, while wielding a shotgun suggestively. Tom has performed the actus reus of section 15(1), with the required mens rea. So we can say that he has committed a *prima facie offence*. Despite this, he will not be convicted since he has a further defence of duress.

The word "defence" can sometimes be misleading, because it tends to be used by lawyers to describe any reason why the defendant should be acquitted. Thus, if the defendant has an alibi, he will rely on this for his defence. More precisely, however, an alibi is not a defence but rather a denial that there was a prima facie offence at all. If the alibi is accepted, it means that the defendant did not do the actus reus. Similarly, automatism is not so much a defence as a denial of voluntariness, and as such a denial of responsibility for the actus reus. Duress and self-defence, by contrast, deny neither actus reus nor mens rea, but rather seek to defend the commission of a prima facie offence by reference to events not contemplated in the actus reus.[71]

Normally, defences reside at large in the common law, and are not expressly set out as part of each offence. Similarly, they are treated in separate chapters of this text. This is because

[70] Cp. *Deller* (1952) 36 Cr App R 184. He would nowadays be guilty of *attempting* to pass forged notes, contrary to s. 1 of the Criminal Attempts Act 1981: see § 9.4 below.

[71] Cp. A.T.H. Smith, "On Actus Reus and Mens Rea" in Glazebrook (ed.), *Reshaping the Criminal Law* (1978) 95, 97ff; Simester, "Mistakes in Defence" (1992) 12 *OJLS* 295, 295–6.

defences are normally of general application to all crimes, unless expressly or impliedly excluded by the statute which creates a particular crime. The fact that defences make up a third element was accepted by Lord Wilberforce in *Lynch*. Duress, he stated:[72]

> "is something which is superimposed on the other ingredients which by themselves would make up an offence, i.e. on the act and the intention. *Coactus volui* sums up the combination: the victim completes the act and knows that he is doing so; but the addition of the element of duress prevents the law from treating what he has done as a crime."

In case it is helpful, we represent this relationship by the following diagram:

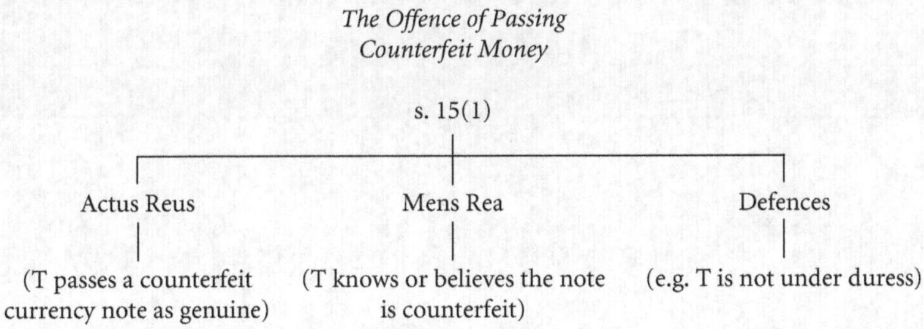


[72] [1975] AC 653, 679–80.

# 2

# THE RULE OF LAW AND THE EUROPEAN CONVENTION ON HUMAN RIGHTS

It is temptingly easy for a government to misuse the criminal justice system as a convenient means of social ordering. The criminal law, in seeking to secure benefits (including security[1]) to society at large, can be a major threat of *in*security for any individual charged with the commission of a crime. Indeed, in some respects the criminal justice system constitutes this country's most potent peacetime threat to the civil rights of those citizens suspected of and prosecuted for crimes. Accordingly, while endeavouring to control and reduce criminal conduct, society must be sensitive to the rights and legitimate expectations of those facing criminal charges, and pay careful attention to the impact that criminalisation will have on citizens' autonomy.

Central to the protection of those rights and expectations is the Rule of Law. The Rule of Law demands that those under the state's control should be dealt with by fixed and knowable law, and not according to the untrammelled discretion of state (including judicial) officials. The Rule of Law embodies a cluster of legal values, including certainty, clarity, and prospectivity. These values have at their heart not merely the constitutional premise that government should operate under the law, but also the ideal that citizens should be able successfully to live within the law, deriving guidance from the law itself.[2] As Gardner summarises that ambition:[3]

> "the law must be such that those subject to it can reliably be guided by it, either to avoid violating it or to build the legal consequences of having violated it into their thinking about what future actions may be open to them. People must be able to find out what the law is and to factor it into their practical deliberations. The law must avoid taking people by surprise. . . ."

This view, in turn, requires that the criminal law must be an organised, ascertainable, system of legal rules—and not *ad hoc* responses to a person's conduct.

The Rule of Law exists, first and foremost, at the level of principle. It comprises values to which the law should aspire, and to which legislators and judges should pay heed when enacting and interpreting law.[4] It is not a legally mandatory doctrine in its own right,

[1] See Ramsay, *The Insecurity State* (2012).

[2] See Raz, *The Authority of Law* (2nd ed., 2009) chap. 11; Colvin, "Criminal Law and the Rule of Law" in Fitzgerald (ed.), *Crime, Justice and Codification* (1986) 125.

[3] See his introduction to Hart, *Punishment and Responsibility* (2nd ed., 2008) xxxvi.

[4] Cp. Law Com. No. 143, *Codification of the Criminal Law* (1985) para. 1.3, where making the criminal law "more accessible, comprehensible, consistent and certain" was regarded as the aim of codification.

save in so far as it operates to inform statutory interpretation.[5] However, with the enactment of the Human Rights Act (HRA) 1998, which allows for direct domestic reliance on parts of the European Convention on Human Rights and Fundamental Freedoms (ECHR), many of the principles associated with the Rule of Law have independent constitutional significance.

(It is worth noting expressly at the outset, because this point is often misunderstood, that the ECHR is an international treaty, not an aspect of the law of the European Union. Accordingly, Brexit has had no impact upon the operation of the HRA or upon the UK's relationship with the European Court of Human Rights (ECtHR).)

In this chapter, we will explore the significance of those principles for the criminal law. More generally, we will consider the impact of the ECHR upon English criminal law.

## § 2.1 No conviction without criminalisation

The first limiting principle is inherent in the definition of criminal law offered at the beginning of Chapter 1: that a crime involves, among other things, an event prohibited by law.[6] This implies that nobody should be convicted of a criminal offence unless what was done is, in law, a crime. This idea is sometimes communicated via the Latin maxim *nullum crimen sine lege* (the *nullum crimen* principle): no crime without law.[7]

Suppose, for example, that D is a visitor from another country where adultery is a criminal offence. While in Wales, D has an affair with a married man. Even though D believes that in law she is committing a crime, she cannot be convicted of any offence, since adultery is not a crime in England and Wales.[8] A similar situation arises where D assumes facts which would make his conduct criminal under an existing offence, but his assumption is wrong. Consider the case of *Deller*.[9] D sold a car, stating as he did so that it was free of encumbrances, meaning that D could deal with the property as he pleased. In fact, D thought the car was encumbered, because he had earlier mortgaged it to a finance company. Unbeknownst to D, however, the earlier mortgage was invalid. Hence, the car *was* unencumbered. By chance, D's pretence was not false. He could, in consequence, not be convicted of the offence of obtaining the proceeds of the car sale under false pretences. He had not satisfied its legal definition.[10]

## § 2.2 Retrospective crimes

A corollary of the *nullum crimen* principle is that there should be no retrospective criminalisation. Citizens should not be convicted on the basis of conduct which was not, *when*

[5] An illustration of its role in statutory interpretation may be seen in Lord Steyn's assertion in *B (A Minor) v DPP* [2000] 2 AC 428, 470 that "in the absence of express words or a truly necessary implication, Parliament must be presumed to legislate on the assumption that the principle of legality will supplement the text".

[6] Above, § 1.1.

[7] Sometimes called the principle of *legality*, especially in the United States. See Hall, *General Principles of Criminal Law* (2nd ed., 1960) chap. 2.

[8] Cp. *Taaffe* [1984] AC 539.

[9] (1952) 36 Cr App R 184 (CA).

[10] Deller could nowadays be convicted of (at least) an attempted fraud by false representation. See below, § 15.3.

*they did it*, an offence. In such cases, it is not enough that the relevant law is to hand at the time of the trial. It would still be true, in such cases, that at the time of D's conduct he had committed no applicable crime. Remedying this legal deficiency by passing a retrospective law, which deemed the offence into existence at the time of its "commission", would be to subvert, rather than uphold, the Rule of Law. Particularly given the dramatic implications of criminal penalties for the lives of individuals, criminal liability is not the sort of nasty surprise that should be sprung on citizens after the fact.

Suppose that an allegation that D caressed V's thigh in 1970 comes to light in 2026. It would obviously be contrary to the Rule of Law to attempt to prosecute D for sexual assault under section 3 of the Sexual Offences Act 2003—an offence that only came into force in 2004. But Rule of Law concerns are not completely allayed by charging D with the predecessor offence of indecent assault, which existed in 1970. If what D did was not indecent by 1970s' standards, but was indecent by the standards of 2026, D would have a legitimate, Rule of Law complaint should the latter understanding of indecency be adopted in his trial.[11] The guidance offered by the concept of indecency (a key part of establishing the precise wrongfulness of D's conduct in 1970) would be frustrated if, *at the time of acting*, D could only guess at what might one day be perceived to be indecent. Citizens should not be put in such situations when criminal liability is in prospect.

A useful contrast might be drawn, in this regard, with the rules of evidence and procedure. The rules regarding the admissibility of several types of evidence (importantly, hearsay and bad character) have changed markedly between 2026 and the 1970s.[12] But D will not have planned his life in 1970 around the existing rules on hearsay and bad character; the rules of evidence are not intended to guide the conduct of citizens living under the criminal law. D thus has no legitimate complaint if his trial in 2026 uses current rules of evidence to assess whether he committed an offence in 1970.

We have argued that it is important to optimise the transparency and efficacy of the substantive criminal law by stating its rules clearly in advance. Fittingly, when interpreting criminal statutes, the common law contains a presumption against retrospective crimes. Although the presumption may be overridden by the express terms of a legislative enactment,[13] it provides protection against that possibility. Moreover, were Parliament expressly to override that presumption, it would also clearly contravene Article 7 of the ECHR, which provides as follows:

> "(1) No one shall be held guilty of any criminal offence on account of any act or omission which did not constitute a criminal offence under national or international law at the time when it was committed. Nor shall a heavier penalty be imposed than the one that was applicable at the time the criminal offence was committed.

[11] The prosecution argued that 2015 standards of indecency should be applied to offending spanning the 1980s to the 2000s in *CPS v Fox*, Westminster Magistrates' Court, 15 December 2015. The Chief Magistrate refused to allow this, on the basis that subsequent changes in attitudes towards touching could not retrospectively make past actions criminal. The prosecution made the valid point that this (surely right) approach could nevertheless lead to problems in prosecuting cases of "historical" sexual offending. Granted, it is difficult to fathom how a juror born in 2008 can reach a meaningful decision in 2026 about whether conduct in 1968 was indecent by the standards of the time.

[12] See Criminal Justice Act 2003, pt. 11.

[13] *Waddington v Miah* [1974] 1 WLR 683 (HL); *Deery* [1977] Crim LR 550 (CA); *Sutcliffe-Williams* [1983] Crim LR 255 (CA).

(2) This Article shall not prejudice the trial and punishment of any person for any act or omission which, at the time when it was committed, was criminal according to the general principles of law recognised by civilised norms."

Article 7 plainly prohibits retroactive criminal law, as well as retroactive increases in the penalties for existing crimes.[14] As things stand, both at common law and under the HRA 1998, courts are required to accept Parliament's will (subject to the tensions and contradictions described below, in § 2.5). Nonetheless, the incorporation of Article 7 via the HRA 1998 should at least ensure that English courts will, in the absence of the clearest statutory language, be loath to interpret a newly created crime, or a statutory increase in penalty, as having retrospective effect. In addition, both the common law presumption against retrospective criminalisation and Article 7 may act as warning signs. Any finding that they are overridden (which could lead to a "declaration of incompatibility", as discussed below) involves public acknowledgement that a part of the criminal law transgresses the Rule of Law and contravenes one of the defendant's basic human rights.

It was not always so. At common law, the courts formerly had the power to create criminal offences: indeed, this is the foundation of many of the oldest crimes—including murder, which remains undefined by legislation.[15] By the twentieth century, however, this power was exercised less frequently and more controversially, since it involved a retrospective deployment of the criminal sanction. In *Shaw v DPP*,[16] for example, D was charged with conspiring to corrupt public morals—an offence that had not existed until he was indicted for it. (Another view is that the offence had fallen into desuetude and was resurrected.) The House of Lords upheld the validity of the indictment. *Whether or not* D's actions were covered by an existing law, it was held that the courts had a residual power to criminalise his conduct. The decision led to outcry among lawyers and academics.[17] It is now accepted that the courts no longer have the power to create new offences,[18] or indeed to abolish old ones.[19] The authority to create or repeal offences nowadays lies solely with Parliament:[20]

> "an important democratic principle in this country [is] that it is for those representing the people of the country in Parliament, not the executive and not the judges, to decide what conduct should be treated as lying so far outside the bounds of what is acceptable in our society as to attract criminal penalties".

[14] On the importance of the principle that penalties should be reasonably predictable, see *Camilleri v Malta* (2013) 57 EHRR 32. Note, however, that the defendant will not necessarily succeed in an appeal against sentence on the ground that, when he is finally sentenced for "historical" offending, the sentence is higher than that which would have been given had the trial proceeded at the time of the offending. A troubling example is *Bell* [2015] EWCA Crim 1426, [2016] 1 WLR 1.

[15] Such powers—which look alarming to modern eyes—must be seen within their historical context. See, further: Williams, *CLGP* 592–6; Kennedy, "Declaring Crimes" (2017) 37 *OJLS* 741.

[16] [1962] AC 220. See Mares, "*Shaw v DPP* (1961)" in Handler, Mares, and Williams (eds.), *Landmark Cases in Criminal Law* (2017) 213.

[17] *Shaw* is objectionable on a second count: it is also discussed in § 16.3, with respect to criminalising *immoral* activity. See, generally: Goodhart, "The *Shaw* Case: The Law and Public Morals" (1961) 77 *LQR* 560; Note (1962) 75 *Harv LR* 1652; Smith, "Judicial Law Making in the Criminal Law" (1984) 100 *LQR* 46.

[18] *Knuller (Publishing, Printing and Promotions) Ltd v DPP* [1973] AC 435; *DPP v Withers* [1975] AC 842.

[19] *Rimmington and Goldstein* [2005] UKHL 63, [2006] 1 AC 459.

[20] *Jones et al.* [2006] UKHL 16, [2007] 1 AC 136, [29] (Lord Bingham). See also [60]–[62] (Lord Hoffmann). In *Jones et al.*, the House rejected the direct incorporation without legislation of new international law crimes into the domestic law of England and Wales.

In principle, the courts do not even have the power to *widen* existing offences, in order to criminalise conduct that previously was permitted.[21] Nevertheless, as the ECtHR has observed,[22]

> "However clearly drafted a legal provision may be, in any system of law, including criminal law, there is an inevitable element of judicial interpretation. There will always be a need for elucidation of doubtful points and for adaptation to changing circumstances. Indeed, in the United Kingdom, as in the other Convention States, the progressive development of the criminal law through judicial lawmaking is a well-entrenched and necessary part of legal tradition. Article 7 of the Convention cannot be read as outlawing the gradual clarification of the rules of criminal liability through judicial interpretation from case to case, provided that the resulting development is consistent with the essence of the offence and could reasonably be foreseen."

There is a clear tension between the evolutionary nature of the common law and the interpretive role of judges generally, and the *nullum crimen* principle. In *R*,[23] for example, the House of Lords abolished an exemption in the common law crime of rape, which had meant that a husband could not be convicted of raping his wife. While that change is to be welcomed as a matter of social and legal policy,[24] the manner in which it was achieved is more controversial, since it led to the defendant's being convicted on the basis of conduct that was apparently immune from the charge of rape when it was performed.[25]

Moreover, the decision of the ECtHR in *SW v UK*[26] shows just how delicate the balance may be between acceptable evolution of common law principles and illegitimate law-making. In the aftermath of *R*, the ECtHR found that there was no breach of Article 7 when the House of Lords ruled against a husband's immunity in rape. There would, the ECtHR observed, have been the clearest breach of Article 7[27] if the House of Lords had acknowledged a current, legally valid immunity, but had decided that it was no longer acceptable and would therefore be abolished. To ensure Article 7 compatibility, the following view must be taken of the House of Lords' decision in *R*: instead of abolishing the exemption, their Lordships ruled that the claim for immunity was unfounded in law. On this view, the House of Lords ruled that, *by the time of the defendant's actions*, the historical immunity for spouses was no longer part of the law. Their Lordships' dissection of the legal and social grounds of the immunity, together with their demonstration of the incoherence and instability of recent case law (which had reluctantly conceded the immunity but, at the same time, had sought to evade its consequences), was the strongest indication available that the day of the immunity was done. Indeed, the ECtHR concluded in *SW* that the decision by the House of Lords in *R* was reasonably predictable. Strictly, however, predictability is not

[21] *DPP v Withers* [1975] AC 842, 863 (Lord Simon); *Rimmington and Goldstein* [2005] UKHL 63, [2006] 1 AC 459, [33] (Lord Bingham). Nonetheless, the House of Lords held in *Rimmington* that the common law offence of public nuisance did not breach Art. 7, if confined to well-established instances of the offence and not used to evade time limits and sentencing restrictions on more specific statutory offences.

[22] *SW v UK* (1996) 21 EHRR 363, [36].

[23] [1992] 1 AC 599.

[24] On the wider context of this legal development, see Travis and Hunt, "The Road to *R v R*: How Feminist Campaigners Abolished the Marital Rape Exemption" [2024] *Crim LR* 154.

[25] See: Giles, "Judicial Law-making in the Criminal Courts: The Case of Marital Rape" [1992] *Crim LR* 680; Stark, "Judicial Development of the Criminal Law by the Supreme Court" (2021) 41 *OJLS* 1, 23–4.

[26] (1995) 21 EHRR 363.

[27] Subject perhaps to the (contested) possibility that the husband's action fell within the exception created by Art. 7(2), noted below in the text.

the point. (It is a separate Rule of Law value, considered in § 2.3.) What blocks a claim of retrospective criminalisation here is a demonstration that the defendant's case was decided on the basis of what the law was *at the time* of the defendant's conduct. The best judgments are not always predictable; Dworkin's perfect judge, Hercules, may surprise everyone, but still get it right.[28] Prior to the decision in *R*, most criminal lawyers would have assumed with justification that the husband's immunity in rape was circumscribed but extant. But, on the understanding of the case being sketched here, this assumption was incorrect *at the time it was made*. Accordingly, as the ECtHR found in *SW*, R's conviction involved no breach of Article 7.

Unfortunately, it is all too easy for a court fixated on the brute merits of a case to shun an analysis of what the law was *at the time of the alleged offence* and slip into plain retroactivity. *R* was decided in 1991. Subsequently, in *C*,[29] a different defendant was convicted in 2002 of raping his wife *in 1970*. Upholding the conviction, the Court of Appeal concluded bluntly that:[30]

> "We need not discuss either the 'declaratory' theory of the effect of judicial decision relating to the development of the common law, nor whether by its decision, the House of Lords was retrospectively creating a new offence where none existed before. The stark fact is that R was convicted. . . . The decision applied to events that had already taken place, as well as those in the future."

This approach effectively abdicates the judicial task. What matters when consulting precedents is not just whether a previous defendant was convicted, but the reasons why. In effect, the Court of Appeal's analysis in *C* implies that *any* development in the law might be applied retrospectively. Such an approach sits badly with the Rule of Law, and with Article 7. Given the acknowledgement of the spouse's exemption in appellate cases between 1970 and 1991,[31] it is tolerably clear that the Lords' conclusion regarding what the law was in 1991 was not applicable to 1970.

The Court of Appeal in *C* disagreed. It asserted, without offering any relevant (and quite a lot of irrelevant) evidence to support its claim, that a solicitor consulted in 1970 would have advised any client that "he might be liable for rape".[32] Even if that were true (which is doubtful), it misses the constitutional point that this is not just a matter of predictability of *future* developments in the criminal law. Lord Bingham saw the distinction in *Rimmington and Goldstein*:[33]

> "There are *two* guiding principles: no one should be punished under a law unless it is sufficiently clear and certain to enable him to know what conduct is forbidden before he does it; and no one should be punished for any act which was not clearly and ascertainably punishable when the act was done."

The first principle concerns fair warning (discussed in the next section). The second principle expresses the *nullum crimen* idea: even if retrospective criminalisation through a later development of the law is predictable, it is still wrong.

[28] See Dworkin, *Law's Empire* (1986) chap. 7.
[29] [2004] EWCA Crim 292, [2004] 1 WLR 2098.
[30] *Ibid.*, [22].
[31] E.g. *Steele* (1977) 65 Cr App R 22 (CA); *Sharples* [1990] Crim LR 198 (CA).
[32] [2004] EWCA Crim 292, [2004] 1 WLR 2098, [19].
[33] [2005] UKHL 63, [2006] 1 AC 459, [33] (emphasis added).

It might have been preferable for the Court of Appeal to acknowledge the revisionary nature of its ruling in *C*, but defend it as an isolated exception—hence specific to rape—on the basis of Article 7(2), which allows for retrospective conviction where a person's act "was criminal according to the general principles of law recognised by civilised nations". Such an approach is not without its own problems,[34] but it would at least confine the reasoning in *C* and mark it out as a special case.

Horder has argued that the above-mentioned problems of retrospectivity are avoided where the Court of Appeal or Supreme Court develops the law via a "declaration" of the criminal law.[35] The most visible "declaratory" mechanism is the Attorney-General's Reference procedure. When a defendant is acquitted, the Attorney-General can seek a clarification of the law concerning his case from the Court of Appeal (with the possibility of a referral or appeal to the Supreme Court).[36] This process leaves the defendant's acquittal unaffected, even if the outcome of the Reference suggests that he ought to have been convicted.[37] Through this system, Horder contends, the appellate courts can state the law *going forwards*, without the usual retrospective harm to the individual defendant involved in changing the law—in a manner detrimental to the defence—during an appeal.

Concerns of retrospectivity nevertheless remain. Even if the individual who was acquitted at the relevant trial's liability is unaffected by an Attorney-General's Reference, that decision will dictate the law for other defendants. For instance, if D has committed an alleged offence and then an Attorney-General's Reference decision is handed down in relation to T's acquittal, D will (presumably) be tried under the law as understood after the decision arising from T's trial. This is so even if the decision in relation to T's acquittal renders criminal (or at least more clearly criminal) what was previously at best ambiguous *at the time of D's allegedly criminal actions*. No "declarative" power can evade concerns of retrospectivity entirely. Such powers should always be subjected to careful scrutiny, and not used liberally by the courts.

## § 2.3 Fair warning

Apart from its constitutional implications, we have noted that the most important reason for requiring criminal offences to be created prospectively is that failure to do so undermines the ability to predict the legal consequences of one's conduct. The Rule of Law mandates that people should be governed by concrete rules that are ascertainable and certain,[38] and which minimise the opportunity for officials to wield arbitrary power.[39] This requires

[34] The *travaux préparatoires* to the ECHR indicate that Art. 7(2) was not intended as a general provision, but merely to ensure that prosecutions for activities that occurred during World War II were not derailed by arguments about retroactivity. This point has been made by the ECtHR: *Kononov v Latvia* (2011) 52 EHRR 21, [186].

[35] Horder, "The Courts' Development of the Criminal Law and the Role of Declarations" (2020) 40 *LS* 42.

[36] Criminal Justice Act 1972, s. 36.

[37] Horder also mentions appeals based on pre-trial decisions and interlocutory appeals. The appellate decisions will nevertheless affect D's trial, raising clear concerns regarding retrospectivity. He also discusses "declaratory" obiter dicta, such as that adopted in *Ivey v Genting Casinos UK Ltd* [2017] UKSC 67, [2018] AC 391, but such dicta may impact on trials for conduct that is alleged to have occurred *before* they were uttered, raising concerns of retrospectivity. See, also, the criticisms of *Ivey* below, § 13.8(iv).

[38] Raz, *The Authority of Law* (2nd ed., 1999) 214–16.

[39] Cp. *R (Gillan) v Commissioner of Police of the Metropolis* [2006] UKHL 12, [2006] 2 AC 307, [75] (Lord Brown), regarding the "in accordance with the law" provision of Art. 8(2) of the ECHR. See, also, *Gillan and Quinton v UK* (2010) 50 EHRR 45, [76]–[77].

both that the rule be stated in advance, and also that it be stated clearly.[40] Clarity is essential if citizens are to have *fair warning* that by their prospective actions they are in danger of incurring a criminal sanction.[41] If individuals understand the law, they will be better able to decide what to do in light of the guidance that the law is meant to provide. Only then can the law act as the deterrent and action-guider it is intended to be. And only then do citizens have a fair opportunity to steer themselves clear of criminal liability.

The law sometimes falls short of this ideal. In *Shaw v DPP* (discussed above), the enterprising Mr Shaw had been assured by his lawyer that his proposed publication, *The Ladies' Directory* (a directory of sex workers), passed muster in legal terms. Yet the House of Lords found that Shaw, with others, had conspired to corrupt public morality. If even competent legal advice cannot predict the unlawfulness of a defendant's conduct, his attempt to live within the law is no easy task.

The importance of security from unexpected prosecution was, by contrast, forcefully recognised by the House of Lords in *R (Purdy) v DPP*.[42] D wished to help his terminally ill partner to travel to Switzerland so that she could receive medical assistance in ending her life. All members of the Appellate Committee considered that what D proposed to do contravened English criminal law, either as assisting suicide (contrary to section 2 of the Suicide Act 1961) or, controversially, as murder. Yet Article 8 of the ECHR (concerning the right to respect for a private and family life) was held by the House of Lords to require the Director of Public Prosecutions to make public the criteria he would use when deciding whether to prosecute in cases of this kind. Doing so would provide adequate *ex ante* guidance to D, V and other persons faced with similar circumstances.[43] If it is the case that persons whose conduct seems in clear breach of law may be *legally* entitled to information relating to the chances of prosecution, the case for protecting persons seeking to conform their conduct to law in cases of legal uncertainty seems stronger.

It is important to notice that, in *Shaw*, predictability was threatened not just because the offence was created retrospectively. Suppose that the Lords rediscovered rather than invented the offence of conspiracy to corrupt public morals, and that the principle against retroactivity was not breached. Either way, the nebulous terms of the offence leave to speculation what kinds of thing one must not conspire to do. Similarly, even if the view of

40 Distinctions are sometimes drawn between different types of clarity: see Stark, "It's Only Words: On Meaning and *Mens Rea*" (2013) 72 *CLJ* 155, 164–6.

41 See the discussion in *Misra* [2004] EWCA Crim 2375, [2005] 1 Cr App R 21, [29]–[37]. Compare, in the United States, *Papachristou v City of Jacksonville* 405 US 156 (1972) (vagrancy ordinance void for vagueness). Fair warning is also relevant to inadvertence-based liability, e.g., for negligence. It is one reason why criminal liability for serious crimes should normally be confined to (subjectively) reckless or intentional wrongdoing. This is because if there were widespread exposure to state interference for inadvertent wrongdoing, then it would be much harder for citizens to plan and get on with their lives, without fearing the unforeseen disruption that facing criminal charges entails. See, e.g., Hart, *Punishment and Responsibility* (2nd ed., 2008) 181–2. However, this argument is not insuperable. To the extent that the Rule of Law enjoins unpredictable interference by the state, liability for negligence is reasonably predictable. Moreover, unless negligence liability is no deterrent, the argument prima facie deprives victims of protection from similarly unlooked-for intrusions by other citizens.

42 [2009] UKHL 45, [2010] 1 AC 345.

43 At the time of the proceedings in *Purdy*, to public knowledge there had been over 150 similar cases, none of which had resulted in prosecution. All that the Director had said publicly was that it should not be assumed that prosecutions would not be brought in such cases. The House of Lords unanimously decided that this uncertainty surrounding prosecution entailed failure of the "quality of law" test required by the ECHR jurisprudence for a lawful interference with the right to respect for private and family life under Art. 8. For further discussion see below, § 18.2(ii)(a).

the ECtHR that *R* involved no retrospective criminalisation were accepted, the decision remains problematic because of its element of surprise.

This shows that non-retroactive criminalisation is not the only standard set by the Rule of Law, and that the need for predictability has more general implications. The criminal law is not there solely to tell police and judges what to do *after* someone offends, but also to tell citizens what not to do *in advance*. As such, it is not enough for there to be a law in place before people can commit a crime. They should also be told about it:[44]

> "Respect for law, which is the most cogent force in prompting orderly conduct in a civilised community, is weakened, if men are punished for acts which according to the general consensus of opinion they were justified in believing to be morally right *and in accordance with law*."

That is the reason why non-publication or unavailability of a statutory instrument may be a defence, if a person is charged with a crime under that instrument while incapable of knowing about its existence.[45] It also explains why the increasing volume, complexity and obscurity of the criminal law is a major threat to basic principles of legal justice.[46]

As a matter of law, the principle of fair warning must nowadays be read in the light of the HRA 1998 and the ECHR.[47] In *Kokkinakis v Greece*, the ECtHR spoke of the principle that:[48]

> "the criminal law must not be extensively construed to the accused's detriment, for instance by analogy; it follows from this that an offence must be clearly defined in law. This condition is satisfied where the individual can know from the wording of the relevant provision and, if need be, with the assistance of the courts' interpretation of it, what acts and omissions will make him liable."

The passage makes clear that judicial creativity and interpretation—the principles of which are considered in Chapter 3—can be reviewed under the terms of Article 7 of the ECHR. As the ECtHR has emphasised, even where there are policy grounds favouring an expansive interpretation, they are secondary to the principle that criminal offences must be unambiguously defined:[49]

> "More specifically . . . the principle that a provision of the criminal law may not be applied extensively to the detriment of the defendant, which is the corollary of the principle of legality in relation to crime and punishment and more generally of the principle of legal certainty, precludes bringing criminal proceedings in respect of conduct not clearly defined as culpable by law. That principle, which is one of the general legal principles underlying the constitutional traditions common to the Member States, has also been enshrined in various international treaties, in particular in Article 7 of the [ECHR] . . ."

44 *State v O'Neil* 126 NW 454, 456 (1910) (emphasis added). See, further: Brett, "Mistake of Law as a Criminal Defence" (1966) 5 *MULR* 179; Ashworth, "Ignorance of the Criminal Law, and Duties to Avoid It" (2011) 74 *MLR* 1.

45 *Burns v Nowell* (1880) 5 QBD 444; *Lim Chin Aik v R.* [1963] AC 160 (PC); *Golden-Brown v Hunt* (1972) 19 Fed LR 438; *Catholique* (1980) 49 CCC (2d) 65; *Grant v Borg* [1982] 1 WLR 638 (HL).

46 Something about which the courts are rightly worried, when neither they nor the enforcement authorities can be sure whether they have to hand the current version of the law: see the extraordinary case of *Chambers* [2008] EWCA Crim 2467.

47 Below, § 2.5.

48 (1994) 17 EHRR 397, [52]. For a summary of the ECtHR's jurisprudence on this point, see *Navalnyye v Russia* (2019) 68 EHRR 25, [54]–[57]. See, also, Bates et al., *Harris, O'Boyle and Warbrick: Law of the European Convention on Human Rights* (5th ed., 2023) chap. 10.

49 *Procura della Republica v X* [1996] ECR I-6609, [25]. See too *Sunday Times v UK* (1979) 2 EHRR 245, [49].

The importance of this passage was acknowledged in the House of Lords,[50] and there is no reason to think that the UK Supreme Court would reject it. Nonetheless, it remains uncertain how far the constraints of Article 7 will be observed in practice.[51]

One consideration appears to be whether imprecision in relation to some aspect of an offence is offset by the presence of other, more precise offence elements.[52] Beyond that, however, there is little guidance regarding what factors will be taken into account when reviewing interpretive decisions for compliance. If conduct has been engaged in on the reasonable assumption that it was lawful, that should count as a factor to be considered by a court. But it may be that the *kind* of conduct at issue should properly influence a court. Hence, if the objection is one of inadequate fair warning rather than a constitutional one of retrospective criminalisation, the decision in *R* is defensible, perhaps, on the footing that R's conduct did constitute a crime when done by anyone else, and the reasons for criminalisation apply just as forcefully to a husband as to anyone else. It should have made no difference had R received an assurance from a lawyer, immediately prior to making his wife submit to intercourse by drawing a knife, that in legal terms he would not be committing rape. That is not, of course, to say that courts may craft new law to catch husbands who treat wives in that fashion. It is merely to say that, in considering what the current law *is*, the fact that the defendant thought it was different has less weight in a context where the defendant's act breached in the most fundamental way his wife's rights to bodily integrity and sexual autonomy. By contrast, if the owner of a factory has done his best to comply with health and safety law and has received professional assurance that he has done enough, this should be recognised when determining whether he has provided a safe system of work "so far as is reasonably practicable".[53]

It is for Parliament to make law and, although judicial interpretation of law may properly be purposive,[54] current legal resources cannot always be stretched to cover a defendant's conduct. The Rule of Law requires a system of legal ordering, not *ad hoc* responses to individuals' conduct. As such, it is particularly important in the criminal law to identify where the law and the jurisdiction of judges runs out. We have seen that, on occasion, judges have gone beyond that point and criminalised conduct they disapproved of even in cases where the policy arguments for criminalisation were not clear-cut. That is contrary to adjudication under law. The incorporation of Article 7 enhances the already compelling case against such judicial activism.

### (i) Use of evaluative concepts

We have argued that a legal system should seek to provide as much guidance and predictability as it can. Realism is required, however, when deciding what degree of certainty

[50] *R (Junttan Oy) v Bristol Magistrates' Court* [2003] UKHL 55, [2004] 2 All ER 555, [21] (Lord Nicholls, dissenting).

[51] An instructive example is the common law offence of cheating, cogently criticised by Ormerod, "Cheating the Public Revenue" [1998] *Crim LR* 627, but held to be compatible with the ECHR in *Pattni* [2001] Crim LR 570 (Crown Court). It is not clear to what extent this finding of compatibility was dependent on the contemporary understanding of dishonesty. See, now, below § 13.8(iv).

[52] Cf. *Hashman and Harrup v United Kingdom* (2000) 30 EHRR 241, where dishonesty offences were distinguished (at [39]) on the basis that the element of dishonesty "is but one element of a more comprehensive definition of the prescribed behaviour".

[53] Health and Safety at Work etc. Act 1974, s. 2.

[54] See below, § 3.1(ii).

is attainable in particular laws. Explicitness is necessarily compromised in offences that involve vague and open-ended concepts such as "unreasonable" and "fraudulent". Similarly, if we drive a car we know (or should know) that we must drive with "due care and attention".[55] The phrase sets a standard for a myriad of driving contexts and inevitably must leave an ultimate assessment to the finder of fact. The phrase gives no more than open-ended guidance, and further glosses on it, such as driving that "falls below what would be expected of a competent and careful driver",[56] hardly help matters. The degree of error or inattention that will turn us into criminals cannot be stated with exactitude. If the criminal law is to involve itself with standards of safety, which it must, it cannot give a rigid specification of the circumstances under which criminal liability will follow.

At the same time, both the legislature and the judiciary should be cautious about the deployment and interpretation of such expressions. Consider, for example, the imposition of negligence-based criminal liability through offences which are typically couched in terms of the "unreasonableness" of the defendant's behaviour. The touchstone, be it "unreasonable" or "negligent", is not susceptible of accurate or formal definition. What is "reasonable"? Nowhere does the law say, and to some extent the individual must judge the law's standard for himself, and take the risk that a court might later disagree.[57] Such gambles ought to be minimised,[58] and where possible these discretionary terms should be replaced by more concrete definitions of what counts as illegal, and what counts as legitimate.

This reservation should not be overstated. It cannot be claimed that such open-textured terms deprive individuals of advance warning altogether. The defendant's judgement is not purely a guess: words such as "reasonable" are not meaningless.[59] We understand them, and know how to apply the implicit judgements they import. The use of broad evaluative terms such as "negligent" and "fraudulent" may well provide an acceptable level of guidance where there is a high degree of social consensus about appropriate behaviour in the area of activity under regulation. One may assume that degree of necessary consensus, for instance, in matters of road safety; accordingly, a requirement to drive with due care and attention may tell us all we really need to know. Furthermore, extra-legal guidance, such as that found in the *Highway Code*, can go some way to solidifying consensus regarding what is considered to be "due care and attention" or the standard of the "competent and careful driver".

Moreover, evaluative standards are useful. Terms like "reasonable" and "dangerous" give the law flexibility to deal with cases that a legislator might not foresee. It is too much to expect a statute to list every single mode of negligent homicide, and meaningful (if open) terms like "unreasonable" save us from being straitjacketed by a rigid specification of the circumstances under which criminal liability will or will not follow. This much has been

55 Road Traffic Act 1988, s. 3.

56 Road Traffic Act 1988, s. 3ZA.

57 Indeed, the judge should not even provide guidance to the jury concerning the ordinary meaning of language used in a statute—which is a matter of fact, not law. See *Brutus v Cozens* [1973] AC 854, 861–2 (Lord Reid). See, also, *Stephens and Mujuru* [2007] EWCA Crim 1249, [2007] 2 Cr App R 26; *Golds* [2016] UKSC 61, [2016] 1 WLR 5231, [37]–[43] (Lord Hughes).

58 "[A] statute which either forbids or requires the doing of an act in terms so vague that men of common intelligence must necessarily guess at its meaning and differ as to its application, violates the first essential of due process of law": *Connally v General Construction Company* 269 US 385, 391 (1926). Cp. Rawls, *A Theory of Justice* (revised ed., 1999) 210: "if the precept of no crime without a law is violated, say by statutes being vague and imprecise, what we are at liberty to do is likewise vague and imprecise".

59 Lucas, "The Philosophy of the Reasonable Man" (1963) 13 *Phil Q* 97.

accepted by the ECtHR, which has observed that "[t]he need to avoid excessive rigidity and to keep pace with changing circumstances means that many laws are inevitably couched in terms which, to a greater or lesser extent, are vague . . ."[60] Indeed, without such flexibility, the law would be unfair and incomplete. There will always be matters that require regulation, but where a degree of imprecision is inevitable. Over many years, for example, the courts sought a legal definition of when an act was sufficiently close to the commission of a crime to constitute an attempt to commit that crime. Various tests were tried; all were unsatisfactory. Nowadays the jury is simply asked whether the defendant's act was "more than merely preparatory" to committing the full offence.[61]

Nonetheless, evaluative terms *are* imprecise, and for that reason, at least in serious crimes, they should normally be used only sparingly and for clear cases of wrongdoing. This is one justification of the common law's requirement that D's negligence be "gross" before D can be found guilty of manslaughter:[62] it is not merely that D's culpability is greater, but also that we can be surer D is culpable.[63] Sometimes, the imprecision is such that these terms ought not to be used at all. It is doubtful whether there is a sufficient degree of consensus about the acceptable contents of literature, plays, and film to render the standard "tend[ing] to deprave and corrupt", employed in obscenity law,[64] a sufficient guide to producers and publishers operating in those fields. If a government wishes to maintain a regulatory presence there, it is better that it regulates by description, expressly identifying those things which are not to be produced, published, or possessed. For instance, it is an offence to possess extreme pornography: an image is extreme if it is "grossly offensive, disgusting or otherwise obscene"; but it *also* must be a realistic depiction of various more specific activities.[65]

Alas, the ECHR seems unlikely to introduce greater rigour into this area. In *Handyside v UK*,[66] the applicant complained that the offence of obscenity in the Obscene Publications Acts 1959–1964 "was so far-reaching and imprecise that it might be applied almost without limit". Under that legislation, items which have a tendency "to deprave and corrupt" are obscene unless they are redeemed by some scientific, educational, literary, or artistic merit.[67] In the absence of a societal consensus on what constitutes obscenity, what kinds of sexual or violent material could be published was essentially a matter of guesswork

[60] *Kokkinakis v Greece* (1994) 17 EHRR 397, [40] (citing *Müller and Others v Switzerland* (1991) 13 EHRR 212, [29]). The Court noted that the potential vagueness of an offence may be ameliorated once the surrounding case law is taken into account.

[61] See below, § 9.3(i).

[62] See below, § 10.7(ii). The use of gross negligence as a culpability standard for manslaughter was held to be compatible with Art. 7 in *Misra* [2004] EWCA Crim 2375, [2005] 1 Cr App R 21.

[63] An interesting discussion is Horder, "Gross Negligence and Criminal Culpability" (1997) 47 *U Toronto LJ* 495.

[64] Obscene Publications Act 1959, s. 1(1). This statutory test differs from that applicable to "obscene" items sent in the post, which are regulated by the Postal Services Act 2000, s. 85(3). The test of "obscenity" in the post is simply that of the word's ordinary meaning, and may include anything that is shocking, lewd, or indecent: *Kirk* [2006] EWCA Crim 725. Yet that standard, too, may be thought rather nebulous; especially since its application is a matter for the jury. Indeed, even in judicial hands the application of evaluative terms may vary. Thus, in *Collins v DPP* [2006] UKHL 40, [2006] 1 WLR 2223, the House of Lords saw fit to overturn a finding by Leicestershire Justices that certain racist telephone messages sent by D were "offensive" but not "grossly offensive". Apparently a reasonable person—but not the Justices—*would* have found the messages to be grossly offensive. Such variation *ipso facto* suggests the need for more detailed legislative guidance.

[65] Such as of sexual interference with a human corpse. See Criminal Justice and Immigration Act 2008, s. 63(7)(c).

[66] (1979–80) 1 EHRR 737.

[67] Obscene Publications Act 1959, s. 4.

about how the particular jury empanelled for the case would respond to the items with which they were presented. Despite this, the ECtHR dismissed the applicant's argument that Article 7 had been violated, stating that "the requirement of certainty in the law cannot mean that the concrete facts giving rise to criminal liability should be set out in the statute concerned".[68] It was enough that the court was provided with a text, a general definition, which it could amplify and make concrete on a case-by-case basis. This glosses the fact that the formula, "to deprave and corrupt" normally involves a finding of fact. It is not subject to judicial amplification and explication. There are merely the *ad hoc* verdicts of different juries.

## § 2.4 Fair labelling

We have seen that the *ex ante* guidance the law is meant to provide requires it to be clearly stated. As Gibson has argued, there are at least three further reasons for expecting clarity in criminal offences, reasons that track distinct temporal stages in the criminal process.[69] When conduct is prohibited, it is essential to be able to communicate to the public what the criminal law has identified as wrongdoing, such that they may plan and respond accordingly. When a crime is alleged, the police, prosecutors, and other criminal justice actors need to know what precise wrongdoing they are considering, and what procedural consequences flow from that classification (e.g., whether the "special measures" available for complainants in sexual offence cases apply[70]). Finally, upon conviction, it is essential that all parties to proceedings, as well as the wider public, know precisely *what* wrongdoing has been proved. All of these reasons provide support for what is known as the principle of fair labelling.[71]

To date, most attention has focussed on the third of these justifications for fair labelling—a fact that Gibson attributes to the conviction's status as the "locus" and "zenith of fair labelling's power".[72] In this respect, the law must make clear what sort of criminal each offender is—what the conviction is *for*. It should communicate this to the defendant, so that he may know exactly what he has done wrong and why he is being punished, in order that his punishment appears meaningful to him, not just an arbitrary harsh treatment. It should also communicate to the victim that her interests were wrongfully set back by the defendant's conduct, and that the state denounces that misconduct. In addition, the law should communicate the crime to the public, so that it too may understand the nature of his transgression. The public record matters. While an employer may have few qualms about hiring a convicted drink driver as an orderly in a children's hospital, it would be an entirely

[68] Council of Europe, *European Convention on Human Rights, Year: 1974* (1976) 290.

[69] See Gibson, "Three Justifications of Fair Labelling" (2024) 140 *LQR* 431.

[70] Youth Justice and Criminal Evidence Act 1999, Pt. 2.

[71] Ashworth, "The Elasticity of *Mens Rea*" in Tapper (ed.), *Crime, Proof and Punishment* (1981) 45, 53–6; Williams, "Convictions and Fair Labelling" (1983) 42 *CLJ* 85; Mitchell, "Multiple Wrongdoing and Offence Structure: A Plea for Consistency and Fair Labelling" (2001) 64 *MLR* 393, 398–400; Chalmers and Leverick, "Fair Labelling in Criminal Law" (2008) 71 *MLR* 217; Tadros, "Fair Labelling and Social Solidarity" in Zedner and Roberts (eds.), *Principles and Values in Criminal Law and Criminal Justice* (2012) 67; Green, *13 Ways to Steal a Bicycle* (2012) 52–4; Gibson, "Deceptive Sexual Relations" (2020) 40 *OJLS* 82, 105–9. See also Stark, "Tort Law, Expression and Duplicative Wrongs" in Oberdiek and Miller (eds.), *Civil Wrongs and Justice in Private Law* (2020) 441.

[72] Gibson, "Three Justifications of Fair Labelling" (2024) 140 *LQR* 431, 451.

different matter to contemplate employing someone who has been convicted of offences related to paedophilia.

Accordingly, if D is publicly convicted of "murder", D should *be* a murderer and not a parking offender. At the same time, it would not be satisfactory for the law simply to label all convicted offenders unspecifically as "criminals", for that would equate the convictions of rapists with those of pickpockets. The criminal law speaks to wider society as well as defendants and complainants when a conviction is returned. It should thus communicate its message with adequate precision, by accurately naming the crime of which the defendant has been convicted.

The need for fair labelling is one reason why we should not merge the separate offences of murder and manslaughter into a single crime of unlawful homicide, as was suggested by Lord Kilbrandon in *Hyam*;[73] or combine arson and vandalism into a single crime of criminal damage, as was once proposed by the Law Commission.[74] In the eyes of society, such offences involve distinct types of wrongdoing, and the communicative function of the law would be impaired were the law to blur these differences.[75]

Underlying this objection is the point that different offences may criminalise *actions* which have differing social significance, and not just *outcomes*. So, for example, it would be a mistake to assimilate vandalism with negligent damage to property.[76] Even though the harm to property is the same, vandalism expresses a certain sort of contempt for society and the victim that negligent damage does not. If the criminal law were not to distinguish the two, a conviction would potentially be misleading.[77]

It must be borne in mind, however, that slavish pursuit of disaggregated offence labels imports its own dangers. Arguably there is something distinctive about causing grievous bodily harm with a knife, as opposed to doing so with one's fists. If that's right, one might therefore contend that fair labelling requires that this distinctiveness be reflected in the criminal law's labels.[78] Such fine distinctions nevertheless risk overcomplicating rather than clarifying the law's messaging about wrongdoing,[79] as well as making trials more time-consuming. There are various considerations that tell against such minute distinctions in offence labels, and these can lend support to the law's present approach of having general offences of causing grievous bodily harm (through whatever means), with the defendant's mens rea making the difference to the ultimate offence label.[80] In the end, a balance must be struck between concerns of accurate labelling and other competing considerations.

[73] [1975] AC 55, 98. For defence of a unitary offence of homicide, see Blom-Cooper and Morris, *With Malice Aforethought* (2004).

[74] Working Paper No. 23, *Malicious Damage* (1969) para. 22.

[75] See Gardner, "Rationality and the Rule of Law in Offences Against the Person" (1994) 53 *CLJ* 502, 504–6, 512–20.

[76] Note that English criminal law adopts the comparatively bland label "criminal damage", rather than "vandalism" (unlike Scotland, which has a specific offence of "vandalism": Criminal Law Consolidation (Scotland) Act 1995, s. 52). See below, § 14.5.

[77] See further below, § 16.6(ii).

[78] For an example, see Horder, "Rethinking Non-fatal Offences against the Person" (1994) 14 *OJLS* 335.

[79] See the juxtaposition of the "law professor's dream" and the "citizen's nightmare" in Husak, "Abetting a Crime" (2014) 33 *Law and Philosophy* 41, 64.

[80] Cornford, "Beyond Fair Labelling" (2022) 42 *OJLS* 985. On such differentiation in the offences against the person, see below, §§ 11.4–11.6.

## § 2.5 The European Convention on Human Rights

The impact of the ECHR and the HRA 1998 on substantive criminal law has been mentioned already in passing. This section discusses the role of the ECHR and HRA 1998 in more detail.[81]

The United Kingdom was one of the original parties to the ECHR. States that contract into the ECHR are obliged (at the level of international law) to secure the enjoyment of ECHR rights for their citizens. Usually, this will require ensuring that state and public officials do not conduct themselves in a manner inimical to ECHR rights. Sometimes, however, positive action may be required; including the creation, amendment, or enforcement of criminal offences.[82] If a country is found to be in breach of one or more Articles of the ECHR, it incurs a treaty obligation to bring its law and practices into step with the ECHR's requirements. Alleged breaches of the ECHR are adjudicated by the ECtHR, which sits in Strasbourg. Since 1966, the UK has allowed individuals to take cases to the Court. On a variety of occasions the ECtHR has found against the UK. A significant number of these adverse judgments concern matters of criminal procedure, criminal law, and sentencing.[83]

The ECHR became of relevance as a matter of domestic law following the HRA 1998, which requires all public authorities (including courts) to act compatibly with Convention obligations.[84] The Act enables the defence and/or the prosecution to raise Convention arguments in any criminal proceedings, whether before the local magistrates or the Supreme Court.[85] Should those arguments be found wanting by the domestic courts, a disappointed individual retains the opportunity to persuade the ECtHR of the merits of her case by making an application directly to it.[86]

From a criminal lawyer's perspective, claims that human rights have been violated are most likely to arise in the contexts of procedure, evidence, and sentencing. Significantly, Article 6 of the ECHR, which guarantees the right to a fair trial and a presumption of innocence, has been construed as having no bearing on the fairness of the substantive law to be

[81] On the law of the ECHR generally, consult Bates et al., *Harris, O'Boyle and Warbrick: Law of the European Convention on Human Rights* (5th ed., 2023). For a (slightly dated, yet still useful) consideration of the ECHR in the context of criminal law, evidence, and procedure see Emmerson, Ashworth, and Macdonald, *Human Rights and Criminal Justice* (3rd ed., 2012).

[82] See Ashworth, *Positive Obligations in Criminal Law* (2013), chap. 8; Lazarus, "Positive Obligations and Criminal Justice: Duties to Protect or Coerce?" in Zedner and Roberts (eds.), *Principles and Values in Criminal Law and Criminal Justice* (2012) 135.

[83] Significant decisions involving findings against the United Kingdom include *Thynne, Wilson and Gunnell v UK* (1991) 13 EHRR 666 (discretionary life-sentencing); *McCann and Others v UK* (1996) 21 EHRR 97 (permissible force in the prevention of crime); *Saunders v UK* (1997) 23 EHRR 313 (compulsory powers of questioning); *Vinter v UK* (2016) 63 EHRR 1 ("whole life" sentences—cf. *Hutchinson v UK* (2015) 61 EHRR 13).

[84] HRA 1998, s. 6. For general discussion of the HRA 1998, see Wade, "The United Kingdom's Bill of Rights" in Cambridge Centre for Public Law, *Constitutional Reform in the United Kingdom* (1998) 61; Bamforth, "The Application of the Human Rights Act 1998 to Public Authorities and Private Bodies" (1999) 58 *CLJ* 159.

[85] For discussion of the HRA 1998 in the context of criminal law, see Smith, "The Human Rights Act and the Criminal Lawyer: The Constitutional Context" [1999] *Crim LR* 251; Arden, "Criminal Law at the Crossroads: The Impact on Human Rights from the Law Commission's Perspective and the Need for a Code" [1999] *Crim LR* 439; Buxton, "The Human Rights Act and the Substantive Criminal Law" [2000] *Crim LR* 331; Ashworth, "The Human Rights Act and the Substantive Criminal Law: A Non-minimalist View" [2000] *Crim LR* 564; Ashworth, "A Decade of Human Rights in Criminal Justice" [2014] *Crim LR* 325.

[86] The passing of the HRA 1998 is without prejudice to a right of individual petition to the ECtHR. However, Art. 35(1) of the ECHR requires that domestic remedies be exhausted before the matter is raised at Strasbourg. Thus ECHR rights must first be asserted in the courts of England and Wales.

applied at the trial.[87] There is no explicit right to a fair substantive criminal law.[88] But this does not mean that the substantive criminal law is immune from scrutiny under the Convention: successful challenges to English criminal offences and defences have been made at Strasbourg.[89] For example, in recent years, various protesters campaigning on issues such as climate change and racism have sought (with limited success) to argue that the right to freedom of expression under Article 10, and the right to freedom of assembly under Article 11, rendered criminalisation of their conduct, or prosecution for it, incompatible with their human rights.[90] Article 10 issues regarding freedom of expression also arise when, for example, a person is charged with making an electronic communication that is "grossly offensive".[91]

The following sections offer a brief account of those ECHR Articles most directly affecting the substantive criminal law. More lengthy consideration will be given to particular human rights issues throughout this work where relevant to the subject matter under discussion. First, however, it is necessary to present an overview of the HRA 1998, in order that the manner and extent to which Convention arguments may be put in the context of criminal proceedings is understood properly.

### *(i) The Human Rights Act 1998—the framework*

At the outset, it should be noted that the HRA 1998 does not elevate the ECHR into a form of higher, fundamental law against which the validity of all other primary legislation may be tested, and those laws invalidated if found wanting.

Instead, the Act obliges courts to interpret legislation, whenever the legislation was passed, "so far as possible . . . in a way which is compatible with the Convention Rights".[92] If there remains any incompatibility that cannot be erased by interpretation, the High Court and appellate courts (the Court of Appeal and the Supreme Court) *may*—not must—make a "declaration of incompatibility" under section 4 of the HRA 1998. Section 4(6) of the HRA 1998 nevertheless provides that a declaration of incompatibility does not affect the

[87] *G v UK* (2011) 53 EHRR SE25; *G* [2008] UKHL 37, [2009] 1 AC 92; *Barnfather v London Borough of Islington and Secretary of State for Education and Skills* [2003] EWHC 418 (Admin), [2003] 1 WLR 2318; *Concannon* [2002] Crim LR 213 (CA); *Z v UK* (2002) 34 EHRR 3.

[88] Cf. Tadros, "A Human Right to a Fair Criminal Law" in Chalmers, Leverick and Farmer (eds.), *Essays in Criminal Law in Honour of Sir Gerald Gordon* (2010) 103.

[89] Notably in: *Dudgeon v UK* (1982) 4 EHRR 149; *McCann and Others v UK* (1996) 21 EHRR 97; *A v UK* (1998) 27 EHRR 611.

[90] See, e.g.: *DPP v Ziegler* [2021] UKSC 23, [2021] 3 WLR 179 (obstruction of the highway under Highways Act 1980, s. 137); *Brown* [2022] EWCA Crim 6 (public nuisance); *Cuciurean* [2022] EWHC 736 (Admin) (aggravated trespass); *Pwr v DPP* [2022] UKSC 2, [2022] 1 WLR 789 (displaying an article in circumstances giving rise to a reasonable suspicion of membership of, or support for, a proscribed organisation); *Attorney-General's Reference (No 1 of 2022)* [2022] EWCA Crim 1259, [2023] KB 73 (criminal damage); *In Re Abortion Services (Safe Access Zones) (Northern Ireland) Bill* [2022] UKSC 32, [2023] AC 505 (prohibition of certain behaviour within "safe access zones" around abortion providers); *Sarti and Others* [2025] EWCA Crim 61, [2025] 1 WLR 3276 (interfering with the use or operation of key national infrastructure); *ABJ* [2026] UKSC 8 (expressing support for a proscribed organisation). For critical engagement with much of this domestic case law, and an argument that it misapprehends the relevant ECtHR jurisprudence, see Martin, "Convicting Peaceful Protesters: Proportionality's Proper Place at Criminal Trial" (2024) 24 *OJLS* 342. See, further, § 14.5(vi)(c) below.

[91] Malicious Communications Act 1988, s 1(1). See *Casserly* [2024] EWCA Crim 25, [2024] 1 WLR 2760.

[92] HRA 1998, s. 3(1). For arguments about how English courts should use the interpretive power conferred by s. 3, see Gearty, "Reconciling Parliamentary Democracy and Human Rights" (2002) 118 *LQR* 248 and Phillipson, "(Mis-)Reading Section 3 of the Human Rights Act" (2003) 119 *LQR* 183.

validity, continuing operation, or enforcement of any incompatible legislation.[93] Instead, a declaration of incompatibility creates political pressure on the legislature to amend the offending legislation.

No explicit provision is made in the HRA 1998 for cases of incompatibility between the common law and the ECHR. One example of a likely incompatibility is the common law defence of insanity, which, at present, is arguably too broad in treating as insane persons with conditions such as epilepsy and diabetes.[94] Some writers have suggested that this practice contravenes Article 5 of the ECHR, which ensures the right to liberty and security of the person.[95] Additionally, it has been claimed that placing the burden of proof on D to prove the elements of the insanity defence on the balance of probabilities contravenes the presumption of innocence guaranteed by Article 6(2).[96]

Suppose that a Crown Court judge is persuaded that an insanity verdict in respect of D will contravene Article 5 or Article 6(2). Can she disregard domestic precedents of the highest authority that require such a verdict in D's case? There is an argument that she *must* now override previous authority. Section 6 of the HRA 1998 imposes a duty on public authorities to act compatibly with Convention rights.[97] It has been argued that, in light of that section, courts—being public bodies—must hand down judgments which are ECHR-compatible, unless precluded from doing so by the clear terms of a statute or other primary legislation. On that view, the statutory duty under section 6 obliges courts of whatever stature to override any common law authority at odds with the ECHR, however high and longstanding that authority may be.[98] (As will be seen in Chapter 19, however, the courts have not impugned the validity of the authorities on insanity.)

### (a) *The interpretative duty*

Although, as we have noted, the HRA 1998 does not confer upon courts the power to invalidate statutes, judges are obliged by section 3(1) to do what they can to render statutes compatible with the ECHR. The injunction "so far as it is possible to do so"[99] indicates both the limits placed on the interpretive process and the extent of the judicial effort that must be made to achieve compatibility. Where a statutory provision potentially contravenes ECHR rights, interpretation is no longer solely a matter of divining the intention of Parliament regarding the meaning of that provision, but instead one of rendering the provision

[93] See, too, HRA 1998, s. 3(2)(b). Subordinate legislation, on the other hand, is likely to be invalid to the extent of any incompatibility with ECHR rights: s. 3(2)(c).

[94] See below, § 19.2(ii)(b).

[95] See Sutherland and Gearty, "Insanity and the European Court of Human Rights" [1992] *Crim LR* 418; Baker, "Human Rights, *McNaghten* and the 1991 Act" [1994] *Crim LR* 84; below, § 19.2(iii). In other respects, the defence is also arguably too narrow, allowing the conviction of some persons in contravention of Art. 3 (interdicting, in addition to torture, "inhuman or degrading treatment or punishment").

[96] See Law Commission, *Insanity and Automatism* (2013) paras. 8.20–1 (critiquing *H v UK* App. No. 15023/89).

[97] It seems that the duty of public authorities to act compatibly with the ECHR may be displaced in circumstances where the UK is obliged under general international law to act in a manner incompatible with an ECHR right. For an example, see the primacy accorded to the UN Charter in *R (Al-Jedda) v Secretary of State for Defence* [2007] UKHL 58, [2008] 1 AC 332.

[98] For an opinion to this effect see HL Debs., 24 Nov. 1997, col. 783 (Lord Chancellor). For a narrower view of the effect of s. 6, see Kentridge, "The Incorporation of the European Convention on Human Rights" in Cambridge Centre for Public Law, *Constitutional Reform in the United Kingdom* (1998) 69. See, also, Phillipson, "The Human Rights Act, 'Horizontal Effect' and the Common Law: a Bang or a Whimper?" (1999) 62 *MLR* 824.

[99] HRA 1998, s. 3(1).

compatible with the relevant ECHR rights (so far as possible). The decision of the House of Lords in *Lambert*[100] illustrates the potential reach of this new power of interpretation. The case concerned a "reverse burden" of proof: to avoid a conviction for possession of a drug with intent to supply, D was required to prove that he did not know, suspect or have reason to suspect that he possessed a controlled drug. By a majority of 4:1, the House of Lords decided that the presumption of innocence enshrined in Article 6(2) of the Convention implied that the word "prove" must be interpreted in future as imposing an *evidential* rather than a legal/persuasive burden on D. In other words, D simply had to *raise evidence* of his lack of knowledge or suspicion, rather than *prove* it on the balance of probabilities.[101] This interpretation of the word "prove" is a remarkable (though welcome) feat of interpretation, notwithstanding the strong terms of section 3(1) of the HRA 1998.

Should courts go even further and "read in" words into statutory provisions in order to ensure compliance with the ECHR? Writing extra-judicially about the likely effect of the incorporated ECHR on the criminal law, Arden LJ (as she then was) entertained as a serious possibility the reading in of words to statutory provisions in order to achieve compatibility.[102] She envisaged, for example, that courts might "write in" due diligence defences for strict liability offences to avoid convictions which otherwise would violate Article 3 (inhuman or degrading treatment or punishment). Save for one Court of Appeal decision later reversed by the House of Lords,[103] the courts have refrained from explicit rewriting of statutes. None the less, they have made decisions going well beyond the canons of interpretation existing prior to the HRA 1998.[104] In *A (No. 2)*,[105] the House of Lords arguably went beyond even the broadest conception of interpretation and into the realm of overriding the statutory text under consideration. In the past, defendants in sexual offence trials have sought to dredge up the complainant's sexual history in an effort to cast doubt on the complainant's credibility.[106] Concern about this practice, and with conviction rates in contested rape trials, led Parliament to place restrictions on the extent to which the complainant in a sexual offence case could be questioned about his or her previous sexual history.[107] The House of Lords has found certain of those restrictions to be in contravention of the guarantee of a fair trial provided by Article 6 of the ECHR, in so far as they sometimes made it impossible for the defendant to mount a credible defence (where, for instance, the previous sexual history evidence concerned acts involving both the defendant and the complainant).[108] Not even the extended power of interpretation allowed by section 3 of the HRA 1998 could massage

100 [2001] UKHL 37, [2002] 2 AC 545.

101 The distinction between evidential and legal burdens is returned to below, § 3.2.

102 "Criminal Law at the Crossroads: the Impact on Human Rights from the Law Commission's Perspective and the Need for a Code" [1999] *Crim LR* 439, 447–51. See also Hooper, "The Impact of the Human Rights Act on Judicial Decision-making" [1998] *EHRLR* 676.

103 *Re W and B; Re W (Care Plan)* [2001] EWCA Civ 757, [2001] 2 FLR 582, reversed in *Re S (Minors) (Care Order: Implementation of Care Plan); Re W (Minors) (Care Order: Adequacy of Care Plan)* [2002] UKHL 10, [2002] 2 AC 291.

104 Perhaps the most notable example is *Ghaidan v Godin-Mendoza* [2004] UKHL 30, [2004] 2 AC 557, where the statutory phrase "husband and wife" was interpreted to include same-sex couples (who, at that time, could not marry).

105 [2001] UKHL 25, [2002] 1 AC 45.

106 For discussion of the myths associated with such evidence, see *Seaboyer* [1991] 2 SCR 577.

107 Youth Justice and Criminal Evidence Act 1999, ss. 41–3.

108 Cf. *Martin* [2004] EWCA Crim 916, [2004] 2 Cr App R 22.

the language of the relevant provisions into a form compatible with Article 6. Instead of making a declaration of incompatibility, however, the House of Lords decided that trial judges must admit evidence of, or allow cross-examination based on, V's previous sexual history if necessary to ensure a fair trial, notwithstanding the clear statutory language disallowing such steps.

Given subsequent cases, the approach to sections 3 and 4 of the HRA 1998 in *A (No. 2)* may be regarded as misguided. In *A (No. 2)*, a declaration of incompatibility was taken to be a thing of very last resort, to be avoided if at all possible.[109] By contrast, in *R (Anderson) v Secretary of State for the Home Department*,[110] the House of Lords straightforwardly made a declaration of incompatibility, after resolving that the statutory provision empowering the Home Secretary to fix the time in prison to be spent by persons serving a mandatory life sentence could not be interpreted in a manner compatible with Article 6. This latter decision comports better with the scheme of the HRA 1998.[111]

Although the HRA 1998 provides for new principles of interpretation, they ought to be exercised in a manner compatible with parliamentary sovereignty. This same point about the sovereignty of Parliament can, however, be used to support an expansive use of section 3 to interpret criminal legislation. According to Lord Bingham in *Attorney-General's Reference (No. 4 of 2002)*:[112]

> "It was argued for the Attorney General that [the contested provision, section 11(2) of the Terrorism Act 2000] could not be read down under section 3 of the [HRA 1998] so as to impose an evidential rather than a legal burden if (contrary to his submissions) the subsection were held to infringe, impermissibly, the presumption of innocence. He submitted that if the presumption of innocence were found to be infringed, a declaration of incompatibility should be made. I cannot accept this submission. . . . In my opinion, reading down section 11(2) so as to impose an evidential instead of a legal burden falls well within the interpretative principles discussed above. . . . Such was not the intention of Parliament when enacting the 2000 Act, but it was the intention of Parliament when enacting section 3 of the [HRA 1998]."

In other words, the interpretation inconsistent with Parliament's intention in the 2000 Act is, in fact, mandated by Parliament's intention as expressed in 1998, and so observes the sovereignty of Parliament. The problem with this sleight-of-hand analysis, as all students of constitutional law will recognise, is that parliamentary sovereignty requires that, where the intentions of Parliament conflict in domestic legislation, the later expression is to be preferred.[113] It is submitted that the possibility of compatible (re)interpretations contemplated in the HRA 1998 extends only to reasonable interpretations of the legislative will, and not far-fetched but "possible" readings, particularly when such "readings" take the form of

[109] Cf. *Ghaidan v Godin-Mendoza* [2004] UKHL 30, [2004] 2 AC 557; *Sheldrake v DPP*; *Attorney-General's Reference (No. 4 of 2002)* [2004] UKHL 43, [2005] 1 AC 264.

[110] [2002] UKHL 46, [2003] 1 AC 837. See, further, the declarations of incompatibility in *Bellinger v Bellinger* [2003] UKHL 21, [2003] 2 AC 467 and *A v Home Secretary* [2004] UKHL 56, [2005] 2 AC 68.

[111] For criticism of the judiciary's reluctance to grant declarations of incompatibility, see Stark, "Facing Facts: Judicial Approaches to Section 4 of the Human Rights Act 1998" (2017) 133 *LQR* 631.

[112] *Sheldrake v DPP*; *Attorney-General's Reference (No. 4 of 2002)* [2004] UKHL 43, [2005] 1 AC 264, [53].

[113] Were it otherwise, the former Parliament could bind the latter: see *Thorburn v Sunderland City Council* [2002] EWHC 195 (Admin), [2003] QB 151, [37]. The controversial exception is where the former Parliament's statute is "constitutional", such as the HRA: these statutes apparently require express overriding by later Parliaments.

re-writings of the legislative text (such as in *A (No. 2)*). The existence of House of Lords and Supreme Court cases where declarations of incompatibility have been made[114] shows that there are boundaries to the realm of the "possible".

*(b) Reviewing legislation "on the face"*

The emphasis of the HRA 1998 on interpreting domestic legislation in a manner compatible with the ECHR indicates that the form of review ought to be "on the face" (a term familiar in US constitutional jurisprudence).[115] That is to say, the reviewing court should look at the impugned statutory provision and evaluate whether the provision, across the range of all of its likely applications, is compatible with the ECHR. By contrast, there is a form of review known as "as applied". Under the latter approach, the issue to be resolved is whether the provision being challenged contravened Convention rights in particular applications.[116]

In its own jurisprudence the ECtHR adopts a particularly narrow version of the "as applied" approach, with its emphasis on whether the rights of the particular applicant have been breached.[117] This is unsurprising, because of the requirement that applicants to the ECtHR be "victims" in the sense defined in Article 34 of the Convention.[118] Yet certain of the ECtHR's decisions are stated in such broad terms as, in effect, to impugn the provision under scrutiny in general terms. For example, in *Saunders v UK*,[119] the ECtHR found that the use, at trial, of evidence obtained from the defendant under powers of compulsory questioning was objectionable *per se* and therefore a breach of Article 6(1) (the right to a fair trial). This apparently amounted to the imposition of a *general* limitation, i.e. one not particular to the case or a particular set of cases.[120] By contrast, in *Salabiaku v France*,[121] where a reverse burden of proof was challenged, the ECtHR—while remarking that reverse burdens were matters of concern and proper issues for judicial scrutiny—found against the appellant on the ground that he had suffered no unfairness in the particular circumstances of the case.

What of the approach in English courts? In *R v Director of Public Prosecutions, ex p Kebilene*,[122] the Divisional Court found certain reverse burdens of proof contained in the Prevention of Terrorism Act 1989 to be in "flagrant" breach of Article 6(2) (which guarantees the presumption of innocence). The finding of the Court was based entirely on the terms of the legislation, i.e. on its face: the Court did not consider whether the particular defendants (or those in a similar position) might have suffered any unfairness. Although,

[114] E.g. *R (Anderson) v Secretary of State for the Home Department* [2002] UKHL 46, [2003] 1 AC 837; *Bellinger v Bellinger* [2003] UKHL 21, [2003] 2 AC 467; *R (T) v Chief Constable of Greater Manchester Police and Others* [2014] UKSC 35, [2015] AC 49; *Re Northern Ireland Human Rights Commission's Application for Judicial Review* [2018] UKSC 27, [2019] 1 All ER 173.

[115] See, further, Fallon, "Fact and Fiction about Facial Challenges" (2011) 99 *Cal LR* 915.

[116] See, further, Stark, "Facing Facts: Judicial Approaches to Section 4 of the Human Rights Act 1998" (2017) 133 *LQR* 631, 635–7.

[117] See, e.g., *Austin v UK* (2012) 55 EHRR 14.

[118] By contrast, in domestic law under the HRA 1998, there need be no determination that the defendant's rights are violated. ECHR questions can arise as collateral issues in criminal trials, without the same requirement of standing. In that context, the appropriate focus is the condition of English law in terms of its compatibility with the ECHR.

[119] (1997) 23 EHRR 313.

[120] Cf. *O'Halloran v UK* (2008) 46 EHRR 21.

[121] (1991) 13 EHRR 379.

[122] [1999] 3 WLR 175 (DC).

on further appeal,[123] the House of Lords decided the case on different grounds, Lords Hope and Hobhouse each demurred from the Divisional Court's approach and indicated that the effect upon the defendants of applying the reverse burden would be relevant matters for consideration. Lord Hobhouse spoke of a necessity "to examine each case on its merits" and "to examine whether the relevant provision has in fact resulted in an injustice to the complainant".[124] This case-specific approach is visible in other decisions.[125] If it were to be adopted generally, the impact of the HRA 1998 on the content of domestic legislation would be considerably diminished—and significantly less predictable. The more general perspective adopted by the Divisional Court and contemplated by Lord Steyn's majority judgment in *Kebilene* better comports with the framework of the HRA 1998. Indeed, in subsequent appeals concerning whether reverse legal burdens within particular offences are in breach of Article 6(2),[126] their Lordships have focused on how such a legal burden will affect trials for the relevant offence *in general*, rather than on the impact of the reverse burden upon the particular appellant's trial. This seems right: it would be odd (and inimical to clarity and consistency in practice) to conclude that a particular statutory offence imposes a reverse legal burden on some defendants and not on others.

That said, whether the applicant's rights have been contravened should not be overlooked when assessing in general terms the Convention compatibility of a legislative provision. In *R (Collins) v Secretary of State for Justice*,[127] the applicant argued that the law relating to the use of self-defence by householders against trespassers present in their home was not compliant with the right to life under Article 2 of the Convention. The applicant had entered D's house as a trespasser and had been caused serious and permanent brain damage when D restrained him for six minutes in a headlock. A prosecution was not brought against D because the CPS took the view that, while the force that D used was arguably disproportionate, householders were entitled to use disproportionate force against trespassers provided the force employed was not grossly disproportionate.[128] The Divisional Court disagreed: under the householder legislation, "disproportionate" but permissible force would still have to be force that was reasonable in the circumstances (a view that was subsequently endorsed by the Court of Appeal).[129] Force that was unreasonable in the circumstances was not protected by the statute. On that basis, the applicant's contention that the legislation

123 [2000] 2 AC 326.

124 *Ibid.*, 397.

125 See, e.g., *Beghal v DPP* [2015] UKSC 49, [2016] AC 88 (considering the specific facts to determine the compatibility of the power to, *inter alia*, detain persons, in ports and at borders, for questioning without reasonable suspicion of involvement in terrorism under Terrorism Act 2000, sched. 7). See, too, *R (Miranda) v Secretary of State for the Home Department* [2016] EWCA Civ 6, [2016] 1 WLR 1505.

126 *Lambert* [2001] UKHL 37, [2002] 2 AC 545; *Johnstone* [2003] UKHL 28, [2003] 1 WLR 1736, [44]–[54] (Lord Nicholls). In *Sheldrake v DPP*; *Attorney-General's Reference (No. 4 of 2002)* [2004] UKHL 43, [2005] 1 AC 264, [21], it was said by Lord Bingham that "[t]he justifiability of any infringement of the presumption of innocence cannot be resolved by any rule of thumb, but on examination of all the facts and circumstances of the particular provision as applied in the particular case". But this assertion needs to be understood in the light of the subsequent discussion by his Lordship, which emphasises the generic facts and circumstances of the offence provision, rather than those of the particular defendant (see, especially, [26] and [30]). The point is that courts must examine each provision afresh, rather than the circumstances of each individual defendant affected by that provision.

127 [2016] EWHC 33 (Admin), [2016] QB 862.

128 The decision not to prosecute was based on an interpretation of s. 76(5A) of the Criminal Justice and Immigration Act 2008, which had been widely understood to allow householders to use any degree of force, falling short of grossly disproportionate force, in defending themselves and others lawfully present in their house.

129 *Ray* [2017] EWCA Crim 1391, [2018] QB 948.

contravened Article 2 failed. What went unexplored was whether the force that D used against the applicant was, despite its magnitude, reasonable in the circumstances.[130]

It is worth noting, in closing, that the law reform process is also influenced by the ECHR. Under section 19 of the HRA 1998, a minister in charge of a Bill must inform Parliament whether he is able to make a statement that the provisions of the Bill are compatible with the ECHR. This usefully ensures that the civil servants and drafters who prepare legislation must consider ECHR questions. Notably, the Law Commission also now pays close attention to ECHR issues when formulating reform proposals.

### *(ii) The interpretation of Convention rights*

In determining the compatibility of statutory provisions and common law with the requirements of the ECHR, some degree of particularity is required concerning the effect and ambit of the various Articles of the ECHR. The terms of the ECHR, an awkward blend of the general and the particular, do not always make the content of the relevant rights self-evident. Additionally, section 2 of the HRA 1998 provides that, when determining a question that arises in connection with an ECHR right, a court must take into account the decisions and judgments of various bodies, in particular the ECtHR, if the court is of the opinion they are relevant to the proceedings.[131]

These interpretive sources are not binding. They are things to be taken into account. This means that, if a court in England and Wales concludes that it ought not to follow a decision by the ECtHR, it may refuse to do so.[132] The circumstances under which this happens, in the criminal law context, tend to be where the ECtHR's judgment appears: to be distinguishable on the facts; to have misunderstood some aspect of English law; to represent merely the latest decision in an unstable line of case law; or, more controversially, to simply be wrong.[133] Such refusals to follow the ECtHR's lead are rare, and are engaged with carefully by Strasbourg.[134] It is more usual, however, for the English and Welsh courts to attempt to "keep pace" with the ECtHR's judgments.[135]

"Keeping pace" implies that the ECtHR is constantly developing its approach to the ECHR. Indeed, the ECHR has been described by the ECtHR as "a living instrument"[136] that is responsive to social and moral change. Accordingly, decisions and opinions of earlier periods may have little or no weight. For instance, early decisions of the European Commis-

[130] The parties to the litigation had agreed that the facts as assumed by the CPS were correct. Hence there was a basis for reviewing whether, on these agreed facts, the force to which D resorted was reasonable in the circumstances. If D's use of force was excessive, then the failure to prosecute would fall short of what is required of the state under Art. 2, which requires active steps to enforce the applicable law on its part to protect persons under its jurisdiction from life threatening force that is not "absolutely necessary": *Osman v UK* (2000) 29 EHRR 245.

[131] In addition to decisions of the ECtHR, earlier opinions and decisions of the European Commission on Human Rights and decisions of the Committee of Ministers should also be taken into account.

[132] Indeed, the court may be bound by a precedent (e.g. a decision of the House of Lords or the Supreme Court) that appears inconsistent with a decision by the ECtHR. Absent "wholly exceptional cases", the court must follow the domestic precedent, leaving it for the appropriate appellate court to consider whether any inconsistency with the ECtHR's jurisprudence should be removed: *R (M) v Secretary of State for Work and Pensions* [2008] UKHL 63, [2009] 1 AC 311, [64] (Lord Neuberger).

[133] See *Horncastle* [2009] UKSC 14, [2010] 2 AC 373; *R (Hallam) v Secretary of State for Justice* [2019] UKSC 2, [2020] AC 279.

[134] See: *Al-Khawaja and Tahery v UK* (2012) 54 EHRR 23; *Nealon v UK* (2024) 79 EHRR 22.

[135] *R (Ullah) v Special Adjudicator* [2004] UKHL 26, [2004] 2 AC 323, [20] (Lord Bingham).

[136] *Tyrer v UK* (1979–80) 2 EHRR 1, [31].

sion of Human Rights found that proscriptions of forms of homosexuality were compatible with the ECHR whereas, more recently, the Commission found that stipulating different ages of consent for heterosexual and homosexual persons contravened both Article 8 (respect for a private and family life) and Article 14 (principle of non-discrimination).[137]

The ECHR is an international treaty, not a constitutional Bill of Rights. It is an undertaking by party states to observe acceptable standards of human rights in their respective jurisdictions. In the light of this, courts, when exercising the jurisdiction instituted by the HRA 1998, should not derogate from the baseline standards clearly set by the ECtHR. The ECtHR authoritatively sets the minimum terms for compliance. However, it does not follow that, when construing the ECHR in a domestic context, English and Welsh courts should go no further to protect rights than does the ECtHR. In its jurisprudence the ECtHR has applied a "margin of appreciation",[138] particularly in cases involving Article 10 (freedom of expression) and Article 11 (freedom of assembly and association). This margin recognises that uniform standards cannot be imposed by an international court on States with different histories and sensitivities. Yet no such restraint is required when judges address human rights issues in their own society.[139] If, say, a judge in England and Wales were to take the view that freedom of speech requires a more robust defence than is found in ECtHR jurisprudence, she is free to give a fuller effect to the terms of Article 10.[140] That said, a degree of deference is due to the legislative will of a democratically elected Parliament, and where an issue is finely balanced, courts should not be too astute to find that legislation breaches the ECHR. Determining whether or not a legislative provision breaches an Article of the ECHR may require consideration of the doctrine of proportionality—is the legislation under consideration a proportionate response in combating the social mischief or advancing the social policy with which the legislation is concerned? Some degree of diminution in the enjoyment of ECHR-protected rights may be an acceptable price for gains in welfare or efficiency, and there may well be trade-offs to be made between different ECHR-protected rights.[141]

When determining whether a breach of the ECHR has occurred, certain rights are guarded more jealously than others. Articles 2 (the right to life), 3 (the right not to be subjected to torture, inhuman or degrading treatment and punishment), and 7 (no retrospective penal law) cannot be derogated from, even in times of war or dire emergency. All the other Articles of the ECHR may be derogated from in such circumstances.[142] When

[137] *Sutherland and Morris v UK* (1996) 22 EHRR CD22.

[138] See Bates et al., *Harris, O'Boyle and Warbrick: Law of the European Convention on Human Rights* (5th ed., 2023) § 1.VII.

[139] In *Kebilene* [2000] 2 AC 326, 380–1, Lord Hope considered that the margin of appreciation doctrine would not be available to English judges when interpreting the ECHR. Of course, as Lord Hope recognised, many ECHR questions will be matters of broad evaluation affected by matters of national culture and subject-matter even in the absence of that doctrine.

[140] It may be noted that s. 12 of the HRA 1998 makes particular reference to freedom of expression, but only in contexts where the court is considering whether to grant any relief.

[141] The doctrine of proportionality does not come into play unless the right is expressed in qualified terms. Some ECHR rights are absolute, for example the right not to be tortured or subjected to inhuman or degrading treatment (Art. 3). As put by Lord Clyde in *de Freitas v Permanent Secretary of Ministry of Agriculture, Fisheries, Lands and Housing* [1999] 1 AC 69, 80 (PC), whether encroachment on a ECHR right is a proportionate legislative response requires consideration of "whether: (i) the legislative objective is sufficiently important to justify limiting a fundamental right; (ii) the measures designed to meet the legislative objective are rationally connected to it; and (iii) the means used to impair the right or freedom are no more than is necessary to accomplish the objective". Cf. *R (Daly) v Secretary of State for Home Department* [2001] UKHL 26, [2001] 2 AC 532, [27] (Lord Steyn).

[142] Art. 15.

the extremities of war and national emergency do not obtain, however, the possibility of derogation does not imply that these other Articles have lesser weight. Article 6 (fair trial, including the presumption of innocence) in particular has been expansively interpreted.[143]

Apart from drastic circumstances permitting derogation, an ECHR right may alternatively be restricted by rulings about its scope. It is fair to say that Article 3 provides an unconditional right: if conduct amounts to torture, or to inhuman or degrading treatment or punishment, it will violate Article 3 whatever the circumstances. However, in respect of Articles 2 and 7, while non-derogation status underlines the importance of the right at issue, it does not preclude argument about the nature and ambit of these rights. For instance, the uncertain state of the English law of obscenity, and judicial abolition of the husband's immunity in rape, arguably involved breaches of Article 7, yet the ECtHR ruled otherwise.[144] Questions concerned with abortions have been raised under Article 2 and, in that context, the ECtHR has applied the margin of appreciation doctrine in light of the considerable differences in the laws of the contracting States.[145] Additionally, even in cases that fall, prima facie, within the general scope of an ECHR right, exceptions may sometimes be justified. In the case of certain Articles, for instance Articles 8 (the right to respect for a private life) and 9 (freedom of thought and religion), the declaration of the right in the ECHR is followed by a statement of the circumstances in which that right may be justifiably interfered with.[146]

### *(iii) The doctrine of "positive obligations"*

Instruments such as the ECHR tend to be viewed as preventing states from engaging in certain actions. State agents must not, for instance, torture individuals (Article 3), or take their lives except in very limited circumstances (Article 2). Such obligations can, in turn, give rise to arguments that the substantive criminal law ought to be amended. For example, it has been argued that English law is too lax in allowing an exemption from criminal liability to law enforcement officials on the basis of a belief in the necessity to use fatal force even in cases where that belief was unreasonable.[147] It is arguable that allowing such latitude to officials contravenes Article 2 (right to life).[148]

An important point captured by such views is that international treaties like the ECHR bind states, not private individuals. A private individual who, without state involvement, tortures another private individual does not—indeed, cannot—violate Article 3. It must be borne in mind, however, that instruments such as the Convention do not merely prohibit the state from acting in particular ways. They also require positive action on the part of the

[143] Bates et al., *Harris, O'Boyle and Warbrick: Law of the European Convention on Human Rights* (5th ed., 2023) chap. 9.

[144] *Handyside v UK* (1979–80) 1 EHRR 737 (obscenity); *SW v UK* (1996) 21 EHRR 363 (marital rape).

[145] "National laws on abortion differ considerably . . . in such a delicate area the contracting states must have a certain discretion": *H v Norway* App. No. 7004/90 (1992).

[146] Arguably, the distinction drawn in ECHR jurisprudence between disputes over the scope of an Article right and over exceptions to that right is spurious. On questions of coherence and uncertainty in ECHR jurisprudence generally, see McHarg, "Reconciling Human Rights and the Public Interest: Conceptual Problems and Doctrinal Uncertainty in the Jurisprudence of the European Court of Human Rights" (1999) 62 *MLR* 671.

[147] Leverick, *Killing in Self-defence* (2006) chap. 10. Cf. Smith, "The Use of Public or Private Defence and Article 2" [2002] *Crim LR* 958.

[148] For further discussion see below, § 21.2(v).

state to sufficiently guarantee enjoyment of relevant rights. For instance, the ECtHR has read into various ECHR rights certain "positive obligations" to set up (and enforce[149]) the criminal law in such a way that private individuals are adequately deterred from engaging in conduct that would violate the Convention if performed by a state agent. If such conduct is effectively (or formally) not subject to criminal sanctions, that very omission can lead to a state's violating the ECHR.[150]

One example of the invocation of Convention arguments to expand the criminal law is *A v UK*,[151] where the ECtHR found that English law's failure to effectively deter inhuman and degrading treatment inflicted by parents in the name of punishing their children violated Article 3. As a result, the scope of the "reasonable chastisement" defence was limited by the legislature, with the aim of securing Article 3 compatibility.[152] This move widened the scope of criminal liability in the context of corporal punishment. Similarly, the criminal law must contain adequate homicide provisions to ensure that private individuals are sufficiently deterred from arbitrarily taking the lives of others, which has implications for the law on self-defence when invoked by such individuals (and, in consequence, the scope of relevant criminal offences).[153] Additionally, "effective deterrence against grave acts such as rape, where fundamental values and essential aspects of private life are at stake, requires efficient criminal law provisions"[154] to prohibit such actions, lest Article 8 of the ECHR (and potentially even Article 3) be violated by the relevant state.

### *(iv) The ECHR and the substantive criminal law*

The above discussion has shown that the ECHR is capable of significantly affecting the substantive criminal law, although some of that capacity remains latent. It may be helpful to list, non-exhaustively, areas of criminal law where, in principle, the ECHR has the potential to have an impact:[155]

Article 2 (right to life): self-defence; force used in the prevention of crime and to make arrests; abortion; assisted suicide and euthanasia.

Article 3 (right not to be subjected to torture or inhuman or degrading treatment and punishment): offences against the person arising from staff (mis)conduct in prison, military and mental health establishments; offences of strict liability, especially 'status' offences; defence of parental chastisement.

Article 5 (right to liberty and security of person): insanity defence; offences against the person in prison, military and mental health establishments.

[149] Accordingly, some failures by the state to investigate criminal allegations adequately can result in violations of the Convention: *Commissioner of Police for the Metropolis v DSD* [2018] UKSC 11, [2019] AC 196.

[150] See, generally, Lavrysen and Mavronicola (eds.), *Coercive Human Rights* (2020).

[151] (1999) 27 EHRR 611. See, further, *R (Williamson) v Secretary of State for Education and Employment* [2005] UKHL 15, [2005] 2 AC 246.

[152] Children Act 2004, s. 58.

[153] The case law on this issue is surveyed in *R (Collins) v Secretary of State for Justice* [2016] EWHC 33 (Admin), [2016] QB 862. See, too, Mavronicola, "Taking Life and Liberty Seriously: Reconsidering Criminal Liability under Article 2 of the ECHR" (2017) 80 *MLR* 1026.

[154] *MC v Bulgaria* (2003) 40 EHRR 20, [150].

[155] See Ashworth, "The European Convention and Criminal Law" in Cambridge Centre for Public Law, *The Human Rights Act and the Criminal and Regulatory Process* (1999) 37.

Article 6 (right to fair hearing and presumption of innocence): reverse burdens of proof; entrapment.

Article 7 (right not to be convicted under retroactive law): offences of dishonesty with broad and vague conduct elements; common law assault; offences of corrupting public morality and of outraging public decency; Protection from Harassment Act 1997.

Article 8 (right to respect for private life): definition of sexual offences; limits of consent to sexual acts; limits of consent to physical injury; ambit of Protection from Harassment Act 1997; Proceeds of Crime Act 2002 (onus to prove provenance of funds).

Article 10 (right to freedom of expression): obscenity, and other offensive conduct; harassment and hate crimes; criminal libel; contempt of court; Official Secrets Act 1989; incitement to disaffection; inviting support for a proscribed organisation.

Article 11 (right to freedom of assembly and association): various offences connected with protests and demonstrations; breach of the peace.

Relevant opportunities for raising Convention issues during criminal trials will be further developed in later chapters, as appropriate.

### *(v) The future of the HRA*

The HRA has been politically controversial for some time. An independent review of the HRA reported to the Lord Chancellor in October 2021 and recommended several clarifications be made to the Act.[156] Previous Conservative governments indicated a desire to go further: a consultation on replacing the HRA with a British Bill of Rights was launched by the Ministry of Justice in December 2021. A Bill of Rights Bill was introduced by the Lord Chancellor in June 2022, but expired with that particular Parliament.[157] So far, the HRA has survived unamended. It is, nonetheless, likely to remain a point of political contention in the years to come.

[156] Ministry of Justice, *The Independent Human Rights Act Review* (CP 586, 2021).
[157] See Ministry of Justice, *Human Rights Act Reform: A Modern Bill of Rights* (CP 588, 2021).

# 3

# INTERPRETATION AND PROOF

## § 3.1 Statutory interpretation

In Chapter 2 we saw how the Rule of Law embodies values such as fair warning—values which are proper aspirations for the criminal law, now partly cast in justiciable form by the European Convention on Human Rights (ECHR) and the Human Rights Act (HRA) 1998. However, neither the Rule of Law nor the ECHR supports demands for unattainable measures of predictability and certainty. A degree of imprecision is inherent in the enterprise of legal ordering. Statutes are necessarily expressed in general terms, and must be interpreted and applied to particular cases. The agent of this process is the court.[1]

In practice, the judicial task is more substantial than it need be. While legislators cannot be expected to foresee every conceivable case that might arise when they create an offence, the standard of draftsmanship in this jurisdiction is such that offences frequently omit to specify quite obvious matters, such as what (if any) mental element an offence requires, on whom the burden of proving certain matters lies, and whether omissions as well as acts are within the conduct proscribed.[2] Moreover, some fundamental aspects of the criminal law, such as causation, are untouched by statute. Consequently, the role of judges is pivotal and powerful.

One way of observing the rights and expectations of citizens under the Rule of Law is for judges to show proper restraint when interpreting the rules of the criminal law. In the civil law—say, a case involving the law of restitution—a judgment may earn praise for the way it reconceptualises the grounds of restitution, thereby vindicating new restitutionary claims. Similar creativity in the criminal law should generally be avoided, especially where the scope for condemnation and punishment might thereby be enlarged.[3] In Chapter 2 we noted the remark by the European Court of Human Rights (ECtHR) that "the criminal law must not be extensively construed to an accused's detriment, for instance by analogy".[4] This

[1] For general discussion, see: Hall, "Strict or Liberal Construction of Penal Statutes" (1935) 48 *Harv LR* 748; Kremnitzer, "Interpretation in Criminal Law" (1986) 21 *Israel LR* 358; Jeffries, "Legality, Vagueness, and the Construction of Penal Statutes" (1985) 71 *Virginia LR* 189; Ashworth, "Interpreting Criminal Statutes: A Crisis of Legality?" (1991) 107 *LQR* 419; MacCormick and Summers (eds.), *Interpreting Statutes* (1991).

[2] This is not necessarily the fault of the people who draft legislation. They can only be as clear as their instructions allow.

[3] Cf. Dworkin, *Taking Rights Seriously* (1977) 100: by contrast with "standard civil cases, when the ruling assumption is that one of the parties has a right to win . . . [t]he accused in a criminal case has a right to a decision in his favor if he is innocent, but the state has no parallel right to a conviction if he is guilty. The court may therefore find in favor of the accused, in some hard case testing rules of evidence, for example, on an argument of policy that does not suppose that the accused has any right to be acquitted." Different considerations may apply when enlarging the scope of defences: see below, § 22.3.

[4] *Kokkinakis v Greece* (1994) 17 EHRR 397, [52]. See above, § 2.3.

need for restraint means that interpreting a criminal statute should involve determining its meaning in an appropriately non-expansive way.

This chapter presents a sketch of that interpretative enterprise. It is useful to begin with a discussion of the sources of the criminal law.

### *(i) The sources of the criminal law*

Until the nineteenth century, the definition of crimes and the rules of criminal responsibility evolved and were developed by judges on a case-by-case basis. Writers of authority—known as the institutional writers—also exerted influence on the law's development. Most notable amongst them are Blackstone, Coke, East, Foster, Hale, and Hawkins. Today, English criminal law is no longer predominantly the result of judicial creativity, and the role of legal commentators is comparatively uninfluential. The criminal law is nowadays primarily enacted through parliamentary statutes and subordinate regulations.[5] Nobody knows how many criminal offences exist on the statute books,[6] and there are methodological, as well as practical, issues inherent in attempts at trying to arrive at a definitive figure.[7] There are, it seems, over 10,000 different criminal offences on the statute books,[8] by far the most important contemporary source of criminal law.[9] This corpus of statutory law reflects, as Glazebrook put it, "two centuries of draftsmanship of very uneven quality . . . the product of changing views of morality and of when and how penal measures should be used in the hope of protecting the community against the violent, the lustful, the avaricious, the selfish and the careless".[10]

It should not be assumed that all criminal offences receive the full scrutiny of Parliament as aspects of primary legislation. Nowadays, criminal offences are quite frequently introduced through secondary legislation,[11] a phenomenon that was historically under-appreciated in discussions of criminalisation.[12]

[5] Prior to Brexit, EU law provided the basis for the creation of a number of criminal offences in England and Wales. Indeed, under section 2(2) of the European Communities Act 1972, the UK *executive* also had a general authority to create criminal offences where this was made necessary by EU legislation. That power was used frequently in the past. While no new offences can be created in this way, any offence that was previously created during the UK's membership of the EU remains in force here unless and until repealed (see, e.g., the mass repeal effected by the Retained EU Law (Revocation and Reform) Act 2023, s. 1).

[6] See, further, Chalmers and Leverick, "Tracking the Creation of Criminal Offences" [2013] *Crim LR* 543; Chalmers, "'Frenzied Law Making': Overcriminalization by Numbers" (2014) 67 *CLP* 483; Chalmers and Leverick, "Quantifying Criminalization" in Duff et al. (eds.), *Criminalization* (2015) 54.

[7] For instance, is fraud one offence (under Fraud Act 2006, s. 1), or three offences (because the s. 1 offence can be committed in three distinct ways, found in ss. 2–4)? Does s. 8 of the Sexual Offences Act 2003, which prohibits the causing *or* inciting of certain sexual activities with children under 13, create one offence or two? (Two, apparently: *Walker* [2006] EWCA Crim 1907.)

[8] Herring, *Criminal Law Statutes* (2012) x.

[9] The proliferation of statutory offences is sometimes presented as a modern problem, but see Chalmers, Leverick and Shaw, "Is Formal Criminalization Really on the Rise? Evidence from the 1950s" [2015] *Crim LR* 177.

[10] Glazebrook, *Blackstone's Statutes on Criminal Law* (9th ed., 1999) xiii. See, further, McBain, "Abolishing Obsolete Legislation on Crimes and Criminal Procedure" (2011) 31 *LS* 96.

[11] The Law Commission rightly expressed concern about this trend, and its expansionist potential, in LCCP No. 195, *Criminal Liability in Regulatory Contexts* (2010) paras. 3.144–3.158. The Commission suggested provisionally that "criminal offences should be created and (other than in relation to minor details) amended only through primary legislation" (para. 3.158). This proposal has not, to date, been taken forward.

[12] See, however, Chalmers and Leverick, "Criminal Law in the Shadows: Creating Offences in Delegated Legislation" (2018) 38 *LS* 221.

The predominance of primary and secondary legislation as sources of the criminal law should not obscure the judiciary's creative role. Statutes have to be interpreted and, as we have mentioned, poor draftsmanship commonly includes failures to specify vital matters such as where the burden of proof lies or even the mens rea requirement(s) in an offence. Inevitably, such issues have to be resolved by judicial interpretation. Even where there is a degree of specificity—e.g. where the offence in question states that intention or recklessness regarding particular elements of the offence is required—in the absence of stipulative definitions for those terms, the judges must resolve their meaning.[13] Moreover, it is still the case that some significant offences, including murder, manslaughter, and assault, remain in large part common law offences. General doctrines affecting criminal liability, such as complicity and causation, remain largely unaffected by statute, and new statutory crimes must be received and absorbed into this common law background.

Even among nations with a common law background, the retention of significant common law offences is nowadays unusual. An influential strand in Enlightenment political theory was the belief that the organs of representative democracy should be more influential than unelected judges in the creation and administration of the criminal law. To that end, criminal codes were promulgated in the hope that they would stipulate with clarity the content of crimes and the conditions of liability, reducing the role of the judge to that of an agent executing the will of the legislature. These hopes were optimistic, yet by no means wholly unfounded, and the vast majority of developed countries now have criminal codes. Codification passed England and Wales by. From time to time, efforts have been made to remedy the situation. The Law Commission, for example, once published a Draft Criminal Code Bill,[14] but neither that draft code nor any future draft is likely to be enacted for England and Wales in the foreseeable future. The political will for codification is simply not there. Indeed, the Law Commission for England and Wales has abandoned the project to codify the criminal law all at once, in favour of a more piecemeal and progressive approach to reform.[15]

Modernisation of English criminal law is long overdue. Certain statutes, such as the practically important Offences Against the Person Act 1861, are riddled with uncertainty and unhelpful overlaps and duplication.[16] Predictably, they are expressed in outmoded, often eccentric, language. Yet reform and rationalisation should not be at the expense of abolishing offences that constitute a valuable cultural endowment. In 1969, a Law Commission draft bill, usefully updating the law of criminal damage, made no provision for an offence of arson.[17] Understandably, in the legislation that ensued, Parliament reinstituted the offence.[18] "Arson" is an evocative term which should not be lost.[19] The same applies to "robbery", rightly preserved in the Theft Act 1968 as a form of acquisitive violence and not

[13] See Stark, "It's Only Words: On Meaning and *Mens Rea*" (2013) 72 *CLJ* 155.
[14] Law Com. No. 177, *A Criminal Code for England and Wales* (1989).
[15] See Law Com. No. 311, *Tenth Programme of Law Reform* (2008) para. 1.6: "Rather than specifically referring to codification as the intended outcome . . . [we will seek] to undertake projects to simplify the criminal law. . . . We see this work as the necessary precursor to any attempts to codify the criminal law." See, further, Dennis, "The Law Commission and the Criminal Law: Reflections on the Codification Project" in Dyson, Lee and Stark (eds.), *Fifty Years of the Law Commissions* (2016) 108.
[16] See *Reform of Offences against the Person* (HC 555, 2015).
[17] See *Malicious Damage*, Working Paper No. 23 (1969) paras. 22, 66.
[18] Criminal Damage Act 1971, s. 1(3).
[19] See the discussion of fair labelling above, § 2.4.

merely retained as an aggravating feature of a general offence of theft.[20] At the same time, the past decade has seen an enormous quantity of legislation relating to the criminal law passed without regard for structure, coherence and guiding principles.[21] The role of the judges will, accordingly, be a powerful one for the foreseeable future. We turn now to their role in interpreting criminal legislation.

### *(ii) The interpretation of criminal statutes*

A text of this nature cannot provide more than an overview of the relevant principles regarding the interpretation of criminal statutes. When questions about the meaning of an offence arise, there are three main steps for a court to take.

#### *(a) Ordinary meaning*

In the first instance, the interpretation of a criminal statute need not differ in technique from the interpretation of any other statute. Modern statutory interpretation should first take the form of ascertaining the *ordinary meaning in context*.[22] The reference to context is particularly important. It is a feature of language that meaning is not merely lexical, but also depends on the surrounding words and the purpose of the writer. A crucial issue in one famous criminal trial was the meaning of the statement "Let him have it, Chris".[23] Was this encouragement to hand over a gun, or to fire it? The latter, thought the jury, and a life as well as an argument was lost. Such uncertainties are not confined to vernacular speech. For example, the former section 20(2) of the Theft Act 1968 made it an offence to procure, by deception, the indorsement of a valuable security by another person.[24] On one meaning, to "indorse" something is to express approval of it. But it was quite clear, both from the lexical context (execution of a valuable security) and the purpose of the offence, that the intended meaning was "to assign by writing".

When determining the ordinary meaning of a provision, the judge may be interpreting a text of considerable age, such as the Offences Against the Person Act 1861. Should the judge interpret the statutory wording by reference to its meaning in 1861, or should current usage dictate the understanding of the statute? It may be that the matter is resolved by previous authority—an appellate case in, say, 1937 may have interpreted the term in a manner clearly applicable to the instant case. But what if there is no such authority? Then it seems the meaning the term bears in present-day English is to be applied, even if it is a meaning clearly not contemplated by the legislature back in 1861. As it was put by the House of Lords in *Ireland*,[25] criminal statutes "are always speaking", and the speech is that of the present day.[26] Accordingly, the court in construing the expression "actual bodily

[20] Cp. Ashworth, "Robbery Reassessed" [2002] *Crim LR* 851, 855–7.

[21] This is not a problem limited to England and Wales. See e.g. Husak, *Overcriminalization* (2007).

[22] See, further, Bell and Engle, *Cross on Statutory Interpretation* (3rd ed., 1995) 31–3, chap. 3. For an interesting analysis of this approach to interpretation, and exploration of how it differs from other ideas that are sometimes presented as being identical with it, see Slocum, *Ordinary Meaning* (2015).

[23] The case of Derek Bentley, who was convicted of murder as an accessory and sentenced to death. Bentley received a posthumous pardon and his conviction was eventually quashed: *Bentley* [2001] 1 Cr App R 21.

[24] Repealed by Fraud Act 2006, sched. 3.

[25] [1998] AC 147.

[26] See too *K* [2001] UKHL 41, [2002] 1 AC 462; *R (Smeaton) v Secretary of State for Health* [2002] EWHC 610 (Admin).

harm" for the purposes of section 47 of the OAPA 1861 (assault occasioning actual bodily harm) was able to conclude that psychiatric injury was a form of bodily harm. Similarly, "grievous bodily harm" has been interpreted to include transmission of HIV.[27] Nobody in 1861 would have included these things within the definition of "actual" or "grievous" bodily harm.[28]

Even the best-drafted statute can require interpretive decisions by the court. If grammatical context as well as lexical meaning is addressed, one meaning will usually emerge as clearly the best suited to express the purposes of the statute or the relevant part thereof. Where it does so, there can be no objection, even in the case of a criminal statute, to an interpretative choice that goes against the defendant.[29] For instance, D commits an offence where, without V's consent, he records an image of V's underwear when it is *beneath* V's clothing.[30] In *Barone*,[31] V was lying asleep across a train seat, with her head on her knees. D took a photograph of V's underwear. D argued that the word "beneath" suggested that the image had to be recorded from close to the floor, whereas the photograph he had taken was achieved merely by adjusting his standing position to see past V's feet. The Court of Appeal rejected this argument, on the basis that it "would exclude a case where a person was, for whatever reason, horizontal . . . which makes no sense at all".[32] Although grammatically plausible, D's argued-for interpretation of the word "beneath" was quite properly rejected by the Court as failing to best suit the purpose of the relevant offence (i.e., to address the phenomenon colloquially known as "up-skirting").

When one interpretation of a statutory provision is tenable and preferable to any competing interpretation, there is nothing particular about the interpretation of criminal statutes. The "ordinary meaning in context" prevails.

### *(b) Legislative background*

Sometimes the meaning of a provision cannot be determined by reference to the ordinary meaning of its words in context. In such cases, the courts have limited powers to consider the legislative background of an Act in order to ascertain Parliament's intention.

An illustration of this process is *A-G's Reference (No. 1 of 1988)*,[33] where determining the ordinary meaning of the statutory words in context left the courts with a choice between two meanings, each of which was "ordinary". In the course of a consultation with a merchant bank, D had been informed on confidential terms that X plc was to be the subject of a takeover bid. D acquired shares in X plc in anticipation of the inevitable rise in its share price. This acquisition would have constituted an offence against insider trading legislation, provided D had "obtained" the information. Had D "obtained" inside information? At trial, he argued successfully that he had not, on the basis that the *Oxford English Dictionary* gave

[27] *Dica* [2004] EWCA Crim 1103, [2004] QB 1257; below, § 11.7.

[28] Sometimes, the courts suggest that the "always speaking" nature of statutes only allows a certain degree of judicial latitude in terms of developing the criminal law, beyond which Parliament must come up with any solution: e.g. *R (Monica) v DPP, ex parte Boyling* [2018] EWHC 3508 (Admin), [2019] QB 1019, [85].

[29] *Choudary* [2016] EWCA Crim 61, [2018] 1 WLR 695, [52].

[30] Sexual Offences Act 2003, s. 67A(2). There are other elements to the offence: D must not reasonably believe that V consents, and D must record the image for one of a specified set of purposes (see s. 67A(3)).

[31] [2025] EWCA Crim 125, [2025] 1 WLR 2143.

[32] *Ibid.*, [17].

[33] [1989] AC 971.

"to acquire by endeavour" as the primary meaning of the term. There had been no effort made to obtain this information; D had merely been informed of it while seeking a banker's advice. If this interpretation were correct, the offence of insider dealing would have been confined to those who actively sought out inside information in order to deal. The legislative history and the overall scheme of the Company Securities (Insider Dealing) Act 1985 was, however, strongly suggestive that chance recipients of insider information were within the scheme of the Act where the informant was a corporate "insider" (as the merchant bank clearly was). Accordingly, the House of Lords subsequently adopted "to get, to come by" (the secondary meaning of "obtained" allowed by the *Oxford English Dictionary*) as the meaning to be applied in relation to this offence.

While the history of a statute can certainly be considered as part of the legislative background that can aid interpretation, there are restrictions on the extent to which parliamentary debates can be investigated, at least in the context of criminal law. The well-known case of *Pepper v Hart*[34] recognised an exceptional and limited permission for judges to seek resolution of ambiguity in a statute by reference to statements made by sponsors of the preceding bill. In *Thet v DPP*, Lord Phillips CJ (as he then was) noted that:[35]

> "[Counsel for the Prosecution] was not able to refer the court to any case in which *Pepper v Hart* has been used in [a criminal trial]. If a criminal statute is ambiguous, I would question whether it is appropriate by the use of *Pepper v Hart* to extend the ambit of the statute so as to impose criminal liability upon a defendant where, in the absence of the parliamentary material, the court would not do so. It seems to me at least arguable that if a criminal statute is ambiguous, the defendant should have the benefit of the ambiguity."

For a time, it appeared that these comments pertained only to use of parliamentary materials by the prosecution, i.e. to *extend* the criminal law. Lord Phillips CJ subsequently qualified his remarks in *Tabnak*: "In this case it is the defendant who seeks to apply *Pepper v Hart* in a criminal process and those comments [in *Thet*] may not have the same force".[36] This prosecution/defence-based distinction is consistent with other areas of the criminal law, but is difficult to square with Lord Phillips' opinion in the subsequent case of *JTB*.[37]

In *JTB*, the question to be resolved was whether the defence of *doli incapax* remained available. If the defence was available then, in addition to any relevant mens rea requirements, for any defendant between the ages of 10 and 14, the prosecution would be required to prove the defendant's awareness that his conduct was wrong (should this issue be raised by the defendant). Formerly, there was a rebuttable presumption that such defendants were incapable of knowing right from wrong. This *presumption* of *doli incapax* was clearly abolished by section 34 of the Crime and Disorder Act 1998, but section 34 said nothing about *the defence* itself. None the less, Lord Phillips concluded that the statute's effect was to abolish the defence as well as the presumption. Invoking *Pepper v Hart*, his Lordship perused the parliamentary debates on the bill that led to the 1998 Act and convinced himself that the sponsors of the bill used the term *doli incapax* to refer to the defence as well as the presump-

[34] [1993] AC 593. In terms of the Rule of Law, consultation of such sources as Hansard is unobjectionable provided the source is adequately made available to the public, so that potential defendants have fair warning of its import. See Evans, *Statutory Interpretation* (1988) 289.

[35] [2006] EWHC 2701 (Admin), [2007] 1 WLR 2022, [15]. See, too, *Massey v Boulden* [2002] EWCA Civ 1634, [2003] 1 WLR 1792, [18]–[19].

[36] [2007] EWCA Crim 380, [2007] 1 WLR 1317, [17].

[37] [2009] UKHL 20, [2009] 1 AC 1310.

tion. On that basis, Lord Phillips declared that section 34 had abolished the defence. This is a troubling application of *Pepper v Hart*, particularly in the context of a provision that went against the young defendant's interests.[38] In effect, Lord Phillips invoked *Pepper v Hart* to subvert the plain language of a statute, to the benefit of the prosecution. This is problematic. The distinction in *Thet v DPP* between prosecution and defence use of parliamentary debates should not have been disregarded so lightly.

Whether or not the legislative history is consulted, even for the benefit of the defendant, often depends upon the inclination of judges. In the notorious case of *Caldwell*,[39] to which we return in Chapter 5, Lord Diplock conceded that there was an issue of interpretation in respect of the meaning to be given to the mens rea term, "reckless". He resolved the issue by recourse to "ordinary" English, which informed him that the term comprehended not only defendants who perceived the likely consequences of their conduct, but also defendants who failed to give thought to the obvious risks involved in that conduct. Lord Diplock did not consider a Law Commission report that stated, unequivocally, that only defendants who actually perceived the risk of damaging or destroying property were to be found reckless in cases of criminal damage.[40] Parliament had not intended to adopt a distinct understanding of recklessness when passing the Criminal Damage Act 1971.[41]

Similarly, in *Khan*,[42] resort to a Law Commission report would have informed the Court of Appeal that their decision about the meaning of "intent" for the crime of attempt was contrary to the meaning envisaged by the Commission when proposing the clause that was subsequently adopted, unamended, by Parliament.[43]

The decisions in *Caldwell* and *Khan* are only two of many instances of expansive interpretation of statutory offences unsupported by judicial examination of the policy and legislative history of the offence interpreted. One may even find different judicial approaches in the same case. In *DPP v Gomez*,[44] the minority in the House of Lords consulted the report of the Criminal Law Revision Committee which had formulated the provisions under review in that case, namely sections 1 and 15 of the Theft Act 1968. That consultation resolved any doubts: on the facts of the case there could have been a conviction under section 15 for obtaining property by deception but there was no theft within the terms of section 1. Untroubled by an engagement with the legislative history, the majority found that there had been a theft, reducing, as Sir John Smith put it, "the actus reus of theft almost to vanishing point".[45]

To demonstrate that sometimes consultation of the legislative history of a provision will carry the day, the unanimous Supreme Court in *Golds*[46] consulted a range of sources

[38] Bennion, "Mens Rea and Defendants below the Age of Discretion" [2009] *Crim LR* 757, 766–8.
[39] [1982] AC 341.
[40] Law Com. No. 29, *Report on Offences of Damage to Property* (1970) para. 44. Lord Edmund-Davies also declined to mention this material, preferring to cite a *different* Law Commission paper in his dissenting opinion: *Caldwell* [1982] AC 341, 357–8.
[41] The decision in *Caldwell* was departed from by the House of Lords in *G* [2003] UKHL 50, [2004] 1 AC 1034. In *G*, their Lordships paid careful attention to Parliament's intention: see [12]–[13], [29] (Lord Bingham), [47]–[50] (Lord Steyn), and [63]–[64] (Lord Bridge).
[42] [1990] 1 WLR 813 (CA). Discussed below, § 9.3(iii)(b).
[43] Law Com. No. 102, *Attempt, and Impossibility in Relation to Attempt, Conspiracy and Incitement* (1980) paras. 2.11–8.
[44] [1993] AC 442. Discussed below, § 13.6(ii).
[45] Commentary at [1993] Crim LR 304, 306.
[46] [2016] UKSC 61, [2016] 1 WLR 5231.

(including the Law Commission's preparatory work) relating to the updating of the defence of diminished responsibility in the Coroners and Justice Act 2009, in order to determine what the word "substantial" meant (a lot, not just more than *de minimis*).[47] Similarly, in *Ivey v Genting Casinos (t/a Crockfords Club)*,[48] the legislative background to the Theft Act 1968 was consulted to clarify the meaning of "dishonesty" in criminal law (albeit that *Ivey* itself was a civil case).

*(c) Constitutional and international law presumptions*

Where, having considered ordinary meaning in context and legislative history, multiple alternative interpretations of a criminal provision are available, an interpretation that conforms to the Rule of Law's requirements of legality and non-retrospectivity,[49] and to the requirements of the ECHR, should be preferred. In general, as we saw in Chapter 2, these presumptions do not override parliamentary legislation: they can be rebutted by the explicit and inescapable language of a statute, which is why a declaration of incompatibility is available to the courts.[50]

In terms of international law, where there is ambiguity in the wording of a statutory offence, the terms of any relevant treaty conventions, and no doubt other sources of international law, can be considered as interpretive aids. Thus there is a rebuttable presumption that domestic law complies with the nation's international obligations:[51]

> "where there is a relevant treaty or ratified convention courts when free to do so will interpret statutory provisions in such a way as to comply with the United Kingdom's international obligations, but that cannot be done when the statutory words are clear, and were enacted in full knowledge of the Convention obligations".

International law cannot, then, effect the repeal of domestic crimes, although it may influence the construction of our substantive law. Under certain circumstances our international obligations can, however, have a procedural impact, and it may be an abuse of process (leading to the permanent cessation of proceedings) to prosecute defendants for conduct that the state was obliged under international law not to criminalise.[52]

Conversely, international criminal law does not directly create crimes in domestic law—they must be imported by specific legislation. Thus, under section 51 of the International Criminal Court Act 2001, it is an offence under domestic English and Welsh law to commit genocide, a crime against humanity or a war crime. Other crimes recognised by international law, such as the crime of aggression, are not offences in England and Wales.[53]

Now that the United Kingdom has exited the European Union, no new offences will be created directly or indirectly by EU law, and no fresh decisions of the Court of Justice of the European Union (CJEU) will bind UK courts. That said, a large number of offences created during the UK's membership of the EU remain in force.[54] Furthermore, decisions by the

[47] See below, § 10.6(ii)(c).
[48] [2017] UKSC 67, [2018] AC 391; below, § 13.8(iv).
[49] Cp. *B (A Minor) v DPP* [2000] 2 AC 428, 470 (Lord Steyn).
[50] Above, § 2.5(i).
[51] *Navabi* [2005] EWCA Crim 2865, [28]; cf. *R (Pepushi) v CPS* [2004] EWHC 798 (Admin), [33].
[52] *Asfaw* [2008] UKHL 31, [2008] 1 AC 1061; *L* [2013] EWCA Crim 991, [2014] 1 All ER 113.
[53] *Jones* [2006] UKHL 16, [2007] 1 AC 136; *R (Al-Rabbat) v City of Westminster Magistrates' Court* [2017] EWHC 1969 (Admin), [2018] 1 WLR 2009.
[54] See, however, the mass repeal effected by the Retained EU Law (Revocation and Reform) Act 2023, s. 1.

CJEU made before the end of the transition period (the end of 2020) will continue to be considered by (and bind lower) UK courts, even if the Court of Appeal and the Supreme Court may now depart from them.[55] To this extent, EU law continues to have some relevance to the interpretation of criminal offences in English law.

### (d) *Strict construction*

Finally if, after examining the ordinary meaning of the words used, the statutory context and its background (including the presumptions and obligations mentioned in the foregoing section), there is still some uncertainty about which interpretation is preferable, then the court should give the benefit of that uncertainty to the defendant: "If a penal provision is reasonably capable of two interpretations, that interpretation which is most favourable to the accused must be adopted."[56]

This is a presumption of strict construction of criminal statutes. It is justified primarily by the requirement to give fair warning,[57] which implies that ambiguity in offences should not be construed so as to generate unpredictable criminal liability. Statutes should not require citizens to guess at their meaning, and so should be construed against imposing liability upon a defendant who reasonably could have thought that she was within the terms of the law.

Fair warning is not the entire rationale for the presumption of strict construction. Its origins are to be found in judicial interpretations *in favorem vitae* ("in favour of life") in times where the number of capital offences was very large:[58] a particularly sharp version of the more general value of parsimony in punishment. As such, the presumption encourages judicial restraint when interpreting not only offences but also defences (and not merely justificatory defences, such as self-defence and necessity, which may guide conduct). Altering the scope of defences alters the scope of criminal liability. Accordingly, it is debatable whether Hughes LJ (as he then was) was correct to dismiss the relevance of strict construction when ruling on the ambit of the partial-defence of diminished responsibility in *Dowds*.[59] This is particularly so because he cited, in support of this approach, the controversial decision of the House of Lords in *JTB*.[60] As noted in § 3.1(ii)(b), a reading of a legislative provision, which the Appellate Committee considered tenable and would have been to the defendant's benefit, was rejected.

In the past, the principle of strict construction has sometimes been read as entailing that the benefit of *any* favourable interpretation which passes a minimal threshold of plausibility must always be given to the defendant.[61] Yet, as Lord Reid recognised in *DPP v Ottewell*,[62] this approach is untenable. A lexically possible meaning should not be adopted

55 European Union (Withdrawal) Act 2018, s. 6; European Union (Withdrawal) Act 2018 (Relevant Court) (Retained EU Case Law) Regulations 2020 (SI 2020/1525), art. 3. "Retained EU Case Law" is now to be referred to as "assimilated case law": Retained EU Law (Revocation and Reform) Act 2023, s. 5.

56 *Sweet v Parsley* [1970] AC 132, 149 (Lord Reid). See, similarly, *Passmore* [2007] EWCA Crim 2053, [2008] 1 Cr App R 12, [18].

57 Above, § 2.3.

58 *CLGP*, 586–92.

59 *Dowds* [2012] EWCA Crim 281, [2012] 1 WLR 2576, [36].

60 [2009] UKHL 20, [2009] 1 AC 1310.

61 E.g. *Harris* (1836) 7 C & P 446, 173 ER 198.

62 [1970] AC 642; cf. *Tuck & Sons v Priester* (1887) 19 QBD 629, 638, where Lord Esher MR required that the favourable alternative must be a "reasonable construction".

if the statutory context makes clear that an alternative interpretation is best suited to the purposes of the statute:[63]

> "The Court of Appeal (Criminal Division) refer to the well-established principle that in doubtful cases a penal provision ought to be given that interpretation which is least unfavourable to the accused. I would never seek to diminish in any way the importance of that principle within its proper sphere. But it only applies where after full inquiry and consideration one is left in real doubt. It is not enough that the provision is ambiguous in the sense that it is capable of having two meanings. The imprecision of the English language (and, so far as I am aware, of any other language) is such that it is extremely difficult to draft any provision which is not ambiguous in that sense. This section is clearly ambiguous in that sense: the Court of Appeal (Criminal Division) attach one meaning to it, and your Lordships are attaching a different meaning to it. But if, after full consideration, your Lordships are satisfied, as I am, that the latter is the meaning which Parliament must have intended the words to convey, then this principle does not prevent us from giving effect to our conclusions."

As a subsidiary principle, then, strict construction is and should be retained in modern criminal law.[64] Nonetheless, it is fair to say that the courts have come to treat the rule of strict construction as one of "last resort",[65] and sometimes have failed to apply it even in a case where it was appropriate. As Glanville Williams observes:[66]

> "The courts cannot manufacture statutes as they manufacture precedents, but they can 'interpret' them. They can cut them down, or expand them. Courts still pay lip-service to the ancient principle that in case of doubt a criminal statute is to be 'strictly construed' in favour of the defendant; but the principle is rarely applied in practice, if there are social reasons for convicting. Indeed, we may make bold to say that the looser the defendant's conduct, the more loosely the judges construe the statute designed to control him."

Indeed.[67] Sometimes, the Rule of Law is displaced by the discretionary rule of individual judges. In *DPP v Gomez*,[68] for example, D was convicted of theft, contrary to section 1 of the Theft Act 1968, on the basis that he had "appropriated" property that he had deceived V into giving him. The conduct was a plain case of obtaining by deception, contrary to section 15 of the same Act. The House of Lords upheld D's conviction for theft, notwithstanding that the "appropriation" was authorised by V and rested upon a construction that wrenched the crime of theft away from (i) a reasonable alternative meaning more favourable to D,[69] which was also (ii) its intended meaning,[70] and (iii) had been unequivocally embraced in an earlier decision by the House of Lords.[71] The problem arose only because D had been charged, inappropriately, with theft rather than obtaining by deception. Their Lordships

[63] *DPP v Ottewell* [1970] AC 642, 649.

[64] Not merely in England and Wales: *Barker* (1983) 153 CLR 338, 350 (Murphy J).

[65] *R (Junttan Oy) v Bristol Magistrates' Court* [2003] UKHL 55, [2004] 2 All ER 555, [84] (Lord Steyn): "If it has a role to play it is as a rule of last resort: it is only to be applied if all other grounds of determining legislative intent have failed."

[66] *TBCL* 12. Cf. Smith, "Codification of the Criminal Law" (1987) 2 *Denning LJ* 137, 143–4.

[67] Compare, e.g., *Duncalf* [1979] 1 WLR 918 (CA); *Delgado* [1984] 1 WLR 89 (CA); *R (Junttan Oy) v Bristol Magistrates' Court* [2003] UKHL 55, [2004] 2 All ER 555, [84] (Lord Steyn): "In the present context there is at stake a cogent countervailing legal policy: the protection of health and safety at work is of overriding importance."

[68] [1993] AC 442, discussed below, § 13.6(ii).

[69] Compare *Hinks* [2001] 2 AC 241, where, unlike *Gomez*, D would otherwise have committed no offence at all.

[70] Cp. Lord Lowry's dissent in *Gomez*.

[71] *Morris* [1984] AC 320.

therefore had the alternatives of acquitting altogether a man obviously guilty of the offence under section 15, or of distorting the law of theft. Convicting one dishonest person was, apparently, more important.

Sometimes, then, the courts disregard the principle of strict construction in cases to which it ought to apply. When they do so, they go wrong. The principle *is* a part of English law, where it operates as a residual doctrine of construction in the way we have described. Moreover, it *ought* not to be ignored. The principle is an important means of upholding the Rule of Law, by making sure that the defendant has fair warning of the scope of the relevant offence, and that (in a case like *Gomez*, where D was plainly guilty of something else)[72] his wrongdoing is fairly labelled. If, after considering ordinary meaning, context and legislative history, a criminal prohibition is reasonably capable of being interpreted in two different ways, the defendant *must* be given the benefit of the doubt. Indeed, as was suggested in Chapter 2, in our view the principle is mandated by Article 7 of the ECHR.[73] A strict approach to construction helps to prevent criminal liability from coming as a surprise to defendants. It ensures that the scope of an offence extends only to those cases where its application, *ex ante*, was clear and predictable. If this approach results in unwanted acquittals, then it is open to Parliament to remedy the problem by amending the relevant law (prospectively).

#### *(e) Summary*

We have argued that the correct approach to statutory interpretation is first to seek the ordinary meaning in context. Where the meaning of a phrase emerges clearly from the context and purpose of the statute, that meaning should be adopted even though it goes against the defendant. Otherwise, if the meaning is not apparent from the Act or the relevant part of the Act, a review of the legislative history should be undertaken. Relevant constitutional presumptions, international rules and (to the extent they remain relevant) EU laws should also be considered. If, at the end of that process, the interpretation of the provision remains a matter of reasonable dispute, the defendant should be given the benefit of the doubt. In practice, as we noted above, the approach argued for here is sometimes vulnerable to judges minded to override interpretive uncertainty in the interests of crime-control. Such vulnerability is unfortunate. Compromising the Rule of Law for the sake of short-term policy objectives (let alone to reach the "right" result in a particular case) is improper adjudication.

#### *(f) The obvious drafting error?*

The above states what we contend is the correct general approach to interpreting criminal statutes. There is apparently one exception—although, in our view, it involves a regrettable compromise of the Rule of Law. The exception concerns the correction of an "obvious drafting error". Consider the case of *R (CPS) v Bow Street Magistrates Court and Others*.[74] There, the defendants were charged under the Identity Cards Act 2006 with possessing a false passport on 4 April 2006. This was formerly an offence under section 5 of the Forgery and Counterfeiting Act 1981.[75] Section 44(2) of the short-lived Identity Cards Act 2006, which

[72] See Shute and Horder, "Thieving and Deceiving: What is the Difference?" (1993) 56 *MLR* 548.
[73] See above, §§ 2.2–3.
[74] [2006] EWHC 1763 (Admin), [2007] 1 WLR 291.
[75] See, now, Identity Documents Act 2010, ss. 4, 6.

came into force on 30 March 2006,[76] repealed the 1981 Act's offences. It was intended that the 1981 offences would be replaced by corresponding provisions in sections 25 and 26 of the 2006 Act. Those new provisions had not, however, themselves come into force by 4 April 2006, because there had not yet been any commencement order. Such an order was necessary because section 44(3) of the 2006 Act suspended the coming into force of most of that Act, although not of section 44 itself:

> This Act (apart from this section and sections 36 and 38) shall come into force on such day as the Secretary of State may by order appoint; and different days may be appointed for different purposes.

There was certainly a slip-up here. By section 44(3), section 44(2) came into force on 30 March 2006 to repeal the offence charged under the 1981 Act; but the replacement offences did not come into force on the same date. Technically, then, the defendants had been convicted of an offence that did not exist at the time they apparently committed it. The Divisional Court nevertheless ruled that their convictions were properly returned. Section 44(3) was interpreted to read as follows:[77]

> This Act (apart from this section, *other than subsection (2) hereof*, and sections 36 and 38) shall come into force on such day as the Secretary of State may by order appoint; and different days may be appointed for different purposes.

The House of Lords laid down three criteria which must be met before such a corrective intervention can be made in *Inco Europe Ltd and others v First Choice Distribution (a Firm) and Others*:[78]

> "This power is confined to plain cases of drafting mistakes. The courts are ever mindful that their constitutional role in this field is interpretative. They must abstain from any course which might have the appearance of judicial legislation. A statute is expressed in language approved and enacted by the legislature. So the courts exercise considerable caution before adding or omitting or substituting words. Before interpreting a statute in this way the court must be abundantly sure of three matters: (1) the intended purpose of the statute or provision in question; (2) that by inadvertence the draftsman and Parliament failed to give effect to that purpose in the provision in question; and (3) the substance of the provision Parliament would have made, although not necessarily the precise words Parliament would have used, had the error in the Bill been noticed."

No doubt those criteria were met in *R (CPS) v Bow Street Magistrates Court and Others*. But *Inco Europe* was a civil case, not a criminal one, and the House of Lords emphasised this point:[79]

> "Sometimes, even when these conditions are met, the court may find itself inhibited from interpreting the statutory provision in accordance with what it is satisfied was the underlying intention of Parliament. The alteration in language may be too far-reaching. . . . Or the subject matter may call for a strict interpretation of the statutory language, as in penal legislation. None of these considerations apply in the present case. Here, the court is able to give effect to a construction of the statute which accords with the intention of the legislature."

[76] The 2006 Act was itself repealed in its entirety by s. 1 of the Identity Documents Act 2010.
[77] See *R (CPS) v Bow Street Magistrates' Court* [2006] EWHC 1763 (Admin), [2007] 1 WLR 291, [44].
[78] [2000] 1 WLR 586, 592 (Lord Nicholls).
[79] *Ibid.*, 592–3.

In construing the Identity Cards Act 2006 in the manner it did, the Divisional Court in *R (CPS) v Bow Street Magistrates Court and Others* wrongly discounted this qualification.[80] Civil law contains no direct equivalent of the *nullum crimen* rule (discussed earlier in §§ 2.1–2). In the criminal law, it is not appropriate to read words into a statute to create an offence that, on the clear meaning of the statute when applying the correct approach outlined on the pages above, does not exist. The "obvious error" rule in *Inco Europe* should be confined to the civil law, and thankfully does not seem to have acted to a criminal defendant's detriment since *R (CPS) v Bow Street Magistrates Court and Others.*

### *(iii) Interpretation and development of common law offences*

Contrasts are frequently made between statutory interpretation, on the one hand, and the creation and development of the common law, on the other. Despite the importance of statutory law for vast tracts of English law, statutes, on this view, do not become part of a general body of law, organically linked to the other statutory and common law norms that already occupy the relevant legal domain. Each statute remains a thing apart, to be interpreted within its own four corners and legislative history and not to be used as a means of extrapolation and analogy for the treatment of issues that do not arise under the statute itself. By contrast, the common law is said to be an entity which subsumes its constituent parts, thereby allowing ideas developed in one branch of the common law to be deployed freely in other branches should cognate issues arise. The self-confident and conscious development of common law rules and doctrines finds no counterpart in statutory interpretation.[81]

Although that account risks parody, it contains a core of truth: for the civil law. The criminal law is different. The criminal branch of the common law is essentially a realm apart.[82] It has not been integrated with contract and property; or even, to any significant extent, with the law of tort.[83] In the criminal law, a comparison between statutory interpretation and the development and interpretation of common law crimes reveals parallel tendencies toward expansive interpretation, usually done in the interests of crime control. One point of difference is that the common law contained rules of such breadth and imprecision that expansive interpretation frequently was not required. In effect, the common law was there ready and waiting to rubber-stamp a prosecutor's decision to proceed.

[80] The Court dealt with the point by opining that the novel construction of s. 44(3) of the 2006 Act did "not inflict any detriment or greater detriment" upon any of the defendants or any other person, because it merely continued the existing law until its replacement by the new provisions, and that no increase in penalty was involved at any stage ([2006] EWHC 1763 (Admin), [2007] 1 WLR 291, [47]–[48]). But of course it did: the interposition of words created an offence where there was otherwise none.

[81] See the classic article by Pound, "Common Law and Legislation" (1907) 21 *Harv LR* 383. The contrast still retains substance, but statutes are no longer treated so circumspectly as formerly they were. As Atiyah has demonstrated ("Common Law and Statute Law" (1985) 48 *MLR* 1), statutes may be used by judges as sources of analogy and policy for legal development generally, though this tends to occur on a haphazard, *ad hoc*, basis. For an example, see *Jogee* [2016] UKSC 8, Jogee; Ruddock, [2017] AC 387, [86] (Lord Toulson), where the Serious Crime Act 2007's provisions on encouraging or assisting crime were thought instructive with regard to the (common) law on accessorial liability.

[82] "The miserable history of crime in England can be shortly told. There is no achievement to trace. Nothing worthwhile was created." With these words, Milsom introduces a chapter in which he demonstrates, by contrast with the rest of the common law, the impoverished development and lack of resources of the law of crime: *Historical Foundations of the Common Law* (2nd ed., 1981) 403.

[83] For interesting essays on this subject, see Dyson (ed.), *Unravelling Tort and Crime* (2014).

Perhaps the best illustration of the flexibility of common law crimes is the common-law version of conspiracy—an agreement between two or more persons to effect some unlawful purpose.[84] Left to judicial devices, "unlawful" was allowed free rein and led to the criminalisation of agreements to do actions which, if done by individuals acting alone, would not have been criminal. This freedom was exercised to large and controversial effect,[85] and at the price of the Rule of Law, until finally limited by the Criminal Law Act 1977.[86] Even so, "elasticity" was not completely forsworn. Common law conspiracies to defraud,[87] to corrupt public morality, and to outrage public decency were retained by the 1977 Act pending their replacement by narrower, statutory offences (which never occurred). These forms of conspiracy are still in rude health, although it is now accepted that their expansion, if any, should be by marginal steps only.[88]

A similar example is the former catch-all offence of "public mischief". In *Manley*,[89] a prosecution was launched against D for deliberately wasting police time. In the absence of anything more suitable to hand, the Court of Criminal Appeal approved the trial judge's resurrection of the offence, a "public mischief" being anything injurious to the public interest. It is perhaps unnecessary to emphasise the extent to which such an offence undermines any aspiration to fair warning[90] in the criminal law. Happily, the offence was infrequently resorted to and eventually consigned to legal history by the House of Lords in *DPP v Withers*.[91]

Whatever criticisms may be made of modern parliaments, it is doubtful whether offences based on phrases so nebulous, extensible, and threatening[92] as "public mischief" or "corrupting public morality" would survive the modern legislative process. Yet even modern parliaments seem disinclined to abolish established, widely phrased offences.[93] In a modern democracy, judges should not have available to them such untrammelled power. Yet we have seen that the phrasing of modern statutes is not always a sufficient constraint on judicial activism,[94] and it seems the internal resources of the criminal law are an insufficient bulwark.

[84] Wright, *Law of Criminal Conspiracies and Agreements* (1873) 63–5.

[85] E.g. *Kamara v DPP* [1974] AC 104.

[86] See below, § 9.2.

[87] Below, § 15.9. Remarkably the Fraud Act 2006, which creates a general fraud offence, does not abolish common law conspiracy to defraud. We can assume that this protean and widely prosecuted offence will be with us for the indefinite future, though it will apparently no longer be extended to criminalise novel forms of activity: *Norris v USA* [2008] UKHL 16, [2008] 1 AC 920.

[88] "If the ambit of a common law offence is to be enlarged, it 'must be done step by step on a case by case basis and not with one large leap'": *Rimmington and Goldstein* [2005] UKHL 63, [2006] 1 AC 459, [33] (Lord Bingham), citing *Clark (Mark)* [2003] EWCA Crim 991, [2003] 2 Cr App R 23, [13]. In the specific context of common law conspiracy to defraud, see *Norris v USA* [2008] UKHL 16, [2008] 1 AC 920; below, § 15.9(iii)(a).

[89] [1933] 1 KB 529 (CCA).

[90] And fair labelling: above, § 2.4.

[91] [1975] AC 842.

[92] Potentially, such phrases permit criminalisation on the basis of immorality rather than harm or offence: see below, § 16.3.

[93] As can be seen in the omission by the Fraud Act 2006 to abolish common law conspiracy to defraud, when reforming the law of fraud. See below, § 15.1.

[94] The *existence* of a statutory offence may, however, displace its common-law antecedent: *Rimmington and Goldstein* [2005] UKHL 63, [2006] 1 AC 459, [30] (Lord Bingham). The interpretation of common-law offences is also subject to international law norms that constrain the construction of statutes: above, § 3.1(ii)(c).

The need for restraint is pressing.[95] Judicial activism is readily visible in cases such as *Ireland*.[96] For hundreds of years, an assault required the threat of imminent violence; that is, the threat of some immediate, unwanted bodily contact. Remarkably, the House of Lords found that this condition could be satisfied in a case involving silent phone calls, despite the caller's being miles away from his victim. As we will see in Chapter 11, the reasoning of the House does not convince. Also remarkably, this decision was reached despite the fact that such conduct would (if repeated) have contravened sections 1 and 2 of the Protection from Harassment Act 1997. Yet the House reached its interpretation not merely to avoid an acquittal in the instant case. It also considered that the penalties provided by the new Act were insufficient and that recourse to the greater penalties provided by the sanctions for aggravated assaults was required. Accordingly, their Lordships decided to customise centuries of common law in order to circumnavigate the new Act. Such judicial activism is undesirable in the context of the criminal law.

Even more problematic is the decision in *Ivey v Genting Casinos (t/a Crockfords Club)*.[97] This was a civil case about, essentially, whether a person who had cheated in a casino was entitled to his winnings. The Supreme Court delved deep into the criminal law's understanding of the word "dishonest", which is employed in a range of property and economic offences.[98] Ultimately, the conclusion was reached that the Court of Appeal (Criminal Division) had made a mistake in the 1982 decision in *Ghosh*,[99] where it had decided that not only must the defendant's conduct be dishonest according to the standards of "reasonable and honest people", but the defendant must additionally *realise* this. In *Ivey*, it was decided that this "subjective" requirement of awareness of the dishonest nature of one's conduct (according to the "objective" standard of the "reasonable and honest people") should be dispensed with. This ruling deprives defendants, in theory, of an argument that could have secured their acquittal, thereby expanding the scope of criminal liability. As this development took place in the context of a civil case, the Supreme Court gave precious little thought to the requirements of fair warning, and Article 7 of the ECHR was not even mentioned. The Court of Appeal (Criminal Division) has since accepted that the Supreme Court can indeed overrule Court of Appeal decisions, even on the criminal law, via sufficiently explicit *obiter dicta*.[100] In so doing, it paid short shrift to Article 7 arguments, notwithstanding that the change in *Ivey* could scarcely be described as predictable, and that it retrospectively widens the scope of criminal liability.[101]

Judicial activism is arguably less problematic when it results in a radical cut-back of criminal liability, which initially seemed likely in the context of accessories following the abolition of the "joint enterprise" doctrine by the Supreme Court in *Jogee*.[102] When there is a joint enterprise to commit one crime, as when P and S agree to burgle the house of V,

95 See, generally, Stark, "Judicial Development of the Criminal Law by the Supreme Court" (2021) 41 *OJLS* 1.
96 [1998] AC 147. See above, § 2.3; below, § 11.2(i)(c).
97 [2017] UKSC 67, [2018] AC 391.
98 See below, § 13.8(iv).
99 [1982] QB 1053 (CA).
100 *Barton* [2020] EWCA Crim 575, [2021] QB 685, [104].
101 *Ibid.*, [117]–[124]; *Bermingham* [2020] EWCA Crim 1662, [2021] 4 WLR 113, [100]–[103]. For critical commentary on this line of case law, see Lamond, "Precedent in English Criminal Law" in Simester (ed.), *Modern Criminal Law* (2024) 287.
102 [2016] UKSC 8; [2017] AC 387. See below, § 7.5.

and burglary is the only crime committed, the fact of joint enterprise does not affect the application of the normal rules relating to complicity. But, if in the course of the burglary, P should kill V with the mens rea for murder, S too was, at least prior to the decision in *Jogee*, also guilty of murder provided that he had foreseen a possibility of P's collateral offence (i.e. that P would deliberately inflict serious violence on V).[103] For the Supreme Court in *Jogee*, the law that allowed S to be convicted of murder on this basis was simply "wrong" and should not be applied in any future case. This "error" was, the Court held, made first by the Privy Council,[104] then in two unanimous decisions by the appellate committee of the House of Lords,[105] and accepted in an earlier Supreme Court decision.[106] But it was not an error in terms of precedent. There was no binding authority that barred the adoption of foresight of possibility as the culpability for offences collateral to the joint enterprise. Those earlier decisions, that is to say, were not *per incuriam*. The Supreme Court's account of history in *Jogee and Ruddock* is deeply unpersuasive.[107] Furthermore, the zeal of the Supreme Court to correct what it regards as "mistakes" should properly be restricted to findings that previous authorities were *per incuriam* or to formal invocations of the power contained in its Practice Directions to depart from previous decisions of the Supreme Court and the House of Lords.[108] *Jogee* may be activism in a good cause, but it is radical activism none the less.

## § 3.2 The burden of proving actus reus and mens rea

In Chapter 1, we argued that convicting an innocent person would be seriously to defame him. Punishing him, of course, compounds the wrong. Because criminal liability is so serious, every citizen has the right not to have the state inflict such liability on him unless he is, in fact, guilty. That right is fundamental: it is profoundly wrong for the state to mistreat an innocent person, and to do so breaches one of the keystones of an individual's relationship with the state. When the state brands someone a criminal, it therefore needs to be sure that it is right—or at least, in the absence of omniscience and unlimited resources, as sure as it can be.[109] For that reason, there is a basic presumption in English law that the defendant in

[103] It was unnecessary for S to foresee that P would *kill* V. See below, § 7.4(iv)(c) (What count as essential matters in murder?).
[104] *Chan Wing-Siu* [1985] AC 168 (PC).
[105] *Powell and English* [1999] 1 AC 1; *Rahman* [2008] UKHL 45, [2009] 1 AC 129.
[106] *Gnango* [2011] UKSC 59, [2012] 1 AC 827.
[107] See, further: Simester, "Accessory Liability and Common Unlawful Purpose" (2017) 133 *LQR* 73, 87–90; Stark, "The Demise of 'Parasitic Accessorial Liability': Substantive Judicial Law Reform, Not Common Law Housekeeping" (2016) 75 *CLJ* 550.
[108] Direction 3.1.3 states that that the terms of the Supreme Court's power to depart from its own decisions and from decisions of the House of Lords will be on the same terms as previously employed by the House of Lords when it empowered itself to depart from its own decisions: Practice Statement (Judicial Precedent) [1966] 1 WLR 1234; cp. *Austin v Mayor and Burgesses of the London Borough of Southwark* [2010] UKSC 28, [2011] 1 AC 355, [24]–[25]. It is worth noting that Direction 3.1.3 requires appellants to give notice if they are to ask the Supreme Court to depart from any of its own decisions or from decisions of the House of Lords so that an enlarged panel of Justices may be convened. No such panel was convened in *Jogee*. See, further, Sullivan, "Law Reform in the Supreme Court" in Krebs (ed.), *Accessorial Liability after* Jogee (2020); Stark, "*Jogee* and the Mechanics of Criminal Law Development" in Graham and Russell (eds.), *Public Law and the Supreme Court* (2025) 46.
[109] Cp. the judgment of Brennan J in *Re Winship* 397 US 358 (1970).

a trial is innocent until proved guilty. On our view, then, the presumption of innocence is not only an answer to the practical question of who must prove what;[110] it is, principally, a response to moral concerns about improper conviction, stigmatisation and punishment.[111] The presumption of innocence is, accordingly, a pervasive and important issue that straddles the divides between evidential, procedural, and substantive law.

The presumption of innocence is codified in Article 6(2) of the ECHR, which provides that a person "charged with a criminal offence shall be presumed innocent until proved guilty according to the law".[112] In the words of the ECtHR:[113]

> "Paragraph 2 embodies the principle of the presumption of innocence. It requires, *inter alia*, that when carrying out their duties, the members of a court should not start with the preconceived idea that the accused has committed the offence charged; the burden of proof is on the prosecution, and any doubt should benefit the accused. It also follows that it is for the prosecution to inform the accused of the case that will be made against him, so that he may prepare and present his defence accordingly, and to adduce evidence sufficient to convict him."

None of this is novel. The presumption of innocence predates the ECHR, and has been a part of English common law at least since *Woolmington v DPP*.[114] In *Woolmington*, a murder case, the trial judge relied on earlier authorities to direct the jury that, once the prosecution had proved that the defendant had killed the deceased, mens rea could be presumed and it was up to the defendant to "satisfy" the jury either that mens rea (the intention to kill or cause serious harm) was absent and the killing had been accidental, or that the killing had been justified (for instance, by self-defence). On this view, the prosecution had to prove only the actus reus, and the burden then lay on the defendant to prove either the lack of mens rea or the existence of a defence. Not so, said the House of Lords:[115]

> "Throughout the web of the English Criminal Law one golden thread is always to be seen, that it is the duty of the prosecution to prove the prisoner's guilt. . . . If, at the end of and on the whole of the case, there is a reasonable doubt, created by the evidence given by either the prosecution or the prisoner, as to whether the prisoner killed the deceased with a malicious intention, the prosecution has not made out the case and the prisoner is entitled to an acquittal. No matter what the charge or where the trial, the principle that the prosecution must prove the guilt of the prisoner is part of the common law of England and no attempt to whittle it down can be entertained."

[110] Cf. Picinali, "The Presumption of Innocence: A Deflationary Account" (2021) 84 *MLR* 708.

[111] See Tomlin, "Extending the Golden Thread? Criminalisation and the Presumption of Innocence" (2013) 21 *Journal of Political Philosophy* 44, 48–52. Cp. Duff's characterisation of (at least one form of) the presumption of innocence as an appropriate form of "civic trust" ("Who Must Presume Whom to be Innocent of What?" (2013) 42 *Netherlands J Legal Philosophy* 170) and Yu's characterisation of the presumption as a "practical" one concerned with how the state ought to relate to individuals ("Putting the Presumption back in the Presumption of Innocence" (2023) 26 *E&P* 342).

[112] It is important to note that the word "charged" (which determines the scope of Article 6(2)) is given a specific meaning in the ECtHR's jurisprudence. The jurisprudence on this point was considered at length in *R (Hallam) v Secretary of State for Justice* [2019] UKSC 2, [2020] AC 279. It is clear that the Supreme Court found some of the ECtHR's decisions on this issue surprising, to put it mildly, and the ECtHR ultimately revisited its jurisprudence in *Nealon v UK* (2024) 79 EHRR 22.

[113] *Barberà, Messegué and Jabardo v Spain* (1989) 11 EHRR 360, [77].

[114] [1935] AC 462.

[115] [1935] AC 462, 481–2 (Viscount Sankey LC). See also *Mancini v DPP* [1942] AC 1, 11–2 (Viscount Simon LC).

It was not for the defendant to demonstrate that the actus reus was an accident; the prosecution must establish mens rea beyond reasonable doubt.

(It should be noted that juries are no longer directed in terms of beyond reasonable doubt. Instead, they are instructed by the trial judge that they must be "sure" of the defendant's guilt.[116] These terms are, apparently, synonymous.[117])

The effect of *Woolmington* may be summarised in the following steps:

(i) The prosecution has the *legal (or "persuasive") burden* to bring evidence which prima facie proves all actus reus and mens rea elements of the offence *beyond reasonable doubt*.

(ii) Once the prosecution has done so, it is then open to the defendant either to raise a reasonable doubt about the evidence the prosecution has brought, or to point to some further evidence which raises a doubt whether the prosecution's evidence is in fact sufficient to prove both actus reus[118] and mens rea beyond reasonable doubt.

(iii) Alternatively, if the prosecution proves both actus reus and mens rea, the defendant has an *evidential burden* to raise any evidence which suggests the credible possibility of a defence.[119] If he does so, or if the evidence introduced by the prosecution does so,[120] then the prosecution incurs the *legal* burden of proving beyond reasonable doubt that the relevant defence is not available in this case.[121] These propositions apply to common law defences with the exception of insanity; there is also an exception for statutory defences. We will consider these exceptions below.

For instance, if D is charged with murdering V, the default position is that the prosecution must prove the elements of murder beyond reasonable doubt: i.e. that (i) D killed V and (ii) D intended to kill, or at least cause serious injury. If D presents evidence that he acted in self-defence (e.g. his own testimony or that of a defence witness), or

[116] Picton et al (eds.), *The Crown Court Compendium: Part I* (2025), § 5(2). On the difficulties of instructing juries on this standard, see Picinali, "The Threshold Lies in the Method: Instructing Jurors about Reasoning Beyond Reasonable Doubt" (2015) 19 *E&P* 139.

[117] Cf. Keane and McKeown, "Time to Abandon 'Beyond Reasonable Doubt' and 'Sure'" [2019] *Crim LR* 505; McKeown, "The Crown Court Compendium and the Criminal Standard of Proof: Suggestions to Aid Juror Comprehension and Help Judges" [2022] *Crim LR* 893; McKeown, Keane and Stares, "Comprehension of 'Sure' as the Description of the Criminal Standard of Proof—An Empirical Study" [2025] *Crim LR* 518.

[118] This includes claims of involuntariness or automatism: *Bratty v A-G for Northern Ireland* [1963] AC 386, 406–7 (Viscount Kilmuir LC), 413–14 (Lord Denning). See below, § 4.3.

[119] *Lobell* [1957] 1 QB 547, 551 (self-defence) (CCA); *Gill* [1963] 1 WLR 841, 845–7 (duress) (CCA). The evidential burden to introduce defences differs from the option to refute evidence of actus reus or mens rea in step (ii). The latter is sometimes called a *tactical burden* on the defendant (referring to the tactical imperative to combat the prosecution's evidence that the offence elements are present). The difference is that, where there is an evidential burden on D to suggest (e.g.) a defence, its absence will be *presumed* by the court unless D discharges that burden. By contrast, a tactical burden involves no presumption. Thus, D may choose not to respond to the prosecution's evidence of actus reus and mens rea, and simply hope that the jury is not convinced by it.

[120] Thus the defence must be considered even if the defendant has not raised it himself: *Palmer v R.* [1971] AC 814, 823 (Lord Morris) (PC); *Wheeler* [1967] 1 WLR 1531, 1533–4 (CA); *Hamand* (1986) 82 Cr App R 65. The same principle applies to partial defences to murder: *Coutts* [2006] UKHL 39, [2006] 1 WLR 2154, [14] (Lord Bingham).

[121] *Lobell* [1957] 1 QB 547 (CA); *Gill* [1963] 2 All ER 688 (CA); *Chan Kau v R* [1955] AC 206, 211 (PC); *Mancini v DPP* [1942] AC 1.

can point to prosecution evidence that raises the issue of self-defence (e.g. testimony by a prosecution witness), then the prosecution will have to prove beyond reasonable doubt that D did *not* act in self-defence. An acquittal should follow if D may: (i) not have killed V; or (ii) not have intended to kill or cause serious injury; or (iii) have acted in self-defence.

The defendant in a criminal trial never has to prove that he is innocent.[122] The jury[123] may think that he is untrustworthy, and be unconvinced by his story. But, save in the exceptional cases of insanity and relevant statutory defences, if the jury thinks there is a reasonable possibility that he is not guilty of the crime charged, the defendant must be acquitted. As the Privy Council put it, in *Jayasena v R.*, "the only burden laid upon the accused in this respect is to collect from the evidence enough material to make it possible for a reasonable jury to acquit".[124]

In practical terms, the effect of the *Woolmington* approach is that a defendant need not collaborate in his own conviction; however strong the grounds of suspicion against him he need not give any account of himself or in any other way assist the prosecution to make its case. As such, the presumption of innocence is an essential counterpart to the defendant's right of non-self-incrimination.

The "beyond reasonable doubt" standard is, thus, crucial to protecting citizens from unjust conviction.[125] It means that the jury must be *sure* that the defendant committed the offence, and acquit if there is a realistic or genuine doubt about the defendant's guilt, although not if the doubt is only vague or fanciful.[126] Such a high standard is needed for the state to be sufficiently sure that it is imposing criminal liability accurately. It is not enough that the defendant "very likely", or even "probably", committed the crime; otherwise there would be too many cases of error and consequent miscarriages of justice, which would—as well as having grave moral costs— endanger public confidence in and support for the criminal justice system. The possibility of error is all the greater when it is also remembered that the state typically has far greater resources with which to conduct a prosecution than the defendant has with which to defend himself. In addition, the high standard of proof acts as a constraint upon the decision to prosecute. Without the presumption of innocence, those who make that decision would have an immense and potentially oppressive power to disrupt the lives of citizens.[127]

122 Perversely, if the defendant is convicted, and that conviction is later quashed, he will have to prove *beyond reasonable doubt* that he was innocent if he wishes to be compensated: Criminal Justice Act 1988, s. 133. Such provisions do not violate Art. 6(2): *R (Hallam) v Secretary of State for Justice* [2019] UKSC 2, [2020] AC 279; *Nealon v UK* (2024) 79 EHRR 22.

123 The finder of fact is the jury in serious cases tried on indictment—the same principles will, however, apply where the defendant is tried summarily in the Magistrates' Court. For the sake of clarity, reference will only be made to "the jury" in the text below.

124 [1970] AC 618, 623 (Lord Devlin).

125 This may be a more stringent standard than that required by Art. 6(2) of the ECHR, which demands evidence "sufficiently strong in the eyes of the law to establish his guilt": *Austria v Italy* 6 YB 740, 784 (1963).

126 *Miller v Minister of Pensions* [1947] 2 All ER 372, 373 (DC).

127 Admittedly, a focus on who proves what at trial can obscure the fact that most defendants plead guilty, thus relieving the prosecution of the burden to prove anything. This practice is compatible with Art. 6(2)—the defendant can waive his right to be proved guilty according to law; see, e.g., *Natsvlishvili v Georgia* (App. No. 9043/05) (2014), [91]—but it represents a challenge to traditional conceptions of the values of the criminal process. See Nobles and Schiff, "Criminal Justice Unhinged" (2019) 39 *OJLS* 100.

### *(i) Cases where the burden of proof is placed on the defendant*

#### *(a) Statutory exceptions*

The first question is whether the legislature intended to "reverse" the burden of proof, in relation to one or more element(s) of the offence, by imposing a legal burden on the defendant.[128] This can be done explicitly or by implication.

An example of an explicit reversal of the burden of proof is found in relation to the offence of child abduction, contrary to section 2 of the Child Abduction Act 1984. Subsection (3) provides that a defence is available (*inter alia*) if the defendant can "prove . . . that, at the time of the alleged offence, he believed that the child had attained the age of sixteen". The word "prove" is clearly intended to reverse the burden of proof. Thus, once the prosecution has proved the other elements of an offence against section 2, the defendant has a legal (and not merely evidential) burden to prove that the conditions of the defence exist. In all such cases, the defendant must prove that such a belief existed to the civil standard of the balance of probabilities.[129] It must, in other words, be more likely than not that he held such a belief.

This is not a textbook on evidence. However, for the reasons given in the last section, explicit statutory exceptions to the presumption of innocence are generally to be deplored.[130] Effectively, they reverse the presumption of innocence, and replace it with a presumption of criminality, whereby the defendant is to be convicted of a crime unless she exculpates herself on the balance of probabilities. As such, they expose the defendant to conviction for a crime without the prosecution being required, at any stage, to lead evidence which proves the *entire* basis for her guilt beyond reasonable doubt. There *may* be occasions when it is apt to require the defendant, in respect of matters that lie peculiarly within her knowledge, to suggest reasons why she should not be convicted.[131] But this is a principle to be sparingly used and only if the prosecution has established a prima facie case of wrongdoing.[132] (This point is all the more important given that, to establish wrongdoing, the prosecution may be able to rely on mechanisms such as the drawing of adverse inferences from the defendant's failure to respond appropriately to police questioning or to give evidence at trial.[133]) Moreover, even then the desired result can usually be achieved by imposing an *evidential* burden to introduce defences upon the defendant, without requiring her to discharge the full legal burden of persuading the court on the balance of probabilities that she is innocent. We think that the defendant should not, on any occasion, be required to prove her innocence to such a standard.

[128] It will be assumed here that D will either have the legal burden as to *all* or *none* of the elements of a defence. For an unsuccessful attempt by counsel to argue for a more nuanced approach, see *K(M)* [2018] EWCA Crim 667, [2019] QB 86.

[129] *Carr-Briant* [1943] KB 607 (CCA). The defendant is *never* required to prove a matter in a criminal trial beyond reasonable doubt.

[130] See, e.g., Roberts, "Taking the Burden of Proof Seriously" [1995] *Crim LR* 783; Jeffries and Stephan, "Defenses, Presumptions and Burden of Proof in Criminal Law" (1979) 88 *Yale LJ* 1325.

[131] Cp. *Jayasena v R* [1970] AC 618, 626–7 (PC). See also the discussion of (and reservations about) strict liability, below, Chapter 6.

[132] Cp. Dennis, "Reverse Onuses and the Presumption of Innocence: In Search of Principle" [2005] *Crim LR* 901. Dennis argues that legal burdens should be imposed on defendants only where the prosecution has established a case of prima facie morally blameworthy behaviour.

[133] See Criminal Justice and Public Order Act 1994, ss. 34–35. The importance of these adverse inferences was emphasised by the Court of Appeal when deciding to "read down" s. 2 of the Prevention of Corruption Act 1916 (now repealed), which was interpreted as imposing only an evidential burden on the defendant regarding the absence of a corrupt motive for giving a gift: *Webster* [2010] EWCA Crim 2819, [2011] 1 Cr App R 16.

Be that as it may, statutory reversal of the burden of proof occurs quite frequently, and is not always explicitly found in the terms of the relevant provision.[134] One situation where the burden of proof is generally reversed by *implication* is in respect of any exonerating circumstances provided for by the statute creating the offence. Where the offence is tried summarily before a Magistrates' Court, section 101 of the Magistrates' Courts Act 1980 provides that the burden of proving any "exception, exemption, proviso, excuse or qualification" shall fall upon the defendant (as always in such cases, to the balance of probabilities). The House of Lords held in *Hunt*[135] that the same rule exists at common law and is applicable to statutory defences to indictable offences as well as to summary proceedings.

Following *Hunt*, the default position is that the defendant must prove statutory defences on the balance of probabilities, even if the relevant statute does not expressly say that this is the case. By contrast, in common law defences such as self-defence and duress (but not insanity) the defendant bears only an evidential burden, and—if this burden is satisfied—the existence of the defence must then be negated beyond reasonable doubt by the prosecution.

The merits of this default position regarding statutory defences may be doubted. It is not always clear what constitutes an aspect of the offence and what constitutes an "exception, exemption, proviso, excuse or qualification". Suppose an (imaginary) statute were to be enacted prohibiting assaults, where "assault" were defined as "the application of force without consent or some other lawful excuse". Is the victim's absence of consent an ingredient of the offence definition, or is consent an "exception, exemption, proviso, excuse or qualification"? There is no easy answer, and the guidance available from the cases is limited[136]—so limited, indeed, that an Australian judge once remarked that "judges are inclined eventually to assert that a case falls on one side of the line or the other without really being able to assign reasons for their view".[137] Given the implications of the categorisation being made, this is a thoroughly unsatisfactory state of affairs.

The discussion so far suggests that a legal burden will, whether expressly or by implication, be placed on the defendant in a wide variety of contexts. Is this approach compatible with the ECHR, particularly Article 6(2), which declares that "Everyone charged with a criminal offence shall be presumed innocent until proved guilty according to law"? In *Lingens v Austria*,[138] the ECtHR ruled that imposing a legal burden on the defendant does not necessarily contravene Article 6(2). Similarly, statutory presumptions of fact, where the burden of rebuttal falls on the accused, have been held consistent with Article 6(2), provided the presumption operates "within reasonable limits which take into account the importance of what is at stake and maintain the rights of the defence".[139] The need for "reasonable

[134] *Hunt* [1987] AC 352, 374 (Lord Griffiths), 379–80 (Lord Ackner). See the survey by Ashworth and Blake, "The Presumption of Innocence in English Criminal Law" [1996] *Crim LR* 306.

[135] *Hunt* [1987] AC 352, (confirming that particular aspect of *Edwards* [1975] QB 27 (CA)). See Smith, "The Presumption of Innocence" (1987) 38 *NILQ* 223.

[136] See *Hunt* [1987] AC 352, 374 (Lord Griffiths). See, also, *Nimmo v Alexander Cowan & Sons Ltd* [1968] AC 107, 135 (Lord Pearson). A useful discussion of this aspect of *Hunt* is Orchard, "The Golden Thread—Somewhat Frayed" (1988) 6 *Otago LR* 615, 624–8.

[137] *Francis v Flood* [1978] 1 NSWLR 113, 119 (Sheppard J).

[138] (1982) 4 EHRR 373.

[139] *Salabiaku v France* (1991) 13 EHRR 379; cp. *X v UK* No. 5124/71, 42 CD 135 (1972). In *Duhs v Sweden* No. 12995/87, 67 DR 204 (1990), the Court held that imposition of a parking fine on the basis of car ownership was within such reasonable limits, and hence was permissible. See also: *A-G of Hong Kong v Lee Kwong-Kut* [1993] AC 951 (PC) (in the context of the Hong Kong Bill of Rights); *Vasquez v R* [1994] 1 WLR 1304 (PC) (Constitution of Belize).

limits" does, at least, offer hope that in extreme cases the imposition of a legal burden on the defendant will be disallowed by Article 6(2). But it seems the case would indeed have to be extreme. In *Salabiaku v France*,[140] D had been found in possession of drugs in the "green" channel (i.e. the route taken by those without imported goods to declare) at Paris airport. He was charged with the serious, imprisonable offence of drug smuggling. Under French law, smuggling was presumed from the fact of possession in such circumstances unless D could establish to the satisfaction of the court that he was unaware of the nature of the items possessed. The ECtHR found that this presumption did not contravene Article 6(2). Similar findings have been made in respect of a presumption that D, a company director, was guilty of an offence if the offence has been proved against his company,[141] and in respect of a presumption that D was living off immoral earnings if it is proved that D was cohabiting with a prostitute.[142]

Fortunately, a series of House of Lords decisions has established a somewhat less permissive attitude to reverse legal burdens.[143] While there is no universal bar to reverse legal burdens, and each offence must be considered on its merits,[144] on some occasions at least a reverse legal burden has been ruled incompatible with Article 6(2). An example is *Lambert*,[145] where, in order to avoid conviction for an offence of drug trafficking under section 5 of the Misuse of Drugs Act 1971, D was required to "prove" that he neither knew, nor suspected, nor had reason to know or suspect, that the substance in his possession was a controlled drug. As a matter of simple statutory interpretation, the use of the word "prove" suggests that Parliament intended to impose a legal burden on a defendant charged with the section 5 offence. In other words, to avoid conviction, he would have to prove on the balance of probabilities that he did not know, suspect, etc., that the substance he had been proved to have possessed was a controlled drug. By a majority of 4:1, the House of Lords decided that, notwithstanding the public interest in prohibiting the trade in illegal drugs, to impose a legal burden on a defendant was a disproportionate legislative response and, consequently, a breach of Article 6(2). It was held that, within the interpretive possibilities allowed for by section 3 of the HRA 1998, the requirement to "prove" lack of knowledge, suspicion, etc., could be reinterpreted to require D merely to raise the possibility that he neither knew nor suspected—merely an evidential burden and not a legal burden. It would then fall to the prosecution to prove beyond reasonable doubt that the defendant *did* know (etc.) that he had proscribed drugs in his possession.

A notable feature of the decision in *Lambert* was a refusal to rely upon any formal distinction between definitional elements of an offence and matters of defence when determining the acceptability of a reverse burden. What mattered was whether D would be found guilty of an offence unless he could prove the particular matter in dispute.

[140] (1991) 13 EHRR 379.
[141] *AG v Malta* No. 16641/90 (1991).
[142] *X v UK* No. 5124/71, 42 CD 135 (1972).
[143] *R v DPP, ex p. Kebilene* [2000] 2 AC 326; *Lambert* [2001] UKHL 37, [2002] 2 AC 545; *Johnstone* [2003] UKHL 28, [2003] 1 WLR 1736; *Sheldrake v DPP; Attorney-General's Reference (No. 4 of 2002)* [2004] UKHL 43, [2005] 1 AC 264.
[144] *Lambert* [2001] UKHL 37, [2002] 2 AC 545, [34] (Lord Steyn), [152] (Lord Clyde); *Sheldrake v DPP; Attorney-General's Reference (No. 4 of 2002)* [2004] UKHL 43, [2005] 1 AC 264, [21] (Lord Bingham).
[145] [2001] UKHL 37, [2002] 2 AC 545.

In so far as the various decisions by their Lordships can be distilled,[146] it seems that the proper approach to the issue of reverse legal burdens is as follows. Where, on ordinary techniques of statutory interpretation (above, § 3.1), a particular piece of legislation imposes expressly or by implication a legal burden on the defendant, the court must then enquire whether doing so is an unjustifiable infringement of the presumption of innocence in Article 6(2).[147] In establishing whether an unjustifiable infringement has occurred, the court will ask whether imposing the reverse legal burden is a proportionate response in pursuit of a legitimate aim. In practice, judicial attention has focussed to date on proportionality, with a legitimate aim generally being assumed. Where a reverse legal burden is a *dis*proportionate response, the presumption of innocence is unjustifiably infringed. In such circumstances, the court must, if possible, reinterpret the legislative provision so as to impose an *evidential* burden.[148] If such an interpretation is precluded by the terms of the legislation, a declaration of incompatibility with the ECHR should be made.[149] Typically, the courts have found it possible to "read down" legislation so as to impose only an evidential burden on the defendant. Resort to a declaration of incompatibility has not yet proved necessary in this context.

When considering whether a reverse legal burden is proportionate, one should balance, on the one hand, society's interest in the effective suppression of the social mischief with which the offence is concerned (and the associated practicalities of proof and enforcement) and, on the other hand, D's right to a fair trial. When weighing up these two competing interests, the courts have emphasised the importance of the seriousness of the offence at issue (usually marked by the severity of the maximum sentence), the relative ease of proof for one party or the other in relation to the element at issue, and the likely risk that the reverse legal burden creates of convicting innocent defendants.

However, the extent to which these considerations are capable of supplying adequate general guidance for future cases has rightly been doubted.[150] The assessments of proportionality in cases to date have been rather *ad hoc*, and it is worth observing that, in the main, reverse legal burdens have been upheld—even in the context of imprisonable offences.[151] In *Williams*,[152] for example, D was charged with the unlawful possession of an imitation firearm that was readily convertible into a weapon capable of firing live ammunition.[153] It is a defence to the charge for D "to show that he did not know and had no reason to suspect that the imitation firearm was so constructed or adapted as to be readily converted into a firearm".[154] The use of the word "show" suggested that Parliament intended to place a legal burden on the defendant,[155] and the Court of Appeal refused to construe the provision as imposing an evidential burden. The Court considered that the public interest in suppressing

[146] See Dennis, "Reverse Onuses and the Presumption of Innocence: In Search of Principle" [2005] *Crim LR* 901; Hamer, "The Presumption of Innocence and Reverse Burdens: A Balancing Act" (2007) 66 *CLJ* 142.

[147] The placing of an evidential burden on the defendant does not infringe Art. 6(2).

[148] Using the procedure outlined in HRA 1998, s. 3; see above, § 2.5(i).

[149] HRA 1998, s. 4.

[150] See Ashworth, "Four Threats to the Presumption of Innocence" (2006) 10 *E&P* 241, 257–70.

[151] See, for example, *Chargot Ltd* [2008] UKHL 73, [2009] 1 WLR 1 (up to two years' imprisonment and an unlimited fine). Cp. *Porter* [2008] EWCA Crim 1271.

[152] [2012] EWCA Crim 2162, [2013] 1 WLR 1200.

[153] Contrary to Firearms Act 1968, s. 5(1).

[154] Firearms Act 1982, s. 1(5).

[155] See, e.g., *Johnstone* [2003] UKHL 28, [2003] 1 WLR 1736.

the possession of firearms made the derogation from the presumption of innocence necessary and proportionate.[156]

It was reasoning of this kind that consistently upheld comparable reverse legal burdens in drug possession cases until the intervention of the House of Lords in *Lambert*. It would be very much in the interests of justice and consistency if the Supreme Court were to resolve more general principles when adjudicating upon reverse burdens. Indeed, it is submitted that the primary general principle should be that, for stigmatic crimes involving proof of culpability and a potential sentence of imprisonment, reverse probative burdens should *always* be reduced to evidential burdens.[157]

It is worth noting, in closing, another important statutory incursion upon the principle that the defendant is not required to prove her innocence. Section 34 of the Criminal Justice and Public Order Act 1994 permits the finder of fact to draw an "adverse inference" from the fact that a defendant failed to mention some fact during police questioning, where she later relies upon that fact in her defence at trial. Likewise, section 35 of the same Act allows (subject to narrow exceptions) the defendant's failure to give evidence at her trial to be put to similar use.[158] As Ashworth has remarked, "if there is to be a presumption that a person is innocent until proved guilty by the prosecution, there appears to be some inconsistency in holding that the defendant can through his or her silence supply an element in that case".[159] The practical effect of modifying a defendant's right to silence is partially to reallocate the burden of proof. For this and other reasons,[160] the provisions of the Criminal Justice and Public Order Act 1994 remain profoundly controversial, even though their broad compatibility with Article 6 has been recognised repeatedly by the ECtHR.[161]

### *(b) The common law exception: insanity*

A second situation in which the legal burden can be on the defendant concerns the defence of insanity. The common law makes a default presumption of sanity.[162] If she wants to rely on the defence of insanity, the defendant must prove it on the balance of probabilities. This is an incongruous anomaly, given that the defendant bears only an evidential burden in respect of other general defences, and that the consequence of prov-

[156] A reverse legal burden indicated by use of the word "show" will not *always* be found to be a proportionate response to a legitimate aim. See, e.g., *Shepherd v Information Commissioner* [2019] EWCA Crim 2, [2019] 4 WLR 50.

[157] See, further, Williams, "The Logic of 'Exceptions'" (1988) 47 *CLJ* 261.

[158] Other provisions in the 1994 Act allow similar adverse inferences to be drawn in different circumstances. See Owusu-Bempah, "Silence in Suspicious Circumstances" [2014] *Crim LR* 126.

[159] *The Criminal Process: An Evaluative Study* (2nd ed., 1998) 96. Cf. *Funke, Cremieux and Miailhe v France* (1993) 16 EHRR 297. For further criticism of the 1994 Act's provisions, see Galligan, "The Right to Silence Reconsidered" (1988) 41 *CLP* 69; Jackson, "Curtailing the Right to Silence: Lessons from Northern Ireland" [1991] *Crim LR* 404; Dennis, "The Criminal Justice and Public Order Act 1994: The Evidence Provisions" [1995] *Crim LR* 4; Birch, "Suffering in Silence: A Cost—Benefit Analysis of Section 34 of the Criminal Justice and Public Order Act 1994" [1999] *Crim LR* 769; Dennis, "Silence in the Police Station: The Marginalisation of Section 34" [2002] *Crim LR* 25.

[160] See, further, Quirk, *The Rise and Fall of the Right to Silence* (2017).

[161] See, e.g., *Murray v UK* (1996) 22 EHRR 29; *O'Donnell v UK* (2015) 61 EHRR 37. The UK has on occasion lost cases concerning the 1994 Act at Strasbourg, but typically on the basis of the trial judge's defective explanation of the adverse inference provisions, rather than the provisions themselves. See, e.g., *Beckles v UK* (2003) 36 EHRR 13.

[162] *M'Naghten* (1843) 10 Cl & F 200, 210, 8 ER 718, 722; *Woolmington v DPP* [1935] AC 462, 475 (Viscount Sankey LC).

ing insanity may be compulsory detention.[163] With that said, a similar rule applies to the statutory defence of diminished responsibility.[164] Note, however, that the need for a defendant to show insanity or diminished responsibility arises only if the prosecution can prove the actus reus (and, in diminished responsibility, the mens rea) beyond reasonable doubt in the normal way. Insanity is discussed in detail in § 19.2; diminished responsibility is considered in § 10.6.

### (c) *Strict liability*

Strict liability is discussed in Chapter 6. To anticipate the discussion there, in offences of strict liability, the prosecution is relieved of the burden of proving mens rea in relation to one or more aspects of the actus reus. The House of Lords and the ECtHR have both held that strict liability offences, of which there are many in English criminal law, are not prohibited by Article 6(2).[165] Typically, the use of strict liability is regarded as a matter of substantive rather than procedural criminal law, even though (as we shall see) this is a false dichotomy: a standard rationale for imposing strict liability is convenience of proof for prosecutors. Strict liability has the capacity almost entirely to circumvent the values protected by the presumption of innocence.[166]

Indeed, as Lord Rodger noted in *Sheldrake*, there is something paradoxical in the existing jurisprudence on reverse burdens of proof.[167] As noted in Chapter 2, there is no right to a fair criminal law; arguments about reverse burdens of proof are arguments about *the procedure* for establishing offences, not the definitions of those offences. This raises the following possibility. Assume there is an offence of, say, knowingly selling food that does not comply with food safety standards. Assume it to be a serious offence with a maximum sentence of, say, 10 years' imprisonment. If the legal burden were placed on D to prove that she did not know the food she sold was non-compliant, the courts could (consistently with section 3 of the HRA 1998) "read down" the legal burden to an evidential one. It would now suffice for D to raise the possibility that she did not know; she would no longer be required to *prove* her lack of knowledge on the balance of probabilities. What if Parliament were to respond to this judicial finding by dropping *any* reference to knowledge and making it an offence simply to sell food, even inadvertently, that is non-compliant with safety standards? Would this imposition of strict liability then remove any potential to present an Article 6 argument about the compatibility of the offence with the Convention? Is it a sufficient response to say that there are no Article 6 presumption-of-innocence implications

[163] See Jones, "Insanity, Automatism, and the Burden of Proof on the Accused" (1995) 111 *LQR* 475.

[164] Homicide Act 1957, s. 2(2). Unsuccessful challenges to the compatibility of this provision with Art. 6(2) were made in *Foye* [2013] EWCA Crim 475 and *Wilcocks* [2016] EWCA Crim 2043, [2017] 4 WLR 39.

[165] *Salabiaku v France* (1991) 13 EHRR 379; *G* [2008] UKHL 37, [2009] 1 AC 92; *G v UK* (2011) 53 EHRR SE25.

[166] For discussion of whether the presumption of innocence does have necessary implications for the imposition of strict liability, see Tadros and Tierney, "The Presumption of Innocence and the Human Rights Act" (2004) 67 *MLR* 402, 422–4; Sullivan, "Strict Liability for Criminal Offences in England and Wales following Incorporation into English Law of the European Convention on Human Rights" in Simester (ed.), *Appraising Strict Liability* (2005) 195; Ashworth, "Four Threats to the Presumption of Innocence" (2006) 10 *E&P* 241; cf. Roberts, "Strict Liability and the Presumption of Innocence: An Exposé of Functionalist Assumptions" in Simester (ed.), *Appraising Strict Liability* (2005) 151.

[167] *Sheldrake v DPP; Attorney-General's Reference (No. 4 of 2002)* [2004] UKHL 43, [2005] 1 AC 264, [71].

because no reverse burden of proof is employed?[168] Some academics have argued that it is not, an answer that opens up the field of strict liability offences for ECHR scrutiny.[169] However, the House of Lords has confined the application of Article 6 to matters of procedural rather than substantive fairness. Thus, reversing the burden to prove some offence element may violate Article 6, but eliminating that element altogether from the offence does not.[170] Their Lordships' logic is impeccable: its moral justification is not.

### *(ii) The "golden thread": somewhat frayed?*[171]

The decision in *Woolmington* was delivered with great rhetorical flourish. Viscount Sankey LC described the burden of proof always falls upon the prosecution as "the one golden thread always to be seen throughout the web of the English criminal law".[172] However, even then it was recognised that insanity was a common law exception, and that Parliament might legislate other exceptions, seemingly without limitation. Article 6(2) of the ECHR has not, to date, generated strict limits on the legislature's power to place legal burdens of proof (to the balance of probabilities) on defendants. On many occasions, the presumption of innocence has been ruled by the ECtHR and the English courts to be compatible with imposing a legal burden of proof on the defendant. There is a multitude of statutory provisions where legal burdens are placed, expressly or by implication, on the defendant. In an illuminating study published in 1996, Ashworth and Blake found that, in 40 per cent of offences triable before the Crown Court, a legal burden on one or more issues was imposed on the defendant.[173] The authors discovered little that was systematic about the allocation of legal burdens; it tended to be happenstance, with similar proof issues allocated differently under different statutes. There is no reason to suspect that the position has improved since then.

Still, the situation is not hopeless. The clear iteration of a presumption of innocence in Article 6(2), combined with decisions such as *Lambert* may one day prompt a better shielding of the presumption of innocence. It cannot be satisfactory, particularly for serious crimes, that D must prove facts crucial to the maintenance of her innocence. This objection is exacerbated by the unsystematic treatment, noted by Ashworth and Blake, of very similar factors in different offences. Moreover, the random variation they describe is not just a matter of statutory stipulation. It is not uncommon, for example, for a defendant charged with

[168] The offence in English law of selling food that is non-compliant with safety standards (Food Safety Act 1990, s. 8) is an offence of strict liability with a maximum penalty of two years' imprisonment. The strict nature of the offence is mitigated by the provision of a due diligence defence with a reverse onus on D (s. 21). From the perspective of effective regulation of a problematic industry, one may hope the offence will withstand ECHR scrutiny. However, there are some offences of strict liability that carry high terms of imprisonment and are not mitigated by any due diligence defence: e.g., unlawful possession of a firearm as interpreted in *Howells* [1977] QB 614 (CA). Such offences are, morally speaking, much more difficult to justify. See below, Chapter 6.

[169] See, e.g., Tadros and Tierney, "The Presumption of Innocence and the Human Rights Act" (2004) 67 *MLR* 402; Tadros, "The Ideal of the Presumption of Innocence" (2014) 8 *Crim Law and Philosophy* 449. Contrast Roberts, "Strict Liability and the Presumption of Innocence: An Exposé of Functionalist Assumptions" in Simester (ed.), *Appraising Strict Liability* (2005) 151.

[170] *G* [2008] UKHL 37, [2009] 1 AC 92 (rape of a child under 13, contrary to s. 5 of the Sexual Offences Act 2003), confirmed (in the context of that offence) by the decision on admissibility in *G v UK* (2011) 53 EHRR SE25.

[171] See Orchard, "The Golden Thread—Somewhat Frayed" (1988) 6 *Otago LR* 615.

[172] *Woolmington v DPP* [1935] AC 462, 481–2 (Viscount Sankey LC).

[173] "The Presumption of Innocence in English Criminal Law" [1996] *Crim LR* 306.

murder to plead in the alternative the defences of loss of control and diminished responsibility. As we shall see,[174] as the law stands it may be very difficult to determine whether particular evidence will give rise to one or other of these defences; it may be too that the evidence will satisfy the differing criteria for each of these defences. But the burden of proof does not reflect these similarities. With loss of control, there is merely an evidential burden upon the defendant: if the issue of loss of control is raised on the evidence, the prosecution must negate the defence beyond reasonable doubt.[175] By contrast, the defendant has the onus of establishing the defence of diminished responsibility on the balance of probabilities.[176] This is not just confusing for juries dealing with the same evidence under different heads of defence. It is unsustainable as a matter of principle.

[174] Below, § 10.6(iii).

[175] Coroners and Justice Act 2009, s. 54(5). The question of how much evidence is required to suggest loss of control has proved controversial: see, e.g., *Drake* [2023] EWCA Crim 1454, [2024] 4 WLR 73.

[176] Homicide Act 1957, s. 2(2).

# 4

# THE ACTUS REUS

In Chapter 1 we discussed some of the reasons why a person cannot and should not be guilty of a crime unless both (a) he has caused or is otherwise responsible for the external event prohibited by law—the actus reus—and (b) he had the required "fault" elements (as specified for the particular crime) with respect to that external event—the mens rea. If D kills V, she may have brought about the actus reus of murder, but it does not follow that she has committed any offence. When the doctor gives a painkiller to her patient, who turns out to be unknowably allergic to it, she may kill that patient: but it is an accident, and no criminal liability will follow. The mens rea is missing. Conversely, if she administers the drug intending it to kill him, and he dies of an unrelated heart attack, she does not murder him.[1] The actus reus is missing. In the next two chapters, we investigate the general principles of criminal law regarding these two elements, beginning with the actus reus.

For the purposes of identifying the constituent elements of an offence, it is conventional to identify the actus reus of a crime with that part of the definition which does not refer to the defendant's mental state.[2] The actus reus can usefully be divided into three types of ingredient: behaviour (or "conduct"), consequences, and circumstances. Often the circumstances or consequences surrounding something the defendant does are relevant to her wrongdoing, and so the offence does not just turn on D's behaviour. It is an essential part of our concept of murder, for instance, that a human being's death is caused. Thus the victim's death—a consequence—is a constitutive part of the actus reus of murder. Such offences are sometimes called "result crimes",[3] because they cannot be committed unless the defendant's actions cause the specified result or consequence actually to occur.

An example of a crime not requiring specific consequences but which is dependent on circumstances is bigamy, which involves D's going through a marriage ceremony (the behaviour) while being married to someone else (the circumstance).

It is important to realise that, since specification of the actus reus of each offence differs, there is no requirement that all three types of ingredient be present in the actus reus of each offence. Hence the actus reus of assault causing actual bodily harm requires that the defendant's assault must cause injury to the victim.[4] By contrast, the actus reus of rape is made out if there is (i) behaviour (D's penetrating V in a particular way), in (ii) circumstances where V does not consent to it. No consequence need be brought about.

[1] *White* [1910] 2 KB 124.

[2] This division of crimes into actus reus and mens rea elements is a helpful expository device but not an analytical necessity. Sometimes, moreover, it is not easy to divide a crime in this way. For instance, as we will see in §§ 4.1(ii)(b) and 5.6(iv), whether D is in "possession" of something may depend both on her physical conduct and on her understandings about that conduct.

[3] The term is from Gordon, *Criminal Law of Scotland* (1967) 61.

[4] Contrary to s. 47 of the OAPA 1861. See below, § 11.4.

## § 4.1 The behaviour element

Normally, the actus reus of any given offence requires an action of some sort: something *done* by the defendant. This is not always obvious. It might sometimes appear as though result crimes such as murder could be specified solely by reference to the consequence, and without the actus reus containing any behavioural element. Thus it is the outcome which is emphasised in Kenny's definition of actus reus: "such result of human conduct as the law seeks to prevent".[5] Consider, for instance, the crime of murder. Surely it is the result, death, which is central to that crime? V's death is the harmful result that, as Kenny puts it, the law seeks to prevent. Without that death, murder is not and cannot be committed. The relevant harm has not occurred.

But the view that it is only the consequence or result that matters is not quite right. The law is not concerned with deaths *per se*, but rather with deaths that other people and, exceptionally, companies and other organisations bring about.[6] The actus reus is *causing* death, not death itself. The result *is* important: it helps to mark out what type of wrongdoing the offence is concerned with. Indeed, it is the nature of the result, rather than of the behaviour which causes it, that gives homicide its special moral and social significance. Murder is murder whether done by knife or poison, and this is why the behaviour element of the actus reus is unspecific. But it exists all the same.

On the other hand, it is possible for an actus reus to consist *only* of behaviour. This is especially true of inchoate crimes, such as attempted murder, where there is no requirement that the attempt be effective.[7] Crimes of this type are sometimes termed "conduct crimes", since the actus reus requires proof only of specified conduct by the defendant and does not specify any particular circumstances or consequences.

### *(i) Behaviour and omissions*

Where behaviour is an element of the actus reus, standard legal doctrine stipulates that it requires a positive action by the defendant. As a general rule, an omission will not do.[8] Thus it is a crime for D deliberately to drown V, but no crime for D gleefully to stand on the beach and watch while her enemy, V, is caught in the tide and drowns nearby.[9]

[5] Turner, *Kenny's Outlines of Criminal Law* (19th ed., 1965) 17.

[6] The Corporate Manslaughter and Homicide Act 2007 creates the offence of corporate manslaughter which only companies and some other organisations such as the NHS and the Prison Service can commit. See below, § 10.7(iv).

[7] Below, § 9.3. Other examples include the offence of false accounting (contrary to s. 17 of the Theft Act 1968), the actus reus of which can be committed merely by omitting to disclose a material particular in a document: *Lancaster* [2010] EWCA Crim 370, [2010] 1 WLR 2558.

[8] Admittedly, the number of exceptions is increasing at the hands of modern lawmakers. For discussion, see Ashworth, "A New Generation of Omissions Offences?" [2018] *Crim LR* 354, 362. For reasons to be discussed in the text, this development is not necessarily a welcome one.

[9] Cp. Stephen, *Digest of the Criminal Law* (4th ed., 1887) Art. 212. Other writing includes Hughes, "Criminal Omissions" (1958) 67 *Yale LJ* 590; Glazebrook, "Criminal Omissions: The Duty Requirement in Offences Against the Person" (1960) 76 *LQR* 386; Ashworth, "The Scope of Criminal Liability for Omissions" (1989) 105 *LQR* 424; Alexander, "Criminal Liability for Omissions: An Inventory of Issues" in Simester and Shute (eds.), *Criminal Law Theory* (2000) 121; Ashworth, "Public Duties and Criminal Omissions: Some Unresolved Questions" (2011) 1 *J Commonwealth Criminal Law* 1; Ashworth, "Manslaughter by Omission and the Rule of Law" [2015] *Crim LR* 563; Ashworth, "Positive Duties, Regulation and the Criminal Sanction" (2017) 133 *LQR* 606.

This standard doctrine comprises two parts. First, behaviour specified in an actus reus can prima facie be satisfied only by a positive act on the part of the defendant, and not by the defendant's omission. Secondly, there are certain exceptions to the requirement for a positive act. These exceptions arise when the defendant has a *duty* to intervene and prevent the prohibited harm from occurring: her failure to act in accordance with that duty counts as an omission satisfying the behavioural element of that actus reus. The first rule is the default one. It is general in nature: the exceptions, and the duties on which they are based, are specific and confined.

The criminal law's approach resembles that of the civil law, which is also generally averse to imposing liability for omissions,[10] and is willing to do so only in special cases where the reasons in favour are strong enough to override that aversion. The distinction between misfeasance and non-feasance is deeply embedded in the common law. Civil law duties to intervene are dependent upon, for example, the defendant's having created the risk of harm[11] or in some other way having assumed responsibility for (avoiding) it.[12] Similarly, an omission to reject a contractual offer cannot constitute its acceptance.[13] Silence is no representation in the tort of deceit;[14] neither is it *per se* a misrepresentation when negotiating a contract.[15]

### *(a) Why omissions are special*

Why *should* the distinction between acts and omissions make any practical difference to criminal liability? One key reason is based upon considerations of autonomy. We value living in a society where citizens are respected as individuals—where they are free to live their own lives and pursue their own priorities without having their choices determined by legal duties to act or intervene. The prohibition of omissions (i.e. the mandating of specified positive acts) is far more intrusive upon individuals' autonomy and freedom than is the prohibition of acts. Hence the systematic imposition of (criminal or civil) liability for failures to act is to be resisted.[16]

[10] *Per* Lord Keith in *Yuen Kun-Yeu v A-G of Hong Kong* [1988] AC 175, 192 (PC), there is no liability in negligence "on the part of one who sees another about to walk over a cliff with his head in the air, and forbears to shout a warning". Cp. *Ancell v McDermott* [1993] 4 All ER 355 (CA); *Alexandrou v Oxford* [1993] 4 All ER 328 (CA); *Hill v Chief Constable of West Yorkshire* [1989] AC 53; *Curran v Northern Ireland Housing Association Ltd* [1987] AC 718; *East Suffolk Catchment Board v Kent* [1941] AC 74; *Gautret v Egerton* (1867) LR 2 CP 371, 375.

[11] *Johnson v Rea* [1962] 1 QB 373 (CA).

[12] E.g. *Dorset Yacht Co v Home Office* [1970] AC 1004; *Barnett v Chelsea and Kensington Hospital Management Committee* [1969] 1 QB 428 (DC).

[13] *Felthouse v Bindley* (1862) 11 CB (NS) 869, 142 ER 1037; cp. *The Leonidas* [1985] 1 WLR 925 (CA); *The Santa Clara* [1996] QB 108 (CA).

[14] *Peek v Gurney* (1873) LR 6 HL 377, 392, 403; *Arkwright v Newbold* (1881) 17 Ch D 301, 318; *Banque Keyser Ullman SA v Skandia UK Insurance Co. Ltd.* [1990] 1 QB 665 (CA).

[15] *Fox v Mackreth* (1791) 2 Cox Eq Cas 320, 321, 30 ER 148, 148–9; *Keates v The Earl of Cadogan* (1851) 10 CB 591, 138 ER 234; *Bell v Lever Bros Ltd* [1932] AC 161, 227 (Lord Atkin).

[16] See, very generally, Simester, *Fundamentals* chap. 6; also the earlier discussion above, §§ 1.2(i), 1.2(ii)(e). There is philosophical controversy whether the act–omission distinction, of and by itself, is morally significant. Nonetheless, it is worth observing that acts usually manifest a greater level of hostility to the interests of others than do omissions, and we tend to feel very differently about killers when compared with non-savers. Omissions are often incidental to the defendant's practical deliberations—they tend to disclose a different and lesser fault, of limited imagination or empathy, rather than malice.

This is not to suggest that there should never be liability for omissions. Those writers who advocate a criminal law duty of easy rescue, for example, have at least an arguable case.[17] Rather, the present argument is that liability for omissions should be exceptional, and not as widespread as liability for actions. At any moment in time, the number of positive actions we are doing is very small. But the number of things we are failing to do is enormous. This is because there are very few ways in which one can do an action, whereas the number of ways in which one can fail to do something is much greater. For example, while D is not saving the drowning swimmer she may be walking, reading a book, playing cricket, etc. But she is unlikely to be able to do these things while she *is* saving the swimmer. The burden the law imposes when it prohibits a person from doing something is therefore lighter and less intrusive than when it orders that person to act. Requiring people to refrain from specified actions involves the sacrifice of fewer options, and is more likely to leave the defendant with a chance of conforming to law without significant disruption. "Compare being banished to Liechtenstein with being banished from Liechtenstein."[18] Or, in a more apposite example, compare being prohibited from drowning the other swimmers when sunbathing at a beach to being required to save them. Wholesale liability for things we fail to do would force us constantly to interrupt our own actions and plans in order to prevent outcomes that are brought about by others: to become, in effect, our brothers' keepers. It would be incompatible with a country's ambition to be a liberal state.

A second consideration is that, if prohibited omissions involve the sacrifice of more options, then they are also likely to require a greater sacrifice of our own interests. If D buys a piece of furniture for his home, why is he not held responsible for the lives that money would save in, say, Ethiopia? One factor is our widespread acceptance that people are to some extent entitled to prefer their own interests, and the interests of those near to them, above the interests of others. A mother who gives her own child pocket-money is not expected to do the same for the child next door. Of course, such a view may be no more than a moral mistake. But if so, it is an inescapable feature of our society, and the law has no choice but to bow to its almost universal acceptance. Moreover, given that individuals exist in different and specific situations, they are typically better placed to assess and contribute to their own lives, and to the lives of those they know, than to the lives of strangers. These points help to explain examples where someone does not save starving children in foreign countries: they limit the extent to which the needs of strangers take precedence over and mandate the sacrifice of our own plans and interests. We cannot do everything, and it would be absurd to expect us to try, especially on pain of a stigmatising conviction and punishment. When we make decisions, we are entitled to acknowledge that our own lives, and the lives of people we are close to, are important to us. So, even apart from questions of autonomy, the law's presumption against penalising omissions can be justified as a simple and workable means by which the law can recognise the priority individuals are entitled to accord to the conduct of their own lives.

[17] See, especially, Ashworth, *Positive Obligations in Criminal Law* (2013), chap. 2; also von Hirsch, "Criminalizing Failure to Rescue: A Matter of 'Solidarity' or Altruism?" in Cruft, Kramer and Reiff (eds.), *Crime, Punishment and Responsibility* (2011) 241.

[18] Bennett, "Morality and Consequences" in McMurrin (ed.), *The Tanner Lectures in Human Values* (1981) 47, 78; cp. Bennett, *The Act Itself* (1995) 92. A similar principle applies in the context of false imprisonment: *Bird v Jones* (1845) 7 QB 742, 115 ER 668.

*(b) The exceptions: situations where criminal liability is imposed for omissions*

*Case 1: Specific statutory and common law offences.*

Many statutes now contain offences which expressly impose liability for an omission.[19] Often these are offences which can *only* be committed by omission, such as failing to provide a breath specimen when asked to do so by a police officer,[20] or failing to file an annual return as required by the Companies Act 2006.[21] Similarly, section 1(2)(a) of the Children and Young Persons Act 1933 requires persons to supply legally dependent children with adequate food, clothing, medical aid, and lodging. An offence is committed when D fails to discharge that duty. The common law also knows some, though very few, offences specifically of omission, such as refusing to assist a police officer when called upon to aid in restoring the peace.[22]

The above offences involve specific reference to a behavioural element on the part of the defendant. A second variety of statutory crime which can be committed, indirectly, by omission is that where the actus reus names no behavioural element at all, and requires only proof of certain events or circumstances. (This type of offence is discussed below, in § 4.1(ii).) Characteristically, offences of the latter sort are an indirect imposition of liability for D's omission to prevent a specified event or outcome occurring—for instance, being in possession of an unlicensed firearm. Of course, in these cases liability will also lie for bringing the outcome about by a positive act. But proof of no such act is *required*.

It merits emphasis that, where an offence criminalises D's omission to prevent something, the courts generally import a requirement that the defendant had the ability or power to stop the relevant outcome from occurring.[23] This kind of restriction, which is grounded in the broader requirement of voluntariness, will be considered further in § 4.3(ii).

*Case 2: Duties imposed due to special relationships of responsibility and dependency.*

Sometimes, even without a specific offence, the law holds that considerations such as autonomy and self-interest are outweighed and the offence is capable of being committed via an omission. This occurs when the defendant is found to be under a more general legal duty, such as the duties of parents to their dependent children. A stranger can stand by and watch a child starve or drown. But that child's parent cannot.

The reason for imposing such duties on parents is that parents are (by default) responsible for their children's welfare, and children are dependent upon their parents. The law does no more than reflect that pre-existing position by imposing legal duties upon parents to intervene on behalf of their children. To some extent these duties now have parallels in statute: we noted in the previous section that the Children and Young Persons Act 1933

[19] Even in the context of homicide: e.g. s. 5(1) of the Domestic Violence, Crime and Victims Act 2004 (causing or allowing, *inter alia*, the death of a child or vulnerable adult).

[20] Contrary to s. 6(6) of the Road Traffic Act 1988. Cp. *Raymond Parry v Department for Work and Pensions* [2005] EWHC 1486 (Admin) (failing to disclose employment when in receipt of an incapacity benefit, contrary to Social Security Administration Act 1992, s. 111A).

[21] An offence contrary to s. 451(1) of that Act.

[22] *Brown* (1841) Car & M 314, 174 ER 522; Nicholson, "The Citizen's Duty to Assist the Police" [1992] *Crim LR* 611. It is also a common law offence of misconduct in a public office for a police constable to refuse to perform his duty to preserve the King's peace: *Dytham* [1979] QB 722 (CA); *A-G's Reference (No. 3 of 2003)* [2004] EWCA Crim 868, [2005] QB 73.

[23] See, e.g., *Tilley* [2009] EWCA Crim 1426, [2010] 1 WLR 605, [36]–[39], citing *Crabtree v Fern Spinning Co. Limited* (1901) 85 LT 549, 552 (in the context of "allowing").

requires legally dependent children to be supplied with adequate food and other necessaries. However, that Act merely creates a particular and confined offence. The common law duties of parents are wider ranging than this, and prima facie apply to any offence (unless it is incapable of commission through omission: see below, § 4.1(i)(c)). Thus a parent's failure to effect an easy rescue of her child would count as the actus reus of murder even though it is scarcely a failure to supply necessaries.[24] And more generally, it is submitted that a parent who willingly permits another to assault his child (when he can prevent this happening) is himself guilty of an assault.[25]

What if the child is 30? Here, although a special relationship still exists between the parent and child, it no longer involves dependency on the part of the child and the same parental commitment to responsibility for the child's welfare.[26] It is these factors that undergird a parent's duty to prevent harm to younger children, and their absence in the case of (most) older children should extinguish that duty. It is thus submitted that parents do not ordinarily owe legal duties to rescue their adult children.[27] Neither do children owe such duties to their parents.[28] This is not to deny that people have moral obligations to their relatives. But it is quite a different matter to hold them criminally liable for failing to discharge those obligations.

These points generalise beyond the context of parent–child relationships. In the old cases governing the relationship of master to apprentice, for instance, the duty of care was said to arise from the master's assumption of responsibility and the apprentice's dependence, so that it was necessary to allege the apprentice was of tender years: "[t]here is a clear distinction between treatment of this sort to a child and to an adult".[29]

The view that, rather than the closeness of their emotional or other relationship, it is D's responsibility for V's welfare, and V's dependency on D, that are the decisive features in finding a duty of care is consistent with the case law regarding legal duties owed toward someone who is in the defendant's care. In *Stone and Dobinson*,[30] S and his mistress D (both of limited intellect) were held to have assumed responsibility for the care of S's sister when

[24] *Handley* (1874) 13 Cox CC 79; *White* (1871) 12 Cox CC 83, 86.

[25] Cp. *Emery* (1993) 14 Cr App R (S) 394 (cruelty); *Russell* [1933] VLR 59 (manslaughter); *Commonwealth v Howard* 402 A 2d 674 (1979) (manslaughter). On the particular question whether assault can be committed by omission, see below, § 4.1(i)(c). The parent would in any case be guilty as a secondary party: below, § 7.4(iii). Liability would very likely also lie under s. 5 of the Domestic Violence, Crime and Victims Act 2004.

[26] Compare s. 1 of the Children and Young Persons Act 1933, the application of which terminates when the child reaches the age of 16 years.

[27] *Smith* (1826) 2 C & P 449, 172 ER 203; *Shepherd* (1862) 9 Cox CC 123; cf. *Chattaway* (1924) 17 Cr App R 7.

[28] Neither do adult children owe such duties to their half-sisters, even if living in the same house and where the half-sister is a minor: *Evans* [2009] EWCA Crim 650, [2009] 1 WLR 1999. However, courts may be astute in circumstances such as *Evans* (which involved drug taking and a drug-related death in the family home) to find a duty of care on other grounds. The half-sister in *Evans* was found guilty of manslaughter of her sibling on the basis of her "contribution", via supply of the drugs, to V's death: see, further, Case 5 below and § 10.7(ii)(a) (Requirement 1).

[29] *Ridley* (1811) 2 Camp 650, 652, 170 ER 1282, 1283; *Friend* (1802) Russ & Ry 20, 168 ER 662. See also *Charlotte Smith* (1865) 10 Cox CC 82 (servant).

[30] [1977] QB 354. Arguably, the Court's finding of an assumed responsibility was doubtful on the facts; see Ashworth, "The Scope of Criminal Liability for Omissions" (1989) 105 *LQR* 424, 443. Strikingly, the ineffectual efforts of the defendants to help V played the dual role of establishing a duty of care and providing evidence of its breach. The case is also unsatisfactory on the question of causation: did the neglect make any difference? Whether V, a person with an extreme eating disorder, could have been helped by anyone was a matter not addressed. Additionally, it is problematic on the question of gross negligence (given the couple's intellectual limitations—compare the discussion of *Elliott v C* [1983] 1 WLR 939 (DC), below, § 5.5(ii)). See also Ashworth, "Public Duties and Criminal Omissions: Some Unresolved Questions" (2011) 1 *J Commonwealth Crim Law* 1, 6–13.

allowing her to lodge with them and making some efforts to assist her while she stayed with them. The sister died from a combination of anorexia nervosa and their incompetent neglect. *Both* S and D were convicted of manslaughter, irrespective of the fact that only S was related to V.[31] The family relationship did not *of itself* impose any duties upon them; they were not obliged to let her stay with them, nor to offer any other form of help. What mattered, the Court of Appeal decided, is that they voluntarily assumed a duty of care toward her, and she was dependent upon them.

Also consistent is *Smith*,[32] in which the Crown Court assumed that the institution of marriage does not itself generate a duty of care between spouses, although an assumption of responsibility for the welfare of one's spouse or partner will readily be inferred, particularly where the parties are cohabiting.[33] If this is right,[34] the Australian decision of *Russell* would not be followed here: R's estranged wife had drowned herself and their sons while R was present, whereupon R was convicted of the manslaughter not only of the sons but also of the wife.[35] By implication, a mutual obligation to protect would not extend to the partners in a casual sexual relationship.[36]

*Case 3: Duties imposed on persons assuming a particular responsibility.*

The cases discussed so far have been concerned with duties arising from a wide-ranging and unspecific responsibility for another's welfare. A more complex relationship is that between a doctor and her patient.[37] This duty is a confined one—a doctor on her way home may drive past the scene of an accident without attracting criminal liability for doing so. The duty applies only to the patients in her care. Where the duty does apply, injury resulting from the doctor's failure to provide proper care is regarded by the criminal law just as if it were brought about by an act of improper treatment.

Even to her patients, however, the doctor's duty is not all-encompassing. She may not kill by positive act, but it appears that she may withdraw care (sometimes only with adequate judicial approval in advance[38]) from a patient in a persistent vegetative state.[39] The duty is

[31] See too *R v West London Coroner, ex p. Gray* [1988] QB 467 (DC); *Condé* (1867) 10 Cox CC 547; *Instan* [1893] 1 QB 450; *Marriott* (1838) 8 C & P 425, 173 ER 559; *Nicholls* (1874) 13 Cox CC 75; *Bubb* (1850) 4 Cox CC 455. See Williams, "Criminal Omissions—The Conventional View" (1991) 107 *LQR* 86, 89–90. A valuable and wide-ranging discussion may be found in the Australian case of *Taktak* (1988) 14 NSWLR 226.

[32] [1979] Crim LR 251 (Crown Court). This decision throws doubt on the assertion made by Horder and McGowan, "Manslaughter by Causing Another's Suicide" [2006] *Crim LR* 1035, 1044, that "[t]here is no doubt that a duty of care exists between spouses". The authors cite the case of *Hood* [2003] EWCA Crim 2772, [2004] 1 Cr App R (S) 73, which in our view illustrates that an assumption of a duty of care between spouses will be readily inferred but not that a duty of care arises from marital status *per se*.

[33] E.g. where D is the sole carer for his disabled wife, as in *Hood* [2003] EWCA Crim 2772, [2004] 1 Cr App R (S) 73.

[34] *Contra Plummer* (1844) 1 C & K 600, 174 ER 954 (estranged spouse).

[35] [1933] VLR 59.

[36] Cp. *People v Beardsley* 113 NW 1128 (1907); discussed by Hughes, "Criminal Omissions" (1958) 67 *Yale LJ* 590, 624. See also *R (Lewin) v CPS* [2002] EWHC 1049 (Admin): D left his intoxicated friend asleep in an unlocked car during a very hot day, with the result that the friend died. The Divisional Court upheld the CPS's decision not to prosecute D for manslaughter.

[37] For another example of role-based responsibility, see *Curtis* (1885) 15 Cox CC 746 (duty of a local authority officer to provide medical assistance to a destitute person).

[38] In practice, judicial authorisation will typically be required where there is a disagreement between the patient's family and doctors. See *An NHS Trust v Y* [2018] UKSC 46, [2019] AC 978.

[39] *Airedale NHS Trust v Bland* [1993] AC 789. See also the note by Finnis, "*Bland*: Crossing the Rubicon?" (1993) 109 *LQR* 329.

not to keep the patient alive, but to make reasonable efforts to do so, consonant with proper medical practice,[40] and only in so far as doing so is in the patient's best interests.[41]

Another source of specific criminal law duties is civil law obligations. The classic case is *Pittwood*.[42] D had been employed by a railway company to manage the gate at a level crossing. He went to lunch forgetting to close the gate. A haycart subsequently entered the crossing and was struck by a train. One of the riders in the cart died. D was convicted of manslaughter. It is not clear whether D's duty depended upon his having been hired to discharge a duty to the public that was owed by his employers,[43] or was grounded in the fact that he was hired to protect other people and that they were likely to be injured by his dereliction. The latter seems to have been the rationale adopted by Wright J,[44] but there is reason to support the former view. Consider a hypothetical case in which D, a nurse, has signed a contract that contains a term requiring her to intervene and save people at large—that is, even when off duty and away from the hospital. In such a case, D's failure to rescue someone when at the beach might be a breach of contract, but should not be a criminal offence.

*Case 4: The continuing act doctrine.*

Sometimes a defendant brings about an actus reus without mens rea but then, while the harmful consequences continue, intentionally omits to remedy or discontinue them. In such cases the "continuing act" doctrine may be applied, and liability imposed without the need to find a legal duty owed by the defendant.[45] In *Fagan v Metropolitan Police Commissioner*,[46] F accidentally drove onto a policeman's foot. When apprised of his action, he refused to move the car. He was convicted of battery on the basis that his refusal to remove the vehicle amounted to a continuation of the original (positive) act of battery,[47] and was not a mere omission. Hence it could satisfy the actus reus requirement (which, the Court had decided, required an *act*),[48] and thus actus reus and mens rea occurred at the same (later) point in time.

A similar case is *Kaitamaki*.[49] D had sexual intercourse with V without her consent. D's evidence was that he became aware V was not consenting only after penetration had occurred. However, he did not then withdraw from intercourse. The trial judge directed the

[40] See *TBCL* 279.

[41] *Airedale NHS Trust v Bland* [1993] AC 789, 868–9 (Lord Goff); *R (Burke) v GMC* [2004] EWHC 1879 (Admin), [2005] QB 424. See also the difficult cases involving the degree of care owed by doctors to disabled neonates: *Arthur* (1981) 12 B Med LR 1; *Re B* [1981] 1 WLR 1421 (CA); *Re F (Mental Patient: Sterilisation)* [1990] 2 AC 1.

[42] (1902) 19 TLR 37. See also *Hughes* (1857) Dears & B 248, 169 ER 996, approved in *Roberts* [1942] 1 All ER 187, 192 (CA); *Kelly v The King* [1923] VLR 704, 708 (reversed on a different ground in (1923) 32 CLR 509).

[43] Compare *Smith* (1869) 11 Cox CC 210, where a watchman who deserted his post was held not liable for manslaughter because his employer had no duty to provide a watchman; also *Singh (Gurphal)* [1999] Crim LR 582 (CA) where D, who was in charge of a lodging house while the landlord was away, was held to owe a duty of care to the tenant such that both D and the landlord were guilty of manslaughter when a faulty gas fire caused the tenant's death by carbon monoxide poisoning. The decision in *Smith* is criticised by Turner in Kenny's *Outlines of Criminal Law* (17th ed., 1958) 169.

[44] *Pittwood* (1902) 19 TLR 37, 38: "The man was paid to keep the gate shut and protect the public. . . . A man might incur criminal liability from a duty arising out of contract".

[45] Compare, in contract, the law governing a representation which later becomes false but where the change of circumstances is not disclosed: *With v O'Flanagan* [1936] Ch 575 ("continuing representation") (CA).

[46] [1969] 1 QB 439 (DC).

[47] Which had not itself been an assault because F lacked mens rea at that time.

[48] See below, § 4.1(i)(c).

[49] [1985] AC 147 (PC). See also *Cooper and Schaub* [1994] Crim LR 531 (CA). Kidnapping is also a continuing act: *Dean* [2021] EWCA Crim 1157, [2022] QB 140; cp. *Vu* [2012] 2 SCR 411.

jury that "if, having realised she is not willing, he continues with the act of intercourse, it then becomes rape".[50] On appeal, the correctness of the direction was affirmed by the Privy Council; it is now replicated in the modern law on sexual offences.[51]

Offences of possession, to which we come shortly,[52] can also be (and generally are) committed on a continuing basis. In *Scott v DPP*,[53] D was held to have encouraged a prisoner, E, to commit an offence by telephoning E while E was in prison and unlawfully in possession there of a mobile telephone.[54] As the Court put it,[55]

> "The concept of possession does not relate only to the initial act or circumstances in which the person first comes into possession of a phone. It extends to the continued knowing control of the phone and involves continuing conduct on the part of the person in possession."

As it happens, E knew all along that he had the mobile telephone with him. In principle, however, if E had acquired it unawares, but then kept it when he realised it was with him, E would have committed the possession offence at that later point. D, in turn, could be guilty of encouraging E's offence at any point while it was ongoing.

Technically—that is, in doctrinal terms—continuing acts are not conceived of as omissions. On occasion, that can be something of a fudge. Liability in *Fagan*, for example, was in reality imposed for something D failed to do: that is, to move his car. (*Kaitamaki* is thus a slightly different case, since it involved something D continued actively to do.) However, the fudge is sometimes doctrinally necessary, to cover offences that cannot be committed by omission. We consider this distinction further in Case 5 below.

*Case 5: Duties imposed on persons with a special relationship to the harm.*

In *Miller*,[56] D, a trespasser, fell asleep whilst smoking a cigarette. His mattress caught fire. He awoke to find the mattress smouldering. Without taking any steps to extinguish the fire, he simply moved to the next room and went to sleep. The house itself caught fire, and D was charged with arson. Upholding D's conviction, the House of Lords ruled that the arson had been committed by D's knowing omission to deal with the fire. D's unintentional starting of the fire had, on this analysis, *created* a legal duty "to take measures that lie within one's power to counteract a danger that one has oneself created".[57] The relevant sorts of "danger" are those which threaten an interest protected by the criminal law—thus the duty arises where, unless D intervenes, his earlier, positive, act (in D's case, of smoking in bed) will bring about the prohibited harm.[58]

Note that a defendant's subsequent failure to deal with the risk he has created will not by itself constitute an offence—it must be accompanied by such other elements of the offence as are required, e.g. mens rea. Neither does *Miller* generate any duty to undo a crime that

[50] *Kaitamaki* [1985] AC 147, 151 (PC).
[51] Sexual Offences Act 2003, s. 79(2).
[52] Below, § 4.1(ii)(b).
[53] [2022] EWHC 91 (Admin), [202] 1 WLR 2231.
[54] Contrary to s. 40D of the Prison Act 1952.
[55] *Scott v DPP* [2022] EWHC 91 (Admin), [2022] 1 Cr App R 16, [39].
[56] [1983] 2 AC 161; see Smith's commentary at [1982] Crim LR 526 and Williams's letter to the editor at [1982] *Crim LR* 773.
[57] [1983] 2 AC 161, 176 (Lord Diplock).
[58] Compare also *Santana-Bermudez* [2003] EWHC 2908 (Admin). D lied to a police officer, before being searched, that there were no needles on him. During the search, the officer was pricked by a needle in D's pocket; a risk that D had created. For an extension of this type of case, see *Speck* [1977] 2 All ER 859 (CA), in which D was convicted of gross indecency because he passively allowed an 8-year-old girl to touch him indecently.

has already occurred.[59] The duty is to take reasonable steps to remedy the self-created risk of a future harm prohibited by the criminal law.

It is important to distinguish the basis of liability in *Miller* from the continuing act doctrine (above). The approach taken in *Miller* is generally to be preferred, and indeed *Fagan* can itself be explained as a case where D created the harm and therefore had a duty to counteract that harm.[60] Nonetheless, it is sometimes necessary to rely on the continuing act doctrine. Because *Miller* imposes liability for an omission, it is inapplicable to those offences that cannot be committed by omission,[61] i.e. where the terms of the offence exclude liability for omissions. Offences of this type are the subject of the next section.

The doctrine in *Miller* was grounded in D's own causation of the fire and consequent damage, and it should be restricted to such cases. On that basis, the subsequent decision in *Evans*[62] is dubious. D lived together with her mother and her half-sister, V. D bought heroin for V, who injected herself with it and became ill. D and her mother decided not to seek medical help for V for fear that they may all "get into trouble". V subsequently died. On these facts, D's conviction for manslaughter was upheld on the basis of her (grossly negligent) failure to aid V once it had become obvious that she was seriously ill.

*Evans* goes beyond Miller in the following way. In *Miller*, D had caused ("created") the risk which he later failed to abate. In *Evans*, D did not *cause* the risk: as the House of Lords has made abundantly clear,[63] causal responsibility for the death lay with V herself, when she freely and deliberately injected herself with the heroin that D supplied. According to the Court of Appeal, however, *Miller*-type duties can now arise "when a person has created *or contributed* to the creation of a state of affairs".[64] As D had *contributed* to the danger V was in, D had a duty to address it.

This extension of *Miller* should be doubted.[65] What kind of non-causal contribution to the danger is required? What about another person, E, who may introduce D (or V) to the heroin dealer? Or F, who lends money to buy the drugs? What about a vendor of alcohol, when he sees the buyer in a drunken altercation? Or a driver who leaves his intoxicated friend sleeping in the car on a hot day, never to awake?[66] All kinds of background acts of facilitation could now underpin potential criminal-law duties as "contributions" to the relevant danger. Part of the point of causation doctrines, which we will consider in § 4.2, is to restrict the ambit of criminal responsibility when things go wrong. *Evans* is a plain attempt to evade the scope of those doctrines. In our view, it represents an illegitimate extension of the otherwise sound principle in *Miller*. It is to be hoped that the Court of Appeal's decision will, *at most*, be confined to cases where D has materially contributed to

[59] This explains the unlawful eviction case, *Ahmad* (1987) 84 Cr App R 64.

[60] Where necessary, however, the two cases can be distinguished, since (unlike *Miller*) in *Fagan* the actus reus (application of force to another) had already occurred (or, rather, begun to occur) by the time D acquired mens rea.

[61] Indeed, this restriction was considered in *Fagan* [1969] 1 QB 439, 444 (DC) itself to apply to the offence of assault: "a mere omission to act cannot amount to an assault". See below, §§ 4.1(i)(c), 11.2(i)(b). Surprisingly, this point was not considered in *Santana-Bermudez* [2003] EWHC 2908 (Admin).

[62] [2009] EWCA Crim 650, [2009] 1 WLR 1999; discussed by Williams, "Gross Negligence Manslaughter and Duty of Care in 'Drugs' Cases: *R. v Evans*" [2009] *Crim LR* 631.

[63] *Kennedy (No. 2)* [2007] UKHL 38, [2008] 1 AC 269. We discuss this rule below, in § 4.2(iii)(b) (Principle 1).

[64] [2009] EWCA Crim 650, [2009] 1 WLR 1999, [31].

[65] See, further, Ashworth, "Manslaughter by Omission and the Rule of Law" [2015] *Crim LR* 563, 575–6; Simester, "Free, Deliberate and Informed?" in Simester (ed.), *Modern Criminal Law* (2024) 3, 9–11.

[66] Cp. *R (Lewin) v CPS* [2002] EWHC 1049 (Admin), where the decision not to prosecute was upheld: "the young man who was left in the unlocked car was an adult, not a small child or dog" (at [24]).

and then intentionally failed to prevent the consequences of a risk arising from intervention by the victim.[67]

In one sense, *Evans* is a special case. The legal difficulty arose in part because D helped P to inflict *self*-harm rather than harm to a third person. Because self-harm is not generally a crime, secondary liability usually does not apply and D cannot be convicted of complicity in P's offence.[68] But general principles of responsibility should not be invented on an *ad hoc* basis to deal with specific problems such as this.

*(c) Statutory restrictions: offences that cannot be committed by omission*

Some offences exclude liability for omissions by specifying the particular type of behaviour that is required. For example, section 32 of the OAPA 1861 makes it an offence (*inter alia*) to "put or throw" objects onto a railway. It would seem that this manner of behaving can only be done by a positive act. Similarly, the actus reus of rape requires active sexual intercourse with, including penetration of, V; an omission cannot suffice.[69]

In these offences, liability for omissions is restricted because the behavioural element of the actus reus has been specified quite precisely by statute. Conversely, omission-based liability should normally be possible where an offence has an unspecific behaviour element, and its actus reus is defined mainly by reference to consequences or circumstances. An example of this is murder, for which, in essence, the actus reus requires the causing of one person's death by another.[70] As such, murder can be committed by omission.[71] But what about other offences? A battery, for example, requires *inter alia* the unlawful application of force to another person.[72] Can this be done by omission? The traditional view (adopted in *Fagan*) is no,[73] but there is contradictory authority on the matter.[74] Consider the following example proposed by *Smith, Hogan, and Ormerod*:[75]

> "It is generally said that D must have done some act and that it is not enough that he stood still and obstructed V's passage like an inanimate object. But suppose D is sitting at the corner of a corridor with his legs stretched across it. He hears V running down the corridor and deliberately remains still with the intention that V, on turning the corner, shall fall over his legs. Why should this not be a battery?"

Williams, however, was doubtful. In his view, this:[76]

> "is a case of special type. The man presumably committed an act when he put his foot there in the first place, though initially it was without wrongful intent. When he later failed to remove his foot, with the requisite mental element, he became guilty of an assault under the rule [in *Miller*]."[77]

67 Note that it must *also* be proved that the subsequent omission to intervene was a cause of death, in that, but for D's omission, V would not have died: below, § 4.1(i)(e). This point was not discussed at all by the Court of Appeal in *Evans* [2009] EWCA Crim 650, [2009] 1 WLR 1999.

68 Below, Chapter 7, esp. § 7.6(i).

69 Sexual Offences Act 2003, s. 1. See also the offence of throwing missiles, contrary to the Football (Offences) Act 1991, s. 2.

70 Cp. *Dyson* [1908] 2 KB 454, 457; see generally below, § 10.2(iii).

71 E.g. *Gibbins and Proctor* (1919) 13 Cr App R 134.

72 Below, §§ 11.1–3.

73 *Fagan* [1969] 1 QB 439, 444 (DC).

74 *Santana-Bermudez* [2003] EWHC 2908 (Admin); *Speck* [1977] 2 All ER 859 (CA).

75 *Smith, Hogan, and Ormerod* § 16.1.5.

76 "What Should the Code Do about Omissions?" (1987) 7 *LS* 92, 116.

77 See above, § 4.1(i)(b) (Case 5).

According to Williams, assault cannot be committed by a pure omission:[78]

> "if a person merely stands stock still, being 'entirely passive like a door or a wall' as it was put in one case, it is not an assault, however inconvenient his presence at that particular spot may have been. . . ."

With respect to Williams, the example cannot be analysed as a *Miller*-type situation, unless perhaps P was already running down the corridor when D (without mens rea) stretched out his legs.

The case proposed by *Smith, Hogan, and Ormerod* should not normally be a battery. However, this is not, *contra* Williams, because assault cannot be committed by omission. Rather, it is for the reasons given earlier, in § 4.1(i): that a stranger generally does not owe duties to act to avert harm to others. By contrast, consider a case where a duty *is* owed. It seems implausible to say that a parent who intentionally trips his child in the way *Smith, Hogan, and Ormerod* describes cannot be convicted of assault. He certainly ought to be. It is submitted that where an offence is unspecific as to the manner of behaviour required, it should be possible to commit that offence by omission. The mere fact that an offence is defined in terms of "action", as such, should not be determinative.[79] Positive action is the default requirement of offences with a behavioural element anyway—the entire sphere of omissions liability is predicated on an exception to that requirement.

Sometimes, as we have seen, the action requirement *is* excluded by linguistic considerations. It would be unfair to convict a defendant for conduct the statutory language clearly excludes.[80] But such instances are and should be rare. There is no judicial compunction about saying that a parent can kill a child by failing to feed it,[81] and it is submitted that linguistic conventions that are unreflective of valid moral principles or distinctions should normally not pre-empt the possibility of liability for omissions.

If such harms as "killing", "obstructing",[82] "harassing",[83] and cheating[84] can be done by omission, and if the law on omissions is not to be arbitrary and piecemeal, then a coherent general approach should be taken. Unless the legislature has demonstrated a contrary intention by using language that necessarily requires an act, a criminal offence should be capable of being committed by omission. This is the only approach capable of producing predictable and consistent rather than random law. Any concern over the width of that approach should be tempered by the knowledge that the defendant would have to be under a legal duty to act, and that mens rea (if any) would still have to be proved.[85]

[78] *TBCL* 179, citing *Innes v Wylie* (1844) 1 C & K 257, 263, 174 ER 800, 803.

[79] *Speck* [1977] 2 All ER 859 (CA). Although it sometimes is: *Ahmad* (1987) 84 Cr App R 64 (in the context of the Protection from Eviction Act 1977).

[80] See the fair warning discussion above, § 2.3. For this reason, Williams argues in a letter to the editor of the *Criminal Law Review* that "the courts should not create liability for omissions without statutory authority. Verbs used in defining offences and prima facie implying active conduct should not be stretched by interpretation to include omissions": [1982] *Crim LR* 773. See also his "Criminal Omissions—The Conventional View" (1991) 107 *LQR* 86, 87–9; "What should the Code do about Omissions?" (1987) 7 *LS* 92, 94–5.

[81] For other examples, see *Shama* [1990] 1 WLR 661 (CA); *Firth* (1990) 91 Cr App R 217.

[82] *Stunt v Bolton* [1972] RTR 435 (DC); *Gully v Smith* (1883) 12 QBD 121.

[83] *Yuthiwattana* (1985) 80 Cr App R 55.

[84] *Mavji* [1987] 1 WLR 1388 (CA); *Tonner* [1985] 1 WLR 344 (CA).

[85] The requirement for mens rea, in particular, seems to meet Williams's concern that "[i]t would be unfair to describe a slack and ineffective tenant who lets the premises burn as an arsonist": *TBCL* 152. Williams's concern is more persuasive in relation to offences of strict liability, but even then it speaks to the problematic nature of such offences: see below, Chapter 6.

As was noted in the previous section, even if omission-based liability is excluded by the terms of the offence, a conviction may still be obtained under the continuing act doctrine (above). Suppose that D and V are having consensual sexual intercourse, during which V withdraws her consent. D deliberately fails to withdraw. This is a continuation of the original act of having sexual intercourse with V. Since that behaviour is no longer consensual, D commits the actus reus of rape.[86]

### (d) *Distinguishing acts from omissions*

Given that, as we have seen, there is normally no liability for omissions, it is important to be able to distinguish acts from omissions in order to decide whether a defendant's behaviour counts as one or the other. Unfortunately, the line between them is not easily drawn:[87]

> "If a doctor is keeping a patient alive by cranking the handle of a machine and the doctor then stops, this looks like a clear case of omission. So, too, if the machine is electrically operated but switches itself off every 24 hours and the doctor deliberately does not restart it. Conversely, switching off a functioning machine looks like an act; but is it any different in substance from the first two cases? On the other hand, is it any different from cutting the high-wire on which a tightrope walker is balancing (which is an act, if ever there was one)? Is the ending of a programme of dialysis an omission, while switching off a ventilator an act? Is the discontinuance of a drip feed, which is keeping a patient alive, by withdrawing the tube, an act, and failure to replace an emptied bag an omission? In theory, it might be possible to distinguish between these cases. It seems offensive if liability for homicide is so heavily dependent on such very fine distinctions of this kind; but it appears that that is the case."

Why is switching off a ventilator an act, and failing to (re)start it an omission? The difference seems to be that the former *requires* certain bodily movements, whereas the latter does not. Switching the ventilator off can be done in only one way,[88] but failing to switch the ventilator on (or off) can be done while doing any number of things—one might be talking to the nurse, reading a journal, taking a walk, booking dinner at a restaurant, etc. Similarly, cranking the handle of a machine and cutting the high-wire are actions because they require very specific behaviour by D: "not cranking the handle" and "not replacing the emptied bag" are not specific about D's behaviour at all.

As we saw earlier, this difference is an important facet of the rationale for separating omissions from acts when it comes to criminalisation. Prohibiting omissions rules out many more options than does prohibiting acts. If D is prohibited by law from striking V, that leaves him with plenty of freedom for legal movement of his arm, not to mention the rest of his body. But if D is *required* to strike V (i.e. prohibited from omitting to do so) then his freedom of movement is severely curtailed. Assuming he wishes to avoid criminal liability, his options are down to one.

[86] *Kaitamaki* [1985] AC 147 (PC); *Cooper and Schaub* [1994] Crim LR 531 (CA). These decisions are now entrenched in legislation by s. 79(2) of the Sexual Offences Act 2003. D will be liable for rape unless D reasonably believes V continues to consent.

[87] *Smith, Hogan, and Ormerod* § 2.4.2.4. See, in respect of the examples, Kennedy, "Switching Off Life Support Machines: The Legal Implications" [1977] *Crim LR* 443; Beynon, "Doctors as Murderers" [1982] *Crim LR* 17. A helpful overview of academic discussion in this area is McGee, "Finding a Way Through the Ethical and Legal Maze: Withdrawal of Medical Treatment and Euthanasia" (2005) 15 *Medical LR* 357.

[88] Or, at most, in only a few ways.

Once a legal duty to act has been recognised, however, the difficulty of separating acts and omissions becomes legally insignificant—either will suffice. With this in mind, we should reconsider *Smith, Hogan, and Ormerod's* remark (above) that "it seems offensive if liability for homicide is so heavily dependent on such very fine distinctions of this kind; but it appears that that is the case". The obvious response is that liability does not *just* depend on the act/omission distinction, but also on the issue in each case whether D is under a legal duty to intervene. What the examples do suggest, though, is that one might be doubtful of the judicial reasoning in life-and-death medical cases. In *Airedale NHS Trust v Bland*,[89] B had been in a persistent vegetative state for 3½ years after being injured in the Hillsborough football stadium disaster. There was no medical hope of improvement. Having obtained parental consent, the hospital applied to the High Court for a declaration that it would be lawful to discontinue artificial feeding and hydration, with the intention that B should be allowed to die. The House of Lords upheld the declaration. Their Lordships affirmed that for the doctors to bring about B's death by lethal injection or suchlike would be murder,[90] but reasoned that (i) what was proposed was an omission rather than an act, and (ii) the legal duty of the doctors did not extend to prolonging treatment of a patient when it was no longer in his best interests to do so.[91]

The difficulty with this reasoning is that ceasing treatment normally involves switching off a ventilator or other life-support machine. Notwithstanding that the House of Lords explicitly countenanced this step in *Bland*,[92] it is an act, not an omission. An intruder who does such a thing commits murder, even though she has no legal duty to save the patient's life. The true explanation of these cases must surely be that there is a limited justification available to doctors, in certain circumstances, to take some quite specific measures toward ending their patients' lives. Those measures can include particular acts as well as omissions; although the permissible scope of such measures remains, of course, a matter of intense and shifting ethical debate.[93]

### (e) Omissions and consequences: causation

One question that arises for omissions is whether or not they can be said to "cause" things. Characteristically, what is significant about omissions is that they fail to prevent *other* factors from bringing about the harm. If D watches from the beach while V drowns, a post mortem will conclude that V's death was caused by drowning. D merely failed to intervene: can she truly be said to have caused V's death? We shall consider this question more fully in § 4.2(iv), when we discuss causation. But it is clear that, in the law, omissions can be causes. If D's intervention would have saved V (and we must be sure of that beyond reasonable doubt), then her failure to intervene was *a* reason why V drowned. And if D had a legal duty to save her, then that failure will be a cause of death in law.

[89] [1993] AC 789. See Keown, "Restoring Moral and Intellectual Shape to the Law after *Bland*" (1997) 113 *LQR* 481.

[90] A conclusion endorsed in *R (Nicklinson) v Ministry of Justice* [2014] UKSC 38, [2015] AC 657.

[91] [1993] AC 789, 868–9 (Lord Goff). Compare *Re A (Children)* [2001] Fam 147 (CA), where surgical intervention was ruled to be a positive act. Cf. McEwan, "Murder by Design: The Feel-good Factor and the Criminal Law" (2001) 9 *Medical LR* 246.

[92] [1993] AC 789, 866 (Lord Goff), 881–2 (Lord Browne-Wilkinson).

[93] Contrast the decisions in *R (Pretty)* [2001] UKHL 61, [2002] 1 AC 800 and *Re B* [2002] EWHC 429 (Fam), [2002] 2 All ER 449. See, further, Jackson and Keown, *Debating Euthanasia* (2011).

### (ii) Crimes with no (explicit) behaviour element

Some academic writers have suggested that there can be no criminal liability without a "voluntary act" on the part of the defendant; meaning by this that there must be (i) a behavioural element specified in every actus reus, which (ii) must be done "voluntarily" by the defendant.[94] For the most part, the second aspect of this suggestion seems right (see below, § 4.3). The first claim, however, is less plausible.

It is certainly true that crimes such as murder, rape, and assault—with which ordinary citizens are most familiar, and which have the greatest moral resonance—are crimes which require wrong*doing*, and necessarily involve some behaviour (whether act or omission) by the defendant. But many other crimes stipulate no behavioural element on the part of the defendant. These are offences which penalise a defendant on the basis of the situation in which she finds herself. It is the circumstances themselves which make up the harm that the criminal law is designed to address, and so it is possible to specify the actus reus of these crimes solely by reference to those circumstances.

For convenience, we can divide offences of this sort into two main types: crimes where the actus reus specifies only the occurrence of some state of affairs; and crimes of possession.

#### (a) Crimes involving states of affairs

Sometimes known as crimes of "situational liability",[95] these are crimes where the actus reus is simply an event or circumstance that is in some way connected to the defendant. An example is provided by section 3(1) of the Prevention of Oil Pollution Act 1971:

> If any oil to which section 1 of this Act applies, or any mixture containing such oil, is discharged into any part of the sea (a) from a pipe-line . . . then, subject to the following provisions of this Act, the owner of the pipe-line . . . shall be guilty of an offence. . . .

Here the actus reus of the offence is apparently complete without the need to prove any act or omission on the part of the defendant.[96]

Of course, it is not enough for a defendant to be criminally liable for an offence just because something bad happens—e.g. because a pipe-line leaks oil into the sea. The defendant must in some way be connected to, and responsible for, the actus reus. Normally this connection is through his having a particular status, or relationship, with respect to that actus reus. If a pipe-line discharges oil, it is the pipe-line's *owner* who is picked out for attention by the criminal law, and not, for instance, every person living or sailing nearby. Situational offences are in this respect similar to offences of omission, in that they raise the problem of attribution to defendants, discussed earlier (§ 1.2(ii)(e)). The potential for overbroad criminalisation makes it important for legislators to restrict the scope of liability to

[94] E.g. Stephen, *A History of the Criminal Law of England* (1883) vol. II, 97; Cross and Jones, *An Introduction to Criminal Law* (3rd ed., 1953) 32; Turner, Kenny's *Outlines of Criminal Law* (17th ed., 1958) 26–7; O'Connor and Fairall, *Criminal Defences* (2nd ed., 1988) 2, 6–7; Moore, *Act and Crime* (1993) chap. 2. The claim made is normally, in fact, even stronger: that there must be a positive (and voluntary) act by the defendant specified in every actus reus. The phrasing in the text is designed to allow for omissions.

[95] Glazebrook, "Situational Liability" in Glazebrook (ed.), *Reshaping the Criminal Law* (1978) 108; Cohen, "The 'Actus Reus' and Offences of 'Situation'" (1972) 7 *Israel LR* 186. Crimes of this sort have sometimes been ruled unconstitutional in the United States: *Robinson v California* 370 US 660 (1962) (being addicted to narcotics); *Papachristou v City of Jacksonville* 405 US 156 (1972) (being a vagrant).

[96] Limited defences are, however, provided by ss. 3(1) and 6 of the same Act.

only those defendants who are responsible for, and in a position to control, the prohibited situation.

The requirement for a particular status or relationship is typically found in a second type of situational liability: the vicarious criminal liability sometimes imposed on employers for the acts of their employees. Vicarious liability is dealt with further in Chapter 8.[97]

A third form of situational liability may be seen in the notorious case of *Larsonneur*.[98] In that case, D was convicted of being found in the United Kingdom when permission for her to enter the country had previously been refused.[99] It was, however, undisputed that the reason for her being back on UK soil was that she had been brought there against her will by the police. Be that as it may, the Court of Criminal Appeal indicated that the circumstances by which she found herself to be in the UK (whether damning or exonerating) were "perfectly immaterial".[100] In convicting her of a situational liability offence, the law picked out Larsonneur because it was she to whom the actus reus happened, and not because of anything she had done.[101]

*Larsonneur* has rightly been widely criticised.[102] But the proper reason for criticising it is less clear. One problem with the case is that the language used in many situational offences appears not to require any mens rea or fault element on the part of the defendant, and thereby imposes what is known as *strict liability*. This is an important criticism, and we shall return to it in § 6.3. But that has not been the only ground of opposition. Ashworth, for instance, once disapproved of "defining an offence in a way that seems to require no act by the defendant as a basis for liability".[103] The objection was that, quite apart from there being no mens rea element, there is no behavioural requirement in the actus reus. However, there is nothing inherently defective or unjust about an offence that contains no specific behaviour element. What matters instead is that the defendant had some measure of control over her being in the proscribed situation.

To see this, *Larsonneur* may be contrasted with the New Zealand case of *Finau v Department of Labour*.[104] D was prosecuted under the Immigration Act 1964 for remaining in New Zealand after the expiry of her visitor's permit. The Court of Appeal upheld D's appeal

[97] See also above, § 1.2(ii)(e).

[98] (1934) 24 Cr App R 74. A later case to similar effect is *Winzar v Chief Constable of Kent*, *The Times*, 28 March 1983 (DC). D, who had been brought to hospital but found merely to be drunk, was subsequently removed by the police to their car parked on the road outside; whereupon he was charged with being found drunk on the highway. His conviction was upheld. Contrast *Winzar* with decisions in other jurisdictions: *O'Sullivan v Fisher* [1954] SASR 33; *Palmer-Brown v Police* [1985] 1 NZLR 365.

[99] A more familiar example of a "presence" offence can be found in s. 4(2) of the Road Traffic Act 1988: being in charge of a vehicle in a public place when unfit to drive through drink or drugs. Cp. *Richardson* [2018] EWHC 428 (Admin), [2019] 4 WLR 46 (where, however, D's conviction was ultimately quashed because the car park in which he was found was not a public one).

[100] (1934) 24 Cr App R 74, 78.

[101] Although see Lanham, "*Larsonneur* Revisited" [1976] *Crim LR* 276, who suggests the possibility of prior fault. While the Court did not take account of that possibility, doing so would allow *Larsonneur* to be read consistently with other English decisions holding that D must have been able to avoid the relevant state of affairs, notably *Robinson-Pierre* [2013] EWCA Crim 2396, [2014] 1 WLR 2638. See below, § 4.3(ii).

[102] E.g. Hall, *GPCL* 329, n. 14; Williams, *CLGP* 11; Howard, *Strict Responsibility* (1963) 47–8.

[103] *Principles of Criminal Law* (2nd ed., 1995) 105. The discussion of *Larsonneur* was modified in later editions, withdrawing the phrasing quoted here.

[104] [1984] 2 NZLR 396. See, also, *Martin v Alabama* 17 So 2d 427 (1944). Contrast the approach of the House of Lords in *Porter v Honey* [1988] 1 WLR 1420, which sought to exculpate a blameless defendant through techniques of statutory interpretation, rather than by reference to impossibility: see below, § 4.3(ii)(b).

against conviction on the basis that it had been impossible for her to leave the country, owing to her pregnancy and the consequent refusal of any airline to carry her.

The result in the New Zealand case demonstrates that there need be no injustice, and there is nothing intrinsically wrong, in criminalising states of affairs, so long as the class of potential defendants is clearly identified. However, *Finau* makes it clear that there is a further requirement under New Zealand law: that the defendant could have done something about the relevant state of affairs' existence. The actus reus, although it specifies no act or omission, must still have been *voluntary*. It is the failure of English law to observe *this* requirement which seems to us the main problem with *Larsonneur*, and the reason why the decision in that case is so objectionable.[105]

At the level of theory,[106] two points emerge from this comparison. First, where the defendant *could* have prevented the actus reus from occurring, then situational liability operates, in effect, just like liability for voluntary omissions. Indirectly, it involves the defendant being prosecuted for her failure or omission to prevent the state of affairs from developing.[107]

Conversely, it is submitted that, unless there is a requirement of voluntariness, situational offences are at odds with the deepest presuppositions of the criminal law. The very notion of a trial, of a plea, assumes putative answerability for something.[108] One is not answerable for a state of affairs (e.g. having red hair), and it should not be the actus reus of an offence, unless one is able to avoid that state of affairs (e.g. by shaving one's head or dyeing the hair another colour).

Turning to matters of doctrine, it is clear that English law allows liability to be imposed for situational offences, without it being necessary to prove a voluntary act or omission by the defendant. We return to this point in detail below (§§ 4.3(ii), 6.2(i)).

### *(b) Crimes of possession*

Possessory offences are creations of statute. They are not found in the common law.[109] There are a number of such offences especially relating to controlled drugs, to weapons, and to tools of crime.[110] According to section 5(2) of the Misuse of Drugs Act 1971, for example,

[105] For an argument that to convict D on facts such as *Larsonneur* contravenes D's right to a fair trial guaranteed by Art 6(1) of the European Convention on Human Rights, see Sullivan, "Strict Liability for Criminal Offences in England and Wales following Incorporation into English Law of the European Convention on Human Rights" in Simester (ed.), *Appraising Strict Liability* (2005) 195, 207–10. An argument that a conviction in such circumstances breaches the presumption of innocence guaranteed by Art. 6(2) of the Convention failed, however, in *Barnfather v London Borough of Islington Education Authority* [2003] EWHC 418 (Admin), [2003] 1 WLR 2318. The literal and intransigent approach of English law to the frequently prosecuted parental truanting offence is vividly exemplified by *Hampshire County Council v E* [2007] EWHC 2584 (Admin), where duress was rejected as a defence on the ground that the behaviour element of the offence was perpetrated by the child rather than the parent. For a comparison of English and New Zealand judicial approaches to offences of this kind, see Sullivan, "Parents and their Truanting Children: An English Lesson in Liability Without Responsibility" (2010) 12 *Otago LR* 285.

[106] See, more generally, Child, "Defense of a Basic Voluntary Act Requirement in Criminal Law from Philosophies of Action" (2020) 23 *New Crim LR* 437; Simester, *Fundamentals* § 8.4.

[107] An illustrative New Zealand case of this sort is *Tifaga v Department of Labour* [1980] 2 NZLR 235. There D *was* convicted of overstaying, following the termination of his temporary entry permit, because his inability to leave the country was due to his own failure to retain sufficient funds to do so.

[108] See Duff, *Answering for Crime* (2007).

[109] Compare, e.g., *Heath* (1810) Russ & Ry 184, 168 ER 750; *Dugdale v R.* (1853) 1 E & B 435, 118 ER 499.

[110] E.g. s. 25 of the Theft Act 1968 (going equipped for stealing); s. 1 of the Firearms Act 1968 (possession of an unlicensed firearm).

"it is an offence for a person to have a controlled drug in his possession". The offence makes no reference to the defendant's conduct.

Characteristically, possession is criminalised as a convenient substitute for the harm that is really objected to, being the *use* of the thing possessed.[111] Criminalisation at an earlier stage both simplifies evidential issues and makes an offence out of behaviour which might otherwise not even count as an *attempt* to do the ultimate crime contemplated. Thus, if offences of this sort did not exist, the police would not be able to intervene at an early stage to prevent many crimes without the prospective offender's escaping the clutches of the criminal law (especially in the context of the illicit trades in proscribed drugs and illegal weapons). It is undesirable as well as wasteful of resources that the police should have to wait until the contraband is about to be used before making an arrest.[112]

In crimes of possession, there is no formal requirement for an act or omission by the defendant.[113] No doubt D put the crowbar in his car before heading out to commit a burglary, but the offence of going equipped for stealing requires only that he *has* it.[114] So far as proving the actus reus is concerned, it does not matter how that situation came about.[115] Nonetheless, like offences of situational liability, possessory offences can normally be thought of as having an implicit behavioural element,[116] albeit one that the prosecution need not prove. In effect, criminalisation of D's possession of the crowbar may be treated as imposing an indirect liability, either for the act of obtaining the crowbar (i.e. acquiring possession) or for the omission by D to dispose of it.[117]

This is why possession offences are continuing in nature.[118] Like situational offences, they contain no formal requirement for proof of a behavioural element on the part of the defendant. Despite this, criminal convictions in these cases can usually be explained in the indirect terms just mentioned: that is, by reference to an implicit act or omission by the

[111] Alternatively, the wrong is sometimes in the *making* of the thing, as in the possession of indecent photographs of children contrary to s. 160(1) of the Criminal Justice Act 1988 (the making of such photographs itself being a criminal offence under s. 1(1) of the Protection of Children Act 1978).

[112] For criticism of this rationale, see Ashworth, *Positive Obligations in the Criminal Law* (2013) chap. 6; Fletcher, *Rethinking Criminal Law* (1978) 197–205. Dubber makes a powerful case for seeing possession offences as a paradigm control mechanism for reinforcing state authority: "The Possession Paradigm: The Special Part and the Police Power Model of the Criminal Process" in Duff and Green (eds.), *Defining Crimes* (2005) 91.

[113] It is otherwise in the United States; § 2.01(4) of the Model Penal Code states that possession is established "if the possessor knowingly procured or received the thing possessed or was aware of his control thereof for a sufficient period to have been able to terminate his possession".

[114] Theft Act 1968, s. 25. The physical nature of the possession requirement varies for different offences. Under s. 25, it is necessary to show that D "has with him" the instrument of theft, burglary, etc.; which requires personal possession, either upon one's person or in one's car nearby: cp. *Doukas* [1978] 1 WLR 372 (CA); *McCalla* (1988) 87 Cr App R 372, 378. By contrast, it will ordinarily be enough for possession that the prohibited item is held by a third party on behalf of D: *Kelt* [1977] 1 WLR 1365 (CA); *Sullivan v Earl of Caithness* [1976] QB 966 (DC). In the case of drugs, the physical element of possession will be established if the substance is present at a place which is subject to D's dominion or control: *Lewis* (1988) 87 Cr App R 270. On the complicated requirements regarding proof that D had a bladed article "with" one in a public place, see *Henderson* [2016] EWCA Crim 965, [2016] 4 WLR 172.

[115] Moreover, the mode of acquisition may be relevant to mens rea. In particular, the possibility of inadvertent possession is usually excluded by the mens rea requirement of knowledge that the courts have held is implicit in the word "possess". Cf. *Cugullere* [1961] 1 WLR 858 (CA); *Warner v Metropolitan Police Commissioner* [1969] 2 AC 256; below, §§ 4.3(ii)(c), 5.6(iv).

[116] Cp. Yaffe, "In Defense of Criminal Possession" (2016) 10 *Crim Law and Philosophy* 441.

[117] Cp. Williams, *CLGP* 8; Moore, *Act and Crime* (1993) 21; *Porter* [2006] EWCA Crim 560, [2006] 1 WLR 2633 (rendering electronic images irretrievable, at least to D).

[118] Above, § 4.1(i)(b) (Case 4); *Scott v DPP* [2022] EWHC 91 (Admin), [2022] 1 WLR 2231.

defendant. Recognition of this implicit element helps to explain some of the more difficult cases where D did not obtain the prohibited item by dint of his own efforts. Suppose that D is stopped while in his car, and is found to have with him a package containing cannabis. He claims, however, that he had nothing to do with the presence of the package in his car, and that it had been placed there by a friend. While that claim would suggest that D is not responsible—and therefore should not be criminally liable[119]—for the fact that the cannabis is in his possession, the law may still be justified in imposing criminal liability because of his voluntary failure to dispose of the item. The difficult cases for this analysis occur when D's possession (whether by acquisition or non-disposal) is *involuntary*. We shall return to this issue in § 4.3(ii).

## § 4.2 Consequences: the need for causation

Not all consequences involve persons. For example, the sudden arrival of a very large meteor is thought to have caused the extinction of dinosaurs; and the collapse of many of San Francisco's buildings in 1906 occurred because of an earthquake. For the purposes of the criminal law, however, consequences are those events or states of affairs which are the result of (i.e. *caused* by) a defendant's behaviour. Thus, whenever a consequence, such as death, is specified as part of the actus reus of an offence, the prosecution must prove both that the consequence occurred and that the defendant's behaviour caused that consequence.

This does not mean that the defendant must in any immediate physical sense cause the consequence. A post-disaster inquiry may find that D was in flagrant breach of his duty in failing to pass on a flood warning to the emergency services of the devastated city. The flooding is the most direct physical cause of the deaths by drowning; but, in law, D's behaviour will also be regarded as *one* of the causes of the deaths of those who would have been saved had he done his duty. It is enough that there is *a* causal link from D's behaviour to the consequence. This point cannot be overemphasised, and we return to it in § 4.2(ii)(c): *there can be multiple legal causes of the same result; D's behaviour need be only one of them.*

The requirement of causation is fundamental to our understanding of the actus reus in criminal law. Suppose, for example, that V dies. The result, death, is an element of the actus reus of murder. But normally it would be wrong to hold someone who does not cause V's death guilty of murder. Imagine B is a bystander who happens to be standing beside V when, suddenly, D rushes up to V and stabs him fatally. Here our criminal law takes a very individualistic approach, emphasising the distinctive responsibility of citizens for their own actions. Even if B had, in fact, been planning to kill V himself, and had delightedly stood aside upon perceiving D's murderous intentions, B would not be a murderer.[120] Neither does the law prosecute D's parents, who brought D up in such a way that he was not adequately instilled with the values that would have stopped him from killing V. In short, there is no doctrine of collective social responsibility in our criminal law. This reflects the nature of our society. Even in team games, such as a football match, the newspaper statistics

[119] See above, § 1.2; below, § 4.3.

[120] B may, however, become guilty of murder if, before D acts, B manifests her delight in a manner which is intended to encourage, and in fact encourages, D to commit the offence. Not all liability for outcomes is predicated on *the defendant's* having caused the outcome; she may be held responsible for the consequence of someone else's actions as a secondary party. See below, Chapter 7.

record the names of those who scored goals. Of course, other approaches are possible.[121] At one time, it was the practice in Greece to hold the entire city punishable for the crimes of its leaders. Similarly, the ancient Chinese doctrine of *tsua-lian* would result in a whole family or village being punished for the wrongdoing of one of its members. But these are not the ways of liberal democracies. Moreover, to impose criminal liability upon someone for the actions of others would not only be out of step with public perceptions, but would also substantially restrict individual liberty.[122]

### *(i) The rule of thumb*

As a matter of doctrine, the starting, and frequently finishing, point of any causation problem is the "but for" or *sine qua non* test: would the consequence specified in the actus reus have occurred *but for* the defendant's behaviour?[123] If it would not have occurred except for the defendant's acting as he did, then prima facie his behaviour caused that consequence. Conversely, if the result would have occurred anyway, that is a reason to deny the existence of causation (and consequently to refrain from holding the defendant criminally liable for the occurrence of the actus reus).

Suppose, for example, that a doctor injects his patient with a painkiller, and the patient subsequently dies. Whether or not the doctor is guilty of manslaughter or murder depends upon a number of factors, but he definitely commits neither offence unless injecting the painkiller caused that patient's death. If the patient would have died when she did whether or not the doctor had injected her (e.g. of an unrelated heart attack), then the *but for* test is not satisfied and we have grounds for saying that the doctor's actions did not cause her death.[124] Conversely, if it can be proved that (subject to a *de minimis* exception[125]) she would not have died *when she did* without the doctor's intervention, then prima facie he caused her death.[126]

Most of the time, the *but for* test will, in the absence of any unusual circumstances, be a reasonable indicator of causation. Indeed, it has become somewhat orthodox (but, as explained below, a mistake) to view but for causation as step one in a two-step analysis, the second step being legal causation (explained in more depth below).[127]

Suppose, for instance, that D invites V to meet her for lunch. Unfortunately, while driving to their rendezvous, V's car is hit by a runaway lorry, the brakes of which have failed. But for D's inviting V to lunch, the accident would not have occurred. Yet in law D did not cause the accident: she was not responsible for the brake failure. Thus D did not cause V's death.

[121] See, e.g., Fauconnet, *La Responsabilité* (1920).

[122] Cp. the argument against liability for omissions, above, § 4.1(i)(a).

[123] This is a particularly important test in the context of omissions: see below, § 4.2(iv).

[124] Cf. *Master* [2007] EWCA Crim 142, where D stabbed V 11 times, aggravating a condition of deep-vein thrombosis from which she died. Although the pre-existing condition might have killed V anyway, D's acts were held to have accelerated her death significantly. Hence causation of V's death was established.

[125] Below, § 4.2(ii)(a).

[126] Cf. *Dalloway* (1847) 2 Cox CC 273; *White* [1910] 2 KB 124 (CA).

[127] Cp. *L* [2010] EWCA Crim 1249, [2011] RTR 19, [9] ("the defendant's driving must have played a part not simply in creating the occasion for the fatal accident, i.e. causation in the 'but for' sense, but in bringing it about"); *Hughes* [2013] UKSC 56, [2013] 1 WLR 2461, [23]. This is old common law: "It must have been the *causa causans*; it is not enough that it may have been the *causa sine qua non*.' *Emperor v Omkar Rampratap* (1902) 4 Bom LR 679, 682.

The *but for* test also misdirects in *Hensler*.[128] D sent V a begging letter in which he misrepresented his plight. V was not deceived, but nevertheless sent D some money. On these facts, although V would not have sent the money but for D's letter, D could not be convicted of obtaining by false pretences, because the false pretence had not caused D to send the money.[129] The presence of *but for* causation does not, then, imply that there is legal causation.[130]

Conversely, the absence of *but for* causation does not imply an absence of legal causation either.[131] In other words, *but for* causation is not a necessary condition of legal causation. Suppose this time that D sets fire to V's house, razing it. It turns out, however, that there was a faulty electrical circuit in the house that was about to overheat and cause a similar fire. We cannot say that, *but for* D's conduct, V's house would not have burned down. Yet despite this, it *is* D who causes the damage by the fire he set. Similarly, imagine that D and E each strike V, causing him to fall to the ground and strike his head. The head injury is fatal. Each blow was sufficient to cause V to fall as he did. Again we are unable to say that, but for D's conduct, V would not have died. Yet D's action causes V's death (as does E's).

The difficulty arises because so-called *but for* "causation" *is not in itself a form of causation at all.* Rather, it is a formula which merely expresses a certain logical relationship between two things: that, in the circumstances, it was impossible for the second event (the "consequence") to happen without the first action (the "cause") having occurred. What matters in the law is not *whether* there is a *but for* relationship between the defendant's behaviour and the prohibited consequence, but *why* (or why not). It is only by investigating that further question that we can decide whether there is a causal relationship *in law*. This is why *but for* "causation" should be treated with care, and seen as being at most an indicator of causation rather than an essential first step in a two-step analysis.

### *(ii) Causation in law*

Some causal relationships are very mechanical, and present no problems for the law. This sort of causation occurs when the action leads to the relevant consequence through the ordinary workings of physics, biochemistry, and the like. Thus the connection between D's knocking over the tumbler and its watery contents pouring out is a simple mechanical one; the consequence follows straightforwardly given the existence of gravity and the fluidity of the liquid inside, without the intervention of subsequent events. The connection between D's shooting V and V's consequential death is normally just as straightforward, something that a pathologist will usually be able to discuss in technical terms.

Difficulties arise when there are other actions, or events of nature, which *also* play a role in bringing about the relevant consequence. Consider, for example, the facts in *Pittwood*.[132] D failed to close the gate at a railway crossing, with the result that a cart entered the crossing

[128] (1870) 11 Cox CC 570.

[129] D was, however, convicted of an attempt to obtain by false pretences. Compare *Mills* (1857) Dears & Bell 205, 169 ER 978. If similar facts arose today, D would be guilty of fraud by false representation, contrary to s. 2 of the Fraud Act 2006. It is enough for that offence to make a false or misleading statement with a view to gain or causing loss: no actual gain or loss need occur. See below, § 15.3.

[130] However, as will be seen in § 4.2(iv) below, *but for* causation remains important as a causative test for omissions.

[131] This point is sometimes obscured by general claims about the "but for" analysis being "the first step in establishing causation": as in *Wallace* [2018] EWCA Crim 690, [2018] 2 Cr App R 22, [53].

[132] (1902) 19 TLR 37.

and was hit by a train. A passenger on the cart was killed. One can say, of this case, that the arrival of the train was itself a causal factor in the accident and thus the passenger's death, and the train's arrival, was independent of D's behaviour. Yet we can still agree that D's negligence caused the crash. Why?

It is not possible to give a definitive analysis of the principles of criminal-law causation here.[133] But over the following pages a number of guiding principles will be suggested. Perhaps the most important point to remember during the discussion which follows is that, while causation frequently depends upon physical, mechanical, relationships between actions and outcomes (such as the relationship that D's firing a gun may bear to V's death a moment later), causation is also often, but not always,[134] a function of moral and policy evaluations about D's responsibility for an event.[135] When we state that Pittwood's dereliction "caused" an accident, we are articulating a view that he was responsible for that accident through his behaviour. In other words, the ascription of causation in *Pittwood* is not so much a *prerequisite* of his being held responsible as it is an expression of the moral *conclusion* that, through his behaviour, he is responsible, and legally answerable, for the accident that resulted. The moral considerations underlying that conclusion find legal expression in the guiding principles outlined below.

*(a) Significant (i.e. non-negligible) cause*

Whatever other causes play a role in bringing the actus reus about, the first requirement is that D's behaviour must contribute in some significant way to its occurrence.[136] In *White*,[137] W gave his mother poison. He had not, however, given her a sufficient dose to cause death. She died of an unrelated heart attack. W was guilty of attempted murder. He did not commit murder because the poison played no role in his mother's death.

The basic point is that the contribution that D makes must be more than insignificant; more than *de minimis*.[138] If a doctor takes a blood sample from a patient who is dying from gunshot wounds, the additional loss of blood for the sample may further weaken the patient and hasten death by a few moments. But the doctor's role in the patient's death is, in this context, causally insignificant, and the law will impute the death solely to the gunshot wounds.[139]

However, the defendant's contribution need only be *significant*.[140] It need not be the, or even a, major factor. In *Hennigan*,[141] for example, a driver emerged inappropriately from a

[133] The classic work is *Hart and Honoré*. See also Kadish, *Blame and Punishment* (1987) chap. 8; Williams, *TBCL* chap. 16. For more philosophical discussion, see Honoré, "Necessary and Sufficient Conditions in Tort Law" in Owen (ed.), *Philosophical Foundations of Tort Law* (1995) 363; Mackie, "Causes and Conditions" in Sosa (ed.), *Causation and Conditionals* (1975) 15; Moore, *Causation and Responsibility* (2009); Simester, *Fundamentals* chap. 5.

[134] *Contra* du Bois-Pedain, "*Novus Actus* and Beyond: Attributing Causal Responsibility in the Criminal Courts" (2021) 80 *CLJ* (Supp) s61. For a straightforward example of physical causation, see *Smith* [1959] 2 QB 35 (C-MAC); discussed below, § 4.2(i)(c) and § 4.2(ii)(c).

[135] *Maybin* [2012] 2 SCR 30, [29].

[136] *Wallace* [2018] EWCA Crim, [2018] 2 Cr App R 22, [64].

[137] [1910] 2 KB 124 (CA).

[138] See *Cato* [1976] 1 WLR 110, 116–7 (CA).

[139] Cf. *Adams*, described in Palmer, "Dr. Adams' Trial for Murder" [1957] Crim LR 365. The direction to the jury by Devlin J is reproduced in Arlidge, "The Trial of Dr David Moor" [2000] *Crim LR* 31, 34–5. Where the role of the doctor is not causally insignificant, the doctor may require a defence, e.g. of necessity: cp. *Re A (Children)* [2001] Fam 147; below, § 21.4.

[140] *Kennedy (No. 2)* [2007] UKHL 38, [2008] 1 AC 269, [7], citing (*inter alia*) *Cato* [1976] 1 WLR 110, 116–7 (CA). For the application of this standard test in the context of omissions, see below, § 4.2(iv).

[141] [1971] 3 All ER 133 (CA). Cp. *Garforth* [1954] Crim LR 936 (CA).

junction and was hit by D, who was speeding. Two passengers were killed in the collision. It was ruled wrong to direct a jury that D was not liable if less than one-fifth to blame for the actus reus. Certainly, D's behaviour need not be the main cause of death. It is enough that her conduct plays a part which is not "minute or negligible",[142] or not "insignificant".[143] Obviously, this test is imprecise, and affords considerable latitude to juries in deciding questions of causation.

*(b) Causal salience*

As well as making a "not insignificant" contribution, D's causal role must also be *salient*. Suppose that D is driving to work at a speed in excess of the speed limit. He slows to the correct speed in advance of an intersection, but is involved in an accident on the intersection with another car. If he had not been speeding he would not have arrived at the intersection when he did, and the accident would not have occurred. But his speeding is not salient with regard to the accident. Although it meant that D was present in a particular place at a particular time, his speeding in no way affected the likelihood of this type of accident's occurring. The risk would have been just as great had he arrived later.[144] Indeed, the accident would not have happened if his speed had been even *more* excessive.

It is sometimes helpful to elucidate the requirement of salience by reference to the question of whether the harm that occurred was "within the risk" unleashed by the defendant's conduct. A good example is offered by Hart and Honoré:[145]

> "If it is negligent of the defendant to hand a child a loaded gun, and the child drops the gun on his foot and injures it, the injury to the foot is not within the risk (shooting) that made it negligent to hand the child the loaded gun. It is also true that the aspect of the defendant's conduct which made it negligent, the fact that the gun was loaded, was not causally relevant to the injury, since that fact did not significantly increase the gun's weight."

Here D, by giving the gun to the child at all (whether loaded or not), played a causal role in V's subsequent injury. But the reasons why D acted wrongfully—which concern the risk that the child will discharge the gun—are in no way salient to the injury that V sustains. Accordingly, D did not cause V's injury in the sense required by the criminal law.

Salience is frequently in point in cases of manslaughter, whether by gross negligence or by an unlawful and dangerous act. In each case, it must be the conduct constituting the gross negligence or the unlawful and dangerous act that caused death. Conversely, it is impermissible for the Crown to prove gross negligence by reference to conduct, even grossly culpable conduct, that is not causatively salient to the fatality. In the New Zealand case of *Fenton*,[146] for example, V had been a passenger D's utility vehicle, and had died in a collision. It was accepted that D's driving had been negligent. The prosecution attempted to prove gross negligence by reference to the following additional factors: D's vehicle lacked a warrant of fitness and registration, D was failing to wear a seatbelt, and D had converted the vehicle without the owner's permission. On the facts, however, none of

142 *Williams* [2010] EWCA Crim 2552, [2011] 1 WLR 588, [33]–[36]; *L* [2010] EWCA Crim 1249, [2011] RTR 19, [9] (not "negligible").

143 *Cato* [1976] 1 WLR 110, 116–7 (CA); *Cheshire* [1991] 1 WLR 844, 852 (CA).

144 Cp. *Berry v Sugar Notch Borough* 43 A 240 (1899); *Hart and Honoré* 168–70; Williams, *TBCL* 387.

145 *Hart and Honoré* lxiii. Cp. *Wrigley* (1829) 1 Lew CC 171, 168 ER 1001; *Gorris v Scott* (1874) LR 9 Ex 125.

146 [2003] 3 NZLR 439, esp. [14]–[15].

these features of the case was relevant to the explanation of why D's conduct had caused V's death: they *may* have been salient causes on a different set of facts, but were not in this case. In particular, the accident occurred because of D's bad driving, not because of any defect in the car.

Similarly, in the English case of *Carey*,[147] the defendants were convicted of affray and of manslaughter by unlawful and dangerous act, after a confrontation in which one of them punched V. Subsequently V, a seemingly healthy 15-year-old girl, died from unexpected ventricular fibrillation triggered, apparently, by her flight. The Court of Appeal quashed the manslaughter convictions. The punch, which was certainly an unlawful and dangerous act, was not the cause of death, for it was not salient in the resulting death. Even if the *affray* was a cause of death, on the other hand, in the view of the Court it was not itself "dangerous", in the technical sense required in the law of manslaughter.[148]

### (c) Multiple causes

The fact that a cause need only be "significant" connects to a further principle, which it can be easy to lose sight of: that there may be multiple causes of the same event. In *Pittwood*,[149] both the arrival of the train and the defendant's failure to close the gate were causes of the accident and the resulting death. This may be true even when more than one person commits an offence.[150] Suppose that D shoots V, who is taken to hospital. While in hospital, V is attended to by E, an inexperienced doctor who negligently fails to recognise the true extent of V's injuries. V dies because those injuries are improperly left untreated. In this case, the actions of both D and E cause V's death, and (depending on mens rea considerations) both D and E may be guilty of homicide-related offences.[151] Similarly, if both A and B simultaneously shoot C fatally through the heart, and C dies instantly, then both A and B kill him; even though we cannot say "but for" each shot, C would not have died (again, *but for* causation is not a necessary component of legal causation).[152] This conclusion follows from the point, noted earlier, that it is enough that the actus reus or consequence can be attributed to the defendant's conduct as *a* cause. It need not be *the* cause, or even the *main* cause. The general test when there are multiple causes is whether the defendant's contribution was, by the time the consequence came about, still a *significant* cause.[153] If so, then it is irrelevant whether that same consequence can also be attributed to other defendants.[154] When considering D's criminal liability, the question to ask is not, *who* caused the relevant harm, but whether the behaviour of *this specific defendant* was *a significant* cause of that harm.

[147] [2006] EWCA Crim 17.

[148] *Ibid.*, [37]. According to the Court, ""it would not have been recognised by a sober and reasonable bystander that an apparently healthy 15 year old (or indeed anyone else present) was at risk of suffering shock as a result of this affray". See below, § 10.7(i)(d).

[149] (1902) 19 TLR 37; above, § 4.1(i)(b) (Case 3).

[150] Cp. *Benge* (1865) 4 F & F 504, 176 ER 665.

[151] It is possible for medical negligence to constitute a *novus actus interveniens*, relieving D of liability for the result, but only in exceptional cases. See below, § 4.2(iii)(c) (Case 3).

[152] *Jones v Commonwealth* 281 SW 2d 920 (1955), 922–3. From a moral and legal perspective, no other conclusion is possible, even though this type of case presents difficulty for philosophical accounts of causation.

[153] See above, § 4.2(ii)(a). The test for omissions works differently: see below, § 4.2(iv).

[154] Cp. *Haines* (1847) 2 Car & K 368, 175 ER 152; *Malcherek* [1981] 1 WLR 690 (CA); *Blaue* [1975] 1 WLR 1411 (CA).

A well-known example of multiple causes is *Smith*.[155] D stabbed V, a fellow soldier, during a fight. V's lung was pierced, an injury that went unrecognised by those who attended to him. While being carried to the medical station, V was dropped twice by a fellow soldier. When he got there, V received "thoroughly bad" treatment from the doctors; had he been properly treated, V would probably have survived. Nonetheless, D's conviction of murder was upheld. The interventions, by V's fellow soldier and the doctors, may have contributed to V's death: from the perspective of *D*'s causal responsibility, however, that was irrelevant. It was irrelevant because, the Court found, the stab wound that D inflicted was still making a significant contribution to V's death when he died—even if that contribution was operating alongside other factors.

It is important to emphasise that, when multiple causes are concurrently at work, there is no requirement that a defendant's conduct must have been sufficient to cause the prohibited outcome by itself.[156] As we shall see on the following pages, there are many cases where the actus reus occurs only in conjunction with a pre-existing condition,[157] or because of the contribution of a third party,[158] or of the victim himself.[159] An example of this is the case of *National Rivers Authority v Yorkshire Water Services*,[160] where the defendant company was charged with causing noxious matter to enter a river. The company regularly and legitimately discharged treated sewage into the river. One night, however, somebody covertly introduced a prohibited substance into the sewer, with the result that when the sewage was discharged, the prohibited material also entered the river. On appeal, the Divisional Court reversed the Crown Court (itself hearing the case on appeal from the Magistrates' Court) and held that the defendant *had* caused the noxious substance to enter the river: the fact that a stranger also caused the pollution was "neither here nor there".[161] This seems correct. Although the defendant did not cause the sewage to become polluted, it did cause the contents of the sewer to enter the river. It was, of course, blameless in doing so, but that is another matter. Where, as here, the pollution occurs only because of the cumulative actions of defendant and vandal, *both* may be said to have caused the harm. Once again, the general test is the same: whether the particular defendant's own conduct was a significant contributor in bringing about the actus reus.

Where there are multiple inputs into a causal scenario, the hard question for criminal lawyers is to determine whether the other inputs operate concurrently—in tandem—with the defendant's contribution, or whether they supersede it. *Yorkshire Water Services* should be distinguished from *National Rivers Authority v Wright Engineering Ltd*.[162] In the latter case, D used a tank to store oil near a brook. Vandals opened a tap on the tank, with the result that the oil flowed into the brook. D was acquitted of causing a noxious substance to enter the brook—again, correctly. This is a case of what is often called a *novus actus interveniens*.[163] By contrast, in *Yorkshire Water Services*, the vandal's intervention was only significant because of the company's subsequent action of processing and discharging the

155 [1959] 2 QB 35 (C–MAC). See below, § 4.2(b)(iii) (Case 3).
156 Cp. *Warburton* [2006] EWCA Crim 627, [21]–[23].
157 E.g. *Master* [2007] EWCA Crim 142 (deep-vein thrombosis); below, § 4.2(iii)(a).
158 E.g. *Pagett* (1983) 76 Cr App R 279; below, § 4.2(iii)(b).
159 E.g. *Roberts* (1972) 56 Cr App R 95; below, § 4.2(iii)(f).
160 [1994] 4 All ER 274 (DC), reversed on another ground by the House of Lords, [1995] 1 AC 444.
161 [1994] 4 All ER 274, 280 (DC).
162 [1994] 4 All ER 281 (DC).
163 Because the intervention was free, deliberate, and informed: see, specifically, below, § 4.2(iii)(b) (Principle 1).

effluent. Thus the latter action remained *a* cause of the pollution. The distinction is not, of course, one that tracks culpability: but it can be vital to questions of causation. We turn now to consider which of various kinds of interventions are likely to count as *novus actus interveniens*, and why.

### *(iii) Intervening causes*

In such cases as *Pittwood* and *National Rivers Authority v Yorkshire Water Services*, the other causal factors operated in tandem with D's conduct to bring about the prohibited harm. Sometimes, however, D's contribution is followed by an action by someone else, or a coincidental event, that is the more immediate (or "proximate") cause of death and which displaces D's causal responsibility for the actus reus: as in *National Rivers Authority v Wright Engineering Ltd*. Consider a variation of the facts in *White*, mentioned earlier.[164] Suppose that in the normal course of events the poison D gave his mother *would* have caused her death.[165] Nonetheless, it was a subsequent, unrelated, heart attack that killed her. In this variant example, the occurrence of the heart attack supervenes over the effects of D's conduct and pre-empts his causal responsibility for her death.

As noted above, when the later event displaces D's responsibility in this way, it is often called a *novus actus interveniens* (or *novus actus*, for short). A *novus actus* is an action or event which "intervenes" to displace existing causal sequences that might otherwise lead from D's behaviour to the eventual harm. Where the prohibited consequence is attributable to a *novus actus* that is not operating in tandem with D's contribution, D is not criminally responsible for bringing about that consequence. His behaviour is no longer a legally significant and operating cause.

Given their role, it is tempting, but misleading, to characterise *novus actus* doctrines as "breaking the causal chain" linking D to the harm.[166] To do so is misleading because a putative causal chain between D's behaviour and the harm simply doesn't exist—it was never there to be broken. At the same time, the phraseology of breaking chains is tempting because, although the law does not attribute responsibility for the result to D, it may still be the case that D's conduct *contributed* to the relevant result. For instance, if D provides V with drugs, which V self-injects, D's act makes a difference. It sets the scene. Yet the law will not hold D responsible for V's resulting death. Legally speaking, it is V's own act that causes her death.

We look now at the main types of intervening causes in more detail.

#### *(a) Natural events*

Where the other causal factors involve natural events rather than persons, the basic rule is that causation is attributed to the defendant *unless* the intervening natural event was not reasonably foreseeable. Another way of putting this test, in the language preferred by Lord Hoffmann, is to say that an intervening natural event is a *novus actus* only if its occurrence

164 Above, § 4.2(ii)(a).

165 In fact, although D probably thought otherwise, it appears that the quantity given was insufficient to cause death, save perhaps as part of a cumulative dose.

166 For criticism of this way of putting things, see Simester, *Fundamentals* § 5.3.1.

is "something extraordinary", rather than an ordinary occurrence or ordinary fact of life.[167] A number of overseas cases have usefully illustrated this point. In *Hart*,[168] D assaulted V, leaving her lying unconscious on a beach below the high-water mark. V was subsequently drowned by the incoming tide. The New Zealand Court of Appeal held that D had caused the death of the victim. It is thought that D would not have caused V's death had she been left lying above the high-water mark and had only drowned because of a freak tidal wave.[169]

The idea here is that the further natural cause of the relevant result is not merely a coincidence. Rather, it is the sort of risk that is created or increased by D's initial actions. The prospect of the prohibited consequence coming about by that further means is one of the reasons we might sensibly give when stating, *ex ante*, why D should not act as he does.[170] For example, in *Gowans and Hillman*,[171] D inflicted serious injuries upon V, sending him into a coma and thereby making V susceptible to a serious infection, which V later contracted and from which he died. It was held that D's conduct, in rendering V especially vulnerable to the further, immediate cause of death, was a sufficient cause for the death to be attributable to D. A contrasting case with different result is *Bush v Commonwealth*.[172] D shot V, who subsequently died of scarlet fever, transmitted to him in hospital by the surgeon who operated on the bullet wound. D was acquitted of unlawful homicide. His attack on V did not substantially increase the risk of V's contracting scarlet fever, nor was that risk a significant reason why we would advise D, *ex ante*, not to engage in his initial actions. A different view might have been taken if D had succumbed from something characteristically associated with his injuries (e.g. sepsis).

There are three important exceptions to the general rule that unforeseeable or extraordinary events are capable of disrupting a defendant's causal responsibility for the eventual outcome.

*Exception 1: Pre-existing conditions.*

For the purpose of analysing causal paths,[173] *pre-existing* natural conditions or vulnerabilities in the victim—"egg-shell skulls"—are treated in law as baselines: "defendants must take [the condition of] their victims as they find them".[174] In *Master*,[175] for example, D inflicted a number of stab wounds upon V, aggravating an existing condition of deep-vein thrombosis. In turn, this triggered a pulmonary embolism, from which V died. D was rightly held to

[167] *Environment Agency v Empress Car Co. (Abertillery) Ltd.* [1999] 2 AC 22, 34–6. Provided it is borne in mind that what must be foreseeable is events of the same *type*, rather than the *particular* intervening event, and that it must be foreseeable to an ordinary person rather than the particular defendant, these alternative ways of phrasing the causation test involve little practical difference.

[168] [1986] 2 NZLR 408. See also *Hallett* [1969] SASR 141; *Phillips* [1971] ALR 740; *Hill* [1953] NZLR 688, 694–5.

[169] Compare Perkins, "The Law of Homicide" (1946) 36 *J Crim L & Crim* 391, 393–4.

[170] See the requirement for salience, above, § 4.2(ii)(b).

[171] [2003] EWCA Crim 3935. For technical reasons not relating to causation, D's convictions were later quashed and a retrial ordered: *Gowans and Hillman* [2015] EWCA Crim 952. See too *Forrest* (1886) 20 SASR 78; *Hood* [2003] EWCA Crim 2772, [2004] 1 Cr App R (S) 73, [6].

[172] 78 Ky 268 (1880).

[173] As opposed to analysing mens rea, where the foreseeability of V's condition will be relevant at least to any finding of negligence (or, in the context of manslaughter, to any finding that D's unlawful act was dangerous: *Carey, Cyeol and Foster* [2006] EWCA Crim 17).

[174] *Blaue* [1975] 1 WLR 1411, 1415 (CA). However, this rule does not apply to actions by the victim: see below, §§ 4.2(iii)(f), 4.2(iv)(b).

[175] [2007] EWCA Crim 142; cp. *M(J)* [2012] EWCA Crim 2293, [2013] 1 WLR 1083.

have caused V's death. It does not matter, in terms of *causation*, whether D ought to have known that V had the relevant condition.

*Exception 2: Concurrent causes.*

The outcome in *Bush v Commonwealth* would have been different if the fever had caused death only *in conjunction with* the fact that V was weakened by the wound D had inflicted. The latter would be a case of *multiple* (concurrent) causes, rather than of *novus actus*, since the original injury would still be making an ongoing (operating) contribution to V's death. This is the kind of case we noted above, in § 4.2(ii)(c).

*Exception 3: Intended effects.*

Finally, a coincidental or fortuitous and unforeseeable route involving natural events will not normally be a *novus actus* when the ultimate result was *intended* by the defendant.[176] For example:

> D shoots at V on a mountainside, meaning to kill him. She misses, but the noise of her shot triggers an avalanche in which V is swept away and killed. D is guilty of murder. She has brought about the intended result, and cannot escape responsibility by pointing to the unexpected causal detour of the means that she herself initiated.

This exception is sometimes described as a rule that "intended consequences are never too remote".[177] It is preferable not to characterise the exception in that way, and indeed to do so would be inaccurate. For example, D's intended contribution to an outcome may sometimes be superseded by the *novus actus* of a third party or an unexpected event. Suppose this time that D leaves V in a small wood, unconscious, intending that V will die of exposure. Subsequently, a helicopter crashes and lands on V, killing him. In such a case D does not cause V's death.[178]

### (b) *Human beings*

There are similarities between the causal status of natural events and the intervening actions of third parties. If D stabs V, and V later dies, D is not causally responsible if V dies because the ambulance within which he was being carried to hospital is crushed by a runaway lorry driven by T. Neither does D kill V if, after being fatally wounded and left for dead, V is chanced upon by his old enemy T, who shoots V, killing him instantly.[179] In these situations, the unforeseeable intervention of another person defeats D's causal responsibility for the eventual outcome. However, there are also significant differences between the attribution of causation where there are intervening natural events and that where there are intervening actions by other persons. In the former case, as we have seen, the main test is one of "ordinariness" or reasonable foreseeability. In the latter, the enquiry is more complex.

[176] E.g. *Anon* ("The Harlot's Case"), Crompton's Justice 24, discussed in *TBCL* 389; *Michael* (1840) 9 C & P 356, 173 ER 867 (where the intervention was by another person); *Demirian* [1989] VR 97, 113–14 (approved in *Royall v R* (1991) 172 CLR 378, 392, 400, 411, 452).

[177] A rule that is sometimes accused of mixing legal policy and metaphysics: Moore, *Causation and Responsibility* (2009) 230.

[178] Cp. the requirement of salience regarding unexpected interventions: above, § 4.2(ii)(b).

[179] Cp. *State v Wood* 53 Vt 558 (1881); *Evans and Gardner* [1976] VR 523, 527–8. See below, § 4.2(iii)(c) (Case 2).

There are three main principles guiding causation when a person other than the defendant intervenes.

*Principle 1: Free, deliberate, and informed human interventions.*

Where T makes a "free, deliberate and informed" intervention, which causes the actus reus, this will normally be a *novus actus* and absolve D of responsibility.[180] This occurs when T *knowingly* intervenes to bring about the prohibited outcome, without her choice to do so being significantly induced, fettered or constrained by the situation D has created. In that situation T assumes full responsibility for the outcome, displacing or pre-empting its attribution to D. The legal correctness of this principle was resoundingly confirmed by the House of Lords in *Kennedy (No. 2)*:[181]

> "The criminal law generally assumes the existence of free will. The law recognises certain exceptions, in the case of the young, those who for any reason are not fully responsible for their actions, and the vulnerable, and it acknowledges situations of duress and necessity, as also of deception and mistake. But, generally speaking, informed adults of sound mind are treated as autonomous beings able to make their own decisions how they will act, and none of the exceptions is relied on as possibly applicable in this case. Thus D is not to be treated as causing V to act in a certain way if V makes a voluntary and informed decision to act in that way rather than another."

In *Kennedy (No. 2)*, D had prepared a heroin mixture for V in a syringe which he then gave to V. V injected himself with the heroin and subsequently died. D was convicted of manslaughter. On appeal,[182] the House quashed D's conviction on the ground that D had not caused V's death. Even though D had played a part in the events leading to V's death, there was an intervening act by another person, V himself, who had self-administered the injection. The intervention by V was free, deliberate, and informed; as such, it was a novus actus, absolving D of causal responsibility for the homicide—even though V's act of self-injection was reasonably foreseeable and would not have occurred without D's contribution.

*Kennedy (No. 2)* was, of course, a case where the intervener was the victim himself. But the point generalises. Suppose that D, a security guard, abandons his post knowing that there are vandals nearby. If the vandals enter and damage the property, D may be liable in private law to make good the damage.[183] But D is not himself a vandal: he does not himself cause the damage; that remains the free, deliberate, and informed choice of the perpetrators. His liability for the offence of criminal damage, if any, belongs to the realm of complicity. (Indeed, much of the law of complicity is predicated on the insight that those who facilitate the free, deliberate, and informed acts of others do not cause those actions.)

[180] *Pagett* (1983) 76 Cr App R 279, 288–9; *Latif* [1996] 1 WLR 104, 115 (Lord Steyn) (HL). See, further, Simester, "Free, Deliberate and Informed?" in Simester (ed.), *Modern Criminal Law* (2024) 3.

[181] [2007] UKHL 38, [2008] 1 AC 269, [14] (Lord Bingham). Cf. the position in Scotland: *MacAngus and Kane v HM Advocate* [2009] HCJAC 8, 2009 SLT 137.

[182] In fact, this was D's second appeal. The first saw his conviction upheld: see *Kennedy* [1999] Crim LR 65 (CA). However, following uncertainty in the subsequent case law, the case was referred back to the Court of Appeal for reconsideration by the Criminal Cases Review Commission: *Kennedy* [2005] EWCA Crim 685, [2005] 1 WLR 2159. For critical analysis of that Court's decision, see the third edition of this work, § 4.2(iii)(e) (Case 2).

[183] Cp. *Stansbie v Troman* [1948] 2 KB 48, where the loss resulted from theft.

The rationale for the free, deliberate, and informed principle is ably expressed by Williams:[184]

> "Underlying this rule there is, undoubtedly, a philosophical attitude. Moralists and lawyers regard the individual's will as the autonomous prime cause of his behaviour. What a person does (if he has reached adult years, is of sound mind and is not acting under mistake, intimidation or similar pressure) is his own responsibility, and is not regarded as having been caused by other people. An intervening act of this kind, therefore, breaks the causal connection that would otherwise have been perceived between previous acts and the forbidden consequence."

It must be emphasised that the extent to which T's intervention is *sufficiently* free, deliberate, and informed is a matter of degree, turning on the particular facts of each case. Very often T's knowing intercession will not meet those criteria. For example, in *Rebelo*,[185] a properly directed jury had reached the conclusion that V's decision to take an overdose of a drug sold to her for dieting purposes by D was not sufficiently "free" because of V's underlying medical conditions (*inter alia*, depression and *bulimia nervosa*).[186]

Similarly, a doctor's intervention in treating V is not free or unconstrained, but rather is a justified response to the need for treatment that D's conduct has engendered. This point can be stated more generally: T's participation in bringing about the actus reus is insufficiently free, and *cannot* be a *novus actus*, when it is impelled by the demands of the situation into which D's conduct has placed her. While T's conduct may itself be a cause of the harm, it is not an *independent* cause that relieves D of responsibility for the relevant outcome; rather, in law, it has the status of being itself a consequence of D's wrongdoing. Thus, instead of T's becoming fully (and exclusively) responsible for the eventual outcome, D remains at least partly responsible for that intervention by T, and criminally responsible for its effects.

Neither will T's input be free, deliberate and informed when T is ignorant of the relevant facts. In this sort of case, T's contribution to the harm is an inadvertent one. Her role may be innocent or accidental, but need not be, and may instead be negligent. Either way, there is no deliberate choice by T to bring (or risk bringing) the harm about, and so she cannot be said to assume full responsibility for that harm to the exclusion of D. The same is in principle true where T lacks the capacity to make informed decisions, being (say) a child or while affected by mental disorder.[187]

[184] *TBCL* 391. Notice that this autonomy-based principle rests upon moral rather than conceptual argument; while endorsed here, it has not been adopted universally. See, e.g., Spencer and Brajeux, "Criminal Liability for Negligence—A Lesson from Across the Channel?" (2010) 59 *ICLQ* 1, 12–13. It seems the position is now also different in Canada, if the unsatisfactory decision in *Maybin* 2012 SCC 24, [2012] 2 SCR 30 is to be believed. In that case, two brothers who started a fight in a bar were said to be causally responsible for the subsequent violence inflicted on V by a bouncer—seemingly on the basis that their actions had "set the tone" for what followed. The decision fails (in [45]–[59]) to recognise the genuinely distinctive nature of the free, deliberate, and informed principle.

[185] [2021] EWCA Crim 306, [2021] 4 WLR 52.

[186] *Rebelo* is nonetheless problematic, in that it fails to consider whether V's unfree actions were reasonably foreseeable: see Principle 2 below.

[187] Compare, in tort, *Corr v IBC Vehicles Ltd* [2008] UKHL 13, [2008] 1 AC 884. In *D* [2006] EWCA Crim 1139, [2006] 2 Cr App R 24, [8], the Court of Appeal noted that "subject to evidence and argument on the critical issue of causation, unlawful violence on an individual with a fragile and vulnerable personality, which is proved to be a material cause of death (even if the result of suicide) would at least arguably, be capable of amounting to manslaughter". It may be in some cases that suicide by the victim is, alternatively, a reasonably foreseeable (or, as Horder and McGowan prefer, "natural") reaction to the defendant's wrong. See below, § 4.2(iii)(f); also Horder and McGowan, "Manslaughter by Causing Another's Suicide" [2006] *Crim LR* 1035.

In the light of the above, the decision in *Wallace* is unsatisfactory.[188] After their relationship foundered, D threw sulphuric acid over her boyfriend, V, saying "If I can't have you, no-one else will". V sustained horrific and permanent injuries to his face and body, and later travelled to Belgium where doctors agreed that he met their criteria for euthanasia (which was lawful under such circumstances in Belgium). A doctor (T) killed V by lethal injection; an intervention that would have been murder in England. On an interlocutory appeal,[189] the Court of Appeal ruled that the question whether D caused V's death should be left to the jury, which should be asked to consider (*inter alia*) whether V's requesting euthanasia was a reasonably foreseeable consequence of D's act.[190] With respect, this is not the principal question that the jury should have been presented with. Had V committed suicide, it might plausibly have been argued that V's action was not sufficiently *free* to count as a *novus actus*. But V did not commit suicide.[191] He was killed by T. The crucial question for the jury, therefore, was whether *T* made a free, deliberate, and informed decision to end V's life. If the answer to that question was yes, D did not cause V's death: *Kennedy (No. 2)* is unequivocal authority for this conclusion. Disregarding that binding authority, however, the Court of Appeal focused on the reasonable foreseeability of V's choice. But D's horrific action, and V's tragic choice, did not contribute to death *in conjunction with* T's intervention. Rather, they led to death only *through* T's act of lethal injection. As such, the Court should have focused on whether T's intervention was free, deliberate, and informed.[192]

Also problematic is the first of the Court of Appeal's decisions in the case of *Field*.[193] D pretended to enter a loving relationship with a vulnerable older man (PF) and, having persuaded PF to change his will in D's favour, then set about bringing about PF's death in a manner that would seem self-inflicted. One evening, D encouraged PF to drink a bottle of 60% proof whisky, pouring out the glasses and handing them to PF. PF died overnight from acute alcohol poisoning. D's conviction of murder was, initially, upheld by the Court of Appeal, on the basis that PF's decision to drink the whisky was not sufficiently *informed*:[194]

> "[He] would have believed that he was drinking 60% proof whisky in the company of someone who loved and would care for him, not someone who wished for his death. As a consequence, PF would not have had an informed appreciation of the truly perilous nature of what was occurring. . . . Engaging in this activity was not, as a consequence, the result of a free, voluntary and informed decision by PF."

Field's conviction was later referred back to the Court of Appeal by the Criminal Cases Review Commission.[195] There, a differently constituted Court recognised that the upholding

[188] *Wallace* [2018] EWCA Crim 690, [2018] 2 Cr App R 22. For discussion of a host of other problems with the decision, see the note by Simester and Sullivan, (2019) 135 *LQR* 21.

[189] This is a form of appeal where the trial is paused until the Court of Appeal has determined a point of law relevant to proceedings.

[190] [2018] EWCA Crim 690, [2018] 2 Cr App R 22, [86].

[191] For an argument to the contrary, see du Bois-Pedain, "*Novus Actus* and Beyond: Attributing Causal Responsibility in the Criminal Courts" (2021) 80 *CLJ*, 80(S1) s. 61, s. 67ff.

[192] Ultimately, D was acquitted of both murder and manslaughter. She was, however, convicted of an offence relating to the throwing of the acid (contrary to OAPA 1861, s. 29) and sentenced to life imprisonment.

[193] [2021] EWCA Crim 380, [2021] 1 WLR 3543. In fact, *Field* has been the subject of three appeals, but the second ([2022] EWCA Crim 315, [2022] 1 WLR 3495) did not engage with the substance of the prosecution's causal argument.

[194] *Ibid.*, [60].

[195] *Field* [2026] EWCA Crim 413.

of Field's conviction for murder could not be reconciled with the ruling in *Kennedy (No. 2)*, which, it must be remembered, is a House of Lords decision. What mattered in *Kennedy* was whether V's action of injecting himself with heroin was deliberate and informed (and it was), *not* whether V knew he was killing himself (presumably not). Similarly, in *Field*, and as the Court accepted on both occasions,[196] PF freely chose to drink the whisky knowing its strength. In each of these cases, the victim was fully informed about the nature of the action that he chose to take (and which directly brought about his death). The defendants in *Kennedy* and *Field* facilitated the victims' acts. But neither of them caused those acts to take place. After quashing Field's conviction following the reference from the Criminal Cases Review Commission, the Court of Appeal permitted the prosecution to appeal to the Supreme Court, in order that an authoritative ruling on the ambit of *Kennedy* can be provided.

The Court of Appeal in *Field* was––at the first time of asking––impressed by an analogy to the case of a weak swimmer, lured to her death by drowning, following an assurance from her companion that he would rescue her should she get into difficulty. D's undisclosed intention not to rescue V demonstrated that V's choice to swim was something far more dangerous than she took it to be: she was led to her death by deceit. This example is, however, importantly different from *Field*. The weak swimmer example involves a positive act of deception with clear causal effect. But there was no comparative deception in *Field*. PF himself chose to drink the whisky he was given, knowing it was 60 per cent proof. The danger of drinking that much whisky remains static regardless of whether D encouraged PF to drink intending that he should die from its effects, or gave PF that amount of whisky simply because PF asked for it. It is hoped that the Supreme Court recognises the problems with the weak swimmer analogy when it hears the appeal in *Field*. It would be desirable for the Court to confirm that the *Kennedy* principle applies in such cases, and therefore that D did not cause PF's death.

*Principle 2: Other human interventions.*

The second main principle applies where, because of ignorance or other reasons, T's intervention does not meet the "free, deliberate and informed" criteria. In that case the intervention is, in effect, no different from a natural event. Thus it is subject to the tests that govern intervention by a natural event: it can only count as a *novus actus* if its occurrence was independent of D's wrongdoing and was not reasonably foreseeable.[197] One new factor in examining this issue will be T's culpability for her conduct: if the harm occurred only following T's gross negligence, it is less likely to be reasonably foreseeable and the sort of risk which provides a reason why D should not have acted as he did in the first place.[198]

The courts have emphasised that "the law does not require that the *particular* circumstances in which a collision occurs should be reasonably foreseeable",[199] for example. It suf-

[196] *Ibid.* For a fuller discussion of the case, see the note by Sullivan and Simester, (2022) 138 *LQR* 11.

[197] Or, in Lord Hoffmann's phrasing, if its occurrence was "extraordinary": above, § 4.2(iii)(a). In *Girdler* [2009] EWCA Crim 2666, [2010] RTR 28, [43], the Court accepted that the language of reasonable foreseeability was apt "for a lawyer", but thought that a jury could more helpfully be asked whether the subsequent events "could sensibly have been anticipated".

[198] Above, § 4.2(iii)(a). Less likely, but not impossible: cp. *Benge* (1865) 4 F & F 504, 176 ER 665, where a railway accident occurred only because the risk created by D's negligence was not counteracted when others also failed to observe proper procedures. See further below, § 4.2(iii)(c) (Case 3).

[199] *A* [2020] EWCA Crim 407, [2020] 1 WLR 2320, [27].

fices that the intervention is of a kind that is *broadly* foreseeable. Thus, if a car is stopped, at night without lights, on the hard shoulder of a motorway, and a truck suddenly swerves onto the hard shoulder and collides with the car, what counts is whether it was reasonably foreseeable that a vehicular collision would follow the car driver's conduct. The precise details or "exact form" of that collision need not themselves be reasonably foreseeable.[200]

*Principle 3: Concurrent causes.*
As with any intervening cause, whether natural or human, a third principle also applies: that even if the intervention was independent of D and unforeseeable, it will be no more than a concurrent cause if D's contribution is still playing a direct, contributory role at the time the harm eventually occurs. This is a straightforward application of the proposition that there can be multiple causes of an outcome.[201]

*(c) Some case studies*

In the following subsections, we will consider these rather abstract principles in the more practical context of the leading cases, and in light of judicial *dicta*.

*Case 1: Foreseeable and innocent interventions.*
Cases where another's intervention is not a *novus actus* occur in a variety of ways. In some of the most dramatic examples, D will still be ascribed with causal responsibility if the contribution of the other party is both predictable (i.e. reasonably foreseeable) and itself innocent.

A famous case of this variety is *Michael.*[202] D wished to murder her illegitimate child, who was in the care of a foster-mother. She gave a bottle of poison to the foster-mother, telling her it was medicine and instructing her to administer it to the baby. The foster-mother decided not to administer the medicine and put it on the mantelpiece. Some days later the foster-mother's own five-year-old child removed the bottle and administered a fatal dose to D's child. D was convicted of murder.[203]

The events in *Michael* involved the input of a young child, undoubtedly an innocent for the purposes of legal responsibility. But they would be treated no differently by the law if T were an adult whose foreseeable intervention was inadvertent and blameless. Suppose, for example, that an altercation occurs between D and V on the pavement of a busy city street. D pushes V, who stumbles onto the road and is run over and killed by a passing car driven by T.[204] In such a case, T's unintended intervention cannot be regarded as a *novus actus*, and D would properly be treated as having caused V's death.

By contrast, the innocent intervention will be regarded as a *novus actus* where it is unforeseeable. In *Martin*,[205] D was held not to have caused death after he offered his child

[200] *Ibid.*, [35]; cp. *Muhammed* [2021] EWCA Crim 802, [2021] 2 Cr App R 17, [34]–[36].
[201] See above, § 4.2(ii)(c). Cp. *Smith* [1959] 2 QB 35 (C-MAC); *Hennigan* [1971] 3 All ER 133 (CA).
[202] (1840) 9 C & P 356, 173 ER 867; see also *Tessymond* (1828) 1 Lew CC 168, 168 ER 1000.
[203] It is thought that T's intervention was reasonably foreseeable. (See *TBCL* 394.) However, even if it were unforeseeable and extraordinary, D's conviction can be justified on the basis that, T's intervention being innocent, it should be treated like a natural event and the rule about intended consequences applied. See above, § 4.2(iii)(a).
[204] *Fleeting (No 1)* [1977] 1 NZLR 343. Cp. *Grey* [2024] EWCA Crim 487 (D gestured at V, who was cycling on the pavement, V lost her balance, fell into the path of T's car and was killed. D was convicted of manslaughter, although the conviction was subsequently quashed for misdirection on other grounds).
[205] (1827) 3 C & P 211, 172 ER 390.

a sip of an alcoholic drink, whereupon the child seized and consumed the entire drink, resulting in the child's death. Similarly, the example in the last paragraph may be compared with a situation in which D assaults V, leaving her unconscious in a quiet and well-lit street. Prima facie, he should not be held responsible for V's death if, subsequently, she is run over by a driver who had ample opportunity to avoid her.[206]

Where T's actions are not inadvertent but instead justified or excused because of the situation D has created, T will effectively be counted as an innocent intervener. T's intervention is itself a consequence of D's actions rather than an independent (i.e. free, deliberate, and informed) cause. This will frequently be the correct analysis regarding the effects of justified medical treatment given in response to injuries D inflicts.[207] Perhaps the most graphic case of this type, however, is *Pagett*.[208] D emerged from a building firing at police and using his hostage as a human shield. The police returned fire in the dark, killing the hostage. The consequence, that the police would—quite understandably—return fire, and so kill the hostage, was an entirely foreseeable upshot of what D did, and so could not disrupt the causal path which led from his behaviour to the hostage's death.

It was said in *Pagett* that the policeman's reaction in returning fire was instinctive and "involuntary". This characterisation was unnecessary (and implausible). In principle, it is enough that the reaction was a reasonable response, justifiable in terms of self-defence. It was not sufficiently "free" to usurp the defendant's causal responsibility for the eventual consequences.[209]

An extension of the principle in *Pagett* may be seen in the earlier tort case of *Scott v Shepherd*.[210] D threw a lighted squib into the market house, where it landed beside T. T, in order to protect himself, threw the squib across the warehouse. It landed beside R, who in turn also threw the squib away, such that it struck P and exploded, blinding P in one eye. D was held to have caused P's injury, on principles that were said in the case to be analogous to those applying in the criminal law.[211] From the point of view of the criminal law, this seems to be right. The case is slightly different from *Pagett*, in that T's (and R's) reaction was arguably excusable rather than justifiable.[212] But it was a reasonably foreseeable response, and moreover one for which T could not be blamed—it was a response induced by the circumstances that D himself had generated through his wrongful conduct. Thus T's reaction is allowed to be a mistake,[213] and unjustified, provided it is a reasonable or understandable response made in the heat or emergency of the moment.

[206] *Knutsen* [1963] Qd R 157.

[207] The difficult cases are where the treatment is itself misjudged. See further below, § 4.2(iii)(c) (Case 3) and the analysis of *Cheshire* in § 4.2(iv)(c).

[208] (1983) 76 Cr App R 279.

[209] A dubious extension of *Pagett* may be seen in *Gnango* [2011] UKSC 59, [2012] 1 AC 827. Without any justification or excuse, P and S exchanged gunfire. P aimed his shot at S but missed. Instead, the bullet hit and killed V, an innocent passer-by. S was held to be guilty of V's murder as either accomplice or principal, *inter alia* on the ground that, by firing at P, he caused P to return fire. For a trenchant critique, see Buxton, "Being an Accessory to One's Own Murder" [2012] *Crim LR* 275. See also Sullivan "Accessories and Principals after *Gnango*" in Reed and Bohlander (eds.), *Participation in Crime* (2013) 25. While the Court of Appeal has since endorsed *Gnango* in the context of *complicity* liability (discussed further in Chapter 7), the case should be treated with great caution in terms of finding *causation* by D (i.e., as a principal).

[210] (1772) 2 Bl W 892, 96 ER 525. Cp. *Tomars* [1978] 2 NZLR 505; *Madison v State* 130 NE 2d 35 (1955).

[211] (1772) 2 Bl W 892, 899, 96 ER 525, 528.

[212] On the distinction between justification and excuse, see below, § 17.2.

[213] Cp. *McKechnie* (1992) 94 Cr App R 51, 58.

One other case worth mention is *Martin*.[214] Intending to cause confusion and terror, D put out the gaslights on a staircase to the exit of a theatre, and placed an iron bar across the exit doorway. In the subsequent panic, a number of persons were seriously injured. D's conviction for inflicting grievous bodily harm was affirmed on appeal. Rightly so. The immediate cause of injury was no doubt the stampeding of the audience. Yet the behaviour of the audience was hardly free, deliberate, and informed. Rather, it was a foreseeable and understandable consequence of the panic induced by D.

*Case 2: Foreseeable and intentional interventions.*
The cases above illustrate the general rule that, where the intervention is both innocent and foreseeable, it will not normally constitute a *novus actus interveniens*. But what if T's free intervention is foreseeable, yet not innocent or blameless? Here things get a little more complicated. The reason for this is the importance of individual autonomy and responsibility in the law. A person's actions are not usually regarded as caused by others, and the law stipulates that a defendant is responsible for her own actions but is normally not responsible for T's wrongdoing even if it was foreseeable, and would not have occurred but for D's contribution. So if D inflicts serious injuries upon V during a mugging, and T later chances upon and shoots V (killing him instantly), then D does not cause V's death, even if it was foreseeable[215] that another person might subsequently kill V. Similarly, the result in *Michael*[216] would have been different if T had been a mature adult who knew the details of D's plans when she administered the poison to D's baby.[217]

Where T's wrongful intervention is itself intentional, something other than causation is required before the outcome can *also* be ascribed to D, the original actor. Characteristically, the extra ingredient is supplied when T's intervention is in some way induced or underwritten by D. In these cases, D's liability is predicated on a derivative, or secondary party basis, rather than upon causation.[218] Thus when D deliberately incites or assists T to commit a crime, D too will be criminally liable, as an accessory, alongside T for its commission. Secondary liability is dealt with separately in Chapter 7.

Sometimes an intervention to bring about the actus reus may be intentional without necessarily being culpable. As we saw in the preceding section, where this occurs because of a justification or excuse arising from D's conduct, T is treated as if his were an innocent intervention. However, where T's intervention is intentional, free, and unconstrained by justificatory or excusatory circumstances, it will usually break the causal link between defendant and outcome. In *Latif*,[219] D was charged, *inter alia*, with importing a controlled drug. The drug was in fact brought into the country by a customs officer with full knowledge of the contents of the packages he carried. The House of Lords held that the officer's voluntary and

[214] (1881) 8 QBD 54. See also the cases involving interventions by the victim: below, § 4.2(iii)(f).

[215] Or even made "likely" by D's actions: *Dalby* [1982] 1 WLR 425 (CA). As Williams states, "[t]he fact that [D's] own conduct, rightful or wrongful, provided the background for a subsequent voluntary act by another does not make him responsible for it. What he does may be a but-for cause of the injurious act, but he did not do it": "*Finis* for *Novus Actus*?" (1989) 48 *CLJ* 391, 391.

[216] Above, § 4.2(iii)(c) (Case 1).

[217] Compare *Hilton* (1838) 2 Lew CC 214, 168 ER 1132, where a stranger's intervention was a *novus actus*, with *Lowe* (1850) 3 Car & Kir 123, 175 ER 489, where the intermediary was an "ignorant boy" and D was not absolved of responsibility. Cp. also *People v Elder* 59 NW 237 (1894); *Commonwealth v Root* 170 A 2d 310 (1961).

[218] Cp. Fletcher, *Rethinking Criminal Law* (1978) 582.

[219] [1996] 1 WLR 104 (HL). To similar effect is *Tse Hung-Lit* [1986] AC 876 (PC). For another, extraordinary, example, see *People v Campbell* 335 NW 2d 27 (1983).

knowing intervention relieved D of causal responsibility for importation of the drugs, and that the most he could be convicted of was an attempt to commit the offence.[220]

*Case 3: Foreseeable and culpable interventions.*

Normally, when there is no *intentional* wrongdoing by the intervener, it is less likely—but not impossible—that the culpable intervention will break the causal link between D and the eventual outcome.[221] This is because, as was stated at the beginning of § 4.2(iii)(b), T cannot be said to have assumed a full responsibility for the effects of her intervention.[222] Nonetheless, it is still possible for T's conduct to disrupt the causal path joining D with the relevant outcome.[223] For example, where V is injured by D, but killed unexpectedly in an accident while being driven to hospital, the fact that the accident was unintended by T, the other driver, is no bar to an application of the *novus actus* doctrine and denial of D's responsibility.

The most instructive legal examples of this variety arise in a medical context, where D inflicts injuries upon V the extent of which are at least exacerbated by the medical treatment V subsequently receives. A case where "palpably" bad medical treatment was held to cause death to the exclusion of D's original actions is *Jordan*.[224] In that case the defendant had stabbed V, who was admitted to hospital and died eight days later. On appeal, evidence was admitted to show that, when he died, V's original injury had substantially healed. V's death was in fact caused by his allergic reaction to the antibiotic he was given in hospital and by the intravenous administration of too much liquid. Moreover, the antibiotic was introduced to prevent infection only after he had shown he was intolerant of it. The Court of Criminal Appeal, in quashing Jordan's conviction, held that the grossly negligent[225] medical treatment broke the causal link between the stabbing and V's death.

While we submit that *Jordan* was rightly decided, it must be regarded as a very unusual case, distinguished by its rather extreme facts. Acknowledging this, the Court was "disposed to accept it as law that death resulting from any normal treatment employed to deal with a felonious injury may be regarded as caused by the felonious injury".[226] Thus, where death results from normal treatment applied to the injury, then both the treatment and the injury are causes of death and the treatment does not negate the causal role of the original injury in bringing about death.

Even if the intervening treatment is abnormal, however, it will not necessarily count as a *novus actus*. Recall the facts of *Smith*,[227] which we described in § 4.2(ii)(c). D stabbed V with a bayonet. V was dropped twice on the way to the medical reception station. There

[220] It is possible that the officer's intervention could be regarded as culpable since the House of Lords treated him as having committed an offence himself. But this was not required in *Horsey* (1862) 3 F & F 287, 176 ER 129.

[221] Cp. *Benge* (1865) 4 F & F 504, 176 ER 665.

[222] Cp. V's death in *Winter* [2010] EWCA Crim 1474, [2011] 1 Cr App R (S) 78. In that case, the defendants stored fireworks in a manner contrary to regulations. A fire broke out, leading to an explosion, in which T (a fireman, carrying out his duties properly) and V (a media awareness officer employed by the fire service, who continued filming after he had been ordered to move back) were killed. T's death is straightforwardly analogous to the situation of the police officers in *Pagett* (Case 1 above). However, the defendants were rightly convicted also for the manslaughter of V.

[223] E.g. *Ledger* (1862) 2 F & F 857, 175 ER 1319.

[224] (1956) 40 Cr App R 152.

[225] See Williams, "Causation in Homicide" [1957] *Crim LR* 429.

[226] (1956) 40 Cr App R 152, 157.

[227] [1959] 2 QB 35 (C–MAC).

the medical officer failed to diagnose the seriousness of the situation and gave the wrong treatment, which very likely increased the risk of death.[228] V died. On appeal, it was held that, where the original injury is still an operating and significant[229] cause of death, then—regardless of other contributing causes—the death can still be attributed to the defendant. It is only if the original wound is merely a *historical setting* for the second injury (here, the treatment), which is then the major operating cause of death, that there can be an absence of causation between that original wounding and the ultimate harm suffered by V.[230] In *Smith* the stab wound and consequent haemorrhage were still immediate medical factors explaining V's death; in *Jordan*, they were not.

There appear, therefore, to be two conditions which must be satisfied before the intervening behaviour can supersede the defendant's causal role. Loosely stated:

(I) The original harm inflicted by D must no longer be contributing to the occurrence of the eventual result (i.e. as a concurrent operating cause). (This is the lesson of *Smith*.)

This condition applies even if T's wrongdoing is intentional. For example, if D inflicts a non-fatal stab wound upon V, then D (as well as T) causes V's death if T later also stabs V and the loss of blood from both wounds is a contributing factor bringing about V's death.[231] Contrast this example with the example mentioned earlier, where D stabs V and T later chances upon V and shoots her, killing her instantly. In that case T causes V's death, not D. The knife wound is merely a historical setting for V's death.

The second condition is as follows:

(II) The relevant intervention by T must be independent (i.e. not itself a consequence) of the original wrongdoing by D.

This condition is conveniently illustrated by the New Zealand case of *Kirikiri*.[232] In that case, V was the victim of a serious assault by D, which caused structural damage to her face. At the hospital where she was first treated, a temporary tracheostomy was performed in order to assist her breathing. She was then transferred to another hospital for reconstructive surgery, which was to take place four days later and was not essential to save her life. Before surgery, however, the inserted tracheal tube slipped. Attempts to replace it failed and V died. The High Court held, on a pre-trial motion, that there was "ample evidence" on these facts for a jury to hold that D caused V's death. This seems right. The immediate cause of death was the failure of the tracheostomy and of the surgeons' attempts to repair it. But the tracheostomy itself was a medically appropriate response, made necessary by the injuries D had inflicted upon V. D might therefore be regarded as causally responsible for the (necessitous, appropriate) intervention that, in turn, led to V's death.

[228] Indeed, it was said in evidence at the trial that V's chances of recovery were 75 per cent given proper treatment.

[229] "Substantial" in the speech of Lord Parker CJ [1959] 2 QB 35, 42–3 (C–MAC). But see above, § 4.2(ii)(a).

[230] Compare *Wallace* [2018] EWCA Crim 690, [2018] 2 Cr App R 22, where the injuries caused to V by D were no longer threatening his life (albeit destroying its quality).

[231] This may be the best explanation of *Dear* [1996] Crim LR 595 (CA).

[232] [1982] 2 NZLR 648. Condition II is also crucial to the explanation of *Cheshire* [1991] 3 All ER 670 (CA), the most important English case on medical interventions. However, because of the complexity of that case its analysis is deferred to the end of our discussion of causation, in § 4.2(iv)(c). For present purposes, *Kirikiri* provides the better illustration.

It may be helpful to illustrate the different legal character of the causal sequences in these cases with diagrams. In *Jordan*, the conduct of the doctor amounted to a *novus actus* independent of D's actions:

*Jordan*: D → stabs V —| T → injects antibiotics → V dies

By contrast, in *Kirikiri* the doctor's intervention was a direct response to the injuries D had inflicted, and thus could be treated as a consequence of D's actions:

*Kirikiri*: D → attacks V → T performs tracheostomy → V dies

In *Smith*, the doctor's conduct made an independent contribution to V's death. But the stab wound inflicted by D remained a concurrent, operating cause of death:

*Smith*: D → stabs V → V dies
T → exacerbates wounds → V dies

One important factor in determining whether the medical intervention counts as a consequence for the purposes of condition II will be the extent to which that treatment is negligent. "Palpably" wrong—i.e. grossly negligent—treatment is obviously not a consequential intervention falling within condition II. (As *Smith* illustrates, the question whether it is a *novus actus interveniens* will then depend upon condition I.) On the other hand, reasonable, even if ultimately incorrect and harmful, treatment *is* a consequence of D's wrongdoing.[233] However, the status of treatment which is negligent, but not grossly negligent, is unclear. Authority on this question is both *obiter* and inconsistent.[234] It is submitted that, by analogy with the principles stated in § 4.2(iii)(c) (Case 1) above and § 4.2(iii)(f) below, medically erroneous treatment that is neither reasonable nor reasonably foreseeable should count as independent action within condition II, relieving D of causal responsibility for the result.

### (d) Distinction from the innocent agent doctrine

Sometimes persons bring about outcomes deliberately through the agency of another person. If D gives V's daughter a lethal draught of poison, telling her it is for V's cold, and the daughter administers the poison to V, D is guilty of murder as if he had administered the poison himself.[235] Similarly, D may be convicted of importing prohibited drugs even though the means of conveyance was an airline.[236] The doctrine of innocent agency renders the intervening participant the mere instrument of D, enabling courts to find that D has committed the offence as a principal offender.

233 *McKechnie* (1992) 94 Cr App R 51, 58; *Kirikiri* [1982] 2 NZLR 648.
234 For a survey of the case law, see *Hart and Honoré* 352–62. The more recent case of *McKechnie* (1992) 94 Cr App R 51 suggests a standard of simple negligence.
235 *Anon* (1634) Kel 53, 84 ER 1079.
236 *White v Ridley* (1978) 140 CLR 342.

Discussion of this doctrine belongs in Chapter 7, on participation in crime. It is mentioned here in order to distinguish it from the causation question that arises upon an innocent third party's intervention. Innocent agency requires that D knowingly uses T as his agent to bring about the prohibited result. Thus *Michael*,[237] where a child later and independently administered the poison that D had instructed V's nurse to give to V, is not a suitable case for application of the doctrine.

Innocent agency and causal principles nonetheless share some common ground. Like causation, innocent agency requires that T should be ignorant of the true nature of her actions. Where this is not so, and T is aware that her conduct constitutes an actus reus, responsibility for her actions and their result cannot then be imputed back to D.[238]

*(e) Two special cases of intervention: pollution and driving*

There are two controversial lines of decisions governing third-party interventions, which we discuss here as special cases that are difficult to reconcile with the cases analysed above.

*Case 1: Pollution and other environmental crimes.*

The first line of cases begins with the decision by the House of Lords in *Environmental Agency v Empress Car Co. (Abertillery) Ltd.*[239] In that case, a company, D, had attached a tap to a diesel tank in its yard. The tap overrode existing barriers designed to contain spillage from the tank, meaning that it was possible for overflows from the tap to drain into the nearby river. Subsequently, the tap was opened by an unknown person, with the result that the entire contents of the tank flowed into the river. D was convicted of "causing polluting matter to enter controlled waters",[240] a conviction that was affirmed by the House of Lords.

The leading judgment, given by Lord Hoffmann, contains a number of useful statements of principle.[241] But it is, in one respect, profoundly unsatisfactory. Apparently, the intervention of the third party was free, deliberate, informed, and indeed malicious. Prima facie, therefore, it was a *novus actus*. But Lord Hoffmann accorded no special status to such interventions and failed to distinguish informed acts by third persons from acts which are either uninformed or unfree, or indeed from interventions of nature. "By parity of reasoning",[242] the same test was said to apply to all cases:[243]

> "The true common sense distinction is, in my view, between acts and events which, although not necessarily foreseeable in the particular case,[244] are in the generality a normal and familiar fact of life, and acts or events which are abnormal and extraordinary."

[237] (1840) 9 C & P 356, 173 ER 867.
[238] In such cases, the question will be whether D is a secondary party to T's offence (below, § 7.4), or has committed the inchoate offence of encouraging or assisting T's offence (see § 9.1).
[239] [1999] 2 AC 22.
[240] Contrary to (the now-repealed) s. 85(1) of the Water Resources Act 1991.
[241] E.g. [1999] 2 AC 22, 29–31.
[242] *Ibid.*, 33.
[243] *Ibid.*, 34.
[244] Thus his Lordship eschewed the language of "foreseeability" in favour of "ordinariness", although the distinction is unlikely to be of great practical significance. See above, § 4.2(iii)(a).

The main effect of this conclusion is to assimilate interventions by human beings with interventions by natural events, thereby extending the appropriate test of the latter (discussed in § 4.2(iii)(a)) also to the former. Hence a normal or foreseeable intervention by a person, even if fully informed and deliberate, would not be a *novus actus interveniens*.

This holding is contrary to both principle and law. At the level of principle, it is unexplained how D's lawful storage of oil on its land had any causal effect. V may lawfully park his car in a street. D may come along and vandalise the vehicle. V inadvertently gives D the opportunity to cause criminal damage, but his parking of his car was not a cause of its being damaged. If the physical location of the car is regarded as a cause of the damage, all other features of the environment which made it possible for D to damage it should also be regarded as causes of the damage. The same reasoning applies to D's storage of the oil in *Empress*. The key point here is that, in the criminal law, a person is responsible for his own autonomous actions and not for those of others. As Williams puts it, "[w]hat a person does . . . is his own responsibility, and is not regarded as having been caused by other people".[245] Otherwise, D's criminal liability for causing an actus reus would not be under his own control, but would instead be subject to the autonomous choice of someone else. Giving other citizens the power to render D guilty of a crime not only disempowers D and undermines his autonomy. It is also contrary to the importance attached in modern English law to an individual's separate identity and responsibility.[246]

The dealer who sells T a gun does not shoot V. T does. It may sometimes be appropriate to criminalise the dealer's actions, but not on the basis of causing harm to V. Similarly, in *Empress*, D did not pollute the river. T did. It was possible for the legislature to make D responsible for that outcome by stipulating vicarious or situational liability; but the legislation did not do that. The statute required causation of the pollution *by D*, in the normal way. The House of Lords lost sight of a fundamental precept of criminal law.

Bad principle, then. Bad law, too. The decision is inconsistent with the reasoning in decisions mentioned earlier,[247] such as *Latif*,[248] *Hilton*,[249] and *Dalby*.[250] Williams's conclusion on *Dalby* holds just as aptly for *Empress*:[251]

> "The fact that [D's] own conduct, rightful or wrongful, provided the background for a subsequent voluntary act by another does not make him responsible for it. What he does may be a but-for cause of the injurious act, but he did not do it."

[245] *TBCL* 391; the passage is quoted more fully above, § 4.2(iii)(b). Cp. *Hart and Honoré* 363–4. Certain jurisdictions take the view that conduct, while remaining free, deliberate, and informed, can be causally influenced by the interventions of other human agents as when, say, P resolves to kill V as a result of being offered £10,000 by D to do so. In Germany, for instance, D would be regarded as "the principal behind the principal" in the murder of V: Fletcher, *Rethinking Criminal Law* (1978) 657–71. Whatever the merits of this less restricted approach, it cannot suddenly be adopted *ad hoc* for England and Wales at the cost of a major disruption in settled doctrine and resulting uncertainty, particularly in the area of parties to crimes. In England and Wales, such a case is properly handled within the law of complicity.

[246] Cp. the principle of personal control argued for in Simester, *Fundamentals* § 5.3.5.

[247] Above, § 4.2(iii)(b). See also *People v Elder* 59 NW 237 (1894); *Commonwealth v Root* 170 A 2d 310 (1961); *People v Campbell* 335 NW 2d 27 (1983); *Horsey* (1862) 3 F & F 287, 176 ER 129. *Empress* is also inconsistent with *Impress (Worcester) Ltd v Rees* [1971] 2 All ER 357, which Lord Hoffmann asserted was wrongly decided, notwithstanding that the result in that case had been endorsed by the House of Lords in *Alphacell v Woodward* [1972] AC 824, 835 (Lord Wilberforce), 847 (Lord Salmon).

[248] [1996] 1 WLR 104 (HL); also *Tse Hung-Lit* [1986] AC 876 (PC).

[249] (1838) 2 Lew CC 214, 168 ER 1132.

[250] [1982] 1 WLR 425 (CA).

[251] "*Finis* for *Novus Actus*?" (1989) 48 *CLJ* 391; above, § 4.2(iii)(b).

In *Empress*, D's storage of oil provided no more than the opportunity for T's vandalous act.[252] Were it otherwise, the law of complicity would be largely redundant. One who assists another to commit a crime could be held to have caused the prohibited harm, and so be convicted of the crime as a principal. Indeed, Lord Hoffmann's analysis virtually demolishes the need for liability of secondary parties. Yet the decision in *Empress* purports to follow law. Unfortunately, in the face of extensive criminal law precedent to the contrary, the only unequivocal authority Lord Hoffmann cited for his conclusion was a tort case.[253] Moreover, his Lordship placed great weight on the statement attributed to Lord Wilberforce in *Alphacell v Woodward* that "the *deliberate* act of a third party does not necessarily negative causal connection".[254] But Lord Wilberforce did not use the word "deliberate". During his speech in *Alphacell v Woodward*. Lord Wilberforce had, *obiter*, merely rejected the proposition that "in every case the act of a third party necessarily interrupts the chain of causation";[255] a warranted rejection that provides no support whatsoever for the reasoning in *Empress*. So: bad principle, bad law, and bad reasoning.

Be that as it may, the decision in *Empress* was confirmed by the House of Lords in *Kennedy (No. 2)*, though only in the particular context of interpreting and applying "a statutory provision imposing strict criminal liability on those who cause pollution of controlled waters".[256] Thus this line of authority appears to be confined to the sphere of regulatory offences, and in particular those governing pollution and, perhaps, other environmental wrongs.[257] That is, in our view, a desirable restriction,[258] albeit one that remains sensitive to the practical difficulties of enforcing environmental crimes.

*Case 2: Being in control of a car involved in an accident?*

Section 3ZB of the Road Traffic Act 1988[259] establishes a crime of causing death by driving when the driver is uninsured, unlicensed, or disqualified. Under the clear terms of the statute, there is no need for the illegal circumstance of D's being unlicensed/uninsured/disqualified to be causally related to the death.[260] In terms of causation, section 3ZB requires

[252] Rather than relying on a finding of causation by D, Horder suggests that it may have been preferable to ground liability in an omission, based upon D's *control* over the premises: a control that generated a duty for D to guard against interference by third parties. See Horder, "Control Over Land and Criminal Pollution: Empress Car Reconsidered" [2024] *Crim LR* 230. However, it seems likely that such a duty would require legislative rather than judicial reform.

[253] *Stansbie v Troman* [1948] 2 KB 48 (CA).

[254] *Empress* [1999] 2 AC 22, 33 (emphasis added). See *Alphacell v Woodward* [1972] AC 824, 835.

[255] *Alphacell v Woodward* [1972] AC 824, 835.

[256] [2007] UKHL 38, [2008] 1 AC 269, [15] (Lord Bingham). See, also, *ibid*., [16].

[257] In *Natural England v Day* [2014] EWCA Crim 2683, [2015] 1 Cr App R (S) 53, [23], the Court of Appeal did not decide the point but noted that "we see strong arguments for following the approach in *Empress Car*" in relation to the Wildlife and Countryside Act 1981.

[258] Even then, however, the analysis will permit some extraordinary conclusions: see, e.g., *L(R) and F(J)* [2008] EWCA Crim 1970, [2009] 1 Cr App R 16, where the *members* of an unincorporated golf club were said to be criminally liable for the same offence as in *Empress*, after an underground pipe supplying oil to the club boiler was fractured when work was done on the ground above by independent building contractors. The Court did not even trouble to enquire whether the intervention was extraordinary, as *Empress* requires (above, § 4.2(iii)(a)). Presumably, if vandals are considered by the judiciary to be an everyday intervener, a fortiori clumsy builders. (And, in Canada, homicidal bouncers: *Maybin* 2012 SCC 24, [2012] 2 SCR 30.)

[259] As amended by the Road Safety Act 2006. The offence carries a maximum sentence of two years' imprisonment.

[260] Thus the offence is a morally illegitimate example of constructive liability: below, § 6.5. See further Hirst, "Causing Death by Driving and Other Offences: A Question of Balance" [2008] *Crim LR* 339.

only that D cause death *by driving a car on the road* whilst not in possession of insurance or a licence, or whilst disqualified.

Initially that causal requirement was liberally interpreted. In *Williams*,[261] for example, D lacked both insurance and a licence. He was otherwise driving lawfully and within the speed limit when V suddenly stepped in front of his car, about three feet away. D was unable to stop in time, and V was killed. In the subsequent case of *Hughes*,[262] D, who was uninsured, was driving at a safe speed on the correct side of the road. V was driving in the opposite direction, exhausted from overwork and disoriented by a cocktail of drugs. After weaving erratically across both sides of the road, V finally veered across the carriageway, collided with D's car, and died. In terms of civil law, the victim in each case was entirely responsible for the accident. Neither defendant was at fault *with regard to V's death*.[263] Yet both defendants were ruled by the Court of Appeal to have caused death by their driving, and as such to have committed the section 3ZB offence.

Indeed, the Court of Appeal was prepared to hold in *Hughes* that "if [V] had ploughed into the respondent's van whilst stationary in a queue of traffic or at a traffic light, [D], it could be said, would have caused the death of [V] by driving a motor vehicle".[264] But in the context of causation, that is to confuse driving with presence,[265] and it is to confuse legal causation with "but for" causation. As was argued in § 4.2(i), the "but for" test is merely an indicator and not a true test of causation in these contexts. D's *presence* was an ingredient in the accident, to be sure, but it does not follow that D's *driving* was a non-negligible cause. Suppose that Jim was walking from his home to the shops when Kevin, who was drunk, lost control of his car, mounted the pavement, and collided with Jim. If Jim died, no one would seriously suggest that Jim's walking is a cause of his own death. But he was there and, on the logic of the Court of Appeal, it did.

Fortunately, this line of objection was accepted by the Supreme Court, which observed that a but-for relationship is not to be equated with legal causation. The Court noted that section 3ZB contains no explicit abrogation of normal causal requirements, and emphasised that any such abrogation would require particular legislative clarity in the context of a homicide offence.[266]

Moreover, the Supreme Court went on to hold that V's death must be connected to something objectively wrong about D's driving: "Juries should thus be directed that it is not necessary for the Crown to prove careless or inconsiderate driving, but that there must be something open to proper criticism in the driving of the defendant, beyond the mere presence of the vehicle on the road, and which contributed in some more than minimal way to the death."[267] In effect, the Court generalised a common-law requirement of causal

[261] [2010] EWCA Crim 2552, [2011] 1 WLR 588.
[262] [2013] UKSC 56, [2013] 1 WLR 2461, on appeal from *MH* [2011] EWCA Crim 1508, [2011] 4 All ER 761.
[263] Cp. *MH* (*ibid.*), [22]: "[i]n terms of civil law, [V] was 100% responsible for causing the accident and [D] was not in any way at fault for the death".
[264] *Ibid.*, [44].
[265] No doubt it is appropriate to regard D as "driving" while stationary on the highway for the purpose of offences like driving with excess blood alcohol; but that legitimate interpretation does not obviate the need to prove causation in offences such as s. 3ZB.
[266] *Hughes* [2013] UKSC 56, [2013] 1 WLR 2461, [26]–[28] (Lords Hughes and Toulson).
[267] *Ibid.*, [33] (Lords Hughes and Toulson).

salience,[268] notwithstanding that section 3ZB was drafted in terms that contained no such requirement. On this analysis, causation requirements in the criminal law are intimately bound up with fault.

The Supreme Court's decision is understandable in the context of a strict liability offence, but it goes too far. When Brandon Lee died tragically during filming of *The Crow*, after an error in preparing the prop gun, it was actor Michael Massee who pulled the trigger.[269] Massee's act was *a* cause of Lee's death despite his lack of fault. The firing of the bullet caused death, and pulling the trigger was a cause of that. By contrast, the "common sense"[270] principle espoused in *Hughes* would lead us to conclude that Massee did not do an act that caused Lee's death. That conclusion should be rejected.

Be that as it may, the fault-based principle in *Hughes* is an appropriate one to apply in the context of offences, like section 3ZB, that contain aggravating consequence elements for which liability is strict. For instance, before Massee could be convicted of Lee's manslaughter, it would need to be proved that he had been grossly negligent. No such independent fault element could save defendants such as Hughes, as indicated by the Court of Appeal's upholding of their convictions. Thus one had to be invented, and smuggled into the concept of legal causation. The extent to which the principle is applicable outside that context, and is generalisable to offences beyond the driving context, remains to be seen.[271] As the Supreme Court itself confirmed in *Hughes*, distinctive causation requirements can be specified by the legislature.[272] Absent that, however, common law doctrines are prima facie of general application.

### *(f) The victim*

What about cases where the intervention is by V himself, rather than by a third party? The general rule is that the consequences of V's intervention are attributable to D provided that:[273]

1. V's intervention was not free, deliberate, and informed; and
2. V's reaction was a reasonably foreseeable possibility.

268 Above, § 4.2(ii)(b).

269 The same analysis applies to Alec Baldwin's shooting of Halyna Hutchins on the set of *Rust* in 2021. Both Baldwin and the person responsible for management of firearms on set were charged with involuntary manslaughter and the latter was convicted (Baldwin's case was dismissed after a prosecution disclosure failure).

270 *Hughes* [2013] UKSC 56, [2013] 1 WLR 2461, [32].

271 *Hughes* was affirmed in *Taylor* [2016] UKSC 5, [2016] 1 WLR 500, in the context of a prosecution for aggravated vehicle taking—i.e. where injury or damage is caused—under s. 12A of the Theft Act 1968. In substance, however, the decision in *Taylor* turned on the Court's finding that s. 12A was not to be construed as imposing strict liability with respect to the aggravating circumstances, rather than on its making a finding of causation premised upon fault. In *Natural England v Day* [2014] EWCA Crim 2683, [2015] 1 Cr App R (S) 53, [23], the Court of Appeal declined counsel's invitation to extend the approach in *Hughes* to environmental offences. While the Court did not decide the point, it considered there were "strong arguments", in the environmental context, for retaining the approach taken in *Environmental Agency v Empress Car Co. (Abertillery) Ltd* [1999] 2 AC 22. (See Case 1 above in this subsection.)

272 *Hughes* [2013] UKSC 56, [2013] 1 WLR 2461, [20] (Lords Hughes and Toulson). See also *Wallace* [2018] EWCA Crim 690, [2018] 2 Cr App R 22, [52].

273 See the discussion in *Wallace* [2018] EWCA 690, [2018] 2 Cr App R 22, [63ff], and the suggested closing question 3(b) for the jury at [86].

The first condition was laid down in *Kennedy (No. 2)*, and need not be further defended here.[274] We focus instead on condition (2). In *Roberts*,[275] D was driving a car, with V as his passenger, when D made sexual advances towards V. V leapt out of the moving vehicle and suffered resulting injuries. D's conviction for assault occasioning actual bodily harm was upheld by the Court of Appeal, which asked whether the injury was "the natural result of what the alleged assailant said and did, in the sense that it was something that could reasonably have been foreseen as the consequence of what he was saying or doing?"[276] The same principle is capable of explaining the American case of *People v Lewis*,[277] in which V, who was dying painfully from a gunshot wound, committed suicide by cutting his throat. D was held to have caused V's death.[278] It would be otherwise, however, if V had killed himself not in reaction to the suffering that D had inflicted,[279] but rather in order to shield D or, indeed, in an attempt to make D liable for a homicide offence. Those kinds of intervention would fail to satisfy condition (1).

The requirement of reasonable foreseeability may not be met where the victim's reaction is disproportionate. Although it is sometimes said that "the victim must be taken as he is found",[280] in *People v Lewis*, D would not have been guilty of murder if the wound had merely been painful rather than life-threatening and, knowing this, V had taken his life only in order to escape pain.[281] In general, V's reaction will not be a *novus actus* where it is "in the foreseeable range",[282] and is not "daft".[283] This remains so even if that reaction is negligent or unlawful.[284]

Analogous to the decision in *Smith*,[285] even an unforeseeable intervention by the victim will not be a novus actus where the original harm inflicted by D is still contributing to the occurrence of the eventual result. In *Wall*,[286] the defendant (a colonial governor) sentenced

[274] [2007] UKHL 38, [2008] 1 AC 269: above, § 4.2(iii)(b) (Principle 1). It is important to emphasise that satisfying condition (1) is not enough to establish causation between D's behaviour and a result: a point missed in *Rebelo* [2021] EWCA Crim 306, [2021] 4 WLR 52. See, especially, at [30], quoting para. 34 of the trial judge's direction to the jury, where condition (2) is missed entirely.

[275] (1972) 56 Cr App R 95. Other cases include *Lewis* [2010] EWCA Crim 151, [25], [39]–[41]; *M* [2000] Crim LR 372 (CA); *DPP v Daley* [1980] AC 237 (PC); *Williams and Davies* [1992] 1 WLR 380 (CA); *Pitts* (1842) Car & M 284, 174 ER 509; *Halliday* [1886–90] All ER 1028, (1889) 61 LT 701. See Elliott, "Frightening a Person into Injuring Himself" [1974] *Crim* LR 15.

[276] (1972) 56 Cr App R 95, 102.

[277] 57 P 470 (1899).

[278] Although the *ratio* of the decision was that V died of multiple causes (the loss of blood from the combined wounds), the Court would have been prepared to decide the case on this ground if the facts had been clear regarding D's motive for cutting his own throat. See also *State v Angelina* 80 SE 141 (1913); *Jones v State* 43 NE 2d 1017 (1942); *Stephenson v State* 179 NE 633 (1932) (torture).

[279] Cp. *D* [2006] EWCA Crim 1139, [2006] 2 Cr App R 24, where the history of abuse may be capable in principle of explaining why V's suicide was a "natural" or intelligible response, taken in circumstances where V's choices are limited by D's acts of oppression. See the discussion by Horder and McGowan, "Manslaughter by Causing Another's Suicide" [2006] *Crim LR* 1035, 1039–43.

[280] E.g. *Blaue* [1975] 1 WLR 1411, 1415 (CA); below, § 4.2(iv)(b).

[281] *Pace* the *obiter dicta* in *D* [2006] EWCA Crim 1139, [2006] 2 Cr App R 24, where it is suggested that a minor assault on a person with a fragile and vulnerable personality (thus not a sufficiently free intervener), who then committed suicide, might be capable of constituting manslaughter. At least in most such cases, deliberate suicide would not be in the foreseeable range of responses to such conduct.

[282] *Corbett* [1996] Crim LR 594 (CA); *pace Dear* [1996] Crim LR 595 (CA). It is submitted that the former case is to be preferred on this point, being consistent with existing case law (see, e.g., § 4.2(iii)(c) (Case 1)).

[283] *Roberts* (1972) 56 Cr App R 95, 102.

[284] Cp. *Walker* (1824) 1 C & P 320, 171 ER 1213; *Swindall and Osborne* (1846) 2 Car & Kir 230, 2 Cox CC 141, 175 ER 95.

[285] [1959] 2 QB 35 (C–MAC); above, §§ 4.2(i)(c) and 4.2(ii)(c).

[286] (1802) 28 St Tr 51, 145. See also *Flynn* (1867) 16 WR 319 (Ir); *Mubila* [1956] SA 31.

V to an illegal flogging of some 800 lashes. V died from the punishment. It appeared that V had drunk alcohol after the flogging, which may well have accelerated his death. If so, it did so in combination with the effects of the flogging, and so would have been no more than a concurrent rather than overriding causal factor. The defendant therefore remained causally responsible for V's death.

### (g) *Summary of approach to intervening causes*

It is impossible to be precise and comprehensive about the principles governing the attribution of causation. The rich detail of the cases defies reduction to a list of simple rules: sometimes when confronting new situations, the best technique may be simply to argue by analogy to one or more decided cases. Nonetheless, at the risk of oversimplification (but not the level of oversimplification that can be found in decisions such as *Empress*[287]), we offer the following general guidelines to causation problems where there are intervening causes.

Begin by considering whether D's original act is still making an ongoing contribution, in its own right, to the prohibited result at the time that result occurs (e.g. where V dies after losing blood from the wound inflicted by D as well as that inflicted by T). If so, the case is like *Smith*: regardless of the other interventions, D's act is a concurrent cause of the result (§ 4.2(ii)(c)) and there is no *novus actus interveniens*. The analysis is concluded.

If the conclusion is not determined by that first step, it then becomes necessary to enquire whether D's original act is a cause of the prohibited result *through the medium of* T's intervention. This question is approached as follows.

First, assuming T is a human agent, consider whether T's intervention is free, deliberate, and informed (§ 4.2(iii)(b)). If it meets these criteria in full, then, regardless of its predictability, T's intervention is a *novus actus interveniens* that pre-empts any causal link between D's original act and the prohibited result. *Pace Empress* (§ 4.2(iii)(e)), D is absolved of causal responsibility and the analysis is concluded.

Alternatively, if T is not a human agent (§ 4.2(iii)(a)) or the intervention was not free, deliberate, and informed, consider whether that intervention was reasonably foreseeable, as opposed to unforeseeable and extraordinary. If it was reasonably foreseeable, then it may be expected not to displace any finding of causation between D's original act and the prohibited result. If it was not reasonably foreseeable, then the intervention is a *novus actus interveniens* and D is not liable for causing it.

## *(iv) Omissions*

### (a) *As causes*

It is sometimes suggested that omissions cannot be causes.[288] This idea is founded on the notion that non-events, like failures to intercede and rescue a drowning victim, cannot bring things about: they are merely failures to prevent things that are already happening.

[287] [1999] 2 AC 22; above, § 4.2(iii)(e) (Case 1).

[288] E.g. Moore, *Act and Crime* (1993) 267–78; Moore, *Causation and Responsibility* (2009) 444–52. For discussion, see Hughes, "Criminal Omissions" (1958) 67 *Yale LJ* 590, 627–31; Husak, *Philosophy of Criminal Law* (1987) chap. 6; Leavens, "A Causation Approach to Omissions" (1988) 76 *Cal LR* 547; Beynon, "Causation, Omissions and Complicity" [1987] *Crim LR* 539; Fletcher, "On the Moral Irrelevance of Bodily Movements" (1994) 142 *U Penn LR* 1443; *Hart and Honoré* 38; Fletcher, *Rethinking Criminal Law* (1978) 589–99; Simester, *Fundamentals* § 5.4.

To some extent this is true. If D watches without intervening while in a position to save V, her causal contribution to V's death is not of the same order as that when D herself holds V's head under water. One thing that is distinctive about omissions is that they do not initiate causal processes. Instead, they permit other causal processes to bring about the harm.

As such, omissions are distinctive in as much as they describe events that did *not* happen but *should* have. Nonetheless, neither ordinary language nor the law has much compunction about attributing causal responsibility to omissions. Both within and outside the courtroom, it is acceptable to say that the railway gatekeeper's failure, in *Pittwood*,[289] to close the gate before the train came through caused the resulting accident. By contrast, it would be misleading just to state that the train's arrival caused the accident, although that was also a causal factor. We tend to reserve the language of causation for those factors which are most relevant to our explanations of an event.

All this reflects the point made earlier in § 4.2(ii), that causation in law is rarely a simple mechanical issue. Rather, it is intimately connected with the process of ascribing *responsibility* for a result. Active intervention, while an obvious means of "causing" harm in the mechanical sense, is not the only way of being involved in bringing that harm about. In law, responsibility for the consequences of omissions involves a twofold test. D is normally held legally responsible for the consequences of an omission when: (i) he has a duty to prevent those consequences from occurring (considered earlier in § 4.1(i)(b));[290] and (ii) his omission to intervene made a difference--that is, *if he had intervened, his intervention would (not might) have made a difference*. Part (ii) is the causal test.[291] For omissions, because of their counterfactual nature, it is usually satisfied by proof of "but for" causation. In other words, D's omission causes an outcome if, but for D's omission, the outcome would *not* have occurred.[292] If there is a reasonable possibility that it might have resulted anyway, then D's omission might have made no difference and D cannot be held causally responsible for that outcome. As an example:

> Suppose that D, a doctor, does not notice that V has stopped breathing and fails to give him artificial respiration. She cannot be held causally responsible for his death unless it can be shown that V would have survived if D had discharged her duty to intervene and artificially respirate him.

A similar example is *Dalloway*,[293] in which D was driving a cart without retaining a proper grip on the reins. A young child ran out in front of the cart and was struck and killed. It was ruled that D could be convicted of manslaughter only if it were proved that, had D been using the reins correctly, the child would have been saved.

[289] (1902) 19 TLR 37. Cp. the discussion in *Hart and Honoré* 32–44; also Feinberg, *Harm to Others* (1984) 171–81.

[290] Note that, in the specific context of gross negligence manslaughter, the requirement of concurrence between actus reus and mens rea (below, § 5.8) has been held to mandate that the causative omission must occur at a time when "there was a serious and obvious risk of death": see, e.g., *Broughton* [2020] EWCA Crim 1093, [2021] 1 WLR 543, [74]. See below, § 10.7(ii)(a) (Requirement 4).

[291] *Quaere* whether this requirement was overlooked in *Stone and Dobinson* [1977] QB 354 (CA).

[292] *Morby* (1882) 8 QBD 571; *Barnett v Chelsea and Kensington Hospital Mgmt Cttee* [1969] 1 QB 428 (DC).

[293] (1847) 2 Cox CC 273.

Note that the prosecution must show, beyond reasonable doubt, that D's intervention *would*—not *might*—have made a difference. This rule is made clear in *Morby*, the facts of which were as follows:[294]

> D's child, aged 8, died of smallpox. Owing to D's religious beliefs, he obtained no medical aid for his son. At trial, it was established that proper medical treatment might have saved or prolonged the child's life, and would certainly have increased his chances of survival; but it could not definitely be said that treatment would have made any difference. It might have been of no avail.

On these facts, the Court for Crown Cases Reserved held unanimously that D's conviction could not be sustained. In this respect the stringency of the causal test for omissions matches that for acts: it must positively be proved that D's conduct *did* cause death, not that it may have done. In the context of *Morby*, this requires the prosecution to prove beyond reasonable doubt that, if D had called for medical assistance, V *would*—not may—have survived.

*Morby* was endorsed by the Court of Appeal in *Broughton*.[295] In that case, D and his girlfriend, V, were at a music festival. D supplied V with a mix of drugs (which she took herself). V became increasingly ill across the evening and, by 9:10pm, was at obvious and serious risk of dying. Yet D, afraid of the legal consequences of supplying drugs, sought no attention for V even though the medical tent was a mere 400 metres away. V died. D's conviction of manslaughter was quashed by the Court of Appeal. Expert testimony averred that, given how little is known about medical responses to bad reactions to the relevant drugs, there was perhaps a 90% chance that, had D sought medical attention, V's life would have been saved.[296] In such circumstances, the judge should not have invited the jury to consider whether D's omission to seek medical attention caused V's death.

It is worth emphasising that even where it can be shown that D's omission is a "but for" cause of the harm, the omission will not be a legal cause if a *novus actus* supervenes. It is also subject to the requirement of sallence.[297] Suppose, for example, that Alice makes a luncheon appointment with James. Later she discovers that she will not be free on the day they have arranged. Unfortunately, she discourteously fails to telephone James and cancel the appointment. While en route to the restaurant, James is killed in an automobile accident. If Alice had remembered to cancel, James would have eaten lunch at his office. Thus, but for Alice's omission, James would not have died. In this situation, however, Alice's omission is not a legal cause of James's death.

*(b) As interventions*

Although this point is often missed in discussions of causation in the criminal law, while an omission by a third party can be a causal factor, it cannot be a *novus actus*. Where D omits to prevent harm, his omission may be a legal cause of that harm, but it is normally

[294] (1882) 8 QBD 571.
[295] [2020] EWCA Crim 1093, [2021] 1 WLR 543.
[296] *Broughton* is reconcilable, but sits uncomfortably, with *Misra and Srivastava* [2004] EWCA Crim 2375, [2005] 1 Cr App R 328. In *Misra*, two doctors failed to give adequate care to the treatment of a patient who subsequently died. Their conviction was affirmed notwithstanding that expert evidence suggested there was (only) a 95% chance that the patient would have survived had the defendants administered proper treatment. It seems that *Misra* now sets the threshold for the question of causation by omission to be left to the jury.
[297] Above, § 4.2(ii)(b).

a *concurrent* cause; that is, alongside those causal processes that the omission has failed to prevent. To illustrate:

> Suppose that D stabs V, who is admitted to hospital with substantial loss of blood and in urgent need of a blood transfusion to save her life. Apart from the loss of blood, V's injuries are not life-threatening. T, the doctor who attends V, recognises that she needs a blood transfusion and prepares to give her one. While waiting for the blood to arrive, he goes to check on another patient. Unfortunately, he is distracted by a conversation with the patient and forgets to return and administer the transfusion to V. V dies from the loss of blood. Had the transfusion been performed, she would have survived.

In this case, *both* D and T cause V's death. Diagrammatically, their actions are multiple concurrent causes:

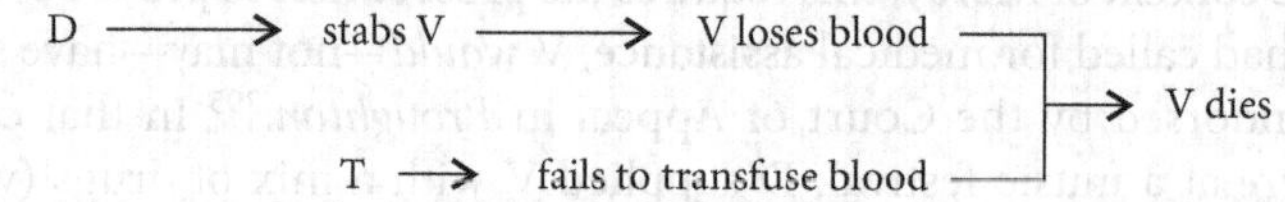


T's omission is not a *novus actus* that intervenes to disrupt the causal path from D's conduct to V's death. The whole reason why T's omission is causally significant is that it *fails to break* the causal sequence from D's action's to V's death. Indeed, we fault T and hold him (as well as D) liable for V's death precisely because he should have intervened before the sequence of events reached its fatal culmination.

The proposition that an omission is normally not a *novus actus interveniens* is the best (though often neglected) explanation of *Blaue*.[298] In that case V was stabbed by D, and was admitted to hospital having lost a large quantity of blood. V was a Jehovah's Witness, and refused the blood transfusion that was necessary to save her life. Consequently, the following day she died. D was convicted of V's manslaughter. He appealed, contending that V's refusal to have a blood transfusion was a *novus actus* that negated D's causal responsibility for V's death.

While it was accepted by the Crown that V's refusal to have a transfusion was *a* cause of her death, the Court of Appeal quite rightly ruled, using an analogy with *Smith*,[299] that the original wound inflicted by D was still an operating cause of V's death. As Lawton LJ explained: "The physical cause of death . . . was the bleeding into the pleural cavity arising from the penetration of the lung. This had not been brought about by any decision made by the deceased but by the stab wound."[300]

Alas, faced with the submission by D's counsel that V's decision was an unreasonable one, and that *therefore* D did not cause V's death, the Court responded that:[301]

> "It has long been the policy of the law that those who use violence on other people must take their victims as they find them. This in our judgment means the whole man, not just the physical man. It does not lie in the mouth of the assailant to say that his victim's religious beliefs which inhibited him from accepting certain kinds of treatment were unreasonable."

[298] [1975] 1 WLR 1411 (CA). It also explains the case of *Holland* (1841) 2 Mood & R 351, 174 ER 313.
[299] See above, § 4.2(iii)(c) (Case 3).
[300] [1975] 1 WLR 1411, 1415 (CA).
[301] *Ibid.*

As a proposition of law, this is not entirely true. Cases such as *Roberts*, discussed in § 4.2(iii)(f), establish that an intervening reaction by V *does* count as a *novus actus* where it is not a reasonably foreseeable possibility—or, as was said in that case, where the reaction is "so daft" that it is really V's own voluntary act.[302] This means that D does not have to take his victim however he finds her, but only in so far as her reaction is a reasonably foreseeable or understandable one.

Suppose, then, that V's refusal of a transfusion *was* "daft", and not a sensible or foreseeable possibility (no such finding was made by the Court in *Blaue*). If the case were like *Roberts*, this would then be a *novus actus* for which D was not responsible. *Blaue*, however, is not like *Roberts*, because V's intervening conduct involved not an act but an omission.[303] Thus, while it played a causal role in bringing about her death, and was a factor (unlike in *Roberts*) for which D was not responsible, it did not disrupt the causal sequence of events that led from the stabbing to V's death. D's appeal, in effect, was that by her refusing to intercept the causal sequence of events D had set in motion, V negated D's responsibility for that very sequence of events. But an omission cannot, by itself, do that.[304] Ultimately, *Blaue* is like *Smith* rather than *Roberts*, in as much as the original wound inflicted by D was still making an operating and substantial contribution to V's death when she died.

The difference between the two cases can be illustrated, once again, with causal diagrams:

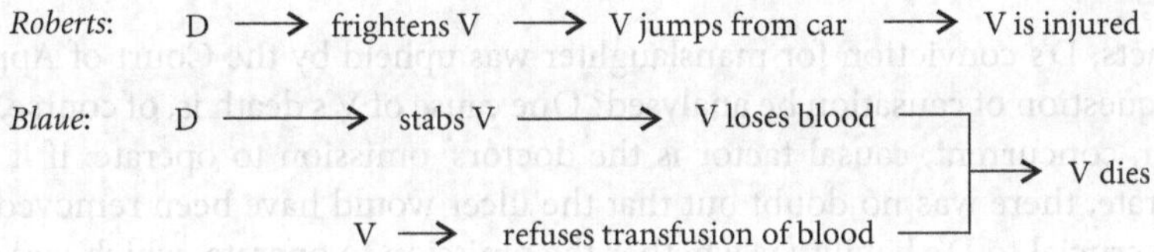


The foregoing account of omissions as causal interventions may seem susceptible to attack by reference to counterexamples. Hart and Honoré imagine a case where V has been stabbed by D, and V's doctor, T, unreasonably fails to give V a blood transfusion, because T would prefer to go and play golf.[305] They conclude that T's omission constitutes a *novus actus*. Not so. What killed V? It would be beyond eccentric to reply, "T's omission and not the stab wound." Both T *and* D killed V. It is a simple, physical truth that V died from the stab wound: this would be so even if T and V were old enemies and T's refusal to intervene was motivated by personal hatred.[306] (Contrast a case where T had smothered V with a pillow so that he could leave early to play golf.) A similar analysis should be applied to cases where V refuses a blood transfusion following a stabbing because of an unreasonable fear or belief

[302] (1972) 56 Cr App R 95, 102.

[303] More precisely, an action (refusal) whose causal role depends upon an omission (non-transfusion).

[304] Occasionally, an omission may form part of a *novus actus* when *combined* with a positive intervention: e.g. when the railway gatekeeper fails to close the gate, causing the ambulance taking V to hospital to be hit by a train. The gatekeeper causes V's death, not V's original assailant.

[305] *Hart and Honoré* 361.

[306] The analysis presented here may be contrasted with the view of Stark, "Omissions, Non-Interventions and Causation: Andrew Simester's Account" [2025] *Sing JLS* 108. Stark argues that omissions can be *novus actus interveniens*, but only where the omission is free, deliberate and informed or not reasonably foreseeable. In most cases, the omission is entirely foreseeable (for instance, in cases of medical distraction).

(a fear of needles, racism towards the medical staff, etc.). In such cases, V *and* D cause V's death; just as in *Blaue* itself.

Imagine too a case where, V, unreasonably terrified by D's frantic gestures,[307] refuses to get out of the way of E's car, which is rolling slowly down a hill towards her. (E has forgotten to put the handbrake on.) If V is injured, what caused that outcome? The answer "V; neither D nor E" is perverse. It was V, D, *and* E. This does not mean that all of these actors are necessarily to be convicted of an offence—that will depend on considerations of mens rea. Our conclusion stands: an omission can be a cause, but it cannot constitute a *novus actus*.

### (c) *Two case studies*

By way of conclusion, it may be helpful to consider two more complex examples of causation. One case that combines both omissions and the issue of medical interventions is *McKechnie*.[308] The facts of the case were as follows:

> D attacked V, inflicting serious head injuries. V was taken, deeply unconscious, to hospital, where he was discovered to be suffering from a duodenal ulcer which required surgery. However, the attending doctors decided not to operate on the ulcer. This decision was taken because, in the doctors' view, administration of the necessary anaesthesia to someone with such extensive head injuries could be fatal. A month later, the ulcer burst, and V died without having regained consciousness.

On these facts, D's conviction for manslaughter was upheld by the Court of Appeal. How should the question of causation be analysed? One cause of V's death is, of course, the ulcer. But another, concurrent, causal factor is the doctors' omission to operate: if it had been safe to operate, there was no doubt but that the ulcer would have been removed.[309] What is therefore crucial to D's liability is whether the omission to operate, which *was* a cause of death, can be said in turn to be a consequence of D's actions in inflicting the head injuries upon V. And it seems clear enough that it was. The doctors' decision not to operate was made precisely because of the injuries D inflicted. Moreover, although expert testimony at trial conflicted over whether it was *possible* to proceed with the operation without endangering V's life, there was no dispute that the decision was a reasonable one to take. Hence it was not a *novus actus*. We may represent the causal analysis as follows:

*McKechnie*:

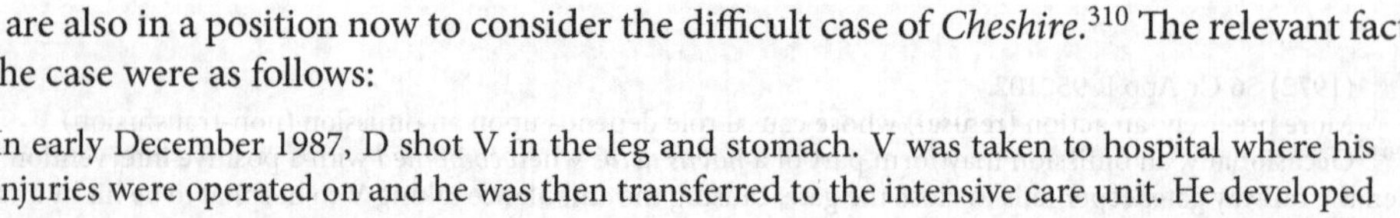


We are also in a position now to consider the difficult case of *Cheshire*.[310] The relevant facts of the case were as follows:

> In early December 1987, D shot V in the leg and stomach. V was taken to hospital where his injuries were operated on and he was then transferred to the intensive care unit. He developed

[307] Compare *Williams* [1992] 1 WLR 380 (CA).
[308] (1992) 94 Cr App R 51.
[309] *Ibid.*, 57.
[310] [1991] 1 WLR 844 (CA).

> respiratory problems and in mid-December a tracheotomy tube was inserted into his windpipe, where it remained for some four weeks. In early February his condition began to improve, and it appears that by this time the injuries inflicted by D's bullets had ceased to threaten V's life. Unfortunately, he then began to develop breathing difficulties. These arose because his windpipe had narrowed near the site of the tracheotomy—a rare but known side-effect of tracheotomies. The medical staff negligently failed to diagnose the cause of the breathing difficulties, and V died in mid-February.

The Court of Appeal upheld D's conviction for murder, and properly so. Both D *and* V's doctors caused V's death. The key point is that the tracheotomy and subsequent complication occurred without negligence by the doctors. Thus there is no disruption of the causal sequence of events linking D's act of shooting V to the narrowing of V's windpipe. This being so, the question then becomes whether the doctors' subsequent negligence is a *novus actus* that negates the causal link between the narrowing of the windpipe and V's death. And the answer to that question is no—because it constitutes an omission. The complaint against the doctors is that they *failed* to prevent the (natural, albeit rare) complication from causing death. Diagrammatically:

*Cheshire*:

D → injures V → T performs tracheotomy → windpipe narrows ┐
                                                                                                    → V dies
T(2) → fails to rectify windpipe ┘

## § 4.3 The requirement of voluntariness

It is a fundamental requirement of the criminal law that D cannot be held liable for the occurrence of an actus reus unless he was *responsible* for it: unless its occurrence can in some way be attributed to D.

We noted in Chapter 1 that when an actus reus occurs (e.g. Jim is killed), the criminal law begins with every member of society as a potential defendant.[311] The legal criteria that define responsibility for an actus reus also help to tell us which members of society are suitable defendants. Suppose that while investigating Jim's death, the police learn that his daughter Alice had secretly wished him dead because she stood to gain from his will. Despite her desires, the need for responsibility means that Alice is not guilty of murder unless she actually played some role in bringing about his death.

In respect of consequences, responsibility is established by showing causation. The police may conclude that although Alice wanted Jim's death, she did not cause it. Hence she did not murder Jim. More generally, causation is necessary to establish a link between D's behaviour and any relevant prohibited consequences. If an actus reus includes specification of such consequences (e.g. a person's death), the prosecution must prove causation in order to show that D's behaviour was responsible for that consequence, as part of showing that the actus reus as a whole can be attributed to D.

However, before she can be criminally liable the defendant must also be responsible for the *behaviour* element of the actus reus. This requirement is met when her behaviour

[311] See §§ 1.2(ii)(e), 7.1.

is voluntary. Suppose that Alice did in fact cause Jim's death, but that she did so while suffering an epileptic seizure, during which her movements caused a heavy object to fall and crush Jim. Alice's behaviour, which causes Jim's death, is not voluntary. She is not responsible for his death, and cannot be convicted of murder.

Very often, an acquittal in these circumstances need not be based upon involuntariness. Crimes such as murder require proof of some mental element on the part of the defendant, i.e. proof of some form of mens rea.[312] Murder itself cannot be committed unless D intends to kill or cause serious injury.[313] Thus, even though Alice's behaviour may have caused death, she lacks the mens rea required to be guilty of murder.

But it is important to emphasise that involuntariness is *not* merely a denial of intention, or of other forms of mens rea, or even a denial of fault in general.[314] Alice does not claim that she killed Jim by *accident*. Her denial is much more profound. It is a claim that the movements of her body which caused Jim's death do not belong to Alice as a reasoning person. It is, as such, a denial of responsibility for the actus reus itself. (Alice is relying on a "failure of proof" argument, in the terms explored in more detail in Chapter 18.)

This point deserves elaboration. As part of our conception of what it is to be a human being, we look for a link between an agent's deliberations and the consequent movements (or non-movements) of her body. Not all movements of one's body can be identified with the person whose body it is that moves. When the doctor tests Simon's reflexes by tapping him on the knee, the swinging of his leg cannot be attributed to Simon. It is merely an event in the history of his body, rather like the lurching of passengers standing in a crowded bus. These are not actions that a person is answerable for doing. They are things that happen to him, over which he has no control, and for which he is not responsible. So it is with Alice in the example above. Her behaviour is part of her body's history, but is not attributable to her as a reasoning person. It is not produced by any exercise of the capacities that identify Alice as a moral agent. In the words of H.L.A. Hart:[315]

> "What is missing in these cases appears to most people as a vital link between mind and body; and both the ordinary man and the lawyer might well insist on this by saying that in these cases there is not 'really' a human action at all and certainly nothing for which anyone should be made criminally responsible however 'strict' legal responsibility may be."

### *(i) Involuntary behaviour*

In general, D's deliberative control over her behaviour can be lost or impaired in two ways. First, D's normal capacity to reason about her behaviour may be suppressed because of an impaired consciousness. Alternatively, even if D is able to reason normally about her actions, she may have lost physical control over the movements of her body. In either case, her actions are not responsive to reason. They are "movements of the body which occurred though the agent had no reason for moving his body in that way".[316]

[312] Below, Chapter 5.
[313] Below, § 10.3(i).
[314] For useful discussion of this point, see Patient, "Some Remarks about the Element of Voluntariness in Offences of Absolute Liability" [1968] *Crim LR* 23.
[315] Hart, *Punishment and Responsibility* (1968) 107.
[316] The definition of involuntariness proposed by Hart, *Punishment and Responsibility* (1968) 255–6.

*(a) Loss of physical control*

Imagine the following scenario:

> Deborah is standing between Vicky and Tanya. Suddenly, Tanya grasps Deborah's arm and forces it into Vicky's midriff. Tanya is more powerful than Deborah, and Deborah has no chance to resist her. Vicky is winded.

In this situation, Deborah does not assault Vicky, because her arm movement is involuntary.[317] The movement does not occur under her control, and she cannot prevent its occurrence. Thus she is not responsible for the actus reus which eventuates. (Indeed, it is Tanya who assaults Vicky, using Deborah's arm.) Comparable instances are where D's arm strikes V as the result of a reflex movement or a muscular convulsion or spasm.[318]

*(b) Impaired consciousness*

It has also been held that if D, while driving, were to be stunned by a blow and rendered incapable of controlling his car, his consequent failure to give way to a pedestrian at a pedestrian crossing would be involuntary and not subject to criminal liability.[319] An analogous situation is sleepwalking. In *Hughes*, a woman had got out of bed during the night and had gone to the kitchen "to peel potatoes". She picked up a knife and returned to the bedroom and stabbed her husband. She was acquitted of wounding with intent.[320]

Sleepwalking is an instructive case, because D's behaviour in this state may well appear purposive,[321] and exhibit many outward signs of intentionality. Williams makes this point vividly:[322]

> "The sleep-walker does not always proceed as the cartoonists imagine him, with eyes tightly closed and arms outstretched. His eyes may be open and he may appear to be in perfect control. He will open a door and turn a corner, walk downstairs, open a drawer, take out a carving-knife, and return to the bedroom where his wife is asleep. But after waking up he will not remember his deed (except sometimes as a dream). Although his acts have a certain purpose (indeed, he may have an understandable reason for killing his wife), it is the purpose of a dream-state. He is not acting with his normal conscious mind."

When Lady Macbeth is observed "washing" her hands at night,[323] her movements are hardly random or completely uncontrolled. They exude purpose. Her actions are, in some sense, a subintentional product of her unconscious or subconscious mind. Certainly they are not mere reflex movements. But the control that Lady Macbeth has over them is in no way a conscious control—indeed, she is incapable of acting intentionally at all. Her "acts" are, in law, involuntary.

317 *Farduto* (1912) 10 DLR 669, 673; compare *O'Sullivan v Fisher* [1954] SASR 33, 39–40.

318 *Bratty v A-G for Northern Ireland* [1963] AC 386, 409 (Lord Denning).

319 *Hill v Baxter* [1958] 1 QB 277, 282–3, 286-7 (DC); *Kay v Butterworth* (1945) 61 TLR 452, 453; *Spurge* [1961] 2 QB 205 (CA); *Bell* [1984] 3 All ER 842, 846–7 (CA).

320 Reported in *The Times*, 3 May 1978, p. 5. Cp. *Bratty v A-G for Northern Ireland* [1963] AC 386, 403 (Viscount Kilmuir), 409 (Lord Denning); *Carpenter*, *The Times*, 14 October 1976; *Carter* [1959] VR 105; *Fain v Commonwealth* 39 Am Rep 213 (1879). Seemingly, the case should have been regarded as one of insane automatism: below, § 19.2(ii)(b).

321 Compare also *Charlson* [1955] 1 WLR 317 (Chester Assizes).

322 *TBCL* 665.

323 *Macbeth*, Act V, scene i.

In the criminal law, these forms of involuntary behaviour are known as automatism. Like Lady Macbeth, the defendant may be unconscious or semi-conscious when she does the actus reus. Where this is so, and her actions are the product of a sufficiently impaired consciousness, those actions are described as automatic. However, as the assault example involving Deborah, Tanya, and Vicky shows, automatism predicated upon unconsciousness or impaired consciousness is not *required* for the defendant to be absolved of responsibility for her behaviour. Whether she was conscious or unconscious, what is essential to the denial of responsibility for a defendant's involuntary behaviour is that *she was unable deliberatively to control that behaviour and to prevent it from occurring.*

In most cases, there will be a connection between consciousness and control: the greater the degree of consciousness a defendant has, the greater the degree of conscious or deliberative control she will have over her actions. This raises a further question. Where D's claim of involuntariness is based upon automatism and an impaired consciousness, must D have lost *all* conscious control over her limbs?

Historically, the law's answer to this question was unclear. One of the leading cases is *A-G's Reference (No. 2 of 1992).*[324] In that case, D was charged with causing death by reckless driving. He had steered his truck onto the hard shoulder of the motorway and then into a stationary vehicle. At the time, D had been driving for six of the past 12 hours. The defence adduced evidence that D had entered a condition known as "driving without awareness", in which a driver's ability to avoid a collision was negated because repetitive stimuli experienced during long motorway journeys induced a trance-like state in which the focal point for forward vision gradually came nearer and nearer until the driver was focusing just ahead of his windscreen. The Court of Appeal held that such evidence could not support a defence of automatism. In the Court's words, "the defence of automatism requires a total destruction of voluntary control on the defendant's part. Impaired, reduced, or partial control is not enough."[325] By contrast, someone driving without awareness "retains some control. He would be able to steer the vehicle and usually to react and return to full awareness when confronted by significant stimuli".[326] The Court observed that although "very little" may intrude upon the driver's consciousness, he is not entirely (just "largely") unaware of steering or of the road ahead.[327]

This standard accords with that in the earlier case of *Watmore v Jenkins*, where automatism was said to connote no "wider or looser concept than involuntary movement of the body or limbs".[328] Similarly, in *Broome v Perkins*, the contrast between normal and automatic driving was described as follows:[329]

> "When driving a motor vehicle, the driver's conscious mind receives signals from his eyes and ears, decides on the appropriate course of action as a result of those signals, and gives directions to the limbs to control the vehicle. When a person's actions are involuntary and automatic his mind is not controlling or directing his limbs."

[324] [1994] QB 91 (CA).
[325] *Ibid.*, 105.
[326] *Ibid.*
[327] *Ibid*, 102.
[328] [1962] 2 QB 572, 586 (DC).
[329] (1987) 85 Cr App R 321, 332 (DC).

On this footing, the defendant Perkins was convicted of driving without due care and attention, albeit in a hypoglycaemic state. Since his erratic driving manifested reaction to stimuli (e.g. veering away from another vehicle, braking behind traffic), his mind must, at least from time to time, have been sufficiently in control of his limbs. During those periods *he was driving*, and therefore, in the view of the Divisional Court, the offence was made out. The defendant in *Watmore v Jenkins* was similarly convicted of dangerous driving despite being in a hypoglycaemic state.[330]

These decisions are somewhat rigid in their approach, and are difficult to reconcile with earlier cases not involving driving offences. In *Charlson*,[331] D was charged with causing grievous bodily harm with intent to his 10-year-old son, whom he had suddenly struck on the head with a mallet and then defenestrated. D may have been suffering from a cerebral tumour, which would render him liable to an outburst of impulsive violence over which he had no control. On these facts, D was permitted to raise a defence of automatism (and found not guilty) even though he could recall hitting V on the head. Similarly, in *Quick*,[332] on a charge of assault D was allowed to raise automatism consequent upon hypoglycaemia, notwithstanding that his condition was one of semi-consciousness. It is hard to see how the same condition, hypoglycaemia, may ground a claim of automatism in *Quick* but not in *Watmore v Jenkins* or *Broome v Perkins*.

In principle, *Charlson* and *Quick* are to be preferred. There seems no reason to require that D be altogether unconscious before an acquittal results.[333] Indeed, what is striking about the driving cases is the simplistic approach of the courts. No middle ground is acknowledged: in which D may not be fully unconscious, yet may have no conscious control over his actions. His limbs may respond to subconscious commands, but not to reason and deliberation. And in the absence of deliberative control, D cannot be regarded as a moral agent with respect to his behaviour. Blaming judgements are inappropriate.[334]

Until quite recently, it seemed that the more Draconian[335] cases on this matter were restricted to contexts involving driving offences. However, in *Coley*,[336] the Court of Appeal followed *Watmore v Jenkins* and *A-G's Reference (No. 2 of 1992)*, and insisted—in the context of an attempted murder charge—that the state of automatism was confined to agents afflicted with "a complete destruction of voluntary control". Strictly speaking, the point was not tested in that case, since the jury had found that D had the mens rea for murder and so was not automatic (albeit that he was under the influence of strong cannabis). Yet the decision suggests, at least for now, that the current law on automatism is stringent in the extreme.

330 *Isitt* (1978) 67 Cr App R 44 may be thought of as a similar authority, in that D's claim of hysterical fugue did not forestall his conviction for dangerous driving. However, on the facts his conduct appears to have involved action for a purpose—merely without moral inhibition (see at 48–9).

331 [1955] 1 WLR 317 (Chester Assizes). Strictly speaking, since D was suffering from an "internal" disorder, the case should be regarded as one of *insane* automatism: below, §§ 4.3(i)(d), 19.1(ii)(b).

332 [1973] QB 910 (CA).

333 The possibility of semi-conscious automatism appears to have been accepted also in *Stripp* (1979) 69 Cr App R 318, 320–1; cp. *Toner* (1991) 93 Cr App R 382; *Carter* [1959] VR 105, 108–9.

334 Except where the involuntariness arises from D's prior fault: below, § 4.3(iii).

335 See, e.g., *Clarke* [2009] EWCA Crim 921, [2010] 1 Cr App R (S) 26, in which a diabetic driver was sentenced to imprisonment for dangerous driving causing death despite, it seems, impeccable management of his condition: Rumbold and Wasik, "Diabetic Drivers, Hypoglycaemic Unawareness, and Automatism" [2011] *Crim LR* 863.

336 [2013] EWCA Crim 223, [22]. Hughes LJ also pointed to the defendant's prior fault in taking a large quantity of strong cannabis, without noticing that attempted murder is a specific intent offence.

This position is an unhappy one for the law to have arrived at. In this context it is helpful to consider *Bratty v Attorney-General for Northern Ireland*, in which Lord Denning stated:[337]

> "No act is punishable if it is done involuntarily: and an involuntary act in this context—some people nowadays prefer to speak of it as 'automatism'—means an act which is done by the muscles without any control of the mind, such as a spasm, a reflex action or a convulsion; or an act done by a person who is not conscious of what he is doing, such as an act done whilst suffering from concussion or whilst sleep-walking."

At first blush, this passage may seem to contemplate only situations where there is a complete loss of consciousness. However, Lord Denning's definition is asserted in order to draw a contrast, later in the same judgment, with an act that the accused merely cannot remember, or which "is unintentional or its consequences are unforeseen".[338] Understood in this context, there is no suggestion that Lord Denning intended to equate involuntariness with unconsciousness; indeed concussion, expressly included in the definition, is a clear case where behaviour is not consciously, but at some lower level, *willed*. Moreover, the judgment goes on to discuss, without reservation on this point, the direction given in *Charlson*,[339] in which (as we saw) D's actions were not only consciously experienced but remembered. The conclusion is inescapable that his Lordship envisaged the conscious, reasoning control of the mind as what must be lacking in automatism.[340]

Moreover, as we noted earlier, this analysis seems correct in principle. What ought to count is the inability *deliberatively* to control one's conduct—that one's movements are not responsive to a capacity to reason and deliberate about one's conduct. Obviously, where the defendant is altogether unconscious her reasoning capacities will be inactive. But a defendant need *not* be unconscious before those capacities may be sufficiently suppressed or inoperative to negate responsibility. A hypnotised patient who carries out the instructions of the hypnotist must be able to comprehend and implement those instructions at some level of consciousness. Yet he lacks capacity to deliberate about what actions to take or his reasons for taking them. He is an automaton, and is not responsible for his behaviour.[341]

Apart from sleepwalking and hypnotism, standard cases of semi-conscious conduct which have previously been accepted as capable of qualifying as automatic and involuntary behaviour include acts done while in a state of concussion,[342] dissociation,[343] and advanced stages of hypoglycaemia.[344] In each of these instances, a loss of the capacity deliberatively

[337] [1963] AC 386, 409. See also the judgment of Viscount Kilmuir LC, at 401.

[338] *Ibid.*, 409.

[339] [1955] 1 WLR 317 (Chester Assizes); see *Bratty* [1963] AC 386, 411. (Lord Denning thought, however, that case should have been regarded as insane rather than sane automatism.)

[340] A conclusion reached by the New Zealand Court of Appeal in *Burr* [1969] NZLR 736, 744–5, when considering the same passage.

[341] For interesting discussion, see Williams, "The Actus Reus of Dr Caligari" (1994) 142 *U Pa L Rev* 1661, 1667–70; also Mason, "The Willed Trance: Volition, Voluntariness and Hypnotised Defendants" (2021) 85 *J Crim Law* 26.

[342] Cp. *Bratty v A-G for Northern Ireland* [1963] AC 386, 403 (Viscount Kilmuir LC); *Quick* [1973] QB 910, 918, 920–2 (CA).

[343] Cp. *Toner* (1991) 93 Cr App R 382; *T* [1990] Crim LR 256 (Crown Court); *Rabey* [1980] 2 SCR 513. Such a possibility was accepted in *Gower* [2025] Crim LR 220 (Crown Court St Alban's), albeit it was ruled in that case that the cause, acute stress, would make it a case of *insane* automatism (see below, § 4.3(i)(d) and, more fully Chapter 19).

[344] *Quick* [1973] QB 910 (CA).

to control D's behaviour should mean that he cannot be held criminally responsible for his actions and their consequences. To the extent that the decision in *Coley* casts doubt on these authorities, it is very much to be regretted.

### *(c) Imperfect deliberative capacity?*

It must be emphasised that where D does in fact form an intention to commit a crime, then however clouded and confused D's awareness may have been, automatism is excluded. Responsibility for behaviour is not denied merely because D's deliberative faculties are "highly confused"[345] or "not working in top gear".[346] "Not thinking clearly" implies that D is still thinking about his actions, even if not very well. He is still exercising some deliberative control over his conduct, and cannot claim that his conduct was involuntary—it is a far cry from this state to one in which D is not reasoning or exercising such control at all. Rather than automatism, the appropriate defence (if applicable) is one of absence of mens rea. An instructive case is *Kingston*, the facts of which were as follows:[347]

> D, who was known by T to have paedophilic desires, was invited by T to a flat for ostensibly innocent purposes. While there, D was given coffee laced with disinhibiting drugs by T. D was then taken into a bedroom where a 15-year-old boy lay, also drugged, on a bed. D touched the boy sexually, and was subsequently charged with an indecent assault. His conviction was upheld by the House of Lords.

It seems likely that D would not have acted as he did had he not (unwittingly) ingested the drugs, which may well have affected his judgement by freeing him of his usual self-restraint. But a disinhibited intent is still an intent, and the explanation cannot amount to a denial of responsibility for D. He acted for reasons—albeit perhaps not reasons that would normally motivate him—and thus was not automatic.[348] More generally, it is no defence that D acted upon an *irresistible impulse*, if he knew what he was doing and acted intentionally.[349] An impulsive action is conscious and intentional—it is action for a reason, not action uncontrolled by reason.

### *(d) Insane automatism*

Whenever a defendant's involuntariness is found to be due to automatism, the court must then determine whether it is to be classified as *sane* or *insane* automatism. This classification depends upon the cause of the automatism. Where the defendant loses consciousness as a result of an "external" cause, such as a blow on the head, his behaviour will be regarded as occurring in a state of sane automatism.[350] By contrast, behaviour occurring as the result

[345] Cp. *Poole* [2003] EWCA Crim 1219, [6].
[346] *Isitt* (1978) 67 Cr App R 44, 48.
[347] [1995] 2 AC 355.
[348] Cp. *Isitt* (1978) 67 Cr App R 44, 49; *A-G for South Australia v Brown* [1960] AC 432 (PC); *Bratty v A-G or Northern Ireland* [1963] AC 386, 409 (Lord Denning); *HM Advocate v Kidd* 1960 JC 61. A similar analysis would apply to loss of control; D's provoked intention is still an intention. Thus the defence functions as an excuse rather than as a denial of voluntariness. See below, § 10.5. For an argument that Kingston might deserve an excusatory defence, see Sullivan, "Making Excuses" in Simester and Smith (eds.), *Harm and Culpability* (1996) 131. See, also, Tadros, *Criminal Responsibility* (2005) 319–20.
[349] *Bratty v A-G for Northern Ireland* [1963] AC 386, 409 (Lord Denning); *A-G for South Australia v Brown* [1960] AC 432 (PC); cp. *Dodd* (1974) 7 SASR 151, 157; *Burr* [1969] NZLR 736, 750.
[350] Cp. *Foye* [2013] EWCA Crim 475, [34]: automatism "may well involve no abnormality of the mind at all".

of an "internal" cause, such as that occurring during an epileptic seizure, will be exculpated on the footing of insane automatism.

The test for differentiating these types of automatism will be discussed in Chapter 19, when we consider the defence of insanity. The importance of the distinction is that sane automatism operates as a straightforward denial of voluntariness and thus leads to an outright acquittal. By contrast, insane automatism is treated in law as a species of insanity, for which there is a special verdict and the burden of proof is placed upon the defendant.

### *(ii) Omissions, states of affairs, and possession*[351]

So far, we have considered involuntariness in the context of positive actions by a defendant. However, we saw earlier in this chapter (§ 4.1) that not every actus reus requires a positive action. For example, if D stands by while her child drowns in the bath, her omission to save him is prima facie the actus reus of murder and manslaughter.[352]

Obviously, the involuntariness of omissions cannot be explained in the same way as actions. It would be odd indeed to talk of a reflex or convulsive omission. Nonetheless, even for omissions the criminal law in general requires that D must be responsible for her behaviour before she commits the actus reus of a crime. D's omission is involuntary, and her responsibility for the actus reus is negated, when she fails to discharge a duty to intervene because it was *impossible* for her to do so. There is extensive authority for this proposition.[353] As Sir William Scott put the point, in *The Generous*:[354]

> "But the law itself, and the administration of it, must yield to that to which everything must bend—to necessity. The law, in its most positive and peremptory injunctions, is understood to disclaim, as it does in its general aphorisms, all intention of compelling them to impossibilities; and the administration of law must adopt that general exception in the consideration of all particular cases."

That general exception was adopted in *Bamber*,[355] where a landowner charged with non-repair of a highway across his land was absolved of liability on the ground that repair of the highway was impossible:[356]

> "Both the road which the defendant is charged with liability to repair, and the land over which it passes, are washed away by the sea. To restore the road, as he is required to do, he must create a part of the earth anew. . . . But here all the materials of which a road could be made have been swept away by the act of God. Under those circumstances can the defendant be liable for not repairing the road? We want an authority for such a proposition; and none has been found."

[351] See, generally, Child, "Defense of a Basic Voluntary Act Requirement in Criminal Law from Philosophies of Action" (2020) 23 *New Crim LR* 437; Simester, *Fundamentals* § 8.4.

[352] Above, § 4.1(i)(b) (Case 2).

[353] *Stockdale v Coulson* [1974] 1 WLR 1192 (DC); *Brown* (1841) Car & M 314, 318, 174 ER 522, 524 ("without any physical impossibility" a proviso); *Hogan* (1851) 2 Den 277, 169 ER 504; *Burns v Bidder* [1967] 2 QB 227 (DC); *Vann* (1851) 2 Denison 325, 169 ER 523. A valuable discussion is Smart, "Criminal Responsibility for Failing to Do the Impossible" (1987) 103 *LQR* 532. See also Williams, *CLGP* 746–8.

[354] (1812) 2 Dods 322, 323, 165 ER 1501, 1501.

[355] (1843) 5 QB 279, 114 ER 1254.

[356] *Ibid.*, 287, 1257.

In the context of a more familiar, criminal wrong, consider the following example:

> After an earthquake, D observes that his daughter is suffocating under a pile of rubble. D fails to rescue her because he is pinned beneath some collapsed masonry from which he cannot escape. D is not responsible for failing to rescue his daughter, and cannot be attributed with the actus reus of a homicide.

This is true even if, for some reason, D had wanted his daughter dead, and would not have rescued her had it been possible to do so.[357]

In such cases, where a defendant would not have complied with the law even if that were possible, it is sometimes important to distinguish between involuntary *behaviour* and unavoidable *consequences*. In the earthquake example, D has no control over his behaviour. But imagine the following case:

> E is sunbathing on the beach when he observes his young daughter, V, entering the sea and starting to swim in shallow water. Unfortunately, V encounters difficulties and is caught in an outgoing tide. E does not lift a finger to help V, despite her cries to him, and watches as she is swept out to sea and drowned.

E may be able to deny responsibility for V's death on the basis of *causation*. In a prosecution for murder or manslaughter, the prosecution must prove that E's omission to intervene caused his daughter's death. If in fact there was a riptide, and E would have been unable to save V anyway, then he is not responsible for the fatal consequence and cannot be convicted of a homicide offence.

The difference between this case and the earthquake example is that E denies responsibility for a *consequence* of his omission, on the basis of causation, while D denies responsibility for his *behaviour*, on the basis of involuntariness. Either way, a vital element of the actus reus of homicide is missing. But unlike D, E may still be criminally liable for any relevant offence where consequences are not part of the actus reus,[358] including an *attempt*. Because E's behaviour was not involuntary, it is capable in principle of constituting the actus reus of an attempted murder.[359] (Whether he would be convicted then depends upon questions of mens rea and proximity.) By contrast, it is impossible for D even to attempt a rescue. Therefore he cannot be held responsible for failing to do so.

### (a) *Omission cases that derogate from principle*

In *Stockdale v Coulson* it was said that "nobody ought to be prosecuted for that which it is impossible to do".[360] Similarly, in *Burns v Nowell*:[361]

> "before a continuous act or proceeding, not originally unlawful, can be treated as unlawful by reason of the passing of an Act of Parliament, . . . a reasonable time must be allowed for its discontinuance. . . ."

[357] Cp. *Starri v SA Police* (1995) 80 A Crim R 197.
[358] Compare *Brown* (1841) Car & M 314, 318, 174 ER 522, 524–5.
[359] Subject to the language of the Criminal Attempts Act 1981, which prima facie requires an "act": below, § 9.3(ii)(c).
[360] [1974] 1 WLR 1192, 1196 (DC).
[361] (1880) 5 QBD 444, 454.

At the level of principle, these sentiments endorse a defence of impossibility in ringing terms. Yet there are cases where such a defence has not been allowed. In *Davey v Towle*,[362] for example, the driver of a car was not excused for failing to produce a test certificate, even though it was impossible for him to do so because the car owner was unable or unwilling to produce the certificate. Such cases should be regarded as exceptional. Derogation from the principle *lex non cogit ad impossibilia* ("the law does not compel a person to do that which is impossible") is not to be encouraged. It is both morally undesirable and inconsistent with a significant body of case law.[363]

It may be that the exceptional cases such as *Davey v Towle* can be explained, and therefore confined. They all involve strict liability offences—especially driving offences—where the defendant chose to engage in a specialist, risk-creating activity, and thereby brought himself within the scope of the relevant criminal law duty. Moreover, the defendant had an opportunity, before doing so (e.g. commencing to drive), to ensure that he had the ability to comply with the law.[364] In such circumstances, it may be reasonable to expect the onus to lie on the defendant to make sure in advance that he has the wherewithal to comply with the law. Failure to do so would then count as a species of antecedent fault (discussed below, § 4.3(iii)).

An additional consideration is that, in *Davey v Towle*, to permit D to shelter behind the recalcitrance of the car owner would undermine the effectiveness and purpose of the offence itself. Provided there is the possibility of ensuring compliance in advance, this would seem a legitimate reason for excluding a defence of impossibility at the time of the infraction. Where, however, the features identified here do not apply, it is submitted that the general rule is that impossibility is a defence to crimes of omission.

*(b) States of affairs*

In principle, the test of responsibility for crimes which specify no behavioural element, and which criminalise states of affairs, ought to be similar to the impossibility test for crimes of omission. This follows from the point made earlier (in § 4.1(ii)(a)) that such offences, while formally needing no proof of particular behaviour by the defendant, can be seen as indirectly imposing liability for a defendant's omission to prevent the actus reus from occurring.

Unfortunately, English courts have not acknowledged this point as a matter of universal principle. Rather, it appears to be incorporated only as a matter of statutory construction. The leading modern decision is *Robinson-Pierre*.[365] D owned a pit bull terrier, a breed that is classified as "dangerous" within the meaning of the Dangerous Dogs Act 1991. Early one morning, police officers executed a search warrant at D's house by breaking down the door without warning and charging into the house. D's dog was locked inside the house at the time. Unsurprisingly, it went berserk, chasing the officers out of the house and continuing to attack and injure them on the street. D was charged with an offence, under section 3 of

[362] [1973] RTR 328 (DC). Cp. *Strowger v John* [1974] RTR 124 (DC); *Pilgram v Dean* [1974] 1 WLR 601 (DC).

[363] See the cases variously discussed and cited in § 4.3(ii) above.

[364] Compare *Strowger v John* [1974] RTR 124, 130 (DC), where, on a charge of failing to display a vehicle excise licence (which had fallen off the windscreen), Lord Widgery CJ observed that it might be different if a stranger had broken into the car and removed the licence without the defendant's knowledge: cp. *Kilbride v Lake* [1962] NZLR 590.

[365] [2013] EWCA Crim 2396, [2014] 1 WLR 2638.

the 1991 Act, of being the owner of a dog which caused injury while dangerously out of control in a public place.[366]

The Court of Appeal quashed D's conviction. While section 3 created an offence of strict liability, it was nevertheless to be presumed that the offence "requires proof by the prosecution of an act or omission of the defendant (with or without fault) that to some (more than minimal) degree caused or permitted the prohibited state of affairs to come about".[367]

A general presumption of this sort is to be welcomed. It is important to emphasise, however, that the voluntariness requirement is presumed *as a matter of statutory interpretation*. Thus it can be excluded by the terms of the statute creating the offence:[368]

> "we have no doubt that the supremacy of Parliament embraces the power to create 'state of affairs' offences in which no causative link between the prohibited state of affairs and the defendant need be established. The legal issue is not, in our view, whether in principle such offences can be created but whether in any particular enactment Parliament intended to create one."

In practice, where the offence specifies no explicit behavioural element at all, the courts have very often regarded such claims as legally irrelevant.

It need not be so. In *Dr Bonham's Case*, Coke CJ spoke words of great power:[369]

> "when an Act of Parliament is against common right and reason, or repugnant, *or impossible to be performed*, the common law will controul it. . . ."

The defence of impossibility, it may be observed, has venerable spiritual heritage: a law that demands the impossible surely is against common right and reason, warranting an exception. Consistently with this, Lord Uthwatt commented in 1948 that a driver who failed to accord precedence at a pedestrian crossing "has, subject only to the application of the principle *Lex non cogit ad impossibilia*, broken the regulation".[370] Yet in 1988 such grand sentiments were nowhere to be found in the Court of Appeal. In *Porter v Honey*,[371] D, an estate agent, was prosecuted for displaying a "for sale" board on a property at a time when a second board was also displayed. D had erected the board at a time when no other board was displayed, and prima facie committed an offence only when (unknown to D) a competing estate agent erected a second "for sale" board on the same property. Faced with this situation, the House of Lords succeeded in exculpating D only by a convoluted (and far-fetched) exercise in statutory interpretation. The moral poverty of this technique was captured, without irony, by Lord Griffiths' first words:[372]

> "the question for your Lordships is whether on the true construction of the relevant legislation an estate agent who lawfully places a 'for sale' board on a property should be held to have committed a criminal offence because another estate agent unlawfully and without the knowledge or consent of the first estate agent places a second 'for sale' board on the same property.

366 The restriction to public places has since been removed by Parliament.
367 *Ibid.*, [42].
368 *Ibid.*, [38].
369 8 Co Rep 113b, 118a, 77 ER 646, 652. Coke CJ's words must now be read in light of the doctrine of parliamentary sovereignty. But there is nothing in that doctrine that prevents recognition of a common law defence of impossibility in the absence of express statutory wording to the contrary.
370 *London Passenger Transport Board v Upson* [1949] AC 155.
371 [1988] 1 WLR 1420 (HL). Compare *Leicester v Pearson* [1952] 2 QB 668 (DC).
372 At 1422.

> I suggest that any layman would not hesitate to answer, 'No, Parliament cannot have intended such an unjust and absurd result'. Unfortunately, the legislation poses a more difficult problem of construction for the lawyer. . . ."

Adoption of this "interpretive", rather than general principle-based, approach has had a significant impact upon situational crimes. In English law, by contrast with other jurisdictions,[373] there is no general defence of impossibility to crimes that impose liability purely for a state of affairs. Authority for this proposition includes *Larsonneur*,[374] discussed earlier, and a number of other cases.[375] In *Larsonneur*, it will be recalled, D was brought into the United Kingdom against her will by the police, and consequently convicted of "being found" in the country when permission for her to enter had previously been refused. A similar case is *Winzar v Chief Constable of Kent*.[376] D, who had been brought to hospital but found merely to be drunk, was later removed by the police to their car parked on the road outside. He was then charged with being found drunk on a highway, and his conviction was upheld by the Divisional Court. "Being found", it was held, refers only to the perceptions or actions of the finder and not to any conduct by the defendant. Given the language used in the statute, the fact that the defendant's involvement was involuntary was said therefore to be immaterial.

Since the defendants were said to be guilty of offences in these cases, presumably the policemen involved should have been found liable as accessories for procuring them.[377] So far as responsibility for the offence is concerned, its commission in each case was brought about by the police and had nothing to do with the defendant.[378] Yet it was the defendant alone who was convicted. Cases such as *Larsonneur* and *Winzar* show a lack of regard for fundamental principles of humanity and justice.[379]

Fortunately, *Robinson-Pierre* points towards a more sympathetic construction of situational offences in the future. Unlike in *Larsonneur* and *Winzar*, the Court in that case was astute to the point that D's dog had only got out into public space because of the unforeseen intervention of a third party. To that extent, the decision is in line with the interpretation of other offences that criminalise D's failure to prevent another person from doing something wrongful: for example, the offence of dishonestly allowing another person (T), who is in receipt of a social security benefit, to refrain from disclosing a change in circumstance that affects T's entitlement to the benefit.[380] In such cases the courts are more likely to read in a requirement that D had the ability to prevent T's wrongful conduct.[381] Underlying this

[373] See, e.g., *O'Sullivan v Fisher* [1954] SASR 33; *Finau v Dept of Labour* [1984] 2 NZLR 396.

[374] (1934) 24 Cr App R 74; above, § 4.1(ii)(a).

[375] E.g. *Hawkins v Holmes* [1974] RTR 436 (DC); *Duck v Peacock* [1949] 1 All ER 318 (DC); *Crump v Gilmore* [1970] Crim LR 28 (CA); *Smedleys Ltd v Breed* [1974] AC 839. See too *Davey v Towle* [1973] RTR 328 (DC); *Strowger v John* [1974] RTR 124 (DC); *Pilgram v Dean* [1974] 1 WLR 601 (DC).

[376] *The Times*, 28 March 1983 (DC).

[377] There is, formally, no defence available to persons who procure crimes in order to later prosecute them. Despite this, *agent provocateurs* never seem to be prosecuted.

[378] Subject to the argument by Lanham, "Larsonneur Revisited" [1976] *Crim LR* 276, that *Larsonneur* involved prior fault; a rationale not, however, relied upon in the Court's decision.

[379] For a consideration of the potential impact of the European Convention of Human Rights on such cases, see Sullivan, "Strict Liability for Criminal Offences in England and Wales following Incorporation into English Law of the European Convention on Human Rights" in Simester (ed.), *Appraising Strict Liability* (2005) 195.

[380] Contrary to s. 111A(1B) of the Social Security Administration Act 1992.

[381] Cp. *Tilley* [2009] EWCA Crim 1426, [2010] 1 WLR 605, [37]–[39]; *Crabtree v Fern Spinning Co. Limited* (1901) 85 LT 549, 552 (KBD).

greater willingness, like the decision in *Porter v Honey* above, is an implicit Rule of Law constraint: that D's liability should not normally lie in the hands of another person, who has the power independently of D's conduct to make D guilty of a crime.[382] It is one thing to say that D failed to prevent harm; it is quite another to say that, although D could do nothing about it, someone else deliberately made her a criminal.

*(c) Involuntary possession*

Like situational offences, criminal possession (e.g. of an instrument of burglary[383] or of a controlled drug[384]) can be established without proving any behaviour by D (above, § 4.1(ii)(b)). The physical element of "being in possession" is a state of affairs in which D has control, with or without custody,[385] of the prohibited item. It is usually sufficient for the actus reus in a possession-based offence to show that the item is at a location where it is subject to D's power of control.[386]

As it happens, most offences of possession are unlikely to raise issues of involuntariness, since they generally require proof of a mental element in addition to proof of the actus reus. Thus, according to Lord Morris in *Warner v Metropolitan Police Commissioner*, possession involves "being *knowingly* in control of a thing in circumstances which have involved an opportunity (whether availed of or not) to learn or discover, at least in a general way, what the thing is".[387] We will consider mens rea issues surrounding possession below, in § 5.6(iv). For present purposes, suppose that D is asleep when another person places controlled drugs in her hand. There is no need to address the question of voluntariness, since D lacks the knowledge required to constitute possession of the drugs.[388]

As we shall see below in § 5.6(iv), the view that "possession" has an embedded mental element has been criticised. If that criticism were to be accepted by the courts, the question of involuntary possession would become more important. However, it is possible to construct situations in which, even if Lord Morris is right, one may involuntarily be in possession of something:

> Imagine that D acquires possession of controlled drugs but not by means of his own voluntary actions—for example, if a visitor to his house leaves the drugs behind when she departs. D may not be responsible for acquiring possession, but normally he is still responsible for *being* in possession because he fails to divest himself of the drugs. Suppose further, however, that D knows that he has been left the drugs yet happens to be bed-ridden through illness and is unable to dispose of them.

It is submitted that, by analogy with offences involving omissions, D should not be held responsible for the actus reus and his involuntary possession should not be attributed to

382 See Simester, *Fundamentals* § 5.3.5.

383 Theft Act 1968, s. 25.

384 Misuse of Drugs Act 1971, s. 5.

385 Compare *Kelt* [1977] 1 WLR 1365 (CA); *Sullivan v Earl of Caithness* [1976] QB 966 (DC) (item held on behalf of D by third party). In some offences control without the availability of imminent custody may not suffice: *Lester* (1955) 39 Cr App R 157.

386 At least in respect of drugs: *Lewis* (1988) 87 Cr App R 270.

387 [1969] 2 AC 256, 289.

388 See, e.g., the hypothetical case posed by Parker LCJ in *Lockyer v Gibb* [1967] 2 QB 243, 248 (DC); discussed by the House of Lords in *Warner v Metropolitan Police Commissioner* [1969] 2 AC 256, 282, 286, 300, 303, 311; below, § 5.6(iv). In addition, even if it were held that D "possessed" the drugs, she could offer the defence of justified ignorance under s. 28 of the Misuse of Drugs Act 1971.

him for the purposes of criminal liability. Indirect authority for this proposition may be inferred from the reasoning of the House of Lords in *Warner*. Presumably the reason Lord Morris required an opportunity to discover possession is in order that the defendant should have the chance to divest himself of contraband unknowingly acquired. It would seem both harsh and unlikely that, the instant some stranger thrusts a package into D's arms while D is out walking, he should be held criminally responsible for possession before he has had even the chance to drop it.[389]

*(d) Distinction between impossibility and ignorance of duty*

Impossibility amounting to involuntariness should be distinguished from situations where D is unaware of the existence of facts that trigger a duty to act in a certain manner.[390] For example, one does not, apparently, commit an offence of remaining in Singapore when one's presence there becomes unlawful pursuant to an unpublished law.[391] Acquittal in such cases does not depend upon any claim of involuntariness, but rather upon the source and sometimes the reasonableness of D's ignorance of law or fact. It is thus a matter for particular defences.

### *(iii) Involuntariness: responsibility by antecedent fault*

Sometimes, even though the actus reus occurs involuntarily, D may still be held criminally responsible. One way in which this may occur is through vicarious liability, which is discussed below in Chapter 8. Leaving that possibility aside, however, D may also be liable for an offence if his involuntariness, and in turn the actus reus, was the consequence of earlier conduct by D in respect of which D was at fault.[392] There are three main situations in which this can occur.

*(a) Voluntary intoxication*

The first is voluntary intoxication. Suppose that D drinks himself into a stupor, and then commits an assault. Even if the court accepts his claim that the assault occurred while D was an automaton, it will not negate his criminal responsibility for the actus reus. In such circumstances, the presence of self-induced intoxication has two roles. First, it precludes the claim of involuntariness. Secondly, it operates as a *substitute* for certain mens rea states, including recklessness (the mens rea element in assault), in so-called basic intent offences. A helpful illustration is provided by *Lipman*,[393] the facts of which were as follows:

> L and his female friend, V, took a quantity of LSD while in V's flat. During the hallucination which followed, L suffocated V by cramming bed sheet into her mouth. He believed when he did so that he was fighting snakes while descending to the centre of the earth.

389 Compare *Wright* (1976) 62 Cr App R 169.

390 See, for example, *Harding v Price* [1948] 1 KB 695 (DC) (failing to report an accident when D did not know it had occurred); *Hampson v Powell* [1970] 1 All ER 929, 931 (DC); *Hardcastle v Bielby* [1892] 1 QB 709; *Simons v Rhodes and Son Ltd* [1956] 1 WLR 642 (CA); *Belling v O'Sullivan* [1950] SASR 43.

391 *Lim Chin Aik* [1963] AC 160 (PC). See below, § 18.2(iii).

392 See Finkelstein, "Involuntary Crimes, Voluntarily Committed" in Shute and Simester (eds.), *Criminal Law Theory* (2000) 143; Robinson, "Causing the Conditions of One's Own Defense: A Study in the Limits of the Criminal Law Doctrine" (1985) 71 *Virginia LR* 1.

393 [1970] 1 QB 152 (CA).

L's behaviour while hallucinating is analogous to sleepwalking. It did not occur under his conscious or deliberative control. However, the automatism was self-induced, and moreover induced by D's own fault in becoming intoxicated. His claim to be exculpated on the basis of automatism was therefore refused, and L was convicted of manslaughter.[394]

The legal ramifications of intoxication will be explored further below, in Chapter 18. It is worth mentioning here, however, that English law on this point is out of line with that prevailing in other common law jurisdictions; where, unless one of the two further exceptions (below, § 4.3(iii)(b)–(c)) applied, automatism would be available and L would not be convicted.[395] The reasoning in other jurisdictions is as follows. Even though L is responsible for his automatism, becoming automatic is not a criminal offence. It thus does *not* follow that he is responsible for the further consequences of his automatism. Before that can be the case, L must have the required mens rea not merely in respect of becoming automatic, but also in respect of those further consequences which make up the actus reus. Thus if an offence requires proof that the defendant foresaw the risk that some element of the actus reus may occur, the claim of automatism or involuntariness denies responsibility unless she actually foresaw the possibility of her incapacity *and* of the resulting actus reus element.[396]

Ignoring such reasoning, English courts have focused on public policy concerns surrounding the inherent dangerousness of the defendant's conduct, and generally impose strict liability for the consequences of voluntary intoxication.[397]

*(b) Recklessness*

The doctrine by which voluntary intoxication overrides a defence of automatism operates only if the intoxication is self-induced through D's taking alcohol or non-soporific drugs (such as LSD). Thus it does not apply in a case such as *Bailey*,[398] where D, a diabetic, failed to take sufficient food after a normal dose of insulin and lapsed into automatism. Similarly, the doctrine does not apply if D's automatism arises from taking Valium, a sedative.[399]

The distinction appears to be that, in the latter cases, the substance that induces automatism is not one with generally recognised tendencies to produce aggressive, dangerous behaviour. Consequently, the public policy considerations that underlie decisions such as *Lipman* are less pressing, and there is no need to regard the defendant as being "on notice" of the dangerous consequences of his becoming intoxicated.

Where the defendant's automatism is not self-induced by alcohol or non-soporific drugs, the test is different. The defendant may rely upon his involuntariness as a defence *unless* he actually foresaw the risk of his behaviour becoming "aggressive, unpredictable

[394] Approved in *DPP v Majewski* [1977] AC 443. See Mackay, "Intoxication as a Factor in Automatism" [1982] *Crim LR* 146; Horder, "Pleading Involuntary Lack of Capacity" (1993) 52 *CLJ* 298, 304–12.

[395] *O'Connor* (1980) 146 CLR 64; *Martin* (1984) 51 ALR 540; *Kamipeli* [1975] 2 NZLR 610; *Cottle* [1958] NZLR 999, 1002, 1007; *Daviault* [1994] 3 SCR 63 (cp. Criminal Code of Canada, s. 33.1); Orchard, "Surviving without *Majewski*—A View from Down Under" [1993] *Crim LR* 426.

[396] *O'Connor* (1980) 146 CLR 64, 73 (Barwick CJ), 103 (Stephen J); cp. *Egan* (1897) 23 VLR 159; *Sione v Labour Dept* [1972] NZLR 278; *Ryan* (1967) 121 CLR 205. In these other jurisdictions, Lipman might have been convicted of manslaughter if the risk of killing someone while under the influence of LSD were such as to make his taking the drug "grossly negligent". (For discussion of the mens rea element(s) in involuntary manslaughter see below, § 10.7.)

[397] See, also, the position in Scotland: *Brennan v HM Advocate* 1977 JC 38.

[398] [1983] 1 WLR 760 (CA).

[399] *Hardie* [1985] 1 WLR 63 (CA).

and uncontrolled with the result that he may cause some injury to others".[400] The standard of prior fault required is essentially that of subjective *recklessness*, which is discussed further in the chapter on mens rea (below, § 5.2).

*(c) Antecedent actus reus*

In each of the above situations, the actus reus occurs while the defendant is automatic, and the defendant is simply precluded in law from claiming that automatism to exculpate herself. A third alternative for prosecutors is to show that the behavioural element of the actus reus occurred *before* the defendant became automatic. One such case arises where D falls asleep while driving and then has an accident. Although D's driving was involuntary at the time of the collision, he will be guilty of careless driving at the earlier time when he continued to drive despite feeling sleepy.[401] Indeed, D will have committed the offence even if no accident should occur.

Another example might be a variety of what is sometimes called "Dutch courage": where D, intending to murder V, drinks himself into a stupor *in order* to perpetrate the killing.[402] The ordinary rule governing intoxication (above, § 4.3(iii)(a)) will make D guilty of manslaughter, but is not sufficient to make him guilty of murder, since the mental element required for murder is intention to kill or cause grievous bodily harm, rather than recklessness regarding those harms. Nonetheless, it is arguable that his conduct in becoming drunk is itself a cause of death, and therefore constitutes part of the actus reus of murder. Hence, rather than focusing upon D's actions while automatic, his responsibility will be based upon his earlier conduct, which caused the prohibited harm, and which was itself accompanied by the fault element required for the crime.

To illustrate this type of analysis, consider the following facts:[403]

> D attempts to rob a jeweller's shop. He threatens those in the shop by pointing a loaded and cocked gun at them with his finger on the trigger. V, the shopkeeper, then springs at him. D is jolted back against the door, causing his finger to depress the trigger involuntarily. V is killed when the gun goes off, and D is charged with murder.

In such a case, D commits murder or manslaughter (depending on his intentions when pointing the gun at V). Even if the immediate cause of death is an involuntary act by D, that is not a *novus actus*; his actions leading up to that point, in threatening V and other people in the shop by pointing a gun at them with his finger on the trigger, are (also) a cause of death.[404] Thus D's earlier conduct, rather than the firing of the gun itself, supplies the causal link needed for the actus reus of murder.

[400] *Bailey* [1983] 1 WLR 760, 764–5 (CA), overruling the earlier decision in *Quick* [1973] QB 910, 922 (CA), where it was said that automatism would not be available where its onset "could have been reasonably foreseen as a result of either doing, or omitting to do something, as, for example, taking alcohol against medical advice after using certain prescribed drugs, or failing to have regular meals while taking insulin". See generally Ashworth, "Reason, Logic and Criminal Liability" (1975) 91 *LQR* 102, 106–9; Robinson, "Causing the Conditions of One's Own Defence: A Study in the Limits of Theory in Criminal Law Doctrine" (1985) 71 *Virginia LR* 1.

[401] *Kay v Butterworth* (1945) 173 LT 191 (KBD); *Spurge* [1961] 2 QB 205 (CA); below, § 5.8(i)(c)–(d). Cp. *Jiminez v The Queen* (1992) 173 CLR 572.

[402] *A-G for Northern Ireland v Gallagher* [1963] AC 349, 382 (Lord Denning).

[403] Taken from *Wickliffe* [1987] 1 NZLR 55, 60, where the approach suggested here was accepted as a possible analysis by the New Zealand Court of Appeal; also by the Australian High Court in *Ryan* (1967) 121 CLR 205, 218–19, 231, 233, 239; cp. Elliott, "Responsibility for Involuntary Acts: *Ryan v The Queen*" (1968) 41 *ALJ* 497. See also the commentary on *Burke* (reported as *Howe* [1987] AC 417) at [1987] Crim LR 480, 484.

[404] See also the discussion of causation earlier in this chapter, § 4.2(iii).

### *(d) Strict liability offences?*

For the sake of clarity, special mention should be made of offences that do not require proof of mens rea regarding each and every aspect of the actus reus. Such offences, involving what is known as strict liability, are considered in Chapter 6. Unless one of the foregoing exceptions applies, it is submitted that because voluntariness is fundamental to D's responsibility for the actus reus, and not merely relevant to mens rea, in principle involuntariness will result in there being no criminal liability for D's conduct:[405]

> "When a man is charged with dangerous driving, it is no defence for him to say, however truly, 'I did not mean to drive dangerously.' There is said to be an absolute prohibition against that offence, whether he had a guilty mind or not, see *Hill v Baxter*[406] by Lord Goddard CJ. But even though it is absolutely prohibited, nevertheless he has a defence if he can show that it was an involuntary act in the sense that he was unconscious at the time and did not know what he was doing, see *H.M. Advocate v Ritchie*,[407] *Reg. v Minor*[408] and *Cooper v McKenna, Ex parte Cooper*.[409]"

The exception, as we saw earlier, is in respect of pure situational offences, which the courts, in cases such as *Larsonneur*,[410] have construed as imposing criminal liability notwithstanding that it may be impossible for D to prevent the actus reus from occurring.

Some strict liability offences dispense with the need for the prosecutor to prove mens rea only for a part of the actus reus, and require proof of mens rea for other parts of the offence. The famous strict liability case of *Woodrow* is a convenient example.[411] D was convicted of possessing adulterated tobacco, even though he did not know it was adulterated. The offence was held to impose strict liability in respect of the fact that the tobacco was adulterated. But there was no suggestion that liability in respect of the *possession* was also strict. Had someone put adulterated tobacco in D's hand while he was sleeping, then involuntariness would have precluded liability in the normal way.[412]

### *(e) Evidential issues*

A claim of involuntariness or automatism is often described by lawyers as a "defence". In terms of substantive legal doctrine, it is not. It is a denial of the actus reus—a "failure of proof" argument—rather than a plea that the defendant's actions were justified or excused. As such, it is for the prosecution to prove voluntariness on the part of the defendant alongside the rest of the actus reus. So far as the burden of proof is concerned, however, automatism is like a defence. In practice, there is a presumption of deliberative capacity to control one's actions, and voluntariness will become an issue only if there is evidence which genuinely raises the issue.[413] Thus, if the defendant wishes to deny responsibility on this basis,

[405] *Bratty v A-G for Northern Ireland* [1963] AC 386, 409–10 (Lord Denning). Cp. *Hill v Baxter* [1958] 1 QB 277 (DC); *O'Connor* (1980) 146 CLR 64; Williams, "Absolute Liability in Traffic Offences" [1967] *Crim LR* 142 and 194, 199–205.

[406] [1958] 1 QB 277, 282 (DC).

[407] 1926 JC 110.

[408] (1955) 15 WWR (NS) 433.

[409] [1960] QLR 406.

[410] Above, § 4.3(ii)(d).

[411] *Woodrow* (1846) 15 M & W 404, 153 ER 907.

[412] See above, § 4.3(ii)(e).

[413] *Bratty v A-G for Northern Ireland* [1963] AC 386, 406–7 (Viscount Kilmuir LC), 413 (Lord Denning), 416–17 (Lord Morris). Similarly for impossibility: cp. *Bailey* [1983] 1 WLR 760, 765–6 (CA). For further discussion of the burden of proof, see above, § 3.2.

she must point to credible evidence that supports her claim. It is said that "blackout is one of the first refuges of a guilty conscience".[414] In general, since it is so easily feigned, the defendant's testimony of automatism will not be accepted unless it is buttressed by relevant evidence of surrounding circumstances or medical conditions.[415] If the evidence of automatism is credible, the prosecution will then have to prove beyond reasonable doubt that the defendant retained some level of deliberative control over her actions. If they fail to do so, the defendant should be acquitted.

[414] *Cooper v McKenna* [1960] Qd R 406, 419; *Bratty v A-G for Northern Ireland* [1963] AC 386, 413–14 (Lord Denning).

[415] *Cook v Atchison* [1968] Crim LR 266 (DC); cp. *Hill v Baxter* [1958] 1 QB 277 (DC); *Stripp* (1979) 69 Cr App R 318; contrast *Budd* [1962] Crim LR 49 (CA).

# 5

# MENS REA

The mens rea of a crime is, generally speaking, that part of the offence which refers to the defendant's mental state.[1] Consider, for example, section 15(1) of the Forgery and Counterfeiting Act 1981:

> It is an offence for a person—
>
> (a) to pass or tender as genuine any thing which is, and which he knows or believes to be, a counterfeit of a currency note or of a protected coin. . . .

When Tom is charged with an offence of passing a counterfeit note under section 15(1)(a), the offence may be established only if Tom *knew or believed that the "note" he passed was counterfeit*. The italicised part of the last sentence is a mens rea requirement.

In the case of section 15(1)(a), the mental element is fairly straightforward. But it is possible for an offence to contain a variety of actus reus elements for which the corresponding mens rea requirements differ, and some actus reus elements may have no corresponding mens rea requirement at all.[2] One such offence is section 3 of the Criminal Damage Act 1971, which provides, in part, that:

> A person who has anything in his custody or under his control intending without lawful excuse to use it . . .
>
> (b) to destroy or damage . . . property in a way which he knows is likely to endanger the life of some other person;
>
> shall be guilty of an offence.

There are two parts to the mens rea for this offence. A defendant must (i) have *intended* to use the item in question to damage property, and (ii) have *known* that doing so was likely to endanger another person's life.

Although mens rea is often regarded as the requirement that the defendant have a "guilty mind", and is taken to contain the fault elements of each offence, in fact mens rea elements serve a number of functions,[3] and it is in practice a rather technical area of law. For a prosecutor, mens rea requires her to establish only that the defendant had the specified mental state(s) toward the actus reus required for that crime. In particular, proof that the defendant has the requisite mens rea of an offence does not mean that she must know her conduct is illegal,[4] or wrong. Similarly, a laudable motive which prompts the defendant deliberately

[1] In this book, we treat negligence as a form of mens rea, notwithstanding that it is only awkwardly characterised as a 'mental state'. See below, § 5.5.

[2] See the discussion of the so-called "correspondence principle" below, § 6.5(i).

[3] Simester, *Fundamentals* §§ 3.1–3.

[4] Ignorance of law is discussed below, § 18.2.

to commit an offence is no defence.[5] In *Smith*,[6] for instance, the defendant offered a bribe to the town mayor. He did so in order to expose the mayor as corrupt. Despite his good motive, Smith was convicted of offering a bribe to a public servant since he had intentionally (the mens rea) offered the bribe (the actus reus). At that stage the offence was complete, and his motive could not help him.[7]

There are three steps to be taken in establishing whether a defendant has mens rea. The first step is to determine what is the minimum mens rea element[8] required in respect of each separate element of the actus reus. The second is to interpret the criteria of those mens rea element(s). Third is the factual question: did the defendant in fact have the mens rea element(s) required?

The present chapter is concerned with the second of those steps; its purpose is to explain the main types of mens rea which the law might require. There is in fact a great variety of possible mens rea states, including purpose, intention, recklessness, wilfulness, knowledge, belief, suspicion, reasonable cause to believe, maliciousness, fraudulence, dishonesty, corruptness, and negligence. However, in this chapter we will confine our discussion to the most common, and most important, types of fault element.

## § 5.1 Intention

The central case of wrongdoing occurs when the defendant's crime is intentional.[9] Both in law and in society at large, praise and blame are most obviously incurred for conduct that a person intends: D typically attracts greater censure if she deliberately breaks V's vase than if she carelessly drops it.

For the majority of offences, it is not necessary to prove that the actus reus was intended, since recklessness––broadly, advertent risk-taking––will normally suffice for a conviction. (Intention will therefore often be more relevant at the sentencing stage.) But this is not always so—murder, for example, requires an intention to kill or cause grievous bodily harm;

[5] For general discussion, see Horder, "On the Irrelevance of Motive in Criminal Law" in Horder (ed.), *Oxford Essays in Jurisprudence; Fourth Series* (2000) 173.

[6] [1960] 2 QB 423 (CA). Cp. *Chandler v DPP* [1964] AC 763.

[7] The decision does not sit well with *Clarke* (1985) 80 Cr App R 344, which holds that a citizen has a defence if acting honestly and solely to reveal crime and recover its proceeds. However, the view that mens rea means no more than the mental element for the offence is endorsed in *Hicklin* (1868) LR 3 QB 360, 370–2; *Yip Chiu-Cheung* [1995] 1 AC 111 (PC); *Kingston* [1995] 2 AC 355; and *Dodman* [1998] 2 Cr App R 338 (C-MAC). This approach, which disconnects a finding of mens rea from the presence of fault, is appropriate only if a suitable range of defences is available. See above, § 1.2(ii); also Brett, *Inquiry into Criminal Guilt* (1960).

[8] As explained below (§ 5.5(i)), mens rea elements exist in a rough hierarchy, and a "higher" mens rea element will satisfy a "lower" mens rea element (for instance, it is no defence to a crime that is based on recklessness that the defendant intended her proscribed action).

[9] See, e.g., Smith, "Intention in Criminal Law" (1974) 27 *CLP* 93; White, "Intention, Purpose, Foresight and Desire" (1976) 92 *LQR* 569; Buzzard, "'Intent'" [1978] *Crim LR* 5; Smith, "'Intent': A Reply" [1978] *Crim LR* 14; Duff, "The Obscure Intentions of the House of Lords" [1986] *Crim LR* 771; Williams, "Oblique Intention" (1987) 46 *CLJ* 417; Buxton, "Some Simple Thoughts on Intention" [1988] *Crim LR* 484; Duff, "Intentions Legal and Philosophical" (1989) 9 *OJLS* 76; Smith, "A Note on 'Intention'" [1990] *Crim LR* 85; Simester and Chan, "Intention Thus Far" [1997] *Crim LR* 704; Norrie, "After *Woollin*" [1999] *Crim LR* 532; Kaveny, "Inferring Intention from Foresight" (2004) 120 *LQR* 81; Moore, "Intention as a Marker of Moral Culpability and Legal Punishability" in Duff and Green (eds.), *Philosophical Foundations of Criminal Law* (2011) 179; Duff, "Intention Revisited" in Baker and Horder (eds.), *The Sanctity of Life and the Criminal Law* (2013) 148. On the earlier history of intention, see Handler, "Criminal Intent in Nineteenth-Century England" (2024) 83 *CLJ* 334.

recklessness regarding those same consequences will not suffice.[10] Other offences requiring proof of intention (to the exclusion of recklessness) include theft, burglary, wounding with intent, conspiracy, and attempt. There are other important reasons for distinguishing intention from recklessness, and we shall return to these later.

There is normally no need for an elaborate definition of intention in order to decide whether an actus reus was intended. A few exceptional situations may present difficulty, but usually the analysis will be intuitively obvious: "[t]he general legal opinion is that 'intention' cannot be satisfactorily defined and does not need a definition, since everybody knows what it means".[11] Indeed, as Lord Bridge explained in *Moloney*, in the run of cases, "[t]he golden rule should be that . . . the judge should avoid any elaboration or paraphrase of what is meant by intent, and leave it to the jury's good sense to decide whether the accused acted with the necessary intent".[12]

Nonetheless, the courts have accepted that sometimes jurors require further guidance about what intention means. Their guidance suggests that English law recognises two alternative categories of intention:

(I) D *intended* the actus reus in the ordinary, core sense of "intention"; or
(II) D recognised[13] that the actus reus was a *virtually certain* consequence of his actions.

The first case, (I), can usefully be described as "direct intention" to distinguish it from the second case, (II), which is commonly described as "indirect" or "oblique" intention. Direct intention is the standard or core variety and largely reflects the ordinary language meaning of "intention". In this paradigm case, D tries (seeks, aims, attempts) to bring about the relevant outcome. For whatever reason, he wants or needs to bring about that outcome, and that is why he acts as he does. By contrast, in the virtual certainty case, (II), D does not act in order to bring about the relevant outcome. He acts for other reasons. However, he knows that the actus reus is a virtually certain consequence of his actions. Though that is not what he is trying to bring about, it is a practically inevitable concomitant. And that, in law, can mean that he intends to bring that particular consequence about.[14]

In the following sections, we will elaborate upon these two categories of intention. In §§ 5.1(i)–(iii), the paradigm category of intention (I) will be discussed. The virtual certainty case (II) is considered in § 5.1(iv).

### (i) *Ways of speaking about intention (in its core, direct sense)*

As a starting point, it may be helpful to consider how "intention" has been paraphrased by judges and academic writers. In *Cunliffe v Goodman*, Asquith LJ stated that intention "connotes a state of affairs which the party 'intending' . . . does more than merely contemplate: it connotes a state of affairs which, on the contrary, he decides, so far as in him lies, to bring

[10] See below, § 10.3.
[11] Williams, *TBCL* 74.
[12] *Moloney* [1985] AC 905, 926. See, also *Belfon* [1976] 1 WLR 741 (CA); *Nedrick* [1986] 1 WLR 1025, 1027 (CA).
[13] Not only must D believe that the actus reus was a virtually certain consequence of his actions; it must *be* such: below, § 5.1(iv)(a).
[14] As noted below, § 5.1(iv), technically the jury is *entitled* for find intention exists in (II); it might elect not to do so if it wishes.

about".[15] In other words, D generally intends an outcome if it is something that he decides, or seeks, to bring about.[16] Additionally, it seems clear that D intends a result if he acts with the *purpose*,[17] or object, of bringing it about. This is the case even if D realises that his chances of success are minuscule. In *Smith, Hogan, and Ormerod*'s useful example:[18]

> "If D has resolved to kill V and he fires a loaded gun at him with the object of killing V, he intends to kill. It is immaterial that he is aware that he is a poor shot, that V is nearly out of range and that his chances of success are small. It is sufficient that killing is D's object or purpose: that D acts in order to kill."

This approach recognises that D intends to kill P if he means to bring about P's death by his actions—if he acts with the aim, object, or purpose of killing P.[19]

Antony Duff has built on this idea. Suppose that D fires a gun knowing that P is nearby, and we are trying to decide whether he intended to kill P. Duff argues that if D aims to cause P's death by his actions, then we can say that D *attempts* to kill P.[20] Furthermore, an attempt can be either a success or a failure. Therefore, Duff shows, one feature of intention (in the core sense) is that a defendant who intends (aims, tries, attempts) to kill P would regard himself as having "failed" in some sense if P does not die.[21] By contrast, if D does not intend P's death (perhaps they are out hunting quail[22]), he would not then think he had failed should P survive. This "test of failure" is another way of diagnosing whether D intended P's death in its core, direct sense.

An illustration of Duff's argument is provided by *Hyam*.[23] Mrs Hyam poured petrol through the letterbox of the house of her love rival, Mrs Booth. Mrs Hyam then set fire to the petrol, intending only to frighten Mrs Booth into moving out of the area, but realising that her actions risked causing death. The resulting fire caused the deaths of two of Mrs Booth's children.[24] Duff remarks:[25]

> "Mrs Hyam intended to set fire to Mrs Booth's house; her action would have failed had the house not caught fire. . . . She intended thereby to frighten Mrs Booth: had the fire not frightened Mrs Booth, her action (though successful as one of 'setting fire to the house') would have failed as one of 'frightening Mrs Booth'. But she did not intend to cause death or injury: though she foresaw death or injury as a likely effect of her action, her action would not have been a failure had no one been killed or injured; death or injury were foreseen side-effects, not intended effects, of her action."

15 [1950] 2 KB 237, 253 (CA).
16 See *Mohan* [1976] QB 1, 11 (CA); *Pearman* (1985) 80 Cr App R 259.
17 *Burke* [1991] 1 AC 135, 147 (HL). Cf. Model Penal Code, § 2.02(2)(a).
18 *Smith, Hogan, and Ormerod* § 3.2.1.
19 See, e.g., *Gollins v Gollins* [1964] AC 644, 663 (Lord Reid); *DPP v Smith* [1961] AC 290, 327 (Viscount Kilmuir LC); *Hyam v DPP* [1975] AC 55, 79 (Lord Hailsham).
20 This point was made by the Court of Appeal in *Moloney*, *The Times*, 22 December 1983 (May LJ) (quoted in *Moloney* [1985] AC 905, 919 (Lord Bridge)). Compare also *Walker* (1990) 90 Cr App R 226, 230: "'[t]rying to kill' is synonymous with purpose. It has never been suggested that a man does not intend what he is trying to achieve."
21 Duff, *Intention, Agency and Criminal Liability* (1990) 61–3. See also his *Criminal Attempts* (1996) chap. 1.
22 For a famous example, see https://en.wikipedia.org/wiki/Dick_Cheney_hunting_accident.
23 [1975] AC 55.
24 As explained below, § 5.7, if D has the mens rea of an offence regarding one individual (e.g. Mrs Booth, in *Hyam*), but the actus reus harms someone else (e.g. Mrs Booth's children), D can still be liable for the complete offence.
25 Duff, *Intention, Agency and Criminal Liability* (1990) 61.

By frightening Mrs Booth, Mrs Hyam would have succeeded in her purpose; her actions would not have been a failure if no one had died, since it was no part of her purpose to kill. Neither, we would say, was she trying to kill anyone. Thus the deaths of Mrs Booth's children were not intended (at least not in the core, direct sense).

### *(ii) A formal definition of intention in its core, direct sense*

The differences noted above between intended and unintended actions can also be set out in terms of means, ends, and side-effects. Things done as means or ends are intended; side-effects are not.[26] Mrs Hyam set fire to the house as a means of frightening Mrs Booth. Hence, both setting fire to the house and frightening Mrs Booth were intended. But the ensuing fatalities were neither a means nor an end. They were side-effects of Mrs Hyam's actions, and as such unintended (in the core, direct sense).[27]

Ideas of means, ends, and purpose point to a more formal way of thinking about intention. The purposes or ends for which one acts are the reasons *why* one acts. They motivate and explain one's action. Intention embraces both these and the intermediate steps (the means) that one undertakes in order to achieve those ends.

Formally, D directly intends to do an action (or to bring about some consequence) if:

(a) She *wants* to do that action (or bring about that consequence), or
(b) She *believes* it is possible for him to achieve something he wants by doing that action (or by bringing about that consequence); and
(c) She behaves as he does *because* of his desire in (a) or his belief in (b).[28]

Again, nothing in this definition requires that D should believe the action or consequence is anything more than merely possible. Again, D can intend to kill P despite believing that the chances of doing so are small.

The combination of (a) with (c) covers actions which are done as ends:

(a) She *wants* to do that action (or to bring about that consequence); and
(b) She behaves as he does *because* of that desire.

Mrs Hyam wanted to frighten Mrs Booth, and she set fire to the house because she wanted to frighten her. Therefore she intended to frighten Mrs Booth. Her desire to frighten, which is the desire contemplated in (a) above, is often termed the defendant's *motive*. But it is important to recognise that a desire, or motive, is not enough by itself to establish intention. Often people want things which they never set out to achieve. If D stands to inherit from his mother's will, he may have a reason for wanting her death to occur. But the mere wish that another person were deceased is not an intention to kill that person: "intention is something quite different from motive or desire".[29] Distinguishing between desire and intention here is (c), the requirement that the defendant act *because* of that motive. A motive is irrelevant to intention unless it is also *why* D did the actus reus.

[26] Finnis, "Intention and Side-effects" in Frey and Morris (eds.), *Liability and Responsibility* (1991) 32. See also Williams, "Oblique Intention" (1987) 46 *CLJ* 417, 421.
[27] As it happens, they were also unintended in the oblique, indirect sense. We come to that category in § 5.1(iv).
[28] Or, at least *in part because*. We consider the possibility of multiple intentions below, § 5.1(vi).
[29] *Moloney* [1985] AC 905, 926 (Lord Bridge).

On the other hand, desire is not an essential component of intention.[30] Often, we bring things about not because we want them, but because they are a *means* to something else (that we do want).[31] The parent who punishes a child for misbehaving may do so regretfully, believing it to be her only option and wishing very much that there were something else she could do; yet she intends to punish him all the same.[32] What she wants (say) is to deter her child from behaving that way again, and she punishes him in order to achieve that aim. But she does not desire his punishment, at least not for its own sake. This sort of case, where the actus reus is done as a means to an end, is captured by the combination of (b) with (c):

(a) She *believes* it is possible for him to achieve something she wants by doing that action (or by bringing about that consequence); and
(b) She behaves as she does *because* of that belief.

In *Smith*,[33] D believed that by bribing the mayor he would be able to expose him as corrupt. This was why he acted as he did. Therefore he intended to bribe[34] the official, even though his ultimate aim was to expose him. It may be helpful to show D's reasoning with a diagram:

*Smith*: S ⟶ bribe mayor$_{\text{Means}}$ ⟶ expose corruption$_{\text{End}}$

Similarly, Mrs Hyam believed that by setting fire to the house she would be able to frighten Mrs Booth. That was why she acted as she did. Therefore she intended to set fire to the house:

*Hyam*: H ⟶ set fire to house$_{\text{Means}}$ ⟶ frighten V$_{\text{End}}$
|
kill V$_{\text{Side-effect}}$

But as this diagram shows, it was no part of her intentions to kill Mrs Booth or do grievous bodily harm to her (or anybody else).

In practice, of course, looking at the defendant's desires and beliefs is an indispensible aid in helping us to ascertain her intentions. Even in (b), the case of doing something as

[30] Cp. *Mohan* [1976] QB 1, 11 (CA): intention is "a decision to bring about, in so far as it lies within the accused's power, the commission of the offence ... no matter whether the accused desired that consequence of his act or not".

[31] See *Hyam* [1975] AC 55, 74 (Lord Hailsham): intention includes "the means as well as the end"; also Williams, *CLGP* 34–6. This point is seen clearly in *Hales* [2005] EWCA Crim 1118, [28]: "The Crown's position was that [D] was prepared to kill in order to escape. It may not have been a gratuitous killing in the sense that the motive was a desire to kill. The motive was that the officer was in the way and that the appellant Hales was prepared to kill in order to escape. That is not a situation which requires any different direction from the conventional one on intent."

[32] Compare *Lang v Lang* [1955] AC 402, 428–9 (PC).

[33] [1960] 2 QB 423 (CA).

[34] Or, more accurately, to "corrupt" the official. In fact s. 1(2) of the (now-repealed) Public Bodies Corrupt Practices Act 1889 required that the defendant act "corruptly". The Court interpreted this to mean only that he must intend to induce a corrupt bargain. See above, § 5; Shyllon, "The Corruption of 'Corruptly'" [1969] *Crim LR* 250.

a means to an end, there must be a motive in the background. And although it does not matter in principle what that background motive is, often it will be important for evidential purposes. "To prove the intention, you may show the motive, and this is a link in the chain of evidence."[35]

### *(iii) Foresight of consequences is not enough*

The key ingredient of any account of intention is (c), that the defendant acts *because* of her desire and/or belief. Without this, there cannot be intention in its core, direct sense. If D foresees an outcome, and indeed welcomes it, but that outcome nonetheless plays no part in her decision to act, then she does not directly intend it.[36] The outcome is, for D, incidental. Mrs Hyam foresaw the possibility of killing Mrs Booth, but she did not set fire to the house because of her belief that doing so might bring about Mrs Booth's death. Hence, although she was reckless about killing Mrs Booth,[37] she did not intend to kill. Similarly, a judge who awards compensatory damages against a defendant may realise that, in so doing, she might cause the bankruptcy of the defendant, but that has nothing to do with why she awards the damages. The bankruptcy is no more than a foreseen but unintended side-effect.

The law has not always been clear on this point. In *Hardy v Motor Insurers' Bureau*, for instance, it was said of the defendant that "he must have foreseen, when he did the act, that it would in all probability injure the other person. Therefore he had the intent to injure the other person."[38] And in *Jakac*, the Supreme Court of Victoria was of similar mind: if the defendant "knew what the consequences were likely to be, and with that knowledge he deliberately did the act and if the consequences in fact did follow, he must be taken to intend them."[39] Indeed, in 1960 the House of Lords in *DPP v Smith* simply presumed (*inter alia*) that the defendant intended whatever he foresaw as potentially flowing from his conduct.[40]

The House of Lords later divided on this question in *Hyam*. Although Lord Hailsham declared it "clear that 'intention' is clearly to be distinguished alike from 'desire' and from foresight of the probable consequences",[41] his Lordship's view did not reflect a consensus. Viscount Dilhorne, for instance, remarked that if someone does an act "knowing when he does it that it is highly probable that grievous bodily harm will result, I think that most people would say and be justified in saying that whatever other intentions he may have had

[35] *Heeson* (1878) 14 Cox CC 40, 44.

[36] A point made by Kenny, "Intention and Purpose in Law" in Summers (ed.), *Essays in Legal Philosophy* (1968) 146, 155.

[37] Below, § 5.2.

[38] [1964] 2 QB 745, 764 (Pearson LJ) (CA); see also at 758 (Lord Denning MR). Cf. Lord Devlin's definition of "purpose" in *Chandler v DPP* [1964] AC 763, 805 to "designate those objects which he knows will probably be achieved by the act, whether he wants them or not".

[39] [1961] VR 367, 371. Cp. Saunders, *Mozley & Whitley's Law Dictionary* (9th ed., 1977) 175: "a person who contemplates any result, as not unlikely to follow from a deliberate act of his own, may be said to intend that result, whether he desire it or not".

[40] [1961] AC 290. At points the Court went even further than that, and presumed that the defendant intended whatever was reasonably foreseeable as a natural consequence of his actions. Cf. Viscount Kilmuir LC, at 326: "the test of what a reasonable man would contemplate as the probable result of his acts, and, therefore, would intend". The reference to the "reasonable man" was highly controversial in that it implied (wrongly) that the test for intention was objective rather than subjective: see now below, § 5.1(ix); also *Ward* [1956] 1 QB 351 (CCA); Kenny, "Intention and Purpose in Law" in Summers (ed.), *Essays in Legal Philosophy* (1968) 146.

[41] [1975] AC 55, 74.

as well, he at least intended grievous bodily harm".[42] Indeed, Lord Diplock felt able, following *Hyam*, to describe the law on this point as "well-settled":[43]

> "Where intention to produce a particular result was a necessary element of an offence, no distinction was to be drawn in law between the state of mind of one who did an act because he desired it to produce that particular result and the state of mind of one who, when he did the act, was aware that it was likely to produce that result but was prepared to take the risk that it might do so."

Subsequently, however, the distinction between intention and foresight came to be accepted by the House of Lords and the Supreme Court. The key House of Lords cases were *Moloney*[44] and *Hancock and Shankland*.[45] In *Moloney*, the defendant was charged with murder after shooting his stepfather during a drunken game. It was not clear that, when he pulled the trigger, he realised the gun was pointing at his stepfather. His conviction was quashed because the trial judge was ruled to have misdirected the jury in stating:[46]

> "a man intends the consequence of his voluntary act (a) when he desires it to happen, whether or not he foresees that it probably will happen, and (b) when he foresees that it will happen, whether he desires it or not."

Contrast that direction with the view of Lord Bridge, who was "firmly of opinion that foresight of consequences, as an element bearing on the issue of intention in murder, or indeed any other crime of specific intent, belongs, not to the substantive law, but to the law of evidence".[47] In other words, foresight of a consequence is merely one piece of evidence from which the existence of intention might be inferred. It is not a "test" for intention in the direct, core sense.

Strictly speaking, Lord Bridge's remarks were *obiter dicta*,[48] since the decisive factor in the decision was that D apparently did not think about the risk of death at all.[49] The case was therefore not one of foresight.[50] The point was not *obiter*, however, in *Hancock and Shankland*.[51] In that case the defendants, miners who were on strike, pushed two pieces of concrete off a bridge onto the motorway below. The blocks struck a taxi ferrying another miner to work. The taxi driver was killed. The defendants, it appears, recognised the dangerousness of their actions but claimed they intended only to frighten the miner and prevent him from breaking the strike, and not to harm anyone (they had, they said, thought the concrete was over the lane *next* to the one occupied by the taxi). Their convictions for murder were quashed. As Lord Scarman put it, "foresight does not necessarily imply the existence of

[42] *Ibid.*, 82.

[43] *Lemon* [1979] AC 617, 638. See also a similar dictum in *Hyam* [1975] AC 55, 86.

[44] [1985] AC 905.

[45] [1986] AC 455.

[46] [1985] AC 905, 917.

[47] *Ibid.*, 928.

[48] Cp. *ibid.*, 920; *Hancock* [1986] AC 455, 460 (CA), [1986] AC 455, 468 (HL).

[49] *Moloney* [1985] AC 905, 920. Their Lordships must have overlooked the jury's finding, in the light of the direction, that D foresaw death or grievous bodily harm as a possible consequence of his conduct.

[50] Thus, strictly, the decision rules only that inadvertence forecloses intention—contra *DPP v Smith* [1961] AC 290. Apart from being undone by s. 8 of the Criminal Justice Act 1967, *DPP v Smith* itself was effectively overruled by the Privy Council in *Frankland and Moore v R* [1987] AC 576 (PC), which held (at 594) that "insofar as [*Smith*] laid down an objective test of the intent in the crime of murder, did not accurately represent the English common law."

[51] [1986] AC 455.

intention".[52] This rule has since been reiterated by the Court of Appeal, in *Nedrick* and in *Matthews*,[53] by the House of Lords in *Woollin*,[54] and by the Supreme Court in *Jogee*.[55] It may safely be regarded as prevailing.[56]

### *(iv) Virtually certain consequences: the second category of (indirect) intention*

Mere foresight of a consequence, then, does not establish an intention. But one question is still not fully resolved: what if the consequence is foreseen not merely as possible, or even probable, but as *certain* or *virtually certain* to occur—does "intention" include such a case?

Consider the following example. V, a fat man, is trapped in the mouth of a cave. The waters in the cave are rapidly rising, and the cave will soon be flooded. The trapped man is immovable, and is preventing the escape and survival of his fellow speleologists. The only way of unblocking the exit is by blowing him up with a stick of dynamite. Can they do so without intending his death?[57] The case can be represented as follows:

*Spelæologist:* S → blow up V → escape and survive
‖
kill V

As this example illustrates, some consequences (in this case, death) which are not themselves sought (as either a means or an end) are nevertheless much too close to the intended effects to be separated off as mere side-effects. V's colleagues would be delighted if they could blow him up, and free themselves, without killing him. But they cannot. It is a certainty that V will die.

This kind of case is regarded as a second variety of intention by the Law Commission, amongst others:[58]

"(1) A person should be taken to intend a result if he or she acts in order to bring it about.
(2) In cases where the judge believes that justice may not be done unless an expanded understanding of intention is given, the jury should be directed as follows: an intention to bring about a result may be found if it is shown that the defendant thought that the result was a virtually certain consequence of his or her action."

52 [1986] AC 455, 472.

53 *Nedrick* [1986] 1 WLR 1025; *Matthews* [2003] EWCA Crim 192, [2003] 2 Cr App R 30.

54 [1999] 1 AC 82.

55 [2016] UKSC 8, [2017] AC 387.

56 Writing extra-judicially in the *Law Quarterly Review*, Lord Goff concluded that "after the journey through *Smith*, *Hyam*, *Moloney* and *Hancock*, the law is really back where it was.... Foresight of consequences is not the same as intent, but is material from which the jury may, having regard to the circumstances of the case, infer that the defendant really had the relevant intent": "The Mental Element in the Crime of Murder" (1988) 104 *LQR* 30, 41.

57 For philosophical discussion of this case, see Geddes, "On the Intrinsic Wrongness of Killing Innocent People" (1973) 33 *Analysis* 93; Duff, "Intentionally Killing the Innocent" (1973) 34 *Analysis* 16; Finnis, "The Rights and Wrongs of Abortion: A Reply to Judith Jarvis Thomson" (1973) 2 *Philosophy and Public Affairs* 117; Hanink, "Some Light on Double Effect" (1975) 35 *Analysis* 147.

58 Law Com. No. 304, *Murder, Manslaughter and Infanticide* (2006) para. 3.27. For earlier proposals, see LCCP No. 177, *A New Homicide Act for England and Wales?* (2006) para. 4.3; and see the discussion in Part 4 generally. See too Law Com. No. 218, *Offences against the Person and General Principles* (1993) paras. 7.1–7.14 and LCCP No. 122, *Offences against the Person and General Principles* (1992) paras. 5.4–5.11.

Limb (2) captures the case of the speleologists. The language of virtual certainty reflects the need for something more than just foresight that the result is likely or possible. Assuming that the defendant had no justification for risking the relevant result's occurrence, the latter would constitute recklessness.

In the past, the courts have been equivocal about cases like that of the speleologists. Although Lord Hailsham did not think that "foresight as such of a high degree of probability is at all the same thing as intention",[59] he nevertheless stated in *Hyam* that intention includes not only those things done as ends or means but also "the inseparable consequences of the end as well as the means".[60] The extension was supported by reference to an example developed by Glanville Williams:[61]

> "suppose that a villain of the deepest dye blows up an aircraft in flight with a time-bomb, merely for the purpose of collecting on insurance. It is not his aim to cause the people on board to perish, but he knows that success in his scheme will inevitably involve their deaths as a side-effect."

According to Lord Hailsham, "if any passengers are killed he is guilty of murder, as their death will be a moral certainty if he carries out his intention".[62] In *Moloney*, Lord Bridge, too, accepted that there may be cases where things which are seemingly not sought as ends or means should be analysed as cases of intention:[63]

> "A man who[,] at London Airport, boards a plane which he knows to be bound for Manchester, clearly intends to travel to Manchester, even though Manchester is the last place he wants to be and his motive for boarding the plane is simply to escape pursuit. . . . By boarding the Manchester plane, the man conclusively demonstrates his intention to go there, because it is a moral certainty that that is where he will arrive."

In such a case the law would say that the "morally certain" consequence is intended. But the basis on which it does so is somewhat unclear.[64] There are two main alternatives: either (1) *by definition*, there is a second category of (indirect) intention involving morally/virtually certain consequences,[65] or (2) moral/virtual certainty is simply evidence of an intention in its core sense. If (2) is the case, there is no second category of intention: foresight of a moral/virtual certainty is no more than a ground for inferring that the consequence was (directly) intended,[66] and that inference may be rebutted by other evidence.

There is something to be said for thinking the link between foresight of virtual certainty and intention is merely evidential, and that there is no second category of intention. Even consequences that, from the perspective of the actor, look certain to occur may appear not to be intended. If D drinks a bottle of whisky one evening, he may be sure that he will get

[59] *Hyam* [1975] AC 55, 77.

[60] *Ibid.*, 74.

[61] "Oblique Intention" (1987) 46 *CLJ* 417, 423; cp. his earlier *The Mental Element in Crime* (1965) 34–5. For discussion of these types of cases and the surrounding literature, see Pedain, "Intention and the Terrorist Example" [2003] *Crim LR* 579. More generally, see also Kugler, *Direct and Oblique Intention in the Criminal Law* (2002).

[62] *Hyam* [1975] AC 55, 74.

[63] *Moloney* [1985] AC 905, 926.

[64] Duff, *Intention, Agency and Criminal Liability* (1990) 21–2. See, also, Duff, "The Obscure Intentions of the House of Lords" [1986] *Crim LR* 771; Kaveny, "Inferring Intention from Foresight" (2004) 120 *LQR* 81.

[65] Cp. Lord Bridge in *Moloney* [1985] AC 905, 925: an overwhelming probability "will *suffice to establish* the necessary intent" (emphasis added). Compare also Lord Bridge's use of "conclusively" in the quotation from *Moloney* recited in the text above in this section.

[66] Cp. *Nedrick* [1986] 1 WLR 1025, 1029 (CA): where D realises that a consequence is inevitable, "the inference *may* be irresistible that he intended that result" (emphasis added).

a hangover in the morning, but he does not intend to have a hangover.[67] Support for this position is found in decisions subsequent to *Moloney*, where the courts frequently tended to read Lord Bridge's remarks as pertaining to evidential matters only. In *Nedrick*, Lord Lane CJ held that "if the jury are satisfied that at the material time the defendant recognised that death or serious harm would be virtually certain (barring some unforeseen intervention) to result from his voluntary act, then that is a fact from which they may find it easy to infer that he intended to kill or do serious bodily harm".[68]

If Lord Lane is right, then the explanation of cases like the flight to Manchester has nothing to do with moral certainty. Rather, such cases should be analysed as instances of *direct* intention. That is to say, the fugitive intentionally travels to Manchester as a *means* of leaving London. She flies to Manchester *because* it is outside of London. This is consistent with the account of intention stated earlier, in § 5.1(ii):

*Traveller*: T ⟶ go to Manchester ⟶ leave London

But this answer does not help to deal with the speleologists, or with the insurance-bombing case proposed by Williams, where the deaths of the airline passengers are clearly not a means to anything. Despite this, it does seem that their deaths are so intimately bound up with the villain's intended actions as to be inseparable, and it would be wrong to call them mere side-effects. It appears, therefore, that the best view of the current law is that there is a special category of intention, which falls outside the standard definition given in § 5.1(ii). This second category arises where the defendant recognises that the additional effect is inseparable from those which he intends. A useful definition of this type of case is the rule proposed by H.L.A. Hart: a foreseen outcome is to be regarded as intended when it "is so immediately and invariably connected with the action done that the suggestion that the action might not have that outcome would by ordinary standards be regarded as absurd, or such as only a mentally abnormal person would seriously entertain".[69] These outcomes are intended even though D is not trying or aiming to bring them about. They represent a supplementary category to the core definition of intention stated in § 5.1(ii).

(We return to this point below, but it is worth emphasising that the evidential thesis is problematic in its practical application. The difficulty is that, if all the thesis means is that the more likely an outcome is foreseen as occurring, the more likely it is that D intended it, this explanation will allow inferences of intention in all kinds of circumstances that are clearly unintended. By contrast if it means that *only* foresight of virtual certainty can do this inferential work, we may as well *define* intention in those terms, rather than saying that from foresight of virtual certainty the jury proceeds to *infer* an intention.)

The law accommodates these virtual certainty cases with a special (albeit imprecise) rule. In *Woollin*,[70] D lost his temper and threw his three-month-old son against a hard surface. The child's skull fractured and death ensued. At D's trial for murder, the prosecution

[67] Duff, *Intention, Agency and Criminal Liability* (1990) 89–90. The temporal delay seems to be important in how we tend to think about examples of this kind.

[68] [1986] 1 WLR 1025 (CA). See also the judgment by Lord Scarman in *Hancock and Shankland* [1986] AC 455.

[69] *Punishment and Responsibility* (1968) 120. See further Simester, *Fundamentals* § 15.3. This is a tighter connection (as with respect it ought to be) than that required by the Canadian Supreme Court in *Chartrand* [1994] 2 SCR 864, 889–95.

[70] [1999] 1 AC 82.

expressly disavowed that D had intended (in the core sense) his son's death or serious injury. His conviction implies, therefore, that foreseeing a result as a virtual certainty is, in law, an alternative category of intention, and not just evidence from which to infer the core definition of intention. On appeal,[71] Lord Steyn accepted this and explicitly rejected the language of inference. His Lordship amended the direction in the earlier case of *Nedrick*[72] to read:[73]

> "in the rare cases where the [standard] direction that it is for the jury simply to decide whether the defendant intended to kill or to do serious bodily harm is not enough, the jury should be directed that they are not entitled to *find* the necessary intention, unless they feel sure that death or serious bodily harm was a virtual certainty (barring some unforeseen intervention) as a result of the defendant's actions and that the defendant appreciated that such was the case."

Although the courts have not always acknowledged it clearly, there are, therefore, two types of intention. First, the normal, core (direct) variety is that defined in § 5.1(ii): where an outcome is sought directly by D (because he wants it for its own sake or as a means to something else). Secondly, there are outcomes which, in D's eyes, are so closely bound to directly intended outcomes that they are virtually certain to occur alongside. Such outcomes may also be regarded as (indirectly) intended.

It should be emphasised, though, that *Woollin* directions are to be given "very exceptionally".[74] Normally, as Lord Steyn said, the jury should receive no elaboration on the meaning of intention. They should simply be left to consider only the core sense of intention,[75] regarding which they should use their own "good sense".[76] The *Woollin* decision gives the prosecution an alternative way of proving that an outcome was intended; it is supplementary to, and not a substitute for, intention in the core sense.[77]

However, while clarifying the independent status of this second legal category of intention, *Woollin* retains opacity in a different aspect. Lord Steyn's model direction is expressed in negative terms: "the jury should be directed that they are not entitled to find the necessary intention, unless they feel sure that death or serious bodily harm was a virtual certainty". This suggests that, although foresight of virtual certainty is *necessary* before the alternative category of intention is satisfied,[78] it may not always be *sufficient*.[79] It seems that, where

[71] Ultimately, D's conviction for murder was quashed and a conviction for manslaughter substituted, because the trial judge had misdirected the jury on the alternative limb by requiring only that D foresaw a "substantial risk" (rather than virtual certainty) of serious injury or death.

[72] [1986] 1 WLR 1025, 1028 (CA).

[73] [1999] 1 AC 82, 96.

[74] *R (Charles) v CCRC* [2017] EWHC 1219 (Admin), [2017] 2 Cr App R 14, [57]. See also *ibid.*, [59].

[75] *Phillips* [2004] EWCA Crim 112, [10]; *Allen* [2005] EWCA Crim 1344, [63]–[64]; *Royle* [2013] EWCA Crim 1461, [17]–[27]; *R (Charles) v CCRC* [2017] EWHC 1219 (Admin), [2017] 2 Cr App R 14, [57]–[61].

[76] *R (Charles) v CCRC* [2017] EWHC 1219 (Admin), [2017] 2 Cr App R 14, [57].

[77] *MD* [2004] EWCA Crim 1391, [29]: "[*Woollin*] is designed to help the prosecution to fill a gap in the rare circumstances in which a defendant does an act which caused the death without the purpose of killing or causing serious injury, but in circumstances where death or serious bodily harm had been a virtual certainty (barring some unforeseen intervention) as a result of the defendant's actions and the defendant had appreciated that such was the case".

[78] In *Thacker* [2021] EWCA Crim 97, [2021] QB 644, [86], the Court of Appeal suggested *obiter* that there may still be some uncertainty whether "whether foresight of 'virtual certainty' as opposed to 'a very high degree of probability' is required". Given that *Woollin* is a House of Lords decision, this is clearly wrong.

[79] Hence the Court of Appeal was right to judge, in *Matthews* [2003] EWCA Crim 192, [2003] 2 Cr App R 30, [43], that "the law has not yet reached a definition of intent in murder in terms of appreciation of a virtual certainty". Foresight of virtual certainty is not the same thing as (indirect) intention, but rather a basis on which it may be found.

there is foresight of virtual certainty, the jury is permitted to conclude that the defendant intended the outcome and, absent any special considerations, the jury should normally so conclude;[80] but they are entitled not to find intention should there be such considerations.[81] For example, a doctor may know that by injecting a terminally ill patient with the morphine necessary to dull pain, incidentally it is virtually certain that she will shorten the patient's life. The doctor does not aim to shorten the patient's life, and does not intend his death in the core sense. In such a case, notwithstanding that it is a virtually certain side-effect, the jury may still conclude that she does not intend his death, even indirectly.[82] This approach to indirect intention thus confers an element of discretion upon the jury.[83] To appropriate the Law Commission's evocative language, *Woollin* allows them some "moral elbow room" to reach appropriate results in certain very difficult cases.[84] (A less charitable interpretation is that *Woollin* devolves responsibility for identifying the precise contours of intention from the judges to juries.[85]) It must be remembered, however, that such instances are rare: *Woollin* directions are exceptional.

### (a) *Objective and subjective virtual certainty?*

There is another oddity about the *Woollin* direction. Lord Steyn requires not only that the defendant *believes* that the outcome is virtually certain; it must also in fact *be* virtually certain. Arguably, however, it is only the former that counts in culpability terms.[86] Intention is a measure of the agent's perceptions and mental state, and should be unaffected by facts of which the agent is unaware. Suppose that D is a fugitive. She accelerates her car toward a policeman who is blocking her escape. The fugitive, let us say, wishes only to escape but thinks it is virtually certain that, by knocking over the policeman, she will cause grievous bodily harm. In fact, there is a 20 per cent chance in such collisions that the victim will not be seriously injured; but D does not know this and, as it happens, the policeman is severely hurt. In our view, D should be held to have intended the injury, despite her error regarding its likelihood.[87]

[80] Compare, e.g., the analysis of the events in *ibid.*, [46]: "If the jury were sure that the appellants appreciated the virtual certainty of Jonathan's death when they threw him from the bridge and also that they then had no intention of saving him from such death, it is impossible to see how the jury could not have found that the appellants intended Jonathan to die".

[81] In its Consultation Paper on homicide, the Law Commission discusses one such case invented by Lord Goff, in which D takes a virtually certain risk of killing or injuring his children by defenestrating them during a house fire, because that is the only chance of saving them: LCCP No. 177, *A New Homicide Act for England and Wales?* (2006) para. 4.21. Clearly, in this situation, the intent is to save rather than to take life. Cp. *Emperor v Dhirajia* AIR 1940 All 486, where D jumped down a well with her baby in order to escape her violent husband.

[82] For a discussion of cases that contain *dicta* to this effect, see Ashworth, "Criminal Liability in a Medical Context: The Treatment of Good Intentions" in Simester and Smith (eds.), *Harm and Culpability* (1996) 173. Cp. *Re A (Children)* [2001] Fam 147, 251–2 (CA).

[83] A result that has found favour with the Law Commission: Law Com. No. 304, *Murder, Manslaughter and Infanticide* (2006) paras. 3.20–3.26. For critical discussion, see Tadros, "The Homicide Ladder" (2006) 69 *MLR* 601.

[84] LCCP No. 177, *A New Homicide Act for England and Wales?* (2006) para. 2.7.

[85] See Ashworth, "Principles, Pragmatism and the Law Commission's Recommendations on Homicide Law Reform" [2007] *Crim LR* 333, 335; also Norrie, *Crime, Reason and History* (3rd ed., 2014) 70–1.

[86] The former is certainly necessary. It is not sufficient that the outcome *be* virtually certain: D must recognise this. Cp. *Stringer* [2008] EWCA Crim 1222, [35]–[36]. As the Court goes on to observe (at [38]), however, the fact that an outcome is virtually certain may also support the inference that D *appreciated* it was virtually certain.

[87] The Law Commission agrees: Law Com. No. 304, *Murder, Manslaughter and Infanticide* (2006) para. 3.27.

*(b) Definitions and evidence*

It is helpful to summarise the argument above regarding the relationship between foresight and the two senses of intention identified by the courts. Where the prosecution seeks to prove that D (directly) intended the actus reus under the standard definition, foresight of a probability is evidence from which that intention may be *inferred*. Notice, however, that reference to probability forms no part of that definition (given in § 5.1(ii)). In terms of the core, direct type of intention, there is no reason to require virtual certainty before inferring (direct) intent. If D aims a pistol at V and pulls the trigger, it may not be virtually certain, or even very likely, that V will die—perhaps it is a difficult shot—yet we would normally infer that D's direct intention was to kill; that he was trying to kill.[88] The connection between (core, direct) intention and foresight of probability is purely evidential.

By contrast, the connection between foresight of a probability and the virtually certain category of (indirect) intention is not evidential. It is non-existent. Without proof that D realised that the relevant outcome was virtually certain to come about as a result of his conduct, the second category of (indirect) intention is simply not in play.

*(c) The reach of* Woollin

*Woollin* was a decision about the meaning of intention in the context of murder, and Lord Steyn expressly limited his analysis of intention to that context.[89] Does this mean that the law's understanding of intention differs depending on the context? As a matter of precedent, yes; but it is significant that *Woollin*'s variety of indirect intention has been applied in other contexts.[90] Furthermore, it is desirable, in terms of clarity and consistency, that mens rea words are used consistently in the criminal law.[91] As such, *Woollin* should be viewed as setting general principles about the law's understanding of intention in those exceptional cases where application of the core, direct sense of intention risks injustice.

### *(v) Intention and circumstances*

The account of intention given so far needs qualification when applied to circumstances which form a part of the actus reus. For example, rape can only be committed by D's having sexual intercourse with V without V's consent. The circumstance, that V does not consent, is part of the actus reus of the offence. There are two main ways in which D's mental state regarding V's non-consent can satisfy the demands of intention. The more straightforward case occurs where D rapes V by intentionally having sexual intercourse with V, *hoping or desiring* that V does not consent. In this case D intends "sexual intercourse without consent" in its core, direct sense, because it is part of his purpose not merely to have sexual inter-

[88] Cp. *MD* [2004] EWCA Crim 1391, [29]: "[*Woollin*] is not designed to make the prosecution's task more difficult. Many murderers whose purpose was to kill or cause serious injury would escape conviction for murder if the jury was given only a [*Woollin*] direction. The man who kills another with a gun would be able to escape liability for murder if he could show that he was such a bad shot that death or serious bodily harm was not a virtual certainty or that the defendant had thought that death or serious bodily harm was not a virtual certainty."

[89] *Woollin* [1999] 1 AC 82, 89.

[90] For instance, in attempts—see below, § 9.4(iii)(c). Cf. Serious Crime Act 2007, s. 44 (where it appears that only the core sense of intention will satisfy the mens rea requirement of intention).

[91] See Stark, "It's Only Words: On Meaning and Mens Rea" (2013) 72 *CLJ* 155. Cp. *Thacker* [2021] EWCA Crim 97, [2021] QB 644.

course with V, but to have it without V's consent. Duff's test of failure shows this clearly:[92] D would regard himself as having "failed" if V did in fact consent to having sexual intercourse with him.

Cases of this first type, however, are likely to be rare. More often, rape is intentional when D *believes* that V does not consent, yet neither intends nor hopes (and does not care) that V is not consenting. In this situation, D intends to have "sexual intercourse without consent", because he intends to have sexual intercourse with V *believing* that V does not consent.

There are two ways of showing that an actus reus is intended when it involves circumstances. The first is by showing that the behaviour and consequences are intended, and that D hopes or desires the circumstances are/will be present. The second is by showing that the behaviour and consequences are intended, and that D believes the circumstances are/will be present.

What does "believing" mean in this context? In our view "believing" has the same legal meaning as "knowing", with one exception. We consider the meaning of knowledge below,[93] but in essence what is required is that the defendant hold a positive belief, amounting to an acceptance, that the circumstance exists. D must believe that V *does not* consent; a belief that V *may not* consent is not sufficient (at least for intention—it may be sufficient for recklessness, discussed below).

The one difference, in law, between knowledge and belief is that a belief need not be correct. The defendant may believe something wrongly, but she cannot "know" something that is false. As Lord Hope once put it:[94]

> "A person cannot know that something is A when it is in fact B. The proposition that a person knows that something is A is based on the premise that it is true that it is A."

Usually the difference will not matter. For example, if D wrongly believes that V does *not* consent to sexual intercourse, when in fact V does consent, then regardless of his mens rea D cannot commit rape, because part of the actus reus is missing. But sometimes it will still be important to establish whether D has mens rea, since even without the actus reus he might nonetheless be guilty of an attempt. In this example, his false belief that V does not consent will be sufficient to help constitute an intention for the purposes of attempted rape.[95]

### *(vi) Multiple intentions*

Very often, a person has more than one reason for acting as he does. By cooking dinner, John might intend not only to assuage his hunger, but also to use up the contents of the fridge, as well as surprise and please his flatmates. All three results are intended. The mere fact that a defendant can point to some other result that he was also trying to achieve does not mean that he cannot have intended the actus reus. It is no answer for a newspaper that deliberately publishes *sub judice* material (i.e. material that is under judicial consideration

92 Above, § 5.1(i).
93 See § 5.4.
94 *Montila* [2004] UKHL 50, [2004] 1 WLR 3141, [27].
95 The claim here is merely that knowledge or belief satisfies the demands of intention. There has in the past been some controversy (discussed in Chapter 9) whether, with respect to circumstances, intention is *required* to establish the mens rea of attempt offences. The decision in *Pace and Rogers* [2014] EWCA Crim 186, [2014] 1 WLR 2867 nowadays suggests that it is. Fortunately, the historical difficulties regarding this question are specific to attempts, and do not carry over to substantive offences.

and should not be discussed publicly) to say that it was *really* trying to increase its circulation. The criminal law asks: whatever else she may have intended by behaving as she did, did D intend the relevant part(s) of the actus reus?

### *(vii) "Ulterior intent" and "future intent" crimes*

Sometimes the intentional doing of an actus reus is not itself an offence, and becomes criminal only when done with some further intention; or, if it is already an offence, it becomes a more serious crime when done with some further intention. For an example of the former, if D carries a crowbar in her bag, she does nothing wrong. If she carries the crowbar with intent to use it in a burglary, she is guilty of an offence: the crime of "going equipped for stealing".[96] An example of the latter is the crime of wounding with intent to do grievous bodily harm. Intentional wounding is itself a crime,[97] but it becomes a much more serious offence, contrary to section 18 of the OAPA 1861, when done with an intention to cause serious bodily injury.[98] Crimes of these sorts require what is often called an "ulterior intent".[99] The main feature of such crimes is that they specify, as part of the mens rea, an intent to do something that is not part of the actus reus. Thus, in the first example above, the actus reus is simple possession of the crowbar—it does not matter whether the crowbar is actually used in a burglary.[100] Similarly, D need not be proved to have caused V grievous bodily harm to be liable for a section 18 offence: causing a wound suffices for the actus reus. This is why such crimes are said to involve "ulterior" intent: because the intention relates to something going beyond the elements of the actus reus.

There is a subtle difference between the two cases of ulterior intent mentioned above, one that appears to have significant legal implications. The section 18 crime involves no further action by the defendant—it is the very act of wounding that must be done with intent to cause serious bodily injury. That intention must be *present* at the time the defendant does the act of wounding. By contrast, in the crime of going equipped, the ulterior intention is a *future* intention to act: that is, an intention, held at the time when D carries the crowbar, to use it in a future burglary. Yet the offence is committed by D at the time she carries the crowbar.

Present ulterior intention cases involve no special doctrinal difficulties. In particular, where a crime specifies a present ulterior intent as part of the mens rea, it seems clear that mere foresight of the further consequence will not do. The crime can be committed only if the defendant intends by his actions to cause that consequence.[101] This is the best explanation of the controversial case of *Steane*.[102] Steane had been compelled, through concern for the safety of his family, to make broadcasts on behalf of the Nazis during the Second World War. He was prosecuted under English wartime regulations for doing an act likely to assist the enemy (the actus reus), "with intent to assist the enemy". The Court of Criminal Appeal quashed his

[96] Theft Act 1968, s. 25. Cp. *Ellames* [1974] 1 WLR 1391 (CA); *Hargreaves* [1985] Crim LR 243 (CA).
[97] OAPA 1861, s. 20.
[98] The offence is considered in detail below, § 11.6.
[99] See generally Horder, "Crimes of Ulterior Intent" in Simester and Smith (eds.), *Harm and Culpability* (1996) 153; Child, "Understanding Ulterior Mens Rea: Future Conduct Intention *is* Conditional Intention" (2017) 76 *CLJ* 311; Child and Hunt, "Beyond the Present-Fault Paradigm: Expanding Mens Rea Definitions in the General Part" (2022) 42 *OJLS* 438.
[100] Cf. *Rodley* [1913] 3 KB 468 (CA).
[101] *Belfon* [1976] 1 WLR 741, 744 (CA).
[102] [1947] KB 997 (CA). See, e.g., Williams, "Oblique Intention" (1987) 46 *CLJ* 417, 428.

conviction for lack of mens rea, and rightly so. Although in making the broadcasts Steane had done an act *likely* to assist the enemy, the prosecution had failed to prove that he intended thereby to assist the enemy (i.e. that assisting the enemy was a part of his purposes in broadcasting). It is important to an understanding of the decision to recognise that the mens rea required was ulterior to the actus reus. The actus reus is "*any act likely* to assist the enemy", and does not involve proof that the defendant in fact did assist the enemy. The mens rea is an intent "to assist the enemy"; which goes beyond the actus reus. Steane intended to make the broadcasts, but his ulterior intent in so doing had been to protect his family. It would be otherwise if the foreseen further consequence were virtually certain to accompany his intended actions; in which case they too could have been found to be (indirectly) intended.[103]

Future ulterior intention cases can pose more difficulty, especially with respect to circumstance elements. Consider the crime of burglary,[104] which can be committed (*inter alia*) by breaking into a house with intent to commit theft of items within it. Suppose that D breaks into V's house with the intention to take an object the ownership of which is disputed between D and V. D is unsure who of them is the rightful owner, but intends to take the object regardless. Does she enter the house *with intent* (i.e. with the future intention) "to take property belonging to another", as the law of theft requires?[105] Child and Hunt argue that she does.[106] Even though, as we saw in § 5.1(v), a *present* intention with respect to circumstances would require that D believes, with no significant doubt, that the circumstance exists (here, that the object belongs to V), a future intention does not. For Child and Hunt, it is enough to establish her future intention that, when she breaks in, D is committed to taking the property *even if* it belongs to V. In the context of circumstance elements accompanying intended future actions, that seems right. As yet, however, it awaits confirmation by the courts.

### *(viii) Conditional intent*

Sometimes a person is willing to commit a crime but her actions will not necessarily result in one. For example, if a thief makes off with a handbag, meaning to keep the contents, she steals those contents only if there are any. In this situation, her intention to take the contents is conditional upon there being anything to steal. Such cases are not uncommon in the criminal law, especially in the context of offences involving a future intent. Indeed, as Child has pointed out, all intentions to do acts or omissions in the future are, strictly speaking, conditional.[107] The general rule is that an intention to do or bring about something only if particular conditions hold is, in law, an intention.[108] Thus a burglar who enters a flat with

103 See above, § 5.1(iv); also *Chartrand* [1994] 2 SCR 864, 889–95.

104 Below, § 14.4.

105 See Chapter 13. For the purposes of the present discussion, we disregard the controversial case of *Turner (No. 2)* [1971] 2 All ER 441 (CA), which is criticised below in § 13.4(iii).

106 "Beyond the Present-Fault Paradigm: Expanding Mens Rea Definitions in the General Part" (2022) 42 *OJLS* 438.

107 Child, "Understanding Ulterior Mens Rea: Future Conduct Intention is Conditional Intention" (2017) 76 *CLJ* 311.

108 One unresolved question is whether intention includes outcomes that are virtually certain to occur if D does come to act as she conditionally intends to do; that is, whether conditional intentions can be of the indirect form discussed above in § 5.1(iii). See Kugler, "Conditional Oblique Intention" [2004] *Crim LR* 284. The doctrinal resolution of this issue may have implications for the scope of complicity liability following *Jogee* [2016] UKSC 8, [2017] AC 387.

intent to steal a television provided there be one to steal, intends to steal.[109] The issue of conditional intention will be returned to later in this book, in the contexts of complicity and attempts.[110]

One point worth emphasising here is that the law on conditional future intentions applies only to future *behaviour* and *consequence* elements. There is no need to prove a conditional intention with respect to future circumstance elements—which is why the proposal by Child and Hunt, discussed in the previous subsection, is a plausible one. What makes circumstance elements of an offence distinctive from consequence elements is that D need not have any control over those circumstance elements in order to satisfy the actus reus. (Sometimes, she may actually have control over whether or not a circumstance element occurs, but the point is that no such control is required.) For instance, to continue the example in the previous subsection, D cannot control whether the vase does in fact belong to him or V. It follows that the law cannot require the prosecution to prove that D *intends* future circumstance elements, conditionally or otherwise. It is enough that D knows or believes, with no significant doubt, that the circumstances will exist. Or, if the courts endorse the extensional claim about intention with respect to future circumstances made in the previous subsection, it would suffice that D commits to performing any future behaviour elements of a crime, and to bringing about any future consequence elements, while believing that any future circumstance elements *may* exist.

### *(ix) No presumption of intention*

Proving a mens rea element such as intention is often difficult. It is impossible to look directly into the minds of defendants in order to know whether they had mens rea at the time of the offence. Usually, if the defendant does not himself confess to having had it, the prosecution will be put to proving the relevant state of mind through supporting evidence, e.g. of the defendant's actions before, during, and after the actus reus occurred. Suppose that D is found to have shot V. If there is evidence that D planned the shooting in advance, this may be admissible to support the allegation that D's actions were intentional. The same is true if it is shown that D took careful aim at V's heart before pulling the trigger. In this case, proof by the prosecution that the prohibited harm (i.e. V's death) was a natural consequence of D's actions will support the inference that D intended it. Similarly, proof that the defendant foresaw the outcome (e.g. because D knew the gun was loaded) may also help to support such a conclusion. Inferences of this variety depend upon a recognition that there is no reasonable interpretation of the evidence other than that the defendant had mens rea.

But such inferences are a matter of evidence only. They are neither irrebuttable, nor are they substantive rules of criminal law. Intention is a subjective concept, and any inference made from the evidence is *not* a presumption. Where the prosecution is obliged to prove mens rea, it must do so beyond reasonable doubt; it must make the fact-finder *sure* about the presence of mens rea. Supporting evidence, e.g. of foresight, is simply a part of what the

[109] *A-G's References (Nos. 1 and 2 of 1979)* [1980] QB 180 (CA), distinguishing and confining *Husseyn* (1978) 67 Cr App R 131; *Walkington* [1979] 1 WLR 1169 (CA); *Buckingham* (1976) 63 Cr App R 159. See Campbell, "Conditional Intention" (1982) 2 *LS* 77.

[110] See § 7.4(iv)(a) (complicity), § 9.3(iii)(d) (attempts).

prosecution may show in order to convince the court that, in light of all the evidence,[111] it may safely conclude, beyond reasonable doubt, that D had the required mens rea.

It was not always so. In *DPP v Smith*,[112] the House of Lords held there was an irrebuttable legal presumption that a person intends the reasonably foreseeable consequences of his acts. Fortunately, this highly controversial decision was reversed by section 8 of the Criminal Justice Act 1967. In any offence requiring the prosecution to prove mens rea on the part of the defendant, section 8 provides that the court:

(a) shall not be bound in law to infer that he intended or foresaw a result of his actions by reason only of its being a natural and probable consequence of those actions; but
(b) shall decide whether he did intend or foresee that result by reference to all the evidence, drawing such inferences from the evidence as appear proper in the circumstances.

The section does not, alas, offer a definition of "intention"—hence the difficulties seen earlier in this chapter. Its only role is to govern, and restrict, evidential rules of inference.

## § 5.2 Recklessness

Often people cause harm without intending to—that is, without acting in order to do so or realising that their conduct is virtually certain to do so. The doctor who injects her patient with a painkiller may unintentionally cause him significant harm, if the patient proves to be allergic to the drug that she injects. But the fact that an injury is unintended does not mean that the person who causes it is blameless; the doctor may have been aware of the risk of injury, a risk that she nevertheless chose to run. In such cases, we would say, she foresaw (but did not intend) the harm.

Not every case of foresight amounts to recklessness. In order for a defendant to be reckless, the choice to run the foreseen risk must also be an unreasonable one.[113] This is sometimes explained in terms of *unjustified* risk-taking. Although in practice the issue of unreasonableness does not often arise in court, the criterion is important. It means that anaesthetists, who knowingly undertake a slight risk that the patient will have a fatal allergic reaction when anaesthetised before an operation, are not necessarily reckless regarding the causing of death. The question of what is reasonable is an objective question, and it is not an issue of whether the defendant thought the risk was reasonable; rather, it is a question whether an ordinary and prudent person would have been prepared to take that risk.[114] To this extent defendants cannot be permitted to judge what is right for themselves. Otherwise precisely the wrong persons—those who cared nothing for the interests of others—might routinely be acquitted.

There are a number of factors for the law to consider when deciding whether a particular risk was a reasonable one to run.[115] These include the probability of the risk occurring, the

[111] Cp. *Hales* [2005] EWCA Crim 1118, [17]: "The jury has to put all the circumstances together, leaving out nothing of potential relevance".
[112] [1961] AC 290. The decision was treated as wrongly decided by the Privy Council in *Frankland* [1987] AC 576.
[113] Cp. *Renouf* [1986] 1 WLR 522 (CA).
[114] See further Alexander and Ferzan, *Crime and Culpability* (2009) 25–71; Stark, *Culpable Carelessness* (2016) 20–25.
[115] For an interesting philosophical treatment of the justification of risk-taking, see Oberdiek, *Imposing Risk* (2017) chap. 5.

nature and gravity of the harm being risked, and the social utility of the defendant's conduct.[116] Driving at 30 mph on a busy road may be reasonable; driving at 50 mph may not be, because of the increased risk of accidents and the more serious injuries that are likely to ensue should there be a crash. Against these considerations should be balanced the value and likelihood of achieving what the defendant was trying to do while running that risk. A high-risk surgical operation may be justified when it is done as a last resort or in an emergency to save the patient's life. But the risks involved may not be acceptable if less dangerous alternatives are available, or if the purpose of the operation is trivial, or if reasonable steps are not taken to reduce those risks to an acceptable level.

One point that should be made here is that the incorporation of a standard of reasonableness means that there is no need for a separate "threshold" criterion of probability or likelihood.[117] Obviously, if a risk is thought to be minimal or only an "outside chance", running that risk is likely to be unobjectionable. But even a very slight risk can be enough for recklessness if the harm being advertently risked is serious enough and the act concerned has no social value. A game of "Russian roulette" would be reckless even if the chances of being killed were thought to be only one in 200.[118] In such cases, it may be necessary to abandon an activity altogether if the defendant cannot eliminate the risk entirely. One example of this is provided by *Chief Constable of Avon and Somerset Constabulary v Shimmen*.[119] D, a martial arts expert, was demonstrating his skill to friends by (as he planned) kicking close to a shop window without breaking it. This experiment in controlled risk-taking failed: Shimmen smashed the window. Even though he thought he had "eliminated as much risk as possible", by stepping back a little way from the window before kicking, Shimmen was held liable for reckless criminal damage: he had chosen to run the slight, yet unjustifiable, risk of property damage that remained. Conversely, there may be a very substantial risk of injury or death in certain "last resort" surgical operations, but those operations are not necessarily unreasonable when undertaken.

There are two definitions of recklessness known to English law: "subjective" or *Cunningham* recklessness, and "objective" or *Caldwell* recklessness.[120] That the defendant's risk-taking was unreasonable is common to both: the difference lies in whether the defendant must herself have adverted to the relevant risk (yes, for subjective recklessness; not necessarily, for objective recklessness). Of the two, subjective recklessness is nowadays the standard variety in English criminal law. Under the subjective definition, D acts recklessly if:

(a) D believes her conduct will risk doing that action; and
(b) It is unreasonable for D to run the risk that she believes to exist.[121]

[116] See *Aubrey* [2017] HCA 18, [49]–[50].
[117] Cp. Stark, *Culpable Carelessness* (2016) 11–20.
[118] Cp. *Vehicle Inspectorate v Nuttall* [1999] 1 WLR 629, 636 (Lord Steyn). Indeed, whether an outcome is sufficiently probable to be, in law, "likely" also depends on the gravity of the outcome at risk: *Whitehouse* [2000] Crim LR 172 (CA).
[119] (1987) 84 Cr App R 7 (DC).
[120] For a detailed history of judicial interpretations of recklessness in English criminal law, see Halpin, *Definition in the Criminal Law* (2004) chap. 3.
[121] There is no further requirement that the risk be obvious and significant: *Brady* [2006] EWCA Crim 2413, [15]–[16]. Note that we are concerned in this discussion with advertent beliefs; thus "belief", "foresight", and "advertence" are generally used interchangeably.

The main difference between intention and (subjective) recklessness is that, while in both cases the defendant must foresee the possibility of realising the actus reus,[122] in recklessness he need not seek or be motivated to bring it about.

The subjective definition of recklessness currently dominates the law. The courts nevertheless suggested for a time that element (a), actual belief in a risk of performing the action, should not always be required, and that an objective definition of recklessness should be adopted. On such an objective understanding of recklessness, element (a) would instead require only that the relevant risk was in fact "obvious and serious". This would mean that a defendant could be accounted reckless in law even if she herself had failed to recognise the relevant risk. We consider this issue in the next section.

### *(i) The need for foresight*

Traditionally, the leading case to require that there be actual foresight of a particular risk before a defendant can be considered reckless is *Cunningham*.[123] In that case, D interfered with the coin-operated gas meter in an unoccupied house in order to steal money from it. The gas escaped, seeped into an adjoining house, and endangered the life of a person living there. Upon his appeal against conviction for maliciously administering a noxious thing so as to endanger life,[124] the Court of Criminal Appeal held that the mens rea term "malice" encapsulated intention and recklessness. In turn, recklessness regarding a particular risk of harm would be present if "the accused has foreseen that the particular kind of harm might be done, and yet has gone on to take the risk of it".[125]

On this view, failing to foresee a risk is not the stuff of recklessness. For example, in *Stephenson*,[126] D lit a fire in order to warm himself while sheltering in a haystack. He was charged with reckless arson after the haystack itself caught fire and was destroyed. Stephenson's conviction was quashed on appeal because (as he suffered from schizophrenia) he might not have recognised at the time that there was a risk of damaging or destroying the haystack.[127] On a subjective understanding of recklessness, the court would have had to be sure that D himself had foreseen the relevant risk before a conviction could follow.

It can be difficult to meet this demanding standard of proof, and the courts accordingly circumnavigate it under particular circumstances. In *Parker*,[128] for example, D slammed down a public telephone receiver with such force that he broke it. The Court rejected his defence that he had been too enraged to think about the risk of damaging the phone. The inherent association of his violent action with its consequence meant that he could be taken to have appreciated the risk without the awareness of that risk being at the forefront of his mind, and without the need for sober or careful deliberation in advance of action.

[122] More precisely, of realising the elements of the actus reus for which recklessness is required.

[123] [1957] 2 QB 396 (CA). Cp. *Briggs* [1977] 1 WLR 605, 608 (CA); *Stephenson* [1979] QB 695, 703 (CA); *Mullins* [1980] Crim LR 37 (CA); *Flack v Hunt* (1980) 70 Cr App R 51 (DC).

[124] Contrary to the Offences Against the Person Act 1861, s. 23.

[125] [1957] 2 QB 396, 399 (CA), quoting with approval from Turner, *Kenny's Outlines of Criminal Law* (16th ed., 1952) 186.

[126] [1979] QB 695 (CA).

[127] Note that on these facts, D might properly have been obliged to plead insanity. Contrast, however, *Harris* (reported with *Coley*) [2013] EWCA Crim 223, where D was allowed to explain his lack of awareness that setting fire to his house endangered the lives of others on the basis of his mental disorder. See further below, § 19.2.

[128] [1977] 1 WLR 600 (CA).

The inference made in *Parker* must arise clearly from the facts if it is to be properly drawn.[129] In *Briggs*,[130] D took hold of the door handle to V's car and tried to open the door, apparently with a normal arm movement. The handle broke. On appeal, the Court of Appeal quashed D's conviction for criminal damage. The trial judge had failed to instruct the jury that, in order to be held reckless regarding the risk of damaging or destroying property belonging to another, D must have given thought to the risk of damaging the door handle; it was possible that D had not done so.

Unlike in *Parker*, the risk created by the defendant in *Briggs* was not so inherent in his actions that it was inevitable that D had appreciated it at the time of acting. *Briggs* reinforces the point that there must be recognition of the risk at some level of the defendant's consciousness before he can be found reckless.[131]

### *(a) An alternative, objective version of recklessness*

The previous section states the established position after *Cunningham*. In 1981 the House of Lords endorsed a second version of recklessness in *Metropolitan Police Commissioner v Caldwell*[132] and the companion case of *Lawrence*.[133] In *Caldwell*, the defendant set fire to a hotel while intoxicated. He was charged, *inter alia*,[134] under section 1(1) of the Criminal Damage Act 1971, which makes it an offence intentionally or recklessly to damage another's property, "being reckless as to whether any such property would be destroyed or damaged". The House of Lords held that a defendant is reckless in law if:[135]

> "(1) he does an act which in fact creates an obvious [and serious][136] risk that property would be destroyed or damaged and (2) when he does the act he either has not given any thought to the possibility of there being any such risk or has recognised that there was some risk involved and has nonetheless gone on to do it."

*Caldwell* deployed a second, objective category of recklessness in criminal law. In addition to the cases of actual foresight covered by *Cunningham*, the defendant would also be treated as reckless if he failed to think of a risk when that risk was a glaring one. In effect, the *Caldwell* definition of recklessness embraces both advertent wrongdoing and (gross) negli-

[129] Indeed, it is arguable that the inference was inappropriate in *Parker* itself: see Stark, *Culpable Carelessness* (2016) 242–3. As such the decision by the Court of Appeal may be a precursor of *Caldwell*, discussed below in the next subsection. If so, however, the approach in *Parker* is narrower than that taken by the House of Lords in *Caldwell*; it would justify inferring recklessness only where D "deliberately closes his mind" to obvious consequences because he is "in a self-induced state of temper", or for a similarly discreditable reason. See *Parker* [1977] 1 WLR 600, 604 (CA).

[130] [1977] 1 WLR 605 (CA).

[131] For excellent discussion of the role of consciousness in recklessness, see Ferzan, "Opaque Recklessness" (2001) 91 *J Crim L & Crim* 597. See also Greenberg, "Awareness and the Recklessness/Negligence Distinction" (2024) 18 *Crim Law and Philosophy* 351.

[132] [1982] AC 341.

[133] [1982] AC 510. See, also, *Miller* [1983] 2 AC 161.

[134] Caldwell was also charged with the aggravated form of criminal damage in s. 1(2), on the basis that he had additionally been reckless whether other people's lives would be endangered. Recklessness was also understood "objectively" by the House of Lords in that context.

[135] [1982] AC 341, 354 (Lord Diplock).

[136] The requirement of "seriousness" was added in *Lawrence* [1982] AC 510, 527 (Lord Diplock). The requirement of obviousness did not apply where the risk was, in fact, foreseen by D: *Reid* [1992] 1 WLR 793, 814 (Lord Goff) (HL).

gence.[137] The main justification for this was, in Lord Diplock's view, the moral equivalence of (some) cases of foresight of risk and (some) cases of missing a risk.[138]

*(b) The predominance of subjective recklessness*

The extension of the criminal law's understanding of recklessness proposed in *Caldwell* was always controversial.[139] Although the decision exercised a considerable influence over English criminal law during the 1980s,[140] its importance quickly diminished, to the point that its application came to be restricted to the offence in *Caldwell* itself (criminal damage and its variants), and to a few other statutory offences.[141] Eventually, in *G*,[142] the House of Lords rejected the application of objective recklessness in criminal damage, reversing the very decision in *Caldwell*. Subjective recklessness is, once more, the dominant—perhaps even the only—form in English and Welsh criminal law.[143]

In *G*, two children aged 11 and 12 had stolen away camping without their parents' permission. During the night they entered the backyard of a shop, where they found some bundles of newspapers. They set fire to some of the newspapers and threw them under a wheelie-bin in the shop's yard. The defendants then left the yard. Subsequently, the fire spread to the bin and to the adjacent shop, causing approximately £1 million worth of damage. The defendants apparently expected the newspapers to burn themselves out on the concrete floor of the yard, and did not foresee the risk that the fire would spread. At trial, following a *Caldwell* direction, they were convicted of reckless arson, a conviction upheld by the Court of Appeal. The House of Lords quashed the convictions. *Caldwell* was overruled: it was held to have misinterpreted Parliament's intention when enacting the Criminal Damage Act 1971. More generally, it was suggested that the objective test of recklessness established in *Caldwell* could offend against the layperson's sense of justice, at least if applied unrelentingly.[144]

Technically, *G* is a decision on the mental element of criminal damage. It therefore remains possible in theory that, in some future context, the courts will interpret a specific statutory requirement of recklessness as entailing *Caldwell* and not *Cunningham* recklessness. Indeed, this possibility was left open by Lords Bingham and Rodger in *G*.[145]

Yet it is generally desirable that the courts should interpret core terms like "recklessness" in a consistent fashion,[146] and the likelihood that courts will ever adopt *Caldwell*

[137] The relationship between gross negligence and *Caldwell* recklessness was never clear. For the modern law on gross negligence, see below, § 5.5(iv). Cf. *Adomako* [1995] 1 AC 171, 187–9 (Lord Mackay).

[138] [1982] AC 341, 352

[139] See, e.g., Smith [1981] Crim LR 393, 410; Williams, "Recklessness Redefined" (1981) 40 *CLJ* 252; Syrota, "A Radical Change in the Law of Recklessness?" [1982] *Crim LR* 97; Duff, "Professor Williams and Conditional Subjectivism" (1982) 41 *CLJ* 273; Williams, "The Unresolved Problem of Recklessness" (1988) 8 *LS* 74.

[140] Contrast other jurisdictions, where *Caldwell* generally failed to take hold: *Smith* (1982) 7 A Crim R 437; *Sansregret* [1985] 1 SCR 570; *Harney* [1987] 2 NZLR 576. See, further, Stark, *Culpable Carelessness* (2016) chap. 2.

[141] E.g. *Large v Mainprize* [1989] Crim LR 213 (DC) (concerning an offence relating to the falsification of records about a fishing vessel's catch).

[142] [2003] UKHL 50, [2004] 1 AC 1034.

[143] One has to search far and wide to find an example of recklessness in England and Wales that does not appear to be limited to the subjective test in *Cunningham* and *G*. See, however, Uranium Enrichment Technology (Prohibition on Disclosure) Regulations 2004 (SI 2004/1818), reg. 2(2).

[144] *G* [2003] UKHL 50, [2004] 1 AC 1034, [57].

[145] *Ibid.*, [28] (Lord Bingham) and [69] (Lord Rodger).

[146] An argument made by Stark, "It's Only Words: On Meaning and Mens Rea" (2013) 72 *CLJ* 155.

recklessness in a statutory interpretation exercise is now remote; notwithstanding the fact that there are some ordinary-language senses of "recklessness" in criminal law which are not subjective (below, § 5.2(ii)). Moreover, while the actual decision in *G* concerns the meaning of recklessness in the context of the Criminal Damage Act 1971, the principles it lays down are general in nature.[147] Unless the statute expressly or by necessary implication precludes it,[148] the fault element for criminal offences should normally be subjective.[149] As the House of Lords itself acknowledged in *G*, convictions of serious crimes should not normally be visited on the inadvertent:[150]

> "But it is not clearly blameworthy to do something involving a risk of injury to another if . . . one genuinely does not perceive the risk. Such a person may fairly be accused of stupidity or lack of imagination, but neither of those failings should expose him to conviction of serious crime or the risk of punishment."

Especially where the defendant suffers from limitations of age, intellect, or the like, to apply the *Caldwell* standard unbendingly would be unfair, since it could lead to the conviction of persons, including children, who lacked the *capacity* to appreciate risks that would be obvious to ordinary adults.[151]

As noted above, the main justification for Lord Diplock's contrary holding in *Caldwell* was that inadvertence to an obvious unreasonable risk frequently is just as blameworthy as choosing to run an unreasonable risk which is foreseen, and so should be treated the same way within the law's understanding of recklessness. There is some force in this: it is an unattractive option to acquit a defendant who did not consider the risks because he was too drunk, too temperamental, or too uncaring a person to bother thinking about them.[152] But, as we shall see in § 5.2(iv), there are already special rules in place which deal with voluntary intoxication. Moreover, a question might be asked whether the moral equation constructed by Lord Diplock will always (or almost always) hold—which ought to be the case before a court makes such a comprehensive extension of the law's understanding of recklessness. In particular, it seems harsh to treat as reckless those whose inadvertence was due to preoccupation or distraction,[153] and who may be utterly horrified when they recognise the consequences of their actions.

One should also recognise an important distinction, in terms of culpability, between advertent and inadvertent wrongdoing. Those who act in the face of risks that they believe to exist *choose* to take those risks. This explains their culpability. They deliber-

[147] Cp. *A-G's Reference (No. 3 of 2003)* [2004] EWCA Crim 868, [2005] QB 73, [12]; *Brady* [2006] EWCA Crim 2413, [15]; *C* [2007] EWCA Crim 1068, [20].

[148] An argument along these lines is advanced by Cartwright in the context of some consumer offences: "Corporate Criminal Liability: Models of Intervention and Liability in Consumer Law", Appendix B of LCCP No. 195, *Criminal Liability in Regulatory Contexts* (2010) paras. B16–17.

[149] The courts now seem to default to subjective recklessness when interpreting statutes. See, e.g., the approach adopted in relation to the offence of recklessly destroying a badger set (contrary to Protection of Badgers Act 1992, s. 3) in *Foster v CPS* [2013] EWHC 3885 (Admin).

[150] *G* [2003] UKHL 50; [2004] 1 AC 1034, [32] (Lord Bingham); see also [55] (Lord Steyn).

[151] *Ibid.*, [33] (Lord Bingham); cp. [52]–[54] (Lord Steyn). The House rejected a modified test, of whether the risk would have been obvious to one with *the defendant's* capacities: *ibid.*, [37]–[38] (Lord Bingham; cp. the earlier case of *Elliott v C (a minor)* [1983] 1 WLR 939 (DC)). See further below, § 5.5(ii).

[152] Cp. *Reid* [1992] 1 WLR 793, 809 (Lord Goff) (HL). This seems to have been the thinking underlying *Parker* (above, § 5.2(i)).

[153] Cp. Griew, "Reckless Damage and Reckless Driving: Living with *Caldwell* and *Lawrence*" [1981] *Crim LR* 743, 747; in tort, *West Ky. Tel. Co. v Pharis* 78 SW 917 (1904).

ately do the wrong thing. Those who fail to note the risks attendant upon their conduct do not choose to take those risks, and so their culpability must stem from something else (perhaps their character, in some sense).[154] *Caldwell* collapsed this important distinction in terms of culpability. Following *G*, this division in the culpability is once again clear: recklessness as a mens rea term is standardly a choice-based mode of culpability, leaving other bases of blame for distinct mens rea states (most prominently, in this context, negligence).

#### *(ii) Recklessness with respect to the behaviour element, rather than circumstances or consequences*

Until 1992, there was a criminal offence known as reckless driving.[155] In *Lawrence*,[156] recklessness was interpreted objectively in the context of that offence. The plausibility of this interpretation rests upon a distinction drawn in Chapter 4.[157] In *Lawrence*, the actus reus of the offence was concerned only with D's *behaviour* (i.e. with his reckless driving). By contrast, in many other offences D's behaviour alone is not sufficient to establish the actus reus. There must be an additional element, e.g. that V is not consenting to what D does (a circumstance), or that V dies as a result of what D does (a consequence). Where an offence involves *circumstances* and *consequences*, it is natural for a lawyer to think of recklessness as a mens rea term, requiring advertence to the specific circumstance or consequence named in that offence. For example, to commit a reckless homicide one has to foresee the possibility of death ensuing. But matters are different when the actus reus is concerned only with the behaviour of the defendant. In relation to an offence of "reckless driving", the court does not ask, "Did the defendant advert to the fact that she was *driving*?" Rather, the main question is whether the *manner* of her behaviour was sufficiently dangerous. "Reckless", in this context, qualified the nature of the behaviour that was needed for the offence. Hence, it was, in that context, an actus reus term. One might, for example, drive in a reckless manner (the *actus*) deliberately (the *mens*).[158] Where recklessness refers to the manner of D's behaviour, the case for an objective interpretation is therefore stronger. That said, it is needlessly confusing to use the same word in different ways in the criminal law: it would be preferable if a different word were used to qualify D's behaviour.[159] The language of the current offence, "dangerous driving", is very much to be preferred.

#### *(iii) Recklessness and circumstances*

Recklessness requires that the defendant foresee a risk that the actus reus element(s) may occur. Hence it requires the defendant to foresee that each relevant element of that actus reus may occur, including the presence of any relevant circumstances. A useful illustration of this is the offence of assault. One requirement of that offence is the victim's lack of

[154] For different versions of this view, see Simester, *Fundamentals* §§ 11.3–5; Stark, *Culpable Carelessness* (2016) chaps. 6–8.
[155] See, now, Road Traffic Act 1988, s. 2 ("dangerous driving").
[156] Above, § 5.2(i)(a).
[157] See §§ 4, 4.1.
[158] Winslade, "Brady on Recklessness" (1972) 33 *Analysis* 31.
[159] Cunningham, "Recklessness: Being Reckless and Acting Recklessly" (2010) 21 *King's College LJ* 445.

consent. The mens rea for this element is (subjective) recklessness.[160] Thus D cannot be guilty if he believes that V consents, and may be convicted only if he goes ahead recognising that V may not be consenting.[161] As Lord Bingham put it in *G*, a person is reckless with respect to a circumstance "when he is aware of a risk that it exists or will exist".[162]

The difference between recklessness and intention can be shown by the following example. If D has sexual intercourse with V recognising (but not caring) that V may not be consenting, then if V does not consent D commits rape, being reckless regarding V's consent.[163] (We assume that his risk-taking is inherently unreasonable.) On the other hand, if D has sexual intercourse *believing* positively that V does not consent, he commits rape, intending that V does not consent. (In either case D commits rape.[164])

Sometimes, this definition of recklessness leads to difficulties where the defendant acts without giving thought to attendant circumstances. This may occur, for example, where D touches V, but claims it did not occur to him that she might not consent. What if D did not think about the possibility because he did not care about V's consent, and would have gone ahead anyway? Should he be acquitted? In order to deal with such situations, the courts have suggested two extensional ways of finding recklessness regarding circumstance elements.

The first is that a defendant may be held reckless about a circumstance, such as non-consent, if he was indifferent to, or could not care less about, whether the victim was consenting. The validity of this approach is nowadays doubtful. Its genesis seems to be the references to indifference found in *Lawrence*. It has been endorsed in a number of decisions, for example *Kimber*, where in the Court of Appeal's words, D's "attitude to [V] was one of indifference to her feelings and wishes. This state of mind is aptly described in the colloquial expression, 'couldn't care less'. In law this is recklessness."[165] But if that proposition was ever correct, it is not now. *Caldwell*, as we have noted, is no longer good law, and *Lawrence* merely echoed that decision. *Kimber* itself was decided in the context of the pre-Sexual Offences Act 2003 law on indecent assault, now repealed, and is no longer of direct application to the law. Mens rea is nowadays not normally concerned with the *attitudes* of defendants;[166] it is concerned with what they intended, knew, believed, etc., and what they did not know, believe, etc. This is why a worthy attitude, or a good motive, is no defence under the criminal law.[167] It is also why, under the subjective approach to recklessness,

[160] Cp. *C* [1992] Crim LR 642 (CA) (indecent assault).

[161] See *DPP v Morgan* [1976] AC 182, discussed below, §§ 18.1(i)–(ii).

[162] [2003] UKHL 50, [2004] 1 AC 1034, [41], quoting from the proposed clause 18(c) in Law. Com. No. 177, *A Draft Code for England and Wales* (1989).

[163] Whether D's recklessness would be sufficient for him to be convicted of an attempt (if V in fact does consent) is discussed below, § 9.4(iii)(b).

[164] Indeed, the mens rea of rape is even wider than recklessness: see below, §§ 12.5–6.

[165] [1983] 1 WLR 1118, 1123 (CA). Cf. *Pigg* [1982] 1 WLR 762 (CA) (reversed on different ground in [1983] 1 WLR 6 (HL)); *Millard* [1987] Crim LR 393 (CA); *Khan* [1990] 1 WLR 813 (CA); *Paine* [1998] 1 Cr App R 36 (C-MAC). Cf. *Vehicle Inspectorate v Nuttall* [1999] 1 WLR 629, 636 (Lord Steyn) (HL). Compare, in Australia, *Tolmie* (1995) 37 NSWLR 660; *Kitchener* (1993) 29 NSWLR 696. The approach in *Tolmie* was endorsed by Callinan J in *Banditt* [2005] HCA 80, (2005) 224 CLR 262, [86], but not by the majority, which favoured a subjective test: see [20], [25], [33]–[36].

[166] This disregard is not a necessary feature of the criminal law. For an alternative approach to recklessness that draws upon the approach in German law, see Duff, "Two Models of Criminal Fault" (2019) 13 *Crim Law and Philosophy* 643.

[167] Cp. *Smith* [1960] 2 QB 423 (CA); above, §§ 5, 5.1(ii). For the rule that a positive attitude, of hoping the actus reus would not happen, supplies no defence, see *Crabbe* (1985) 156 CLR 464, 470.

defendants are not to be convicted merely on the basis of an unworthy attitude or bad motive, e.g. for indifference to a particular risk. Correspondingly, the law should not be concerned to enquire whether D's failure to foresee a risk was because he did not care or exhibited some other indifferent attitude.[168] Such fine nuances have no practical place in the law.

The second extension to recklessness regarding circumstances is more plausible. On this test, D will be held reckless about a circumstantial element in an offence *unless* he has a positive belief that the circumstance is absent. Thus, if D deliberately touches V, he is reckless regarding V's consent unless he believes positively that V consents. More generally, where recklessness about non-consent is required to establish mens rea, it suffices *either* if D recognised V might not be consenting, *or* if D did *not* believe that she was consenting. This test was accepted by the House of Lords' decision in *B (A Minor) v DPP*.[169] In effect, the prosecution need prove only that D lacked a genuine belief that V consented, without having to prove, in addition, that he positively believed there was a risk that she did not consent.

This extension to subjective recklessness will not convict defendants who wrongly assume that V consents, but will catch those who proceed to harm V without positively believing they have V's agreement. The advantage of this test is that (like *Cunningham*) its focus is restricted to D's cognitive beliefs, whereas the test suggested in *Kimber* requires consideration of D's attitude—with all the uncertainties that come with that inquiry. Moreover, *Kimber* itself also falls within this second category. An attitudinal test for recklessness in this context is thus unnecessary to secure warranted convictions.

### *(iv) Voluntary intoxication and the presumption of recklessness*

In general, the prosecution is obliged to prove recklessness without the assistance of irrebuttable inferences or presumptions.[170] The prosecution may rely on evidential inferences in the normal way: for example, the fact that D took precautions, say by wearing fire-resistant clothing when dealing with flammable materials, may be relied on to suggest that he recognised the risk existed of starting a fire. However, there is no rule of substantive law by which the defendant is deemed to have foreseen a consequence merely because it was likely or obvious.[171] The defendant should benefit from any reasonable doubt over whether he in fact believed a risk of that consequence existed.

This generalisation is subject to one exception, which arises when the defendant fails to foresee the relevant risk due to a state of voluntary intoxication. If the defendant would have foreseen the relevant risk had she been sober, she may be treated, in law, as having

[168] Moreover, as Norrie points out, there are different kinds of indifferent attitude: "Between Orthodox Subjectivism and Moral Contextualism: Intention and the Consultation Paper" [2006] *Crim LR* 486, 492–3. Thus the objection is compounded by ambiguity about *which* standard to apply.

[169] [2000] 2 AC 428, 459 (Lord Mackay), 466 (Lord Nicholls). Cp. *K* [2001] UKHL 41, [2002] 1 AC 462, [16] (Lord Bingham), [38] (Lord Hobhouse); *Satnam and Kewal Singh* (1984) 78 Cr App R 149. Contrast, however, the quotation from Lord Bingham in *G* [2003] UKHL 50, [2004] 1 AC 1034, [41], above in the text of this subsection ("when he is aware of a risk that it exists or will exist").

[170] See s. 8 of the Criminal Justice Act 1967; above, § 5.1(ix).

[171] *Caldwell* [1982] AC 341, discussed earlier in § 5.2(i), was not such a decision; rather, it held that for the objective variety of recklessness actual foresight by the defendant was not a required element.

foreseen that risk at the time of her conduct.[172] So, for instance, D cannot argue that she was too drunk to foresee the risks attendant upon waving her arms about wildly on a crowded dancefloor when she makes physical contact with another reveller. Voluntary intoxication can lead, as a matter of law, to a finding of recklessness—including *Cunningham* recklessness—in such circumstances. The legal significance of intoxication will be discussed in more detail below, in Chapter 18.

## § 5.3 Why distinguish intention from recklessness?

In practice, recklessness satisfies the mens rea requirement in most crimes. This raises an obvious question: why bother discussing a separate category of intention at all? There are at least three reasons for doing so. First, some actions can only be done with intention. For example, a person attempts to harm another only if he intends to do so. It would be a misuse of language to describe a knowing risk-taker as "attempting" to inflict harm.

Often this linguistic difference reflects a moral distinction,[173] because the presence of intention can alter the very nature of what is done. As Glanville Williams once pointed out, "[t]he act constituting a crime may in some circumstances be objectively innocent, and take its criminal colouring entirely from the intent with which it is done".[174] It was the defendant's intention which changed the action from simple assault to indecent assault in *Court*,[175] a case where D spanked a young girl on the seat of her shorts. He was convicted of indecent assault because he had done so for sexual gratification—his intention made the behaviour "indecent".[176] Similarly, the difference between negligent appropriation of property and theft lies not merely in the degree of culpability but also in the nature of the action itself (even though the physical harm may be the same). Theft cannot fully be defined in terms of its physical components because the wrong of theft expresses a certain sort of contempt for property rights, and for the victim, which the mere appropriation of property does not.

The second rationale for distinguishing intention from recklessness is that, as we have seen, recklessness is established only if the defendant risked doing the actus reus *unreasonably*. By contrast, there is no condition of unreasonableness attaching to intention. Neither is there a general defence known to the criminal law of reasonable action.[177]

The third reason to distinguish intention from recklessness also involves defences. As the law presently stands, in order to claim a defence such as self-defence, the defendant must *intend* to defend himself when he does the actus reus. This point is illustrated by the well-known case of *Dadson*,[178] in which a policeman shot and wounded a thief who was

[172] *Bennett* [1995] Crim LR 877 (CA); *Brady* [2006] EWCA Crim 2413.

[173] See, e.g., Duff, "Attempted Homicide" (1995) 1 *Legal Theory* 149; Horder, "Crimes of Ulterior Intent" in Simester and Smith (eds.), *Harm and Culpability* (1996) 153.

[174] *CLGP* 22. See also Lynch, "The Mental Element in the Actus Reus" (1982) 98 *LQR* 109.

[175] [1989] AC 28. See Sullivan, "The Need for a Crime of Sexual Assault" [1989] *Crim LR* 331.

[176] *Per* Lord Ackner (at 43), "[t]o decide whether or not right-minded persons might think that the assault was indecent, the following factors were clearly relevant: the relationship of the defendant to this victim . . ., how had the defendant come to embark on this conduct and *why* was he behaving in this way?"

[177] Cp. *Yip Chiu-cheung* [1995] 1 AC 111 (PC). For a discussion of this point in the context of medical necessity, see Ashworth, "Criminal Liability in a Medical Context: the Treatment of Good Intentions" in Simester and Smith (eds.), *Harm and Culpability* (1996) 173.

[178] (1850) 4 Cox CC 358; below, § 17.2.

stealing wood. It was then, as now, an offence intentionally to shoot another, and both the actus reus and mens rea were made out in Dadson's case. However, the thief was in fact a felon, and a lawful-arrest defence existed at that time to the effect that the policeman would be justified in shooting to prevent the escape of a felon. The difficulty was that the policeman had not realised that the person he was shooting was a felon. Hence, although he intended to shoot V, he did not intend to use this justification: i.e. to prevent the escape of a felon. Therefore, the Court ruled, he was not entitled to claim the defence, and he was convicted. The same rule applies if D had recognised that V may be a felon, but that was not why he shot V (perhaps V also happened to be D's sworn enemy). In such a case, the defence of preventing the escape of a felon would also have been unavailable.[179]

## § 5.4 Knowledge

Where an offence is formulated so as to require that the defendant act "knowing" that some circumstance exists, this demands a positive (and correct)[180] belief on the part of the defendant that the relevant circumstance exists.[181] Legally speaking, "knowledge means true belief".[182] If Tom purchases goods suspecting they may well be stolen, he commits no offence of handling stolen goods because he does not "know" in law that they are stolen—he merely suspects they are.[183] Belief or knowledge that a circumstance *may* obtain, which would be sufficient for recklessness, is neither knowledge nor belief that it *does* obtain. Hence it is inadequate to satisfy the mens rea of any offence which requires knowledge or intention that some circumstance exists.[184]

What is not necessary, however, is that the defendant should think that the relevant circumstance exists with provable certainty.[185] In law, it is sufficient that the defendant accepts, or assumes, and has no serious doubt, at the time he acts, that the circumstance is present.[186] (Or, if the circumstance lies in the future, that it will be present when the time comes.) Hence if Tom refrains from investigating further whether or not the goods are indeed stolen, and goes ahead with the purchase believing that they may well be, he is not guilty of handling. It is not enough for him to believe there is a possibility or likelihood that they are stolen.[187] But if, despite the fact that he has not actually seen proof of another's

[179] See also *Thain* [1985] NI 457; Sullivan, "Bad Thoughts and Bad Acts" [1990] *Crim LR* 559; Hogan, "The *Dadson* Principle" [1989] *Crim LR* 679.

[180] *USA v Dynar* [1997] 2 SCR 462, [41]–[47].

[181] See generally Shute, "Knowledge and Belief in the Criminal Law" and Sullivan, "Knowledge, Belief and Culpability" in Shute and Simester (eds.), *Criminal Law Theory* (2002) 171 and 207 respectively; also Stark, "Against Knowledge (in the Criminal Law)" in Simester (ed.), *Modern Criminal Law* (2024) 25.

[182] *Saik* [2006] UKHL 18, [2007] 1 AC 18, [26] (Lord Nicholls). Technically, this definition was specific to the context of money laundering, but in principle it can be generalised. Cf. *Montila* [2004] UKHL 50, [2004] 1 WLR 3141.

[183] *Grainge* [1974] 1 WLR 619 (CA). In law, a "suspicion" involves believing there is a genuine possibility that the circumstance exists: *Da Silva* [2006] EWCA Crim 1654, [2007] 1 WLR 303, [16].

[184] *Hall* (1985) 81 Cr App R 260; *Ismael* [1977] Crim LR 557 (CA).

[185] Cp. *Godir* [2018] EWCA Crim 2294, [15]: "In simple terms, one can be said to *know* something if one is absolutely sure that it is so".

[186] See, similarly, Smith, noting *MPC v Charles* [1977] Crim LR 615, 620 (HL): "doubts are inconsistent with belief"—at least if those doubts are serious ones. See the interesting discussion by Griew, "Consistency, Communication and Codification—Reflections on Two Mens Rea Words" in Glazebrook (ed.), *Reshaping the Criminal Law* (1978) 57, 69–76.

[187] *Griffiths* (1974) 60 Cr App R 14; *Woods* [1969] 1 QB 447 (CA).

ownership, he accepts the vendor's disclosure to him that the goods are purloined, then he handles them when he goes ahead with the purchase.

### *(i) Wilful blindness*

The situation where Tom realises there is a chance the goods are stolen, yet deliberately refrains from checking his suspicion, raises the issue of "wilful blindness". Cases of wilful blindness often appear to fall between the mens rea alternatives (i) recklessness as to the circumstance, and (ii) (actual) knowledge, which satisfies a requirement of intention when applied to circumstance elements. The first alternative is straightforward. *Every* case where a defendant realises or suspects the circumstance might exist and refrains from investigating further is a case of (i), recklessness (assuming it is unreasonable for D to proceed given that perceived risk). Even without further investigation, the defendant believes already that there is a risk that the circumstance is present. So if the mens rea of an offence requires only recklessness, then the defendant may be convicted.[188]

Finding actual knowledge is more difficult. In some cases of deliberate non-inquiry by a defendant, the court will invoke what is known as the doctrine of wilful blindness. This doctrine applies where the defendant intentionally chooses not to inquire whether something is true because he has no real doubt what the answer is going to be. Its effect is to attribute knowledge of the circumstance to the defendant. In other words, where the wilful blindness doctrine applies, the law will treat the defendant as having *actual* knowledge.

The conditions under which the doctrine applies are not capable of being stated precisely.[189] Broadly speaking, if there is an obvious way of finding something out and the defendant deliberately shuts his eyes to a risk by failing to find out, he will not be permitted to exculpate himself by claiming that he did not know the truth. Wilful blindness covers the case where D "deliberately refrained from making inquiries the results of which he might not care to have".[190] Or, as the House of Lords stated in *Westminster CC v Croyalgrange Ltd*:[191]

> "it is always open to the tribunal of fact, when knowledge on the part of a defendant is required to be proved, to base a finding of knowledge on evidence that the defendant had deliberately shut his eyes to the obvious or refrained from enquiry because he suspected the truth but did not want to have his suspicion confirmed."

On the other hand, wilful blindness cannot be invoked just because D *should* have inquired further into the facts,[192] or even if he suspected the truth;[193] otherwise knowledge would

[188] Above, § 5.2(iii).

[189] See Wasik and Thompson, "Turning a Blind Eye as Constituting Mens Rea" (1981) 32 *NILQ* 328; Williams, *CLGP* 157–9; Lanham, "Wilful Blindness and the Criminal Law" (1985) 9 *Crim LJ* 261; Ryan, "Reckless Transmission of HIV: Knowledge and Culpability" [2006] *Crim LR* 981, 984–9. For an account premised on duties of "reasonable investigation", see Sarch, *Criminally Ignorant: Why the Law Pretends We Know What We Don't* (2019) chap. 4. See also Yaffe, "The Point of Mens Rea: The Case of Willful Ignorance" (2018) 12 *Crim Law and Philosophy* 19.

[190] *Roper v Taylor's Central Garages Ltd* [1951] 2 TLR 284, 288 (DC), quoting from *Evans v Dell* [1937] 1 All ER 349, 353–4 (DC).

[191] *Westminster CC v Croyalgrange Ltd* [1986] 1 WLR 674, 684 (Lord Bridge).

[192] Sometimes, perhaps misleadingly, called "constructive knowledge", but not to be assimilated with knowledge: cf. *Flintshire County Council v Reynolds* [2006] EWHC 195 (Admin), [17], endorsing Devlin J's judgment in *Roper v Taylor's Central Garages Ltd* [1951] 2 TLR 284 (DC).

[193] *Griffiths* (1974) 60 Cr App R 14; *Court* [1954] Crim LR 622 (CA); *Havard* (1916) 11 Cr App R 2. Cf. *Saik* [2006] UKHL 18, [2007] 1 AC 18, [32] (Lord Nicholls), [78] (Lord Hope), and [120] (Lord Brown).

effectively be indistinguishable from recklessness. However, the line between recklessness and wilful blindness is a fine one. It appears that the defendant is wilfully blind in two situations. The first is if he shuts his eyes and fails to enquire because he is virtually certain what the answer will be.[194] This approach squares with the test once proposed by the Law Commission:[195]

> "The standard test of knowledge is—Did the person whose conduct is in issue either know of the relevant circumstances or have no substantial doubt of their existence?"

Alternatively, the wilful blindness doctrine will also apply if the means of knowledge are easily to hand, and D realises the likely truth of a matter but refrains from enquiry *in order* not to attain knowledge. In such circumstances, although D in fact lacks knowledge there are clear normative grounds for inculpation. This type of case is helpfully elucidated by the judgment of Lord Sumner in *The Zamora*:[196]

> "There are two senses in which a man is said not to know something because he does not want to know it. A thing may be troublesome to learn, and the knowledge of it, when acquired, may be uninteresting or distasteful. To refuse to know any more about the subject or anything at all is then a wilful but a real ignorance. On the other hand, a man is said not to know because he does not want to know, where the substance of the thing is borne in upon his mind with a conviction that full details or precise proofs may be dangerous, because they may embarrass his denials or compromise his protests. In such a case he flatters himself that where ignorance is safe, 'tis folly to be wise, but there he is wrong, for he has been put upon notice and his further ignorance . . . is a mere affectation and disguise."

It should be emphasised that wilful blindness is a doctrine of substantive rather than evidential law. It imputes knowledge to the defendant for legal purposes where there is not, in fact, such knowledge.[197] Even if the doctrine does not apply, however, there remains the further possibility that a jury may *infer* actual knowledge on the part of the defendant (i.e. that in fact she accepted the truth and had no serious doubt), from evidence that she recognised the likely circumstances and made no further enquiry.[198] Nonetheless, proof of the latter does not constitute proof of the former.

## § 5.5 Negligence

Unlike mens rea varieties such as recklessness, intention, and knowledge, negligence does not presuppose any particular state of mind on the part of the defendant. It is, however, a standard that reflects fault on the part of the defendant, and so it is appropriately discussed alongside the other mens rea categories. The main feature distinguishing negligence from

[194] E.g. *Ross v Moss* [1965] 2 QB 396 (DC).

[195] Draft Criminal Liability (Mental Element) Bill, Law Com. No. 89 (1978) cl. 3(1). This is a more demanding test than that finally endorsed by the Law Commission: Law Com. No. 177, *A Criminal Code for England and Wales* (1989) cl. 18(a).

[196] [1921] 1 AC 801, 812. See *Borthwick-Norton v Romney Warwick Estates Ltd* [1950] 1 All ER 362, 365–6 (CA); *Redgate v Haynes* (1876) 1 QBD 89; *Somerset v Wade* [1894] 1 QB 574. Cp. *Sansregret* [1985] 1 SCR 570, 584–7; *Barbeau* (1996) 110 CCC (3d) 69, 92–5.

[197] For a contrary view, see Dsouza, "Criminally Ignorant—An Invitation for Broader Evaluation" (2021) 12 *Jurisprudence* 226.

[198] *Smith (Albert)* (1977) 64 Cr App R 217.

the categories we have mentioned so far is that, in negligence, there is no requirement that the defendant foresee the risk that the actus reus might occur. Sometimes we blame people precisely because they have *failed* to think about something—because they were careless or thoughtless.[199] It is this sort of case that is captured by negligence.

### *(i) The test for negligence*

Because negligence permits the finding of fault for inadvertent wrongdoing, it does not matter whether the defendant actually adverts to the risks. As Glanville Williams asserts, "the essential question, at any rate for legal purposes, is whether it was reasonable for you to go ahead with your conduct in the circumstances".[200] Of course, normally one who foresees and runs an unreasonable risk will be reckless as well as negligent. Negligence does not, however, *require* inadvertence. This is for two reasons. The first is that in the criminal law, the lesser fault standard incorporates the greater. A defendant should not be able to exculpate herself by pleading that her actions were reckless or intentional rather than negligent. (Similarly, she should be unable to escape an allegation of recklessness by pleading that her actions were intended.) It follows that where negligence regarding an offence element is enough for criminal liability, then, *a fortiori*, there is liability for intention or recklessness.

The second reason is that, as we mentioned earlier, a defendant can foresee the actus reus without being reckless, yet may still be negligent. For example, an anaesthetist who recognises there is a slight risk of killing his patient is not normally reckless, because taking that risk will normally be justified. But if he has unknowingly miscalculated the dose, then he may be negligent even though not reckless. Recklessness involves an objective assessment of running the subjectively perceived risk. Negligence involves an objective assessment of running an objectively recognisable risk.[201]

So the emphasis is on the unreasonableness of the defendant's behaviour. Formally, the defendant is negligent in law if a reasonable person in the same circumstances: (a) would have been aware of the risks of doing the actus reus; and (b) would not have run those risks.[202] It does not matter if the defendant herself was unaware of the risks. What counts is that her behaviour falls short of the standard of conduct that we would expect of a reasonable person; that she failed to take reasonable precautions against the harm specified in the actus reus. In general, such cases are *distinctively* negligent (rather than reckless or intentional) because D failed to form beliefs about the risks that she could reasonably have been expected to form (for instance, about V's consent to sexual activity); because she failed to foresee risks that a reasonable person would have foreseen.[203]

[199] For philosophical treatments of this topic, see Sher, *Who Knew?* (2009); Levi, *Consciousness and Moral Responsibility* (2014); Shiffrin, "The Moral Neglect of Negligence" (2017) 3 *Oxford Studies in Political Philosophy* 197.

[200] Williams in Fitzpatrick and Williams, "Carelessness, Indifference and Recklessness: Two Replies" (1962) 25 *MLR* 49, 57.

[201] This proposition will be qualified below, in § 5.5(ii).

[202] Note that this is a statement of the contemporary doctrinal position in English criminal law. In criminal theory, accounts of criminal negligence are more complicated. See Stark, *Culpable Carelessness* (2016) chaps. 7–8.

[203] For consideration of defendants who *forget* about the risks attendant upon their conduct prior to unleashing them, see Husak, "Negligence, Belief, Blame and Criminal Liability: The Special Case of Forgetting" (2011) 5 *Crim Law and Philosophy* 199.

*(a) Ordinary or gross negligence?*

The criminal law knows two types of negligence: "ordinary" negligence and "gross" negligence. Each of these standards can be imposed by the law either explicitly or implicitly. One example of an offence implicitly requiring ordinary negligence is that of driving without due care and attention, contrary to section 3 of the Road Traffic Act 1988. D commits an offence by making an error while driving that "falls below what would be expected of a competent and careful driver";[204] in other words, by driving in a manner which involves a risk of harm that the reasonable person would regard as unjustifiable to take. A standard of ordinary negligence may also be imported indirectly: an example is section 21 of the Food Safety Act 1990, which introduces a defence of "due diligence" for offences under that Act. Alternatively, there may be a direct reference to the reasonableness of D's mental state: in rape, and other sexual offences, it is sufficient that D "does not reasonably believe" that V consents.[205] In these cases, it is enough that D has failed to exercise a reasonable level of care in forming beliefs about V's consent. This is a form of negligence.

Sometimes, however, the mens rea of an offence cannot be satisfied by anything less than gross negligence. For example, the Road Traffic Act 1988 also contains the offence of dangerous driving, which is committed by a defendant if:[206]

(a) the way he drives falls far below what would be expected of a competent and careful driver, and
(b) it would be obvious to a competent and careful driver that driving in that way would be dangerous.

The standard is that of gross rather than ordinary negligence. The difference between the two is a matter of degree and judgement in each case. Broadly speaking, negligence will be gross if the defendant's conduct not merely fails to meet the standard set by the reasonable-person test, but falls short of that standard by a considerable margin—i.e. if the defendant's conduct is not merely unreasonable, but *very* unreasonable:[207]

> "in order to establish criminal liability the facts must be such that, in the opinion of the jury, the negligence of the accused went beyond a mere matter of compensation between subjects and showed such disregard for the life and safety of others as to amount to a crime against the State and conduct deserving punishment."

It may be negligent to drive around a particular bend at 50 mph; if so, it is likely to be grossly negligent to do so at 80 mph. Hart puts the test another way: "Negligence is gross if the precautions to be taken against harm are very simple, such as persons who are but poorly endowed with physical and mental capacities can easily take."[208]

At common law, a conviction for manslaughter may be predicated on gross negligence. One example is provided by *Adomako*.[209] D, an anaesthetist, was attending an operation when the tube supplying oxygen to the patient became dislodged. D failed to notice the

204 Road Traffic Act 1988, s. 3ZA. See, also, *Simpson v Peat* [1952] 2 QB 24, 27 (DC).
205 See below, § 12.5.
206 Road Traffic Act 1988, s. 2A.
207 *Bateman* (1927) 19 Cr App R 8, 11–12. In manslaughter, this is a demanding standard: *Sellu* [2016] EWCA Crim 1716, [2017] 4 WLR 64, [144]–[155].
208 *Punishment and Responsibility* (1968) 149.
209 [1995] 1 AC 171.

signs of disconnection, in consequence of which the patient, some nine minutes later, suffered cardiac arrest and subsequently died. D was convicted of manslaughter, on the footing that his failure to notice and remedy the problem was a gross dereliction of the standard of care that may reasonably be expected from a competent anaesthetist.

*(b) Emergency*

One of the features of *Adomako* was that the situation was urgent: the defendant, in his own testimony, stated that "after things went wrong I think I did panic a bit".[210] The test of negligence has sometimes been criticised for being insensitive to circumstances, and for assessing emergency decision-making in the cold light of the courtroom. Jeremy Horder has argued that in such situations we should not demand clinical accuracy, and that legitimate emotions such as fear and compassion, which sometimes lead us to make mistakes, are not properly allowed for by the orthodox test of negligence.[211] But this underestimates the legal test. We usually excuse a prima facie "negligent" mistake because it was not unreasonable *in the circumstances*. Although the evaluation of a defendant's conduct is done in a courtroom, in each case it must be done in the light of the defendant's particular circumstances and of normal social and personal values—including those of compassion and self-preservation. This is why it is sometimes reasonable to get things wrong.[212] The law does make allowance for emergencies: as Holmes J once noted, "detached reflection cannot be demanded in the presence of an uplifted knife".[213] A nice illustration of this principle is given in *Simpson v Peat*:[214]

> "Suppose a driver is confronted with a sudden emergency through no fault of his own; in an endeavour to avert a collision he swerves to his right—it is shown that had he swerved to the left the accident would not have happened: that is being wise after the event and, if the driver was in fact exercising the degree of care and attention which a reasonably prudent driver would exercise, he ought not to be convicted, even though another and perhaps more highly skilled driver would have acted differently."

Horder claims that negligence in such cases "is not culpable". But if it is not culpable, this will be because the conduct involved is in the circumstances reasonable and, accordingly, not negligent at all.

### *(ii) Does the reasonable person share any of the defendant's characteristics?*

The tests of negligence that we have identified seem at first blush to be objective.[215] We complain of the defendant's *conduct*, and decide that she was negligent simply by determining that her conduct does not match a standard of behaviour that would have been acceptable in the circumstances. The same approach can be taken with regard to the defendant's beliefs. However, if negligence truly is a measure of culpability, there would seem to be a problem

[210] [1995] 1 AC 171, 182.

[211] "Cognition, Emotion and Criminal Culpability" (1990) 106 *LQR* 469, 482. Compare Williams, "Offences and Defences" (1982) 2 *LS* 233, 242. See also Merry and McCall-Smith, *Errors, Medicine and the Law* (2001) 58–64.

[212] As Bernard Williams notes: *Ethics and the Limits of Philosophy* (1985) 185.

[213] *Brown v US* 256 US 335, 343 (1921). More prosaically, see *Wood v Richards* (1977) 65 Cr App R 300; also Williams, *TBCL* 90.

[214] [1952] 2 QB 24, 28 (DC).

[215] Contrast Moran, *Rethinking the Reasonable Person* (2003).

with this approach. In other categories of mens rea, the defendant is blameworthy because she *knowingly* does (or risks doing) the wrong thing—not merely because her behaviour is wrong. But that ground of fault cannot apply here. In negligence, the law says that the defendant *should* have done whatever the reasonable person would have done, and should have foreseen what the reasonable person would have foreseen: but why? Why should the defendant be regarded as blameworthy, and attract the odium of criminal culpability, just because her behaviour causes some harm that she did not foresee?

The law's response is to assume that the reasonable-person test incorporates the requirements of blame. If the defendant's conduct is objectively unreasonable, then it manifests a failing on the part of the defendant for which she may properly be blamed. Putting things the other way around, had she not been deserving of blame, her behaviour (and, by implication, her belief-formation processes) would not have failed the reasonable-person test.

Most of the time this is a satisfactory answer. For example, if D had been a properly attentive and caring parent, she would not have left her child unattended by the swimming pool—we may hold her negligent, and blame her, for doing so where a reasonable parent would not. And the fact that D was not a naturally caring parent is no excuse! But not every case is so straightforward. What if D is in some way distinctive? Suppose, for example, that D fails to observe a child climbing into the pool. A normal person would have seen the child. Is D negligent? Perhaps not, if D is blind. The example suggests that, although the reasonable-person test is mostly independent of the particular defendant, it is not entirely so. We do not expect D to behave as if she were sighted, but rather as a reasonable blind person would.

Generally speaking, the law states that behaviour is negligent if it involves a failure to exercise that "care and caution which a reasonable and prudent person ordinarily would exercise under like conditions or circumstances".[216] But what exactly is meant by the "reasonable and prudent person"? The illustration above suggests that we do not replace the defendant altogether with objective characteristics, otherwise the youngest child would receive no allowance for immaturity,[217] and the blind would be expected to see.[218] *Smith, Hogan, and Ormerod*, however, considers it to be orthodoxy that where D has less capacity for foresight than the reasonable person, this will not generally help him.[219] Similarly, asked "What if the defendant is substandard in abilities?", Williams responds, "The reasonable man is not imagined to be substandard in intelligence or foresight."[220]

We disagree. The test is mostly objective, but it can, if properly and sensitively applied, be in part subjective.[221] As a minimum, the test should comprise a reasonable person of

[216] *Cordas v Peerless Transportation Co* 27 NYS 2d 198, 4 Am LR 2d 147 (1941).

[217] An allowance that is made under current law: *R (on the application of The Royal Society for the Prevention of Cruelty to Animals) v C* [2006] EWHC 1069 (Admin). Cf., in tort, Gray, "The Standard of Care for Children Revisited" (1980) 45 *Missouri LR* 597; Shulman, "The Standard of Care Required of Children" (1928) 37 *Yale LJ* 618. See e.g. *McHale v Watson* (1966) 115 CLR 199; *Yorkton Agricultural Assoc v Morley* (1967) 66 DLR (2d) 37. Compare *DPP v Camplin* [1978] AC 705, 718 (Lord Diplock) (provocation).

[218] Compare, in tort law, *Bernard v Russell* 164 A 2d 577 (1960); *Keith v Worcester St R.R.* 82 NE 680 (1907); *Balcom v City of Independence* 160 NW 305 (1921). See Weisiger, "Negligence of the Physically Infirm" (1946) 24 *NCLR* 187; James, "The Qualities of the Reasonable Man in Negligence Cases" (1951) 16 *Missouri LR* 1, 17–22; Lowry, "The Blind and the Law of Tort" (1972) 20 *Chittys LJ* 253.

[219] *Smith, Hogan, and Ormerod* § 4.1.2.2.

[220] *TBCL* 94.

[221] For an account of the reasonable person that would incorporate *all* of the defendant's subjective characteristics except for her individual level of respect for the values involved in the relevant offence, see Westen, "Individualizing the Reasonable Person in Criminal Law" (2008) 2 *Crim Law and Philosophy* 137.

the same age and gender as the defendant's, to the extent that such matters are relevant.[222] These are, after all, not distinctive features in any way: they are ordinary qualities that we all have. Beyond this, in our view the reasonable person should be endowed with any peculiar physical characteristic of the defendant—including sight and hearing.[223] If his colleague's electrocution could have been avoided simply by throwing the mains switch, D is not negligent if he fails to do so because he is a person with paraplegia. Similarly, it would be bizarre to require a blind person to see, or even to behave as if sighted. She ought to behave like a reasonable blind person.[224]

Sometimes this approach can work against the defendant. If she has *additional* knowledge, over and above that which a reasonable person would possess, she should be held to the standard of that extra knowledge.[225] Thus a driver with exceptionally good vision should be expected to avoid the cyclist she notices ahead of her even if drivers with normal vision would not see that cyclist in time. And a professional, acting in a professional capacity,[226] will be judged by the standard of a reasonably skilful and competent practitioner;[227] not by the standard of a layperson.

In what other ways is the reasonable-person test to be influenced by facts about the particular defendant? Often, we can accommodate the defendant's personal situation by asking what a reasonable person, *in the circumstances of the defendant*, would have perceived (and done).[228] Within that rubric, the reasonable person may be taken to have the same levels of training, experience and knowledge that are possessed by the defendant herself. In *Price*,[229] for example, in the context of a prosecution under the Armed Forces Act 2006, the Court of Appeal held that D's conduct was to be measured against that of a reasonable serviceman with D's (lack of) training, knowledge and experience. The Court's approach sets the standard of a reasonable person who is placed in the same position as the defendant. Moreover, it remains fundamentally objective, in as much as it takes no cognisance of the defendant's own lack of skill,[230] or indeed of her above-average skill.[231]

*Price* involved a specialist field of activity (namely, overseeing the handling of machine guns by other soldiers). In that sense, it resembles other specialist activities such as, say,

[222] *RSPCA v C* [2006] EWHC 1069 (Admin). See too Ashworth, *Positive Obligations in the Criminal Law* (2013) 193–4.

[223] Cp. *S.A. Ambulance v Waldheim* (1948) 77 CLR 215.

[224] *Smith, Hogan, and Ormerod* asserts (§ 4.1.2.2) that "it is doubtful that the courts would entertain such a radical qualification of the objective standard" as to accommodate "characteristics such as age, hearing, sight, cognitive capacity, etc." The difficult case of intellectual limitations is discussed below. But the claim that, say, a blind person would be expected by the law to see is a serious error, both morally and legally. It is not true even in tort: see n. 218 above.

[225] Cp. *Lamb* [1967] 2 QB 981 (CA); *Haynes v Swain* [1975] RTR 40 (DC); *Gossett* [1993] 3 SCR 76, 96–9; Road Traffic Act 1988, s. 3ZA(3).

[226] This constraint may not apply in tort: *McComiskey v McDermott* [1974] IR 75.

[227] *Bateman* (1927) 19 Cr App R 8, 12–13; *Adomako* [1995] 1 AC 171, 188 (Lord Mackay LC). As will be noted in the next paragraph, the standard is also sensitive to D's level of training and experience.

[228] For an argument regarding this being a "hopeless" test to use in the context of the criminal law, see King, "Against Personifying the Reasonable Person" (2017) 11 *Crim Law and Philosophy* 725.

[229] *Price* [2014] EWCA Crim 229, [2014] 1 WLR 3501 (C-MAC).

[230] *Ibid*., [20].

[231] See, e.g., *Bannister* [2009] EWCA Crim 1571, [2010] 1 WLR 870, where D argued (unsuccessfully) that his driving skills meant it would not be negligent for him to take risks that it would undeniably be negligent for someone without his training to take. As was noted in the previous paragraph, where D is acting in a professional capacity she will be held to the average standard of skills expected from a reasonably competent practitioner. This applies even if D's own abilities are *above* that average: hence the rule for skills differs from that for knowledge.

operating a crane. It could hardly be an answer for D to say, "I'm sorry, but I am just a bad crane operator." To permit such a response would undermine the law's regulatory role. Thus we can summarise the position for professionals or other specialists as follows: the specialist, acting in a specialist capacity, is held to the standard of a reasonably competent specialist with D's level of training and experience, blessed with any additional knowledge that D happens to have.

Yet does that mean we should disregard the defendant's own capacities *altogether*, even in non-specialist activities? In order to answer that question, consider why we would expect the apparently "objective" standard in negligence to be affected by a defendant's physical limitations. The reason is that to convict a blind person for failing to see would be wrong and unfair. The blind do not deserve blame for failing to see. This, it is submitted, is the right way to approach the question of objectivity in negligence. The reasonable-person test should be objective to the extent that the defendant's shortcomings disclose fault. This principle can, of course, work against the defendant. For instance, a voluntarily intoxicated defendant should not be held to the standard of conduct of the "reasonable drunk person". Neither does the criminal law know "a reasonable selfish person". Conversely, however, the reasonable-person test should be *subjective* to the extent that the defendant's shortcomings do *not* disclose fault. Consider a failing for which an abnormal defendant should not be blamed: intelligence. Regard the facts of *Elliott v C (a minor)*.[232] C, a 14-year-old girl of low intelligence, had wandered away from home and spent the night outdoors without sleep before ending up in a garden shed. There she found some white spirit, which she poured onto the floor and ignited by dropping lighted matches on it. The shed was destroyed in the ensuing fire, and C was charged with arson (i.e., criminal damage by fire). Although someone without C's disability would no doubt have appreciated the risk of burning down the shed, it was found as a fact that the risk would not have been obvious to a person of her limited capacities, even if she had stopped to think about it.[233] Under the objective, *Caldwell*-based test of recklessness prevailing at the time, C was convicted of criminal damage.[234] But this seems to us highly problematic. It is submitted that to regard her even as having destroyed the shed *negligently* would be wrong.

That having been said, it is not clear whether the criminal law currently makes any allowance for low intelligence when assessing negligence. Academic argument favours taking account of personal incapacities. H.L.A. Hart proposed a general precondition for criminal liability of the form, "*could* the accused, given his mental and physical capacities have taken [the required] precautions?"[235] Although the Canadian Supreme Court has approved a similar requirement,[236] there is *obiter dicta* from the High Court of Australia endorsing an objective test, one that disregards individual capacities.[237] In England there is little relevant legal authority. The suggestion of a test like Hart's may be found in *Hudson*,[238] where the

232 [1983] 1 WLR 939 (DC).

233 *Ibid.*, 945 ("in the circumstances this risk [that the shed would be destroyed] would not have been obvious to her or appreciated by her if she had given thought to the matter").

234 By application of the *Caldwell* definition of recklessness, now reversed by the House of Lords in *G*: above, § 5.2(i)(a)–(b).

235 *Punishment and Responsibility* (1968) 154. See also Simester, "Can Negligence Be Culpable?" in Horder (ed.), *Oxford Essays in Jurisprudence* (Fourth Series, 2000) 85.

236 *Creighton* [1993] 3 SCR 3.

237 *Lavender* [2005] HCA 37, (2005) 222 CLR 67, [128].

238 [1966] 1 QB 448 (CA). See also *Hardie* [1985] 1 WLR 64 (CA).

defendant was charged with the former offence of having "sexual intercourse with a woman who is a defective".[239] It was a defence to this charge that the defendant "[did] not know and [had] no reason to suspect [the woman] to be a defective". In adjudicating the defence, the court was prepared to consider the limitations of the particular defendant:[240]

> "There may be cases, of which this is not one, where there is evidence before the jury that the accused himself is a person of limited intelligence, or possibly suffering from some handicap [*sic*] which would prevent him from appreciating the state of affairs which an ordinary man might realise."

Similarly, low intelligence was considered by the Court of Appeal in *Wawrzyniak* to be relevant to the question whether D used appropriate force in the context of perceived necessity.[241] By contrast, subjective allowances were excluded by the Divisional Court in *Elliott v C* (above),[242] where C was held to have acted recklessly on the *Caldwell* standard because the risk was obvious to a reasonable adult. An objective standard of negligence has also been applied in the context of causing unnecessary suffering to animals and failing to ensure their welfare,[243] notwithstanding that (as in *Elliott v C*) the offences were imprisonable. The Court of Appeal also excluded the defendant's schizophrenia in *C (Sean Peter)*,[244] when determining whether, under section 1(2) of the Protection from Harassment Act 1997, a reasonable person would think that threatening letters sent by the defendant to his local MP amounted to harassment.[245] Similarly, in *B*, delusional beliefs arising from a schizophrenic disorder were excluded, *obiter*, from the range of reasonable beliefs in consent under section 1 of the Sexual Offences Act 2003: "A delusional belief in consent, if entertained, would be by definition irrational and thus *un*reasonable, not reasonable".[246]

Notably, however, the Court of Appeal in *B* restricted its analysis to cases where the defendant's belief was irrational, arising from delusional personality disorders and the like. By contrast:[247]

> "It does not follow that there will not be cases in which the personality or abilities of the defendant may be relevant to whether his positive belief in consent was reasonable. It may be that cases could arise in which the reasonableness of such belief depends on the reading by the defendant of subtle social signals, and in which his impaired ability to do so is relevant to

[239] *Sic*: contrary to the (now-repealed) Sexual Offences Act 1956, s. 7, as amended by s. 127 of the Mental Health Act 1959.

[240] [1966] 1 QB 448, 455 (CA).

[241] [2017] EWCA Crim 2008. D wrongly thought that shaking his baby was the best way to save her life after she stopped breathing.

[242] [1983] 1 WLR 939 (DC), above, § 5.2(i); also *R (Stephen)* (1984) 79 Cr App R 334; *Stone and Dobinson* [1977] QB 354 (CA); *Ward* [1956] 1 QB 351 (CA).

[243] Contrary to ss. 4, 9 of the Animal Welfare Act 2006—see *R. (Gray) v The Crown Court Aylesbury* [2013] EWHC 500 (Admin), [2014] 1 WLR 818.

[244] [2001] EWCA Crim 1251. See also below, § 11.10. The decision is perhaps explicable on policy grounds specific to the statute (at [18]–[19]): "The conduct at which the Act is aimed, and from which it seeks to provide protection, is particularly likely to be conduct pursued by those of obsessive or otherwise unusual psychological make-up and very frequently by those suffering from an identifiable mental illness. . . . We are satisfied that to give the Act the construction for which [counsel] contends would be to remove from its protection a very large number of victims and indeed to run the risk of significantly thwarting the purpose of the Act."

[245] A similarly hard line with regard to schizophrenia was adopted in the tort case, *Dunnage v Randall* [2015] EWCA Civ 673, [2016] QB 639.

[246] *B* [2013] EWCA Crim 3, [2013] 1 Cr App R 36, [35].

[247] *Ibid.*, [41]. Cp. *Jacobs* [2023] EWCA Crim 1503, [2024] 1 Cr App R 13.

> the reasonableness of his belief. We do not attempt exhaustively to foresee the circumstances which might arise in which a belief might be held which is not in any sense irrational, even though most people would not have held it. Whether (for example) a particular defendant of less than ordinary intelligence or with demonstrated inability to recognise behavioural cues might be such a case, or whether his belief ought properly to be characterised as unreasonable, must await a decision on specific facts. It is possible, we think, that beliefs generated by such factors may not properly be described as irrational and might be judged by a jury not to be unreasonable on their particular facts. But once a belief could be judged reasonable only by a process which labelled a plainly irrational belief as reasonable, it is clear that it cannot be open to the jury so to determine without stepping outside the Act."

Even if these decisions can be reconciled, they raise questions that require definitive resolution by the Supreme Court. Moreover, there are signs of a more compassionate approach in some House of Lords decisions. Lord Mackay suggested in *Adomako* that gross negligence involves conduct so bad that it may be characterised as reckless "in the ordinary connotation of that word".[248] In *Elliott v C*, C was surely not "reckless" in ordinary language. There are also *dicta* in *Reid* to the effect that fault should be assessed by reference to the capacities of the particular defendant: Lord Keith made it clear that a defendant should not be liable where his inadvertence is owing to "some condition not involving fault on his part",[249] while Lord Goff referred to "illness or shock",[250] and Lord Browne-Wilkinson to "sudden disability".[251] Subsequently, in *G*, the House of Lords was plainly hostile to the unfairness of convicting of arson "a defendant (least of all a child) on the strength of what someone else would have apprehended".[252] In Lord Steyn's view:[253]

> "it is contrary to art 40(1) [of the United Nations Convention on the Rights of the Child] to ignore in a crime punishable by life imprisonment, or detention during Her Majesty's pleasure, the age of a child in judging whether the mental element has been satisfied. . . . If it is wrong to ignore the special characteristics of children in the context of recklessness under s 1 of the 1971 [Criminal Damage] Act, an adult who suffers from a lack of mental capacity or a relevant personality disorder may be entitled to the same standard of justice. Recognising the special characteristics of children and mentally disabled people goes some way towards reducing the scope of s 1 of the 1971 Act for producing unjust results which are inherent in the objective mould into which the *Caldwell* analysis forced recklessness."

There remains room, therefore, for some optimism that ultimately the approach of the Court of Criminal Appeal in *Hudson* will prevail, at least in the context of low intelligence. As a matter of justice, it is submitted that significantly below-average intelligence *should* be considered when assessing the reasonableness of the defendant's conduct or beliefs.

248 [1995] 1 AC 171, 187. See Gardner, "Manslaughter by Gross Negligence" (1995) 111 *LQR* 22, 23–4.

249 [1992] 1 WLR 793, 796 (HL). But D's paranoid schizophrenia was disregarded by the Court of Appeal in *Colohan* [2001] EWCA Crim 1251, when determining whether D ought to have known that his conduct amounted to harassment contrary to s. 1 of the Protection from Harassment Act 1997. On the other hand, it was said in *Khan* [2009] EWCA Crim 2, [2009] 1 WLR 2036, [33] that the defendant's own vulnerability may be allowed for when determining what can reasonably be expected of *that* defendant in the context of a charge under s. 5(1) of the Domestic Violence, Crime and Victims Act 2004 of allowing the death of a vulnerable adult.

250 [1992] 1 WLR 793, 813 (HL).

251 *Ibid.*, 819.

252 [2003] UKHL 50, [2004] 1 AC 1034, [33] (Lord Bingham).

253 *Ibid.*, [53]–[54].

### *(iii) Negligence with respect to behaviour rather than consequences or circumstances*

As with recklessness, negligence sometimes operates like an actus reus term.[254] It does so when it qualifies the *behavioural* element in the actus reus, as opposed to elements of consequence or circumstance. So, for example, in an offence of careless driving the carelessness—i.e. the negligence—of the driving is not a mens rea term meaning that a reasonable person would (and the defendant should) have realised that he was driving, or even that he was driving in a substandard manner. Rather, it is effectively an actus reus term: meaning that the defendant was driving in a *manner* that fell short of the standard a reasonable person would set. Thus careless driving is a different type of negligence offence from that involved in rape, where the law's concern is not so much with the manner of the defendant's action as with the fact that the defendant proceeded with an unreasonable belief regarding the complainant's consent.

Most of the time the difference will not be important, since even as a mens rea term negligence is assessed by reference to the defendant's conduct. However, it seems that the subjective elements of the reasonable-person test may not apply when negligence is operating as an actus reus standard. Hence in *McCrone v Riding* it was said that the standard of care in driving:[255]

> "is an objective standard, impersonal and universal, fixed in relation to the safety of other users of the highway. It is in no way related to the degree of proficiency or degree of experience to be attained by the individual driver."

In other words, it is irrelevant to assessment of the quality of D's driving that D is a driver of below-average ability, or indeed of above-average ability.[256] This sets an even more stringent standard than the demands made of specialists when negligence operates as a mens rea term: in those cases, account can be taken of D's own levels of training and experience.[257] As we noted in § 5.5(ii), part of the justification for imposing impersonal standards lies in the need for the law to discharge its regulatory functions when governing specialist activities. In the context of driving, the even more objective, actus reus standard of negligence also helps to establish a co-operative regime that other drivers can rely upon. Driving is a voluntary activity, and those who engage in it may be thought to hold themselves out to their fellow drivers as being reasonably competent to do so.

### *(iv) The place of negligence*

A number of writers have argued that people should never be subject to criminal liability on the basis of negligence,[258] and that its place lies properly in the arena of torts and compensation rather than of crimes and punishment. There is force in this argument, since it would

[254] Indeed, Cunningham has argued that "reckless" conduct is in truth negligent conduct: Cunningham, "Recklessness: Being Reckless and Acting Recklessly" (2010) 21 *King's College LJ* 445.

[255] [1938] All ER 157, 158 (DC). See too *Gosney* [1971] 2 QB 674, 680 (CA); *R v Preston Justices, ex p Lyons* [1982] RTR 173 (DC); Wasik, "A Learner's Careless Driving" [1982] *Crim LR* 411.

[256] *Bannister* [2009] EWCA Crim 1571, [2010] 1 WLR 870.

[257] *Price* [2014] EWCA Crim 229, [2014] 1 WLR 3501; above, § 5.5(ii).

[258] Hall, "Negligent Behaviour Should be Excluded from Penal Liability" (1963) 63 *Columbia LR* 632; Turner, "The Mental Element in Crimes at Common Law" in Radzinowicz and Turner (eds.), *The Modern Approach to Criminal Law* (1948) 195, 207–11; Hall, *General Principles of Criminal Law* (2nd ed., 1960) 138. Hart's refutation of Turner's argument is convincing: *Punishment and Responsibility* (1968) chap. 6. More recently, see Alexander and Ferzan, *Crime and Culpability* (2009) chap. 3; Moore and Hurd, "Punishing the Awkward, the Stupid, the Weak, and the Selfish: the Culpability of Negligence" (2011) 5 *Crim Law and Philosophy* 147.

normally be harsh to equate those who do wrong inadvertently with others who break the law intentionally or recklessly. There can also be concerns about fair warning in negligence offences.[259] The person who inadvertently does harm might well have refrained from doing so, had she only realised the risk before acting. But the fact that negligence is often not as bad as recklessness or intention does not mean that it is not culpable at all,[260] or that it is never serious enough to warrant criminalisation. Baker's example is instructive:[261]

> "Carelessly handling loaded firearms in a crowded area, or speeding through a school zone at lunch hour oblivious to the dangers to others because one is absorbed in an interesting conversation, is more culpable . . . than deliberately taking a $0.50 store item without payment or than many other knowing offences against property."

Sometimes, one who knowingly takes the risk of a minor crime is not so deserving of a criminal sanction as another who carelessly risks serious harm. It would be wrong for the criminal law only ever to convict in the former case.

Such instances are properly exceptional, and the law has traditionally been reluctant to inflict serious criminal (rather than civil) sanctions upon people who have merely been negligent. Nonetheless, it would be a mistake to discount the significance of negligence.[262] While not a staple mens rea standard in traditional common-law offences, it has become very important indeed in modern criminal law. Quite apart from setting a key mens rea standard for manslaughter and some other very serious crimes,[263] it does the same for innumerable statutory offences, especially in the context of specialist activities; many of which are imprisonable or allow for very large fines. Negligence also remains very important in the context of defences, both common law and statutory. For example, duress is available only if the defendant's reaction is reasonable, while in many health and safety offences the defendant may be exculpated if found to have taken reasonable precautions against injury or death.[264]

## § 5.6 Other mens rea states

We have mentioned that there is a variety of other mens rea terms used in the criminal law. Some of these, such as "dishonestly",[265] occur primarily in the context of property crimes such as theft, and will be explored in some detail when we come to look at the specific offences. Here, we briefly outline certain other mens rea states.

### *(i) "With a view to"*

The phrase, "with a view to", introduces a form of ulterior intention. A person does X with a view to Y when Y supplies one of the reasons why she does X.[266] Foresight that Y is likely to

[259] See, e.g., Gardner, 'Wrongs and Faults' in Simester (ed.), *Appraising Strict Liability* (2005) 51, 70–2; Simester, *Fundamentals* § 3.3.

[260] See, e.g., Baron, "Negligence, *Mens Rea*, and What We Want the Element to *Mens Rea* to Provide (2020) 14 *Crim Law and Philosophy* 69.

[261] Baker, "Mens Rea, Negligence and Criminal Law Reform" (1987) 6 *Law and Philosophy* 53, 81; see too Leipold, "A Case for Criminal Negligence" (2010) 29 *Law and Philosophy* 455.

[262] See Stark, *Culpable Carelessness* (2016) chap. 8.

[263] Compare, for example, its use in the context of sexual offences: below, § 12.5.

[264] See ss. 2 and 3 of the Health and Safety at Work Act 1974, read together with s. 40 (placing the burden of proof on the defendant).

[265] Below, § 13.8.

[266] *Dooley* [2005] EWCA Crim 3093, [2006] 1 WLR 775, [14].

occur is insufficient.[267] On the other hand, it is not necessary that Y be the ultimate motive, or even the dominant objective, behind the doing of X.[268] It is enough that it be *one* of the objectives or intentions with which X is done.

To make this less abstract, consider the offence regarding the taking of indecent photographs of children under section 1 of the Protection of Children Act 1978. D commits an offence if (*inter alia*) he has "in his possession . . . indecent photographs . . . with a view to their being distributed or shown by himself or others".[269] The future possibility of showing the photographs to other people (Y) must be part of D's reason for having them in his possession (X). D may also intend to look at the picture himself later—such an intention is not incompatible with his being convicted of the offence, so long as he also has them in order to be able to show them to another person. If, however, D merely thinks it is possible that he will show the pictures to others, he does not commit the offence.

As such, the phrase "with a view to" is cognate to (future) intention rather than recklessness, and overlaps considerably with "with an intention to". It goes beyond intention, however, in that there is no requirement for any crystallized intention to be formed by D. It is enough if, for example, X is done *in case* Y will later be sought. Thus the phrase is apt to capture preparatory conduct such as taking certain preliminary steps (X) in readiness for the possibility of later pursuing an unlawful objective (Y), an objective that D is still undecided upon.

### *(ii) Wilfulness*

Historically, the case law regarding the meaning of "wilfulness" was inconsistent.[270] Fortunately, its meaning has been clarified over time, beginning with the House of Lords' decision in *Sheppard*.[271] The defendants in that case were charged with wilfully neglecting their young child.[272] They had failed to ensure adequate medical care for the child, but apparently had not realised how ill he was. At trial, the judge directed the jury that wilful neglect was established if a reasonable parent would have appreciated the danger to the child in the same circumstances. On appeal, the House of Lords quashed the defendants' convictions. Wilfulness in such circumstances, it was held, requires either a deliberate decision to neglect the child, by refraining from calling a doctor when it is known that a doctor is needed; or a failure to call the doctor because the defendant does not care whether the child may need a medical examination. In essence, this meant that wilfulness was akin to being a form of objective recklessness, and was satisfied if the defendant either consciously disregarded the child's needs or ignored those needs because he was indifferent to the child's welfare.

The link between wilfulness and recklessness was perhaps not surprising in a decision handed down only a few months before *Caldwell* (discussed in § 5.1(i)(a)). More recently,

[267] Whether this holds if Y is seen as virtually certain was left open in *ibid.*, [17].
[268] Cp. *J. Lyons and Sons v Wilkins* [1899] 1 Ch 255, 269; *Bevans* (1988) 87 Cr App R 64.
[269] Protection of Children Act 1978, s. 1(1)(c).
[270] Andrews, "Wilfulness: A Lesson in Ambiguity" (1981) 1 *LS* 303, 315–22.
[271] [1981] AC 394.
[272] The context was therefore one of omission rather than positive act. But the reasoning did not turn on this distinction, and it seems that nothing is to be made of it: *Daniels* [2008] EWCA Crim 2360, [15], [21].

however, wilfulness has become restricted to situations where the defendant actually foresees the risk of the prohibited outcome. Thus it is now more akin to subjective recklessness. In *A-G's Reference (No. 3 of 2003)*, the Court of Appeal asserted that the principles behind the rejection of *Caldwell* in *G* (discussed above) applied to wilfulness too:[273]

> "We do not accept the submission that *Sheppard* imposes a lower duty on the prosecution than does *G*. Indeed, we do not accept the submission that, in the present context, there is any material difference between them and, in our view, the approach to recklessness in *G* can be incorporated into a direction on wilfulness in relation to this offence."

Subsequent decisions confirm that wilfulness now requires intention or subjective recklessness.[274] Indeed, support for the subjectivist reading can be found in *Sheppard* itself, where, according to Lord Keith:[275]

> "The primary meaning of 'wilful' is 'deliberate'. So a parent who knows that his child needs medical care and deliberately, that is by conscious decision, refrains from calling a doctor, is guilty under the subsection. As a matter of general principle, recklessness is to be equiparated with deliberation."

Lord Keith's analogy with deliberateness does, however, raise a question. Recklessness, we saw earlier, requires that the occurrence of the actus reus be an unreasonable risk for the defendant to take. Is it possible that "wilfully", like "deliberately", imports no such requirement? If so, a surgeon who carries out a risky yet medically justified operation might be said to injure her patient wilfully, even though she is not reckless. It is submitted, however, that in the context of the criminal law "wilfully" should bear the more restricted meaning, i.e. of subjective recklessness. The defendant who, without intending the actus reus, takes a reasonable risk of bringing that actus about should not be regarded as having brought it about wilfully. In short, wilfully, nowadays means intentionally or with subjective recklessness. As will be seen in the next section, the same conclusion has been reached with regard to "malice".

### *(iii) Malice*

Many older statutes use the term "maliciously" when specifying crimes. Section 48 of the Malicious Damage Act 1861, for instance, provides that "whosoever shall unlawfully and maliciously cut away, cast adrift, remove, alter, deface, sink, or destroy . . . any boat, buoy, buoy rope, perch, or mark used or intended for the guidance of seamen" commits an offence imprisonable for up to seven years. It is settled law that "maliciously" comprises intention or subjective, *Cunningham* recklessness.[276] Inadvertence, even *Caldwell* recklessness, will

[273] [2004] EWCA Crim 868, [2005] QB 73, [27]. See above, § 5.2(i)(b).

[274] *Emma W* [2006] EWCA Crim 2723; *D* [2008] EWCA Crim 2360; *Patel* [2013] EWCA Crim 965; *Turbill* [2013] EWCA Crim 1422, [2014] 1 Cr App R 7. Some earlier case law also supports a subjective interpretation of wilfulness, including *Holroyd* (1841) 2 M & Rob 339, 174 ER 308; *Eaton v Cobb* [1950] 1 All ER 1016 (DC); *Bullock v Turnbull* [1952] 2 Lloyd's Rep 303 (DC); *Wilmott v Attack* [1977] QB 498 (DC); *Ostler v Elliott* [1980] Crim LR 584 (DC). Contrast *Cotterill v Penn* [1936] 1 KB 53 (DC), rightly criticised by Andrews, "Wilfulness: A Lesson in Ambiguity" (1981) 1 *LS* 303, 319–20; *McPherson* [1980] Crim LR 654 (Crown Court (Leicester)), criticised in a letter to the editor by Williams, [1981] *Crim LR* 796.

[275] [1981] AC 394, 418.

[276] *Cunningham* [1957] 2 QB 396, 399 (CA); *Savage; Parmenter* [1992] 1 AC 699; Williams, *CLGP* 72–5; Turner, *Kenny's Outlines of Criminal Law* (16th ed., 1952) 186.

not do. On the other hand, there is no requirement that D's actions must be accompanied by "malice" in the ordinary sense of that term (i.e. by animosity or spite).[277] A choice to run a foreseen (and unreasonable) risk of the relevant outcome, or an intention to bring it about, is sufficient.

One special case is section 20 of the OAPA 1861, which provides that "whosoever shall unlawfully and maliciously wound or inflict any grievous bodily harm upon any other person" commits an offence. Although it is clear that "maliciously" in section 20 requires subjective foresight of harm, *how severe* the harm the must be foreseen remains controversial, and the courts have accepted that D need not foresee a wounding or grievous bodily harm.[278] The rule makes a crucial part of the offence—the occurrence of an injury more serious than mere bodily harm—effectively a matter of strict liability. Furthermore, given the distance between what must be foreseen and what must occur for the offence to be made out, this interpretation of section 20 is not justifiable as an example of constructive liability (a concept discussed below in § 6.5). Quite apart from distorting the meaning of "maliciously", such a departure from principle[279] is particularly undesirable in the context of a serious crime like that in section 20. Fortunately, the definition of malice has not suffered from similar judicial creativity when appearing in other offences.

### *(iv) Possession*

Although primarily an actus reus term,[280] "possession" typically imports into the offence a concomitant mental ingredient. The leading decision, at least in the context of drug offences, is *Warner*.[281] D was convicted of unauthorised possession of a controlled drug, contrary to section 1 of the (now-repealed) Misuse of Drugs Act 1964, after being found with a box containing 20,000 amphetamine tablets. He claimed that he had thought the box contained scent. The House of Lords upheld his conviction. Although a *ratio decidendi* is difficult to distil from the judgments, it appears that a majority of their Lordships were prepared to accept that the mens rea of possession requires only that D should know he is in possession of *something*, provided the something he thinks he possesses is not completely different from the thing he actually has. In other words, D need not know the precise nature of the material he possesses, so long as he knows that he has control of *it*. Thus, if D had thought the box was empty, he would not have been in possession of its contents—yet since, on the facts, he thought it contained scent, he had sufficient mens rea to be in possession of

[277] *Solanke* [1970[1 WLR 1 (CA). Neither is it required that the risk foreseen be "obvious and significant": *Brady* [2006] EWCA Crim 2413.

[278] Cp. *Mowatt* [1968] 1 QB 421 (CA); *Savage; Parmenter* [1992] 1 AC 699; *Rushworth* (1992) 95 Cr App R 252 (some harm); a higher standard is required in *ML* [2018] EWCA Crim 2536, [19]: "the accused must either have intended or harm foreseen that his unlawful act . . . might cause physical harm of the gravity implicit in a section 20 offence". The offence is discussed in detail below, § 11.5.

[279] Cf. "the ordinary principle that, where it is required that an offence should have been knowingly committed, the requisite knowledge must embrace all the elements of the offence": *Westminster City Council v Croyalgrange Ltd* [1985] 1 All ER 740, 744 (DC) (affirmed in [1986] 1 WLR 674 (HL)).

[280] Above, § 4.1(ii)(b).

[281] [1969] 2 AC 256; cp. *McNamara* (1988) 87 Cr App R 246. Amongst earlier cases, see *Southern* (1821) R & R 444, 168 ER 889; *Woodrow* (1846) 15 M & W 404, 153 ER 907; *Pearson* (1908) 1 Cr App R 77.

the drugs (because scent, apparently, is not sufficiently different from drugs). Lord Pearce summarised the law as follows:[282]

> "I think that the term 'possession' is satisfied by a knowledge only of the existence of the thing itself and not its qualities, and that ignorance or mistake as to its qualities is not an excuse. This would comply with the general understanding of the word 'possess'. Though I reasonably believe the tablet which I possess to be aspirin, yet if they turn out to be heroin I am in possession of heroin tablets. This would be so I think even if I believed them to be sweets."

Where the contraband is not in a container, the rule is the same. Suppose that a stranger plants a cannabis cigarette in D's handbag or car, without D's knowledge. According to *Warner*, D would lack the mental element required to be in possession of the cannabis: "if someone surreptitiously puts something into my pocket, I am not in possession of it until I know it is there".[283]

A similar approach has been adopted in other contexts, but with degrees of stringency that vary across those contexts. For instance, with regard to the offence of "conveying" prohibited items into or out of prison,[284] D must know that she has control of *something prohibited* with her, even if she is not aware of its precise nature, let alone its precise classification under the relevant legislation.[285] The result is a narrower mens rea standard than that found in *Warner*. The approach in *Warner* was, however, significantly broadened in *Tinarwo*,[286] in the context of a charge of possessing a prohibited firearm. D was in possession of a bag, which contained a prohibited firearm, but claimed that the firearm had been planted without his knowledge. It was concluded that:[287]

> "The effect of the authorities is that ignorance of the contents of a bag of which a person is in possession can afford no defence where the contents include a firearm. It makes no difference whether there is something in the bag that the carrier is unaware of, or is mistaken to its nature, or does not know that the bag has any contents, far less that it contains a gun. In each case the question for the jury for consideration relates to possession, which in turn depends on control."

D's conviction was, accordingly, safe—even if his planting story were true. This is a startling conclusion, which the Court of Appeal recognised may be thought to be "harsh".[288] Responsibility for addressing any deficiency here rests, the Court concluded, with Parliament.

As well as being applied inconsistently, the rule in *Warner* is also subject to certain qualifications. First, even though D does not realise he is in physical possession of something, he will nevertheless be in legal possession if he invited receipt of the thing. In *Peaston*,[289] D ordered a delivery of amphetamines, which arrived in the post. He was held to be in possession

[282] [1969] 2 AC 256, 305. Lord Pearce's subsequent qualification, that "it would be otherwise if I believed them to be something of a wholly different nature", is hard to justify and has not been observed in subsequent cases: *Marriott* [1971] 1 WLR 187 (CA); *McNamara* (1988) 87 Cr App R 246.

[283] [1969] 2 AC 256, 299 (Lord Guest). Cp. *ibid.*, 305 (Lord Pearce); *Ashton-Rickhardt* [1978] 1 WLR 37 (CA); *Irving* [1970] Crim LR 642 (CA); *Cugullere* [1961] 1 WLR 858 (CA) ("having with him an offensive weapon").

[284] Prison Act 1952, ss. 40B, 40C.

[285] *Johnson* [2017] EWCA Crim 189, [2018] 1 WLR 19.

[286] [2014] EWCA Crim 1409.

[287] *Ibid.*, [12].

[288] *Ibid.*, [13].

[289] (1979) 69 Cr App R 203.

of the drugs as soon as the envelope was delivered through his letterbox, even though he was not yet aware it had arrived.

Secondly, certain passages in *Warner* suggest that as well as knowing one is in possession of something, one must also have had a right or opportunity to discover the nature of that thing, e.g. (in *Warner* itself) by opening the box. Lord Morris characterised possession as "being knowingly in control of a thing in circumstances which have involved an opportunity (whether availed of or not) to learn or to discover, at least in a general way, what the thing is".[290] This additional requirement became redundant when the Misuse of Drugs Act 1971, section 28, enacted a defence that the defendant neither believed, suspected, nor had reason to suspect that the thing in his possession was a controlled drug; it was abandoned by the Court of Appeal in *McNamara*.[291] However, in *Lewis*,[292] the requirement was resurrected, not as a necessary (i.e. exculpatory) condition of possession, but as a sufficient (i.e. inculpatory) one. The Court of Appeal held in that case that the sole tenant of a house may be in possession of drugs found there even though he visited the house infrequently and did not know they were on the premises, provided he had an opportunity to find out that they were present. The decision is unfortunate and should not be followed. It seriously misconstrues Lord Morris's words by turning a dual requirement, for knowledge of the thing's being within his physical custody (whatever it might be) *and* opportunity to discover its nature, into *alternative* inculpatory tests, of knowledge *or* opportunity to discover the drug.

By now, it may be apparent that *Warner* is a deeply problematic decision. Unfortunately, the section under which D was charged contained no explicit mens rea requirement. With the exception of Lord Reid, who was prepared to imply a requirement for mens rea into the offence as a whole, their Lordships therefore saw themselves as constrained to choose between the options of: (i) making drug possession a no-fault, strict liability, offence; or (ii) implying a mental ingredient into the term "possession" itself. The House resorted to a fictional, artificial, construction rather than face squarely the true source of the difficulty, i.e. the absence of an express mens rea element in the statute. Smith's analysis encapsulates the problem nicely:[293]

> "The difficulty arises because possession has become the criterion of guilt, yet possession is a neutral concept, not involving blame or fault. We shrink from saying that the lady with the shopping basket is in possession of the packet slipped in without her knowledge because it contains controlled drugs. If it were a box of chocolates dropped in by a friend as a birthday present, would any of the judges in *Warner* have hesitated to hold that she was in possession of it? If it were removed by a thief would they have had any doubt that it was stolen from her . . . ? Of course not. So far as the question of possession is concerned, there should be no distinction between the drugs and the chocolates. If the House in *Warner* had followed the lead of Lord Reid, these difficulties would have been largely if not entirely avoided. . . ."

[290] [1969] 2 AC 256, 289.
[291] (1988) 87 Cr App R 246.
[292] (1988) 87 Cr App R 270, criticised in [1988] Crim LR 518–19. An instructive contrast is the language of the otherwise wide-ranging Terrorism Act 2000, s. 57(3): possession is established if the relevant article was either on any premises at the same time as the accused or on premises of which the accused was the occupier or which he habitually used otherwise than as a member of the public *unless* he did not know of its presence on the premises or he had no control over it.
[293] [1988] Crim LR 519.

One clear limitation, at least, on the scope of possession is helpfully articulated in *Kousar*,[294] a valuable counterweight to *Lewis*. D's husband was a market trader who sold counterfeit goods, a large quantity of which were stored in the loft of the matrimonial home. D's conviction under the Trade Marks Act 1994 was quashed. The goods belonged to her husband and were not joint property. D may have known about and acquiesced in their storage, and may have had the *ability* to control the stored goods. But what is necessary for her, as well as her husband, to have possession is that she *exercises* control (or otherwise has personal possession or custody of them). Knowledge is not enough:[295]

> "In the course of argument some discussion was engendered about the normal domestic situation: is a husband or wife to be regarded as in joint possession of items in that house which are in fact the property of the other spouse? Is a husband to be regarded as in possession of clothing and cosmetics, for example, of which his wife is both the owner and the possessor? We venture to suggest that that concept is quite inappropriate. One is not in possession of one's spouse's personal property in that sense. The term 'permission' has been used, that she permitted this property to be in the house. Permission may be something more than an acquiescence but even then is not in our judgment sufficient to render the permittor a person in possession of the goods. In the field of drugs offences, there is a specific offence of permitting premises to be used for certain activities but there is no equivalent in the legislation with which we are concerned. A finding of being able to exercise a measure of control, which is the basis upon which this issue was in due course left to the jury, is not the same as a finding that she did exercise control."

The decision emphasises a long-established point,[296] that merely knowing another person possesses the relevant goods does not suffice to make one personally in possession.

## § 5.7 "Transferring" mens rea

Until now, we have considered situations where the occurrence of the actus reus is straightforwardly aligned with the defendant's mens rea: D intends, and manages, to kill V; D foresees a risk of damaging, and does damage, V's property. What happens when D's actions misfire yet still produce an actus reus? Consider the following example:

> Suppose that Dorit takes aim at Tom with intent to kill him, and pulls the trigger. Just as Dorit shoots, however, Tom bends down to pick a flower. Dorit's shot misses Tom and hits Bill, who was standing behind Tom. Bill is killed instantly.

In this situation Dorit is guilty of murdering Bill, notwithstanding that she did not foresee that possible outcome. The actus reus of murder is to kill a person.[297] Thus, although Dorit intended to kill Tom rather than Bill, she had the mens rea for murder since she intended to kill a person; the identity of that person is immaterial to the definition of the offence.

[294] [2009] EWCA Crim 139, [2009] 2 Cr App R 5.
[295] *Ibid*, [18].
[296] See, e.g., *Searle* [1971] Crim LR 592 (CA).
[297] *Gore* (1611) 9 Co Rep 81, 77 ER 853; *A-G's Reference (No. 3 of 1994)* [1996] QB 581 (CA); *Hopwood* (1913) 8 Cr App R 143.

This type of example is usually said to be governed by the "doctrine" of "transferred malice".[298] This "doctrine" is not confined to murder,[299] or indeed *intention*. Imagine, this time, that Jane bears a grudge against Daniel. She throws a stone at the brickwork of his house, No. 6 King Street. She recognises that the stone may break one of Daniel's windows, although she does not intend it to do so. As it happens, the stone misses the windows of No. 6 but ricochets off the brickwork and breaks Pat's window at No. 8. Jane's recklessness is sufficient mens rea for criminal damage,[300] and it corresponds to the (otherwise unanticipated) result: damage to *Pat's* property.

As well as being "transferred", the defendant's mens rea can also be "recycled". Suppose, for example, that D shoots at V. She misses, but hits and kills T, D can be convicted of T's murder (a "transfer" of mens rea) *and* of V's attempted murder. Accordingly, there is no requirement that the defendant's planned target escapes harm before mens rea can be "transferred". Consider the following example:[301]

> Allan and Gavin's business is haemorrhaging money. They decide to place barrels of petrol in the basement of their business premises, and then start a fire that will destroy the building. They hope to then claim an insurance payment. They are aware that Val, an associate, knows of their plan. Allan and Gavin arrange for Val to be in the premises when the fire starts, intending that she will be killed in the blaze. The fire is more violent than Allan and Gavin expected and causes a large explosion. Val is killed, and so are the family in the flat above the business premises.

Allan and Gavin did not intend to kill or cause serious bodily harm to the family in the "core" sense of (direct) intention discussed above in § 5.1: their plan would not have failed if the family had survived. Neither did they believe that it was virtually certain that the family would be killed or seriously injured as a result of the fire. Indeed, they may have been entirely ignorant of the family's presence. There is, however, no difficulty in convicting Allan and Gavin of the family's murder. Allan and Gavin intended to kill a human being (Val), and that will satisfy the mens rea requirement for murder in relation to any and all deaths caused by the fire.

It has been objected that such results grossly inflate the defendant's culpability beyond retributive limits, and unfairly label the defendant who intended to kill one person as a multiple murderer.[302] Yet the "recycling" of malice in this way is permitted as a matter of law.

[298] For critical discussion, see Ashworth, "Transferred Malice and Punishment for Unforeseen Consequences" in Glazebrook (ed.), *Reshaping the Criminal Law* (1978) 77; Ashworth, "The Elasticity of Mens Rea" in Tapper (ed.), *Crime, Proof and Punishment* (1981) 45; Williams, "Convictions and Fair Labelling" (1983) 42 *CLJ* 85; Horder, "Transferred Malice and the Remoteness of Unexpected Outcomes from Intentions" [2006] *Crim LR* 383; Bohlander, "Transferred Malice and Transferred Defenses: A Critique of the Traditional Doctrine and Arguments for a Change in Paradigm" (2010) 13 *New Criminal LR* 555; Eldar, "The Limits of Transferred Malice" (2012) 32 *OJLS* 633. For more abstract treatments, see Husak, "Transferred Intent" (1996) 10 *Notre Dame Journal of Legal Ethics and Public Policy* 65; Dillof, "Transferred Intent: an Enquiry into the Nature of Criminal Culpability" (1998) 1 *Buffalo Crim LR* 501.

[299] E.g. *Mitchell* [1983] QB 741 (CA) (unlawful act manslaughter); *Gross* (1913) 23 Cox CC 455 (voluntary manslaughter); *Latimer* (1886) 17 QBD 359 (wounding); *McCullum* (1973) 57 Cr App R 645 (handling stolen goods).

[300] Criminal Damage Act 1971, s. 1(1).

[301] Cp. *Kurd, Ali and Hassan*, Leicester Crown Court, 2018: reported in *The Times*, 29 December 2018.

[302] Stark, "Recycled Malice" (2023) 82 *CLJ* 509.

Although there is little case-law authority on the point, it seems that defences can also "transfer".[303] Suppose that Dorit attempts to shoot Tom only because she believes, correctly, that Tom is attacking her and that her life is in peril. Unfortunately, Dorit's shot misses and unexpectedly kills Bill. Dorit's intention to kill may be transferred, and it seems right that so too should be her claim of self-defence. Accordingly, she ought not to be guilty of murder.[304] The same should be true of excuse-based defences, such as duress. If David threatens Sandy with serious injury unless Sandy burgles Veronica's house, and a reasonable person would have given in to that threat, Sandy should have a defence if he mistakenly burgles Violet's house instead of Veronica's.

In the foregoing examples, the divergence between actus reus and mens rea was irrelevant to the definition of the offence. In general, however, it is not possible to convict someone on the basis of an actus reus for one offence accompanied by the mens rea for a different offence: that would not be *transference* but *exchange*. If Jane were to throw a stone at Daniel and miss but inadvertently break his window, she is not guilty of criminal damage (unless she foresaw a risk to the window when throwing the stone at Daniel and ran that risk unreasonably).[305] Her intent to injure Daniel does not satisfy the mens rea requirement for damage to property. Conversely, if Ted fires a shot at Ellie but misses and kills her dachshund, Ted cannot be held liable for criminal damage on the basis of his intention to kill. It would have to be shown, quite separately, that Ted had the mens rea for the latter offence (e.g. that Ted foresaw the risk of hitting the dog when firing, and took that risk without adequate justification).

Although the transferred malice "doctrine" has been criticised,[306] in its modern incarnation (i.e. as stated here) it is unobjectionable. Indeed, it is not really a doctrine at all. It is instead recognition of the fact that some variations in the way in which a crime is committed are, legally, immaterial. The causal miscarriage of D's actions in "transferred malice" cases has exactly the same legal status as, for example, cases of immaterial mistake. If Ian steals a cheap painting because he thinks it is a valuable Constable, he has the mens rea (and commits the actus reus) of theft since the specific identity of the property stolen forms no necessary part of the offence definition. It is enough that he takes "property belonging to another", whether or not that property is of great value.[307] Similarly, if Callum strikes the person in front of him, thinking her to be his enemy, Anne, it does not matter—in terms of his criminal liability—that he is in fact hitting Fiona. The precise identity of the victim is immaterial to the legal definition of battery. As long as Callum intends to strike, and manages to strike, a human being, he is guilty of that offence.

Rather than elevating matters to the level of a bespoke "doctrine", it may be preferable to express them in terms of the following basic principle: where D's actions cause an outcome

303 The authority typically cited in this context is *Gross* (1913) 23 Cox CC 455, which concerned provocation. See, too, the infanticide example discussed in Eldar, "The Limits of Transferred Malice" (2012) 32 *OJLS* 633, 642.

304 Note that the transfer of a defence will not necessarily preclude liability for an independent offence. It may, for example, have been grossly negligent to shoot at Tom because of the risk of hitting Bill, meaning Dorit may be liable for Bill's manslaughter.

305 Compare *Pembliton* (1874) LR 2 CCC 119; *Taaffe* [1984] AC 539. Jane could, of course, have been convicted straightforwardly if she had foreseen the risk of breaking the window. Compare, however, *Ellis and Street* (1986) 84 Cr App R 235, which pays lip service to the principle that the actus reus and mens rea must correspond, but at the same time subverts that fundamental requirement for the sake of enforcement convenience.

306 See, e.g., *A-G's Reference (No. 3 of 1994)* [1998] AC 245, 259–62 (Lord Mustill); below, § 10.2(i)(a).

307 Cf. *Wrigley* [1957] Crim LR 57 (Crown Court).

that is in some way unexpected,[308] but not in a way relevant to the offence definition,[309] D can still be found guilty of the offence.

The point is clearly illustrated in *Grant*.[310] The defendants were chasing B, who ran into a shop to escape them. They then fired two shots into the shop, missing B but seriously injuring two other customers in the shop, S and T. The defendants were straightforwardly convicted of the attempted murder of B. They were *also* convicted on two further counts of causing grievous bodily harm with intent to S and T, contrary to section 18 of the OAPA 1861.[311] Rightly so, affirmed the Court of Appeal. The attempt to kill B implied that the defendants had an intent to cause grievous bodily harm (to B). Hence, when they caused serious injury to each of S and T, they did so with the mens rea for the section 18 offence.

Even so, the problems with "recycling" malice arise here too.[312] Technically, it would appear that the defendants in *Grant* could have been convicted of three counts of attempted murder (B's, S's, and T's). This would, in effect, be to impute an intention to kill a third human being when, in reality, only two such intentions existed. Neither is the difficulty resolved by convicting of grievous bodily harm with intent in two cases, with attempted murder reserved for the intended target of the attack. Much as it does not matter *which* human being the defendants intended to hit, it does seem to matter *how many*—although not, apparently, to the law of England and Wales.

### (i) "Incompatible" or "remote" transfers where the offence elements are satisfied?

Lord Mustill has observed of transferring mens rea that "to make any sense of this process there must, as it seems to me, be some compatibility between the original intention and the actual occurrence, and this is, indeed, what one finds in the cases".[313] We have suggested above that the need for compatibility is satisfied when the variation is immaterial to the definition of the offence. However, Horder has suggested an additional limitation, which would sometimes prevent the transfer of mens rea even though the appropriate mens rea and actus reus elements are present. In his view, an outcome is too "remote" for mens rea to be transferred if: (i) the victim was not the intended victim; and (ii) the victim was killed

[308] A proviso: transferred malice is unproblematic only if causal principles are properly observed. This explains the otherwise troubling case of *Heigho* 18 Idaho 566 (1910), criticised for its "mechanical reasoning" in Williams, *TBCL* 181 n. 1. In that case, D assaulted W, and an onlooker died of fright. D was convicted of the manslaughter of W. It is submitted the conviction was wrong because D was not causally responsible for the onlooker's death. Horder disagrees with this view ("Transferred Malice and the Remoteness of Unexpected Outcomes from Intentions" [2006] *Crim LR* 383, 389–90), but one of the criteria of causal responsibility here is that the intervening event be reasonably foreseeable: above, § 4.2(iii)(a)–(b).

[309] Cf. *Wrigley* [1957] Crim LR 57 (Crown Court). This analysis would allow variations where the greater incorporates the lesser, as in Ashworth's example of an assault committed while intending to wound: discussed by Eldar, "The Limits of Transferred Malice" (2012) 32 *OJLS* 633, 641. Yet Eldar would go beyond that, contending that mens rea may generally be transferred if the difference in what actually happened was *morally* immaterial and was reasonably foreseeable. Perhaps, then, we might contemplate liability for offence X where D commits the actus reus of offence X, with the mens rea for offence Y, *and the two offences criminalise (in different actus reus forms) the same wrong*. Such pairs of offences are surely, hopefully, rare. Moreover, as we noted in §§ 2.1–2, even then there is a constitutional-law difficulty about extending liability to cases falling outside the definition of an offence.

[310] [2014] EWCA Crim 143.

[311] The elements of this crime are set out in § 11.6.

[312] Stark, "Recycled Malice" (2023) 82 *CLJ* 509.

[313] *A-G's Reference (No. 3 of 1994)* [1998] AC 245, 262.

in an unexpected way, i.e. in a manner unforeseen by the defendant.[314] Thus consider the following example:

> Emily shoots at Vlad, intending to kill him. The bullet misses, but enters a factory behind Vlad. There, it strikes an electrical transformer, causing the transformer to explode. The explosion kills a factory worker, Thomas.

There is general agreement that the intention to kill Vlad cannot be transferred to any charge of criminal damage involving the unanticipated explosion. At the same time, on the analysis set out in the previous section, Emily is straightforwardly guilty of murder, since by her act she intended to, and did, kill a human being. However, if we were to accept Horder's limiting principle of "remoteness" or "incompatibility", it seems that Emily would not be convicted of Thomas's murder but, rather, of the attempted murder of Vlad and of the manslaughter of Thomas.[315]

In our view, such a limiting principle should be rejected. First, it promotes uncertainty. When is the manner in which an outcome is caused sufficiently different and unexpected to count as incompatible? One might think that causation doctrines already have this in hand, but Horder's principle is meant to apply *after* causal responsibility for V2's death is established. It is undesirable to compound the complexity of the enquiry into D's guilt, since the criteria of any additional limitation do not seem susceptible of clear enunciation. Moreover, the moral case for a limitation seems unmeritorious. Suppose that the unexpected explosion had, in fact, killed Vlad. Convicting Emily of murder is then straightforward. Why should it make all the difference that it was Thomas instead who died? Both are human beings. All the elements of the offence are present. As was observed in *Mitchell*, "the criminality of the doer of the act is precisely the same whether it is A or B who dies".[316] To convict Emily of unlawful-act manslaughter, on the basis of an attempted murder causing death, is an unnecessary sophistication.

## § 5.8 Concurrence

As a general rule, the actus reus and mens rea of a crime must coincide in time. That is, the behavioural and circumstantial elements of the actus reus must occur at the same time as the mens rea requirements are satisfied. Unless there is a moment in time, a *scintilla temporis*, at which these elements are all present, the crime is not committed.[317] Consider the following illustration:

> D is an assassin who has been hired to kill V. One evening she drives over to V's house in order to shoot him when he comes home. On the way, however, she is involved in an accident when she collides with a cyclist who has suddenly cut in front of her car. Upon getting out of the car,

[314] "Transferred Malice and the Remoteness of Unexpected Outcomes from Intentions" [2006] *Crim LR* 383, 388–9.

[315] In this Horder aligns himself with Ashworth: "Transferred Malice and Punishment for Unforeseen Consequences" in Glazebrook (ed.), *Reshaping the Criminal Law* (1978) 77.

[316] [1983] QB 741, 748 (CA). The same objection applies to Eldar's argument for a limitation of (reasonable) foreseeability: "The Limits of Transferred Malice" (2012) 32 *OJLS* 633, 649–57. Suppose that D sets out to damage T's property. In an unforeseeable turn of events, it is V's property that she harms. Although Eldar suggests (at 657) that circumstantial variations may be different from consequential ones, there seems no merit in the distinction.

[317] *Fowler v Padget* (1798) 7 Term Rep 509, 101 ER 1103.

D recognises that the cyclist is V. Thinking V is unconscious but alive, she shoots him through the heart. V, however, was already dead as a result of the accident.

D has not murdered V. Although she may have caused his death (the actus reus) by driving into him, when she did so she did not have a present intention to kill. Later, when she shot V, she had the mens rea for murder but her behaviour did not cause his death, so could not constitute the actus reus. Thus there is no moment in time at which both the actus reus and mens rea of murder are present. (V does, however, commit attempted murder at the later time.[318])

Neither can an antecedent mens rea be added to a subsequent actus reus in order to support a conviction. For example:

D takes a new umbrella to the law library one morning. When she departs, she cannot remember exactly what her umbrella looked like. Seeing an attractive umbrella in the stand, she decides to take and keep that one instead—not realising that it is in fact her own umbrella. Later, she begins to feel guilty. She returns to the law library, and replaces the attractive umbrella. In its place, she takes with her a different umbrella which she mistakenly thinks is the one she originally came with.

When D first leaves the library, she attempts to steal an umbrella but fails to commit a theft because the one she takes is her own. She has the mens rea for that offence but does not commit the actus reus.[319] Later, when she departs for a second time, she commits the actus reus of theft by taking another person's umbrella, but does so innocently—without an "intention of permanently depriving the other".[320] There is no moment in time at which all elements of the definition of theft are co-existent.

A striking illustration of this principle is supplied by *Wright*.[321] D was charged with possessing a Class B drug with intent to supply. At the time of his arrest, the many cannabis plants in his possession were too immature to qualify as a Class B drug within the meaning of section 5(3) of the Misuse of Drugs Act 1971. Since D's intended supply related to the harvested end-product and not to the immature plants, there was no temporal concurrence and his conviction was quashed.

Where the actus reus includes consequences, the requirement for concurrence applies to the behavioural element rather than its consequence. If D deliberately poisons V, and V takes some hours to die, the fact that D repents in the meantime will not absolve her of murder.[322] Conversely, if D is driving and accidentally hits a cyclist, the fact that she realises the cyclist is V, her enemy, and rejoices while he is dying of his injuries will not make her guilty of a homicide offence. For the purposes of concurrence, the actus reus has already occurred.

Although concurrence is a standard requirement for offences involving mens rea, there are some situations where the need for concurrence does not operate or can be circumnavigated.[323] We consider these below.

[318] As explained below in § 9.4(i) so long as D *believed* that V was alive, the fact that V was already dead is not a barrier to conviction for attempted murder.
[319] The umbrella is not property belonging to another: Theft Act 1968, s. 1(1).
[320] Theft Act 1968, ss. 1(1), 5.
[321] [2011] EWCA Crim 1180, [2011] 2 Cr App R 15.
[322] Cp. *Jakeman* (1983) 76 Cr App R 223.
[323] Marston, "Contemporaneity of Act and Intention in Crimes" (1970) 86 *LQR* 208. See also White, "The Identity and Time of the Actus Reus" [1977] *Crim LR* 148.

### *(i) Circumventing the concurrence requirement*

#### *(a) Fresh acts, continuing acts, and subsequent omissions*

Where an actus reus by D precedes her having mens rea, one technique available to the prosecutor is to show another, later, occurrence of the actus reus which coincides with D's mens rea—i.e. to look for a different moment in time at which the offence can be proved to have occurred.

A standard, if unusual, case of this would be where D does a second positive act which also brings about the actus reus. Suppose, in the days when tort actions died with the plaintiff,[324] that while driving D accidentally runs over V. V, fatally injured, lies dying. D is uninsured and, panicking, she backs up hoping thereby to avoid tortious liability. If the further injuries D inflicts by reversing over V play any causal role by accelerating V's death then D becomes guilty of murder, on the basis of the second and not the first incident.

Absent a fresh causative act by the defendant, the prosecution may try instead to show a *continuing* act: that the actus reus, although initiated by D without mens rea, is still occurring or being perpetrated by D at a later moment when D now has the required mens rea. This type of case was discussed above, in § 4.1(i)(b).[325] It is exemplified by *Fagan v Metropolitan Police Commissioner*,[326] in which D accidentally stopped his car on a police officer's foot. That itself was no assault, since D did not yet have mens rea. However, when D deliberately refrained from moving his car, an assault was established. On the court's analysis, there was an ongoing application of force to the police officer by D (the actus reus), which was now accompanied by mens rea.[327]

Alternatively, the prosecution can try to bring its case within the ambit of *Miller*.[328] In this situation, D's failure to prevent a danger from crystallising into harm may constitute an actus reus if that danger was created (however innocently) by D's own earlier actions. *Miller* is also discussed above, in § 4.1(i)(b).[329]

#### *(b) The complex single transaction*

The law is different when the actus reus of an offence occurs *after* D has mens rea. Here it will sometimes be possible to convict D on the basis that the particular act that caused harm was part of a larger, complex series of actions which should be viewed as a whole, where D has mens rea at some earlier point during that "transaction".

The classic case is *Thabo Meli*.[330] In that case, four defendants conspired to kill V and dispose of his body in a manner that would make it look like V had died accidentally. In accordance with their plan, they struck V on the head (with intent thereby to kill him). Thinking him dead, they rolled him over a cliff. In fact, V was not killed by the blow and died from exposure suffered after being rolled over the cliff. Prima facie, the act of disposal, which caused V's death, was unaccompanied by the mens rea for murder since the defendants believed he was already dead. Nonetheless, the Privy Council upheld their convictions

[324] Winfield, "Death as Affecting Liability in Tort" (1929) 29 *Columbia LR* 239.
[325] See Case 4.
[326] [1969] 1 QB 439 (DC).
[327] See also *Kaitamaki* [1985] AC 147 (PC); *Cooper and Schaub* [1994] Crim LR 531 (CA).
[328] [1983] 2 AC 161.
[329] See Case 5.
[330] [1954] 1 WLR 228 (PC).

for murder. The defence sought to slice up the events into component moments of time and then point to the absence of a single moment at which actus reus and mens rea coincided. The Privy Council was unpersuaded:[331]

> "It appears to their Lordships impossible to divide up what was really one series of acts in this way. There is no doubt that the accused set out to do all these acts in order to achieve their plan, and as parts of their plan; and it is much too refined a ground of judgment to say that, because they were under a misapprehension at one stage and thought that their guilty purpose was achieved before, in fact, it was achieved, therefore they are to escape the penalties of the law."

It is hard to disagree with this decision, which represents a genuine exception to the concurrence requirement.[332] The defendants did exactly what they planned to do, and brought about exactly the result they had intended. The fact that the manner in which their success occurred was unexpected seems no ground for exculpation in such circumstances.

As the quotation above emphasises, the actions of the defendants were deliberate and pursuant to a preconceived plan. However, these elements of preplanning and intent have not been required in subsequent cases. In *Church*,[333] the defendant knocked the victim unconscious during a fight and, mistakenly believing he had killed her, threw her into a river where she drowned. His conviction for manslaughter was upheld on the basis of the single transaction principle. Similarly, in *Le Brun*,[334] D knocked his wife unconscious during an argument and, while attempting to drag her body away, dropped her on her head and killed her. On appeal, the trial judge was held correctly to have directed the jury that they could convict D of murder or manslaughter (depending on the intention with which he first struck his wife) if D had accidentally dropped her while either attempting to move her to her home against her known wishes, and/or attempting to dispose of the body, or to cover up the assault. In such circumstances, English law holds that the sequence of wrongful acts by the defendant may be regarded as elements of a single episode of unlawful conduct, where the transaction as a whole incorporates both the mens rea and actus reus elements of a crime.

*Le Brun* does suggest one limitation to the *Thabo Meli* principle. The Court of Appeal appeared to acquiesce in the trial judge's direction that:[335]

> "if the fatal injury had happened in the course of . . . well-intentioned efforts to help her, he would be guilty neither of murder nor manslaughter . . . the distinction I am drawing [is] between as it were an extension or a furtherance or a continuation of the unlawful conduct and a different tack where whatever he has done to her before he is trying his best to help or comfort her even if in a misguided way."

According to Lord Lane CJ, "the judge was drawing a sharp distinction between actions by the appellant which were designed to help his wife and actions which were not so designed".[336]

331 *Ibid.*, 230.
332 It is worth noting, however, that the case could have been decided on a more straightforward causation basis, to be discussed in § 5.8(i)(c). The same could be said of *Church*, considered below in the next paragraph. Arguably, *Le Brun* (also considered below) is the only case where the transactional analysis was actually needed.
333 [1966] 1 QB 59 (CA).
334 [1992] QB 61 (CA). See also *Moore and Dorn* [1975] Crim LR 229 (CA); *A-G's Reference (No. 4 of 1980)* [1981] 1 WLR 705 (CA). For discussion, see Sullivan, "Cause and the Contemporaneity of *Actus Reus* and *Mens Rea*" (1993) 52 *CLJ* 487, 495–9.
335 [1992] QB 61 (CA).
336 *Ibid.*, 71.

This suggests the *Thabo Meli* doctrine will apply only where the ongoing actions are still tainted by D's unlawful purpose, so that there is a moral congruence between D's earlier culpability and his subsequent conduct.[337] Had D dropped his wife while carrying her to hospital, his doing so would have been a separate incident, divisible from the earlier, unlawful transaction. This may seem a vague test, but it has achieved intuitively acceptable results in the decided cases.

*(c) A causation approach*

Where the defendant's mens rea precedes the action that most obviously constitutes the actus reus, another way of circumventing concurrence difficulties is to show that some earlier action by the defendant, done at the time when he had mens rea, was *also* a cause of the prohibited harm. The clearest illustrations of this approach are to be found in overseas cases. In *McKinnon*,[338] D assaulted V and knocked him unconscious. D then manhandled V, apparently causing an accidental nose-bleed, before leaving V lying on the ground and running off. While V was lying unconscious, the blood from his nose entered his lungs and he suffocated. The New Zealand Court of Appeal upheld D's conviction for murder. Although D may not have had the required mens rea when he caused the injury to V's nose, he did have mens rea when he struck V and knocked him unconscious. Moreover, the Court ruled, D's striking V was a contributory cause of his death, in combination with the nose-bleed, since it rendered V unable to deal with the bleeding. Thus there was no need to invoke a "transactional" analysis, of the sort found in *Thabo Meli*, since there was already a *scintilla temporis* at which both an actus reus and the mens rea of murder were present.

Indeed, it is arguable that *Thabo Meli* could itself have been decided on a causation basis: after all, V would have been able to seek shelter from the elements had he not been rendered unconscious by the defendants.[339] On this approach, the *Thabo Meli* doctrine would still be necessary in some cases, but only where the second event was overwhelmingly the cause of death, and D's earlier action was not a concurrent cause on the facts (e.g. where V is killed instantly by the impact after he is thrown over a cliff).[340] Conversely, the causation analysis will be necessary in situations where *Thabo Meli* cannot apply, for example because D's second intervention was innocent and well-meaning, or where the intervention is by a stranger rather than by D.

*(d) Involuntariness and antecedent fault*

If D perpetrates an actus reus while in an automatic state, normally the concurrence requirement will not be satisfied. Exceptionally, however, it may be possible to convict D, on the basis that his automatism is a consequence of his own earlier actions which occurred at a time when he had the mens rea for the offence. This type of case is discussed more fully

337 Another illustration is the Singaporean case of *Muhammad Radi v PP* [1994] 2 SLR 146, where D's follow-up conduct involved an attempt to conceal the evidence.

338 [1980] 2 NZLR 31. Compare *S v Masilela* 1968 (2) SA 558. For discussion of multiple causes see above, § 4.2(ii)(c).

339 Adams, "Homicide and the Supposed Corpse" (1968) 1 *Otago LR* 278, 287; Marston, "Contemporaneity of Act and Intention in Crimes" (1970) 86 *LQR* 208, 218–19; *McKinnon* [1980] 2 NZLR 31, 36–7. The thought in such cases is that V died from concurrent causes, i.e. a combination of being thrown over the cliff and being unable (because unconscious) to save himself.

340 Compare *Le Brun* [1992] QB 61 (CA).

above, in § 4.3(iii). Suppose, for example, that David is a diabetic. One day he deliberately takes insulin without eating any food. He does this in the hope of reducing himself into a semi-conscious state, where he knows that he is likely to become violent and assault his flatmate whom he does not like. Should his plan be successful, David will be guilty of an intentional assault, notwithstanding his automatism at the time the assault occurs.

Sometimes the offence may be proved without reference to the defendant's subsequent, involuntary conduct. In *Kay v Butterworth*,[341] D fell asleep while driving and collided with soldiers marching on the road. He was convicted of careless driving, but not because he drove into the soldiers. (At that time he was asleep and his behaviour was involuntary.) Rather, the offence was complete when he continued to drive while drowsy—that, in itself, was careless driving. Indeed, D would have committed the offence even if he had not run into the soldiers.[342] Williams illustrates this point in a lucid example:[343]

> "When, for example, a driver proceeds along Church Lane in a sleepy condition, and falls asleep at the wheel just before entering High Street, where he is involved in an accident, he cannot be convicted of careless driving in High Street, because in contemplation of law he did not 'drive' in High Street, and it makes no difference that his involuntary accident in High Street was the result of his own previous fault. He can, indeed, be convicted of careless driving, but this must be laid as having taken place in Church Lane, when the driver was undoubtedly 'driving.'"

The offence occurs in Church Lane.

[341] (1945) 61 TLR 452 (DC). Cf. *Moses v Winder* [1981] RTR 37 (DC). For a rather more dramatic example, see *People v Decina* 2 NY 2d 133 (1956).

[342] *Spurge* [1961] 2 QB 205, 210 (CA).

[343] *TBCL* 682. Obviously, this analysis works only if the timeframe for commission of the actus reus is sufficiently elastic, and not tied to a particular incident. Contrast *Burns v Bidder* [1967] 2 QB 227 (DC) (failing to accord precedence at a pedestrian crossing).

# 6

# STRICT AND CONSTRUCTIVE LIABILITY

We argued in Chapter 1 that serious criminal offences, where considerable public stigma attaches to a conviction, should always stipulate some form of mens rea that must be proved in relation to the actus reus before the defendant may be convicted. Such a scheme helps to avoid inflicting "the disgrace of criminality"[1] upon defendants who are not at fault when harm occurs. However, not every offence against the criminal law involves the sort of public condemnation that is implicit in a conviction for theft or homicide. A speeding offence, for example, involves little or no stigma, so the need for mens rea with regard to the actus reus is not as pressing.[2] In recognition of this fact, there are many offences of a regulatory nature which lack a mens rea ingredient with regard to one or more elements of the actus reus.[3] These offences involve strict liability.[4]

(Strict liability is sometimes called absolute liability in England and Wales, but—due to the fact that a distinction between these terms is recognised elsewhere in the Anglo-American world[5]—that terminology will be eschewed in this chapter.)

To see strict liability in action, consider *Pharmaceutical Society of Great Britain v Storkwain Ltd*.[6] There, the defendant chemists were convicted of (the now-repealed version of) the offence of selling controlled medicines without prescription even though they neither knew nor had reason to suspect that the "prescriptions" they filled were forgeries.[7] No mens rea element was required with regard to that aspect of the actus reus. This does not mean that the offence contains no mens rea element at all. It had to be shown that D intended to sell controlled medicines. In principle, if a chemist were to pick up the wrong packet, and hand over controlled medicines thinking they were over-the-counter headache

[1] *Warner v Metropolitan Police Commissioner* [1969] 2 AC 256, 272 (Lord Reid).

[2] Cp. "acts not criminal in any real sense": *Sherras v De Rutzen* [1895] 1 QB 918, 922.

[3] See Reid, "Strict Liability: Some Principles for Parliament" (2008) 29 *Statute LR* 173; Simester (ed.), *Appraising Strict Liability* (2005); Horder, "Strict Liability, Statutory Construction, and the Spirit of Liberty" (2002) 118 *LQR* 458; Richardson, "Strict Liability for Regulatory Crime: The Empirical Research" [1987] *Crim LR* 295; Leigh, *Strict and Vicarious Liability* (1982); Howard, *Strict Responsibility* (1963); Kadish, "Some Observations on the Use of Criminal Sanctions in Enforcing Economic Regulations" (1963) 30 *U Chicago LR* 423; Sayre, "Public Welfare Offenses" (1933) 33 *Col LR* 55.

[4] A similar definition of strict liability—found in Smith and Hogan, *Criminal Law* (4th ed., 1978) 79—was endorsed in *Lemon* [1979] AC 617, 656 (Lord Edmund-Davies). Other understandings of the term are possible: see, e.g., Moore, "The Strictness of Strict Liability" (2018) 12 *Crim Law and Philosophy* 513, 514–21. The focus of this chapter is on domestic principles regarding strict liability. For discussion of the European Court of Justice's approach to strict liability, which influenced the interpretation of some offences prior to the United Kingdom's departure from the European Union, see *R (Highbury Poultry Farm Produce Ltd) v Telford Magistrates' Court* [2020] UKSC 39, [2020] 1 WLR 4309.

[5] See below, § 6.4.

[6] [1986] 1 WLR 903 (HL).

[7] See, now, the Human Medicines Regulations 2012/1916, reg. 214.

tablets, he could not be convicted should his mistake vitiate the contract of sale. Other cases can be analysed similarly. In *Woodrow*,[8] a dealer was held to be guilty of possessing adulterated tobacco even though he had no ground for suspecting the tobacco was adulterated, and could only have discovered it to be so by a chemical analysis that it would be unreasonable to expect of dealers (thus the dealer was not even negligent with regard to the nature of the tobacco). The sale itself would have to be intentional, but no fault was required with regard to the adulteration of the tobacco. Similarly, in *Cundy v Le Cocq*,[9] D, a landlord, was convicted of selling intoxicating liquor to a drunken person, contrary to section 13 of the Licensing Act 1872, which provided that "if any licensed person . . . sells any intoxicating liquor to any drunken person, he shall be liable to a penalty".[10] D and his staff neither knew nor had reason to suspect the buyer was drunk—he had "been quiet in his demeanour and had done nothing to indicate insobriety".[11] The Divisional Court held that no mens rea was required with regard to that element of the actus reus. An intentional sale of intoxicating liquor to a person who was, in fact, drunk was enough to secure liability. Finally, in *Pwr and Others v DPP*,[12] the defendants were charged with an offence under section 13 of the Terrorism Act 2000, on the basis that they had displayed a flag "in such a way or in such circumstances as to arouse reasonable suspicion that [they were] member[s] or supporter[s] of a proscribed organisation". The Supreme Court held that this offence required the defendants to know that they were displaying the relevant article. In consequence: "If persons were to stick a flag into or onto a defendant's backpack without the defendant's knowledge that he or she is doing so, the defendant would not be guilty of the offence".[13] By contrast, no mens rea element was required regarding the proscribed nature of the relevant organisation represented on the flag. Accordingly, the prosecution did not need to prove, for instance, that DD knew, or even suspected, that the flag contained the symbol of a proscribed organisation.[14]

Strict liability is a controversial, though common, element of modern criminal law statutes, and there is a presumption that mens rea is required as to each and every aspect of the actus reus. This presumption, and the factors that can overcome it in relation to a particular criminal offence, are considered in § 6.1. The relationship between strict liability and defences will then be considered in § 6.2, before the more general question of whether strict liability should be used in the criminal law is covered in § 6.3. As this is an area where opinions differ around the Anglo-American world, § 6.4 considers comparative approaches to the issue of strict liability. Finally, § 6.5 discusses the concept of "constructive liability",

[8] (1846) 15 M & W 404, 153 ER 907. The case is said to be the first to impose strict liability, although doubt is cast on this view by Singer, "The Resurgence of Mens Rea: III—The Rise and Fall of Strict Criminal Liability" (1989) 30 *Boston College LR* 337, 340–45.

[9] (1884) 13 QBD 207.

[10] See, now, Licensing Act 2003, s. 141.

[11] *Cundy v Le Cocq* (1884) 13 QBD 207, 207.

[12] [2022] UKSC 2, [2022] 1 WLR 789.

[13] [2022] UKSC 2, [2022] 1 WLR 789, [26].

[14] See, similarly, *ABJ* [2024] EWCA Crim 1597, [2025] 1 WLR 1909. Oddly, in *Pwr v DPP* the Supreme Court expressed the view that, because D could prove the absence of a terroristic purpose and thus avoid liability, the relevant offence was not one of strict liability ([2022] UKSC 2, [2022] 1 WLR 789, [48]). Yet the point remains that the prosecution was not required to prove mens rea regarding every aspect of the actus reus—the classic definition of strict liability in English criminal law.

which is at times difficult to distinguish from strict liability, but can be—in theory—more readily defended as part of the criminal law.

## § 6.1 Recognition of strict liability in a statutory offence

With isolated exceptions (most now consigned to history),[15] strict liability offences are a creation of statute rather than the common law. The opportunity to impose strict liability generally arises from the fact that criminal legislation may be (and all too frequently is) silent regarding the mens rea element(s) pertaining to each element of the actus reus, leaving it to the courts either to imply a mens rea requirement or to interpret the offence as one involving strict liability.

Originally, the courts recognised a principle that in such cases mens rea was to be implied as to each element of the actus reus: "Acts of Parliament are to be so construed, as no man that is innocent, or free from injury or wrong, be by a literal construction punished or endamaged."[16] Although operation of the principle could be overridden by Parliament itself, the legislation would have to be clear on the point:[17]

> "it is contrary to the whole established law of England (unless the legislation on the subject has clearly enacted it), to say that a person can be guilty of a crime in England without a wrongful intent—without an attempt to do that which the law has forbidden."

Extensive authority can be found in support of this proposition, which applied even to summary offences.[18] Indeed, as we shall see, it remains the point of departure for courts when determining whether a particular statute creates an offence of strict liability or one requiring mens rea as to every aspect of the actus reus.[19] But the presumption of mens rea is not always decisive, and the courts are often willing to read statutes without implying a mens rea requirement as to every aspect of the actus reus.

The seeds of this willingness were sown during the later part of the nineteenth century, when strict liability offences tried summarily in magistrates' courts began to emerge as a convenient and—compared with creating special administrative or industrial courts—an inexpensive means of dealing with rapidly changing social and industrial practices.[20] Most often they owe their existence to a perception that the need to protect the public from harm

[15] The common law exceptions included an employer's liability for public nuisance and the former crime of criminal libel (abolished by the Coroners and Justice Act 2009, s. 73). Common-law contempt of court, once thought to be a matter of strict liability, is now said, *obiter*, to require mens rea: *Yousaf v Luton Crown Court* [2006] EWCA Crim 469, [19].

[16] *Margate Pier Co v Hannam* (1819) 3 B & Ald 266, 270, 106 ER 661, 663, quoting Coke. See, also, *Tolson* (1889) 23 QBD 168, 187.

[17] *Attorney-General v Bradlaugh* (1885) 14 QBD 667, 689. See, also, *Chisholm v Doulton* (1889) 22 QBD 736, 741.

[18] E.g. *Fowler v Padget* (1798) 7 Term Rep 509, 101 ER 1103; *Hearne v Garton and Stone* (1859) 2 El & El 66, 121 ER 26; *Batting v Bristol and Exeter Ry Co* (1860) 3 LT 665; *Sleep* (1861) L & C 44, 169 ER 1296; *Core v James* (1871–2) LR 7 QB 135; *Sherras v de Rutzen* [1895] 1 QB 918; *Paul v Hargreaves* [1908] 2 KB 289.

[19] An exception found in some contexts is where an aspect of the actus reus is evaluative. This point is discussed in § 6.1(ii)(d) below.

[20] See, e.g., Carson, "Symbolic and Instrumental Dimensions of Early Factory Legislation" in Hood (ed.), *Crime, Criminology and Public Policy* (1974) 107; Carson, "The Conventionalisation of Early Factory Crime" (1979) 7 *Int J Soc Law* 37.

might on occasion justify convicting people of criminal offences even where they were not necessarily at fault;[21] especially, though not invariably, where the harm involved resulted from a specialised activity, one which might naturally lend itself to control by regulatory rather than "truly criminal" prohibitions. Even the enforcement of such offences tends to be distinctive. They are frequently the responsibility not of the police, but of specialist agencies created to monitor and control the effects of particular types of activity such as those that risk pollution and physical injury. Habits of prosecution also differ. Regulatory agencies tend to prosecute only recurring or very serious breaches of the law. Characteristically, in the hands of regulatory agencies, the fact that an offence imposes strict liability operates as an important background consideration in compliance negotiations.[22]

The discussion of mens rea and strict liability has so far concentrated on defining the leading terms. But a further question arises every time we consider a particular offence. *Which* mens rea state is required to satisfy *that* offence? The answer varies from offence to offence. For assault, recklessness about the apprehension of immediate unlawful violence will suffice.[23] For murder, an intention to kill or cause grievous bodily harm is required.[24] Driving while disqualified, by contrast, is an offence of strict liability: no fault as to the fact of disqualification need be proved; all that D must be proved to have done is deliberately driven a vehicle on a public highway.[25]

Often the answer to the question of what type of mens rea is required with regard to each element of the actus reus will be found straightforwardly in the explicit words of the statute that creates the offence. For example, section 2 of the Explosive Substances Act 1883 makes it an offence "maliciously" to cause an explosion likely to endanger life or property: the offence cannot be committed without awareness of such potential consequences.[26] But, frequently, a statute will specify only the actus reus elements, and be silent regarding whether a form of mens rea is required as to each element, and—if so—*what* variety of mens rea will do. For example, section 47 of the Offences Against the Person Act 1861 prohibits "any assault occasioning actual bodily harm", without mentioning any mens rea state.[27] In such instances the courts must decide whether an offence involves strict liability.

The first point to consider is whether the mens rea standard has been settled by judicial precedent. As noted above, the offence of driving while disqualified has been held to impose strict liability with regard to the fact of disqualification. Unless the offence becomes altered by legislation,[28] there would seem to be no reason for another court to reconsider the question in the future.

[21] Cp. *Hobbs v Winchester Corporation* [1910] 2 KB 471, 484: "the natural inference from the statute and its object is that the peril to the butcher from innocently selling unsound meat is deemed by the legislature to be much less than the peril to the public which would follow from the necessity in each case of proving a *mens rea*".

[22] See, e.g., Hawkins, *Law as Last Resort* (2003); Hutter, *The Reasonable Arm of the Law?* (1988); Hawkins, *Environment and Enforcement* (1984); Reiss, "Selecting Strategies of Social Control over Organizational Life" in Hawkins and Thomas (eds.), *Enforcing Regulation* (1984) 25. But the discretionary nature of prosecutions in such instances is not without Rule of Law problems: Simester, "Is Strict Liability Always Wrong?" in Simester (ed.), *Appraising Strict Liability* (2005) 21, 32–3.

[23] *Spratt* [1990] 1 WLR 1073 (CA); *Savage* [1992] 1 AC 699.

[24] *Cunningham* [1982] AC 566.

[25] *Bowsher* [1973] RTR 202 (CA); *Miller* [1974] 1 WLR 1222 (CA).

[26] Malice incorporates both intention and "subjective" recklessness: *Cunningham* [1957] 2 QB 396 (CA).

[27] The mens rea of this offence is analysed below, § 11.4(ii).

[28] The offence, formerly contained in Road Traffic Act 1972, s. 99, was re-enacted by Road Traffic Act 1988, s. 103, without substantive change.

If the mens rea standard for the offence is not settled by statute or case law, the court will have to make a fresh decision. The guiding principles (to the extent that these exist) affecting that decision are stated in the following subsections. By way of introduction, however, it is helpful to quote from the Privy Council's summary of those principles in *Gammon Ltd v A-G of Hong Kong*:[29]

> "(1) there is a presumption of law that mens rea is required before a person can be held guilty of a criminal offence; (2) the presumption is particularly strong where the offence is 'truly criminal' in character; (3) the presumption applies to statutory offences, and can be displaced only if this is clearly or by necessary implication the effect of the statute; (4) the only situation in which the presumption can be displaced is where the statute is concerned with an issue of social concern, and public safety is such an issue; (5) mens rea stands unless it can also be shown that the creation of strict liability will be effective to promote the objects of the statute by encouraging greater vigilance to prevent the commission of the prohibited act."

This makes things sound simple. As will be seen, establishing what, if any, mens rea is required with regard to an element of an offence's actus reus is often far from easy.

### *(i) The initial presumption*

The presumption from which one starts is that mens rea is required for each and every element of the actus reus. It should be emphasised that the presumption of mens rea generally imports intention or (subjective) recklessness (or, as appropriate, knowledge or belief). Thus in *Sweet v Parsley*,[30] the House of Lords regarded itself as able to choose only between strict liability and advertent mens rea (in that case, knowledge).[31] Negligence is not, apparently, on the common-law table.

The presumption of mens rea has in the past been controversial.[32] Its place was secured by the House of Lords in two leading decisions on strict liability, *Sweet v Parsley*[33] and *B (A Minor) v DPP*,[34] and the starting presumption of mens rea is nowadays recognised as a "well established"[35] and "totally fundamental point".[36] The presumption of mens rea has been described as a matter of "great importance",[37] and even as a "constitutional principle".[38]

29 [1985] AC 1, 14.
30 [1970] AC 132.
31 Cp. Lord Diplock's discussion of negligence and duties of care in *ibid.*, 162–5. See Devlin's discussion of this point in *Samples of Lawmaking* (1962) 67–82. For a suggestion that due diligence (i.e. no-negligence) defences may be "read in" to comply with Art. 3 of the ECHR, see Arden, "Criminal Law at the Crossroads: The Impact on Human Rights from the Law Commission's Perspective and the Need for a Code" [1999] *Crim LR* 439, 450. Contrast, however, *Salabiaku v France* (1991) 13 EHRR 379.
32 E.g. "in construing a modern statute this presumption as to mens rea does not exist": *Hobbs v Winchester Corporation* [1910] 2 KB 471, 483; *St Margaret's Trust Ltd* [1958] 1 WLR 522 (CA). Cp. *Brend v Wood* (1946) 175 LT 306, 307 (DC); *Harding v Price* [1948] 1 KB 695, 700–1 (CA); *Reynolds v G.H. Austin and Sons* [1951] 2 KB 135 (DC).
33 [1970] AC 132.
34 [2000] 2 AC 428.
35 *Lane* [2018] UKSC 36, [2018] 1 WLR 3647, [8].
36 *Nurse v Trinidad and Tobago* [2019] UKPC 43, [2021] AC 1, [20].
37 *Attorney-General's Reference (No 1 of 2020)* [2020] EWCA Crim 1665, [2021] QB 441, [42].
38 See *Brown* [2013] UKSC 43, [2013] 4 All ER 860, [26]–[29] (Lord Kerr). See, also, the central role played by the presumption of mens rea in *Taylor* [2016] UKSC 5, [2016] 1 WLR 500.

In *Sweet v Parsley*, a schoolteacher was prosecuted for "being concerned in the management of premises used for the purpose of smoking cannabis".[39] She had sublet her farmhouse to a group of students who, without her knowledge, smoked cannabis there. Even though the terms of the statute prima facie were satisfied—she was concerned in the management of the premises, and cannabis was smoked there—the House of Lords quashed her conviction. They decided that knowledge that cannabis was being smoked on the premises was an, albeit unstated, element of the offence:[40]

> "there has for centuries been a presumption that Parliament did not intend to make criminals of persons who were in no way blameworthy in what they did. This means that, whenever a section is silent as to mens rea there is a presumption that, in order to give effect to the will of Parliament, we must read in words appropriate to require mens rea."

The justification for this starting-point rests in the issues discussed in Chapter 1 and in § 3.2. According to Lord Diplock:[41]

> "the mere fact that Parliament has made the conduct a criminal offence gives rise to *some* implication about the mental element of the conduct proscribed. . . . This implication stems from the principle that it is contrary to a rational and civilised criminal code, such as Parliament must be presumed to have intended, to penalise one who has performed his duty as a citizen to ascertain what acts are prohibited by law (ignorantia juris non excusat) and has taken all proper care to inform himself of any facts which would make his conduct lawful."

Parliament normally does not, and indeed should not, intend to make criminals of those who are not blameworthy regarding the actus reus. Such persons do not warrant that label. Thus, according to Lord Reid in *Sweet v Parsley*:[42]

> "it is a universal principle that if a penal provision is reasonably capable of two interpretations, that interpretation which is most favourable to the accused must be adopted".

*B (A Minor) v DPP*[43] appeared to strengthen the presumption of mens rea further. During a bus journey, B, a boy aged 15, persistently requested that a 13-year-old girl perform oral sex on him. He was charged with the (now-repealed) offence of inciting a girl under 14 to commit an act of gross indecency.[44] B claimed that he had honestly believed that the girl was over 14. However, the Youth Court justices ruled, following the leading early case of *Prince*,[45] that the offence was one of strict liability in respect of the victim's age. B's state of mind concerning her age was irrelevant. B appealed ultimately to the House of Lords, arguing that since the Act did not specify a mens rea requirement, the common law presumption that mens rea was necessary should apply. Since he had thought the girl was over 14, B argued that he lacked the intent, knowledge or recklessness presumptively required.

[39] Contrary to s. 5(b) of the (now superseded) Dangerous Drugs Act 1965.
[40] [1970] AC 132, 148 (Lord Reid).
[41] *Ibid.*, 162–3. See also at 153 (Lord Morris).
[42] *Ibid.*, 149.
[43] [2000] 2 AC 428.
[44] Contrary to the Indecency with Children Act 1960, s. 1(1).
[45] (1875) LR 2 CCR 154. In *Prince*, D was convicted of an offence against s. 55 of the OAPA 1861, which enacted that "whosoever shall unlawfully take . . . any unmarried girl, being under the age of sixteen years, out of the possession and against the will of her father or mother . . . shall be guilty of a misdemeanour". D did exactly that, but reasonably believed the girl's age was 18. The Court for Crown Cases Reserved held that the age of the girl was a matter of strict liability, so that D's belief was irrelevant. Notwithstanding that *Prince* was a leading decision for 125 years, its authority must be regarded as doubtful in light of *B (A Minor) v DPP*.

The House of Lords allowed B's appeal.[46] It ruled that the common-law presumption of mens rea applied:[47]

> "In these circumstances the starting point for a court is the established common law presumption that a mental element, traditionally labelled mens rea, is an essential ingredient unless Parliament has indicated a contrary intention either expressly or by necessary implication. The common law presumes that, unless Parliament indicated otherwise, the appropriate mental element is an unexpressed ingredient of every statutory offence."

The presumption is only to be overridden, according to their Lordships, if there is a *necessary* implication that Parliament intended the offence to be strict:[48]

> "[T]he test is not whether it is a reasonable implication that the statute rules out mens rea as a constituent part of the crime–the test is whether it is a *necessary* implication."

Necessary implication means, in this context:[49]

> "[A]n implication that is compellingly clear from the language used, the nature of the offence, the mischief sought to be prevented and any other circumstances which may assist in determining Parliament's intention".

As will be seen, this ostensibly "high hurdle"[50] is not always that difficult for the prosecution to overcome. Frequently, the courts have ruled that the only reasonable construction of regulatory offences is that they are intended to be of strict liability, and they remain willing to do so notwithstanding *B (A Minor) v DPP*.[51] But, at least for serious crimes, *B* sets down an important marker in the law of strict liability (although not, alas, in the new law of sexual offences).[52] In *K*,[53] decided shortly afterwards, the defendant, aged 26, indecently assaulted V contrary to (the now repealed) section 14 of the Sexual Offences Act 1956. V was aged 14, and by section 14(2) of the 1956 Act a girl under the age of 16 could not in law consent to an indecent assault. However, K believed that V was aged 16: she had told him so. The Court of Appeal upheld K's conviction, refusing to overrule previous decisions that liability is strict as to age in the offence of indecent assault.[54] This decision is not inconsistent with *B (A Minor) v DPP*. In *K*, the Court of Appeal rightly started with a presumption that the offence in section 14 required mens rea as to all elements, but was led by various factors (in particular, the statutory history) to conclude that the presumption was overridden in respect of age where the victim was under 16, and that Parliament had intended that particular element of the offence to be one of strict liability.

[46] For criticism of the decision, see Horder, "How Culpability Can, and Cannot, be Denied in Under-age Sex Crimes" [2001] *Crim LR* 15; Glazebrook, "How Old Did You Think She Was?" (2001) 60 *CLJ* 26.

[47] [2000] 2 AC 428, 460 (Lord Nicholls), citing the passage from Lord Reid's judgment (above in the text) in *Sweet v Parsley* [1970] AC 132, 148–9.

[48] [2000] 2 AC 428, 481 (Lord Hutton: emphasis in original). This requirement was said to be fulfilled only if such a reading is "compellingly clear" (Lord Nicholls (464), with whom Lord Irvine agreed), "sufficiently clear" (Lord Steyn (474)), or "necessary" (Lord Hutton (479), whose speech Lord Steyn also endorsed).

[49] *Bailey* [2022] EWHC 3302 (Admin), [2023] KB 392, [17].

[50] *Nurse v Trinidad and Tobago* [2019] UKPC 43, [2020] 2 WLR 131, [24].

[51] See, e.g., *Muhamad* [2002] EWCA Crim 1856, [2003] QB 1031 (materially contributing to insolvency by gambling); *Hart v Anglian Water Services Ltd* [2003] EWCA Crim 2243, [2004] 1 Cr App R (S) 62 (causing a discharge of effluent); *Matudi* [2003] EWCA Crim 697, [2003] EHLR 13 (importing contrabanded animal products); *G* [2008] UKHL 37, [2009] 1 AC 92 (rape of a child under 13; below, § 12.11(i)).

[52] As will be seen in § 12.11, the Sexual Offences Act 2003 subsequently introduced a regime of designedly strict liability offences with respect to sexual offences involving children aged under 13 years.

[53] [2001] UKHL 41, [2002] 1 AC 462.

[54] *K* [2001] 1 Cr App R 35.

Despite this, the House of Lords overruled the Court of Appeal. Notwithstanding the history, it was not a *necessary* implication of the legislation that, in respect of V's age, the offence was one of strict liability. Given the strength of the arguments in favour of the view that section 14 imposed strict liability (indeed, as Lord Millett noted, that was clearly Parliament's intention), their Lordships' decision in *K* signals clearly that, in serious criminal offences, the courts will strive to uphold the presumption in favour of mens rea.[55]

*K* reinforces the strength of the presumption of mens rea as a principle of statutory interpretation in the context of the criminal law. At the same time, it remains merely a presumption under English law. The presumption of mens rea is simply a point of departure, and can be outweighed by other factors.[56] Even imprisonable offences have on occasion been held to be of strict liability.

That this is so is demonstrated by G.[57] G was charged with the offence of rape of a child under 13, contrary to section 5 of the Sexual Offences Act 2003. One element of this offence is that the complainant is under 13 years of age. When G's case reached the House of Lords it was held that the intention of Parliament, as manifested in the scheme of the statute, excluded mens rea with regard to that element of the offence.[58] G's mistake as to V's age—G had been told by V that she was, like him, 15 years old—was, accordingly, legally irrelevant. G's conviction for rape of a child under 13 was, thus, upheld (it being no defence that V willingly participated in sexual activity with G). Unfortunately, though inevitably, the courts in *G* went on to rule further that this interpretation was consistent with the presumption of innocence guaranteed by Article 6(2) of the ECHR.[59] The imposition of strict liability is still a matter of statutory interpretation, rather than a question of the defendant's right to a fair trial.

In summary, although the presumption of mens rea is assured as a judicial starting point, it can be overcome. In ascertaining whether the presumption of mens rea will be overcome in relation to one or more elements of a criminal offence, the courts have emphasised the importance of several factors. These factors—which interact, and can exist in tension, with each another—are considered in the following sections.

### *(ii) Factor 1: The nature of the offence*

#### *(a) The nature of the offence in general*

The first, and perhaps most important, concern is whether the offence is "serious" or "truly criminal", as opposed to a "quasi-criminal",[60] "public welfare", or "regulatory" offence.[61] At

[55] Compare *Kumar* [2004] EWCA Crim 3207, [2005] 1 WLR 1352, where the Court of Appeal cited both *B (A Minor)* and *K* in ruling that, in the former offence of buggery contrary to s. 12 of the Sexual Offences Act 1956, a mens rea requirement with respect to C's age had been neither expressly nor necessarily excluded by the legislation.

[56] A point emphasised in *Lane* [2018] UKSC 36, [2018] 1 WLR 3647, [9] (Lord Hughes).

[57] [2008] UKHL 37, [2009] 1 AC 92.

[58] Below, § 12.11(i).

[59] A ruling confirmed (in the context of that offence) in *G v UK* (2011) 53 EHRR SE25. Cf. *Deyemi and Edwards* [2007] EWCA Crim 2060, [2008] 1 Cr App R 25, [26]–[27]; *O'Riordan v DPP* [2005] EWHC 1240 (Admin). Contrast the law in Canada, at least where the offence imports the possibility of imprisonment (including in the event of failure to pay a fine): *Reference re Section 94(2) of the Motor Vehicle Act* [1985] 2 SCR 486; *Pontes* [1995] 3 SCR 44.

[60] *Pearks, Gunston & Tee Ltd v Ward* [1902] 2 KB 1, 11 (Channell J). Cp. *London Borough of Harrow v Shah* [2000] 1 WLR 83, 89 ("not truly criminal in character") (DC).

[61] Strict liability offences are typically "founded on collective convenience rather than moral imperatives": *Taylor* [2016] UKSC 5, [2016] 1 WLR 500, [26] (Lord Sumption).

the heart of this (sometimes very difficult, yet apparently sufficiently clear[62]) distinction is the nature of the mischief that the offence is designed to suppress. An offence will be of the truly criminal variety, and require a mens rea element for every element of the actus reus, when it prohibits an activity that is, in itself, overtly wrongful (e.g. murder, assault, and the like).[63] In these cases the activity may occasion moral condemnation even without being criminalised, and a conviction is therefore likely to attract a substantial level of moral stigma. By contrast, where conviction for the offence is likely to occasion little or no public stigma (as in the case of speeding),[64] the courts will be more willing to impose strict liability. Such instances are said to fall within the "class of acts . . . which are not criminal in any real sense, but are acts which in the public interest are prohibited under a penalty".[65]

*(b) Specialist activities*

More problematic are cases where the defendant's activity is not necessarily or inherently wrongful, but becomes the actus reus of an offence when done in a particular manner. Such offences often involve strict liability. Driving a vehicle may be a legitimate activity, but driving a vehicle without insurance is a strict liability offence—the defendant does not need to know, or even be reckless, about his lack of insurance.[66] Factors relevant to the assessment of such offences include whether the offence is directed at regulating trades, activities, and the like, especially those which involve specialist skills and those for which one must be licensed. Where this is the case, it is more likely to be treated as a public welfare offence, i.e. as one that regulates and controls excesses in an otherwise acceptable practice, and strict liability is more likely to be imposed.

The fact that the activity is a specialist one also increases the probability that its regulation will involve strict liability. One reason for this is that the use of strict liability simplifies prosecutions, increasing the chances of effective enforcement of the criminal law. This factor is especially salient when the defendant may be expected to know far better than the prosecutor what went wrong and how it could have been prevented. In such circumstances, it may be unreasonable to suppose that the prosecutor will be able to acquire sufficiently accurate knowledge of the workings of the defendant's business organisation or activity to prove mens rea for each element of the actus reus. As Lord Salmon commented in *Alphacell Ltd v Woodward*, on a charge brought under a now-repealed offence under the Rivers (Prevention of Pollution) Act 1951:[67]

> "If . . . no conviction could be obtained under the 1951 Act unless the prosecution could discharge the often impossible onus of proving that the pollution was caused intentionally or negligently, a great deal of pollution would go unpunished and undeterred to the relief of many riparian factory owners."

This reasoning is reinforced (at least in the eyes of the courts) by the fact that regulation of a voluntary specialist activity does not lead to the conviction of citizens for doing ordinary

[62] *R (Mohamed) v Waltham Forest LBC* [2020] EWHC 1083 (Admin), [2020] 1 WLR 2929, [37].
[63] Note, however, that murder does not require mens rea as to the causing of death: an intention to cause grievous bodily harm will suffice. Murder is an example of constructive liability, discussed in § 6.5 below.
[64] Road Traffic Regulation Act 1984, s. 89(1). The only argument open to defendants who are ignorant of the speed limit is that the relevant signage did not comply with the requirements of the 1988 Act.
[65] *Sherras v De Rutzen* [1895] 1 QB 918, 922.
[66] Road Traffic Act 1988, s. 143(2); *Tapsell v Maslen* [1967] Crim LR 53 (DC).
[67] [1972] AC 824. Cp. *Woodrow* (1846) 15 M & W 404, 417, 153 ER 907, 913.

things without being on notice that their conduct risked breaching the criminal law. Concerns about fair warning[68] are (the argument goes) less pressing where the defendant may be said to some extent to have assumed the risks of liability by voluntarily bringing herself within the particular sphere of operation of a regulatory law. In *Hobbs v Winchester Corporation*, for example, a butcher suing for compensation in respect of unsound meat that had been destroyed was held to have been in default, and so barred from recovering, even though he had no reasonable means of discovering the condition of the meat:[69]

> "the policy of the Act is this: that if a man chooses for profit to engage in a business which involves offering for sale of that which may be deadly or injurious to health he must take that risk, and that it is not a sufficient defence for anyone who chooses to embark on such a business to say 'I could not have discovered the disease unless I had an analyst on the premises'".

A similar point was made in *Sweet v Parsley* by Lord Diplock:[70]

> "Where penal provisions are of general application to the conduct of ordinary citizens in the course of their every day life, the presumption is that the standard of care required of them in informing themselves of facts which would make their conduct unlawful, is that of the familiar common law duty of care. But where the subject-matter of a statute is the regulation of a particular activity involving potential danger to public health, safety or morals, in which citizens have a choice whether they participate or not, the court may feel driven to infer an intention of Parliament to impose, by penal sanctions, a higher duty of care on those who choose to participate."

Whether this is a *good* argument for imposing strict liability will be considered below, in § 6.3. For the moment it is sufficient to note that some judges think it is, and will be more willing to find strict liability where the statute governs a specialist activity.

### *(c) The danger posed by the relevant conduct*

As Lord Diplock contemplates in the quotation above, the likelihood that strict liability will be read into an offence is also increased if the activities it regulates have a tendency to endanger sections of the public[71] or the environment.[72] Obvious places for such laws are regulations governing the quality of food products,[73] the distribution of drugs,[74] and safety on the road[75] or in the workplace. An important instance of the last type is *Gammon (Hong Kong) Ltd v A-G for Hong Kong*.[76] Following the collapse of construction work on a building site, the defendants responsible for the site were charged with deviating in a material way from the approved

[68] See above, § 2.3.
[69] [1910] 2 KB 471, 484–85 (CA).
[70] [1970] AC 132, 163. One interesting philosophical discussion which makes a point of this type is Honoré, "Responsibility and Luck: The Moral Basis of Strict Liability" (1988) 104 *LQR* 530.
[71] Or, it seems, the economy: *St Margaret's Trust Ltd* [1958] 1 WLR 522, 527 (CA): "The present generation has witnessed the collapse of the currency in other countries and the consequent chaos, misery and widespread ruin".
[72] Cf. *Alphacell Ltd v Woodward* [1972] AC 824, 848 (Lord Salmon): "many rivers which are now filthy would become filthier still and many rivers which are now clean would lose their cleanliness"; *Kirkland v Robinson* [1987] Crim LR 643 (DC). This approach is still adopted, notwithstanding the fact that environmental offences now involve significant social stigma.
[73] Especially prior to the introduction of a statutory "due diligence" defence in Food Safety Act 1990, s. 21. Cf. *Lim Chin Aik* [1963] AC 160, 174 (PC); Williams, *CLGP* 218–27.
[74] *Pharmaceutical Society of Great Britain v Storkwain Ltd* [1986] 1 WLR 903 (HL); *Warner v Metropolitan Police Commissioner* [1969] 2 AC 256.
[75] *Bowsher* [1973] RTR 202 (CA); *Reynolds v GH Austin & Sons* [1951] 2 KB 135 (DC).
[76] [1985] AC 1 (PC).

plan, contrary to local construction regulations. The offence carried a substantial fine and possible imprisonment for up to three years. Noting that the presumption of mens rea is "particularly strong" in such circumstances, since the offence did appear to be "truly criminal" in character, the Privy Council nonetheless advised that the offence was one of strict liability. Lord Scarman highlighted the importance of the danger that the offence sought to guard against: "the only situation in which the presumption can be displaced is where the statute is concerned with an issue of social concern, and public safety is such an issue".[77]

Lord Scarman went on to describe an additional condition that should be met: efficacy. Overriding the presumption of mens rea should not be done simply as a matter of convenience—something more substantial must be gained by doing so:[78]

> "Even where a statute is concerned with such an issue [of social concern], the presumption of mens rea stands unless it can also be shown that the creation of strict liability will be effective to promote the objects of the statute by encouraging greater vigilance to prevent the commission of the prohibited act."

### *(d) Legal assessment of the defendant's conduct*

Another factor relevant to strict liability is that, if one element of the actus reus involves the arbitrary drawing of a line over such matters as time, quantity, or size, mens rea may be less likely to be required in respect of it. The most obvious case is a speeding offence, where the difference between 30 and 31 m.p.h. may have a significance that is purely the result of law.[79] It would be indulgent to require proof of knowledge of one's speed in such cases, and in the absence of a default negligence standard, strict liability becomes the leading alternative.[80]

Sometimes the law will not draw determinative lines, but will rather seek to evaluate the defendant's conduct with regard to evaluative criteria such as "reasonableness". If an element of the actus reus involves the legal evaluation of certain facts, then the defendant need possess only whatever mens rea is required regarding the facts themselves. She need not be aware of the legal evaluation itself,[81] which is a legal conclusion in the nature of a normative value judgement that the defendant is not permitted to second-guess.[82] For example, it is not

[77] *Ibid.*, 14.

[78] *Ibid.* Cf. *Lim Chin Aik* [1963] AC 160, 175 (PC); *Sweet v Parsley* [1970] AC 132, 163 (Lord Diplock); *Reynolds v GH Austin & Sons* [1951] 2 KB 135, 150 (DC).

[79] This principle does not apply to age, at least in the context of sexual offences—where V's age has independent moral significance: *B (A Minor) v DPP* [2000] 2 AC 428.

[80] Sometimes, the bluntness of this approach can be tempered by police and/or prosecutorial discretion—for instance, it may be that only drivers who exceed the speed limit by an appreciable manner will be prosecuted for speeding.

[81] A notable exception was, until recently, "dishonesty", where the defendant had to be aware that her conduct would be considered "dishonest" by the standards of reasonable and honest people: *Ghosh* [1982] QB 1053 (CA). This aspect of *Ghosh* was disapproved in *Ivey v Genting Casinos UK Ltd (t/a Crockfords Club)* [2017] UKSC 67, [2018] AC 391. See below, § 13.8(iv).

[82] As in *Doring* [2002] EWCA Crim 1695, [2003] 1 Cr App R 9 (being concerned in the management of a company while being an undisclosed bankrupt). D had been involved in the publicity, promotion, and design activities of the company, but had neither hired nor fired staff and made no financial decisions or contracts for the company. Apparently, D believed that in doing so she was not directly or indirectly managing the company. The Court of Appeal upheld her conviction, ruling that it was a matter of strict liability whether her acts, objectively understood, amounted to being concerned in the management of the company. Cp. *Lemon and Gay News Ltd* [1979] AC 617 (whether a statement is "calculated to outrage the feelings of Christians"); also the discussion of evaluative terms, above, § 2.3(i). But compare the dissent on this point by Barwick CJ in *Iannella v French* (1968) 119 CLR 84, 97.

determinative whether, in the circumstances as she perceived them, a defendant believed she was using "*reasonable* force" in self-defence: it is for the court to decide whether the force she used was reasonable.[83] (Indeed, sometimes a failure to recognise the status of one's actions—e.g. that the force one uses is excessive—may itself disclose culpability.[84]) Neither is the defendant's own perspective, about whether his conduct is "sexual", determinative.[85] The presence of a legal evaluation within the actus reus raises conflicting concerns between the need to prevent individuals from undermining the law's values, and the need to give them fair warning of the criminal implications of their conduct. We will return to this issue in the discussion of ignorance of law.[86]

*(e) The severity of punishment*

In asking whether an offence requires mens rea for each element of the actus reus, the range and severity of punishments prescribed upon conviction is taken into account. In *Gammon*, for example, the fact that the maximum penalty for the offence was a substantial fine and imprisonment for three years was said by the Privy Council to be a "formidable point"[87] militating against strict liability. The severity of punishment might inform the court about the nature of the offence: the potential for imprisonment is often an indication that an offence is "truly criminal" rather than merely "regulatory" in character. In such cases, the presumption of mens rea normally should not be displaced.

The courts do not, however, regard the mere prospect of imprisonment as enough to make a crime "serious". In *Muhamad*,[88] the offence of materially contributing to one's insolvency by gambling, contrary to a now repealed offence under the Insolvency Act 1986, was held to involve strict liability notwithstanding the maximum sentence of two years' imprisonment. In the view of Dyson LJ:[89]

> "The starting point, therefore, is to determine how serious an offence is created by section 362(1)(a), and accordingly how much weight, if any, should be attached to the presumption. Some weight must undoubtedly be given to the presumption, but in our judgment it can be readily displaced. As we have said, the maximum sentence indicates that Parliament considered this to be an offence of some significance, but not one of the utmost seriousness. This is not surprising. We do not believe that great stigma attaches to a conviction of this offence."

It is not clear why an offence must be of "the utmost seriousness" if the presumption of mens rea is to remain in place. There is much to be said for the approach adopted in the Model Penal Code, which asserts that the possibility of imprisonment for any term should be a conclusive reason against imposing strict liability.[90] Nonetheless, the English courts and the Privy Council have ruled some quite substantial maximum sentences to be consistent with the imposition of strict liability, after taking into account such considerations

[83] *Owino* [1996] 2 Cr App R 128; Criminal Justice and Immigration Act 2008, s. 76(6). See, further, below, § 21.2(iii).
[84] For brief discussion of this point, see Simester, "Is Strict Liability Always Wrong?" in Simester (ed.), *Appraising Strict Liability* (2005) 21, 42–4.
[85] *Attorney-General's Reference (No. 1 of 2020)* [2020] EWCA Crim 1665, [2021] QB 441.
[86] Below, § 18.2.
[87] [1985] AC 1, 17 (PC).
[88] [2002] EWCA Crim 1856, [2003] QB 1031.
[89] *Ibid*, [16]. Cp. *Lim Chin Aik* [1963] AC 160, 174-5 (PC).
[90] § 6.02(4). Cp., in Canada, *Reference re Section 94(2) of the Motor Vehicle Act* [1985] 2 SCR 486.

as the interest (e.g. public safety) being protected,[91] and, more controversially, the need to ensure compliance with the law.[92] These include the offence in *Gammon* itself, where the Privy Council, immediately after acknowledging the severity of the maximum penalties, continued with a "but": "there is nothing inconsistent with the purpose of the Ordinance in imposing severe penalties for offences of strict liability".[93]

One may ask whether the Privy Council missed the point. The mere fact that strict liability is "not inconsistent" with the purpose of the statute is hardly a reason to impose it, and in no way meets the objection that in *Gammon* the maximum penalties were severe, which points towards the "truly criminal" nature of the offence. Neither does the logic in *Gammon* conform to the requirement—laid down in *B (A Minor) v DPP*[94]—that the imposition of strict liability must be a *necessary implication* of the statute, and not merely *consistent* with it. It is to be hoped that decisions such as *Gammon* will be rarer in the future.

That having been said, the potential for heavy penalties in an offence gives rise to a tension. Severe sanctions generally give the offence a criminal character, yet they may also reflect the fact that the subject matter of the offence—the social danger or harm involved—is itself substantial, a factor (as seen above) weighing in favour of strict liability. The type of offence most suitable for strict liability would involve substantial ultimate public harm or inconvenience (whether directly or cumulatively), and relatively little stigma for an individual offence. This may occur, for example, in certain road traffic offences. Similarly, the offence in *Alphacell Ltd v Woodward*[95] of causing polluted material to enter a stream, which carried a low maximum penalty, was also relatively well suited to strict liability; especially in 1972, when pollution offences tended to be regarded as "acts not criminal in any real sense".[96] It is clear from the foregoing discussion that in practice the courts have extended their recognition of strict liability well beyond these examples. Moreover, attitudes change. Destruction and despoliation of the natural environment is now a very salient concern and acts degrading and threatening the environment would now readily be regarded as "truly criminal". On the face of it, that would give greater weight to the presumption in favour of mens rea for offences in this area, a move not likely to be favoured by anyone committed to optimum enforcement of environmental law.[97]

### *(iii) Factor 2: The language of the legislation*

Sometimes, rather than being presumed or explicit, or established by the judicial history, the legislature's intent to include or exclude a mens rea requirement can be implied directly from the words or scheme of the statute. This may occur in a number of ways.[98]

[91] E.g. *R v Wells Street Magistrates' Court and Martin, ex p Westminster City Council* [1986] 1 WLR 1046 (DC) (1 year's imprisonment); *Pharmaceutical Society of Great Britain v Storkwain Ltd* [1986] 1 WLR 903 (HL) (2 years' imprisonment); *Howells* [1977] QB 614 (CA) (5 years' imprisonment). Indeed, English courts have even imposed strict liability in crimes attracting a *mandatory* minimum term of imprisonment, such as Firearms Act 1968, s. 5 (if D is over 18, 5 years' imprisonment—s. 51A(5)): see, e.g., *Zahid* [2010] EWCA Crim 2158.

[92] E.g. *Nurse v Trinidad and Tobago* [2019] UKPC 43, [2020] 2 WLR 131, [47].

[93] [1985] AC 1, 17 (PC).

[94] [2000] 2 AC 428.

[95] [1972] AC 824.

[96] *Sherras v De Rutzen* [1895] 1 QB 918, 922 (Wright J).

[97] For an interesting perspective on the practical enforceability of environmental crimes, see Tromans, "Environmental Crime at Ambridge" [2019] 6 *Archbold Review* 4.

[98] See, further, Manchester, "Knowledge, Due Diligence and Strict Liability in Regulatory Offences" [2006] *Crim LR* 213, 216–19, 223–7.

First, a verb specifying part of the actus reus may import a mental element. An example of this is "possession", the meaning of which was discussed in § 5.6(iv). According to the House of Lords,[99] D is not in possession of an article unless she is *aware* that she possesses it.[100] Similarly, it has been held that "permitting" another to use a vehicle when equipped with defective brakes can only be done knowingly. As a matter of ordinary language, the Divisional Court said, permitting "in our opinion, at once imports a state of mind".[101] Thus it is impossible, at least in that offence, to "permit" inadvertently.[102] A similar argument can be made in respect of "allowing".[103]

### *(iv) Factor 3: The scheme of the legislation*

A third factor in establishing whether an offence involves strict liability is the scheme of the statute. Some of the earliest strict liability cases turned on this point. In *Betts v Armstead*,[104] the defendant was charged with selling adulterated bread, contrary to section 6 of the Sale of Food and Drugs Act 1875. He was apparently unaware the loaf was adulterated; nonetheless, he was convicted, since under section 5 an absence of relevant knowledge had expressly been made a defence to offences enacted by sections 2–4, but not to the section 6 offence.

The validity of this type of inference was, however, subsequently doubted by Lord Goddard CJ,[105] since verbal distinctions of this sort may arise from the consolidation of earlier statutes without thematic revision, the vagaries of parliamentary amendment, or even imperfect drafting. The present situation appears to be that linguistic difference between sections is a factor that may be taken into account, but is not itself decisive:[106]

> "It is also firmly established that the fact that other sections of the Act expressly require mens rea, for example because they contain the word 'knowingly', is not itself sufficient to justify a decision that a section which is silent as to mens rea creates an absolute offence."

Similarly, some offences have a defence of non-negligence (due diligence) attached to them.[107] Such a defence would be otiose if the offence were to require proof of mens rea

[99] *Warner v Metropolitan Police Commissioner* [1969] 2 AC 256.

[100] Although she need not be aware of the item's precise character; to that extent, therefore, a possession offence which specifies no further mens rea element can be regarded, in substance, as an offence of strict liability. In *Tinarwo* [2014] EWCA Crim 1409, for instance, T was held liable for possession of a firearm on the basis that the bag that he was in (knowing) possession of contained a handgun, which he claimed had been "planted" without his knowledge. In upholding T's conviction, the Court of Appeal conceded that "this may or may not be harsh", but noted that it could not rewrite the relevant statutory wording (at [13]). Cf. *Johnson* [2017] EWCA Crim 189, [2018] 1 WLR 19, where it was held that, although D need not know exactly what prohibited item he possessed, D had to be proved to know that he was carrying *something* prohibited.

[101] *James & Son Ltd v Smee* [1955] 1 QB 78, 91 (DC).

[102] Although the same may not hold for other offences: *DPP v Fisher* [1992] RTR 93 (DC) (permitting a vehicle to be used without insurance a strict liability offence). The meaning of "permit" appears to depend on the context and may vary across offences: contrast, e.g., *Vehicle Inspectorate v Nuttall* [1999] 1 WLR 629 (HL); *Brock* [2001] 1 WLR 1159 (CA).

[103] Edwards, *Mens Rea in Statutory Offences* (1955) 162–3. See, also, *CPS v M* [2009] EWCA Crim 2615, [2011] 1 WLR 822 ("throwing" held to import mens rea).

[104] (1888) 20 QBD 771. Cf. *Parker v Alder* [1899] 1 QB 20; *Fitzpatrick v Kelly* (1873) LR 8 QB 337.

[105] *Lines v Hersom* [1951] 2 KB 682, 686–7 (DC).

[106] *Sweet v Parsley* [1970] AC 132, 149 (Lord Reid). This factor will be particularly weak if the statute is a consolidation of previous statutes passed at different times: cp. *K* [2002] 1 AC 462, 467 (Lord Bingham).

[107] See Parry, "Judicial Approaches to Due Diligence" [1995] *Crim LR* 695.

regarding the relevant part(s) of the actus reus. Section 21 of the Food Safety Act 1990, for example, provides, in respect of offences created by sections 1–20 of the Act, that "it shall . . . be a defence for the person charged to prove that he took all reasonable precautions and exercised all due diligence to avoid the commission of the offence". By implication, the offences enacted in those preceding sections are otherwise of strict liability. This type of statutory "due diligence" defence is now a common feature of regulatory offences.[108]

The difference is more likely to be decisive, however, where the relevant statute was drawn up as a coherent regime, especially where the legislature has created parallel pairs of offences only one of which specifies a mens rea requirement. An example is the Sexual Offences Act 2003, which—as Chapter 12 explains—aims to set out a coherent scheme of sexual offences. Differences in the drafting of sections of the 2003 Act can therefore help to uncover strict liability. Consider section 9, which creates an offence of "sexual activity with a child". Section 9 provides that, if the child is between 13 and 15 years of age, the defendant must be proved not to have reasonably believed that the child was over 16: a negligence-based standard. If the child is under 13, however, no fault element is mentioned. It can be assumed that Parliament intended to draw a distinction between cases involving 13- to 15-year-olds (where fault is required) and children under 13 (where no fault is required). Further support for this proposition can be taken from the offence under section 5 ("rape of a child under 13"). Again, no fault element is mentioned with regard to the age of the child, and it has been held that Parliament intended this to engage strict liability.[109] It would be odd, in a statute enacted so recently and with aspirations of consistency, for Parliament to have intended strict liability in section 5, and then—with the same wording in the parallel part of section 9—intended there to be a requirement of fault. This example demonstrates both how internal reasoning (within section 9) and analogical reasoning (from section 5) can help uncover whether a particular offence within a coherent statute involves strict liability.[110]

### *(v) The need to avoid judicial legislation?*

A fourth—dubious—factor considered by the courts is whether they regard it as possible to discern a precise fault element relating to a particular aspect of the actus reus, or whether this would be an unduly speculative endeavour. In the latter scenario, the court will be "wary of arrogating to itself the role of Parliament by drafting the definition of the offence itself".[111]

For instance, in *Pwr v DPP*,[112] the Supreme Court confessed its inability to discern which particular fault element might be required regarding the fact that the defendant's conduct gave rise to a "reasonable suspicion" of membership of, or support for, a proscribed

[108] See, e.g., Simester and Roberts, "Strict Liability in UK Regulation" in Macrory, *Regulatory Justice* (2006) annex E.

[109] *G* [2008] UKHL 37, [2009] 1 AC 92.

[110] See, similarly, *Pwr v DPP* [2022] UKSC 2, [2022] 1 WLR 789, where it was noted (at [45]–[46]) that, if an offence under s. 13(1) of the Terrorism Act 2000 required subjective mens rea regarding the proscribed nature of the relevant organisation, it would entirely overlap with other offences in the same legislation.

[111] *Bailey* [2022] EWHC 3302 (Admin), [2023] KB 392, [44].

[112] [2022] UKSC 2, [2022] 1 WLR 789.

organisation.[113] Would it, for example, be knowledge, belief, suspicion, or recklessness? Trying to answer such questions was viewed as going beyond the judicial role:[114]

> "[Counsel for the defence] argued that it was the role of this court to articulate an appropriate mens rea and that he was merely making suggestions as to possibilities so as to try to assist the court. We accept, of course, that it is the role of the court to interpret correctly what Parliament has enacted. But it is not the role of the court, in applying the law on the presumption of mens rea, to rewrite the statute, still less to do so in a way that contradicts the express words used. We also regard it as falling outside the judicial role for this court to accept [counsel's] invitation to embark on a speculative exercise to divine what Parliament may have intended as mens rea."

For this and other reasons, the relevant matter was held to be one of strict liability.

Similarly, in *DPP v Bailey*,[115] the question for the Divisional Court was whether the offence of aggravated trespass[116] required mens rea regarding the defendant's status as a trespasser. The trial judge had decided that proof was required of the defendant's intention to trespass, or recklessness regarding the defendant's status as a trespasser, but the Divisional Court held that it was "not at all clear why that should be so; nor were we offered any principled or reasoned argument for that particular formulation".[117] Here, as in *Pwr*, it may again be questioned whether recklessness is the appropriate mens rea here, or whether it would be more appropriate to require proof of at least knowledge or belief. Parliament had not clearly indicated any view on this point, and the Court refused to perform that task on its behalf. For this and other reasons, it was held that the defendant's status as a trespasser was a matter of strict liability.

Although this rationale about speculation and appropriate fault elements is now adopted by the courts, it does present a quandary. Debates about strict liability arise *precisely because* Parliament has remained silent on the matter of mens rea regarding one or more aspects of the actus reus. *Some* judicial imagination is therefore required unless all such offences are to be found to be ones of strict liability. Accordingly, the courts have often grasped the nettle and endorsed a particular mens rea concept—typically knowledge or recklessness—regarding a particular element of the actus reus. The refusal to engage in such an exercise in *Pwr* and *Bailey* is an abdication of this judicial function. It has the potential to reduce significantly the strength of the presumption of mens rea.

It would have been preferable if the courts in *Pwr* and *Bailey* had relied exclusively on the other factors that they thought pointed in favour of strict liability, and not relied on the apparent need for judicial creativity in deciding which precise mens rea concept might require to be proved. For instance, in *Pwr* the defendant was arguing that mens rea should be proved in relation to a legal assessment of his conduct (whether it gave rise to the relevant reasonable suspicion). As explained above (in § 6.1(ii)(d)), such assessments tend to be matters of strict liability. In relation to *Bailey*, the Divisional Court considered the scheme of the relevant legislation, and noted that Parliament had expended significant effort on setting out the mens rea for other aspects of the aggravated trespass offence,

113 Terrorism Act 2000, s. 13.
114 *Pwr v DPP* [2022] UKSC 2, [2022] 1 WLR 789, [40].
115 [2022] EWHC 3302 (Admin), [2023] KB 392.
116 Criminal Justice and Public Order Act 1994, s. 68.
117 *Bailey v DPP* [2022] EWHC 3302 (Admin), [2023] KB 392, [44].

suggesting that it had intended for the fact that D was a trespasser to be a matter of strict liability.

### *(vi) The ability of others to affect D's liability?*

In overseas jurisdictions, it has sometimes been said that if strict liability is to be imposed at all, it should be done only in offences that are set out in the clearest terms, so that it is possible for a defendant to know in advance what are the boundaries of the offence: "When there is absolute liability there ought to be absolute certainty as to the ingredients of the offence so that the offender cannot say that he was unable beforehand to conduct himself so as to avoid the offence".[118] As part of this general approach, the New Zealand courts have been reluctant to ascribe strict liability in cases where the defendant's activity is affected by what others are doing. Thus, in *Jackson v Attorney-General*,[119] the High Court held that one reason for not imposing strict liability for the (now-repealed) offence of possessing cannabis in a prison cell, contrary to section 32 of the Penal Institutions Act 1954 (NZ), was that imposition of strict liability would tend to encourage inmates to take retribution against another inmate by placing cannabis or other drugs in the other's cell.[120]

The potential for third parties to bring D within the scope of an offence should not normally be accompanied by strict liability on D's part.[121] These considerations, which involve principles applicable to the common law generally, deserve also to be given weight by English courts when determining whether a particular offence imposes strict liability. To date, they have not been mentioned.

## § 6.2 The availability of common law defences

If an offence is found to involve strict liability, this can impact upon the arguments available to D. Obviously, D may not plead an absence of mens rea regarding strict liability elements of an offence. It appears that D may still, however, plead common law defences, in addition to any specific statutory defences that have been created. For instance, there is modern appellate authority recognising that duress, whether by threats or circumstances, is available as a defence to the strict liability offence of driving while disqualified.[122] Defences such

[118] *Re Wairarapa Election Petition* [1988] 2 NZLR 74, 117.

[119] [2006] 2 NZLR 534, [36(d)].

[120] Compare, too, *Police v Creedon* [1976] 1 NZLR 571, 573, a prosecution for failing to yield the right of way at an intersection, where the Court of Appeal emphasised the importance of the fact that "the regulation requires a driver of a motor vehicle to take a specific course of action if, and only if, something else is being done by someone else". By contrast with (say) failing to stop at an intersection governed by a stop sign, the offence in *Creedon* does "not impose an omnipresent and unvarying obligation" (*ibid.*, 574). Its uncertain boundaries were said therefore to militate against strict liability.

[121] Cp. *Re Wairarapa Election Petition* [1988] 2 NZLR 74, 117. For related discussion of this point, see Simester, "The Mental Element in Complicity" (2006) 122 *LQR* 578, 580–1.

[122] *Martin* [1989] 1 All ER 652 (CA); though see *Cichon v DPP* (DC), noted and criticised at [1994] Crim LR 918. Neither was the defence doubted (except on the facts) in *DPP v Mullally* [2006] EWHC 3448 (Admin). See, further, *Pipe v DPP* [2012] EWHC 1821 (Admin) (duress of circumstances a defence to speeding). Canadian authority supports the availability of such defences as a general proposition: *Cancoil Thermal Corp and Parkinson* (1986) 27 CCC (3d) 295, 301–2; *Walker* (1979) 48 CCC (2d) 126, 134–5; *Kennedy* (1972) 7 CCC (2d) 42; *Breau* (1959) 125 CCC 84. There is a brief discussion of these questions in Sayre, "Public Welfare Offences" (1933) 33 *Col LR* 55, 75–8.

as duress, necessity, and self-defence therefore seem to be available. We saw in Chapter 4 that the same is true for automatism and involuntariness.[123]

The position was, until recently, less clear regarding insanity. In *DPP v H*, McCowan LJ stated that:[124]

> "The [insanity] defence is based on the absence of mens rea, but none is required for the offence of driving with an excess of alcohol. Hence the defence of insanity has no relevance to such a charge as it is an offence of strict liability."

This is simply wrong,[125] and fortunately the error has now been noticed by the Divisional Court. In *Loake v CPS*,[126] the Court noted that insanity, in law, is not based on the absence of mens rea. It is a much more profound denial of the defendant's moral agency; of moral responsibility for the actus reus.[127] As we shall see in Chapter 19, the defence of insanity comes in two main forms: either as (effectively) insane automatism or as incapacity to recognise the wrongness of one's act. Regarding the first variety of insanity: automatism—whether sane or insane—is not merely a denial of mens rea, as a matter either of law or of principle. It is clearly established that automatism is a general defence to strict liability as well as other offences, and there was Court of Appeal authority from before *H* that this includes insane automatism[128]—which, at the level of principle and as recognised in *Loake*, is right. Regarding the second variety of insanity: there is no denial of mens rea at all. The defendant *has* mens rea, and is simply incapable of recognising that his actions (of which he is aware) are wrong. It is therefore impossible for insanity to be "based on the absence of mens rea". The confirmation in *Loake* that insanity is available in relation to offences of strict liability is, accordingly, welcome.

### *(i) Exception for situational offences*

In Chapter 4, during the discussion of involuntariness, a distinction was drawn between state-of affairs offences and other types of offences, e.g. those involving an act or omission by the defendant. As we saw in § 4.3(ii)(b), it appears that automatism and impossibility are not available in relation to offences that comprise purely a state of affairs, and which make no reference to the defendant's behaviour. It may be that the same is true for common law defences such as duress. If so, then although duress seems generally to be available for strict liability offences, it would not be available when the particular strict liability offence criminalises a pure state of affairs. The point appears to be undecided.[129]

A second distinction reinforces the suspicion that duress is not a defence in relation to offences based exclusively on the existence of a state of affairs. In those strict liability cases

[123] Above, § 4.3(i).

[124] [1997] 1 WLR 1406, 1409 (DC). See, further, *R. v Horseferry Road Magistrates' Court, ex parte K* [1997] QB 23 (DC).

[125] See Ward, "Magistrates, Insanity and the Common Law" [1997] *Crim LR* 796, 800–2.

[126] [2017] EWHC 2855 (Admin), [2018] QB 998.

[127] Simester, "On Justifications and Excuses" in Zedner and Roberts (eds.), *Principles and Values in Criminal Law and Criminal Justice* (2012) 95, 96–7.

[128] *Hennessy* [1989] 1 WLR 287 (CA); *Isitt* (1978) 67 Cr App R 44; cp. *Hill v Baxter* [1958] 1 QB 277, 283, 285–6 (DC).

[129] In this respect, *Larsonneur* (1934) 24 Cr App R 74 is authority only that *lawful* compulsion by another would be no defence.

where a common law defence has been recognised, the offence has always been a mixed one, containing a strict liability element together with one or more actus reus elements for which mens rea is required. However, where the offence is mixed, defences such as duress will be available anyway, since they can attach in respect of the components that require mens rea. By contrast, strict liability offences which criminalise states of affairs *simpliciter* are likely to contain no mens rea element whatsoever. There is no case of this type in which a common law defence has been allowed, and *obiter* authority to the contrary. In the context of the strict liability crime of being a parent of a child who fails to attend school regularly,[130] Richards LJ was most sceptical:[131]

> "I am reluctant to decide this point on the basis of a late short argument from one side and without the benefit of contrary submissions. I have to say, for my part, that I am very doubtful whether the terms of s 444(1) admit of the possibility of a defence of duress of circumstances at all. The subsection looks not to the conduct of the parent or even to the parent's failure to act, but simply to whether the child has failed to attend regularly at school and whether the defendant is the parent of that child. There is no obvious scope for a defence that the parent acted or failed to act by reason of some necessity or duress of circumstances. In my view, this was not the kind of offence that Rose LJ can have had in mind when formulating his broad proposition in *R v Abdul-Hussain and Others* [1999] Crim LR 570 as to the cases in which the defence is available. In *Abdul-Hussain* he went on to say that:
>
> 'Imminent peril of death or serious injury to the defendant or those to whom the defendant had responsibility is an essential element in the defence and that the perils operated on the mind of the defendant at the time that he commenced the otherwise criminal act so as to overbear his will.'
>
> That reference to the will being overborne reinforces my concern about the availability of the defence in the context of a strict liability offence of this nature."

In our view, the legal and moral case for excepting situational offences from the reach of duress should be rejected. For one thing, it is founded on a category error, a false assimilation of defences with mens rea. Especially given the technical nature of mens rea requirements,[132] the two are quite separate kinds of liability element. Secondly, as will be seen in Chapter 20, duress is *not* a refutation of "will"—rather, it explains why D (reasonably) made the choice *that D wilfully made*. Thirdly, and most importantly, there is no moral basis for drawing a distinction that deprives situational liability offences, as opposed to other strict liability crimes, of access to the common-law defences. As we noted earlier,[133] situational liability is simply a convenient and indirect way of imposing liability for D's failure to prevent the "situation"—i.e., the actus reus—from occurring. If the offence had been phrased in terms of that failure to prevent, the defences would be available.

## § 6.3 The justification of strict liability

Like it or not, strict liability appears to be well entrenched in our legal system. Indeed, studies have suggested that approximately half of all offences involve at least one strict liability

[130] Contrary to the Education Act 1996, s. 444(1).
[131] *Hampshire County Council v E* [2007] EWHC 2584 (Admin), [2008] ELR 260, [10]–[11].
[132] Above, Chapter 5.
[133] Above, §§ 4.1(ii)(a), 4.3(ii)(b).

element.[134] But is it ever *morally* right to impose strict liability for a criminal offence? Without a mens rea requirement being required in relation to the entirety of the actus reus, strict liability characteristically licenses the conviction of the blameless. Can doing so ever be justified?[135]

In the following sections, we argue that the answer is "no": strict liability should be replaced with a requirement that the prosecution proves at least negligence with regard to the relevant actus reus element, or—if that is unrealistic—strict liability offences should systematically allow for "due diligence" (i.e. no negligence) defences, with a legal burden being placed on the defendant.

### *(i) The need for public protection*

The first argument that is often given for abandoning a mens rea requirement with regard to one or more aspects of the actus reus is that protection of the public sometimes requires a high standard of care on the part of those who undertake risk-creating activities.[136] Proper care needs to be taken by such persons, and without strict liability the careless will be able to transfer the considerable costs of their foolishness to the rest of society, without having any serious incentive to reduce or eliminate those risks. The threat of strict criminal liability supplies a motive for persons in risk-generating activities to adopt precautions, which might not otherwise be taken, in order to ensure that unforeseen mishaps and errors are eliminated.[137] Lady Wootton's writing is a useful example of this type of argument:[138]

> "If the law says that certain things are not to be done, it is illogical to confine this prohibition to occasions on which they are done from malice aforethought; for at least the material consequences of an action, and the reasons for prohibiting it are the same whether it is the result of sinister malicious plotting, of negligence, or of sheer accident. . . . [I]n the modern world . . . as much and more damage is done by negligence, or by indifference to the welfare or safety of others, as by deliberate wickedness."

In practice, such deterrence-based reasoning seems to be reflected in the law, since, as we have observed already, regulatory offences are often found where there is a need to protect the public from risks created by industrial and other specialist activities. Particularly where the harmful impact of the actus reus is severe and widespread, the law has reason to provide incentives through criminalisation for persons not only to refrain from advertent wrongdoing, but also to take care against inadvertent harms.

Two responses are available to this argument. First, it is unclear why *criminal* rather than civil sanctions should be used to regulate the activities involved and deter risk-takers. Even if private individuals cannot pursue a claim for damages, it may be open to the state,

[134] Ashworth and Blake, "The Presumption of Innocence in English Criminal Law" [1996] *Crim LR* 306; JUSTICE, *Breaking the Rules* (1980). Although these studies are now showing their age, there is no reason to suspect the situation has improved.

[135] See, further, Simester, *Fundamentals* chap. 13.

[136] See Honoré, "Responsibility and Luck: The Moral Basis of Strict Liability" (1988) 104 *LQR* 530.

[137] *R v City of Sault Ste. Marie* [1978] 2 SCR 1299, 1310–1311. Cp. the criterion of efficacy, above, § 6.1(ii)(c).

[138] *Crime and the Criminal Law* (2nd ed., 1981) 46, 50. The claim of illogicality is, incidentally, false. Sometimes the presence of mens rea (and particularly intention) is crucial to the wrongfulness of what is done: above, § 5.3. Wootton's argument therefore applies only to those harms whose nature is independent of the mens rea with which they are caused, and which (as such) are sufficiently severe to warrant criminalisation.

by legislative reform, to pursue miscreants through an administrative system of regulations that applies a standard of strict liability without the accompanying connotations of a criminal conviction—a move that was once contemplated by the Cabinet Office.[139] Arguably, as things stand now, the moral authority of the criminal law is being undermined by the extension of liability to what are, in essence, mere regulatory violations.[140]

Against this response it may be noted that the description, "mere regulatory violations", somewhat underplays the vital public protection role that construction standards, work-safety standards, pollution standards, etc., discharge. Setting up a new system to try these matters as civil infractions rather than crimes would, admittedly, be a major task, and might be seen as downgrading the importance of effective regulation. There is little evidence that the proliferation of regulatory crimes has blunted the distinction between doing wrong and getting something wrong.

Yet, even if an alternative system to deal with such activities is rejected, why we should prefer strict liability to negligence? It is true that regulatory offences seek to deter those entering into specialist activities from inflicting harm upon others, and by criminalising negligence such offences may help to deter the careless and indifferent and not merely the malicious or wicked. But strict liability goes beyond that, by criminalising accidents and reasonable conduct. This goes further than is necessary or desirable.

It is foolish for the law to demand that defendants do more than what is reasonable.[141] There is no evidence that strict liability is a more effective deterrent than mens rea- or negligence-based offences,[142] and where it *does* deter, it does so in an extremely clumsy manner.[143] The effect of demanding perfection (i.e. the unreasonable) through strict liability is to force a person either: (i) to desist from the risk-creating activity altogether; or (ii) to persist and accept that she must run all risks, however esoteric and unlikely, of the prohibited harm occurring, and incur the ensuing conviction if disaster occurs.[144] The first option cannot be taken seriously. It is surely not the intention of the law to discourage people from entering into productive activity altogether. The nation's economy would not last very long if that were the outcome. It is presumably also not the aim of the law to discourage those who take criminal liability very seriously from business, whilst those who view it as just

[139] Macrory, *Regulatory Justice* (2006). The Macrory Review recommended introducing a complementary regime of Monetary Administrative Penalties, using strict liability to enforce regulatory breaches outside the criminal law.

[140] Compare Robinson, "The Criminal–Civil Distinction and the Utility of Desert" (1996) 76 *Boston ULR* 201, 212–14.

[141] Strict liability "encourages riparian factory owners not only to take reasonable steps to prevent pollution but to do everything possible to ensure that they do not cause it": *Alphacell Ltd v Woodward* [1972] AC 824, 848–9 (Lord Salmon). See, also, in *St Margaret's Trust Ltd* [1958] 1 WLR 522, 527 (CA): "[t]here would be little point in enacting that no one should breach the defences against a flood, and at the same time excusing any one who did it innocently".

[142] See Jackson, "*Storkwain*: A Case Study in Strict liability and Self-Regulation" [1991] *Crim LR* 892; Baldwin, "Why Rules Don't Work" (1990) 53 *MLR* 321; Richardson, "Strict Liability for Regulatory Crime: The Empirical Research" [1987] *Crim LR* 295; Hall, *General Principles of Criminal Law* (2nd ed., 1960) 344–7. In terms of economic incentives, it is possible that strict liability may lead to reduced rather than increased deterrence: Simester, "Is Strict Liability Always Wrong?" in Simester (ed.), *Appraising Strict Liability* (2005) 21, 30–1.

[143] Alexander, "Is There a Case for Strict Liability?" (2018) 12 *Crim Law and Philosophy* 531, 533–4; Hasnas, "Reflections on *Prince*, Public Welfare Offenses, *American Cyanamid*, and the Wisdom of the Common Law" (2018) 12 *Crim Law and Philosophy* 427, 434–7.

[144] Cp. Lord Sumption's point that strict liability should be imposed only where practical steps against the occurrence of the actus reus can realistically be taken: *Taylor* [2016] UKSC 6, [2016] 1 WLR 500, [26].

another cost remain.[145] Rather, the aim of regulatory laws must be to discourage people from entering into an activity (or from executing it in a manner) which creates *unreasonable* risks of the unwanted harm occurring. But *that* aim can be achieved by imposing negligence liability. Strict liability forces the blameless defendant to become a gratuitous risk-taker, subject to a criminal legal lottery over which he has no reasonable control. If she is unlucky, she will be convicted. A lottery is no basis on which to attribute criminal liability. Such a Draconian system, moreover, is likely to promote cynicism and disrespect for the law, particularly among innocent people who are labelled criminal "offenders" by their conviction.[146]

### *(ii) The distinction between "real" crimes and quasi-criminal offences*

Another point about the deterrence (or public protection) argument for strict liability is that it cannot possibly succeed by itself. The public needs also to be protected from assaults, damage to property, and the like, yet these are not strict liability offences; they require proof of mens rea in the ordinary way.[147] The difference, it is said, is that assault is a "true" crime, conviction for which entails serious social stigma—hence the need for a higher standard of fault, which partially overrides the deterrence argument—whereas regulatory offences control "quasi-" (i.e. not truly) criminal actions.[148] This leads to a second argument in favour of strict liability: that it is legitimate to use it when the offence under consideration is not "truly criminal".

As noted above, in the context of strict liability both the House of Lords and the Privy Council have recognised a distinction between "truly criminal" and "regulatory" offences.[149] Danger nevertheless lies in the fact that, if a defendant's interests are to be subordinated to those of the general public in "regulatory" offences, the line between such offences and "true" crimes is not always easy to draw. We have seen already (§ 6.1) that categorising offences is a difficult exercise, involving conflicting factors whose force is not readily quantified. Indeed, the courts have sometimes imposed strict liability for offences that are punishable by imprisonment;[150] an indicator of a serious rather than a minor transgression.[151] If a clear distinction between "regulatory" and "truly criminal" offences cannot be drawn, or if that distinction fails to capture the public imagination, then the arguments[152] for retain-

[145] For an interesting comparative perspective, see Lerner and Yahya, "'Left Behind' after Sarbanes-Oxley" (2007) 44 *American Crim LR* 1383.

[146] For an argument that strict liability can undermine the credibility of the criminal law more generally, see Robinson, "Strict Liability's Criminogenic Effect" (2018) 12 *Crim Law and Philosophy* 411, 415–26.

[147] Cp. Mannheim, "Mens Rea in German and English Criminal Law III" (1936) 18 *J Comp Leg* 78, 90: "the number of larcenies committed, e.g., is also very great; nevertheless, nobody would suggest that acts of larceny should be punished when committed without mens rea".

[148] See above, § 6.1(ii). See, also, the interesting discussion by Lamond, "What is a Crime?" (2007) 27 *OJLS* 609, 629–31, where he suggests that strict liability can sometimes perform a valuable role in co-ordinating behaviour so as to minimise risk.

[149] *Sweet v Parsley* [1970] AC 132, 149 (Lord Reid), 163 (Lord Diplock); *Alphacell Ltd v Woodward* [1972] AC 824, 839 (Viscount Dilhorne), 848 (Lord Salmon); *Gammon (Hong Kong) Ltd v A-G for Hong Kong* [1985] AC 1, 12–14 (PC).

[150] Above, § 6.1(ii)(e).

[151] It is worth noting that the US Model Penal Code eschews such a possibility, asserting that the possibility of imprisonment should be a conclusive reason against imposing strict liability: § 6.02(4). A contrary statute would not, however, be unconstitutional: *US v Freed* 401 US 601 (1971).

[152] See above, § 3.2.

ing the presumption of innocence—and for always requiring proof of mens rea—are much harder to surmount.

Furthermore, it may be responded that transgressors for so-called "regulatory" crimes still suffer the rigours of the criminal process, with associated costs and loss of time, not to mention the fact of a conviction and a criminal record. And—once again—if the conviction is a trivial consideration, why make the wrongdoing a criminal rather than civil or administrative matter? A regime of civil sanctions would help safeguard the moral force of the criminal law.[153] "When it becomes respectable to be convicted, the vitality of the criminal law has been sapped."[154]

#### *(iii) The practicalities of proof and the need for efficiency*

Another argument frequently wheeled out in support of strict liability concerns the practicalities of proof. Very often, the activities controlled by regulatory offences involve the commercial behaviour of corporations rather than the private conduct of individuals. Strict liability seems particularly useful where the offence is directed toward controlling the activity of corporations. There are three reasons for this. First, corporate convictions do not normally involve the same level of stigma as do those attaching to individuals, nor the same practical implications. Secondly, corporate activity is characteristically on a larger scale than that by individuals, and correspondingly creates greater levels of social threat. Finally, and most importantly for present purposes, the proof of mens rea (particularly subjective mens rea) presents special difficulty in the context of corporate bodies, since there may be no one person who can be identified as the agent when a corporation acts.[155] Strict liability, by contrast, is much more easily applied to companies and the like, since it can be administered without reference to the defendant's mental state, or even its negligence. Administration of justice would be more expensive and greatly slowed if the prosecution were put to proving fault—even negligence—in respect of every element of a minor offence before the court. This is especially true in areas regulated by public welfare offences, where the defendant may be far better placed to understand the nature of her own specialist activity, and thus to prevent the occurrence of harm, than is the prosecutor to learn the nature of the defendant's activity in order to prove fault; all the more so in the case of activities (and transgressions) by large and complex corporations.

Admittedly, regulatory enforcement needs to be done efficiently—a government cannot afford to spend large amounts of money on prosecutions, especially where the offences involved are common and individually involve no serious harm or even any harm at all. (Where substantial harm does ensue for individual transgressions, the prosecution should in any event be for a more serious crime involving mens rea and greater penalties.) Moreover, individual offences that involve no serious stigma can protect against a cumulative harm that may be very substantial indeed. These costs of controlling economic activity

[153] Progress has been made in this direction with the passing of the Regulatory Enforcement and Sanctions Act 2008, though we have a long way to go before we match the sophistication of French and German regimes: see Spencer and Pedain, "Approaches to Strict and Constructive Liability in Continental Criminal Law" in Simester (ed.), *Appraising Strict Liability* (2005) 237.

[154] Sayre, "The Present Significance of *Mens Rea* in the Criminal Law" in Pound (ed.), *Harvard Legal Essays* (1934) 399, 409.

[155] On the need for such identification in most cases of corporate criminal liability, see below, § 8.2(iii)(b).

are, in truth, part of the costs of carrying on that activity, and it therefore makes some economic sense that the burden of criminal penalties should be borne as a form of production expense by those who voluntarily initiate risk-creating activities.[156]

Again, however, negligence would seem to fit the bill better than strict liability. Negligence can be established with relative ease compared to subjective mens rea elements, in as much as it need not involve proving the state of mind of a controlling officer. Negligence is measured, typically, in terms of conduct.[157] It is, of course, true that even that form of negligence obliges the prosecution to establish behaviour by the employee that can be attributed to the company—but the same constraint applies to strict liability.

More generally, there is a profound moral problem with the efficacy argument: it presents an issue of *procedural* convenience as a reason to change *substantive* law. The better answer is to change the procedure: by reversing the burden of proof.[158] This approach has been taken elsewhere in the Commonwealth, where "strict liability" offences require the prosecution to prove the actus reus beyond reasonable doubt, and the defendant may exculpate himself by proving absence of fault (i.e. a "no-negligence" defence) on the balance of probabilities. Moreover, the question whether the defendant is at fault in a strict liability offence will still be relevant to any common-law defence and, in particular, to sentencing. Indeed, fault is likely to be relevant even to the decision to prosecute.[159] In the light of this, it seems that the evidence may as well be heard straightforwardly before conviction.[160] The judge certainly cannot pass sentence without deciding whether the offence was committed knowingly, negligently, or blamelessly.[161] Even if the defendant pleads guilty, where the facts are disputed, a further hearing will be held to determine them for the purposes of sentencing.[162] Given the advantage the defendant may have, of familiarity with the nature of his specialist activity, it is arguable that, as well as being more efficient, shifting the burden of proof may also result in better justice. This may sound counter-intuitive, but insisting on the provision of at least a no-negligence defence, with attendant legal burden of proof on the defendant, in offences of strict liability would not only be compatible with Article 6(2) of the ECHR (which guarantees the presumption of innocence),[163] but be more compatible with its spirit. At present, defendants have no real means of defending themselves against

156 "In the case of a minor pollution . . . a comparatively nominal fine will no doubt be imposed. This may be regarded as a not unfair hazard of carrying on a business which may cause pollution on the banks of a river": *Alphacell Ltd v Woodward* [1972] AC 824, 848 (Lord Salmon).

157 This is not always the case. Negligence sometimes attaches to a defendant's beliefs, as in the main non-consensual sexual offences—see below, § 12.5.

158 See above, §§ 2.5(i), 3.2(i)(a).

159 Richardson, Ogus, and Burrows, *Policing Pollution* (1982); Hutter, *The Reasonable Arm of the Law* (1988); *Smedleys Ltd v Breed* [1974] AC 839, 856 (Viscount Dilhorne); *James & Son v Smee* [1955] 1 QB 78, 93 (DC). Compare *Hart v Bex* [1957] Crim LR 622 (DC), where the Court upheld the conviction but thought that a prosecution should not have been brought.

160 As things stand, such evidence is inadmissible and its introduction may lead to the quashing of D's conviction of a strict liability offence, because of its potentially prejudicial effect: cp. *Sandhu* [1997] Crim LR 288 (CA). Some of the difficulty this generates may be observed in *Hill* [1997] 2 Cr App R (S) 243.

161 See, e.g., *Smedleys Ltd v Breed* [1974] AC 839, 857 (Viscount Dilhorne); *Lester* (1976) 63 Cr App R 144. Compare *Attorney-General's References (Nos. 74 and 83 of 2007)* [2007] EWCA Crim 2550, [2008] 1 Cr App R (S) 110. In one case (*Fenn*) following conviction for rape of a child under 13, contrary to s. 5(1) of the Sexual Offences Act 2003, it was regarded as relevant to the sentence that V had "ostensibly consented" and that his appearance was "significantly older than 13".

162 See *Newton* (1983) 77 Cr App R 13.

163 See above, § 3.2.

criminal liability for strict liability offences; again, they are punished however reasonable their conduct was. Insisting on the existence of a no-negligence defence, with an associated reverse legal burden, in strict liability offences would thus *improve* the defendant's position relative to the status quo.

In summary, it is doubtful whether there are any significant advantages to be gained from the device of strict liability, and significant moral costs. It is wrong to convict those who acted entirely reasonably, whilst pursuing a socially valuable activity. To do so is a misuse of criminal law, the most condemnatory institution available to society. If someone does not deserve to be convicted, then they should not be. To convict such people violates this most basic tenet of criminal liability.[164] It also arguably breaches the requirement for fair warning. Although citizens can know the activities to which strict liability attaches (assuming they have been publicised adequately, etc.), citizens have no way of predicting reliably when they may be about to incur criminal liability; too much is left to chance.[165] No doubt the public need to be protected from the harms that regulatory offences are designed to prevent. But the public also need to be protected from random liability. Either the prosecution should be required to prove at least negligence as to each element of the actus reus, or the defendant should be afforded the opportunity to prove the absence of negligence in order to secure an acquittal.

## § 6.4 Taking the middle ground: strict liability in the Commonwealth

In parts of the Commonwealth, a distinction is drawn between the terms "strict liability" and "absolute liability". In "strict liability" offences, the prosecution is required to prove the actus reus but, in relation to one or more elements of the actus reus, there is no mens rea element to prove. Nonetheless, the defendant can prove absence of fault in order to escape liability. In essence, the offences are negligence-based, but with a reversed burden of proof, such as the one argued for in the previous section. "Absolute liability", by contrast, refers to what in England is known as "strict liability". There is no need to prove fault in relation to at least one part of the actus reus, and the defendant cannot claim an absence of fault in his own defence.

In the leading case of *R v City of Sault Ste Marie*,[166] the Supreme Court of Canada decided that although mens rea need not be an essential ingredient of an offence, an alternative to absolute liability was nonetheless possible: there might be a defence available of "total absence of fault", the onus of proof for which would lie on the defendant. This third category, which the Court named strict liability, was characterised as follows:[167]

> "the doing of the prohibited act *prima facie* imports the offence, leaving it open to the accused to avoid liability by proving that he took all reasonable care. This involves consideration of what

[164] See above, § 1.2(ii)(a).

[165] Cp. above, § 2.3.

[166] [1978] 2 SCR 1299 (water pollution). See Hutchinson, "*Sault Ste. Marie*, Mens Rea and the Halfway House: Public Welfare Offences Get a Home of Their Own" (1979) 17 *Osgoode Hall LJ* 415.

[167] [1978] 2 SCR 1299, 1326. Compare, in Australia, *Proudman v Dayman* (1941) 67 CLR 536, 540; Howard, "Strict Responsibility in the High Court of Australia" (1960) 76 *LQR* 547. See also Brett, "Strict Responsibility: Possible Solutions" (1974) 37 *MLR* 417; Orchard, "The Defence of Absence of Fault in Australasia and Canada" in Smith (ed.), *Criminal Law: Essays in Honour of J.C. Smith* (1987) 114.

> a reasonable man would have done in the circumstances. The defence will be available if the accused reasonably believed in a mistaken set of facts which, if true, would render the act or omission innocent, or if he took all reasonable steps to avoid the particular event."

The Supreme Court of Canada thus claimed a middle ground that the House of Lords denied itself in *Sweet v Parsley*.[168] Indeed, the Supreme Court of Canada went further and held that regulatory offences, if they were not found to require proof of full mens rea, should presumptively involve "strict" rather than "absolute" liability.[169] Absolute liability is now a rare phenomenon in Canada and other Commonwealth jurisdictions, such as New Zealand: as a matter of principle, it should be applied only if imposed by the legislation "in clear terms or by necessary implication".[170]

The Law Commission has itself advocated that the English courts should have a general power to apply a defence of due diligence when a statutory offence is silent about mens rea.[171] Such a move is likely to require legislative reform. Yet why did the House of Lords reject the possibility of a negligence-based middle ground? The answer is that, although a "halfway house" between mens rea and "absolute" liability was looked upon favourably by many of their Lordships in *Sweet v Parsley*,[172] the House regarded the imposition of a persuasive burden of proof upon the defendant as inconsistent with *Woolmington*. In *Woolmington*, Viscount Sankey LC had said that, saving insanity and express statutory exceptions, the prosecution was required to prove guilt "no matter what the charge or where the trial".[173] The objection raised by the House is not merely of technical precedent: the Commonwealth version of strict liability contravenes the fundamental principle espoused in *Woolmington* that the prosecution must prove the whole of its case, and it is not for the defendant to prove his innocence. The irony of this is surely obvious, even if lost upon their Lordships.[174] *Woolmington* is, and was meant to be, a bastion for the defendant, a fortress against conviction of the innocent. How extraordinary that, in *Sweet v Parsley*, it led to an "absolute" liability doctrine whereby the innocent defendant is denied even the *opportunity* to exculpate himself.

It is, moreover, not clear that the English view of strict liability was genuinely entailed by the precedent set by *Woolmington*. First, the point made by the Supreme Court in *Sault Ste Marie*, that *Woolmington* (a murder case) was concerned with "criminal offences in the true sense", and not with regulatory offences,[175] has much force. There is no reason to suppose that Viscount Sankey intended or even envisaged the implication later drawn from his words. Secondly, if it comes to judicial creativity, the House of Lords showed little compunction about trampling upon *Woolmington* in *Hunt*, when (as we saw in § 3.2(i)(a)) it ruled that the defendant bears the onus of proving any statutory exceptions to an offence, even where the statute does not expressly impose that burden. Finally, if *Woolmington* really

[168] [1970] AC 132; above, § 6.1(i).

[169] [1978] 2 SCR 1299, 1326. The policy reasons for preferring strict liability are stated at 1311–12.

[170] *Millar v MOT* [1986] 1 NZLR 660, 668.

[171] LCCP No. 195, *Criminal Liability in Regulatory Contexts* (2010) Part 6.

[172] [1970] AC 132, 150 (Lord Reid), 158 (Lord Pearce), 164 (Lord Diplock).

[173] [1935] AC 462, 481; above, § 3.2. Cf. *Mancini v DPP* [1942] AC 1, 11 (Viscount Simon LC): the rule is "of general application in all charges under the criminal law".

[174] Not, however, upon others: *R v City of Sault Ste Marie* [1978] 2 SCR 1299, 1316; *Millar v MOT* [1986] 1 NZLR 660, 666; Lord Cooke, *Turning Points of the Common Law* (1997) 47.

[175] [1978] 2 SCR 1299, 1316; cf. *Civil Aviation Dept v MacKenzie* [1983] NZLR 78, 84–5.

does foreclose the Commonwealth version of strict liability, alternatives are available. In particular, a defence of absence of fault where the *evidential* (rather than persuasive) burden lies on the defendant is consistent with *Woolmington* (and the European Convention), and was favoured by Lord Diplock in *Sweet v Parsley*.[176] But the House preferred to impose a knowledge requirement in that case, and foreclosed the option of developing an approach to strict liability such as that embraced in *Sault St Marie*. Although they achieved justice in *Sweet v Parsley*, the Lords' refusal to engage with due diligence defences leaves English law looking extremely harsh when compared with some of its Commonwealth equivalents. Again, things being as they are, any change in this regard is likely to require the intervention of Parliament.[177]

## § 6.5 The correspondence principle, moral luck, and constructive liability

This chapter has outlined several objections to strict liability. One such objection concerns the fact that strict liability leads to the imposition of criminal liability based on luck: the defendant has, in respect of the relevant aspect(s) of the actus reus, entered a punishment lottery. Even if she exercises reasonable care to avoid the occurrence of the relevant part(s) of the actus reus, she can still be convicted. If she wishes to avoid that risk, she must abstain from the relevant activity altogether.

This objection to strict liability needs to be probed further, because there is a closely related species of criminal liability—constructive liability—that is less susceptible to this argument about luck. Constructive liability is difficult to define precisely (and the courts have never defined it). Like strict liability, it exists where the prosecution is relieved of the burden of proving that the defendant was at fault with regard to an element of the actus reus. By contrast to strict liability, however, constructive liability arises in two parts: a "gateway" wrong[178] and an aggravating part. The actus reus of the gateway wrong has a corresponding mens rea requirement, while the aggravating part is a matter of strict liability.[179] Moreover, at least in legitimate versions of constructive liability, the risk of that further, constructive-liability part will be connected (in ways explored below) to the defendant's gateway wrong.[180] Consider the offence of murder: D need not intend (or even foresee a risk of) killing V an intention to cause serious injury ("GBH") suffices.[181] Although no mens rea element need be proved formally with regard to V's death, D must be at fault in relation to a closely related matter (the causing of GBH). On that footing, "GBH murder" is not *just*

[176] [1970] AC 132, 164. More accurately, the defence was said to be one of "honest and reasonable belief in a state of affairs which, had it existed, would have made his act innocent" (in effect, an absence of fault). Lord Diplock's preference was subsequently adopted by the New Zealand Court of Appeal in *Strawbridge* [1970] NZLR 909, but that decision is now superseded: *Millar v MOT* [1986] 1 NZLR 660, 668.

[177] The Privy Council refused to say this explicitly, in the context of the law of Trinidad and Tobago, in *Nurse v Trinidad and Tobago* [2019] UKPC 43, [2020] 2 WLR 131, [60].

[178] Cp. Horder, "Reconsidering Psychic Assault" [1998] *Crim LR* 392, 402–3. One might also refer to these as "'X+Y' crimes", where it is an offence to do X (with a corresponding mens rea element) in circumstance Y or with consequence Y (a matter of strict liability): Simester, *Fundamentals* 315.

[179] Simester, "Intoxication Is Never a Defence" [2009] *Crim LR* 3, 7.

[180] Indeed, many intuitively appealing instances of constructive liability seem plausibly to involve the defendant's negligence regarding the ultimate consequence. See Stark, "Deconstructing Constructive Liability" [2023] *Crim LR* 115.

[181] *Cunningham* [1982] AC 566.

strict liability, and there is a respectable argument that it can be a defensible instance of constructive liability; but that argument does not support all forms of constructive liability. In order to work towards a defensible distinction between acceptable and unacceptable uses of constructive liability, it is necessary to consider what has become known as the "correspondence principle".

### *(i) The correspondence principle*

In § 5.8, we discussed a requirement of *concurrence*: that the actus reus and mens rea of an offence must coincide in time. The concurrence requirement reflects a more general principle, of *correspondence*, in criminal law. Loosely stated, the standard version of the correspondence principle maintains that for every offence there should be mens rea elements relating to the whole of the actus reus, and that all of these elements must simultaneously be satisfied before the offence is committed.

The correspondence principle has an ancient pedigree.[182] As long ago as 1798 Lord Kenyon described it as "a principle of natural justice, and of our law, that *actus non facit reum nisi mens sit rea*. The intent and the act must both concur to constitute the crime."[183] Before that, references to the principle may be found in Bracton and Coke. According to Bracton, for example:[184]

> "For take away the will and every act will be indifferent, because it is your intent which gives meaning to your act, and a crime is not committed unless an intent to injure exists; neither is a theft committed without the intention to steal."

Certainly in the centuries after Coke,[185] these early sentiments had become so entrenched in the common law that mens rea could properly be described as "one of the fundamental requisites of criminality".[186] "The general rule of English law is, that no crime can be committed unless there is mens rea."[187] Criminal conviction, therefore, required something more than the mere occurrence of harm. Subject to limited exceptions whose genesis, we have observed, lay in the nineteenth century,[188] strict liability would not do.

Understood in this way, the principle of correspondence is a limited ethical principle, one that recognises that criminal liability should depend not only upon a person's acts but also upon her moral culpability (as indicated by the presence of mens rea) with respect to those acts. However, some writers have claimed a larger role for the correspondence principle. They defend what may be termed a "rigid version" of the principle.[189] According to

[182] Horder, "Two Histories and Four Hidden Principles of Mens Rea" (1997) 113 *LQR* 95.
[183] *Fowler v Padget* (1798) 7 Term Rep 509, 514, 101 ER 1103, 1106.
[184] *De Legibus et Consuetudinibus Angliae*, 101b. Cp. Coke, *Third Institute* (1641) 6, 107.
[185] For discussion see Sayre, "*Mens Rea*" (1932) 45 *Harv LR* 974.
[186] Sayre, "The Present Significance of Mens Rea in the Criminal Law" in Pound (ed.), *Harvard Legal Essays* (1934) 399, 399.
[187] *Williamson v Norris* [1899] 1 QB 7, 14.
[188] "It is true that there are cases where the Legislature in its wisdom has declared that, in the particular class of cases dealt with, a man is to be treated as guilty of the offence in question, although he has not acted with negligence, and had no guilty mind. There are several such cases, but they form an exception to the general rule of law": *ibid.*
[189] There are, in fact, multiple versions of the correspondence principle: see Tadros, *Criminal Responsibility* (2005) 93–5.

the rigid version, for *every* actus reus element there should be a corresponding mens rea element, every one of which should simultaneously be satisfied before the offence is committed. Thus, according to Ashworth:[190]

> "if the conduct element of a crime is 'causing serious injury', the principle of correspondence demands that the fault element should be intention or recklessness as to causing serious injury, and not intention or recklessness as to some lesser harm such as a mere assault. Another example . . . is the law of murder: in English law a person may be convicted of murder if he either intended to kill or intended to cause grievous bodily harm. However, the latter species of fault breaches the principle of correspondence: the fault element does not correspond with the conduct element (which is, causing death), and so a person is liable to conviction for a higher crime than contemplated."

Another offence that violates the rigid version of the correspondence principle is section 1 of the Road Traffic Act 1988, causing death by dangerous driving. Once the preliminary offence of dangerous driving is committed,[191] liability for the greater offence in section 1 becomes a matter of strict liability, because the only difference in the definitions of these two offences is whether D causes someone's death; and that is an actus reus element for which no additional mens rea element is required.[192]

In many such constructive offences, the aggravating element involves a death. For example, one well-known constructive liability offence is manslaughter by an unlawful act. If D commits a gateway offence which creates a reasonably foreseeable risk of some injury to another person, D becomes guilty of manslaughter should her gateway offending cause someone's death.[193] This form of manslaughter contains no mens rea ingredient referring to the crucial actus reus element, death.

Constructive liability of the type seen here breaches the correspondence principle, at least in its rigid form. But is constructive liability necessarily a bad thing, or is slavish adherence to the correspondence principle overrated? The answer is a bit of both. The rigid version of the correspondence principle is not and never has been a part of the criminal law.[194] On the other hand, the case for the standard version of the correspondence principle is much stronger. The maxim *actus non facit reum nisi mens sit rea* is rightly a venerable one because we want convictions for causing harm to be a matter of culpability and not of luck. We have seen that strict liability is objectionable because it exposes defendants to convictions purely on the basis of luck rather than fault. Is constructive liability vulnerable to the same objection? The answer to be defended here is "sometimes but not always". To discriminate between cases of legitimate and illegitimate use of constructive liability, we must first address the problem of moral luck.

[190] *Principles of Criminal Law* (6th ed., 2009) 76. See Horder, "A Critique of the Correspondence Principle in Criminal Law" [1995] *Crim LR* 759; Mitchell, "In Defence of a Principle of Correspondence" [1999] *Crim LR* 195; Horder, "Questioning the Correspondence Principle—A Reply" [1999] *Crim LR* 206.

[191] Road Traffic Act 1988, s. 2.

[192] One worry about this sort of example is that dangerous driving (which the prosecution must prove) is a *de facto* demonstration of negligence, if not gross negligence, regarding the causing of death, securing fault regarding the relevant result. See Stark, "Deconstructing Constructive Liability" [2023] *Crim LR* 115, 127. The situation is less clear with careless and inconsiderate driving, but such conduct still plausibly demonstrates negligence with regard to the risk of causing death.

[193] Below, § 10.7(i). See especially the critique in § 10.7(i)(f).

[194] Gardner, "Rationality and the Rule of Law in Offences Against the Person" (1994) 53 *CLJ* 502, 509.

### *(ii) Moral luck*

Luck is integral to the criminal law. If D shoots at V and misses, for example, the most she can be guilty of is attempted murder. If V dies, D becomes liable for murder; a different conviction with different penal consequences. Yet, once D has pulled the trigger, the outcome is a matter of luck. "We never do more than move our bodies: the rest is up to nature."[195]

The problem is as follows. Luck, it may be thought, is involuntary—the antithesis of control. And culpability, it may be thought, should be dependent upon control rather than luck.[196] As Nagel puts it:[197]

> "Prior to reflection it is intuitively plausible that people cannot be morally assessed for what is not their fault, or for what is due to factors beyond their control. [Moral] judgment is different from the evaluation of something as a good or bad thing, or state of affairs. The latter may be present in addition to moral judgment, but when we blame someone for his actions we are not merely saying it is bad that they happened, or bad that he exists: we are judging *him*, saying he is bad. . . . Without being able to explain exactly why, we feel that the appropriateness of moral assessment is easily undermined by the discovery that the act or attribute, no matter how good or bad, is not under the person's control."

If that is so, there is an obvious difficulty because outcomes—harms—unavoidably involve luck. Nagel continues:[198]

> "Whether we succeed or fail in what we try to do nearly always depends to some extent on factors beyond our control. This is true of murder, altruism, revolution, the sacrifice of certain interests for the sake of others—almost any morally important act. What has been done, and what is morally judged, is partly determined by other factors. However jewel-like[[199]] the good will may be in its own right, there is a morally significant difference between rescuing someone from a burning building and dropping him from a twelfth-storey window while trying to rescue him. Similarly, there is a morally significant difference between reckless driving and manslaughter. But whether a reckless driver hits a pedestrian depends on the presence of the pedestrian at the point where he recklessly passes a red light."

And that, we have noted, is a matter of luck.

Ashworth, amongst others, has used this type of point to oppose segregating attempts liability: where the difference is merely down to luck, a failed attempt to kill ought to be

[195] Davidson, *Essays on Actions and Events* (1980) 59. Cp. Ashworth, "Taking the Consequences" in Shute, Gardner and Horder (eds.), *Action and Value in Criminal Law* (1993) 107.

[196] For discussion of this problem, see: Edwards and Simester, "Crime, Blameworthiness, and Outcomes" (2019) 39 *OJLS* 50; Cornford, "Resultant Luck and Criminal Liability" in Duff et al. (eds.), *The Structures of Criminal Law* (2011) 36; Alexander and Ferzan, *Crime and Culpability* (2009), chap. 5; Duff, "Whose Luck is it Anyway?" in Clarkson and Cunningham (eds.), *Criminal Liability for Non-aggressive Death* (2008) 61; Honoré, "Responsibility and Luck: The Moral Basis of Strict Liability" (1989) 104 *LQR* 530; Mandil, "Chance, Freedom and Criminal Liability" (1987) 87 *Col LR* 125; Williams, "Moral Luck" in *Moral Luck* (1981) 20; Schulhofer, "Harm and Punishment: A Critique of Emphasis on the Results of Conduct in the Criminal Law" (1974) 122 *U Pa LR* 1497; Smith, "The Element of Chance in Criminal Liability" [1971] *Crim LR* 63.

[197] *Mortal Questions* (1979) 25.

[198] *Ibid.*

[199] A reference to Kant, *Groundwork of the Metaphysics of Morals* (1785) § 1: if "only the good will were to remain . . . then, like a jewel, it would still shine by itself, as something that has its full worth in itself".

punished just as severely as if it had succeeded, and vice versa.[200] On Ashworth's view, any substantive offence, such as murder, is analogous to a constructive liability offence: the gateway crime committed by D is attempted murder, and what elevates D's crime to murder is (like dangerous driving causing death) merely the actus reus element of causing death—for which no additional mens rea element is required.

It is not possible, in a book of this nature, to answer these objections in full; here, we can only sketch a defence of moral luck in the criminal law. The key point is that in causing death by dangerous driving, like in murder, death is not *merely* a matter of luck. To see this, consider the following example proposed by Smith:[201]

> "the daughter of a business executive has been assigned a science project of investigating the distribution of blood-types within the population. To assist her, the executive asks his secretary to survey the office staff and prepare a report on their blood-types by noon. Instead of carrying out this request, the secretary reads a spy novel. At 11:45 a co-worker suffers massive bleeding as a result of an office accident. Paramedics arrive, and could start a transfusion immediately if the workers' blood-type were known. Unfortunately he is unconscious, cannot provide this information, and so dies before the transfusion can be started. Had the secretary followed her boss's orders, she would have known the worker's blood-type and his life would have been saved. Her failure to obtain this information is both objectively wrong *and* culpable, and it led to her inability to save her co-worker's life. But [there is] no inclination to say that the secretary is to blame for the co-worker's death."

Contrast Smith's example with a different type of case:

> Edgar is driving through a village at a speed 20 miles per hour in excess of the speed limit. Unexpectedly he loses control of his car, mounts the pavement, and kills Allan, who had been walking quietly toward the corner shop in order to buy a newspaper.

Driving through the village at such excessive speed is, we may conclude, dangerous driving. As such, Edgar commits the offence of causing death by dangerous driving notwithstanding that he does not foresee Allan's death.[202] As noted earlier, the offence imposes constructive liability. But there need be nothing wrong with that. Certainly it is, in one sense, a matter of luck that Allan was killed. But the luck is not random or unrelated in the way it was for Smith's delinquent secretary. Here, the possibility of this type of outcome forms part of the very reason why dangerous driving is wrongful—and itself criminalised.[203]

[200] "Criminal Attempts and the Role of Resulting Harm under the Code and in Common Law" (1988) 19 *Rutgers LJ* 725; "Belief, Intent, and Criminal Liability" in Eekelaar and Bell (eds.), *Oxford Essays in Jurisprudence* (3rd Series, 1987) 1. The argument is restricted to "complete" rather than "incomplete" attempts: Duff, "Subjectivism, Objectivism and Criminal Attempts" in Simester and Smith (eds.), *Harm and Culpability* (1996) 19. For an interesting discussion of these issues, see Lewis, "The Punishment that Leaves Something to Chance" (1989) 18 *Philosophy & Public Affairs* 53. See also below, § 9.3(vi).

[201] "Culpable Ignorance" (1983) 92 *Philosophical Review* 543, 550–51.

[202] Indeed, whether the relevant consequence was foreseeable is not determinative of whether the defendant is properly found to be culpable for it on the view presented here. See Simester, *Fundamentals* § 13.5.1; contrast Stark, "Deconstructing Constructive Liability" [2023] *Crim LR* 155, 127–31.

[203] For further development of this distinction, see Simester, *Fundamentals* 318–23. Again, a worry one might raise regarding this sort of example is that dangerous driving can plausibly be seen as a *de facto* demonstration of negligence, if not gross negligence, regarding the causing of death, rendering an "x + y" analysis strictly unnecessary. D's responsibility for the fatal outcome could instead, on such a view, be explained on the basis of his negligent fault regarding it.

A comparison between Edgar's case and Smith's delinquent secretary example highlights the potential importance of distinguishing between two types of luck: intrinsic and extrinsic.[204] The secretary is not blameworthy for the coworker's death because that risk was *extrinsic* to the reasons why her conduct was wrongful. Such risks affect the outcome, and perhaps affect our retrospective judgements about what D *did*, but they are not the relevant factors when deciding, *in advance*, what it would be wrongful for D to do. By contrast, in Edgar's case, the risk of death was *intrinsic* in the sense that it formed part of the reason why, even *ex ante*, Edgar's behaviour was wrong. The same can be said of "GBH murder" cases: the risk of killing a person is *intrinsic* to why it is wrongful for D to intentionally cause serious injury to V. Mounting such attacks is to be avoided, in part, *because* they can easily result in an unintended fatality.[205] The risk of death is a core reason why intentionally causing someone serious harm is wrongful and criminalised.

Ashworth and Nagel are right to observe that many factors affecting an outcome are beyond our control. But this does not imply that the outcome itself is beyond our control. It is only *given* D's behaviour that the outcome is—thereafter—beyond her control. D does have control over the outcome; she exercises that control *through* her behaviour. It is D's dangerous driving, or her pulling the trigger, or her intentionally causing V serious harm, that brings the uncontrolled factors into play, and makes the luck relevant. Where that luck is intrinsic, holding D responsible and culpable for the outcome is a long way away from imposing strict liability or opening her liability to the vagaries of fortune.[206] Constructive liability, this argument goes, may be defensible in such circumstances.

Moreover, constructive liability in such circumstances is consistent with the Rule of Law. Where such offences are predicated on intrinsic luck, they do not defeat the desire to give fair warning in criminal law.[207] Indeed, D may be regarded as already warned, since she has committed the gateway crime (e.g. causing GBH) with mens rea;[208] and the intrinsic luck forms part of the rationale for blaming D and regarding that gateway crime as wrong.[209]

At the same time, such constructive liability can advance the goal of representative labelling in the law.[210] If D intentionally shoots and kills V, we do not reprove the attack and, separately, regret V's death. We reprove the murder. It does not sufficiently describe

[204] Williams, *Moral Luck* (1981) 25–6. This distinction supports a better analysis of Horder's gun-cleaning example than the author himself offers: "A Critique of the Correspondence Principle in Criminal Law" [1995] *Crim LR* 759, 764. Suppose D cleans her gun outside *in order* to upset V. Although D's deliberate wrong changes her normative position, it does not does not do so with respect to extrinsic risks such as an accidental discharge that causes V's death by shock. The distinction also takes the account sketched here outside the version of "moderate constructivism" critiqued by Ashworth, "A Change of Normative Position: Determining the Contours of Culpability in Criminal Law" (2008) 11 *New Criminal LR* 232. Ashworth himself associates *Simester and Sullivan* with moderate constructivism (*ibid.*, 241), quoting not from the present section but from a previous version of the discussion of joint enterprise in Chapter 7.

[205] Much depends, of course, on how GBH is interpreted; not all "serious injury" plausibly threatens life. As presently defined, the English law of murder arguably goes further than the account outlined here allows.

[206] Our concern here is primarily with the issue of liability rather than punishment. Simons rightly observes that, even if liability is appropriate, quantifying the amount of deserved punishment in constructive liability cases remains a deep problem: "Is Strict Criminal Liability in the Grading of Offences Consistent with Retributive Desert?" (2012) 32 *OJLS* 445.

[207] Discussed above, § 2.3.

[208] See Gardner, "Rationality and the Rule of Law in Offences Against the Person" (1994) 53 *CLJ* 502, 521–3.

[209] This further point presupposes that the goal of giving potential offenders fair warning of their crimes does not always require advertence by defendants to the actus reus. Crimes of negligence are capable, on this view, of giving fair warning.

[210] Above, § 2.4. See, further, Edwards and Simester, "Crime, Blameworthiness and Luck" (2019) 39 *OJLS* 50.

D's act to say that she attempted to murder V. She murdered him. Similarly, it would be incomplete and therefore inaccurate to describe Edgar's conduct merely as dangerous driving. Even where the mens rea for two offences is the same, fair labelling in the criminal law is constrained by harm. Why are reckless endangerment by dangerous driving, attempts to kill, and the like wrongful? The answer is not because they involve any direct (e.g. physical) harm to the victim, but because D wrongfully manipulates, subordinates, attacks, or endangers V's interests and autonomy. But when an attempt succeeds, when dangerous driving kills, or when serious bodily harm results in a fatality, the harm is rather different. V is dead. Only by acknowledging that fact can the criminal law adequately communicate what D has done.

To be clear, some offences under English law push the boundaries of constructive liability too far, even on the account explored here, because they pay insufficient attention to the distinction between intrinsic and extrinsic luck. One example is the offence of manslaughter by an unlawful act. As we noted above, and will see in Chapter 10, if D commits a crime (with mens rea)[211] which creates a reasonably foreseeable risk of *some* harm to V, D becomes guilty of manslaughter should his gateway crime in fact cause V's death. This form of manslaughter contains no mens rea ingredient referring to the key actus reus element, death. The difficulty with imposing homicide-based liability in such circumstances is that the defendant's initial criminal act might not be prohibited because of its close relationship with death, but merely because of a connection with *some* physical harm. Consider a case where D throws a rock through V's window, intending to break it, and disaster (not to mention the rock) strikes. Should V die as a result of being hit, D will be liable for manslaughter. True, there must have been *some* foreseeable risk of injury as a consequence of D's action; that risk supplies one reason not to perpetrate criminal damage. But that risk did not supply the reason why D's act of criminal damage was wrong—and neither did the risk that someone would die. This point can be elucidated by considering D's position *ex ante*. Imagine that T had stopped D before he threw the rock and sought to counsel him against doing so. T would emphasise the breaking of V's window. Doubtless T would accept, if pressed, that there is a risk of killing someone. However, given its unlikelihood, this seems an eccentric thing to emphasise. This suggests in turn, that the link between risks of death and the wrongfulness of criminal damage is an extrinsic one. Consequently, the offence of unlawful act manslaughter should be reformed.[212]

[211] If the "base crime" in this form of manslaughter can be one of strict liability, then this offence is doubly problematic. See below, § 10.7(i)(c).

[212] Below, § 10.7(i)(f).

# 7
# SECONDARY PARTICIPATION

## § 7.1 The possibility of derivative liability

In Chapter 1, we considered the following example:[1]

> One fine September morning, Jim is discovered dead in his home. His skull has been crushed by a blow inflicted with a heavy object. The police are called. Upon investigation, they establish that he was murdered by his daughter, Alice, who killed him in order to receive her inheritance under his will.

This, as we said earlier, is a paradigm case of criminal wrongdoing by Alice, involving deliberate, culpable infliction of the sort of serious harm that the criminal law seeks to prevent. Alice is precisely the sort of person who deserves the condemnation of a criminal conviction. But she may not be the only person responsible for Jim's death. Imagine the following additional details:

> During the course of their investigation, the police unearth a number of related facts. Frank, Jim's cousin, had learned by accident of Alice's plan to murder Jim, but had done nothing because he, too, stood to inherit under the will. Alice had planned the murder with the help of Gertrude, whom she had consulted about possible methods of carrying out the killing. The baseball bat that Alice eventually used belongs to Harry, who lent it to Alice for the purpose of killing Jim.

When an offence is committed it is not only the immediate perpetrator of the actus reus (also referred to as the "principal") who may incur criminal liability. Others may also be held accountable by the criminal law. Usually, this will occur when those others have participated in the commission of the crime, albeit without directly perpetrating the actus reus.[2] Such persons, when they are held to be criminally accountable, are said to be *parties* to the offence.

The difficult questions, for both theory and doctrine in criminal law, are *when* and *why* persons other than the perpetrator of a crime should be held liable, along with the perpetrator, for the offence itself. Theoretically, when Jim dies every legally competent person within the jurisdiction is a potential defendant, yet it is inappropriate to regard every member of society as involved in the crime that Alice commits. But how do we narrow the field in a principled way? In short, when a crime occurs, who are the appropriate defendants?

[1] Above, § 1.2 and, especially, § 1.2(ii)(e).

[2] Note, however, occasional suggestions of a causal approach to participants' liability in the case law and literature, the logic of which threatens to undermine this proposition—and in turn, much of the rationale for secondary liability. See below, § 7.7(i).

In Chapter 4 we considered the criminal law's doctrines of omissions and causation, which play a vital role in identifying those persons who may be ascribed with legal responsibility for committing a crime. Because of the law relating to omissions, for example, Frank will not be held responsible for Jim's death. By contrast, although Gertrude and Harry did not cause Jim's death, their actions will make them complicit in Alice's crime.[3] All three will be guilty of murder.

In this and the following chapter, we consider the doctrines by which a defendant may be held responsible for a crime she does not herself commit.[4] There are two main ways in which this may occur. The first, which we explore in this chapter, gives rise to *secondary liability*. Although they did not perpetrate the crime, Gertrude and Harry have participated in Jim's murder by rendering aid and encouragement to Alice. Hence, they are known as secondary parties to the murder and are guilty of the offence alongside Alice. The second doctrine of responsibility occurs when a person is held responsible, at large, for the various acts of another person. This is known as *vicarious liability* and is much more common in civil than in criminal law. For example, an employer may sometimes be sued in tort for the damage its employee causes to V's property, but cannot itself be prosecuted for criminal damage. Vicarious liability is considered in § 8.1.

Both forms of liability are *derivative*. The defendant is indirectly held responsible for a crime committed by another and, as such, her liability is dependent upon the criminal actions of that other person. If no crime is committed, there is generally nothing of a criminal character that can be secondarily or vicariously attributed to the defendant.[5] As was noted in § 1.2(ii)(e), and will be seen below, the fact that liability is derived from the crime of another raises difficult questions of principle and policy. The level of involvement required to make S[6] guilty when P commits a crime must balance the consideration that S is often just as culpable as P (and indeed sometimes more culpable), even though it was not D who pulled the trigger, against the difficulty that derivative liability casts the net of guilt well beyond the direct infliction of criminal harms, to catch ostensibly innocent conduct such as lending (or selling[7]) Alice a baseball bat, or even sitting as a passenger in a car.[8] It is for this reason that the mens rea requirements of secondary liability, in particular, are generally more complex than those of principal liability for the underlying offence.

[3] See above, § 4.2; also below, § 7.7(i). Their assistance need not even be a *sine qua non* of the crime—Alice, we may suppose, would have received the same advice and aid from others had Gertrude and Harry been unavailable or unwilling.

[4] A classic discussion is Sayre, "Criminal Responsibility for the Acts of Another" (1930) 43 *Harv LR* 678. Other American writings include Perkins, "Parties to Crime" (1941) 89 *U Pa LR* 581; Dressler, "Reassessing the Theoretical Underpinnings of Accomplice Liability: New Solutions to an Old Problem" (1985) 37 *Hastings LJ* 91.

[5] Kadish, *Blame and Punishment* (1987) 146ff. This proposition is subject to certain exceptions, e.g. where S has procured P to do the actus reus of an offence without mens rea, or under duress: see below, § 7.6(ii).

[6] For the sake of clarity of exposition, this chapter uses S and P to designate the secondary party and principal, respectively. Additionally, and for the same reason, where pronouns are used, S is deemed to be female and P to be male.

[7] *NCB v Gamble* [1959] 1 QB 11 (DC). See, e.g., Duff, "'Can I Help You?' Accessorial Liability and the Intention to Assist" (1990) 10 *LS* 165; Williams, "Complicity, Purpose and the Draft Code" [1990] *Crim LR* 4.

[8] E.g. *Du Cros v Lambourne* [1907] 1 KB 40; below, § 7.4(iii).

## § 7.2 Modes of participation

The law recognises two main varieties of participation in a crime. For convenience, we begin with a summary. Participation in an offence may occur in the following ways:

(i) As principal (the person who carries out the offence); or
(ii) As secondary party who assists or encourages the offence—by aiding, abetting, counselling, or procuring the commission of that offence.[9]

Suppose that P commits an assault by hitting V during an argument. In this case, P acts as the *principal*—the person who actually commits the crime. In general, P will be a principal offender if he personally fulfils the actus reus and mens rea requirements of the crime.

Alternatively, the crime itself may be done by the principal (P), but another person (S) may be involved as a *secondary party*. Secondary parties are those persons whose role in giving assistance or encouragement to P is sufficient to make them participants in, and guilty of, the crime committed by P, notwithstanding that they do not themselves satisfy the actus reus and mens rea elements of the crime. *Per* section 8 of the Accessories and Abettors Act 1861, as amended by the Criminal Law Act 1977:

> Whosoever shall aid, abet, counsel or procure the commission of any indictable offence,[10] whether the same be an offence at common law or by virtue of any Act passed or to be passed, shall be liable to be tried, indicted, and punished as a principal offender.

A secondary party should be distinguished from a person who assists someone else (who may be either a principal or secondary party) who has committed an offence *after* the crime has been completed. Such a person does not participate in the crime itself, and his liability is not for the original crime committed, but instead arises independently as an offence under section 4 of the Criminal Law Act 1967.[11] By contrast, participation by a party to an offence must occur before or during the commission of that offence.[12]

A secondary party should also be distinguished from someone who commits an inchoate offence by encouraging or assisting a crime. Suppose that D encourages another person to commit a crime. She may, by giving such encouragement, commit a distinct inchoate offence under the Serious Crime Act 2007.[13] The inchoate offence is committed by D as principal, and it is committed whether or not the encouraged crime later occurs. Should

[9] Strictly speaking, procurement is a form of contribution distinct from assistance or encouragement. See below, § 7.4(i).

[10] Similar rules apply to summary trials: Magistrates' Courts Act 1980, s. 44.

[11] See Williams, "Evading Justice" [1975] *Crim LR* 430. This rule differs from the common law, which was repealed by the Criminal Law Act 1967. At common law, whenever D subsequently gave assistance to any person committing or party to a felony, which assistance tended to and had the object of enabling that person to avoid arrest, trial, or conviction, D also became a party (an "accessory after the fact") to the original felony and did not commit an independent offence.

[12] *King* (1817) Russ & Ry 332, 168 ER 830; *Stally* [1960] 1 WLR 79 (CCA). In the case of a continuing offence, such as rape (cp. Sexual Offences Act 2003, s. 79(2); *Kaitamaki* [1985] AC 147 (PC)), the participation may occur after commencement of the offence but must happen before its completion (i.e. prior to withdrawal by the rapist): *Mok Wei Tak v R* [1990] 2 AC 333 (PC); *Mayberry* [1973] Qd R 211. Cp. *BXQ* [2025] EWCA Crim 1088, [2025] 4 WLR 98 (joining an attack that caused grievous bodily harm); also *Scott v DPP* [2022] EWHC 91 (Admin), [2022] 1 WLR 2231, a prosecution for encouragement of a (possession) offence, contrary to s. 45 of the Serious Crime Act 2007.

[13] See below, § 7.7 and, for a detailed analysis of assistance and encouragement as inchoate offences, § 9.1.

the encouraged crime ultimately be perpetrated, however, D will *also* become guilty of *that* crime—as a secondary party. By contrast with inchoate liability, the conviction of a secondary party is *for the principal's crime*; it is derived from one person's participation in the crime actually committed by another.

The formal distinction between principals and secondary offenders is now of little practical significance when it comes to the verdict, because—by virtue of section 8 (above)—each is deemed to be guilty of the full offence.[14] Thus it will not affect his resulting conviction for, say, murder, whether D himself killed another person or was simply a secondary party who, say, supplied P with the murder weapon. Indeed, it can be very difficult on the facts of some cases to differentiate between principals and secondary parties,[15] and under current law the form of charge need not specify the nature of D's participation, but may simply allege guilt.[16] This practice is somewhat in tension with the ECHR, as Article 6(1) has been held to require that an offender should be able to understand clearly the basis on which she is convicted.[17] The full ramifications of that ruling for English law remain to be seen.[18]

Certainly, differentiation between principals and secondary parties is still to be found in the case law. One reason for this is that the distinction is still crucial to the operation of section 8 itself. If the defendant was not a principal, the enquiry whether she was a secondary party will depend in part upon the existence of a principal who *did* perpetrate the offence,[19] and will take a different form—with a different actus reus and different mens rea—from the enquiry into the principal's liability. The elements of the principal's liability are specific to each offence: in murder, for example, the prosecution must prove an intent to kill or inflict grievous bodily injury (Chapter 10), while strict liability offences require no proof of mens rea on the part of a principal (Chapter 6). By contrast, for both types of offence the elements of *secondary* liability, including the mens rea requirements, are the same; they are as set out in this chapter *whatever* the main offence.

The difference between principals and secondary parties matters for at least two other reasons. First, some offences are defined so that certain participants are excluded from liability, either because only a named class of persons may commit the offence as a principal

[14] As is observed in the leading case of *Jogee* [2016] UKSC 8; *Ruddock* [2016] UKPC 7, [2017] AC 387, [6], s. 8 is essentially a procedural provision. However, this does not mean that it lacks substantive implications. While s. 8 did not change the law governing what *constitutes* aiding, abetting, counselling, or procuring, it did formalise their importance. For discussion, see below, § 7.4(i).

[15] See, e.g., *Giannetto* [1997] 1 Cr App 1; *Du Cros v Lambourne* [1907] 1 KB 40; *Swindall and Osborne* (1846) 2 C & K 230, 175 ER 95.

[16] A practice that is said to be compatible with Art. 6(3)(a) of the ECHR: *Mercer* [2001] EWCA Crim 638, [2001] All ER (D) 187 (Mar) (CA). However, it is desirable wherever possible for the prosecution to specify the form of participation when laying the charge: *DPP for Northern Ireland v Maxwell* [1978] 1 WLR 1350, 1352 (HL).

[17] *Taxquet v Belgium* (2012) 54 EHRR 26.

[18] The practice was thought compatible with Art. 6 of the ECHR in *Mercer* [2001] EWCA Crim 638, [2001] All ER (D) 187 (Mar) and *Concannon* [2002] Crim LR 213 (CA); but see Ashworth, "A Decade of Human Rights in Criminal Justice" [2014] *Crim LR* 325, 327. The Scottish system of jury trial was said to pass muster in *Judge v UK* (2011) 52 EHRR SE17, especially in light of other features (details in the indictment; directions by the judge; the right to appeal for a miscarriage of justice) that conveyed information to the defendant despite the lack of reasons for the jury verdict itself. Whether that bill of health would extend to a case where D's participatory basis went unspecified remains to be seen.

[19] There must *be* a principal, even if unidentified: cp. the commentary to *Bristow* [2013] EWCA Crim 1540, [2014] Crim LR 457, 461.

or (more rarely) because the possibility of secondary participation is excluded.[20] Secondly, there is no vicarious liability for the acts of secondary parties.[21]

## § 7.3 The principal

Before considering the varieties of secondary participation falling within section 8, it is necessary to make some observations regarding the liability of principal offenders. First, there may be more than one principal offender. If P and Q assault V by jointly raining blows on him, they are each principals. If V dies from the combination of blows, they will each be guilty, as principals, of manslaughter or murder.[22] There are two ways in which multiple defendants may be held to be principals. First, each may separately satisfy all the required ingredients of the relevant offence. In the above example, P and Q are each independently guilty of an assault. Alternatively, each may separately satisfy *some* part of the actus reus for the offence where their actions, in combination, fulfil the complete actus reus requirement and each has the requisite mens rea. The latter is a true case of joint principals, in that it is sufficient for liability that each party does a part of the actus reus.[23]

Note, however, that there must be *some* contribution to the occurrence of the actus reus before one can be held to have committed the offence as a principal.[24] Thus, if S and P attack V in concert yet it is a particular blow by P that causes death, independently of the effect of the earlier blows by S, then S cannot be convicted of murder as a principal and may only be convicted as a secondary party. While the outcome may be the same (depending on their mens rea, each could be convicted of murder), the importance of this is that the actus reus and mens rea elements required to be proved in order to convict S as a secondary party are different from those required to convict P.

### *(i) Innocent agents*

Sometimes the actus reus is not perpetrated personally by the defendant, who instead organises for it to be brought about by a third party (T), who is unaware of the true nature of his (T's) actions. Where the defendant deliberately[25] organises for an "innocent agent" to bring about the actus reus, the participation of the intervening actor is disregarded[26] and the law treats the defendant as the principal.[27] Conceptually, it is as if the defendant "stands

[20] See below, § 7.6(iv).

[21] *Ferguson v Weaving* [1951] 1 KB 814 (DC).

[22] Cp. *Langman v Valentine* [1952] 2 All ER 803 (DC) (joint drivers).

[23] E.g. *Bingley* (1821) Russ & Ry 446 (each forged part of a banknote). See Lanham, "Complicity, Concert and Conspiracy" (1980) 4 *Crim LJ* 276.

[24] "The essential ingredient for joint principal offending is a contribution to the cause of the actus reus. If this is absent, the fact that there is a common purpose . . . cannot transform the offending into joint principal liability." *Gnango* [2011] UKSC 59, [2012] AC 827, [129] (Lord Kerr).

[25] Exceptionally, an actus reus brought about by an innocent agent may also be attributed to D if it resulted from D's negligence, when negligence is sufficient to establish mens rea: *Tessymond* (1828) 1 Lewin 169.

[26] For an argument that the law's disregarding of T is disrespectful to T's dignity—an independent wrong that ought to be recognised by the criminal law—see Eldar, "Human Dignity and the Innocent Agent" (2024) 18 *Crim Law and Philosophy* 617.

[27] For discussion, see Alldridge, "The Doctrine of Innocent Agency" (1990) 2 *Crim L Forum* 45; Williams, "Innocent Agency and Causation" (1992) 3 *Crim L Forum* 289; Alldridge, "Common Sense, Innocent Agency, and Causation" (1992) 3 *Crim L Forum* 299. By contrast, secondary liability is thought to depend upon the existence of a principal offender: a striking illustration is *Demirian* [1989] VR 97. This requirement is considered below, § 7.6(i).

in the shoes" of the innocent agent. An example is when D, the host at a party, gives a waiter, T, a glass of wine to take out to V. D knows, but T does not know, that the wine contains poison. Although T gives V poison, T is merely an innocent agent and it is D who is the perpetrator of the crime.[28]

The doctrine of innocent agency does not apply if the intervening agent is herself guilty of the offence; consequently, it is normally inapplicable to strict liability offences.[29] Further, the doctrine may only be invoked, and the agent can only be categorised as an *innocent* agent, either if she does not know that she is committing the actus reus or if she lacks criminal capacity, in particular through being insane[30] or falling within the legal defence of infancy.[31]

There are also some crimes for which the doctrine is excluded altogether because, by the very nature of those crimes, direct perpetration of the crime is required of the principal offender. This will depend upon the interpretation of each particular offence, but in general such cases are of two types.[32]

First, innocent agency is more likely to be excluded where the essence of the crime is specified *behaviour* by the criminal, rather than the bringing about of some *consequence*.[33] In bigamy, for example, it seems impossible to say that P has gone through a ceremony of marriage with V (the actus reus) when he has procured T to do so. The same is true for rape (notwithstanding the contrary decision, to be discussed below, in *Cogan and Leak*[34]), and for crimes such as careless driving[35] and driving with excess alcohol.[36] The doctrine of innocent agency operates only where it is possible for P to fulfil the elements of the actus reus by the instrument of some other person. That is straightforwardly done where the actus reus does not specify particular behaviour by the perpetrator. For example, in murder, which requires the causing of another's death, it is apt to view P as having killed V herself, even though (as in the example above) she in fact procures T to deliver the poison.[37] It is rather less easy to treat P as having done the actus reus personally when the gist of the wrong is T's actual conduct, rather than its consequence.

However, while the distinction may seem clear enough in principle, the question whether the conduct element of a particular offence requires P's direct, personal involvement can

[28] Cp. *Anon* (1634) Kel 53, 84 ER 1079; *Johnson* (1805) 7 East 65, 103 ER 26; *Butcher* (1858) Bell 6, 169 ER 1145; *Butt* (1884) 15 Cox CC 56; *White v Ridley* (1978) 140 CLR 342.

[29] Where, despite her innocence, the intervening agent is guilty of an offence, D should be convicted as a secondary party: *A-G's Reference (No. 1 of 1975)* [1975] QB 773 (CA); below, § 7.4(i)(d).

[30] *Tyler* (1838) 8 C & P 616, 173 ER 643—notwithstanding that the insane "innocent agent" in that case was the ringleader!

[31] *Manley* (1844) 1 Cox CC 104; *Mazeau* (1840) 9 C & P 676, 173 ER 1006.

[32] Kadish, "Complicity, Cause and Blame" in *Essays in the Criminal Law* (1987) 135, 171ff.

[33] See the distinction made between behavioural, circumstantial, and consequential elements of the actus reus, above, § 4.

[34] [1976] QB 217 (CA); see the commentary in [1975] Crim LR 584. *Cogan and Leak* was followed by the Victorian Court of Appeal in *Hewitt* (1996) 84 A Crim R 440, but should now be explained on the basis of procurement: below, § 7.6(ii)(b).

[35] *Thornton v Mitchell* [1940] 1 All ER 339 (DC), considered in *CLGP* § 129 n. 11. Cf. *Millward* [1994] Crim LR 527 (CA). Both cases are discussed in the text below, §§ 7.6(i), 7.6(ii)(b).

[36] Cp. *A-G's Reference (No. 1 of 1975)* [1975] QB 773 (CA), in which D secretly laced P's drink. (Note that the offence in that case was held to be one of strict liability, and that P was therefore guilty of committing the offence as a principal, notwithstanding his "innocence". D, in turn, was a secondary party.)

[37] Cp. *Butt* (1884) 15 Cox CC 56 (D guilty as principal of falsifying his employer's accounts by making a false statement to the employer's innocent bookkeeper).

involve fine—indeed, seemingly arbitrary—distinctions. For instance, it is apparently possible to "enter" premises as a burglar through the agency of another,[38] or for senior executives of a bank to make false statements in a prospectus issued by that bank;[39] but one cannot "buy" liquor on licensed premises unless personally present on those premises.[40] Thus the range of offences to which the innocent agent doctrine applies is somewhat uncertain.

Secondly, innocent agency is also excluded if P is not a member of the class of persons eligible to commit the offence as a principal. A typical example is an offence that can only be committed by a licensee. A useful illustration of this sort of offence, though not one involving innocent agency, is *Morris v Tolman*:[41]

> P obtained a licence to use his vehicle on the highway. S, his employee, then used the vehicle for a purpose not covered by the licence. It was a statutory offence for the licensee to use the vehicle outside the terms of the licence.

On these facts, no offence was committed by either P or S. P had not used the vehicle himself (hence no actus reus by P). S had used the vehicle, but could not be guilty of the offence since he was not the licensee (hence no actus reus by S).

Suppose, instead, that by a trick S procures P, the innocent licensee, to use the vehicle (as S knows) outside the terms of the licence. Because he is not the licensee, S is incapable of committing the offence personally; therefore the innocent agency doctrine cannot apply and he cannot be convicted as principal. P commits a crime in such cases only if the main offence is one of strict liability; in which case S, in turn, is guilty as a secondary party on the basis that he procured the offence.

## § 7.4 Secondary parties who assist or encourage crime

Section 8 applies to persons who involve themselves in a crime by giving assistance or encouragement to its commission. The section mentions four varieties of conduct counting as secondary participation: aiding, abetting, counselling, and procuring. These are the standard categories of participation recognised at common law.[42] Because, as we shall see, the categories overlap, it appears that they include the actus reus of virtually any form of assistance, encouragement, or contribution toward a crime by the principal.

Historically, there was a fifth variety of secondary participation, sometimes called "joint enterprise" (or "parasitic accessorial liability"), which arose through S's forming a *common unlawful purpose* with the principal. Following the now-leading Supreme Court decision in *Jogee*,[43] liability based on a common purpose is abolished. (This former ground of liability, and the reasons for its abolition, are outlined in § 7.5 below.)

[38] Hale 1 PC 555 (1736).

[39] *Varley* [2019] EWCA Crim 1074, [2020] Lloyd's Rep FC 281 (where, however, the defendants were acquitted on a retrial). Cp. *Brisac* (1803) 4 East 164, 102 ER 792 (conspiracy to cheat).

[40] Hence, in *Woby v B and O* [1986] Crim LR 183 (DC), the two defendant minors, who had sent an adult into an off-licence to buy lager on their behalf, were ruled not to be guilty of "buying intoxicating liquor on licensed premises, being aged under 18 years" since they were not on the premises when they did so. Similarly, in *Pratt v Martin* [1911] 2 KB 90 (DC), D was held not to have effected "entry" within the meaning of the Game Act 1831, s. 30, when he sent a dog onto land.

[41] [1923] 1 KB 166 (DC).

[42] *Benford v Sims* [1898] 2 QB 641.

[43] *Jogee* [2016] UKSC 8; *Ruddock* [2016] UKPC 7, [2017] AC 387.

### *(i) The conduct element*

Although section 8 of the Accessories and Abettors Act 1861 mentions four types of conduct constituting participation, it is not necessary in the charge to specify which type of conduct is relied on, and all four verbs may also be used together.[44] Indeed, to some extent the overlap in meanings between the words makes this a sensible practice,[45] and it is slightly artificial to analyse the terms as independent, alternative, actus reus elements. Indeed, the overlap is such that the Law Commission has proposed a formal simplification, by replacing the traditional language with "assisting or encouraging".[46] Moreover, that simplification was in effect adopted by the Supreme Court in *Jogee*,[47] which, throughout its judgment, characterises the actus reus of secondary participation in terms of "assistance or encouragement".

That phrasing is convenient; it is deployed in this chapter too. But it is no more than a shorthand, one that must be used with care *because it is misleading*. (Perhaps a better shorthand phrase would have been "encouragement or contribution".) As will be seen, "counselling" could be omitted without loss from the traditional section 8 formula. But "procuring" cannot be—and this point was missed in *Jogee*. There are forms of procuring that are neither assistance nor encouragement; moreover, procurement requires a distinct causal relationship to the principal's crime that the other forms of complicity lack.

Part of the difficulty lies in how one understands the role of section 8 itself. As was noted in *Jogee*,[48] the purpose behind the enactment of section 8 was to simplify the prosecution of secondary parties (by allowing them to be charged as if principals). The section was not intended to establish a new substantive code governing the modes of participation. But it does not follow from this insight that the words have no distinct meanings. They certainly did at the time (being tied, in part, to whether S's involvement preceded P's crime);[49] moreover, distinctions between each term have sometimes been identified in later cases (albeit ones preceding *Jogee*).[50] Each of "aid", "abet", and "procure" involves a particular form of contribution to or involvement in the principal's crime that cannot be completely assimilated with its counterparts. Therefore, while the generic "assistance or encouragement" is a convenient encapsulation of the actus reus of secondary liability, it remains necessary to examine the traditional forms of conduct separately.

#### *(a) Aiding*

S aids P by assisting, helping, or giving material support to P in the commission of a crime.[51] There must be actual assistance: merely trying to help is not enough for complicity

[44] *Ferguson v Weaving* [1951] KB 814 (DC).

[45] Albeit not a desirable one in cases where the evidence allows the particular form of participation to be specified: *Maxwell* [1978] 1 WLR 1350 (HL); *Gaughan* [1990] Crim LR 880 (CA).

[46] Law Com. No. 305, *Participation in Crime* (2007) paras. 3.9–3.10. This move would necessitate separate provision for certain instances of procurement where S causes P to commit an offence: *ibid.*, part 4; below, § 7.4(i).

[47] *Jogee* [2016] UKSC 8; *Ruddock* [2016] UKPC 7, [2017] AC 387.

[48] *Ibid.*, [6].

[49] That traditional distinction between aiders and abettors (present at the time of the offence) and counsellors and procurers (accessories before the fact) is no longer of legal effect. See below, § 7.4(i)(a).

[50] Indeed, in *A-G's Reference (No. 1 of 1975)* [1975] 1 QB 773, 779 (CA), Lord Widgery CJ instructed that the four terms are, in so far as possible, to be interpreted according to their ordinary meanings. For criticism, see Smith, "Aid, Abet, Counsel, or Procure" in Glazebrook (ed.), *Reshaping the Criminal Law* (1978) 120, 125.

[51] E.g. *Bainbridge* [1960] 1 QB 129 (CCA) (supplying oxygen cutting equipment for use in a burglary); *Stansfeld & Co v Andrews* (1909) 22 Cox 84 (supplying beer for illegal sale).

liability.[52] If S, knowing that P intends to rob a bank, plans to lend P her gun, she does not aid the offence if her car breaks down on the way over to P's house, and P leaves to commit the robbery before S arrives. On the other hand, the assistance need not be substantial. If T acts as lookout for P during the bank robbery, he is a party to the robbery even should there be no need to give a warning.[53]

It is no longer necessary that the assistance should be rendered at the scene of the offence.[54] Traditionally, the common law divided secondary parties into two groups. Aiders and abettors were said to be "principals in the second degree", and distinguished from counsellors and procurers—"accessories before the fact"—by their actual or constructive presence *at the time* the offence is committed.[55] The division is now only of historical interest, and the former requirements of presence for aiders and abettors, and conversely the former requirements of absence for counsellors and procurers, have all disappeared.[56]

Although the aid must be rendered to P, the aid need not be essential to P's commission of the crime. In particular, it need not be a "but for" cause of P's committing the crime.[57] Neither is it required that P should be aware of S's assistance, provided P is in fact assisted.[58] Suppose that P plans a robbery, intending to use his gun. The day before the robbery takes place, S notices that P's gun has not been cleaned properly, such that it might malfunction. Without telling P, S places her own gun, an identical model, in the drawer for P to use instead. P carries out the robbery using S's gun. In this case S has aided P and is a party to the robbery even though P is ignorant of S's contribution. A well-known illustration is the American case of *State v Tally*.[59] Judge Tally, whose brothers-in-law were pursuing and planning to kill V, prevented a third party from warning V of the danger, thereby making it easier for the pursuers to kill V. Tally had aided the murder (and thus was guilty of

[52] See Smith, "Secondary Participation and Inchoate Offences" in Tapper (ed.), *Crime, Proof and Punishment* (1981) 21, 36–9. Cp. *A-G v Able* [1984] QB 795, 812 (Woolf J) (DC): no offence unless the reader "was assisted or encouraged by so reading the booklet to take or attempt to take his own life, otherwise the alleged offender cannot be guilty of more than an attempt". Note that there is no general offence of attempting to aid another to commit a crime: Criminal Law Act 1977, s. 1(4)(b). Conviction for an inchoate offence may, however, be possible under the Serious Crime Act 2007: see below, § 9.1.

[53] "The assistance given, however, need not contribute to the criminal result in the sense that but for it the result would not have ensued. It is quite sufficient if it facilitated a result that would have transpired without it": *State v Tally* 102 Ala 25, 15 So 722 (1894). Cp. *Gogerly* (1818) R & R 343, 168 ER 836.

[54] *Blakely v DPP* [1991] RTR 405, 411 (DC); *Thambiah v R.* [1966] AC 37 (PC).

[55] *Ferguson v Weaving* [1951] 1 KB 814, 819 (DC); *Bowker v Premier Drug Co* [1928] 1 KB 217 (DC). "Constructive" presence tended to be interpreted broadly. It included any assistance rendered while the offence was being carried out, even if such assistance was from afar—compare *State v Tally* 102 Ala 25, 15 So 722 (1894); as well as being near enough to render assistance if called upon, cf. *Betts* (1930) 22 Cr App R 148. For discussion, see Smith, "Aid, Abet, Counsel, or Procure" in Glazebrook (ed.), *Reshaping the Criminal Law* (1978) 120, 125ff; Williams, *CLGP* § 120.

[56] Compare *A-G v Able* [1984] QB 795 (DC), where advice given in advance was regarded as within the scope of aiding and abetting, with *Bainbridge* [1960] 1 QB 129 (CA), where it was treated as counselling or procuring.

[57] *Stringer* [2011] EWCA 1396, [2012] QB 160, [48]. (On so-called "but for" causation, see § 4.2(i).) On the kind of connection that is required between S's conduct and P's offending, see § 7.4(ii) below.

[58] Cp. *Fury* [2006] EWCA Crim 1258, [15]; *Kupferberg* (1918) 13 Cr App R 166, 168. *Per* Turner, *Russell on Crime* (12th ed., 1964) 147, "it is quite possible for a complete stranger to be guilty of aiding and abetting a crime committed by a principal offender who does not even know that he is being aided". This passage was approved by Martin JA in *Hobart v R* (1982) 25 CR (3d) 214, 236 (Ont CA).

[59] 102 Ala 25, 15 So 722 (1894).

murder as a secondary party), notwithstanding that his brothers-in-law were unaware of the assistance.[60]

*(b) Abetting*

The core idea of abetment is encouragement.[61] In practice, such encouragement can overlap with other forms of participation in crime. For example, in cases where S is alleged to have "assisted" P by offering support (e.g. as a lookout) on which P relies, the reliance itself may be sufficient encouragement for P to be abetted, whether or not any assistance was in fact necessary. Similarly, encouragement of P to commit an offence is likely also to constitute counselling.[62] A secondary party can, in other words, encourage *by* aiding, counselling, or procuring. But whether or not S does those other things, what counts for abetment is whether S's actions give encouragement to P.

Whether S's actions communicate encouragement is always a question of fact,[63] and there are no specified forms of qualifying behaviour.[64] The encouragement may be by words[65] or conduct—nodding one's head in endorsement of a crime may be just as effective as a verbal indication of agreement. Indeed, mere presence may constitute abetment where that presence supplies an incentive to P to go ahead. For example, in *Coney*,[66] it was said that attendance at an illegal prizefight might be evidence of abetting battery by the fighters, since, as Mathew J observed:[67]

> "The chief incentive to the wretched combatants to fight on until (as happens too often) dreadful injuries have been inflicted and life endangered or sacrificed, is the presence of spectators watching with keen interest every incident of the fight."

Simply by watching, S may encourage the fighters. (Although, as we shall see below, the mens rea requirement means that S must also *intend* to encourage them.[68]) Similarly, joining P in a chase after V could amount to encouraging P's use of violence against V when they caught up with him.[69] Presence can lend moral support, for example, "by contributing to the force of numbers in a hostile confrontation".[70]

[60] See also *Larkins v Police* [1987] 2 NZLR 282, where S spontaneously decided to act as lookout during a robbery. *Per* Eichelbaum J (at 290), "the appellant's action in providing the principal offenders with, as counsel put it, an extra pair of eyes was at least evidence of actual assistance regardless whether those offenders were aware of its availability".

[61] Cp. *Clarkson* [1971] 1 WLR 1402 (C-MAC).

[62] As noted in § 7.4(i)(a), historically the main difference between abetting and counselling lay in the timing of the encouragement. If it occurred prior to the crime, S would be an "accessory before the fact" (counsellor or procurer) rather than a "principal in the second degree" (abettor or aider). See, e.g., the discussion in *A-G v Able* [1984] QB 795, 809 (DC).

[63] *Stringer* [2011] EWCA Crim 1396, [2012] QB 160, [51].

[64] This well-established point is confirmed in *Jogee* [2016] UKSC 8; *Ruddock* [2016] UKPC 7, [2017] AC 387, [11], [89].

[65] *Royce* (1767) 4 Burr 2073, 2082, 98 ER 81, 86.

[66] (1882) 8 QBD 534.

[67] *Ibid.*, 544 (dissenting).

[68] Cp. *N* [2019] EWCA Crim 2280, [2020] 4 WLR 64, [14]. It is submitted that this point was not taken sufficiently seriously by the Supreme Court in the bizarre case of *Gnango* [2011] UKSC 59, [2012] 1 AC 827: see below, § 7.4(d).

[69] *Stringer* [2011] EWCA Crim 1396, [2012] QB 160.

[70] *Jogee* [2016] UKSC 8; *Ruddock* [2016] UKPC 7, [2017] AC 387, [89]; *N* [2019] EWCA Crim 2280, [2020] 4 WLR 64, [15].

However, such cases are exceptional, because it is necessary to show that S did *in fact* communicate encouragement to P.[71] A good illustration of this principle is *Clarkson*.[72] Two soldiers, hearing noises emanating from a room at their barracks, entered the room where they found other soldiers raping a young woman. The two remained in the room to watch. Apparently, they neither did nor said anything, either to encourage or discourage continuance of the rape. The Court of Appeal, sitting as the Courts-Martial Appeal Court, quashed their convictions for aiding and abetting, because the Judge-advocate had not clearly stated that it must be proved the appellants intended to and did encourage the commission of the crime. While the Court acknowledged it was possible that the rapists *might* in fact have received encouragement from the appellants' presence,[73] that encouragement had to be proved beyond reasonable doubt. Mere presence *which does not by itself encourage* is insufficient: "[t]here must be an intention to encourage; and there must also be encouragement in fact".[74] Edmund Davies J, giving the judgment of the Court of Criminal Appeal in *Allan*, stated the point as follows:[75]

> "In our judgment, before a jury can properly convict an accused person of being [an accessory to the offence], they must be convinced by the evidence that, at the very least, he by some means or other encouraged the participants. To hold otherwise would be, in effect, as counsel for the appellants rightly expressed it, to convict a man on his thoughts, unaccompanied by any physical act other than the fact of his mere presence."

In practice, therefore, the inference of encouragement will usually require something further, such as proof of some additional action by S (e.g. words or gestures) or of a particular circumstance that implies support,[76] for example that P and S are members of the same gang or that S's presence is pursuant to some prior arrangement.[77] Alternatively, as in *Coney* (above), it may be sufficient that S is part of a group offering encouragement, and that P is aware of the group's behaviour, albeit unaware of S's individual conduct.

Indeed, there could even be situations where the presence of a particular individual—say, a trusted confidant or a superior officer—reassures and encourages P's commission of a crime. This is not to say that their *mere* presence constitutes abetment: it does not.[78] But the additional consideration that, say, S is someone in whom P places great faith may suffice to establish the required encouragement, and the question remains one of fact for each case.

By contrast with aid, which can be rendered to P without P's knowledge (above, § 7.4(i)(a)), it is essential to abetment that the encouragement be communicated successfully to P. There cannot be "encouragement in fact" by S unless P knows of it. Suppose, for example,

[71] "It is, however, important to make clear to juries that mere approval of (ie 'assent' to, or 'concurrence' in) the offence by a bystander who gives no assistance, does not without more amount to aiding." *Robinson* [2011] UKPC 3, [14]. Cp. *Coney* (1882) 8 QBD 534; *Young* (1838) 8 C & P 644, 173 ER 655; *Atkinson* (1869) 11 Cox CC 330; below, §§ 7.4(ii), (iii).

[72] [1971] 1 WLR 1402 (C-MAC).

[73] *Ibid*., 1406.

[74] *Ibid*., 1407. Cf. *Smith v Baker* [1971] RTR 350 (DC). (S, a passenger, does not abet driving without insurance merely by sitting in the car. For cases where S also owns the car, see below, § 7.4(iii).)

[75] [1965] 1 QB 130, 138.

[76] See also *Wilcox v Jeffery* [1951] 1 All ER 464 (DC), where S attended a concert by Coleman Hawkins in his capacity as a jazz critic and, further, paid a fee to attend. The concert was unlawful since Hawkins was an American who did not have a work permit. S was held to have abetted P's contravention of the Aliens Order 1920: "his presence and his payment to go there was an encouragement" (at 466 *per* Lord Goddard CJ).

[77] E.g. *Smith v Reynolds* [1986] Crim LR 559 (DC) (presence pursuant to a prior agreement).

[78] As was emphasised in *Willett* [2010] EWCA Crim 1620 (brother).

that S knows P intends to commit a robbery. S posts a letter to P in which she encourages P to commit the robbery, but the letter is never delivered. On these facts alone, S cannot be a party to the robbery because her encouragement, although offered, is not received by P.[79]

This point, which applies also to counselling, is considered further below (§ 7.4(ii)). But it is important to emphasise that the requirement, that S's encouragement be communicated to P, is not a requirement that the encouragement had any effect upon P, by inducing him to commit the offence. It is unnecessary to show that P would not have offended but for the encouragement, or even that P was in any way influenced by it. P must be aware of his being encouraged (the encouragement must be communicated), but it need not make a difference to P's decision to offend.[80]

*(c) Counselling*

"Counselling" has two varieties of meaning. First, it includes the provision of advice or information,[81] though such conduct may also amount to aiding or abetting.[82] Alternatively, counselling may contemplate "urging" someone to commit an offence[83]—in which sense the overlap is with abetting and, to a lesser extent, procuring.

The upshot of these overlaps is that "counselling" occupies no independent space as a conduct element of secondary participation. Every case of counselling constitutes, at the same time, one or more of assisting, encouraging, or procuring. Hence, as a general matter, we shall not refer specifically to this form of participation in what follows.

*(d) Procuring*

Most cases of secondary participation involve acts of assistance or encouragement by S, and it is understandable that these forms of complicity have received more attention from the courts in recent years. But procurement remains a distinctive, if less common, way of contributing to P's offence. By contrast with the other varieties of participation, procurement of an offence requires that S deliberately *induces* or *influences* P to commit the offence. Therefore the requisite connection between S and the commission of the offence by P must be rather stronger than for aiding or abetting. By contrast with those other terms, which require only that S play some part in the crime:[84]

> "To procure means to produce by endeavour. You procure a thing by setting out to see that it happens and taking the appropriate steps to produce that happening."

[79] Cp. *Stringer* [2011] EWCA Crim 1396, [2012] QB 160, [49]. There may, however, be inchoate liability for encouraging or assisting crime under the Serious Crime Act 2007: below, § 9.1.

[80] Compare the facts of *Wilcox v Jeffery* [1951] 1 All ER 464 (DC). This proposition is accepted in *Jogee* [2016] UKSC 8; *Ruddock* [2016] UKPC 7, [2017] AC 387, [10]; citing *Calhaem* [1985] QB 808 (CA), which is discussed below, § 7.4(ii).

[81] A classic example is *Baker* (1909) 28 NZLR 536, where S wrote to P with advice how to break into a safe using explosives. The case is criticised by Williams, *CLGP* § 125, but only on the issue of mens rea.

[82] Cp. *A-G v Able* [1984] QB 795, 809 (DC), where it was noted that "[i]gnorance how to commit suicide must by itself be a deterrent. . . . The contents of the booklet provide information as to methods which are less likely to result in an unsuccessful attempt. This assistance must encourage some readers to commit or attempt to commit suicide."

[83] *Calhaem* [1985] QB 808 (CA); cp. *Stuart v R* (1976) 134 CLR 426.

[84] *A-G's Reference (No. 1 of 1975)* [1975] QB 773 (CA). See also *Millward* [1994] Crim LR 527 (CA); *Beck* [1985] 1 WLR 22 (CA); *Reed* [1982] Crim LR 819 (CA); *Broadfoot* [1976] 3 All ER 753 (CA); *Bryce* [2004] EWCA Crim 1231.

Thus the perpetration of P's crime must in some sense be a consequence of the procurement by S.[85] However, S's contribution need not be a decisive or *sine qua non* ingredient of the decision by P to commit the offence: it is enough that the procurement was influential. Even if there were other reasons why, without S's contribution, P might have chosen to commit the offence anyway, that does not matter. Provided that S's conduct in fact played *some* part in influencing P, S will be guilty of P's offence on the basis that she procured it.[86]

Normally, procurement by S will take the form of persuasion, inducement, or threats. Sometimes, however, S's contribution may operate without influencing P's reasons; indeed, P may be entirely ignorant of S's role. In cases where an offence can be committed without mens rea, and the innocent agent doctrine does not apply,[87] S may become a secondary party to an offence by causing P to commit it. In *A-G's Reference (No. 1 of 1975)*[88] S secretly laced the drinks of P, who was subsequently convicted of driving with excess alcohol (a strict liability offence). S had procured P's offence, and was thus a secondary party to it.

### *(ii) The need for a connection*

Secondary liability is derived from S's *involvement* in the principal offence, and not merely her attempt to become involved. It follows that S's conduct must somehow be connected to the commission of the offence by P. As we have seen, in the case of aiding this requirement is manifested by the need to demonstrate that assistance of some sort *was in fact* provided to P; in the case of procuring, it is reflected in the need to show a link of influence or inducement between S's conduct and perpetration of the offence. A link must also exist for abetting (and counselling). Although causation need not be shown (otherwise S would normally be a principal),[89] and S's contribution need not be "substantial" or "measurable",[90] a sufficient degree of connection between S's conduct and the actus reus of P's offence must be proved. It must be established by the prosecution that the principal *received* encouragement, urging, or advice, before S's conduct may count as participation falling within section 8.[91]

This point is fundamental to the nature of secondary participation. Derivative liability is *not* a form of inchoate liability. Liability is not *for S's act* of encouragement (for example)

[85] See the summary by Smith, "Aid, Abet, Counsel, or Procure" in Glazebrook (ed.), *Reshaping the Criminal Law* (1978) 120, 134.

[86] For a civil law illustration see *Barton v Armstrong* [1976] AC 104, 121 (execution of deed voidable for duress, even though P had other reasons to execute the deed apart from D's threat): "the illegitimate means used was a reason (not the reason, nor the predominant reason nor the clinching reason) why the complainant acted as he did. We are also prepared to accept that a decisive answer is not obtainable by asking the question whether the contract would have been made even if there had been no threats because, even if the answer to this question is affirmative, that does not prove that the contract was not made because of the threats."

[87] Above, § 7.3(i).

[88] [1975] QB 773 (CA). The decision has considerable untapped potential for the liability of hosts and publicans: see below, § 7.4(iv)(a).

[89] See the discussion in *Luffman and Briscoe* [2008] EWCA Crim 1739. The Court of Appeal retreated on this point in *Stringer* [2011] EWCA Crim 1396, [2012] QB 160, [47ff], from its earlier suggestion in *Mendez v R* [2010] EWCA Crim 516, [2011] QB 876, [18] that "secondary liability is founded on a principle of causation". Gardner argues for a causal relationship but in a very attenuated sense rarely encountered in legal discourse: "Complicity and Causality" (2007) 1 *Crim Law and Philosophy* 127. Cf. Sullivan, "First Degree Murder and Complicity" (2007) 1 *Crim Law and Philosophy* 271.

[90] Indeed, the Court of Appeal "had some difficulty understanding exactly what is meant" by these terms in *Hussain* [2023] EWCA Crim 697, [84].

[91] *Clarkson* [1971] 1 WLR 1402 (C-MAC) (abetting); *Calhaem* [1985] QB 808 (CA) (counselling). Cf. Smith, "Aid, Abet, Counsel, or Procure" in Glazebrook (ed.), *Reshaping the Criminal Law* (1978) 120, 131–4.

*per se*, as it is in inchoate offences.[92] Rather, it is derived from S's *participation in* the offence perpetrated by P. If P is not aware of the encouragement, urging, or advice, S necessarily fails to participate in the commission of the offence. In such a case, S cannot be a party to its commission.

The result is the same if the encouragement was so long ago that P has forgotten about it by the time she resolves to commit the offence, in which case S will not be a party to the offence.[93] This type of "forgotten advice" case is covered by a further *connection-based* requirement, suggested in the extraordinary case of *Calhaem*:[94] P must not only be aware of S's encouragement (for example), but he must also act in accordance with, or within the scope of,[95] the endorsement provided by S's encouragement. The Court of Appeal provided the following illustration:[96]

> "For example, if the principal offender happened to be involved in a football riot in the course of which he laid about him with a weapon of some sort and killed someone who, unknown to him, was the person whom he had been counselled to kill, he would not, in our view, have been acting within the scope of his authority; he would have been acting outside it, albeit what he had done was what he had been counselled to do."

Again, this is not to require that the encouragement actually "made a difference" in influencing P to commit the offence. As Woolf J stated in *A-G v Able*, "it does not make any difference that the person [encouraged] would have tried to commit suicide anyway".[97] P must have received and been aware of, say, encouragement by S, but the encouragement need not have played any further role.

### *(iii) Omissions*

S may aid or abet an offence by omission.[98] Most obviously, this may occur where S's failure to discharge a legal duty assists P to commit an offence: for example, when the security guard at a warehouse deliberately fails to lock a door, intending that P may readily gain entry into the building and steal some of the goods stored inside. If P then uses that door to carry out the burglary, the security guard will be an accessory to that crime.

Rather more problematic are cases where a person is held liable as a party for omitting to interfere and prevent an offence when she has a duty to do so and/or a right of control over the principal or the victim, together with an opportunity to discharge that duty or to

[92] Most notably, as in the inchoate crimes of encouraging or assisting crime contrary to ss. 44–46 of the Serious Crime Act 2007: below, § 9.1.

[93] Cp. *A-G v Able* [1984] QB 795 (DC).

[94] [1985] QB 808 (CA). S had hired P to murder her rival V. It was said that P, after having second thoughts, had decided not to kill V but went to V's house in order to act out a pretence so that both S and V would think an attempt had been made to kill V. However, after V screamed, P apparently went "berserk" and killed V by hitting her several times with a hammer. On these facts, the Court of Appeal upheld S's conviction for counselling murder.

[95] See also the discussion in § 7.4(iv)(c).

[96] [1985] QB 808, 813 (CA). The connection is "a matter of fact and degree": *Jogee* [2016] UKSC 8; *Ruddock* [2016] UKPC 7, [2017] AC 387, [12].

[97] *A-G v Able* [1984] QB 795, 812 (DC). See too *Stringer* [2011] EWCA Crim 1396, [2012] QB 160, [48].

[98] Sullivan, "Conduct and Complicity: Liability Based on Omission and Risk" (2008) 39 *Cambrian LR* 687.

exercise that right.[99] Standard examples of this variety of abetment are said to occur if a parent permits another to commit an offence against her child,[100] or if the owner of a car, while sitting in a passenger seat, permits the driver to break the law. However, these are not the same type of case.

Consider, first, the case where S and his son, V, are at the local park. P, a stranger, unexpectedly attacks V, inflicting fatal injuries. S, who never liked V, permits P to inflict those injuries despite being in a position to prevent the attack. It is sometimes suggested that such a person would be party to murder or manslaughter (as the case may be) if, by not intervening, S encouraged (and—the mens rea element—intended to encourage) P's offence.[101] As far as secondary liability is concerned, however, this seems to understate the position. It is submitted that where S has (i) a legal duty and (ii) the present ability[102] to prevent V's death by taking reasonable steps, his failure to do so, *in itself*, constitutes *aiding*, and not merely evidence of encouragement.[103] (Hence there would be no need to show an additional intention thereby to encourage P's crime.) The case is analogous to that of the warehouse security guard (above); in both examples, the conduct would be aiding whether or not P knew of the decision by S to refrain from performing his duty.[104]

Indeed, arguably S is not merely a secondary party; he may be independently guilty as a principal. Provided his intervention would have been causally efficacious in preventing the actus reus from occurring, it seems open to conclude that death results from his culpable failure to discharge his duty as a parent to take reasonable steps to intervene,[105] in which case this is a plain case of direct liability for murder or manslaughter resulting from his omission to perform a legal duty.[106]

At the other end of the scale is the case where S, a stranger, chances upon the commission of a crime and remains to watch. As we have noted already, such facts by themselves are insufficient to make S a party to the crime. This point is illustrated by *Clarkson*,[107]

[99] The duty or power is not sufficient by itself; it must be proved that S had an opportunity to intervene: *Webster* [2006] EWCA Crim 415, [2006] 2 Cr App R 6, [27]–[29].

[100] Many such cases will nowadays also fall within the compass of s. 5 of the Domestic Violence, Crime and Victims Act 2004, which makes it an offence to allow (*inter alia*) the death of a child or vulnerable adult within one's household.

[101] E.g. *Foreman and Ford* [1988] Crim LR 677 (Crown Court) (police officer); *Witika* (1991) 7 CRNZ 621(CA); *Nixon* (1990) 57 CCC (3d) 97, 109–10; cf. *Witika* [1993] 2 NZLR 424 (CA). For discussion, see Finn, "Culpable Non-Intervention: Reconsidering the Basis for Party Liability by Omission" (1994) 18 *Crim LJ* 90.

[102] Cp. *Webster* [2006] EWCA Crim 415, [2006] 2 Cr App R 6; *Tilley* [2009] EWCA Crim 1426, [2010] 1 WLR 605 ("allows").

[103] This appears to be the analysis in *Russell* [1933] VLR 59, 66 (Cussen ACJ), 76 (Mann J) (Vic SC); *Popen* (1981) 60 CCC (2d) 232 (Ont CA). Cf. *Rubie v Faulkner* [1940] 1 KB 571 (DC); *Russell and Russell* (1987) 85 Cr App R 388.

[104] In *Russell* [1933] VLR 59, 67, Cussen ACJ suggested that S must have known of S's acquiescence: see above, § 4.1(i)(b) (Case 2). (S's wife drowned herself and their sons in S's presence, wherefore S was convicted of manslaughter.) In principle, however, P need not be aware of S's contribution when it constitutes aiding: above, § 7.4(i)(a).

[105] This would require analysis of the case as involving concurrent causes (i.e. P's action and S's omission), rather than a novus actus by P. Yet such an approach seems plausible, provided that S is able to prevent P's conduct.

[106] See the judgment of McArthur J in *Russell* [1933] VLR 59. The existence of such a duty is discussed above, § 4.1(i)(b) (Case 2). The failure of household member to prevent a child's death may also be an offence, committed directly as principal, of causing or allowing the death of a child or vulnerable adult, contrary to s. 5 of The Domestic Violence, Crime and Victims Act 2004. See below, § 10.10.

[107] [1971] 1 WLR 1402 (C-MAC).

which was discussed in § 7.4(i)(b). Two soldiers entered a room where a rape was taking place. They stayed to observe the events, but it was not proved that they had encouraged the commission of the offence. The Courts-Martial Appeal Court quashed their convictions for rape. In the absence of proof of actual and intended encouragement, their failure to intervene attracted no criminal liability, since they were under no legal duty to intervene.

The difficult case arises when S is not under a legal duty but has a specific legal right to control P's activity. Consider the facts of *Du Cros v Lambourne*.[108] S was the owner of a car that had been driven dangerously, but it was not clear whether S or his companion, P, was driving at the time. Nonetheless, S was convicted of being a party to dangerous driving, it being irrelevant (in terms of his formal conviction) whether he was principal or abettor. If P was driving, S had the legal right as owner to direct the manner in which P drove; his acquiescence in the manner of P's driving was therefore held to constitute abetment of the offence of dangerous driving.

*Du Cros v Lambourne* was regarded by the Court of Appeal in *Webster* as authority for the proposition that a deliberate failure by S to exercise a legal right (not duty) of control over P's activity may be, without more, constitutive of secondary participation in crime:[109]

> "*Du Cros v Lambourne* . . . establishes that a defendant might be convicted of aiding and abetting dangerous driving if the driver drives dangerously in the owner's presence and with the owner's consent and approval. The owner was in control and ought to have prevented or attempted to prevent the driver driving in a dangerous manner."

In other words, there is no need to show that S's non-intervention actually assisted or encouraged P. However, the judgments in *Du Cros* are equivocal on the point,[110] and the point was *obiter* in *Webster*, where it was not established that the owner-passenger had any opportunity to intervene. Moreover, in *Cassady v Reg. Morris Transport Ltd* it was held that an employer's failure to forbid an offence by its employee was merely *evidence* (and not itself constitutive) of encouragement.[111] Thus, strictly speaking, it remains open for S to argue that where she has a mere right, not only must there be a failure to intervene, but the non-intervention must in fact encourage (and be intended to encourage) P in his commission of an offence.[112] Support for that conclusion can also be found in a number of possession cases, usually involving drugs or counterfeit goods. Suppose that S lives with P, who keeps contraband on the premises. While a cohabitee may well have a right to demand that

[108] [1907] 1 KB 40. See generally on this topic Smith, *A Modern Treatise on the Law of Criminal Complicity* (1991) 39ff.

[109] *Webster* [2006] EWCA Crim 415, [2006] 2 Cr App R 6, [28].

[110] Darling J appears to have regarded non-intervention as abetment *per se* ([1907] 1 KB 40, 46–7); Lord Alverstone CJ, with whom Ridley J agreed, refused to "attempt to lay down any general rule or principle, but having regard to these findings of fact, it is, in my opinion, impossible to say that there was in this case no evidence of aiding and abetting" (at 46). It appears that in *Webster* the matter was not subject to argument from counsel.

[111] [1975] RTR 470 (DC). Cf. *Duxley v Gilmore* (1959) 123 JP 331, but contrast *Ferguson v Weaving* [1951] 1 KB 814, 819 (DC); *Thomas v Lindop* [1950] 1 All ER 966, 968 (DC).

[112] Cf. *Martin* [2010] EWCA Crim 1450, [32] ("D intended to assist or encourage P to drive in this manner and D did in fact by his presence and failure to intervene encourage P to drive dangerously").

contraband be removed from the shared premises, the courts have required more than the mere right to establish either that S herself jointly possesses the goods with P (i.e. commits the offence as principal) or that she aids and abets P to do so. Thus S must do something *more* than simply acquiesce. Sir John Smith's commentary to *McNamara* helpfully summarises the position:[113]

> "The evidence must be sufficient to satisfy a jury either that each party was in possession . . . or that someone [else] was and the defendant not only knew that he was but also assisted or encouraged him."

Hence in *Bland*,[114] where S was living with P, a drug-dealer, her conviction, as an accomplice, for possession of a controlled drug with intent to supply was quashed notwithstanding that she knew of P's activities.

In any event, the gulf between specific right and duty is easily bridged. Where S has a supervisory role, e.g. as the instructor of a learner-driver, it seems clear that a mere omission to intervene is sufficient to establish liability as a secondary party, and that the instructor is under a legal *duty* (and does not merely have a right) to intervene and prevent a dangerous manoeuvre by the learner-driver.[115] And in *Tuck v Robson*,[116] a public house licensee was held to have assisted others in drinking after hours through "passive assistance", which the Court defined as "presence with no steps being taken to enforce his right either to eject the customers or at any rate to revoke their licence to be on the premises".[117] The decision is problematic: although the Court relied upon the publican's "right" and did not use the language of duties, the decision effectively recognised a duty on the publican to revoke his customers' licence. Seemingly, that duty rested on nothing other than the existence of a corresponding right.

In light of these cases, it appears that the current law regarding secondary liability for omissions is as follows:

(i) If S has a *legal duty* to prevent an offence (e.g. in the case of a parent to protect his child), then a failure by S to take reasonable steps to intervene *in itself* constitutes the actus reus of aiding and abetting. (Indeed, if causation between S's failure and the relevant result can be established, S may be guilty as a principal.)

(ii) If S has a specific right of control over P, but no particular legal duty, it seems that the position is the same as in (i): a failure by S to take reasonable steps to intervene *in itself* constitutes the actus reus of aiding and abetting.

(iii) If S has neither a duty nor a particular right, then he must intend by his non-intervention to encourage P, and, in fact, his inaction must also communicate encouragement to P.

113 [1998] Crim LR 278; a summary endorsed in *Kousar* [2009] EWCA Crim 139, [2009] 2 Cr App R 5, [16], where D was charged as a principal; above, § 5.6(iv).

114 (1987) 151 JP 857, [1988] Crim LR 41 (CA).

115 *Rubie v Faulkner* [1940] 1 KB 571, 575 (DC): "For him to refrain from doing anything when he could see that an unlawful act was about to be done, and his duty was to prevent an unlawful act if he could, was for him to aid and abet". See also *Harris* [1964] Crim LR 54 (CA); Wasik, "A Learner's Careless Driving" [1982] *Crim LR* 411; Lanham, "Drivers, Control, and Accomplices" [1982] *Crim LR* 419.

116 [1970] 1 WLR 741.

117 *Ibid.*, 746.

That said, the matter is finely balanced. If, in future, *Cassady* came to be seen as representing the better view, the position of those such as the owner-passenger in (ii) would be identical in law to that in (iii), i.e. the owner-passenger would be in the same legal position as the onlookers to the rape in *Clarkson*, or the casual spectators at the prizefight in *Coney*.[118] Of course, in that event the existence of a right of control would remain potentially relevant to an allegation that, by her acquiescence, S *in fact* encouraged P. Even though, under the approach in *Cassady*, it would not constitute abetment in law, known acquiescence by an authoritative figure could still be the "something further" that supports the inference of encouragement required for such cases.[119]

There are arguments in favour of *Cassady*, arguments strong enough to convince the Law Commission.[120] To impose liability in such cases is, effectively, to extend criminal liability for omissions. As we saw in § 4.1, the criminal law is reluctant to impose liability for omissions, and for good reason. Forcing persons to intervene and regulate the actions of others (e.g. requiring property-owners to police the actions of users) substantially widens the scope of criminal responsibility for wrongdoing and, in turn, risks intruding severely upon the autonomy of citizens.[121] This point is particularly significant when one takes into account the fact that *everyone* has a general right to use reasonable force to forestall the criminal activities of others, by virtue of section 3(1) of the Criminal Law Act 1967.[122] If a mere such right were sufficient to make S an accomplice, then anyone, stranger or friend, who is in position to intervene with reasonable force to prevent a crime would become an accessory to that crime. *That*, surely, cannot be allowed, since it would entirely subvert the policy of the law against generally criminalising omissions.

On the other hand, in the difficult case, S is not a mere stranger, a passer-by who stumbles upon a crime that she is under no duty to prevent. An important distinction can be drawn between the background general right to use reasonable force to prevent crimes, under section 3(1) of the Criminal Law Act 1967, and the more specific rights of control at issue in cases such as *Du Cros v Lambourne*: it is only in the latter cases that S is entitled to control P's activity *whether or not* an offence is being committed. Although there is no general obligation to prevent crime,[123] it seems reasonable to conclude that those with specific legal rights to prevent a crime *do* contribute to—hence, participate in—the wrongdoing by refraining from exercising their authority and, thus, permitting that crime to occur.

As with active forms of secondary participation, the omission to intervene must occur at a time when S also has the requisite mens rea—e.g., as we see below, when S has knowledge of the essential matters of P's crime. In the specific context of omissions, however, it is worth re-emphasising that S's mens rea must arise at a point when she has an opportunity to intervene. Mere knowledge of P's misconduct is not enough if it is too late for S to prevent it.

[118] (1882) 8 QBD 534.

[119] Above, § 7.4(i)(b).

[120] Law Com. No. 305, *Participation in Crime* (2007) paras. 3.39–41, citing the second edition of this book.

[121] For elaboration of this argument, see above, §§ 4.1(i)(a), 1.2(i)(b), 1.2(ii)(e). See also Bronitt, "Defending *Giorgianni*—Part Two: New Solutions for Old Problems in Complicity" (1993) 17 *Crim LJ* 305, 310–11. *Contra*, Ashworth makes a powerful argument for limited duties to prevent crime in "The Scope of Criminal Liability for Omissions" (1989) 105 *LQR* 424.

[122] "A person may use such force as is reasonable in the circumstances in the prevention of crime, or in effecting or assisting in the lawful arrest of offenders or suspected offenders or of persons unlawfully at large."

[123] Cp. *Allan* [1965] 1 QB 130 (CCA).

### *(iv) Mens rea for participation by assistance or encouragement*

To have the mens rea for secondary participation, S must intend to assist in (or encourage or procure, as the case may be) the crime committed by P.[124] Stated in this way, the fault element appears straightforward. Misleadingly so. It is in fact quite complex, because the mens rea element must relate to two different matters: (i) S's own conduct, in assisting or encouraging P; and (ii) the nature of P's (criminal) actions.

Moreover, S's intention to help (etc.) P to commit a crime may be either *direct* or *indirect* ("*oblique*"). It is sufficient mens rea either for S to act *in order to help (etc.) P to do the essential matters of P's crime*, or for S to act *knowing that P will thereby be helped (etc.) to do the essential matters of P's crime*. Hence we may summarise the mens rea requirement for secondary liability as follows:

(i) S must intend her own contribution (i.e. to do the thing that assists, encourages P); and

(ii) *either*

 (a) *Direct intent*: One of S's purposes when making her own contribution is to assist (or encourage or procure, as the case may be) P to do the essential matters of P's crime; *or*

 (a) *Indirect intent*: S must appreciate the nature of P's actions. That is, S must know about the essential matters relating to P's actions which make those actions an offence.[125]

Accordingly, if S is proved to have provided P with a baseball bat, which P uses to deliberately cause grievous bodily harm to V, S is guilty alongside P of an offence contrary to section 18 of the Offences against the Person Act 1861 if: (i) S intended to provide the bat to P; and (ii)(a) one of S's *purposes* in so doing was to assist P to cause grievous bodily harm; *or* (ii)(b) S *knew* that her action *would* assist P to do so. In both (ii)(a) and (ii)(b), S's purpose or knowledge must relate to the deliberate causing of grievous bodily harm, if she is to be guilty of the section 18 offence as a secondary party. If, for instance, S intended to assist P merely to cause *actual* bodily harm, she could not be convicted of a section 18 offence.[126]

#### *(a) S's own contribution: the intention to aid, abet, or counsel*

Let us start with the core forms of complicity: aiding and abetting. (As explained earlier, counselling has little independent significance; we consider procurement separately, below.) The essence of aiding and abetting is intentional help or encouragement.[127] This means that not only must S intend her actions ((i), above), but she must also act with the intent thereby

[124] *Jogee* [2016] UKSC 8; *Ruddock* [2016] UKPC 7, [2017] AC 387, [9].

[125] Technically, as this is a species of "indirect" intention, it is *open* to the jury to find the relevant intention in such circumstances; the jury is not *required* to do so. See above, § 5.1(iv).

[126] We consider the position where S has in mind an offence different from the one P commits in § 7.4(iv)(c) below.

[127] This was settled law well before being confirmed in *Jogee* [2016] UKSC 8; *Ruddock* [2016] UKPC 7, [2017] AC 387, [9]–[10], [90ff]. See generally Dennis, "The Mental Element for Accessories" in Smith (ed.), *Criminal Law: Essays in Honour of J.C. Smith* (1987) 40; Smith, *A Modern Treatise on Criminal Complicity* (1991) part II; Sullivan, "Intent, Purpose and Complicity" [1988] *Crim LR* 641; Dennis, "Intention and Complicity: A Reply" [1988] *Crim LR* 649.

to aid or abet P's conduct, or knowledge that her actions *will* aid or abet P's conduct ((ii), above).[128] This requirement counts as a specific intention requirement for the purposes of the voluntary intoxication rules.[129]

In terms of (i) above, i.e. intending one's own conduct, consider a simple example where S accidentally leaves her gun cabinet unlocked, and P opportunistically steals S's gun and uses it to commit murder. S is not liable because S did not *intend* to do the thing that assisted P, never mind intend *that* it assist P in committing murder.

In practice, (i) is unlikely to be a difficult requirement for the prosecution to satisfy in most cases. More attention is likely to centre on the second requirement, elaborated in (ii) above: S's intention or knowledge regarding the aiding or abetting of P's conduct. Its role can be seen in the following example. Suppose that S had just got into and started her car, which is parked on the driveway of her house, when she remembered that she had left her wallet in the house. S then left her car running, with the keys in the ignition, while she went back into the house to collect the wallet. An opportunistic thief stole the car. S intended *to leave the car running*, which was an action that assisted the theft. But she did not intend *to assist the theft*. Neither did S *know* that her action *would* aid or abet P's crime. If she lived in an area where such thefts are relatively common, we might conclude that she knew the theft was likely to happen. Yet that is not sufficient to render her a secondary party to theft.

The criteria of intention were discussed in detail in § 5.1. As we have noted here, they include both direct and indirect (or "oblique") intention. Complicity law covers cases where S acts as she does *in order* to help (or encourage) P, as well as cases where S acts as she does knowing that P *will* be aided (or encouraged) by her conduct. The latter type of case is a form of indirectly intended aid (or encouragement). Consider, however, the following example:

> Sally sees Paul's car broken down in a dangerous area of town. Motivated by concern for his welfare, she stops and helps Paul to repair his car. She knows, because Paul tells her, that Paul will use the car that afternoon to commit a robbery, but she does not endorse criminal activity and that is not why she helps Paul.

It is submitted that this is a situation in which it is open for the jury to "find" an (indirect) intention to help Paul: equally, the jury is not required to do so.[130] Such cases, however, are likely to be rare. In practice, in cases where S did not directly intend to assist or encourage P's offending, the courts tend to focus on whether S knew that P *would* be encouraged or assisted by her conduct, and treat that as sufficient to establish S's indirect intention to aid or abet P.

It is necessary to say a little more about how the foregoing criteria apply.

In the context of secondary parties, the plain case is where S *wants* P to commit the relevant offence, and acts with the purpose of helping (or encouraging) P to do so. Suppose that S wants V dead, and encourages P to kill him. Assuming that P does then murder V, this would be a straightforward case of directly intended abetment, even if, at the time of encouraging P, S was unsure whether P would actually carry out the killing. Just as a golfer

[128] For criticism of the Supreme Court's failure to consider this requirement in *Gnango* [2011] UKSC 59, [2012] 1 AC 827, see Buxton, "Being an Accessory to One's Own Murder" [2012] *Crim LR* 275, 276–8.

[129] *McNamara* [2009] EWCA Crim 2530: see below, § 18.4, for discussion of intoxication rules. This point was noted (albeit implicitly) in *Mohamadi* [2020] EWCA Crim 327, in relation to secondary liability for rape.

[130] Cp. *Woollin* [1999] 1 AC 82; above, § 5.1(iv).

can directly intend to hit a hole in one, whilst realising this is most unlikely to happen, S can think there is a high chance that P will not go ahead, but still *directly* intend to assist or encourage P's offending. In terms of the criteria stated earlier, S has (i) intended her own act of encouragement, and (ii) done so *in order to* encourage P to commit the murder.

Direct intent of this kind may be straightforward, but it is not required for secondary liability. In other cases, S may have no purpose to assist or encourage P to commit a crime. Nonetheless, S may become guilty of P's crime on the basis of her *indirect* intent to aid or abet: that is, because she knows—i.e. has no significant doubt—that her conduct *will* assist or encourage P to commit an offence. In this second type of case, there is no requirement for S to desire that P commit the offence she aids (abets, etc.). It is the *assistance* or the *encouragement*, not P's perpetration of the ultimate crime, that must be intended by S.[131] Consider, for example, the following facts, which are based on *Cafferata v Wilson*:[132]

> Stephen is a firearms wholesaler. He sells a firearm to Pamela, a general shopkeeper. Stephen knows that Pamela will resell the firearm in her shop, and that Pamela does not have a licence to deal in firearms. Stephen does not sell the firearm to Pamela because he wants her to resell it, but rather because he wants the money that Pamela is prepared to pay for it. He would be entirely happy if Pamela kept the firearm locked in a box in her attic for the remainder of her life.

The claim that Stephen does not want Pamela to resell the firearm is irrelevant. It may be characterised as a claim about Stephen's motive, or ultimate purpose, which is of course to make money. But what matters is whether he (directly) intended to assist Pamela, or *knew* he *would* be assisting Pamela, in committing that crime. The answer to that question is, yes: Stephen intended to sell the gun to Pamela, and he knew that the result of his deliberate behaviour would be the provision of an ingredient essential to Pamela's reselling of a firearm. It is this facilitation, not the ultimate offence, that must be intended; whether that aid is itself rendered for the further purpose of bringing about the offence is, legally, beside the point. Indeed, any requirement that *P's commission of the offence* must be intended by S would deprive secondary liability of much of its current scope.

On the other hand, the help or encouragement must be *intended*, directly or indirectly. Recklessness is insufficient.[133] Thus, in a case where S does not have the purpose of assisting P, it would not be enough for secondary liability that S merely thinks it is *likely* that P may be assisted. Suppose, for example, the following variation:

> Susan is an auctioneer of various goods. She sells an unlabelled box of goods to Peter, a wholesaler. Because the goods are in bond, she is unsure (i.e. reckless) whether the goods are toy pistols or real guns. Susan knows that Peter does not have a licence to deal in firearms.

On these facts, Susan lacks the mens rea for secondary participation because she is merely reckless whether Peter is assisted or encouraged by her conduct. She does not have the purpose of assisting Peter to make an unlicensed sale of a firearm, or the knowledge that

[131] See *Bryce* [2004] EWCA Crim 1231, [61], citing this proposition from the first edition. Cp. *National Coal Board v Gamble* [1959] 1 QB 11, 23 (DC); *Lynch v DPP for Northern Ireland* [1975] AC 653, 678 (HL); *A-G v Able* [1984] QB 795 (DC); *Clarke* (1984) 80 Cr App R 344; *Jogee* [2016] UKSC 8; *Ruddock* [2016] UKPC 7, [2017] AC 387, [10]. Note that the connection is necessarily tighter in cases of participation by procurement. We turn to that difference below in this section (S's own contribution: the intention to procure).

[132] [1936] 3 All ER 149 (DC).

[133] *Scott* (1978) 68 Cr App R 164 (suspicion not enough).

the sale *will* (or, at least, is virtually certain to) assist Peter to make an unlicensed sale of a firearm.

*"Conditional" (direct) intentions?*

Intentions may, of course, be conditional. As was noted in § 5.1(vii), the general rule is that an intention to do or bring about something only if particular conditions hold is, in law, an intention. Much was made of this point by the Supreme Court in *Jogee*.[134] However, care is required here. *Direct* intentions can be conditional, but indirect ones, and knowledge more generally, cannot be. Consider the following example:

> Steffi is a firearms wholesaler. She sells a handgun to Pavlov, whom she suspects to be a member of a local violent gang. Steffi is certain that, if Pavlov is indeed a member of the gang, he will use the handgun to shoot a rival gang member. However, she is unsure whether Pavlov is in fact a member of the gang.

On these facts, there is no "conditional intent" that, *if* Pavlov is a gang member, Steffi's conduct will assist in the shooting. The case is simply one of being reckless whether she is helping Pavlov to carry out a shooting. If Pavlov is a member of the gang, and uses the gun to shoot a rival gang member, Steffi should *not* be held liable for his offence as an accessory.

It would be otherwise if Steffi directly intended to help, as in the following example:

> Stephanie sells a handgun to Pavlov, whom she suspects to be a member of a local violent gang. Stephanie thinks it likely that, if Pavlov is indeed a member of the gang, he will use the handgun to shoot a rival gang member. She is unsure whether Pavlov is in fact a member of the gang. However, Stephanie herself bears a grudge against the rival gang and she sells the gun to Pavlov in the hope that he will use it as envisaged.

On these revised facts, Stephanie directly intends to assist Pavlov to shoot a rival gang member. Whether he *is* in fact assisted is a conditional matter. But she acts with the direct intention that he be assisted and, if he does go on to shoot the rival gang member, Stephanie is liable to be convicted as a secondary party to that offence.

Once again, it is important to be clear here about what it is that must be intended. In cases of aiding and abetting,[135] S does not have to intend *that P commit the relevant crime*. (Apart from in cases of procurement, which is considered below, S typically has no control over P's actions at all; so she cannot *intend* that P commit the offence.) S only has to intend *to assist (or encourage) P to commit the relevant crime*. Strictly speaking, therefore, even the second of the examples above is not a case of conditional intent. Stephanie has a *present* intention by her actions to help Pavlov, albeit that the help will come to fruition conditionally and in the future.[136]

It may be helpful to elaborate upon this argument. A conditional intention is a species of future intention, in the sense that one holds a conditional intention to do X when one holds an intention to do X should the relevant condition be met at some time in the future. Such an intention imports two key constraints. First, X must lie in the future, in that one is not

[134] *Jogee* [2016] UKSC 8; *Ruddock* [2016] UKPC 7, [2017] AC 387, esp. [92]–[95].

[135] We consider the special case of procuring in the next subsection.

[136] The following paragraphs are drawn from an extended critique of the Supreme Court's handling of intention and conditional intention in Simester, "Accessory Liability and Common Unlawful Purposes" (2017) 133 *LQR* 73, 82–6. See also Child, "Understanding Ulterior Mens Rea: Future Conduct Intention Is Conditional Intention" (2017) 76 *CLJ* 311.

yet actually doing X, although that moment may be close at hand. Secondly, whatever else it relates to, S's intention must also relate to an action *by S*. Someone who opens the back door of a lorry intending to steal the contents should they be valuable still has an action to do (i.e. steal the contents). Hence they can have a conditional intention to steal the contents at the point when they open the door.

By contrast, once S has performed her act of aiding or abetting, *she* has nothing left to do. The gun that S has handed to P is literally out of S's hands. What lies in the future is P's action. And that action is up to P, not S. Save in the special case of procuring, S normally does not, and need not, intend *that P will do X*. S can, of course, act *in order* to help or encourage P to do X: S can intend her own act of *helping* or *encouraging* P's action. But S need not intend P's action: because, at least normally, she has no control over it.[137] Neither, normally, can S intend P's mens rea.[138] And so she cannot conditionally intend these matters, either.

None of this is to deny the possibility of conditionally intending to help another. However, that would be a case where S has not yet rendered help, and means to do so only if some further condition is met (e.g. if P pays the agreed fee, or turns out to be a friend). In such a case, the actus reus of S's aiding has not yet occurred, so participation cannot be established. By contrast, once the help is rendered—the gun is passed to P—that help is either intended or not. It cannot be conditionally intended: it is done. Of course, there are still conditions to be met before we can say that S did actually aid P to commit, say, murder. Notably, P must go on to kill V. But that is an actus reus condition relating to P's crime, not a mens rea one relating to S's contribution.

These nuanced points were missed in *Jogee*, and have yet to be captured in its wake.

*S's own contribution: the intention to procure.*
To aid or abet, as we have seen, S must *intend* to help or assist P's criminal actions. Similarly, to be a procurer S must intend by her actions to *procure* P's criminal conduct. None the less, in respect of S's intending her own contribution, procurement is a special case. By contrast with assistance and encouragement, the connection to P's crime is necessarily tighter. S must still be proved to have intended her act of procurement. However, because procurement requires a contribution that actually influences or induces P to commit the crime, it follows that S must *directly* intend to help bring it about that P will commit the crime itself. For this reason, it was said by the Court of Appeal in *A-G's Reference (No. 1 of 1975)*[139] that, unlike aiding or abetting (or counselling), procuring an offence requires an "endeavour" or

[137] On the control requirement in intention, see, e.g., Duff, *Intention, Agency and Criminal Liability* (1990) 56; Simester, "Paradigm Intention" (1992) 11 *Law and Philosophy* 235, 246–50. I intend things that I act in order to bring about; conversely, if I believe that I have no control over whether the thing occurs, I cannot intend to bring it about. This is not to claim that S can *never* act in order to bring about an action by P, or have the requisite degree of control over P's actions; indeed, procurement allows for such cases. The point is, however, that neither aiding nor abetting require such control. Ergo, they cannot require the corresponding intention about P's actions (or mental state).

[138] This point is misunderstood by Ormerod and Laird, "*Jogee*: Not the End of a Legal Saga but the Start of One?" [2016] *Crim LR* 539, 540. The authors are drawn into error here by an oversimplification (at 544): "Knowledge speaks to the present and intention to the future." But not all intentions are future-related. (Neither is all knowledge about the present.) One may intend a punch even as one throws it. The more important distinction here is between consequences and circumstances. In standard cases of aiding and abetting, from S's perspective, P's mens rea is a circumstance and need not itself be intended. Indeed, one *cannot* intend a circumstance or future fact over which one has no control.

[139] [1975] QB 773, 779 (CA).

"setting out" to cause the commission of the offence. This special feature of procurement was not noted in *Jogee*,[140] but it is well established, and nothing the Supreme Court said is incompatible with it.

*An exception for duress or necessity?*

Suppose that S aids P for some further reason, such as out of fear. This may, of course, give rise to a supervening defence of duress or necessity. Sometimes, however, the courts have treated such circumstances as vitiating S's mens rea. In *Gillick*,[141] the House of Lords appeared to hold that a doctor who gives contraceptive advice or treatment to a girl aged under 16 years for clinical reasons, while recognising that this would facilitate acts of unlawful sexual intercourse, would lack the mens rea required to aid and abet unlawful sexual intercourse. Similarly, in *Fretwell*,[142] S reluctantly supplied an abortifacient to a woman who had threatened to kill herself should S not do so. Although S hoped P would not take the drug, she did so and died. S was held not liable for murder as an accessory (to the then-crime of *felo de se*, or "self-murder") because he was "unwilling that the woman should take the poison".[143]

The analysis in these decisions is understandable—Fretwell, in particular, faced the death penalty—but problematic. Notwithstanding the language of the judgments, in both cases the aid *was* intended by S. Like the example of Susan and Peter above, in both *Fretwell* and *Gillick* S may have hoped that P would not ultimately engage in the criminal conduct. Nonetheless, S's own help was at least indirectly intended: it was reluctant, justified, and deliberate. The very purpose of an abortifacient is to induce an abortion;[144] similarly, the very purpose of contraception is to facilitate sexual intercourse with a reduced risk of pregnancy. Contrast the analysis in *Lynch v DPP for Northern Ireland* where, under duress, S drove P to a garage where P planned to murder a policeman. According to Lord Morris:[145]

> "If in the present case the jury were satisfied that the car was driven towards the garage in pursuance of a murderous plan and that the appellant knew that was the plan and intentionally drove the car in execution of that plan he could be held to have aided and abetted even though he regretted the plan or indeed was horrified by it."

[140] *Jogee* [2016] UKSC 8; *Ruddock* [2016] UKPC 7, [2017] AC 387: where the distinctive character of procurement was not in issue.

[141] *Gillick v West Norfolk and Wisbech Area Health Authority* [1986] AC 112, adopting Woolf J's views on the criminal law aspects of the case (which was brought as a civil action for a declaration) at [1984] QB 581, 589 (QBD). Cp. *Janaway v Salford Health Authority* [1989] AC 537, 550–1 (Slade LJ), 558 (Stocker LJ), CA; contrast at 572 (Lord Keith), 572–3 (Lord Lowry), HL. For general discussion, see Ashworth, "Criminal Liability in a Medical Context: The Treatment of Good Intentions" in Simester and Smith (eds.), *Harm and Culpability* (1996) 173; Smith, *Justification and Excuse in the Criminal Law* (1989) 64–70; Spencer, "Trying to Help Another Person Commit a Crime" in Smith (ed.), *Criminal Law: Essays in Honour of J.C. Smith* (1987) 148.

[142] (1862) Le & Ca 161, 169 ER 1345. *Per* Woolf J, in *A-G v Able* [1984] QB 795 (DC), *Fretwell* should be regarded as "confined to its own facts".

[143] (1862) Le & Ca 161, 164, 169 ER 1345, 1346.

[144] Admittedly, S did not intend either directly or indirectly to assist in a self-murder. It was neither his purpose nor virtually certain that P would die. However, under the old law of felony murder, such a finding was not required: death was a constructive liability element of P's crime and, from the perspective of S's liability, not an essential matter. See below, § 7.4(iv)(c) (Constructive liability elements of P's crime). Fortunately, felony-murder doctrines are no longer a part of the law, having been abolished for England and Wales by s. 1 of the Homicide Act 1957.

[145] [1975] AC 653, 678.

The better approach in cases such as *Fretwell* and *Lynch* is to accept that S has the mens rea to aid and abet P's offence, but to allow S a defence based on duress or necessity. This was precisely the view taken by Lord Morris in *Lynch*. His Lordship continued:[146]

> "But if that intention and all that he did only came about because of the compulsion of duress of the nature that I have described he would, in my view, have a defence."

The decisions in *Fretwell* and *Gillick* were constrained from taking such an enlightened approach by the fact that, at the time, it was thought that the defences of duress and necessity did not cover those cases.[147] It is to be hoped that the fiction of denying an intent by S will not be required in future and that, in particular, the scope of the necessity defence will ultimately be accepted as embracing such instances of *bona fide* medical treatment.

*An exception for performance of a duty?*

Consider the following facts, which occurred in *National Coal Board v Gamble*:[148]

> S (the National Coal Board) sold P's employer a large quantity of coal. P, a lorry driver, was despatched to collect some of the coal. Once loaded, the lorry was weighed before leaving the colliery. S's employee, the weighbridge clerk, realised the load exceeded that permitted to be carried on the highway. He drew P's attention to the illegality. P said that he was prepared to take the risk of being caught, whereupon the clerk issued P with a weighbridge ticket. The weighbridge clerk's function in issuing the ticket to P was to record how much coal had been taken, in order that S could then charge the buyer for that amount of coal, and also to pass title in the coal to the buyer. Had S not issued the ticket, P would not have been permitted to leave the colliery with the coal.

On these facts, it was held by a majority of the Divisional Court[149] that S, through its employee, was an accessory to the offence committed by P. In handing over the ticket and passing title to the coal, S aided P by enabling the lorry to depart from the colliery with the coal (and thereby to commit an offence). The fact that the clerk was motivated only by considerations of accounting was irrelevant to the question whether he (indirectly) intended that aid.

In the majority judgments, a great deal was made of the fact that ownership of the coal had not passed before the clerk handed over the weighbridge ticket. Implicit in this is the proposition that if P already owns some item possessed by S, then by handing the item over, S merely performs her legal duty to deliver up possession to P; she does not aid or abet P to commit an offence with that item. Regard the facts of *Lomas*:[150]

> S has possession of a jemmy, which she borrowed from P. S knows that P is a professional burglar. P asks for return of the jemmy and S gives it to him. P then uses the jemmy to commit a burglary.

[146] *Ibid*. Cp. *Hibbert* (1995) 99 CCC (3d) 193. Note that duress is no longer available as a defence to participation in murder: below, § 20.1(i)(d).

[147] For discussion of the current scope of these defences, see below, §§ 20.1, 21.4. The scenario in *Gillick* would now be covered by the specific exceptions provided for in s. 73 of the Sexual Offences Act 2003.

[148] [1959] 1 QB 11 (DC). See Duff, "'Can I Help You?' Accessorial Liability and the Intention to Assist" (1990) 10 *LS* 165; Williams, "Complicity, Purpose and the Draft Code" [1990] *Crim LR* 4.

[149] Lord Goddard CJ and Devlin J; Slade J dissenting.

[150] (1913) 9 Cr App R 220; discussed in *Bullock* [1955] 1 WLR 1 (CCA).

S was held not to be a party to P's crime. Properly so, observed Devlin J in *NCB v Gamble*:[151]

> "In a sense a man who gives up to a criminal a weapon which the latter has a right to demand from him aids in the commission of the crime as much as if he sold or lent the article, but this has never been held to be aiding in law. . . . In the transfer of property there must be either a physical delivery or a positive act of assent to a taking. But a man who hands over to another his own property on demand, although he may physically be performing a positive act, in law is only refraining from detinue. Thus in law the former act is one of assistance voluntarily given and the latter is only a failure to prevent the commission of a crime by means of forcible detention."

By contrast, the act of a shopkeeper who knows P's criminal purpose before selling P the jemmy would be an act "of assistance voluntarily given":[152]

> "If one man deliberately sells to another a gun to be used for murdering a third, he may be indifferent about whether the third man lives or dies and interested only in the cash profit to be made out of the sale, but he can still be an aider and abettor. To hold otherwise would be to negative the rule that mens rea is a matter of intent only and does not depend on desire or motive."

Prima facie, then, the law after *NCB v Gamble* is as follows: S intentionally aids P to commit a crime when she intentionally provides material assistance (e.g. by handing over an instrument of burglary), believing that P will commit that crime, *except* when P has a legal right to receive that assistance from S, and S renders the assistance only because she owes a legal duty to do so.

Unfortunately, this summary of the law involves a false distinction. The underlying rationale identified by Devlin J is spurious. Whether or not P owns the jemmy, he is aided when S gives it to him, because he now has possession when before he did not. In both cases (i.e. owned and unowned), the aid itself is intended. The fact that the jemmy belongs to P is relevant, once again, only to motive. Therefore, while S does not act *in order to* facilitate P's crime, she has an indirect intention to do so: she *knows* that handing over the jemmy will help P.

Neither does P's ownership establish a legal duty on S to hand over the jemmy. While there is normally a civil law duty on bailees-at-will to return borrowed property upon demand, it is defeated by the duty not to commit a crime. Just as it is "incumbent on a court of equity to act by such rule as tends most to discountenance the crime",[153] so it is that the rules of the civil law must always be subject to exception whenever they would tend to undermine the criminal law. This point was recognised by Parker LCJ in *Garrett v Arthur Churchill (Glass) Ltd*:[154]

> "albeit there was a legal duty in ordinary circumstances to hand over the goblet to the owners once the agency was determined, I do not think that an action would lie for breach of that duty if the handing over would constitute the offence of being knowingly concerned in its exportation."

[151] [1959] 1 QB 11, 20 (DC).
[152] *Ibid*., 23.
[153] *Bridgman v Green* (1855) 2 Ves Sen 627, 628, 28 ER 399. Cp. *Amicable Society v Bolland* (1830) 4 Bligh (NS) 194, 211, 5 ER 70; *Re Estate of Crippen, decd.* [1911] P 108, 112; Smith, "Civil Law Concepts in the Criminal Law" [1972B] *CLJ* 197, 208–11.
[154] [1970] 1 QB 92, 99 (DC). To similar effect, see *K Ltd v National Westminster Bank* [2006] EWCA Civ 1039, [2007] 1 WLR 311, [10]; below, § 9.1(iv).

The inevitable conclusion must be that, in terms of legal principle, ownership makes no difference. Assuming in each case that S knows the essential matters of P's offence, there is no distinction to be drawn between the situation in *Lomas* and that in *NCB v Gamble*. Both cases, moreover, are inseparable from the case of a shopkeeper who sells a jemmy to P knowing his purpose. Notwithstanding the distinction laid down in *NCB v Gamble*, in principle all three situations ought to result in the same outcome: the conviction of S.

*Civil liberties and the interests of victims.*

Accordingly, liability for complicity is a real possibility for persons who are merely performing the routines of their jobs or trades. Given this possibility, it is important to consider whether, morally speaking, an exception *ought* to be allowed in such cases as those of the weighbridge clerk, the bailee, and/or the shopkeeper? Williams argues that, at least in the case of the shopkeeper, there should be an exception:[155]

> "From the point of view of policy the question is one of some complexity. On the one side are the policy of repressing crime, and the difficulty of distinguishing between the merchant who knowingly assists a crime and the ordinary accessory before the fact. On the other side stand the undesirability of giving too great an extension to the criminal law, and the inconvenience to legitimate trade of requiring a merchant to concern himself with the affairs of his customers. ... It is submitted that ... the seller of an ordinary marketable commodity is not his buyer's keeper in criminal law unless he is specifically made so by statute. Any other rule would be too wide an extension of criminal responsibility."

Williams suggests that the exception should be confined to sellers of "an ordinary marketable commodity". In respect of bailment cases like *Lomas*, a further possibility would be to create an exception covering those who return property to its owner, provided that it is not S's purpose thereby to assist the owner to commit a crime, and that the contemplated crime is not a serious one (say, a crime triable only on indictment).[156]

In our view, the criminal law should take priority over the civil law in this matter. Sometimes, where criminal and civil law overlap, the criminal law must perforce follow the civil law, e.g. where it is the civil law that defines the relevant harm. An example is the law of theft; where property rights, the interests being safeguarded by the criminal law, are a creature of civil law.[157] But complicity is not like theft. When S hands P a weapon, P is aided, and V's rights are put at risk, equally, *whoever* of them owns it.

The argument against our view is a strong one. Williams highlights the inconvenience to shopkeepers if they are required to concern themselves with the affairs of their customers. A similar point may be made regarding ordinary citizens who return the belongings of others. It is important that persons engaging in ordinary activities should be able to perform those activities—i.e. to live their lives—without being harassed by the criminal law, especially if the harassment requires them to modify their own activities because of the plans and conduct of others, and not because of anything they have done themselves. It is significant that

[155] *CLGP* § 124. See also Alexander and Ferzan, *Reflections on Crime and Culpability* (2018) 40–3; Hurd and Moore, "Untying the Gordian Knot of Mens Rea Requirements for Accomplices" (2016) 32 *Social Philosophy and Policy* 161.

[156] Williams, "Obedience to Law as a Crime" (1990) 53 *MLR* 445; Sullivan, "The Law Commission Consultation Paper on Complicity: Fault Elements and Joint Enterprise" [1994] *Crim LR* 252.

[157] For discussion of this proposition, and of derogations from it by the courts, see below, Chapter 13.

the duty not to help P arises out of P's intentions, and not from S's conduct or plans. Thus, as Williams objects (in the context of the weighbridge operator's case):[158]

> "It seems a strong thing to hold that a man who is simply pursuing his ordinary and lawful vocation, and takes no special steps to assist illegalities, becomes involved as a third party to a crime committed by the customer merely because he realises that his customer will be enabled by what he himself does to commit a crime."

Consider also the case of *A-G's Reference (No. 1 of 1975)*,[159] mentioned earlier, in which S was convicted of procuring P to drive with excess alcohol after secretly lacing P's drinks. Although P was ignorant of S's actions in that case, one possible implication of the decision is that publicans—and, indeed, generous hosts at a dinner party—could be regarded as having aided and abetted whenever their customers or guests then drive home drunk.[160] Williams's objection may be extended to these cases too, and one should hesitate before allowing the criminal law to reach so far into the ordinary commercial and private activities of citizens.

Nonetheless, while Williams's reasoning is powerful, it is not in our view conclusive. These are not cases where S stands by passively and omits to prevent P's crime. S *actively and intentionally helps* P to commit that crime. Indeed, S's aid may even be an indispensable feature of P's wrongdoing.[161] The rights of victims not to be burgled, assaulted, etc. mean that it is sometimes necessary to curtail the liberty of citizens to intervene and assist criminals, as well as the liberty of shopkeepers to sell goods to anyone at will. Those rights should prevail here. Moreover, the intrusive implications of this position for the lives of citizens are not as great as they may seem. S's duty is not to refuse aid to those suspected of having a criminal purpose; the duty arises only if S *knows or wants* that a crime will be committed.[162] Thus S is not required to police the actions of P. She does not have to enquire into P's purpose; neither must she take active steps, either to stop P or to inform the police. She is simply not free to assist P deliberately when she realises that P plans to take advantage of her contribution in order to commit a crime.

There is room for compromise, one which balances individual liberty against the need to prevent crime. The potential intrusiveness of criminal liability for ordinary activities—including the activities of bailees otherwise mandated by the civil law—would be reduced by excluding party liability for persons who assist or encourage summary offences.[163] A similar restriction applies for attempts liability,[164] and there seems little reason not to carry the logic over to complicity.[165] Apart from fostering individual autonomy, such a move would give due recognition to the seriousness of the underlying offence and the interests being

[158] *TBCL* 342.

[159] [1975] QB 773 (CA); above, § 7.4(i)(d).

[160] Williams, *TBCL* 338–41. Widgery LCJ refers to the question of hosts in the case itself, and argues that they are unaffected by the decision, since where the provision of alcohol is overt rather than by lacing, guests make up their own minds whether or not to take drink—hence, no procurement by the host. Unfortunately, this reasoning is unconvincing since it applies only to the case of secondary participation by procurement; and not to assistance or encouragement, which lack a requirement of causation: above, § 7.4(i)(d).

[161] As in *NCB v Gamble* [1959] 1 QB 11 (DC).

[162] For discussion of the trade-off between a stringent mens rea requirement and the reach of criminalisation, see Simester, "The Mental Element in Complicity" (2006) 122 *LQR* 578, 591–2.

[163] Cp. Williams, *TBCL* 343; Spencer, "Trying to Help Another Person Commit a Crime" in Smith (ed.), *Criminal Law: Essays in Honour of J.C. Smith* (1987) 148, 162.

[164] Below, § 9.3(ii)(a); but not to conspiracy.

[165] Compare *NCB v Gamble* [1959] 1 QB 11, 20 (DC) ("except in the case of a felony" *per* Devlin J).

protected by that offence, while avoiding the uncertainties of "balance of evils" or "reasonable conduct" defences[166] in these difficult cases.

*(b) P's criminal conduct: S must have knowledge or purpose regarding the essential matters of S's offending*

Sometimes, as we have said in § 7.4(iv)(a), S offers assistance or encouragement *in order that* doing so will facilitate some criminal act by P, without being certain what P actually means to do. Of such a case, we can say straightforwardly that S (directly) intends to aid or abet P's (potential) crime. However, very often S has no particular intent concerning what P will do. In those cases, it suffices that she intends to help or encourage P, *knowing* what it is that P will do: this is a case of indirect intent to aid or abet P. The classic statement of this latter requirement is to be found in *Johnson v Youden*, where it was said that:[167]

> "Before a person can be convicted of aiding and abetting the commission of an offence he must at least know the essential matters which constitute that offence."

Two issues arise from this traditional requirement: (i) is "knowledge" by S really required or is foresight of a risk of P's offending sufficient, and (ii) what "essential matters" of an offence must S's purpose or knowledge relate to?

The meaning of "knowledge" is considered earlier, in § 5.4: S must accept, or assume, and have no substantial doubt that the relevant facts are true. There must be actual knowledge: it is not enough that S *ought* to have known the facts.[168] Neither is it sufficient if S suspects that they may well be true, even if accompanied by a negligent[169] or reckless failure to enquire into the facts;[170] although in the more extreme case of wilful blindness, S will be treated as having knowledge.[171]

*Johnson v Youden* is still good law. Thus the requirement for knowledge would exclude from liability a person who renders assistance to P believing that P *may* be about to commit a crime but not knowing that he *will* (and without wanting him to do so). Mere belief in the possible existence of a set of facts is the stuff of recklessness, not intention.[172] Consider the following variant of an example used in section § 7.4(iv)(a):

> S is a firearms wholesaler. She sells a firearm to P, a general shopkeeper. S knows that P does not have a licence to deal in firearms. S does not sell the firearm to P because she wants him to resell it, but rather because she wants the money that P is prepared to pay for it. However, (this time) S is unsure whether P intends to resell the firearm in his shop or to keep the firearm for his own use. In fact, P does resell the firearm.

On these facts, S does not act with the purpose of helping P to sell the firearm. Assuming S does not satisfy the criteria of wilful blindness,[173] she also does not *know* the firearm will be

[166] A defence of acting reasonably is now available to the inchoate offences of assisting or encouraging crime: Serious Crime Act 2007, s. 50; below, § 9.1(iv)(b).
[167] [1950] 1 KB 544, 546 (DC).
[168] *Webster* [2006] EWCA Crim 415, [25].
[169] Cp. *Callow v Tillstone* (1900) 64 JP 823.
[170] *Bainbridge* [1960] 1 QB 129, 134; *DPP for Northern Ireland v Maxwell* [1978] 1 WLR 1350, 1357–59 (Lord Hailsham) (HL).
[171] *Antonelli* (1905) 70 JP 4. The doctrine of wilful blindness is examined above, § 5.4(i).
[172] See above, §§ 5.2(iii), 5.4.
[173] Above, § 5.4(i).

resold. S is merely reckless about whether her action will assist P to resell the firearm without a licence. As such, according to the criteria laid down in *Johnson v Youden*, S is innocent of secondary participation in P's crime.

In the context of indirectly intended participation, the requirement of knowledge has been adopted expressly in numerous cases,[174] and has received the endorsement of the House of Lords.[175] However, for a while its importance was doubted. In its 1993 Consultation Paper on *Assisting and Encouraging Crime*, the Law Commission suggested that notwithstanding the dicta in *Johnson v Youden*, whenever a case has turned on the point, recklessness regarding whether P will commit an offence has been sufficient to convict the accessory:[176]

> "there is no case which rejects the awareness of a mere possibility of the commission of the principal offence as a ground of accessorial liability, and at least some authority that seems to support that analysis."

One such authority appears to be *Carter v Richardson*,[177] where S was supervising P, a learner driver, who was driving with excess alcohol. Even though it was impossible for S to know precisely P's blood-alcohol level, S was convicted of aiding and abetting the offence committed by P. On a case stated, the Divisional Court held that "it was sufficient if the defendant was aware that the principal offender had consumed excessive alcohol even though the precise amount had not been determined";[178] a test satisfied, Lord Widgery CJ continued, if S "*knew* that [P] had been drinking to such an extent that it was *probable* that his blood alcohol content was over the limit".[179] The first statement is unobjectionable. However, it seems that the second part of the quotation pitches the standard lower than "knowledge" in that, prima facie, it does not require S to have a settled belief, or no substantial doubt, that P's blood alcohol content was over the limit (and thus P would commit an offence by driving). To the extent that this is so, the test shades into (subjective[180]) recklessness.[181]

Subsequent decisions of the Court of Appeal supported the proposition that foresight of the probable existence of the essential matters of P's crime satisfied the mens rea requirement of aiding and abetting. Such a standard was endorsed by the Court of Appeal in *Rook*,[182] where contemplation or foresight of P's committing the crime "as a real or serious risk" was

[174] E.g. *Ackroyds Air Travel Ltd v DPP* [1950] 1 All ER 933 (DC); *Thomas v Lindop* [1950] 1 All ER 966 (DC); *Ferguson v Weaving* [1951] 1 KB 814 (DC); *Smith v Jenner* [1968] Crim LR 99 (DC); *Patel* [1970] Crim LR 274 (CA). Compare *Webster* [2006] EWCA Crim 415, [21]; *Martin* [2010] EWCA Crim 1450, [2011] RTR 4, [35].

[175] *Churchill* [1967] 2 AC 224, 236–7; *Maxwell v DPP for Northern Ireland* [1978] 1 WLR 1350 (HL). Cp. the decision by the High Court of Australia in *Giorgianni v R* (1984) 156 CLR 473.

[176] LCCP No. 131 (1993) para. 2.58. The Law Commission's final Report prefers a requirement that S intend (directly or obliquely) that P will commit the offence: Law Com. No. 305, *Participating in Crime* (2007).

[177] [1974] RTR 314 (DC). Contrast *Tinsley* [1963] Crim LR 520 (CCA).

[178] [1974] RTR 314, 318 (Lord Widgery CJ) (DC).

[179] *Ibid.* (emphasis added).

[180] Objective or *Caldwell*-recklessness was never sufficient: *Blakely and Sutton v DPP* [1991] RTR 405 (DC).

[181] It is not clear that, on the facts of *Carter v Richardson*, the Court needed to go so far as this. The case seems better analysed as a situation where (given, e.g., S's awareness of P's behaviour and of the amount of alcohol consumed by P) the court could readily infer from the facts of the case that S had no substantial doubt that, whatever the precise blood-alcohol measurement, it was in excess of the permitted level. Indeed, S had originally pretended he himself was the driver, presumably for this very reason. Cp. *Crampton v Fish* [1970] Crim LR 235 (DC), where "the evidence was apparently so overwhelming that no reasonable magistrate could fail to be satisfied of the accused's knowledge".

[182] [1993] 1 WLR 1005, 1009–10 (CA).

said to suffice; in *Reardon*,[183] where foresight by S of the "strong possibility" of P's committing the relevant crime was sufficient; and in *Bryce*,[184] where (following *Rook*) a "real or substantial risk" of P going ahead would do. Although the (*obiter*) reasoning in those cases was criticised trenchantly,[185] for a period this position came to be regarded as orthodox.

In a welcome return to principle, however, the law stated in *Johnson v Youden*—and defended consistently across previous editions of this book—was re-established by the Supreme Court and Privy Council in *Jogee*:[186]

> "the mental element in assisting or encouraging is an intention to assist or encourage the commission of the crime and this requires knowledge of any existing facts necessary for it to be criminal."

The Court cited a number of leading cases in support of this position,[187] besides endorsing *Johnson v Youden* itself.[188] Disappointingly, it did so without reference to the contrary body of case law that had built up in decisions such as *Rook*, *Reardon*, and *Bryce*. Yet the Supreme Court's decision seems right in principle, and decisions such as *Rook*, *Reardon*, and *Bryce* should be viewed as bad law. As we saw in § 5.1(v), "intending" to do some action requires an intention with respect to the *behavioural* and *consequential* elements of that action, but is generally satisfied by knowledge or settled belief (with no significant doubt) regarding the action's *circumstance* elements. The same distinction applies here. It is sufficient to establish S's intention to assist or encourage P's crime if she intends her own contribution, knowing what P will do—the latter is, from S's perspective, analogous to a circumstance element that accompanies and need not be brought about by S's behaviour.

To be clear, where it is S's *purpose* to encourage or assist P to commit an offence, S can be liable even where she thinks that P might not go ahead. The rule in *Johnson v Youden* is limited to cases where encouraging or assisting P's offending is not one of S's purposes when acting.

*The merits of requiring less than knowledge.*
Still, perhaps a broadening of the law on this point is desirable? An argument for the merits of requiring less than knowledge of the principal's crime might be summarised as follows:

> Why should knowledge (or settled belief) be necessary for there to be secondary liability? No doubt S should be required to know of any relevant circumstance where knowledge is required of P. But it does *not* follow that recklessness should be insufficient for S's liability when it suffices for P's. Otherwise, S would escape liability in many cases where she willingly assists P to commit a crime, and has the same mens rea, i.e. recklessness, toward that crime as has P; and there is no merit in that. Surely S has crossed the threshold justifying conviction, both in terms of her culpability and her conduct?

Despite the attractiveness of this argument, in our view the relaxation of the requirement for "knowledge" into one of foresight, let alone foresight of a mere possibility, should be

[183] [1999] Crim LR 392 (CA).
[184] [2004] EWCA Crim 1231, [71].
[185] See Simester, "The Mental Element in Complicity" (2006) 122 *LQR* 578, 583–8.
[186] *Jogee* [2016] UKSC 8; *Ruddock* [2016] UKPC 7, [2017] AC 387, [9].
[187] *National Coal Board v Gamble* [1959] 1 QB 11 (DC); *Attorney-General v Able* [1984] QB 795 (DC); *Gillick v West Norfolk and Wisbech Area Health Authority* [1986] AC 112; *Director of Public Prosecutions for Northern Ireland v Maxwell* [1978] 1 WLR 1350 (HL).
[188] *Jogee* [2016] UKSC 8; *Ruddock* [2016] UKPC 7, [2017] AC 387, [16].

avoided.[189] The basis of secondary liability is different from that of a principal. There is no requirement that the secondary party actually commits the offence herself or that she personally satisfies the actus reus of the relevant crime. The actus reus element of secondary participation is entirely independent of the actus reus of the principal offence. This being so, there seems no reason why the mens rea requirement for participation should be determined by that principal offence.

Moreover, derivative liability of any variety involves widening the net of the criminal law beyond those who actually perpetrate offences: not only may S not strike V, she may not do anything to help anyone else strike V either.[190] Because of this widening, the grounds of derivative liability ought correspondingly to be constricted, in order to prevent excessive criminalisation of conduct that does not itself cause a criminal harm. If something less than knowledge were required in cases where S lacks a direct intent (a purpose) to assist or encourage P's crime, the legitimate activities of people like shopkeepers, trading in products with potentially illicit usages, could be significantly compromised. It is one thing to convict a shopkeeper of selling a baseball bat or kitchen knife that she *knows will* be used in a criminal assault. It is quite another to convict her just because she foresees that risk.[191] Computer sellers, who know there is a real risk their hardware will be used to pirate music, would be forced out of business. More generally, over-criminalisation through weakening the mens rea requirement has the potential to lead, in turn, to a disproportionate intrusion upon the freedoms of citizens who do not themselves commit crimes. Respectable citizens such as shopkeepers should not be obliged to stop trading, on pain of risking convictions, whenever they realise that P may put his purchases to criminal use.[192] The same goes for ordinary citizens going about their everyday activities, just because they realise there is a *risk* some miscreant will exploit what they do.

*Future facts?*

In *Webster*, S allowed P to drive S's car, which P then drove dangerously. The Court of Appeal drew a distinction between present and future facts. It opined that, where P's conduct was not at hand but lay further into the future, in order to establish S's aiding and abetting of P's dangerous driving the prosecution must prove that S "foresaw that [P] was *likely* to drive in a dangerous manner".[193] Alternatively, if S had *not* foreseen that likelihood when allowing P to take the wheel, the Court noted that it would be open to establish that S abetted P, by allowing P to remain at the wheel while P was actually driving dangerously. In

[189] See Simester, *Fundamentals* § 7.4.

[190] Above, § 1.2(ii)(e).

[191] See the discussion of *National Coal Board v Gamble* [1959] 1 QB 11 (DC) and related cases, above, § 7.4(iv)(a).

[192] One compromise possibility, discussed in the fifth edition of this work, might be to moderate the traditional requirement for knowledge to one of *recklessness*. Since recklessness is only established when the risk taken by the defendant is unreasonable, this may help to keep reasonable conduct by shopkeepers and the like outside the scope of the criminal law; they are not obliged to stop trading, on pain of risking convictions, *whenever* they realise that P may put his purchases to criminal use. Even that compromise would, however, significantly impinge upon the liberties of law-abiding persons to conduct their day-to-day activities, and tend to make them legal risk-takers; all the more so given the likely assumption, once P has actually committed a crime aided by S, that a jury would retrospectively adjudge that risk an unreasonable one.

[193] [2006] EWCA Crim 415, [26] (emphasis added).

that situation, where S's abetment occurred *at the time* P's conduct was occurring, the Court asserted that S must *know* the essential matters of P's crime:[194]

> "In pursuance of this second approach, we conclude that the prosecution had to prove that [S] knew that [P] was, by virtue of the speed the vehicle was travelling, driving dangerously at a time when there was an opportunity to intervene."

The latter position is now uncontroversial. But is foresight of likelihood sufficient for *future* facts? The matter was not addressed in *Jogee*, which refers only to knowledge of "existing facts".[195] An analogous distinction, between knowledge of present facts and beliefs about future ones, has been drawn in New Zealand, where a lesser degree of confidence suffices for the latter.[196] One might, then, seek to defend a foresight requirement in England and Wales on the ground that it is impossible to "know" future facts.[197] As it happens, that ground is dubious. It does seem possible for one to know about a future event: to know, for instance, that the sun will rise tomorrow.[198] But more importantly, there is no *legal* difficulty here. As we noted earlier in this section, a requirement of knowledge is—as always[199]—satisfied whenever S holds a settled belief, with no substantial doubt, that the fact exists or, in the case of future facts, will exist.[200] So the distinction drawn in *Webster* between present and future facts is unnecessary.

Again, uncertainty about future facts is, of course, no barrier to S's liability where the aid or encouragement is directly intended. Suppose that S lends P a knife in order to help P to kill V, *should V be found*. As noted in § 7.4(iv)(a), and as the Supreme Court made clear in *Jogee*,[201] if V is indeed killed, S will be complicit in the murder.

*Strict liability offences.*

One implication of the analysis above is that an intention to assist or encourage, and knowledge of essential matters, is still required notwithstanding that the principal offence may be one of negligence or even strict liability. The classic authority for this proposition is *Callow v Tillstone*.[202] In that case, P, a butcher, was convicted of the strict liability offence of exposing unsound meat for sale. P had offered the meat for sale only after asking S, a veterinary surgeon, to examine the meat and certify whether it was sound. S had performed the examination negligently, and wrongly certified the meat as sound. Despite his negligence, S's conviction for abetting P's offence was quashed because S did not know the meat was unsound.

194 *Ibid.*, [29]. Cf. *Martin* [2010] EWCA Crim 1450, [2011] RTR 4.

195 *Jogee* [2016] UKSC 8; *Ruddock* [2016] UKPC 7, [2017] AC 387, [9]. For discussion of some of the difficulties here, see Child and Hunt, "Beyond the Present-Fault Paradigm: Expanding *Mens Rea* Definitions in the General Part" (2022) 42 *OJLS* 438, § 4.

196 *Cooper v MOT* [1991] 2 NZLR 693: knowledge is required with respect to present facts, but knowledge of the probable existence of future (or otherwise unknowable) facts suffices.

197 Something that seems to have troubled Lord Nicholls in *Saik* [2006] UKHL 18, [2007] 1 AC 18, [20]. Cf. *Bryce* [2004] EWCA Crim 1231, [49]. See too Ormerod and Laird, "*Jogee*: Not the End of a Legal Saga but the Start of One?" [2016] *Crim LR* 539, 544: "Knowledge speaks to the present and intention to the future."

198 See on this point Shute, "Knowledge and Belief in the Criminal Law" and Sullivan, "Knowledge, Belief and Culpability" in Shute and Simester (eds.), *Criminal Law Theory* (2002) 184, 186–7 and 207, 214–15 respectively.

199 Above, § 5.4.

200 For an argument that the language of "knowledge" is liable to mislead here, and it is preferable to speak in terms of settled beliefs, see Stark, "Against Knowledge (In the Criminal Law)" in Simester (ed.), *Modern Criminal Law* (2024) 25.

201 *Jogee* [2016] UKSC 8; *Ruddock* [2016] UKPC 7, [2017] AC 387, [92]–[95]. See also below, § 7.4(iv)(c) (What count as essential matters in murder and manslaughter?).

202 (1900) 64 JP 823. See also below, § 7.4(iv)(c) (Constructive liability elements of P's crime).

The result in *Callow v Tillstone* seems odd. P, who lacked fault, was convicted while S, whose negligence induced the offence, was acquitted. Once again, however, it is important to note that, unlike P, S did not commit the actus reus of any offence. (The doctrine of innocent agency was ruled out by the fact that S fell outside the class of persons who could commit that offence.) The anomalous-looking outcome in the case should be attributed not to the law governing secondary parties, but rather to the morally indefensible phenomenon of strict liability (with no defence of due diligence) for principals.[203]

*(c) P's criminal conduct: what "essential matters" must S intend or know about?*

It is also a difficult question what aspects of P's crime count as "essential matters",[204] such that they must be known about by S (or be part of S's purpose). The following propositions may be discerned from the authorities.

First, S must appreciate that P will do actions that constitute the actus reus of an offence, although S need not recognise that those actions in fact constitute an offence.[205] Secondly, S need not know all the details of the envisaged offence, such as the time or place of its commission.[206] However, mere purpose or knowledge that "something illegal" occur is not enough. S must have the purpose of assisting or encouraging, or know that her conduct will assist or encourage, either:

(i) the *type* of offence committed by P; or
(ii) the commission by P of one of a number of offences, the "list" of which includes the type of offence that eventually was committed.

The first of these possibilities was explained in *Bainbridge*;[207] the second was introduced in *Maxwell*.[208] Let us take them in turn.[209]

*The type of offence.*

In *Bainbridge*, S supplied oxygen-cutting equipment to P, who later used it to break into the Midland Bank at Stoke Newington. S claimed that he had suspected P wanted the equipment for some illegal purpose (e.g. to break up stolen goods), but had not known it would be used to break into a bank, let alone the Midland Bank at Stoke Newington. While his claim failed on the evidence, the Court of Criminal Appeal ruled that, on those facts, S would have lacked mens rea. His knowledge that he was aiding "some illegal venture" would

[203] See Chapter 6.

[204] An "essential matters" approach is effectively endorsed in *Jogee* [2016] UKSC 8; *Ruddock* [2016] UKPC 7, [2017] AC 387, [9]: "the mental element in assisting or encouraging is an intention to assist or encourage the commission of the crime and this requires knowledge of any existing facts *necessary for it to be criminal*." And at [16]: "an intention to assist or encourage the commission of an offence requires knowledge by D2 of any facts *necessary to give the principal's conduct or intended conduct its criminal character*." (Emphases added.) Cp. [99] ("necessary for it to be a prohibited act"). The Court of Appeal referred to an "essential necessary condition" in *Pop* [2026] EWCA Crim 774, [36]. See also the discussion of constructive liability offences below in this section.

[205] *Johnson v Youden* [1950] 1 KB 544, 546 (DC): "[h]e need not actually know that an offence has been committed, because he may not know that the facts constitute an offence and ignorance of the law is not a defence".

[206] *Bainbridge* [1960] 1 QB 129 (CA); *Bullock* [1955] 1 WLR 1 (CCA); cf. *Lomas* [1913] 9 Cr App R 220.

[207] [1960] 1 QB 129 (CA).

[208] [1978] 1 WLR 1350 (HL).

[209] See, further, Simester and Stark, "Overwhelming Supervening Acts – A Corrective" (2025) 84 *CLJ* 345.

be insufficient:[210] he had to know what *type* of crime would be committed by P. On the other hand, S need only appreciate the type and not the details. It was sufficient that S knew P intended to break and enter, and steal. S did not have to know the particulars of the plan, e.g. that the target was a particular bank in Stoke Newington.

On one view, *Bainbridge* merely re-states the "essential matters" concept introduced above. In general, a crime is of different type when it has different essential elements. Another way of putting this is to say that it is not enough to prove that S knew about the essential matters of crime X (say) when the charge is complicity in crime Y and the two crimes have different essential elements. In such a case, the prosecution must prove that S knew about *all* the essential elements of crime Y.

An example may be helpful. Suppose that S is charged with aiding and abetting a burglary.[211] S had encouraged P to steal V's wallet, but had not anticipated that P would steal the wallet from V's house. In such a case, it would be a misdirection for the trial judge to state that S need not know that P intended to steal from the house. Trespassory entry into a building is an essential element of the offence of burglary; indeed, it is the distinguishing feature of that offence. It follows that burglary cannot be regarded as being the same *type* of offence as simple theft. S can only be convicted as a party to burglary if, as well as knowing that P contemplated a theft, he also realised that P contemplated doing so within a building.

Accordingly, "type" should not be read broadly to refer to the sort of crime—for instance, "a property offence", "a sexual offence"—but to a *precise* combination of actus reus and mens rea elements.[212] A useful analogy can be drawn here with the law of conspiracy. Where D1 agrees to commit theft, but D2 and D3 agree to commit theft with violence, as we will see in § 9.2(ii)(b) (Case 1), D1 is rightly not guilty of conspiracy to commit robbery.[213] It makes no difference that both crimes can be, and often are, categorised as property offences.[214] Similarly, if S aids P to commit theft by informing P of where V keeps her laptop, it is submitted that application of the principle in *Bainbridge* means that S does not become liable for robbery if P uses force to relieve V of her laptop.

*A list of offences.*

The reasoning in *Bainbridge* was extended by the House of Lords in *DPP for Northern Ireland v Maxwell*.[215] In that case, S was a member of the Ulster Volunteer Force (UVF), a terrorist organisation. One night he was called upon to drive a car guiding other UVF members to a public house. He did so knowing that a terrorist attack was planned, though uncertain whether the attack was to be perpetrated by bomb, gun, or other means. In fact,

[210] [1960] 1 QB 129, 133 (CA); *Scott* (1978) 68 Cr App R 164; *Patel* [1970] Crim LR 274 (CA).

[211] Contrary to s. 9 of the Theft Act 1968; below, § 14.4.

[212] Of course, some actus reus and mens rea combinations are extremely broad. Consider the following example from *Smith, Hogan, and Ormerod* § 6.4.2.3: S provides V with a jimmy to break into V's home in order to steal; P uses the jimmy to break in but does so in order to cause grievous bodily harm. Both scenarios involve the same crime (burglary), yet does P's differing ulterior intention render these offences of a different "type"? No clear answer is found in the case law. Arguably, however, the answer is "No".

[213] *Barnard* (1980) 70 Cr App R 28 (CA).

[214] Robbery and theft are, for example, in the same "category" of offences for the purposes of the rules on bad character evidence: Criminal Justice Act 2003 (Categories of Offences) Order 2004, SI 2004/3346, sched. 1, pt. 1.

[215] [1978] 1 WLR 1350; endorsed in *Jogee* [2016] UKSC 8; *Ruddock* [2016] UKPC 7, [2017] AC 387, [15]–[16].

the attack was carried out using a bomb. S was guilty of aiding two offences against the Explosive Substances Act 1883, since these offences were within the range of types of crime that S contemplated P would commit. According to Lord Scarman, the accessory:[216]

> "may have in contemplation only one [type of[217]] offence, or several; and the several which he contemplates he may see as alternatives. An accessory who leaves it to his principal to choose is liable, provided always the choice is made from the range of offences from which the accessory contemplates the choice will be made. Although the court's formulation of the principle goes further than [*Bainbridge*], it is a sound development of the law and in no way inconsistent. . . ."

Thus S would instead have been guilty of murder if, alternatively, P had killed the publican by shooting him. Conversely, and odd as it might seem, S would not have been liable had the principals entered the pub and stolen a bottle of whiskey—notwithstanding that the latter offence is so much lesser than those actually contemplated by S.[218] The point of *Maxwell* is to extend liability to a case where S has the purpose of assisting or encouraging, or knows that P *will* be assisted or encouraged, to commit one of crimes X, Y, or Z, but has no firm belief regarding which of them it will be.[219]

*The* Calhaem *principle.*
For the most part, variations *within* a type will not, then, affect secondary liability. Suppose that P plans to set fire to V's house. Knowing the details of the plan, S helps P by giving him V's address. P goes to the house, then changes his mind and instead sets fire to V's car.[220] Is S guilty of arson? Yes. As cases like *Bainbridge* establish, incidental variations of detail such as time and place are immaterial since they do not alter the type of crime committed by P (and assisted by S). Therefore, because P commits the same offence—arson—either way, S's liability is normally unaffected by this variation.

The exception is if S's contribution is *directed* specifically to the aspect of P's offence that was varied, and that such variation was a deliberate choice by P. In such cases, even though that aspect may be legally immaterial to P's guilt, it becomes essential to S's complicity. For example:

> S counsels P to murder a particular person, V. P, having set out to kill V, then changes his mind and decides instead to kill W. S is not a party to the murder of W.[221]

It is otherwise if the identity of the victim to be killed—or the identity of the property to be fired, in our earlier example—were of no particular relevance to S's intervention. Thus, for instance, if P were to obtain S's help with obtaining a weapon in order to kill someone ("as it happens, X"), S would still be liable when Y is shot instead.

[216] [1978] 1 WLR 1350, 1363 (Lord Scarman).
[217] The insertion is an implication of *Bainbridge*.
[218] It is an interesting question why the correspondence principle (above, § 6.5) is observed even when, as here, D is prepared to do an actus reus more heinous (albeit of a different type) than he in fact does. The point perhaps deserves closer attention than it has yet received in the literature.
[219] For a helpful analogy to liability under s. 46 of the Serious Crime Act 2007, see Virgo, "The Relationship between Inchoate and Accessorial Liability after *Jogee*" [2016] 9 *Archbold Review* 6.
[220] The facts of *Dunning and Graham* (unreported, Preston Crown Court Preston, Dec. 1985), discussed in *Smith, Hogan, and Ormerod* § 6.4.2.3.
[221] *Saunders and Archer* (1573) 2 Plowd 473, 75 ER 706; *Leahy* [1985] Crim LR 99; (Crown Court); *S v Robinson* 1968 (1) SA 666; Hawkins, 2 PC ch. 29, §§ 20, 21; Foster, *Crown Law* 369; Stephen, *Digest* art. 43. For criticism of this rule, see Smith, *A Modern Treatise on the Law of Criminal Complicity* (1991) 200ff; Clarkson, "Complicity, *Powell* and Manslaughter" [1998] *Crim LR* 556, 559.

At first glance, although this states the law, the law looks somewhat odd. Since the difference between shooting V and shooting W is immaterial to the definition of murder, the variation would seem to be a simple case of what is sometimes called "transferred mens rea".[222] It is murder of any human being, and participation therein, that the law criminalises; not murder of a particular person. In principle, since the identity of the victim does not matter to P's liability for murder, prima facie neither should it make a difference to the liability of S.

Notwithstanding its apparent oddity, however, the exception is defensible on the basis of the *Calhaem* principle: that P must act within the scope of the encouragement.[223] As such, it is arguable that the rule applies to encouragement and not assistance; a distinction that is consistent with the case law. On that view, assistance should always allow for the transference of liability across victims,[224] but encouragement (say) to murder V can be expressed in such confined terms that it does not encourage murder generally, i.e. of anyone else; in which case the *Calhaem* principle may appropriately displace S's liability.[225] (In such a case, S would in any event be exposed to a conviction for the inchoate offence of encouraging or assisting crime.[226])

*Calhaem* is a narrow restriction upon the requirements of secondary liability. It is, in our view, a justified one. Secondary liability is an inherently problematic area because it places S's liability in P's hands.[227] The *Calhaem* principle means that S can set parameters on her encouragement or instruction, and thus "delimit the scope of [her] participation in an intended crime"[228] even if it remains, legally, the same type of offence envisaged by S.

Importantly, S remains liable, if the variation in P's offending is unintentional. Suppose that P does not change his mind, and carries out his attempt to shoot V. Unfortunately, he mistakes W for V and kills W. Here, the "transference" of mens rea applies to S as well as P. Both S and P are guilty of murdering W.[229]

*Mens rea of the principal.*

P's mens rea is also an essential matter. S must know, or act with the purpose, that P will do the actus reus with the level of mens rea required for it to amount to an offence.[230] S cannot abet murder, for example, if S recognises that P is about to kill V negligently,[231] since negligence is insufficient mens rea for P to be guilty of murder. Similarly, if P's offence requires proof of an ulterior intention, S must be aware of that intent by P.[232] To illustrate: in order to be found to have abetted possession of a controlled drug with intent to supply,[233] S would have to be proved to have acted in order that, or known that, her conduct would assist or

[222] Above, § 5.7.
[223] Above, § 7.4(ii).
[224] Cp. *BHV* [2022] EWCA Crim 1690.
[225] This distinction would support S's conviction in *Reardon* [1999] Crim LR 392 (CA).
[226] Below, § 9.1.
[227] Simester, *Fundamentals* 119–21, 157.
[228] Williams, *TBCL* 356.
[229] Hawkins, 2 PC ch. 29, § 22; Foster, *Crown Law* 370; Stephen, *Digest* art. 41.
[230] Cp. *A, B, C and D v R* [2010] EWCA Crim 1622, [2011] QB 841.
[231] *Cruse* (1838) 8 C & P 541, 173 ER 610; *Quick* [1973] QB 910, 923 (CA); Dennis, "The Mental Element for Accessories" in Smith (ed.), *Criminal Law: Essays in Honour of J.C. Smith* (1987) 40, 46–7, 55.
[232] *DPP for Northern Ireland v Maxwell* [1978] 1 WLR 1350 (HL).
[233] Contrary to s. 5(3) of the Misuse of Drugs Act 1971.

encourage P's possession, *and* also to have had the purpose, or knowledge, that P would be assisted or encouraged to possess the drugs *with the intent to supply* them to another person.[234]

It has been claimed post-*Jogee* that, rather than knowledge, S *must* intend P's mens rea.[235] That is wrong. Normally, S will have no control over P's mental state: without that, S cannot intend what P's mental state should be. From S's perspective, P's mental state is a (future) circumstance and, as with intentions and circumstances generally,[236] it suffices either that S's purpose is that P should be assisted or encouraged to act with mens rea or that S knows (i.e. believes with no significant doubt) that P *will* be so assisted or encouraged.

More generally, any insistence that S must *intend* P act with mens rea is mistaken at a deeper level. To recall what was said in § 7.4(iv), S must intend to *help* (encourage; procure) P to commit a crime. What must be intended is the help (etc.): even in cases of directly intended help (etc.), S does not have to intend *that P commit the relevant crime*—let alone that P act with the requisite mens rea. She has to intend, by her action, *to help (encourage; procure) P to commit the relevant crime*. She must have, that is to say, a *present* intention about her own action; not a future intention, whether direct or indirect, about P's. With respect to P's actions and mental states, knowledge is sufficient.

This point was not seen clearly in *Jogee*, where the Court stated:[237]

> "If [S] joins with a group which he realises is out to cause serious injury, the jury may well infer that he intended [i] to encourage or assist the deliberate infliction of serious bodily injury and/ or [ii] intended that that should happen if necessary."

The "and/or" is inappropriate. A finding that S intended (i) to encourage or assist the killing or deliberate infliction of serious bodily injury is indeed essential if S is to be convicted of murder. However, a finding that S intended (ii) that the killing or deliberate infliction of serious bodily injury "should happen if necessary" adds nothing. S need not have (ii) an intention that serious injury should occur in order to incur secondary liability for murder. And if she *did* have the intention in (ii), she would necessarily have (i) the intention to encourage or assist that crime. What counts in all cases of aiding and abetting liability is (i), not (ii).

*Constructive liability elements of P's crime.*

Many offences contain a mixture of actus reus elements where, for some of those elements, the prosecution must prove mens rea on P's part and, for other actus reus elements, no mens rea is required. In the context of secondary liability, where the actus reus of P's offence requires his conduct to cause particular consequences but does not require P to have any mens rea regarding those consequences, the same applies for S: she need have no mens rea going to such consequences.[238] Effectively, those strict-liability consequences are not regarded as part of the essential matters of P's conduct that S must be aiming to assist or encourage, or knowingly assisting or encouraging.

234 Cf. *Samuels* [1985] 1 NZLR 350.
235 See, e.g., Ormerod and Laird, "*Jogee*: Not the End of a Legal Saga but the Start of One?" [2016] *Crim LR* 539, 544.
236 See above, § 5.1(v).
237 *Jogee* [2016] UKSC 8; *Ruddock* [2016] UKPC 7, [2017] AC 387, [95].
238 *Ibid.*, [99].

For example, S need not anticipate the consequence (death) in order to abet the offence of "causing death by dangerous driving".[239] For the purposes of secondary participation, only the dangerous driving counts as an essential element.[240] Similarly, if S aids or abets P to inflict a common assault upon V, and V dies, both S and P are guilty of manslaughter even though neither may have contemplated the prospect of V's death. P is guilty because causing death by an unlawful act satisfies the required elements of manslaughter as a principal;[241] upon proof of the criminal assault, death is a constructive liability element. Correspondingly, death is not an "essential matter" and S need not contemplate V's death for the purposes of secondary liability.[242] Thus V's death need be anticipated by neither P nor S.

This doctrine sits poorly with cases such as *Callow v Tillstone*,[243] discussed earlier. It will be remembered that P, a butcher, was convicted of the strict liability offence of exposing unsound meat for sale, whereas S—a veterinary surgeon—who had negligently certified the meat as sound, was ruled not to be an accessory because he did not know the meat was unsound. Yet the unsoundness of the meat was a matter of strict liability for P: why, then, must S know about it?

There are two possible ways of explaining cases such as *Callow v Tillstone*. The first, less satisfactory basis is that what was at issue in that case was a circumstance element (that the meat was unsound), whereas in dangerous driving causing death and other constructive homicide offences the aggravating feature is a *consequence* element (death). But that would require, in the context of unlawful-act manslaughter, that S must subjectively recognise the dangerousness of P's unlawful act (a circumstance), which is contrary to current law. A second, more plausible explanation is that what is key in these constructive liability offences is that S knowingly abets or assists P to *do an unlawful act*, and the relevant aggravating factor in P's liability (death) is merely a constructive liability element: thus it is strict for S as well as for P. The latter analysis comports with the position taken in *Jogee*:[244]

> "Where the offence charged does not require mens rea, the only mens rea required of the secondary party is that he intended to encourage or assist the perpetrator to do the prohibited act, with knowledge of any facts and circumstances necessary for it to be a prohibited act: *National Coal Board v Gamble*."

What counts, then, is whether S has intentionally assisted or encouraged "a prohibited act": the unlawful act in manslaughter cases; the intentional infliction of (at least) grievous bodily harm in murder; or the dangerous driving in causing death by dangerous driving. In principle, this approach is not restricted to consequence elements.[245] For example, the offence of assaulting a constable, contrary to section 89 of the Police Act 1996, imposes strict

[239] Road Traffic Act 1988, s. 1.

[240] *Robert Millar (Contractors) Ltd* [1970] 2 QB 54 (CA); *Harris* [1964] Crim LR 54 (CCA). This point was left open by the Court in *Martin* [2010] EWCA Crim 1450, but it is submitted that the applicable legal principle is a settled one, albeit it is more familiar in the context of unlawful-act manslaughter. See Cunningham, "Complicating Complicity: Aiding and Abetting Causing Death by Dangerous Driving in *R v Martin*" (2011) 74 *MLR* 767.

[241] See below, Chapter 10.

[242] *Creamer* [1966] 1 QB 72 (CCA); *Buck* (1960) 44 Cr App R 213; *Baldessare* (1930) 22 Cr App R 70; *Reid* (1976) 62 Cr App R 109; *Swindall and Osborne* (1846) 2 C & K 230, 175 ER 95.

[243] (1900) 64 JP 823; above, § 7.4(iv)(b) (Strict liability offences).

[244] *Jogee* [2016] UKSC 8; *Ruddock* [2016] UKPC 7, [2017] AC 387, [99].

[245] Cp. the element of dangerousness in the context of unlawful-act manslaughter, which S need not anticipate: *Jogee* [2016] UKSC 8; *Ruddock* [2016] UKPC 7, [2017] AC 387, [96].

liability with respect to the fact that the victim is a constable.[246] It would seem to follow that S participates in the section 89 offence by intentionally assisting or encouraging P to commit an assault on any person who—however unexpectedly—turns out to be a constable.

*What count as essential matters in murder?*

Given the number of cases on complicity that involve homicides, it is worth explicating further what elements count as essential in the specific context of murder and manslaughter. In murder, S must (directly or obliquely) intend to assist or encourage at least the deliberate causing by P of grievous bodily harm. Where V dies as a result of P's attack, both P and S are liable for murder, even if the thought that V might die never entered the mind of either.

Where S's intention is direct, it may be conditional, in as much as S recognises that the need to cause grievous bodily harm may not arise.[247] As it was put in *Jogee*, in a passage quoted earlier in this section:[248]

> "If D2 joins with a group which he realises is out to cause serious injury, the jury may well infer that *he intended to encourage or assist the deliberate infliction of serious bodily injury* and/or intended that that should happen if necessary. In that case, if D1 acts with intent to cause serious bodily injury and death results, D1 and D2 will each be guilty of murder."

By contrast, where it is not S's purpose, in offering assistance or encouragement, to facilitate the deliberate causing by P of grievous bodily harm, S must know (have a settled belief) that P *will* cause such injury before S can be an accessory.

*What count as essential matters in unlawful-act manslaughter?*

In unlawful-act manslaughter,[249] only the unlawful act counts as an essential matter for the purposes of secondary liability:[250]

> "If a person . . . participates by encouragement or assistance in any other unlawful act which all sober and reasonable people would realise carried the risk of some harm (not necessarily serious) to another, and death in fact results. . . . The test is objective."

But care is needed here in cases where violence escalates. Consider the rest of the foregoing paragraph from *Jogee*:[251]

> "If a person is a party to a violent attack on another, without an intent to assist in the causing of death or really serious harm, but the violence escalates and results in death, he will be not guilty of murder but guilty of manslaughter."

Not necessarily. Suppose that S encourages P to commit an assault. P, however, goes on to commit murder by deliberately inflicting serious injuries that cause death. It does not follow that S has intentionally encouraged the type of act that caused death—and that would need to be proved. Admittedly, murder and manslaughter are constructive crimes. But that truth

[246] *Forbes and Webb* (1865) 10 Cox CC 362; *Maxwell* (1909) 2 Cr App R 26; *Mark* [1961] Crim LR 173 (Central Criminal Court).

[247] See the discussion in § 7.4(iv)(a) (Conditional (direct) intentions?).

[248] *Jogee* [2016] UKSC 8; *Ruddock* [2016] UKPC 7, [2017] AC 387, [95] (emphasis added); above, § 7.4(iv)(c) (Mens rea of the principal).

[249] Below, § 10.7(i).

[250] *Jogee* [2016] UKSC 8; *Ruddock* [2016] UKPC 7, [2017] AC 387, [96], citing *Church* [1966] 1 QB 59 (CCA); *DPP v Newbury* [1977] AC 500; *F(J) & E(N)* [2015] EWCA Crim 351, [2015] 2 Cr App R 5. See also below, § 10.7(i) (d).

[251] *Jogee* [2016] UKSC 8; *Ruddock* [2016] UKPC 7, [2017] AC 387, [96].

does not permit us to bypass the requirement that secondary parties must have encouraged *the type of act that caused death*, and that they must have done so intentionally. Where the injuries actually inflicted by P are serious ones, and they are the exclusive cause of death, it seems that, unless S has assisted or encouraged the infliction of injuries of that type, S cannot be a party to manslaughter. This possibility involves what has been characterised as an "overwhelming supervening act" that relegates S's contributions to history.[252] However, what counts as such an act has proved controversial in the case law since *Jogee*. We explore that controversy below in section § 7.6(iii)(a).

*What count as essential matters in gross negligence manslaughter?*

The position is different for manslaughter predicated on gross negligence rather than on an independently unlawful act. Both the death and P's gross negligence should in principle count as essential matters in such situations, because they constitute the very basis of P's liability; whereas for unlawful-act manslaughter it is the unlawful act that generates P's culpability for the homicide offence.

*(d) The case of mutual confrontations:* Gnango

In *Gnango*,[253] G, armed with a loaded handgun, went to a housing estate car park in search of a man with a red bandana. Shortly thereafter, P—wearing a red bandana—appeared on steps leading to the car park. (It was not established whether P's appearance was spontaneous or by arrangement, or whether P was in fact the person for whom G was searching.) P, also armed, began shooting at G, who began shooting back. One of P's shots hit and killed V, a passer-by. P was clearly guilty of murder by application of transferred malice principles,[254] but escaped without being identified. G did not, and was convicted of the murder of V.

The Supreme Court upheld G's conviction on the basis of abetment:[255] G had encouraged P to fire the shot (at G) that killed V. The encouragement arose, it was said, because G and P had formed a mutual agreement (perhaps on the spot[256]) to have a gun fight in which each would attempt to kill or seriously injure the other, and P accidentally killed V pursuant to that encouragement.[257]

Even without an agreement, formal or informal, it seems in principle possible that G's conduct encouraged P to shoot at him. But what is less plausible is that G *intended* by that conduct to encourage P to shoot at him.[258] An indirect intention to encourage would, of course, suffice: but that would have to be proved on the facts, and—absent a prior agreement—it seems a stretch to conclude that, by going in search for P, G knew he was *virtually certain* to encourage P to fire at him.[259]

[252] *Ibid.*, [97]; cp. *Tas* [2018] EWCA Crim 2603, [2019] 4 WLR 14, [38]–[41].
[253] [2011] UKSC 59, [2012] 1 AC 827.
[254] Above, § 5.7.
[255] In fact, the Supreme Court upheld *Gnango*'s conviction on various competing bases. See Stark, "'A Most Difficult Case': on the Ratio of *Gnango*" (2013) 3 *The UK Supreme Court Yearbook* 55.
[256] [2011] UKSC 59, [2012] 1 AC 827, [57] (Lord Phillips and Lord Judge), [66] (Lord Brown), For an example involving what was, in effect, a prearranged knife duel (albeit at short notice), see *Riley and Robinson* [2018] EWCA Crim 1000.
[257] [2011] UKSC 59, [2012] 1 AC 827, [58], [64] (Lord Phillips and Lord Judge), [71] (Lord Brown), [81] Lord Clarke, [103] (Lord Dyson).
[258] For criticism, see Buxton, "Being an Accessory to One's Own Murder" [2012] *Crim LR* 275, 276–8; Sullivan, "Accessories and Principals after Gnango" in Reed and Bohlander (eds.), *Participation in Crime* (2013) 37, 43–6.
[259] This point was decisive in *ARU, ACC and BHL* [2024] EWCA Crim 1101.

One may harbour doubts about the particular facts. Yet the *law* governing such confrontations, as stated in *Gnango*, has since been invoked without criticism by the Court of Appeal in a number of cases, and it may now be regarded as settled. In *Seed and others*,[260] for instance, V and three fellow gang members had gone "riding out" into another gang's territory intending to cause at least serious injury to members of that other gang. A gunfight ensued, during which V was killed. *V's own gang members* were convicted of V's murder. In the view of the Court of Appeal:[261]

> "the necessary agreement to shoot and be shot at may properly be inferred where two or more persons engage in, or assist or encourage, shooting at each other, each knowing that it was a virtual certainty that the other(s) would be armed and would either open or return fire, and each intending to kill or to cause really serious injury. It may or may not be helpful to refer to such a situation as a 'shoot out': at best, that may be a convenient but imprecise shorthand description of a situation which will have to be analysed with care by a jury before the necessary agreement to shoot and be shot at can be inferred. It may be thought that the term implies the reciprocity which is a feature of the agreement which must be proved. But be that as it may, the whole purpose of each party shooting in such a situation is to kill or to cause serious injury, and it can be no defence for one party to say that the victim of the shooting was a member of his own side."

Confrontation cases of this kind invite a reading of the facts that brings them within the scope of, and in principle makes them compatible with, *Jogee*.[262] At the same time, it is essential in every such case for the prosecution to prove that there was *actual* encouragement of P, *with* direct or indirect intention, to perpetrate the essential elements of P's crime. Absent such proof, conviction of participants in such confrontations (on either side) has the potential to reincarnate a form of joint enterprise liability, now abolished, and to which we now turn.

## § 7.5 Secondary parties pursuant to common unlawful purpose ("joint enterprise"; "parasitic accessory liability")

In § 7.4, we considered the standard forms of secondary participation; those which are mentioned expressly by section 8 of the Accessories and Abettors Act 1861.[263] In these standard cases, liability is established on the basis that S assists or encourages the principal by aiding, abetting, counselling, or procuring the relevant offence. As an accessory, S knows the essential facts of the offence charged and she intends to assist or encourage P in committing that offence.

Prior to its abolition in *Jogee*,[264] a second form of participation was known to the common law: where S and P embarked on a *common purpose* to commit a crime. If that crime was actually committed by P during their venture, S too was guilty of it. It is worthwhile briefly to elaborate on this mode of liability, in order to set out the background regarding

[260] [2024] EWCA Crim 650.
[261] *Ibid.*, [71].
[262] *Jogee* [2016] UKSC 8; *Ruddock* [2016] UKPC 7, [2017] AC 387, [99]. The shooting must, of course, be within the scope of the agreement: cp. *Morgan* [2021] EWCA Crim 895, where, in a confrontation between S and others (including P), S's associate was shot while sitting in a car. If the targeting of V were deliberate, and it lay outside the scope of the agreement between S and P, S would not be an accomplice: cp. *Saunders and Archer* (1573) 2 Plowd 473, 75 ER 706. See above, § 7.4(iv)(c) (The *Calhaem* principle).
[263] Set out in the text above, § 7.2.
[264] *Jogee* [2016] UKSC 8; *Ruddock* [2016] UKPC 7, [2017] AC 387, [99].

some concepts that, we shall argue, should not have survived its abolition (most prominently, the doctrine of "overwhelming supervening act").[265]

Common-purpose liability was an ancient form of secondary participation.[266] In its most basic form, sometimes described as the "plain vanilla" variety of joint enterprise,[267] it was uncontroversial and added nothing to aiding and abetting, which we considered in § 7.4 above. The standard forms of complicity are expressed by reference to a single offence: i.e. the offence that is deliberately aided or encouraged by S and which ultimately is committed by P. By forming a common purpose with P to commit that offence, S effectively abets it.[268] Indeed, in *Jogee* it was reiterated that evidence of a common purpose between P and S to commit an offence is strong evidence that S abetted P's crime.[269]

What was much more controversial, however, was the twin-crime scenario of common-purpose liability, which gave rise to what was sometimes called "parasitic accessory liability".[270] This more complicated scenario involved *two* crimes: an offence (A) that was the subject of a common purpose between S and P,[271] and a further offence (B) then committed by P alone. S did not need to have specifically assisted or encouraged offence B to become liable for its commission. She became a party to the offence if she had foreseen that its commission was a possible consequence of proceeding with the original plan to commit offence A; even though she may not have intended or even been directly involved in the commission of that further, or "collateral", offence B that was perpetrated by P. For example:

> P and S agree to commit a burglary. Together they break into V's home. In the course of the burglary, P is challenged by V, whom he attacks and injures. S does not participate physically in the assault. However, S knew when they agreed to burgle that P has a propensity toward violence, and realised that P might well assault the occupier of the house were they to be confronted.

Under the law before *Jogee*, S was guilty, with P, of assault occasioning actual bodily harm (as well as the burglary). It mattered not that S did not intend that an assault should be committed; nor that S was uncertain whether the assault would occur; nor that S did not intend to help or encourage its commission. Liability arose because S participated in a criminal enterprise to commit burglary with P, pursuant to which P has committed a further, "collateral", offence (assault occasioning actual bodily harm) which S foresaw might occur. In simple terms, we might say that the parties set out to commit one crime and become liable for another one. The difference between the two varieties of secondary participation, in so far as the conduct element is concerned, is that there was *no need to show specifically that S assisted or encouraged the second offence*. This is key to understanding the distinctiveness of this (former) type of participatory liability: it had a different actus reus from the variety of secondary liability discussed earlier in this chapter.

[265] Below, § 7.6(iii)(a).

[266] For discussion of some of the older cases, see Smith, *A Modern Treatise on the Law of Criminal Complicity* (1991) chap. 8; Stark, "The Demise of 'Parasitic Accessorial Liability': Substantive Judicial Law Reform, Not Common Law Housekeeping" (2016) 75 *CLJ* 550; Simester, "Accessory Liability and Common Unlawful Purposes" (2017) 133 *LQR* 73, 76–81.

[267] *Brown and Isaac v The State* [2003] UKPC 10, [13] (Lord Hoffmann).

[268] Unless, of course, P commits it outside the scope of that abetment: above, § 7.4(ii).

[269] *Jogee* [2016] UKSC 8; *Ruddock* [2016] UKPC 7, [2017] AC 387, [78].

[270] *Gnango* [2011] UKSC 59, [2012] 1 AC 827, [42]–[43], [94]–[96]. The phrase is attributable to Smith, "Criminal Liability of Accessories: Law and Law Reform" (1997) 113 *LQR* 453.

[271] Note there is no requirement in joint enterprise liability for offence B that offence A must successfully be perpetrated. Obviously, if it is perpetrated by P, joint enterprise liability would also apply, although S will normally be liable anyway for the offence on standard principles of abetment.

As the burglary example illustrates, the idea of a common purpose had a strong affinity with the inchoate offence of conspiracy. The elements of this more complicated, twin-crime form of secondary participation were as follows:[272]

(i) S and P jointly embark on the commission of crime A.
(ii) S foresees that, in the course of the joint enterprise to commit crime A, P may commit crime B.
(iii) P commits crime B.
(iv) The commission of crime B occurs as an incident of the joint enterprise, and not in a manner that is fundamentally different from the possibility foreseen by S.
(v) P's commission of crime B occurs at a point in time when the joint enterprise is still ongoing, and S has not withdrawn from it.

If these requirements were met, then in addition to any liability S may have had for conspiracy to commit a crime, and as a (principal or secondary) party to crime A, S became liable as a party to crime B. Indeed, where S and P formed a common purpose to commit a crime, S potentially became liable for any offence that she contemplated might be committed by P in furtherance of that purpose. It all then depended on what P did.

Notwithstanding its endorsement in multiple decisions by our most senior courts,[273] in the wake of *Jogee*, common purpose is no longer a distinct basis of secondary liability—at least, not in England and Wales.[274] The Supreme Court in *Jogee* rejected those earlier decisions, but not by invoking superior authority. Indeed, there was no binding authority that barred twin crime scenarios at common law.[275] Those earlier decisions were not *per incuriam*. Rather, they were rejected because the Court in *Jogee* considered their reasoning to be wanting. Overruling those earlier decisions is constitutionally possible, but requires reference to the power contained in the Court's Practice Directions to depart from previous decisions of the Supreme Court and the House of Lords.[276] No such reference occurred in *Jogee*.[277]

Constitutional worries aside, the main implications of abolishing common-purpose liability are outlined below.

[272] For a fuller discussion, see § 7.5 of the fifth edition of this work.

[273] Including *Chan Wing-Siu* [1985] AC 168 (PC); *Hui Chi-Ming v R* [1992] 1 AC 34 (PC); *Powell; English* [1999] 1 AC 1; *Rahman* [2008] UKHL 45, [2009] 1 AC 129. Cp. *Gnango* [2011] UKSC 59, [2012] 1 AC 827, [42]–[43] (Lords Phillips and Judge, Lord Wilson concurring) and [94]-[96] (Lord Dyson), where the Supreme Court upheld secondary liability on the basis of aiding and abetting while rejecting what their Lordships called "parasitic accessory liability" on the facts; thus distinguishing the two bases.

[274] But it continues to exist in the common law of other jurisdictions, notably within Australia and in Hong Kong: *Miller v The Queen; Smith v The Queen; Presley v DPP for South Australia* [2016] HCA 30, (2016) 259 CLR 380; *HKSAR v Chan Kam Shing* [2016] HKCFA 87. Joint enterprise liability continues also in New Zealand, where it is entrenched in s. 66(2) of the Crimes Act 1961 (NZ): see *Uhrle v R* [2016] NZSC 64, (2016) 28 CRNZ 270, [5].

[275] Stark, "The Demise of 'Parasitic Accessorial Liability': Substantive Judicial Law Reform, Not Common Law Housekeeping" (2016) 75 *CLJ* 550; see also Simester, "Accessory Liability and Common Unlawful Purposes" (2017) 133 *LQR* 73.

[276] Direction 3.1.3 (incorporating Practice Statement (Judicial Precedent) [1966] 1 WLR 1234).

[277] A point made by Sullivan: "Law Reform and the Supreme Court: The Abolition of Joint Enterprise Liability?" in Krebs (ed.), *Accessorial Liability after Jogee* (2020) 7. See, further, Stark, "Judicial Development of the Criminal Law by the Supreme Court" (2021) 41 *OJLS* 1; Stark, "*Jogee* and the Mechanics of Criminal Law Development" in Russell and Graham (eds.), *Public Law and the UK Supreme Court* (2025) 46.

### (i) The main doctrinal differences

Formerly, the actus reus requirements of common-purpose-based liability differed in twin-crime scenarios from those applying to participation by assistance or encouragement. In the "plain vanilla", single-crime scenario,[278] the shared purpose necessarily constituted abetment of crime A. In a twin-crime situation, however, it did not. It was settled law that S may form a common purpose to commit crime A while opposing crime B; and that liability for crime B nonetheless could follow if S had foreseen its potential commission as part of the enterprise. Liability for crime B followed without S's having assisted or encouraged it.[279] Suppose S participates in a burglary knowing P has both a knife and a propensity for violence. S, however, makes it clear to P that she is opposed to his using the knife. If P, confronted during the burglary, stabs his victim, the stabbing is neither assisted nor encouraged. It is merely foreseen. In such cases, the courts held prior to *Jogee* that S was a party to the stabbing,[280] notwithstanding that she did not aid, abet, counsel, or procure it.

The mens rea requirement also differed. As *Jogee* itself has clarified, liability for aiding or abetting any crime requires purpose or knowledge concerning the essential facts of that crime.[281] By contrast, the law applicable to twin-crime scenarios clearly required only that S foresaw the possibility[282] that P *might* commit the relevant "collateral" crime (with mens rea). In *Powell*,[283] for example, S1 and S2 went with P to buy drugs from V, a drug dealer. Before the transaction could take place, the dealer was shot dead using a gun carried by P. S1 and S2 knew that P was armed, and had realised P might use the gun to kill or inflict grievous bodily injury on V. On these facts the House upheld their convictions for murder. Notwithstanding that the mens rea for murder as principal is *intention* to kill or inflict grievous bodily injury, it was sufficient if secondary parties to a joint unlawful enterprise *foresaw* that murder, or the intentional infliction of grievous bodily harm, by P was a possible offshoot of their criminal enterprise. In so holding, their Lordships followed the lead taken in a number of decisions by the Court of Appeal and Privy Council.[284]

### (ii) The underlying structural and normative differences

The twin-crime scenario was fundamentally, structurally different from ordinary assistance, encouragement, or procurement. In cases of aiding and abetting, and now for all

[278] *Brown and Isaac v The State* [2003] UKPC 10, [13] (Lord Hoffmann).

[279] Toulson LJ finessed this point in *Mendez v R* [2010] EWCA Crim 516, [2011] QB 876, [36], suggesting that "by going along with P in the criminal venture knowing that P may commit murder, D encourages or assists P to place himself in the position where that may occur". But that is obviously not the same thing as encouraging or assisting the murder itself.

[280] *Powell; English* [1999] 1 AC 1, 19–20; *Hui Chi-Ming v R* [1992] 1 AC 34, 53 (PC); *Hyde* [1991] 1 QB 134, 139 (CA). Cp. *Rahman* [2008] UKHL 45, [2009] 1 AC 129, [36] (Lord Rodger); also *Day* [2001] Crim LR 984 (CA), where S's conviction was upheld because he foresaw that P might kick V in the head, notwithstanding that apparently he did not approve of it.

[281] *Jogee* [2016] UKSC 8; *Ruddock* [2016] UKPC 7, [2017] AC 387, [9], [16], [99]; above, § 7.4(iv).

[282] Not probability: cp. *Powell; English* [1999] 1 AC 1, 14 (Lord Steyn), 30–1 (Lord Hutton).

[283] *Ibid.*

[284] *Smith (Wesley)* [1963] 3 All ER 597 (CCA); *Anderson and Morris* [1966] 2 QB 110 (CCA); *Chan Wing-Siu v R* [1985] AC 168 (PC); *Hui Chi-ming v R* [1992] 1 AC 34 (PC). See Smith, "Criminal Liability of Accessories: Law and Law Reform" (1997) 113 *LQR* 453.

forms of complicity post-*Jogee*, S's liability for any crime by P is considered purely in terms of her involvement in and mental state regarding that particular crime.[285] S directly participates in each crime by her intended act of aiding or abetting that very crime. The wrong which makes S responsible for each crime is that deliberate assistance or encouragement: it is her act of directly connecting herself with P's crime. In common-purpose cases, by contrast, the wrong was the agreement or confederacy.[286] The agreement (to commit crime A) opened a wider door to liability; it exposed S to conviction for any foreseen crimes B, C, D, etc., committed by P in the course of executing the agreement. As such, S's connection to crime B (etc.) was *indirect*. Its legal significance depended upon the agreement to commit crime A.

It is important to recognise that the doctrines governing aiding, abetting, counselling, and procuring are not doctrines that operate as ends in themselves. They exist as channels via which the law sets aside the normal limitations of autonomy, individual responsibility, and causation doctrines in order to ascribe one person with responsibility for a crime committed by another. There is no in-principle objection, therefore, to the law's recognising complementary doctrines where a similar rationale for extending responsibility applies.[287] Common-purpose liability, in the form of "parasitic accessorial liability", presented just that situation.

Even so, we should ask, *why* should the agreement or confederacy make such a difference?[288] Clearly, the law regarded the common unlawful purpose as an aggravating factor, such that S became liable to be convicted of crimes to which she had not actually contributed.

There is little discussion of the normative merits in *Jogee* itself. However, the Court worried that common-purpose liability imported "the striking anomaly of requiring a lower mental threshold for guilt in the case of the accessory than in the case of the principal."[289] Yet there is no *a priori* reason why S and P should have identical mens rea requirements. The basis of P's liability is different: he is liable because he satisfies the actus reus and mens rea requirements of the relevant crime. S was liable because she satisfies the actus reus and mens rea requirements of common-purpose liability (and note that this meant she must foresee not only the prospect of P's acts, but also that they will be done with mens rea; it is not enough even to foresee, say, the possibility that death may result

[285] Although, of course, crime A may be committed on more than one occasion; as when P uses the jemmy supplied by S to commit several burglaries.

[286] Compare the American rule that one who enters into a conspiracy thereby becomes liable for every reasonably foreseeable crime committed by his co-conspirators in furtherance of the conspiracy: *Pinkerton v United States* 328 US 640 (1946); Johnson, "The Unnecessary Crime of Conspiracy" (1973) 61 *Calif LR* 1137, 1146ff. The (overbroad) rule is not found in the Model Penal Code (see § 2.06).

[287] Admittedly, a pragmatic consideration is whether to do so would over-complicate the law and associated jury directions: cp. *Clayton* [2006] HCA 58, [113]–[117] (Kirby J, dissenting). On the other hand, common purpose doctrine offers real practical gains in overcoming the evidential difficulties, where there is concerted action, of distinguishing between the contributions made by individual actors and of establishing precisely what part was taken by each member of the combination.

[288] In particular, the free use—overuse—of common-purpose liability in spontaneous group-fight cases had meant that, in practice, individuals peripherally associated with such events could be convicted more or less just for being there. But that should not have been happening. It ought to have been crucially important to prove, positively, the existence of a *shared* unlawful purpose—a conspiracy—on the part of S.

[289] *Jogee* [2016] UKSC 8; *Ruddock* [2016] UKPC 7, [2017] AC 387, [85].

as an incident of the plan). Since the actus reus requirements are different, logic does not compel the mens rea requirements to be the same. Quite the opposite: even after *Jogee*, S still does not have to possess the "same" mens rea as P to be convicted of murder. Suppose that S gives P a crowbar, intending that this will assist P in intentionally causing grievous bodily harm to V. As seen above,[290] S does not need to intend that grievous bodily harm actually be caused to V. So S's mens rea is different from P's, yet S too is a murderer, even after *Jogee*.

Of course, opinions may differ on, say, whether purpose or knowledge regarding the causing of grievous bodily harm is sufficient culpability for convicting *anyone* of murder, whether as principal or accessory. But the key normative question here is not whether S is identically, or even *equally*, guilty as P. What counts is whether S is *sufficiently* culpable to be held responsible for the crime perpetrated by P. The answer to that question depends on how much significance is given to the fact that S's common purpose was *unlawful*. Prior to *Jogee*, the law saw S's commitment to a common unlawful purpose as adding the crucial extra normative ingredient, justifying the law's requiring only that S must foresee the possibility of P's crime. This is a very different normative ground from that in aiding and abetting, where S's actions need not be in themselves wrongful.

Let us explain. In standard cases of aid or abetment, lending P (an adult) a knife is unproblematic *until* we know that P's plans for its use are wrongful. What makes S's actions the stuff of criminal liability, in other words, is her mens rea with respect to P's conduct. In turn, that is why we should be wary of criminalising secondary participation by someone who merely foresees a risk of P's criminality. As we observed in § 7.4(iv), relaxing the stringent mens rea requirements for secondary liability through assistance and encouragement would reduce an ordinary citizen's freedom to do things that may happen to help others to commit crimes. It seems most undesirable to hold someone liable for doing something otherwise ordinary and lawful—say, selling a knife or a baseball bat—merely because she realised it was *possible* that P may have a crime in mind. No case has ever held this.[291] It would mean a massive expansion of the criminal law into the lives of private citizens. Perhaps this increased scope of criminalisation would be justified, although that is doubtful. Certainly, however, the implications of such a rule for ordinary citizens needed to be more carefully considered before the distinction between aiding/abetting and common-purpose liability was so blithely abandoned in *Jogee*: because one probable effect of abandoning that distinction is to increase the pressure to dilute those mens rea requirements for aiding and abetting.[292]

The same worry had less force in the pursuit of common unlawful purposes—to conspiracies acted out.[293] By entering into a common unlawful purpose, S became, through her

[290] § 7.4(iv).

[291] Although, prior to the decision in *Jogee*, certain Court of Appeal cases seemed to be converging on that position: see above, § 7.4(iv)(b). It is that very possibility that, prior to *Jogee*, made distinguishing joint enterprise liability so important—i.e., in order to prevent the watering down of the mens rea requirements for secondary participation by assistance or encouragement,

[292] As *Jogee* itself confirmed, those requirements involve proof of intention and/or knowledge by S: above, § 7.4(iv). The requirements for procurement are more tightly bound to S's intention: see § 7.4(iv)(a).

[293] Simester, "The Mental Element in Complicity" (2006) 122 *LQR* 578, 592–600; an argument accepted by the High Court of Australia: *Clayton v R* [2006] HCA 58, [20].

own deliberate choice, a participant in a group action to commit a crime.[294] Moreover, her new status can be viewed as having moral significance: she allies herself with the conduct of the other members of the group in a way that the mere aider or abettor, who remains an independent character throughout the episode, does not.[295] The law has a particular hostility to criminal groups. As with the inchoate crime of conspiracy, the rationale is partly one of dangerousness: "Experience has shown that joint criminal enterprises only too readily escalate into the commission of greater offences."[296] Criminal associations are dangerous. They present a threat to public safety that ordinary criminal prohibitions, addressed to individual actors, do not entirely address. Moreover, the danger is not just of an immediately physical nature. A group is a form of society, and a group constituted by a joint unlawful enterprise is a form of society that has set itself against the law and order of society at large. Individuals offending alone do not do this. Thus concerted wrongdoing imports additional and special reasons for the law to intervene. It is regrettable that English law no longer accommodates those reasons.

## § 7.6 General principles applying to all secondary parties

Secondary liability is subject to certain general doctrines governing the nature of the link required between the participant's actions and the commission of the offence to which she is party. These doctrines are discussed below.

### *(i) Liability is normally dependent on commission of the offence*

As we have observed already, and unlike inchoate crimes of assisting and encouraging crime and conspiracy, the forms of secondary participation liability are derivative and not themselves offences. Rather, they involve S in being ascribed with legal responsibility for the offence that P commits. It follows that, subject to certain exceptions, S may only be attributed with that offence *if it actually is committed.*[297] For example:

> S urges P to shoot V, a common enemy. P purchases a rifle, but before he has the opportunity to purchase any ammunition the gun dealer becomes suspicious and alerts the police, who cancel P's gun licence and confiscate the weapon.

[294] In *Clayton* [2006] HCA 58, [107], Kirby J (dissenting) rejects this argument: "The law may indeed dislike anti-social activities, particularly where they result in death. But a rational and just legal system will dislike such activities equally, whether the conduct charged is prosecuted as an offence of acting in concert or of aiding and abetting others in carrying out the group activity." (See also Sullivan, "Complicity for First Degree Murder and Complicity in an Unlawful Killing" [2006] *Crim LR* 502, 509–10.) Yet the point being made here in the text is that S's activity is not merely "anti-social" but independently *criminal.* By contrast, aiding and abetting need involve no otherwise criminal conduct; it is S's intention to aid, abet, etc. that turns her otherwise lawful conduct into the stuff of criminality. Hence a rational legal system may distinguish between the two, especially with respect to the mens rea requirement.

[295] In "Joint Criminal Enterprise" (2010) 73 *MLR* 578, 599, Krebs worries that the sharing of an unlawful purpose would make S guilty of crimes that P does alone. Not so: P's crime needed to be an incident of his pursuing their common purpose, a purpose in which S must be a participant.

[296] *Powell; English* [1999] 1 AC 1, 14 (Lord Steyn); cf. *Rahman* [2007] EWCA Crim 342, [61]; Marshall, Webb and Tilley, *Rationalisation of Current Research on Guns, Gangs and other Weapons: Phase 1* (2005) § 3.4.

[297] *A, B, C and D* [2010] EWCA Crim 1622, [2011] QB 841, [37]; cp. *Rahman* [2008] UKHL 45, [2009] 1 AC 129, [21] (Lord Bingham).

S is guilty of the inchoate offence of encouraging a crime (murder),[298] but since P does not actually commit any crime, S cannot be a party to murder.[299] In these standard examples, there can be no secondary liability because there is no actus reus by the principal.[300] Consider the facts of *Thornton v Mitchell*:[301]

> S, a bus conductor, negligently directed the bus driver to reverse. Two pedestrians were in consequence hit by the bus. However, the driver was acquitted of careless driving, since he had quite properly relied upon the instructions of the conductor.

In these circumstances, S was acquitted of aiding and abetting the offence of careless driving. There was no actus reus by the bus driver—he had not been driving carelessly[302]—and thus no criminal conduct from which S's liability might derive.

### *(ii) Exceptions: secondary liability without the primary offence*

The case is straightforward where P does not commit an actus reus at all. However, where that actus reus has occurred, there are some situations in which S can be convicted despite P's not being guilty of the full offence. The first occurs when P commits the actus reus of the offence, but is not criminally responsible for doing so because of legal infancy or insanity. To illustrate, consider the following facts from the Australian case of *Schultz v Pettitt*:[303]

> S allowed P, his five-year-old daughter, to operate a power boat. P pushed the throttle too far and the boat ploughed into another boat. S was charged with carelessly operating the boat.

Prima facie, P "operated" the boat, not S. However, as we shall see in Chapter 19, P could not be convicted because of her age. Therefore, no offence was committed by P. Despite this, Cox J would have been willing to uphold S's conviction as a secondary party. This analysis seems right in principle;[304] although in many cases of this kind it will be unnecessary, because it will be possible also to convict S as a principal.[305]

English law recognises at least two further exceptions to the requirement that P be guilty of an offence, although the scope of these exceptions is not fully settled. We consider them in the following subsections.

[298] Serious Crime Act 2007, s. 44; discussed below, § 9.1.

[299] Cp. *Demirian* [1989] VR 97; Lanham, "Primary and Derivative Criminal Liability: An Australian Perspective" [2000] *Crim LR* 707.

[300] A proposition confirmed, if confirmation be needed, in *Kenning* [2008] EWCA Crim 1534, [26].

[301] [1940] 1 All ER 339 (DC). See also *Loukes* [1996] Crim LR 341 (CA); Taylor, "Complicity and Excuses" [1983] *Crim LR* 656. In *Pickford* [1995] QB 203, 213 the Court of Appeal noted, *obiter*, that S could not be convicted of aiding or abetting an offence by P if P was not a member of the class of persons who, in law, could commit the offence.

[302] For explanation, see above, § 5.5(iii).

[303] (1980) 25 SASR 427.

[304] As it happened, this ground for upholding the conviction failed on the facts, because the father apparently lacked the mens rea required for secondary participation.

[305] Potentially on the basis of statutory construction (S was "operating" the boat while P was driving); or an anterior actus reus (S was operating the boat when he put P in charge); or via the doctrine of innocent agency. Note that in *Schultz v Pettitt* itself, the innocent agency doctrine was held not to apply: see §§ 7.3(i), 7.6(ii)(b).

### (a) When S is responsible for P's excuse

The first exception is for other possible defences, apart from legal infancy and insanity, that P may claim but which do not negate S's liability as a party. There is at least one such general defence:[306] that of duress, when S is the source of the duress. In *Bourne*,[307] S forced his wife to have sexual connection with an animal. S was convicted of abetting her to commit buggery notwithstanding that it was assumed his wife, had she been charged with the same offence, would have been acquitted owing to the availability of a defence of duress.[308] It appears that this defence operates only as a personal excuse in such circumstances.[309] Similar reasoning would not, therefore, carry over to make S liable in situations where (for example) P acts lawfully to prevent a crime.

### (b) When S procures P to act without mens rea

The second exception arises when P does the actus reus of an offence but lacks mens rea.[310] In limited circumstances, S may be liable as a secondary party when she procures P to commit the actus reus of an offence for which P lacks mens rea. In *Cogan and Leak*,[311] P had sexual intercourse with V, S's wife, apparently believing (on the basis of what S told him) that V was consenting. On appeal, P's conviction for rape was quashed, but S's conviction was upheld. The Court of Appeal explained that its main ground for upholding his conviction was that P was an innocent agent through whom S had acted as a principal in committing the offence. However, that analysis is problematic, in so far as rape is one of a number of offences that cannot be committed through an innocent agent.[312]

Alternatively, the Court of Appeal reasoned that S was guilty of procuring V's rape, since even though P could not be convicted, V had "clearly" been raped: "Cogan had sexual intercourse with her without her consent. The fact that Cogan was innocent of rape because he believed that she was consenting does not affect the position that she was raped."[313]

This, with respect, is misconceived. Rape is not an absolute liability crime, constituted simply by its actus reus. The unfortunate truth that P lacked mens rea under the

[306] And see also below, § 7.6(iii).

[307] (1952) 36 Cr App R 125. See Edwards, "Duress and Aiding and Abetting" (1953) 69 *LQR* 227; Cross, "Duress and Aiding and Abetting (A Reply)" (1953) 69 *LQR* 354.

[308] Strictly, the appropriate defence would have been marital coercion, a special, extended, variety of the duress defence, formerly available to wives who committed crimes in the presence of their husbands.

[309] Compare *Howe* [1987] AC 417, 458, where Lord Mackay highlighted the fact that duress involved a "reason special to [P] himself". Note that this was not the reasoning used by the Court in *Bourne* itself: see discussion of the limitations of such reasoning in the text and footnotes below, § 7.6(ii)(b). The best explanation of *Bourne* is that highlighted by Lord Mackay and adopted here. For discussion of the distinction between justification and excuse see below, § 17.2.

[310] Cp. *DPP v K and B* [1997] 1 Cr App R 36 (DC), in which two girls, B and K, used threats of violence to order V to have sexual intercourse with P, an unknown boy apparently under 14 years of age. Note, however, that the analysis in that case is flawed. The Divisional Court treated P as lacking mens rea on the basis of the *doli incapax* presumption (*ibid.*, 42). This was wrong: the *doli incapax* presumption was not against mens rea but against P's having the capacity to distinguish right from wrong (below, § 19.3(ii)). It was therefore a denial of criminal responsibility, like insanity and the irrebuttable presumption of *doli incapax* for children below 10 years of age. For criticism, see the commentary at [1997] Crim LR 121.

[311] [1976] QB 217 (CA).

[312] See above, § 7.3(i). This common-law limitation upon the scope of rape is preserved in s. 1 of the Sexual Offences Act 2003; below, § 12.6.

[313] *Cogan and Leak* [1976] QB 217, 223 (CA).

then-prevailing law[314] means that, for the purposes of the criminal law (and by contrast with ordinary language), no rape occurred.[315] Nonetheless, S's conviction seems a just result, albeit reached by a piece of tortured reasoning. Given that P lacked mens rea, the better explanation of *Cogan and Leak* is that, where S *procures* P to commit the actus reus of an offence without mens rea, S may be convicted of procuring that offence. The Court of Appeal subsequently accepted this approach in *Millward*,[316] the facts of which were as follows:

> S instructed P, his employee, to drive S's tractor on the highway. The tractor was in a defective condition, and by driving it on the highway P (the Court assumed[317]) committed the actus reus of reckless driving. S knew, and P did not know, that the vehicle was unroadworthy. While on the highway, the tractor's condition caused an accident, killing the passenger of another car.

On these facts, P was acquitted of causing death by reckless driving but S was convicted as a party to the offence. The Court of Appeal upheld S's conviction explicitly on the basis that he had procured commission of the actus reus by P.

The propriety of this exception to the rule that P must be guilty of the offence has been doubted.[318] Be that as it may, such cases will be rare, since whenever the actus reus involves consequences, S may normally be convicted as a principal offender: either on the basis of having caused the actus reus personally or by means of the innocent agent doctrine.[319] Appeal to a procurement-based analysis may remain necessary, though, where the crime charged is one that cannot be committed through an innocent agent.[320]

### *(iii) Conviction for different offences with the same actus reus*

A variant situation arises when there are two offences constituted by the same actus reus, and differentiated only by their respective mens rea requirements. The leading example of this is murder and manslaughter. Suppose, for instance, the following situation:

> S lends P a cosh, which he knows P plans to use to in order to assault V. S knows that the blow may cause V's death, but believes P intends only to knock V out temporarily and does not mean to kill him. In this, however, S is mistaken. P intends to kill V. Unfortunately, although P hits V no harder than agreed, she succeeds in her aim of killing him.

[314] The mens rea requirement in rape has since been expanded to include negligence by the Sexual Offences Act 2003: P would surely now be found guilty. See below, § 12.5.

[315] A similar example of this reasoning appears in *Bourne* (1952) 36 Cr App R 125, discussed in the previous section. Lord Goddard asserted (at 128) that the fact that P would have been acquitted of buggery presented no impediment to S's conviction for complicity because "that [P] could have set up duress . . . means that she admits that she has committed the crime but prays to be excused from punishment". Yet an acquittal would mean that she committed no crime.

[316] [1994] Crim LR 527 (CA); see also *Wheelhouse* [1994] Crim LR 756 (CA).

[317] Erroneously. In fact, the case was like *Thornton v Mitchell*, discussed above in § 7.6(i), where no actus reus occurred. Cp. the acceptance of this criticism of *Millward* by Smith, in his discussion of *Loukes* [1996] Crim LR 341, 343.

[318] See, e.g., Kadish, "Complicity, Cause and Blame" in *Essays in the Criminal Law* (1987) 135, 180; Law Com. No. 305, *Participation in Crime* (2007) para. 2.16.

[319] The Law Commission's preference is to deal with such cases by an extended statutory doctrine of innocent agency (§ 7.3(i) above) together with a specific new offence of causing another to commit a strict liability crime. See Law Com. No. 305, *Participation in Crime* (2007) part 4.

[320] See § 7.3(i).

In cases of this sort, S and P need not be convicted of the same offence. Where P is guilty of murder, it is possible to convict S only of manslaughter, provided P's acts are within the scope of the assistance or encouragement lent by S.[321] This issue, amongst others, arose in *Yemoh*,[322] the relevant facts of which were as follows:

> S joined with others in an attack on V, during the course of which V was fatally stabbed. By implication of the jury finding,[323] S realised that P might use a knife to cause injury, but may not have realised that P intended to kill or inflict really serious injury.

On these facts, the Court of Appeal upheld S's conviction for manslaughter. P was convicted of murder.

The rationale for S's lesser conviction in such cases is that S's participation was done with the intention of assisting or encouraging P whose proposed conduct was such that, were V to die, P would be guilty of manslaughter; in circumstances where, ultimately, P performed the envisaged conduct with sufficient mens rea for murder.[324]

The fact that murder and manslaughter share the same actus reus means that, in cases such as *Yemoh*, any incursion upon the principle that S's liability is derivative upon P's is minimal. Indeed, manslaughter may be regarded as a lesser included offence within murder.[325] Moreover, arguably the jury has a constitutional power on a charge of murder (improperly) to return a verdict of manslaughter, even though the jury is satisfied that every element necessary to constitute the crime of murder has been established.[326]

However, the reverse is not true, and it does not follow from the above that S may be convicted of murder if P is guilty only of manslaughter. Imagine the following example:

> S encourages P to punch V. S knows, and P does not, that V has an "egg-shell skull", and she hopes that the blow will cause V's death. P strikes V, killing him.

P is guilty of manslaughter. But is S guilty of murder, or only of manslaughter? In *Richards*,[327] the Court of Appeal first suggested that S could only be guilty of manslaughter. The facts of that case were as follows:

> S hired P1 and P2 to beat up V, her husband, badly enough to hospitalise him for a month. P1 and P2 then attacked V and inflicted a minor, but not serious, wound. The principals were acquitted of wounding with intent to cause grievous bodily harm and convicted instead of

[321] Above, § 7.4(ii). If outside the scope, S is generally entitled to a complete acquittal in respect of P's crime.

[322] [2009] EWCA Crim 930.

[323] *Ibid*., [124].

[324] Cp. *Gilmour* [2000] 2 Cr App R 407; *Murtagh and Kennedy* (1955) 39 Cr App R 72.

[325] Thus a verdict of manslaughter may be returned on a charge of murder: Criminal Law Act 1967, s. 6(2)(a).

[326] See, e.g., *Gammage v R* (1969) 122 CLR 444, 450–1, 453, 460, 463, 465. English courts have not determined the point authoritatively, but in *Shipley* (1784) 4 Doug KB 73, 178, 99 ER 774, 828, Ashurst J drew a distinction similar to that accepted by the Australian High Court in *Gammage*: "I admit the jury have the power of finding a verdict against the law, and so they have of finding a verdict against the evidence, but I deny that they have a right to do so". In *Meany* (1862) L & C 213, 216, 169 ER 1368, 1370, Pollock CB noted that the judge "is not bound to receive their verdict unless they insist upon his doing so". A manslaughter verdict contrary to direction has been accepted, reluctantly, by the judge in at least one case, noted (1942) 86 *Sol LJ* 251; see also *Soanes* [1948] 1 All ER 289, 290 (CCA) (infanticide); *Clement v Blunt* (1623) 2 Rolle 460, 81 ER 916. In *Smith*, *The Times*, 14 January 1804 (discussed by Williams, "Homicide and the Supernatural" (1949) 65 *LQR* 491, 500–3), however, the Court refused to receive the jury's first verdict of manslaughter, and sent the jury back out with a direction to convict of murder or acquit; see also Snelling, "The Alternative Verdict of Manslaughter" (1958) 32 *ALJ* 137.

[327] [1974] QB 776 (CA).

unlawful wounding, a lesser offence. S was convicted of wounding with intent to cause grievous bodily harm.

The Court of Appeal quashed S's conviction, and substituted a conviction for unlawful wounding. However, the decision has been powerfully criticised,[328] and was disapproved by both the Court of Appeal and the House of Lords in *Howe*.[329] It appears, therefore, that under current law S may be found guilty of the greater offence (e.g. murder) even though, because of lack of mens rea, P is guilty of only of the lesser offence (e.g. manslaughter).

It may be the law, but does the position after *Howe* accord with principle? One might worry that, on the view taken in *Howe*, the accomplice's liability can no longer derive from the principal's crime—it is driven more by the accomplice's personal culpability than by his participation in the principal's crime.

Certainly, P has acted without the mens rea for the more serious offence of murder. Prior to *Howe* the only permitted exception in such cases (i.e. where S may be convicted despite P's lacking mens rea) was restricted to situations in which S has actively procured the actus reus through P;[330] and that is a special case, justified by analogy with the doctrine of innocent agency. The exception approved in *Howe* can claim no such analogy.

Nonetheless, there are reasons why S should be convicted of murder. It is misleading to present murder and manslaughter as independent offences. Although the wrong in each is not *precisely* the same (there are some reasons against killing someone deliberately which do not apply to killing someone inadvertently, and vice versa), the core of the wrong is identical. The dominant rationale for each offence is the protection of life. Indeed, it is generally appropriate to think of manslaughter as an alternative rather than separate charge, available when the mens rea of murder cannot be proved or when the defendant has some limited defence such as loss of control.[331] Arguably, therefore, it is wrong to characterise the theory underlying the *dicta* in *Howe* as a matter of culpability triumphing over the principles of derivative liability; in the context of derivation, these offences should not be regarded as separate.

As we observed in § 7.5(ii), the principles of derivative liability do not have a life of their own. They exist only for a further purpose: to supplement ordinary actus reus doctrines (governing omissions, causation, etc.) by identifying other persons who are answerable when a criminal wrong is done. Once we consider this underlying rationale, it becomes apparent that S *can* be attributed with responsibility for the actus reus of murder in these cases. At least arguably, the underlying function of derivative liability doctrines is properly served by the ruling in *Howe*.

In any event, there is one further, uncontroversial, exception. Consistent with the case of duress above (§ 7.6(ii)(a)), it arises when there is a personal excusatory defence available to P. Culpable homicide admits of palliative defences: especially, for loss of control,[332]

[328] E.g. [1974] *Crim LR* 96; Smith, "Aid, Abet, Counsel, or Procure" in Glazebrook (ed.), *Reshaping the Criminal Law* (1978) 120, 128–30; Williams, *TBCL* § 15.18. Contrast Kadish, "Complicity, Cause and Blame" in *Blame and Punishment* (1987) 135, 184–6.

[329] [1987] AC 417 (HL), *sub nom. Burke* [1986] QB 626, 641–2 (CA).

[330] Above, § 7.6(ii)(c). Where S's participation is by procurement, it may even be possible in such cases to convict her as principal on ordinary principles of causation. See Alldridge, "The Doctrine of Innocent Agency" (1990) 2 *Crim L Forum* 45, 61ff.

[331] See s. 6(2)(a) of the Criminal Law Act 1967.

[332] Coroners and Justice Act 2009, ss. 54–55.

diminished responsibility,[333] suicide pacts,[334] and infanticide.[335] Where such a defence is open to P, S's liability for murder (or manslaughter, in the case of infanticide) will not correspondingly be reduced.[336]

*(a) A "simple escalation"[337] or an "overwhelming supervening act"?*

One special case needs discussion.[338] It arises where P unexpectedly goes beyond the envisaged conduct (i.e. beyond a mere unlawful and dangerous act) by, say, pulling out a knife and stabbing V dead. This kind of case has been described as one of "overwhelming supervening act"—a different type of act from anything assisted or encouraged by S.[339] In such a case, S will generally not be liable as a party to either murder or manslaughter, because S did not intentionally aid or abet the *type of act* that caused death. (It would be otherwise, and S would still be guilty of manslaughter, if V died from a combination of the punches that S originally envisaged and the subsequent knife wound.)

That, at least, is the position in principle. Indeed, in doctrinal terms, there is nothing special about an overwhelming supervening act. That is to say, "overwhelming supervening act" is not a distinctive category of complicity liability that involves any unusual rules. It is simply one type of case amongst others in which S fails to satisfy the standard criteria of secondary liability. Contrast the facts of *Grant*:[340]

> S, P, and others set out on an expedition to inflict serious bodily injury on V. The boot of their car, which was being driven by P, contained a number of weapons intended for that purpose: knives, a sledgehammer, and a baseball bat. Espying V, however, P accelerated the car and drove straight into him with intention to kill. V was killed in the collision.

On these facts, the Court of Appeal confirmed S's conviction of murder. S abetted P knowing that P intended to inflict serious injury (an intention that S shared). P killed V in pursuance of the criminal project that S abetted.[341] P simply used a different weapon. As such, it can defensibly be regarded as a mere variation within the type of activity that S was abetting.[342] As the Court of Appeal put matters, in the subsequent case of *Ayre*, "it is not necessary to prove that the secondary party encouraged or assisted the principal to commit the crime *in a particular way*".[343]

Rather more difficult are situations in which S participates with P in an attack upon V, where S does not contemplate the prospect of serious injury, but where the contemplated attack would constitute unlawful act manslaughter should V die in consequence. Suppose that S's understanding was that S and P would beat up V with their fists but, to S's surprise,

333 Homicide Act 1957, s. 2(4).
334 Homicide Act 1957, s. 4(1).
335 Infanticide Act 1938, s. 1(1).
336 The same defence may, however, be available to the secondary party personally. See, for example, Homicide Act 1957, s. 2(1) (diminished responsibility).
337 *Tas* [2018] EWCA Crim 2603, [2019] 4 WLR 14, [40]; cp. *Jogee* [2016] UKSC 8; *Ruddock* [2016] UKPC 7, [2017] AC 387, [33].
338 This type of case was flagged up earlier, in § 7.4(iv)(c) (What count as essential matters in unlawful-act manslaughter?). See, further, Simester and Stark, "Overwhelming Supervening Acts – A Corrective" (2025) 84 *CLJ* 345.
339 *Jogee* [2016] UKSC 8; *Ruddock* [2016] UKPC 7, [2017] AC 387, [97]. Cp. *Tas* [2018] EWCA Crim 2603, [2019] 4 WLR 14, [38]–[41].
340 [2021] EWCA Crim 1243, [2022] 2 WLR 321.
341 That is to say, it is not a *Calhaem*-type case: above, § 7.4(ii).
342 See above, § 7.4(iv)(c).
343 [2025] EWCA Crim 255, [45]. (Emphasis added.)

while they are fighting, P suddenly pulls out a knife and stabs V to death. Is S guilty of murder or manslaughter? In principle, neither. S did not intend to assist or encourage P to do an act of causing grievous bodily harm with intent, so she does not satisfy the mens rea requirements for participation in murder. Moreover, although she was a party to an assault (i.e. to an unlawful and dangerous act), *that assault* did not cause V's death.[344]

Indeed, even under the former law of joint enterprise, discussed in section 7.5, S would not be liable for P's foreseen offending if it were perpetrated in a manner "fundamentally different" from what S had foreseen. To adapt our example, if S and P agreed to beat up V with their fists (say, occasioning actual bodily harm), and S foresaw that P might go "too far" and deliberately cause greater injury (say, grievous bodily harm), then S would have been guilty under the old joint enterprise law of a section 18 offence if that is what P went on to commit. If, however, during the attack on V, P produced a knife (that S did not previously know about) and stabbed V, causing grievous bodily harm, then S would not have been liable for P's further offending.[345] To be clear: in such scenarios, S was guilty neither of murder *nor* of manslaughter.

What the Supreme Court should have done in *Jogee* was disavow the doctrine of "fundamental difference" and taken the logic of its reasoning regarding secondary liability to its natural conclusion: if S did not assist or encourage *the act* that caused death, with the intention to provide such assistance or encouragement, she should not be held liable for an offence of homicide. Alas, the Supreme Court allowed the "fundamental difference" doctrine to linger on, in the form of a doctrine of "overwhelming supervening act".[346] The Court of Appeal has enthusiastically seized the baton from the Supreme Court and created an unjustified, new inculpatory doctrine for homicide cases.

What matters in so-called "escalation" cases, it was said in *Jogee* (and has been reiterated by the Court of Appeal), is whether death was caused "by some overwhelming supervening act by the perpetrator which nobody in the defendant's shoes could have contemplated might happen and is of such a character as to relegate his acts to history".[347] If it was so caused, then no liability for manslaughter can follow. Otherwise, liability seems, for the Court of Appeal, to flow automatically. Admittedly, that test is based on a direct quotation from *Jogee*. But that test invites the following misreading of the law: Where P does something that was not reasonably foreseeable following S's intended contribution, then P's act is fundamentally different from the one that S intended to assist/encourage; it is an overwhelming supervening act and S is not liable. *Otherwise*, S is liable for P's offence. Indeed, the very idea of a "supervening event" appears to presuppose that S is already prima facie liable for P's full offending, unless a reason for acquitting S arises.[348] But this is to bypass

[344] The facts of this example follow those in *Anderson and Morris* [1966] 2 QB 110 (CCA), in which S's conviction of manslaughter was quashed. The case is cited in *Jogee* [2016] UKSC 8; *Ruddock* [2016] UKPC 7, [2017] AC 387, [69], [97] as an example of the kind of unexpected ("overwhelming supervening") act by P that could leave S guilty of neither murder nor manslaughter.

[345] *Powell; English* [1999] 1 AC 1. S would still be guilty of a section 47 offence, but *not* of the section 18 offence.

[346] The Supreme Court envisaged "overwhelming supervening acts" as being a surviving example of the "fundamental difference" (or "fundamental departure") rule: *Jogee* [2016] UKSC 8; *Ruddock* [2016] UKPC 7, [2017] AC 387, [98].

[347] *Jogee; Ruddock*, *ibid.*, [97]. See, especially, *Tas* [2018] EWCA Crim 2603, [2019] 4 WLR 14; also *Harper* [2019] EWCA Crim 343, [2019] 4 WLR 39; *Lanning* [2021] EWCA Crim 450.

[348] References to "overwhelming supervening acts" as "exclusions" of liability are equally liable to mislead, but see *Rowe* [2022] EWCA Crim 27, [130].

the basic requirements of the actus reus and mens rea of secondary liability. The fact of the matter is that S typically has not satisfied those basic liability elements in "escalation" cases, and should be acquitted of P's offence. There is no room, post-*Jogee*, for a doctrine premised on P's going *further* than S intended to encourage or assist him to go.[349]

The irony here is considerable. The decision in *Jogee* to abolish a distinct legal category of joint enterprise was motivated by a perception that it is unfair to predicate convictions of homicide crimes upon mere foresight of a possible escalation in violence. Now, however, such foresight is no longer required. According to the Court of Appeal, if S is present and abetting an unlawful activity, a conviction of manslaughter will follow if escalation was *foreseeable*.

As things stand, then, if S goes into a fistfight with P against others, envisaging some but not serious injury, and during the fight P unexpectedly pulls out a knife and stabs V to death, S will be guilty of at least manslaughter. That represents a significant expansion of pre-*Jogee* law.[350] It is hoped that, should the Supreme Court be given the opportunity to disavow the doctrines of "overwhelming supervening acts" and "escalation" in the future, it does so. The focus should *solely* be on whether S assisted or encouraged the act that caused death, intending to do so. If not, S should not be convicted of a homicide offence, however foreseeable it was that P may go further than assisted or encouraged. "Overwhelming supervening acts" and "escalations" are distractions, and harmful ones at that.

### *(iv) Limitations on secondary liability*

#### *(a) The* Tyrrell *principle*

The common law contains a limited exemption from secondary liability for victims of crime. The exemption arises in respect of offences that exist for the *protection* of a certain class of person, i.e. persons who are regarded by the statute as victims rather than co-offenders. Such persons are treated as incapable of participating in crimes against themselves. The leading case is *Tyrrell*, where it was held that D, a girl under the age of 16 years, could not be convicted of abetting unlawful sexual intercourse with herself, because the Act that created the offence "was passed for the purpose of protecting women and girls against themselves".[351] The common law principle espoused in *Tyrrell* is of limited scope,[352] and its application may be doubtful in areas other than offences against young persons and persons with a disability. Indeed, its place even in sexual offences involving the young is now uncertain, following enactment of the Sexual Offences Act 2003. That Act, while not explicitly excluding the *Tyrrell* principle,[353] frequently fails to identify with consistency or

[349] For an extended discussion of this point, see Simester and Stark, "Overwhelming Supervening Acts—A Corrective" (2025) 84 *CLJ* 345.

[350] Cp. *Rafferty* [2007] EWCA Crim 1846; *Uddin* [1998] EWCA Crim 999, [1999] QB 431.

[351] [1894] 1 QB 710, 712 (Lord Coleridge CJ). See also *Whitehouse* [1977] QB 868 (CA); *Pickford* [1995] 1 Cr App R 420, 428; *Congdon* [1990] NLJR 1221. However, while these three cases were decided on the basis of the *Tyrrell* principle, they are better analysed as falling within the next type of exceptions (§ 7.6(iv)(b)), where liability is excluded as a matter of statutory interpretation. See Williams, "Victims and Other Exempt Parties in Crime" (1990) 10 *LS* 245, 249–50.

[352] Williams, "Victims and Other Exempt Parties in Crime" (1990) 10 *LS* 245; Hogan, "Victims as Parties to Crime" [1962] *Crim LR* 683; Williams, "Victims as Parties to Crimes—A Further Comment" [1964] *Crim LR* 686; Heydon, "The Corroboration of Accomplices" [1973] *Crim LR* 264, 274.

[353] See s. 73(3), which preserves existing exceptions to complicity liability.

clarity whether its various offences are designed to protect particular classes of persons, and allows that young persons can commit many of the Act's offences even as principals.[354] Consequently, we must await future rulings about which, if any, of its offences remain subject to the common law exception.[355]

The possibility of applying the *Tyrrell* principle depends on the purpose of the relevant legislation, and arises only if the statute is directed toward protecting an identified class of persons.[356] There is certainly no *general* exception for victims of crime.[357] Thus if, for example, in the course of a sadomasochistic episode S asks P to inflict injury on him, it appears that both P and S commit an offence of assault occasioning actual bodily harm contrary to section 47 of the Offences Against the Person Act 1861, since that offence protects the public at large.[358]

*(b) Specific legislation*

Quite apart from situations where the policy of a statute invokes the *Tyrrell* principle, the relevant primary offence may also be defined by legislation in such a way that it delimits the class of persons who may commit that offence. In such instances, secondary participation is excluded except in so far as such participants qualify within the class stipulated by the primary offence. One example of a statutory restriction on the range of secondary participants was suggested, *obiter*, by Lord Parker CJ in *Carmichael & Sons Ltd v Cottle*.[359] The Lord Chief Justice observed that, in the context of regulations prohibiting the use or causing or permitting of use of a defective vehicle on the road, since "normally, 'using' is applicable to the actual driver" it may follow that:

> "when the words used are 'using or causing or permitting [to be used]', there is no room for the application of the principle in regard to aiders and abettors. The statute in other words itself provides the alternatives, and, if a person is to be charged as an aider and abettor or an accessory, he should be so charged, and under these provisions should be specifically charged with causing or permitting the user."

However, such cases are rare. More commonly, the statute may define a class of persons who may commit the offence *as a principal*, without restricting the class of persons who may be guilty of the offence as a secondary party.[360] An example is the offence of rape, which can

354 Below, Chapter 12.

355 Bohlander, "The Sexual Offences Act 2003 and the *Tyrrell* Principle—Criminalising the Victims?" [2005] *Crim LR* 701.

356 Cf. *Gnango* [2011] UKSC 59, [2012] 1 AC 827, [17]–[18], [48]–[49]. A similar restriction is favoured by the Law Commission: Law Com. No. 305, *Participation in Crime* (2007) paras. 5.24–5.39.

357 *Wright's Case* (1603) 1 Co. Lit. 127a: D agreed to cut off V's hand so that V could beg more effectively. Both D and V were convicted of mayhem.

358 Cp. *Brown* [1994] 1 AC 212. Interestingly, since the rhetoric of the majority judgments in that case emphasises the paternalistic aspect of not allowing the masochist legally to consent to violence perpetrated by the sadist, arguably it follows that the masochist ought to be treated as a victim falling within the protected class to which the *Tyrrell* principle applies. It is legal moralism, not paternalism, that indicts the masochist.

359 [1971] RTR 11, 14 (DC). Cp. *Crawford v Haughton* [1972] WLR 572 (DC); *Farr* [1982] Crim LR 745 (CA). Arguably, *Sockett* (1908) 72 JP 428 should have been treated as such a case: see Williams, *TBCL* § 15.15 n. 11. S, who was not pregnant, was convicted of aiding and abetting P to use an instrument on S with intent to procure a miscarriage; even though the statute made it no offence for someone not pregnant to use such an instrument on herself, so that S fell outside the class of persons who could commit the offence as principal.

360 Cp. the actual decision in *Sockett*, *ibid.*; also *Mok Wei Tak v R* [1990] 2 AC 333 (PC); Heydon, "The Corroboration of Accomplices" [1973] *Crim LR* 264, 271.

generally only be committed by a male.[361] This criterion means that a female cannot normally commit rape as a principal. But she may nonetheless aid and abet a rape committed by someone else.[362]

*(c) Law enforcement*

One exception of uncertain scope is law enforcement.[363] Suppose that S is a police officer (or indeed a private individual)[364] who assists P to commit a crime in order to gather evidence against P. Is S too guilty of the crime? The answer appears to depend on the nature of S's participation. Consider first the case where S instigates the crime herself. According to the House of Lords in *Sang*, in that case S has no defence:[365]

> "I would now refer to what is, I believe and hope, the unusual case in which a dishonest policeman, anxious to improve his detection record, tries very hard with the help of an *agent provocateur* to induce a young man with no criminal tendencies to commit a serious crime, and ultimately the young man succumbs to the inducement. . . . The policeman and the informer who acted together in inciting him to commit the crime should . . . both be prosecuted and suitably punished."

(So too, added their Lordships, should the young man.) By contrast, where P has instigated the offence and S then participates solely in order to trap P, or to prevent the offence from coming to fruition,[366] S appears to be exempted from liability as a secondary party even though he may satisfy the actus reus and mens rea elements required for liability. According to the Court of Appeal in *Birtles*:[367]

> "It is one thing for the police to make use of information concerning an offence that is already laid on. In such a case the police are clearly entitled, and indeed it is their duty, to mitigate the consequences of the proposed offence, for example, to protect the proposed victim, and to that end it may be perfectly proper for them to encourage the informer to take part in the offence or for the police officer himself to do so. But it is quite another thing, and something of which this court thoroughly disapproves, to use an informer to encourage another to commit an offence or indeed an offence of a more serious character, which he would not otherwise commit."

There is difficult middle ground.[368] In *Williams v DPP*,[369] police officers exposed cartons of cigarettes, apparently unguarded, in the back of a van parked in the street. P helped himself

[361] More precisely, rape can only be committed by a person with a penis: Sexual Offences Act 2003, s. 1. See § 12.6.

[362] See *Ram* (1893) 17 Cox CC 609.

[363] The Law Commission has recommended a somewhat complex statutory defence of acting to prevent an offence or to limit harm, provided that S's conduct is reasonable in the circumstances: Law Com. No. 305, *Participating in Crime* (2007) paras. 5.10–5.23.

[364] "Paedophile hunters", who pose as children to ensnare paedophiles online and via messaging apps, seem routinely to fulfil the requirements of secondary liability, yet are never prosecuted alongside their targets. For a discussion of the wider legal issues raised by such activities, see Purshouse, "'Paedophile Hunters', Criminal Procedure, and Fundamental Human Rights" (2020) 47 *J Law and Society* 384.

[365] [1980] AC 402 (Lord Salmon).

[366] As in *Gillick v West Norfolk and Wisbech Area Health Authority* [1986] AC 112. Such cases are, perhaps, better dealt with under the rubric of necessity: see below, § 21.4.

[367] [1969] 2 All ER 1131n, 1132 (Lord Parker CJ). Cp. *Bainbridge* [1991] Crim LR 535 (CA); *Clarke* (1984) 80 Cr App R 344; *McEvilly* (1973) 60 Cr App R 150; *McCann* (1971) 56 Cr App R 359.

[368] See Ashworth, "Testing Fidelity to Legal Values: Official Involvement and Criminal Justice" in Shute and Simester (eds.), *Criminal Law Theory* (2002) 299.

[369] (1993) 98 Cr App R 209.

to some of them, and was prosecuted for interfering with a vehicle, or something carried in it, with intent to commit theft.[370] While there is much to be said for allowing the police to use temptation-based methods to trap criminals, such cases do present difficulties for complicity law. The Divisional Court in *Williams* stated that the police had not aided or abetted P's crime; yet it is arguable that they did so. Provision of the "bait" constituted an essential ingredient of the crime, not to mention encouragement. Perhaps there is a subtle distinction to be drawn between "instigation" and mere "temptation"; a distinction favourably construed where S's motive is law enforcement. It is impossible, in a text of this nature, to resolve the many difficulties raised by these cases. Suffice it to note, however, that the judgment in *Birtles* is very difficult to reconcile with decisions such as *Yip Chiu-Cheung v R*,[371] where an undercover police officer (who was not charged) was said by the Privy Council to be a co-conspirator with D to export heroin, even though the officer had entered into the conspiracy solely in order to expose the operation. A look behind the judgments is revealing. By ruling the officer a conspirator in *Yip*, their Lordships secured D's conviction for conspiracy. By ruling the officer a non-participant in *Birtles*, the Court of Appeal freed him from the rules constraining evidence given by accomplices, so that his evidence against D did not need a warning about corroboration.[372] Making law for ulterior purposes like these, it must be said, is following a recipe for bad law.

### (v) *Secondary liability and inchoate offences*

We have observed that secondary participation is not *per se* a crime. Its doctrines do not create offences. They operate as a conduit to S's responsibility for some other form of criminal wrongdoing. Therefore, since secondary participation is not an offence, it follows that S cannot commit the inchoate crime of attempting to be a party to an offence.[373] (By contrast, it is possible to attempt to commit the distinct, inchoate offences of encouraging or assisting crime.[374]) If there were ever any doubt about attempted participation at common law, it has been resolved by section 1(4)(b) of the Criminal Attempts Act 1981, which expressly excludes aiding, abetting, counselling, and procuring from the ambit of the crime of attempting to commit an offence.[375]

Similarly, neither may one commit an offence of conspiring to aid and abet. Although the question had been left open by the House of Lords in *Hollinshead*,[376] the position was confirmed by the Court of Appeal in *Kenning*,[377] and may for now be regarded as settled.

Conceptually, the view that there can be no liability in attempts or conspiracy for attempted participation in crime seems right. If S has failed to participate in a crime, she

[370] Criminal Attempts Act 1981, s. 9.
[371] [1995] 1 AC 111 (PC); below, § 9.2(v)(b). Cp. *Latif* [1996] 1 WLR 104 (HL); above, § 4.2(iii)(c) (Case 2).
[372] Prior to 1994, such jury warnings were mandated. See, now, Criminal Justice and Public Order Act 1994, s. 32; *Makanjuola* [1995] 1 WLR 1348 (CA).
[373] Smith, "Secondary Participation and Inchoate Offences" in Tapper (ed.), *Crime, Proof and Punishment* (1981) 21. See also Spencer, "Trying to Help Another Person Commit a Crime" in Smith (ed.), *Criminal Law: Essays in Honour of J.C. Smith* (1987) 148; below, § 7.7. Contrast the Model Penal Code, § 2.06(3)(a)(ii).
[374] Below, § 9.1(ii)(d) (Inchoate offences).
[375] Cp. *Dunnington* [1984] QB 472 (CA).
[376] *Hollinshead* [1985] AC 975.
[377] *Kenning* [2008] EWCA Crim 1534; endorsing the Court's own conclusion in *Hollinshead* [1985] 1 All ER 850, 857–8 (CA).

has no connection with it and should not be convicted. Her conduct is, one might say, too remote from manifest criminality to warrant the attention of the criminal law—attention that would be tantamount to punishing for little more than wrongful thoughts.[378] Conversely, however, the inchoate offences *are* offences in themselves, independent of the further crime that is attempted or conspired toward. Therefore, S may be a party to (aid, abet, etc.) an attempt[379] or a conspiracy[380] by P to commit an offence. So, if S provides P with a gun, intending to assist in the murder of V, but P's shot misses V, S *and* P are liable for attempted murder.

An exception to the general rule that there is no inchoate liability for participation arises if assistance or encouragement is itself made a substantive offence by legislation. In *McShane*,[381] D visited her mother in hospital where they discussed the possibility of the mother's suicide. D was convicted of attempting to counsel or procure her mother's suicide. She appealed on the ground that no such offence was known to law. However, the Court of Appeal dismissed the appeal. The relevant substantive offence at that time was enacted by section 2(1) of the Suicide Act 1961 in the following terms:

> A person who aids, abets, counsels or procures the suicide of another, or an attempt by another to commit suicide, shall be liable on conviction to imprisonment for a term not exceeding 14 years.

Under this section, the counselling or procuring was not a secondary form of participation in some further offence; it constituted an offence in its own right. Consequently, there could be an inchoate offence of attempting to commit an offence against that section, and D was rightly convicted of attempting to counsel or procure another's suicide.[382]

In 2007, the government generalised this last technique, by making assisting or encouraging crime an inchoate offence *in its own right*, independently of the perpetration of the principal's crime. Under sections 44–6 of the Serious Crime Act, one who, say, encourages P to commit a murder (and satisfies the complex mens rea requirements) becomes, herself, immediately guilty of an inchoate offence of *encouraging or assisting crime*. The new offences are inchoate, in that S's guilt does not depend on the occurrence of the substantive crime; and the conviction is for an offence under one of sections 44–6, not for murder (or any other homicide offence). Thus these new offences are complementary to, and do not displace, secondary liability. If, subsequently, P then carries out the crime as encouraged, complicity doctrines would operate to make S guilty of murder. These new inchoate offences are noted further in § 7.7. They are considered in detail in Chapter 9.

### *(vi) Withdrawal*

When perpetrating the principal offence, P cannot undo his crime. Once the elements of the offence are concurrently satisfied, the offence is committed and cannot be "uncommitted".

[378] *Per* Fletcher, *Rethinking Criminal Law* (1978) 680–1: "there is no social wrong in acting to aid the crime of another, unless the aid actually furthers the criminal objective".

[379] *Hapgood v Wyatt* (1870) LR 1 CCR 221, 11 Cox CC 471; *Clayton* (1843) 1 C & K 128, 174 ER 743. Cf. *Mackie* [1957] NZLR 669 (CA).

[380] *Anderson* (1984) 80 Cr App R 64; cp. *McNamara (No. 1)* (1981) 56 CCC (2d) 193.

[381] (1977) 66 Cr App R 97.

[382] The relevant substantive offence would now be encouraging or assisting suicide, contrary to s. 59 of the Coroners and Justice Act 2009—an offence which cannot be attempted. See below, § 10.11(ii).

By contrast, secondary participation *can* be undone.[383] S may withdraw her participation,[384] although she must do so before the crime is committed by P:[385]

> "A person who unequivocally withdraws from the joint enterprise before the moment of the actual commission of the crime by the principal ... should not be liable for that crime, although his acts before withdrawing may render him liable for other offences."

Withdrawal, however, is not easy. Repentance is insufficient.[386] The participation must not merely be discontinued. It must be countermanded.[387]

What this means in practical terms is that mere cessation of further participatory activity will be insufficient.[388] Withdrawal may only be effected by taking steps to counteract the effect of S's previous actions. What steps are sufficient will therefore depend upon the circumstances and upon the extent of S's prior participation: the greater the involvement, the more S must do to withdraw.[389] Encouragement can normally be undone by an express statement to the opposite effect.[390] However, any such communication of withdrawal, whether made by words or actions,[391] must be "unequivocal";[392] a perfunctory disclaimer is likely to be insufficient,[393] as is merely leaving the scene,[394] or simply not turning up to a prearranged criminal enterprise.[395]

If material assistance has been rendered, the steps required to withdraw are likely to be more onerous, and some form of physical intervention to impede the crime may be required. For example, S may have to try to recover the knife loaned to P or attempt to protect the victim, perhaps even by restraining P physically.[396] On the other hand, the provision of aid via advice or other information cannot as such be undone: in such cases, it may be countermanded by attempts to dissuade P from proceeding with the crime. In *Grundy*,[397] S had provided P1 and P2 with information about premises they were planning to burgle. Two weeks before the burglary was to be committed, however, S apparently had a change of heart and thereafter had been trying to stop the principals from carrying out

383 However, any concomitant liability for the inchoate offences of encouraging or assisting crime (under ss. 44–46 of the Serious Crime Act 2007) cannot be undone.

384 Confirmed, if confirmation be needed, in *Mitchell* [2018] EWCA Crim 2687.

385 *O'Flaherty* [2004] EWCA Crim 526, [2004] 2 Cr App R 20, [58].

386 *Croft* [1944] 1 KB 295 (CCA); *Becerra and Cooper* (1976) 62 Cr App R 212; Hale, 1 PC 618.

387 Compare the Law Commission's report, which describes withdrawal in terms of "negating" the effect of S's participation: Law Com. No. 305, *Participating in Crime* (2007) paras. 3.60ff.

388 *Johnson and Jones* (1841) Car & M 218, 174 ER 479.

389 Australian case law requires that S take "all reasonable steps" to undo the impact of his participation: *Menniti* [1985] 1 Qd R 520, noted at (1986) 10 *Crim LJ* 236; *Wilton* (1993) 64 A Crim R 359. The proposition that S must seek to "neutralise" the effect of previous assistance was left undecided by the Court of Appeal in *Rook* [1993] 1 WLR 1005, 1011–12, but seems implicit in *Becerra and Cooper* (1976) 62 Cr App R 212, 219: where S handed over the knife to P, "something vastly different and vastly more effective" than an announced departure was required to constitute withdrawal.

390 *Saunders and Archer* (1573) 2 Plowd 473, 75 ER 706. Cp. *Croft* [1944] KB 295; *Rook* [1993] 1 WLR 1005 (CA).

391 E.g., by S's action of quitting the company he has joined: *Hyde* (1672) 1 Hale PC 537; Foster, *Crown Law* 354; *Edmeades* (1828) 3 C & P 390, 392, 172 ER 469, 470. *Hyde* and Foster are endorsed in *Jogee* [2016] UKSC 8; *Ruddock* [2016] UKPC 7, [2017] AC 387, [13], suggesting that the law on this point has not changed.

392 *Rook* [1993] 1 WLR 1005, 1012 (CA); *Baker* [1994] Crim LR 444 (CA).

393 Cp. *Fletcher* [1962] Crim LR 551 (CCA).

394 *Becerra and Cooper* (1976) 62 Cr App R 212.

395 *Goodspeed* (1911) 6 Cr App R 133; *Rook* [1993] 1 WLR 1005.

396 *Becerra and Cooper* (1976) 62 Cr App R 212; *Baker* [1994] Crim LR 444 (CA).

397 [1977] Crim LR 543 (CA); cf. *Whitefield* (1984) 79 Cr App R 36.

their plan. The Court of Appeal ruled that the trial judge had erred by refusing to leave S's claim of withdrawal to the jury.

There is no general requirement that S must, in addition to countermanding her own participation, also take reasonable steps to prevent P from committing the offence.[398] However, where the situation is such that withdrawing by other means is impossible or impractical, withdrawal may alternatively be effected by taking steps to prevent the commission of the offence, e.g. by warning the victim or the police.[399] There may come a point when events are so far advanced that efficacious withdrawal by S is impossible.[400]

It is worth re-emphasising that the withdrawal must be timely, occurring before the crime is committed, and perhaps before its commission is even commenced.[401] As such, even where withdrawal is effected by S, it will not preclude liability if the actus reus of P's crime occurs prior to that withdrawal. In *Campbell (André)*,[402] S engaged in a joint attack with P and others upon V. Subsequently, P continued the assault on the other side of the road. While S may not have been a secondary party to that continuation of the assault, his conviction was upheld on the alternative basis that the events during the earlier attack, to which he was a party, were themselves a contributing (concurrent) cause of death.

## § 7.7 Do we need complicity?

Should the day ever arrive when England and Wales join with the rest of the civilised world in codifying their criminal law, Peter Glazebrook has suggested that we might dispense with doctrines of complicity.[403] Glazebrook would simply specify the various modes of involvement in crimes—i.e. modes by which one may become guilty of committing a crime—without drawing a formal distinction between principals and accessories.

It is certainly possible to express a person's involvement in wrongs that are perpetrated by others without resorting to a formal notion of complicity, as the law on joint tortfeasors demonstrates. Removing the labels, however, may not dissolve the reasons that begat them. Even on Glazebrook's draft provisions,[404] helping and encouraging crime are only modes of committing an offence *if* some other person (let us call her the "principal") actually commits that offence. So the liability of the helper or encourager remains dependent on the wrongdoing of someone else. Moreover, the actus reus of offending by helping will necessarily differ from the actus reus of offending by committing (i.e. as principal). It looks as if distinct principles will still be needed in order to identify separately those who

[398] *O'Flaherty* [2004] EWCA Crim 526, [2004] 2 Cr App R 20, [60]–[61]. Compare, however, *Gallant* [2008] EWCA Crim 1111, [14], where the Court took note of the fact that S was the instigator of the attack: "In those circumstances, assuming that the attack started as a joint enterprise, he clearly would have had to do more than merely walk away in order to demonstrate that he was withdrawing from any further participation". This more onerous standard may be justified on the basis that, as well as withdrawing from the common purpose, an instigator needs also to countermand the encouragement given: § 7.6(vi)(b).

[399] *Becerra and Cooper* (1976) 62 Cr App R 212. See Lanham, "Accomplices and Withdrawal" (1981) 97 *LQR* 575, 580ff; *Eldredge v United States* (1932) 62 F 2d 449; *Commonwealth v Huber* (1958) 15 D & C 2d 726.

[400] As appears to have occurred in *White v Ridley* (1978) 140 CLR 342.

[401] A possibility raised in *Perman* [1996] 1 Cr App R 24, 34.

[402] [2009] EWCA Crim 50.

[403] "Structuring the Criminal Code: Functional Approaches to Complicity, Incomplete Offences and General Offences" in Simester and Smith (eds.), *Harm and Culpability* (1996) 195.

[404] *Ibid.*, 211–12.

independently commit the offence and those who commit it only by helping or encouraging another.

As noted already, Parliament has, however, gone even further than Glazebrook's proposal, and has chosen to supplement the law of complicity with three inchoate offences of assisting and encouraging crime, contrary to sections 44–46 of the Serious Crime Act 2007.[405] S's liability for these inchoate offences is constituted by her own actions, intentions, and beliefs: it arises independently of whether the relevant substantive offence is, ultimately, committed by P. The attraction of such a proposal is that, like any inchoate offence, it would reduce the element of luck in S's conviction. The point is made by Spencer:[406]

> "If you commit the crime I knew you intended with my help to commit, I am likely to be an accessory, but if you do not, I may well commit no offence at all. . . . This is very strange. In either case, I have done all that I have to do to incur criminal liability. It is no fault of mine—or to be accurate, it is not due to any lack of fault on my part—that the crime was never committed. If my behaviour was bad enough to punish where you actually made use of the help I gave you, it was surely bad enough to punish where I fully expected you to use it but you got caught before you had the chance."

In principle, the existence of these offences takes some of the pressure off the law of complicity since, for many of the more difficult cases, an alternative conviction will be available under the Serious Crime Act—which imports a potential maximum sentence corresponding to the principal's envisaged crime, even where that offence is ultimately not committed.

At the same time, there remains a place for complicity doctrine. The inchoate offences generate a stand-alone conviction under the Serious Crime Act. By contrast, secondary liability generates a conviction *for the principal offence*. If S supplies an automatic weapon to P for the purpose of murdering V, and P uses it accordingly, a conviction of murder may better represent S's criminality than one of "intentionally encouraging or assisting an offence".[407]

Admittedly, one upshot of preserving complicity liability is the phenomenon to which Spencer, and presumably subjectivists such as Ashworth,[408] would object: that S's liability becomes a matter of moral luck. So far as S is concerned, it is no more than luck that determines whether she becomes guilty of burglary as a secondary party.[409] S has made a complete attempt to aid P's offence. Therefore, the subjectivists would say, she *deserves* to be convicted; and, under the Serious Crime Act, she can be.

405 Below, § 9.1. Cp. Law Com. No. 300, *Inchoate Liability for Assisting and Encouraging Crime* (2006). When these offences were first contemplated by the Law Commission, they were intended to replace rather than supplement complicity: LCCP No. 131 (1993). See Sullivan, "Inchoate Liability for Assisting and Encouraging Crime—The Law Commission Report" [2006] *Crim LR* 1047.

406 "Trying to Help Another Person Commit a Crime" in Smith (ed.), *Criminal Law: Essays in Honour of J.C. Smith* (1987) 148, 148. Stark and Bock argue that it may be legitimate to criminalise attempted abetment whilst allowing attempted aid to be non-criminal, because the risks that the substantive crime will actually be perpetrated are (they suggest) generally higher in encouragement cases than in assistance cases: "Preparatory Offences" in Ambos *et al.* (eds.), *Core Concepts in Criminal Law and Justice* (2020) 54, 67–68.

407 An advantage of complicity liability more generally: Simester, "The Mental Element in Complicity" (2006) 122 *LQR* 578, 582.

408 Ashworth, "Taking the Consequences" in Shute, Gardner, and Horder (eds.), *Action and Value in Criminal Law* (1993) 107.

409 It might be thought that this is less true of cases in which S is present at the crime, rather than participating in it beforehand. That was, of course, part of the point of joint enterprise liability: Simester, "Accessory Liability and Common Unlawful Purposes" (2017) 133 *LQR* 73, 86–9.

The issue of moral luck was considered earlier, in § 6.5(ii). Suffice it to say here that moral luck of this variety is an indispensable aspect both of ordinary life and of the criminal law. It establishes what action S *does*, and therefore what S is guilty *for doing*.[410] Correspondingly, convicting S for complicity in a particular crime (when P commits it) captures the moral quality of the events in which S was involved better than would her conviction for an inchoate offence.[411] The difference between being convicted, say, of attempted murder and of murder may be a matter of luck (e.g. whether the defendant's shot misses; whether the bomb fails to explode). But it matters nonetheless. So too in secondary participation. Moreover, the luck is not random. The defendant *makes* her guilt a matter of luck, by attempting to kill or by attempting to aid another's crime. If other areas of the criminal law are properly subject to moral luck, so too is secondary liability.

### *(i) A causation analysis?*

An even more radical suggestion would be to embrace the "causal" analysis of complicity, identified by K.J.M. Smith.[412] Smith suggests that complicity liability is best understood as resting on a causal basis, i.e. that S is liable because of her causal contribution to the crime that P commits.[413] More recently, Michael Moore has argued that derivative liability is at odds with the fundamental principle that criminal liability should be based on findings of *personal* responsibility for one's own acts and omissions.[414] To be sure, the effects of one's conduct on the conduct of others can be taken into account, but only in terms of what one is personally responsible for. It should be added that, in terms of causal theory, Moore contends that it is perfectly possible to hold that something done by S can be a cause of something voluntarily done by P, such as when P kills V because he has been paid to do so by S.[415] On that relaxed view of causation in interpersonal relations, much of the territory currently covered by complicity could be remapped as forms of direct liability as a principal.

To adopt such an approach would require a much wider notion of causation than is usually employed by the criminal law. This would be implausible, as a matter of doctrine.[416] Even the most generous and broad version of causation is absent in some cases of secondary liability—at least, absent in any sense that leaves causation a meaningful concept. S abets P to offend, for instance, by communicating encouragement to P, whether or not the encouragement makes any difference to P.[417] Of course, surrounding complicity doctrine could be

[410] Edwards and Simester, "Crime, Blameworthiness, and Outcomes" (2019) 39 *OJLS* 50, 63–5.

[411] For a valuable general discussion of these questions, see Kadish, "Complicity, Cause and Blame" in *Blame and Punishment* (1987) 135.

[412] *A Modern Treatise on the Law of Criminal Complicity* (1991).

[413] The idea that liability should arise directly for D's *contributions* to causings of harm is also found in Kaiserman, "Against Accomplice Liability" (2021) *Oxford Studies in Philosophy of Law* 124, where it is developed in a rich philosophical context. Kaiserman argues for the replacement of complicity liability with a regime of substantive-inchoate offences, predicated upon D's "making a contribution" to the occurrence of harms such as death, grievous bodily injury, and the like.

[414] *Causation and Responsibility* (2009) chap. 13. See also Sullivan, "Doing Without Complicity" [2012] *J Commonwealth Crim Law* 199.

[415] *Causation and Responsibility* (2009) chaps. 11, 12.

[416] A causal analysis is rejected, for instance, by Smith, "Aid, Abet, Counsel, or Procure" in Glazebrook (ed.), *Reshaping the Criminal Law* (1978) 120; also *Hart and Honoré* 377–88.

[417] See, e.g., *Wilcox v Jeffery* [1951] 1 All ER 464 (DC); above, §§ 7.4(i)(b), 7.4(ii).

narrowed to compensate for a wider notion of causation, but a normative case for doing so would need to be presented. In our view, this case is not made out: a person may be sufficiently involved in the crime of another to merit condemnation and punishment without that involvement's generating any causal ripples.

Nonetheless, it is worth noting that the case law has sometimes suggested just such a widening of causation, of the sort that Smith's analysis would require. In *Empress*,[418] D was charged with causing a pollutant to enter the nearby river.[419] D had removed a protective device which would otherwise have contained overflows from the drum in which the pollutant was contained. Subsequently, an unknown person (T) opened the tap on the drum, whereupon the contents poured out and overflowed into the river. D's conviction was upheld by the House of Lords. T also caused the pollution, but his act was not a *novus actus* because, according to Lord Hoffmann, it was not "extraordinary":[420]

> "If the defendant did something which produced a situation in which the polluting matter could escape but a necessary condition of the actual escape which happened was also the act of a third party or a natural event, the justices should consider whether that act or event should be regarded as a normal fact of life or something extraordinary. If it was in the general run of things a matter of ordinary occurrence, it will not negative the causal effect of the defendant's acts, even if it was not foreseeable that it would happen to that particular defendant or take that particular form. If it can be regarded as something extraordinary, it will be open to the justices to hold that the defendant did not cause the pollution."

With respect to his Lordship, if this were a correct statement of the criminal law on causation, it would undermine almost entirely the need for complicity liability. The action of P will virtually never count as extraordinary where it is aided or abetted by S, and so will not count as a *novus actus*. Therefore it would almost always be possible to convict S as a principal for the crime that P commits.

Fortunately, as we saw when discussing *Empress* in § 4.2(iii)(e), the passage quoted is not a correct statement of the law. Notwithstanding Lord Hoffmann's purported denial, T's action was a *novus actus*. It was free, deliberate, and informed,[421] and met all the criteria of a fresh intervening act outlined in § 4.2(iii)(b). The reasoning in *Empress* is inconsistent with the case law discussed in that section;[422] it is, quite simply, wrong. The decision is also restricted to its specific statutory context.[423]

The core of Lord Hoffmann's error is his likening of deliberate intervening acts *by persons* to the interventions of nature. They are not the same, and are not governed by the same rules. Lord Hoffmann has correctly stated the relevant test for whether a natural event[424] (or a third party's action which is not free, deliberate, and informed)[425] counts as a *novus actus*. However, when T's intervention is free, deliberate, and informed, it is causally independent *whether or not* it is predictable, foreseeable, or ordinary.

418 *Empress Car Co (Abertillery) Ltd v National Rivers Authority* [1999] 2 AC 22.
419 Contrary to the then s. 85(1) of the Water Resources Act 1991.
420 [1999] 2 AC 22, 36.
421 *Kennedy (No. 2)* [2007] UKHL 38, [2008] 1 AC 269; *Pagett* (1983) 76 Cr App R 279, 288–9.
422 E.g. *Latif* [1996] 1 WLR 104, noted in § 4.2(iii)(c) (Case 2).
423 *Kennedy (No. 2)* [2007] UKHL 38, [2008] 1 AC 269, [15]–[16]; above, § 4.2(iii)(e).
424 Above, § 4.2(iii)(a).
425 Above, § 4.2(iii)(b).

The rationale for distinguishing human from natural intervention was discussed in § 4.2(iii)(b). In the context of secondary liability, recall the example with which we began this chapter:

> One fine September morning, Jim is discovered dead in his home. His skull has been crushed by a blow inflicted with a heavy object. The police are called. Upon investigation, they establish that he was murdered by his daughter, Alice, who killed him in order to receive her inheritance under his will. The baseball bat that Alice used to murder Jim belongs to Harry, who lent it to Alice for the purpose.

It matters who killed Jim. Alice did, not Harry. Neither was it a joint murder. Without special causal rules of some form for intervening human agents, we would be forced to say that both Harry and Alice caused Jim's death. But to do so would disregard the claim Harry and Alice each has to be treated as a separate, human, moral agent.

Why is secondary liability special? The answer is that, normally, liability ought to depend on a person's own actions and mental states. Rightly, the law is profoundly reluctant to put one person's criminal liability at the mercy of another person's deliberate choice. This is true as a general proposition. Consider, for example, the question posed by *Smith, Hogan, and Ormerod* in the context of liability for omissions:[426]

> "It is generally said that D must have done some act and that it is not enough that he stood still and obstructed V's passage like an inanimate object. But suppose D is sitting at the corner of a corridor with his legs stretched across it. He hears V running down the corridor and deliberately remains still with the intention that V, on turning the corner, shall fall over his legs. Why should this not be a battery?"

But if D has a duty to remove his leg, then V is granted a power to put D under that duty, simply by running toward him. The law that facilitates this has become a tool by which V may subject D's will to his own. More generally, under a legal system of this sort, D's choices and liability would be governed not merely by his own goals and values but equally by the whims of others.

So, too, for principles of causation and secondary liability. Free, deliberate, and informed interventions by third parties have a distinctive causal status because we do not want T to have the power to choose that D shall become guilty of a crime.[427] Secondary liability is a special case. The aider, the abettor, the counsellor, and the procurer each places her liability in the hands of P deliberately by her actions, and cannot complain when responsibility for P's crime is attributed also to her. However, S does not commit the offence as a principal, in the way that causation-based approaches to her liability may suggest. It *is* a special case, properly constituted by actus reus and mens rea elements that are quite distinct from those applying to the principal.

426 Above, § 4.1(i)(c).
427 Simester, "The Mental Element in Complicity" (2006) 122 *LQR* 578, 580–1.

# 8

# VICARIOUS AND CORPORATE LIABILITY

The previous chapter introduced the idea of one person's being held criminally responsible on the basis of conduct performed by another human agent. This chapter introduces two further forms of criminal liability via which D is held liable on the basis of conduct performed by a distinct agent, E.

The first is vicarious liability. To take a classic example (albeit that the law on this precise topic has moved on[1]), imagine that D is the licence holder at a pub, and E, one of her employees, serves alcohol to someone outside of the terms permitted by that licence. D can rightly claim that *she* has not personally performed the actus reus of an offence. She may just as convincingly establish doubt over whether she encouraged or assisted E's conduct, or even knew about it. Compounding matters, as far as secondary liability is concerned, criminal offences pertaining to licences can often only be perpetrated by the licence holder. In such situations, E *cannot* commit the offence: it follows that D cannot be a secondary party to its commission by E.[2] These difficulties had the potential to make criminal laws unenforceable around licensing requirements. In order to deal with these and similar problems, the criminal law has developed a limited doctrine whereby, under certain conditions, E's actus reus and mens rea could be attributed to D *vicariously*, making D liable for the relevant offence. The narrow limits of vicarious criminal liability are explored in § 8.1.

The remainder of the chapter considers a related phenomenon: corporate criminal liability. Suppose that D plc's employee, E, commits fraud in the course of her employment, with the intention of securing a lucrative contract for D plc. It might be thought insufficient simply to convict E of the relevant offence and leave it at that. After all, E is not necessarily "going rogue" (indeed, such wrongdoing might be common at D plc). Furthermore, D plc's competitors may have committed resources to avoiding precisely the wrongdoing that E has engaged in, thereby incurring an economic disadvantage. English criminal law has responded to such concerns but has shied away from a general doctrine of vicarious liability in the corporate context.[3] Instead, it requires proof of fault on the part of D plc before D plc can be convicted of a crime requiring mens rea.[4] Yet D plc is a legal construct: it cannot *itself* form mens rea states. The law has addressed this difficulty by permitting the fault of certain human agents—typically those concerned in its higher management—to be ascribed to the corporation, in order to hold the latter criminally liable. The principles under which such attributions can occur under English criminal law will be considered in § 8.2. It will also be

[1] See Licensing Act 2003, s. 136.

[2] Unless one of the exceptional cases of secondary liability noted in § 7.6(ii) applies.

[3] This position is in stark contrast to that adopted in the United States of America, on which see Silver, "When Should the Master Answer? Respondeat Superior and the Criminal Law" (2024) 18 *Crim Law and Philosophy* 89.

[4] As explained below, the position is more straightforward where D Ltd is accused of an offence of strict liability.

noted there that, in recent times, the legislature has sought to expand corporate criminal liability, particularly in the arena of economic crime.[5] These reforms fit awkwardly with the common law's traditional approach to corporate criminal liability.

## § 8.1 Vicarious liability

Tort law imposes extensive liability upon employers for torts committed by employees in the course of their employment[6] and for similar acts of those in positions akin to employment.[7] By contrast, "[t]he general principle is that in criminal law, in contrast to tort law, there is no doctrine of vicarious liability",[8] and so developments in tort are irrelevant for current purposes.[9] This difference in approach is unsurprising. The law of negligence, the mainstay of tort, aims predominantly to provide compensation for injury. It may well be unjust to an injured party for a judgment debt against the employee to go unsatisfied because of the employee's lack of means (what is known as a defendant's being "judgment proof"). Thus, the employer (who presumably will have the required means, or suitable insurance) is held liable to the injured party as well. There is no equivalent pressure to forge a general doctrine of vicarious liability in the criminal law. The traditional concern of the criminal law is with *individuals* who perpetrate or participate in crimes.[10]

The judicial disinclination to create a general, common law doctrine of vicarious criminal liability is clearly visible in *Huggins*.[11] D, the governor of a prison, was charged with aiding and abetting E, a warder, to murder V, a prisoner who had died on account of E's mistreatment. D was open to considerable criticism in the manner in which he discharged his office. Yet D had not caused V's death. Neither had he ordered, assisted, or encouraged E's mistreatment of V. In the absence of such personal involvement, D could not be liable for V's murder:[12]

> "It is not a point to be disputed . . . that in criminal cases the principal is not answerable for the act of the deputy, as he is in civil cases; they must each answer for their own acts and stand or fall by their own behaviour."

Despite this statement of general principle, it is inaccurate to state that there is *no* doctrine of criminal vicarious liability at common law. One example[13] of such liability is found in

[5] See the discussion of the Economic Crime and Corporate Transparency Act 2023, s. 196; below, § 8.2(v).

[6] See Atiyah, *Vicarious Liability* (1969); Giliker, *Vicarious Liability in Tort* (2013).

[7] For the Supreme Court's most recent restatement of the law on this area, see *Trustees of the Barry Congregation of Jehovah's Witnesses v BXB* [2023] UKSC 15, [2024] AC 567.

[8] *Smart Planning Limited v Brentwood Borough Council* [2018] EWHC 2372 (Admin), [24].

[9] On vicarious criminal liability generally, see Glazebrook, "Situational Liability" in Glazebrook (ed.), *Reshaping the Criminal Law* (1978) 108; Leigh, *Strict and Vicarious Liability* (1982); Williams, *CLGP* chap. 7.

[10] For critiques of the criminal law's preoccupation with individuals and its presuppositions of liability see Norrie, *Crime, Reason and History* (3rd ed., 2014) chaps. 2, 3; Wells, *Corporations and Criminal Responsibility* (2nd ed., 2001) chap. 3; Norrie, "'Simulacra of Morality?' Beyond the Ideal/Actual Antinomies of Criminal Justice" in Duff (ed.), *Philosophy and the Criminal Law* (1998) 101.

[11] (1730) 2 Str 883, 93 ER 915.

[12] *Ibid.*, 885, 917.

[13] At one time, the offence of criminal libel imposed vicarious liability on owners of newspapers for libels published by employees without requiring proof of any knowledge or instruction on the part of the proprietor: *Walter* (1799) 3 Esp 21, 170 ER 524; *Gutch, Fisher and Alexander* (1829) Mood & M 432, 173 ER 1214. That crime was abolished by Coroners and Justice Act 2009, s. 73.

the crime of public nuisance, where some authorities suggest that an employer may be liable for the act of an employee despite the lack of any instruction or knowledge in respect of the employee's act.[14] The authorities are not, however, univocal on the extent to which vicarious liability is available in cases of public nuisance.[15] Furthermore, public nuisance is an anomalous crime, which in some respects has more affinity with the law of tort than the law of crime.[16]

The position regarding statutory offences is more settled. There, it seems that there are now four ways in which vicarious or quasi-vicarious liability may arise:

(i) By express legislation.
(ii) Where the employee/agent's actions are, in civil law, the actions of the employer/principal (e.g. selling or possessing something in the course of employment). Properly, this is not an instance of vicarious liability, since it requires no attribution of another person's actus reus to the defendant. It may, however, be described loosely as generating vicarious liability, in the sense that D's liability is triggered by the conduct of another person. These cases generally involve offences of strict liability.
(iii) By the delegation doctrine. This arises where a licence is granted to a named individual to manage a property or activity within the terms of that licence. Should the individual to whom the licence is awarded delegate the performance of the terms of the licence to another person, then, in matters relevant to the licence, the conduct *and state of mind* of the other person is attributed to the delegator.[17]
(iv) Finally, there is a fourth, anomalous, category of cases where vicarious liability for acts of employees has been imposed without delegation.

In the following sections, we consider the defensibility of each of these categories of vicarious liability.

### *(i) Express legislation*

Parliament can explicitly impose vicarious liability, and sometimes this is done. For example, in relation to certain minor traffic offences, Parliament has passed legislation conclusively presuming the owner of a vehicle to have been the driver of that vehicle at the time of the offence.[18]

### *(ii) When the act of an employee/agent is that of the employer/principal*

There is a group of cases which are sometimes said to involve vicarious liability but which, on ultimate analysis, are cases of *strict* liability. Unfortunately, as we discussed in Chapter 6,

[14] *Stephens* (1865–6) LR 1 QB 702. The decision in *Stephens* is limited carefully: the court was anxious to avoid disturbing "the general rule that a principal is not answerable for the act of his agent" (at 709). See, also, *Medley* (1834) 6 C & P 292, [1824–34] All ER Rep 123.

[15] See, e.g., *Chisholm v Doulton* (1889) 22 QBD 736.

[16] In *Stephens* (1865–6) LR 1 QB 702, the proceedings were said to be civil "in substance" (708).

[17] *Allen v Whitehead* [1930] 1 KB 211 (DC); *Mullins v Collins* (1874) LR 9 QB 292.

[18] Road Traffic Offenders Act 1988, s. 64(5). An exception is made if D's car had been stolen: s. 64(6). See also the Highways Act 1980, s. 168(1).

English law quite often allows conviction without the need to establish mens rea on the part of D as to every aspect of the actus reus. The unfairness of strict liability can be exacerbated when the trigger for liability is a third party's conduct. Consider the offence of being the parent of a child of compulsory school age who fails to attend regularly at school.[19] In *Crump v Gilmore*,[20] the Divisional Court confirmed the conviction of D, the parent of E, where E made too few appearances at school. The Court took the offence to be one of strict liability, and therefore it was irrelevant that D neither knew nor had reason to know of E's sporadic school attendances.[21] Accordingly, D's liability was attributable to E's conduct but it was not truly vicarious; she was *directly* responsible on the basis of her involuntary acquisition of a particular status.[22] It is not unnatural to perceive such liability as vicarious, because D's liability arises out of the conduct of a third party. Legally, however, D's liability is imposed directly.

A similar analysis applies where D Ltd, a company, sells food not complying with food safety standards and thereby contravenes section 8 of the Food Safety Act 1990. Liability ensues if it can be proved the seller sold non-compliant food; there is no need to demonstrate any form of knowledge, recklessness, or negligence by anyone.[23] D Ltd sells food each time one of its shop assistants makes a sale to a customer and, if the food is non-compliant, D Ltd commits the offence. This situation is often described as an instance of vicarious liability, with liability imposed on the company in respect of the act of its assistant. But, structurally, the scenario may be analysed in the same manner as the facts of *Crump v Gilmore*. Each time a sale is made by an assistant to a customer, the company, as legal owner of the item sold, is selling to the customer. Thus the company commits the offence *directly*. An illustration is *Coppen v Moore (No. 2)*,[24] where a shop assistant sold food under a false description to a customer. The sale, in the legal sense of the term, was made by D, the employer and owner of the goods sold. The employer "was the seller, although not the actual salesman".[25] Consequently, since the offence of selling goods under a false trade description did not require any form of knowledge, recklessness, or negligence with regard to the falsity to be proved against D, liability was established against him on proof that the assistant had deliberately sold the item in the course of employment and a false description had been given of it. Strict liability offences concerning workplace health and safety can be analysed identically.[26]

[19] Formerly Education Act 1944, s. 39(1); now Education Act 1996, s. 444(1). For critical discussion of the line of authority imposing this extreme form of strict liability, see Horder, "Whose Values Should Determine when Liability Is Strict?" in Simester (ed.), *Appraising Strict Liability* (2005) 105; Sullivan, "Parents and Their Truanting Children: An English Lesson in Liability without Responsibility" (2010) 12 *Otago LR* 285.

[20] [1970] Crim LR 28 (DC).

[21] In *Barnfather v London Borough of Islington and Secretary of State for Education and Skills* [2003] EWHC 418 (Admin), [2003] 1 WLR 2318, D argued that to convict parents who were blameless with respect to their child's truanting contravened the presumption of innocence guaranteed by Art. 6(2) of the ECHR. The argument failed on the basis that the presumption of innocence does not engage with the elements of criminal liability, but merely with proof of those elements. It failed despite the recognition by Elias J ([50]–[57]) that parents would then be convicted of this stigmatic offence, with its implications of irresponsible parenting, in circumstances where securing regular attendance of their child at school was for practical purposes impossible.

[22] See the discussion in Glazebrook, "Situational Liability" in Glazebrook (ed.), *Reshaping the Criminal Law* (1978) 108, 108–14.

[23] Although s. 21 of the Act provides for a defence of due diligence with a reverse burden of proof.

[24] [1898] 2 QB 306.

[25] *Ibid.*, 313.

[26] See, e.g., *Gateway Foodmarkets Ltd* [1997] 3 All ER 78 (CA). See, further, Almond, "The Health and Safety at Work Act at 50: A 'Long Revolution' in Workplace Criminal Liability" [2025] *Crim LR* 377, 386–8.

That these are not cases of true vicarious liability can be demonstrated by a contrasting example of a selling offence requiring proof of mens rea. Consider, for instance, the old offence of selling intoxicating liquor to an under-age person.[27] Here D, the owner of the liquor (and the licensee), made a sale each time liquor was sold by one of his employees. D would, however, only have been liable for the offence if *he* knew that the customer was under-age (direct personal liability), or if he had delegated the running of the licensed premises to the employee who then knowingly sold intoxicating liquor to an under-age customer (a case of true vicarious liability, as explained in the next section).

A difficult point is raised where the employee acts outside the scope of guidance given by the employer. In *Coppen v Moore*, the employer had expressly instructed his employees to describe the ham as "breakfast ham", rather than ham from a specific region. An employee sold the meat as a regional ("Scotch") ham. The employer's express instructions did not prevent liability from being imposed upon him. It was still *he* who (in law) had made the sale. What is clear, however, is that where an employee does something she has *no* right to do, liability will not be imposed upon the employer.[28] In *Adams v Camfoni*,[29] for example, it was held that a master was not liable when a servant boy, who had no authority to do so, supplied his master's liquor to a customer out of hours. Similarly, if a cleaner, lacking any authority to do so, opens a hotel bar outside the legal hours and sells liquor to customers, the licensee will not be liable.[30] The cleaner's acts are clearly outside the scope of his employment or any implicit permission from the licensee who employs him. Contrast the employee in *Coppen v Moore*, who was arguably acting closely enough to the manner in which he was employed to act to justify the vicarious imposition of liability to his employer.

### *(iii) Delegation*

Vicarious liability based on the principle of delegation is a judicial response to a perceived legislative deficiency. Suppose that, pursuant to legislation, a licence is granted to a named person of presumed good character. Typically, the legislation will be silent about the legal position if the licence holder devolves responsibility for compliance with the terms of that licence to someone else. Of course, if the legislation allows criminal liability for breaches of the licence terms to be imposed on the delegate, enforcing such offences is possible notwithstanding the fact of delegation.[31] Frequently, however, the only person who may commit the offence is the licensee. For instance, section 44 of the Metropolitan Police Act 1839 states that it is an offence for:

> "every person who shall have or keep any house, shop, room or place of public resort within the metropolitan police district wherein . . . refreshments of any kind shall be sold . . . and who shall knowingly permit or suffer prostitutes or persons of notoriously bad character to meet together and remain therein."

[27] See, now, Licensing Act 2003, s. 146 (no knowledge of the purchaser's age is required).

[28] This parallels the position in tort law: see *Various Claimants v Wm Morrison Supermarkets plc* [2020] UKSC 12, [2020] AC 989.

[29] [1929] 1 KB 95 (DC).

[30] See *Jull v Treanor* (1896) 14 NZLR 513.

[31] For instance, the Licensing Act 2003, which repeals much but not all of the previous licensing legislation, creates offences relating to the sale of alcohol on licensed premises which can be committed by bar staff as well as the licensee, removing the need to resort to the delegation principle to enforce the terms of the licence.

It will be noted that the persons who may commit offences under this provision are the owner, tenant, or keeper of a house, shop, room, or place of public resort. Prima facie, it must be a person within that class who *knowingly* permits or suffers prostitutes, etc. In the leading case of *Allen v Whitehead*,[32] D, the occupier and licensee of a café, was charged with an offence under section 44, and defended himself on the basis that, as an occasional visitor to his own café, he was unaware that his manager (E) was allowing prostitutes to remain on the premises. Indeed, D had instructed E not to allow this to happen and had arranged for notices to be placed in the café warning prostitutes off. Confirming D's conviction, Lord Hewart CJ held that, if D had delegated to E the conduct of the café, "knowledge in the manager was knowledge in the keeper of the house". Were it otherwise, the Chief Justice reasoned, "this statute would be rendered nugatory".[33] *Allen v Whitehead* is therefore best understood as being a decision based on the practicalities of enforcement, and the belief that licencees should not be able to evade their responsibilities by delegating duties to someone else.

In so ruling, Lord Hewart CJ confirmed a line of authority that, though varying in expression and emphasis, can best be explained as imposing vicarious liability based on a delegation principle. This line of authority was reviewed by the House of Lords in *Vane v Yiannopoullos*.[34] E, a waitress employed by D, knowingly sold drinks to customers who were not ordering a meal, in contravention of the terms of D's licence. Once again, D had not encouraged or known about E's behaviour. The Lords did not accept the delegation principle enthusiastically. Lords Reid, Evershed and Morris suggested that the delegation principle was a judicial gloss designed to respond to the practicalities of enforcement,[35] whilst Lord Donovan opined that difficulties in convicting licence holders should be resolved by Parliament, not the courts.[36] Lord Hodson expressed no view on the legitimacy of the delegation principle. As it happens, all these opinions were *obiter* since it was found on the facts that no delegation had occurred: D, the licensee, remained on the premises, albeit on the upper floor of his restaurant, while E served the drinks two floors below. Their Lordships took the view that a delegation required a *total* devolvement to someone else of responsibility for keeping to the terms of the licence. This was not the case here. D was involved in the running of his business, even if he could not be everywhere at once. Accordingly, he had not contravened the terms of his licence because he was unaware of the illicit sales by E. Only if he had *totally* delegated management to E would E's knowledge have been attributed to him.[37]

This limitation is sound. Even the most conscientious of persons cannot be attending to their legal responsibilities at all hours. If D has gone to bed to sleep, or has left her post to pick up her children from school, she will not normally have made a complete delegation of her responsibilities to someone else, even if she leaves a deputy in charge in the meantime. Ultimate authority and recourse will remain with her. In *Bradshaw v Ewart-James*,[38]

[32] [1930] 1 KB 211.
[33] *Ibid.*, 220.
[34] [1965] AC 486.
[35] *Ibid.*, 496 (Lord Reid), 500, 504 (Lord Evershed), 507 (Lord Morris).
[36] *Ibid.*, 512.
[37] See, too, *Winson* [1969] 1 QB 371 (CA).
[38] [1983] QB 671 (DC).

for example, it was held that a ship's master had not delegated his responsibilities as master when he took himself off to bed leaving the first mate with temporary responsibility for the vessel. Such temporary delegations are not enough for vicarious criminal liability to arise. Again: only a complete delegation of authority will suffice. This approach to delegation has been attacked.[39] It has been regarded as paradoxical that, if D is miles away, she should be fixed with knowledge on the basis of delegation, but can evade the attribution of her employee's knowledge when she is much closer to the action. But there is no paradox. Let us accept, for the moment, the legitimacy of vicarious criminal liability based on delegation. Where D, the licence holder, remains involved in the management of the licensed premises, it is entirely appropriate that his criminal liability be determined by reference to his own culpability. If liability requires knowledge, D must be proved to have knowledge. By contrast, if D accepts the obligations of a licence by becoming a licence holder, but leaves it to another person to ensure compliance with its terms, there need be no inconsistency in fixing D with the delegate's knowledge. D has assumed the risk. That said, such reasoning will not always resolve liabilities fairly. D1 may take great care in appointing a delegate but be fixed with any knowledge the delegate acquires. Contrast D2, who remains on the premises but manages them very slackly. The knowledge of D2's employees cannot be imputed to her. It cannot be said, then, that the delegation principle ensures an even-handed pattern of enforcement of licence conditions.

Given the potential harshness of the doctrine of vicarious liability via delegation, it is unsurprising that it has come under attack in the courtroom as well as in the literature. In *Winson*,[40] defence counsel argued that, given the division of opinion amongst their Lordships in *Vane* concerning the propriety of the doctrine, the Court of Appeal was free to reject it. The Court of Appeal demurred, ruling that vicarious liability based on delegation was too firmly established to have been unsettled by the *obiter* doubts expressed in *Vane*. Further, the Court opined that the doctrine was justified by the need to prevent a licensee from evading her responsibilities by delegating them to another.[41] As long as the relevant statute can be construed consistently with the doctrine of delegation, then vicarious liability remains a possibility.[42]

From the above discussion, two principles can be discerned. First, the delegation approach will be employed only where the statutory provision would otherwise be impractical to enforce. Secondly, the delegation principle will only be applied where there was a total delegation of authority from D to another person.

These principles cast significant doubt on the correctness of the decision of the Divisional Court in *Howker v Robinson*.[43] In that case, D's conviction for knowingly selling alcohol to a person under the age of 18 was upheld. The sale was made by E, an employee who served in the lounge bar. At the time of the sale, D was in the public bar. The first problem is that the offence in question was an offence not exclusive to licensees; it could also be committed by employees, undermining the "rendered nugatory" rationale of vicarious liability

[39] Pace, "Delegation: A Doctrine in Search of a Definition" [1982] *Crim LR* 627.
[40] [1969] 1 QB 371 (CA).
[41] *Ibid.*, 382.
[42] See, further, *St Regis Paper Company Ltd* [2011] EWCA Crim 2527, [2012] 1 Cr App R 14, [28].
[43] [1973] QB 178 (DC).

discussed above. It is useful to contrast *Howker* with the case of *Qureshi*.[44] D, a landlord, was charged with interfering with the peace and comfort of a residential occupier.[45] The acts complained of were done by members of D's family, not by D. The offence can, however, be committed by the landlord or a landlord's "agent". The Court of Appeal ruled that D's family members were his agents, precluding any possibility of vicarious liability for the offence on the part of D.[46] A similar approach should have been adopted in *Howker*.

The second difficulty with *Howker* is that the magistrates had made a finding of fact that there had been a delegation of authority to E in respect of the lounge bar, a finding which the Divisional Court refused to disturb on the ground that the finding was not plainly unreasonable. Yet it emerges from the discussion above that, as a matter of law, the delegation principle will come into play only if D has *completely* devolved to another his obligation to ensure compliance with the terms of the licence. There seems to have been no evidence of that in *Howker*. D was serving in the public bar while E was in the lounge bar. There was nothing in the facts to suggest that the lounge bar was in any sense E's "domain", where he enjoyed total managerial authority. D could not be everywhere; E was just a barman. *Howker* is wrong and should not be followed.

### *(iv) Anomalous cases of liability for an employee's act*

We turn now to consider other, anomalous, cases in which an employer has been found liable for the conduct of an employee. In straightforward cases such as selling or possession there can be no objection to attributing an actus reus to D. Activities like "selling" and "possessing" are, in law, technical terms. They are legally constructed activities whose application is determined by the civil law. Thus it comes as no surprise that, legally, one can sell or possess through the instrumentality of others. The injustice, if any, does not arise from the way in which the actus reus is established. Rather, it arises from the imposition of strict liability.

The picture changes where the actus reus is not a technical legal act, but seemingly something that requires personal conduct on the part of D. That necessary element of liability is missing if the conduct proved was the conduct of someone else. If D is charged as a principal offender with a driving offence, she can quite properly complain if the driving in question was E's driving and not her own. The courts have therefore required the driving to be by D if she is to be convicted as a principal offender of a driving offence.[47]

Unfortunately, the courts have not always adopted this sensible approach. In *James & Son Ltd v Smee*,[48] D, a company, claimed that "using" a vehicle required the same degree of personal involvement as driving a vehicle. A company employee had used a vehicle with defective brakes in the course of his employment. The condition of the brakes was not known to (the management of) the defendant company. The company was charged under the Motor Vehicles (Construction and Use) Regulations 1951 with "using or causing or permitting to be used . . . a motor vehicle which did not comply with [these] regulations". The company conceded that it may have "caused" or "permitted" the vehicle to be used, but liability could

[44] [2011] EWCA Crim 1584, [2012] 1 WLR 694.
[45] Contrary to s. 1(3A) of the Protection from Eviction Act 1977.
[46] Of course, D might have been liable as a secondary party to his agent's offence, but that was not argued by the prosecution.
[47] *Richmond London Borough Council v Pinn & Wheeler Ltd* [1989] RTR 354 (DC).
[48] [1955] 1 QB 78 (DC).

not be imposed under those heads because, under the statute, proof of causing or permitting a vehicle to be used in a defective condition required proof that D was aware of the condition of the vehicle. Nonetheless, the Divisional Court imposed liability on the company for "using" the vehicle.[49] That term, as the Court interpreted it, simply required the vehicle to be used by an employee in the course of employment. It did not require any knowledge, on the part of the company's management, of the state of the vehicle. In its statutory context, this is a strained interpretation. The juxtaposition of the term "using" and "causing or permitting to be used" strongly suggests that a personal physical act (D himself/itself using) is being contrasted with a permitting or causing of the same physical act (of using by another person). This interpretation would have required that the vehicle was being driven by someone sufficiently senior within the company to be identified with it (using the principles discussed in § 8.2(iii), below). This would have rendered corporate liability for the "use" limb of the offence extremely narrow. In the event, the Divisional Court seemingly ignored this aspect of corporate liability and considered that a use of the vehicle by an employee in the course of employment was also a use by the employer company.

The decision in *James & Son Ltd v Smee* appears to be confined to the employer–employee relationship. It has been held that the owner of a vehicle does not "use" it when he lends it to a friend,[50] nor when it is taken by a stranger and used for an unlicensed purpose.[51] This suggests that *James & Son Ltd v Smee* is a case of true vicarious liability, and one outside the sphere of managerial delegation. It is a case of an attributed actus reus, not an example of an actus reus requirement that can be fulfilled by the conduct of someone other than the defendant.

An even starker example of this phenomenon is *Slatcher v George Mence Smith Ltd*,[52] where the "act" of an employee was taken, in law, to be the "act" of the employer. One could not imagine a word more redolent of personal involvement than "act". In the pungent words of Glanville Williams, "a mere statement of this decision is sufficient to show that something must have gone wrong with the reasoning".[53]

As a result of the decision of the House of Lords in *Environmental Agency v Empress Car Co. (Abertillery) Ltd*,[54] in substance the scope of unacknowledged vicarious liability has been extended even beyond employees. Recall that the defendant company was found to have "caused" pollution to a river when the immediate cause of the pollution was the act of an unknown intruder who had turned the tap of the oil tank sited on the company's land. We will not rehearse again here our criticisms of the finding that the mere presence of oil on the company's land was a cause of the pollution. It suffices to say that, if those criticisms are well founded, then in substance the company was made vicariously liable for the intruder's act. Such a finding is deeply unsettling, in the absence of any prior relationship between D

[49] See, too, *Evans v Dell* [1937] 1 All ER 349 (DC).
[50] *Crawford v Haughton* [1972] 1 WLR 572 (DC).
[51] *Strutt v Cliff* [1911] 1 KB 1 (DC).
[52] [1951] 2 KB 631 (DC). In a prosecution under s. 2 of the Merchandise Marks Act 1887, D was entitled to a defence (per s. 2(2)(c)) if he could establish "that otherwise he had acted innocently". The Divisional Court disallowed the defence because, although D personally had acted innocently, its employee had not. See also *Sopp v Long* [1970] 1 QB 518 (DC), where D "caused" a customer to receive an illegal measurement of whisky, even though it was E (a barmaid whom D had never met) who had poured the drink (in an establishment that D had never entered).
[53] *CLGP* 222–3.
[54] [1999] 2 AC 22; discussed above, § 4.2(iii)(e).

and the person whose conduct is to be attributed to her/it. This is particularly true when that person might have been attempting to harm, rather than further, D's interests.

### *(v) Summary*

We have argued that the occurrence of true vicarious liability is confined to: (i) statutes which expressly impose such liability; and (ii) to situations where a duty of compliance with the requirements of a licence or other regulatory regime has been completely delegated, and vicarious liability is required to ensure the practical enforcement of the relevant statutory provision. There are some cases of strict liability which may be described as cases of vicarious liability, but these merely demonstrate that certain activities, such as selling or possessing, can be done through the agency of others. By contrast, other verbs imply personal involvement. A company, for instance, can sell a car through a salesperson but does not itself "use" or "drive" a car when a company car is used or driven by a company employee.

However, even in cases where the actus reus seemingly requires personal agency, D has sometimes been held vicariously liable without there being any finding of delegation. Decisions such as *James & Son Ltd v Smee* have attributed to D the actus reus of an offence which requires personal involvement even though D was not personally involved. Such cases involve a form of vicarious liability. An activity such as driving can only be *attributed* to a person who was not in fact driving. This last form of vicarious criminal liability is *ad hoc* and unacknowledged even when imposed. It ought not to exist as part of English criminal law.

### *(vi) Reform*

In its Draft Criminal Code, the Law Commission provided no statutory version of the delegation principle. Under the Code, vicarious liability would only be imposed through express statutory wording.[55] This change would have been welcome. The judicial creation of the delegation principle is an undiscriminating way of enforcing the duties of licensees. As we have acknowledged, there is some reason to discriminate between cases where D retains a responsibility for complying with the terms of the licence, and cases where he wholly delegates the discharging of his duties to another person. Yet this is, ultimately, an unsatisfactory distinction. As noted above, D1 may remain on his premises, manage his business inattentively, and take no care in the discharge of his legal duties. Conversely, D2 may take particular care in appointing a delegate and have good reason to think that the appointed person will be scrupulous in her observance of the delegated duties. Yet the former case is treated more indulgently than the latter.

The Law Commission scrutinised the delegation principle further in a 2010 consultation paper.[56] It proposed there that criminal liability based on the fact of delegation, without

[55] Law Com. No. 177, *A Criminal Code for England and Wales* (1989) cl. 29(2).

[56] LCCP No. 195, *Criminal Liability in Regulatory Contexts* (2010) part 7. At the time of writing, some aspects of the Commission's proposals have been implemented through Government guidance to departments. Other aspects of the project were placed on hold until a project on corporate liability could be undertaken. That project produced a discussion paper and an options paper, rather than proceeding to a full report with full-throated recommendations for reform: see *Corporate Criminal Liability: A Discussion Paper* (2021); *Corporate Criminal Liability: An Options Paper* (2022). As explained further below, the result has been a failure by the legislature to grasp the nettle and bring coherence to this area of the law. Indeed, as explained below in § 8.2(v), the position has if anything worsened in the aftermath of the options paper.

more, should be abolished. In its place should be an offence of failing to prevent an offence by a person to whom the running of the business has been delegated.[57] The proposal was influenced by the offence of failure by a commercial organisation to prevent bribery done on its behalf.[58] Under that offence, the commercial organisation incurs liability if its failure to prevent bribery reflects an omission to have adequate procedures to prevent persons associated with the organisation from committing bribery offences on its behalf. Although the culpability for this offence is of a lower order than the culpability for bribery itself, at least some form of managerial failure (in effect, structural negligence) is required. If applied generally (and not just in relation to specified offences, which is the legislature's present approach[59]), this technique would therefore represent an improvement on present liability based upon the mere fact of delegation.[60]

## § 8.2 Corporate liability[61]

### *(i) The justification of corporate liability*

Since the mid-nineteenth century, it has been established that companies may commit crimes of strict liability.[62] Unless there is a clear legislative intent to the contrary,[63] the word "person" in legislation includes "a body of persons corporate or unincorporate".[64] Where no culpability is required in the definition of the offence, the fact that a company is, in law, a separate "person" distinct from its directors, employees, and shareholders presents no barrier to the imposition of criminal liability. For example, environmental legislation may require that the carbon levels of smoke emissions must not exceed a given level, a matter of strict liability.[65] If the smoke emissions of a factory owned by D plc should exceed permitted levels, then D plc, as owner of the factory, will be liable straightforwardly for the offence.

Historically, there was a view that companies, by virtue of their artificial nature, were incapable of being guilty of any crime because guilt was perceived to be exclusively a human

57 LCCP No. 195, *Criminal Liability in Regulatory Contexts* (2010) para. 7.58.

58 Bribery Act 2010, s. 7. See Sullivan, "The Bribery Act 2010—An Overview" [2011] *Crim LR* 87, 95–6, 98; Gentle, "The Corporate Offence" [2011] *Crim LR* 101.

59 Alongside the corporate bribery offence, there now exist offences concerning the failure to prevent tax evasion and fraud: Criminal Finances Act 2017, ss. 45–46; Economic Crime and Corporate Transparency Act 2023, s. 199.

60 Cp. Ashworth, "A New Generation of Omissions Offences?" [2018] *Crim LR* 354. See, further, Horder and Watts, "The Scope of Liability for Failure to Prevent Economic Crime" [2021] *Crim LR* 851.

61 Wells, "Corporate Criminal Liability: A Ten Year Review" [2014] *Crim LR* 849; List and Pettit, *Group Agency* (2011); Gobert and Punch, *Rethinking Corporate Crime* (2003); Wells, *Corporations and Criminal Responsibility* (2nd ed., 2001); Clarkson, "Kicking Corporate Bodies and Damning Their Souls" (1996) 59 *MLR* 557; Sullivan, "The Attribution of Culpability to Limited Companies" (1996) 55 *CLJ* 515; Sullivan, "Expressing Corporate Guilt" (1995) 15 *OJLS* 281; Gobert, "Corporate Criminality: New Crimes for the Times" [1994] *Crim LR* 722; Fisse and Braithwaite, *Corporations, Crime and Accountability* (1993). Corporate criminal liability was, and in some cases continues to be, resisted to a far greater extent in civil law jurisdictions. See: Pieth and Ivory (eds.), *Corporate Criminal Liability* (2011); Dsouza and Schmitt-Leonardy, "Old and New Tracks for Corporate Criminal Liability" in Duff et al (eds.), *Core Concepts in Criminal Law and Criminal Justice* (Vol. 3, 2025) 179.

62 *Birmingham and Gloucester Railway Co.* (1842) 3 QB 223, 114 ER 492.

63 For discussion of whether a contrary statutory intention exists in the context of harassment, contrary to s. 2(1) of the Protection from Harassment Act 1997, see *Kosar v Bank of Scotland plc T/A Halifax* [2011] EWHC 1050 (Admin).

64 Interpretation Act 1978, sched. 1, pt. 1.

65 Clean Air Act 1993, s. 2.

property.[66] That view did not survive long into the era of industrialisation and the advent of the joint-stock company. The application of regulatory law to limited companies is now almost completely uncontroversial. It is arguable whether such regulation should ever take the form of strict liability, but hardly anyone objects specifically to the fact that *companies* are held liable for such offences. Indeed, given the overwhelming predominance of the limited company in industrial, transport, and commercial activity,[67] corporate liability is essential for the efficacy of any legislation concerned with pollution, health, safety, and trading standards.

Nonetheless, some writers have queried the need for any form of corporate criminal liability, even with respect to regulatory law.[68] It has been objected that the fines paid by the company ultimately will be borne by the shareholders who are not, in any sense, responsible for the offence. However, this stance overlooks the nature of an investment as a shareholder in a limited company. An investment on the terms of limited liability is a legally created privilege, and the terms on which sums of capital can be aggregated and deployed have, from the controversial inception of limited companies, been a matter of continuing legislative scrutiny and revision. The funds of limited companies are subject to a host of different financial constraints imposed in (what is taken to be) the public interest. Investments must be made on the assumption that companies will not seek illegitimate competitive advantages by non-compliance with regulatory law. From that perspective, there is no difference in principle between fines and other forms of financial exaction (e.g. by a regulator for underperformance on agreed targets). The impact of fines on investors, arising from non-compliance with the law, even the criminal law, is merely one of a large number of investment risks. In our view, it is not enough to punish the individuals responsible for breaching regulations. In fairness to those companies which commit resources to meet their legal obligations, companies found in breach should be fined at least to the extent necessary to correct any competitive advantage gained thereby.

In principle, then, corporations should be capable of being held criminally liable. The next sections explain how, practically, such liability is imposed under English law. As we shall see, this is an area rife with conceptual confusion.

### *(ii) Crimes of strict liability*

For crimes of strict liability, the artificial personality of a limited company poses few conceptual difficulties in imposing corporate liability. In one sense, all corporate liability can be spoken of as vicarious liability, because corporate conduct is ultimately referable to some form of human conduct.[69] When the corporately owned factory chimney belches pollution, it does so as a product of a set of acts and omissions by human agents. In legal terms,

[66] In the famous words of Edward, First Baron Thurlow, a company has "no soul to be damned and no body to be kicked": Mencken, *A New Dictionary of Quotations* (1942) 223.

[67] As of September 2025, there are over 4.5 million incorporated companies in England and Wales: https://www.gov.uk/government/statistics/incorporated-companies-in-the-uk-july-to-september-2025/incorporated-companies-in-the-uk-july-to-september-2025.

[68] See, e.g., the view of the former authors of Smith and Hogan, *Criminal Law* (10th ed., 2002) 207: "the necessity for corporate criminal liability awaits demonstration".

[69] Although this claim may be disputed, a matter to be discussed below, § 8.2(vi).

however, companies will commit offences of strict liability directly.[70] The company, itself, will fulfil the offence specifications of regulatory crimes (in terms of selling, leasing, possessing, using, etc.), if done in the course of the business of the company.[71] This type of case is discussed in more detail above, in § 8.1(ii).

### *(iii) Crimes of mens rea*

#### *(a) The policy issue: how is corporate culpability possible?*

For crimes where forms of mens rea are required—defrauding the revenue, acting dishonestly when appropriating property belonging to another with an intent permanently to deprive, killing V by an act of gross negligence, etc.—some legal means of attributing the requisite mens rea to the company is required. This raises a potential issue. The view might be taken that "culpability", in the non-legal sense of the term, is an entirely human property; something that a corporation, with its inherently artificial form, cannot possess.[72] Acceptance of that view leads to two possible approaches to corporate liability for crimes of mens rea. On the first view, any attempt to hold companies responsible for what may be termed "culpability crimes" is regarded as a mistake. On the second view, corporate liability for such crimes is allowed, but it is recognised that the attribution of culpability to companies is a matter of form rather than substance (for companies cannot *really* be culpable). This fiction is engaged in in order to secure whatever consequentialist returns may be had. On this second approach (the approach by and large taken by English law), the conduct and state of mind of an individual is attributed to the company, thus becoming *corporate* conduct and a *corporate* state of mind (while remaining also, for legal purposes, the conduct and state of mind of the given individual). So, to take defrauding the revenue as an example, if E, an employee of D plc, submits a dishonest tax return by misrepresenting D plc's income in the course of his employment with D plc, it may be possible to attribute E's conduct and culpability to D plc, allowing both D plc and E to be convicted of tax fraud.[73] In so doing, the law does not claim that D plc *actually* itself exhibited culpability.

A radically different approach is in order if the view is taken, as increasingly it is, that companies are culpability-bearing agents in their own right, manifesting an inherently *corporate* agency, and a distinct culpability not reducible to human agency. If corporations *as corporations* can possess intentionality, concoct schemes to injure or defraud, etc., then rules and doctrines must be crafted to capture (in a forensically manageable way) this form of culpability.

In the next sections, we consider how liability for crimes of mens rea is imposed on companies in English law, noting its traditional adoption of the view that corporations

[70] Although the courts do always not seem particularly concerned with this technical detail—see, e.g., *R (Highbury Poultry Farm Produce Ltd) v Telford Magistrates' Court and CPS* [2018] EWHC 3122 (Admin), [94]: "Ultimately, I do not think that it really matters whether the conceptual route to corporate liability under the [relevant] provision is seen as being vicarious or direct".

[71] There is also, often, the potential for officers of the corporation to be held liable for such offences if they were committed by the corporation with their consent or connivance, or as a result of their neglect. See, e.g., Legal Services Act 2007, s. 197(1).

[72] Wolf, "The Legal and Moral Responsibility of Organisations" in Pennock and Chapman (eds.), *Criminal Justice* (1985) 267.

[73] *DPP v Kent and Sussex Contractors, Limited* [1944] KB 146 (DC).

themselves cannot commit crimes (and so human agents' conduct and culpability must be ascribed to the corporation) and its more recent moves in the direction of recognising corporate fault as a distinct conceptual possibility.

### (b) *Attributing culpability to corporations: the doctrine of identification*

The idea that forms the basis of the identification doctrine is a simple one. The identification doctrine, sometimes known as the *alter ego* or "directing mind" principle, takes the conduct and state of mind of certain high-ranking corporate officials to be the conduct and state of mind of the corporation itself. If, for example, a company director, of sufficient stature to be regarded as a corporate *alter ego*, were to form a dishonest intent in the course of transacting company business, his company would possess that same dishonest intent.[74]

This anthropomorphic doctrine first surfaced in the civil case of *Lennards Carrying Co Ltd v Asiatic Petroleum Ltd*.[75] The defendants were being sued by plaintiff cargo-owners for the loss of cargo caused by the unseaworthiness of a vessel managed by Lennards. Under applicable legislation, Lennards' liability in damages would have been capped unless it could be proved that the loss was attributable to their "fault". As interpreted by Lord Haldane for the Privy Council, "fault" required personal fault on the part of Lennards, the company that managed the ship on behalf of its owners. This fault was supplied by Mr Lennard, the managing director of Lennards, who was aware of the condition of the vessel yet permitted it to be taken to sea. According to Lord Haldane:[76]

> "Mr Lennard was the directing mind of the company . . . his action was the action of the company itself . . . [his] fault is not merely that of a servant or agent for whom the company is liable upon the footing *respondent superior* but somebody for whom the company is liable because his action is the very action of the company itself."

This identification of high-ranking officials with the company itself was adopted into the criminal law in the cases of *DPP v Kent and Sussex Contractors*,[77] *ICR Haulage Ltd*,[78] and *Moore v Bresler*.[79] In those cases, companies were held liable (for intending to deceive the revenue and for conspiracy to defraud) after the court identified the culpable states of mind of corporate officials with their companies. The decision in *Moore* is particularly noteworthy because of the flexible manner in which the identification doctrine was applied: the tax returns that implicated the company were made by a company secretary and a branch sales manager. (As will be seen below, there is reason to think that such flexibility would no longer be needed under the identification doctrine;[80] such cases nowadays may well be caught by supplementary legislative rules.)

74 A prosecution of the company on this basis would not be an abuse of process if the relevant director was not himself charged with an offence: *Alstom Network UK Ltd* [2019] EWCA Crim 1318, [2019] 2 Cr App R 34.
75 [1915] AC 705 (PC).
76 *Ibid.*, 713, 714.
77 [1944] KB 146 (DC).
78 [1944] KB 551 (CA).
79 [1944] 2 All ER 515 (DC).
80 The decision in *Moore* was viewed sceptically in *St Regis Paper Company Ltd* [2011] EWCA Crim 2527, [2012] 1 Cr App R 14, [24]–[25].

Over time, the identification doctrine became well embedded into both civil and criminal law, and an increasingly liberal approach was taken to the question of which corporate officials could be identified with the company.[81] This liberality was checked by the House of Lords in *Tesco Supermarkets Ltd v Nattrass*.[82] There, it was ruled that only individuals at the apex of the corporate hierarchy could be identified with the company. Lord Diplock took a rigid and formal approach to this question: only officials granted plenary authority (i.e. the power to take decisions) over a company's affairs in the articles of association (basically, the company's constitution) could be so identified. For him, that would include the board of directors making decisions on behalf of the company, together with the chief executive and, possibly, any other executive possessing a plenary authority for the activity at issue in a particular case.[83] Lord Reid, too, required a plenary authority, but was prepared to look at substance as well as form. He did not make a grant of authority in the articles of association a precondition for identification.[84]

The narrowness of the identification doctrine post-*Tesco Supermarkets Ltd v Nattrass* is exemplified by the decision in *Redfern*.[85] There, Dunlop (Europe) Ltd was charged with knowingly exporting combat equipment to Iran in contravention of an embargo that formed part of agreed sanctions. The relevant facts were known to the European sales manager, but he was considered insufficiently important in Dunlop's scheme of things to be identified with the company. Similarly, in *P&O European Ferries (Dover) Ltd*,[86] P&O Ltd was charged with manslaughter following the 1987 Zeebrugge ferry disaster (in which the *Herald of Free Enterprise* sank, resulting in the drowning of 193 passengers and crew). The ship's master was ruled not to be sufficiently senior within P&O Ltd to be identified with the company.

One thing in favour of the identification doctrine is that, provided it is confined to the very top echelon of corporate officials, the doctrine operates with a fair measure of predictability. In *Tesco*, Lord Diplock reasoned that this exclusive focus on top management was integral to the very nature of the doctrine.[87] He insisted that it involved a form of *direct* corporate responsibility in contradistinction to vicarious liability. As the doctrine identifies the very state of mind of the company itself, that entity is to be located solely at the top—the very "brain and nerve centre" of the company in Lord Denning's quaint idiom.[88] Yet scrutiny of the way that the doctrine works reveals it, in substance, to be very close to vicarious liability. The company's culpability is a derivative of human culpability. Within the doctrine's own terms, a finding that the company possessed the mens rea for an offence may only be made if some decision-making organ or individual of sufficient seniority possessed the mens rea for the offence. This narrowness is the doctrine's major limitation in terms of obtaining corporate convictions,[89] and the driver of modern reform.

[81] E.g. *The Lady Gwendolen* [1965] 3 WLR 91 (CA).
[82] [1972] AC 153.
[83] *Ibid*., 199.
[84] *Ibid*., 171.
[85] (1992) 13 Cr App R (S) 709.
[86] (1991) 93 Cr App R 72.
[87] [1972] AC 153, 199–200.
[88] *Bolton (Engineering) Co Ltd v Graham & Sons* [1957] 1 QB 159, 172 (CA).
[89] For critical discussion, see Dsouza, "The Corporate Agent in Criminal Law—An Argument for Comprehensive Identification" (2020) 79 *CLJ* 91. Dsouza contends that corporations should be "identified" with all their officers and employees, so long as they were acting within the scope of their authority. As will be explained below, the law has never gone this far.

*(c) Vicarious corporate liability*

It has been seen that the narrowness of the identification doctrine frustrates effective prosecution of corporations for offences involving mens rea. Perhaps understandably, the courts have at times sought to evade the strictures of the identification doctrine. In *Tesco Supermarkets plc v Brent LBC*,[90] an issue arose concerning whether Tesco "knew or had reasonable cause to believe" that a hirer of an age-restricted video was under the age of 18. This was a matter of culpability which, one would have suspected, would be resolved under the terms of the identification doctrine.[91] The Divisional Court nevertheless confirmed the company's conviction, ruling that the state of mind of the checkout assistant could be identified with Tesco. Staughton LJ blithely distinguished the earlier *Tesco* decision on the basis that it concerned a provision in a different statute. The House of Lords took a similar line in *Director General of Fair Trading v Pioneer Concrete (UK) Ltd*,[92] finding that the knowledge and conduct of a company's sales force sufficed to place the company in contempt of court.

These, and other decisions, may give the impression that identification was—due to its limitations—in the process of being supplanted by vicarious liability. Yet prospects of an orderly demise were confounded by the decision of the House of Lords in *Seaboard Offshore Ltd v Secretary of State for Transport*.[93] A company was charged with failing to take reasonable steps to secure maritime safety. The human fault lay with a company engineer, who allowed a ship to sail despite an inadequate inspection of the engines. One might expect that, in a regulatory offence concerned with safety standards, vicarious liability might be imposed. Instead, the identification principle was applied, and the company was acquitted due to the engineer being insufficiently senior to generate criminal liability for the company. Consequently, there is now considerable confusion over the appropriate rule of attribution to employ when resolving corporate liability for a regulatory offence that requires proof of some form of culpability.

*(d) A middle road*

This uncertainty in the law was directly addressed by Lord Hoffmann in the Privy Council case of *Meridian Global Funds Management Asia Ltd v Securities Commission*.[94] After conducting a broad review of previous authority, Lord Hoffmann concluded that there is no general theory of attribution in the matter of assigning culpability to companies. Instead, there are specific rules of attribution tailored for the terms and policies of the statutory or common law offence at issue in particular cases. What were previously thought to be leading cases on the theory of attribution—*Tesco Supermarkets Ltd* and *Asiatic Petroleum Ltd*—were thus downgraded by Lord Hoffmann to authorities dealing with specific statutory provisions.[95] For his Lordship, the way to proceed in determining a question of corporate criminal liability is, first, to resolve whether the offence in question is an offence that may be committed by a company. If it is, one then moves on to consider the level in the corporate

[90] [1993] 1 WLR 1037 (DC).
[91] See Smith's commentary on the case at [1993] Crim LR 624, 626.
[92] [1995] AC 456.
[93] [1994] 1 WLR 541 (PC).
[94] [1995] 2 AC 500 (PC).
[95] Trade Descriptions Act 1968 (*Tesco*); Merchant Shipping Act 1894 (*Asiatic Petroleum*).

hierarchy where culpability should be located in order best to give expression to the terms and policy of the offence under consideration.[96]

According to the *Meridian* analysis, the identification doctrine on the one hand and vicarious liability on the other are the two polar extremes of a range of different rules of attribution. One must allow this as a theoretical possibility. Yet the case law does not disclose a spectrum of choices; it suggests a binary distinction between identification and vicarious liability. It is not difficult to understand why choices made to date divide into these two possibilities. If uppermost in a court's mind is the need for an effective law that maximises deterrence of companies, the broad-based inculpation offered by vicarious liability becomes attractive. Thus, in *Meridian* itself, the issue was whether the company "knew" that it had acquired a shareholding in another company.[97] The knowledge of a fund manager of insufficient status to be identified with the company was, nonetheless, found to be knowledge attributable to the company. The Privy Council advised that the statutory policy informing the offence—the need for prompt disclosure of acquisitions to provide transparency in securities markets—required the imposition of vicarious liability.[98]

Militating against a wholesale adoption of vicarious liability is the concern to be fair to companies and to their constituencies. The more serious the offence, the greater the potential for damage to corporate reputation and the more compelling the value of fairness. Restraint in the imposition of corporate liability for serious offences has been expressed by the courts, until now, by insisting on the applicability of the identification doctrine. After *Meridian*, we must now allow the possibility of some judicial *via media* between vicarious liability and identification.[99]

To date there has been no judicial experiment along those lines, and—if anything—the Court of Appeal has proved unwilling to depart from the principle of identification when invited to do so. In *St Regis Paper Company Ltd*,[100] for example, the company was charged with "intentionally making a false entry" as to the amount of solids it was discharging into a river. The record keeper was the company's waste disposal manager, the person who supervised the company's discharge of waste products. The doctrine of identification was applied and, under its strictures, the waste disposal manager was found to be an insufficiently senior officer for the purposes of identification—he was too far down the chain of decision-making in the company. Lord Hoffmann's judgment in *Meridian* formed the basis of the prosecution's argument for a more flexible approach; but his Lordship's judgment, despite its range and depth, was taken to be no more than authority on the legislative provisions at issue in that case.[101] Similarly, in *A Ltd and Others*,[102] the Court of Appeal appeared to view the broader approach to corporate liability in *Meridian* as exceptional, with the identification principle being the law's general approach. The Court said nothing, however, to clarify precisely when particular statutory provisions will allow the latitude offered by *Meridian* to be utilised.

[96] [1995] 2 AC 500, 507 (PC).
[97] Securities Amendment Act 1988 (New Zealand), s. 20(4)(e).
[98] [1995] 2 AC 500, 511 (PC).
[99] See, however, the discussion of the statutory "senior manager" model, below § 8.2(v).
[100] [2011] EWCA Crim 2527, [2012] 1 Cr App R 14.
[101] *Ibid*, [22].
[102] [2016] EWCA Crim 1469, [2016] 4 WLR 176, [27].

Unfortunately, then, the question of how criminal liability might be attributed to a company is now to be addressed on a case-by-case basis, with clear principles proving evasive.

#### *(iv) Summary*

It is useful, before delineating the recent statutory reforms in this area, to give a tentative overview of the common-law principles of corporate criminal liability introduced above. As will be seen imminently, the recent statutory reforms sit uneasily with these principles:

(i) If an offence is of a regulatory nature, makes no reference to mens rea, and concerns activities which can straightforwardly be attributed to corporations ("selling", "possession", "polluting", etc.), corporate liability will be a simple exercise in the imposition of strict liability.

(ii) Vicarious liability will be imposed for mens rea offences concerned with compliance with the terms of a licence should it be found that the corporation has completely delegated to another the task of compliance with its duties. This follows on ordinary vicarious liability principles (discussed above), which are applicable to corporate and individual defendants alike.

(iii) Even in the absence of total delegation, mens rea may be attributed to a corporation on the basis of vicarious corporate liability if the offence concerns retail regulation (*Tesco Supermarkets v Brent*)[103] or market regulation (*Meridian*).[104]

(iv) In the light of *Seaboard Offshore*[105] and *St Regis*,[106] it cannot be assumed that vicarious liability will always be the rule of attribution for corporate defendants, even where the offence is of a regulatory nature. As these decisions show, if a regulatory offence requires mens rea, the identification doctrine can be chosen as the rule of attribution. There is a depressing lack of theory and system in the matter of regulatory crimes requiring proof of mens rea. The identification doctrine may be departed from, but only as a matter of *ad hoc* statutory interpretation.

This summary leaves open the question of when, if ever, the doctrine of identification will be put aside by the courts where serious, stigmatic criminal offences are involved. Recall that, in *Pioneer Concrete*,[107] the House of Lords found companies to be in contempt of court on the basis of vicarious liability. Contempt is a matter of grave reputational consequence and may give rise to unlimited fines. But its nature is too anomalous to warrant any general conclusions. It may well be the case that identification will remain the principal, perhaps even the sole, common law basis of attribution of culpability for serious, stigmatic crimes. It is simply not clear.

[103] [1993] 1 WLR 1037 (DC).
[104] [1995] 2 AC 500 (PC).
[105] [1994] 1 WLR 541 (HL).
[106] [2011] EWCA Crim 2527, [2012] 1 Cr App R 14.
[107] *Director General of Fair Trading v Pioneer Concrete (UK) Ltd* [1995] 1 AC 456.

### *(v) The "senior manager" regime under the Economic Crime and Corporate Transparency Act 2023*

The law on corporate criminal liability has been complicated even further by the legislature via section 196 of the Economic Crime and Corporate Transparency Act 2023. Section 196 provides that where a "senior manager" of a body corporate or partnership commits a "relevant offence"[108] whilst "acting within the actual or apparent scope of their authority", the body corporate or partnership is *also* liable for that offence.[109] The list of "relevant offences" in Schedule 12 of the Act includes economic offences running the gamut from theft to fund-raising for a proscribed terrorist organisation.

The explanatory notes accompanying the 2023 Act make plain that section 196 is "a new statutory route to corporate liability",[110] which is not meant to supplant (or interfere with) the operation of the identification doctrine. How radically this model differs from the judicially created identification doctrine is currently uncertain,[111] and will depend on how widely the concept of "senior manager" comes to be applied. The legislation defines a "senior manager" as being either "an individual who plays a significant role in the making of decisions about how the whole or a substantial part of the activities of the body corporate or . . . partnership are managed or organised" or an individual who organises "the whole or a substantial part of those activities".[112] Although it is clear that this definition extends beyond the realm of the "directing mind and will" of the corporation, the question of who is, and who is not, a senior manager is likely to be a matter of significant debate, which raises Rule of Law difficulties.[113] As noted above, one of the benefits of the identification doctrine is its relative clarity concerning which offences can be ascribed to corporations.

Section 196 sits uncomfortably, not just next to the identification doctrine, but also adjacent to offences such as the failure to prevent bribery.[114] In the latter context, the corporation can avoid liability for offences perpetrated by employees by proving on the balance of probabilities that it had adequate procedures in place to prevent bribery.[115] In the case of bribery offences perpetrated by "senior managers", however, such a defence seems unavailable under section 196. It must be queried whether it is fair to label *the corporation* as committing the relevant offence if it had expressly disavowed such offending and had in place policies reasonably capable of preventing it.[116] No such policies can ever be totally effective in preventing offending by employees, even "senior" ones.

As Horder puts matters, the reform in section 196 is "half-hearted, and founded on conceptual confusion".[117] It is therefore regrettable that section 250 of the Crime and Policing

[108] See Economic Crime and Corporate Transparency Act 2023, sched. 12, as supplemented by s. 196(2).
[109] *Ibid.*, s. 196(1).
[110] Economic Crime and Corporate Transparency Act 2023: Explanatory Notes, para. 824.
[111] For further doubts, see Dsouza and Schmitt-Leonardy, "Old and New Tracks for Corporate Criminal Liability" in Duff et al (eds.), *Core Concepts in Criminal Law and Criminal Justice* (Vol. 3, 2025) 179, 184–5.
[112] Economic Crime and Corporate Transparency Act 2023, s. 196(4).
[113] Horder, "Corporate Criminal Liability under the Economic Crime and Corporate Transparency Act 2023" (2025) 45 *LS* 133, 135.
[114] Bribery Act 2010, s. 7.
[115] *Ibid.*, s. 7(2).
[116] Horder, "Corporate Criminal Liability under the Economic Crime and Corporate Transparency Act 2023" (2025) 45 *LS* 133, 140–2.
[117] *Ibid.*, 134.

Act 2026 will, when in force, expand the 2023 Act's regime still further, to encompass all offences committed by "senior managers" acting within the actual or apparent scope of their authority. This expanded version of section 196 will be difficult to reconcile, not just with the identification doctrine and the failure-to-prevent model of offences, but also with the law on corporate liability for strict liability offences and vicarious liability more generally (at least where offences are committed by "senior managers").[118]

In sum, section 196 adds another poorly considered response to the existing mix and section 250 exacerbates matters. Consideration naturally turns next to how this area of the law might best be reformed.

### *(vi) Reform: new conceptions of corporate action and responsibility*

The previous sections have outlined the sorry state of the law on corporate criminal liability in England and Wales. There is a growing strand of opinion that the unsatisfactory state of the law regarding corporate criminal liability is in large part explained by a failure to ask the right questions. To date in English law, the approach has been to ask questions first about the culpability of *individuals* associated with companies, and then to ask further questions concerning how the culpability of these individuals has implications for the culpability of their companies. To proceed in this way, it may be argued, overlooks the crucial fact that there is such a thing as genuine corporate agency and, in turn, corporate culpability—a free-standing culpability that need not be derived from the faults of individuals associated with the corporation.[119] Indeed, it has been asserted that corporate culpability may be present even if no one associated individual has been in any degree at fault.[120] Three attempts to capture this form of culpability will now be examined.[121]

#### *(a) Reactive fault*

"Reactive fault" is a proposal by Fisse and Braithwaite for a new basis of corporate liability.[122] They are committed to the view that corporations, in moral terms, amount to something more than the sum of the individuals associated with them; that something important

[118] See, further, Horder, "Corporate Criminal Liability under the Crime and Policing Bill 2025: A Critique of the 'Senior Manager' Regime" [2025] *Crim LR* 452.

[119] French, *Collective and Corporate Responsibility* (1984) esp. 30–65. French appears to claim that the structure and practice of decision-making in companies may constitute a distinctive form of corporate intentionality which is not reducible to the mental states, past and present, of human agents associated with companies. For a view that French is offering merely a semantic account of the agency of companies see Ouyang and Shiner, "Organizations and Agency" (1995) 1 *Legal Theory* 283.

[120] Dan-Cohen, *Rights, Persons and Organisations* (1986) chap. 3.

[121] To the extent that any account of distinct corporate fault conceives of corporations as moral agents, there is an argument that this commits the proponent to granting corporations certain human rights protections, which may serve to limit, rather than enhance, corporate responsibility. See Friedman, "Corporations as Moral Agents: Trade-offs in Criminal Liability and Human Rights for Corporations" (2020) 83 *MLR* 255.

[122] See Fisse and Braithwaite, *Corporations, Crime and Accountability* (1993); Fisse and Braithwaite, "The Allocation of Responsibility for Corporate Crime: Individualism, Collectivism and Accountability" (1988) 11 *Sydney LR* 468. Cf. French, "Fishing the Red Herrings out of a Sea of Moral Responsibility" in LePore and McLaughlin (eds.), *Actions and Events: Perspectives on the Philosophy of Donald Davidson* (1985) 73.

is lost if corporate conduct is represented exclusively as a function of human conduct.[123] This perspective forms the backdrop of their proposal. They do not, however, try to devise a new regime that gives direct expression to an intrinsically corporate form of culpability. Their proposal dispenses entirely with the need to establish culpability at the time of the actus reus. The fault of the corporation is to be found in terms of its reaction, or lack of reaction, to the commission of the actus reus.[124] In their words:[125]

> "Reactive fault [is an] . . . unreasonable corporate failure to devise and undertake satisfactory preventative or corrective measures in response to the commission of the actus reus of the offence."

Finding culpability from acts, omissions, and states of mind which arise *after* the commission of the actus reus is a radical departure from the norm. Yet we would not have left behind the appraisal of the conduct of human beings. Let us assume that the actus reus is the death of a worker caused, say, during the course of building activities undertaken by D Ltd. There would, of course, have to be an initial investigation of the incident that resulted in death. There would follow an examination of what could and should have been done, in order to make the working practices of D Ltd safer for the future. It is hard to see how the conduct of individuals associated with D Ltd would not form a key element at the trial. There are other, allied, problems. What charge would be brought against D Ltd? Would it (could it) depend on the degree of reactive fault found to be present? How would it be determined whether the degree of reactive fault proved against D Ltd merited a conviction for manslaughter? If the jury brought in a verdict of manslaughter against D Ltd, what would be the position of individuals associated with D Ltd whose conduct was found to be wanting? Would there be a possibility of complicity charges and, if so, on what conceptual basis? If such charges are not to be brought, would and should any civil law consequences follow for individuals closely associated with the guilty verdict against the company?

The adoption of reactive fault would signal an enormous change in corporate liability. Deaths or injuries occurring in the context of manufacturing, construction, mining, air, rail and sea transport activities, road accidents involving corporately owned vehicles, etc., potentially involve serious criminal liability on the part of companies. The issues arising at trial would not turn on the culpability at the time of a particular incident but instead would require a review of corporate safety and other procedures within an open-ended timeframe.[126] The prosecutorial and forensic burden would be enormous. Reactive fault is an untenable basis for corporate liability.

[123] Fisse and Braithwaite, *Corporations, Crime and Accountability* (1993) chap. 2.

[124] It should be noted that one factor telling in favour of the prosecution of a corporation is that "[t]he company had been previously subject to warning, sanctions or criminal charges and had nonetheless failed to take adequate action to prevent future unlawful conduct, and/or had continued to engage in the conduct". Against prosecution is a "genuinely proactive approach adopted by the corporate management team when the offending is brought to their notice, involving self-reporting and remedial actions, including the compensation of victims": CPS, *Corporate Prosecutions*, available at https://www.cps.gov.uk/prosecution-guidance/corporate-prosecutions.

[125] Fisse and Braithwaite, *Corporations, Crime and Accountability* (1993) 48.

[126] The efficacy and acceptability of trial by jury comes under increasing pressure the more protracted and complex the issue to be resolved, as is evidenced by the difficulties experienced in effectively prosecuting serious fraud. See Sullivan, "The Particularity of Serious Fraud" in Birks (ed.), *Pressing Problems in the Law: Vol. 1—Criminal*

### *(b) The theory of aggregation*

Under this theory,[127] the faults of any two or more persons associated with the company may be aggregated and attributed, as a whole, to the company. A judgement then has to be made as to whether the totality of this consolidated fault constitutes, for the company, the culpability required for the offence. If one or more of the associated individuals possessed the culpability the offence requires, the aggregation theory will not, in that particular application, extend beyond vicarious liability. The theory comes into its own when it cannot be said of any associated individual that she possessed the culpability the offence requires. This theory can attain some degree of metaphysical coherence only if one assumes that the company has the moral and agency properties of a real person, absorbing, over time and space, the faults of those associated with it. In that sense, the theory of aggregation is a theory genuinely concerned with *corporate* guilt.

The theory of aggregation can be seen as potentially more efficacious in securing convictions against corporations than the identification doctrine. If we confine our attention to charges of manslaughter, by 2005 there had been only 34 prosecutions for manslaughter brought against companies, with no convictions against companies of any size or complexity.[128] Successful prosecutions were confined to small companies where the top management ran the company in a "hands on" manner. In any larger company, it is exceedingly unlikely that an official of sufficient stature to count as an *alter ego* of the company would be found grossly negligent in respect of the risk of causing death. The failed prosecution of P&O Ltd (a "body corporate infected with the disease of sloppiness")[129] after the sinking of the *Herald of Free Enterprise* demonstrates that. Notwithstanding increasing public concern with corporate safety standards through the 1980s and 1990s, the Court of Appeal confirmed in *Attorney-General's Reference (No. 2 of 1999)*[130] that liability for gross negligence manslaughter could only be imposed on a company under the principle of identification.

The legislature's response to this difficulty endorses, to an extent, the theory of aggregation.[131] Aggregation is an element in the scheme of liability for the distinct offence of corporate manslaughter, created by the Corporate Manslaughter and Homicide Act 2007. The specifics of this offence will be examined below.[132] For now we should note that a company will be liable for corporate manslaughter if it causes a person's death as a consequence of a gross breach of a relevant duty of care.[133] A gross breach of a duty of care will be established if "the conduct of [the organisation] falls far below what can reasonably be expected of the organisation in the circumstances".[134] In resolving that issue, the jury may consider the

*Justice and Human Rights* (1995) 99, 102–3. Legislation that would have allowed complex and serious fraud cases to be tried without a jury was passed in 2003, but the provisions were never brought into force, and were eventually repealed by Protection of Freedoms Act 2012, sched. 9, pt. 12.

[127] See Wells, *Corporations and Criminal Responsibility* (2nd ed., 2001) 156. It is important not to conflate such models with those that would seek, for example, to aggregate the *knowledge* of various actors when assessing what a corporation itself "knew". See, further, Sarch, "Collective Knowledge and the Limits of the Expanded Identification Doctrine" (2024) 44 *OJLS* 920.

[128] Home Office, *Corporate Manslaughter: The Government's Draft Bill for Reform*, Cm. 6497 (2005).

[129] *Report of Court No. 8074* (HMSO, 1987) para. 14.1 ("Sheen Report").

[130] [2000] QB 796 (CA).

[131] The 2007 Act also contains elements of the organisational approach discussed in the next section.

[132] See below, § 10.7(iv).

[133] Corporate Manslaughter and Corporate Homicide Act 2007, s. 1(1).

[134] *Ibid.*, s. 1(4)(b).

conduct of the entirety of the workforce, the safety policies and practices of the company, and any failures to comply with health and safety legislation.[135] However, a full version of aggregation is not adopted by the 2007 Act. Although the elements just referred to must be weighed when determining whether the company's conduct in relation to causing V's death fell far below what should have been reasonably expected, the organisation will be guilty of the offence only if the way in which its activities are managed or organised by its senior management was a "substantial element" in the breach of the duty of care.[136] The 2007 Act thus in reality represents "an uneasy no man's land between competing approaches to corporate criminal liability".[137]

Even in this modified form, however, one may have reservations about the implications for individuals of the aggregation approach. The practical implementation of that approach will inevitably be linked to criticisms made against the company's personnel. Persons connected with the company who have been subjected to criticism at public trials will be closely linked to any guilty verdict sustained by the company, with possible adverse legal consequences, at least at civil law.[138] There is a danger that they will be tainted with the stigma of a homicide offence without any necessary proof of their *personal* culpability commensurate with a serious criminal offence.[139] Given the relatively small number of successful prosecutions for the distinct offence of corporate manslaughter to date,[140] it is not clear how much of a concern this is in practice.

*(c) The organisational model*

An alternative conception of corporate fault can be premised on a corporation's structures—i.e. its policies and practices.[141] For instance, in dealing with the Zeebrugge ferry disaster, the question for an organisational fault proponent would not be whether P&O's senior management had culpability (the identification doctrine), or whether culpability could be found through the consideration of various actors within the corporation (the aggregation approach). Rather, the question would be whether "the corporation can be blamed because its system, its operating policies, displayed a reckless attitude to safety".[142]

[135] *Ibid.*, s. 8.

[136] *Ibid.*, s. 1(3).

[137] Wells, "Corporate Criminal Liability: A Ten Year Review" [2014] *Crim LR* 849, 865. See, too, Norrie, *Crime, Reason and History* (3rd ed., 2014) 125–6. For discussion of the law's operation in practice, see: Hebert, Bittle. and Tombs, "Obscuring Corporate Violence: Corporate Manslaughter in Action" (2019) 58 *Howard Journal of Criminal Justice* 554; Roper, "The Corporate Manslaughter and Corporate Homicide Act 2007: A Re-evaluation 10 Years On From the First Case" [2022] *Crim LR* 290.

[138] The Act confines criminal liability to organisations. Individuals cannot be criminally liable for corporate manslaughter either as principals or accessories: Corporate Manslaughter and Corporate Homicide Act 2007, s. 18.

[139] Interestingly, it appears that public attitudes towards *work-related* deaths are perhaps less punitive than those regarding fatalities in other contexts: Almond, "Public Perceptions of Work-related Fatality Cases: Reaching the Outer Limits of 'Populist Punitiveness'?" (2008) 48 *Brit J Criminology* 448.

[140] The Act came into force on 6 April 2008. For a survey of cases under the old and new regimes, see Wells, "Corporate Criminal Liability: A Ten Year Review" [2014] *Crim LR* 849, 860–2. Statistics released by the CPS in response to a freedom of information request suggest that between 2011 and 2023 there were, on average, around three prosecutions for corporate manslaughter per annum: CPS, "Prosecutions Relating to Corporate Manslaughter" (2024), https://www.cps.gov.uk/foi/2024/prosecutions-relating-corporate-manslaughter.

[141] Wells, *Corporations and Criminal Responsibility* (2nd ed., 2001) chap. 8.

[142] *Ibid.*, 158.

Such an organisational approach has been adopted in the Australian Capital Territory.[143] There, alongside the identification doctrine, sit alternative modes of corporate fault that involve "proving that a corporate culture existed within the corporation that directed, encouraged, tolerated or led to noncompliance with the . . . law" or "proving that the corporation failed to create and maintain a corporate culture requiring compliance with the contravened law". This culture-based approach is similar to Wells' organisational model, but has not yet been adopted expressly in England and Wales (even if aspects of it are visible in the offence of corporate manslaughter).[144] This is fortunate. The corporate culture model is inherently vague, despite Wells' best efforts to explain it in terms that would satisfy the requirements of the Rule of Law.

*(d) The future of corporate liability*

On one view, the Corporate Manslaughter and Corporate Homicide Act 2007 (which covers "organisations", which is a wider concept than "corporation")[145] broke new conceptual ground. We now have an offence where the grounds of corporate liability for a serious offence are not dependent on establishing that any individual associated with the company possessed the culpability for the crime.

For those who favour this development, and indeed in going further in the aggregation or organisational fault direction, the question is whether this idea of aggregation or organisational culpability can be implemented for other crimes. That may prove difficult. Corporate manslaughter has a close affinity with manslaughter by gross negligence and, whatever the reservations expressed above, the negligence standard—which is assessed primarily by reference to a defendant's conduct—is well adapted to a holistic appraisal of the company's performance in safety matters. Many other serious offences have states of mind such as intent, dishonesty, or recklessness as definitional elements. Posing questions relating to general corporate performance would less clearly capture these states of mind. Attributing intentionality and other states of mind to a company directly, without any mediation through the intentions and states of mind of persons connected with it, would require full adoption of the view that companies are, sufficient unto themselves, moral agents or "intelligent machines".

This seems an unlikely prospect. In line with English traditions of empiricism is the assertion of Lord Hoffmann that "there is no such thing as the company itself, no ding an sich".[146]

[143] Criminal Code 2002, s. 51. See, too, Criminal Code Act 1995, s. 12.3 (which applies to federal criminal law in Australia).

[144] Cf. Bribery Act 2010, s. 7(2): "it is a defence for [a commercial organisation] to prove that [it] had in place adequate procedures designed to prevent persons associated with [it] from" committing an offence of bribery for the benefit of the commercial organisation.

[145] The Corporate Manslaughter and Homicide Act 2007 takes organisational culpability beyond companies, which are of course legal persons in their own right. The Act includes within the purview of the corporate manslaughter offence non-corporate entities such as partnerships, health trusts, prisons, and the emergency services. One may note too an increasing willingness on the part of the judiciary to interpret regulatory statutes in a manner that imposes criminal liability on non-corporate entities, such as partnerships and unincorporated associations: e.g. *Stevenson and Sons* [2008] EWCA Crim 273, [2008] 2 Cr App R 14 (partnership); *L(R) and F(J)* [2008] EWCA Crim 1970, [2009] 1 Cr App R 16 (golf club organised as an unincorporated association).

[146] *Meridian Global Funds Management Asia Ltd v Securities Commission* [1995] 2 AC 500, 507 (*sic*) (PC). In Kantian philosophy, *Ding an sich* refers to a thing that has not been mediated through perception or conceptualisation.

The traditional view of English company law is that companies are inherently and exclusively *legal* regimes with no transcendent reality beyond the merely legal realm.[147] That view of companies fits well with a rejection of the claim that human agency may be submerged and transmuted by social and bureaucratic structures. Instead, one may assert that companies, in terms of their activities and planning, depend on human agency and are not, in terms of conduct and states of mind, some form of non-human sentient creature.[148] This perspective does not need to deny the force of corporate culture on behavioural patterns. It merely insists that those cultures emanate from the interactions, past and present, of human beings.[149]

On this view, the gateway to corporate liability lies through the conduct and states of mind of persons connected with the company. If it is thought right to convict companies for serious offences on a broader front than is currently the case, the most straightforward way of doing this would be to convict companies on the basis of vicarious liability. It may be objected that this would be too undiscriminating: why, it might be asked, should, say, a reputable insurance company be found guilty of fraud by false representation because one of its sales force on a particular occasion made false and dishonest statements when selling a policy to a customer? This objection has considerable force. Vicarious liability would be far more acceptable if companies were allowed a due diligence defence.[150] In the insurance company example, the company should be exonerated if it could demonstrate that its recruiting, training, and monitoring practices emphasised and supported honesty in sales and penalised or otherwise deterred dishonesty.

Even if more inventive approaches are not adopted in England and Wales, something should be done to clarify the mechanisms for establishing corporate liability for offences involving mens rea. In 2010, the Law Commission proposed that Parliament should expressly state what the rule of attribution was if an offence was intended to apply to companies and that for the meantime courts should not assume that the doctrine of identification was the predominant principle.[151] Alas, this sensible proposal has not been taken forward. As noted above, the Court of Appeal in *St Regis Paper Company Ltd*[152] and *A Ltd and Others*[153] was of the view that, for any offence involving proof of culpability, there was a strong presumption that the identification doctrine provided the applicable rule of attribution. It

[147] See Hart, "Definition and Theory in Jurisprudence" (1954) 70 *LQR* 37.

[148] A perspective identified as "methodological individualism": Popper, *The Poverty of Historicism* (1957); Watkins, "Historical Explanation in the Social Sciences" (1957) 8 *British Journal for the Philosophy of Science* 104.

[149] For an account which accepts methodological individualism but which emphasises the formative influence of group and social structures in creating forms of "collective intentionality" see Searle, *The Construction of Social Reality* (1995).

[150] Cp. Bribery Act 2010, s. 7. The Law Commission consulted on a recommendation that a due diligence defence be provided in respect of all regulatory strict liability, offences: LCCP No. 195, *Criminal Liability in Regulatory Contexts* (2010) para. 6.95. There is much to be said for extending this proposal to corporate liability for any offence, including mens rea offences, thereby allowing a company to demonstrate that the offence was committed on the initiative of an individual employee rather than a by-product of the company's policies and practices.

[151] LCCP No. 195, *Criminal Liability in Regulatory Contexts* (2010) para. 5.110.

[152] [2011] EWCA Crim 2527, [2012] 1 Cr App R 14.

[153] [2016] EWCA Crim 1469, [2016] 4 WLR 176.

seems unlikely that, following the piecemeal development of specific offences[154] targeting bribery,[155] tax evasion,[156] and corporate manslaughter,[157] a general restatement of the law on corporate liability is now possible or likely.[158]

The Law Commission's "options paper" on corporate criminal liability, published in 2022, examined a range of models that could be adopted generally to resolve this muddle.[159] Rather than reaching a firm recommendation,[160] the Commission left the options of a clarified identification doctrine and a "senior manager" model open to policy-makers. These were viewed as *alternatives*, however, and it was not the Law Commission's hope that the "senior manager" approach would simply be grafted onto an unreformed identification doctrine.[161] The conceptual mess that the Law Commission encountered has, as a result of Parliament's response, only become worse. When section 196 is extended to cover all offences, it is likely to eclipse the identification doctrine entirely. If this is the direction Parliament wishes to go in, it would be sensible if the identification doctrine were expressly abolished by statute. The history of corporate criminal liability in England and Wales nevertheless suggests that this nettle will not be grasped.

### *(vi) Punishing Corporations*

If corporations are regularly to be convicted for serious offences, it is necessary to consider what forms of sanction are appropriate. It should be uncontroversial that companies, by way of fines, should be stripped of any illicit gains and of any quantifiable competitive advantage attributable to the crimes and breaches of regulation occurring in the course of their activities. But what level of sanction beyond that? There is an intractable tension between imposing monetary penalties aimed at deterrence[162] and avoiding adverse consequences for employees, creditors, and shareholders not implicated in the wrongdoing. If the company is forced into liquidation, a valuable source of employment and goods and services may be lost. Adaptation of monetary penalties such as the "equity" fine and non-monetary alternatives such as corporate probation have been suggested but are fraught with difficulty in both theory and practice.[163] These problems have yet to be resolved. Corporate

[154] On the problems of such piecemeal offences, see Dsouza, "The Corporate Agent in Criminal Law—An Argument for Comprehensive Identification" (2020) 79 *CLJ* 91, 95–96.

[155] Bribery Act 2010, s. 7.

[156] Criminal Finances Act 2017, ss. 45–46.

[157] Corporate Manslaughter and Corporate Homicide Act 2007, s. 1.

[158] LCCP No. 195, *Criminal Liability in Regulatory Contexts* (2010) para. 5.91. Indeed, it may be that the most practical way forwards is to argue for the duplication of these bespoke solutions in cognate areas: e.g. Wells, "Corporate Failure to Prevent Economic Crime: A Proposal" [2017] *Crim LR* 426; cf. Clifford and Reurts, "Corporate Criminal Liability in the Supply Chain: A Coherent Divergence?" [2018] *Crim LR* 633. See, further, Horder and Watts, "The Scope of Liability for Failure to Prevent Economic Crime" [2021] *Crim LR* 851.

[159] *Corporate Criminal Liability: An Options Paper* (2022). See, further, Lööf, "The Law Commission Options Paper: Doubtful Progress on Reforming Corporate Criminal Liability" [2022] *Crim LR* 814.

[160] *Corporate Criminal Liability: An Options Paper* (2022), para. 1.36.

[161] The Law Commission claims that s. 192 "reformed the identification doctrine": https://lawcom.gov.uk/project/corporate-criminal-liability/. The two models in fact exist awkwardly alongside one another.

[162] And fines should, in principle, be large enough to encourage management and shareholders to ensure future compliance: *Thames Water Utilities Ltd* [2015] EWCA Crim 960, [2015] 1 WLR 4411.

[163] For discussion of the forms of sanction that may be deployed against companies see Wells, *Corporations and Criminal Responsibility* (2nd ed., 2001) 31–9, 165–8; Coffee, "No Soul to Damn: No Body to Kick: An Unscandalized Inquiry into the Problem of Corporate Punishment" (1981) 79 *Michigan LR* 386.

punishment, like corporate liability, remains a rich source of philosophical and economic challenges.[164]

### *(vii) Deferred Prosecution Agreements*

A modern discussion of the topic of corporate liability should not ignore the fact that prosecutors and defendants can nowadays hope to circumnavigate the legal quagmire explained above, via a deferred prosecution agreement (DPA).[165] DPAs began life in England and Wales in 2014, and are agreed in relation to certain offences[166] between "a body corporate, a partnership or an unincorporated association" and a prosecutor.[167] DPAs suspend the threat of prosecution for a period, on the condition that the corporation fulfils the conditions detailed within the agreement. Typically, these conditions will involve addressing the causes of the criminality mentioned in the agreement, cooperating with investigations into the alleged and admitted wrongdoing, and paying compensation to victims.[168] There will also be a financial penalty, commensurate with the fine that would have been imposed had the defendant pleaded guilty to the wrongdoing admitted in the DPA.[169] The DPA must be approved by a judge of the Crown Court,[170] who must find that the DPA is in the interests of justice, and that its terms are fair, reasonable, and proportionate.[171]

If it is proved on the balance of probabilities that the DPA has been breached before its expiry, further negotiations may take place or the agreement may be terminated, with the consequence that the defendant will (presumably) be prosecuted.[172] If the DPA is complied with, then after its period of application has ended, the prosecutor should give notice to the Crown Court that it wishes to discontinue proceedings against the defendant. The result of this is that the defendant will not be prosecuted for the relevant offending.[173]

Part of the motivation for the creation of DPAs was to promote self-reporting and cooperation on the part of corporations who discover criminality within their organisation. And, to that extent, they appear to work: DPAs have been agreed after self-reporting.[174] They are, however, controversial. Despite their reference to *deferment* of prosecution, DPAs are *alternatives* to prosecution, albeit conditional ones.[175] They thus permit corporate

[164] See Lederman, "Models for Imposing Corporate Criminal Liability: From Adaptation and Imitation towards Aggregation and the Search for Self-identity" (2000) 4 *Buffalo Crim LR* 641 for a thoughtful account of theorising in the area.

[165] Crime and Courts Act 2013, sched. 17. See, further, Serious Fraud Office and Crown Prosecution Service, *Deferred Prosecution Agreements Code of Practice* (2014), available at https://www.sfo.gov.uk/?wpdmdl=1447.

[166] The list of common law and statutory offences that can form the basis of a DPA is set out in Crime and Courts Act 2013, sched. 17, pt. 2.

[167] Crime and Courts Act 2013, sched. 17, para 4(1).

[168] *Ibid.*, sched. 17, para 5(3).

[169] *Ibid.*, sched. 17, para 5(4).

[170] This judicial oversight means that some of the problems with the form of DPA used in the USA are avoided. For a useful comparative account, see Davis, "Judicial Review of Deferred Prosecution Agreements" (2022) 60 *Columbia Journal of Transnational Law* 751.

[171] Crime and Courts Act 2013, sched. 17, para 8(1). On the judge's role with regard to the evidential basis of the DPA, see *SFO v Amec Foster Wheeler Energy Ltd* [2021] Lloyd's Rep FC 353 (Crown Court).

[172] Crime and Courts Act 2013, sched. 17, para 9.

[173] There are limited exceptions: see Crime and Courts Act 2013, sched. 17, para 10.

[174] For instance, *SFO v Standard Bank Plc* [2016] Lloyd's Rep FC 102 (Crown Court).

[175] It remains possible to prosecute *individuals* for their wrongdoing, even if a DPA spares the corporation from the same fate.

defendants to negotiate and pay their way out of potential criminal liability, which might be thought to generate Rule of Law worries. There are also concerns regarding how consistent the courts have been in their approach to DPAs, a matter which cannot be explored in detail here.[176] And, of course, creating a mechanism to evade the strictures and pitfalls of the system of corporate criminal liability does nothing to address the underlying problems with that system.

[176] See King and Lord, "Deferred Prosecution Agreements in England and Wales: Castles Built on Sand?" [2020] *PL* 307.

# 9

# THE INCHOATE OFFENCES

The offences of encouraging and assisting a crime, conspiracy to commit a crime, and attempting a crime are known as the inchoate offences because liability for these crimes may arise before, and often without, the commission of any substantive offence.[1] The essentials of these offences are clear. D will be liable for encouraging theft as soon as he urges P to steal property from V, even if P ignores him. D will be liable for assisting theft as soon as he helps the would-be thief by telling P where V's property is located, even if P does not steal the property. Both D and P will be liable for a conspiracy to commit theft the moment P agrees with D that D should steal from V, even if they do not carry out the agreement. D will be guilty of attempted theft from V when, intending to steal from V, she does anything that comes sufficiently close to appropriating property from V.

The virtue of inchoate offences is that they permit the lawful restraint and arrest of aspirant criminals prior to the realisation of any actual harm, and so reduce the risk of the commission of substantive offences.[2] If D, lacking any justification or excuse, were to shoot at V with an intent to kill her, it is a matter of great relief should the bullet miss V and harmlessly fall to the ground. Yet it would be a remarkably indulgent system of criminal law that allowed the absence of harm to preclude any criminal liability of D. From a consequentialist perspective, D's liability for attempted murder is justified by society's need to restrain and deter dangerous people. Provided there was a clear and present danger of the violation of a protected interest of any innocent person, the use of restraining and punitive measures against D is justified. Indeed, to subject an innocent person to an unwarranted risk of death may properly be considered *in itself* to constitute the harmful violation of a protected interest.

From a retributivist position, moreover, many "desert" theorists would maintain that a person who tries to do harm but fails to achieve his objective is, in terms of culpability, not materially different from the person who tries and succeeds.[3] Further, even theorists who insist that the occurrence of harm has moral significance (i.e. that it matters to D's culpability whether she succeeds or fails) would not question the restraint and punishment of a

[1] The terms "substantive offence", "full offence", and "principal offence" will be used in this chapter to denote the crime that is the objective of the encourager, assister, conspirator, or attemptor.

[2] Bock and Stark, "Preparatory Offences" in Ambos, Duff, Roberts, Weigend, and Heinze (eds.), *Core Concepts in Criminal Law and Criminal Justice* (2019) vol. 2, 64. Despite the evident utility of these offences, they have been criticised for their potential to punish conduct too remote from the realisation of any concrete harm. Some of these criticisms will be addressed later in this chapter. For a general critical survey, see Husak, "The Nature and Justifiability of Nonconsummate Offences" (1995) 37 *Arizona LR* 151.

[3] Ashworth, "Criminal Attempts and the Role of Resulting Harm under the Code and in the Common Law" (1988) 19 *Rutgers LJ* 725. Perhaps the most extreme example of this view is Alexander and Ferzan, *Crime and Culpability* (2009) chap. 5.

person who has unequivocally tried to harm another; they merely dispute whether failure should be penalised as heavily as success.[4]

The consequentialist and retributivist justifications for inchoate offences are most graphically demonstrated when, as in our shooting example, D has done everything that he intends to do in his attempt to harm V. In that case, D's attempt can be considered to be complete. The appropriateness, however, of penalising conduct which is of a more preliminary nature is controversial; the further away D's conduct is from the commission of a completed offence the more difficult it is to consider criminalising D's conduct as a proportionate state response.[5] For instance, there has been considerable debate as to whether agreeing with another to commit a crime at some future date warrants criminalisation.[6] In the United States, certain state jurisdictions and federal law require, before liability for conspiracy may arise, that at least one overt act in pursuance of the criminal objective must have been carried out by a party to the agreement.[7] In England and Wales, however, the law of conspiracy does not require proof of any overt act in carrying out the agreement and permits restraint well before the commission of the agreed substantive offence. The legitimacy of having a crime of conspiracy was considered by the Law Commission, which concluded that it is justifiable to have an offence founded on the making of an agreement without the need to prove that anything was done in pursuance of the objective, since the relevant culpability can be inferred from the fact that the agreement was made with the parties intending that the agreement be carried out.[8] Indeed, a policy of early intervention is not confined to inchoate crimes. Many substantive offences, particularly those which proscribe possession of such things as guns, explosives, and drugs, are designed indirectly to prevent future harms.[9]

## § 9.1 Incitement and encouraging or assisting crime

At common law, there existed an offence of incitement, where D urged or persuaded others to perpetrate crimes.[10] This offence was committed at the point when D had successfully communicated with P.[11] Although there was some uncertainty about the interpretation of the crime of incitement, especially concerning the relevant mens rea, the offence was

[4] Duff, *Criminal Attempts* (1996) chap. 4; Edwards and Simester, "Crime, Blameworthiness, and Outcomes" (2019) 39 *OJLS* 50. For further discussion and references, see below, § 9.3(vi).

[5] Bock and Stark, "Preparatory Offences" in Ambos, Duff, Roberts, Weigend, and Heinze (eds.), *Core Concepts in Criminal Law and Criminal Justice* (2019) vol. 1, 56.

[6] Johnson, "The Unnecessary Crime of Conspiracy" (1973) 61 *Cal LR* 1137; Marcus, "Criminal Conspiracy Law: Time to Turn Back from an Ever Expanding, Ever More Troubling Area" (1992) 1 *William and Mary Bill of Rights J* 1.

[7] Perkins and Boyce, *Criminal Law* (3rd ed., 1982) 685–7. Except where the agreement is to commit a felony, a similar requirement is found in the Model Penal Code, § 5.03(5).

[8] Law Com. No. 318, *Conspiracy and Attempts* (2009) para. 2.33.

[9] To this category, one might add crimes involving the proscription of conduct associated with drink-driving, and forms of sexual conduct and obscenity, which are frequently justified by reference to the ultimate impact that such conduct may have on the social order. The link between the proscribed activities and such generalised further or underlying harm may be tenuous. For discussion of the role of remote harms in the creation of criminal offences, see Simester and von Hirsch, *Crimes, Harms, and Wrongs* (2011) chaps. 5–6.

[10] *Higgins* (1801) 2 East 5, 102 ER 269.

[11] *Banks* (1873) 12 Cox CC 393.

generally workable and acceptable. There was, however, a significant gap in the law[12] where a person sought to assist the commission of a crime but did not communicate to anybody a desire that the offence should be committed. If the substantive offence was committed, D could be convicted as an accessory; but, if no substantive offence was committed, D could not be guilty of any offence. So, if D placed poison in a drink knowing that P would administer that drink to V, but P tripped and spilled the drink before it could be administered, D would not be guilty of a crime. D could not be an accessory to administration of the poison, since accessorial liability turns on the substantive offence being committed. D could not be guilty of an attempt, since her actions were not sufficiently proximate to the commission of the substantive offence. D could not be guilty of a conspiracy, since there had been no agreement with P. D could not be guilty of incitement, since there had been no communication with P. The absence of criminal liability in such a case was difficult to justify in terms of culpability and social defence.

The Law Commission[13] considered this to be a major gap in the law and recommended the creation of a new inchoate offence of assisting the commission of a crime and replacing the common law offence of incitement with a new inchoate offence of encouraging crime. These recommendations were rapidly enacted in the Serious Crime Act 2007, albeit in a different form from that recommended by the Law Commission. Section 59 of that statute abolished the common law offence of incitement. It does not follow, however, that crimes of incitement no longer exist in English law, since a number of statutory offences use the language of inciting crimes, or similar language. For example, there are various incitement offences within the Sexual Offences Act 2003, including inciting a child under 13 to engage in sexual activity.[14] Further, section 4 of the Offences Against the Person Act 1861 criminalises the solicitation, encouragement, persuasion, or proposal of murder;[15] the Incitement to Disaffection Act 1934 creates an offence of endeavouring to seduce members of the armed forces from their duty or allegiance; the Terrorism Act 2006, section 1(2) creates an offence of encouraging or inducing terrorism; and the Crime and Policing Act 2026, section 135 creates an offence of encouraging or assisting serious self-harm.

### *(i) The Serious Crime Act 2007 offences*

Part 2 of the Serious Crime Act 2007 creates new inchoate offences of encouraging or assisting another person to commit a crime.[16] Although this statutory scheme purported to implement the recommendations of the Law Commission,[17] the eventual scheme is very

[12] Identified by Spencer, "Trying to Help Another Person Commit a Crime" in Smith (ed.), *Criminal Law: Essays in Honour of J C. Smith* (1987) 148.

[13] Law Com. No. 300, *Inchoate Liability for Assisting and Encouraging Crime* (2006).

[14] Sexual Offences Act 2003, s. 8. See *Jones* [2007] EWCA Crim 1118, [2008] QB 460 (no specific child needs to be identified).

[15] The Law Commission recommended that there is still a need for this offence, despite the general inchoate offences of encouraging and assisting crime, because the solicitation offence may be needed where D has incited groups or where advice to kill is only intended to be followed in certain circumstances. The Law Commission recommended that this offence be called "encouraging murder": Law Com. No. 316, *Reform of Offences Against the Person* (2015).

[16] Spencer and Virgo, "Encouraging and Assisting Crime: Legislate in Haste, Repent at Leisure" [2008] 9 *Arch. News* 7; Ormerod and Fortson, "Serious Crime Act 2007: The Part 2 Offences" [2009] *Crim LR* 389.

[17] Law Com. No. 300, *Inchoate Liability for Assisting and Encouraging Crime* (2006).

different from that which had been recommended, involving the creation of three offences in an unnecessarily prolix and complex way. Each of these offences requires that D perform an act which is capable of encouraging or assisting the commission by another person of a substantive offence. They are distinguished by their mens rea requirements. D's conduct becomes an offence when he acts:

(i) with intent to encourage or assist the commission of the substantive offence (section 44);
(ii) believing that the substantive offence will be committed *and* that the act will encourage or assist its commission (section 45); or
(iii) where the act is capable of encouraging or assisting the commission of one or more of a number of principal offences, believing that one or more of those offences will be committed *and* that D's act will encourage or assist one or more of them (section 46).

Each of these inchoate offences can be committed even though the substantive offence is not committed,[18] and even though there has been no effective encouragement or assistance of P, who might have had no idea that D has done any act of encouragement or assistance. The maximum penalty upon conviction for one of these statutory inchoate offences will be the same as for the anticipated substantive offence,[19] save that the penalty for encouraging or assisting murder is a discretionary, rather than a mandatory, sentence of life imprisonment.[20] These new offences expand the ambit of inchoate liability significantly. It is sufficient that D does an act which is capable of encouraging or assisting the commission of a substantive offence,[21] without needing to prove that it has encouraged or assisted P in any way, so the identification of any relevant potential harm becomes increasingly difficult. The fact that D's unsuccessful attempt to get another person to commit a crime is sufficient in itself for criminal liability has not escaped criticism, on the grounds of the remoteness of D's conduct from the commission of any substantive offence.[22] In creating new offences of encouraging and assisting crime, Parliament clearly considered that this form of liability is not too remote from the commission of a substantive offence to prevent D from being convicted.

Further, this legislative regime is inherently complex and overlaps substantially with existing criminal liability, notably conspiracy and accessorial liability. Many parties to a conspiracy will have encouraged the commission of a crime and so could be convicted of the encouragement offence. Similarly, if D assists P's substantive offence, D could be convicted either of assistance or—assuming P actually commits the offence—as an accessory.

[18] Serious Crime Act 2007, s. 49(1). D can also be convicted of one of the statutory inchoate offences if it can be proved that D must have committed either the inchoate offence or the relevant substantive offence as principal, but not as accessory, but it is not proved which offence D committed: *Ibid.*, s. 56.

[19] Or the anticipated substantive offence with the longest maximum term if s. 46 applies: *ibid.*, s. 58(4)–(7).

[20] *Ibid.*, s. 58.

[21] Notably, by virtue of s. 1(4) of the Criminal Attempts Act 1981, one cannot attempt to commit a summary offence; and the permission of the Director of Public Prosecutions is required in order to prosecute a conspiracy to commit a summary offence. Yet the encouraging or assisting crime provisions have no such restrictions.

[22] For a critique of the old offence of incitement see Robbins, "Double Inchoate Crimes" (1989) 26 *Harv J Legis* 1. Robbins argues that incitement essentially penalised attempts to conspire and, consequently, targeted conduct too remote from the principal offence. There is some force in his critique, and more so in respect of the new statutory inchoate offences of assisting and encouraging.

For a significant time after Part 2 of the Serious Crime Act 2007 was brought into force, the offences were rarely charged. Following riots in England in 2011, however, the crimes of encouraging and assisting proved to be particularly significant. The fact that some defendants, who placed messages on social media encouraging riot and other offences, were convicted of the encouraging offence and received sentences of four years' imprisonment,[23] showed that these offences could have a very significant role to play in the criminal justice system. The Court of Appeal recognised that "the abuse of modern technology for criminal purposes extends to and includes incitement of very many people by a single step".[24] The offences may also have a significant role to play in relation to serious organised crime in dealing with the background figures who organise the criminal activities of others,[25] and in relation to activities relating to terrorism. There are, however, few reported cases relating to the encouragement and assistance offences.

### *(ii) Actus reus*

#### *(a) Encouragement*

Encouragement is not defined by the Serious Crime Act 2007, so it is appropriate to assume that the cases which defined the actus reus of the common law offence of incitement remain relevant to the interpretation of the actus reus of the new statutory offences. The essence of encouragement is consequently some communication or gesture on the part of D which might persuade, induce, or influence P to commit a crime. It is not necessary for D's encouragement to have any effect on the intentions or conduct of others. It is consequently immaterial if, as in *DPP v Armstrong*,[26] P is an undercover police officer who is not influenced by D's encouragement. The target of the encouragement may be either a particular individual or people generally—as when D addresses a meeting, writes a newspaper article, or creates a public post on social media.[27]

Whether D's conduct is capable of encouraging a crime requires careful analysis of the context of the particular act. In *Scott v DPP*,[28] D was convicted of encouraging P (a prisoner) to possess an unauthorised mobile telephone in prison. D's acts of encouragement consisted of exchanging telephone calls and text messages with P. If D had not made or received calls or messages, the DPP successfully argued, it was less likely that P would continue to possess the phone. Encouragement was also found to be present, for purposes of the crime of incitement, in *Invicta Plastics v Clare*,[29] where D, a company, advertised in a motoring magazine a device, "Radatec", which indicated the presence of a police radar device monitoring traffic speed. It was illegal for private persons to install such devices.[30] Pictorial detail in the advertisement illustrated the utility of "Radatec" in avoiding detection for speeding. The company was endeavouring to persuade motorists to acquire the device in order to assist purchasers to contravene the laws against speeding and so the Divisional Court confirmed

[23] See *Blackshaw et al* [2011] EWCA Crim 2312, [2012] 1 WLR 1126.
[24] *Ibid.*, [73].
[25] *Sadique (No 2)* [2013] EWCA Crim 1150, [2014] 1 WLR 986.
[26] [2000] Crim LR 379 (DC).
[27] *Most* (1881) 7 QBD 244. See also *Jones* [2007] EWCA Crim 1118, [2008] QB 460.
[28] [2022] EWHC 91 (Admin), [2022] 1 WLR 2231.
[29] [1976] RTR 251 (DC).
[30] Wireless Telegraphy Act 1949, s. 1(1) (now repealed). The successor 2006 Act has a narrower scope.

D's conviction for inciting the commission of speeding offences. In *Marlow*,[31] D was convicted of incitement on the basis of publishing instructions on the growing of cannabis, something which clearly might encourage others to follow suit.[32]

A more dubious decision is *Goldman*,[33] where D was held to have incited E by responding positively to an advertisement placed by E, which offered the sale of indecent photographs of children. That E's advertisement constituted encouragement to others to possess child pornography is not in doubt. D's role, however, seems to have been confined to that of a willing recipient of E's criminal services. D's encouragement allegedly took the form of "arousing [E's] cupidity", yet D did nothing more than show himself to be a purchaser of E's child pornography. It would be perverse to think that we encourage the sale of a sweater by Marks & Spencer when we present the item for payment. On the facts of *Goldman*, the crucial element of inducement or persuasion appears to be missing. It is difficult to overlook the fact that the Court of Appeal's rather strained analysis enabled D to be found criminally liable for conduct in England in respect of seeking to access child pornography supplied from overseas. An understandable zeal to curb this vile trade seems to have distorted the natural meaning of encouraging a crime.

The same impetus may explain *O'Shea v Coventry Magistrates' Court*,[34] where D had accessed internet sites featuring child pornography. He was charged with inciting P, who ran the site, to distribute indecent photographs of children. D's defence was that he had incited no one, merely downloaded images from his computer. The Divisional Court confirmed D's conviction on the basis that, by accessing the site, D would have encouraged P to maintain the site. It seems that no evidence was required that P was aware that D had visited the site. This stretches any reasonable conception of encouragement beyond its limits. Today, under the Serious Crime Act 2007, actual encouragement is not required—it is sufficient that D's act *be capable of* encouraging P.[35] That seems straightforward: without buyers, the child pornographer cannot sell his illegal wares. The artificial extension of the meaning of encouragement in the earlier cases might consequently be explained on the basis that an inchoate offence of assistance did not exist until the enactment of the Serious Crime Act 2007.

Lord Denning, when determining the scope of the statutory offence of incitement to racial hatred in *Race Relations Board v Applin*,[36] considered that threats fell within the legal conception of incitement.[37] That encouragement includes threatening or putting pressure on another to commit an offence is specifically recognised by the Serious Crime Act 2007.[38] Although, as a matter of ordinary language, we would not describe coercion or threats as "encouragement", to confine that word to its ordinary meaning in this context would be perverse. Take a case where D seeks to persuade her employee P to commit an offence

[31] [1997] Crim LR 897 (CA).

[32] A challenge against the decision in *Marlow* on the ground that it contravened D's right to freedom of expression guaranteed by Art. 10 ECHR was held by the European Court to be inadmissible on the ground that the derogation from that freedom was in pursuit of the legitimate aim of suppressing the foreseeable commission of crimes: (2001) 4 EHRLR 444.

[33] [2001] Crim LR 822 (CA).

[34] CO/6342/2003.

[35] See below, § 9.1(ii)(c).

[36] [1973] QB 815 (CA).

[37] *Ibid.*, 827.

[38] Serious Crime Act 2007, s. 65(1).

within the course of his employment. If she offers a rise in salary by way of inducement, she unequivocally encourages P to commit the offence. The same must surely follow if she uses instead the stick of redundancy. Threats are a mode of influence, and it is conduct which seeks to induce and influence the commission of crimes that constitutes the legal conception of encouragement.

Although the point is undecided, D's attitude or motivation may be relevant to the identification of encouragement. For instance, P may ask D whether V, P's wife, is still seeing E. D answers truthfully that V is, although D is aware that this information will lead to P's killing V. If D simply felt constrained to tell P the truth, arguably no encouragement of murder arises. Contrast the case where D seeks P out to impart this information in order to deceive P into thinking that V is seeing E; depending on D's mens rea, this could constitute the crime of encouraging murder.

Finally, the encouragement of P can be via an intermediary.[39] Suppose that D writes a letter encouraging P to kill V, and gives the letter to X with the instruction that she should pass it to P. If X does so, D's actions will constitute encouragement of P to murder V.

*(b) Assistance*

Assistance is not defined by the Serious Crime Act 2007, so its interpretation will be a matter for the courts, presumably with reference to the interpretation of aiding in accessorial liability.[40] The essence of assistance is conduct which can be considered to make it easier for the substantive offence to be committed. As with encouragement, it is possible to provide assistance indirectly through an intermediary.[41] For example, if D gives to X the combination number for V's safe and asks X to pass this on to P, who is intending to steal from the safe, the necessary act of assistance can be established if X does so.

*(c) An act capable of encouraging or assisting*

The offences of encouragement and assistance are committed once D has done any act which is capable of encouraging or assisting the crime to be committed. This requires an act that might at some future point encourage or assist the commission of a crime by another person.[42] Presumably, this need not be a substantial act, and neither will it be necessary to establish any communication or interaction with P. In *Banks*,[43] for example, D's letter to P advising P to kill V was intercepted in the post. D was convicted of attempting to incite murder, but today his behaviour would be sufficient to constitute the crime of encouraging murder, because sending such a letter is capable of encouraging P to commit that offence. Although it would not be necessary to show that the letter had been received by P, presumably it would be required to show that the letter had been posted, this being the act performed by D which is capable of encouraging the crime. Although this act would not actually have encouraged P before P had read the letter, the focus of the actus reus is on D's act and its capability rather than on its actual effect, so the posting alone would be sufficient. The earlier act of writing the letter might also be analysed as constituting an act which is

[39] *Ibid.*, s. 66.
[40] See above, § 7.4(i)(a).
[41] Serious Crime Act 2007, s. 66.
[42] *Scott v DPP* [2022] EWHC 91 (Admin), [2022] 1 WLR 2231.
[43] (1873) 12 Cox CC 393.

capable of encouraging the crime; but, since D must do further acts, including posting it, before this capability can be realised, the preferable view is that this is not a sufficient act. D might instead be guilty of attempting to encourage a crime, but that would require the writing of the letter to be considered a more than merely preparatory act towards the commission of the encouragement offence.[44] The notion of an act which is capable of encouraging or assisting a crime is fraught with ambiguity, since there is no reference to any notion of remoteness within the statute. The courts will undoubtedly be required to impose some remoteness limitation to make sense of the provision: ideally, that D has performed the last act which is capable of encouraging or assisting the crime without D's having to perform any other acts.

The relevant act can include a course of conduct[45] and also the taking of steps which reduce the possibility of proceedings being brought in respect of the substantive offence.[46] So, for example, D would be guilty of assisting theft if she tripped up a police officer who was chasing a thief from the scene of the crime, although only because the act of theft would be continuing.[47] D cannot be regarded as encouraging or assisting an offence that has already been completed. Further, an act which is capable of encouraging or assisting a crime includes an omission where D has failed to take reasonable steps to discharge a duty to act.[48] So, for example, D, a security guard, who fails to switch on a burglar alarm with the intent to assist a burglary, will have assisted by the failure to act because she was under a duty to act by virtue of her employment.

*(d) The conduct encouraged or assisted*

*Substantive offences.*
D will be guilty if the conduct he encourages or assists would constitute any offence on the part of P: save that the crime of corporate manslaughter[49] cannot be encouraged or assisted; the offence contrary to section 44 cannot be committed in respect of encouraging or assisting suicide;[50] and the offences contrary to sections 45 and 46 cannot be committed in respect of certain substantive offences.[51]

At common law, the offence of incitement could only be committed if the conduct D encouraged involved the commission of an offence by P in the capacity of a principal offender.[52] There is no such limitation in respect of the statutory offences of encouraging or assisting, so it is possible to encourage or assist P to do something which will involve P's liability as an accessory. For example, if D provides P with a knife, intending that P will then deliberately provide this to T to assist in a robbery, D is liable for encouraging or assisting P to become an accessory to robbery.

An offence can be encouraged or assisted even where the offending by P has already commenced at the time of D's act, as long as the encouragement or assistance relates to the

44 See below, § 9.3(i)(c).
45 Serious Crime Act 2007, s. 67.
46 *Ibid.*, s. 65(2)(a).
47 See below, § 13.6(iv).
48 Serious Crime Act 2007, s. 65(2)(b).
49 Corporate Manslaughter and Corporate Homicide Act 2007, s. 18(1A).
50 Serious Crime Act 2007, s. 51A.
51 Listed in sched. 3.
52 *Bodin* [1979] Crim LR 176.

continuation of the offending by P. So, in *Scott v DPP*,[53] D's act of making and receiving phone calls from P's unauthorised phone in prison encouraged P to continue to commit the offence of being in possession of the phone. D was convicted of an offence contrary to section 45, although a conviction as an accessory would also have been appropriate: P did, after all, commit the offence that D had intentionally encouraged.

*Inchoate offences.*

Logically, there is nothing to preclude bringing a charge of encouragement or assistance in respect of another inchoate offence (e.g. D's encouraging T to encourage P to commit an offence or to conspire with X to commit an offence). Reservations may be had, however, about criminalising conduct which might be considered too remote from the commission of a substantive offence. In the context of encouraging or assisting inchoate offences, Parliament has given only partial effect to these reservations.

The inchoate offence of encouraging or assisting a crime with intent that the crime be committed, contrary to section 44, can be committed in respect of any inchoate offence including itself. So it is possible for D1 to encourage or assist D2 to encourage or assist P to commit a substantive offence; or for D1 to encourage or assist D2 to conspire with X; or for D1 to encourage or assist D2 to attempt an offence, so long as, in each case, D1 intends D2 to encourage, assist, conspire to commit, or attempt the substantive offence. For example, suppose that D1 urges D2 to attend a clandestine meeting of terrorists and advocate the immediate resumption of a bombing strategy. For reasons of security, D1 instructs D2 to leave immediately after he has addressed the meeting and on no account to enter into any conversation with any of the other parties. D1 will have encouraged D2 to encourage the others to commit a terrorist offence. Alternatively, D1 may require D2 to make calls on individual terrorists and obtain their respective agreements to resume bombing activities. D1 will be guilty of encouraging a conspiracy to be made. Similarly, suppose that D1 orders D2 to enter V's bedroom at night and shoot V in his bed. D1 knows that V is already dead; she wants the unwitting D2 to shoot a bullet into V's corpse to obfuscate the true cause of death. D2 would be guilty of attempted murder if she fired the shot not knowing that V was already dead.[54] D1, with her knowledge of the true facts, should be guilty of encouraging attempted murder. She would not be guilty of encouraging murder, since she was aware that murder was impossible and so was not seeking, through the agency of D2, to bring about that crime. Nonetheless, she was encouraging conduct which would constitute attempted murder on D2's part, and a conviction for encouraging D2's attempt appropriately reflects her culpability.[55]

It is not, however, possible to commit the inchoate offences contrary to sections 45 and 46 (involving doing something believed to be capable of assisting and encouraging another to commit an offence, and believing that one or more substantive offences will be committed) in respect of any of the inchoate offences.[56] Consequently, where the mens rea in respect of the principal offence is one of belief rather than intent that the offence will be

[53] [2022] EWHC 91 (Admin), [2022] 1 WLR 2231. See also above, § 4.1(i)(b) (Case 4).

[54] Notwithstanding the impossibility of D2's attempt: below, § 9.4(iii).

[55] *Hapgood* (1870) LR 1 CCR 221 indicates that D1 would also be liable as a secondary party to D2's attempt. See further Smith, "Secondary Participation and Inchoate Offences" in Tapper (ed.), *Crime, Proof and Punishment* (1981) 21, 26–7.

[56] Serious Crime Act 2007, s. 49(5).

committed, the remoteness from the commission of the substantive offence negates liability. For example, if D1 believes that giving D2 a knife is capable of encouraging D2 to assist P to murder V, and that this is what D2 and P will do, he is not liable under section 45 for encouraging D2 to commit the offence of assisting murder.

*(e) Encouraging or assisting an actus reus*

In our discussion of the liability of accessories, we saw that the perpetration of a mere actus reus by P may sometimes ground a charge of complicity against D.[57] Recall that if, say, D persuades P to have intercourse with V by alleging that V's genuine protestations will be feigned, D may yet be an accomplice to rape even if P is acquitted of the substantive offence because of lack of proof of mens rea.[58] D's conviction as an accessory to rape is appropriate because D has procured the occurrence of the harm associated with commission of the substantive offence. This reasoning carries over to the inchoate offences of encouragement and assistance. On the facts above, D may have perpetrated the actus reus of encouraging rape as soon as he persuades P to have intercourse with V, whether or not P goes on to rape V, because the harm of rape, i.e. non-consensual sexual activity, is still being sought through D's actions. D's persuasion is certainly capable of encouraging the offence of rape, although it will be necessary to establish that D had the appropriate mens rea for the encouragement offence.[59]

*(f) Future crimes*

It is immaterial that the crime D encourages or assists will become possible only at some time in the future. For example, D will be liable for encouraging murder if he urges the killing, at birth, of a baby yet to be born[60] or the handling of goods yet to be stolen.[61]

### *(iii) Mens rea*

The mens rea for the encouraging and assistance offences is complex.[62] First, it is presumably necessary to establish that D intended to do the act which is capable of encouraging or assisting P. Thus a security guard who negligently fails to close a door, leading to a subsequent theft, does not commit an offence of encouraging or assisting crime.

Secondly, it is necessary to consider D's mens rea, if any, in respect of P's offence which D is alleged to have encouraged or assisted. This second requirement is the complicated one. There are three alternative ways of satisfying it. In straightforward cases, either intention or belief that D's act will encourage or assist P's offence will suffice, depending on the particular inchoate offence with which D is charged.

[57] Above, § 7.6(ii)(b).

[58] Although this is unlikely under the Sexual Offences Act 2003, because the relevant mens rea is absence of a reasonable belief in consent.

[59] This will be established through the operation of the Serious Crime Act 2007, s. 47(5)(a)(iii): if D had committed the actus reus of rape he would have done so with the necessary fault. See below, § 9.1(iii).

[60] *Banks* (1873) 12 Cox CC 393.

[61] *McDonough* (1962) 47 Cr App R 37.

[62] See Child, "Exploring the Mens Rea Requirements of the Serious Crime Act 2007 Assisting and Encouraging Offences" (2012) 76 *J Crim Law* 220.

### (a) Intention

The section 44 offence will be committed where D intends to encourage or assist the commission of an offence. It is unclear whether D's mental state relates only to the act of encouraging or assisting or whether it must also be shown that D means the specific offence to be committed. In practice, D's intention will usually relate both to the encouragement or assistance and to the commission of the substantive offence; but there may be cases where D intends merely to encourage or assist and does not care whether the specific offence will be committed. This uncertainty does not arise in respect of sections 45 and 46, which expressly requires proof that D believed that the relevant offence will be committed. Although no such requirement is spelled out in section 44, one might reasonably infer that what is required for the section 44 offence is that D either directly or (subject to what is said below) obliquely intends to assist or encourage P's offence. As such, D would have to intend his own act of encouragement or assistance, and do so either *in order* to encourage or assist P's crime or knowing that it will do so. This interpretation would align with the requirements in the law of complicity.[63]

Unfortunately, this straightforward reading of section 44 conflicts with section 47 of the Serious Crime Act 2007. Section 47(5), in particular,[64] waters down D's mens rea requirements regarding P's crime. The provision substitutes two requirements. The first concerns D's mens rea regarding *P's mens rea* for P's crime. D must have *believed* that, if P acted on the assistance or encouragement received from D, P would do so with the fault required for that offence; or D must have been *reckless* whether P would do the act with this fault; or, if D had himself done the act that he had assisted or encouraged, he would have done so with the necessary fault for the substantive crime. The second substituted requirement concerns D's mens rea regarding any *consequence or circumstance elements* of P's crime. D must intend, believe, or be reckless whether any such consequence and circumstance elements will be present. By contrast, section 47(2) appears to require that any *behaviour* ("act") element of P's crime must be (directly or indirectly) intended by D.

Section 44(2) states that D must not be found to have had the necessary intent merely because encouragement or assistance of an offence was a foreseeable consequence of his act. It is unclear whether the effect of this provision is simply that it is not possible to assume intention because encouragement or assistance of an offence was objectively foreseeable, or that subjective recklessness is not sufficient evidence of intent, both of which would appear to be obvious. An alternative interpretation is that oblique intent, involving foresight of a virtually certain consequence, does not constitute an intent for purposes of the section 44 offence. There is much to be said for this interpretation of the provision,[65] especially because the case where D foresees (but does not intend) the encouragement or assistance of a substantive crime, whether virtually certain or otherwise, might be read as being impliedly excluded from section 44 by the high standard of foresight (that the offence *will* occur) in sections 45 and 46.

### (b) Belief

The offence contrary to sections 45 will be committed where D believes: (i) that the substantive offence will be committed; and (ii) that his act will encourage or assist that offence. It is

[63] Above, § 7.4(iv).
[64] Taken together with s. 47(7). See further below, § 9.1(iii)(d).
[65] Stark, "It's Only Words: On Meaning and Mens Rea" (2013) 72 *CLJ* 155, 157.

not sufficient that D believes that the offence *might* or even *probably will* be committed. D will have the relevant mens rea even if he believes that an offence will be committed only if certain conditions are met, such as that P manages to locate V.[66]

### *(c) Believing that one or more offence may be committed*

The section 46 offence applies in situations where D believes that his act *might* encourage or assist a number of offences to be committed and that his act *will* encourage or assist one or more of those offences, but he has no belief as to which. Its operation is illustrated by *Blackshaw et al.*,[67] where one defendant had posted messages on Facebook encouraging people to meet at a particular location and time generally to wreak havoc in a town. The defendant was convicted of the Section 46 offence even though he believed that a number of different offences might be committed, including riot, burglary, and criminal damage, it being sufficient that he believed at least one of those offences *would* be encouraged or assisted by his conduct, and *would* be committed.

Section 46 is needed to ensure that D should not be acquitted of encouraging or assisting a crime simply because his act might encourage or assist a variety of offences, rather than just one specific offence, and therefore it is difficult to prove that D believed the relevant offences *would* be encouraged or assisted *and* committed.[68]

The operation of section 46 was considered by the Court of Appeal in *Sadique (No.1)*,[69] where D had been charged with assisting in the supply of Class A and/or Class B drugs by supplying various chemical cutting agents. The key issue in that case was whether the section 46 offence was incompatible with Article 7 of the ECHR on the ground that it was too vague and uncertain. In confirming its compatibility, the Court of Appeal sought to make sense of the offence; but, in doing so held that each of the identified offences will be committed. This interpretation was rejected by the Court of Appeal in *Sadique (No. 2)*,[70] which held that the section 46 offence required D to believe that *one or more* of the offences which are capable of being committed *will* be committed, but this perceived inevitability of commission is not required in respect of *each* offence. This is emphasised by the fact that section 46(1)(b)(i) adds in parentheses "(but has no belief as to which)" offence will be committed. Further, as regards the requirement that D believes that his act will encourage or assist one or more of the offences which are capable of being encouraged or assisted, it is specifically recognised[71] that it is immaterial whether he believes that a particular offence will be assisted or encouraged, it consequently being sufficient that D believes that *an* offence will be assisted or encouraged.[72] In addition, section 46(3) makes specific provision for the charging of an offence contrary to section 46. The indictment must specify the reference offences which are capable of being assisted or encouraged by D's act. This need not be a comprehensive list of all the possible offences which could be assisted or encouraged, but

[66] Serious Crime Act 2007, s. 49(7).

[67] [2011] EWCA Crim 2312, [2012] 1 WLR 1126.

[68] A similar result is obtained in the law of complicity. See *DPP for Northern Ireland v Maxwell* [1978] 1 WLR 1350. See above, § 7.4(iv)(c).

[69] [2011] EWCA Crim 2872, [2012] 1 WLR 1700. See Virgo, "Encouraging or Assisting More Than One Offence" (2012) 2 *Arch Rev* 6; Virgo, "Part 2 of the Serious Crime Act 2007—Enough Is Enough" (2013) 3 *Arch Rev* 7.

[70] [2013] EWCA Crim 1150; [2014] 1 WLR 986. See Virgo, "Making Sense of Section 46 of the Serious Crime Act 2007" [2013] 7 *Arch Rev* 4.

[71] Serious Crimes Act 2007, s. 462(2).

[72] Which can include a lesser included offence of an offence specified in the indictment: ibid., s. 57(2), (3).

just those which are identified for the purposes of the charge.[73] Nothing is stated about each of the reference offences being identified in separate counts. Consequently, section 46 creates a single offence and not a number of individual offences depending on the number of reference offences which are identified. It followed that, on the facts of *Sadique*, D would be guilty of a section 46 offence in supplying chemical cutting agents if he believed that the chemicals would be used to supply drugs but was not sure whether these would be Class A or Class B, but would be one of them.

It might be thought that this interpretation of section 46 creates a problem for sentencing. If D is convicted of the single section 46 offence, what will be the maximum sentence where he believes that one of the range of offences will be committed but has no belief as to the commission of any specific offence? Reinforcing the interpretation adopted in *Sadique (No. 2)*, this question is answered specifically by section 58(4)–(7), the effect of which is that, where the defendant is convicted under section 46 by reference to more than one offence, the maximum prison sentence is that of the reference offence which has the longest term.[74] Admittedly, this has the potential to generate harsh results. Suppose that D lends P a jemmy. D thinks that P will use it to commit burglary, assault, or murder, but is not sure which. Since D contemplates that P might use the jemmy to commit murder, and since this is the most serious offence contemplated, D is liable upon conviction for the section 46 offence to life imprisonment. Whilst this is a shocking result, it is one that is explicitly acknowledged by the Serious Crime Act 2007.[75] Note, however, that this is only the maximum sentence; the trial judge will undoubtedly exercise appropriate discretion when sentencing. Moreover, it must not be forgotten that D has willingly provided P with a jemmy contemplating that she might thereby be helped to commit, and in fact commit, murder. D has done all that he can to assist P in her criminal enterprise: D's conduct is certainly wrongful, and it is of a kind that section 46 was intended to prohibit. If, however, P does commit murder, D would be subject to the mandatory life sentence as an accessory, but only, after *Jogee*,[76] if D intended or knew what P would do; whereas, for section 46, it is sufficient that D foresaw that murder might be committed but believed that another offence would be committed. It is most undesirable that D can be convicted of an inchoate offence relating to murder with less culpability than is required for accessorial liability. But this is a consequence of the Draconian approach to inchoate offences expressed by Parliament in the Serious Crime Act, and of the failure of the Supreme Court to appreciate the disconnect created in *Jogee* between accessorial and inchoate liability.[77]

### *(d) Intention or belief relating only to the behaviour element of the offence*

Suppose that it is not possible to prove an intention to encourage or assist a specific offence for section 44 or a belief that an offence will be encouraged or assisted for either section 45 or 46. It may still may be possible to convict D of encouraging or assisting if he intended to encourage or assist the doing of an "act" which would amount to the commission of the

[73] Ibid., s. 46(3)(b).
[74] Where one of the reference offences is murder, the maximum term is life imprisonment: Serious Crime Act 2007, s. 58(5).
[75] Serious Crime Act 2007, s. 58(5).
[76] *Jogee* [2016] UKSC 8; *Ruddock* [2016] UKPC 7, [2017] AC 387.
[77] See further Virgo, "The Relationship between Inchoate and Accessorial Liability After *Jogee*" [2016] 9 *Arch Rev* 6.

crime for the purposes of section 44.[78] Similarly, it may be possible to convict D under section 45 if he believed that P would do the act amounting to the crime and that D's act would encourage or assist P's act,[79] or one or more acts within the scope of section 46.[80]

The notion of an "act" is widely defined to include a failure to act, the continuation of an act which has already begun, and an attempt to do an act.[81] In other words, rather than proving an intention or a belief in respect of the encouragement or assistance of the commission of a crime by P, it may be sufficient to prove that D only intended to encourage or assist the behaviour element of P's crime, and believed that this element would be committed.

For example, if D provides P with a knife, intending to encourage or assist him to stab V, this will be sufficient proof of mens rea regarding the behavioural element of murder. In such a case it is necessary to prove additional mens rea elements concerning: (i) the circumstances or consequences of P's behaviour, to the extent that they form part of the actus reus of P's substantive offence; and (ii) P's mens rea for the substantive offence. These need to be considered separately.

*Circumstances or consequences of P's anticipated crime.*

Where the substantive offence requires proof of particular circumstances or consequences or both, it is necessary to prove that D believed[82] or was reckless[83] as to whether the act would be done in those circumstances or with those consequences. So, to be guilty of encouraging murder contrary to section 44 where D does not intend to encourage that specific crime, it must be shown that D had intended to encourage the doing of an act by P, such as stabbing V, which D believed would result in death, or thought that it might have that consequence and proceeded without justification. For example, in *A-G's Reference (No. 39 of 2011)*,[84] D had been convicted of intentionally encouraging aggravated criminal damage, for which it had to be proved that D intended arson to be committed in circumstances where P would be reckless about whether life was endangered, the latter element was, in effect, treated as a circumstance of the substantive offence (although it is better treated as an ulterior mens rea element).[85]

*Mens rea in offences requiring proof of fault.*

If the substantive offence is one which requires proof of fault on P's part, it will be necessary to prove an additional fault element on the part of D,[86] by virtue of section 47(5)(a), being:

(I) a belief that the act would be done with the requisite mens rea for the substantive offence; or

(II) recklessness as to whether P would have the relevant mens rea for the substantive offence; or

(III) D's state of mind was such that, had he committed the act, he would have the appropriate mens rea for that substantive offence.[87]

[78] Serious Crime Act 2007, s. 47(2).

[79] *Ibid.*, s. 47(3).

[80] *Ibid.*, s. 47(4).

[81] *Ibid.*, s. 47(8). The language of s. 47(8) does at least seem to preclude liability for assisting or encouraging situational crimes which have no behavioural element at all: above, § 4.1(ii)(a).

[82] Intention or belief suffices for the s. 44 offence: Serious Crime Act 2007, s. 47(7).

[83] *Ibid.*, s. 47(5)(b).

[84] [2011] EWCA Crim 2617.

[85] Child, "The Structure, Coherence and Limits of Inchoate Liability: The New *Ulterior* Element" (2014) 34 *LS* 537. See further below, § 9.3(iii)(c).

[86] And not the other party: *Sadique (No. 1)* [2011] EWCA Crim 2872, [2012] 1 WLR 1700, [64].

[87] Or for one of them, if charged under section 46: Serious Crime Act 2007, s. 48(2).

So, if D does not intend to encourage P to commit murder but intends to encourage P to do an act which he believed might cause V's death, or thought that it might have that consequence and proceeded without justification, D could be convicted of encouraging murder contrary to section 44, but only if one of the three additional mens rea elements is proved, namely: a belief that P would intend to kill or cause serious injury; recklessness as to whether P would have such mens rea;[88] or, if D had done the act himself, he would have intended to kill or cause serious injury.

These requirements have no application where the substantive offence is one of strict liability: in which case D's mens rea need only relate to his own act and to P's actus reus, and section 47(5)(a) is not engaged. Where the substantive offence does require proof of fault, section 47(5)(a) may influence the offence which D will have assisted or encouraged. Thus, if D does not intend P to commit murder but intends to encourage P to do an act which, D realises, might cause V's death,[89] that may be sufficient for D to be convicted of encouraging murder provided that D foresaw a risk that P might act with intent to kill or cause serious injury (option II). Alternatively, it may be sufficient for D to be convicted of encouraging manslaughter provided that, were D himself to do the act he intends P will do, that would be grossly negligent regarding a serious and obvious risk of V's death (option III).

While section 47 is described in the statute as a provision concerning the proof of sections 44–6, subsection (5) radically expands the ambit of these offences. Sections 44–6 have a requirement that D intends or believes that he will encourage or assist P *to commit an offence*; but that requirement is immediately dispensed with in section 47, since D could be guilty of one of the inchoate offences if he only intends or believes that P will do the act which amounts to the commission of the offence.

*(e) Application of the mens rea provisions*

The implications of these absurdly complex provisions can best be appreciated with reference to some hypothetical examples.

D offers P a necklace which D has stolen. D believes that P knows the necklace to be stolen, but in fact P believes that D acquired it honestly. In such circumstances, D will clearly be guilty of assisting P to handle stolen goods contrary to section 45. This is because D believes that P will commit the substantive offence of handling with mens rea due to his belief as to her knowledge of the provenance of the jewellery and his act of giving her the jewellery will assist her to commit the crime. Being an inchoate offence, it is irrelevant that P's lack of knowledge or belief as to the provenance of the jewellery means that she will not be guilty of the substantive offence.

If, however, D believes that P thinks that D has acquired the necklace honestly, it might be assumed that D cannot be guilty of assisting the crime of handling stolen goods contrary to section 45 because he does not believe that his act will assist her to commit the offence. But, since D does believe that his act will assist P to commit the behavioural element of the substantive offence, namely to handle goods, it is necessary to consider section 47(5). D does believe that the relevant circumstance of the substantive offence, namely that the

[88] That recklessness might be sufficient mens rea for the s. 44 offence was not appreciated by the Supreme Court in *Jogee* [2016] UKSC 8; *Ruddock* [2016] UKPC 7, [2017] AC 387 where Lords Hughes and Toulson said, at [86], "that Parliament has provided that foresight is not sufficient mens rea for the offence of intentionally encouraging or assisting another to commit an offence". In the light of s. 47(5)(a), this is incorrect.

[89] Serious Crime Act 2007, s. 47(5)(b)(ii).

goods are stolen, will be satisfied, this being a circumstance which D must believe or be reckless regarding.[90] D does not, however, believe or is reckless that P will have the mens rea for the substantive offence. But, if D committed the actus reus of the substantive offence himself, he would have the mens rea for that crime since he knows that the necklace is stolen.[91] Consequently he will be guilty of assisting P to handle stolen goods contrary to section 45.

If D encourages P to beat up V and intends that P will do so, D could be guilty of encouraging murder contrary to section 44 if she: (i) believes that V will die, or is reckless as to whether V might die, as a result of P's attack,[92] this being the relevant consequence of the substantive offence; and (ii) believes that P will, or is reckless as to whether P would, have the relevant mens rea for murder, or, if D did the act of beating up V herself, she would have intended to kill V or to cause him serious injury. Similarly, D would assist murder contrary to section 44 if D supplied P with a poisoned drink intending P to do the act of administering the drink to V, and D: (i) believed that V would die, or foresaw that V might die (and proceeded without adequate justification) and (ii) believed that P would intend to kill or cause serious injury, or was reckless whether P might kill with this fault, or, had D himself supplied V with the drink, D would have had the necessary mens rea for murder. In both cases D could therefore be convicted of encouraging or assisting murder, for which a sentence of life imprisonment is potentially available, even though D did not intend or believe that P would commit murder.

Further, if D encourages P to have consensual sex with V, in circumstances where D both knows that V is 15 but also knows that P reasonably believes that V is 16, whether D is guilty of encouraging P to commit the offence of sexual activity with a child[93] involves a convoluted analysis of D's mens rea. Since D thinks that P will be reasonably mistaken as to the age of V, D does not intend or believe that the offence of sexual activity with a child will be committed. But, since that offence requires proof of fault (namely intentional touching and that the defendant did not reasonably believe that the child was 16 or older) section 47(5)(a) is engaged. Since D does not believe that P would have no reasonable belief that V was 16, and D is not reckless as regards whether P might have no reasonable belief that V was 16, the question then is whether, were D to have sexual activity with P, he would not reasonably believe that V was 16 or older. Since D knew that V is actually 15 he would not have such a belief and so the offence of encouraging sexual activity with a child would be made out.

Apart from the tortuous path which needs to be followed through the statutory provisions to reach such conclusions, which makes jury directions very difficult, the fact that D could be convicted of an inchoate offence relating to a serious crime, in circumstances where D might not contemplate that the substantive offence would actually be committed by P, means that the ambit of inchoate criminal liability is far removed from the commission of any substantive offence. The ambit of criminal liability has been extended far beyond its legitimate limits. Bock and Stark have consequently argued that, for inchoate offences such as this, D should be required to be *more* culpable than the completed substantive offence

[90] *Ibid.*, s. 47(5)(b).
[91] *Ibid.*, s. 47(5)(a).
[92] *Ibid.*, s. 47(5)(b).
[93] Sexual Offences Act 2003, s. 9. See below, § 12.11(ii).

requires, so as to make up for the deficit in harm that is present in the inchoate offence;[94] but this does not reflect the law.

### *(iv) Defences*

#### *(a) Withdrawal?*

Since the inchoate offences of encouragement and assistance are complete at the point when D has done the act which is capable of encouraging or assisting the crime, any countermanding or withdrawal of her initial encouragement or assistance by D should count, at most, as mitigation. It cannot undo the crime she has already committed. In the cognate sphere of complicity, if D counsels P to commit an offence but then, prior to the commission of that offence, effectively revokes her earlier counselling or contacts an appropriate person in authority, she will no longer be a party to the offence if P goes on to commit it.[95] No such defence of revocation or withdrawal applies to the offences of encouragement and assistance, but should it have been made available? Encouragement and counselling are not precisely parallel. D will not be an accomplice until the principal commits the substantive offence, whereas encouragement is complete once D has done the act which is capable of encouraging a crime. Yet the counsellor and the encourager are in other senses very much alike. In each case, all the elements of liability personal to D are present as soon as the encouragement is given. The public policy considerations that allow a withdrawal defence where the charge is one of complicity also seem germane to a charge of encouragement, and also of assistance. Furthermore, it will undermine the policy behind the withdrawal defence in complicity if the prosecution could obviate it by charging an inchoate offence of encouragement or assistance on the same facts. In our view, the encourager or assister should have been allowed a defence if, prior to the commission of the offence encouraged or assisted, she countermanded the encouragement or assistance of the crime to the person she encouraged or assisted, or informed an appropriate authority (such as the police) of the details of her conduct.[96]

#### *(b) Acting reasonably*

Section 50 of the Serious Crime Act 2007 recognises a defence of acting reasonably. This defence takes two forms:

(i) where D knew that certain circumstances existed and it was reasonable for D to act as he did in those circumstances;[97] and
(ii) where D reasonably believed certain circumstances existed and it was reasonable for D to act as he did in the circumstances as he believed them to be.[98]

The second version will be relevant where D is mistaken as to the circumstances, though his mistake must be a reasonable one. Various factors are identified to determine whether D

[94] Bock and Stark, "Preparatory Offences" in Ambos *et al.* (eds.), *Core Concepts in Criminal Law and Criminal Justice* (2019) vol. 1, 79.
[95] See the discussion above, § 7.6(vi).
[96] See further Bock and Stark, "Preparatory Offences" in Ambos *et al.* (eds), *Core Concepts in Criminal Law and Criminal Justice* (2019) vol. 1, 84.
[97] Serious Crime Act 2007, s. 50(1).
[98] *Ibid.*, s. 50(2).

had acted reasonably, including the seriousness of the anticipated offence; the purposes for which D was acting, which would presumably include preventing a crime; and any authority by which D claims to have been acting, such as through being a police officer. The defence operates when D did the act capable of encouraging or assisting P to commit a crime. The fact that D subsequently may have acted reasonably cannot be taken into account. Consequently, the defence cannot be interpreted to incorporate a defence of withdrawal.

The potential application of the defence can be illustrated with reference to the facts of *Shaw*,[99] which concerned the old common law offence of incitement. D incited P and other fellow employees to commit thefts against their employer. D's motivation, apparently, was to bring deficiencies in the firm's security system to the notice of their employer. It was held that D's motivation was incompatible with liability for incitement to steal and D was acquitted. Yet what P was persuaded by D to do was clearly theft,[100] and D was aware of all the material circumstances which rendered P's conduct theft. For the crime of conspiracy, the Privy Council in *Yip Chiu-Cheung* assumed that D would commit a serious drugs offence even though his sole motivation in importing drugs was to expose the activities of drug traffickers.[101] The approach of English law, though not beyond criticism,[102] is that mens rea may be present even though D's conduct may lack moral culpability; indeed, it may be present even if his conduct merits praise. The decision in *Shaw* is incompatible with this stance; there are no particular features of inchoate offences which justify a different approach. Accordingly, *Shaw* should be regarded as wrongly decided. At the very least it has been regarded as authoritative only in terms of the wording of the charge: in *DPP v Armstrong*,[103] the decision in *Shaw* was given guarded approval only because D in that case was charged with *dishonestly* inciting P to commit theft. The reference to dishonesty in the charge was otiose, since dishonesty was not a constituent element of incitement. If the facts of *Shaw* arose today and D was charged with encouraging theft, he would probably not have a defence of acting reasonably. Although he may reasonably have believed that there were deficiencies in the employer's security system, his actions in encouraging theft were seemingly not reasonable: the anticipated offence was serious, he was not acting to prevent a crime, and he was not acting under any particular authority.

This reasonableness defence is unsatisfactory in a variety of ways,[104] most notably because the burden of proof is placed on D and because its application depends on the vagueness of what is "reasonable". For example, if D is a shop assistant who sells a knife to P, whom she believes will use it to commit murder so that the section 45 offence is engaged, is it possible to conclude that she acted reasonably in selling the knife to P, bearing in mind that she was under a contractual obligation to her employer to do so? In assessing the reasonableness of D's conduct, it is necessary to have regard to the seriousness of the crime that she believes P will commit, but is it relevant that she was employed to sell the knife? In *K Ltd v National Westminster Bank plc*,[105] in the context of the distinct crime of facilitating

[99] [1994] Crim LR 365 (CA).

[100] Note that P, unlike D, was dishonest since he was unaware of D's reason for encouraging the thefts.

[101] [1995] 1 AC 111.

[102] See above, § 1.2(ii); § 5.

[103] [2000] Crim LR 379 (DC).

[104] See Ormerod and Forston, "Serious Crime Act 2007: The Part 2 Offences" [2009] *Crim LR* 389, 411.

[105] [2006] EWCA Civ 1039, [2007] 1 WLR 311; see also above, § 7.4(iv)(a) (An exception for performance of a duty?).

the use or control of criminal property, it was recognised that D had no defence that he was contractually obliged to use the property. Similar reasoning would mean that D would have no defence to encouraging or assisting a crime when selling a knife to P.

The "reasonableness defence" is inadequate if it is being used as a sop to counteract the breadth of liability for the inchoate offences. Bearing in mind the detailed complexity of the definition of mens rea for the inchoate offences, it is unacceptable that the statutory defence has been left so vague. It is inevitable that the courts will at some point be required to set limits on the defence and to identify more detailed principles against which the notion of reasonableness can be assessed.

*(c) Victims*

D will have a defence if she would be the victim of the substantive offence that she assists or encourages,[106] provided that the relevant substantive offence is a "protective offence" and that D falls within the relevant protected category of person. It follows that D, a child under 13, who encourages P, an adult, to have sex with them, will not be guilty of assisting or encouraging the offence of rape of a child under 13.[107] That offence exists to protect D and it would be an odd form of protection to then convict D of assisting or encouraging it.

This defence is a statutory parallel to the so-called *Tyrrell* exception to complicity liability.[108] However, as with its common law counterpart, determining whether an offence is a protective offence for the purposes of the Serious Crime Act 2007, and whether D falls within the protected category of persons, will not always be clear. This was considered by the Supreme Court in *Gnango*,[109] as regards complicity, but will be significant to the inchoate offences as well. Lords Phillips and Judge[110] described section 51 as giving a "limited exemption" from liability. They considered that masochists, who have consented to be injured by sadists,[111] could be convicted of aiding and abetting the infliction of injuries on themselves because they did not fall within the protected category. It would follow that the masochists could also be guilty of encouraging the offences against the person committed on themselves, because they would not fall within the statutory exception, since those offences do not exist to protect masochists.

***(v) The future of Part 2 of the Serious Crime Act 2007***

The intentions behind the enactment of Part 2 of the Serious Crime Act were good. Since the common law offence of incitement did not extend to conduct which purported to assist a crime, there was a gap in the law which needed to be plugged. The significance of this is illustrated by the conviction secured in *Sadique (No. 2)*[112] for assisting the supply of drugs, which could not have been prosecuted before Part 2 of the Serious Crime Act was enacted. If a statutory offence of assisting was to be created, it was entirely appropriate to codify the crime of incitement at the same time, to ensure consistency between the two offences. But,

[106] Serious Crime Act 2007, s. 51.
[107] Sexual Offences Act 2003, s. 13; below, § 12.11(ii).
[108] Described above, § 7.6(iv)(a).
[109] [2011] UKSC 59, [2012] 1 AC 827.
[110] *Ibid.*, [52].
[111] As in *Brown* [1994] 1 AC 212. See below, § 11.9.
[112] [2013] EWCA Crim 1150; [2014] 1 WLR 986.

whereas the common law offence of incitement could be expressed very simply and was a body of law about which there was little uncertainty, that is not true of the offences which replaced it. The key point of principle relating to the legitimacy of Part 2 of the Serious Crime Act 2007 relates to the appropriate formulation of criminal legislation, which needs to be certain, clear, and readily explicable. The success of a new criminal offence should not be judged simply by the intellectual satisfaction derived from providing solutions to unlikely problems. The application of the law in the real world by the police, prosecutors, judges, and legal advisers must be considered as well. Judged in this way, Part 2 is not fit for purpose. Further, the growing disconnect between the breadth of inchoate liability and the restrictive interpretation of accessorial liability, especially following the decision of the Supreme Court in *Jogee*,[113] is a cause of particular concern, especially since this might mean that prosecutors prefer to prosecute D for the inchoate offence of encouraging or assisting despite the commission of the substantive offence, safe in the knowledge that the maximum penalty available will be identical in both cases.[114]

The real problem with Part 2 of the Serious Crime Act 2007 is that it is seeking to do far too much, by providing for a wide variety of different circumstances and resulting in the criminalisation of conduct artificially. Where, for example, D encourages P to handle goods in circumstances where D knows that the goods are stolen, D should only be guilty of encouraging the offence if she knows or believes that P will commit it. What is required is radical, but simple, reform. Part 2 of the Act needs to be replaced with one new offence of encouraging or assisting another to commit an offence, intending or believing that the other would commit that offence. Provision would also need to be made for the situation where D believes that one offence from a list of offences will be committed, but is not sure which. Whilst the coverage of these new provisions would not be quite as wide as the existing offences in Part 2, that is no bad thing. Moreover, these reforms would facilitate greater consistency between inchoate and accessorial liability, thereby helping to ensure that the inchoate offences involving encouragement and assistance are fit for purpose.

## § 9.2 Conspiracy

Conspiracy is predominantly a statutory offence, defined by section 1 of the Criminal Law Act 1977. The essence of statutory conspiracy is an agreement between two or more people which, if carried out in accordance with the intentions of the parties, will result in the commission of a statutory or common law crime by at least one of the parties to the agreement.

### *(i) Common law conspiracy*

There are some forms of conspiracy which survive at common law. Prior to the enactment of the Criminal Law Act 1977, the Law Commission examined the common law of conspiracy and prepared a Bill which, with some significant alterations by Parliament, became

[113] *Jogee* [2016] UKSC 8; *Ruddock* [2016] UKSC 7, [2017] AC 387. See above, § 7.4(iv)(b)–(c).
[114] Save for murder, where a *discretionary* life sentence would be available, rather than a *mandatory* one.

the substance of the 1977 Act.[115] The aspiration of the Law Commission, echoed in ministerial statements, was ultimately to replace entirely common law conspiracy by a statutory offence. However, at the time the Act was passed, abolition in its entirety of common law conspiracy was not regarded as feasible.[116] Three heads of common law conspiracy were felt to be indispensable until new offences, as yet unresolved, were created to replace them. The common law conspiracies retained were: (i) to outrage public decency; (ii) to corrupt public morality; and (iii) to defraud. Accordingly, common law conspiracy, to this diminished extent, still exists alongside the statutory offence.[117]

These three heads of common law conspiracy were retained because it was unclear to what extent they criminalise agreements to carry out conduct that would not be criminal if done by an individual acting alone. Statutory conspiracy is confined to agreements *to commit crimes*. Rightly or otherwise, it was the opinion of Parliament at the time that provision for common law conspiracy was required in these three areas, even if that required penalising conduct which would not be criminal but for the presence of a conspiracy. However, since the enactment of the 1977 Act, *Gibson*[118] has resolved that conduct outraging public decency constitutes a substantive offence in its own right, which can be committed by an individual acting alone. Accordingly, an agreement to outrage public decency will now fall within the ambit of statutory conspiracy.[119] The position in respect of corrupting public morality is less clear, but is probably the same as for outraging public decency.[120] Consequently these offences are now covered by statutory conspiracy and will not be further considered here.

By contrast, in the case of conspiracy to defraud, it is incontrovertibly the case that forms of dishonest conduct which would not otherwise be criminal are rendered criminal only by virtue of the common law conspiracy.[121] This form of conspiracy, which is of enormous breadth, is frequently resorted to, particularly in the sphere of large-scale fraud, such as motor insurance fraud.[122] It was widely anticipated that the Fraud Act 2006 would abolish the offence, but the Government did not do so, fearful, it seems, of leaving gaps in the coverage of dishonest conduct.[123] Conspiracy to defraud will be considered in detail below, in the context of property offences.[124]

[115] Law Com. No. 76, *Conspiracy and Criminal Law Reform* (1976).
[116] HL Vol. 379, col. 206 (Lord Harris of Greenwich).
[117] Criminal Law Act 1977, s. 5.
[118] [1990] 2 QB 619 (CA).
[119] Under the terms of s. 5(3) of the Criminal Law Act 1977, if there is a substantive offence of outraging public decency, as now appears to be the case, an agreement to commit that offence must be charged as a statutory conspiracy, falling within s. 1 of the Act, and may not be charged as a common law conspiracy.
[120] In *Shaw v DPP* [1962] AC 220, the Court of Criminal Appeal had held that there was a substantive offence of corrupting public morality. However, the House of Lords confirmed the appellant's conviction for conspiracy to corrupt public morality and did not go on to confirm whether or not there was a substantive offence.
[121] Conduct which clearly falls within the ambit of a substantive offence involving dishonesty, such as theft, will almost invariably fall within the ambit of conspiracy to defraud if two or more persons are involved. Section 12 of the Criminal Justice Act 1987, resolving an interpretative conflict that had arisen over the effect of s. 5(2) of the Criminal Law Act 1977, provides that in such circumstances the conduct may be charged as either a statutory conspiracy or a common law conspiracy. Contrast s. 5(3) of the Criminal Law Act 1977, which clearly provides that, if corrupting public morality or outraging public decency constitute substantive offences, only a charge of statutory conspiracy may be brought in respect of any agreement to commit such offences.
[122] *McKenzie* [2013] EWCA Crim 1544, [2014] 1 Cr App R (S) 68.
[123] Ormerod, "The Fraud Act 2006: Criminalising Lying?" [2007] *Crim LR* 193, 194.
[124] § 15.9.

### *(ii) Statutory conspiracy—definition and ambit*

In this chapter, we will examine the elements of statutory conspiracy. Unfortunately, as we shall see, the Criminal Law Act 1977 does not provide clear answers to many of the points of interpretation that arise.[125] It may consequently sometimes be necessary to refer to pre-Act common law authority to assist with the resolution of difficulties of interpretation.

Section 1 of the Criminal Law Act 1977 provides that:

> if a person agrees with any other person or persons that a course of conduct will be pursued which, if the agreement is carried out in accordance with their intentions, either—
> (a) will necessarily amount to or involve the commission of any offence or offences by one or more parties to the agreement, or
> (b) would do so but for the existence of facts which render the commission of the offence or any offences impossible, he is guilty of conspiracy to commit the offence or offences in question.

At the core of statutory conspiracy is an agreement between two or more persons which will necessarily involve the commission of an offence by one or more of the parties[126] should the agreement be carried out in accordance with their intentions. The agreed offence may be common law or statutory, indictable or summary.[127] It is not necessary to establish that the conspirators have done anything to carry out the agreement. The offence is complete once the agreement has been made with the necessary intention.[128] If a conspirator subsequently repents this does not operate as a defence but is only relevant to the mitigation of sentence.[129]

### *(iii) The agreement*

Agreement[130] is the essence of conspiracy.[131] Yet the term must be regarded with some caution, particularly by lawyers familiar with the concept of agreement as used in other areas of law, such as contract. Indeed, the formalities of a conventional contract are not required to establish an agreement for a conspiracy, which is a straightforward concept[132] which should not be complicated with reference to ideas derived from the civil law of contract.

The Criminal Law Act 1977 provides no definition of agreement.[133] Accordingly, we may assume that the Act intends no change from the common law regarding the nature of the agreement required for conspiracy. The Canadian case of *Sokoloski*[134] provides a useful

[125] See Smith, "Conspiracy under the Criminal Law Act 1977" [1977] *Crim LR* 598 and 638.

[126] The actus reus of the offence might be brought about by an innocent agent: *Varley* [2019] EWCA Crim 1074, [89].

[127] In the case of conspiracies to commit a summary offence, prosecutions may be brought only with the consent of the Director of Public Prosecutions: Criminal Law Act 1977, s. 4.

[128] *Maxey* [2025] EWCA Crim 472, [2025] 2 Cr App R 7, [21].

[129] *Oni* [2025] EWCA Crim 12, [2025] 4 WLR 19, [74].

[130] Orchard, "Agreement in Criminal Conspiracy" [1974] *Crim LR* 297, 335; Marcus, "The Criminal Agreement in Theory and in Practice" (1977) 65 *Geo LJ* 925; Jarvis and Bisgrove, "The Use and Abuse of Conspiracy" [2014] *Crim LR* 261.

[131] *Oni* [2025] EWCA Crim 12, [2025] 4 WLR 19, [73].

[132] *Ibid.*

[133] The Law Commission has recommended that a conspiracy should be defined as involving an agreement between at least two people to engage in the conduct element of an offence and, where relevant, to bring about the consequences of that offence: Law Com. No. 318, *Conspiracy and Attempts* (2009) para. 2.45.

[134] [1977] 2 SCR 523.

illustration of an agreement directed at criminal activity which falls short of a criminal conspiracy. D and E arranged a rendezvous at which D could hand over drugs to E in exchange for cash. The selling of drugs by D constituted the crime of drug-trafficking on his part. E was charged with conspiracy with D to traffic in drugs. On appeal, it was held that there was no drug-trafficking conspiracy between D and E. Selling drugs for cash was D's project, and his alone. The fact that E agreed arrangements with D which enabled D to sell drugs did not alter the fact that E's role in these arrangements was that of a buyer of drugs, an activity which did not constitute drug trafficking. But for this limitation on the kind of agreement required for conspiracy, all manner of consumption of illegal services could be brought within the net of conspiracy.[135]

*(a) Conspiracy as common purpose*

It is not enough that D and E agree a course of conduct which necessarily involves the commission of an offence. The commission of that offence must constitute a project that they have in common; their agreement must be indicative of a collaboration to achieve that end. The collaborative nature of the agreement necessary for a criminal conspiracy was usefully highlighted by the Court of Appeal in *Mehta*,[136] where Toulson LJ recognised the following propositions:

> "1. A conspiracy requires that the parties to it have a common unlawful purpose or design.
> 2. A common design means a shared design. It is not the same as similar but separate designs."

It is not necessary to prove that all conspirators have met either in person or online.[137]

The need for collaboration means that the conspirators might not all be party to the same agreement. There may be different agreements between different parties, involving distinct conspiracy offences. This was recognised by Toulson LJ in *Mehta*:[138]

> "In criminal law (as in civil law) there may be an umbrella agreement pursuant to which the parties enter into any further agreements which may include parties who are not parties to the umbrella agreement. So, A and B may enter into an umbrella agreement pursuant to which they enter into a further agreement between A, B and C, and a further agreement between A, B and D, and so on. In that example, C and D will not be conspirators with each other."

So-called "chain" and "wheel" conspiracies have been recognised. A chain conspiracy was described by Lord Hewart CJ in *Meyrick and Ribuffi* as arising where "A communicates with B, B with C, C with D, and so on to the end of the list of conspirators".[139] He described a wheel conspiracy as involving "one person . . . round whom the rest revolve". Whether the chain conspiracy or a wheel conspiracy is a single conspiracy or a number of different conspiracies will depend on whether a shared design can be identified between the conspirators.[140] This requirement of commonality of purpose was lacking in *Meyrick and Ribuffi*.[141] D and E separately owned nightclubs occupying adjacent premises. D and E, each acting

135 Note the criticism of just such a development in the law of encouragement above, § 9.1(i)(a).
136 [2012] EWCA Crim 2824, [36]. See also *Ardalan* [1972] 2 All ER 257, 261; (CA); *Shillam* [2013] EWCA Crim 160, [19] (Toulson LJ).
137 *Oni* [2025] EWCA Crim 12, [2025] 4 WLR 19, [75].
138 [2012] EWCA Crim 2824, [36]. See *D* [2009] EWCA Crim 584.
139 (1930) 21 Cr App R 94, 102 (CA).
140 *Oni* [2025] EWCA Crim 12, [2025] 4 WLR 19, [75].
141 (1930) 21 Cr App R 94 (CA).

on his own initiative, paid bribes to the same police officer in return for non-enforcement of the licensing laws in respect of their own premises. Notwithstanding the lack of any personal communication between D and E regarding the bribes, a verdict of conspiracy to corrupt was reached on the basis that "each well knew what the other was doing".[142] *Griffiths*[143] provides a useful contrast with *Meyrick*. In *Griffiths*, the defendants were all farmers who purchased lime from the same supplier. The supplier had instructed the defendants in various ways of dishonestly obtaining subsidies from the Ministry of Agriculture. The Court of Appeal found that, while individual defendants may have been aware that fellow defendants were acting on the instructions of the same supplier to similar fraudulent effect, this did not of itself make them conspirators: each was engaging in fraudulent conduct in the course of his own affairs. *Meyrick* was "explained" in *Griffiths* on the basis of the proximity of the respective premises. But why should that matter? If D and E, both shoplifters, should notice what the other is doing, that would not make for a conspiracy to steal, however close together they stood. *Meyrick* should be regarded as wrong, both in light of the decision in *Griffiths* and by reference to the statement of general principle in *Mehta* (quoted above) of a shared design. The essence of liability for conspiracy in such cases was summarised by Toulson LJ in *Shillam*:[144]

> "although each conspirator need not necessarily know of the identity or even the existence of all the other conspirators, there must be shared criminal purpose of design in which all have joined, rather than merely similar or parallel ones."

In *Griffiths* the criminal designs were parallel rather than joint. D and the police officer had formed a conspiracy, and separately E had formed a conspiracy with the police officer. There were two conspiracies, not one. Crucially, just because D is party to a sub-agreement it does not necessarily follow that they are party to an overarching agreement; they must share the criminal purpose of the parties to that overarching agreement.[145]

If the purpose of the conspirators is narrower than what the prosecution allege, it is possible to convict them of the narrow conspiracy, the smaller purpose being included in the larger. As Toulson LJ recognised in *Mehta*:[146]

> "Conspiracy requires a common design, but it is not a bed of Procrustes whose minimum dimensions are fixed by the prosecution's initial measurements."

So, for example, if A and B are charged with a conspiracy to rob but it can only be established that they conspired to steal, they should be convicted of a conspiracy to commit the lesser offence.[147] Similarly, if A, B and C are charged with conspiracy to import drugs illegally in years 1, 2 and 3 and the evidence leaves the jury unsure as to whether A was party to such a conspiracy, but there is evidence that B and C agreed to import drugs in years 2 and 3, B and C should be convicted of that conspiracy.[148] Further, if some parties intend to kill and others intend to cause grievous bodily harm there cannot be a single

142 *Ibid.*, 102.
143 (1965) 49 Cr App R 279 (CA).
144 [2013] EWCA Crim 160, [20].
145 *Johnson* [2020] EWCA Crim 482.
146 [2012] EWCA Crim 2824, [45].
147 By virtue of section 6(3) of the Criminal Law Act 1967.
148 See *Mehta* [2012] EWCA Crim 2824, [43].

conspiracy, but rather two conspiracies, one to commit murder and the other to cause grievous bodily harm.[149]

The existence of a common purpose may be questioned when D's role is merely to supply some weapon or other object to be used in the commission of the offence. If D agrees with E that V should be killed and volunteers to provide a weapon, clearly D is E's partner in the project of killing V. But this appears not to be the case where D supplies a weapon to E for cash, aware that E intends to use the weapon to kill V but without agreeing with E that V should be killed. In *Gemmell*,[150] the Court of Appeal of New Zealand held that, where D knows that other persons have agreed to commit a crime but he is not a party to their agreement, he does not become a party to the conspiracy if he does certain acts intended to assist the commission of the crime. *Gemmell* lays down the correct approach. D may well be a secondary party to the substantive offence if and when it is committed, but he is not involved in the conspiracy. If the substantive offence is not committed, D can instead be convicted of assisting the commission of the offence intending or believing that it will be committed contrary to sections 44 or 45 of the Serious Crime Act 2007.

*(b) Differences between the parties over what has been agreed*

To what extent can it be said that D and E have reached agreement on a course of conduct when the evidence reveals differences between them as to the content of their agreement? Two situations must be distinguished: (i) where D and E have different offences in mind; and (ii) where the differences between D and E do not preclude an agreement to commit the same offence.

*Case 1: Different offences in mind.*

In *Barnard*,[151] E and F (and others) agreed to commit robbery. D agreed to assist them, but he thought the scheme was to commit the less serious offence of theft. The Court of Appeal held that D was not guilty of conspiracy to rob; an intention to agree to the lesser offence of theft was not equivalent to an intention to agree to commit robbery. In *Patel*,[152] Woolf LJ considered, *obiter*, the converse situation; he instanced circumstances where D took himself to be agreeing to the importation of heroin, whereas his fellow conspirators planned to import cannabis, a lesser offence. Given that the offences were of the same type, Woolf LJ considered that the greater incorporated the lesser and D could not disassociate himself from the conspiracy merely because the crime to be committed was less serious than the offence he had contemplated. Woolf LJ's view receives support from *dicta* of the Court of Appeal in *Taylor (Robert John)*,[153] where the Court held that an agreement to import Class B drugs would not encompass the importation of Class A drugs, a more serious offence. However, the converse did not apply: if D agreed to import Class A drugs he would be liable for a conspiracy to import Class B drugs, a less serious offence, if that was what his co-conspirators had agreed to do. In terms of policy, this conclusion is entirely reasonable; D has demonstrated his preparedness to do something that was cognate with, yet

[149] *Oni* [2025] EWCA Crim 12, [2025] 4 WLR 19, [82].
[150] [1985] 2 NZLR 740.
[151] (1980) 70 Cr App R 28 (CA).
[152] Unreported, 7 August 1991 (CA). Transcript 89/4351/51.
[153] [2001] EWCA Crim 1044.

even more serious than, the crime his fellow conspirators had in mind. The problem with this culpability-driven approach, however, is that it blurs the line between actus reus (the agreement) and mens rea (the intention to commit a particular crime). In strict terms, the presence of an agreement—a meeting of minds—should be established first and only then should one move on to determine whether the mens rea of each party is consonant with that agreement. If there is no meeting of minds, there is no actus reus.

In *Barnard*, the conduct of the parties, assessed objectively, amounted to the formation of an agreement, an agreement to which D was a party, so the actus reus of conspiracy objectively was present. The reason D was not guilty of the offence was that he lacked mens rea; a readiness to thieve was not equivalent to a willingness to rob. Likewise, in the situation discussed by Woolf LJ in *Patel*, there was a conspiracy to import cannabis which D had, by his actions, joined; unlike Barnard, D would be guilty of conspiracy to import cannabis, since an intent to import heroin was sufficient mens rea for the smuggling offence with which he was charged.[154] In some cases, however, differences between the parties may preclude the formation of an agreement if an objective approach is taken. Suppose that D and E agree to import drugs; D assumes the agreement concerns a consignment of heroin, a Class A drug, whereas E has in mind a consignment of cannabis, a Class B drug. It may be that, objectively, one view of their agreement is more reasonable than the other; on the evidence, a court may find that this was a conspiracy to import heroin or it was a conspiracy to import cannabis, as the case may be. There will consequently be an objective act of agreement ascribable to both parties and their ultimate liability will hinge on their respective states of mind and whether it suffices for liability for the crime each had in mind to commit. Alternatively, their actions may be considered to be genuinely ambiguous, so that both views of the agreement are plausible. If the presence of agreement is to be judged objectively, then in this case no act of agreement can be established.

Understandably, a criminal court may be reluctant to reach such a conclusion as it would involve the acquittal of persons who had demonstrated a commitment to perpetrate crimes. There would be a natural temptation to reason that each defendant is to be judged from his own, subjective, perspective; even if, in the light of their differing perspectives, there is no agreement in the strict contractual sense. A less strict approach would, in our example, enable a court to find D guilty of conspiracy to import heroin and E guilty of conspiracy to import cannabis. Both parties have the mens rea for importation contrary to section 170 of the Customs and Excise Management Act 1979, and no great injustice is done if they are convicted of conspiracy to commit an offence of importation of drugs, provided the punishment that each party receives is appropriate to their mens rea.

*Case 2: Same offence in mind.*

In *Broad*,[155] D and E agreed to manufacture drugs. D believed their agreement was to produce heroin, whereas E thought they had arranged to produce cocaine. The Court of Appeal held the difference to be immaterial: on either view of the agreement, the objective would constitute the same offence, i.e. production of a Class A drug. *Broad* should be read as

[154] Importation of a controlled drug contravenes s. 170 of the Customs and Excise Management Act 1979. As interpreted, the mens rea for the offence is awareness that some form of contraband is being imported even though penalties vary markedly (potentially life imprisonment for importing a Class A drug) according to the objects actually imported: *Taafe* [1984] AC 539.

[155] [1997] Crim LR 666 (CA).

recognising a general principle that differences over the content of their agreement between the parties do not vitiate any agreement between them if the respective course of conduct that each party contemplates will result in the commission of the same offence.

Smith, however, queried the generality of *Broad*.[156] He contrasted the facts of that case with a hypothetical situation where D thought he was agreeing with E to murder V and is subsequently horrified to learn that E's intended victim is W. Smith suggested that differences regarding the kind of Class A drug to be manufactured are immaterial, but the identity of the victim is a matter of substance. On that view, D would not be liable for conspiracy to murder. This conclusion may be doubted. The mens rea for murder takes no account of the identity of the victim; all that is required is an intention to kill or cause serious injury to a human being. In the terms of section 1 of the Criminal Law Act 1977, D had agreed a course of conduct which "will necessarily amount to or involve the commission of [an] offence". Accordingly, differences between the parties as to the particulars of their agreement should not preclude liability for conspiracy if, notwithstanding those differences, the parties have agreed to commit the same offence.[157] If, on account of such differences, there are variations in the moral standing of the respective defendants, normally they can be taken into account at the sentencing stage.

### *(c) Conditional agreements*

The parties must conclude an agreement before liability for conspiracy can arise. This means that, if D makes the resolution of certain matters a precondition to final agreement,[158] there is no conspiracy; as in *Walker*,[159] where D agreed in principle to robbery but then withdrew because of unresolved differences between himself and the other parties on how the robbery was to be carried out. The Court of Appeal quashed D's conviction for conspiracy to commit robbery, reasoning that he had not concluded a final agreement with the other parties because his conditions for joining their criminal project had not been met.

If, however, the parties have unequivocally agreed a criminal project, liability arises at that point. Such liability is unaffected by its being contingent on future events. In *O'Hadhmaill*,[160] the defendants, members of the Irish Republican Army ("the IRA"), resolved to carry out a bombing campaign. They agreed not to give effect to this project unless and until the IRA abandoned a ceasefire policy. In confirming the defendants' convictions for conspiracy to cause explosions, the Court of Appeal held that this condition did not preclude the formation of an agreement on a course of conduct which, in the words of section 1 of the Criminal Law Act 1977, "if carried out in accordance with their intentions . . . will necessarily amount to or involve the commission of any offence". The agreement was in no sense equivocal. It was the intention of the parties to carry it out should a particular state of affairs arise. *O'Hadhmaill* is salutary. Practically all future projects will be subject to implicit conditions. For instance, suppose D and E agree to steal from a bank. They are asked by some third party what they will do should they find the bank surrounded by armed police at the time they propose to steal from it. A reply that they would then abandon their scheme in no

156 *Ibid.*, 668.
157 Cp. the discussion of *Bainbridge* [1960] 1 QB 129 (CA), in the context of complicity, above in § 7.4(iv)(c).
158 Broderick, "Conditional Objectives of Conspiracies" (1985) 94 *Yale LJ* 895.
159 [1962] Crim LR 458 (CA).
160 [1996] Crim LR 509 (CA).

way alters the fact that they have unequivocally agreed to steal from a bank. They are liable for a conspiracy to commit theft.

The reasoning in *O'Hadhmaill* clearly applies where the project of D and E is intrinsically criminal, e.g. to cause explosions or to steal from banks. According to dicta in *Reed*,[161] such reasoning does not extend to situations where D and E conceive an objective which may be realised lawfully but agree to act in a criminal manner should that prove necessary in order to attain their goal. The following example was given in *Reed*:[162]

> "A and B agree to drive from London to Edinburgh in a time which can be achieved without exceeding the speed limits, but only if the traffic which they encounter is exceptionally light. Their agreement will not necessarily involve the commission of any offence, even if it is carried out in accordance with their intentions, and they do arrive from London to Edinburgh in the stated time."

Apparently, conditional agreements of that description fall outside the ambit of statutory conspiracy. This conclusion rests on a questionable interpretation of the phrase, "course of conduct" which appears in section 1 of the Criminal Law Act 1977; the matter will be dealt with more fully below, in § 9.2(iv), when we examine the meaning of that phrase.

### *(d) The sufficiency of agreement*

Liability for conspiracy arises as soon as a course of conduct is agreed which is sufficiently specific to identify the crime(s) that would be committed should the agreement be carried out. Consequently, conduct which is very remote from the commission of a substantive offence may constitute a conspiracy. Suppose D and E agree to hire themselves out as "contract killers". From that point, they are parties to a conspiracy to murder notwithstanding that vital matters such as clients, victims, and rates of payment have yet to be resolved. In certain jurisdictions, there is a further requirement for an overt act done in pursuit of the agreed criminal objective before liability in conspiracy can arise.[163] This requirement has much to commend it. The overt act is evidence that the agreement is a serious one and constitutes a real social threat. Moreover, such a requirement has the potential to lessen reliance on confessions as a mode of proof. The overt act requirement has not, however, been received into English law to date and its introduction has not been proposed by any law reform body.

In principle, once liability for conspiracy has arisen, it cannot be undone through any voluntary revocation of the agreement by all the parties to it or, in terms of the liability of specific individuals, through any voluntary withdrawal by a party to the agreement. In *Walker*,[164] D's conviction for conspiracy was quashed on the basis that he withdrew from negotiations with other parties *prior* to reaching an agreement with them; the Court of Appeal indicated, *obiter*, that, had the point of agreement already been reached, a subsequent voluntary withdrawal would have provided at most mitigation of sentence and not a defence.[165] As we have seen, a voluntary withdrawal defence is allowed for accessories.[166]

161 [1982] Crim LR 819 (CA).
162 *Ibid.*, 820.
163 As in Texas; Texas Penal Code § 15.02(a)(2).
164 [1962] Crim LR 458 (CA).
165 See also *Oni* [2025] EWCA Crim 12, [2025] 4 WLR 19, [74].
166 Above, § 7.6(vi).

Although the conceptual bases of conspiracy and complicity differ—conspiracy is a form of direct liability which arises at the point of agreement; complicity is a form of derivative liability which arises on the commission of a substantive offence by another person—providing an incentive to withdraw from a criminal project prior to the commission of the substantive offence is equally significant for conspiracy. Moreover, many accessories will be parties to a conspiracy made with the principal offender. In terms of policy, it seems inconsistent to allow D a defence of voluntary withdrawal in respect of a complicity charge yet to impose liability upon D as a conspirator. Such a defence has not, however, been created for the inchoate offences involving encouraging and assisting,[167] and it has been confirmed by the Court of Appeal that withdrawal from a conspiracy is only relevant in mitigation of sentence.[168]

### *(iv) The "course of conduct"*

Under the terms of section 1(1) of the Criminal Law Act 1977, the parties must agree that:

> a course of conduct shall be pursued which, if the agreement is carried out in accordance with their intentions, . . . will necessarily amount to or involve the commission of any offence or offences.

On the face of it, this requirement is straightforward: it demands proof of what the parties had agreed to do and proof that doing what had been agreed would *necessarily* have involved the commission of one or more crimes by at least one party to the agreement. Unfortunately, the position is not as straightforward as it should be. Interpretative difficulties have arisen over the phrase, "course of conduct". Two areas of ambiguity will be discussed: (i) how broadly or narrowly should the phrase be construed? and (ii) how many courses of conduct may a particular episode of conduct contain?

#### *(a) A broad or narrow construction?*

At its broadest, "course of conduct" may be construed as including any acts or omissions the parties propose to do, any consequences that will arise from the perpetration of those acts or omissions and the necessary circumstances. At its narrowest, the reference to conduct could be read as signifying simply the acts or omissions the parties propose without reference to ensuing consequences or the necessary circumstances. The broad interpretation is most consistent with the language of the Act and the rationale of conspiracy. The Act speaks of a "course of conduct . . . carried out *in accordance with their intentions*", which seems to imply that the consequences the parties intend to bring about are to be included within the expression, "course of conduct", as well as the necessary circumstances. Suppose that D and E agree to tamper with the brakes of V's car with the intention that it should crash and V be killed. That agreement is, surely, a conspiracy to murder, a judgment confirmed if "course of conduct" includes the results that D and E intend their conduct to achieve. If that is the correct interpretation of the phrase, then the course of conduct they have agreed, "will *necessarily* amount to or involve the commission of [an] offence". However, if the narrow interpretation prevails and the course of conduct that D and E have agreed is confined to

[167] Above, § 9.1(iv)(a).
[168] *Oni* [2025] EWCA Crim 12, [2025] 4 WLR 19, [74].

the physical interference with the brakes of the car, it cannot be said that their conduct will necessarily cause the death of V. V might survive any ensuing crash, the tampering might prove ineffective, and so on. The narrow interpretation attains a measure of plausibility from the fact that it is common practice to break down the elements of "result" crimes into a tripartite division of conduct (or "behaviour") elements, circumstance elements, and consequence elements; where the "conduct" element encompasses only the physical movements of D.[169] But that is merely done for the purposes of exposition and in no sense determines the correct interpretation of section 1(1). In ordinary English speech, it is perfectly permissible to describe the same incident in a manner whereby D's conduct includes consequential results (as in "D killed V by shooting him") or in a manner which separates D's conduct from its consequence (as in "D fired a gun at V causing V to die").[170] Therefore, in terms of the wording of the Act and an effective law of conspiracy, the broader interpretation should be adopted so that the conduct of the parties is taken to include the intended consequences of their agreed acts and omissions and the necessary circumstances. There is no theory of language nor legal principle which precludes this interpretation.

Unfortunately, the approach argued for here is contrary to that adopted by the House of Lords in *Nock*.[171] That case involved common law conspiracy, on which the Criminal Law Act 1977 has no bearing. Lord Scarman, however, adverted to the defining elements of statutory conspiracy and regarded them as an effective summary of the common law position for conspiracies where the objective of the conspiracy was the commission of a crime. D and E had attempted to produce cocaine from a set of materials which, unknown to them, did not contain any coca-base, rendering their project impossible. Lord Scarman construed the phrase "course of conduct" as a reference to what D and E physically proposed to do, i.e. to apply certain chemical procedures to the material they had. The consequence they intended to bring about from applying these procedures was not, itself, to be taken as part of their course of conduct; it was the objective of their agreed course of conduct but was not part of it.[172] Accordingly, D and E were not parties to a conspiracy to produce cocaine because the implementation of what they had agreed would not "necessarily" involve the commission of a crime. Indeed, it could not.

The actual decision in *Nock* was reversed by an amendment of the Criminal Law Act 1977. It now suffices that an offence would have been committed, "but for the existence of facts which render the commission of the offence . . . impossible".[173] Lord Scarman's reasoning has therefore been displaced for cases of impossibility. Seemingly, however, it remains in place for cases where attainable objectives are pursued by ineffectual means. On this view, D and E would now be conspirators on the original facts of *Nock* but not in circumstances, say, where it was *possible* to manufacture cocaine from the materials D and E possessed but not in the time available to them to do so.

This conclusion is so perverse that one is tempted peremptorily to reject it. However, if the interpretation we have argued for—that the course of conduct includes the consequences the parties intend to achieve—is correct, the amendment to the Act for the case

[169] See above, § 4.

[170] Feinberg describes this as the "accordion effect": "Action and Responsibility" in Black (ed.), *Philosophy in America* (1965) 134.

[171] [1978] AC 979.

[172] *Ibid.*, 995–6, 998.

[173] Section 1(1)(b) of the Criminal Law Act 1977, as amended by the Criminal Attempts Act 1981.

of impossibility was unnecessary. Under our preferred interpretation, a course of conduct includes intended consequences and it is thus irrelevant whether those consequences are possible or impossible of attainment.

Lord Scarman's analysis in *Nock* may be contrasted with the decision of the Court of Appeal in *Bolton*,[174] which concerned a dishonest scheme agreed between D and E to obtain a mortgage advance from a building society. They anticipated that they would receive the advance by way of a cheque, a valuable security, but, because of changes in the society's payments system, they received the advance by way of electronic transfer, a method that did not involve the creation of a valuable security. It was held that they had conspired to procure the execution of a valuable security as their expectation of receiving a cheque was to be regarded as part of the "course of conduct" they had agreed. Unfortunately, Lord Scarman's contrary analysis of this phrase was not considered by the Court of Appeal. Recall that, although Lord Scarman construed the terms of the Act, he was taking the Act as a guide to the common law. His Lordship's reading of section 1(1) is of only persuasive authority, but the analysis in *Bolton* is to be preferred. Further, the amendment of the Criminal Law Act 1977 relating to cases of impossibility should be treated as being intended to remove the long-standing common law defence of impossibility to the crime of statutory conspiracy. It should not be regarded as confirming Lord Scarman's analysis by way of creating a special exemption to it. The "course of conduct" in statutory conspiracy should be read to include agreed consequences of the defendants' agreed acts. This has now been affirmed by the decision of the Court of Appeal in *Maxey*,[175] which held that the parties were guilty of a conspiracy to cause public nuisance by flying drones near an airport intending to close the airport. It was irrelevant that the closure of the airport was not inevitable; it was sufficient that the closure of the airport was the intended consequence, and the closure would necessarily have constituted a public nuisance.

*(b) How many courses of conduct?*

Suppose that D and E agree to commit a burglary and contingently agree also to commit some further offence, such as murder, should they encounter opposition in the course of the burglary. It may be asked how many conspiracies arise in such a case. Clearly, there is a conspiracy to commit burglary. Is there an additional conspiracy to commit murder? If we characterise their agreement as an agreement involving but one agreed course of conduct—to commit burglary—then there is no conspiracy to murder. They may successfully conclude the burglary without necessarily committing murder. However, it is possible to separate the strands of their overall agreement: an agreement to burgle and an agreement to murder on a particular eventuality. Linguistically, it is perfectly apt to regard them as two separate agreements to pursue two different courses of conduct. It is true that their project is burglary rather than murder: the murder, if it should occur, would be but a means to an end, namely to successfully complete the burglary or to escape. But that has no bearing on the wrongfulness of agreeing to murder someone. *O'Hadhmaill*[176] held that it is no answer to a charge of conspiracy that the implementation of an agreement was subject to a condition which may not be fulfilled, provided the parties have unequivocally agreed to pursue

174 (1992) 94 Cr App R 74 (CA).
175 [2025] EWCA Crim 472, [2025] 2 Cr App R 7. See below, § 9.2(v)(a).
176 [1966] Crim LR 509 (DC).

a criminal course of conduct should the terms of the condition be fulfilled. It is submitted that in such circumstances there are as many separate courses of conduct as there are crimes the parties have unequivocally agreed to commit. This conclusion is supported by *A-G's Reference (No. 4 of 2003)*,[177] where the Court of Appeal was sympathetic to the view that, if D and others agree to steal a particular item and resolve that, should it be necessary, they will commit burglary or robbery to get it, there are conspiracies for theft, burglary, and robbery.

Recall, however, our discussion of the "driving to Edinburgh" example put by Lord Lane in *Reed*.[178] Lord Lane took the view that if the objective of D and E—arriving in Edinburgh in time, say, for lunch—could be achieved by driving within speed limits, their agreement to exceed those limits, should it be necessary, did not constitute a conspiracy to exceed statutory limits. Their course of conduct could reach a successful conclusion without necessarily involving the commission of a crime. His view appears to be that courses of conduct are identified by reference to the ultimate objective of the parties and to any means employed to attain that objective which are intrinsically necessary and not merely contingently necessary. On that view, the Edinburgh agreement takes in lunching and driving to lunch, two separate courses of conduct, but not speeding to lunch which is not a requirement of the agreement.

Employing a distinction between intrinsically necessary means and contingently necessary means to delimit the ambit of conspiracy entails some fine distinctions. Suppose that D and E agree to obtain money from V. They agree to try first to obtain the money by a hard-luck story; should that not succeed, they agree to kill V and then take his money. Here the distinction between intrinsically necessary means and contingently necessary means does not apply. They contemplate the possibility of having to try two means to the same end, plan A and plan B. Surely there is a conspiracy to commit fraud *and* a conspiracy to murder? Distinguishing between situations such as the lunch in Edinburgh scenario and the money plot is too refined for the practical concerns of the criminal law. It is submitted that, in the spirit of the decision in *O'Hadhmaill*, if the parties have unequivocally agreed to commit an offence should a particular eventuality arise, they have agreed "a course of conduct shall be pursued which . . . will necessarily . . . involve the commission of an offence". The dictum to the contrary of Lord Lane in *Reed* should not be followed.

### *(v) The mens rea of conspiracy*

There is an element of contrivance in subdividing the constituents of conspiracy into sections dealing with actus reus—the agreement—on the one hand, and mens rea on the other. After all, an agreement involves a mental operation through the meeting of minds. That said, the presence of a consensus does not exhaust what is required by way of a mental element for this offence. Agreements operate on the surface of things and the fact of agreement may co-exist with secret reservations or betrayals that one or more of the parties may have in mind. For example, suppose D and E agree to meet later that night in order to carry out a burglary at the house of V. D has no intention of showing up. He agrees with E because he is disinclined to admit that he lacks the courage to commit burglary. E, on the other hand, is an undercover policeman who plans to arrest D before the burglary is committed. If neither D nor E is guilty of conspiracy, as is likely the case, it will be because each lacks mens rea, rather than because no objective agreement had been formed.

177 [2004] EWCA Crim 1944, [2005] 1 WLR 1574.
178 [1982] Crim LR 819 (CA). See above, § 9.2(iii)(c).

*(a) Intended consequences of the agreed course of conduct*

Section 1 of the Criminal Law Act 1977 refers to an agreement which, if carried out in accordance with the intentions of the parties, will necessarily amount to or involve the commission of any offence. This requires the jury to consider what the consequences of the parties' course of conduct would be if the agreement was carried out in accordance with their intentions. The jury should be concerned with the legal quality of the intended outcome rather than the inevitability of the outcome resulting.[179] So, for example, in *Maxey*[180] the defendants agreed to fly drones within the five-kilometre Flight Restriction Zone of London Heathrow airport in order to close the airport, as part of a protest against the proposed expansion of the airport. The defendants were convicted of conspiracy to cause a public nuisance. They appealed on the ground that, if the flying of the drones would not necessarily have closed the airport, they could not be convicted of the conspiracy. The appeal was dismissed because their intended outcome was the closure of the airport, which would necessarily constitute a public nuisance. It was irrelevant that the closure was not inevitable; it was what they were setting out to achieve.

What offence the parties are agreeing to commit will be determined by the consequence they are intending. So, for example, as regards a conspiracy to commit murder, it is necessary to prove an intention to kill; an intention to cause grievous bodily harm will not be sufficient.[181] This is because it is necessary to prove an intention that the result of the substantive offence occurs. However, an intention to kill will be sufficient to establish a conspiracy to cause grievous bodily harm, because the intention to cause the lesser harm would be included in the greater harm.[182] Consequently where some members of a gang planned to kill and others only to cause grievous bodily harm, there were two conspiracies, one to commit murder and one to cause grievous bodily harm with intent, but those who intended to kill could also be guilty of the conspiracy to cause grievous bodily harm.

*(b) Intention to carry out the agreement*

The reference to an agreement "carried out in accordance with the" parties' intentions in section 1 of the Criminal Law Act 1977 indicates that liability in conspiracy is predicated on the intention of the parties to carry out their agreement. The requirement for this form of intention is a matter of implication rather than express stipulation. The Law Commission recommended that there should be express stipulation on the matter. It drafted the following provision:[183]

> "both he and the other person or persons with whom he agrees must intend to bring about any consequence which is an element of that offence, even where the offence in question may be committed without that consequence actually being intended by the person committing it."

In the debates on the Bill that became the Criminal Law Act 1977, this provision was rejected on the ground of excessive complexity. Nonetheless, the Lord Chancellor, when

179 *Maxey* [2025] EWCA Crim 472, [2025] 2 Cr App R 7.
180 *Ibid.*
181 *Oni* [2025] EWCA Crim 12, [2025] 4 WLR 19, [77].
182 *Ibid*, [82].
183 Law Com. No. 76, *Conspiracy and Criminal Law Reform* (1976); Law Com. No. 177, *A Criminal Code for England and Wales* (1989) cl. 1(3). The Law Commission has now recommended that a specific statutory provision is required which states that a conspirator must intend that both the conduct and consequence elements of the substantive offence should be brought about: Law Com. No. 318, *Conspiracy and Attempts* (2009) para. 2.56.

agreeing to the deletion of the clause, stated that what is now section 1 of the Criminal Law Act 1977 required "full intention and knowledge before conspiracy can be established".[184]

This legislative history needs to be borne in mind[185] when considering the implications of the House of Lords decision in *Anderson*.[186] Seemingly, the Lords unanimously decided that an intention to carry out the agreed course of conduct was not a defining element of conspiracy. It sufficed that D had agreed a criminal project with others and intended to play his assigned part in it; nothing else was required. In particular, the prosecution did not need to establish that D intended that the agreement be carried through to completion.

The ruling in *Anderson* was novel. Previously, it had never been suggested, let alone decided, that an intention to carry out the agreement and realise the objective of the conspiracy was not essential to liability as a conspirator.[187] The elements of liability will, of course, be the same for each conspirator. Consequently, *Anderson* raises the possibility of liability for conspiracy in circumstances where none of the parties to a particular agreement intends that it be carried out in full. So radical is this interpretation, and so out of accord with the legislative history of statutory conspiracy and the history of conspiracy generally, that it is necessary to examine the facts of *Anderson* to see if any limitations or special considerations can be brought to bear on the ambit of the decision:

> The appellant, D, had been a prisoner, along with E and F. E and F conceived a plan to effect the escape from prison of G. D agreed with E and F to help effect G's escape and undertook that when D was released from prison he would procure some diamond cutting equipment and arrange for it to be smuggled into the prison. D sought to defend himself from liability for conspiracy on the basis that his sole interest in this venture was to make some money from selling the equipment to E and F. He claimed that he envisaged no prospect that E and F would succeed in their plan.

D had apparently entered into an agreement with E and F, the object of which was to bring about the escape of G. The plot was a real one in the sense that D knew that E and F would try to put it into effect. But, since D did not anticipate that the plan would be successful, he could not be considered to have intended the agreement to be carried out such that the consequence of G's escape would be effected, and so he should not have been convicted of conspiracy. Today, if the facts arose, he could be convicted of encouraging a conspiracy to be made contrary to section 44 of the Serious Crime Act 2007.

Whilst the decision in Anderson has not been overruled, a number of subsequent decisions are not consistent with it. For example, in *McPhillips*,[188] Lowry LCJ, giving judgment for the Court of Appeal of Northern Ireland, ruled that section 1(1) of the Criminal Law Act 1977 required an intention on the part of a conspirator that the object of the conspiracy be carried out. Accordingly, D was not liable for conspiracy to murder in *McPhillips* because he intended to alert the relevant authorities prior to the explosion of the bomb which he and his partners had set. Lord Lowry distinguished the decision in *Anderson* on the basis that, on the facts of that case, D had had no intention of frustrating the plans of his fellow conspirators to effect the escape of a prisoner. The facts of the respective cases do differ in

[184] HL Debs, vol. 379, col. 55.
[185] Including reference to Ministerial statements to Parliament, pursuant to *Pepper v Hart* [1993] AC 593.
[186] [1986] AC 27.
[187] In *Thomson* (1965) 50 Cr App R 1, for example, the Court of Criminal Appeal had held that to be guilty of conspiracy a person must not only agree a criminal project but also intend that the project be carried out.
[188] [1989] NI 360.

the manner indicated by his Lordship. Yet, if one were to remain faithful to the decision in *Anderson*, it is unclear why this factual difference should be of any consequence. By becoming a party to an agreement to murder and intending to play a part (indeed playing a part) in carrying out the agreement, the appellant in *McPhillips* fulfilled the requirements for liability in conspiracy as set down by Lord Bridge in *Anderson*, but it is right that the appellant in *McPhillips* was not liable for conspiracy.

In other cases, too, Lord Bridge's requirements have not been taken as either a necessary or a sufficient basis for liability in conspiracy. Rather, it has been held that D must intend for the agreement to be pursued to completion before liability for conspiracy arises. In *Edwards*,[189] the Court of Appeal ruled that D could incur liability for conspiracy to supply amphetamine only if he intended that amphetamine be supplied. No reference to *Anderson* was made in the judgment. In *Yip Chiu-Cheung*, again without reference to *Anderson*, Lord Griffiths in the Privy Council stated that "the crime of conspiracy requires an agreement between two or more persons to commit an unlawful act with the intention of carrying it out. *It is the intention to carry out the crime* that constitutes the mens rea of the offence."[190] Finally, in *Saik*,[191] Lord Nicholls recognised, albeit *obiter* and without reference to *Anderson*, that conspirators must intend to do the act which is prohibited by the substantive offence.

Of course, this post-*Anderson* case law comprising, as it does, a decision of the Court of Appeal of Northern Ireland, a *per incuriam* decision of the Court of Appeal, dicta of the Privy Council, and an *obiter dictum* from the House of Lords, cannot overturn an unequivocal ruling of the House of Lords. Yet, in estimating the future influence of the *Anderson* ruling, it is pertinent to recall our previous discussion of the legislative history of statutory conspiracy. That history clearly indicates that it was not the intention of Parliament, when enacting section 1(1) of the Criminal Law Act 1977, to dispense with the venerable requirement of an intention that the agreement be carried out; section 1(1) was understood to require proof of such an intention. Furthermore, as will be seen below, section 1(2) requires proof of intent or knowledge with respect to any circumstances necessary for the commission of the substantive offence. It would have been quite bizarre for Parliament to insist on full mens rea as to circumstance elements of the substantive offence while, at the same time, dispensing with mens rea as to any consequence element required to establish the substantive offence. In the light of this analysis it is submitted, with some confidence, that to be a guilty party to a conspiracy, D must intend that the course of conduct that the parties have agreed should be carried out in circumstances which would necessarily amount to the commission of an offence by at least one of the parties to the agreement.

### (c) *Intention and foresight of certainty*

Where the substantive offence is the very object of the conspiracy, mens rea is straightforward. For example, there will undoubtedly be a conspiracy to murder where D and E agree to firebomb V's house with the objective of killing V. Suppose, however, that D and E conceive of a plan to explode a bomb on a plane in mid-flight, in order to make a fraudulent insurance claim for destruction of the plane. They appreciate the life-threatening potential of their projected conduct, yet the prospect of death to the passengers is not a motivating

[189] [1991] Crim LR 45 (CA).
[190] [1995] 1 AC 111, 118 (PC) (emphasis added). See too *Harvey* [1999] Crim LR 70 (CA).
[191] [2006] UKHL 18, [2007] 1 AC 18, [4].

factor in the making of their agreement. From the perspective of potential conspiracy charges, there are obvious charges in relation to their fraudulent objective. On the assumption that it can be proved both that death is a virtually certain consequence and that D and E foresee the death of passengers as a virtual certainty if the course of conduct they have agreed is carried out according to their intentions, can we say that their agreement is also a conspiracy to murder?

English criminal law consistently, though not invariably, permits findings of intent to be drawn with respect to side-effects which are the virtually certain outcome of D's conduct, if D foresaw the outcome as virtually certain.[192] At common law, the identification of intention with reference to the foresight of virtually certain consequences has been carried over to conspiracy. For example, in *Cooke*,[193] D and other railway employees were found guilty of conspiracy to defraud British Rail on the basis that, in scheming to sell their own food and drink to British Rail customers, they intended to cause loss to their employer (who also sold food and drink to customers). Of course, it was no part of D's purpose to cause loss; that was merely the inevitable concomitant of making such gains. It may well be that the same analysis will be made in the context of statutory conspiracy.[194] Should that prove to be the case, then in our plane bombing example D and E would be liable for conspiracy to murder.

Intention, as always, must be distinguished from motive. In *Yip Chiu-Cheung*,[195] it was the view of the Privy Council that D would incur liability for conspiracy to import drugs to Sydney from Hong Kong if he intended that the agreement be carried out, notwithstanding his secret role as an undercover police officer and his desire to bring his fellow conspirators to justice. If, however, he had planned to secure the arrest of the others prior to the implementation of the agreement he would not have been guilty of conspiracy, since he would have lacked an intention to carry out the agreement. In either of those scenarios, the timing of any arrests may depend on contingencies which would have no bearing on the moral quality of D's conduct. Despite this, English courts regard mens rea as a technical legal description of D's state of mind which need not necessarily involve any culpability on the part of D.[196] Accordingly, the analysis in *Yip* reflects the current state of English law.[197]

*(d) Intention to take some part in carrying out the agreement*

As we have discussed, the decision in *Anderson* sought to dispense with the requirement of an intent that the agreement be carried out such that an offence will be committed.

[192] See above, § 5.1(iv).
[193] [1986] AC 909.
[194] Cf. *Walker* (1990) 90 Cr App R 226 (CA), where a similar analysis was adopted in respect of statutory attempt.
[195] [1995] 1 AC 111.
[196] See also the discussion earlier, § 5.
[197] In *Somchai Liangsiriprasert v US Government* (1991) 92 Cr App R 77, 82 the Privy Council had left open the question whether law enforcement officials should be given dispensation to enter conspiracies in order to frustrate criminal objectives, but *Yip Chiu-Cheung* suggests no such dispensation will be given. For valuable discussion of the issues of principle and policy in condoning illegal actions in the interests of law enforcement see Ashworth, "Testing Fidelity to Legal Values: Official Involvement and Criminal Justice" in Shute and Simester (eds.), *Criminal Law Theory* (2002) 299.

According to Lord Bridge, the relevant intent to be established is simply an intent by D to take some part in carrying out the agreement:[198]

> "But, beyond the mere fact of agreement, the necessary mens rea of the crime is, in my opinion, established if, and only if, it is shown that the accused, when he entered into the agreement, intended to play some part in the agreed course of conduct in furtherance of the criminal purpose which the agreed course of conduct was intended to achieve. Nothing less will suffice; nothing more is required."

Prior to *Anderson*, a requirement that D must intend to play some part in carrying out the agreement was unknown to English law. From the origin of the offence liability for conspiracy has been founded on the fact of agreement.[199] Suppose, for the moment, we take *Anderson* at face value and accept that the requirement of an intention to play some part in implementing the agreement is a part of English law. It appears that D, for instance, would no longer be liable for conspiracy to murder if he induced E and F to agree to kill V by offering a financial incentive.[200] D's conduct would have brought about an agreement to kill to which she was a party but, assuming the validity of *Anderson*, she cannot incur liability for conspiracy unless she intended to play some part in implementing this agreement.

What does "taking some part" require by way of conduct? In our agreement-to-murder example in the last paragraph, it would be enough, by analogy with the facts of *Anderson*, for D to intend to provide some practical assistance to E and F, such as providing them with a weapon. Presumably, it would also suffice if D, say, intended to inform E and F of V's whereabouts. But, if D was to have no active role to play in implementing the agreement, he would not be liable for conspiracy. Yet surely one can be party to an agreement—and thus a member of a conspiracy—without being allocated an active role in its implementation? The test in *Anderson* apportions liability on the basis of differences that are irrelevant to the gist of conspiracy. The gist of conspiracy is the entry into the agreement and the intention that it be carried out, even if by others.

With that in mind, the approach of the Court of Appeal in *Siracusa*[201] is to be welcomed. D had recruited and agreed with E and others that offences be committed in contravention of section 170(2)(b) of the Customs and Excise Management Act 1979. It could not be proved against him that he intended to play an active part in implementing this agreement. O'Connor LJ confirmed his conviction for conspiracy on the basis that his "intention to participate in the furtherance of the criminal purpose is . . . established by his failure to stop the unlawful activity. Lord Bridge's dictum does not require anything more".[202] On O'Connor LJ's approach, D, in our agreement-to-kill example, would intend to play some part in carrying out the agreement if she did not intend to frustrate the conspiracy, for example by reporting their agreement to the police.

O'Connor LJ's analysis is artificial: not preventing an offence is hardly "playing a part" in its commission. But the artificiality is forced by the need to pay lip-service to *Anderson*. O'Connor LJ departed from the view of the law held by Lord Bridge under the guise of

[198] [1986] AC 27, 39.
[199] *Poulterer's Case* (1611) 9 Co Rep 55b, 77 ER 813; *Starling* (1664) 1 Sid 174, 82 ER 1039.
[200] Although D could be convicted of encouraging murder contrary to the Serious Crime Act 2007; above, § 9.1(i).
[201] (1990) 90 Cr App R 340 (CA).
[202] *Ibid.*, 349.

complying with it, but, as Lord Bridge's conception of the mental element in conspiracy is so novel and so destructive of the rationale of conspiracy, O'Connor LJ's "interpretation" of Lord Bridge should prevail.

*(e) Intention or knowledge regarding facts or circumstances necessary for the commission of the offence*

Section 1(2) of the Criminal Law Act 1977 provides:

> Where liability for any offence may be incurred without knowledge on the part of the person committing it of any particular fact or circumstance necessary for the commission of the offence, a person shall nevertheless not be guilty of conspiracy to commit that offence by virtue of subsection (1) above unless he and at least one other party to the agreement intend or know that that fact or circumstance shall or will exist at the time when the conduct constituting the offence is to take place.

Section 1(2) is the only provision of the Act which deals explicitly with the mens rea requirements for conspiracy. Ostensibly, its terms are of limited effect. It deals with the situation where liability for the substantive offence may be incurred without knowledge on the part of D of any particular fact or circumstance necessary for the commission of the offence; for example, where the substantive offence is one of strict liability. If a conspiracy charge relating to an agreement to commit an offence of strict liability is brought, section 1(2) makes clear that intention or knowledge regarding the facts or circumstances of the substantive offence is required, even if such proof would not be required for the substantive offence itself. This intention or knowledge relates to the actus reus of the substantive offence.[203] In *Ali*,[204] the conspiracy related to the crime of assisting the unlawful immigration of people who were not citizens of the EU. For the substantive offence, it is sufficient that D knew or had reasonable cause to believe that the immigrants were not EU citizens. For the conspiracy, D had either to intend that the assistance would help non-EU citizens, if they had not yet been identified, or knew this, if they had been identified.

Does the provision have any wider effect? No reference is made to any conduct or consequence elements of the substantive offence. No indication is given about the mens rea required for conspiracy when the substantive offence does require proof of knowledge of any particular fact or circumstance necessary for the commission of the offence. A basic principle of statutory interpretation is that, if express provision is made for a particular matter or issue and no provision is made for cognate matters or issues falling outside the situation expressly provided for, the inference to be drawn is that the same provision does not extend to those cognate matters or issues.[205] Prima facie, applying that rule of construction, we reach what has been described as a "scandalous paradox":[206] on a conspiracy charge, knowledge or intent must be proved for any particular fact or circumstance necessary for the commission of the offence if such knowledge or intent would *not* be required in a trial for the substantive offence, but proof of such knowledge or intent may be dispensed with where such knowledge or intent *is* required for the substantive offence. Furthermore, on a conspiracy charge, no mens rea need be proved with respect to conduct and consequence

[203] *Ali* [2019] EWCA Crim 2448, [2020] 4 WLR 33.
[204] *Ibid.*
[205] "*Expressio unius est exclusio alterius*"—"the mention of one thing is the exclusion of another".
[206] Elliot, "Mens Rea in Statutory Conspiracy" [1978] *Crim LR* 202, 204.

elements of the substantive offence, regardless of whether mens rea is required for the substantive offence.

This *prima facie* conclusion defies logic and cannot be defended in terms of policy. It is relevant to refer again to the legislative history of the Act. Recall that the original Bill put before Parliament contained a clause that provided for proof of intention as to any consequence elements necessary for commission of the substantive offence on a charge of conspiracy. Although the clause was deleted on the ground that it was excessively complex, the Lord Chancellor assured Parliament that what is now section 1(1) of the Criminal Law Act 1977 required proof of "full intention and knowledge before conspiracy can be established". If these words are taken as an authoritative guide to the interpretation of section 1(1), intention or knowledge should be required as to all elements that make up the substantive offence. That is the position at common law;[207] one would have anticipated express provision in the Act were the well-established and long-standing common law position to be departed from. If, therefore, we accept that section 1(1) requires intention or knowledge for all elements of the substantive offence, then section 1(2) may be regarded as a provision inserted to avoid any doubt that the same level of intention or knowledge is required on a conspiracy charge even when it is not required by the substantive offence. The word "nevertheless" adds force to this interpretation; it may be taken to stress that, even in cases where there is an element of strict liability within the substantive offence, mens rea as to those elements is required for conspiracy; *a fortiori* such intention or knowledge is required when proof of such intention or knowledge is required for the substantive offence. This reading, originally proposed by Sir John Smith,[208] was endorsed by the House of Lords in *Saik*[209] and can now be taken as established.

Accordingly, D will not be liable for conspiracy unless she intends or knows of any particular fact or circumstance necessary for the commission of the substantive offence. Recklessness, even of the *Cunningham* variety,[210] as regards the actus reus of the substantive offence will not suffice for conspiracy. Suppose D and E agree to cut down a tree that they think may belong either to E or to V. Should it be the case that the ownership of the tree is V's, destruction of the tree by D and E would constitute criminal damage on their part, recklessness regarding the ownership of the tree being sufficient culpability for the offence.[211] Yet there would not be a conspiracy to commit criminal damage: they would neither know[212] nor intend that the tree belongs to V.

The rule is different concerning any mens rea ingredients of the substantive offence that are ulterior where those ingredients are unrelated to the actus reus.[213] To be guilty of a conspiracy in respect of such an offence, D and E must themselves also satisfy those ulterior mental elements, even if they involve recklessness. So, for example, if D and E are charged with conspiracy to commit criminal damage being reckless as to whether life is

[207] See below, § 15.9(iv), regarding the mens rea for conspiracy to defraud.
[208] "Mens Rea in Statutory Conspiracy: (3) Some Answers" [1978] *Crim LR* 210.
[209] [2006] UKHL 18, [2007] 1 AC 18, [16]–[21] (Lord Nicholls).
[210] [1957] 2 QB 396 (CA).
[211] Criminal Damage Act 1971, s. 1(1). We assume, for the purposes of the example, that it is unreasonable to take the risk that the tree belongs to someone else.
[212] Above, § 5.4. For general discussion of knowledge as a culpability term in criminal law, see Shute, "Knowledge and Belief in the Criminal Law" and Sullivan, "Knowledge, Belief and Culpability" in Shute and Simester (eds.), *Criminal Law Theory* (2002) 184 and 207 respectively.
[213] *Saik* [2006] UKHL 18, [2007] 1 AC 18, [4] (Lord Nicholls).

endangered,[214] since it need not be proved that life is actually endangered, this need not be intended or known and recklessness as to endangerment suffices for the conspiracy since this is the ulterior mens rea.

*(f) Future facts*

Under the terms of section 1(2), D must intend or know that "facts or circumstances necessary for the commission of [the substantive offence] shall or will exist at the time when the conduct constituting the offence is to take place". It is possible to intend a future fact or circumstance. If D invites V for dinner next Saturday, he intends to have dinner with V on that day. Suppose that D and E agree to invite V to dinner next Saturday and to kill him when he comes on that day. D and E are guilty of conspiracy to murder as they intend a fact necessary for the commission of the crime—the presence of V for dinner—to occur.

Ordinarily, however, one would not say that D *knows* V will come to dinner next Saturday, at least until V responds affirmatively to the invitation. It is therefore possible to conceive of situations where D and E plan to kill V and it cannot be said that they intend or know of V's necessary presence. For example, suppose that D and E are aware that V always drives home by either route A or route B. They agree that, should V take route B next Saturday, they will intercept him and kill him. Strictly, they cannot *intend* the presence of V unless they have (or think they have) some means of influencing V to take route B. Moreover, they do not *know* which route V will take. Accordingly, on a literal interpretation of section 1(2), there is no conspiracy.

Such a literal interpretation would seriously undermine the law of conspiracy. As we saw earlier, when discussing conditional agreements (§ 9.2(iii)(c)), the successful implementation of an agreement will often require the presence of facts or circumstances which can neither be known nor intended when the agreement is struck. Since it is generally not possible to "know" the future outcome of unresolved contingencies,[215] the interpretation of "intend" becomes crucial. It is submitted that, for the purpose of section 1(2), D's intention must embrace the preconditions of that intention, such that D should be taken to intend the existence of those facts or circumstances which he contemplates as necessary for the commission of the intended substantive offence.[216]

Subject to that qualification, whatever the mens rea requirements for the substantive offence, or the lack thereof, to be convicted of conspiracy D must know of or intend the presence of any material circumstances necessary for proof of the substantive offence. The decision in *Sakavickas*[217] is, however, in flat contradiction of this statement of the law. The money-laundering offences at issue in that case required proof of knowledge or suspicion

[214] Contrary to the Criminal Damage Act 1977, s. 1(2).

[215] Above, § 5.4. Cf. *Sunair Holidays Ltd* [1973] 2 All ER 1233, where the Court of Appeal held that D could not be taken to "know" the existence of a future, contingent fact (the date of completion of a swimming-pool).

[216] Such an interpretation must underlie decisions such as *O'Hadhmaill* [1996] Crim LR 509 (CA), discussed above in § 9.2(iii)(c). In that case, D and others agreed to resume a bombing campaign if and when a ceasefire was revoked. Strictly, they could neither have known nor intended that hostilities would restart (the matter was not for them to decide). Their conviction for conspiracy indicates that it was enough for them to *contemplate* circumstances whereupon their agreement would take effect.

[217] [2004] EWCA Crim 2686 and see too *Ali* [2005] EWCA Crim 87.

of the illegal provenance of funds: the Court of Appeal held that D and E were guilty of conspiracy to commit these offences on the basis of their *suspicion* that the funds they had agreed to process were the proceeds of drug trafficking or other illegal activity. Happily, we need not consider the tortuous reasoning behind the decision.[218] In *Saik*,[219] the House of Lords ruled that, even where liability for an offence could be incurred without knowledge on the part of the person committing it of any particular fact or circumstance necessary for the commission of the offence, section 1(2) of the 1977 Act required proof that every conspirator knew or intended that the fact or circumstance "shall or will" exist when the conspiracy was put into effect. Baroness Hale, dissenting, considered that D would intend in a conditional sense the fact of the illegal provenance of the funds if he agreed to accept them for changing into another currency despite his suspicions.[220] But the concept of conditional intent is best reserved for where D resolves a course of action subject to a contingency as in, "I will steal that necklace if those are real diamonds".[221] To adapt the concept in the manner of Baroness Hale is to render it a synonym for suspicion and to water down the mens rea of conspiracy significantly.

Special mention should be made of cases involving conspiracies to import or deal in controlled drugs. It seems that, if D takes himself to be agreeing to the importation of a Class A drug, he will be liable for conspiracy to import a Class B or C drug if that is what his co-conspirators take themselves to have agreed.[222] Even though importation of a Class A drug is a different and more serious offence from importation of a Class B or Class C drug, the mens rea for each different importation offence is the same. It suffices that there was awareness that the item in possession was some form of contraband.[223] Yet, strictly speaking, D neither knew nor intended the existence of the facts necessary for the commission of this lesser offence. The finding of conspiracy to commit the lesser offence can be defended if we are prepared to say in this context that the greater offence can comprehend the lesser, so that an intention to import a Class A drug can be taken to be an intent to import a Class B or Class C drug.

*(g) Mens rea for statutory conspiracy—a summary*

It is helpful to summarise our conclusions on the mental element required for conspiracy:

(i) D must intend that the agreement to which she is a party should be carried out. This encompasses an intention that any relevant conduct be engaged in and any relevant consequences brought about by at least one party to the agreement.
(ii) D must intend or know of the existence of any fact or circumstance necessary for the commission of the agreed offence.

[218] Critically dissected by Ormerod, "Making Sense of Mens Rea in Statutory Conspiracies" (2006) 59 *Current Legal Problems* 185, an analysis endorsed by Lord Nicholls in *Saik* [2006] UKHL 18, [2007] 1 AC 18, [37].
[219] *Ibid.* See also *Suchedina* [2006] EWCA Crim 2543, [2007] 1 Cr App R 23; *K* [2007] EWCA Crim 1888, [2008] 1 Cr App R 1.
[220] *Saik* [2006] UKHL 18, [2007] 1 AC 18, [97]–[100].
[221] Child has called this "future conduct intention" relating to what D would intend their conduct to be if the condition was satisfied: "Understanding Ulterior Mens Rea: Future Conduct Intention *is* Conditional Intention" (2017) 76 CLJ 323.
[222] *Patel*, unreported, 7 August 1991 (CA), transcript 89/4351/51; *Taylor* [2002] Crim LR 205 (CA).
[223] *Taafe* [1984] AC 539.

(iii) Where a fact or circumstance necessary for the commission of the agreed offence is not in existence at the time of the agreement, D must intend or know (i.e. have a settled belief[224]) that any such fact or circumstance will exist at the time the offence takes place.

(iv) If D is to be guilty of conspiracy, at least one other party to the agreement must satisfy conditions (i) through (iii) above.

(v) It is not necessary for D to intend to play any active part in carrying out the agreement; it is sufficient that D does not intend to frustrate the agreement from being carried out.

### *(h) Reform of the mens rea of conspiracy*

The Law Commission[225] reviewed the appropriate mens rea for conspiracy relating to the circumstance elements of the substantive offence and recommended that it should be reformed so that: (i) where the substantive offence requires proof of no fault or only negligence as regards circumstance elements, it should be sufficient to prove recklessness as regards such elements for the conspiracy; and (ii) where the substantive offence requires proof of subjective fault as regards circumstance elements, that fault element should also apply as regards such elements for the conspiracy.

The adoption of such a reform to the law of conspiracy would be a significant change. It would result in an approach to mens rea which has sometimes been adopted for attempt[226] and would avoid the artificial restriction of a conspiracy to where D and E intended or knew that a relevant circumstance would or does exist, for there is culpability in agreeing to do something suspecting that the circumstance might exist and a need for social protection in such circumstances. Further, the line between conditional intent and recklessness is already narrow and increasingly difficult to draw, making the case for recognising recklessness for conspiracy even stronger.

The significance of this reform is illustrated by conspiracy to rape. As the law stands, for D and E to be guilty of conspiracy to rape they must intend one of them to have sex with V intending or knowing that V would not be consenting to intercourse. This would be particularly difficult to prove; D and E lack much control over whether V consents or not, and probably do not "know" she does not consent in advance. However, since the mens rea of rape with respect to consent is absence of reasonable belief—a form of negligence—if the law of conspiracy was reformed as the Law Commission recommends, D and E could be convicted of conspiracy to rape if they suspected that there was a possibility that V might not be consenting and took that risk without adequate justification. An agreement to have sex even if V might not be consenting is properly characterised as a criminal conspiracy to commit rape. Similarly, the effect of this reform would be that the defendant in *Saik* would be guilty of conspiring to launder money if he suspected that the money might be the proceeds of crime (and took that risk without adequate justification), since suspicion is the applicable mens rea for the substantive offence.

[224] Above, § 5.4.

[225] Law Com. No. 318, *Conspiracy and Attempts* (2009) paras. 2.137 and 2.146.

[226] Below, § 9.3(iii)(b). It is inconsistent with the approach to the mens rea for attempt recognised by the Court of Appeal in *Pace and Rogers* [2014] EWCA Crim 186, [2014] 1 WLR 2867, but consistent with the approach of that Court in *Pop* [2026] EWCA Crim 774.

### *(vi) D's co-conspirators: some limitations*

Once it has been proved that D is a party to an agreement to commit a crime and is possessed of the necessary mens rea, and that at least one other party to the agreement has mens rea, liability for conspiracy will normally ensue against D and any other party with mens rea.[227] However, liability will not arise if that other party is the only other party to the agreement and is: (a) D's spouse or civil partner; (b) a person under the age of criminal responsibility; (c) a victim of the intended substantive offence; or (d) a limited company. We must also consider the position (e) when the only other party to the agreement is acquitted.

#### *(a) Spouses and civil partners*

It was probably a rule at common law that an agreement between a husband and wife alone to commit a crime did not constitute a conspiracy. The common law was based upon the legal fiction that husband and wife constituted a single legal person.[228] In *R*,[229] the House of Lords decided that the same fiction no longer had any role to play in providing the husband with a defence to a charge of raping his wife. The view expressed in *R*, that this fiction was fundamentally at odds with the status of women in modern English life, is of general application and would enable common law conspiracy charges to be brought on the basis of agreements confined to a husband and wife.[230] However, section 2(2) of the Criminal Law Act 1977 expressly provides that an agreement confined to a spouse or to a civil partner[231] will not constitute a statutory conspiracy.

This provision was endorsed by the Law Commission as safeguarding "the stability of marriage".[232] One might think there are more serious threats to a marriage than conspiracy charges and, in any event, one spouse may be charged as a secondary party to the other spouse's crimes should the conspiracy be carried out. A spouse may also incur liability under section 4 of the Criminal Law Act 1967 if anything is done with intent to impede the apprehension or prosecution of the principal offender. Be that as it may, section 2(2) is unequivocal. Its terms are, however, confined to agreements where the parties are the spouse or civil partners alone. Should they be joined by any other party, such as a child of the marriage over the age of criminal responsibility, all parties will be liable for conspiracy.[233]

The immunity in respect of conspiracy is anomalous and anachronistic and the Law Commission has subsequently acknowledged that spousal immunity is outdated and has recommended its removal.[234]

227 Although there is no rule of law which requires all parties to the conspiracy to be charged: *Rowan* [2023] EWCA Crim 205, [2023] 1 WLR 4523, [35].

228 Williams, *CLGP* 799–803.

229 [1992] 1 AC 599.

230 There is no English decision which rules that husband and wife cannot conspire at common law, although there is a statement to that effect in Hawkins 1 PC, ch. 27, § 8 and dicta in *Mawji v R* [1957] AC 126 (PC). In the civil law, a husband and wife can conspire: *Midland Bank Trust Co Ltd v Green (No 3)* [1979] Ch 496.

231 Civil Partnership Act 2004, sched. 27, para. 56. The exception does not apply to agreements between "de facto" partners, who are living together as a couple but not in a formal marriage or civil partnership: *Suski* [2016] EWCA Crim 24.

232 Law Com. No. 76, *Conspiracy and Criminal Law Reform* (1976) paras. 1.46–1.49.

233 *Chrastny* [1991] 1 WLR 1381 (CA).

234 Law Com. No. 318, *Conspiracy and Attempts* (2009) para. 5.16.

*(b) Persons under the age of criminal responsibility*

Section 2(2) further provides that D will not be guilty of conspiracy if the only other person with whom he agrees is a person under the age of criminal responsibility. If E is under the age of 10, E has a complete defence to a charge of statutory conspiracy.[235] Section 2(2) makes it clear that, if E is the only party to the conspiracy, D too is exempt from liability in conspiracy. It is not obvious why E's lack of criminal capacity should also provide immunity for D if E was capable of entering into an agreement with an intention that the agreement be carried out. However, arguably persons under 10 are generally incapable in any meaningful sense of making criminal agreements; if so, one way of justifying the subsection is to see it as a form of conclusive presumption against the existence of a conspiracy. On that view, there would be no agreement to which D can be a party in any case where E, the only other party, is under 10.

The Law Commission has recommended that this rule should not be changed,[236] but has recognised that the adult D could be guilty of encouraging or assisting a conspiracy under the Serious Crime Act 2007, since the Law Commission considers that it is sufficient that D has done an act which is capable of encouraging or assisting the offence, it being irrelevant that this substantive offence has not been and cannot be committed because E is under 10.[237] It is not, however, clear that any of the inchoate encouraging or assisting offences will have been committed in such circumstances, because D will not have committed an act which is capable of encouraging or assisting an offence to be committed by E, since E lacks the capacity to commit any such offence.

*(c) Where the only other party is a victim*

At common law, where D would otherwise be party to a conspiracy with E, D will not be liable if she is to be regarded as the victim of the agreed crime. So, in *Tyrrell*,[238] D, a girl under the age of 14, was not a conspirator with E in the crime of unlawful sexual intercourse despite her readiness to participate. Section 2(2) confirms this immunity for statutory conspiracy. It also provides that E, too, is not liable for statutory conspiracy if the only other party to the agreement is an "intended victim" of the agreed offence. It is difficult to appreciate why this should be so. If D, notwithstanding her victim status, possesses the capacity to enter agreements with intent that they be carried out, there is a sufficient actus reus for E's liability to be assessed by reference to his own culpability. The rule in *Tyrrell* is protective of victims and, it is submitted, should confer no immunity on non-victim participants in the criminal activity. The effect of section 2(2) is to pass on the protection accorded to victims to persons who are fully accountable for the agreements they enter.

The range of persons who fall within the category of victim is not defined by the Act. At common law, in the context of immunity from charges of complicity and conspiracy, a "victim" has always been a member of a defined, vulnerable class, such as a young person below the age of consent or a statutorily protected tenant.[239] The absence of such limiting characteristics specified in section 2(2)—there is simply an unqualified reference to "intended

[235] The defence of legal infancy is discussed below, § 19.3.
[236] Law Com. No. 318, *Conspiracy and Attempts* (2009) para. 5.39.
[237] See above, § 9.1(ii)(e).
[238] [1894] 1 QB 710. See above, § 7.6(iv)(a).
[239] *Grace Rymer Investment v Waite* [1958] Ch 831.

victim"—invites consideration whether the term is to be taken in a broader sense. This was considered by the Supreme Court in *Gnango*,[240] where Lords Phillips and Judge[241] recognised that the word "victim" might be interpreted broadly to mean any person who would be harmed by the offence. They went on, however, to emphasise that the word "victim" in section 2(2) had not previously received judicial consideration and the adoption of the broad interpretation could produce surprising results. For example, an agreement between D and E to commit mass murder through a terrorist atrocity by E acting as a suicide bomber would not be a criminal conspiracy, because E would be characterised as a victim since he was intended to be killed. Similarly, a conspiracy between D and E to set fire to E's house fraudulently to obtain insurance money would not be a conspiracy, because E would suffer property damage and so would be characterised as a victim. In the light of such results, Lords Phillips and Judge suggested that "victim" for the purposes of section 2(2) should be interpreted narrowly so as to be confined to the person who was intended to be protected by the offence. This would be consistent with the interpretation of "victim" for the inchoate offences involving encouraging and assisting[242] and for complicity.[243] Further, as the policy of section 2(2) is questionable, a narrow interpretation of "victim" should be adopted, and, preferably, and as the Law Commission has recommended, it should exempt the victim only and not any other party to the conspiracy.[244]

The express provision in section 2(2) for the cases of children under the age of criminal responsibility (above, § 9.2(vi)(b)) and for victims indicates that D will otherwise be liable for conspiracy in any situation where the only other party to the agreement is exempt from prosecution on some other ground (provided the ground of exemption is compatible with the capacity to enter an agreement with the intention that it be carried out). An illustration from the common law is provided by *Duguid*,[245] where D agreed with E, the mother of a child, to remove the child from the possession of the lawful guardian. Had the agreement been carried out, D would have been liable for an offence under section 56 of the Offences Against the Person Act 1861, but not E, as it was provided that a mother could not be prosecuted for taking her own child. It was held that E's immunity from prosecution for the substantive offence did not preclude D from being convicted for conspiracy to commit the offence. The same should follow for statutory conspiracy except in the situations expressly envisaged by section 2(2).

### *(d) Corporate liability*

The position of companies as parties to conspiracies is not dealt with by the Act. It may be assumed that the common law rules will apply to statutory conspiracies.

As seen in Chapter 8, companies, as legal persons with an identity separate from that of shareholders and directors,[246] may commit crimes in their own right. It has been held that companies may become parties to conspiracies provided an agreement on behalf of the

240 [2011] UKSC 59, [2012] 1 AC 827.
241 *Ibid.*, [49].
242 Serious Crime Act 2007, s. 51; above, § 9.1(iii)(c). This is also the recommendation of the Law Commission: Law Com. No. 318, *Conspiracy and Attempts* (2009) para. 5.35.
243 *Gnango* [2011] UKSC 59, [2012] 1 AC 827; above, § 7.6(iv)(a).
244 Law Com. No. 318, *Conspiracy and Attempts* (2009) para. 5.35.
245 (1906) 70 JP 294.
246 *Salomon v Salomon* [1897] AC 22.

company is made by a person sufficiently senior to be identified with the company.[247] In *McDonnell*,[248] Nield J ruled there was no conspiracy where D, the managing director and sole shareholder in E Ltd, arranged the tax affairs of E Ltd so as to evade fraudulently the payment of corporation tax. For Nield J, conspiracy required the involvement of at least two human agents; he rejected the view that E Ltd could be regarded as possessing a mind separate from D's as "too artificial".

It may be noted that if, in *McDonnell*, D had enlisted the help of, say, F, an accountant, to create the fraudulent scheme of corporate tax evasion, a conviction of D, F, and E Ltd for conspiracy to evade corporation tax would have been possible. Yet a conviction of E Ltd for conspiracy in those circumstances would involve the same degree of artificiality which the judge found unacceptable on the facts of *McDonnell*. The conviction of E Ltd would be on the basis that D's agreement with F entailed the agreement of E Ltd. Whenever a company is convicted of conspiracy, an artificial duality is involved, since the state of mind of D (a person of requisite seniority) is not merely her own state of mind but, additionally, a state of mind attributable to the company. The same logic can be carried over to one-person companies, as the Privy Council decision in *Lee v Lee's Air Farming*,[249] a civil case, demonstrates. In the civil law it is possible to identify a conspiracy where the company is alleged to have conspired with only one human agent, who is the very person identified with that company;[250] there is no reason of principle or logic why the position in criminal law should be any different. By virtue of the separate legal identity of the sole shareholder and the company, it would be appropriate for the criminal law to follow civil law so that a conspiracy between the sole shareholder and the company should result in liability under both regimes.[251]

*(e) Acquittal of the only other party*

Suppose that D and E are jointly tried for conspiracy and no other persons are alleged to have conspired with them. At one time the common law rule was that the acquittal of one of the alleged conspirators entailed the acquittal of the other. The reasoning behind this rule was that the acquittal of one conspirator and the conviction of the other in circumstances where only two persons had been charged with conspiracy would be incompatible with the requirement that two or more parties are necessary to constitute a conspiracy. The rule was criticised for confusing the requirements of formal legal proof with actual facts in the world. It may be the case, for example, that a confession or hearsay evidence is admissible against D but not against E,[252] resulting in proof beyond reasonable doubt against D but not against E. This criticism of the common law proved decisive for the House of Lords in *DPP v Shannon*.[253] Thereafter, the acquittal of one party to the conspiracy was no bar to the conviction of the other even for cases where only two parties were alleged to have formed a

247 *DPP v Kent and Sussex Contractors Ltd* [1944] KB 146 (DC).

248 [1966] 1 QB 233 (Assizes (Bristol)). See also *AAH Pharmaceuticals v Birdi* [2011] EWHC 1625 (QB), [31] (Coulson J).

249 [1961] AC 12 (PC). It was held that Mr Lee could be identified with his company in his capacity as managing director and could be regarded as an employee, under the direction of the company, in his capacity as the company's one and only pilot. According to Lord Morris, "such is the logic of *Salomon*".

250 *Barclay Pharmaceuticals Ltd v Waypharm LP* [2012] EWHC 306 (Comm), paras. 227–9 (Gloster J); *Twentieth Century Fox Film Corp. v Harris* [2014] EWHC 1568 (Ch), [151] (Barling J).

251 Virgo, "'We Do This in the Criminal Law and That in the Law of Tort': A New Fusion Debate" in Pitel, Neyers, and Chamberlain (eds.), *Tort Law: Challenging Orthodoxy* (2013) 95, 114.

252 Williams, *CLGP* 678–9. As a general rule, confessions are admissible evidence only against their maker.

253 [1975] AC 717.

conspiracy. The Criminal Law Act 1977, in section 5(8) and (9), confirms the rule in *Shannon* for both statutory and common law conspiracies. So long as the jury is sure that D entered into an agreement with *someone* (even if not E) and both parties had the requisite mens rea, a conviction for conspiracy would be permissible.

### *(vii) Conspiracies involving the commission of more than one offence*

Section 1(1) of the Criminal Law Act 1977 refers to a course of conduct involving "the commission of any offence or *offences*", indicating that a course of conduct charged as a single conspiracy may have as its objective the commission of two or more offences. It is even permissible for a number of offences of differing degrees of seriousness to be charged in a single conspiracy; provided it can be proved against each conspirator that she agreed to the commission of the most serious offences referred to in the indictment. The effect of this proviso can be seen in *Roberts*,[254] where there was evidence that some of the defendants had agreed to acts of aggravated criminal damage, being at least reckless as to the endangerment of the lives of others, whereas other defendants had agreed only to acts of simple criminal damage. The Court of Appeal ruled that the defendants in the latter group were not parties to the conspiracy as charged, namely to commit aggravated criminal damage. Presumably, they would have been parties if the indictment had charged only a conspiracy to commit acts of simple criminal damage.

When an agreement to commit two or more crimes is charged as a single conspiracy, particular care must be taken not to bring into association parties who are not truly partners in the same objectives. For example, D and E may agree to rob V and W banks but decide that they will need the assistance of F with a further robbery of X bank. Accordingly, they enlist F for the X bank project. In a trial where only D and E are the defendants, the most appropriate course may be to charge D and E with a single conspiracy to rob V, W, and X banks. Such a course may be more economical of court-time and provide a jury with a better overall perspective of their wrongdoing. If F is joined too as a defendant, he may only properly be charged with conspiring to rob X bank, thus precluding the use against him of evidence that relates only to the robbery of V and W banks.

Although multi-offence conspiracies may be charged as a single conspiracy, there is nothing to preclude several, distinct conspiracy charges. In *Lavercombe*,[255] D and E agreed to buy cannabis in Thailand for importing into the United Kingdom. Although already convicted in Thailand for conspiracy to possess cannabis, the Court of Appeal confirmed their liability for conspiracy to import cannabis into the United Kingdom. Since there were two distinct offences there could be two distinct conspiracies and it was immaterial that both conspiracies were constituted by the one agreement on a course of conduct.

### *(viii) Conspiracy to commit murder—duress*

Duress is not a defence to murder, either for a principal or for an accessory,[256] nor to attempted murder.[257] It has, however, been recognised at first instance that duress is a

[254] [1998] 1 Cr App R 441 (CA).
[255] [1988] Crim LR 435 (CA).
[256] *Howe* [1987] AC 417. See below, § 20.1(i).
[257] *Gotts* [1992] 2 AC 412.

defence to conspiracy to commit murder,[258] apparently because conspiracy is considered to be more remote from the completed offence than attempt,[259] so there is greater opportunity for repentance and failure. If duress is available to conspiracy to murder, it should also be a defence to encouraging or assisting murder. The Privy Council in *Moss*[260] assumed that duress is a defence to conspiracy to commit murder, although it could not be established on the facts, and the Board declined to give an opinion on whether the defence should be available. If focus is placed on the culpability of D, this categorical distinction in the operation of the defence of duress for different inchoate offences is difficult to defend, because for each inchoate offence relating to murder there must be an intention that V be killed. It was because the mens rea for attempted murder is an intention to kill that duress was denied to that offence, and conspiracy to commit murder requires a similar intent. But, if the focus is placed on potential harm, that harm is more remote where there is a conspiracy to murder rather than an attempt, so it is possible, albeit artificial, to distinguish between the different inchoate offences.[261] It would be preferable to allow the defence of duress in respect of all inchoate offences to commit murder, and even to murder itself.[262]

### *(ix) Secondary liability*

"Commission of any offence" is a term appropriate to acts of perpetration of a crime but is unsuited to convey complicity in the offence of another. An agreement between and *confined* to D and E to assist the commission of an offence by P will consequently not constitute a statutory conspiracy on the part of D and E to be accessories to the offence.[263] The fact that section 1 of the Criminal Law Act 1977 contemplates that only "*one* or more parties to the agreement" may commit the agreed crime strengthens this view. Further, even if all the acts are performed as the conspirators have agreed, no offence will be committed unless the principal, who is not party to the conspiracy, commits the substantive offence, and there is no certainty that she will do so; consequently the conspirators' agreed course of conduct will not *necessarily* amount to an offence as section 1(1) of the Criminal Law Act 1977 requires. Of course, if D and E agree, for example, to assist P in the commission of burglary and P is party to that agreement, this will constitute a conspiracy on the part of all of them to commit burglary.

### *(x) Inchoate offences*

The phrase "commission of any offence" employed in section 1 of the Criminal Law Act 1977 is perfectly apt to cover inchoate offences. Accordingly, it is possible to conspire to commit the inchoate offences of assisting or encouraging a crime contrary to Part 2 of the Serious Crime Act 2007. This was recognised in *Russo*,[264] where the defendants were convicted of conspiracy to do an act capable of encouraging or assisting the commission

[258] *Ness and Awan* [2011] Crim LR 645 (Crown Court (Newcastle)).
[259] *Gotts* [1991] 1 QB 660, 668 (CA).
[260] [2023] UKPC 28, [54] (Lord Stephens).
[261] *Ness and Awan* [2011] Crim LR 645, [29] (McCombe J).
[262] See Law Commission, *Murder, Manslaughter and Infanticide* No. 304 (2006), Part 6.
[263] *Kenning* [2008] EWCA Crim 1534, [2009] QB 221. See also *Dang* [2014] EWCA Crim 348.
[264] [2025] EWCA Crim 472, [2026] KB 89.

of more than one offence:[265] namely an agreement to supply encrypted communication devices to others knowing that this would encourage or assist them to import and supply drugs. The defendants had argued that, if conspiracy to be an accessory was not an offence known to the law, then neither should the offence of conspiracy to encourage or assist. This argument was rejected on the unconvincing ground that the inchoate offence of encouraging and assisting was completed by doing the act which was capable of encouraging or assisting the crime, whereas accessorial liability depended on the principal committing the substantive offence. One implication of the recognition of the conspiracy to commit the inchoate offence of encouraging or assisting is that the reach of the criminal law will extend far back from the point of commission of the substantive offence. Serious doubts may be entertained about the propriety of such charges for conduct so remote from the substantive crime,[266] yet there is now no legal impediment to such a prosecution. But, by virtue of the wide definition of the encouraging and assisting offence, it may not be necessary to charge a conspiracy to commit the offence because the parties will have encouraged or assisted the substantive offence to be committed. This was the case in *Russo.*

Similarly, in principle there are no legal difficulties precluding charges of conspiracy to conspire or conspiracy to attempt. However, such charges will rarely be apt. It is hard to envisage a conspiracy to conspire which is not, more straightforwardly, a conspiracy to commit a substantive offence. Likewise, a conspiracy to attempt will be a conspiracy to commit the substantive offence, save for some very rare cases where D is aware that it is impossible to commit the substantive offence;[267] in which case, as was seen above in § 9.2(v), D will lack mens rea.

### *(xi) Conspiracy—an unnecessary offence?*

If statutory conspiracy were to be abolished,[268] persons who agreed to commit a crime would be beyond the reach of the criminal law only until they encouraged or assisted others to commit crimes, committed some offence of a preliminary or possessory kind by way of preparation for the offence agreed, or engaged in conduct sufficiently proximate to the substantive offence to constitute an attempt. The ground covered by conspiracy and conspiracy alone is narrow and it may be practically non-existent following the enactment of the Serious Crime Act 2007. The only possible ground covered exclusively by conspiracy is limited to some non-consummated agreements where D's agreement with E that E should commit a crime does not constitute any form of encouragement or assistance in relation to the projected offence; usually the very act of making an agreement will constitute some form of encouragement in respect of the commission of the substantive offence and so be covered by the Serious Crime Act 2007. In practical terms, such conspiracies that have manifested themselves in nothing more than the fact of agreement are rarely prosecuted. Such bare

[265] An inchoate offence contrary to the Serious Crime Act 2007, s. 46.

[266] For critical discussion, see Johnson, "The Unnecessary Crime of Conspiracy" (1973) 61 *California LR* 1137; Marcus, "Criminal Conspiracy Law: Time to Turn Back from an Ever Expanding, Ever More Troubling Area" (1992) 1 *William and Mary Bill of Rights J* 1.

[267] See the discussion above, § 9.1(ii)(d) (encouragement and assistance offences); the example given there could be adapted to conspiracy.

[268] Johnson, "The Unnecessary Crime of Conspiracy" (1973) 61 *Cal LR* 1137; Dennis, "The Rationale of Criminal Conspiracy" (1977) 93 *LQR* 39.

agreements will seldom come to light, since criminals do not plan their crimes on the public record. Typically, evidence of a conspiracy is inferred from concerted criminal activity.[269] Moreover, when a crime has been committed, anyone who has agreed to its commission will, almost invariably, be an accomplice of the principal offender(s) and thus equally liable for their offending. It may be doubted whether it is worth retaining such a complex body of law merely to proscribe non-consummated agreements.

Against that view, those who wish to retain conspiracy would argue that multi-party agreements to commit crimes are more dangerous and subversive than commitments to crime on the part of individuals.[270] There is a degree of plausibility in that claim, especially because, after a period when prosecutions were seldom brought in respect of conspiracies which did not result in the commission of substantive offences, non-consummated conspiracies are increasingly prosecuted as, for example, terrorist conspiracies to cause explosions which are intercepted by police at a preparatory stage. A joint trial of principals and accomplices in respect of the substantive offences actually committed or attempted enables the prosecution to lay appropriate stress on the dangers that may be posed by well-organised criminal activity.

At common law, conspiracy was employed for what has been described as its "useful elasticity". When conspiracy was entirely a common law crime, prosecutors were allowed to use conspiracy charges to evade time limits, sentencing restrictions, and procedural requirements imposed in respect of particular statutory offences. Happily, such elasticity is no longer permitted; the Criminal Law Act 1977 ensures that the penalty for conspiracy cannot exceed that imposed for the substantive offence[271] and that any time or procedural requirements associated with the substantive offence equally apply to conspiracies to commit that offence.[272] As we noted at the outset of this discussion of conspiracy, one form of elasticity remains. It is still the case that some forms of conduct which would not be criminal if perpetrated by an individual may become criminal at common law if done in pursuance of an agreement by two or more persons to defraud.[273] It is very much a matter for regret that the Fraud Act 2006 did not abolish conspiracy to defraud despite the Law Commission's intention that it should.[274]

Supporters of conspiracy charges emphasise their procedural and evidential advantages. Following an allegation of conspiracy, each alleged conspirator may be treated as the agent of his co-defendants. Accordingly, evidence pertaining to one particular defendant becomes admissible against all other defendants for the purposes of the conspiracy charge that yokes them together.[275] Conspiracy counts, it is claimed, give proper emphasis to the group character of multi-party offending and allow the jury a clearer, more rounded, picture of what the defendants have done.[276] This is particularly useful, it is said, where the role played by one or more of the parties in the perpetration of the substantive offences is

[269] *Mulcahy* (1868) LR 3 HL 306, 317; *Hammersley* (1958) 42 Cr App R 207 (CA).

[270] *Griffiths* [1966] 1 QB 589 (CA).

[271] Criminal Law Act 1977, s. 3.

[272] *Ibid.*, s. 4.

[273] Below, § 15.9.

[274] Law Com. Consultation Paper No. 155, *Fraud and Deception* (1999).

[275] Cf. *Griffiths* [1966] 1 QB 589 (CA). See, too, the exception to the hearsay rule preserved by Criminal Justice Act 2003, s 118 (Rule 7).

[276] *Cox and Mead*, *The Times*, 6 December 1984, discussed in Law Com. No. 104, *Conspiracy to Defraud* (1987) para. 6.6; *Simmonds* [1969] 1 QB 685, 690 (CA).

unclear. Yet, as Williams pointed out many years ago, these benefits are equally accessible if defendants are charged with being each other's accomplices,[277] although that depends on establishing the commission of a substantive offence by the principal. It is habit of mind and long-standing practice that favours recourse to conspiracy rather than any unique advantage that the charge brings.

In 2009, the Law Commission reviewed the law of conspiracy, particularly in the light of the creation of inchoate offences of encouragement and assistance, and concluded that there is still a role for the offence.[278] The Law Commission did, however, find the existing offence wanting in certain respects. As has already been observed, it proposed amending the mens rea of the offence and certain aspects of the law concerning which parties can be exempt from liability. Further, from a desire to attain some measure of consistency between conspiracy and the inchoate offences of encouragement and assistance, it recommended that the defence of acting reasonably should be available for conspiracy in the same form as it appears in section 50 of the Serious Crime Act 2007.[279] Whilst consistency between the inchoate offences is desirable, the case for consistency is less strong when the defence of acting reasonably is so far from satisfactory.[280]

## § 9.3 Attempt

The inchoate offence of attempt[281] penalises conduct which is sufficiently proximate to the commission of an indictable offence, when done with intent to commit that offence. At common law, attempt was a complex, vacillating body of law.[282] Considerable, albeit imperfect, simplification has been achieved by the Criminal Attempts Act 1981, which abolishes the common law offence and replaces it with the following statutory offence, contained in section 1:[283]

> If, with intent to commit an offence to which this section applies, a person does an act which is more than merely preparatory to the commission of the offence, he is guilty of an attempt to commit the offence.

The most obvious justification for having a general law of attempts is to allow the timely prevention of future criminal harms. A concern with harms yet to be realised can be seen even in the early development of the common law. For instance, burglary, from its emergence in the twelfth century, penalised individuals who entered walled cities or inhabited premises at night with felonious intent. The threat to security from such entry called for intervention; it was not necessary to demonstrate that the felony D had in mind was ultimately committed.[284] Likewise, the offence of assault was devised to proscribe threats of immediate violence, supplementing the earlier offence of battery which penalised the actual

[277] *The Proof of Guilt* (2nd ed., 1958) chap. 9.
[278] Law Com. No. 318, *Conspiracy and Attempts* (2009).
[279] *Ibid.*, para. 6.56.
[280] Above, § 9.1(iv)(b).
[281] Duff, *Criminal Attempts* (1996).
[282] See the definitive account in Williams, *CLGP*, chap. 14.
[283] The Act broadly gives effect to the recommendations in Law Com. No. 102, *Attempt and Impossibility in Relation to Attempt, Conspiracy and Incitement* (1980).
[284] Kenny, *Outlines of the Criminal Law* (1902) 170–1.

use of force.[285] The crime of attempt itself, dealing in general terms with threatened harms, did not emerge until much later. We owe to the Star Chamber the notion that, if a crime exists, it is also an offence to attempt to commit that crime.[286] This idea was received into the common law and by the early nineteenth century it was possible to speak in terms of a general common law crime of attempt,[287] now replaced by the present statutory offence.

### *(i) Actus reus: the requirement of proximity*

Resolving when conduct is sufficiently close to the commission of an offence to constitute an attempt has been a matter of intractable difficulty for English law.[288] It would be unfair to characterise this failure to devise a simple and clear test of proximity as a matter of judicial ineptitude. Ordinary language supplies little help in distinguishing conduct that is merely preparatory from conduct that is close enough to harm to constitute an attempt.[289] We would not say of D, a high jumper, that she was attempting to clear the bar until she had commenced her run-up to the jump. We can assume a general agreement that earlier conduct (warm-up, removal of track suit, etc.) is conduct preliminary to an attempt to clear the bar. Thereafter, dispute may arise. Some may argue that an attempt to clear the bar does not begin until D launches herself upwards, whereas others may insist that we are within the ambit of an attempt once the run-up commences. In terms of the rules of athletic competitions, the latter group would win the argument if the rule for competitions is that a run-up to the bar, however faltering and incomplete, constitutes an attempt at a jump. It will be readily appreciated that this rule would be a matter of stipulation and does not rest on any "correct" view of what, in any natural or philosophical sense, constitutes an attempt at jumping obstacles.

#### *(a) The proximity requirement at common law*

Unsurprisingly, the common law failed to identify a general test of sufficient proximity. Consensus on a test for proximity has been undermined by an unresolved tension between the claims of social protection, on the one hand, and an insistence that criminal liability should be confined to those who have perpetrated some wrongful deed, on the other. The latter approach was given its best expression in what was known as the "last act" test.[290] Under that test, D would not be liable for the attempted murder of V until, say, she had aimed the gun and squeezed the trigger (i.e. D had done the last act required of her to commit the crime). The test has its attractions. It allows certainty of application and confines liability to those who have perpetrated a wrong. From the perspective of V, however, the test has grave limitations. Provided we can be sure that D has resolved to kill V, there is much to be said for intervening and stopping D well before V's life is imperilled by D's actually firing at him.

Such concerns were reflected in alternative formulations to the last act test such as the "substantial step"[291] test and the "unequivocal act" test.[292] Under the substantial step test, D

[285] Hawkins, *Pleas of the Crown*, chap. 62, § 1.

[286] Stephen, *History of the Criminal Law of England* (1883) vol. 2, 221–3.

[287] *Higgins* (1801) 2 East 5, 102 ER 269.

[288] Duff, *Criminal Attempts* (1996) chap. 2; Smith, "Proximity in Attempt: Lord Lane's Midway Course" [1991] *Crim LR* 576; Stuart, "The Actus Reus in Attempts" [1970] *Crim LR* 505.

[289] For instructive discussion see Duff, *Criminal Attempts* (1996) 33–5.

[290] *Eagleton* (1855) 6 Cox CC 559.

[291] *Roberts* (1855) Dears 539, 169 ER 836.

[292] *Davey v Lee* [1968] 1 QB 366 (DC).

could be convicted of attempted arson on the basis of, say, walking towards a haystack with matches in his pocket (should it be proved that he intended to set fire to the stack). Objections to D's conviction could be raised on the basis that, until he strikes a match in order to ignite the stack, he has done nothing wrong; there is nothing reprehensible about walking in a field with matches in one's pocket.[293] An additional objection is that convictions in such circumstances may be unduly dependent on confession evidence to prove D's intention. The "unequivocal act" test addressed these concerns. Under its terms, in our arson example, D would not commit attempted arson until his extrinsic conduct indicated in the clearest terms that his immediate project was arson. In application, however, this test was not consistently or strictly applied, and resort to D's state of mind was permitted to resolve the ambiguities of his conduct.[294]

*(b) The proximity requirement under statute*

No particular test achieved primacy at common law, although it is fair to say that the predominant trend in the thirty years or so prior to the Criminal Attempts Act 1981 was toward a restrictive rather than expansive approach to the test of sufficient proximity.[295] Following recommendations of the Law Commission, the Criminal Attempts Act 1981 dispenses with any formal legal test of proximity. Instead, it addresses the proximity issue in terms of a question of fact to be placed before the jury: did D do an act which was "more than merely preparatory to the commission of the offence"?[296]

The Act provides explicitly that whether an act by D is more than merely preparatory "is a question of fact"[297] to be answered by the jury, provided that there is evidence sufficient in law to support such a finding. Accordingly, a judge must satisfy herself that the prosecution has adduced enough evidence to support a finding that D's act was more than merely preparatory to the commission of an offence. If the judge is satisfied, the question of sufficient proximity is put to the jury, the members of which must then make their own decision on the issue. However compellingly obvious it may seem that particular conduct is more than merely preparatory, it is a misdirection for a judge to instruct a jury that they *must* find the actus reus is proved.[298]

*(c) The approach in the cases*

The long title to the Criminal Attempts Act 1981 indicates that it was enacted to reform the previous law.[299] Accordingly, it would be reasonable to suppose that the common law on the issue of sufficient proximity was superseded. Despite this, in the early cases decided under the Act, reference was made to pre-Act case law when addressing the question of sufficient

[293] On this view, punishing D might well be regarded as a form of preventative detention and a violation of D's rights.

[294] In *Davey v Lee* [1968] 1 QB 366, the Court of Criminal Appeal adopted the unequivocal act test and, at the same time, permitted resort to confession evidence in order to clarify D's otherwise ambiguous conduct.

[295] E.g. *Kyprianou v Reynolds* [1969] Crim LR 656 (DC); *Comer v Bloomfield* (1971) 55 Cr App R 305 (DC).

[296] Criminal Attempts Act 1981, s. 1(1).

[297] *Ibid.*, s. 4(3).

[298] See *Stonehouse* [1978] AC 55, which resolved the position under the common law. The reasoning in *Stonehouse* is *a fortiori* applicable to the position under the Criminal Attempts Act 1981 which provides explicitly that the question of proximity is one of fact.

[299] "An Act to amend the Law of England and Wales as to attempt to commit offences . . ."

proximity.[300] By contrast, later cases, most notably *Jones*,[301] stressed that the words "more than merely preparatory" must be allowed their natural meaning and not be expansively or restrictively glossed by reference to cases decided before the Act. This seems now to be the law. It follows that an appellate court, when reviewing a conviction for attempt, must satisfy itself simply that there was sufficient evidence to sustain the finding that D's conduct was more than merely preparatory. On the face of it, that is a question of evaluating the facts of each particular case. In *Geddes*, however, Lord Bingham CJ introduced a degree of rigour into the question by insisting that the necessary proximity would not occur until D reached the stage of trying to commit the offence:[302]

> "It is, we think, an accurate paraphrase of the statutory test and not an illegitimate gloss upon it to ask whether the available evidence, if accepted, could show that a defendant has done an act which shows that he has actually tried to commit the offence in question, or whether he has only got ready or put himself in a position or equipped himself to do so."

In *Geddes*, D was a trespasser who has been seen entering a school lavatory while in possession of a knife, rope, and binding tape. There was compelling reason to believe that D intended to abduct a pupil of the school. D was convicted at trial of attempted false imprisonment, but, applying Lord Bingham's test, his conviction was unsafe, and was accordingly quashed on appeal, because he had not tried before his arrest to detain any victim. In *MS*,[303] the distinction between D placing herself in a position to commit an offence, which is a mere preparatory act, and attempting to commit the offence, was confirmed. Crucially, it was emphasised that whether D had done a more than a merely preparatory act will depend on the ingredients of the offence and the facts of the case. Further, no single factor will constitute a uniform test which will apply to all cases. This point is illustrated by the factor of "geographical proximity". The fact that D is some physical distance away from V would be relevant to the crimes of attempted murder and robbery, for example, and might well indicate that D had not gone beyond placing herself in a position to commit the offence.[304] However, in *MS*, which concerned the crime of attempting to abduct a child, geographical proximity was not considered to have the same significance. In that case, D had been stopped by the police 85 miles away from the port of Dover, from where she intended to leave on a ferry to France with her child, at which point the crime of child abduction would have been committed (since the removal of her child from the country would have been in breach of a court order). It was held that the question of whether D had done a more than merely preparatory act should have been left to the jury, especially in the light of the other evidence including forging documents and booking accommodation and tickets for the onward journey.

In light of *Geddes* and *MS*, a person does not reach the stage of trying to commit the offence until he broaches commission of the actus reus of the substantive offence, as occurred in *Jones*,[305] where D was convicted of attempted murder upon unlocking the

300 *Widdowsen* (1985) 82 Cr App R 314 (CA); *Boyle* (1987) 84 Cr App R 270 (CA).

301 [1990] 3 All ER 886 (CA).

302 [1996] Crim LR 894, 895 (CA). In *Gullefer* (1990) 91 Cr App R 356 (CA) the appropriate test had been described as being whether the defendant had "embarked on the crime proper".

303 [2021] EWCA Crim 600, [2021] 1 WLR 5019.

304 See Clarkson, "Attempt: The Conduct Requirement" (2009) 29 *OJLS* 25, 26, who concludes that in most cases there will have been an attempt where there has been a confrontation with the victim or property.

305 (1990) 91 Cr App R 351 (CA). Contrast at common law, *Stevens* [1985] LRC (Crim) 17, noted (1986) 50 *J Crim L* 247.

safety-catch and pointing a loaded firearm at V, and in *A-G's Reference (No. 1 of 1992)*,[306] where a conviction for attempted rape was upheld after D had thrown V to the ground and exposed his penis. In *Mason v DPP*,[307] by contrast, D's conviction for attempting to drive a motor vehicle while under the influence of alcohol was quashed where D, being twice over the legal limit for alcohol consumption, had opened his car door intending to drive the vehicle, which was then stolen from him. D was not considered to have embarked on the crime proper; but he would apparently have done so had he managed to turn the engine on before the car was stolen. Similarly, in *Campbell*,[308] D, in possession of an imitation firearm, was arrested just before entering a Post Office which he intended to rob. The quashing of his conviction for attempted robbery followed from the fact that, however close he came to committing robbery, he had yet to commence those acts which would constitute theft by force or the threat of force—which is the actus reus of robbery.

Less easily explained in terms of Lord Bingham's test is *Tosti*.[309] D was observed concealing oxyacetylene equipment behind a hedge, approaching a barn door, and bending down to examine a padlock. His conviction for attempted burglary was sustained by the Court of Appeal, because, although his act was preparatory, it was not "merely" so. The line dividing *Campbell* from *Tosti* may be considered so faint as to be invisible. It could, perhaps, be asserted that, by examining the padlock in *Tosti*, D was getting physically to grips with committing the crime itself, something that had yet to occur in *Campbell*. That at least was the view of Beldam LJ, who described the defendant in *Tosti* as taking "the first steps in the commission of the offence".[310]

Broadly, the approach to the question of sufficient proximity taken by Lord Bingham in *Geddes* is to be welcomed. In insisting that D must have commenced that series of acts which will constitute, if and when completed, the actus reus of the substantive offence, liability for attempt is confined to those who have demonstrated by their overt conduct that they are prepared to commit crimes. Moreover, a law of attempt cast in these restrictive terms is less dependent on confession evidence for convictions than would be the case under a more expansive test. To be sure, as in many areas of law, there will be decisions not easy to reconcile, as the contrasting decisions in *Campbell* and *Tosti* demonstrate. Yet, in general terms, the current law governing sufficient proximity in attempt is far more straightforward than it was under the common law, where incompatible legal tests competed for supremacy.

### *(ii) The scope of the actus reus of attempt*

#### *(a) Summary offences*

To be guilty of an attempt, D must intend to commit an offence to which section 1 of the Criminal Attempts Act 1981 applies.[311] Section 1(4) of the Act provides that the offence must be an offence that would be triable in England and Wales as an indictable offence. In general terms, therefore, there is no offence of attempting to commit a summary offence. This must

306 [1993] 2 All ER 190 (CA).
307 [2009] EWHC 2198 (Admin).
308 (1990) 93 Cr App R 350 (CA).
309 [1997] Crim LR 746 (CA).
310 *Ibid.*, 747.
311 Section 1(1).

reflect the legislative view that attempts are systemically less serious than the perpetration of substantive offences and do not merit criminalisation where the substantive crime is of a minor nature. There are, however, a number of specific statutory offences of attempting to commit particular summary offences.[312] Furthermore, the offence of attempted battery was recognised in *Nelson*,[313] even though the substantive offence is a summary offence.[314] This was because, exceptionally, battery (and common assault) can be tried on indictment where it is part of a series of offences of the same or similar character as an indictable offence.[315] Consequently attempted battery can be charged, but only if the indictment also charges indictable offences or attempts to commit indictable offences.

*(b) Attempt, conspiracy, and complicity*

Section 1(4) additionally provides that the offence of attempt does not apply to common law or statutory conspiracy, nor to aiding, abetting, counselling, procuring, or suborning (meaning "inducing") the commission of an offence. The reasoning lying behind these exceptions appears, in the case of conspiracy, to be its remoteness from any substantive offence and, in the case of secondary participation, because of the need to avoid unprincipled results arising from the peculiar nature of secondary liability. Complicity is not an offence known to English law; rather, the accessory is convicted of the same offence as the principal. But where D has tried to assist or encourage P to commit a substantive offence, P may still have a number of acts still to do before that crime is committed, so that to say that D has attempted to commit that substantive offence, albeit as a secondary party, "stretches the language of attempts beyond acceptable limits".[316] If, for example, D had sent a gun to P to kill V but the police intercepted the gun before P could shoot V, it would be odd to convict D of attempting to assist P to commit murder as P could not even be convicted of attempted murder because she had not done a more than merely preparatory act towards the commission of that offence. If attempted complicity was confined instead to where the substantive offence had been committed but D had failed actually to encourage or assist it, D's liability for attempt would be unprincipled. If, for example, P had committed murder as a principal but it could not be shown that D's act had assisted P to commit the crime (because, for example, the gun was sent to but not received by P), whether D had done a more than merely preparatory act towards being an accessory could not be determined at the point when D had sent the gun, but would depend on whether P had gone on to commit the substantive offence. Adopting such a "wait and see" approach is not consistent with the principle which requires liability for attempt to be determined at the point of doing a more than merely preparatory act, and not in the light of subsequent events.[317] In both these cases it would now be possible to convict D, but by reference to an inchoate offence involving assisting rather than complicity. In the

[312] Section 3 of the Criminal Attempts Act 1981 provides that, if any special statutory provision permits a charge of attempt in respect of a summary offence, liability for such an attempt will be governed by the same principles that apply to charges of attempt brought under the 1981 Act.

[313] [2013] EWCA Crim 30, [2013] 1 Cr App R 30.

[314] Criminal Justice Act 1988, s. 39.

[315] *Ibid.*, s. 40.

[316] Child, "The Difference Between Attempted Complicity and Inchoate Assisting and Encouraging—A Reply to Professor Bohlander" [2010] *Crim LR* 924, 926.

[317] See Smith, "Secondary Participants and Inchoate Offences" in Tapper (ed.), *Crime, Proof and Punishment: Essays in Memory of Sir Rupert Cross* (1981) 38.

example where D sent a gun to P but it was intercepted by the police, D had in fact committed an inchoate offence by doing an act which was capable of assisting the crime. If D had not supplied the gun to P but had done a more than merely preparatory act towards the supply of the gun (such as packing it in a parcel and taking it to the Post Office when he was stopped by the police), there is no objection to D being convicted of attempting to commit one of the inchoate offence involving assistance, since this does not relate in any way to the commission of an offence by P, and this is not excluded by section 1(4) of the Criminal Attempts Act 1981.

Complicitous conduct may also be made the gravamen of a specific substantive offence, as in the statutory crimes of encouraging or assisting suicide and of procuring an act of gross indecency. These statutory offences can, in turn, be attempted.[318]

*(c) Omissions*

Section 1 of the Act makes reference to "a person who does an act which is more than merely preparatory". There is authority that statutory phrases which make reference to the "doing of acts" import a legislative intent to preclude liability for omission.[319] In the context of attempts, the practical effect of this limitation is likely to be limited. On occasion, however, it may leave unpunished conduct which should be censured. Suppose that D, a carer who is wholly responsible for the welfare of the bedridden V, intentionally omits to provide food and drink for him. All other things being equal, it would be appropriate to find D liable for attempted murder if and when V's health becomes seriously impaired by a lack of sustenance.[320] Under the terms of the Criminal Attempts Act 1981, however, D will not be liable for attempted murder, notwithstanding how parlous V's condition may become, because D has not acted. The Law Commission has recommended that it should be possible to be liable for an attempt by omission, but only in the context of attempted murder.[321] It would follow that the carer who omitted to provide food and drink to V would be guilty of attempt if she intended to kill, but not if she only intended to cause serious harm to V. This is a highly artificial distinction to draw and it would have been preferable had the Law Commission simply recommended that it should be possible to attempt by omission regardless of the offence attempted.

*(d) Offences of negligence and strict liability*

As will be discussed below in § 9.3(iii), liability for attempt requires proof of an intent to commit the substantive offence. It has been argued that this requirement places limits on the kind of offences that can be attempted:[322]

> "The requirement of an intent to commit the substantive offence whose attempt is charged means that a charge of attempt to commit involuntary manslaughter is inappropriate because the prosecution would have to prove an intent to kill and if they did this they would establish attempted murder."

318 *McShane* (1977) 66 Cr App R 97 (CA).

319 *Ahmad* (1986) 84 Cr App R 64 (CA).

320 The possibility of liability for attempts by omission may give rise to difficult questions of proximity. Suppose that V falls down a hole and D is under a duty to rescue V. D, however, walks away hoping that V will not be found and will perish of starvation. Does D's conduct amount to an attempt as soon as she walks away, or must V first come close to death?

321 Law Com. No 318, *Conspiracy and Attempts* (2009) para. 8.151.

322 Card and Molloy, *Card, Cross & Jones: Criminal Law* (22nd ed., 2016) 577.

Not so. Admittedly, it would be odd to charge, say, attempted manslaughter by gross negligence. Negligence is a failure to attain reasonable standards and a person intentionally flouting such standards is acting culpably but not in a manner we would ordinarily call "negligent". To say that one is attempting to be negligent is, for most practical purposes, a contradiction in terms.[323] The oddity arises, however, not because manslaughter is an offence of negligence, but because, if the actus reus of manslaughter is intended, the appropriate offence is normally murder (since manslaughter and murder share the same actus reus and are differentiated by gradations of mens rea).[324] Even so, there is nothing that prevents an intentional killing from being charged as manslaughter—the greater offence includes the lesser.[325] The lesser forms of culpability provided for manslaughter are sufficient but not necessary conditions of liability. Accordingly, a charge of attempted manslaughter[326] is not a contradiction in terms, but must be proved by evidence which establishes an intent to kill. The fact that such evidence would satisfy the requirements of attempted murder does not preclude the lesser charge from being brought.

The point at issue here is simple but important. Most substantive offences do not require proof of an intent to commit them—many offences require no proof of culpability at all.[327] If they can be tried on indictment, these crimes can be attempted, provided that D intended to commit the crime. For example, if D takes a vehicle which is in a dangerous condition onto the highway, she will commit the offence of dangerous driving if the state of the vehicle should have been obvious to a careful and competent driver.[328] For the substantive offence, it is irrelevant that D herself was unaware of the danger her vehicle posed. Suppose she were to be stopped immediately prior to driving onto the highway and her vehicle examined. In principle, she would be guilty of attempted dangerous driving should she be aware of the dangerous condition of her vehicle, but not otherwise.

### *(iii) The mens rea of attempt*

The mens rea requirement of attempt is simply stated: according to the Criminal Attempts Act 1981, D must act "with intent to commit [the substantive] offence".[329] Alas, judicial interpretation has rendered the explication of this requirement much less straightforward than it should be. It will assist our discussion if we look at the question of intent sequentially in respect of the separate elements that may make up the actus reus of a substantive offence. Almost invariably an offence will require some form of *conduct* (i.e., physical behaviour) on the part of D,[330] and usually conduct perpetrated in particular *circumstances*. For some offences, an additional *consequence* element is required; it must be proved that D's conduct caused a particular result, such as a wound or a death. The concept of intent is not the same

[323] For some unusual possibilities where that would not be so, see Yaffe, *Attempts* (2010) chap. 6.

[324] See below, Chapter 10.

[325] Not infrequently, prosecutors lay manslaughter charges where the evidence would support a charge of murder. They may do so for a variety of reasons, including evasion of time-consuming trial issues and avoidance of the mandatory sentence associated with murder. For discussion, see Farrier, "The Distinction between Murder and Manslaughter in its Procedure Context" (1976) 39 *MLR* 415, esp. at 430–1.

[326] Particularly of the constructive variety: below, § 10.7(i).

[327] See above, Chapter 6.

[328] Road Traffic Act 1988, s. 2, as substituted by s. 1 of the Road Traffic Act 1991.

[329] Section 1(1).

[330] For possible exceptions see above, § 4.1(ii).

across these three elements.[331] Hence, we need to discuss the intent required for attempt liability by reference to each of these elements separately.

### *(a) Conduct*

By "conduct", we mean those movements on the part of D which are required of her as part of the actus reus of the substantive offence. In a case of murder by shooting, for example, the conduct element would include D's aiming of the gun and squeezing the trigger. Typically, such conduct will speak for itself in terms of it being intended.[332] Were we to observe D picking up the gun and aiming it at V, we would thereby directly observe her intention to act in that way. Generally, we would only be unsure whether or not her conduct was intended were we to be told that, despite her appearance of consciousness, she was, say, sleepwalking or in a hypnotic trance. Outside such very special cases, and the more common cases of altered states of consciousness induced by drink or drugs, the intention to engage in certain conduct will be straightforwardly established.

### *(b) Circumstances*

Conduct will rarely constitute an actus reus by itself. Attendant circumstances will need to be present. Frequently, the presence or absence of such circumstances will be matters beyond the control of D and, consequently, matters beyond the scope of his intention. Consider the case of D who finds a book on a seat in an airport lounge. Make two alternative assumptions: (i) the book was deliberately abandoned by its owner V, thereby divesting V of ownership; or (ii) V left the book inadvertently and would recover it if he could, so that ownership would remain with V. Suppose that D is about to deface the book but is prevented from doing so by the intervention of X. The substantive offence of criminal damage would have been possible only if the book were property belonging to another, e.g. on the facts of assumption (ii).[333] Whether or not the book belongs to V is a circumstance that, strictly, D cannot have intentions about—the facts are whatever they are. If the facts are those of assumption (ii) and D is aware of those facts, then clearly he intends to damage property belonging to another and is guilty of an attempt. His *knowledge* of the circumstances makes for an intention to damage someone else's property.[334] That intention would also subsist if D has a firm *belief* that the facts were those of assumption (ii).[335] His belief similarly entails an intent to damage property belonging to another. The same applies even if D has a settled but *false* belief that the facts are as in (ii), where the truth is that V has indeed abandoned the book. Under the Criminal Attempts Act 1981, even in this last case

[331] See generally Child, "Wrong on Many Levels: Understanding Crimes Across and Between Events" [2024] *Crim LR* 378.

[332] See Duff, *Intention, Agency and Criminal Liability* (1990) 116–20, where it is argued that intentions may take a form which can be directly observed and are inappropriately characterised as inner mental states severable from the conduct of the agent.

[333] On assumption (i), ownership in the book would not vest in the owners or tenants of the airport lounge but in the first person taking possession of the book intending to keep it: *Parker v British Airways Board* [1982] QB 1004; below, § 13.4(v).

[334] Unless he made a mistake of civil law and believed that he was entitled to assume ownership of the book in such circumstances: cf. *Smith* [1974] QB 354 (CA).

[335] As a general proposition, a settled belief—while falling short of knowledge in ordinary language—satisfies requirements of "knowledge" in the criminal law: above, § 5.4.

D is guilty of an attempt—notwithstanding that the full offence is impossible to commit.[336] His false belief makes for an *intention* to damage property belonging to another. And that suffices for the mens rea of an attempt.

But what if D lacks knowledge or any settled (true or false) belief? He observes V leaving for his flight and is unsure whether V has abandoned or inadvertently left the book. If he takes the book, lacking any knowledge or belief about its ownership, it could not be said that he intends to steal property belonging to another—that would not be his purpose; neither would interfering with another's property rights be something that he foresees as virtually certain. Here we should say that he is merely reckless about stealing *another's* property. He apparently lacks the intent that the Act requires. This conclusion is supported by section 1(3) of the Criminal Attempts Act 1981, which provides that, where D's intent would not be regarded as an intent to commit an offence, D shall be regarded as having the necessary intent to commit the offence, "if the facts of the case had been as he *believed* them to be" (emphasis added). These words demonstrate that, even where V has in fact abandoned the book, D may still be convicted of attempted theft if, *and only if*, he has a *belief* that the property is owned by another. Unfortunately, there is no express provision covering the position where the facts are as D believes them to be; but as a matter of general principle it may be said that only a belief (here a correct belief) that the property is owned by another should allow a conviction for attempted theft. Recklessness or suspicion should not suffice. That was the position taken by the Law Commission when proposing what became section 1(3).[337]

The proper interpretation of the mens rea relating to circumstances was considered by the Court of Appeal in *Pace and Rogers*,[338] which concerned a police operation to test whether scrap yards were prepared to buy stolen metal. The police offered scrap metal for sale to the defendants who purchased it. Had the metal been stolen, the defendants would have been guilty of converting criminal property[339] if they had suspected that the metal had been stolen.[340] In fact, the metal was the property of the police and so not stolen. Hence the defendants were charged with attempting to convert stolen property. The trial judge had held that it was sufficient for the attempt that the defendants had *suspected* that the metal was stolen. The Court of Appeal disagreed. It was held that the mental element for attempt according to section 1(1) required D to intend *all* the elements of the substantive offence; in the Court's view, there was no linguistic or purposive basis for any alternative interpretation.[341] Consequently, D had to intend the metal to be stolen. Since this had not been established, the convictions were quashed.

336 Criminal Attempts Act 1981, s. 1(2).

337 Law Com. No. 102, *Attempt and Impossibility in Relation to Attempt, Conspiracy and Incitement* (1980) paras. 214–18. Note that the Law Commission later changed its mind on the underlying policy questions: Law. Com. No. 177, *A Criminal Code for England and Wales* (1989) cl. 49(2).

338 [2014] EWCA Crim 186, [2014] 1 WLR 2867. See Virgo, "Criminal Attempts—The Law of Unintended Circumstances" [2014] *CLJ* 244; Simester, "The Mens Rea of Criminal Attempts" (2015) 131 *LQR* 169; Stark, "The Mens Rea of a Criminal Attempt" [2014] 3 *Arch Rev* 7; Dyson, "Scrapping Khan" [2014] *Crim LR* 445; Mirfield, "Intention and Criminal Attempts" [2015] *Crim LR* 142; Bruneau and Taylor, "In Defence of *Pace and Rogers*" [2015] 8 *Arch Rev* 6.

339 Proceeds of Crime Act 2002, s. 327.

340 *Ibid.*, s. 340(3)(b).

341 This analysis is defended by Mirfield, "Intention and Criminal Attempts" [2015] *Crim LR* 142, 148.

The decision in *Pace* has proved to be controversial, primarily for two reasons. First, that the insistence on intention as to all elements of the substantive offence faces difficulties when engaging with the circumstance elements of a crime, a problem highlighted by our example (above) of the book found in the airport lounge. As a matter both of statutory interpretation and of principle the intention to commit an offence should connote an intention with respect to the conduct or consequence elements of the offence, whereas it is knowledge or belief which should operate with respect to the circumstance elements of the offence.[342] The Court of Appeal in *Pace* did in fact acknowledge that knowledge or belief could be relevant to an attempt, despite its earlier insistence that intention is required for all elements of the offence, when it was recognised that the defendants could have been charged with attempting to handle stolen goods, for which the relevant mens rea relating to the goods' being stolen is knowledge or belief.[343] It follows that it is legitimate to interpret the Court of Appeal's insistence on intention as to all the elements of the offence to include knowledge or belief as to circumstances.

The second controversial feature of the decision in *Pace* is that it is inconsistent with earlier decisions of the Court of Appeal about the mens rea for attempt. The first of these was *Khan*,[344] where D had attempted to have sexual intercourse with V, aware that she might not consent to the act. On the interpretation of the mens rea in respect of circumstances adopted in *Pace*, D would be liable for attempted rape only if he intended to have sex with V intending that she did not consent; lack of consent being a circumstance element of rape. But in *Khan*, D was found to have been reckless about V's consent: that is, aware that she might not consent and proceeding unreasonably. In confirming D's conviction for attempted rape, the Court of Appeal in *Khan* ruled that, provided D possessed an intention with respect to the conduct element of the full offence (and D clearly intended to have sex), proof of recklessness regarding the absence of consent would permit a finding that D intended to commit rape within the meaning of section 1 of the Criminal Attempts Act 1981. The Court emphasised that the mens rea for rape and attempted rape were the same,[345] since at the time recklessness as to absence of consent was the required mens rea for rape.[346]

Conceptually, the Court's reasoning in *Khan* is unconvincing.[347] Where D lacks knowledge or belief regarding the absence of V's consent, D intends to rape only if it is his purpose "to have sexual intercourse without consent"—i.e. if it was *part* of his design that V should not consent.[348] Alternatively, if D's purpose was simply "to have sex", it being incidental to him whether V consents, then he would certainly intend "to have sex" but would intend "to have sex without consent" only if he knew or believed that V would not consent.

342 Simester, "The Mens Rea of Criminal Attempts" (2015) 131 *LQR* 169, 171.
343 [2014] EWCA Crim 186, [2014] 1 WLR 2867, [81].
344 [1990] 1 WLR 813 (CA). The other decision is *A-G's Reference (No. 3 of 1992)* [1994] 1 WLR 409 (CA): below, § 9.3(iii)(c).
345 [1990] 1 WLR 813, 819 (CA).
346 See now the Sexual Offences Act 2003, s. 1(1).
347 See Sullivan, "Intent, Subjective Recklessness and Culpability" (1992) 12 *OJLS* 380, where the reasoning but not the outcome in *Khan* is criticised. For a defence and rigorous explication of the reasoning in *Khan*, see Duff, "The Circumstances of an Attempt" (1991) 50 *CLJ* 100. *Khan* was, however, followed by the Court of Appeal for attempted rape in *Pop* [2026] EWCA Crim 774.
348 Above, § 5.1(v).

In confirming the conviction in *Khan*, the Court was heavily influenced by the fact that, had D succeeded in having intercourse, he would have been liable for the full offence of rape, an offence which could then be committed intentionally or recklessly with respect to V's non-consent. In the interests of public protection, the Court of Appeal considered that the mens rea for attempt should be aligned as closely as possible with the mens rea for the substantive offence. This is a powerful consideration. Undeniably, the conduct involved in *Khan* was gravely wrong and a considerable gap in social protection would have been allowed had his conviction been quashed. Nonetheless, the Court of Appeal seems in *Khan* to have departed from the statutory requirement of an intent to commit the full offence.[349]

*Khan* was tentatively distinguished in *Pace* on the grounds that the mens rea for rape at the time *Khan* was decided was recklessness and also because, had D succeeded in his act of penetration, he would have been guilty of rape, whereas the defendants in *Pace* could never have successfully converted stolen property because the property was not stolen. But neither ground is convincing. Although the relevant mens rea for the substantive offence in *Khan* was recklessness, which is different from the relevant mens rea of suspicion in *Pace*, since recklessness requires D to foresee a risk which it is unreasonable to take, recklessness and suspicion are not in this context significantly different. Further, no indication was given as to why the existence of recklessness as a mens rea for the substantive offence should result in a different approach, especially where that approach is inconsistent with the mens rea requirement for circumstances as interpreted by the Court in *Pace*. Additionally, whilst it is certainly the case that rape in *Khan* was possible, since V was not consenting to sex, and the conversion of stolen property in *Pace* was not possible, because the property was not stolen, it is unclear why this should make any difference to the mens rea requirement for attempt. There is consequently an inconsistency in the two decisions of the Court of Appeal Criminal Division, one which needs to be resolved by the Supreme Court. The interpretation adopted in *Pace* appears consistent with the mens rea requirement explicitly articulated in the Criminal Attempts Act 1981. It follows that the mens rea for attempted rape is preferably analysed as being that D must have intended to have intercourse with V, knowing or believing that V did not or would not consent,[350] even though this is not what *Khan* decided. The decision in *Khan*, however, is more acceptable in the interests of public protection. It might be defended on the ground that the Criminal Attempts Act 1981 only identifies intention as the mens rea for attempt. This can be contrasted with the Criminal Law Act 1977 which identifies intention and knowledge. If it is concluded that it is not possible to intend the existence of circumstances, it follows that no provision is made by the statute for circumstances such that the mens rea for the substantive offence should apply. It

[349] Furthermore, the Law Commission, reversing the position it took at the time the Criminal Attempts Act 1981 was framed (Law Com. No. 102, *Attempt and Impossibility in Relation to Attempt, Conspiracy and Incitement* (1980)), adopted the reasoning in *Khan* in its proposed Criminal Code: Law Com. No. 177, *A Criminal Code for England and Wales* (1989) cl. 49(2). The Law Commission has since recommended that, for substantive offences which have circumstance elements but no corresponding fault element or have a fault element of negligence, D should only be convicted of attempting the offence if he is subjectively reckless as to those circumstance elements: Law Com. No. 318, *Conspiracy and Attempts* (2009) para. 8.133. Further, for those substantive offences which have fault elements not requiring negligence as regards facts or circumstances, D should only be convicted of attempting that offence if he possesses that fault element: *ibid.*, para. 8.137. These proposals are consistent with the Law Commission's recommendations for the reform of statutory conspiracy: above, § 9.2(v)(h).

[350] See now *Pop* [2026] EWCA Crim 774 where the Court of Appeal followed *Khan* and distinguished *Pace* and *Rogers* on the ground that that case concerned an impossible attempt: [20]. Yang, "Recklessness and Circumstances in Criminal Attempts" (2023) 17 *Crim Law and Philosophy* 359 argues that a distinct endangerment offence should be created to deal with cases such as *Khan*, for which recklessness would be sufficient.

would follow that the mens rea for attempted rape is the same as for rape, namely intention to have sexual intercourse with no reasonable belief in consent. But this requires a restrictive interpretation of intention, one which was not adopted in *Pace*, but which was adopted by the Court of Appeal in *Pop*.

*(c) Consequences*

Prior to the Criminal Attempts Act 1981, in order to be liable for attempt D had to intend to cause any consequence specified in the actus reus of the full offence. A leading pre-Act case is *Whybrow*,[351] where D was charged with the attempted murder of his wife. Asserting that, in the case of attempt, "intent becomes the principal ingredient of the crime", Goddard LCJ ruled that, for D to be guilty of attempted murder, he must have intended to cause the death of V. He explicitly rejected the argument that, because an intent to cause grievous bodily harm would suffice for the full offence, it would also suffice for the attempt to commit it. The centrality of intent to attempt liability was confirmed in another pre-Act case, *Mohan*, where James LJ spoke of:[352]

> "a decision to bring about, in so far as it lies within the accused's power, the commission of the offence which it is alleged the accused attempted to commit, no matter whether the accused desired that consequence of his act or not."

In *Pearman*,[353] the Court of Appeal stated that this passage remained an authoritative guide to the interpretation of intent under the Criminal Attempts Act 1981, and the vital significance of intention to consequences was confirmed in *Pace*.[354]

The words employed by James LJ in *Mohan* comprehend not only the primary meaning of the term intent (what is sometimes called direct intent), but also foresight that a consequence was a virtual certainty. This was confirmed in *Pearman*, where it was stated that:[355]

> "a man who is cornered by the police when he is in a car may have the primary purpose of simply escaping from that situation. If he drives straight at police officers at high speed, a jury is likely to conclude that he intended to injure a police officer and maybe cause him serious grievous bodily harm."

In the light of the House of Lords decision in *Woollin*,[356] where the consequence is not directly intended by D a jury should be invited to make a finding of intent only where that consequence was a virtually certain result of D's conduct and where D was aware of this virtual certainty. Only then, in the words of James LJ, can we speak convincingly of a "decision to bring about, in so far as it lies within the accused's power, the commission of the offence which it is alleged the accused attempted to commit".

It has been argued that this constitutes too broad a view of what is required for a finding of intent as to consequences in the law of attempt. The argument runs that the term "attempt" is synonymous with "trying" and it can only be said that D is attempting to achieve a consequence if he is acting in order to bring about that consequence.[357] But

351 (1951) 35 Cr App R 141 (CA).
352 [1976] QB 1, 3 (CA).
353 (1984) 80 Cr App R 259 (CA).
354 [2014] EWCA Crim 186, [2014] 1 WLR 2867, [46]–[47].
355 (1984) 80 Cr App R 259, 263.
356 [1999] 1 AC 82.
357 Fletcher, *Rethinking Criminal Law* (1978) 161.

ordinary English usage is not always clear-cut in these matters, and need not foreclose discussion of issues of principle or policy in criminal law. Suppose, to use Glanville Williams's example,[358] that D places a bomb in the hold of a departing passenger plane. When asked why, he may truthfully reply that he was looking to make an insurance claim based on the loss of the plane and deny that his purpose was to take life. Yet he knows that success in his objective is inseparable from the sacrifice of people's lives. It is not open to D to deny, even on ordinary language grounds, that he was trying to kill—only to deny that this was his ultimate motive. Moreover, the grave wrongdoing involved and the requirements of social protection supply compelling reasons to treat such a case as one of attempted murder. This conclusion is supported by *Mohan*, by *Pearman*, and by the Court of Appeal decision in *Walker and Hayles*.[359]

Thus far, the mens rea required for consequence elements seems straightforward—direct intent or an acknowledged virtual certainty, which is consistent with the language of the Criminal Attempts Act as interpreted in *Pace*. However, the decision of the Court of Appeal in *Pace* is inconsistent with an earlier decision of the Court of Appeal, *A-G's Reference (No. 3 of 1992)*,[360] which might be interpreted to support recklessness sometimes being sufficient in respect of the consequence element of a substantive offence. In that case D and others had thrown lighted petrol bombs at a car in which V and others were passengers. The bombs missed the car and smashed against a wall. D was charged with attempted arson being reckless whether life be endangered, contrary to section 1(2) of the Criminal Damage Act 1971. The trial judge directed that D would not be guilty of this aggravated form of attempted criminal damage unless it were proved that he *intended* that V's life be endangered. The Court of Appeal, much influenced by its earlier decision in *Khan*,[361] disagreed. It adopted what has been called the "missing element"[362] analysis of the intent requirement in attempt:[363]

> "If the facts are that, although the defendant had one of the appropriate states of mind required for the complete offence, but the physical element required for the commission of the complete offence is missing, the defendant is not to be convicted unless it can be shown that he intended to supply the physical element."

The Court effectively divided the actus reus of an attempt into those elements of the substantive offence that D had satisfied, and those elements that were still "missing". For the former, whatever mens rea was required by the substantive offence would suffice also for the attempt. For the latter, intent would be required. Applying this analysis to the facts of *A-G's Reference* itself, the only element missing from commission of the full offence was damage to property, an element which, in the quaint language of the court, D was doing his best to supply. This was the only element that D was required to intend. So far as the remaining elements were required, for the full offence it sufficed at the time that D be *Caldwell*-reckless whether life would be endangered by his conduct. The Court ruled that *Caldwell* recklessness would equally suffice for the attempt.

358 Above, § 5.1(iv).
359 (1989) 90 Cr App R 226 (CA).
360 [1994] 1 WLR 409 (CA).
361 [1990] 1 WLR 813 (CA): above, § 9.3(iii)(b). See also *Pop* [2026] EWCA Crim 774.
362 Stannard, "Making up for the Missing Element: A Sideways Look at Attempts" (1987) 7 *LS* 194.
363 [1994] 1 WLR 409, 417.

*A-G's Reference (No. 3 of 1992)* could be read as deciding that, on a charge of attempt, recklessness may suffice for any "present" consequence element of the full offence (where it suffices for that element in the substantive offence itself), provided that D intends to bring about any "missing" consequence or other element. The cases decided prior to *A-G's Reference* are reconcilable on the basis that, in the earlier decisions, the relevant consequence had always been a "missing element", i.e. something that had not materialised. An intention to bring about a non-realised consequence is still required, if this reading of *A-G's Reference* is accepted.

An alternative explanation of the result of the case, though not of the reasoning adopted, arises from dicta of Lord Nicholls in *Saik* in the context of conspiracy,[364] namely that it is not necessary for the substantive offence to show that life had actually been endangered, only that D was reckless whether the criminal damage would endanger life, such that it is an ulterior mens rea requirement which is not related to an actus reus element of the offence. The consequence for conspiracy is that the mens rea for conspiring to commit criminal damage being reckless whether life is endangered is an intent to damage property and recklessness as to endangerment. *A-G's Reference (No. 3 of 1992)* could be analysed as reaching the same conclusion for an attempt to commit this offence, so recklessness as to endangerment is sufficient, not because it was a "present" consequence but simply because it was an ulterior mental ingredient of the substantive offence. In other words, the case should not be read as considering the mens rea in respect of the consequence element of the substantive offence. Rather, the requirement of endangering life should be treated as neither a conduct, consequence nor a circumstance of the substantive offence, but as an ulterior mens rea element.[365] If the recommendations of the Law Commission as to the mens rea for attempt were to be adopted,[366] the result in *A-G's Reference* would be confirmed, since the mens rea for the substantive offence relating to whether life was endangered should apply to the attempt. This reform would at least ensure consistency between the results in cases and the relevant legislation.

We are, however, left with dicta in *A-G's Reference* which adopts "the missing physical element test". These dicta were described in *Pace* as elliptical if not self-contradictory.[367] They are best forgotten and, indeed, in *Pace* the decision was mentioned but then ignored. That is appropriate: if intention were required only for those elements of the full offence which D has not brought about, the scope of attempt would be considerably enlarged. A noteworthy feature of *A-G's Reference* was that *Caldwell* recklessness (which was at that time sufficient mens rea for the substantive offence of arson) was found to constitute adequate culpability in the context of attempts liability. It is hardly any step further to allow negligence to suffice.[368] Suppose that D, who is driving a dangerous vehicle, is stopped

[364] [2006] UKHL 18, [2007] AC 18, [4] (Lord Nicholls); above, § 9.2(v)(e).

[365] See Child, "The Structure, Coherence and Limits of Inchoate Liability: The New *Ulterior* Element" (2014) 34 *LS* 537. Child rationalises this, at 558, on the basis that D's knowledge of her own recklessness constitutes an intention that she should be reckless as to life being endangered; but he then acknowledges that this is best interpreted as a simple requirement of recklessness regarding the ulterior element.

[366] Law Com. No. 318, *Conspiracy and Attempts* (2009) para. 8.133.

[367] [2014] EWCA Crim 186, [2014] 1 WLR 2867, [53].

[368] See above, § 5.2(i). The abolition of *Caldwell* recklessness in *G* [2003] UKHL 50, [2004] 1 AC 1034 and the endorsement by the House of Lords of a subjective approach to mens rea in serious offences may make such a prospect less likely; but in *Misra* [2004] EWCA Crim 2375, [2005] 1 Cr App R 21 it was held that the decision in *G* had no implications for gross negligence manslaughter. The Law Commission has recommended that negligence should not suffice for an attempt: Law Com. No. 318, *Conspiracy and Attempts* (2009) para. 8.133.

immediately before joining the highway. It is established that he intended to drive onto the highway, but the evidence falls short of proof that he was aware of the condition of his car. If, however, a careful competent driver would have been aware, then D intended to bring about the missing element of driving on the highway and possessed the culpability for other elements required for the full offence, namely that the vehicle is dangerous.[369] On the authority of *A-G's Reference*, D would be guilty of attempting to drive dangerously. This is a very odd result. Doubtless there is something to be said for this approach in terms of public safety, but it goes beyond anything Parliament intended when passing the Criminal Attempts Act 1981 and it is clearly inconsistent with the decision in *Pace* and so, like *Khan*, *A-G's Reference (No. 3 of 1992)* is preferably treated as incorrect, but its overruling would require a decision of the Supreme Court.

*(d) Conditional intent*

Does a "conditional intent" satisfy the intent requirement for attempt?[370] In *Husseyn*,[371] D was charged with attempting to steal sub-aqua equipment. He had been on the point of opening a holdall which contained the equipment. His conviction for attempted theft was quashed on the basis that he was searching for something that, for him, would be worth taking. A "present" intent to steal would not arise until D determined to take some particular item of property. By contrast, an intent to steal if and when some precondition should be satisfied was not sufficient for an attempt: it was not a "present" intent to steal.

The ramifications of *Husseyn* were considerable.[372] Many people enter property with intent to steal but propose only to steal things which are valuable, concealable, and portable, such as money or jewellery. Prima facie, on the reasoning in *Husseyn*, such people would not be burglars until they encountered some property that they resolved to steal since, until then, there is no "present" intent to steal. However, a subsequent Court of Appeal decision, *A-G's Reference (Nos. 1 and 2 of 1979)*,[373] held that a conditional intent to steal is a "present" intent for the purposes of burglary.

How are the decisions in *Husseyn* and *A-G's Reference (Nos. 1 and 2 of 1979)* to be reconciled? In the latter case, the Court of Appeal put forward an explanation of *Husseyn* in procedural terms. In *Husseyn*, D had been charged with attempting to steal sub-aqua equipment. Such a charge could not succeed as D never formed an intent to steal sub-aqua equipment as such. Had he been charged with attempting to steal "some or all of the contents of the holdall", a conviction for attempted theft would have been sustainable. Yet, as observed in *Smith, Hogan, and Ormerod*, unless it could be proved that D would have taken something from the receptacle, the issue found to be decisive in *Husseyn* is left intact.[374] In the circumstances that arose in that case, it is suggested that D should have been charged with "attempting to steal from a holdall".

Yet, even if that procedural solution is accepted, a further difficulty may remain. Liability for attempt still requires an act of sufficient proximity which, in the case of attempted theft,

369 Under s. 2 of the Road Traffic Act 1988, as substituted by s. 1 of the Road Traffic Act 1991, it suffices that the dangerous condition of the vehicle "would be obvious to a competent and careful driver".

370 See, generally, Child, "Understanding Ulterior Mens Rea: Future Conduct Intention *is* Conditional Intention" (2017) 76 *CLJ* 311.

371 (1977) 67 Cr App R 131 (CA). See also below, § 13.7(i)(f).

372 See Williams, "Three Rogues' Charters" [1980] *Crim LR* 263.

373 [1980] QB 180 (CA). And see too *Toothill* [1998] Crim LR 876 (CA).

374 *Smith, Hogan and Ormerod* 454.

implies an act that is proximate to the appropriation of someone else's property.[375] If D has demonstrated that he does not want *that* property—for example, he opens the door to a room and then closes it without taking its contents—how close has D come to appropriating *those* contents? Proving a sufficiently proximate act in these circumstances requires a fictional supposition that D did intend to acquire the items which, in reality, he went on to reject.[376]

The Law Commission has proposed that the Criminal Attempts Act 1981 should be amended to make clear that an intent to commit a crime includes a conditional intent to commit it.[377] This would be an appropriate clarification of the law.

*(e) Mens rea for attempt—a summary*

Regarding the mens rea for attempt, the Criminal Attempts Act 1981 merely refers to "an intent to commit the offence". We can now appreciate that this beguilingly simple statement requires considerable explication in the light of contradictory case law. It is not possible to reconcile the trilogy of Court of Appeal cases which have considered the mens rea for attempt. However, if it is assumed that *Pace* broadly reflects the appropriate mens rea, it is possible to summarise the preferred interpretation of the law as follows:

(i) D must intend to perpetrate any conduct element specified for the full offence.
(ii) For any circumstance elements of the full offence, it is sufficient if D intends, knows, or believes that those circumstances are or will be present at the time of her conduct, even if that circumstance will never exist in reality.
(iii) For consequence elements it must be proved that D intended to realise that consequence.
(iv) Finally, a conditional intent should be a sufficient mens rea provided that D has resolved to commit the crime at issue should the condition be satisfied.[378]

In *Pace*, the Court of Appeal justified the restrictive interpretation of the mens rea of attempt on the ground that it was in accordance with the principle that a higher level of mens rea should be required for an attempt than for the substantive offence.[379] No attempt was made to justify this principle, although it can be assumed that it was because the criminality of inchoate offences turns on culpability rather than harm caused.

***(iv) Voluntary withdrawal***

In the case of substantive offences, full repentance and restoration after commission of the offence will be merely matters of mitigation of sentence. If D surreptitiously picks up an item in a shop, dishonestly intending to avoid paying for it, he commits theft notwithstanding

[375] The problem does not arise in burglary, the offence at issue in *A-G's Reference (Nos. 1 and 2 of 1979)*; there the intent to steal can be established in general terms; there is no need to prove that D came close to stealing something in particular.

[376] Fictional, or counterfactual, assumptions of this sort may properly be used to resolve the issue of proximity in cases where it is impossible to commit the substantive crime: Criminal Attempts Act 1981, s. 1(3), and see further below, § 9.4. This provision does not, however, apply to cases of property not wanted by D, since it is clearly possible to steal such property.

[377] Law Com. No. 318, *Conspiracy and Attempts* (2009) para. 8.106.

[378] Although, as noted above in § 9.3(iii)(d), there may be difficulties with the actus reus requirement of proximity in such cases.

[379] [2014] EWCA Crim 186, [2014] 1 WLR 2867, [74]. An argument rejected by the Court of Appeal at least for attempted rape: *Pop* [2026] EWCA Crim 774.

a subsequent pang of conscience which leads him to put it back. What if that change of heart should strike D as he reaches for the item but before he makes contact with it?[380] The answer is the same. Analytically, if the actus reus and mens rea of attempted theft are present, he has reached the point of no return. In conceptual terms, liability for attempt should ensue if actus reus and mens rea are present, save where D can lay claim to any justification or excuse for his conduct.

In the case of attempts, however, there is something inapt about such an unyielding analysis. Although attempt is a crime in its own right, its principal rationales are to allow timely interventions by law enforcement personnel prior to the realisation of any harm and to allow lawful restraint of the socially dangerous. A genuine change of heart by D prior to bringing about harm indicates that intervention and restraint were not required for that occasion. Further, some voluntary withdrawals can considerably reduce D's culpability. As we shall argue in the next section, should D take aim at V and shoot with intent to kill, D's innate culpability remains the same whether or not she succeeds in killing V. Yet, if D should take aim and then voluntarily desist, the survival of V is to D's credit. Besides, from a purely instrumental perspective, there is something to be said for the law's giving D an incentive for voluntary withdrawal in such cases. Further, withdrawal is available as a defence to accessorial liability.[381] Krebs has argued that the same should be true of the principal offender who voluntarily abandons further commission of the attempted crime.[382] She justifies this on the ground that, although D has crossed the threshold towards wrongdoing and done so culpably, the subsequent repentance removes the need for society to step in and punish.

Such English case law as touches on voluntary withdrawal in attempt is inconclusive on whether, currently, a "change of heart" defence is allowed.[383] Ideally a defence should be created by legislation.[384] The main problem about providing such a defence concerns the difficulty of differentiating between voluntary and involuntary desistance. In *Page*,[385] for instance, D was observed climbing a ladder and inserting the point of a crowbar under a window frame. He then withdrew the implement and climbed down the ladder. He claimed that thoughts of his mother had brought him back to his good self. An alternative explanation was that he had become aware of police observation. To obviate these difficulties of establishing true motive, there is something to be said for placing the onus of proof of a change of mind, on a balance of probabilities, on the defendant. As a matter of general principle, the burden of proving constituent elements of the crime and of disproving any excuse or justification arising from the facts should lie with the prosecution.[386] Yet the defence proposed is highly exceptional. It would be raised where the formal elements of guilt were present and where there was nothing to suggest that the defendant lacked the capacity to choose to conform her conduct to law. Accordingly, a reverse burden of proof would not cause undue hardship and may encourage acceptance of such a defence.

[380] See Wasik, "Abandoning Criminal Intent" [1980] *Crim LR* 785.

[381] Above, § 7.6(vi).

[382] Krebs, "Withdrawal from Attempts" in Simester (ed.), *Modern Criminal Law* (2024) 177.

[383] For discussion of English and Commonwealth authority, see Stuart, "The *Actus Reus* in Attempts" [1970] *Crim LR* 505, 519–21.

[384] However, the Law Commission made no such recommendation in its review of the law of attempt, and specifically rejected such a defence for conspiracy: Law Com. No. 318, *Conspiracy and Attempts* (2009).

[385] [1933] Argus LR 374 (Victoria). Cf. *Taylor* (1859) 1 F & F 511, 175 ER 831; *Lankford* [1959] Crim LR 209 (CA).

[386] See Roberts, "Taking the Burden of Proof Seriously" [1995] *Crim LR* 783.

### *(v) Liability for attempt and commission of the full offence*

Failure is implicit in the ordinary notion of an attempt. When we watch a high jump competitor sail effortlessly over the bar, we do not describe her effort as a "commendable attempt" to clear the bar. For the purposes of legal analysis, it has been argued that the offence of attempt is subsumed and eclipsed by commission of the full offence.[387] If this idea of merger is taken literally then were D, say, to be charged with attempted murder, she would be able to answer the charge by demonstrating that she had, in fact, committed murder. Attempt liability would no longer subsist, as it would have been eclipsed by the commission of the full offence.

This argument has found favour in some jurisdictions,[388] but is manifestly unsatisfactory. As a matter of ordinary English usage, the term "attempt" may imply a failure to complete but there is no need here slavishly to follow the contours of ordinary language when addressing issues of principle and policy. For the purposes of the criminal law, "attempt" need not be construed as a description of D's conduct as a whole, but should be regarded as a description of the kind of liability his conduct will attract at a particular stage in his sequence of acts.[389] That liability, once established, remains free-standing and is not subsumed within any subsequent liability for the full offence. This analysis is supported by section 6(4) of the Criminal Law Act 1967, which provides that D may be convicted for an attempt "notwithstanding that he is shown to be guilty of the completed offence". Indeed, attempt charges have been permitted in circumstances where the evidence supporting the charge was unequivocally evidence of the full offence. Such was the case in *Cox*,[390] a case of "mercy killing" by a doctor. The evidence of poisoning which secured a conviction for attempted murder, the only charge preferred, was overwhelming evidence that V had met her death by poisoning.[391] A charge of attempted murder may have been preferred in order to avoid confronting the jury with a decision to convict for the full offence of murder—a decision that would result in the imposition of a mandatory life sentence—rather than leaving the sentence to the discretion of the judge, as is the case for attempted murder, in a case where the defendant had acted on the request of and from compassion for his patient. Whatever the merits of this prosecutorial decision, the conviction of Dr Cox suggests that liability for the attempt survives the commission of the full offence. This is consistent with the law of conspiracy where a conviction for conspiracy will be available even if the substantive offence has been committed.

### *(vi) Attempt, luck, and punishment*

Consider the following scenarios:

> D leaves a house heavily intoxicated. He makes for his car in the driveway but is so drunk that he stumbles before he reaches the driveway and falls asleep. Alternatively, he may succeed in getting to his car but be so befuddled by drink that he cannot fit his key into the ignition. Or,

[387] Hall, *General Principles of Criminal Law* (2nd ed., 1960) 577; Fletcher, *Rethinking Criminal Law* (1978) 131.

[388] E.g. *Commonwealth v Crow* (1931) 303 Pa 91.

[389] See Donnelly-Lazarov, *A Philosophy of Criminal Attempts* (2015) 82.

[390] (1992) 12 BMLR 38.

[391] On the facts of *Cox*, V was unquestionably alive when the poison was administered, and the dosage was sufficient to kill anyone instantly, whatever their state of health. See too *Burke* [2000] Crim LR 413 (CA), where there was a conviction for attempt despite evidence of commission of the full offence.

he may manage to drive his car onto the road and, despite his intoxicated condition, reach his destination without mishap. On the other hand, he may be involved in a collision with another vehicle and deaths or injuries might ensue. Why was D drunk? He may be an alcoholic and that condition may have arisen because of a genetic disposition, the vagaries of life, weakness of will, or any combination thereof. Or he may be an overseas visitor, unfamiliar with alcohol, who is taken completely unawares by the effect it has on him.

The possible narratives sketched above reflect the all-pervasive influence of chance factors on the prospect of criminal liability, the kind of offence committed, and what punishment, if any, will be received. Certain forms of contingency are so intrinsic to the very substance of life that a system of criminal law must merely take them as read, and can seek no form of accommodation with them.[392] Social circumstances, the particularities of character, and the patterns of opportunity for criminal acts constitute the most powerful crimogenic factors in play—but only exceptionally will they generate matters to be taken into account when determining whether D has committed a crime. Critical theorists such as Kelman[393] and Norrie[394] rebuke the failure of the criminal law to take account of these background factors, particularly the question of social disadvantage. Other theorists, such as Ashworth,[395] accept that the criminal law as currently theorised and practised must, save for exceptional circumstances, assume that persons subjected to the criminal law are capable of autonomous choice. Nonetheless, indeed because of that assumption, Ashworth insists that a rational criminal law should seek to eradicate, so far as practicable, the influence of luck on a person's criminal liability and punishment. In our drunken driver scenario, what would matter for Ashworth is that D attempted to drive while in a condition that posed a serious threat to others: provided he committed an act sufficiently proximate to driving the car, his culpability would hold constant; irrespective of whether he succeeded in driving, whether he was involved in an accident, and whether fatalities or injuries ensued from the accident. In Ashworth's view, D should be punished in a manner commensurate with his culpability and his just punishment should not be affected by the vagaries of chance.[396]

The impact of luck is particularly marked in the sphere of liability for attempt. A Chicago-based study revealed that over 45 per cent of gunshot victims struck in the head by a high-calibre bullet survive their ordeal.[397] If D shoots V in the head with premeditated intent to kill him and succeeds, in some US jurisdictions he will face the prospect of the death penalty and in England he will receive a mandatory life sentence. Should V survive,

[392] See above, § 6.5(i). On the appropriate treatment of chance and contingency in the making of moral judgements see, especially, Williams, "Moral Luck" in *Moral Luck* (1981) 20; Nagel, "Moral Luck" in *Mortal Questions* (1979) 24; and, in the criminal law context, Edwards and Simester, "Crime, Blameworthiness, and Outcomes" (2019) 39 *OJLS* 50.

[393] Kelman, "Interpretative Construction in the Substantive Criminal Law" (1981) 33 *Stanford LR* 591.

[394] *Crime, Reason and History* (3rd ed., 2014) chap. 3; also his "'Simulacra of Morality'? Beyond the Ideal/Actual Antimonies of Criminal Justice" in Duff (ed.), *Philosophy of Criminal Law* (1998) 101.

[395] "Criminal Attempts and the Role of Resulting Harm under the Code and in the Common Law" (1988) 19 *Rutgers LJ* 19; "Taking the Consequences" in Shute, Gardner, and Horder (eds.), *Action and Value in Criminal Law* (1993) 107.

[396] See also Donnelly-Lazarov, *A Philosophy of Criminal Attempts* (2015) chap. 7; Alexander and Ferzan, *Crime and Culpability* (2009) chap. 5.

[397] Zimring, "The Medium is the Message: Firearm Caliber as a Determinant of Death from Assault" (1972) 1 *J Legal Studies* 97, 104.

D will not be a murderer and, in general, will receive a lesser sentence.[398] Here Ashworth's "culpability holds constant" argument has particular force: it is not obvious how contingencies, such as the availability of timely and skilled surgery, put D in a different moral position even if the deftness of a surgeon allows him to evade the status of murderer. Still, on one scenario D will have killed and brought into the world such harms as the loss of a life, feelings of loss and grief for those persons close to V, the elimination of a productive member of society, etc.; whereas if death does not ensue, the harm actually brought about by D will be significantly less. Duff, in his exhaustive and richly layered treatise on criminal attempts, argues forcefully from a deontological perspective that results do matter morally; that the greater the harm we bring about, the deeper our culpability.[399] On this perspective, differential punishment for attempts and completed crimes is justified.

To minimise the influence of luck upon the imposition of blame and punishment is attractive, even if contrary to popular sentiment. Kant argued for the primacy of trying, in contradistinction to succeeding, in making moral judgments. Assuming the presence of autonomy and the capacity for choice, an agent is in control of her decisions but is not in control of outcomes. If moral judgement is to be based on the quality of our autonomous choices, outcomes matter for such judgments only in so far as they cast light on our choices and indicate our resolve. That said, outcomes matter enormously in terms of human welfare and our relations with others. We may invite a friend for dinner and laugh with relief when he catches reflexively a bottle he has carelessly elbowed from the table. Laughter may be absent for a while should a mop and bucket be needed. Clearly, if a bad outcome does not arise, the emotional drive to impose full severity of sanction loses force. That is no cause for concern—in fact the opposite. Merely because D has put himself in a position where he may be justly punished does not, *pace* Kant, entail that he must be punished to the full measure of his culpability.[400] If all just punishment were fully exacted, the world would be even worse than it already is.[401] Indeed, a much greater cause for concern is excessive punishment. Frequently, outcome-specific sanctions, such as mandatory life sentences, inflict a punishment which exceeds D's innate culpability.[402] That is of more concern than any undue leniency offered to those guilty of attempts.

### *(vii) Reform of the law of attempt*

Inherent in the very idea of an attempt is something done that is proximate to commission of a full criminal offence. This necessary proximity was found to be lacking in *Geddes*,[403] where D, a trespasser who apparently intended to abduct a pupil of the school, had entered a

[398] Attempts are consistently punished less severely than the equivalent full offence. For a defence of this practice, see Robinson and Darley, "Objectivist Versus Subjectivist View of Criminality: A Study in the Role of Social Science in Criminal Law Theory" (1998) 18 *OJLS* 409.

[399] *Criminal Attempts* (1996) chap. 12.

[400] Kant, *Philosophy of Law* (1796; transl. Clarke, 1887). Kant believed that mercy had no place in criminal justice and should be confined to dealings between individuals. In his view, the State is under a duty not to pardon or forgive crimes.

[401] For attempts to justify acts of mercy under specified circumstances in criminal justice settings, see Smart, "Mercy" (1968) 43 *Philosophy* 345; Card, "Mercy" (1972) 81 *Philosophical Review* 182.

[402] See the discussion below, § 10.3(ii).

[403] [1996] Crim LR 894 (CA).

school lavatory while in possession of a kitchen knife, rope, and binding tape. The Court of Appeal ruled that D's conduct did not constitute attempted false imprisonment because he had not tried to restrict anyone's movements. Similarly, in *Campbell*,[404] D was not convicted of attempted robbery when he was arrested just as he was entering a Post Office with an imitation firearm. Not unreasonably, both decisions could be castigated as failures to afford adequate social protection to victims of serious crimes. In *Geddes*, had D trespassed in the school building with intent to steal or inflict grievous bodily harm, or cause damage to property, he could have been convicted of burglary;[405] and in *Campbell*, D could also have been convicted of burglary had he actually entered the Post Office. Prior to the Criminal Attempts Act 1981, Geddes could have been convicted of procuring an instrument to commit a crime,[406] were it the case that he obtained the knife, rope, or tape as aids to abduction.

The Law Commission reviewed this gap in social protection and, in a Consultation Paper, recommended that the law of attempt should be split into two separate inchoate offences.[407] The first would be committed where D had committed the last acts necessary to commit the intended offence, but this would not be limited to the commission of the very last act, so it would encompass D, who, wanting to kill V, aimed a gun at V but still had to remove the safety catch and pull the trigger. The second would be a newly created offence of criminal preparation where D had done acts of preparation which form part of the execution of the plan to commit the intended offence, such as gaining entry to a building, interfering with a lock, or lying in wait for V. This recommendation was not intended to extend the ambit of the law of attempt but simply to reflect society's understanding of attempt and the intention of Parliament when enacting the 1981 statute. The recommendation was subject to much criticism,[408] primarily that the two offences do not involve sufficiently distinct wrongdoing,[409] and consequently the Law Commission concluded in its report[410] that there is no need for any subdivision of attempt and that the existing definition of the actus reus is workable and satisfactory.

Nonetheless, it remains a matter of concern that there is a gap in social protection where D clearly intends to commit a crime and has started to prepare for the commission of that crime but has not done more than a merely preparatory act for its commission. The appropriate response to this gap is not to reintroduce a general offence of procuring materials to commit a crime nor to relax the interpretation of the proximity requirement in attempt. If we were to take the former path, any paedophile would obtain items like a rope or a kitchen knife at his peril. Likewise, if we were to extend the actus reus of attempted false imprisonment to encompass any step, however preliminary, towards the commission of the offence, his freedom from arrest would be threatened whenever he was in the vicinity of children. Such steps, if taken to fill the gap exposed by *Geddes* and *Campbell*, carry an undue risk of oppressive policing and unsafe convictions based on dubious confessions. That said, intervention at a stage earlier than currently allowed by the law of attempt is warranted, despite

[404] (1990) 93 Cr App R 350 (CA).

[405] Theft Act 1968, s. 9.

[406] As in *Gurmit Singh* [1966] 2 QB 53 (Assizes (Leeds)); but see now s. 6 of the Criminal Attempts Act 1981.

[407] LCCP No. 183, *Conspiracy and Attempts* (2007).

[408] See Clarkson, "Attempt: The Conduct Element" (2009) 29 *OJLS* 25; Rogers, "The Codification of Attempts and the Case for 'Preparation'" [2008] *Crim LR* 937.

[409] Clarkson, *ibid.*, 32.

[410] Law Com. No. 318, *Conspiracy and Attempts* (2009).

the conclusions of the Law Commission, in respect of situations notoriously associated with particular kinds of harm. We are aware that we acquire such things as guns or explosives at our peril should we lack a licence or justification to do so. If we drive a car, we should know that we will be in trouble if we drive dangerously or allow our vehicle to become unsafe, even if no accident results. Convictions for offences of this kind do not violate legitimate expectations of fair warning nor require undue reliance on confession evidence. The way forward is to craft specific offences for particular situations which presage the occurrence of serious harm. In circumstances such as *Geddes* it might be possible to convict D of being in possession of a blade in a public place,[411] or carrying an offensive weapon in a public place, if the weapon was made, adapted, or intended to be used to cause injury to the person.[412] In *Campbell*, D was in fact convicted for possession of an imitation firearm.[413] Following *Geddes*, there has been specific legislative reform in the form of section 63 of the Sexual Offences Act 2003, which creates an offence of trespass with intent to commit a sexual offence;[414] and it would be appropriate to create a new offence of trespass with intent to imprison falsely or kidnap, where a sexual offence cannot be proved to have been intended.[415] It is better to proceed in this piecemeal way than to resort to a broad and vague law of attempt susceptible to uncertainties of interpretation and oppressive modes of enforcement.

Unquestionably, resolving when the criminal law should intervene to restrain and punish D at a point before she has committed any material harm is a sensitive and difficult matter. Serious crimes should require proof of culpability. It has been forcefully argued that culpability does not arise until D's conduct releases a risk of harm to a legally protected interest of V, in circumstances where D cannot control the realisation of the risk. On that view, D is not culpable when he strikes the match to light the fuse, but he is culpable when he lights the fuse.[416] Whatever the merits of that view, its implementation would not be politically feasible for societies understandably concerned with risk and security.

## § 9.4 Impossibility and inchoate offences

### *(i) The principle of an impossibility defence*

In principle, if the substantive offence is impossible to commit, this need not preclude liability for encouragement, assistance, conspiracy, or attempt. V may already be dead, but that does not rule out the possibility that D and E, unaware of his death, could make an agreement to kill V. The question then arises whether this agreement constitutes a criminal conspiracy. Prior to 1981, the common law position was that, if the full offence was impossible to commit, there could be no liability for any incitement, conspiracy, or attempt to commit it. Since 1981, the position has changed for attempts[417] and statutory conspiracy,[418] but impossibil-

[411] Criminal Justice Act 1988, s. 139.
[412] Prevention of Crime Act 1953.
[413] Firearms Act 1968, s. 16A.
[414] Note also the offence contrary to s. 62 of the Sexual Offences Act 2003 of committing an offence (e.g. battery) with intent to commit a relevant sexual offence (e.g. rape).
[415] Note also the crime of preparing to commit an act of terrorism: Terrorism Act 2006, s. 5(1)(a).
[416] Alexander and Ferzan, *Crime and Culpability* (2009) chap. 6.
[417] Criminal Attempts Act 1981, s. 1(2).
[418] Criminal Law Act 1977, s. 1(1)(b) as amended by the Criminal Attempts Act 1981.

ity remains a defence to common law conspiracy. The Serious Crime Act 2007 makes no reference to a defence of impossibility to the inchoate offences involving encouragement and assistance. However, for reasons of consistency with the statutory inchoate offences of attempt and conspiracy, and because encouragement and assistance can be committed if D does an act which is capable of encouraging or assisting a crime without any requirement that there be actual encouragement or assistance of any offence, the better view is that impossibility is not a defence to encouragement or assistance either.[419] That said, however, the requirement of an act which is *capable* of encouraging or assisting an offence could imply a defence of impossibility in some circumstances. Suppose, for example, that D tells E to kill V and, unknown to D and E, V is already dead. Has D done an act which is capable of encouraging murder? It is capable only on the assumption that V is still alive. If capability is assessed with reference to the real world, it is not capable of encouraging murder because V cannot be murdered. In such circumstances, none the less, it would be possible to convict D of attempting to encourage murder, since it is clear that impossibility is not a defence to attempt. In the context of the inchoate offences of encouraging and assisting, however, it is unfortunate that a statute which contains so much detail about the encouragement and assistance offences fails to make any reference to whether they are subject to a defence of impossibility.

It seems therefore that, apart from common law conspiracy, impossibility is not a defence to the inchoate offences. Nonetheless it remains important to consider whether impossibility should preclude liability for all inchoate offences.

In the case law and voluminous literature that the impossibility issue has generated, no predominant rationale for the existence of a defence of impossibility has emerged. It has been argued that impossibility necessarily provides a defence to a charge of attempt on grounds of lack of proximity to the completion of the substantive offence, yet this explanation does not carry over to encouragement, assistance, and conspiracy. Besides, the proximity objection is circular. It implicitly assumes the conclusion that impossibility should provide a defence: if we allow liability to be proved on the basis of facts that D assumes, then his act may have been sufficiently proximate on the facts mistakenly assumed. More persuasive is the view that, since no harm was in fact threatened, the matter is insufficiently serious to warrant criminal liability; a conclusion attractive for those theorists who assert that criminal liability should be for conduct which causes harm or threatens harm and should not be imposed just because of one's character, however bad that may be.[420] On this view, when D and E agree to kill V, a person already dead, the agreement does not give rise to any social danger. Yet impossibility defences have previously been allowed even when danger beckoned. Picking an empty pocket has been regarded as a case of impossibility,[421] yet such conduct is menacing. Moreover, conduct may deserve censure irrespective of its propensity for harm: trying to kill someone without justification or excuse, for instance, is a very bad thing to do and merits punishment for its badness alone, whatever danger, if any, was threatened. The lack of a consistent rationale has given rise to unstable and shifting case law in jurisdictions which recognise an impossibility defence.[422]

[419] This is the view of the Law Commission: Law Com. No. 318, *Conspiracy and Attempts* (2009) para. 5.42.

[420] For a robust statement of this view see Hogan, "The Criminal Attempts Act and Attempting the Impossible" [1984] *Crim LR* 584.

[421] *Collins* (1864) Le & Ca 471, 169 ER 1477; but contrast *Ring* (1892) 61 LJMC 116.

[422] For a discussion of cases from a variety of US jurisdictions see Perkins and Boyle, *Criminal Law* (3rd ed., 1982) 627–35.

This lack of focus has created difficulties in the legal application of impossibility defences. Insufficiency of means to attain an achievable end will generally not constitute an impossibility defence, yet radical insufficiency of means may do so. Further distinctions have been drawn concerning the relevance of the success or failure of D's project. Where D's project was to obtain a video recorder as cheaply as possible, it was ruled by the House of Lords that D did not attempt to handle stolen goods when she acquired a second-hand recorder which, erroneously, she thought was stolen.[423] On the other hand, D was subsequently held to be guilty of attempting to traffic in heroin when he acquired a substance which he took to be heroin but which in fact was snuff, thereby frustrating his scheme to acquire the drug.[424] One way to defend the acquittal of a defendant is to maintain that a project brought to fruition without committing a crime cannot be regarded as an attempt to commit a crime, rendering irrelevant the question of impossibility as a defence.[425] Alternatively, some theorists acknowledge that in both situations an issue of impossibility arises but that only in the case of the failure to obtain drugs can there be said to be an intent to commit an offence.[426] These matters will require more discussion below. Enough has been said for now to indicate the vagaries and complexity of the topic of impossibility; a topic which, thankfully, has diminished in importance since the 1981 and subsequent statutory reforms.

The impossibility at issue here concerns matters of fact and law, but not impossibility relating to the very existence of an offence. There is a broad consensus that this latter form of impossibility should not lead to criminal liability. It is impossible in England to attempt to commit, say, the crime of adultery, because adultery is not a crime. In *Taaffe*[427] it was held that D could not be guilty of attempting to import foreign currency, since the importation of foreign currency was not a crime, even though D thought that it was. The consensus is not, perhaps, uniform: it has been claimed that it is inconsistent to deny a defence of impossibility and yet acquit someone who commits adultery in the belief that he is committing a crime.[428] Yet the principle of legality requires that attempt liability take its bounds from the norms of the substantive criminal law.[429] Non-existent crimes are an entirely different case from a crime which, in particular circumstances, it may be impossible to commit.

Less straightforward is the situation where D considers his conduct to fall within the boundaries of an extant offence because he is mistaken about the ambit of the offence. Suppose that D "borrows" V's lawnmower for the weekend when V is away, aware that V would not have given D permission to use it had he asked. On the basis of a conversation with E (a confused law student), D believes that dishonestly borrowing the mower constitutes theft despite his lack of intention to deprive V permanently of the mower. D has demonstrated that he is prepared to do something which he assumes is theft, a crime that assuredly exists. Yet, legally, he is in the same case as our adulterer. He believes that dishonestly borrowing a lawnmower is a crime: it is not. Even more complex is the case where the mistake as to the ambit of a crime is the product of a mistake of civil law. For exculpatory purposes, a mistake

423 *Anderton v Ryan* [1985] 1 AC 560; below, § 9.4(iii).
424 *Shivpuri* [1987] AC 1; below, § 9.4(iii).
425 Hogan, "The Criminal Attempts Act and Attempting the Impossible" [1984] *Crim LR* 584; *Anderton v Ryan* [1985] 1 AC 560.
426 Duff, *Criminal Attempts* (1996) 112–13.
427 [1984] AC 539.
428 Gross, *A Theory of Criminal Justice* (1979) 209.
429 See Williams, *CLGP* 633–5.

of civil law is put on the same footing as a mistake of fact[430] and, arguably, this should cut both ways. Suppose that D cuts down a particular tree that he mistakenly thinks belongs to V. The fence separating D's land from V's had been moved by V without D noticing this change for six years, and D assumes that ownership in the tree is vested in V because he believes that ownership of land is acquired by adverse possession after six years; whereas the legally effective period for registered land is ten years. If D's belief were true, he would be intentionally destroying property belonging to another, a clear case of criminal damage. There seems little difference here from the situation where D makes a valid contract for the acquisition of an item in the mistaken belief that it was stolen. Both cases should come out the same way on the question whether an inchoate offence has been committed. But which way remains a matter of controversy, as we shall see.

### *(ii) Impossibility at common law*

The House of Lords decisions in *Haughton v Smith*[431] and *DPP v Nock*[432] established a defence of impossibility for inchoate offences at common law. These decisions still govern common law conspiracy. Three distinctive situations were identified in *Haughton* and confirmed in *Nock*. They will be discussed in turn.

#### *(a) Inefficient and insufficient means*

Seeking an attainable end in a manner which will not attain success is not to be regarded as a case of impossibility. That D and E dishonestly agree to relieve V of money through a scheme never likely to fool V will not preclude a conviction for conspiracy to defraud. In practice this category is straightforward and uncontroversial. At the theoretical level, however, it might be considered that in those rare cases where D commits himself to a criminal endeavour by means which are radically deficient and which threaten no one's interests, this degree of deficiency of means should be classified as intrinsically impossible. So if D, who believed in voodoo, wished to kill V by sticking pins into an effigy of V, one may be inclined not to take the matter seriously—however convinced D may be of her diabolical powers. As a matter of principle, it might appear natural to dismiss any charge of attempted murder in such a case on the ground of impossibility. On the other hand, since the particular result *is* achievable, by some means or other, and is genuinely, if ineffectually, striven for, the situation does seem to be one of ineffective means and so the issue of impossibility would not even arise.

Duff suggests that this sort of case should be dealt with by providing for an acquittal if the conduct alleged "failed to engage with the world as an attempt to commit [the] offence".[433] As matters stand, since impossibility is not a defence to attempt, one would have to rely on prosecutorial discretion. Given the absence of reported cases, the employment

[430] *Smith* [1974] QB 354 (CA).

[431] [1975] AC 476.

[432] [1978] AC 979.

[433] *Criminal Attempts* (1996) 398. See also Bock and Stark, "Preparatory Offences" in Ambos *et al.* (eds.), *Core Concepts in Criminal Law and Criminal Justice* (2019) vol. 1, 77: no liability if it was obvious that there was no substantial risk that the conduct would culminate in the commission of the threatened offence.

of radically deficient means does not appear to attract prosecution, perhaps because it does not normally come to light or is not taken seriously when it does.[434]

*(b) Physical impossibility*

Perhaps the voodoo doll case should be treated as a case involving physical impossibility, so the availability of the defence of impossibility at common law would matter. In *Nock*,[435] D and others were in possession of a mixture of substances from which they attempted to obtain cocaine. The mixture was incapable of yielding cocaine whatever processes it was subjected to. The House of Lords held that should a particular objective be physically impossible, whatever the means employed, the defence of impossibility applied. Suppose that V falsely informs D and E that he has a large credit balance at X bank. In fact, V has no funds at all at the bank. If D and E contrive a dishonest scheme in an attempt to access V's supposed account, they have a defence of impossibility to conspiracy to defraud.

This head of impossibility has given rise to great dissatisfaction. In the example above, V may have suspected the dishonest designs of D and E and led them a false trail in order to entrap them. Should this be regarded as a case of physical impossibility if V had the large balance he claimed, but at the Y bank? In the past, it has been held to be a case of impossibility when D shot at a tree stump thinking it was a human being,[436] but not a case of impossibility when D shoots into an empty room while V is located elsewhere in the house.[437] The "empty pocket" cases, too, have divided courts,[438] with exceptional variables (such as property situated elsewhere on the victim or the proximity of other victims) generating convictions for attempted theft against the general trend of acquittals. There are few academic defenders of acquittals in cases of physical impossibility (subject to Duff's "engagement with the world" reservation referred to earlier) and the matter is much less important than it was following the intervention of statute for most inchoate offences. Nonetheless, the continuing presence of this defence for common law conspiracies underscores the desirability of statutory intervention in respect of these offences.

*(c) Completion of intended conduct without the commission of a substantive offence*

This category is exemplified by *Haughton*,[439] where D arranged to take possession of corned beef that he assumed would be stolen. When he did take possession, the beef was no longer stolen as it had been taken into police custody[440] and then released under police supervision in order to entrap D. The House of Lords ruled that D was not guilty of attempting to handle stolen goods. His physical conduct was "objectively innocent" and his belief that the goods were stolen did not alter that fact.

[434] In a study conducted by Finkel *et al.*, subjects almost unanimously considered that a case involving radically deficient means (pins in a wax effigy) did not merit prosecution: "Lay Perspectives on Legal Conundrums: Impossible and Mistaken Act Cases" (1995) 19 *Law and Human Behaviour* 593.

[435] [1978] AC 979.

[436] *McPherson* (1857) 7 Cox CC 281, 169 ER 975 (CCR).

[437] *State v Mitchell* (1902) 170 Mo 633.

[438] Contrast *Collins* (1864) Le & Ca 471, 169 ER 1477 with *Ring* (1892) 61 LJMC 116.

[439] [1975] AC 476.

[440] Theft Act 1968, s. 24(3).

This notion of "objective innocence" has proved tenacious. Indeed, for some time it even withstood the statutory abolition of an impossibility defence in attempt and statutory conspiracy (discussed in the next section). Two arguments supported acquittals in these cases. First, it was claimed that situations which consist of D achieving everything he set out to do are ineptly described as attempts, which imply some form of miscarriage or failure. Secondly, where the conduct is "objectively innocent", convictions in these cases may arguably be castigated as involving punishment for thought alone. It is submitted that neither claim is defensible. As we noted earlier (§ 9.3(v)), "attempt" as a legal term of art need not imply any form of failure. Moreover, "impossible" attempts are no more thought crimes than are other attempts. D must do some act which is more than merely preparatory on the facts that he assumed.

### *(iii) Impossibility in attempt, statutory conspiracy, encouragement, and assistance*

Decisions such as *Haughton* and *Nock* were subjected to considerable criticism, principally on the ground that people who unequivocally embarked on criminal projects, such as receiving stolen goods on a large scale or producing cocaine for trafficking purposes, were evading justified censure and restraint because of flukes which, although precluding concrete harm on particular occasions, allowed dangerous actors to remain at large.[441] This sentiment ultimately proved decisive and the Criminal Attempts Act 1981 abolished the impossibility defence for statutory conspiracy and attempt. For both offences it is provided that D may conspire or attempt to commit an offence, "even though the facts are such that the commission of the offence is impossible".[442] Those words seem apt to eradicate the defence of impossibility in all its forms and, although no explicit provision is made in the Serious Crime Act 2007, it is consistent with that statute to assume that the defence is not available either for encouragement and assistance either. D will encourage P to traffic in a Class A drug even if the suitcase which D instructs P to collect contains snuff and not, as D believes, heroin. Similarly, D and E will be guilty of conspiracy to traffic in the drugs if they both believe the suitcase to contain heroin, even though it does not. D will attempt to handle stolen corned beef, notwithstanding that the beef has ceased to be stolen property, if D thinks it is stolen. In the case of attempt, for the avoidance of any conceivable doubt, it is provided that D's intention is to be judged as if "the facts of the case had been as he believed them to be".[443] This renders completely untenable the always fallacious argument which took the form, on facts such as *Haughton*, that "D intended to handle that particular consignment of beef: that particular consignment of beef was not stolen beef; accordingly, D did not intend to handle stolen beef".

Yet even the most clearly drafted legislation, emerging from a transparent and easily verifiable legislative history,[444] may not defeat firmly entrenched judicial views. In *Anderton v*

[441] See the discussion in Law Com. No. 102, *Attempt and Impossibility in Relation to Attempt, Conspiracy and Incitement* (1980) paras. 2.85–2.100.

[442] Criminal Attempts Act 1981, s. 1(2); Criminal Law Act 1977, s. 1(1)(b).

[443] Criminal Attempts Act 1981, s. 1(3)(b).

[444] In the discussion in Law Com. No. 102, *Attempt and Impossibility in Relation to Attempt, Conspiracy and Incitement* (1980) paras. 2.85–2.100, no distinction was drawn between the fact patterns of cases such as *Anderton* and cases such as *Shivpuri*. The provisions in the Law Commission's draft Bill, reflecting this analysis, were adopted unchanged by Parliament.

*Ryan*,[445] D was questioned by police about her acquisition of a video recorder at a low price. She admitted that she believed the item was stolen, although it was never proved that it had been. She was charged with attempted handling of stolen goods. Clearly what D did was not intrinsically a criminal project. The project was the acquisition of a video recorder and D was not so perverse as to prefer a recorder that was actually stolen. Moreover, there was no evidence that she was a trader in stolen goods, rendering her prosecution heavy-handed, if not oppressive. Yet, according to the Criminal Attempts Act 1981, her conviction would seem assured. If the facts had been as she believed them to be, she would have acquired a stolen item. Judging her intent against the facts she believed them to be, she intended to handle stolen goods.

A unanimous House of Lords quashed D's conviction. The language of the 1981 Act was not so much interpreted as swept aside by the idea of "objective innocence". She had done everything she had wanted to do, it was said, and she had not been proved to have committed a crime. How could every day, lawful acts such as acquiring goods for payment be turned into crimes by mere beliefs which could not be shown to correspond with the facts? The conduct was not of the sort intended to be regulated by the Criminal Attempts Act 1981 and, accordingly, application of the impossibility provisions to D's conduct seemingly did not arise.

Within a matter of months, in *Shivpuri*,[446] the House of Lords was confronted with facts from a very different milieu from *Anderton*. D was a suspected drug trafficker. In the context of an undercover police operation, he was induced to take possession of a suitcase full of tobacco snuff which he had been assured contained heroin, and he was subsequently charged with attempting to commit the offence of being knowingly concerned with dealing in controlled drugs. Here D's project was intrinsically criminal. The absence of heroin entailed the failure of his project. Moreover, it is clearly in the public interest that "sting" operations should be carried out, where possible, with the aid of such props as powder masquerading as a drug, fake firearms, or explosives, etc., without risking circulation of the real things. It is not surprising then, that D's conviction for attempted drug trafficking was upheld by a unanimous House of Lords. More surprising, perhaps, was that *Anderton v Ryan* was overruled. A majority of the House considered that differing outcomes in these cases could not be reconciled. Interestingly, two Law Lords considered that the two cases could be reconciled,[447] but they were not prepared to take this opinion to the point of dissent.

That there are differences between the facts of *Shivpuri* and *Anderton* is undeniable. But, as the majority in *Shivpuri* recognised, these differences can gain no purchase on the language of the 1981 Act.[448] If we judge Ryan on the facts that she believed to exist, she would have obtained a stolen item and would have intended to obtain a stolen item. The fact that this criminal act (on the supposed facts) was not done for its own sake but to gain some

[445] [1985] 1 AC 560.

[446] [1987] AC 1.

[447] Lords Hailsham and Mackay took the view that in *Shivpuri* D intended to deal in drugs whereas in *Anderton* D merely believed the recorder was stolen and did not intend to acquire a stolen recorder. It is submitted that, although there certainly is a distinction between the cases, the difference is one of motive rather than a lack of intention.

[448] Lord Bridge, in giving judgment for the House, acknowledged his indebtedness to an article by Glanville Williams, "The Lords and Impossible Attempts" (1986) 45 *CLJ* 33.

ulterior advantage is true of a great many acts which are indubitably criminal. That Ryan did not in fact obtain a stolen item (or could not be proved to have done so) prompts reactions of indulgence for her case. Yet it has not proved feasible to draft legislation on impossibility which leaves out a Ryan but includes a Shivpuri.

Duff unconvincingly maintains that the two cases can and should have different outcomes and, moreover, that different outcomes are compatible with the language of the Criminal Attempts Act 1981.[449] His position is that while Shivpuri intended to traffick in drugs, Ryan did not intend to handle stolen goods. According to Duff, Ryan lacked the requisite intent as obtaining a stolen recorder played no motivational part in her conduct. She wanted a cheap recorder, nothing else, and therefore the stolen quality which she mistakenly attributed to the item she acquired was not part, as Duff terms it, of the "content" of her intent. He does acknowledge, however, that had her belief been congruent with the facts, she would have intended to obtain a stolen item.

Duff's explication of this perceived difference is complex and subtle. Suffice it here to say that he would draw distinctions which, however fine-grained, do not necessarily carry moral weight. He says of D who intends to kill V, a person he takes to be the prime minister but whose identity is immaterial to D (a contract killer, say), that D intends to kill the prime minister if V is the prime minister but not if D mistakenly takes V to be the prime minister. Either way, of course, D is guilty of murder. But surely, in either case, he intends to kill the prime minister? Duff ties "intent" too tightly to "motive". Intention is a cognitive as well as a motivational state: the "content" of one's intent includes circumstances that are known about or believed even when not desired. Moreover, the claim that the content of one's intentions depends upon what actually happens is profoundly implausible. Intention is a mental state, a subjective phenomenon. We intend those acts and results which provide us with a reason for which we act—it is hard to see how those reasons could be constituted by unknown truths.

## § 9.5 Jurisdiction and inchoate offences

At common law, the dependence of jurisdiction upon territory ensured that "all crime is local".[450] For statutory crimes, there is a very strong presumption that criminal statutes are concerned only with the regulation of acts or omissions perpetrated within the jurisdiction.[451] There are, however, some long-standing statutory exceptions to the territoriality principle[452] and, in recent times, significant further exceptions have been enacted in response to the transnational character of some forms of criminality.[453]

### *(i) Inchoate offences abroad to commit offences in England and Wales*

In principle, inchoate offences need not be constrained by the territoriality principle, provided the inchoate offence in question relates to an offence to be perpetrated in England

449 Duff, *Criminal Attempts* (1996) 378–84.

450 Williams, "Venue and Ambit of the Criminal Law" (1965) 81 *LQR* 276, 395, 518.

451 *Cox v Army Council* [1963] AC 48; *Air India v Wiggins* [1980] 1 WLR 815 (HL).

452 Notably murder, manslaughter, and bigamy: OAPA 1861, ss. 9, 57.

453 E.g. Criminal Justice Act 1993, part 1; Suppression of Terrorism Act 1978, s. 4; Taking of Hostages Act 1982, s. 1(1).

or Wales. As Lord Salmon observed, what difference does it make if a plan to rob a bank in London is hatched in Birmingham or Brussels?[454] In that spirit, the Privy Council in *Somchai Liangsiriprasert v United States*[455] considered that parties to agreements made abroad to perpetrate offences in England are subject to English criminal jurisdiction, notwithstanding the absence of any steps taken in England to put the agreements into effect. The Court of Appeal has made similar rulings in *Sansom*[456] and *Naini*.[457]

The position established for conspiracy may well apply also to attempt. In *DPP v Stonehouse*,[458] D faked his death by drowning in Miami so that his wife, who was not involved in the fraud, could claim on life assurance policies. The House of Lords asserted jurisdiction over this attempted criminal deception. The majority of the House justified the assumption of jurisdiction on the basis that "effects" (reports in the press) of D's conduct in Miami were felt in England.[459] Lord Diplock, however, asserted jurisdiction on a different basis: that D's conduct abroad was sufficiently proximate to the commission of an offence of criminal deception in England. His Lordship's more straightforward approach gains strength from the subsequent adoption, in cases such as *Sansom*,[460] of the same approach to cases of conspiracy. If attempts or conspiracies are focused on substantive crimes which are themselves triable in England or Wales, there is no reason in principle why the attempt or conspiracy should take place in England or Wales. This has now been recognised explicitly for encouragement and assistance, so that, if D knows or believes that the act amounting to the commission of the substantive offence might take place wholly or partly in England or Wales, he can be guilty of inchoate offences involving encouragement or assistance regardless of where he was at the relevant time.[461]

For most offences of fraud and dishonesty, it is now clearly the case, following the implementation of Part I of the Criminal Justice Act 1993,[462] that conspiracies, attempts, encouragement, and assistance directed at those offences need not take place in England and Wales provided that English courts would have jurisdiction over the substantive offence.[463] As we have seen, that position has been established judicially for conspiracy in general, applies generally by statute for encouragement and assistance, and probably extends generally for attempts too.

### *(ii) Inchoate offences in England and Wales relating to the commission of crimes abroad*

We now turn to the converse case of inchoate offences in England and Wales to commit crimes within foreign jurisdictions. Classically, inchoate activity directed at breaching foreign laws did not constitute an offence under English law.[464] An exception is recognised

[454] *DPP v Doot* [1973] AC 807.
[455] [1991] AC 225.
[456] [1991] 2 QB 130 (CA).
[457] [1999] 2 Cr App R 398 (CA) (common law conspiracy to defraud).
[458] [1978] AC 55. See now Part I of the Criminal Justice Act 1993.
[459] For criticism of that approach see Sullivan, "Crossing the Rubicon in Miami" (1978) 41 *MLR* 215.
[460] [1991] 2 QB 130 (CA).
[461] Serious Crime Act 2007, s. 52(1).
[462] SI 1999 No. 1189 (32); SI 1999 No. 1499 (42). For discussion of Part 1 of the Criminal Justice Act 1993 in relation to substantive offences of fraud and dishonesty, see below, § 13.9.
[463] Criminal Justice Act 1993, ss. 3, 4.
[464] *Board of Trade v Owen* [1957] AC 602; *Abu Hamza* [2006] EWCA Crim 2918, [2007] QB 659.

for the crime of soliciting murder contrary to section 4 of the Offences Against the Person Act 1861,[465] such that it is possible to solicit murder to be committed abroad from within England and Wales, even if the potential victim is not a British citizen. It is also a statutory offence to incite in England and Wales the commission of an act of terrorism outside the United Kingdom.[466] For conspiracy, too, the classical position is radically changed by section 1A of the Criminal Law Act 1977,[467] which provides jurisdiction over conspiracies notwithstanding that implementation of the agreement will involve an act or event by one or more of the parties taking place outside England or Wales. The act or event must constitute an offence in the country where it is to take place and must also constitute an offence under English law were the act or event to take place in England or Wales. Jurisdiction is triggered if "anything" relating to the conspiracy—e.g. the posting of a letter—is done in England by a party to the conspiracy or by the "agent" of a party, either before or after the agreement was made. The breadth of coverage is enormous. For instance, D and E, Australian tourists passing through London, could be tried for conspiracy were they to agree in a London pub to cheat on the Paris Metro. The Attorney-General must give consent to any prosecution under section 1A.

The Serious Crime Act 2007 also gives the English courts jurisdiction over offences involving encouragement or assistance if the act of encouragement or assistance was committed wholly or partly in England or Wales and D knew or believed that the conduct element of the substantive offence might occur abroad, and the offence would be triable in England and Wales were it committed there,[468] or would be an offence in the place where it was committed.[469] So, for example, if D writes a letter in England, which is posted to P in France, encouraging P to kill V, who might be in England or France, the English court would have jurisdiction over D. This is because the English court has jurisdiction over murder if P is a British citizen.[470] Alternatively, the English court would have jurisdiction over D even if her act of encouragement or assistance occurred wholly outside England and Wales, if she believed that the conduct element of the substantive offence might occur abroad and D would be guilty of the offence were she to commit it in that country.[471] So, if D, a British citizen, was on holiday in Japan and encouraged P to commit rape there, the English courts would have jurisdiction over D's encouragement because, if he had committed rape in Japan, the English court would have jurisdiction to try him.[472] The only limitation on jurisdiction over encouragement and assessment offences would be where the act of encouragement or assistance was committed wholly abroad and the English court would have no jurisdiction over D were she to commit the offence there. So, if D encouraged P in Brazil to assault V there, the English court would not have jurisdiction.

[465] *Abu Hamza*, *ibid.*

[466] Terrorism Act 2006, s. 59.

[467] Interpolated by s. 5 of the Criminal Justice (Terrorism and Conspiracy) Act 1998, as amended by the Coroners and Justice Act 2009, s. 72(1). No provision is made for attempt. Note, also, s. 5 of the Criminal Justice Act 1993, which extends conspiracy to defraud to commit specified offences of fraud and dishonesty to situations where the fraudulent or dishonest conduct will take place outside England and Wales.

[468] Serious Crime Act 2007, sched. 4, para. 1. For the purposes of this provision it is to be assumed that the person assisted or encouraged satisfies any conditions of citizenship, nationality, or residence which must be met in order for the English court to have jurisdiction.

[469] *Ibid.*, para. 2.

[470] Offences Against the Person Act 1861, s. 9.

[471] Serious Crime Act 2007, sched. 4, para. 3.

[472] Sexual Offences Act 2003, s. 72 and sched. 2.

The Law Commission has recommended that the jurisdictional code relating to conspiracy should be clarified, so that:

(i) Statute should recognise that the English court has jurisdiction over a conspiracy made abroad where D knew or believed that the conduct or circumstance element of the substantive offence might occur in England and Wales.[473] This accords with the position at common law.

(ii) The English court should have jurisdiction where a conspiracy is intended to be carried out abroad in circumstances broadly consistent with the regime under the Serious Crime Act 2007. So, for example, there would be jurisdiction in England and Wales if D made a communication in England and Wales leading to the formation of a conspiracy abroad, D knew or believed that the conduct or circumstances of the offence might be committed abroad, and to do so would be a crime in that country.[474]

There is no recommendation that these jurisdictional reforms should encompass attempt as well, since there is very little scope for a more than merely preparatory act to be committed in England and Wales in respect of an offence committed abroad.[475] Nevertheless, D, who posts a fraudulent letter in England with a view to making a false insurance claim in France, will have committed a more than merely preparatory act in respect of fraud by false representation, but the English court would not have jurisdiction in such circumstances.

[473] Law Com No. 318, *Conspiracy and Attempts* (2009) para. 7.49.

[474] *Ibid.*, para. 7.56. See also paras. 7.60 and 7.65.

[475] However, it would be appropriate to confirm by statute that there is jurisdiction in England and Wales where an attempt is committed abroad in respect of a substantive offence which is intended to be committed in England and Wales.

# 10

# HOMICIDE

## § 10.1 Death and liability

Homicide is the death of a human being in circumstances where the death can be attributed to the conduct of one or more other human beings, or exceptionally to a corporation or other organisation.[1] A homicide may be lawful or unlawful. An example of lawful homicide is where D kills V in justifiable self-defence.[2] If the homicide is unlawful it may constitute one of a variety of offences: in this chapter we will consider murder, manslaughter, and some related offences.

If D is found to be causally responsible for V's death, important penal consequences may follow that are unparalleled elsewhere in the criminal law. For instance, in *Mallet*,[3] D quarrelled with his neighbour V and punched V in the face. Ordinarily, this would have been a case of battery, as the punch itself inflicted no injury upon V. Unfortunately, V fell awkwardly and died as a result of striking his head on a paving stone. The events therefore constituted, as will be explained later, manslaughter.[4] The Court of Appeal confirmed D's custodial sentence[5] even though D had not intended to cause V's death or foreseen it. If a motorist, by his dangerous driving, were to cause dreadful but non-fatal injuries, he would receive, at most, a five-year prison sentence.[6] If his driving were to cause death, the maximum sentence would extend to life imprisonment.[7] A person may cause another individual serious injury by grossly negligent conduct and usually such conduct will not result in criminal liability. Should death ensue, however, liability may be incurred for manslaughter.[8] Formerly, all persons found guilty of murder would receive a mandatory death sentence.[9] Nowadays, the mandatory sentence is life imprisonment,[10] a unique case of penal inflexibility for a crime which, like many other offences, can encompass substantial variations

[1] See below, § 10.7(iv).

[2] At one time the common law formally distinguished between justifiable homicides and merely excusable homicides. While an acquittal followed upon verdicts either of justifiable or excusable homicide, in the case of the latter D's goods were forfeited. In 1828 forfeiture was abolished and, so far as D is concerned, there is no difference between the various defences to homicide (or to any other crime).

[3] [1972] Crim LR 260 (CA).

[4] Below, § 10.7.

[5] Imprisonment for one year.

[6] Road Traffic Offenders Act 1988, sched. 2, as amended by Legal Aid, Sentencing and Punishment of Offenders Act 2012, s. 143(5).

[7] Road Traffic Offenders Act 1988, sched. 2, as amended by Police, Crime, Sentencing and Courts Act 2022, s. 86(2).

[8] *Adomako* [1995] 1 AC 171.

[9] That is, until s. 5 of the Homicide Act 1957 (now repealed) created a distinction between capital and non-capital murder. Non-capital murder attracted a mandatory life sentence.

[10] Murder (Abolition of Death Penalty) Act 1965.

of culpability in its range of applications. For manslaughter, the full range of sentencing options is available, including life imprisonment but at the discretion of the judge.[11] A final introductory point is that a conviction for manslaughter does not necessarily preclude a conviction on the same facts for murder.[12] So, for example, if the jury convicted of manslaughter and was unable to reach a verdict on murder, it may be possible to have a retrial of the murder charge.

Of course, the criminal law must take killings seriously. By its very finality, death is an irremediable harm and even if V is killed instantly and painlessly in circumstances which did not cause her any prior anxiety, she will normally have been done a very great wrong. Yet it is a mistake to hold that death as a harm will invariably transcend all other harms. True, death is the negation of life, and life is a precondition for all other forms of value and disvalue. Yet it does not follow that death is always the worst alternative. There may be circumstances where death is the preferred outcome for a particular person for reasons that strike us as rational, whereas only in the most bizarre circumstances would a person welcome the infliction upon herself of significant disablement or other forms of serious harm. Death is special in terms of the impact it has on those with strong emotional[13] and material bonds with the person deceased. The anger and resentment of these "secondary" victims,[14] amplified in the media, is perhaps the most potent factor inhibiting a more equable penal response to causing death. As this chapter will show, causing death may involve morally debatable forms of liability and risk exposure to excessive punishment.

## § 10.2 Homicide defined

A homicide must contain the following elements:

(a) The victim must be a human being.
(b) Death must be caused through the act or omission of one or more human beings, or exceptionally by a corporation or other organisation.
(c) Death must occur within the King's peace.

We will now examine these elements.

### *(i) Human beings*

Homicide is defined in terms of the taking of human life. In certain rare situations, a dispute may arise about the human status of a victim of an alleged homicide. First, until birth, the interests of a foetus are protected by laws falling outside the law of homicide.[15] Secondly,

[11] The Sentencing Council issued guidelines on sentencing for manslaughter in 2018: *Manslaughter: Definitive Guideline*. See Wasik, "Reflections on the Manslaughter Sentencing Guidelines" [2019] *Crim LR* 315.

[12] *ANL* [2025] EWCA Crim 969, [2026] 2 WLR 339.

[13] For a searching study of impact on family and significant others see Rock, *After Homicide* (1998).

[14] It may be noted that close relatives of persons deceased have been treated as "victims" for the purposes of bringing actions before the European Court of Human Rights (*McCann and Others v UK* (1996) 21 EHRR 97) in order to contest the legality of State action resulting in fatalities.

[15] Infant Life (Preservation) Act 1929; OAPA 1861, s. 58 (administering poison or using instruments with intent to procure a miscarriage). On the latter offence see Quirk, "Abortion and the Process and Politics of (de-) Criminalisation" [2023] *Crim LR* 489.

advances in medical techniques have undermined the certainty with which we can apply or disapply the concept of death to persons with profound and permanent disabilities whose existence is sustained by artificial means.[16] Accordingly, homicide law requires criteria by which to establish the presence of independent human life at the time of birth and to determine the life/death status of persons who may exhibit one or more of the traditional indicia of life, but only by virtue of technological intervention.

### *(a) Life at birth*

In *A-G's Reference (No. 3 of 1994)*,[17] the House of Lords confirmed, *obiter*, that to destroy a viable foetus, however late in term, does not constitute any form of homicide. This is so whether the act of destruction terminates the life of the foetus in the womb or causes the foetus to be stillborn. For a live foetus to attain full personhood in the criminal law's eyes, the whole body of the child must emerge into the world and must sustain an existence independently of the mother, for however brief a period of time. There is no modern case law on what constitutes an existence independently of the mother.[18] The preponderance of nineteenth-century authority on the topic favours a test of independent respiration,[19] which provides a serviceable criterion for the existence of human life.[20]

Although the criterion of independent existence has sometimes been accepted,[21] it is controversial. It was regarded by Lord Mustill in *A-G's Reference (No. 3 of 1994)*[22] as a contradiction of incontrovertible biological fact. From an early stage in pregnancy, a foetus becomes an entity unto itself, whose habitat is the womb. Indeed, after eight months of pregnancy, no further metamorphic development of the foetus occurs, and from then on the difference between a foetus and a neonate is purely a matter of location.[23] The legal conferment of personhood reflects dated perceptions which are not underpinned by biological data. This results in some uncomfortable anomalies. If a late-term viable foetus is destroyed in the womb without justification or excuse, the applicable offences are child destruction or unlawfully procuring a miscarriage.[24] If, however, the pre-term attempt to destroy the foetus in the womb is unsuccessful and a birth ensues, and the neonate dies as a consequence of injuries sustained in the earlier attempt to destroy it, a verdict of murder or manslaughter may ensue.[25] Similarly, a lawful abortion may be performed outside the normally permitted period of 24 weeks if it seems likely that a child, if born, would be "seriously handicapped".[26]

[16] See Skegg, *Law, Ethics and Medicine* (1985) chap. 9.

[17] [1998] AC 245.

[18] For general discussion see Temkin, "Pre-Natal Injury, Homicide and the Draft Criminal Code" (1986) 45 *CLJ* 414.

[19] *Poulton* (1832) 5 C & P 329, 172 ER 997; *Brain* (1834) 6 C & P 349, 172 ER 1272; *West* (1848) 2 Cox CC 500; *Crutchley* (1857) 7 C & P 814, 173 ER 355.

[20] The Criminal Law Revision Committee, in its Fourteenth Report, *Offences Against the Person* Cmnd. 7844 (1980), did not recommend any statutory change in the law.

[21] A view adopted by the Court of Appeal in *A-G's Reference (No. 3 of 1994)* [1996] 2 All ER 10, 18.

[22] [1998] AC 245, 256.

[23] Although the location of a foetus does have implications when the interests of the foetus are irreconcilable with respect for the autonomous choices of the pregnant woman: *St George's Health Care NHS Trust v S* [1998] 3 All ER 673 (CA).

[24] Infant Life (Preservation) Act 1929; OAPA 1861, s. 58.

[25] Confirmed by the House of Lords in *A-G's Reference (No. 3 of 1994)* [1998] AC 245.

[26] Abortion Act 1967, s. 1(1)(d).

By contrast, if a pre-term child is sustained alive outside the womb, the destruction of the child would be regarded as the destruction of a human being, however disabled the child.[27]

Debate about the appropriate legal status of the late-term foetus has arisen in other jurisdictions, most notably in the United States.[28] South Carolina has legislated that a late-term foetus is legally to be regarded as a full human subject.[29] A considerable number of states have enacted "feticide" statutes, which fall short of attributing personhood to foetuses but which stipulate that the non-therapeutic destruction of a foetus is to be regarded as equivalent to the taking of human life.[30] In England, however, a late-term foetus is never regarded as a person. The House of Lords in *A-G's Reference (No. 3 of 1994)*[31] regarded this matter as beyond argument, and would have refused to uphold a conviction of murder where D had stabbed E when she was pregnant, with the intent only to injure E. The stabbing caused E to go into premature labour. The child survived for four months before dying, it was assumed, as a consequence of the premature birth induced by D's stabbing of E. The House of Lords considered that it would be extending the concept of transferred malice too far to transfer the intention to injure first from the mother to the foetus and then to the child that the foetus subsequently became at birth. Although the ruling was expressed in terms of discountenancing a "double" transfer of malice, that objection could not have been sustained had there not been a perceived discontinuity between the status of the foetus and that of the child.[32] Furthermore, in a civil case, it has been ruled unlawful to make a woman submit to surgery in order to save the life of the foetus (and her own life) at the time of confinement.[33] Such an assertion of autonomy would be difficult to sustain in legal terms had the claimant been regarded as the mother of a child rather than of a foetus.

Moreover, the Infant Life Preservation Act 1929 reinforces the non-person status of a late-term foetus. The Act was passed on the assumption that to destroy a foetus in the process of birth would not constitute a homicide offence unless it could be proved that the child had taken breath after complete emergence from the mother. Therefore, it may be asserted with some confidence that the recognition of a late-term foetus as a full person would require legislative intervention.[34] Any such initiative should proceed cautiously. As

[27] There are civil cases, such as *Re C* [1990] Fam 26 (CA) and *Re J* [1990] 3 All ER 930 (CA), and the criminal trial case of *Arthur* (1981) 12 B Med LR 1 (Crown Court (Leicester)) which indicate that lesser degrees of medical care may be owed to profoundly disabled neonates, but the deliberate killing of any person is murder regardless of the state of disability: *Airedale National Health Trust v Bland* [1993] AC 789. In the very special circumstances of *Re A (Children) (Conjoined Twins: Surgical Separation)* [2001] 1 Fam 147 (CA), the separation of conjoined twins was held to be a lawful procedure even though it was known that it would entail the death of the weaker twin. The difficulty and significance of the case arise from the fact that the weaker, profoundly handicapped twin was, properly, accorded full human status: see further § 21.4(ii)(e). In the case of late-term abortions, a foetus may be delivered capable of survival outside the womb but, particularly in a case of "serious handicap", be allowed to die.

[28] There are decisions to the effect that the common law recognises the personhood of a late-term viable foetus: *Commonwealth v Lawrence* (1998) 404 Mass 378.

[29] Code of Laws of South Carolina, Offenses Against the Person, s. 16-3-90.

[30] Schott, "Fetal Protection—An Overview of Recent State Legislative Responses" (1991) 22 *Memphis State University LR* 119; Kaufman, "Legal Recognition of Independent Fetal Rights" (1997) 17 *Children's Legal Rights J* 20.

[31] [1998] AC 245.

[32] Even then, one might doubt the outcome of the case. An argument can be made that D intended to cause grievous bodily harm to a human being and, in acting with that intention, he did cause the death of a human being. As such, on ordinary principles of transferred malice (above, § 5.7), he satisfies the actus reus and mens rea of murder. We return to this point in the next section.

[33] *St George's Healthcare NHS Trust v S* [1998] 3 All ER 673 (CA).

[34] Currently, the jurisprudence on Art. 2 of the ECHR seems unlikely to require any judge-made change to the law: *Vo v France* (2005) 40 EHRR 259.

we have discussed, the present law gives rise to some anomalous distinctions when tested against the biological facts. Yet the reception of a child into the world after the point of birth is an event of enormous cultural significance, laden with symbolism. These social facts may weigh more heavily than biological facts when resolving the parameters of the law of homicide.[35]

*Post-natal deaths from pre-natal injuries.*

Once a child has an existence independent of the mother, the death of the child by the agency of another person will constitute homicide. This includes where a pre-birth injury causes a post-birth death. In *Senior*,[36] for instance, D, a midwife, ineptly supervised a birth. As a consequence, the child died shortly after being born and D was successfully prosecuted for manslaughter by gross negligence.

There are, however, limits to the scope of liability based on pre-birth injuries. In *A-G's Reference (No. 3 of 1994)*, D stabbed a pregnant woman, and this caused her baby to be born prematurely. It was assumed that the baby died as a result of its premature birth. In such cases, if D intends to destroy a foetus in the womb, he will lack an intent to kill *a person* and therefore will lack the mens rea for murder. Consequently, should the foetus survive D's destructive efforts but die some time after the birth as a consequence of them, a murder charge would be ruled out. D will be liable for murder only if he inflicts a pre-birth injury intending to cause the child to die after the birth[37] or to be born with a serious injury.[38] On the facts of *A-G's Reference (No. 3 of 1994)*, D did not direct his violence at the foetus. His target was the pregnant woman. The House of Lords considered D guilty of manslaughter of the kind known as constructive manslaughter,[39] which merely requires a dangerous criminal act causally associated with the death. It is not necessary that the dangerous act be targeted at the deceased.[40]

In ruling that D would be guilty of manslaughter, the House of Lords differed from the Court of Appeal,[41] which had thought that a murder verdict was possible on the basis of the transferred malice principle.[42] D had intended to cause grievous bodily harm to the pregnant woman, and with that intention he had done an act causing the subsequent death of the child. Lord Mustill, in rejecting this view, expressed his dislike both of the rule that intent to cause grievous bodily harm sufficed as mens rea for murder and of the transferred malice principle. He accepted that these grounds of inculpation were too well entrenched to remove. Yet he declined to "extend" the transferred intent principle to "double" transfers (first from the mother to the foetus, then from the foetus to the child it became).[43]

A wide range of pre-birth conduct on the part of pregnant women may be associated with the deaths of infants, including substance abuse. In English case law, at the present time,

[35] Becker, "Human Being: The Boundaries of the Concept" (1974) 4 *Philosophy & Public Affairs* 334; Engelhardt, "The Ontology of Abortion" (1973) 84 *Ethics* 217.

[36] (1832) 1 Mood CC 346, 168 ER 1298.

[37] According to Lord Mustill, in these circumstances D's mens rea may be regarded as not directed to the foetus but to the human being if and when it comes into existence: *A–G's Reference (No. 3 of 1994)* [1998] AC 245, 261.

[38] This should follow from the rule that an intent to cause grievous bodily harm is sufficient mens rea for murder.

[39] See further below, § 10.7(i).

[40] *Mitchell* [1983] QB 741 (CA), confirmed in *A-G's Reference (No. 3 of 1994)* [1998] AC 245, 270.

[41] [1996] 2 All ER 10 (CA).

[42] Above, § 5.7.

[43] [1998] AC 245, 261.

there is no reported case of a prosecution for homicide arising from such circumstances. There may be a very understandable ambivalence on the part of prosecuting authorities in seeking penal sanctions against persons who are in thrall to addictions of various kinds or burdened by other forms of social dysfunction, but in principle such prosecutions are possible.[44] Section 241 of the Crime and Policing Act 2026 removes criminal liability for abortion from a woman in respect of any act in relation to her own pregnancy.

### (b) Death[45]

In most circumstances, death means the irreversible cessation of respiration and heartbeat. But complex cases arise where respiration and heartbeat are sustained by artificial means. Are such persons alive or dead? The answer to this question will depend on the condition of the patient. It may be that, because of the length of time that the patient's brain was deprived of oxygen, the condition known as "brainstem death" has arisen.[46] This is an irreversible condition involving the complete non-functioning of the brain stem.[47] This condition can be confirmed by a flat printout from an electroencephalography (EEG) machine.[48] There is an international medical consensus that brainstem death is death *ipso facto* and many jurisdictions have passed legislation stipulating brainstem death as a criterion of death.[49] There has been no legislative response for England and Wales. However, in *Bland*,[50] three Law Lords assumed that destruction of the brain stem entailed death.[51] In *Re A (a minor)*,[52] a civil case, there was a first instance ruling that brain-stem-death was, for legal purposes, death. It would be surprising if a contrary view were to be taken in the criminal law.

Nonetheless, it is not universally agreed that brainstem dead persons sustained mechanically are to be regarded as dead.[53] Certainly the body of a continuously respirated brainstem dead person is a living organism. Should terminating the vitality of such an organism be regarded as causing the death of a human being? Current medical practice assumes that such organisms are no longer persons.[54] Considerable expense would be incurred and beneficent transplant and grafting surgery precluded were an appellate court to rule that brain-dead persons are live persons. It is not easy to see what value such a judgment would advance and, accordingly, we will assume here that brainstem death is death in every case.

Any condition affecting the brain which is less radical than brainstem death is unlikely to be legally designated a form of death. The House of Lords in *Bland*[55] decided that a person in a persistent vegetative state ("PVS") was alive and made the same assumption for

[44] Prosecutions and civil law injunctions have been sought against substance-abusing pregnant women in the United States: Jos, Marshall and Perlmutter, "The Charleston Policy on Cocaine Use during Pregnancy: A Cautionary Tale" (1995) 23 *J Law, Medicine and Ethics* 120; Glaze, "Combatting Prenatal Substance Abuse: Court Ordered Protective Custody of the Fetus" (1997) 80 *Marquette LR* 793.

[45] Cp. Laing and McHale (eds.), *Principles of Medical Law* (5th ed., 2025) chap. 21 ("Death").

[46] See *Dance v Barts Health NHS Trust* [2022] EWCA Civ 1106.

[47] The brain stem controls reflexive functions of the body including breathing and heartbeat.

[48] "Criteria for the Diagnosis of Brain Stem Death" (1995) 29 *J Royal College of Physicians* 381.

[49] For references to international legislation, see Giesen, *International Medical Malpractice Law* (1988) 612, n. 73.

[50] [1993] 1 AC 789.

[51] *Ibid.*, 856 (Lord Keith), 863 (Lord Goff), 878 (Lord Browne-Wilkinson).

[52] [1992] 3 Med L Rev 303 (CA).

[53] See, for example, Stringer, *Rethinking Life and Death* (1995) 24.

[54] "Death" in Laing and McHale (eds), *Principles of Medical Law* (5th ed., 2025) paras. 21-24–21-33.

[55] [1993] 1 AC 789.

persons in profound and permanent coma. One may ponder whether persons permanently lacking any form of sentient life, wholly cut off from any form of interaction with other people, are a morally different case from persons who are brainstem dead. Yet there are strong pragmatic reasons for drawing a distinction between brainstem death and other forms of non-sentience. There are reliable and easily applied criteria for determining the presence of brainstem death.[56] The condition is completely irreversible. By contrast, diagnosis of the profundity and duration of states which fall short of brainstem death is far less certain. Questions about the appropriate treatment of PVS and comatose patients can and should be debated in terms of the quality and meaning of life, a debate which should not be foreclosed by any stipulative definition of death.[57] Accordingly, it is submitted that any mental condition which does not amount to brainstem death should be regarded as compatible with the presence of life.

### *(ii) Causation in homicide*

We have already discussed principles of causation in criminal law.[58] There are no principles of causation distinctive to homicide, but homicide cases provide some striking examples of cases where causal principles are taken to their limits—and even beyond. When a person who is at fault is somehow connected to a result so grave as death, there is a disposition to attribute causal responsibility to that person. This sometimes results in strained causal attributions, particularly in cases where some other person, not morally at fault, seems more directly responsible for causing the death. This is examined in detail in Chapter 4.

### *(iii) Acts, omissions, and homicide*

Well-known definitions of murder and manslaughter given by institutional authors such as Coke employ the terms "kill" and "killing" in their formulations of the conduct to be proved against D.[59] Accordingly, at one time, there was scope for an argument that "merely" allowing V to die could not constitute the actus reus of either murder or manslaughter, even if it could be established that D owed V a duty to act. This argument was put forward in *Gibbins and Proctor*,[60] where D was charged with murder on the basis of a deliberate failure to feed her infant stepdaughter. Unsurprisingly, on the facts of the case, the argument failed. A deliberate strategy to starve someone to death can legitimately be described as a killing— "I killed him by starving him to death" is a perfectly sensible statement. By contrast, failures to provide essential sustenance by mismanagement and incompetence, as in *Instan*,[61] or failures of supervision, such as the negligent failure of the railway crossing keeper in *Pittwood* to close the gates before the arrival of the train,[62] are less obviously designated "killings".

[56] "Criteria for the Diagnosis of Brain Stem Death" (1995) 29 *J Royal College of Physicians* 381.
[57] Dworkin, *Life's Dominion* (1993) chap. 7.
[58] Above, § 4.2.
[59] "Murder is when a man of sound memory, and of the age of discretion, unlawfully killeth within any county of the realm any reasonable creature in *rerum natura* under the king's peace, with malice aforethought, either expressed by the party or implied by law": Coke, 3 Inst 47.
[60] (1918) 13 Cr App R 134.
[61] [1893] 1 QB 450.
[62] (1902) 19 TLR 37.

The conviction for manslaughter in each of these cases indicates that the expressions "kill" and "killing" are not to be taken too literally. They should be regarded as synonymous with "cause death" and "causing death".[63] The notion of cause will accommodate failures by D to prevent the avoidable death of V where it can be maintained that it was D's duty to prevent V's death and that she possessed the capacity to do so.

Accordingly, the distinction between acts and omissions presents no difficulties that are peculiar to homicide. That said, *ad hoc* use of the act/omissions distinction has sometimes been judicially employed in order to contain the scope of certain forms of homicide. The form of manslaughter known as constructive manslaughter is, as we shall see below, of very wide ambit. It would be broader still had not unlawful omissions been excluded from its scope by the definitional fiat of the Court of Appeal in *Lowe*.[64] In the same vein, it appears that V does not commit suicide should he refuse food or essential medical treatment while aware that refusal entails his certain death;[65] a matter of great moment for those caring for V, who might otherwise find themselves assisters in his suicide.[66] Likewise, V does not commit suicide should she ask to be removed from a life-support system;[67] but V will be asking for help in an act of suicide should she request assistance to take a substance that will end her life.[68] In both cases, the exercise of V's autonomy requires the assistance of others. However, the former situation is characterised as the refusal of treatment: her physical removal from life support is said, legally, to be an omission to provide further treatment, whereas active assistance in the taking of a fatal substance remains an illegal act.[69]

Particularly in medical contexts, D may find herself under a duty to sustain V's life in the first instance but then be relieved of that duty should it be determined by the court that V's best interests do not require the sustaining of his life.[70] The cessation of the duty to keep V alive is without prejudice to the overarching duty imposed on us all not to cause the death of others by a positive act.[71] That latter duty sits awkwardly with the well-established practice of closing down systems of life support in the light of a patient's wishes or a decision that the patient's best interests no longer require the sustaining of his life. On the face of it, the step-by-step procedure involved in shutting down a life-support system seems, indubitably, an act of commission comparable, say, to the simpler task of switching off a television. Be that as it may, Lord Goff in *Bland* considered that the removal of life support was to be regarded as an omission: in such cases the cause of death is attributed to the underlying pathology which necessitated life support, and the removal of life support

[63] Stephen, *Digest of Criminal Law* (4th ed., 1887) 138, cited with approval in *A-G's Reference (No. 3 of 1994)* [1998] AC 245 (HL).

[64] [1973] QB 702 (CA).

[65] *Secretary of State v Robb* [1995] 1 All ER 677 (CA).

[66] Suicide Act 1961, s. 2.

[67] *Re B (adult: refusal of Medical Treatment)* [2002] 2 All ER 449 (HC (Fam)).

[68] *R (on the application of Pretty) v DPP* [2002] 1 All ER 1 (HL).

[69] For critical discussion see Tur, "Legislative Technique and Human Rights: The Sad Case of Assisted Suicide" [2003] *Crim LR* 3.

[70] *Airedale NHS Trust v Bland* [1993] AC 789; *Aintree University Hospitals NHS Foundation Trust v James* [2013] UKSC 67, [2014] AC 591, [18]–[22] (Baroness Hale). Where medical professionals and V's family agree that clinically assisted nutrition and hydration can be withdrawn, this does not require recourse to the courts: *An NHS Trust v Y* [2018] UKSC 46, [2019] AC 978.

[71] All the judgments in *Bland* emphasise that, although it may be in a patient's best interests not to be kept alive, no patient, whatever her condition and whatever her wishes, may be actively killed. See too *Cox* (1992) 12 BMLR 38.

is merely a failure to suppress this underlying cause.[72] In *Nicklinson v Ministry of Justice*,[73] Lord Neuberger confirmed the distinction between a doctor who switches a life support machine off, which he characterised as an omission, and an interloper who maliciously switches the machine off, which he characterised as an act. Hence the interloper would be liable for a homicide offence, depending on his mens rea. The distinction is highly artificial and analytically unconvincing, but it does have the instrumental value of protecting medical personnel from liability for murder or manslaughter when carrying out what are now routine procedures of terminating life support.

### *(iv) Abolition of the year and a day rule*

At common law, in order for D to be held responsible for V's death, the death had to occur within one year and a day of the act or omission by D that caused it.[74] The rule was of great antiquity and obscure in origin and rationale.[75] By early modern times, the rule was justified in terms of the difficulty of proving that D's conduct was a cause of V's death after the lapse of such a period of time. The current wide availability of life-support technology for the seriously injured renders such a rationalisation untenable, and the rule was abolished by the Law Reform (Year and a Day Rule) Act 1996[76] in respect of offences concerned with the causing of death and of suicide.

The Act brings homicide cases into line with other indictable offences. However, there are potentially oppressive situations for an accused person which may arise in homicide contexts. There may be a considerable lapse of time occurring between the injury caused by D and the ultimate death of V. During that time D will face the prospect of prosecution for some form of homicide in circumstances where he may already have been tried and convicted for an offence arising from the initial injury. Accordingly, the Act provides that proceedings in respect of a "fatal offence" may be instituted only if the Attorney-General gives consent whenever the injury that causes death is sustained more than three years before death occurs or if the accused has previously been convicted of an offence in circumstances alleged to be connected with the death.[77]

### *(v) The King's Peace*

Any human being can be the victim of homicide with the exception of persons who are not "under the King's Peace". Accordingly, causing the deaths of alien enemies in the course of war supplies no ground for a homicide prosecution.[78] The same probably applies to rebels who, at the time they were killed, were engaged in hostile operations against the Crown.[79]

[72] [1993] AC 789, 866.
[73] [2014] UKSC 38, [2015] AC 657, [22].
[74] In the classic definition of murder given by Coke, V must die "of the wound or hurt, etc., within a year or a day of the same": 3 Inst 47.
[75] Yale, "A Year and a Day in Homicide" (1989) 48 *CLJ* 202.
[76] Section 1.
[77] Section 2.
[78] See Rowe, "The Criminal Liability of a British Soldier Merely for Participating in the Iraq War 2003: a Response to Chilcot Evidence" [2010] *Crim LR* 752, 753–4. It is homicide if an enemy alien is killed other than in the course of war: *Maria v Hall* (1807) 1 Taunt 33, 36, 127 ER 741.
[79] 1 Hale PC 433; *Page* [1954] 1 QB 170, 175 (CMAC).

As a matter of history, operations of war involving subjects of the Crown have been predominantly carried out overseas. On normal rules of criminal jurisdiction, which apply a territoriality principle, killings perpetrated overseas would in any event not be justiciable in England and Wales. However, section 9 of the OAPA 1861 provides that any murder or manslaughter committed by any subject of the Crown on land out of the United Kingdom may be tried and punished in England.[80] The specific exception for those not under the King's Peace is therefore essential.

## § 10.3 Murder

### *(i) The mental element in murder*[81]

The traditional definition of murder is that it is a homicide committed with "malice aforethought". This definition is no longer useful; neither malice[82] nor forethought[83] is necessary, or sufficient, for the mens rea of murder. For many years, malice aforethought has been a purely technical expression meaning nothing more than those mental states recognised by the common law as sufficiently culpable to make a homicide murder. Before the Homicide Act 1957, there were three kinds of malice aforethought—"express", "implied", and "constructive". Express malice required an intent to cause death. Implied malice was established by proof of an intention to cause grievous bodily harm. Constructive malice was present if D caused death while committing or attempting to commit a felony or when resisting lawful arrest. If a causal connection between the causing of death and commission of the felony or resistance to the arrest was established, it was immaterial that D intended neither to kill nor to cause grievous bodily harm.

Constructive malice was taken to be too indiscriminate in its operation[84] and was abolished by section 1 of the Homicide Act 1957. That Act makes clear that implied as well as express malice survives the abolition of constructive malice.[85] We will not further employ these anachronistic terms; it is better simply to refer to *an intent to cause death* and *an intent to cause grievous bodily harm* as the two forms of mental element currently sufficient under English law to constitute the mens rea of murder.

[80] Section 4 of the Suppression of Terrorism Act 1978 gives the English court jurisdiction if a murder is committed in a country which is a party to the European Convention on Human Rights, regardless of whether D or the victim is a British citizen. So, in *Venclovas* [2013] EWCA Crim 2182, it was possible to convict D, a Lithuanian, of murder even though it was unclear whether the victim was killed in England or in Poland (where her body was found). This expands the jurisdiction of the English court significantly, although the assertion of jurisdiction under the 1978 Act requires the consent of the Attorney-General.

[81] Goff, "The Mental Element in the Crime of Murder" (1988) 104 *LQR* 30; Williams, "The Mens Rea for Murder: Leave it Alone" (1989) 105 *LQR* 387; Wilson, "A Plea for Rationality in the Law of Murder" (1990) 10 *LS* 307; House of Lords, Report of the Select Committee on Murder and Life Imprisonment (Session 1988–89) HL Paper 78, paras. 30–8.

[82] It is murder, for example, if D's intentional killing of V is done from motives of compassion, say because V has a painful, terminal illness.

[83] A spontaneous intentional killing is murder in the absence of any justification, excuse, or extenuation.

[84] *Royal Commission on Capital Punishment* Cmnd. 8932 (1953) 24–8.

[85] Homicide Act 1957, s. 1: "where a person kills another in the course or furtherance of some other offence, the killing shall not amount to murder unless done with the same malice aforethought (*express or implied*) as is required for a killing or to amount to murder when not done in the course or furtherance of some other offence" (emphasis added).

*(a) Intent to cause grievous bodily harm*

An intent to cause grievous bodily harm, in the sense of really serious harm,[86] remains sufficient mens rea for murder, and it has survived several attempts to unseat it.

In *Hyam*,[87] where the House of Lords sought to resolve the definition of the mens rea for murder, Lord Diplock, with the assent of Lord Kilbrandon, rejected as a sufficient mental element the mere intent to cause grievous bodily harm. He considered that, historically, the erstwhile constructive malice doctrine had unduly inhibited the development and refinement of the mental element for murder. Without that restraint, he considered that judges would have confined murder to circumstances where D either intended to kill or intentionally caused grievous bodily harm knowing that his conduct threatened the life of the victim.[88] With constructive malice abolished, Lord Diplock concluded that the House was free to express the mens rea for murder in the form it would have attained without the constraint of the felony/murder rule.

Of the three remaining Law Lords in *Hyam*, Lords Hailsham and Dilhorne refused to go along with Lord Diplock's striking version of counterfactual history. Remarkably, the fifth judge, Lord Cross, refused to make a decision on the matter, acknowledging force in both positions. Instead, he confirmed the verdict of murder on the "assumption" that an intent to cause grievous bodily harm constituted sufficient mens rea.[89] This lack of resolution entailed a subsequent appeal on the matter in *Cunningham*.[90] Here, a differently constituted House of Lords ruled by a majority that an intent to cause grievous bodily harm was sufficient mens rea for murder. Criticism continues at the highest judicial level of a law of murder which allows convictions for this grave offence without proof of any mens rea element that refers to the element of death—a "fiction" according to Lord Mustill.[91] The criticism has particular force in circumstances where the harm in question, although "really serious", is not harm which constitutes, of itself, a threat to life. As Lord Edmund-Davies observed in his dissenting speech in *Cunningham*, a broken arm is "really serious"[92] but an intent to inflict such an injury should be regarded as insufficient for murder, the most serious of crimes.[93] Yet, despite the continuing vein of judicial criticism,[94] the law is settled by *Cunningham* and was approved by the House of Lords in *Rahman*.[95] Any future change to the mens rea for murder will require legislation. Such a change had been recommended by the Law Commission,[96] so that a person who caused death but only intended to cause serious

[86] In *Sidhu* [2019] EWCA Crim 1034, [19] the language of serious harm was used but it was accepted that there were degrees of such harm and for murder the intent must relate to the higher level of such serious injury. This includes an intention to incapacitate V by drugging: *Cristea* [2021] EWCA Crim 1597.

[87] [1975] AC 55.

[88] *Ibid.*, 89–93.

[89] *Ibid.*, 97–8.

[90] [1982] AC 566.

[91] *A-G's Reference (No. 3 of 1994)* [1998] AC 245, 262.

[92] The interpretation of grievous bodily harm given in *DPP v Smith* [1961] AC 290, 334. See too *Bollom* [2003] EWCA Crim 2846, where the Court of Appeal confirmed that harm which raised no risk to the life of V could constitute serious bodily harm.

[93] [1982] AC 566, 582–3. In terms of the discussion of moral luck above, § 6.5(i), this would be an injury where consequent death was a matter of extrinsic rather than intrinsic luck.

[94] *Powell, Daniels and English* [1999] 1 AC 1, 11 (Lord Mustill), 14–15 (Lord Steyn); *Woollin* [1999] AC 82, 90 (Lord Steyn).

[95] [2008] UKHL 45, [2009] 1 AC 129, [51] (Lord Brown).

[96] Law Com. No. 304, *Murder, Manslaughter and Infanticide* (2006) para. 1.69. See also Law Com. CP No. 277, *Homicide Offences* (2026)

injury would be guilty of second degree murder—which would not attract the mandatory life sentence. This recommendation was not adopted by Parliament. It is notable that the Law Commission is presently engaged in another review of the law of homicide.

*(b) Intent is subjective*

The intent to be proved in a case of murder is the intent possessed by D herself at the time of the acts or omissions alleged to be the cause of death.[97] This may appear so obvious a requirement as not to be worth stating. Such a statement of the obvious needs to be made, however, because of the notorious decision of the House of Lords in *DPP v Smith*.[98] The House of Lords held that D could be presumed to have intended to cause death or grievous bodily harm to V if a reasonable person, placed in the same situation as D and with D's knowledge of the surrounding circumstances, would have foreseen the causing of death or grievous bodily harm to V as a natural and probable consequence of D's conduct. What precisely this formulation conveyed was a matter of intense debate.[99] An entirely tenable view of the decision was that it allowed a conviction for murder on the basis of negligence, on the foresight of the reasonable person rather than the accused. The controversy the decision aroused led to the preparation of a two-clause Bill by the Law Commission which, had it been enacted as it stood, would clearly have overturned *Smith*.[100] However, only one clause was enacted, being the clause that subsequently became section 8 of the Criminal Justice Act 1967. The clause that focused directly on the decision in *Smith* was dropped.

It will be recalled that section 8 deals with *proof* of intent and foresight;[101] it has nothing to say on the definition of these terms, or about when intent or foresight need be proved. On one reading of this legislative history, the decision in *Smith* remained intact, Parliament having explicitly rejected a provision that would have reversed it. If *Smith* still stood, it followed that murder was defined in a manner that did not require proof of intent or foresight on the part of D. Accordingly, section 8 would be irrelevant to the issue of the culpability required for murder; the section applies only when the definition of an offence requires proof of intent or foresight on the part of D.

Whatever the force of this reasoning, from the moment section 8 came into force, appellate courts regarded *Smith* as overturned[102] and this conclusion has been uncritically reiterated many times, most recently by the House of Lords in *Woollin*.[103] Furthermore, the Privy Council in *Frankland*[104] advised that *Smith* had been based on a misunderstanding of the common law and should no longer be followed, even in a common law jurisdiction which did not possess the equivalent of section 8. *Smith*, it seems, has been remaindered safely to legal history: the intent required for murder is an intent that the accused herself must be proved to have possessed.

[97] Even if D was intoxicated, since a drunken intent is still an intent: *Aidid* [2021] EWCA Crim 581, [2021] 1 WLR 4939. See below, § 18.4.

[98] [1961] AC 290.

[99] Contrast Denning, *Responsibility Before the Law* (1961) with Williams, *The Mental Element in Crime* (1965) chap. 1.

[100] Law Com. No. 10, *Imported Criminal Intent (Director of Public Prosecutions v Smith)* (1967) 17.

[101] See above, § 5.1(ix), where s. 8 is quoted in the text.

[102] *Wallett* [1968] 2 QB 367 (CA).

[103] [1999] AC 82.

[104] [1987] AC 576.

*(c) The meaning of intent in murder*

Following our discussion in Chapter 5 of intention, D intends to cause V's death or grievous bodily harm, in the core or primary sense, if he acts in order to cause death or grievous bodily harm to V, or if he causes death or grievous bodily harm as a necessary means to some other end. When D acts in one of these states of mind, his conduct will normally take the form of a direct physical attack on V. In such cases Lord Bridge's "Golden Rule" applies:[105]

> "When directing a jury on the mental element necessary in a crime of specific intent, the judge should avoid any elaboration or paraphrase of what is meant by intent and leave it to the jury's good sense to decide whether the accused acted with the necessary intent."

This approach is commendably straightforward. Where V has died following an attack by D with a gun, knife, or heavy implement, a very strong inference arises that D attacked in order to kill or seriously hurt V. The jury may be safely left to draw that inference in the absence of any reason why they should not do so.

Such an uncomplicated approach is impossible where there is no compelling evidence that D intended to kill or cause grievous bodily harm in this core, direct sense. Take a case where D sets fire to a house in order to make a fraudulent insurance claim in respect of the damage he will cause. He is aware that the house is occupied by V and that it is virtually certain that V will perish in the fire. Here there may be no evidence that D intends the death of V in the core sense of that term. He may be wholly indifferent whether V lives or dies. The existence or non-existence of V may have no bearing whatever on the success of his fraudulent claim. Consequently, were D to be charged with the murder of V, this would be one of those "rare cases" where a direction on intention of the kind laid down by the House of Lords in *Woollin* would be required:[106]

> "the jury should be directed that they are not entitled to find the necessary intention, unless they feel sure that death or serious injury was a virtual certainty (barring some unforeseen intervention) as a result of the defendant's actions and that the defendant appreciated that such was the case."

As we saw above in § 5.1(iv), *Woollin* establishes that foresight of a virtually certain outcome is the basis of finding intention in the secondary, non-core sense. Ideally, *Woollin* should be read as establishing that proof of foresight on the part of D that it is virtually certain he will cause death or grievous bodily harm to V constitutes an intent, in the secondary, indirect (or "oblique") sense, to cause death or grievous bodily harm.[107] But, as previously discussed, because of the way the *Woollin* direction is expressed and because of pre-*Woollin* case law, there is space for an interpretation to the effect that proof of the state of mind which the direction identifies is merely evidence from which intent may be inferred and does not constitute intent *per se*.[108] Such a reading was endorsed by the Court of Appeal in *Matthews and Alleyne*.[109] To read the decision in *Woollin* in this manner is unfortunate. It is when we lack evidence of direct intent that a *Woollin* direction is required. It would be puzzling to insist that foresight that an outcome is virtually certain is

[105] *Moloney* [1985] AC 905, 926.
[106] [1999] AC 82, 90.
[107] Simester, "Murder, Mens Rea and the House of Lords—Again" (1999) 115 *LQR* 17.
[108] Above, § 5.1(iv). See also Norrie, "After *Woollin*" [1999] *Crim LR* 532.
[109] [2003] 2 Cr App R 30 (CA).

mere evidence on which a finding of indirect intent to cause that outcome may be based. Far better to hold that appreciation on the part of D that his conduct is virtually certain to cause a particular result constitutes an indirect intent to cause that result, otherwise we are in the dark as to what constitutes this alternative form of intent. This is exemplified by *Matthews and Alleyne* itself. D and others threw V into a river when it was in mid-winter flood, despite their awareness that V could not swim. The trial judge directed the jury that they should convict D of murder if D appreciated that V's death by drowning was a virtual certainty. That was held to be a misdirection. The jury should have been told that they were entitled to find D guilty of murder should they choose to do so. Yet the conviction for murder was confirmed on the basis that any reasonable jury properly directed would have convicted on such evidence. Why such certainty? Because the jury could have had no doubt that D knew V was virtually certain to drown. So it seems that for indirect intent there is in reality nothing beyond the accurate perception of a practical certainty; it is unfortunate that obfuscation was not put to one side.

To conclude, we can say that D will have the mens rea for murder if:

(i) he acts in order to kill or cause grievous bodily harm; or
(ii) he kills or causes grievous bodily harm as a means to some other end he is seeking to achieve.

Additionally, members of the jury can be told that they are entitled to make a finding of intent against D if:

(iii) his conduct is virtually certain to cause death or grievous bodily harm and he appreciates that his conduct is virtually certain to cause death or grievous bodily harm.

There may be one situation, however, where the state of mind identified in (iii) may not suffice for murder. In *Bland*, Lord Goff considered that a doctor administering pain-relieving drugs to a terminal patient would not be guilty of murder, or any other offence, if the patient's death were accelerated as a known side-effect of this palliative care.[110] *Dicta* from other appellate cases[111] indicate that a doctor will not be criminally responsible for any consequences brought about as a side-effect of treatment given in what a responsible body of medical opinion would consider the best interests of the patient. Indeed, in *Gillick*, Lord Scarman went so far as to state that "the bona fide exercise by a doctor of his clinical judgment must be a complete negation of the guilty mind".[112] Whatever scope is given to that statement, in the context of murder it is clear that any exemption for medical personnel from the scope of the offence is confined to the side-effects of treatment and does not embrace fatal means to a desired objective. If, as in *Cox*,[113] the acceleration of death is used as a means of terminating pain, liability will be incurred irrespective of the gravity of the pain, the lack of any other means of palliation, and the considered wishes of the patient. Whether a distinction between means and side-effects should be accorded such decisive effect in these distressing cases is, of course, a matter of intense ethical debate.

[110] [1993] AC 789.
[111] *Re J* [1990] 3 All ER 930, 938 (CA).
[112] [1986] 1 AC 112, 190.
[113] (1992) 12 BMLR 38 (CA).

The Law Commission has in substance recommended codifying the law relating to intent in murder.[114] Under its proposals, D would be taken to intend a result if she acts in order to bring it about and, additionally, a jury "may" make a finding of intent if it is shown that D "thought the result was a virtually certain consequence of his or her action". A welcome advance on the current position is that D need only think a result to have been virtually certain: the prosecution would not have to prove that the result was in fact virtually certain, so ensuring an exclusive focus on the culpability of D. But, as under the current law, the jury in this case of indirect intent may choose whether or not to make the ultimate finding of intent. The basis of such a finding is left a deliberate blank by the Law Commission, which favours unstructured moral evaluations as a basis for findings of intent. Although Parliament subsequently reformed aspects of the law of homicide, it did not use the opportunity to adopt the Law Commission's proposed codification of the law relating to intent in murder. As noted already, the Law Commission is presently engaged in another review of the law of homicide.

### *(ii) The ambit of murder—an evaluation*

Any evaluation of the defining elements of murder cannot leave out of account the mandatory sentence of life imprisonment that the offence attracts.[115] Many offences are defined in very general terms and encompass conduct that varies enormously in terms of its content and its culpability. Theft, for instance, ranges from taking an apple from an orchard to sophisticated deceptions involving the electronic manipulation of huge sums of money. Of course, the apple thief and the large-scale fraudster will receive very different treatment at the hands of the court, a latitude facilitated by the discretionary sentencing scheme provided in the event of a conviction for theft.[116] By contrast, because each murder receives the same Draconian penalty, in principle there ought to be a large degree of similarity in the culpability evinced by each particular murder. A moment's reflection, however, reveals that murder, like other offences, spans a range of differing culpabilities:[117]

> "Murder, as every practitioner of the law knows, though often described as one of the utmost heinousness, is not in fact necessarily so, but consists in a whole bundle of offences of vastly differing degrees of culpability, ranging from brutal, cynical and repeated offences like the so-called Moors murders (*R v Brady and Hindley* (6 May 1966, unreported)) to the almost venial, if objectively immoral, 'mercy killing' of a beloved partner."

Why, then, the unyielding fixed penalty? The origin of the mandatory life sentence is to be found in the political process that led to the passing of the Murder (Abolition of Death Penalty) Act 1965. There would not have been a Parliamentary majority for the abolition of the death penalty in murder had not the supporters of abolition undertaken that each and every conviction for murder should attract a mandatory life sentence.[118] There was then, and remains now, a strong public sentiment that murder is a special offence which should be marked on each occasion by a special penalty. Those who argue for retention of the mandatory life sentence (or for reintroduction of the death penalty) assert that the intentional

[114] Law Com. No. 304, *Murder, Manslaughter and Infanticide* (2006). For discussion, see Norrie, "Between Orthodox and Moral Contextualism" [2006] *Crim LR* 486.

[115] Murder (Abolition of the Death Penalty) Act 1965.

[116] From an absolute discharge to 7 years' imprisonment: Criminal Justice Act 1991, s. 26.

[117] *Howe* [1987] AC 417, 433.

[118] The Bill that became the Murder (Abolition of Death Penalty) Act 1965 was a private member's Bill passed on a free vote.

taking of any life merits a life sentence and/or that an unyielding and Draconian response is an effective deterrent for those who would otherwise kill. Against this, two authoritative committees which have investigated the issue found neither argument persuasive and recommended a discretionary sentencing regime for the offence.[119] Nonetheless, the Government has indicated its intention to retain the mandatory sentence,[120] even where D kills but only intended to cause grievous bodily harm.

There have been other proposals to limit the effects of the mandatory life sentence for murder. One, proposed by Spencer,[121] was that the jury should be given the power to add to a verdict of guilty of murder that they found "extenuating circumstances" so that the judge would not be obliged to impose a mandatory life sentence. The proposal has not, however, been adopted.

The continuation of the mandatory life sentence for the indefinite future makes it all the more important that the definition of murder should be focused on the most culpable forms of killing.[122] The current definition of murder includes many persons convicted of the offence who do not merit a life sentence. Even though legal forms of extenuation, such as the partial defences of loss of control and diminished responsibility, take outside the ambit of murder some defendants who would otherwise be convicted of the offence, murder remains too inclusive an offence. It may be argued that the situation is not as Draconian as it might seem because a prisoner serving a mandatory life term will rarely spend the rest of his life in prison. Nonetheless, the position of a person serving a mandatory life sentence is unenviable. A life sentence contains a literal truth in that any release is a release on licence that may be revoked only by administrative rather than judicial decision. The release decision for a mandatory lifer is entrusted to the Parole Board rather than the Home Secretary, following reform of the mandatory life-sentencing process instituted by the Criminal Justice Act 2003 and now governed by the Sentencing Act 2020.[123] Under this scheme, the trial judge must recommend a minimum term of years which D should serve by way of retribution for his offence. Although what period of time should be served on this retributive basis is ultimately a matter for the judge,[124] there is a strong statutory presumption that the term should be at least 15 years[125] or, according to aggravating features such as the motive or mode of killing, 25 years, 30 years, or whole life. The last will be appropriate, for example, if the murder was the result of premeditated planning of at least two people, the murder of a child following abduction of the child or sexual or sadistic motivation or a substantial degree of premeditation or planning, the murder of a police, prison or probation officer in the course of their duty, or where D sought to advance a political, religious, racial, or ideological cause.[126] A term of 30 years would be appropriate, for example, if the murder involved a firearm or explosive, was done for gain, involved two or more victims

[119] Report of the Advisory Council on the Penal System: *Sentences of Imprisonment* (1978) paras. 235–44; House of Lords, Select Committee on Murder and Life Imprisonment (Session 1988–89) HL Paper 78, paras. 108–18.

[120] *Hansard*, HL, 11 June 1997, WA 83.

[121] (2009) 173 *Criminal Law and Justice Weekly* 165.

[122] Child and Sullivan, "The Current State of Murder in English Law" in Reed and Bohlander (eds.), *Homicide in Criminal Law* (2019) 62.

[123] Section 321 and sched. 21. See Roberts and Saunders, "Sentencing for Murder" [2020] *Crim LR* 900.

[124] *Sullivan* [2004] EWCA Crim 1762, [2005] 1 Cr App R 3.

[125] Sentencing Act 2020, sched. 21, para 5. If D was under 18 at the time of the offence the minimum term will be lower depending on D's age: sched. 21, para. 5A.

[126] *Ibid*, sched. 21, para 2, as amended by the Sentencing Act 2026, s. 11.

or was aggravated by hostility related to race, sexual orientation, disability, or transgender identity.[127] If D had taken a knife or other weapon with him which he used to commit murder, the starting point for the assessment of sentence is 25 years' imprisonment.[128]

When the retributive part of the sentence is served, the Parole Board may delay release on licence if the prisoner's release is considered a risk for particular persons or the public generally. This regime is severe. Unlike prisoners serving a fixed term of years who are normally released after serving one-half of the term, persons subject to a mandatory life sentence must serve the retributive period of the sentence in full. It is imperative, therefore, that the scope of the offence of murder ensures as far as is possible that only those who warrant such treatment are convicted of the offence.

Criticism of the current scope of murder predominantly focuses on the fact that, in addition to an intention to kill, an intention to cause grievous bodily harm will suffice as mens rea. Those who support the current position argue that a person who acts with an intention to cause serious harm is sufficiently heinous to warrant full responsibility for the fact of death, should that occur. Yet, even if this is sometimes true, as a general proposition it is too broad; it may, for example, be murder if V dies as an untoward consequence of D's act of deliberately breaking V's arm, arising for example from poor treatment of the injury. In the light of judicial criticism of this form of culpability,[129] it is surprising that grievous bodily harm has not been reinterpreted in the context of murder to require the causing of harm that is intrinsically dangerous to life.[130] Yet, even if that were done, there remains force in the argument that an offence designed to pick out the worst kinds of killings should require some advertence to the chance of causing death.

The Law Commission proposed an offence of first-degree murder along these lines.[131] As recommended, it would be first-degree murder either to kill with intent to kill or to kill with intent to cause serious injury when D was aware of a serious risk of causing death.[132] Only first-degree murder with this welcome narrowing of culpability would attract a mandatory life sentence. The Law Commission also proposed an offence of second-degree murder defined in terms of killings done with intent to cause serious injury or intended to cause injury or fear or risk of injury if D was aware of a serious risk of causing death. Additionally, it would be second-degree murder if D successfully raised diminished responsibility or loss of control to a charge of first-degree murder. This second-degree form of murder would not attract the mandatory penalty but could be punished with a life term if appropriate.

Suppose the mens rea for the form of murder attracting a mandatory sentence were to be reformulated along these lines. The range of culpability falling within the compass of the offence of first-degree murder, though significantly narrower than the current offence, nonetheless would remain extensive, as the range of circumstances where the mens rea for the offence may arise would still be considerable. At one time, English law looked to features

[127] *Ibid.*, sched. 21, para. 3.

[128] *Ibid.*, sched. 21, para. 4.

[129] *Cunningham* [1982] AC 566, 582–3 (Lord Edmund-Davies); *Powell and Daniels and English* [1999] 1 AC 1, 11 (Lord Mustill), 14–15 (Lord Steyn); *Woollin* [1999] AC 82, 90 (Lord Steyn).

[130] Although this might be consistent with the narrow approach to the definition of grievous bodily harm in *Sidhu* [2019] EWCA Crim 1034. Above, § 10.3(i)(a).

[131] Law Com. No. 304, *Murder, Manslaughter and Infanticide* (2006).

[132] For discussion, see Wilson, "The Structure of Criminal Homicide" [2006] *Crim LR* 471.

beyond mens rea in an attempt to identify what forms of murder should attract a capital sentence. The same technique might be employed to determine which kinds of murder should attract a mandatory life sentence. Under now-repealed provisions of the Homicide Act 1957, factors such as killing a police officer or use of a firearm would make the offence a capital one.[133] Other jurisdictions make reference to such matters as the use of torture,[134] the use of poison,[135] a sexual motive, or the age of the victim.[136] However, in England and Wales, such an approach proved unsatisfactory. The grounds of aggravation of murder were controversial and it was generally agreed that these subdivisions of the offence entailed fine distinctions which did not reliably track gradations of culpability.[137] Because, for political reasons, the mandatory penalty of life imprisonment seems set to remain for the indefinite future, there is much to be said for a definition of first-degree murder confined to killings done with intent to kill and it is to be regretted that the Law Commission did not remain faithful to its original proposal to this effect.[138] However, when Parliament subsequently took the opportunity to reform the law of murder, it did not adopt the Law Commission's recommendations concerning first- and second-degree murder. Consequently, the partial defences to murder of loss of control and diminished responsibility, which Parliament did revise, will be important palliatives for an offence punished in such a rigid fashion. As noted above, the Law Commission is conducting a further review of the law relating to homicide offences, including full and partial defences and the existing sentencing framework for murder,[139] although the review will assume the continued existence of the mandatory life sentence for murder (or for the most serious form of murder if a tiered structure is again recommended). The final report is due to be published in 2028.

## § 10.4 Manslaughter

### *(i) Introduction*

At one time, under the common law, any killing which was unlawful but insufficiently grave to amount to murder would be designated manslaughter.[140] Nowadays, the element of unlawfulness attendant on the killing of V by D no longer suffices *per se*. The unlawfulness must take particular forms if a verdict of manslaughter is to follow. Yet, even in its modern form, manslaughter is a crime of enormous scope. It is an offence that can be committed with several differing forms of culpability. Between these various ways of committing what is but a

133 Section 5(1) provided that murders done in furtherance of theft, by shooting or explosion, when avoiding arrest or escaping from custody, or of police officers and prison officers (and those assisting them) would constitute capital murder.

134 See, e.g., New York Penal Law, s. 125.26.

135 California Penal Code, s. 189.

136 Ariz. Rev. Stat. Ann; s. 13-604.01(A). Cp. the German Criminal Code: *Strafgesetzbuch* §§ 211–212.

137 The class of capital murder in England and Wales was designed to capture not so much the worst killings in terms of innate culpability but those killings which most threatened order and stability, thereby warranting maximum deterrence. But this approach became discredited precisely because the line between capital and non-capital murder did not reliably track differing degrees of heinousness.

138 LCCP No. 177.

139 https://lawcom.gov.uk/project/law-of-homicide/.

140 Up to the nineteenth century manslaughter was regarded as the residual category of homicide, into which fell all killings that were not justified, excusable, or murder: see Turner, *Kenny's Outlines of Criminal Law* (16th ed., 1952) 139–40.

single offence, there is a major divide: the division between voluntary and involuntary manslaughter. Voluntary manslaughter refers to those killings perpetrated with an intent to kill or to cause grievous bodily harm, but where there is some form of legally recognised extenuation, established at trial, which reduces what would otherwise be murder to manslaughter. Involuntary manslaughter does not require proof of an intent to kill or cause grievous bodily harm. In the sphere of involuntary manslaughter, gross negligence, or the commission of certain "dangerous" criminal acts, provides a sufficient culpability for a manslaughter conviction.

### *(ii) Voluntary manslaughter*

There are three forms of voluntary manslaughter: committing a *prima facie* murder in response to some incident or event which constitutes loss of control; committing a *prima facie* murder when afflicted by one or more of the conditions specified in section 2 of the Homicide Act 1957 (diminished responsibility); and committing *prima facie* murder in pursuance of a suicide pact. In each case, these grounds of mitigation will be relevant as legal extenuation only if it is established that D acted with intent to cause death or to cause grievous bodily harm.

Evidence of loss of control or of diminished responsibility may also be used to throw reasonable doubt on whether D did intend to kill or cause grievous bodily harm.[141] If proof of the mens rea for murder is not established, evidence of loss of control or mental disorder may still be relevant, but only at the sentencing stage following a verdict of involuntary manslaughter. But that is not our present concern, which is with legal extenuation; that is, situations where all the elements of murder are made out and loss of control, diminished responsibility, or membership of a suicide pact is adduced to reduce the conviction to manslaughter.

At this juncture, only loss of control and diminished responsibility will be considered. Membership of suicide pacts will be discussed when we consider the legal response to suicide and to those who assist it.[142]

## § 10.5 Loss of control

For many centuries, English law has partially condoned killings when done in a state of anger aroused by some form of provocation. The origins of this form of extenuation have been traced back to verdicts of medieval juries whereby certain spontaneous angry killings were treated, indulgently, as killing *se defendendo*, thereby avoiding a verdict of murder and all its consequences.[143] From these beginnings, provocation ultimately emerged as a distinct partial defence to murder at common law and generated its own body of principles and rules.[144] This defence proved controversial and, following recommendations of the

[141] As was pointed out in the context of the previous common law defence of provocation in *Richens* [1993] 4 All ER 877 (CA), the loss of self-control has to be compatible with proof of an intent to kill or to cause grievous bodily harm.

[142] Below, § 10.11.

[143] Horder, *Provocation and Responsibility* (1992) chap. 1.

[144] Ashworth, "The Doctrine of Provocation" (1976) 35 *CLJ* 292; Horder, *Provocation and Responsibility* (1992); Sullivan, "Anger and Excuse: Reassessing Provocation" (1992) 12 *OJLS* 380.

Law Commission,[145] was abolished by section 56 of the Coroners and Justice Act 2009, being replaced with a new, narrower, defence of loss of control. The statutory defence has been described as "self-contained",[146] in the sense that the ambit of the defence is encompassed within the statutory provisions, unaffected by its common law heritage, and also as being more restrictive than the provocation defence.[147] Nevertheless, to understand the operation of the defence, it is important to be aware of the operation of the common law defence of provocation and why the Law Commission and Parliament considered that it needed to be replaced. Further, although the authorities on the old common law defence have no influence on the interpretation of the new defence, it remains useful to apply the new defence to the facts of the old cases in order to determine how the new defence will operate, and what has changed. In doing so, it will be seen, as the Court of Appeal has observed, that there are aspects of the legislation which are "likely to produce surprising results".[148]

### (i) *The former defence of provocation*

The common law defence of provocation[149] was only available as a defence to murder.[150] When the defence was raised, the relevant issues fell within two tests. The first, subjective test concerned whether D had lost self-control suddenly and temporarily because of something said or done. The second, objective test concerned whether a reasonable person would have lost control on account of the provocation and would have acted as D did. The interpretation of both tests proved to be controversial. As regards the subjective test, the need for a "sudden and temporary loss of self-control" indicated that there had to be something in the nature of a spontaneous response to the provocation if it was to be claimed that D lost self-control.[151] Any indication of a plan or design to kill V would sit uncomfortably with a plea that the killing was something beyond D's control. Similarly, any lapse of time between the last provocative incident and D's reaction would undermine D's claim to have lost control. There were, however, a series of cases in which trial judges allowed the defence to go to the jury despite significant passages of time between the killing and the provocative incident. In none of these cases did the Court of Appeal deprecate this more accommodating approach.[152] These decisions changed the significance of lapse of time from being a formal legal barrier into an item of evidence relevant to the subjective issue of whether D did, in fact, lose self-control.

[145] Law Com. No. 304, *Murder, Manslaughter and Infanticide* (2006). Although the details of the new statutory defence are not closely linked to the recommendations of the Law Commission.

[146] *Clinton* [2012] EWCA Crim 2, [2013] QB 1, [2]; *Gurpinar* [2015] EWCA Crim 178, [2015] 1 WLR 3442, [4].

[147] *Goodwin* [2018] EWCA Crim 2287, [2018] 4 WLR 165, [35].

[148] *Clinton* [2012] EWCA Crim 2, [2013] QB 1, [2].

[149] Although it was supplemented by s. 3 of the Homicide Act 1957.

[150] In *Cunningham* [1958] 3 All ER 711 (CA), where a charge of wounding with intent to cause grievous bodily harm was brought, and in *Bruzas* [1972] Crim LR 367 (Crown Court (Lewes)), which concerned a charge of attempted murder, it was confirmed that provocation could not be argued at trial in order to avoid conviction for the offence charged: outwith murder, provocation was relevant only at the sentencing stage as a possible ground of mitigation. Contrast, for example, the Indian Penal Code, ss. 334–5 (a partial defence to voluntarily causing hurt and grievous hurt).

[151] *Ibrams* (1982) 74 Cr App R 154 (CA).

[152] In particular cases involving so-called "battered woman syndrome", such as *Ahluwalia* [1992] 4 All ER 889 (CA) and *Thornton (No. 2)* [1996] 2 All ER 1023 (CA).

The chief controversy relating to the objective test concerned the identification of any characteristics of D which could be taken into account when assessing the impact that the provocation would have had on a reasonable person. This reasonable person standard was a judicial device to prevent what were seen as undeserving pleas from being placed before a jury. The reasonable person was an ordinary person from whom a normal capacity to exercise self-control should be expected.[153] In evaluating D's response by reference to the standard of the ordinary person, there might be particular facets of D's person or character which explain the loss of self-control and its fatal consequences. D might be unusually pugnacious, abnormally sensitive, mocked about a particular form of affliction, and so on. The question thus arose as to what characteristics associated with D could be attributed to the reasonable person when assessing whether the reasonable person would have acted as D did.

Two distinct lines of authority developed. First, the defence was premised on the reactions of people capable of an ordinary level of self-restraint, so an objective standard of expectation applied, mediated only by the age or sex of the particular defendant.[154] However, when considering the weight or sting of the provocation, particular facets of D's person or character could be attributed to the reasonable person if germane to the weight of the provocation at issue in the case. For instance, a taunt about D's height might be more provocative to D if she was extremely short; or an adolescent may have less capacity for self-control than a mature adult.[155]

The second line of authority took into account conditions which were relevant on account of the effect they had on D's capacity for self-control in general, such as a personality disorder[156] or a mental impairment such as "battered woman syndrome",[157] even if the provocation was not directed at those characteristics. This second approach was criticised by the Privy Council,[158] but was endorsed by the House of Lords.[159] This approach was eventually rejected by the Privy Council in *A-G for Jersey v Holley*,[160] where it was considered that D's alcoholism might have been a relevant consideration in evaluating the provocative sting of V's conduct, had his quarrel with V related to his state of addiction, but that his addiction had no relevance to the level of self-control to be expected of him. On that matter the only variables that the jury should have taken into account were age and sex. A consequence of this appeared to be that if D was, for example, a woman who was suffering from "battered woman syndrome" as a result of years of domestic abuse from her partner, whom she had killed, the syndrome would not usually be relevant when evaluating whether the reasonable person would have killed, since the syndrome would relate to the ability to exercise self-control rather than to the gravity of the provocation. This implication of the decision in *Holley* was a matter of particular concern and proved ultimately significant in the decision of Parliament that the law needed to be reformed; although, as will be seen, the decision in *Holley* has effectively been replicated in the new defence of loss of control.

[153] *Morhall* [1996] AC 90, 97–8 (Lord Goff).
[154] *Camplin* [1978] AC 705, 718 (Lord Diplock).
[155] *Ibid.*
[156] *Dryden* [1995] 4 All ER 987 (CA).
[157] *Ahluwalia* [1992] 4 All ER 889 (CA); *Thornton (No. 2)* [1996] 2 All ER 1023 (CA); *Humphreys* [1995] 4 All ER 1008 (CA).
[158] *Luc Thiet Thuan* [1997] AC 131 (PC).
[159] *Smith* [2001] 1 AC 146.
[160] [2005] UKPC 23, [2005] 2 AC 580.

### *(ii) A critique of provocation*

The defence of provocation was subject to widespread criticism, most notably from Horder, who recommended the abolition of the defence.[161] Subsequently, as a Law Commissioner, he was responsible for the report which made a similar recommendation.[162] There were many aspects of the defence which proved to be a cause for concern, but ultimately its key failing was that no acceptable rationale for it could be readily identified.

A condition of angry loss of self-control was at the core of provocation. Yet anger is a criminogenic emotion and one of the key deterrent tasks of the criminal law is to provide incentives for citizens to curb violent responses induced by their angry states. A person disposed to respond to frustrations and setbacks with an angry loss of control culminating in serious violence would thereby demonstrate a dangerous and deficient character and should not be accorded any form of condonation of their conduct. Moreover, the partial condonation of angry violence through a provocation defence came with an inbuilt sex bias because it clearly privileged people with the capacity and disposition spontaneously to kill others, and such people were typically men. Such killings occur frequently in domestic contexts against physically vulnerable members of the household.[163] The historical origins of provocation lay in a perception, long discarded as part of the law, that killings which emerged from sudden falling-outs ("chance-medleys") were less heinous than killings which were the product of premeditation. From the early modern period the continuation of the defence was reinforced by an acceptance that male honour can (even should) be vindicated by acts of retaliatory violence.[164] These paradigms are unsuited to a modern liberal democracy.

Attempts were made to offer a modern rationale for the defence. McAuley[165] defended the extenuating force of provocation on the basis of what he termed "partial justification". For him, there needed to be some element of the victim's "asking for it", so that blame for the killing is in some sense shared between defendant and victim. As McAuley observed himself, such a rationale could not underpin the English version of the provocation defence, because provocation could apply where the victim was someone other than the provocateur and, more importantly, the defence was available if D was provoked by anything, such as the crying of a baby or a predictable reaction to his own unlawful or offensive behaviour. These are not cases where the victim "asks for it". In any event, the notion of partial justification is incoherent. Conduct is either justified, all things considered, or it is not (although in the latter case it may be condonable). Even in the case of the gravest provocation—say D has just witnessed the murder of his wife by V, and some other, non-lethal response is warranted—D's *killing* V cannot be justified. Understandable, yes. Excusable, perhaps. But not justified. Viewed from the perspective of a general rule of conduct, his action is clearly wrong and impermissible.

Dressler[166] located the rationale of the provocation defence in the realm of excuse, the excuse consisting of D's reduced capacity to conform his conduct to law when induced to lose self-control in angry reaction to provocation. But, as he recognised, our reaction to

[161] *Provocation and Responsibility* (1992) chap. 9.

[162] Law Com. No. 304, *Murder, Manslaughter and Infanticide* (2006) part 5.

[163] In 2024/25 40% of female homicide victims were killed by a partner or ex-partner, whereas 4% of male homicide victims were killed by a partner or ex-partner: Office for National Statistics, *Homicide in England and Wales: Year Ending March 2025* (2026).

[164] Horder, *Provocation and Responsibility* (1992) chaps. 1–3.

[165] "Anticipating the Past: The Defence of Provocation in Irish Law" (1987) 50 *MLR* 133.

[166] "Rethinking Heat of Passion: A Defence in Search of a Rationale" (1982) 73 *J Crim L and Criminology* 421.

loss of control greatly depends on the nature of the conduct which caused the reaction. In the example where V kills D's wife, we readily condone, at least in part, D's response. By contrast, where the precipitating incident is trivial, we may, quite reasonably, see E's loss of self-control as a ground of censure. Yet the emotions gripping E may be just as strong, just as choice-constraining, as the emotions aroused in a person who has endured grave provocation. The loss of self-control does not in itself explain why we feel blame is extenuated in some cases. Indeed, in some cases where murder verdicts have been sustained because of insufficient evidence of loss of self-control, there may be a strong case for extenuation, even in a case of considered, deliberate killing.

The rigidity of the mandatory life sentence for murder calls for flexible, fact-sensitive grounds of extenuation. Some members of the judiciary sought to make provocation more flexible and fact-sensitive, particularly through reception of syndrome evidence. In so doing, they created an awkward overlap with the grounds of extenuation afforded by diminished responsibility, undermining the coherence of provocation as a defence available for reasonable people. That tendency was halted by the decision in *Holley*; but this swapped one set of concerns for another. Take, for instance, the post-*Holley* decision in *Mohammed*.[167] D had killed his daughter V, enraged that she was continuing a relationship with a man after he had ordered her to end the connection. Not merely was this defiance but, according to the version of the Muslim faith to which D subscribed, it was in breach of V's religious obligation to obey her father, placing her beyond the bounds of her community. In an accurate rendering of the post-*Holley* law, the trial judge, in a direction approved by the Court of Appeal, instructed the jury that they should consider D's religion and culture in determining how gravely a reasonable person so situated would have regarded V's defiance of her father. When it came to evaluating how a reasonable person would have reacted to the defiance (on discovering the couple in his house), the test to be employed was the likely reaction of a person of ordinary stability and temperament. This awkward amalgam of cultural relativism and mainstream expectations concerning self-control was not easy material with which a jury could achieve justice.

Cases such as *Mohammed* raised the question whether a soundly based defence of provocation could be worked out or whether the defence should be abolished. After careful consideration of the law and searching for a rationale for the defence, the Law Commission recommended its abolition and replacement with a new defence of loss of control.[168] These recommendations were incorporated, subject to certain key amendments, in the Coroners and Justice Act 2009.

### *(iii) Loss of control*

The defence of loss of control is defined by sections 54 and 55 of the Coroners and Justice Act 2009.[169] The heading to these provisions describes the defence as a "partial defence

[167] [2005] EWCA Crim 1880.

[168] Law Com. No. 304, *Murder, Manslaughter and Infanticide* (2006), part 5. The proposals are in substance the same as recommended in LCCP No. 177, *A New Homicide Act for England and Wales?* (2005), part 6, on which see Mackay and Mitchell, "But Is this Provocation? Some Thoughts on the Law Commission's Report on Partial Defences to Murder" [2005] *Crim LR* 44; Quick and Wells "Getting Tough with Defences" [2006] *Crim LR* 514.

[169] See Norrie, "The Coroners and Justice Act 2009—Partial Defences to Murder (1) Loss of Control" [2010] *Crim LR* 275; Withey, "Loss of Control: Loss of Opportunity?" [2011] *Crim LR* 263; Sullivan, Crombag, and Child, "Loss of Control in the Appeal Courts" (2021) 72 *NILQ* 200.

to murder". As with the old common law defence of provocation, loss of control is only available for the crime of murder and if the defence succeeds it results in D's being liable to conviction for manslaughter,[170] thus avoiding the mandatory life sentence. The defence is available whether D is the principal offender who killed V, or an accessory who was party to V's killing.[171]

To establish the defence, there must be sufficient evidence that:

(a) D actually lost self-control because of a triggering event;
(b) the triggering event was a qualifying one;
(c) the loss of self-control was objectively understandable, in that a "normal" person might also have lost self-control in the circumstances.

All three components need to be identified; if one is proved to be absent, the defence fails. Although the components should be analysed sequentially and separately, typically they will arise simultaneously at the point when the fatal violence is used.[172]

The defendant does not bear the burden of proof to establish the defence. In line with mainstream full defences such as self-defence, once it has become a live issue at trial, the burden falls upon the prosecution to negate at least one necessary element of the defence beyond reasonable doubt.[173] It is enough to establish the defence, therefore, if there is a reasonable possibility that its elements are satisfied.[174] The trial judge must leave the defence to the jury, even if D has not raised the defence or given any evidence of loss of self-control, but only if sufficient evidence is adduced to raise an issue with respect to each[175] of the components of the defence on which, in the opinion of the judge, a properly directed jury could reasonably conclude that the defence might apply.[176] The judge has a gatekeeping role in assessing the evidence, but must not usurp the function of the jury;[177] rather the judge should determine whether it would be open to the jury to determine that the elements of the defence may have been satisfied.[178] If the defence is left to the jury, its members must assume that the requirements of the defence are satisfied unless the prosecution proves beyond reasonable doubt that they are not.[179] D may wish to plead both the full defence of self-defence and the partial defence of loss of control, in which case self-defence should be considered by the jury first and, if it is rejected, they should then consider loss of control.[180]

*(a) D's loss of self-control*

It must first be established that D's acts and omissions in killing V or being a party to V's killing resulted from D's loss of self-control.[181] Loss of self-control is not defined in the

[170] Coroners and Justice Act 2009, s. 54(7).
[171] *Ibid.*, s. 54(1). If the defence is successful for one party to the killing this does not affect the liability of any other party to the murder: s. 54(8).
[172] *Clinton* [2012] EWCA Crim 2, [2013] QB 1, [9].
[173] *Dawes* [2013] EWCA Crim 322, [49].
[174] See § 3.2 above.
[175] *Gurpinar* [2015] EWCA Crim 178, [2015] 1 WLR 3442, [22].
[176] Coroners and Justice Act 2009, s. 54(6). This requires more rigorous evaluation of the evidence by the trial judge than was required under the old defence of provocation: *Goodwin* [2018] EWCA Crim 2287, [2018] 4 WLR 165, [33].
[177] *Turner* [2023] EWCA Crim 1626, [39].
[178] *Ibid.*
[179] Coroners and Justice Act 2009, s. 54(5).
[180] *Drake* [2023] EWCA Crim 1454, [2024] 4 WLR 73, [59].
[181] Coroners and Justice Act 2009, s. 54(1)(a).

legislation but it has been interpreted by the courts as involving "D's loss of ability to maintain his actions in accordance with considered judgment or [where] he had lost normal powers of reasoning".[182] This is a subjective test which focuses on D's reaction, and it is necessary to establish that a causative link between the loss of self-control and the relevant act or omission may have existed. Exactly what psychological state represents a loss of self-control cannot precisely be pinned down. In *Gurpinar*[183] the Court of Appeal considered that what constituted a loss of self-control was generally fact-sensitive. In *Martin*,[184] however, the Court of Appeal indicated that a panicked and scared response to the aggressive act of another was not of itself indicative of loss of control. Loss of self-control does not require proof of a frenzied attack,[185] and in *Dawson*[186] it was recognised that a frenzied attack involving multiple injuries did not itself provide sufficient evidence of loss of self-control. This is because it might have been the result of revenge, sadism, a wish to intimidate others, or simply because it took a long time to achieve the desired outcome of the victim's death.

Loss of self-control was also a key requirement of the old defence of provocation. So, in *Cocker*,[187] where D killed his terminally ill wife in response to her incessant requests for him to do so, no issue of provocation arose. The circumstances of the killing indicated calm deliberation. The "classic" direction on the matter given by Devlin J in *Duffy*,[188] in respect of the defence of provocation, referred to "a loss of self-control, rendering the accused so subject to passion as to make him or her not master of his [*sic*] mind". Obviously, then, D had to be in some extremity of anger, but the anger need not be so overwhelming as to render D incapable of knowing what she was doing. In principle, if D's anger was as radically destabilising as that, she could claim that she lacked the mens rea for murder. In *Richens*[189] it was stressed that awareness of the nature and quality of one's actions and of the consequences that will ensue from them was compatible with a successful plea of the old defence of provocation. All that was required was that D must be so angry that he was unable to restrain himself. Presumably this remains the case in respect of the defence of loss of control.

Whereas the old defence of provocation required the loss of self-control to be sudden and temporary, for the new statutory defence the loss of control need not be sudden.[190] Although it might appear that this reform dramatically widens the ambit of the defence, so that a killing which occurs days or even weeks after a particular triggering event might still be one which resulted from loss of self-control, the reform is not as radical as it might first appear. This is for four reasons. First, although there remained a formal requirement of sudden and temporary loss of self-control for the defence of provocation, whether this was satisfied was a question of fact for the jury, meaning that longer gaps between a provocative event and killing would not necessarily mean that the defence failed. Secondly, the loss of

[182] See *Jewell* [2014] EWCA Crim 414, [24].
[183] [2015] EWCA Crim 178, [2015] 1 WLR 3442, [20].
[184] [2017] EWCA Crim 1359.
[185] *Islam* [2019] EWCA Crim 2419, [28].
[186] [2021] EWCA Crim 40. In *Goodwin* [2018] EWCA Crim 2287, [2018] 4 WLR 165, an attack involving 18 blows was not considered sufficient to make loss of self-control a live issue, such that the defence had to be left to the jury.
[187] [1989] Crim LR 740 (CA).
[188] [1949] 1 All ER 932 (CA).
[189] [1993] 4 All ER 877 (CA).
[190] Coroners and Justice Act 2009, s. 54(2).

control defence will only operate where a person with "a normal degree of tolerance and self-restraint" might have acted in a similar way. Consequently, the fact that the loss of self-control is not sudden may be relevant to a jury's concluding that a normal person would not have acted as D did. Thirdly, the defence will not be available where D has "acted in a considered desire for revenge".[191] The longer the gap between a triggering event and the killing, the more likely it will be that the jury concludes that the killing was motivated by revenge. The Court of Appeal has recognised that a jury was properly directed about the relevance of a considered desire for revenge when the trial judge referred to a "deliberate and considered decision . . . one that has been thought about" by D.[192]

Fourthly, although the judge should not withdraw the defence from the jury merely because of the delay between a relevant triggering event and the loss of control, the jury may still legitimately conclude that the lapse of time means that there was no operative loss of control at the time of the killing. For example, in *Ibrams*,[193] which concerned the defence of provocation, the last provocative act perpetrated by V occurred on 7 October. On 10 October, D planned with others the killing of V. The attack was successfully carried out on 12 October. On such facts, the trial judge ruled that there was no evidence of any loss of self-control. It is submitted that the important feature in *Ibrams* was the planning and deliberation, with the lapse of time underscoring the organised nature of the killing. This would presumably be decided the same way under the new defence of loss of control. But evidence of premeditation and planning may not necessarily be incompatible with a finding of loss of self-control. In *Thornton (No. 2)*,[194] for instance, D declared her intention of killing V, her brutal husband, and went into another room to obtain and sharpen a knife, before returning and stabbing him. Similarly, in *Ahluwalia*,[195] D waited until her abusive husband V was asleep, fetched a can of petrol, doused his bed with fuel, and then set it alight. Most strikingly, in *Pearson*,[196] D and E had armed themselves with weapons and killed their abusive father in the course of a planned joint enterprise. In each of these cases, the jury was asked to consider whether D had acted in a state of loss of control. This insistence upon a finding of loss of self-control has been criticised—a criticism founded on a very understandable concern with the nature of the provocation endured by the defendants in these cases.[197] But provocation had a requirement that there must be a loss of self-control, and this has not changed under the new defence. Similarly, for the old defence it was possible to have regard to the cumulative impact of earlier events to assess whether D had lost self-control. Such cumulative impact remains relevant to the statutory defence of loss of control.[198]

[191] *Ibid.*, s. 54(4).
[192] *Clinton* [2012] EWCA Crim 2, [2013] QB 1, [131].
[193] (1982) 74 Cr App R 154 (CA).
[194] [1996] 2 All ER 1023 (CA).
[195] [1992] 4 All ER 889 (CA).
[196] [1992] Crim LR 193 (CA).
[197] O'Donovan, "Defences for Battered Women Who Kill" (1991) 18 *J Law and Soc* 219; Nicholson, "Telling Tales: Gender Discrimination Gender Construction and Battered Women Who Kill" (1995) 3 *Feminist Leg Stud* 185; McColgan, "In Defence of Battered Women Who Kill" (1993) 130 *J Law and Soc* 508; Wells, "Battered Women Syndrome and Defences to Homicide: Where Now?" (1994) 14 *LS* 266; Dressler, "Battered Women Who Kill Their Sleeping Tormenters: Reflections on Maintaining Respect for Human Life while Killing Moral Monsters" in Shute and Simester (eds.), *Criminal Law Theory* (2002) 259.
[198] *Dawes* [2013] EWCA Crim 322, [2014] 1 WLR 947, [54].

*(b) Qualifying trigger*

Provocation required the defendant's loss of self-control to arise from something said or done. There is no such requirement for the loss of control defence; it is sufficient that D lost self-control and this need not arise from human agency. For example, D, a farmer, might look out upon his flood-devastated land and feel a great surge of anger towards V, his prosperous neighbour, who farms on higher ground. Should D's resentment lead him to kill V, loss of control would not be ruled out *merely* because it arose from nothing done or said. Instead, the loss of control defence would be ruled out by the second requirement needed to establish it: D's loss of self-control must have a recognised qualifying trigger.[199] There are two alternative qualifying triggers, which may be deployed in combination.[200] The qualifying triggers limit the circumstances where the defence of loss of control can operate when compared with the old defence of provocation,[201] but, as the Court of Appeal correctly observed in *Clinton*:[202]

> "There is no point in pretending that the practical application of [the qualifying trigger provision] will not create considerable difficulties."

*Fear of serious violence.*

The loss of self-control will have a qualifying trigger if it was "attributable to D's fear of serious violence from V against D or another identified person".[203]

This trigger seems entirely suitable to cover domestic violence cases such as *Thornton (No. 2)*[204] and *Ahluwalia*.[205] Furthermore, it repairs the failure of English law to provide some extenuation for cases where there is a right to use some force in self-defence, but where that right was abused by D's recourse to excessive force, so that the complete defence of self-defence will not be available.[206] If the defence of self-defence fails, it does not follow that this qualifying trigger for loss of control is necessarily absent.[207]

But, whereas the defence of self-defence applies where there is a threat of any violence, the qualifying trigger will only be engaged where D fears serious violence. This fear of serious violence is to be disregarded to the extent that the fear itself was caused by a thing which D incited to be done or said for the purpose of providing an excuse to use violence.[208] This restriction on the trigger embodies the notion that D cannot rely on a self-induced loss of control, at least when D's purpose was to create a situation where he could resort to violence. Further, the defence is not available where, even though D feared serious violence, he "acted in a considered desire for revenge".[209] But this qualifying trigger would appear to be satisfied if the facts of *Johnson*[210] arose again, where D was allowed to raise the defence

199 Coroners and Justice Act 2009, s. 54(1)(b).
200 *Ibid.*, s. 55(5).
201 *Dawes* [2013] EWCA Crim 322, [2014] 1 WLR 947, [60].
202 [2012] EWCA Crim 2, [2013] QB 1, [11].
203 Coroners and Justice Act 2009, s. 55(3).
204 [1996] 2 All ER 1023 (CA).
205 [1992] 4 All ER 889 (CA).
206 *Clegg* [1995] 1 AC 482.
207 *Goodwin* [2018] EWCA Crim 2287, [2018] 4 WLR 165.
208 Coroners and Justice Act 2009, s. 55(6)(a).
209 *Ibid.*, s. 54(4).
210 [1989] 1 WLR 740 (CA).

of provocation in respect of V's extreme but predictable reaction to D's own objectionable and aggressive behaviour. This was confirmed by the Court of Appeal in *Dawes*,[211] where it was held that the mere fact that D was behaving badly and was looking for and provoking trouble does not necessarily lead to the absence of a qualifying trigger. It is only where D intended that his actions would provide him with the excuse or opportunity to use violence that the qualifying trigger will not operate.

*Sense of being seriously wronged by things done or said.*
The loss of self-control will alternatively have a qualifying trigger if it was attributable to something done or said or both which:[212]

(a) constituted circumstances of an extremely grave character, and
(b) caused D to have a justifiable sense of being seriously wronged.

A sense of being seriously wronged by something done or said will not be justifiable, however, where D has incited what was done or said, in order to provide an excuse to use violence.[213]

Both the scope and the interpretation of this second qualifying trigger are troubling, with much of the concern being focused on the meaning of the phrases "extremely grave character" and "justifiable sense of being seriously wronged". Whether D has a sense of having been seriously wronged is a subjective test to be assessed with reference to D's own perception.[214] But, whether the circumstances were extremely grave, whether D was seriously wronged, and whether D's sense of grievance was justifiable, are to be evaluated objectively.[215] In *Dawson*,[216] irritating acts performed by the victim and even low-level criminality were considered to be a source for anger on D's part, but were not considered sufficient to constitute circumstances of an extremely grave character.

It remains unclear when D's sense of being seriously wronged can be considered to be justifiable rather than being merely excusable or understandable. In particular, when determining whether the sense of being seriously wronged is justifiable, it is not clear whether D's own circumstances can be taken into account or whether this is simply a matter for the jury to determine without regard to those circumstances.

The effect of this trigger is that certain cases where the old defence of provocation applied will not fall within the loss of control defence. So, for example, the defence of provocation was available in *Doughty*,[217] where D killed his crying baby. Such a defendant would not now have a defence of loss of control, since he would have no fear of serious violence and, even if the circumstances are extremely grave (which is unlikely), he has no justifiable sense of being seriously wronged by the crying. However, the defendant in *Mohammed*[218] might establish such a qualifying trigger by virtue of his daughter's continuation of a relationship which he had forbidden, arguably an "extremely grave" matter, and, having regard to the

[211] [2013] EWCA Crim 322, [2014] 1 WLR 947, [58].
[212] Coroners and Justice Act 2009, s. 55(4).
[213] *Ibid.*, s 55(6)(b). This has been called "self-induced loss of control": *Clinton* [2012] EWCA Crim 2, [2013] QB 1, [13].
[214] *Ibid.*, [12].
[215] *Ibid.*; *Dawes* [2013] EWCA Crim 322, [2014] 1 WLR 681, [61].
[216] [2021] EWCA Crim 40.
[217] (1986) 83 Cr App R 319 (CA).
[218] [2005] EWCA Crim 1880.

norms of his religion and culture, he might be characterised as having a justifiable sense of being seriously wronged. The prospect of the defence of loss of control being available in such cases of so-called "honour killings" is at least curtailed if D "acted in a considered desire for revenge",[219] although much will turn on whether D's motive can really be characterised as revenge. Alternatively, the defence would not succeed in such a case if the daughter's continuance of the relationship is not considered to be of "an extremely grave character", which is an objective test and does not turn on what D himself considered to be extremely grave. Further, the defence would only succeed if the third component of the defence is satisfied, namely that a person of a normal degree of tolerance and self-restraint might have reacted in a similar way. As we will see below, when determining how such a person might have reacted, the circumstances of D should be taken into account. If those circumstances include D's religious and cultural norms, as they did in *Mohammed* itself, the objective standard might potentially be regarded as satisfied by a particular jury.

*Mistaken triggers?*

In principle, loss of control can be established even where it arises from a mistake made by D. For the common law defence of provocation it was recognised that, where D had mistakenly assumed that V had done something to him amounting to provocation, he was entitled to be tried on the basis that his mistaken assumptions were true.[220] The same should be true under the loss of control defence, even if the mistake was induced by alcohol, as was also the case at common law.[221] Consequently, even loss of self-control arising from an honest but unreasonable mistake should suffice. This position can be justified because a successful plea of loss of control merely extenuates D's liability and does not completely excuse.

*Sexual infidelity*

One of the areas traditionally covered by the old defence of provocation was where D lost his self-control by virtue of his partner's infidelity and killed either the partner or her lover, or both of them. The second qualifying trigger in the loss of control defence might be considered to apply to such situations. The infidelity could be characterised as being "of an extremely grave character" and D could be considered to have a justifiable sense of being seriously wronged by the betrayal. Under the statute, however, the fact that what was done or said "constituted sexual infidelity" must be disregarded when considering this qualifying trigger.[222]

The interpretation of this exclusion was examined by the Court of Appeal in *Clinton*.[223] The Court emphasised that there was no definition of "sexual infidelity" in the legislation. It was acknowledged that the concept should be interpreted restrictively to confine it to conduct which relates directly and exclusively to sexual activity, so that words and acts

[219] Coroners and Justice Act 2009, s. 54(4).

[220] *Brown* (1776) 1 Leach 148, 168 ER 177.

[221] *Letenock* (1917) 12 Cr App R 221 (CA); *Wardrope* [1960] Crim LR 770 (Central Criminal Court). Intoxication is not generally relevant to the third component of the defence if it relates to D's capacity for tolerance and self-restraint (*Asmelash* [2013] EWCA Crim 157, [2014] QB 103), but that should not exclude it from being relevant to the first component, i.e. whether D had lost self-control.

[222] *Ibid.*, s. 55(6)(c). See Reed and Wake, "Sexual Infidelity Killings" in Reed and Bohlander (eds.), *Loss of Control and Diminished Responsibility* (2011) 117.

[223] [2012] EWCA Crim 2, [2013] QB 1.

constituting sexual activity would count, but the effects of infidelity would not, such as envy, jealousy or possessiveness. The inclusion of the word "infidelity" would suggest that there needs to be a relationship of some kind to which one party could be unfaithful,[224] although the relationship need not be a legally recognised one through marriage or a civil partnership. Consequently, on the facts of the Australian case *Stingel*,[225] the exclusion would not apply where a stalker found his victim having sexual intercourse; there was no infidelity by the victim. Further, the infidelity must be sexual. So, for example, if one partner told the other that she considered their relationship to be at an end and that she considered herself free to have sexual intercourse with anyone she wished, this would not be considered to be "sexual infidelity", because the sex would take place after the relationship had ended. It would, presumably, be different if she had sex with others whilst she continued in an ostensibly exclusive relationship with her partner.

A further difficulty of interpretation relates to the treatment of things "said" constituting sexual infidelity. Whilst this might encompass D who overhears her partner tell his lover, "I love you", it is not clear that this necessarily constitutes infidelity which is "sexual", but equally it is not clear that it necessarily "constitutes" sexual infidelity; that would depend on the context and the circumstances in which it was said.[226] A further difficulty arises where the words said are untrue. This would apparently not constitute sexual infidelity, so could not be excluded when considering the qualifying trigger, but a truthful statement would be excluded. As the Court of Appeal recognised in *Clinton*, such a distinction would be "illogical".[227] For this reason, the Court sensibly held that "things said" include admissions of sexual infidelity, true or untrue, and reports by others of sexual infidelity, accurate or inaccurate.

Whilst the legislation appears to prevent sexual infidelity from constituting a qualifying trigger, the Court of Appeal recognised in *Clinton* that, to avoid injustice and absurd results, a more subtle interpretation must be adopted. The provision was interpreted as excluding sexual infidelity when it is the *only* trigger of D's loss of self-control. But this is not a blanket exclusion, since events cannot be isolated from their context. Where sexual infidelity is integral to and forms an essential part of the context surrounding *another* potential qualifying trigger, evidence of sexual infidelity cannot be excluded, and must be taken into account in order to evaluate whether other circumstances relevant to that other potential qualifying trigger are grave and establish a justifiable sense of being wronged.[228] Consider the facts of *Clinton* itself. D had an argument with his wife following realisation that their marriage was at an end. During the argument, D's wife informed him that she was having an affair and had had sexual intercourse with a number of other men, which she described in graphic detail. D's wife taunted him about his previous failed attempts to commit suicide. D then killed his wife. The trial judge had withdrawn the defence of loss of control from the jury, on the ground that the defence was founded on sexual infidelity. The Court of Appeal considered this to be a misdirection because D's wife's confession of sexual infidelity was relevant to the evaluation of the taunts about D's attempts to commit suicide. A retrial was ordered, at which D pleaded guilty to murder, so the jury did not have the opportunity to

[224] *Ibid.*, [17].
[225] [1990] 171 CLR 313.
[226] *Clinton* [2012] EWCA Crim 2, [2013] QB 1, [25].
[227] *Ibid.*, [26].
[228] *Ibid.*, [39].

consider whether the totality of the evidence, including sexual infidelity, was sufficient to establish the existence of a qualifying trigger.

The exclusion of sexual infidelity as a circumstance that could establish a qualifying trigger was motivated by a concern that evidence of sexual infidelity had been abused when establishing the old defence of provocation. It is nevertheless unclear why it was felt that express provision was required for the exclusion of sexual infidelity, when the defence of loss of control will only be available where a person of a normal degree of tolerance and self-restraint might have acted as D did. Surely this objective standard provides a sufficient safeguard against potential abuse of the defence of loss of control: if the "normal person" might have acted as D did had she found her partner having an extramarital affair, the defence ought to be available.

*(c) Objectively understandable*

Thirdly, D's loss of control must be judged by reference to an objective standard, namely whether "a person of D's sex and age, with a normal degree of tolerance and self-restraint and in the circumstances of D, might have reacted in the same or in a similar way to D".[229] The reference to D's circumstances is a "reference to all D's circumstances other than those whose only relevance to D's conduct is that they bear on D's general capacity for tolerance or self-restraint".[230]

This test broadly replicates the test at common law after the decision in *Holley*,[231] although without reference to "the reasonable person" and replacing the language of "characteristics" with that of "circumstances". This is because personal characteristics of D relating to her general capacity for tolerance or self-restraint are to be excluded from this test. Consequently the effect of the line of authority ultimately endorsed in *Smith*, that mental disorder was relevant when evaluating D's conduct on the ground that it affected the capacity to exercise self-control, has not been adopted for the new defence.

All other circumstances of D are relevant, including D's social, religious and cultural context, and any circumstance which relates to the effect of the triggering event on D. If the facts of *Holley* arose today, the fact that D was an alcoholic would not be a relevant circumstance for this test since it related only to D's general capacity for tolerance and self-restraint. Things would be different had D been taunted about his alcoholism, in which case D's alcoholism would *also* have been relevant to the question of whether there existed a qualifying trigger: moreover, once that test had been passed, it would also have been relevant when assessing the impact of that qualifying trigger on the normal person. It follows that, if D was addicted to solvents and was taunted by V about the addiction,[232] this would be a relevant circumstance for the defence of loss of control, as would D's ethnicity, sexual orientation, impotence,[233] or eczema[234] if he was taunted about that, and even though the latter condition might be temporary. The age of D continues to be relevant as well. Consequently, *Camplin*[235] would be decided in the same way in respect of the defence of loss of

[229] Coroners and Justice Act 2009, s. 54(1)(c).
[230] *Ibid.*, s. 54(3).
[231] [2005] 2 AC 580.
[232] *Morhall* [1996] AC 90. See also *Asmelash* [2013] EWCA Crim 157, [2014] QB 103, [25].
[233] Cf. *Bedder* [1954] 2 All ER 801 (HL).
[234] *Morhall* [1996] AC 90, 99 (Lord Goff).
[235] [1978] AC 705.

control. In that case D, a 15-year-old boy, struck and killed V after V had sodomised and subsequently mocked him. The House of Lords recognised that the jury should be allowed to take into account D's age when determining the degree of self-control reasonably to be expected of him, since an adolescent would typically be more sensitive and volatile, when mocked, than would be a person of more mature years. Further, presumably a qualifying trigger could be identified on the basis of grave circumstances giving rise to a justifiable sense of being seriously wronged.

All circumstances other than those bearing on D's general capacity for tolerance or self-restraint can be taken into account. This will be particularly significant where D is suffering from mental disorder and it is necessary to determine whether this is a circumstance which can be taken into account. In *Rejmanski; Gassman*,[236] the Court of Appeal considered that, if the mental disorders in the conjoined appeals (namely post-traumatic stress disorder and an emotionally unstable personality disorder respectively) only reduced D's general capacity for tolerance or self-restraint they would not be relevant to the assessment of the objective test. But, if a mental disorder had relevance to D's conduct other than by bearing on her general capacity for tolerance or self-restraint, the jury could then take it into account. This should not, however, be used to undermine the principle that whether D's reaction was understandable is to be judged against "normal" standards, rather than the abnormal standard of the individual D. An example of a scenario where a mental disorder *would* be a relevant circumstance which could be taken into account is where a personality disorder had caused D to attempt suicide and he had then been taunted by the deceased about his failure to commit suicide. In *Sargeant*,[237] D's history of being abused, isolated, and feeling trapped was considered to be relevant when she had killed her abusive mother, but the mental disorder resulting from that abuse was not relevant to the objective test because it affected her general capacity for tolerance or self-restraint, even though it was considered to be relevant to the gravity of the qualifying trigger.

*Distinguishing two parts of the objectively understandable test*

There are some fine distinctions at work here, and much room for confusion. It may be helpful to think about the operation of this test in terms of the following three-step inquiry.

First, determine what is the applicable *expected standard of self-control* in the case at hand: that is, what level of self-control the law demands of this particular defendant. This step is objective, and is fairly straightforward. D is expected to exhibit the ordinary powers of self-restraint that would be normal for any ordinary person of the same age and sex as D. In practice, most cases will involve a uniform expectation based on an ordinary adult; but if D is young, as in *Camplin*, the expected standard of self-control may be lower, and should reflect what level of self-control a child of D's age would ordinarily possess. But any other considerations, such as the mental disorder in *Rejmanski*, are excluded from the expected standard.

Secondly, evaluate the likely gravity or seriousness of the taunts or other triggering events that are bound up with the qualifying triggers (such as the sexual infidelity in *Clinton*). This second inquiry is more personalised. It asks how much impact would those taunts or triggering events have had *for D*? To answer this question, we can take into account all of D's circumstances, including personal characteristics going beyond age and sex. Thus, the fact that in *Camplin* D had just been sodomised by V was a relevant factor to consider when

[236] [2017] EWCA Crim 2061, [2018] 1 WLR 2721.
[237] [2019] EWCA Crim 1088.

evaluating how severe were V's taunts about D's sexuality. And in *Sergeant*, D's history of abuse could be taken into consideration when evaluating just how grave was her mother's most recent abusive act.

Finally, we must measure the gravity of the taunts or other triggering events (the second inquiry) against the expected standard of self-control (the first inquiry). If the overall gravity of the taunts or other triggering events upon *a person such as D* meets or exceeds the expected standard of self-control, the defence can be available. It is an admittedly artificial comparison, but this is what the law requires. In effect, we ask how *provocative* the taunts or other triggering events would have been to somebody in D's shoes; then ask, might *any* event of similar provocativeness have caused an ordinary person of D's age and sex to lose self-control?

*Some case studies.*
The significance of this objective test which excludes circumstances bearing on D's general capacity for tolerance or self-restraint can be assessed by reference to the facts of some of the cases relating to the operation of the old defence of provocation. For example, in *McArthy*,[238] D lost control after receiving an unwelcome sexual request from V. The jury was entitled to consider the fact that, some 20 minutes earlier, V had indecently assaulted D. Similarly, in both *Thornton*[239] and *Ahluwalia*,[240] the whole course of marital discord endured by the respective defendants was admitted as evidence relevant to the weight of the provocation and the impact it would have had. But the recognition in those cases that "battered woman syndrome" was a relevant characteristic for the defence of provocation would appear not to be relevant to the objective test for the defence of loss of control, because the syndrome relates to the ability to exercise self-control, although it would be relevant to the qualifying trigger of circumstances of an extremely grave character and being seriously wronged.[241] The same applies to *Humphreys*,[242] which concerned immaturity and attention seeking by self-harm, and *Dryden*,[243] involving D's "obsessive and eccentric" personality. Common to all these cases was the presence of expert testimony indicating that these conditions were beyond the normal range of personality variation and constituted discrete syndromes. But they were considered to be relevant solely because they affected D's ability to exercise self-control. In other words, their only relevance is to "D's general capacity for tolerance or self-restraint" and so must now be ignored when assessing whether an ordinary person might have reacted as D did. Such a conclusion is consistent with the approach adopted in *Roberts*,[244] where, although expert witnesses were prepared to testify that pre-lingual deaf persons typically experienced raised anger levels because of the frustrations inherent in coping with their disability, such evidence was not considered to be relevant to the provocation defence. The degree of self-control to be required of such a defendant was the same degree of self-control to be expected of any ordinary person of D's age and sex. Similarly, the decision of the Privy Council in *Luc Thiet-Thuan*,[245] that D's brain damage, which induced

[238] [1954] 2 QB 105 (CCA).
[239] [1992] 1 All ER 306 (CA).
[240] [1992] 4 All ER 889 (CA).
[241] For criticism of the relevance of this syndrome and the related notion of learned helplessness to defences, including loss of control, on the ground that its recognition lacks sufficient scientific integrity, see Loveless, "*R v GAC*: Battered Woman 'Syndromization'" [2014] *Crim LR* 655.
[242] [1995] 4 All ER 1008 (CA).
[243] [1995] 4 All ER 987 (CA).
[244] [1990] Crim LR 122 (CA).
[245] [1997] AC 131 (PC).

impulsive behaviour in D, should not be taken into account remains relevant for the defence of loss of control. Once the loss of control and the qualifying trigger have been established (for which D's brain damage can be taken into account), D's reaction must be measured against that of someone without such brain damage. The decision of the House of Lords in *Smith*[246] would, however, now be different. In that case it was held that D's depression was relevant to the defence of provocation, even though the quarrel leading to V's death at the hands of D did not involve any pejorative reference by V to D's depressed condition. The depression simply affected D's capacity to exercise self-control and so would not now be relevant to the third objective stage of the loss of control defence. Further, intoxication is generally not a relevant circumstance, because it relates to D's capacity for tolerance and self-restraint;[247] similarly if D was suffering from withdrawal symptoms.

Crucially, the fact that all circumstances other than those bearing on D's general capacity for tolerance or self-restraint can be taken into account when assessing the objective test means that sexual infidelity is relevant at this stage of the analysis, even if it has been excluded when considering the second qualifying trigger. This was confirmed by the Court of Appeal in *Clinton*.[248] This emphasises the absurdity of the exclusion of "sexual infidelity" in the first place. If this can be taken into account when considering the objectively understandable test but may be excluded as being a qualifying trigger, this makes the task of the judge in directing the jury very difficult, and the task of the jury almost impossible. As the Court said in *Clinton*:[249]

> "there will be occasions when the jury would be both disregarding and considering the same evidence. That is, to put it neutrally, counter intuitive."

It is simply not possible to compartmentalise evidence of sexual infidelity so that it is only considered at the stage of evaluating the objectively understandable nature of D's reactions. If evidence of such infidelity is adduced, it will inevitably also be taken into account when evaluating the qualifying trigger.

### (d) *Critique of the loss of control defence*

It is clear that the application of the defence of loss of control will be more limited than the defence of provocation, largely because of the need to establish a qualifying trigger. However, the reality is likely to be that in many cases the same result would be achieved whether at common law or under the statute, but some cases would be decided differently under the new defence. This can be assessed with reference to the case of a woman who, having been abused for many years by her partner, suffers from a recognised psychological syndrome and then deliberately kills her abusive partner. In determining whether she will have a defence of loss of control,[250] it is necessary to consider the three requirements in turn. First, she must have killed as the result of a loss of self-control. Importantly, this

[246] [2001] 1 AC 146. For critical commentary on *Smith* see Gardner and Macklem, "Compassion without Respect? Nine Fallacies in *R. v Smith*" [2001] *Crim LR* 623.

[247] *Asmelash* [2013] EWCA Crim 157, [2014] QB 103. Intoxication might, however, be relevant where D has made a mistake because then it is not only relevant to D's capacity for tolerance and self-restraint: see Ashworth's commentary at [2013] Crim LR 599, 601.

[248] [2012] EWCA Crim 2, [2013] QB 1.

[249] *Ibid.*, [32].

[250] Self-defence as a complete defence would be a preferred plea, but this is rarely successful for women who kill their abuser: Howes, Williams, and Wistrich, "Women Who Kill: Why Self-defence Rarely Works for Women Who Kill their Abuser" [2021] *Crim LR* 945.

need not happen as a sudden response to a particular event. Secondly, the relevant trigger is most likely to be that her loss of self-control was attributable to her fear of serious violence from V, although this may be difficult to establish where D has suffered from coercive and controlling behaviour. Finally, it must be considered whether a woman of her age and in her circumstances with normal tolerance and self-restraint would have reacted in a similar way. The key question is whether it is relevant that she has been abused for a long time and suffers from a syndrome as a consequence. If the syndrome relates exclusively to D's general capacity for tolerance or self-restraint, then it cannot be taken into account when determining whether the third objective test is satisfied. However, it is likely that the history of abuse will support the existence, and explain the impact, of the relevant qualifying trigger. Further, it has been recognised that evidence of coercive control by V over D, which involves systemic coercion, degradation, and control,[251] may be taken into account when applying the objective test.[252] Crucially, however, it is not obvious that a woman who suffers from a recognised psychological condition following an extended period of domestic abuse who kills her abusive partner is any more likely to have a successful partial defence of loss of control than she would have had a defence of provocation at common law.

The structure of the defence of loss of control is complicated: the meaning of the qualifying triggers is opaque, especially as regards a justifiable sense of being seriously wronged; moreover, the objective test, while avoiding the language of the reasonable person and D's characteristics, will still be difficult for the jury to apply, especially as the jury must disregard those circumstances of D which relate exclusively to a general capacity for tolerance and self-restraint. Judicial directions to the jury relating to this defence are likely to be excessively complicated. The Law Commission is reviewing the partial defence of loss of control as part of its review of the law of homicide, with particular, but not exclusive, reference to the consideration of the defence (and other defences) for the victims of abuse who kill their abuser in the light of the modern understanding of domestic abuse on victims. The Law Commission is expected to report in 2028.

## § 10.6 Diminished responsibility

Diminished responsibility is a statutory partial defence to murder, first introduced into English law by section 2 of the Homicide Act 1957. Subsection (1) of section 2 was amended by section 52 of the Coroners and Justice Act 2009,[253] and now reads as follows:

> (1) A person ("D") who kills or is a party to the killing of another is not to be convicted of murder if D was suffering from an abnormality of mental functioning which—
>
> (a) arose from a recognised medical condition,
> (b) substantially impaired D's ability to do one or more of the things mentioned in subsection (1A), and
> (c) provides an explanation for D's acts and omissions in doing or being a party to the killing.

[251] And is an offence in its own right: Serious Crime Act 2015, s. 76.
[252] *Challen* [2019] EWCA Crim 916.
[253] Mackay, "The New Diminished Responsibility Plea" [2010] *Crim LR* 290; Mackay, "The New Diminished Responsibility Plea: More than Mere Modernisation?; Fortson, "The Modern Partial Defence of Diminished Responsibility" in Reed and Bohlander (eds.), *Loss of Control and Diminished Responsibility* (2011) 21.

(1A) Those things are—

(a) to understand the nature of D's conduct;
(b) to form a rational judgement;
(c) to exercise self-control.

(1B) For the purposes of subsection (1)(c), an abnormality of mental functioning provides an explanation for D's conduct if it causes, or is a significant contributory factor in causing, D to carry out that conduct.

Unlike an insanity plea,[254] a successful defence of diminished responsibility does not secure an outright acquittal. The effect is to reduce the offence from murder to voluntary manslaughter, avoiding the mandatory life sentence attached to the former.[255] For offences other than murder, there is no defence of diminished responsibility, and matters which would fall within section 2 in the context of murder become matters of mitigation of sentence, not defence.[256]

A large range of culpability falls within the provision. One defendant may successfully plead the defence and receive a non-custodial sentence such as a hospital order with or even without restriction, whereas another defendant may receive a very substantial term of imprisonment. Each outcome may be justifiable in its own terms, varying by the degree of D's impaired capacity and his future dangerousness. It is also possible for courts to provide an order for hospital treatment within a prison sentence. Section 45A of the Mental Health Act 1983 empowers a court to hand down a sentence of imprisonment but direct that D goes first to hospital for treatment. Under the section 45A regime, D remains a prisoner rather than a patient and any release is a matter for the Parole Board, the decisions of which are based on public safety rather than the interests of D. In *Vowles*,[257] the Court of Appeal stressed what it saw as the virtue of section 45A, relative to other forms of disposal.[258]

### *(i) The burden of proof*

Section 2(2) places the burden of proof on the defence.[259] On general principles, any burden placed on the defence is discharged on a balance of probabilities.[260] The burden was placed on the defence as it was thought that it would be anomalous to arrange the matter any differently from the position prevailing for insanity. It remains unclear why insanity and diminished responsibility should be treated any differently from defences such as self-defence or duress in the matter of proof. The determining factor has been considered to be the presumption of sanity, but that presumption could surely have been displaced on the basis of evidential onus rather than the imposition of a full probative burden.[261]

[254] Below, § 19.2.
[255] Homicide Act 1957, s. 2(3).
[256] For a proposal that a defence of diminished responsibility be more widely available, see Horder, "Pleading Involuntary Lack of Capacity" (1993) 52 *CLJ* 298. See, also, Brink, *Fair Opportunity and Responsibility* (2021).
[257] [2015] EWCA Crim 45, [2015] 1 WLR 5131.
[258] For criticism of *Vowles*, see Peay, "Responsibility, Culpability and the Sentencing of Mentally Disordered Offenders: Objectives in Conflict" [2016] *Crim LR* 152.
[259] Homicide Act 1957, s. 2(2).
[260] *Carr-Briant* [1943] KB 607 (CA).
[261] See below, § 19.2(i)(c).

Be that as it may, the Court of Appeal has held that there is no breach of Article 6(2) of the ECHR in placing the burden of proof on D, ruling it not to be disproportionate principally because the burden did not fall to D until the prosecution had established a *prima facie* case of murder.[262] In practice, this is problematic. The same facts may, on occasion, raise issues of both diminished responsibility and loss of control. In the case of the latter, a burden of disproof falls to the prosecution.[263] It cannot be easy for juries to assess the same facts raising two separate but overlapping issues under different standards of proof. In *Wilcocks*,[264] this difference was justified on the ground that diminished responsibility relates to D's internal mental condition. Yet the same could be said, for example, when D denies theft when he claims to have picked up V's watch merely to look at it rather than to keep it. Nonetheless, the prosecution has to prove an intent permanently to deprive in such cases, and rightly so. Furthermore, in practice evidence about D's mental state will be given by medical experts who have examined D, rather than D himself. Nevertheless, Article 6(2) compatibility has been affirmed consistently by the courts.

### *(ii) The elements of diminished responsibility*

According to the statute, there are four elements to the defence:

*Element 1*: There must be an abnormality of mental functioning.
*Element 2*: The abnormality must arise from a recognised medical condition.
*Element 3*: The abnormality must give rise to a substantial impairment of mental ability.
*Element 4*: This impairment must provide an explanation for D's acts or omissions in doing or being a party to the killing.

By contrast with the insanity defence, there is no formal legal requirement that medical evidence must be submitted as a condition of raising the defence. However, it can be readily appreciated that expert medical evidence is a practical necessity if the defence is to be successful.[265] Despite the greater medicalisation of the diminished responsibility defence, whether the elements of the defence are satisfied remains a question for the jury. A count on the indictment alleging murder will therefore be withdrawn from the jury only in exceptional cases, where unanimous expert evidence confirming the elements of the defence is left entirely unchallenged by the prosecution. *Brennan*[266] provides one example of such an exceptional case: the Court of Appeal ruled that, in the light of unchallenged expert evidence establishing diminished responsibility, the trial judge was wrong not to withdraw the charge of murder. This ruling was endorsed by the Supreme Court in *Golds*: "If the jury is to be invited to reject expert opinion some rational basis for doing so must be suggested."[267] However, in cases where expert evidence is contested, including cases where unanimous expert evidence is capable of being rebutted by other evidence considered in the round, a charge of murder should be left for the jury to consider. This was usefully illustrated in

[262] *Lambert* [2002] QB 1112 (CA).
[263] Coroners and Justice Act 2009, s. 54(5).
[264] [2016] EWCA Crim 2043, [2017] 4 WLR 39.
[265] *Bunch* [2013] EWCA Crim 2498.
[266] [2014] EWCA Crim 2387, [2015] 1 WLR 2060.
[267] [2016] UKSC 61, [2016] 1 WLR 5231, [49].

*Hussain*,[268] where the Court of Appeal held that the trial judge was correct not to withdraw the allegation of murder, despite unanimous expert evidence suggesting D satisfied the requirements of diminished responsibility.

Prior to the 2009 reformulation of the defence, the ultimate question was whether D's *responsibility* for the killing of V was substantially impaired, essentially a matter for the moral sense of the jury—a judgment informed but not compelled by the medical evidence. Indeed, in the early days of the defence, trial judges were wont to direct the jury to consider whether D was on the borderline of insanity. The Supreme Court has rejected that approach: "It is not usually helpful to direct juries whether [at the time of D's act] he was on the borderline of insanity."[269] The ultimate question is now more fact-specific: is it more likely than not that the recognised medical condition (which must substantially impair either D's understanding of the nature of his conduct, or D's ability to form a rational judgement, or D's ability to exercise self-control) provides an *explanation* for D's acts or omissions? That is a question amenable to psychiatric testimony, allowing expert witnesses to give their opinion on whether the relevant mental abilities were substantially impaired.

### *(a) Element 1: An abnormality of mental functioning*

Abnormality of mental functioning is a free-standing element of the defence but, as will be examined below, there must also be proof that there was a substantial impairment of one or more of D's capacities to understand the nature of his conduct, to form a rational judgement, or to exercise self-control.[270] In cases where there is substantial impairment of the capacity to understand one's conduct or to make rational judgements, that of itself will very likely establish abnormality of mental functioning. Less obvious will be cases where D claims that his ability to exercise self-control was substantially impaired due to psychopathy or forms of personality disorder, but D lacks any delusional beliefs and is not afflicted by auditory or visual hallucinations.[271] The objects of D's desires may be reprehensible, but that does not entail that they arise from an abnormality of mental functioning. In such cases the line between a substantially impaired capacity to control oneself and a simple failure to control oneself may be very fine,[272] and a jury's perception that D is abnormal and by that token not fully responsible for his acts may be significant.

In *Blackman*,[273] for example, D, a sergeant, whilst serving in Afghanistan, killed a wounded but no longer dangerous insurgent by shooting him in the presence of the platoon D commanded. The verdict of murder he received when court-martialled was controversial for several newspapers, but understandable. D had ensured that his killing of V was off-camera and advised his troops to keep the incident to themselves because, as he said, "I've just broken the Geneva Convention."[274] His motive was to avenge friends and colleagues killed

[268] [2019] EWCA Crim 666.

[269] *Golds* [2016] UKSC 61, [2016] 1 WLR 5231, [12].] (Lord Hughes).

[270] Homicide Act 1957, s. 2(1A).

[271] In *Gower* [2025] *Crim LR* 220, a temporary dissociative state in response to overwhelming stress was sufficient to establish diminished responsibility.

[272] Wootton, "Diminished Responsibility: A Layman's View" [1960] *LQR* 224. Although the article deals with the previous version of the defence, the same problem of differentiating between the difficulties of self-control that can beset anyone and those failures of self-control that partially excuse are present in the current law.

[273] [2017] EWCA Crim 190 (C–MAC).

[274] *Ibid.*, [22].

or seriously injured by insurgents—a very understandable emotion, in no way abnormal. On appeal, D's conviction was quashed and a verdict of voluntary manslaughter on the ground of diminished responsibility substituted, because insufficient note had been taken at court-martial of his "adjustment disorder of moderate severity" brought about by the conditions of his military service, a lack of workplace support, and the recent death of his father.[275] This apparently substantially impaired his abilities to make a rational judgement about taking revenge and to exercise self-control.[276] As such, a finding of diminished responsibility was appropriate. Yet in *Blackman*, we are a long way away from conditions such as schizophrenia and bipolar disorder. *Blackman* should be considered to be a borderline case.

*(b) Element 2: Arising from a recognised medical condition*

The abnormality of mental functioning must arise from a recognised medical condition.[277] Although the defence of diminished responsibility most readily brings to mind forms of mental disorder such as schizophrenia or bipolar disorder, transient disorders of the mind brought about by conditions such as diabetes and arteriosclerosis should also readily fall within the category of recognised medical condition. Mere stress brought about by, say, the protracted suffering of a gravely ill partner will not suffice unless the stress induces a recognised medical condition such as depression. Again, this requirement underscores the practical necessity for expert medical evidence.

There is no approved list of recognised medical conditions. This allows the defence to be sensitive to advances in the expert consensus about what amounts to a medical condition. There may be disputes among experts over what amounts to a medical condition. In resolving those disputes, reference will typically be made to the World Health Organization's *International Statistical Classification of Diseases and Related Health Problems* (ICD-11) and the American Medical Association's *Diagnostic and Statistical Manual* (DSM-5). Given the prestige of these glossaries, it would be tempting for courts to assume that, if a particular condition relating to D is described in one or both of these compilations as a medical condition, it is a recognised medical condition for the purposes of the diminished responsibility defence. That temptation should be resisted. The term "recognised medical condition" is a statutory term and is ultimately a question of law to be resolved by the judge. For instance, DSM-5 lists "intermittent explosive disorder" as a medical condition.[278] It is far from obvious whether this should be accepted as a recognised medical condition for the purposes of the defence of diminished responsibility. As Hughes LJ observed of this particular medical condition in *Dowds*, "any suggestion that it could give rise to a defence, whether because it amounted to an impairment of mental functioning or otherwise, would, to say the least, demand extremely careful attention".[279]

The decision in *Dowds* demonstrates that the ICD-11 and DSM-5 are merely indicative and not conclusive regarding what in law makes for a recognised medical condition. In that case D had killed his wife when he was acutely intoxicated. He was a binge drinker but not alcohol-dependent. It was argued for D that a state of acute intoxication was of

275 *Ibid.*, [32].
276 *Ibid.*, [101].
277 Homicide Act 1957, s. 2(1)(a).
278 Also listed are other criminogenic conditions such as kleptomania and sexual sadism.
279 *Dowds* [2012] EWCA Crim 281, [2012] 1 WLR 2576, [31].

itself a recognised medical condition because it was listed as such in both the ICD and DSM.[280] The Court of Appeal held that the diminished responsibility defence had to be read against the well-established principle that voluntary intoxication was only relevant to dis-proof of mens rea in murder cases.[281] Consequently, acute voluntary intoxication was not a recognised medical condition for the purposes of the law.[282] *Dowds* follows the position taken by the House of Lords in *Dietschmann*[283] on the law of diminished responsibility prior to its 2009 reformulation: voluntary intoxication will neither assist nor prevent a defence of diminished responsibility. The question is, *putting the state of intoxication to one side*, whether the elements of the defence are made out.[284] For example, in the combined cases of *Joyce and Kay*,[285] the Court of Appeal considered and distinguished two cases in both of which D was intoxicated and schizophrenic. In the first case, D1's defence of diminished responsibility was rejected because his schizophrenia did not have a substantial impact on his conduct, whilst his intoxication, which did have a significant impact, was voluntary in that his condition did not cause a compulsion to drink. D2, however, successfully raised diminished responsibility. He was voluntarily intoxicated, but his schizophrenia played a substantial part in explaining his killing of V. The same approach is taken where D's medical condition is directly related to intoxication, as long is that condition can be distinguished from the state of intoxication. In *Lindo*,[286] for example, the Court of Appeal distinguished voluntary intoxication from drug- or alcohol-induced psychosis, a condition that can last days or even months after drugs are no longer active in D's system. Drug- or alcohol-induced psychosis is a recognised medical condition on which a plea of diminished responsibility may be based. So too for drug or alcohol addiction. Addiction is indisputably a medical condition. The question, again, is whether that underlying condition is capable of explaining or causing D's conduct, ignoring any intoxicants in D's system at the time of the offence.[287] Causal distinctions of this kind are far from straightforward; and they continue to generate problems for the courts in practice.[288]

Although inclusion as a medical condition in ICD-11 or DSM-5 does not guarantee that any particular condition relating to D will be regarded as a recognised medical condition, neither should the absence of the condition from the lists entail its dismissal as a recognised medical condition. If satisfied that a reputable body of medical experts considers D's condition to be a medical condition, the judge can classify it as a recognised medical condition.[289] That said, there will be some facets of D's psychological dispositions or state of development which may have a bearing on her responsibility for her acts but which cannot be plausibly medicalised so as to bring her case within the parameters of the defence. Under the previous law, provision was made for "arrested or retarded development of mind" and the Law

[280] *Ibid.*, [33].
[281] Below, § 18.4. See Simester, "Intoxication Is Never a Defence" [2009] *Crim LR* 3.
[282] *Dowds* [2012] EWCA Crim 281, [2012] 1 WLR 2576, [34–35].
[283] [2003] UKHL 10, [2003] 1 AC 1209.
[284] Sullivan, "Intoxicants and Diminished Responsibility" [1994] *Crim LR* 156; cf. Gibson, "Intoxicants and Diminished Responsibility: The Impact of the Coroners and Justice Act 2009" [2011] *Crim LR* 909.
[285] [2017] EWCA Crim 647, [2017] 4 WLR 121.
[286] [2016] EWCA Crim 1940.
[287] See *Wood* [2008] EWCA Crim 1305; *Stewart* [2010] EWCA Crim 2159.
[288] See, for example, *Nijhawan* [2022] EWCA Crim 10 (causative role of prescription medication); *Foy* [2020] EWCA Crim 270 (mental disorder and intoxication).
[289] Criminal courts would find guidance on what may be considered a reputable if minority medical opinion from the tort cases of *Bolam v Friern Hospital Management Committee* [1957] 1 WLR 582 (DC) and *Bolitho v City and Hackney Health Authority* [1998] AC 232.

Commission recommended that any reformulated version of the defence should make provision for developmental immaturity for persons under the age of 18.[290] That proposal was explicitly rejected by the government, which was of the view that conditions such as autism and learning disabilities were sufficiently accommodated within the term "recognised medical condition".[291] Because of this determination, the fact that D is, say, eleven years old, immature for her age, and therefore suggestible will not assist her. There is potential for injustice in cases of this kind.

*(c) Element 3: Substantial impairment of mental functioning*

As the definition in the reformulated section 2(1) of the Homicide Act 1957 makes clear, diminished responsibility requires that D must have a substantially impaired ability to understand the nature of her conduct, form a rational judgement, or exercise self-control.[292] It suffices for this third element that at least one of these abilities is substantially impaired.

*Substantial.*

Prior to 2009, the old diminished responsibility defence required proof of a "substantial impairment" of D's responsibility for his acts or omissions, and so jurisprudence already existed on the meaning of the term "substantial" in this context. In *R*,[293] Judge LCJ considered that the meaning of substantial should not typically be further explained to a jury, but added that use of the word indicated that the impact of conditions which were "trivial and insignificant" were not sufficient to establish the defence. He also added that the "defence should be available without the defendant having to show that his mental responsibility for his actions was so grossly impaired as to be extinguished". It was initially thought that the same approach would apply to the amended defence. However, in *Golds*,[294] Elias LJ identified a tension between two cases decided under the pre-2009 law, namely *Lloyd*[295] and *Simcox*.[296] On his Lordship's reading of these cases, there remained an unresolved question: is it the case that any impairment that is more than trivial and insignificant should be treated as "substantial", or is it the case that something more than trivial and insignificant might still not be "substantial"?

This matter was reviewed by the Supreme Court in *Golds*.[297] The Court advised that in many cases where evidence in favour of diminished responsibility was accepted, it would be clear from this evidence that the impairment was substantial. Where guidance was needed, it should take this form:[298]

> "It is not the law that any impairment beyond the merely trivial will suffice. The impairment must of course pass the merely trivial to be considered, just as it need not reach the total, but whether, when it has passed the trivial, it can properly be regarded as substantial, is a matter for the jury in the individual case, aided as it will be by the experts' exposition of the kind of impairment which the condition under consideration may have generated in the accused."

290 Law Com. No. 304, *Murder, Manslaughter and Infanticide* (2006) paras. 5.125–5.137.

291 Ministry of Justice, *Murder, Manslaughter and Infanticide: Proposals for Reform of the Law. Summary of Responses and Government Position*, Response to Consultation, CP(R) 19/08 (2009).

292 Homicide Act 1957, s. 2(1A).

293 [2010] EWCA Crim 194, *sub nom Ramchurn* [2010] 2 Cr App R 3, [15].

294 [2014] EWCA Crim 748, [2015] 1 WLR 1030.

295 [1967] 1 QB 175 (CA).

296 [1964] Crim LR 402 (CA).

297 [2016] UKSC 61, [2016] 1 WLR 5231.

298 *Ibid.*, [41].

This guidance has attracted criticism on the ground that it has narrowed the scope of the partial defence.[299] This may well be the case. It is also unfortunate that the term "substantial" should have a different meaning here (significant or weighty) than it does when used in the context of a "substantial cause" (something that is more than *de minimis*).[300] However, the guidance is consistent with the ordinary understanding of the word (as in "a substantial rise in salary" or a "substantial delay"), and the merits of tracking common usage in terms addressed to a jury should not be underestimated.

In *Squelch*,[301] the three forensic psychiatric witnesses were agreed that D suffered from paranoid personality disorder and that, when he killed V, this disorder affected his ability to understand the nature of his conduct, his ability to form a rational judgement, and to exercise self-control. Two of these experts opined that his impaired ability to do these things was substantial, yet the third expert disagreed. Therefore, a jury direction on the meaning of substantial was required. It took this form: "'Substantially' is an ordinary English word on which you will reach a conclusion in this case, based upon you own experience of ordinary life. It means less than total and more than trivial. Where you the jury draw the line is a matter for your collective judgment."[302] The Court of Appeal commended this direction for reflecting the Supreme Court's judgment in *Golds* in a clear and concise way.

*Three categories of mental functioning.*
The three categories of mental functioning specified in section 2(1A) are distinct,[303] and a substantial impairment of any one may suffice to establish the defence of diminished responsibility. However, it may well be the case that D's mental abnormality substantially impairs more than one of the categories of mental functioning. In *Blackman*,[304] for example, D's adjustment disorder substantially impaired both his capacity to make a rational judgement and his capacity for self-control.

The first category, an impaired capacity to understand the nature of one's conduct, is reminiscent of the first limb of the *M'Naghten* Rules defining insanity, which, as we will see, has received a very narrow interpretation.[305] Indeed, in the Law Commission report that preceded the reform of the diminished responsibility defence,[306] the example used to illustrate this category was of a 10-year-old boy who did not understand the physical consequences of his harmful actions.[307]

By contrast, the second category—the ability to form a rational judgement—on its face is much wider than the requirements for the insanity defence. The Law Commission clearly intended the impairment of this ability to be found in cases which fall outside the insanity

[299] Gibson, "Diminished Responsibility in *Golds* and Beyond: Insights and Implications" [2017] *Crim LR* 543; Mackay, "*R* v *Golds*" [2017] *Archbold Review* 4.
[300] Above, § 4.2.
[301] [2017] EWCA Crim 204.
[302] *Ibid.*, [37].
[303] Mackay, "The Impairment Factors in the New Diminished Responsibility Plea" [2018] *Crim LR* 462.
[304] [2017] EWCA Crim 190.
[305] Below, § 19.2(ii)(c).
[306] Law Com. No. 304, *Murder, Manslaughter and Infanticide* (2006).
[307] In the example, the boy has been left to play violent video games for much of his life and he loses his temper and kills another child who attempts to steal his game. He assumes that his victim can be later revived, as happens in the game: *ibid.*, para. 5.121(1)(a).

defence.[308] It is important to understand that what is rational in this context refers primarily to the ability for sequential and ordered thought about obtaining an objective, and is not concerned with whether persons of normal sensibility and morals would seek the objective that D sought when he killed V. To use an example from *Conroy*:[309] D, a gangland boss, may demonstrate his capacity for rational thought by carefully planning the capture and killing of his rival, V. Yet the capacity to plan and execute a certain outcome will not necessarily establish a capacity for rational thought. To take another example from *Conroy*: D, a paranoid schizophrenic, may consider his neighbour V to be a dangerous Martian, and kill him after planning carefully how and when to do so. It would be possible for a jury to find this killing an irrational act induced by an abnormality of mind, despite the planned nature of the killing. In *Conroy* itself, D was autistic. He was sexually attracted to V and conceived a plan to strangle her in her bed, take her body to his room, perform sexual acts on her body, and then return her body to her bedroom. D carried out this plan to the extent of killing V by strangulation and was then interrupted. Defence experts testified that the use of such means to obtain sexual gratification indicated substantially impaired rationality. The prosecution expert was of the opinion that D's planning demonstrated a capacity for rational thought in the matter of killing V. The Court of Appeal, confirming D's conviction for murder, ruled that the trial judge was correct in allowing the jury to resolve for themselves whether D was sufficiently capable of rational thought when planning to kill and in killing V.

The third category of mental functioning--impairment of the ability to exercise self-control--also covers territory beyond the insanity defence, which—as will be seen below, § 19.2—makes no accommodation for volitional incapacity. In *Byrne*,[310] a successful defence of diminished responsibility under the old law was founded on evidence of perverted sexual urges which, according to expert testimony, were more difficult to control than normal sexual desires. Such a case would go to the jury under the current law if there was expert testimony that D's perverted sexual urges arose from a recognised medical condition and were substantially more difficult to control than ordinary sexual desires. In this manner, courts and juries are required to mark a difficult distinction between impaired capacity to exercise self-control (qualifying) and simple loss of temper (not qualifying). This was usefully illustrated in *Sargeant*,[311] where the Court of Appeal accepted that the prosecution had advanced a rational basis for the claim that D's apparent loss of control was the result of a loss of temper following a dispute over money with her mother, whom D then killed.

It can be concluded with some confidence that, in determining whether D has a substantial impairment of mental functioning, the courts will give an interpretation attuned to the rationale of this partial defence—which is not concerned with defendants who lack culpability, but with defendants who lack *sufficient* culpability for a murder conviction, and

[308] As an example of an impairment to make a rational judgement, the Law Commission instanced a depressed man who has been a long-term carer for his terminally ill wife. She has requested many times that he kill her and he finally complies because "I felt that I would never think straight again until I had given her what she wanted" (*ibid.*, para. 5.121(2)(c)). It is doubtful whether a defence of insanity could be raised on those facts.

[309] [2017] EWCA Crim 81, [2017] 2 Cr App R 26.

[310] [1960] 2 QB 396 (CA).

[311] [2019] EWCA Crim 1088

who are appropriately excepted from the mandatory life sentence that follows it. Moreover, it must always be borne in mind, when assessing whether D has a substantial impairment of mental functioning, that the impairment of mental functioning of itself does not ground the defence. The final question is whether the impairment provides an explanation for D's acts and omissions in doing (or being a party to) the killing.

*(d) Element 4: An abnormality of mental functioning that provides an explanation for D's conduct*

The requirements of the diminished responsibility defence are, in an important sense, *less* accommodating than those of insanity.[312] D's insanity defence will succeed if he proves that, as a result of a "disease of the mind", he did not know his conduct was wrong or that he did not understand the nature and quality of his actions. In the case of diminished responsibility, however, it will not suffice to prove that a recognised medical condition undermined D's rationality or powers of understanding, even if those faculties are substantially impaired. The disability alone does not suffice: it must provide an *explanation* for the acts or omissions related to D's killing of V.[313] That explanation must establish, on the balance of probabilities, that D's abnormality of mental functioning "causes, or is a significant contributory factor in causing, D to carry out the conduct".[314]

On the face of it, the statutory language provides that the linkage between the substantial impairment of mental functioning and the killing must be causal. That was the view of the government,[315] and is the natural reading of the provision. However, there could have been more explicitness on this important matter. The provision contains no locution such as "if and only if". Mackay and Hughes argue that the requirement for a causal link is unprincipled and impractical, and so the provision should be read—using the language of "explanation"—to apply as expansively as possible beyond a strict causal nexus between the other features of diminished responsibility and the killing.[316] But this argument lacks support from either the statute or the case law. There is no mention of non-causal explanations in the statute. Their omission suggests that a causal linkage is indeed necessary. It is notable in this regard that a unanimous Supreme Court in *Golds* noted, albeit *obiter*, that the Law Commission "was concerned to ensure that a requirement for causation was explicitly incorporated into the proposed statutory test, *as it now has been*".[317]

In terms of causal doctrine, no distinction should be drawn between a "cause" of an event and a "significant contributory factor in causing" an event. A significant contributory factor is clearly some input into bringing about the event which is more than *de minimis* and is

[312] Below, § 19.2.

[313] Homicide Act 1957, s. 2(1)(c). Mackay and Hughes, "Explaining the 'Explanation' Requirement in the New Diminished Responsibility Plea" [2021] *Crim LR* 461.

[314] Homicide Act 1957, s. 2(1B).

[315] "We do not believe that this partial defence should succeed when random coincidence has brought together the activity of the person and the recognised medical condition . . . there must have been at least a significant contributory factor in causing the defendant to act as he did. We do not require the defence to prove that it was the only cause or the main cause or the most important factor, but there must be something that is more than a merely trivial factor." *Hansard*, HC, 4 March 2009, col. 416.

[316] Mackay and Hughes, "Explaining the 'Explanation' Requirement in the New Diminished Responsibility Plea" [2021] *Crim LR* 461.

[317] [2016] UKSC 61, [2016] 1 WLR 5231, [32] (Lord Hughes) (emphasis added).

therefore a cause of the event in the eye of the law, even if more dominant causal features are also in play.[318] Normally, it would be said that the reasons which motivated D to kill V (say, because D wanted V's money) explain rather than "cause" D's killing, as voluntary human conduct is regarded as uncaused.[319] However, because, under the terms of section 2, the explanation must take a causal form, it seems that a motivation to kill arising from an abnormality of mental functioning (etc.) is to be regarded in this context as a cause of D's actions.

### *(iii) Relationship between loss of control and diminished responsibility*

There may be circumstances where the defences of loss of control and of diminished responsibility will be raised in the same proceedings. Any diagnosable personality disorder or mental impairment falls within section 2 of the Homicide Act 1957 provided it is a "recognised medical condition". This may well lead a jury to conclude that D's responsibility for his acts was substantially impaired within the terms of that section where she had a personality disorder or mental impairment which was medically recognised. Equally, such evidence might be relevant to a plea of loss of control,[320] at least to the extent that it has a relevance to D's conduct other than as regards D's general capacity for tolerance or self-restraint. In an appropriate case, therefore, both defences may have to be left to the jury. This points up a major anomaly: for diminished responsibility, the burden of proof, on the balance of probabilities, lies on the defendant;[321] for loss of control, the burden of disproof is on the prosecution once sufficient evidence has been adduced to raise an issue in respect of it.[322] This burden is discharged by proof beyond reasonable doubt.[323] It cannot be easy, even for the most conscientious and capable jury, to deal with the same evidence under different heads, applying different burdens and standards of proof. A further difficulty for the jury, as recognised in *Clinton*,[324] is that evidence of sexual infidelity may be relevant to the defence of diminished responsibility, since the discovery of sexual infidelity may lead to a recognised medical condition such as severe depression and impair D's ability to form a rational judgement, but it may be excluded for the purposes of the defence of loss of control. One of the reasons why it has been held that self-induced intoxication is not a relevant circumstance when assessing the objective test for the defence of loss of control[325] is that self-induced intoxication is not relevant to the assessment of diminished responsibility,[326] and "the potential for uncertainty and confusion which would follow the necessarily very different directions on the issue of intoxication, depending on which partial defence was under consideration, does not bear

[318] See above, § 4.2(ii)(c).
[319] Above, § 4.2(iii)(b).
[320] In *Ahluwalia* [1992] 4 All ER 889 (CA) and *Thornton (No. 2)* [1996] 2 All ER 1023 (CA), evidence of "battered woman syndrome" was taken to be relevant to provocation and diminished responsibility. Coercive control was considered to be relevant to both defences in *Challen* [2019] EWCA Crim 916.
[321] Homicide Act 1957 s. 2(2).
[322] Coroners and Justice Act 2009, s. 54(6).
[323] *Ibid.*, s. 54(5).
[324] [2012] EWCA Crim 2, [2013] QB 1, [33].
[325] *Asmelash* [2013] EWCA Crim 157, [2014] QB 103.
[326] *Dowds* [2012] EWCA Crim 281, [2012] 1 WLR 2576.

contemplation".[327] But such uncertainty and confusion does need to be contemplated for other aspects of the two defences.

## § 10.7 Involuntary manslaughter

The term "involuntary manslaughter" refers to those killings made criminal at common law notwithstanding a lack of intention to kill or cause grievous bodily harm.[328] The ambit of involuntary manslaughter is wide, ranging from killings which have a strong affinity with murder to situations where D would lack the culpability for any serious criminal offence had he not caused death. Nowhere is the role of chance factors more prevalent. For instance, assault is a summary offence;[329] should a death be causally linked to an assault a manslaughter verdict will likely ensue, however unexpected the death may have been.[330] Certain forms of sexual behaviour, not in themselves criminal, may attract a manslaughter verdict should death inadvertently occur.[331] The various ways in which liability for involuntary manslaughter may arise are not explicable by reference to any coherent conceptual scheme or overarching principle. They merely reflect the assessments of judges down the years of which killings that are not murder nevertheless merit a punitive response. To an extent, the wide scope of involuntary manslaughter is a function of the complete sentencing discretion that judges are permitted at common law: D may receive anything from life imprisonment to an absolute discharge. If judges had accepted as a restraining principle that the minimum culpability requirement for manslaughter should, at least normally, be such as to merit a substantial custodial sentence, we would have a narrower and more defensible law of manslaughter.

It is impossible to state the ambit of involuntary manslaughter with precision. Four broad areas of liability can be identified and will now be discussed.

### *(i) Constructive manslaughter*

What is now known as constructive manslaughter, or "unlawful act" manslaughter,[332] used to be the manslaughter counterpart of the felony/murder rule. If the unlawful act responsible for the death was not a felony but involved any other form of unlawful conduct, criminal or civil, then the perpetrator of the unlawful act was automatically guilty of manslaughter.[333] The extraordinary breadth of this form of liability needs no emphasis. Unfortunately, unlike the felony-murder rule itself, constructive manslaughter has not been abolished. The kinds of unlawful act on which a manslaughter verdict may be based have, however,

[327] *Asmelash* [2013] EWCA Crim 157, [2014] QB 103, [24].
[328] 1 Russ 611–33 (views about the scope of manslaughter from Coke, Hale, Hawkins, Forster, Black, and East). See generally on manslaughter Ashworth, "Manslaughter: Generic or Nominate Offences?" in Clarkson and Cunningham (eds.), *Criminal Liability for Non-Aggressive Deaths* (2008) chap. 11.
[329] Criminal Justice Act 1988, s. 39.
[330] See the facts of *Mallett* [1972] Crim LR 260 (CA).
[331] *Pike* [1961] Crim LR 547.
[332] Kenny, *Outlines of Criminal Law* (1902) 119–20.
[333] Buxton, "By Any Unlawful Act" (1966) 82 *LQR* 174.

been significantly narrowed since the eighteenth century, yet it remains a broad and frequently unpredictable ground of liability. Constructive manslaughter requires:

(i) a criminal act which causes death;
(ii) an act which is criminal *per se*; and
(iii) an act which is dangerous.

*(a) A criminal act*

In *Franklin*,[334] D was strolling along Brighton Pier and threw a stallholder's empty wooden beer crate into the sea. The crate struck and killed V, who was swimming in the sea below. The prosecution argued that liability for constructive manslaughter followed from the trespass to goods perpetrated by D on taking and disposing of the stallholder's crate. Field J rejected this argument by insisting that the unlawful act that causes V's death must be a crime. While merely a trial direction, it has been widely cited as authoritative; since *Franklin* there has been no imposition of liability for constructive manslaughter on the basis of mere civil law wrongdoing.[335]

The criminal act constitutes the base offence for constructive manslaughter. Consequently, the offence must be identified and proved. So, for example, in *Grey*,[336] where D had swung her arm towards V who was cycling towards D on the pavement and V swerved, fell into the road and was killed by a car, D's conviction for manslaughter was quashed. It had not been established that D had committed a battery since she had not touched V. Neither had assault been established, because it had not been established that V apprehended immediate unlawful force or that D had the appropriate mens rea, namely intention or recklessness as regards V's apprehension.

When considering whether a criminal act has been committed, it will also be necessary to determine whether D has a defence which negates liability. In some cases involving homicide during sexual activity, D has sought to argue that V consented to what has been called "rough sex", and that this is what resulted in V's death. In an attempt to negate such a plea, Parliament has enacted section 71 of the Domestic Abuse Act 2021, which states that, for offences involving "serious harm",[337] it is not a defence that V consented to the infliction of serious harm for the purposes of some person's obtaining sexual gratification. Consequently the commission of an offence against V involving serious harm can constitute the criminal act for constructive manslaughter even if V consented to the harm.[338] It appears that this provision will not, however, extend to the case where V consents to sexual activity which involves the risk of such harm being caused,[339] and even if V's consent is not established it

[334] (1883) 15 Cox CC 163.

[335] In *Lamb* [1967] 2 QB 981, a case of horseplay involving a gun but not involving any assault, Sachs LJ held that it was a misdirection to speak in general terms of "an unlawful and dangerous act" and "not in point to consider whether an act is unlawful merely from the angle of civil liabilities". What was required was an act "unlawful in the criminal sense of the word".

[336] [2024] EWCA Crim 487.

[337] Namely sections 18, 20, and 47 of the Offences Against the Person Act 1861. See below, §§ 11.4, 11.5, and 11.6. It is notable that "serious harm" is the standard definition of grievous bodily harm in English criminal law, but in this formulation it also covers actual bodily harm.

[338] Which was already the case following the decision of the House of Lords in *Brown* [1994] 1 AC 212.

[339] As occurred in *Slingsby* [1995] Crim LR 570.

will still be necessary to show that D had the mens rea for the substantive offence, either intention to cause serious harm or recklessness in respect of the harm, which may be difficult to establish.[340]

### *(b) An act of commission*

Since the Court of Appeal decision in *Lowe*,[341] it appears that the criminal act must take the form of an act rather than an omission. D was found to have wilfully neglected her child contrary to section 1 of the Children and Young Persons Act 1933 by her failure to arrange for medical treatment despite the obvious need of her child for medical attention. Phillimore LJ drew a sharp distinction between a child's dying as the result of a parent's blow and death resulting from parental neglect of the child. The former incident but not the latter will attract liability for constructive manslaughter. His Lordship did not offer any defence of this distinction and it is not obvious why indifference and neglect of one's parental duties to catastrophic effect is systemically less culpable than parental violence. But we are dealing here with *constructive* liability, in the sense that there need be no mens rea regarding death (or, indeed, anything more than "some harm"): if the ruling had been the other way, *all* child deaths associated with wilful neglect would constitute manslaughter without any necessity to demonstrate parental culpability in respect of the risk of death. Cases of egregious parental neglect resulting in the death of children can be charged as manslaughter on the basis of the gross negligence of the parents.[342] For that form of manslaughter, the negligence must relate to the risk of death.[343] With this in mind, the decision in *Lowe* may be welcomed. It is regrettable enough that the causing of inadvertent death by a positive criminal act may frequently sustain a charge of manslaughter; there is no virtue in imposing this harsh doctrine on omissions, even on the assumption that, other things being equal, acts and omissions are morally equivalent.[344]

### *(c) An act criminal per se*

The sheer number of criminal offences, particularly regulatory offences, leaves enormous scope for constructive manslaughter. A random example is the selling of food non-compliant with food safety standards, an offence of strict liability.[345] Each year, deaths ensue from food-poisoning. The lack of manslaughter verdicts associated with such deaths is, in part, attributable to the decision of the House of Lords in *Andrews*.[346] D had committed the offence of dangerous driving, and in so doing had caused the death of V. According to Lord Atkin, a verdict of manslaughter did not necessarily flow from such facts. For constructive manslaughter there had to be an underlying crime which was intrinsically criminal and

[340] Ormerod, "The Domestic Abuse Bill 2021" [2021] *Crim LR* 423.

[341] [1973] QB 702; disapproving *Senior* [1899] 1 QB 283. Although *Lowe* has been superseded in other respects by *Sheppard* [1981] AC 394, it has been considered to be authoritative on the present point. But note Taylor, "The Contours of Involuntary Manslaughter. A Place for Unlawful Act by Omission" [2019] *Crim LR* 205, who argues that the *dictum* about omission was *obiter* because the decision turned on the relevant unlawful act being one of strict liability which is not sufficient to establish unlawful act manslaughter.

[342] See also the offence contrary to s. 5 of the Domestic Violence, Crime and Victims Act 2004; below, § 10.10.

[343] See below, § 10.7(ii).

[344] On the question of equivalence, see the penetrating discussion in Bennett, *The Act Itself* (1995) 139–42.

[345] Food Safety Act 1990, s. 8. A defence of due diligence, with an onus of proof on D, is provided by s. 21.

[346] [1937] AC 576.

not merely "a lawful act [done] with a degree of carelessness which the legislature makes criminal".[347] The distinction is not an easy one but in practical terms the effect of *Andrews* has been to take driving offences and regulatory offences concerned with public and workplace safety outside the ambit of constructive manslaughter.[348] Serious transgressions in those areas which result in death may, instead, constitute manslaughter by gross negligence. Otherwise there is increasing statutory regulation concerning deaths by driving[349] and in the workplace.[350]

Although the practical effect of *Andrews* is easily grasped, its conceptual underpinning is problematic. Lord Atkin's informing idea is straightforward: driving is not of itself illegal; it becomes illegal if done carelessly or dangerously. Therefore, dangerous or careless driving does not, of itself, provide a basis for manslaughter. But this distinction soon runs into difficulties. What if D takes his car on to the public roads with a blood alcohol level above the permitted limit or uses a mobile phone while driving a vehicle in contravention of section 41D of the Road Traffic Act 1988? And why is it the case that driving in a manner which is dangerous or, indeed, which exceeds the speed limit, is not something intrinsically illegal? There is a host of things which are otherwise legal but which become illegal if done the wrong way or with the wrong motivation, and it is odd to base any classificatory scheme on this otherwise unremarkable fact. Here, we may discern judicial policy masquerading as a conceptually driven distinction. As we will see, constructive manslaughter is allowed free rein over such conduct as fighting, vandalism, drug-taking, and exotic sexual practices. It does not spill over to the quotidian criminalities of the majority population. This, it must be stressed, is not an argument for employing constructive manslaughter to its full extent.[351] It is an argument for abolition of this form of liability.[352]

Some writers have interpreted *Andrews* as authority for a much simpler proposition: that the unlawful act must be not merely a crime, but a crime of more than negligence or strict liability.[353] Strictly speaking, this is a misreading of the distinction drawn by Lord Atkin. But it is perhaps defensible to read the decision in this way, since doing so provides a better underpinning to the practical distinction Lord Atkin sought to make. Nevertheless, in

[347] *Ibid.*, 585.

[348] Many accidental deaths in workplace and road-traffic situations will involve criminal offences, yet the number of prosecutions for manslaughter form a tiny percentage of prosecutions compared with the prosecutions for health and safety offences and road traffic offences that may be brought following death from unnatural causes.

[349] Notably, causing death by dangerous driving (Road Traffic Act 1998, s. 1), but also causing death by careless or inconsiderate driving (Road Traffic Act 1988, s. 2B), causing death by careless driving whilst under the influence of drink or drugs (Road Traffic Act 1988, s. 3A) and causing death by unlawful driving where D was an unlicensed, uninsured, or disqualified driver (Road Traffic Act 1988, ss. 3ZB and 3ZC). See generally Cunningham, "Has Law Reform Policy Been Driven in the Right Direction? How the New Causing Death by Driving Offences Are Operating in Practice" [2013] *Crim LR* 711.

[350] Notably, the Health and Safety at Work Act 1974. See *Chargot Ltd* [2008] UKHL 73, [2009] 1 WLR 1, where it was held that liability for failure to ensure health and safety at work is strict, with the burden placed on D to prove that it was not reasonably practicable for her to prevent the accident. The Health and Safety (Offences) Act 2008 enables the court to impose custodial sentences of up to two years' imprisonment for committing an offence under the 1974 Act.

[351] But see Wells, *Corporations and Criminal Responsibility* (2nd ed., 2001) 75–8, who argues for more frequent resort to this category of manslaughter in the interests of industrial and transportation safety.

[352] As recommended by the Law Commission in Law Com. No. 237, *Involuntary Manslaughter* (1996) 127. Unfortunately, as will be discussed below, the Commission then substantially reversed its earlier position in Law Com. No. 304 (2006).

[353] See, e.g., *Smith, Hogan and Ormerod* 611.

a later case also called *Andrews*,[354] D was convicted of unlawful act manslaughter where he injected V with insulin contrary to the Medicines Act 1968, even though this was a strict liability offence. Similarly, in *Meeking*,[355] D was convicted of unlawful act manslaughter where she had interfered with a motor vehicle by pulling on the handbrake, thereby endangering road users contrary to the Road Traffic Act 1988, even though this is an offence of negligence since it had to be obvious to a reasonable person that the conduct was dangerous. In this latter case at least, as the unlawful act was one of negligence it would have been preferable to base the prosecution on gross negligence manslaughter,[356] since liability would then depend on the negligence being characterised as gross, which would have been established on the facts.[357]

*(d) A dangerous criminal act*

The House of Lords in *Newbury*[358] confirmed earlier authority to the effect that the criminal act in question must also be "dangerous". The House adopted an earlier statement of the law made by the Court of Appeal in *Church*:[359]

> "the unlawful act must be such that all sober and reasonable people would inevitably recognise it as an act which must subject the other person to at least the risk of some harm resulting therefrom albeit not serious harm."

Two points may be made about this passage. First, the dangerousness of the act need not be perceived by D; it is a matter of objective appraisal from the perspective of a reasonable person. Secondly, the danger in question need not relate to a risk of death or even serious bodily harm; the risk of minor physical harm is sufficient. Thus the constructive nature of unlawful act manslaughter is mitigated only to a slight degree by the dangerousness requirement. Indeed, in many cases the dangerousness requirement will be superfluous: presumably it is always foreseeable that a battery could result in "some harm".

Nonetheless, there are cases where the requirement for a dangerous act has prevented a conviction for manslaughter from being returned. In *Dawson*,[360] D pointed an imitation firearm at V in the course of a robbery. V, a middle-aged man with coronary illness, suffered a fatal heart attack induced by the fright engendered by his confrontation with D. This was held not to be a case of constructive manslaughter. The reasonable person would have foreseen that V would be frightened, even extremely frightened, but fright *per se* (falling short of psychiatric injury) was not a form of harm within the *Church* formulation. According to the Court of Appeal, it was clear that some form of foreseeable bodily harm is required. A coronary thrombosis was to be regarded as a form of bodily harm, but the reasonable person would not inevitably have recognised the risk of that eventuality arising from these circumstances. The reasonable person was to be invested with the knowledge available to

[354] [2002] EWCA Crim 3021.
[355] [2012] EWCA Crim 1641, [2012] 1 WLR 3349.
[356] Below, § 10.7(ii).
[357] [2012] EWCA Crim 1641, [2012] 1 WLR 3349, [14].
[358] [1977] AC 500.
[359] [1966] 1 QB 59, 70 (CA).
[360] (1985) 81 Cr App R 150 (CA).

D at the time of his act, no less, no more.[361] Middle-aged men did not comprise a class of individuals susceptible to heart attacks induced by fright.

By contrast, in *Watson*,[362] *Dawson* was distinguished on facts where an 87-year-old man died as a result of a coronary thrombosis induced by the stress of D's burglarious entry into his home. Elderly men did comprise a class of individuals susceptible to stress-induced heart attacks. D knew his victim to be an elderly man, so it followed that the reasonable person test should be applied with that in mind. *Dawson* was also distinguished in *JM and SM*,[363] where the defendants fought with a doorman who died from an undiagnosed heart defect as a result of shock and a surge in blood pressure caused by the fight. It was accepted that the fight was a cause of V's death. The trial judge had directed the jury that the prosecution had to prove both that the reasonable person would have foreseen the risk of some harm *and* that the victim died as a result of the sort of harm that a reasonable person would realise that the unlawful act risked causing. This would have constituted a significant (and defensible) restriction on the operation of unlawful act manslaughter. This direction was, however, rejected by the Court of Appeal, which held that it was not necessary to establish that the reasonable person would have foreseen the risk of the type of harm suffered by V; it was sufficient that some harm would have been foreseen, namely the physical harm to V arising from his restraining the defendants during the fight, even though the effect of the heart defect would not have been foreseen. *Dawson* was different because, on the facts of that case, no physical harm would have been foreseen arising from threatening with an imitation firearm.

*Dawson* was also distinguished, questionably, in *Ball*.[364] D was quarrelling with V and reached into his pocket to take a cartridge which he placed in his shotgun. He fired the gun, killing V. The pocket contained live and blank cartridges. D claimed that he had intended to load his gun with a blank cartridge. His counsel argued that the reasoning in *Dawson* obliged the judge to direct the jury that, in applying the reasonable person test, the reasonable person must be taken to assume the presence of a blank cartridge in the gun because that was the assumption made by D. The Court of Appeal dismissed this argument on the ground that *Dawson* was a case concerned with the vulnerability of the victim, whereas the facts of *Ball* involved a question about the inherent danger of D's act. In the latter kind of case the jury was entitled to appraise the dangerousness of the act in the light of all the circumstances actually present at the time of D's act, not merely those circumstances known to D himself. Yet this distinction would lead to absurd consequences. Suppose that, on facts otherwise similar to *Ball*, D had bought a carton of blank cartridges which, due to a packaging mishap of which he was unaware, contained some live cartridges. In those circumstances, surely, the reasonable person should be invested with the same assumption as D; the assumption that the gun was loaded with a blank cartridge. Moreover, distinguishing *Dawson* was unnecessary. On the facts of *Ball*, D was aware that his pocket contained live cartridges as well as blanks and that he might have placed a live cartridge in the shotgun. His manslaughter conviction is entirely in keeping with the reasoning of *Dawson*: D's act was dangerous given the facts that D knew, including facts about the risks involved in his

[361] *Ibid.*, 157.
[362] (1989) 89 Cr App R 211 (CA).
[363] [2012] EWCA Crim 2293, [2013] 1 WLR 1083.
[364] [1989] Crim LR 730.

conduct. The argument of defence counsel in *Ball*, as sketched here, was a fallacious reading of *Dawson*. It should have been dismissed on that ground.

An alternative reading[365] of the decision of the House of Lords in *Andrews*,[366] particularly the judgment of Lord Atkin, is that there must be equivalent culpability between constructive manslaughter and gross negligence manslaughter. Today[367] this would require proof that D was grossly negligent in relation to a serious and obvious risk of death, rather than merely reasonable foreseeability of "some harm". Whilst attractive in terms of result, especially because logically it would mean that constructive manslaughter would have no independent existence and would be subsumed into gross negligence manslaughter, this reading of *Andrews* was not (and conceivably cannot now) be adopted by the courts. Reform must be left to Parliament.

*(e) No "aimed at" requirement*

In the now discredited case of *DPP v Smith*,[368] the House of Lords used the language of an act "aimed at the victim" as a defining element of the crime of murder. That requirement, if such it ever was, did not survive the later decision of the House in *Hyam*.[369] Yet in *Dalby*,[370] Waller LJ, giving the judgment of the Court of Appeal, incorporated this limitation into the definition of constructive manslaughter. D unlawfully supplied V with drugs contrary to section 4 of the Misuse of Drugs Act 1971. V injected the drugs intravenously and subsequently died from their effects. The illegal supply of drugs was not a sufficient unlawful act for a verdict of manslaughter because, according to Waller LJ, it lacked the quality of being "directed at the victim".[371] The validity of this requirement was soon tested against the facts of *Mitchell*,[372] where D began a fight with E in a crowded Post Office. In the ensuing fracas, V, a frail old lady, was crushed to death. D's manslaughter conviction was confirmed by the Court of Appeal notwithstanding that D's violence was directed at E and not V. All that was required was a criminal and dangerous act which was a legal cause of V's death, an approach followed by the Court of Appeal in *Goodfellow*[373] and vindicated by the House of Lords in *A-G's Reference (No. 3 of 1994)*.[374]

Despite the rejection of the "aimed at" requirement, the result in *Dalby* can now be defended on the basis of the absence of a causal nexus between D's act of supply and V's subsequent death. Following the decision of the House of Lords in *Kennedy (No. 2)*,[375] the fully informed and voluntary decision of V in injecting drugs into his bloodstream will break the chain of causation between D's supplying V with drugs and V's death.

365 See Stark, "Re-reading *Andrews v DPP*" [2024] *Crim LR* 831.

366 [1937] AC 576.

367 In the 1930s, the fault element for gross negligence manslaughter was different from what it is today, requiring gross negligence regarding the lives or "safety" of others: Stark, "Re-reading *Andrews v DPP*" [2024] *Crim LR* 831, 837–9.

368 [1961] AC 290. In *Frankland* [1987] AC 576, the Privy Council ruled that *Smith* had been based on a misunderstanding of the law of murder.

369 [1975] AC 55.

370 [1982] 1 All ER 916 (CA).

371 *Ibid.*, 919.

372 [1983] QB 741 (CA).

373 (1986) 83 Cr App R 23 (CA).

374 [1998] AC 245.

375 [2007] UKHL 38, [2008] 2 AC 269; above, § 4.2(iii)(b) (Principle 1).

### *(f) Constructive manslaughter—a critique*

In the late Victorian case of *Franklin*,[376] Field J expressed a "horror" of constructive crime. Such a reaction is by no means universal. In *Cato*,[377] two drug addicts, D and V, obtained heroin of a high degree of purity. As was their practice, they consensually injected heroin into each other. Each of them became comatose. Because of contingencies with no bearing on the respective culpability of each actor, D received medical treatment and survived, whereas V died. D was successfully prosecuted for V's manslaughter, receiving five years' imprisonment. At trial, the unlawful act was found to be the malicious administration of a noxious substance.[378] On appeal, Lord Widgery CJ suppressed his doubts about the propriety of that finding[379] by ruling that, alternatively, the unlawful act was "injecting [V] with a mixture of heroin and water which at the time of the injection and for the purposes of the injection [D] had unlawfully taken into his possession".[380] The difficulty about the latter "offence", a difficulty which should have daunted even a judge so robust as Lord Widgery CJ, is that no such crime is known to English law.[381]

What drove Lord Widgery CJ's judgment is an abhorrence of drug-taking and a determination to impose penal consequences on those involved in it. It is hard to discern any moral or social difference between drugs taken by an individual and those taken with the assistance of a mutual addict. Yet it was only the latter feature that created scope for a conviction for constructive manslaughter in *Cato* (and even then the decision is hard to justify in legal terms). A striking feature is the fortuity surrounding the verdict. Both V and D may easily have died; equally likely was joint survival or the sole death of D.

In our discussion of the law of attempt, we acknowledged both the impossibility of eradicating "outcome luck" from the criminal law, and the plausibility of the view that outcome luck could have legitimate implications for the grading of offences and the quantum of punishment.[382] But luck is too potent a factor in the imposition of liability for constructive manslaughter. It can turn a "trivial" assault between quarrelling neighbours into a serious crime involving a custodial sentence where, as in *Mallett*,[383] V falls awkwardly and fatally bumps his head on concrete. Such a verdict can be defended only on the basis that, if D engages in criminal conduct, he must take responsibility for the consequences of his criminality, whatever those consequences may be. No doubt such reasoning may have its place where D's conduct gives rise to a clear and vivid danger that death may occur.[384] Yet, in constructive manslaughter, the connection between the unlawfulness of D's act and its dangerousness may be extremely tenuous. In *Arobieke*,[385] D terrified V by following him closely

[376] (1883) 15 Cox CC 163.
[377] [1976] 1 All ER 260 (CA). See the valuable note by Wells (1976) 39 *MLR* 474.
[378] OAPA 1861, s. 23.
[379] The effect of V's consent to the injection was insufficiently considered at trial in relation to a conviction under s. 23. Difficult questions would require resolution—particularly, now, concerning the impact of the House of Lords decision in *Brown* [1994] 1 AC 212 about whether, as a question of public policy, V could legitimately consent to the injection.
[380] [1976] 1 All ER 260, 267.
[381] While *possession* and *supply* of controlled drugs are criminalised, it is not an offence to, without more, *administer* a controlled drug.
[382] Above, § 9.3(vi). See also above, § 6.5 (ii).
[383] [1972] Crim LR 260 (CA).
[384] See further Stark, "Deconstructing Constructive Liability" [2023] *Crim LR* 118, 127.
[385] [1988] Crim LR 314 (CA).

to the railway station and then searching for him on the train V had boarded. V had good reason to fear serious violence at the hands of D and, in his fear, sought to escape across the live tracks, thereby electrocuting himself. A conviction of constructive manslaughter against D was ruled out because, *inter alia*, the facts disclosed no unlawful act on his part, although it is unclear why an assault could not have been established. Contrast *Mallett*, where there was no threat of serious violence, but D was nonetheless convicted of manslaughter.

Unfortunately, there is no likelihood that the legislature will abolish constructive manslaughter. Rather, the Government does not hesitate to impose heavy penalties based substantially on the fact of causing death: witness the increase in the maximum penalty for causing death by dangerous driving from five years' then to 14 years' and now to life imprisonment.[386] The (in many ways admirable) heightened concern with the wrongs suffered by the victims of crime and the relatives of those victims appears for now to militate against rational appraisals of culpability in the face of death.[387] The most recent Law Commission proposals[388] recommend the creation of an offence of unlawful dangerous act manslaughter, with an additional requirement that D must have intended to cause some injury or was reckless as to whether some injury was caused. Although the trigger for liability would be a subjective state of mind, a conviction for an offence which carries a possible penalty of life imprisonment would be possible without proof of any culpability relating to death or even substantial harm.[389] Even if this reform was enacted, therefore, it would maintain the unprincipled nature of this form of manslaughter.

### *(ii) Manslaughter by gross negligence*

Carelessness may be thought to be a problematic form of culpability for a serious criminal offence. The breadth of constructive manslaughter has been criticised. Nonetheless, liability for that form of manslaughter will be triggered by some form of chosen, criminal conduct. By contrast, gross negligence manslaughter requires no advertent wrongdoing and may penalise a person who lacks any violent or predatory designs on the persons or property of others. To be convicted of manslaughter by gross negligence, D must cause the death of V by doing something or omitting to do something in circumstances which reveal a very clear failure to exhibit minimum standards of competence or concern in the face of a serious and obvious risk of death. Such standards are largely objective.[390] It was no answer for D to claim, in *Stone and Dobinson*,[391] that his intelligence and skills were so deficient as to preclude performance of the most basic of social tasks. Yet if we do not pay heed to such deficiencies, what is the basis of our censure?[392] If a person is capable of attaining basic

[386] Road Traffic Offenders Act 1988, sched. 2, as amended by the Police, Crime, Sentencing and Courts Act 2022, s. 85(2). The sentence for causing death by careless or inconsiderate driving is five years, although when under the influence of drink or drugs the maximum sentence is life imprisonment (Police, Crime, Sentencing and Courts Act 2022, s. 85(3)). Contrast the maximum penalty for dangerous driving *simpliciter* (contrary to s. 2 of the Road Traffic Act 1988), which remains pegged at two years' imprisonment.

[387] See also *A-G's Reference (No. 60 of 2009)* [2009] EWCA Crim 2693, [2010] 2 Cr App R (S) 311, [22] (Lord Judge).

[388] Law Com. CP No. 277, *Homicide Offences* (2026), para. 8.102.

[389] See further Freer, "We Need to Talk about Charlie: Putting the Brakes on Unlawful Act Manslaughter" [2018] *Crim LR* 612.

[390] There is, however, uncertainty whether the standards are *entirely* objective: above, § 5.5(ii).

[391] [1977] QB 354 (CA).

[392] See too the facts of *Elliott v C (a minor)* [1983] 1 WLR 939 (DC).

skills and competence, then it is conventional and acceptable to criticise her for failure to exercise that competence. If the consequences of such failure are minor, criticism should normally be restrained. She would rightly be aggrieved to receive the same degree of censure for carelessly losing another person's £10 note as for dishonestly taking it. Yet what if D, a child-minder, allows V, an infant in her care, to wander with fatal consequences onto a busy road because she was preoccupied by a conversation with E? The urge to punish would arise. Would it be in point that D was distraught at what she had allowed to happen? If the child had survived, however badly injured, no criminal offence would have been committed by D. Should the impact of death override the lack of subjective recklessness or intent? Or should gross negligence receive criminal censure on a broader and more consistent basis than it now does?[393] The answer to such questions depends ultimately on value judgements which are psychologically grounded, lying beyond proof and refutation.[394]

*(a) The elements of gross negligence manslaughter*

To cause or allow the death of another negligently will not, of itself, incur liability for manslaughter. The failure of care or concern must be more egregious than is required for civil liability. According to Lord Hewart CJ in *Bateman*, it must be the case that:[395]

> "in the opinion of the jury, the negligence of the accused went beyond a mere matter of compensation between subjects and showed such disregard for the life and safety of others, as to amount to a crime against the state and conduct deserving of punishment."

This dictum has been criticised for vacuity, yet it usefully stresses that juries should be cautious when attributing criminality to a defendant who has neither intended nor foreseen that she would cause or allow harm to another. The dictum was approved by the House of Lords in *Andrews*[396] and reflects a consistent pattern of jury directions. Exemplifying this approach is the decision in *Finney*,[397] where D, a lunatic asylum attendant, was found not guilty of manslaughter even though he made no visual check to see if his patient, V, had left the bath following D's direction to do so. V had remained in the bath and had been killed when, for cleaning purposes, D released scalding water into it. The evidence fell short of establishing the abject failure of care necessary to justify a finding of gross negligence with penal consequences.

Sometimes, the courts equate gross negligence with a form of recklessness. For instance, Lord Atkin opined in *Andrews* that a useful synonym for gross negligence was the term recklessness. It is clear from the context (the approval of the decision in *Bateman*) that Lord Atkin was not in any sense seeking to dilute the degree of egregiousness required for a finding of gross negligence.[398] However, the House of Lords went further in *Seymour*.[399] Lord Roskill, in giving judgment for the House, took recklessness to be the most suitable

[393] As is argued in Schulhofer, "Harm and Punishment: A Critique of the Emphasis on the Results of Conduct in the Criminal Law" (1974) 122 *U Pa L Rev* 1497, 1605.

[394] Acceptance of the salience of psychological reactions as precipitates for moral judgments entails the rejection of moral realism but not an acceptance of moral relativism. On psychological reactions and moral judgements see Bennett, *The Act Itself* (1995) 12–16.

[395] (1925) 19 Cr App R 8, 11 (CA).

[396] [1937] AC 576, 582–3.

[397] (1874) 12 Cox CC 625.

[398] [1937] AC 576, 583.

[399] [1983] 2 AC 493.

term to express the kind of culpability required for this head of manslaughter. Moreover, he ruled that the recklessness required should be of the kind expounded in *Caldwell*[400] and *Lawrence*,[401] and that recklessness as to the risk of any degree of harm would suffice.[402] The upshot was an enormously wide form of manslaughter. Liability would ensue if D's conduct had given rise to an obvious and serious risk of physical harm, a risk which D had either foreseen or failed to give any thought to. The breadth of this new approach is readily appreciated if we return to the facts of *Finney*; a manslaughter verdict would seem assured were a jury to be directed along the lines indicated by Lord Roskill.

In *Adomako*,[403] the House of Lords reviewed the fundamentals of this form of manslaughter and restated the essential ingredients. *Seymour* was not overruled but was seen as no longer relevant. Lord Mackay noted that the House in *Seymour* was concerned with liability for the offence of causing death by reckless driving alongside liability for manslaughter. Indeed it was, and one of the most telling criticisms of *Seymour* was that Lord Roskill took the constituents of each offence exactly to correspond. According to Lord Mackay, the statutory abolition of causing death by reckless driving therefore remaindered *Seymour* to legal history. Unfortunately, he did not explain the mystery of how the abolition of the offence of reckless driving had also undone what *Seymour* had decided about manslaughter. It would have been far better to have departed from that decision by using the 1966 Practice Direction. Judicial comity restrains judicial candour.

*Adomako* asserts the continuing relevance of the approach taken in *Andrews* and *Bateman* and reinstates gross negligence as the required form of culpability, albeit that reasonable foreseeability of the risk of death is a key component of this. To incur liability for this form of manslaughter, there are five requirements:

1. D owes V a duty of care
2. D breaches that duty
3. In circumstances where there was reasonable foreseeability of an obvious and serious risk of death
4. D's breach of duty caused V's death
5. D's breach of duty displayed "gross" negligence

*Requirement 1: Duty of care.*

D must owe a duty of care to V. This is a question of law for the judge, who should direct the jury that a duty of care is owed if certain facts are established, the determination of those facts being for the jury.[404] For example, in *Zaman*,[405] the owner of a restaurant was found to have owed a duty of care to the victim who had a peanut allergy and who had been assured that his food contained no peanuts, but who died as a result of eating food which did contain traces of nuts.

400 [1982] AC 341.

401 [1982] AC 510.

402 [1983] 2 AC 493, 505 where the elements of reckless manslaughter are assimilated to the elements of reckless driving.

403 [1995] 1 AC 171. For valuable notes discussing the decision see Smith [1994] *Crim LR* 758; Virgo (1995) 54 *CLJ* 14; and Gardner (1995) 111 *LQR* 22.

404 *Evans* [2009] EWCA Crim 650, [2009] 1 WLR 1999.

405 [2017] EWCA Crim 1783.

Although the civil law of negligence is to be applied to determine whether a duty of care was owed, some of the rules relating to tortious liability will not be relevant. So, for example, if D and V are engaged on a joint criminal enterprise—such as illegal immigration[406] or arson of a building[407]—D may be liable for the manslaughter of V on the basis of his gross negligence irrespective of the fact that public policy might preclude a successful civil action in negligence against V.

While there is a general duty imposed on us all not to cause death by a positive act, the duty requirement requires closer attention where the allegation of gross negligence relates to D's omission rather than actions.[408] In such cases it is necessary to identify a legal duty to act as distinct from a duty of care,[409] with reference to the established categories of duties to act,[410] but, once a duty *to act* has been identified, it will be necessary to identify that a duty *of care* was owed to V, although this will usually follow inexorably from the duty to act. So, in *Pittwood*,[411] where D had failed to close a railway-crossing gate, D's liability for manslaughter rested on a finding that he had a contractual duty owed to his employer to close the gate and a general duty of care which was owed to the users of the crossing. Similarly, in *Evans*,[412] D had supplied heroin to her half-sister, who had then self-injected and died from an overdose. D owed a duty to obtain medical assistance because she had contributed to the creation of a state of affairs by the supply of drugs which she ought to have known was life threatening. The duty to act meant that she also owed a duty of care towards her sister. Her failure to take the reasonable step of obtaining medical assistance constituted a breach of this duty that was considered to be grossly negligent and so she was guilty of manslaughter. As was seen in Chapter 4,[413] the identification of a duty to act in *Evans* is controversial. Although the recognition of the duty was founded on *Miller*,[414] in that case D had created the dangerous situation and was aware of having done so, whereas in *Evans* it was sufficient that D had contributed to the creation of the risk of the danger occurring and ought to have known this. D could not be considered to have created the dangerous situation because, following the decision of the House of Lords in *Kennedy (No. 2)*,[415] V's self-injection broke the chain of causation; it was V's own act of injection that created the danger.

*Requirement 2: Breach of duty.*

D must have negligently breached the duty of care. This question falls to be decided under the ordinary principles of the tort of negligence and requires consideration of whether D has failed to comply with the reasonable standards of care expected of them. Where D is a professional they are expected to exhibit the standard of care that is reasonable to that profession. So, for example, a medical professional is expected to exhibit the standard of care

406 *Wacker* [2003] 1 Cr App R 22.
407 *Willoughby* [2004] EWCA Crim 3365.
408 See generally Ashworth, "Manslaughter by Omission and the Rule of Law" [2015] *Crim LR* 563.
409 *Evans* [2009] EWCA Crim 650, [2009] 1 WLR 1999, [21].
410 Above, § 4.1(i)(b).
411 (1902) 19 TLR 37; above, § 4.1(i)(b) (Case 3).
412 [2009] EWCA Crim 650, [2009] 1 WLR 1999.
413 § 4.1(i)(b) (Case 5).
414 [1983] 2 AC 161.
415 [2007] UKHL 38, [2008] 2 AC 269.

of a reasonable medical professional. Failure to exhibit such care will constitute a breach of duty.

*Requirement 3: Reasonable foreseeability of an obvious and serious risk of death.*

The jury must consider whether a reasonably prudent person possessed of the information known to D would have foreseen[416] that D's actions or omissions which constitute the breach of duty would give rise to an obvious and serious risk of death, and not simply a risk of serious injury or illness.[417] A serious risk is one that is much more than minimal or remote.[418] An obvious risk of death is a risk which is present, clear, and unambiguous; it is immediately apparent, striking, and glaring rather than something which might become apparent on future investigation.[419] The risk of death need not relate to V specifically but to the class of which V is a member.[420] So, in *Kuddus*,[421] where D had supplied food to V containing peanuts, to which V was allergic, it was not necessary to show an obvious and serious risk of V's death specifically, but rather that D's conduct posed such a risk to the class of nut allergy sufferers. It was, accordingly, irrelevant that the risk to V herself was low, or was a risk only of injury rather than death. On the facts, however, D was acquitted because he was unaware of V's nut allergy, and so consequently the reasonable person would not have foreseen a serious risk of death, so it was therefore not an *obvious* risk.

Crucially, in *Rose*,[422] it was held that when determining foreseeability of risk it is not appropriate to take into account information which would, could, or should have been available to D had there not been a breach of duty. The test is objective and prospective, with regard to what D knew at the time of the breach, and not retrospective with reference to what D would have known had further investigation been undertaken. The reasonable foreseeability test is to be determined at the time of the breach of duty. This was summarised by the Court of Appeal in *Rose* as follows:[423]

> "The test of reasonable foreseeability simply requires the notional objective exercise of putting a reasonably prudent professional in the shoes of the person whose conduct is under scrutiny and asking whether, at the moment of breach of the duty on which the prosecution rely, that person ought reasonably (ie objectively) to have foreseen an obvious and serious risk of death."

The significance of this interpretation of an obvious and serious risk of death which is reasonably foreseeable is illustrated by *Rudling*.[424] D was a GP who had received a phone call from the mother of V, a child who was unwell. Despite the mother describing V's symptoms on the phone, D failed to follow up by examining V face-to-face, which was considered to be a breach of duty. Had D examined the child she would have discovered that he was suffering from a life-threatening illness, namely Addison's disease, which is very rare in

416 In *Broughton* [2020] EWCA Crim 1093, [2021] 1 WLR 543 reasonable foreseeability was considered to be a separate requirement from the risk being obvious and serious (although it was acknowledged that they would rarely require separate articulation), but they are preferably treated as a single requirement. Indeed, an obvious and serious risk of death should be considered to be reasonably foreseeable.

417 *Rudling* [2016] EWCA Crim 741; *Kuddus* [2019] EWCA Crim 837, [2019] 1 WLR 5199,

418 *Broughton* [2020] EWCA Crim 1093, [2021] 1 WLR 543, [5].

419 *Ibid.*

420 *Kuddus* [2019] EWCA Crim 837, [2019] 1 WLR 5199.

421 *Ibid.*

422 [2017] EWCA Crim 1168, [2018] QB 328, [78].

423 *Ibid.*, [84].

424 [2016] EWCA Crim 741.

children. It was held that, at the time of the phone call, there was not an obvious and serious risk of death and so D was found not to have been grossly negligent. Similarly, in *Rose*,[425] where D, an optometrist, examined V's eye without conducting an internal examination, which constituted a breach of a statutory duty of care, and consequently failed to detect that he was suffering from an illness from which he died five months later. This was held not to be grossly negligent because, even though it was negligent for D not to have conducted the internal eye examination, gross negligence regarding *death* was to be determined with reference to whether there was a present risk of death which was clear and unambiguous at the time of the examination, and not one which might have become apparent on further investigation, albeit that the reasonable optometrist would have conducted such an investigation. Crucially V had not presented with any symptoms of the illness, which, had he done so, would have meant that failing to investigate those present symptoms could have been characterised as grossly negligent.

These cases can be contrasted with *Winterton*,[426] where V had died following the collapse of a trench on a building site. D was responsible for health and safety on the site and so owed a duty of care to V throughout the construction of the trench. The dangerous construction of the trench was such that it was considered to be a question of "when" rather than "if" the trench would collapse, and consequently an obvious and serious risk of death was reasonably foreseeable. *Rose* and *Rudling* were distinguished because both those defendants were not sufficiently alerted to the risk of death on the facts which were available to them when they broke their respective duties of care. *Winterton* was different because the warning signs were such that an obvious and serious risk was present for D to see without any need for further investigation. As the Court found, D either did see the warning signs and ignored them, or failed to see them in circumstances where the reasonable site manager would have.

The implications of these decisions is that the ambit of liability for gross negligence manslaughter has been restricted, but this does produce results which might be considered to be counter-intuitive. It means, for example, that in a case such as *Rose*, if D had actually conducted the internal eye investigation but had failed to detect the symptoms of the disease, there might be considered to have been an obvious and serious risk of death which was reasonably foreseeable, whereas D who failed to conduct the investigation at all, which is arguably a more egregious breach of duty involving greater culpability will not be liable.[427]

*Requirement 4: Causation.*

The breach of the duty of care must have caused V's death.[428] Causation is discussed at length in § 4.2.[429] If, for example V's act was free, deliberate, and informed, any prior breach of duty by D will not be considered to be a cause of V's death.[430] Causation is to be determined from the moment of breach when there was an obvious and serious risk of death.

425 [2017] EWCA Crim 1168, [2018] QB 328.

426 [2018] EWCA Crim 2435, [2019] 2 Cr App R 12.

427 Laird, "The Evolution of Gross Negligence Manslaughter" (2018) 1 *Archbold Review* 8. But see Stark, "In Praise of *Rose*" [2019] 8 *Archbold Review* 7, who suggests different ways of responding to this disincentive to act, such as by regulatory measures. See also Greenberg, "Why Criminal Responsibility for Negligence Cannot Be Indirect" (2021) 80 *CLJ* 489, 507 who suggests that where D fails to conduct an investigation, she might be wilfully blind to the relevant risks, and consequently be liable for gross negligence manslaughter.

428 *Broughton* [2020] EWCA Crim 1093, [2021] 1 WLR 543; *Wood Treatment Ltd* [2021] EWCA Crim 618.

429 Note too the requirement that D's negligence must have been a *salient* cause of V's death: above, § 4.2(ii)(b).

430 *Rebelo* [2021] EWCA Crim 306, [2021] 4 WLR 52.

In *Broughton*,[431] D's breach of duty was held not to have been a substantial contributory cause of V's death, where the breach involved failing to seek medical assistance after V had overdosed on drugs supplied by D: it had not been established that, at the time that an obvious and serious risk of V's death arose, her life could have been saved by any medical assistance sought by D. This outcome can be contrasted with that in *Evans*.[432] It can also be contrasted with *Broadhurst*,[433] where D was guilty of gross negligence manslaughter having failed to obtain medical assistance for V following injuries arising from consensual sado-masochistic activities.

*Requirement 5: "Gross" negligence.*
The final question for the jury[434] to consider is whether, having regard to the risk of death, D's conduct was so bad in all the circumstances of the case as to amount to a criminal act or omission. This has been described as requiring "truly exceptionally bad" conduct rather than very serious mistakes or lapses of conduct.[435] "Badness" in this context is not a matter of evil disposition or even indifference to the victim's welfare. It is a matter of D's conduct. In one of the cases disposed of in *Adomako* where a conviction for gross negligence manslaughter was confirmed, an anaesthetist had failed for 11 minutes or so to identify the cause of the patient's respiratory difficulty as a dislodged endotracheal tube. Other means of restoring the supply of oxygen were frantically tried but the simple and obvious procedure of reattaching the tube was not performed, something that, according to expert evidence, would have been done by a competent anaesthetist within 30 seconds of observing the patient's difficulties. As a qualified professional person, he was required to demonstrate competence. His incompetence was so bad as to allow his conviction for manslaughter to be confirmed.

### (b) A critique of gross negligence manslaughter

Whether negligence, however gross, is a sufficient form of culpability for a serious offence is a matter that has divided theorists.[436] In the light of the House of Lords decision in *G*,[437] which rejected objective recklessness as a suitable form of culpability for serious offences, the optimistic argument was put in *Misra*[438] that abolition of objective recklessness in criminal damage implied the abolition of gross negligence as a form of culpability for an offence as serious as manslaughter. The argument predictably failed,[439] since gross negligence manslaughter has been well established for decades and had been endorsed and redefined by the House of Lords in *Adomako*. Moreover, there is clearly ground for serious criticism of D if she has failed to conduct herself to the standard that she is reasonably capable of achieving; equally so were she to attempt a task that she knows she is incapable of achieving. It has been argued that penal consequences in respect of negligence are pointless because the thoughtless and the careless cannot be deterred, whereas reckless or intentional criminality can be influenced by the prospect of hard treatment. The point has been put as a matter of logic, but it is a question

431 [2020] EWCA Crim 1093, [2021] 1 WLR 543.
432 [2009] EWCA Crim 650, [2009] 1 WLR 1999 (above, § 10.7(ii)(a) (Requirement 1)).
433 [2019] EWCA Crim 2026.
434 *Sellu* [2016] EWCA Crim 1716, [2017] 4 WLR 64, [155].
435 *Ibid.*, [152]. See also *Bawa-Garba* [2016] EWCA Crim 1841.
436 See above, § 5.5(iv).
437 [2004] 1 AC 1034; above, § 5.2(i)(b).
438 [2005] 1 Cr App R 21.
439 As was also the case in *Mark* [2004] EWCA Crim 2490.

of fact. We all have prudential reasons to drive carefully because, if we do, our chances of being killed or injured on the road are diminished. Another reason for driving carefully is to avoid liability for the crime of driving without due care and attention.[440] Whether that offence and other motoring offences improve driving standards on a significant scale is something to be investigated and not dismissed out of hand. The argument from deterrence has gained force recently, particularly by way of reaction to several large transportation disasters.[441]

In 2006, the Law Commission, reversing an earlier stance, took the view that there is a valid role for gross negligence manslaughter in English law.[442] Further, gross negligence—"conduct falling far below what can reasonably be expected"—was the informing idea behind the creation of the offence of corporate manslaughter.[443] Yet legitimate concern with effective deterrence should not override an insistence that convictions for serious, stigmatic offences should be based on a sufficient degree of culpability. Should an anaesthetist, assuming he is doing his inadequate best, receive a custodial sentence for the disastrous consequences of his ineptitude? Yes, it might be answered, if he was capable of doing better or had reason to know that he was not up to the demands of his job. But if he was a normally careful professional who on this occasion made an isolated blunder, the moral position is less clear. The sad truth is that everyone, however normally careful, makes occasional mistakes, particularly when (as frequently in hospitals) they are working under stress, and it is questionable—to put it mildly—whether the threat of prosecution and possible imprisonment reduces the likelihood of medical professionals making the occasional mistake. In 2015 the manslaughter conviction of a junior paediatrician for death resulting from a blunder made after some 12 or 13 hours on duty without a break[444] caused an outcry in the medical profession. In response to this the Minister of Health ordered an official review of medical manslaughter prosecutions, which recommended (among other things) "revised guidance" for investigators and prosecutors, to ensure that "systemic issues and human factors" are taken into account before medical professionals are prosecuted.[445]

In their book, *Errors, Medicine and the Law*, Merry and McCall-Smith suggest that the law should make a distinction between "slips"—medical mishaps that result from simple human error—and "violations"—those resulting from a conscious decision by the medical professional to disobey an accepted rule of proper practice.[446] As an illustration they contrast the facts of *Adomako*, where an unconscious patient died because the defendant anaesthetist had failed to notice that the patient's endotracheal breathing tube had become disconnected, and the hypothetical case of a patient who dies in the same way when the anaesthetist, contrary to a basic rule of practice, leaves him in the theatre unattended. Applying this distinction, a conviction for manslaughter by gross negligence would be possible in the second case, but not the first. This distinction was suggested in the context of

440 Road Traffic Act 1988, s. 3.

441 Which proved influential regarding the creation of the new crime of corporate manslaughter: below, § 10.7(iv).

442 Law Com. No. 304, para. 9.9. Confirmed in 2026: *Homicide Offences* Law Com. CP No. 227, para. 8.123.

443 Below, § 10.7(iv).

444 Her appeal against conviction was rejected: see *Bawa-Garba* [2016] EWCA Crim 1841; but after further litigation she was eventually permitted to resume practice: *Bawa-Garba v General Medical Council* [2018] EWCA Crim 1879. For a summary, see Spencer, "Prosecuting Medical Professionals for Manslaughter" [2019] 2 *Archbold Review* 9.

445 *Gross Negligence Manslaughter in Healthcare—The Report of a Rapid Policy Review* (2018). See also the *Independent Review of Gross Negligence Manslaughter and Culpable Homicide* (2019) commissioned by the General Medical Council.

446 (2nd ed., 2017), ch. 4.

medical negligence, but it is capable of wider application. The driver who drives through a red traffic light deliberately is, *ceteris paribus*, obviously more blameworthy than the one who merely fails to see it; the employer who deliberately disregards the requirements of health and safety law in order to save money is obviously more blameworthy than the one who simply fails to understand them; and the riparian owner who intentionally discharges toxic waste into a river is obviously more blameworthy than the one who allows that to happen by careless oversight. As such, it is a distinction that could be adopted, instead of the current *Bateman* test, as the general criterion for determining whether a given piece of negligence was "gross". Under the *Bateman* test, as we saw earlier, negligence is "gross" if the jury in the case considers that it "went beyond a mere matter of compensation between subjects and showed such disregard for the life and safety of others as to amount to a crime". This test is circular and unpredictable, leaving wide scope for different verdicts on similar facts, to the point where it is barely compatible with the fair-notice requirements of Article 7 of the ECHR.[447] By contrast, the distinction proposed by Merry and McCall-Smith would have the merit of much greater certainty.

### *(iii) Reckless manslaughter*

In *Hyam*,[448] the House of Lords ruled by a majority that a high degree of *Cunningham* recklessness—foresight of the probability of death or grievous bodily harm—sufficed for malice aforethought in murder. *Hyam* was, in substance, reversed by *Moloney*,[449] where the House decided that nothing less than an intent to kill or cause grievous bodily harm would suffice as the culpability required for murder. The dissenting judges in *Hyam* assumed that the more culpable form of recklessness that the majority found sufficient for murder would suffice to support a verdict of manslaughter. This must surely be the case, at least where D foresees he may kill or seriously injure V; yet there is little authority on subjective recklessness as a form of culpability for manslaughter. In the vast majority of cases when there is foresight on the part of D that his conduct may unjustifiably or inexcusably kill or seriously injure V, his conduct will involve the commission of some offence, irrespective of the causing of any injury or death to V. In *Hyam* itself, D had perpetrated arson. Consequently, a conviction for constructive manslaughter would straightforwardly be obtained on facts such as those without regard to the question whether D foresaw death or serious injury to another.

There may, nonetheless, occasionally be circumstances where D is subjectively reckless as to the causing of death or serious injury but where his conduct would not involve liability for constructive manslaughter. For instance, D, an archer, might continue with his target practice even though V is present within the vicinity. When aiming at the target, D would not necessarily commit any offence against V.[450] Accordingly, if V were killed by D's overshooting arrow, it might not be a case of constructive manslaughter but it would be reckless manslaughter if D foresaw a risk of causing death or serious bodily harm.

Does foresight of harm of a lesser magnitude than death or serious harm suffice? In *Adomako*, Lord Mackay gave his approval to earlier *dicta* which suggest that the mens rea

[447] An argument raised by the defendants, unsuccessfully, in *Misra* [2004] EWCA Crim 2375, [2005] 1 Cr App R 21.
[448] [1975] AC 55.
[449] [1985] AC 905.
[450] There might be an assault if V were made apprehensive by D's continuing to shoot his arrows and D was aware that this was the case, but not otherwise.

for manslaughter will be present in circumstances where D foresees that his acts or omissions may cause physical harm to V or where D is indifferent to the effects of his conduct upon V's health or welfare.[451] It is unfortunate that Lord Mackay approved these *dicta*, which are vaguely expressed and of uncertain ambit. In any event, they are no more than *obiter dicta*: the cases wherein they occur involved questions of gross negligence regarding V's death.[452] There is nothing to preclude the adoption of a rule that the mens rea for reckless manslaughter is foresight of an unwarranted risk of death or grievous bodily harm. In *Lidar*,[453] where the Court of Appeal appeared to recognise subjectively reckless manslaughter, it was assumed that foresight of death or serious harm was required.

This form of manslaughter has rarely been prosecuted, because any qualifying cases are likely also to fall within the ambit of either constructive manslaughter or gross negligence manslaughter. In *A-G's Reference (No. 2 of 1999)*,[454] Rose LJ considered that recklessness in the form of advertence to risk or indifference to risk, might lead to a finding of gross negligence in the criminal law; confirming the view that there is very little scope, if any, for a distinct species of manslaughter based exclusively on recklessness. Indeed, in *Heath*,[455] the trial judge ruled that a distinct count of subjective reckless manslaughter should be dismissed in favour of a count of gross negligence manslaughter, and that *Lidar* was "incapable of doing the jurisprudential lifting" to recognise reckless manslaughter, with the recklessness in that case properly being relevant to the assessment of gross negligence.[456]

It is true that a finding of gross negligence must rest on a finding that D's conduct was "so bad in all the circumstances as to amount to a criminal act or omission", but that quality is surely present where D takes or is indifferent to an unwarranted risk of causing death or serious bodily harm. It seems negligent as well as reckless to take a known risk—and frequently grossly negligent. The only discrete ground covered by this variant of manslaughter would be situations where D knowingly takes an unwarranted risk of causing serious bodily harm but is not grossly negligent as to causing V's death, essentially a theoretical rather than practical possibility. In 2006 in the Law Commission's final report on the reform of homicide, no provision was made for a statutory version of reckless manslaughter. However, in its 2026 Consultation Paper the Law Commission has proposed a distinct category of reckless manslaughter which would apply where the defendant was aware of the risk of serious injury or death and unreasonably ran that risk, causing death. This proposal is welcome in distinguishing the culpability of recklessness from other forms of manslaughter.[457]

### *(iv) Corporate manslaughter*

There is no reason in principle why a company cannot be convicted of manslaughter, since a company has legal personality in its own right.[458] But securing convictions of companies proved difficult at common law by virtue of the attribution theory of corporate criminal

451 [1995] 1 AC 171, 187.
452 *Stone and Dobinson* [1977] QB 354 (CA); *West London Coroner, Ex parte Gray* [1988] QB 467 (CA).
453 [2000] 4 Archbold News (CA).
454 [2000] 3 All ER 182 (CA).
455 22 March 2022.
456 See also Stark, "Reckless Manslaughter" [2017] *Crim LR* 763.
457 *Homicide Offences* Law Com. No. 227 (2026), para. 8.163.
458 See above, § 8.2.

liability,[459] whereby one or more senior managers[460] in the corporate hierarchy had to be identified whose fault could be attributed to the company.[461] That it could be established that there was widespread negligence in the management of the company was not sufficient to impose corporate liability for manslaughter. It was only in very rare cases that it could be shown that, for example, a senior manager was personally grossly negligent for the purposes of establishing corporate liability.

The Corporate Manslaughter and Corporate Homicide Act 2007[462] was enacted as a result. This statute creates corporate liability for what is in effect gross negligence manslaughter but without the need to rely on the attribution theory. Consequently, instead of needing to show that, for example, a particular manager possessed sufficient culpability for the crime, it is sufficient now to show that there was general culpability in the management or organisation of the company.[463]

Although the statute creates a new offence of corporate manslaughter and abolishes corporate manslaughter by gross negligence at common law,[464] the reach of liability encompasses a variety of organisations other than companies, including most corporations, partnerships, trade unions, police forces, and various government departments.[465]

An organisation will be guilty of corporate manslaughter if the way its activities are managed or organised causes a person's death and amounts to a gross breach of a relevant duty owed by that organisation to the deceased.[466] The organisation will only be liable if the way its activities are managed or organised by its senior management[467] is a substantial element in the breach of duty.[468] Key to this offence is the need to identify a relevant duty of care and whether the breach of it was "gross". A variety of relevant duties of care in the tort of negligence are specifically identified, including duties owed by virtue of being an employer, the occupier of premises, the supplier of goods or services, construction or maintenance, use of plant or vehicle, or the carrying on of any activity on a commercial basis.[469] Whether a duty of care is owed is a question of law for the judge,[470] as is also the case for the common law offence of gross negligence manslaughter. The range of the relevant duties is extensive and encompasses, for example, duties relating to building, transport, and even leisure activities; it does not, however, include duties of care owed by a public authority relating to matters of public policy, such as the allocation of resources or the weighing of competing public interests.[471] So, a government department which implements a policy of extensive reductions in public spending will not be guilty of the offence if deaths result from that implementation.[472]

[459] See above, § 8.2(iii)(b).

[460] *P & O European Ferries (Dover) Ltd* (1990) 93 Cr App R 72 (CA).

[461] *Tesco Supermarkets Ltd v Nattrass* [1972] AC 153; *A-G's Reference (No. 2 of 1999)* [2000] 1 QB 796 (CA).

[462] Ormerod and Taylor, "The Corporate Manslaughter and Corporate Homicide Act 2007" [2008] *Crim LR* 589.

[463] By section 254 of the Crime and Policing Act 2026 a company or a partnership is liable for any crime committed by a senior manager of the company or partnership within the actual or apparent scope of their authority. See above, § 8.2(v).

[464] Corporate Manslaughter and Corporate Homicide Act 2007, s. 20.

[465] *Ibid.*, s. 1(2) and sched. 1.

[466] *Ibid.*, s. 1(1).

[467] People are "senior management" if they play significant roles in making decisions about how the organisation's activities are managed or organised or actually manage or organise those activities: *ibid.*, s. 1(4)(c).

[468] *Ibid.*, s. 1(3).

[469] *Ibid.*, s. 2(1). The Act extends to duties owed to people in custody (s. 2(2)).

[470] *Ibid.*, s. 2(5).

[471] *Ibid.*, s. 3(1).

[472] There are further statutory exclusions for statutory inspections (s. 3(3)), certain military activities (s. 4), certain policing activities (s. 5), and certain organisations which respond to emergency circumstances (s. 6).

Once a duty of care has been established, it is then necessary to show that its breach is gross—something defined as conduct which "falls far below what can reasonably be expected of the organisation in the circumstances".[473] This mirrors the standard of gross negligence employed in gross negligence manslaughter. However, the statute identifies certain factors which the jury should take into account when deciding whether there was a gross breach of duty.[474] These factors include whether there was a serious failure to comply with health and safety legislation and the consequent risk of death, and the existence of attitudes, policies, systems, or accepted practices within the organisation which are likely to have encouraged failure to comply with health and safety legislation, or tolerance of such failures. This gross breach of duty must also be shown to have caused V's death. For instance, if death may have been caused by a gross breach of duty, but there is a possibility that death was caused by something independent of that breach, an acquittal for corporate manslaughter should result.[475]

The liability created by this offence is fixed only on the corporation itself. Consequently, it is not possible for an individual, such as a director of the company, to be an accessory to corporate manslaughter,[476] although directors continue to be prosecuted for manslaughter or breach of health and safety legislation in their own right.[477]

The 2007 Act was a significant piece of legislation for corporate liability, although prosecutions under it are not common, being confined to the clearer cases of gross negligence since proceedings cannot be commenced without the consent of the Director of Public Prosecutions.[478] The first company to be convicted of this offence was Cotswold Geotechnical Holdings Ltd,[479] a small family-run business, with the prosecution arising from the death of an employee who was working in a deep and unsupported pit which collapsed. This case is typical of those where a company has been convicted of corporate manslaughter, with regard to the small size of the company, its simple management structure, and the fact that the death was of an employee acting in the course of their employment.[480] The fact that prosecutions are uncommon is likely to be due to the complex enforcement environment, especially since other charges under health and safety and other legislation are available and may be easier to establish, particularly in the case of large organisations.[481]

## § 10.8 Reform of the law of homicide

In 2006 the Law Commission published a major review of the English law of homicide, focusing on the partial defences to murder[482] and the structure and content of the law

[473] *Ibid.*, s. 1(4)(b).
[474] *Ibid.*, s. 8.
[475] *Wood Treatment Ltd* [2021] EWCA Crim 618.
[476] Corporate Manslaughter and Corporate Homicide Act 2007, s. 18(1).
[477] See Antrobus, "The Criminal Liability of Directors for Health and Safety Breaches and Manslaughter" [2013] *Crim LR* 309.
[478] Corporate Manslaughter and Corporate Homicide Act 2007, s. 17(a).
[479] [2011] EWCA Crim 1337.
[480] Roper, "The Corporate Manslaughter and Corporate Homicide Act 2007: A Re-evaluation 10 Years on from the First Case" [2022] *Crim LR* 290. See, too, Hébert, Bittle and Tombs, "Obscuring Corporate Violence: Corporate Manslaughter in Action" (2019) 58 *Howard Journal of Criminal Justice* 554.
[481] *Ibid.*
[482] LCCP No. 173, *Partial Defences to Murder* (2003); Law Com. No. 290, *Partial Defences to Murder* (2004).

of homicide.[483] Looking in the round at this body of work,[484] and without repeating our earlier remarks on specific aspects of the proposals, the principal impression is how much the future envisaged by the Commission is similar to the present. There would be a crime of murder—first-degree murder—with a mandatory penalty of life imprisonment. There would be partial defences of loss of control and diminished responsibility, reducing first-degree murder to second-degree murder and so displacing the mandatory penalty in favour of a discretionary life sentence. Gross negligence manslaughter would be retained and the proposal for an offence of criminal act manslaughter has a large affinity with the current constructive manslaughter. To be sure, there are some significant changes. First-degree murder would require some degree of subjective culpability as to the risk of causing death, and duress would be a defence to first-degree and second-degree murder, albeit with a reverse burden of proof. Second-degree murder would also encompass killings done with intent to cause serious injury or intended to cause injury or fear or risk of injury if D was aware of a serious risk of causing death. The subsequent statutory reform of the partial defences, which departs in some significant ways from what the Commission proposed, was essentially a refurbishment rather than a new blueprint for these defences. The defence of diminished responsibility is essentially unchanged and the new defence of loss of control is not as radical as might first be thought, with a large degree of codification of aspects of the common law, especially regarding the objective test.

The crucial decision was the retention of one form of murder attracting a mandatory penalty. Much of the design and content of the new dispensation follows from that. A radical, simplifying reform, suggested by Lord Kilbrandon in *Hyam*,[485] would be to reduce all the categories of homicide to one: a general, all-embracing offence of unlawful homicide. This proposal has been defended and elaborated by Blom-Cooper and Morris.[486] Certainly, many of the post-*Hyam* appeals on the demarcation of the murder/manslaughter boundary, the limits of what has become the loss of control defence, and the applicability of duress to murder would have been unnecessary had this bold proposal been taken up by the legislature. The principal casualty of such a change would be a distinct crime of murder. The pay-off would be radical simplification of a complex body of law and a sentencing discretion for every case of homicide.

These are powerful attractions, yet it may cogently be objected that to scrap all the current gradations of homicide would bring under one label an enormous range of differing conduct with very different forms of culpability. Besides, there is a strong sentiment to retain the evocative term murder; a feeling that an important cultural value would be lost if the worst killings did not attract that label. That sentiment proved decisive for the Law Commission.[487] It remains to be seen what price must be paid in terms of appeals and complexity should these wider reforms ever be implemented. Enlightenment seems unlikely since, when Parliament had the opportunity to reform the law of homicide, it chose to concentrate on reforming the partial defences to murder; ignoring the recommendations of the Law Commission for structural changes to the law.

483 LCCP No. 177, *A New Homicide Act for England and Wales?* (2003); Law Com. No. 304, *Murder, Manslaughter and Infanticide* (2006).

484 For reviews, see Wilson, "The Structure of Criminal Homicide" [2006] *Crim LR* 471; Ashworth, "Principles, Pragmatism and the Law Commission's Recommendations on Homicide Law Reform" [2007] *Crim LR* 345.

485 [1975] AC 55, 98.

486 *With Malice Aforethought* (2004) and *Fine Lines and Distinctions* (2011).

487 Law Com. No. 304, part 2.

However, the Law Commission announced in 2025 that it is conducting a further review of the law relating to homicide offences and published a Consultation Paper in 2026.[488] The Law Commission proposes a structural reform of the law of homicide which largely replicates what it proposed in 2006. Consequently, the Law Commission proposes three tiers of homicide offences: an offence of first-degree murder where D unlawfully killed with an intention to kill; second-degree murder (for which a discretionary life sentence would be available) where D unlawfully killed with an intention to cause serious injury or where D is charged with first-degree murder and a partial defence is successful; and manslaughter of three types, namely unlawful dangerous act, gross negligence (involving conduct which was "truly exceptionally bad") and reckless. Other matters on which the Law Commission is consulting include whether the term "manslaughter" should be retained, whether a specific offence should be created of supplying unlawful drugs resulting in the death of a person and of controlling or coercive behaviour in an intimate or family relationship which contributes to V's death by suicide. The final report will be published in 2028. If the initial recommendations are confirmed and adopted by Parliament this will constitute radical changes to the law of homicide.

## § 10.9 Infanticide

Conceptually, infanticide is not simply a defence but a distinct category of homicide: applying as a stand-alone offence in its own right, as well as a form of partial defence when D's conduct satisfies the elements of murder or manslaughter (i.e. reducing murder or manslaughter to infanticide).[489] As was affirmed in *Tunstill*,[490] the point of infanticide is "to ameliorate the potential harshness of the offence of murder" in particular,[491] with its mandatory life sentence. The offence of infanticide under the Infanticide Act 1938 is committed if D, the mother of V, a child under the age of 12 months, kills V when the balance of D's mind is disturbed by reason of her not having fully recovered from the effect of giving birth to V, or by reason of the effect of lactation consequent upon V's birth.

The offence provides, within its limited terms of reference, a more accommodating ground of mitigation than diminished responsibility. There is no requirement that the balance of D's mind should be disturbed by a condition amounting to a recognised medical disorder.[492] The jury may return a verdict of infanticide as an alternative to a finding of murder or of manslaughter,[493] or the offence may be charged in its own right. If the issue is contested, it seems that D need not prove that the balance of her mind was disturbed but must merely point to sufficient evidence to make this a live issue.[494] Most verdicts of infanticide arise from a plea of guilty to the offence. The scale of punishment is the same as manslaughter, so the maximum sentence is life imprisonment, but usually culpability is

[488] *Homicide Offences* Law Com. CP No. 277 (2026).

[489] Mackay, *Mental Condition Defences in the Criminal Law* (1995) 207–14; Maier-Katkin and Ogle, "A Rationale for Infanticide Laws" [1993] *Crim LR* 903; Loughnan, "The 'Strange' Case of the Infanticide Doctrine (2012) 32 *OJLS* 685.

[490] [2018] EWCA Crim 1696, [2019] 1 WLR 416.

[491] *Ibid.*, [31].

[492] From a study of 23 persons convicted of infanticide, only two could be considered mentally ill: d'Orban, "Women Who Kill Their Children" (1974) 134 *British Journal of Psychiatry* 560.

[493] Infanticide Act 1938, s. 1(2), as amended by the Coroners and Justice Act 2009.

[494] The Act makes no reference to a burden of proof on D.

treated at the lower end, with custodial sentences starting at two years' imprisonment, and typically non-custodial orders are made.[495]

Studies of the working of the Infanticide Act 1938 indicate that a plea of guilty to infanticide will readily be accepted in cases where a mother kills her child when the child is under the age of 12 months if there is evidence of emotional disturbance at the time of the killing.[496] This liberal approach in practice contrasts with the restrictive terms of the Act. According to the statute, D's mind must be disturbed by (i) not having fully recovered from the effect of giving birth or (ii) by reason of the effect of lactation consequent upon the birth of the child. The latter condition is medically controversial.[497] The first is also *potentially* problematic because, strictly, D's disturbance must be the result of the birth process and not owing to pressures, economic or emotional, arising from the introduction of a new child into D's domestic environment. In the informal world of guilty pleas, it would appear that such fine discriminations are not made.

The position is different if the conditions of the offence are contested in court. In *Kai-Whitewind*,[498] Judge LJ, for the Court of Appeal, insisted that under the terms of the Infanticide Act 1938, the only question for the jury was whether the effects of giving birth or of lactation disturbed the balance of D's mind. Pre-existing mental disorders, unconnected with giving birth, could not be referenced as evidence of disturbance of mind. Semantically, this seems correct: the statutory phrase "by reason of her not having fully recovered from the effect of having given birth to the child or by reason of the effect of lactation" would seem to exclude disturbances of mind caused by other factors.

A very different view was taken in *Tunstill*,[499] where D killed her child almost immediately after giving birth. Prior to the birth, there was evidence suggestive that D had Asperger's syndrome and was very depressed. There was also evidence that she experienced a "stress reaction" to the birth process. The trial judge ruled that only the stress reaction could be taken into account and D was convicted of murder. The Court of Appeal ordered a retrial, on the basis that the phrase "by reason of" did not mean "solely by reason of". Rather, "as long as a failure to recover from the effects of birth is an operative and substantial cause of the disturbance of [D's] balance of mind, that should be sufficient even if there are underlying mental problems (perhaps falling short of diminished responsibility) which are part of the overall picture".[500] The Court of Appeal drew a comparison with the House of Lords' decision in *Dietschmann*,[501] where D was permitted to put forward his extreme grief reaction as evidence of diminished responsibility, irrespective of the fact that, but for his intoxication, he would not have attacked and killed V. As the Court recognised, this analogy is far from exact.[502]

[495] https://insights.doughtystreet.co.uk/post/102jl6z/an-update-on-the-law-of-infanticide-a-review-of-cases-over-the-past-20-years-by.

[496] Mackay, "The Consequences of Killing Very Young Children" [1993] *Crim LR* 21.

[497] Bluglass, "Infanticide" [1978] *Bulletin of the Royal College of Psychiatrists* 14. In Law Com. No. 304, *Murder, Manslaughter and Infanticide* (2006) para. 826, reference is made to a yet-unpublished study reporting a link between lactation and dopamine sensitivity which may trigger psychosis. Maier-Katkin and Ogle note that childbirth itself can give rise to mental disturbance, although social and familial pressures are more important causes of subsequent instability: "A Rationale for Infanticide Laws" [1993] *Crim LR* 903.

[498] [2005] EWCA Crim 1092, [2005] 2 Cr App R 31.

[499] [2018] EWCA Crim 1696, [2019] 1 WLR 416.

[500] *Ibid.*, [31].

[501] [2003] UKHL 10, [2003] 1 AC 1209.

[502] [2018] EWCA Crim 1696, [2019] 1 WLR 416, [32].

There is much to be said for *Kai-Whitewind* in terms of an unforced reading of section 1(1) of the Infanticide Act 1938. Yet the reading in *Tunstill* is surely preferable in terms of capturing the rationale underlying the statute. In this context, it is worth noting the Law Commission's proposed Criminal Code formulation:[503]

> "A woman who, but for this section, would be guilty of murder or manslaughter of her child is not guilty of murder or manslaughter, but is guilty of infanticide, if her act is done when the child is under the age of twelve months and when the balance of her mind was disturbed by reason of the effect of giving birth [together with circumstances present before the birth, yet also present at the time of birth and any further circumstances] consequent upon that birth."

Even under that formulation, however, restrictions would remain which could operate with arbitrary effect. The offence would still require that the child killed be under 12 months of age and could only be committed by women. It is perhaps no surprise therefore that, more recently, the Law Commission has recommended that the offence should be retained as it is.[504] Yet it would improve a far from perfectly conceived offence to adopt the Law Commission's earlier formulation, with amendments to extend its scope by time and sex.

## § 10.10 Causing the death of a child or vulnerable adult

There have been difficult cases where it is clear that a child has been killed by a parent, but it cannot be proved whether it was the mother or the father, or indeed another person in the same household, who killed the child, or that one person was at least an accomplice to the other: so none is convicted. To ensure a conviction in such circumstances, a new offence was created by section 5(1) of the Domestic Violence, Crime and Victims Act 2004 where D failed to take reasonable steps to protect V. To establish this offence, it must be shown that V, who is a child or a vulnerable adult,[505] was killed[506] as the result of an unlawful act by somebody who was a member of the same household and who had frequent contact with V, and that there was a significant risk of serious physical harm being caused to V by such a person. This risk of serious physical harm must be in existence before harm was caused.[507] D will be guilty of the offence if, as well as being a member of the same household as V and having frequent contact with him, she either

(i) caused V's death; or
(ii) was aware, or ought to have been aware, of the risk of serious harm to V; she failed to take reasonable steps to protect V from the risk;[508] and the unlawful act occurred in circumstances of the kind which D foresaw or ought to have foreseen.

503 Law Com. No. 177, *A Criminal Code for England and Wales* (1989) cl. 64(1); Law Com. No. 304, *Murder, Manslaughter and Infanticide* (2006) Part 8.

504 Law Com CP No. 277, *Homicide Offences* (2026) para. 9.49.

505 The state of vulnerability need not be long-standing and may arise from injury, illness, or circumstance, such as being a recent immigrant who does not speak any English and who is utterly dependent on others in the household (*Khan* [2009] EWCA Crim 2, [2009] 1 WLR 2036), or may arise from external factors such as being the victim of sexual or domestic abuse or modern slavery (*Uddin* [2017] EWCA Crim 1072, [2017] 1 WLR 4739).

506 The offence was extended to cases where V suffers serious physical harm by the Domestic Violence, Crime and Victims (Amendment) Act 2012, s. 1.

507 *ATT* [2024] EWCA Crim 460, [2025] KB 225. In that case poor parenting did not give rise to a risk of serious physical harm.

508 Morrison, "Should there be a Domestic Violence Defence to the Offence of Familial Homicide?" [2013] *Crim LR* 826, 830 considers this reasonable steps test to constitute both actus reus and mens rea, sine it determines both breach of duty and fault.

The Act imposes a penalty upon conviction of up to 14 years' imprisonment.

Although the offence appears complex, its application is clear. Suppose, for example, that D is the mother of V, a baby. She lives with her partner, P, who has physically abused V on a number of occasions. P murders V. D would be guilty of the section 5 offence if: she was aware, or should have been aware, of the significant risk of physical harm being caused to V by P; she failed to take reasonable steps to protect V from the risk, such as contacting the social services; and the murder occurred in circumstances which D did foresee or should have foreseen. It is notable that D's liability can depend on an objective assessment of risk and takes the form of liability for an omission, the statute creating a duty to act if there is no pre-existing legal duty to do so. There would, however, be such a pre-existing duty in the case of a parent and their child.

It has been suggested that there is a danger that this offence will criminalise mothers of abused children who are themselves victims of domestic abuse.[509] This concern was discounted in *Khan*[510] on the ground that D would only be liable if she had failed to take reasonable steps to protect her child; what is reasonable being assessed with reference to D's own circumstances and attributes, having regard to her own suffering of domestic abuse.[511]

## § 10.11 Suicide, encouraging or assisting suicide, and suicide pacts

### *(i) Suicide*

For centuries, death by suicide entailed for the deceased a form of post-mortem disgrace. Burial rites were prohibited and real and personal property were forfeit to the Crown.[512] That stigma was reflected in law. Until the passing of the Suicide Act 1961, it was an offence at common law to attempt suicide. Because of the Act, however, a survivor of a suicide attempt will no longer attract criminal liability for her self-directed conduct.[513] In *Nicklinson v Ministry of Justice*,[514] Lord Sumption noted that the move to decriminalise suicide was taken not because suicide had become morally acceptable, but rather because the imposition of criminal sanctions on those who had attempted suicide was perceived as inhumane and ineffective.

As will be seen, it remains criminal to encourage or assist the suicide of others, whether by urging or helping others to kill themselves or simply by doing an act which is capable of encouraging or assisting another to commit suicide (even if no suicide is ultimately attempted).[515]

The residual criminality still associated with suicide requires some attempt at determining what acts are to be regarded as suicides.[516] In *Bland*,[517] Lord Goff took the view that a

509 Herring, "Familial Homicide, Failure to Protect and Domestic Violence—Who's the Victim?" [2007] *Crim LR* 923.

510 *Khan (Uzuma)* [2009] EWCA Crim 2, [2009] 1 WLR 2036, [33].

511 See further Morrison, "Should There Be a Domestic Violence Defence to the Offence of Familial Homicide?" [2013] *Crim LR* 826; Freer, "'Causing or Allowing the Death of a Child': Challenges to Working Out 'Which of You Did It'" [2016] *Crim LR* 618.

512 Kenny, *Outlines of Criminal Law* (1902) 112–14.

513 Suicide Act 1961, s. 1.

514 [2014] UKSC 38, [2015] AC 657, [212].

515 Suicide Act 1961, s. 2.

516 See also Wheat, "The Law's Treatment of the Suicidal" [2000] *Med LR* 182.

517 [1993] AC 789, 864.

person was legitimately entitled to insist on the cessation of forms of life support such as mechanical respiration. Such an exercise of autonomy was not to be regarded as a form of suicide, merely a refusal of medical treatment. Lord Goff did not explain why, in particular circumstances, to decline further treatment is not to opt for suicide. It is not obvious why a request to be taken off life support is not a form of suicide in circumstances where the removal of support entails a rapid and certain death. Prima facie, it seems to be a case of opting for non-existence by rejecting an unacceptable form of life. Be that as it may, Lord Goff's denial that such a choice was equivalent to suicide both ensures patient autonomy and shields doctors and other medical personnel from the possibility of criminal liability in respect of assisting suicide. It remains the case that the taking of any drug or poison to end life will be suicide whatever the degree of pain and disability the patient must otherwise endure. That position has not changed following the incorporation of the ECHR into English law.[518]

In *Bland*, Hoffmann LJ took the decriminalisation of suicide to be a recognition of the principle of self-determination.[519] If this is indicative of a right in the strict sense, it should follow that if a person of sufficient maturity and competent decision-making capacity has resolved to take her life, any physical intervention to prevent her from doing so will constitute an assault. This analysis throws into question the legality of such interventions as non-consensual medical treatment to prevent loss of life following a suicide attempt. It may be doubted, however, whether there is a right to commit suicide, at least in the full sense. If there were such a right, the right-holder should be entitled to call upon others to help her in the vindication of the right. But it is quite clear that if others were to help her they would become liable for assisting suicide, contrary to section 2 of the Suicide Act 1961. The existence of section 2 rather suggests that the abolition of the offence of attempted suicide does not make the choice to commit suicide a legally protected sphere of autonomy, merely that such a choice will not incur a criminal sanction. On the other hand, the mere fact that life-preserving intervention *may* be lawful does not mean that it *should* be employed in every possible case.

### *(ii) Encouraging or assisting suicide*

Following the decision of the House of Lords in *Kennedy (No. 2)*,[520] V's voluntary act of committing suicide is likely to break the chain of causation so that persons who encourage or assist V are not liable as a principal for a homicide offence in respect of V's death.[521] Rather, liability is under section 2 of the Suicide Act 1961.[522] When first enacted, section 2 created an offence of aiding, abetting, counselling, or procuring suicide or attempted suicide. This involved the standard complicity formula and it required proof that V had

518 In *Re B (Adult: refusal of medical treatment)* [2002] 2 All ER 449, the Court of Appeal ruled that the continuation of life support should cease on notification by a competent patient that such treatment was no longer wanted. However, assisting a person wishing to die by providing a substance that will terminate life is unlawfully to assist that person's suicide: *R (on the application of Pretty)* [2002] 1 All ER 1. For critical discussion, see Tur, "Legislative Technique and Human Rights: The Sad Case of Assisted Suicide" [2003] *Crim LR* 3.

519 [1993] AC 789, 827.

520 [2007] UKHL 38, [2008] 2 AC 269.

521 But compare *Dhaliwal* [2006] EWCA Crim 1139, [2006] 2 Cr App R 24 and *Wallace* [2018] EWCA Crim 690, [2018] 2 Cr App R 22. *Wallace* is further criticised in § 4.2(iii)(b) (Principle 1).

522 There is no such liability in Scotland, as confirmed in *Ross v Lord Advocate* [2016] CSIH 12.

committed suicide and that D had done an act which helped, encouraged, or procured this offence with the necessary mens rea for accessorial liability. However, the section created a free-standing crime, not a way of participating in the crime of another, since V's act of committing suicide or attempting suicide is not an offence in its own right.

This original offence of complicity in suicide has now been replaced by what is, in effect, a new offence of doing an act which is capable of encouraging or assisting suicide, contrary to section 2(1) of the Suicide Act 1961.[523] Whereas the old offence required proof of suicide or a suicide attempt, under the new version of the offence it is not necessary to prove that any suicide or attempted suicide has occurred.[524] This version uses the language of the new inchoate offences of encouraging and assisting a crime,[525] and it is an inchoate offence too. The maximum sentence following conviction for this offence is imprisonment for 14 years.[526] The old complicity offence could be attempted, whereas it is not possible to attempt the new offence,[527] so it is unlikely that the scope of liability will be expanded by this reform, since an act which is capable of encouraging or assisting suicide is likely to have been a more than merely preparatory act in respect of the aiding, abetting, counselling, or procuring of a suicide or a suicide attempt.

The actus reus of this offence requires D to do an act which is capable of encouraging or assisting suicide or attempted suicide of another person. The encouragement and assistance need not relate to a specific person or class of person known to D or even identified by her. So a person who writes an article in a blog which advocates those readers who are terminally ill to commit suicide would in principle be guilty of the offence. Encouragement is defined as including the making of threats or putting pressure on a person to commit suicide.[528] It is possible to encourage or assist indirectly by arranging for D2 to do the act of encouraging or assisting.[529] As with the Serious Crime Act offences of encouraging and assisting crime, it is not necessary to show that D's act had any effect on V; D may be guilty of the offence even if V is unaware of D's act, so long as it was *capable* of encouraging or assisting V's suicide or attempted suicide.

The mens rea of the offence is an intent by D's act to encourage or assist suicide or attempted suicide.[530] For encouraging or assisting crime under section 44 of the Serious Crime Act 2007, foresight does not constitute intent, so oblique intent appears not to be sufficient; but no similar provision is made for encouraging or assisting suicide, so presumably foresight of a proven virtually certain consequence of D's conduct will suffice.

If D's act is not actually capable of encouraging or assisting suicide, the facts should be judged as D believed that they were or would be, and, in the light of D's belief, it should be determined whether the act was capable of encouraging or assisting suicide.[531] The effect of this qualification is that factual impossibility should not defeat liability for this offence. So,

[523] Inserted by s. 59 of the Coroners and Justice Act 2009.
[524] Suicide Act 1961, s. 2(1B).
[525] Serious Crime Act 2007, Part 2. See above, § 9.1.
[526] Suicide Act 1961, s. 2(1C).
[527] Criminal Attempts Act 1981, s. 1(4)(ba). Neither is it possible to commit the offence of encouraging or assisting contrary to section 44 of the Serious Crime Act 2007 in respect of the offence of encouraging or assisting suicide: Serious Crime Act 2007, s. 51A.
[528] Suicide Act 1961, s. 2A(3).
[529] *Ibid.*, s. 2A(1). D2 must in fact do the act arranged by D1 for such liability to arise.
[530] *Ibid.*, s. 2(1)(b).
[531] *Ibid.*, s. 2A(2).

for example, if D writes a letter to encourage V to commit suicide but, unknown to D, V had already killed himself, D's act of sending the letter should be treated as capable of encouraging suicide on the facts as she believed them to be.

Under the previous law, where D aided or abetted V to commit suicide in a country abroad where suicide is lawful, there was some doubt as to whether English courts would have jurisdiction over D.[532] There can be no doubts about this under section 2. This is because, as long as D does the act which is capable of encouraging or assisting suicide in England, it is irrelevant that it has no effect on V and equally irrelevant that any possible suicide might be committed abroad.

Although in medical contexts life-sustaining treatment can be withdrawn or refused without embroiling medical or caring personnel in assisting suicide charges, outside these contexts D's encouraging V's self-determination to cause death via V's omission will result in potential liability for D. So, if V determines to die by way of starvation, D may incur liability under section 2 were he to encourage and strengthen her resolve not to take food during the critical period. However, if V were to go on a hunger strike to make a political point, it is by no means obvious that persons strengthening her resolve up to the point of death will incur liability under section 2. It may well be that the doctrine of double effect will operate in this context,[533] so that D's liability will depend on whether he intended V to die or merely foresaw death as a side-effect. However, if he foresaw suicide as a virtually certain consequence, this may well be sufficient for liability under section 2. In *Nicklinson v Ministry of Justice*,[534] Lord Sumption recognised that, whilst a doctor cannot advise a patient on how to kill herself, there is no danger of criminal liability if the doctor provides advice about the clinical options, such as sedation and other palliative care, available to a patient who wishes to kill herself. This constitutes an impossibly fine line between the doctor's legitimate duty of care of the patient and the illegitimate encouragement or assistance of suicide.

The section 2 offence can only be prosecuted with the consent of the Director of Public Prosecutions (DPP).[535] The exercise of the DPP's discretion to prosecute has proved controversial. In *Pretty v DPP*,[536] the claimant sought a declaration of immunity from prosecution if her husband subsequently aided her suicide. The House of Lords refused to require the DPP to grant such an exemption. Subsequently, in *R (On the application of Purdy) v DPP*[537] the claimant sought and obtained an order requiring the DPP to specify the facts and circumstances which he would take into account when considering whether to prosecute for assisting suicide.

Consequently, the DPP issued a policy document identifying the factors he will take into account when determining whether to prosecute.[538] Relevant factors in favour of

[532] This was considered by some of the judges in *R (On the application of Purdy) v DPP* [2009] UKHL 45, [2010] 1 AC 345, but was left open.

[533] *Secretary of State for the Home Department v Robb* [1995] 1 All ER 677; *Nicklinson v Ministry of Justice* [2014] UKSC 38, [2015] AC 657, [18] (Lord Neuberger).

[534] *Ibid.*, [255(3)].

[535] Suicide Act 1961, s. 2(4).

[536] [2002] 1 All ER 1 (HL).

[537] [2009] UKHL 45, [2010] 1 AC 345. Heywood, "Clarification on Assisted Suicide" (2010) 126 *LQR* 5.

[538] *Policy for Prosecutors in Respect of Cases of Encouraging or Assisting Suicide* (2010), updated October 2014. See Daw and Solomon, "Assisted Suicide and Identifying the Public Interest in the Decision to Prosecute" [2010] *Crim LR* 737; Rogers, "Prosecutorial Policies, Prosecutorial Systems, and the Purdy Litigation" [2010] *Crim LR* 543; Sanders, "The CPS, Policy-Making and Assisted Dying: Towards a 'Freedom' Approach" in Child and Duff (eds.), *Criminal Law Reform Now* (2019) 133.

prosecution include that: V was under 18; V had not reached a voluntary, clear, settled, and informed decision to commit suicide before D's intervention; D was not wholly motivated by compassion; D was acting as a healthcare professional, a professional carer, or as a person in authority, such as a prison officer, and V was in his care; or D pressured V to commit suicide. The purpose of such a policy document, as identified by the House of Lords, is that it will enable V to make an informed decision when, at some future date, she wishes to die but needs assistance to do so.[539] The essence of the DPP's policy, consistent with the attitude of the House of Lords in *Purdy*, is that the autonomy of V should prevail, and D should not be prosecuted for assisting V's suicide, where V had a settled and clear intent to die for reasons of debilitating illness and had the clear capacity to make such a decision. The uncertainty of this policy was later challenged in *Nicklinson v Ministry of Justice*,[540] but the Supreme Court held that the policy did not require clarification and it would be inappropriate for the court to dictate to the DPP what the policy on prosecution should be; the court could review that policy, and its compatibility with human rights, but could not dictate its terms.

In *Nicklinson v Ministry of Justice*,[541] the Supreme Court acknowledged that the criminalisation of assisted suicide is not necessarily incompatible with the right to private life under Article 8 of the European Convention on Human Rights, because interference with that right has to be balanced against the interests of society in protecting vulnerable people from being pressured into suicide.[542] The Court concluded that it was not able to declare such incompatibility on the evidence before it, although some of their Lordships did not rule out such a declaration in the future if Parliament refused to debate seriously the issue of assisted suicide. Others of their Lordships considered that reform of the crime of assisted suicide was a matter for Parliament and not the courts. Subsequently, in *Conway*,[543] a panel of Supreme Court justices (Lady Hale, Lord Reed, and Lord Kerr) refused permission to appeal to the Court on the question of whether the applicant's medical circumstances (motor neurone disease) might make it permissible for him to receive assistance in suicide. The panel considered that the prospects for a successful appeal (from the Court of Appeal's ruling that any such assistance would be unlawful) were too slight to justify an appeal. It seems unlikely that there will be any further decisions of the Supreme Court on assisted suicide for quite some time. The focus has now shifted to Parliament. In 2024 a private member's Bill was introduced to allow adults who are terminally ill to request and be provided with assistance to end their own life.[544] The Bill was controversial and was subject to numerous amendments. It failed to be enacted but is likely to be brought back in a future parliamentary session.

[539] [2009] UKHL 45, [2010] 1 AC 345, [30] (Lord Hope).
[540] [2014] UKSC 38, [2015] AC 657.
[541] *Ibid.*
[542] In *R (Conway) v Justice Secretary* [2018] EWCA Civ 1431, [2020] QB 1, [201], respect for the sanctity of life and promotion of trust between patient and doctor in the care relationship were also acknowledged to be legitimate objectives.
[543] *R (Conway) v Secretary of State for Justice*, Supreme Court, 27 November 2018; refusing leave to appeal from *R (Conway) v Justice Secretary* [2018] EWCA Civ 1431, [2020] QB 1.
[544] Terminally Ill Adults (End of Life) Bill.

### *(iii) Suicide pacts*

If D kills V with the "settled intention" of dying too in pursuance of a suicide pact between herself and V, D will be guilty of voluntary manslaughter rather than murder by virtue of section 4 of the Homicide Act 1957; this provision operates as a partial defence to murder. To be a member of such a pact, one must intend to die in pursuance of the pact. If that is not the case, D will be guilty of murder. It is not a defining element of a suicide pact that each member of it must intend to die on the same occasion. Accordingly, D should be entitled to a verdict of manslaughter even if a time comes when she no longer intends to fulfil the pact, provided she intended to observe the pact at the time she killed V. One aspect of the extenuation that underlines section 4 is that D's mental state is assumed to be so desperate as to induce a decision to commit suicide *at the time of the killing*. It is irrelevant that the relevant condition may pass.

For obvious reasons, it may be difficult to resolve what part the survivor of a suicide pact played in enacting the pact. The Suicide Act 1961 provides that, on a charge of murder or manslaughter in pursuance of the pact, a verdict of encouraging or assisting suicide may be given.[545]

[545] Suicide Act 1961, s. 2(2).

# 11

# NON-FATAL OFFENCES AGAINST THE PERSON

Non-fatal offences against the person cover an enormous spectrum of human conduct. D commits battery if he takes hold of V's arm, should V have made it clear that she objects to such contact by D.[1] Or D may shoot and seriously injure V and thereby commit serious offences such as attempted murder or wounding with intent. What links the arm-holding with the shooting is the right of all persons not to be subjected to any unwarranted intrusion upon the body.[2] This most basic of rights is jealously guarded by the criminal law and, because of this, the concept of personal interference employed in the foundation offences of assault and battery extends to the mere touching of the clothes of the victim and even to the threat of such touching.[3] This is not overreaction: the right not to be physically touched, outside the sphere of consensual touchings and the exigencies of normal life, is fundamental to ordered liberty. Even where no harm occurs, the raw battery or assault in itself violates D's right to be left alone and not be interfered with by others. This shows that there is a further dimension to the offences against the person, additional to the concern for personal integrity and our right not to be hurt. This further dimension is a matter of privacy. The very act of interfering with another's person is a wrong; not because of any harmful consequences, but because it violates one of the core interests implicated in the right to respect for a private life, guaranteed by Article 8 of the ECHR.

There are a considerable number of offences which deal with personal interference, some of which involve the infliction or the threat of violence. Many of them are to be found in the Offences Against the Person Act 1861,[4] a statute which remains of central importance today. The Act did not create a brand new codification of non-fatal offences against the person, but was a consolidation of a disparate collection of existing statutory offences. There is consequently much overlap and inconsistent terminology within the 1861 Act. Even at the time of its enactment it was castigated as "singularly fragmentary and unsystematic".[5]

[1] *Collins v Wilcock* [1984] 3 All ER 374 (CA).

[2] The right inheres in all persons capable of autonomous choices, however irrational the choice made by the particular agent: *St George's Healthcare NHS Trust v S* [1998] 3 All ER 673 (CA). By contrast, if a person is considered unable to choose, quite drastic physical interventions may become lawful, such as the sterilisation of a learning-disabled woman: *F v West Berkshire Health Authority* [1990] 2 AC 1.

[3] *Day* (1845) 1 Cox CC 207; *Thomas* (1985) 81 Cr App R 331 (CA).

[4] Non-fatal offences continue to be created in other legislation. For example, the Domestic Abuse Act 2021 inserts a new offence of strangulation or suffocation into the Serious Crime Act 2015, s. 75A. See below, § 11.3(iv)).

[5] Greaves, *The Criminal Law Consolidation and Amendment Acts* (2nd ed., 1862) 3–4.

Yet it remains, today, at the centre of the law's response to offences against the person[6] and continues to generate a stream of appellate, interpretative case law.

In this chapter, no attempt will be made at a comprehensive coverage of the non-fatal offences. We will look first at the two basic offences, assault and battery, which police the frontier between lawful conduct and unlawful acts. Then we will turn to offences involving some form of bodily harm, including psychiatric harm, namely assault occasioning actual bodily harm, malicious wounding or infliction of grievous bodily harm, and wounding or causing of grievous bodily harm with intent to do grievous bodily harm. We will also examine when the victim's consent operates to negate liability. As we shall see, these offences have been extended to include the intentional and reckless transmission of diseases and infection. Following that, we will briefly consider offences concerned with poisons and noxious substances and then go on to consider harassment offences. Finally, we will examine versions of these offences aggravated by racial or religious hostility.

## § 11.1 Assault and battery

Assault and battery are two distinct offences. V is assaulted if she *apprehends* the possibility of imminent unlawful harm: if D has "done something of a physical kind which causes someone else to apprehend that they are about to be struck".[7] A battery is inflicted upon V if unlawful harm is *inflicted* upon her.[8] The former tends to be called "common assault" and the latter "assault by beating".[9] The distinction may seem odd. Ordinary people, and lawyers too, would naturally describe D's punching V simply as an assault. It would seem pedantic to insist that, if V saw the punch coming, she was first assaulted as she apprehended its impact and subsequently battered when the punch landed. The pedant might add for good measure that if D struck V without warning from behind, D would be guilty of battery but not of assault. It would be far better to do away with such nit-picking and use the single word "assault" to cover situations where V *either* apprehends *or* suffers harm (in the latter case, whether she apprehended it or not). The term battery (or even "assault" with the addition of "by beating") could be allowed to wither away as an archaism. Indeed, in 1980, the Criminal Law Revision Committee took the view that the term "assault" could be safely used in legal discourse to cover assaults in the narrow sense (i.e. causing an apprehension of harm) and in the sense of inflicting harm, rendering the term battery otiose.[10] A similar position was taken by the Law Commission, although it recommended distinguishing between threatened and physical assault.[11]

[6] It is assumed that "person" is a reference to a human being and that pre-natal injury does not fall within provisions relating to the causing of injury. There is no authority or dictum to the contrary and no reason of principle why the law relating to non-fatal offences against the person should differ on this point from the law of homicide (see above, § 10.2(i)(a)). If V should be born in an injured condition because of something done by D prior to V's birth, then, applying the reasoning in *A-G's Reference* (*No. 3 of 1994*) [1998] AC 245, in principle a charge against D under a suitable provision of the OAPA 1861 should be possible.

[7] *Nelson* [2013] EWCA Crim 30, [2013] 1 WLR 2861, [3]. See *Logdon* [1976] Crim LR 121 (DC) for an example of a "pure" assault, i.e. a situation where D intended V to apprehend harm by showing him a gun in a desk drawer but lacked any present intention to inflict harm.

[8] *Nelson* [2013] EWCA Crim 30, [2013] 1 WLR 2861, [3].

[9] *Ibid.*

[10] Criminal Law Revision Committee, Fourteenth Report, *Offences Against the Person* Cmnd. 7844 (1980).

[11] Law Com. No. 361, *Reform of Offences Against the Person* (2015); discussed below, § 11.12.

Unfortunately, pedantry has survived, thanks to *DPP v Little*.[12] The information laid against D charged that he "did unlawfully assault and batter [V] contrary to [section 39 of the Criminal Justice Act 1988]". The Divisional Court ruled that the information was bad for duplicity because it charged two separate offences instead of the permissible single offence. Assault, said the Court, was to cause an apprehension of violence and battery was to inflict violence, which does not require proof of any apprehension by V.[13] If assault *and* battery were to be charged, they would have to be laid by separate informations.

In historical terms, the decision in *Little* is correct. Battery emerged as a crime from the tort of trespass to the person.[14] The etymology of assault—*adsaltare*, to jump at—indicates the focus on frightening rather than hitting people. Yet it is remarkably inconvenient to revert to the medieval origins of these offences. For example, section 47 of the OAPA 1861 penalises "any *assault* occasioning actual bodily harm". There is no reference whatever to battery. By far and away the most common incident giving rise to a charge under section 47 is a direct physical attack by D on V. The standard form of indictment for such an occurrence is "D assaulted V, thereby occasioning him actual bodily harm". If V apprehended the attack, the reference to assault is sustainable in terms of the presence of the elements of that offence. Yet it is the battery rather than the assault that occasions the actual bodily harm. What if D succeeds in striking V without first causing him apprehension? (Suppose V is looking the other way or is asleep.) This would still constitute a section 47 offence.

In *Little*, the Divisional Court accepted that the legislature, in section 47 and in other provisions, used the term "assault" to embrace both assault in the pure sense of the term and the offence of battery. It follows that the standard form of indictment referred to above, used in respect of section 47, is duplicitous, in that the term "assault" when used in that section is a reference to the two distinct offences of assault or battery. To avoid this problem it would be appropriate for prosecutors to make it clear that the section 47 charge involves an assault or battery, but not both. It has, however, been recognised that if D is charged with "common assault", this is properly treated as an abbreviation for assault and battery and therefore incorporates a battery.[15] Thus, if D is charged with "common assault", it is acceptable for the prosecution to establish this by evidence of battery. Such an approach avoids the duplicity identified in *DPP v Little*, since only one offence is charged, but it provides the prosecution with the opportunity to prove either assault or battery to secure a conviction. This is neither transparent nor fair to D since he is not given sufficient notice of the case he has to meet, but it is at least consistent with the approach adopted to establish assault occasioning actual bodily harm. In all cases, however, it would be preferable to distinguish explicitly between assault and battery, at least until the long-overdue reform of offences against the person has occurred.[16]

The maximum punishment for assault and battery is six months' imprisonment.[17] Where, however, V is an emergency worker acting in the exercise of her functions as such

[12] [1992] QB 645 (DC).

[13] See also *Nelson* [2013] EWCA Crim 30, [2013] 1 WLR 2861, [7].

[14] Milsom, *Historical Foundations of the Common Law* (2nd ed., 1981) chap. 11.

[15] *R (Ward) v Black Country Magistrates' Court* [2020] EWHC 680 (Admin).

[16] See below, § 11.12.

[17] Criminal Justice Act 1988, s. 39. Although it is presumed that such a sentence will be suspended: Sentencing Act 2026, s. 1.

a worker, the maximum sentence is increased to two years' imprisonment.[18] An emergency worker includes a police officer,[19] a prison officer, somebody working for fire and rescue, and also somebody working for the National Health Service. It is not necessary to prove that D was aware that V was or might be an emergency worker.

## § 11.2 Assault

### *(i) The actus reus*

Although *Little*[20] recognised that assault is a statutory offence, charged properly under section 39 of the Criminal Justice Act 1988, no definition of assault is to be found in that provision. We must turn to the common law in order to delineate the nature and ambit of the offence, notwithstanding that the practice after *Little* is for information to refer to assault as an offence charged under section 39.[21]

The actus reus of assault is any act by D that causes V to apprehend immediate and unlawful personal violence, although sometimes the language of "force" is used instead of "violence"[22] (and the former is more accurate: see § 11.(3)(i) below). There is high authority endorsing this statement of the actus reus in assault.[23] However, as we shall see, key elements of this judicially derived formula have been expansively interpreted. Before turning to those elements, some general remarks concerning the actus reus need to be made.

#### *(a) Unlawfulness and consent*

The violence or force that V apprehends must be *unlawful*. Sometimes, the application of force may be lawful, as in the application of defensive or preventive force.[24] Consent of the victim, too, may legitimate what would otherwise be unlawful violence. Although consent is further discussed below,[25] given the crucial role that it may play in determining whether an assault has been committed, some additional discussion of that element is appropriate here.

[18] Assaults on Emergency Workers (Offences) Act 2018, s. 1. Section 45 of the Crime and Policing Act 2026 creates a new offence of assault of a retail worker at work.

[19] Who does not need to be executing a duty as a police officer, it being sufficient that they are exercising an emergency function as a police officer: *Campbell* [2020] EWHC 3868 (Admin); *Ahmed* [2021] EWHC 2122 (Admin), [2022] 1 WLR 314. If a police constable is assaulted in the execution of duty there is a distinct offence under the Police Act 1996, s. 89(1), although the maximum sentence is six months' imprisonment, albeit it is presumed that this will be suspended sentence (the same as for assault and battery).

[20] [1992] QB 645 (DC).

[21] Subsequently, the Court of Appeal has left open the question whether assault and battery should be regarded as separate statutory offences: *Lynsey* [1995] 3 All ER 654. Further, in *Haystead v Chief Constable of Derbyshire* [2000] 3 All ER 890, Laws LJ observed that assault and battery were "in truth" common law offences. However, unless and until *Little* is overruled, charges of assault and battery should be brought under s. 39 of the Criminal Justice Act 1988.

[22] *DPP v Ahmed* [2021] EWHC 2122 (Admin), [2022] 1 WLR 314, [13].

[23] *Ireland* [1998] AC 147.

[24] Below, § 21.2. This includes reasonable force as self-help to recover property from a trespasser: *Burns* [2010] EWCA Crim 1023, [2010] 1 WLR 2694.

[25] § 11.9.

There is some uncertainty whether lack of consent is an element of the actus reus of assault or a defence to assault.[26] In principle, the former is the better view, even if it does not represent the current law. The threshold of violence or force in assault is, properly, set at a very low level. V suffers the actus reus of an assault if she apprehends an imminent touching by D to which she has not consented and which is not an inevitable concomitant of ordinary life (like being jostled on a crowded train). Because an assault may include the threat of things that (should they happen) will not even hurt, we can see that lack of consent, and D's corresponding disrespect for V's autonomy and privacy, are at the heart of the wrong that constitutes an assault.[27] Certain forceful interventions may be well intentioned and, from a paternalist standpoint, be in the interests of V. But it is for V to decide what is in her interest. In *St George's Trust*,[28] a tort case, D performed an operation to save V's life and the late-term foetus she was carrying. However, he did so despite V's lack of consent. This was held to be trespass to V's person and, undoubtedly, was also an assault, as well as a battery.

Consequently, it is not necessary for V in any sense to be *frightened* by what D intends to do. It is enough that she does not want D to do it. If D threatens any form of immediate touching which V has not consented to, or which need not be tolerated as an incident of everyday life, D commits the actus reus of assault.

*(b) The conduct element in assault*

In *Fagan v MPC*,[29] the Divisional Court reiterated the traditional view that assault requires a positive act and that a mere omission will not suffice. In *Fagan*, D's conviction for assault[30] was confirmed on the basis of intentional failure to remove the wheel of a car which he had inadvertently parked on V's foot. The decision demonstrates that the act requirement will be fulfilled if D persists with a threatening posture that he may have adopted without any intent to cause apprehension of harm. Suppose that D, believing himself to be alone in a railway carriage, puts on a "horror" mask to amuse himself. In fact there is another passenger, V, in the carriage, and donning the mask causes V to fear an imminent attack from D. The actus reus of assault has occurred: and it continues while D does not remove the mask. Thus, it will be possible for D to commit the offence later, once he becomes aware of V's presence (and of V's fear).

[26] In *Brown* [1994] 1 AC 212, Lords Jauncey, Lowry, and Templeman considered consent to be a defence to assault, whereas Lords Mustill and Slynn considered the absence of consent to be part of the harm that constituted the offence. However, the views expressed on this point were *obiter* in respect of simple assault, since the case involved the causing of actual bodily harm—which in the circumstances was taken by the majority to negative the relevance of consent altogether (below, § 11.9(iii)). In *Kimber* [1983] 3 All ER 316, the Court of Appeal considered absence of consent to be an integral element of the actus reus in assault. However, the decision in *Brown* has now been confirmed by statute (the Domestic Abuse Act 2021, s. 71) where the language of a defence is used.

[27] Consequently, in principle there should be no finding of *assault*, even where D has caused significant physical harm to V, if D acts with V's consent. (There may well be liability for other offences which do not require an assault upon V, such as ss. 18 and 20 of the OAPA 1861.) However, this may not be the position under English law at present; on the majority view in *Brown* (see previous note), the most minor of apprehended contacts will constitute the actus reus of assault and consent is simply a qualified defence.

[28] [1998] 3 All ER 673 (CA).

[29] [1969] 1 QB 439 (DC); above, § 4.1(i)(b) (Case 4). This point was not taken, however, in *Santana-Bermudez* [2003] EWHC 2908 (Admin).

[30] Strictly, the case involved battery rather than assault, as it was concerned with the application of force and not the threat of force. The Divisional Court spoke in terms of assault and there is no reason to suppose that its reasoning does not extend to assault in the pure sense of that term.

The act requirement will not be satisfied, however, if D's *lawful* presence, without more, is perceived as a threat by V. Suppose that D enters an enclosed railway carriage on a train. The only other occupant is V, a lone woman. D notes that V seems agitated: moments later she says, "Please do not touch me". It would be appropriate socially for D to remove himself from the carriage at the first safe opportunity, but his failure to do so should not constitute the actus reus of assault. Arguably, this conclusion would not hold if D had knowingly entered a "women-only" carriage, i.e. if D were a trespasser. In *Smith v Superintendent of Woking Police Station*,[31] D had trespassed onto enclosed grounds and looked through the window of a ground-floor bedroom. V, undressing for sleep, was terrified when she saw him standing there; conduct which constituted an act of assault.

To speak is clearly an act. Formerly, there were dicta to the effect that "mere words" would not constitute an assault.[32] Applying such *dicta*, the Court of Appeal of British Columbia ruled in *Byrne* that to say, threateningly, "I've got a gun, give me all your money or I will shoot" did not constitute an assault.[33] The court insisted on some form of physical act. This remarkable indulgence is no longer available in England and Wales. The decision in *Smith*, above, holds that mere presence in unlawful threatening circumstances may constitute an assault. Those features were present in *Byrne* and, in addition, there were threatening words, making *Byrne* an *a fortiori* case from the standpoint of *Smith*. Any remaining doubt on the matter is resolved by the decision of the House of Lords in *Ireland*.[34] One of the matters requiring resolution was whether silent telephone calls could, *in principle*, constitute an assault. (The ruling was in principle because D had pleaded guilty to a charge of assault occasioning actual bodily harm, in the sense of psychiatric harm by silent telephone calls; accordingly the facts of the case were not under review.) The court ruled unanimously that a silent telephone call would constitute an assault if, *inter alia*, it caused V to apprehend the possibility of immediate unlawful violence. Although it would be possible to draw a distinction between telephone calls *per se* and "mere words", the two full judgments given in *Ireland* take their decision to have abolished the rule that mere words cannot constitute an assault if it ever truly existed in English law.[35] Similarly, in *Constanza*,[36] (discussed below), the Court of Appeal held that written threats by letter could found an assault. Presumably this would extend to threats communicated by text message or social media.

### (c) *A threat of immediate violence*

Assault in its pure form is a *threat* offence, whereas battery is a *contact* offence. Although they have differing histories, the two offences are closely linked. The actus reus of assault is the threat of an immediate battery. But it would be a mistake to describe assault as an attempted battery. To be guilty of assault, D need not possess any intention to inflict violence on V; it is enough that he intentionally or recklessly causes V *to apprehend* immediate

[31] (1983) 76 Cr App R 234 (DC).
[32] *Meade and Belt* (1823) 1 Lew CC 184.
[33] *Byrne* [1968] 3 CCC 179.
[34] [1998] AC 147 (HL).
[35] *Ibid.*, 161–2 (Lord Steyn), 166 (Lord Hope).
[36] [1997] 2 Cr App R 492 (CA).

violence.[37] On the other hand, a threat to inflict violence later is not enough. So, if D were to say, "I will come round next Monday and cut your right leg off", he would not have assaulted V, notwithstanding V's state of terror, because the violence which was threatened was not intended to occur immediately. Presumably this is to recognise that V could readily escape the threat, for example by going to the police.

An understandable judicial concern with the life-wrecking consequences of the abusive conduct familiarly called "harassment" has led to a significant attenuation of the immediacy requirement in assault, making for considerable doubt about the current scope of the offence. In *Constanza*, the Court of Appeal reviewed D's conviction for assault occasioning actual bodily harm arising from circumstances where D, among other things, sent threatening letters to V. Confirming D's conviction, the Court noted that D lived in the same neighbourhood as V and that it was enough to prove "fear of violence at some time not excluding the immediate future".[38] These words are not conspicuously clear but, in the context of the case, they appear to mean that it sufficed that among the fears that V entertained was the fear of a possible imminent attack. That this is enough is confirmed by the House of Lords in *Ireland* where Lord Steyn, speaking for the judicial committee, concluded that the immediacy requirement was made out if D's conduct caused V to apprehend the "possibility" of an immediate attack.[39]

In *Ireland*, D's conduct took the form of silent telephone calls which were made miles from the homes of his victims. As mentioned already, their Lordships did not decide whether the actual calls placed by D constituted assaults; in the light of D's guilty plea it merely had to be decided whether silent calls could in principle constitute assaults. Of course, on particular facts, a silent call might cause a fear of an immediate attack (e.g. where V believes the caller is phoning from outside their front door). Yet, even though V may know that the caller is many miles away, she may still be reduced to a state of great fear. It seems from *Ireland* that in such cases the issue of assault may now be put to the jury; whether V is put in fear of the possibility of an immediate attack is a question of fact. Nonetheless, Lord Steyn recommended that trial judges might advise juries that, if they found that V was put in fear, they should consider "what, if not the possibility of imminent personal violence, was the victim terrified about?"[40]

This relaxes the imminence requirement in assault beyond any point previously contemplated. It is simply not the case that a state of fear is, necessarily, a fear of the possibility of imminent attack. It is perfectly possible to experience fear and simultaneously be aware that one is perfectly safe, as anyone who has watched a well-crafted horror film well knows. Many recipients of threatening letters or calls may be traumatised by the experience, particularly if it is an extended one, yet at no time fear an *immediate* attack. Certainly, there should be legal protection from such conduct.[41] But the law of assault is the wrong medium

[37] *Logdon* [1976] Crim LR 121 (DC). For a discussion of assaults not culminating in bodily contact, see Horder, "Reconsidering Psychic Assault" [1998] *Crim LR* 392.

[38] [1997] 2 Cr App R 492, 494 (CA).

[39] [1998] AC 147, 162.

[40] *Ibid.*, 162. See also *DPP v Ramos* [2000] Crim LR 768 (DC).

[41] Including under the Protection from Harassment Act 1997 and the Communications Act 2003, s. 127. On the latter see *DPP v Collins* [2005] Crim LR 794 (DC).

(as Lord Steyn seemingly conceded at one point in his judgment in *Ireland*).[42] In cases involving threatening calls or letters, it is submitted that judges should refrain from leaving assault-based offences to juries unless there is some evidence that V was actually put in fear of the possibility of an immediate attack. *Pace* Lord Steyn, evidence of fear of something inchoate or non-immediate should not be placed before juries with an invitation to find that the only plausible basis for the fear was the threat of immediate attack.

### *(d) Conditional threats*

There is some authority that a "conditional" threat cannot constitute an assault. In *Blake v Barnard*,[43] there was held to be no assault where D pointed a pistol at V's head with the words, "Shut up or I will blow your brains out". The reasoning behind this remarkable decision was that there was no threat of immediate violence because V could negate the threat by doing what he was told.

Several criticisms may be made. In *Blake*, the famous civil case of *Tuberville v Savage*[44] was perceived to be in point. This was an error. In *Tuberville*, D touched the handle of his sword and informed V that "If it were not assize time, I would not take such language". We can see that D was informing V that, despite V's impertinence, D was not going to use his sword for fear of being tried, by the judges who were in the neighbourhood, and hanged:[45] a case of a non-threat rather than a conditional threat. Moreover, as already discussed, assault is as much about the protection of autonomy as protection from hurt. In *Blake*, D had no right to put such a coercive condition to V. Accordingly, V was under no duty to comply with the threat and was being confronted with a risk of violence should he assert his right to speak. In principle, such threats should normally constitute assaults. Indeed, there are *dicta* in the later case of *Read v Coker* to that effect.[46]

### *(ii) The mens rea for assault*

The mental element for the crime of assault is that D must intend that V should fear the possibility of immediate violence, or recklessly cause V to fear the possibility of immediate violence.[47] Intention bears its ordinary meaning in this context.[48] The recklessness in question is *Cunningham* recklessness:[49] accordingly, D must intend or foresee a risk that V will fear the possibility of immediate violence, and take that risk unreasonably.

Because assault is a crime which may be committed recklessly, it is, in the confusing terminology employed by the courts, a crime of "basic" intent and therefore a crime

[42] [1998] AC 147, 162.

[43] (1840) 9 C & P 626, 173 ER 985.

[44] (1669) 1 Mod Rep 3, 86 ER 684.

[45] Assuming, as the Court seemingly did, that D's words were a reliable indication that V was in no immediate danger. It is easy to imagine circumstances where reaching for a weapon is construed as a threat of immediate violence despite placatory words.

[46] (1853) 13 CB 850, 138 ER 1437.

[47] *Savage* [1992] 1 AC 699. If non-consent is treated as an element of the actus reus of assault (above, § 11.2(i)(a)), D would also have to be at least reckless about V's non-consent.

[48] See above, § 5.1.

[49] *Spratt* [1991] 2 All ER 210 (CA); *Parmenter* [1992] 1 AC 699 (HL). *Dicta* in the House of Lords in *Savage* (which overruled *Spratt* and *Parmenter* on other grounds) assume that advertence is required for assault: [1992] 1 AC 699, 736 (Lord Ackner).

where the liability of voluntarily intoxicated persons is resolved under the principles of *Majewski*.[50]

## § 11.3 Battery

### *(i) Actus reus*

The actus reus of battery is the infliction of violence, or preferably "force",[51] on V by D. It has emerged from our discussion of assault that "violence" is used in a very extended sense, reflecting the values of autonomy and privacy as well as protection from physical harm. Accordingly, D commits battery if he makes contact with V in any fashion to which she has not consented, expressly or impliedly, or which is not a contact in keeping with the normal expectations of the relevant time and place.[52] To kiss someone without consent has been considered a battery,[53] as has the act of spitting upon someone,[54] and the unauthorised cutting of hair.[55] If D makes contact with clothes that V is wearing, that will also suffice for battery.[56]

If one wishes to have the benefits of moving about in a modern society, one must accept the inevitable bodily contacts arising therefrom. Suppose that V has a horror of bodily contact with strangers but must take a train at rush hour in order to get to work. She cannot complain of battery when she is crushed together with others in the carriage. However, she is entitled to resist what would otherwise be normal lawful contact provided she has made it clear to D that she does not want such contact with him and it is practicable for him to desist from such contact.[57] Further, where social distancing is encouraged as a way of minimising the spread of a respiratory infection, the notion of normal lawful contact is likely to be interpreted more restrictively, and this will certainly be the case if social distancing has been mandated by law.

There is dispute about how direct the contact with V must be to constitute battery. Person-to-person contact is obviously sufficient but not necessary. Using any form of weapon will suffice. Just as a knife wielded in the hand is within the offence, so too a knife that is thrown. As *Scott v Shepherd* illustrates,[58] it does not matter if a dangerous weapon, such as a grenade, passes through several panic-stricken hands after being thrown by D prior to the impact on V. Such a response would not constitute a *novus actus interveniens*. Extending the offence further, there are *dicta* to the effect that to set a booby trap[59] or

50 [1977] AC 443; discussed below, § 18.4.

51 *DPP v Ahmed* [2021] EWHC 2122 (Admin), [2022] 1 WLR 314, [13]; *Marland v DPP* [2023] EWHC 1046 (Admin), [2023] 2 Cr App R 5, [8].

52 "An assault [*sic.* meaning "battery"] is an intentional touching of another person without the consent of that person and without lawful excuse": *Faulkner v Talbot* [1981] 3 All ER 468, 471 (DC); applied in *Thomas* (1985) 81 Cr App R 331 (CA).

53 *Dungey* (1864) 4 F & F 99, 102, 176 ER 487. Nowadays, it may also be a sexual assault, contrary to s. 3 of the Sexual Offences Act 2003; cp. *Lamb* [2007] EWCA Crim 1766.

54 *Smith* (1866) F & F 1066, 176 ER 910.

55 *Smith* [2006] EWHC 94 (Admin), [2006] 1 WLR 1571.

56 *Day* (1845) 1 Cox CC 207.

57 *Collins v Wilcock* [1984] 3 All ER 374 (CA).

58 (1773) 3 Wils 403, 96 ER 525; above, § 4.2(iii)(c) (Case 1). *Scott v Shepherd* is a civil case but there is no reason why a narrower conception should be adopted in the criminal law.

59 *Clarence* (1888) 22 QBD 23, 36 (Wills J), 45 (Stephen J).

to cause crushing by inducing panic amongst a crowd of people[60] may constitute battery. There seems a clear public interest in including such events within the scope of the offence; it should not matter in principle whether D causes violence to the person of V by direct or indirect means, provided the causing of violence is attributable to some act by D.

As with assault, battery usually requires an act, but the normal rules on omissions are applicable, so that the defendant will be liable for failing to act where they were under a duty to do so.[61] For example, in *Santana-Bermudez*,[62] V's finger was pierced by a syringe-needle lying in D's pocket. Prior to searching D, V (a police officer) asked if D had any needles on his person, and D replied "No". The danger that D had created was found to come within the decision in *Miller*;[63] on the Divisional Court's reading of that decision, his failure to inform V was a breach of duty to act sufficient to satisfy the conduct element of battery.

It follows that battery encompasses the indirect causing of harm through the application of force, albeit that the force derived from V. However, in *Ireland*, Lord Steyn strongly discountenanced any assumption that a battery had occurred on the facts of that case where there was no application of force. The silent telephone calls had caused psychiatric injury to V, injury which was taken to constitute bodily harm. The prosecution had argued that causing such bodily harm through the medium of the telephone was a form of battery. This was decisively rejected, on the ground that the concept of battery could not accommodate the causing of psychiatric injury by telephone.[64] Moreover, in *Wilson*,[65] the House of Lords had earlier ruled that the statutory offence of maliciously inflicting a wound or grievous bodily harm would encompass percussive and impact injuries whether directly or indirectly caused. In so ruling, their Lordships had considered that, so construed, the offence of malicious wounding[66] would take in a broader swathe of conduct than battery. The cases which take a broader view of battery are not binding on the House of Lords.[67] In the one decision directly in point (and uncomplicated by any creative use of the *Miller* principle), *DPP v K*,[68] the Divisional Court held that a battery had occurred where D had secreted acid in a hand-dryer, causing V to be burnt with acid upon using the machine. It is submitted that the Divisional Court was correct. Particularly in cases where such means are intentionally employed to cause harm, it would be absurd to draw any distinction between indirect methods and more standard forms of weapon. The idea that battery requires a very direct form of violence gains force from the term "inflict", which features in standard formulations of the offence. Yet the same verb also features in the statutory offence of malicious wounding and, in that context, is no longer taken to require that the injury be an immediate consequence of D's action.[69] Indeed in *Burstow*, an appeal heard jointly with *Ireland*, the House of Lords approved (in the context of maliciously inflicting grievous bodily harm) a reading of inflict

[60] *Martin* (1881) 8 QBD 54 (CCR); see also *Lewis* [1970] Crim LR 647 (CA).
[61] Above, § 4.1(i).
[62] [2003] EWHC 2908 (Admin).
[63] [1983] 2 AC 161. See above, § 4.1(i)(b) (Case 5).
[64] [1998] AC 147, 161. The conduct was held to constitute an assault.
[65] [1984] AC 242; followed in *Mandair* [1995] 1 AC 208.
[66] OAPA 1861, s. 20.
[67] *Martin* (1881) 8 QBD 54 and *Lewis* [1970] Crim LR 647 (CA) did involve assumptions that a battery had occurred, as the view was taken in those cases that a conviction under s. 20 of the OAPA 1861 required proof of a battery; an assumption no longer tenable in the light of *Wilson* [1984] AC 242 and *Mandair* [1995] 1 AC 208.
[68] [1990] 1 All ER 331 (DC).
[69] See *Wilson* [1984] AC 242 and *Mandair* [1995] 1 AC 208.

as a synonym for cause when the harm consisted of psychiatric injury.[70] The restrictive view of battery taken in *Ireland* was *obiter*.[71] It is submitted that, in cases of physical contact, the more relaxed reading of inflict in *Wilson*[72] should be extended to battery. It follows that the causation of violence through the application of force, directly or indirectly, should suffice for battery.[73]

#### *(ii) Hostility*

In *Brown*,[74] the House of Lords confirmed that the contact required for battery was a "hostile" contact. This requirement is not straightforwardly classified as an element of either actus reus or mens rea. The presence of hostility is a function of the motivation and attitude of D (seemingly a matter of mens rea) but which serves to fix and identify the nature of the conduct itself (prima facie, a matter of actus reus). A hand placed on V's shoulder in friendship is different in kind from a hand that will pull V into the violent clutches of D, notwithstanding that the force applied in the initial placing of the hand may be the same.

The requirement for hostility has come under strong judicial and academic attack. Lord Goff, in particular, has criticised the requirement as too vague and restrictive. For him, the boundaries of "physical contact which is generally acceptable in the ordinary conduct of daily life" should inform decisions concerning the ambit of battery.[75] But does this provide a clearer cutting edge? Suppose V is embraced by D, an exuberant stranger, in a crowded bar one minute after midnight on New Year's Day. V does not like it. Is this a battery or, in the context of the time and place (with no expectation of social distancing), an "acceptable standard of conduct"? If one takes the view that a *faux pas* should not necessarily entail criminal liability, there may be something to be said for a requirement of hostility.

While the majority in *Brown* endorsed the need for hostility in battery, it has been remarked that, in the context of that case, the word was interpreted in such a way as to deprive it of any meaning.[76] In *Brown*, all the defendants had fully consented to participation in sadomasochistic activities. Nonetheless, the hostility requirement was found to be satisfied. The contacts between the defendants in *Brown* caused actual bodily harm or wounds and were intended to do so. They were more than mere batteries. From *Brown*, we may infer that conduct intentionally causing that degree of harm for a purpose not judicially recognised as acceptable will *ipso facto* be found to be hostile.[77] In such cases the requirement adds nothing. That still leaves a possible role for the hostility requirement in cases where the contact does not cause bodily harm or where bodily harm was unintended

[70] [1998] AC 147, 160 (Lord Steyn), 164 (Lord Hope).

[71] The convictions were sustained on a finding of assault.

[72] [1984] AC 242.

[73] For a view that this conclusion, while desirable in terms of policy, is untenable on the state of the authorities, see Hirst, "Assault, Battery and Indirect Violence" [1999] *Crim LR* 557. But see also *Haystead v Chief Constable of Derbyshire* [2000] 3 All ER 890 (DC), where D caused V, a baby, to fall to the floor by hitting V's mother who was carrying V. Laws LJ took the view that battery did not require a directly inflicted injury. Although this opinion was strictly *obiter* (on the facts there was, on analysis, a directly inflicted injury), Laws LJ made it clear that he would have confirmed D's conviction even had he found V's injuries to be indirectly inflicted.

[74] [1994] 1 AC 212. A requirement for hostility was also endorsed by the Court of Appeal in the civil case of *Wilson v Pringle* [1987] QB 237.

[75] *Collins v Wilcock* [1984] 3 All ER 374, 378 (CA); see too *F v West Berkshire Health Authority* [1990] 2 AC 1.

[76] *Ashworth's Principles of Criminal Law* (10th ed., 2022) 360.

[77] But see *Wilson* [1997] QB 47 (CA); discussed below, § 11.9(iii)(b).

and unforeseen. For the tort of battery, the requirement of hostility has been decisively rejected by the Court of Appeal, with reference to cases in the criminal law;[78] the language of hostility should be rejected for the crime of battery as well.

### *(iii) Mens rea*

The mens rea for battery is analogous to the mens rea for assault. D must intend to inflict unlawful violence or do so recklessly.[79] The recklessness is *Cunningham* recklessness.[80] D must actually have foreseen the risk of inflicting violence upon V and taken it without adequate justification. Battery is an offence of basic intent under the *Majewski* rules regarding voluntary intoxication.[81]

### *(iv) Non-fatal strangulation or suffocation*

The offence of strangulation or suffocation, contrary to section 75A of the Serious Crime Act 2015,[82] constitutes an aggravated form of battery, involving conduct that does, or is likely to, interfere with V's breathing or blood circulation.[83] Although the offence is gender-neutral in its definition, it is more likely to be committed by a man rather than a woman.

Section 75A creates a single non-fatal offence that can be committed in two distinct ways.[84] The first way is where D intentionally strangles V. Here, there is no need to prove an intention on D's part to cause harm to V. In *Jones*,[85] strangulation was considered to encompass compression of V's neck, whether by the hand, a ligature, or the pressure of a body part or an object across the neck, provided that the means employed is, by its nature, likely to, and usually will, restrict the victim's ability to breathe. Secondly, the offence is committed where D batters V and thereby affects V's ability to breathe. In *Jones*, this second route to liability was considered to cover the use of means to affect V's ability to breathe other than the compression of V's neck. Since the conduct for this form of the offence must involve battery, it follows that this form of the offence can be committed while being reckless regarding the risk of contact with V,[86] although presumably the interference with V's breathing is a matter of strict liability. Although the Court of Appeal in *Jones* recognised that the offence could be charged as "intentional strangulation or suffocation", the reference to intention is inappropriate as regards the second form of the offence involving a battery.

It is a defence[87] to the section 75A offence that V consents to the strangulation or the suffocation, save where V suffered serious harm and D either intended to cause serious

[78] *FXS v Mulberry Bush Organisation Ltd* [2026] EWCA Civ 415, [31].

[79] In principle, this requirement would include recklessness about any circumstances that render the force used unlawful. Depending on the facts of the case, this might include, for example, V's non-consent.

[80] *Savage* [1992] 1 AC 699; *Fagan v Metropolitan Police Commissioner* [1969] 1 QB 439 (DC). The cases do not discriminate between the separate offences of assault and battery when discussing mens rea issues; it is safe to assume equivalence.

[81] Below, § 18.4(ii).

[82] Inserted by the Domestic Abuse Act 2021, s. 70. See Kelly and Ormerod, "Non-fatal Strangulation and Suffocation" [2021] *Crim LR* 532.

[83] *Jones* [2025] EWCA Crim 195, [2025] KB 539, [6].

[84] *Ibid.*

[85] *Ibid.*, [6].

[86] *Ibid.*, [24].

[87] Serious Crime Act 2015, s. 75A (2).

harm to V or was reckless as to whether V would suffer serious harm.[88] Serious harm in this context, as opposed to the definition of serious harm for other non-fatal offences, encompasses grievous *and* actual bodily harm *and* wounding.[89] D's genuine but mistaken belief in V's consent is described as a defence, but it is preferable to regard consent as operating to negate the offence for lack of mens rea, consistent with the approach to consent for non-fatal offences against the person.[90] The offence is triable either way; on indictment the maximum sentence is five years.

As noted already, section 75A offence can be seen as an aggravated form of battery, since it is not necessary to prove that V suffered any injury or harm. Where injury is caused, D will be likely to have perpetrated one of the offences discussed in the next subsections. Liability in such circumstances remains justified because the act of strangulation or suffocation creates a real and justified fear of death, even where no injury is in fact caused.[91]

## § 11.4 Assault occasioning actual bodily harm

A second form of aggravated assault or battery is found in section 47 of the OAPA 1861, which provides:

> whosoever shall be convicted upon an indictment of any assault occasioning actual bodily harm shall be liable to be imprisoned for any term not exceeding five years.

### *(i) Actus reus*

The term assault is used here as an umbrella term to cover the discrete offence of assault, in the technical sense of that term, and the offence of battery.[92] By far and away the most common form of this offence will be a battery which causes the requisite degree of bodily harm. However, it is possible for a technical assault to occasion bodily harm; in *Lewis*,[93] for instance, a frightened V was injured when escaping the threatened violence of D.

In "fright" cases such as *Lewis*, where harm arises in the course of a reaction to a threat of violence, a causal link between D's threatening conduct and V's injury exists even though V's frightened reaction may be considered ill-advised. It is unrealistic to expect frightened people to take measured responses and it is quite foreseeable that they will not do so. In the leading case of *Roberts*,[94] where V jumped from a moving car in order to escape the sexual gropings of D, causal responsibility for V's injuries was attributed to D on the footing that

[88] *Ibid*., s. 75A(3).

[89] *Ibid*., s.. 75A(6).

[90] Below, § 11.9(iv). Kelly and Ormerod, "Non-fatal Strangulation and Belief in Consent" [2025] *Crim LR* 22. Cp. Nott and Simmons, "Crossing the Rubicon: Implications of s. 75A of the Serious Crime Act 2015 for Consent and Reasonable Belief in Consent in Sexual Offences Act 2003 Offences" [2023] *Crim LR* 512, who argue that such a defence should not be available for reasons of statutory construction and consistency with the offences under Sexual Offences Act 2003, ss. 1–4.

[91] *Cook* [2023] EWCA Crim 452, [2023] 4 WLR 71, [4].

[92] In *Savage* [1992] 1 AC 699, 736, 740, Lord Ackner described the mens rea for s. 47 in terms of the mens rea for assault and in terms of the mens rea for battery: we can safely assume that in this context, the term "assault" covers "pure" assault and battery.

[93] [1970] Crim LR 647 (CA); see also *Cartledge v Allen* [1973] Crim LR 530 (DC).

[94] (1971) 56 Cr App R 95 (CA).

V's reaction was not so "daft" as to be unforeseeable.[95] There seems, in this context, to be no difference between "occasioning" bodily harm and "causing" bodily harm.[96]

What constitutes actual bodily harm is set at a very low threshold: "any hurt or injury calculated to interfere with the health or comfort of [V]", provided it is more than "transient and trifling".[97] Bruisings, abrasions, blooded noses, etc., will be enough, as will momentary unconsciousness.[98] Practically any sustained attack or fighting will involve occasioning actual bodily harm. Enormous scope is thus afforded to prosecutorial discretion. Various factors may be relevant in determining whether to prosecute, but in particular whether significant medical intervention is required (such as a need for a number of stitches or a hospital procedure under anaesthetic) and/or whether permanent effects have resulted. The vast majority of the common assaults that are tried summarily by virtue of section 39 of the Criminal Justice Act 1988 are also triable on indictment under section 47 of the OAPA 1861, with the maximum term of imprisonment inflated from six months to five years. The gravity of the injury is but one of the many variables determining whether a violent incident is tried summarily or on indictment, or, indeed, tried at all.[99]

The expression *actual* bodily harm might be taken to signify that only physical harm will fall within the section. However, as interpreted in *Miller*, the expression includes "a hysterical and nervous condition".[100] In *Chan-Fook*,[101] the Court of Appeal asserted that non-physical harm falls within section 47 provided that it constitutes some form of psychiatric injury attested to by expert evidence. This ruling was confirmed by the House of Lords in *Burstow*.[102] Accordingly, mere fright will not constitute bodily harm, even where a nervous or hysterical condition is induced, unless there is accepted expert testimony that V's state constitutes a form of psychiatric injury.[103] The CPS charging standard recognises that psychological injury may suffice as actual bodily harm but it must amount to a recognisable psychiatric illness.[104] Finch has convincingly argued that confining non-physical harm to recognised and diagnosed psychiatric injury is too restrictive and the focus should instead be on the symptoms suffered by V, with the jury being asked to determine whether they constitute sufficient harm to constitute actual bodily harm.[105] It would follow that emotional harm, which is more than transient emotion, could constitute actual bodily harm. This is properly described as psychological harm, which is the language now used in the CPS charging standard. This would reflect contemporary

[95] *Ibid.*, 102. *Williams* [1992] 2 All ER 183 (CA) adopts the same approach to causation in homicide. For discussion of interventions by victims see above, § 4.2(iii)(f).

[96] Gardner claimed that "occasion" is a broader term than "cause" and includes liability for outcomes which would not be attributed on the basis of a causal analysis: "Rationality and the Rule of Law in Offences against the Person" [1994] *CLJ* 502, 509–10. No authority is cited for this claim; he merely stated that the distinction between "occasion" and "cause" was "neglected" in *Roberts*.

[97] *Donovan* [1934] 2 KB 498 (CA).

[98] *T v DPP* [2003] EWHC 266 (Admin).

[99] For an illuminating study, in the context of assaults, of which factors determine a decision to prosecute and for what offence, see Clarkson, Cretney, Davis, and Shepherd, "Assaults: The Relationship between Seriousness, Criminalisation and Punishment" [1994] *Crim LR* 4.

[100] *Miller* [1954] 2 QB 282, 292 (Assizes (Winchester)).

[101] [1994] 2 All ER 552 (CA).

[102] [1998] AC 147.

[103] In *Morris* [1998] 1 Cr App R 386 (CA), evidence from a general practitioner that V suffered anxiety, fear, and sleeplessness was held to be insufficient to establish actual bodily harm.

[104] Crown Prosecution Service, *Offences Against the Person, Incorporating the Charging Standard*.

[105] Finch, "Psychological Injury: Where's the Harm In It?" [2022] *Crim LR* 358.

medical knowledge and terminology and would enable degrees of psychological harm to be identified as constituting actual bodily harm, or even grievous bodily harm, if it was seriously harmful.

The inclusion of psychiatric and psychological injury as a harm within the sphere of offences against the person has considerable ramifications, discussed in more detail below.[106] In the context of section 47, the range of conduct penalised which caused psychological injury is limited by the need for an assault or battery: D must threaten or inflict unlawful violence on V. Only if psychological injury ensues from those circumstances is a charge under section 47 in order.

### *(ii) Mens rea*

The mens rea for section 47 is the mens rea for assault or battery, discussed previously. There is no need to prove any mental element with respect to occasioning bodily harm.[107] Accordingly, this is an offence of constructive liability.[108] Once the "gateway wrong" of assault or battery is proved to have been perpetrated with adequate mens rea, the aggravating consequence of the causing of actual bodily harm is an element of strict liability.

In the context of aggravated offences of violence, constructive liability seems wrong in principle. This is disputed by Gardner, who explains that the law could be seen as taking the view that persons who threaten or use violence cross a moral threshold when they do so, and occupy a position of responsibility for any consequences that ensue from such conduct.[109] Gardner's suggestion finds great support in popular sentiments and from some judges. By contrast, in the context of offences against the person, the correspondence principle mandates that sufficient culpability is most reliably evidenced by proof that D intended or at least foresaw those consequences of her conduct which are elements of the offence with which she is charged.[110] There is room in the criminal law for liability based on negligence (even, perhaps, strict liability for minor regulatory offences),[111] but not when the crimes are concerned with violence. It is true that many cases of assault occasioning actual bodily harm will arise spontaneously in street and recreational settings, quite often where D has consumed significant quantities of drink or drugs. Difficulties of proving mens rea in such circumstances are considerably eased by the special regime for the voluntarily intoxicated.[112] Since assault occasioning actual bodily harm is the least serious of the aggravated offences of violence, it may be that on proof of mens rea for the *assault* element, negligence as to the consequence—the infliction of actual bodily harm—would be an acceptable form of culpability, but there should be some form of culpability for the aggravating element of the offence.

106 § 11.5(i).

107 *Savage* [1992] 1 AC 699, affirming *Roberts* (1971) 56 Cr App R 95 (CA), overruling *Spratt* [1991] 2 All ER 210 (CA) and *Parmenter* [1992] 1 AC 699 (CA).

108 Above, § 6.5.

109 "Rationality and the Rule of Law in Offences Against the Person" (1994) 53 *CLJ* 502. For different views on the merits of the correspondence principle, see Horder, "A Critique of the Correspondence Principle" [1995] *Crim LR* 759 and Mitchell, "In Defence of the Correspondence Principle" [1999] *Crim LR* 195.

110 Above, § 6.5.

111 Though see above, § 6.3, for a full discussion of this issue.

112 See below, § 18.4.

## § 11.5 Maliciously wounding or inflicting grievous bodily harm

Section 20 of the OAPA 1861 provides:

> whosoever shall unlawfully and maliciously wound or inflict any grievous bodily harm upon any other person, either with or without any weapon or instrument, shall be guilty of an offence, and being convicted thereof shall be liable . . . to imprisonment for a term not exceeding five years.

It is noteworthy that the maximum penalty for this offence, five years, is the same penalty provided under section 47. In practice, section 20 is regarded as the more serious offence. Further, in terms of punishment, the sentences handed down in respect of section 20 convictions are typically in a higher range than are the sentences imposed in respect of section 47.[113]

### *(i) Actus reus*

#### *(a) Wounds or inflicts grievous bodily harm*

The harm element of the offence is present if D wounds or inflicts grievous bodily harm on V. A wound requires all layers of the skin to be pierced.[114] Internal ruptures, even if they cause significant internal bleeding, are not wounds.[115] Even so, the range of what counts as a wound is considerable. If sufficiently serious, a wound may also constitute grievous bodily harm while, at the other end of the spectrum, even a very minor injury may count as a wound, such as a pin prick.

In *Metheram*,[116] the phrase "really serious harm" was thought best to express the meaning of grievous bodily harm. The harm does not have to be permanent or dangerous to constitute really serious injury; ultimately it is for the jury to assess the harm applying contemporary social standards.[117] As explained in *Grundy*,[118] the totality of the injuries suffered by V should be taken into account; it may be that no one particular injury is really serious, and yet, taken as a whole, V's injuries may amount to grievous bodily harm. This approach was confirmed in *Bollom*,[119] where it was applied with the sensible observation that far less by way of bodily harm would constitute serious harm if V were a young child, or elderly, or unwell, or psychiatrically vulnerable. According to the Crown Prosecution Service's charging standard,[120] grievous bodily harm includes life-changing injuries and may include injuries for which significant or sustained medical treatment is required, such as intensive care or a blood transfusion, even if a full, or a relatively full, recovery occurs.

[113] Sentencing Council, *Inflicting Grievous Bodily Harm/Unlawful Wounding* (2021).
[114] Both the dermis and the epidermis must be broken: *Moriarty v Brooks* (1834) 6 C & P 684, 172 ER 1419; a break in the outer skin is insufficient: *M'Loughlin* (1838) 8 C & P 635, 173 ER 651.
[115] *JCC (a minor) v Eisenhower* (1984) 78 Cr App R 48 (DC).
[116] [1961] 3 All ER 200 (CA). See also *Sidhu* [2019] EWCA Crim 1034, [19] concerning the intention to cause really serious injury for the crime of murder.
[117] *Golding* [2014] EWCA Crim 889: genital herpes could be grievous bodily harm.
[118] [1977] Crim LR 543 (CA).
[119] [2003] EWCA Crim 2846, [2004] 2 Cr App R6.
[120] *Offences Against the Person, Incorporating the Charging Standard.*

It has been recognised that infection with the Human Immunodeficiency Virus (HIV) can constitute grievous bodily harm.[121] In *Burstow*,[122] the House of Lords confirmed that psychiatric injury, attested to by expert evidence, could constitute *bodily* harm. Further, if the adverse psychiatric condition inflicted on V by D were sufficiently serious, it would constitute grievous bodily harm falling within section 20 (and section 18) of the OAPA 1861. In the context of psychiatric injury, it was ruled in *Burstow* that D would "inflict" such harm if his conduct was a cause of V's psychiatric condition, a matter to be determined on normal causal principles.[123]

The effect of *Burstow* is to enlarge significantly the kinds of setback to personal well-being that fall within grievous bodily harm and, consequentially, the kinds of conduct coming within the scope of section 20 (and section 18). On the facts of *Burstow*, there was no physical contact that impacted upon V, directly or indirectly. V had endured a long process of harassment by D, which included such abuses as threatening letters and telephone calls, following, photographing, etc. A reading of the case leaves no doubt about the extent of V's suffering and the wrongfulness of D's conduct. There can be no qualms about the actual decision in the case. However, the limits of the decision are difficult to identify.[124]

In *Burstow*, psychiatric injury was held to be a form of *bodily* injury. If no distinction is to be taken between psychiatric and physical injury *in general*, the effects of the decision could be profound. For example, suppose that D, an employer, wishes to terminate the contract of V, her employee. D has good reason to consider V's job performance unacceptable. Of course, in no circumstances whatsoever may D inflict physical harm on V to force his resignation. Instead of that, however, she calls V to her office, gives him three months' salary in lieu of notice, and explains that he is sacked. She is aware of V's previous psychiatric history and foresees that his mental health will once again break down if sacked. That proves to be the case. On these facts, D has caused V psychiatric injury and foresaw that she would do so. Has a section 20 offence been committed? One's initial response is to stress that section 20 requires *unlawful* conduct on the part of D. How can a legitimate termination of employment be unlawful? The answer, if one takes literally the finding in *Burstow*, is that any course of conduct whereby D foresees that she will cause V some *bodily* harm cannot be legitimate conduct unless she is acting in self-defence.

It is unlikely that the limits of *Burstow* will be tested in this way. The Crown Prosecution Service will probably not prosecute in those cases where such commonplaces as adultery, verbal cruelty, termination of employment, promises made for the purposes of seduction, and the like, cause serious mental distress amounting to psychiatric injury. These things will be tolerated as part of "normal" life, as they should be. Any attempt rigorously to police such matters would make for an intolerable society. There would need to be something extreme and visible—the kind of conduct that occurred in *Burstow* or, perhaps, sustained classroom or workplace bullying, to trigger a police investigation and a file of evidence for the Crown Prosecution Service. Psychiatric injury may have devastating consequences,

[121] *Dica* [2004] EWCA Crim 1103, [2004] QB 1257; *Konzani* [2005] EWCA Crim 706, [2005] 2 Cr App R 14; *B* [2006] EWCA Crim 2945, [2007] 1 WLR 1567. As can the transmission of genital herpes: *Golding* [2014] EWCA Crim 889.

[122] [1998] AC 147.

[123] *Ibid.*, 160, 164.

[124] For an incisive discussion see Gardner, "Stalking" (1998) 114 *LQR* 33.

but it is *different* from physical injury. Policing the causing of psychiatric injury by way of nineteenth-century laws focused on physical harm is not the way forward. New legislation is required which should pay particular attention to the kind of conduct which is to be penalised.[125]

*(b) Inflict*

The verb "inflict", which features in section 20, was for a very long time thought to include a narrower range of conduct than would be captured by employing the term "cause". In the context of psychological injury, *Burstow* held that inflict is to be interpreted as a synonym for cause.[126] We will consider first the meaning of inflict derived in cases of physical injury, and then consider whether the extensive interpretation adopted in *Burstow* has implications for such cases.

For many years, *Clarence*[127] was regarded as the leading case on the meaning of "inflict". D had been charged with the malicious infliction of grievous bodily harm upon V, on account of his infecting her with gonorrhoea. Despite V's ignorance of D's infected state, her consent to intercourse was taken to be valid; accordingly, the bodily contact involved in intercourse did not constitute a battery by D. For the majority, this ruled out a conviction under section 20 because of the need for:[128]

> "[a] direct causing of some grievous injury to the body itself with a weapon, as by a cut with a knife, or without a weapon, as by a blow with the fist, or by pushing a person down. Indeed, ['inflict' implies] an assault and battery of which a wound or grievous bodily harm is the manifest immediate and obvious result."

The restrictive definition in *Clarence* was relaxed to a degree in cases such as *Martin*[129] and *Halliday*.[130] Subsequently, the House of Lords in *Wilson* held, *contra Clarence*, that section 20 did not require the commission of an assault or battery:[131]

> "grievous bodily harm may be inflicted where the accused has directly or violently inflicted it by assaulting the victim or where the accused has 'inflicted' it by doing something intentionally which though it is not in itself a direct application of force to the body of the victim does directly result in some force being applied violently to the body of the victim so that he suffers grievous bodily harm."

This passage was subsequently endorsed by the House of Lords in *Mandair*.[132] An injury caused by way of an "infliction" is an injury caused by an impact or percussion set in motion by D. The injury must arise directly from the impact but the impact itself need not be something that D's action has immediately caused; any direct or indirectly caused impact or percussive connection will suffice. Returning to the facts of *Clarence*, we can now appreciate

[125] To some extent, the Protection from Harassment Act 1997 provides appropriate protection from conduct of this kind: see below, § 11.10.
[126] [1998] AC 147.
[127] (1888) 22 QBD 23.
[128] *Ibid.*, 41 (Stephen J).
[129] (1881) 8 QBD 54 (D held to have inflicted grievous bodily harm by causing victims to rush to locked exits).
[130] [1886–90] All ER 1028 (CA) (D held to have inflicted grievous bodily harm when V was injured in the course of escaping the threatened violence of D).
[131] [1984] AC 242.
[132] [1995] 1 AC 208.

that if an assault or battery is not required, the fact of consensual intercourse will not be a barrier to a conviction. Yet to convict on the facts of *Clarence*, we must still find that "force [was] applied violently" and that, because of the violent application of force, injury (infection) was sustained. Even if we regard consensual intercourse as involving the violent application of force (which is doubtful), the injury is not caused by the application of force but by the process of infection.

To allow diseases and infections within the scope of section 20, "inflict" must be interpreted as a synonym for cause. That, as we know, was the course taken in the context of psychological injury in *Burstow*, where there had been no physical contact between D and V. Lord Hope[133] considered that inflict and cause are not exactly synonymous (a possible difference is that the consequences of infliction might be more likely to be unpleasant or harmful), but the approach of the House of Lords effectively assimilates "inflict" to "cause", and would ensure a conviction on facts such as *Clarence*. Lord Steyn, whose judgment was that of the majority, was more circumspect. He did not consider the two terms to be synonymous but took it to be natural to speak of inflicting psychological injury without implying, in that context, any direct or indirect violent contact.[134] In the important decisions of *Dica*[135] and *Konzani*,[136] the Court of Appeal took the analysis of Lord Hope to be of general application. Departing from the ruling in *Clarence*, it was held in both cases that, for D to pass on a sexually transmitted disease to his sexual partner V, where V was unaware and had not consented to the risk of infection, was conduct falling within section 20 (mens rea would also have to be proved before D could be convicted). These cases have considerable ramifications for the scope of some key sexual offences, for questions relating to what constitutes a valid consent to harm, and for the appropriateness of using laws designed to curb violence to penalise sexual risk-taking. The first issue will be treated below in Chapter 12, and the latter two matters later in this chapter (§ 11.7); for now, we need merely note that, unless and until they are overruled by the House of Lords, *Dica* and *Konzani* resolve that "inflict" should be treated as a synonym for "cause" for the purposes of section 20.

### *(ii) Mens rea*

In modern English criminal law, malice is interpreted as intention or recklessness. The recklessness is *Cunningham* recklessness.[137] However, the intention or foresight required for this offence is not intention or foresight on the part of D that he will wound or inflict grievous bodily harm on V. It is enough, according to a line of authority originating in *Mowatt*,[138] and endorsed by the House of Lords in *Savage and Parmenter*,[139] that D intends or foresees that he may[140] inflict some, even minor, bodily harm on V. This violation of the correspondence principle is unacceptable in the context of a serious offence of violence.[141]

[133] [1998] AC 147.
[134] *Ibid.*, 160–1.
[135] [2004] EWCA Crim 1103, [2004] QB 1257.
[136] [2005] EWCA Crim 706, [2005] 2 Cr App R 14.
[137] *Savage* [1992] 1 AC 699.
[138] [1968] 1 QB 421 (CA).
[139] [1992] 1 AC 699.
[140] *Rushworth* (1992) 95 Cr App R 252, 255 (CA), dismissing an argument that D *must* foresee that some harm to V will result from his conduct.
[141] See Stark, 'Deconstructing Constructive Liability' [2023] *Crim LR* 118, 127.

Most section 20 cases will involve physical attacks. The Court of Appeal sensibly ruled in *Beeson*[142] that, if a wound or grievous bodily harm is caused by a direct attack inherently likely to cause physical harm, no guidance to the jury on the meaning of malice is necessary. Guidance should be given only if D raises an argument that his conduct was in some sense mistaken or accidental or that, for some other reason, he failed to recognise that he might cause harm.

## § 11.6 Wounding or causing grievous bodily harm with intent

Section 18 of the OAPA 1861 provides:

> Whosoever shall unlawfully and maliciously by any means whatsoever wound or cause grievous bodily harm to any person . . . with intent . . . to do some . . . grievous bodily harm to any person, or with intent to resist or prevent the lawful apprehension or detainer of any person, shall be guilty of an offence, and being convicted thereof shall be liable . . . to imprisonment for life.

Section 18 creates one offence with four different modes of commission, as follows:

(a) unlawfully and maliciously wounding, with intent to do grievous bodily harm;
(b) unlawfully and maliciously wounding, with intent to resist or prevent the lawful apprehension or detainer of any person;
(c) unlawfully and maliciously causing grievous bodily harm, with intent to do grievous bodily harm;
(d) unlawfully and maliciously causing grievous bodily harm, with intent to resist or prevent the lawful apprehension or detainer of any person.

### *(i) Actus reus*

We are already familiar with the meanings of "wounding" and "grievous bodily harm".[143] As we have discussed, the term "grievous bodily harm" includes serious psychological injury and serious infection or disease. In the context of section 18, where the culpability requirement is intention to cause grievous bodily harm, there may be less concern about the extension of liability into these areas. The requirement of such an intention will narrow and focus the potential range of conduct that may be penalised and ensure a culpability that warrants a criminal sanction. What constitutes "lawful apprehension or detention" will depend on the validity of the arrest and detention, a matter dependent on the particular facts of each case.

With the omission of the verb "inflict", the former uncertainties associated with that term in section 20[144] are avoided. It is necessary only that D wounds or causes serious injury. Normal principles of causation apply.[145]

142 *Beeson* [1994] Crim LR 190 (CA).
143 Above, § 11.5(i)(a).
144 Now resolved: above, § 11.5(i)(b).
145 See above, § 4.2.

### *(ii) Mens rea*

The core of the section 18 offence is intention. In variants (a), (b), and (d) (set out above), this is an ulterior intent,[146] while in variant (c) the required intent coincides with the actus reus. The most common variants of the offence are (a) where D wounds V with intent to cause grievous bodily harm, and (c) where D causes V grievous bodily harm with intent to cause grievous bodily harm.

In variant (c), where mens rea coincides with actus reus, if the grievous bodily harm is caused by way of a direct attack, the jury should simply be invited to consider whether D intended that result: there is no need for any direction on the meaning of intent.[147] By contrast, where D has caused V grievous bodily harm by some dangerous act not in the nature of a direct attack, and asserts that she did not act in order to cause such harm, it will be sufficient for the matter to go to the jury if she foresaw that harm is virtually certain to occur.[148] In both of the cases under discussion—direct attack causing grievous bodily harm and a dangerous act causing grievous bodily harm—the term "maliciously", which appears in section 18, is redundant. The mens rea issue is whether D intended grievous bodily harm: if she did, a fortiori it was done maliciously in the sense that term carries in modern English criminal law.

Under variant (a), where the section 18 offence takes the form of a wound falling short of grievous bodily harm, an ulterior intent to cause grievous bodily harm must be proved. In practice, there is no room in this kind of case for intent proved on the basis of foresight that the grievous bodily harm was a virtual certainty: if grievous bodily harm did not arise, that is powerful evidence that it was not a virtually certain result of D's actual conduct. Accordingly, it must be proved that D acted with intent in the core sense[149] to cause V grievous bodily harm. Again, the term maliciously is redundant; if D acted in order to cause serious harm, a fortiori he acted maliciously with respect to that consequence.

The requirement of malice may have a role to play in variants (b) and (d), where D's intent is to prevent or resist the lawful apprehension or detention of any person. In principle, the requirement of malice in section 18 entails that D must at least foresee the possibility that she might cause a wound or grievous bodily harm in cases where her intent is to resist arrest or detention.[150]

In variants (b) and (d), it is clear from the terms of section 18 that D must *intend* to resist an apprehension or detention. Section 18 further requires that D must intend to resist a *lawful* apprehension or detention. In principle, what is needed is that, in the circumstances that D believes to exist, the arrest is lawful. Thus if D wrongly believes in facts which, if true, would have made the arrest unlawful, he lacks mens rea for the section 18 offence. On the other hand, if D has made no mistake about the circumstances, it suffices that the

[146] Above, § 5.1(vii).
[147] *Moloney* [1985] AC 905, 926.
[148] *Woollin* [1999] AC 82; above, § 5.1(iv). Although *Woollin* is a decision about obliquely intended grievous bodily harm in the context of murder, the reasoning carries over straightforwardly to the context of s. 18.
[149] Above, § 5.1.
[150] *Morrison* (1989) 89 Cr App R 17 (CA). The case confirms that the test is actual foresight of injury on the part of D but it did not rehearse the question whether the foresight must be of a wound or grievous bodily harm. In principle it should; but see *Mowatt* [1968] 1 QB 421 (CA).

apprehension or detention is, in fact, lawful. It would not go to liability, merely mitigation, that D believed the apprehension or detention was unlawful.[151]

## § 11.7 Transmitting diseases and infection

Towards the end of the twentieth century, concern about the spread of Acquired Immune Deficiency Syndrome (AIDS) led to consideration whether current offences against the person can apply to conduct associated with transmission of HIV.[152] More generally, as we will see, there are justified concerns over the appropriateness of the existing range of offences that protect the person in the context of harms inflicted by the transmission of diseases and infection. Our discussion will focus on AIDS and HIV; there are, of course, implications for other forms of transmission of disease and infection, whether transmitted sexually or otherwise.

### *(i) Cases where harm was intended*

The most straightforward situation will be where V dies as a consequence of AIDS and it can be proved that D infected V with HIV in order that she should die. With the abolition of the year-and-a-day rule,[153] there is no impediment to a charge of murder. Such cases are likely to be very rare (although they are not unknown).

What offences, if any, are committed if D intentionally causes V to become HIV-positive? From the decisions in *Dica*[154] and *Konzani*,[155] we know that to be made HIV-positive is to be seriously harmed in a bodily sense. If the infection is intentionally transmitted there is no impediment to a conviction under section 18 of the OAPA 1861.[156] Although the condition of being HIV-positive is compatible with years of normal healthy existence, given access to suitable drugs, the condition is a significant setback to the interests of the person so afflicted and the setback is, in a broad sense, to bodily integrity. Whatever reservations there may be concerning the extension of bodily harm to psychological injury,[157] it would, in the light of that extension, have been perverse to hold that the condition of being HIV-positive did not amount to grievous bodily harm. That said, the expression is not a natural one to employ in this context, pointing up the need for specific legislation. The Law Commission has, however, recommended that specific offences concerning the transmission of disease should not simply be enacted; rather, there should be a wider review of the law, in consultation with health professionals, to determine whether specific offences should be created.[158]

151 Cf. *Bentley* (1850) 4 Cox CC 406. Such a mistake should be characterised as a mistake of law, discussed below, § 18.2.

152 Bronitt, "Spreading Disease and the Criminal Law" [1994] *Crim LR* 21.

153 Law Reform (Year and a Day Rule) Act 1996; discussed above, § 10.2(iv).

154 [2004] EWCA Crim 1103, [2004] QB 1257.

155 [2005] EWCA Crim 706, [2005] 2 Cr App R 14.

156 In *Rowe* [2018] EWCA Crim 2688, [2019] 1 Cr App R (S) 38, life imprisonment was imposed on D, who had intentionally infected others with HIV. Rowe was also convicted of *attempting* the section 18 offence in cases where his plan to infect others with HIV had failed.

157 *Burstow* [1998] AC 147; *Chan-Fook* [1994] 2 All ER 552 (CA).

158 Law Com. No. 361, *Reform of Offences Against the Person* (2015).

### *(ii) Cases where the harm was knowingly risked*

Far more common than intentionally transmitting infection will be taking risks relating to infection, notably through forms of unprotected sexual activity engaged in by persons who are aware that they have a condition that can be passed on by sexual contact. By reading "inflict" as synonymous with cause, the Court of Appeal in *Dica* and *Konzani* laid the ground for straightforward convictions of maliciously inflicting grievous bodily harm, within the terms of section 20, in cases where D infects his sexual partner having foreseen the risk of doing so, and where V has not given an informed consent to that risk. Section 71(4) of the Domestic Abuse Act 2021 confirms that, where D has infected V with a sexually transmitted infection in the course of sexual activity, it is a defence that V consented to that activity in the knowledge or belief that D had the sexually transmitted infection. This defence of informed consent will not apply where V only suspected that D *might* have the infection.

In *Dica*, on the facts assumed for the purposes of the appeal, and on the facts themselves in *Konzani*, V had not consented to the risk of infection. In light of the decision of the House of Lords in *Brown*,[159] however, it might be considered that whether V had actually consented was irrelevant, since it was held in that case that, save for special circumstances,[160] valid consent is restricted to the infliction of harms falling short of actual bodily harm, and the harm in *Dica* and *Konzani* was much more serious than that. Since, however, the victims in *Dica* and *Konzani* clearly had not consented to the *deliberate* infliction of actual bodily harm or worse, it followed that *Brown* was not engaged. Consequently, if they had consented to the *risk* of the disease being transmitted, this might have negated D's liability. In *Dica*, reference was made to a couple trying to start a family and to another couple organising their sex life without contraception according to the strictures of the Roman Catholic church. The assumption was made that, in those circumstances, it would be legitimate for D to take the risk of V becoming HIV-positive. More significantly, however, following *Konzani*, if D was aware that he might be HIV-positive and did not disclose this to V, V's consent to unprotected sexual intercourse would be assumed not to be an informed consent, so liability would be possible.[161] In such circumstances, should V subsequently die, D could face a charge of manslaughter of the constructive or gross negligence varieties.[162]

### *(iii) Administering noxious things*

Finally, mention should be made of section 23 of the OAPA 1861, which concerns the malicious administration (or causing to be administered or taken) of noxious things which endanger life or inflict grievous bodily harm. It has been suggested that bodily fluids containing HIV are "noxious" things and that sexual transmission of fluids can be regarded as an "administration" or a "taking" within the meaning of this section.[163] These are by

[159] [1994] 1 AC 212, discussed below, § 11.9(iii).

[160] Such as organised sport; one may safely assume that sexual activity would not in itself qualify as a special circumstance. See below, § 11.9(iii)(d).

[161] Ryan, "'Active Deception' v Non-disclosure: HIV Transmission, Non-fatal Offences and Criminal Responsibility" [2019] *Crim LR* 4, argues that D who is HIV-positive should only be liable for transmitting the disease if he actively deceived V about the disease, this being consistent with "public health messages about individual responsibility for sexual health" (*ibid.*, 5), which prioritises safe sex over non-disclosure.

[162] See the discussion of these ways of committing manslaughter in Chapter 10.

[163] Bronnitt, "Spreading Disease and the Criminal Law" [1994] *Crim LR* 21.

no means untenable claims and, if this interpretation is accepted, a defendant could be convicted on the basis of having unprotected sex knowing or suspecting himself to be HIV-positive, since that fact would be life-endangering to an HIV-negative person. Under the section, the element of malice (recklessness) merely relates to the administration of the noxious substance; it need not be proved that D foresaw life endangerment or the infliction of grievous bodily harm.[164]

Save for cases involving the intentional transmission of disease, it is submitted that the vigorous application of the laws regulating physical and sexual violence to cases involving transmission of diseases would be a far from ideal response to a difficult area of social and health policy, where confident and confidential reporting of an HIV status is at least as important as deterring sexual irresponsibility.[165]

## § 11.8 The defence of chastisement

At common law, disciplinary chastisement of an apprentice, servant, or child was permitted provided it was done by a person with the authority to do so and was of a "moderate, reasonable nature".[166] Nowadays, it may be asserted confidently that the age of legal corporal punishment for apprentices and junior employees has long gone. The social and legal substrata permitting force against persons in these categories have completely disappeared, and with them any colour of justification for disciplinary force.

At one time it looked as if there might be a general revocation in the United Kingdom of the right to chastise, but the Government resiled from this step in the light of public consultations reporting that a majority of adults favoured a right to chastise children.[167] It seems that there is no cogent evidence that chastisement produces good parents or good children.[168]

Parents and persons *in loco parentis* are still allowed a common law power of reasonable and moderate chastisement.[169] In 1994, a stepfather (D) who frequently and severely beat his stepson (V) with a garden cane was acquitted of assault occasioning actual bodily harm by a jury on the ground of reasonable chastisement. An application on behalf of the boy was made to Strasbourg where the ECtHR ruled that the common law provided insufficient protection for children, since it had exculpated (in that case) a degree of chastisement that constituted "inhuman and degrading treatment" within the terms of Article 3 of

[164] *Cato* [1976] 1 All ER 260. The Law Commission recommends that the poisoning offences in the OAPA 1861 should be replaced with a single offence of knowingly or recklessly administering a substance which is capable of causing injury: Law Com. No. 361, *Reform of Offences Against the Person* (2015). It would not be necessary to prove that injury was caused.

[165] A position acknowledged by the Law Commission in Law Com. No. 361, *Reform of Offences Against the Person* (2015). See the critiques in Weait, "Taking the Blame: Criminal Law, Social Responsibility and the Sexual Transmission of HIV" (2001) 23 *Journal of Social Welfare and Family Law* 441 and Weait, "Knowledge, Autonomy and Consent: *R v Konzani*" [2005] *Crim LR* 763. The sensitivities of prosecution of such cases is also acknowledged by the Crown Prosecution Service in *Intentional or Reckless Sexual Transmission of Infection* (2007).

[166] Kenny, *Outlines of Criminal Law* (1st ed., 1902) 108–9.

[167] See the discussion by Rogers, "A Criminal Lawyer's Response to Chastisement in the European Court of Human Rights" [2002] *Crim LR* 98.

[168] For a full legal and policy discussion see Keating, "Protecting or Punishing Children: Physical Punishment, Human Rights and English Law Reform" (2006) 26 *LS* 394.

[169] *Hopley* (1860) 2 F & F 202, 175 ER 1024; *Clearly v Booth* [1893] 1 QB 465.

the Convention.[170] Under the Human Rights Act 1998, English courts are obliged to limit permissible chastisement to force not proscribed by Article 3. What degree of force falls outside Article 3 is unclear.[171] Using a cane "with considerable force" to cause significant bruising is now clearly interdicted by the ECHR. But physical punishment *per se* is not banished.[172] What physical punishment remains allowable under the Convention is a matter of conjecture.

The limits of the current defence, for parents in England at least, has been usefully clarified within section 58 of the Children Act 2004, which excludes the defence of chastisement if actual bodily harm (or worse) is caused. The section also requires that the force used by D must be reasonable and proportionate in the circumstances, and involve no cruelty. Parents cannot rely on any religious belief or practice to chastise beyond these limits,[173] and the same must surely apply to reliance on any cultural norms or practices. We highlight section 58 as a clarification of the defence in *England* because, in 2022, the defence of chastisement was abolished in its entirety in Wales.[174] The change represents an important milestone in the likely phasing out of the chastisement defence more generally, as well as a significant expression of Welsh devolutionary powers in the criminal law context.

Schoolteachers are the largest class of persons who are regularly *in loco parentis* to children. Under pressure of earlier ECtHR rulings, there has been legislation relating to the use of corporal punishment by teachers,[175] which has effectively revoked the right of teachers to use corporal punishment as a form of discipline.

## § 11.9 Consent

Consent is not mentioned in the statutory definitions of offences relating to actual and grievous bodily harm in the OAPA 1861. However, whether V consented to the harmful acts of D is an essential point of enquiry when assessing D's liability for those offences and the other non-fatal offences against the person. The potential for consent to negate liability is essential for basic human interactions, such as shaking hands and the hustle and bustle of communal living, events otherwise caught within the expansive terms of assault and battery.[176] Even where D causes serious harm, it is the element of V's consent that allows us to distinguish beneficial conduct in medical care and sports, for example, from acts of criminal violence. In this section we consider the role and definition of consent as it may apply to undermine D's liability, first where V consents in a legally recognised way, and, secondly, where D believes that V has consented.

170 *A v UK* [1998] Crim LR 892. The breach of Art. 3 by the United Kingdom was on the basis of allowing too broad a defence of chastisement which might allow the inhuman and degrading treatment of children. Exception was taken to the fact that it was for the prosecution to prove that the chastisement was not reasonable and moderate.

171 *Ibid.*

172 *H* [2002] 1 Cr App R 59 (CA); Rogers, "A Criminal Lawyer's Response to Chastisement in the European Court of Human Rights" [2002] *Crim LR* 98.

173 *R (Williamson) v Secretary of State for Education* [2005] UKHL 15, [2005] 2 AC 246.

174 Children (Abolition of Defence of Reasonable Punishment) (Wales) Act 2020. The defence was also abolished in Scotland: Children (Equal Protection from Assault) (Scotland) Act 2019, s. 1.

175 Children and Young Persons Act 1933, s. 1; Education Act 1996, ss. 548, 549.

176 *Collins v Wilcock* [1984] 3 All ER 374 (DC).

Across different criminal law contexts, the challenge to identify and to apply a workable definition of consent remains formidable.[177] There is no general legal definition of consent, and the common law remains (as we shall see) replete with doctrinal and normative inconsistency.[178] However, at a level of abstraction, it is useful to highlight three related points of enquiry that provide some structure for the discussion that follows: (i) the giving of V's consent; (ii) the genuineness of V's consent, examining V's knowledge and freedom of choice; and (iii) the nature of the activity consented to. A classic liberalist approach to this area might well discount the last of these points of enquiry, but the law has embraced a more paternalistic approach. The most important expression of such paternalism lies in the distinction drawn by the law between (a) offences of assault and battery, where a genuine consent by V will negate liability generally, and (b) offences involving (or risking) actual or grievous bodily harm, where V's consent will be legally valid only if the consented-to activity falls within certain recognised categories.[179]

Despite the important role of consent, there is no uniformity at common law as to whether consent is best perceived as a supervening defence (which would mean that the issue of consent only arises once the *actus reus* had been proved) or whether V's non-consent should be analysed as an offence element (in which case, consent would negate the *actus reus*). The law on this question depends upon the type of offence involved. In the context of most sexual offences, for example, lack of consent is a defining element of the actus reus.[180] Similarly in the context of battery, where D's harmful conduct amounts to a mere consensual touching, such as shaking hands with V, the language of "defence" seems inappropriate: establishing a *prima facie* criminal wrong in such cases appears to require non-consensual touching. The same intuitions are less pronounced, however, where D's conduct causes actual or grievous bodily harm, and this is where much of the academic and judicial comment has focused.[181] The predominant view, has been that V's consent (where it is legally valid) operates as a supervening defence.[182] Continued uncertainty on this point is regrettable. The Law Commission has announced a project to view the law of consent, although work on this has not yet started.[183]

### *(i) Element 1: Communication of consent*

Straightforward examples of consent involve explicit communication from V, such as agreeing to join a game of football with D. But in many cases of physical interaction, V's consent will be implied. This includes, for example, consenting to the hustle and bustle of communal living: V may not much like being brushed past on the pavement, or tapped on the

[177] See also below, § 21.1. There is a vast literature on the meaning and application of consent. See, e.g., Law Com. Consultation Paper No. 139, *Consent in the Criminal Law* (1995); Roberts, "The Philosophical Foundations of Consent in the Criminal Law" (1997) 17 *OJLS* 389; Reed et al (eds.) *Consent* (2017).

[178] Dripps, "For a Negative, Normative Model of Consent, with a Comment on Preference Skepticism" (1996) 2 *Legal Theory* 113.

[179] Below, § 11.9(iii).

[180] On consent and sexual offending, see below § 12.4.

[181] Compare, e.g., Williams, who argued that it is "inherent in the concept of assault and battery that the victim does not consent." ("Consent and Public Policy" [1962] Crim LR 74, 75) with the language of defences preferred by the Law Commission in LCCP No. 139, *Consent in the Criminal Law* (1995).

[182] This was the approach preferred by a bare majority in *Brown* [1994] AC 212: Lord Jauncey, Lord Lowry and Lord Templeman analysed consent as a defence; Lord Mustill and Lord Slynn considered non-consent as part of the offence. See, Shute, "Something Old, Something New, Something Borrowed" [1996] *Crim LR* 684.

[183] https://lawcom.gov.uk/project/consent-in-the-criminal-law/.

shoulder for attention,[184] but these (and similar) interactions are implicitly consented to within our society.[185] Moreover, when considering our explicit consent example of joining a game of football, the limits of V's consent are likely to be defined implicitly. As we discuss further below, when V consents to a contact sport she is clearly consenting to the physical contact and potential harms within the rules of that game; but it has also been held that she is implicitly consenting to non-intentional harms caused by foul play.[186] Particularly where V is consenting to an amateur sport, the risks of poorly timed tackles and accidental harms are, unfortunately, part and parcel of the activity.

There are important limits to V's implied consent. Implied consent to a tap on the shoulder does not equate to implied consent to more forceful physical restraint.[187] Neither does an implied consent to accidental foul play in football equate to a consent to intentional foul play.[188] Nor is it possible to rely on implied consent on the basis that D was acting in V's best interests to ensure she was safe because V was extremely intoxicated, when D knew that V was not consenting to be grabbed and D moved V towards his car against her will; this was physical restraint rather than a touch to attract V's attention.[189] It is also important to distinguish between implied consent to harm and foresight of harm. In *H v CPS*,[190] for example, V (a teacher) was aware of the risk of physical assault when working in a school for children with special educational needs and behavioural problems. However, as the Divisional Court accepted, such foresight did not amount to an implied consent when he was later assaulted by a student.

### *(ii) Element 2: Genuineness of consent*

For V's consent to be legally valid, it must be genuine in the sense that V must: (a) have capacity to give consent; (b) be sufficiently well informed to understand what she is consenting to; and (c) be free of fraud and coercion. If V was aware of the essential features of what she was consenting to, and was not deceived or coerced by D, a finding of valid consent should normally follow, unless the conduct involved is, in the eye of the law, something that even a competent adult cannot validly consent to do (element 3).[191] That third element, however, does not become relevant unless the consent involved a sufficiently free and informed choice.

#### *(a) Capacity*

In order to provide legally valid consent, V must possess a sufficiently mature capacity to understand the nature of the interaction that D proposes. V may lack capacity for a variety

184 Discussed in *Donnelly v Jackman* [1970] 1 WLR 562 (DC).

185 *Collins v Wilcock* [1984] 3 All ER 374 (DC). The limits of this category will reflect the cultural norms of any particular society, including different expectations around physical interactions. It is alternatively possible to analyse activities in this category—the hustle and bustle of social living—as being *exempted* from the offences against the person, rather than implicitly consented-to. This analysis is acknowledged in *Re F (Mental Patient: Sterilisation)* [1990] 2 AC 1, 72–73 (Lord Goff), and has the advantage of better explaining why D's ordinary social contact with V will not give rise to liability even where V lacks capacity to consent (e.g., due to youth or mental disorder).

186 *Barnes* [2004] EWCA Crim 3246, [2005] 1 WLR 910.

187 *Wood v DPP* [2008] EWHC 1056 (Admin): no implicit consent where a police officer restrained D for the purpose of establishing his identity (i.e., not part of lawful arrest); thus, D was entitled to resist.

188 *Bradshaw* (1878) Cox CC 83; *Barnes* [2005] 1 WLR 910.

189 *Marland v DPP* [2023] EWHC 1046 (Amin), [2023] 2 Cr App R 5.

190 [2010] EWHC 1374 (Admin), [2012] QB 257.

191 See below, § 11.9(iii).

of reasons, including infancy, mental disorder, or learning difficulty; or because of shorter-term conditions such as acute intoxication. In these cases, courts are required by legislation to assess V's capacity with an individual and decision-specific focus, avoiding status-based tests that simply (and potentially inaccurately) equate certain conditions with a lack of decision-making capacity.[192]

The relationship between V's age and her capacity provides a useful illustration. For medical treatment, consent given at the age of 16 is taken to be legally effective, other things being equal.[193] It does not follow that the consent of a younger person will be legally ineffective. As the House of Lords explained in *Gillick*,[194] a person under that age may nonetheless give legally valid consent to treatment which is in her best interests if she has sufficient maturity and understanding to assess those interests.

It was widely assumed that a "*Gillick*-competent" young person under 16 could also refuse consent to treatment. Donaldson MR thought differently in *Re R*,[195] when he ordered treatment for a 15-year-old girl with an eating disorder, even though he accepted that her refusal of treatment was a refusal on the part of a *Gillick*-competent person. He introduced the notion of "joint key-holders"; she could unlock the door, making her treatment lawful by virtue of her consent, but so too could other competent persons, such as the court when exercising its wardship jurisdiction on her behalf. This asymmetry between refusal of treatment and consent to treatment has been widely attacked and, indeed, it would be hard to defend if the sole value informing *Gillick*-competence were personal autonomy.[196] But it is not. *Gillick* was, *inter alia*, a case concerned to ensure that treatment in the best interests of a patient was delivered. The leading consideration in *Gillick* was ensuring that sexually active girls under the age of 16 received contraception, even in circumstances where parents or guardians would not be involved in the decision-making (and even in cases where those parties might object to such treatment). In *Re R*, similarly, the underlying concern was that a patient with volatile mood swings would receive therapy that would (and did) save her life. The cases reflect the fact that the consequences of accepting treatment are typically beneficent, whereas the outcomes ensuing from the refusal of treatment may be catastrophic. In that sense, the decisions in *Gillick* and *Re R* have a greater affinity than may at first appear.[197]

These cases illustrate two important points. The first is that courts, where they deem it appropriate, can examine issues of competence with an individual, decision-specific focus. Secondly, normative (as well as clinical) factors play a role when considering if such examination is appropriate. If, on policy or moral grounds, the court disapproves of the interaction between D and V, it may be astute to find a lack of competence on the ground of the relevant party's age. For instance, in *Burrell v Harmer*,[198] D tattooed V, a 13-year-old boy, for payment. According to the Divisional Court, this constituted an assault on V, a conclusion

[192] Criminal courts have been particularly influenced by the Mental Capacity Act 2005, s. 1 of which provides that "a person lacks capacity in relation to a matter if at the material time he is unable to make a decision for himself in relation to the matter because of an impairment, or a disturbance in the functioning of, the mind or brain." Section 4 goes on to caution that determinations of capacity should not be inferred from V's "age or appearance" or "a condition of his, or an aspect of his behaviour, which might lead others to make unjustified assumptions about what might be in his best interests."

[193] Family Law Reform Act 1969, s. 8.

[194] [1986] AC 112.

[195] [1992] Fam 11 (CA).

[196] Grubb, "Treatment Decisions; Keeping it in the Family" in Grubb (ed.), *Choices and Decisions in Health Care* (1993) 37, 54–68.

[197] See further Teff, *Reasonable Care* (1994) 146–52.

[198] [1967] Crim LR 169 (DC).

predicated on the questionable finding that he did not understand the nature of the act that D had performed upon him.[199]

*(b) Information*

V must also possess sufficient information to understand what he is consenting to. Where V accepts D's offer for a drink, for example, this acceptance will not extend to drugs secretly laced within that drink. D should provide V with sufficient information so that V may choose whether to consent to particular harms or risks of harm. D need not provide complete information of all conceivable risks, as that would be impractical.[200] Rather, particularly where more serious harms are at issue, D is expected to provide sufficient information for V to make an informed decision about the risks involved, including any unusual or inflated risks that D might have special knowledge of.

A useful illustration is *Konzani*.[201] D engaged in consensual unprotected sexual intercourse with three women, knowing (but not informing them) that he was HIV-positive. Each of the women contracted the virus. In line with the earlier decision in *Dica*,[202] the Court of Appeal entertained no doubt that V could give a valid consent to sexual activity with D despite a failure by D to disclose his HIV-positive status. The gravamen of D's wrong in such circumstances was taken to be the infection of V, rather than non-consensual sexual intercourse. Thus, in *Konzani*, it was ruled that, by passing on HIV to the women without fully informing them of his positive status, D had maliciously inflicted grievous bodily harm contrary to section 20 of the OAPA 1861.

When considering cases such as *Konzani*, and questions of informed consent, three situations are usefully distinguished. In the first, a particular risk is present (e.g. D is HIV-positive), but D is neither aware of this fact nor wilfully blind to the risk. In these circumstances, D cannot be expected to disclose information that he does not possess, and so V's consent to intercourse and associated risks would not be undermined. In the second situation, D is aware of the particular risk, but informs V of the necessary facts prior to intercourse. In these circumstances, even where V contracts the virus, her informed consent to the risk of infection means that her consent remains legally effective.[203] It is only in the third situation, where D is aware of the particular risk and fails to inform V of it prior to intercourse (as occurred in *Konzani*) where V will not be held to have given legally valid consent to the risk of transmission.

*(c) Freedom*

The genuineness of V's consent may be negated by fraud or coercion that undermines V's freedom to choose as she wishes. These factors have proved particularly difficult for the courts to apply in a principled and consistent manner.[204]

199 D's conduct would now be more straightforwardly dealt with under the Tattooing of Minors Act 1969.

200 There may be other drawbacks as well, such as therapeutic concerns where a medical patient is informed of all possible extreme (albeit unlikely) complications or side-effects.

201 [2005] EWCA Crim 706, [2005] 2 Cr App R 14. See Weait, "Knowledge, Autonomy and Consent" [2005] *Crim LR* 673.

202 [2004] EWCA Crim 1103, [2004] QB 1257.

203 Discussed in *Dica* [2004] EWCA Crim 1103; [2004] QB 1257, [47]–[52], and now codified in the Domestic Abuse Act 2021, s. 71(4).

204 As have the equivalent requirements for sexual consent: below, § 12.4.

It is clear that coercion is capable of undermining V's consent. Paradigm cases arise where V "consents" to a lesser assault in order to avoid the threat of a more serious harm, including non-physical harms such as dismissal from employment,[205] or implied threats from a person in a position of authority.[206] The precise nature of the test of coercion remains unclear; including, for example, whether V is expected to demonstrate reasonable steadfastness in the face of threats from D, and how the courts would deal with V whose consent is motivated by several reasons including (but not limited to) D's coercion.

Issues of fraud are no less challenging. These can arise where V is deceived as to the nature of the conduct to which she is consenting (e.g. where D tells V that it is within the rules to punch the opposition when playing football). Courts have adopted a conservative approach to cases within this category, interpreting the nature of the relevant conduct narrowly such that only extreme deceptions (as in our example) are likely to undermine consent. We have seen this above, for example, where D's deception as to his HIV-positive status did not undermine V's consent to sexual intercourse: the nature of that conduct was not, the courts have held, changed by D's known infection.[207]

Apparent consent may also be undermined by a fraud regarding D's identity. This is clearly the case where, for example, D pretends to be another person in order to trick V into giving consent. However, beyond this, matters relating to the status or qualifications of D may also be germane to consent. In *Richardson*,[208] at trial it was held that V had made the equivalent to a mistake of identity when she submitted to dental treatment by D, assuming her to be a qualified dentist whereas D was in fact suspended from practice. On appeal, however, D's conviction was quashed on the ground that the finding unduly distorted the natural meaning of "identity". In this manner, as we saw with the nature of D's conduct, a narrow reading of identity restricted the potential for deception to undermine consent.

*Richardson* appears to be inconsistent with the subsequent case of *Melin*.[209] D administered Botox injections to V, who suffered serious facial burns as a consequence. The injections were intended to produce cosmetic enhancement. It was found that D foresaw the risk of causing some harm to V and he was convicted of maliciously inflicting serious bodily harm upon V, contrary to section 20 of the OAPA 1861. D appealed on the ground that V had given a valid consent to the injections. For the Court of Appeal, no question of law arose, merely the application of settled principles to the facts. *Richardson* was taken to be correct on its particular facts. Crucially, in *Melin*, V had asked D whether he was a doctor and D had lied that he was. V testified that she would not have consented to the injections but for her belief that D was a doctor. The Court of Appeal, confirming the conviction, found that, because of the importance that V attached to a medical qualification, it was a defining part of D's identity.[210] Seemingly, it is now safe to assume that if D lies to V about a qualification relevant to the procedure for which V's consent is necessary, V's apparent consent will be vitiated. However, the position in cases of non-disclosure of matters that would have led V to withhold consent remains obscure.[211]

205 *McCoy* 1953 (2) SA 4.
206 *Nichol* (1807) Russ & Ry 130: between teacher and student.
207 *Konzani* [2005] EWCA Crim 706, [2005] 2 Cr App R 14.
208 [1999] QB 444 (CA).
209 [2019] EWCA Crim 557, [2019] QB 1063.
210 *Ibid.*, [33]. No qualifications of any kind are required to make administering Botox injections lawful.
211 In particular, the Court noted in *Melin* (*ibid.*) that D had merely failed to disclose her disqualification in *Richardson*.

### *(iii) Element 3: Nature of the activity consented to*

The third element required for the determination of a legally valid consent does not relate to V's understanding of D's conduct, but to the circumstances of that conduct itself. It is here that a critical distinction has been made at common law between consent to offences of assault and battery on the one hand, and consent to more serious offences involving actual or grievous bodily harm on the other. For assault or battery, so long as V's consent is genuinely given within the terms of elements 1 and 2 discussed above, V's consent will be legally valid, and D will not have committed an offence. It is only for the second category of more serious offences involving bodily harm, that this final element of consent is engaged. Indeed, it is typically said that V *cannot* consent to more serious offences of this kind, albeit there are limited exemptions from this more general prohibition. Unfortunately, determining the boundaries of such exceptions is not easy. As we shall see, English law is internally inconsistent, and, on occasion, irrational, when determining whether consent to the risk[212] of significant harm is effective.

This distinction between assault/battery and more serious non-fatal offences raises difficulties where D is charged with assault occasioning actual bodily harm contrary section 47 and raises the issue of consent to undermine the base crime of assault or battery necessary for liability. Will element 3 be required here, because of the ABH charge, or is it possible to establish consent on the basis of elements 1 and 2 alone, because the focus is on D's base offence of assault or battery? The answer, it seems, will depend on D's foresight of the risk of ABH eventuating. If D foresees the possibility of ABH then V's consent will only be valid if it satisfies all three elements to determine the relevance of consent;[213] but, if D does not foresee the possibility of ABH, V's consent will be valid on the basis of elements 1 and 2 alone.[214]

The leading case on element 3 is *Brown*.[215] By a three-to-two majority, the House of Lords held that consensual sado-masochistic activity does not fall within any recognised exception to the general legal principle that V's consent affords no defence to D should the harm foreseen be actual bodily harm or worse. None of the majority judgments satisfactorily explains why consent should be irrelevant in these circumstances. In those judgments, one can discern two different principles justifying state intervention in respect of such sexual activity. First, there is a strand of legal moralism: the view that if conduct is sufficiently immoral or degrading, that *of itself* merits the punishing of persons who engage in such conduct, despite the consensual nature and self-regarding quality of the acts concerned.[216] Secondly, we find an attitude of paternalism: the view that the criminal law may be used to protect persons from themselves. These two principles are sometimes expressed in the same judgment in *Brown*.[217] While not contradictory principles, they tend to support differing

[212] For example, in *Slingsby* [1995] Crim LR 570 (CA), V's consent to "vigorous" sexual activity was sufficient to negate D's liability, notwithstanding, following unforeseen injury and subsequent infection, V's death.

[213] *Donovan* [1934] 2 KB 498 (CA).

[214] *Meachen* [2006] EWCA Crim 2414.

[215] [1994] 1 AC 212.

[216] "Pleasure derived from the infliction of pain is an evil thing. Cruelty is uncivilised": [1994] 1 AC 212, 237 (Lord Templeman).

[217] "There were obvious dangers of serious personal injury or blood infection. . . . It is fortunate that there were no permanent injuries to a victim. . . . Such violence is injurious to the participants and unpredictably dangerous": *ibid*., 236 (Lord Templeman).

conclusions, something the majority judgments do not address: if intervention in personal preferences is based on paternalism, one may well differentiate, in the context of the facts arising in *Brown*, between those who endure the pain and those who inflict it,[218] whereas legal moralism would draw no such distinction.[219]

The parameters of legally valid consent are unstable and contestable. There are, nonetheless, clear cases where it can be said that a freely given and sufficiently informed consent by V will preclude any finding of liability against D. Conversely, there are clear cases where V's consent is legally irrelevant. It is in the middle ground that the lack of guiding principles is exposed. Below we consider various groups of activities where V's consent has been recognised as legally valid in relation to ABH or worse, highlighting and exploring the special circumstances required to satisfy this final element of legally valid consent: (a) medical care; (b) tattooing, piercing, and more minor of body modification; (c) harms relating to religious or cultural practices; (d) sports; (e) horseplay; and (f) sexual pleasure.

### (a) *Medical treatment*

Medical treatments, including surgery, provide perhaps the most straightforward example of an activity that can be validly consented to and might otherwise constitute a serious offence against the person.[220] Therapeutic surgery is clearly lawful, at least where the objective of the surgery is to improve the health and functionality of the patient in commonly understood terms.[221] So too, it seems, is non-therapeutic plastic surgery (being non-therapeutic in the sense of making bodily changes which, rather than remedy some bodily feature that is a cause of distress, will in the patient's opinion increase his attractiveness); likewise for contraceptive surgery and gender reassignment surgery.[222]

### (b) *Tattooing, piercing, and certain forms of body modification*

This grouping includes routine activities such as haircutting (which, as noted above, can constitute ABH), as well as prevalent and clearly lawful practices such as body piercing and tattooing.[223] In most cases such acts will be performed by licensed professionals, but (unlike the category of medical treatment) this need not always be so. The case of *Wilson*

[218] A paternalist might respond by saying that punishing those masochists who may be exploited by sadists reduces the number of people who submit to sadists, thereby advancing welfare overall. But, even in its own terms, the response is problematic. It would be very difficult to measure what further increments of deterrence are achieved by punishing masochists in addition to sadists. Further, the punishment of a member of the protected class is a disvalue to be set against any advance in welfare achieved for that individual and in the quantum of welfare generally.

[219] In *Gnango* [2011] UKSC 59, [44]–[53], Lord Phillips considered that in the case of "willing" victims, only where the offence charged was for the protection of a defined class of vulnerable persons, such as underage sex offences (the *Tyrrell* principle: above, § 7.6(iv)(a)), would the victim not be implicated as an accessory in the crime of the perpetrator. For his Lordship, both the sadists and the masochists in *Brown* [1994] 1 AC 212 should be treated as guilty of the offences charged.

[220] Skegg, "Medical Procedures and the Crime of Battery" [1974] *Crim LR* 693; "Consent to Medical Procedures on Minors" (1973) 36 *MLR* 370.

[221] Certain patients may seek extraordinary surgical interventions: as in the case of a person afflicted with Bodily Integrity Disorder, a condition that can give rise to an intense desire to have a healthy limb amputated, such that amputation may bring about a degree of calm and stability. Such an intervention might be regarded as legitimate surgery: Bayne and Levy, "Amputees by Choice: Bodily Integrity Disorder and the Ethics of Amputation" (2005) 22 *J Applied Phil* 75, although after *BM* [2018] EWCA Crim 560, [2019] QB 1, discussed next, this will be more difficult to regard as legitimate surgery, although whether D is a qualified medical practitioner will be a relevant consideration.

[222] Discussed in LCCP No. 139, *Consent in the Criminal Law* (1995) Part VIII.

[223] *Ibid.*, part IX.

provides a vivid example of this:[224] D branded his initials onto the buttock of his wife (V) at her request, causing injuries that required medical care. Despite D's initial conviction for a section 47 offence, the Court of Appeal held that V's consent should have been regarded as effective, and that D's conduct was akin to lawful tattooing. Indeed, the Court gave short shrift to the prosecution case, making clear that the criminal law should not be engaging with consensual activities of this kind performed in private. Whilst the approach here may be defensible, its contrast with the House of Lords decision in *Brown* (where permissive analogies to acts such as genital piercing were not forthcoming) has attracted considerable academic scrutiny,[225] and in *Hobday*,[226] a case involving cutting of an initial into V's buttock with a knife, *Wilson* was distinguished, and described as being "hard to justify as an application of the rule in *Brown*".[227] Accordingly, V's consent to the cutting was not effective. In the light of the decision in *Hobday*, it is likely that, if the facts of *Wilson* arose today, D would be convicted of the section 47 offence despite V's consent.

The courts have also considered the legality of more extreme forms of body modification. In *BM*,[228] D, a self-described "body modification artist", removed, respectively, an ear and a nipple from two consenting clients, and divided the tongue of a third consenting client. His conviction under section 18 of the OAPA 1861 was upheld by the Court of Appeal, which described his conduct as "extreme cosmetic surgery".[229] The decision provides some important clarification regarding the boundaries of consent within this category of activities, although significant problems remain. First, the decision clarifies some cases at each end of the spectrum (routine piercing is legal, but the procedures in *BM* are not). However, the Court offered no guidance about the host of procedures lying between those extremes, such as scarification (scratching designs into the skin to create raised scars), branding, beading (inserting beads under the skin) and skin peels. Secondly, although the activities in *BM* are clearly outside that which can be consented to, the factors underpinning that conclusion were left uncertain. The Court considered a number of potentially relevant factors, including whether the conduct resulted in actual or grievous bodily harm; whether the harms gave rise to further risks of infection; and whether the activity was properly regulated. Yet, despite highlighting these factors, the Court failed to articulate which (if any) were determinative; and failed to identify their threshold limits (if any).[230] It may well be correct for the courts to defer to Parliament on the creation of new groups of consensual activities within this element of the test for legally valid consent,[231] but there are powerful Rule of Law reasons, notably concerning fair warning,[232] why the courts should do more to clarify the boundaries of acceptable conduct. It seems especially urgent to clarify the legality of procedures being advertised and performed in tattoo studios across the country.[233]

224 [1997] QB 47 (CA).
225 Discussed below, § 11.9(v).
226 [2025] EWCA Crim 46, [2025] 2 Cr App R 11. See below § 11.9(v).
227 *Ibid.*, [40].
228 [2018] EWCA Crim 560, [2019] QB 1.
229 *Ibid.*, [37].
230 E.g., the Court did not express an opinion on whether such "body modifications" could ever be lawful but ruled that they were unlawful if carried out by a person such as D who lacked relevant medical qualifications.
231 *BM* [2018] EWCA Crim 560, [2019] QB 1, [45].
232 Above, § 2.3.
233 Pegg, "Not So Clear Cut: The Lawfulness of Body Modifications" [2019] *Crim LR* 579; Williams, "Body Modification and the Limits of Consent to Injury" (2019) 135 *LQR* 19; Clement, "Consent to Body Modification in Criminal Law" (2018) 77 *CLJ* 451.

*(c) Harms relating to religious or cultural practices*

Several religious or cultural practices involve causing physical harms, from religious flagellation (ritual beating or whipping) to circumcision. In terms of legality, there are few consistent principles at work, but rather *ad hoc* reasoning and intervention. Female circumcision is clearly unlawful because of legislative intervention,[234] although we must still assume that religiously ordained male circumcision is lawful.[235] The legality of customary and tribal scarification and markings is debatable, particularly in the case of minors.

*(d) Sports*

*Brown* confirmed earlier authority that, in the course of "properly organised sports", V could lawfully take the risk of being seriously hurt by D. The extent of this exception is far from clear. Obviously well-established sports with rule-making bodies, such as football, rugby, hockey, and cricket, fall within this exception. In a very useful review of the sports exception in *Barnes*,[236] Lord Woolf emphasised the importance of open public performance, rules of the game, and disciplinary and governing bodies. The better regulated is the "zone of toleration", the more secure are the participants from interference under the general law. Yet, as the Law Commission observed, the position of so-called minority sports (especially those with less structured oversight and regulation), such as Thai boxing and full contact karate, is less secure.[237]

The case law on sports injuries and criminal liability also draws a distinction between injuries, including foreseen injuries which are a by-product of play, and intentionally inflicted injuries. In *Bradshaw*,[238] it was said that an act intended to cause serious injury would be unlawful even if it complied with the rules of the game. At the same time, provided there is no intent to cause injury, there may be effective consent to injuries inflicted outside the rules of the game. In *Barnes*,[239] the Court of Appeal confirmed the category of what may be called the conventional foul, the kind of thing that players should expect and thereby consent to when they participate in a particular kind of game.

Intent seems to be the key. If the move by D is intended to cause V injury, it may well constitute an offence against the person regardless of whether D's play is within or outside the rules of the game. Notoriously, however, the sport of boxing does not fit this picture.[240] The causing of serious injury with a direct intent to cause such injury seems to be at the heart of that sport, notwithstanding pious references to the "noble art of self-defence". Lord Mustill, a dissentient in *Brown*, was at a loss to understand how intentionally causing serious injury for financial gain could be considered lawful, whereas inflicting painful but non-serious injury for sexual gratification, as in some of the activity in *Brown*, was illegal.[241] The legality of boxing does not rest on any statute or well-regarded appellate case. In favour of the legality of boxing is its openness, its rule book, its governing bodies—factors given salience for sport generally in *Barnes*—and, above all, the generally held assumption of legality

[234] The Prohibition of Female Circumcision Act 1985.
[235] LCCP No. 139, *Consent in the Criminal Law* (1995) para. 9.2.
[236] [2004] EWCA Crim 3246, [2005] 1 WLR 910.
[237] LCCP No. 139, *Consent in the Criminal Law* (1995) Part XII.
[238] (1878) Cox CC 83.
[239] [2004] EWCA Crim 3246, [2005] 1 WLR 910.
[240] Gunn and Ormerod, "The Legality of Boxing" (1995) 15 *LS* 181.
[241] [1994] 1 AC 212.

that has stood for many years.[242] Were boxing suddenly to be regarded as illegal in the course of criminal litigation, there would be a real question of retroactive law-making and grounds for challenge under Article 7 of the ECHR. But, just as with the former immunity granted to husbands who raped their wives,[243] the legality of boxing could crumble without the need for legislation should public and judicial opinion turn decisively against the sport as an acceptable form of activity within the moral framework of current society. There is no indication that any such stage has been reached.

We tentatively offer the following summary:

(i) In games that do not involve fighting as the defining activity: where the injury is intentionally inflicted, criminal liability may arise even if the incident falls within the rules of the particular game.

(ii) In games that do not involve fighting as the defining activity: where the injury is non-intentional and a foreseeable consequence of playing the game, the rules of the game may be considered very strong evidence of what risks are consented to by the players. Further, incidents falling beyond the rules of the game but within its bounds of tolerance—e.g. marginally late tackles in rugby or football—will also fall within the boundaries of effective consent.

(iii) In the anomalous case of sports that involve rule-governed fighting, all manner of injury, up to and including death, would seem to be within the purview of effective consent, provided the injury is inflicted within the rules of the sport. This rule is offered with confidence only for fighting sports long tolerated and openly presented and organised, such as boxing and wrestling, when conducted under the auspices of the relevant controlling bodies. Intentional injuries in newer fighting sports or fighting sports new to this jurisdiction, e.g. free- or cage-fighting and Thai boxing, are of more doubtful legality notwithstanding their public performance and extensive media coverage.

(iv) Intentionally inflicted injuries falling outside the rules of any game (including its bounds of tolerance) should lead straightforwardly to criminal liability. The intention may be either direct or oblique.

### *(e) Horseplay*

In addition to organised sport, "rough, undisciplined play" allows scope for consent even to the risk of serious harm of the kind that occurred in *Aitken*,[244] where air force officers in an after-dinner mess game amused themselves, *inter alia*, by dousing each other with fuel and setting it alight. The idea, apparently, was to test the fire-resistant properties of their flying-suits. As all concerned had consented to this exceedingly dangerous activity, it was held that no offence had been committed against V, a participant, who suffered horrendous burns. The activity must, however, constitute "play": if injury is intentionally inflicted, the conduct will lose its character as play.

[242] In *BM* [2018] EWCA Crim 560, [2019] QB 1, Burnett LCJ remarked (*obiter*, at [38]) that boxing was "undoubtedly lawful when organised properly". This assurance rests on social facts rather than legal rules: compare Simpson, "The Common Law and Legal Theory" in Twining (ed.), *Legal Theory and Common Law* (1986) 8.

[243] *R* [1992] 1AC 599; above, § 2.2.

[244] *Aitken, Bennett and Barson* [1992] 1 WLR 1066 (CA). See too *Jones* (1986) 83 Cr App R 375 (CA).

*(f) Sexual pleasure*

The potential for sexual pleasure to provide legal validation for V's consent, alongside sporting pleasure and horseplay, remains hotly contested. We have already identified one relatively narrow exception that could be placed within this category: where V knowingly consents to the risk of infection from unprotected sexual intercourse with an HIV-positive D. The validity of V's consent here, including to the risk of death, was acknowledged by the Court of Appeal in *Dica*.[245] As the Court observed, as long as V is informed of the relevant risks, her decision is "pre-eminently private" and any attempt at criminalisation would suffer a "impracticality of enforcement."[246] This position is now codified by section 71(4) of the Domestic Abuse Act 2021.

As noted earlier, however, the same position is not taken where sexual pleasure is derived from the infliction and/or receipt of pain: so-called sado-masochism.[247] This was the stance of the House of Lords in *Brown*,[248] and it has not been displaced since. In *Emmett*,[249] D and V, a couple soon to be married, engaged in two episodes of consensual sexual risk-taking, involving setting fire to lighter fluid on V's breasts and her partial suffocation with a plastic bag. Both episodes resulted in actual bodily harm. The harm, unlike the harm in *Brown*, was not intended, though the risk of harm was clearly present. The Court of Appeal confirmed D's conviction for assault occasioning actual bodily harm. *Wilson* was unconvincingly distinguished as a tattooing case. The position in *Brown* regarding sexual gratification has been codified by section 71 of the Domestic Abuse Act 2021.

***(iv) Belief in consent***

If D acts with an honest belief that V is consenting (i.e. believes that all relevant elements of consent are satisfied), then he does not commit a non-fatal offence against the person, regardless of whether V is consenting in fact. This can be analysed as a negation of mens rea or as a standalone defence of belief in consent, depending on whether non-consent is treated as an element of the actus reus in the offence at issue. In *Jones and Others*,[250] for example, the defendants (schoolboys) were initially convicted of section 20 GBH offences for harms caused to two victims (also schoolboys) after they were thrown into the air as part of—what the defence described as—rough play. The defendants claimed, *inter alia*, that they genuinely believed that both victims were consenting, but changed their pleas to guilty when the trial judge declined to direct the jury regarding this potential line of defence. On appeal, the defendants' convictions were quashed. The Court of Appeal highlighted that the defence of honest belief in consent may well have failed on the facts of the case, but that the trial judge was wrong not to put it to the jury for consideration. The defence of belief in consent is rarely pursued in practice.

245 [2004] EWCA Crim 1103; [2004] QB 1257.
246 *Ibid.*, [51].
247 Bamforth, "Sadomasochism and Consent" [1994] *Crim LR* 661; Leigh, "Sado-Masochism, Consent and the Reform of the Criminal Law" (1976) 39 *MLR* 130.
248 [1994] 1 AC 212.
249 *Emmett (Stephen Roy), The Times*, 15 October 1999 (CA).
250 (1986) 83 Cr App R 375 (CA).

### *(v) The limits of consent—a critique*

Any account of consent that seeks an acceptable degree of consistent principle and policy is confounded by the *ad hoc* nature of the legal materials to hand.[251] The confusing nature of the current situation can best be exemplified by comparing the decision of the House of Lords in *Brown*[252] with the subsequent Court of Appeal decision in *Wilson*[253] and, 30 years later, with the decision of the Court of Appeal in *Hobday*.[254]

In *Brown*, an organised group of homosexual men had devised elaborate and ritualised methods of inflicting pain on consenting group members. Although bodily harm was inflicted, no member of the group required medical assistance as a consequence of these activities. In *Wilson*, a wife requested that her husband brand his initials on her buttocks. She required medical treatment to salve the burns that he inflicted with her consent. In *Hobday*, V, a 17-year old girl who was seeking drugs, consented to sexual activity with D, during which D carved the letter M (the first letter of D's name) on her buttock with a sharp knife. The cuts constituted a wound but they were superficial and it was not clear whether a permanent scar would be left. In *Brown*, there were convictions for assault occasioning ABH and malicious wounding; in *Hobday*, a conviction for assault occasioning ABH; in *Wilson*, the defendant was acquitted. Why the difference?

The decision in *Brown*, although controversial in policy terms, at least can be expressed straightforwardly. The House of Lords confirmed the general rule that effective consent could not be given if the harm amounted to actual bodily harm or worse. The value of free sexual expression between consenting adults did not weigh sufficiently to displace the general rule. This general rule was characterised as a rule about the control of violence, and the infliction of harm to that degree was considered a token of violence. The sexual motivation of the defendants did not override the violence and change its nature to private sexual conduct; an opinion confirmed by the European Court of Human Rights in finding that the conviction of the defendants did not infringe their right to respect for a private life under Article 8 of the ECHR,[255] and a position now codified in statute.[256] The Court of Appeal in *Wilson* found three grounds of differentiation from *Brown*.[257] First, in *Wilson*, there was no "aggressive intent", as had been present in *Brown*. The distinction is spurious. If a person were to be branded without consent, it would be a violent act. In both *Brown* and *Wilson* there was no aggressive intent because of V's consent. Secondly, the Court of Appeal described *Brown* as a "truly extreme" case, involving "physical torture". Yet only in *Wilson* was medical attention needed. Finally, the branding procedure was characterised as a form of tattooing and not, like the various acts in *Brown*, as acts of violence. Further, in *Wilson*, the Court of Appeal emphasised the significance of D and V being married and the activity occurring within the marital home.

In *Hobday*, the justifications for the acquittal in *Wilson* were not found to be convincing. *Wilson* was considered to be difficult to justify as an application of the rule in *Brown*, and

[251] Kell, "Social Disutility and the Law of Consent" (1994) 14 *OJLS* 121.
[252] [1994] 1 AC 212.
[253] [1997] QB 47 (CA).
[254] [2025] EWCA Crim 46, [2025] 2 Cr App 11.
[255] *Laskey et al. v United Kingdom* (1997) 24 EHRR 39.
[256] Domestic Abuse Act 2021, s. 71.
[257] *Wilson* [1997] QB 47, 50 (CA).

the exception for tattooing was not extended to include cutting of the skin, even though the superficial cut in *Hobday* might be considered to be closer to tattooing than the act of branding. The analogy between branding and tattooing was also found to be difficult to justify.[258] The Court in *Hobday* specifically rejected the relevance of the marital status of D and V. Crucially, *Hobday* was decided 30 years after *Wilson*. In *Hobday* the Court noted that, today, there is much less enthusiasm for deterring a police investigation into possible criminal activity on the ground that the partes were in a domestic relationship with each other,[259] especially given the potential for coercive control within a domestic setting. The Court emphasised the relevance of an imbalance of power between D and V, as well as the risk of additional harm arising from the activity (such as the risk of infection), as being factors relevant to determining whether an exception to *Brown* should be recognised. A further policy factor was that cutting of the skin is a form of self-harm to which the young and vulnerable are especially prone and, in the light of this, there were good reasons why D should not be permitted to do that to V, regardless of V's consent.[260] Ultimately, the Court in *Hobday* acknowledged that the exceptions to *Brown* are not fixed in time and can be developed in response to changes in social attitudes or with increased knowledge of associated risks.[261] *Wilson* might be considered to be a judgment of its time (albeit it was decided only a few years after the decision of the House of Lords in *Brown*). Social attitudes can be considered to have changed since then, with a more paternalistic approach accordingly being adopted by the courts. In the light of this, if the facts of *Wilson* arose today, it is likely that D would be convicted despite V's consent.

When looked at as a whole, the existing body of case law defies classification and conceptional analysis. Why injury, often serious, risked in sport (and in the case of boxing intentionally inflicted), horseplay, or ornamentation, has an acceptability denied to sexual fulfilment lies beyond rational explanation.[262] All that can be done is to note the decisions of the courts as and when they arise. As Burnett LCJ remarked in *BM*: "The special categories [that exempt from the general rule] hitherto identified in the cases do not lend themselves to a coherent statement of underlying principle. They are at best *ad hoc*."[263]

A law employing such distinctions is a law ripe for change. The Law Commission's Second Consultation Paper on the role of consent in the criminal law provided a useful agenda for reform. The core suggestion of the Commission's Report was that consent to harm on the part of competent persons should be effective in all spheres of activity provided the harm consented to falls short of serious injury.[264] This strikes a balance between the values of paternalism and autonomy, allowing greater weight to the latter but denying validity to

258 [2025] EWCA Crim 46, [2025] 2 Cr App R 11, [40].
259 *Ibid.*, [30].
260 *Ibid.*, [22]
261 *Ibid.*, [23].
262 "The position is unprincipled and incoherent. . . . [R]ecognition of individual autonomy [concerns] the right of individuals of sufficient understanding to make their own decisions about what is good for them. In principle, this should apply to people's sexual preferences. Indeed, it is hard to see how the interest (whether public or private) in allowing people to express their sexuality, which forms a fundamental part of people's personality, could be less important than the interest in allowing people to play sports": Feldman, *Civil Liberties and Human Rights* (1993) 517.
263 [2018] EWCA Crim 560, [2019] QB 1, [74].
264 LCCP No. 139, *Consent in the Criminal Law* (1995) paras. 4.46–53.

choices that favour the infliction of serious injury on the basis that an agent opting for harm of that gravity can be assumed not to be acting in her own best interests.

With that said, the Law Commission's recommendation has itself been attacked as a muddled and unstable compromise. Roberts, for instance, has argued that the only principled stance for a modern, heterogeneous democracy is thorough-going liberalism, a liberalism that would enjoin respect and freedom for *any* self-regarding choice made by a competent agent.[265] Certainly the liberal position in its pure form is cut and dried. In terms of individual choice, the freedom to choose is maximised and the shadow of the criminal law removed. The self-regarding (genuine) choice of a competent agent precludes any finding of a wrong done to the agent and, in the absence of any wrong, any ground of state intervention for the consistent liberal. Yet if persons are to be allowed complete freedom to choose, inevitably some very dark choices will be made; such as the choices of Bernd Brandes and Armin Miewes, that the latter should make a meal of parts of the former's body, some parts to be mutually consumed while Brandes was being hacked by Miewes to his inevitable death, the rest for Miewes later.[266] Given that neither Miewes nor Brandes were incompetent decision-makers in terms of their mental capacities,[267] the sentence of life imprisonment for murder handed down by a German court was a great injustice to Miewes from the classic liberal perspective. From that vantage, the consent of Brandes entailed that no wrong had been done to him and that should have entailed that Miewes had committed no crime.

Yet even many liberals, on learning of Miewes's sentence, will not experience the sense of indignation that is the typical reaction on encountering an injustice. Indeed, the real and imagined horrors that may flow from unrestrained choice led Feinberg, the leading philosopher on the application of liberal principles to the criminal law, to concede that the criminal law could intervene to suppress what he termed "free floating evils".[268] One token of such an evil acknowledged by Feinberg was a commercially sponsored gladiatorial contest to the death. If such a contest is to be regarded as evil, then for Feinberg it is of the free-floating kind, as the consent of the contestants entails that no one has been wronged. But he allows that a society that permits such public events debases itself, loses civic virtue, and that it may be permissible to depart from the liberal framework to suppress such evils in the general societal interest. Other commentators have striven to bring proscription of extreme choices within the liberal paradigm by challenging the claim that a freely chosen harm by an autonomous agent can never constitute a wrong to the agent.

Duff maintains that the gladiatorial contestants have been wronged: their interests as human subjects have been set back, as even chosen participation degrades and dehumanises those involved. For a state not to intervene to prevent the degradation of the participants would itself be a wrong by that state. Preventing such contests advances the interests of those who would otherwise have participated.[269] In similar vein, Dan-Cohen

265 Roberts, "The Philosophical Foundations of Consent in the Criminal Law" (1997) 17 *OJLS* 389.

266 This macabre case is discussed by Bergelson, "The Right to be Hurt. Testing the Boundaries of Consent" (2007) 75 *George Washington LR* 165, 167.

267 Consistent liberalism is constantly challenged by inferring from bizarre choices that the chooser in making such a choice has demonstrated his mental incapacity and hence his ineligibility for autonomous agency. If that temptation is avoided in the cases of Brandes and Miewes, there was nothing to cast doubt on their mental capacities.

268 *Harmless Wrongdoing* (1988) 3–33.

269 Duff, "Harms and Wrongs" (2001) 5 *Buffalo Crim LR* 13, 39.

maintains that to allow participation in such spectacles is to disrespect the participants, to regard them as lacking moral worth.[270] Whether the liberal framework is left intact after such adjustments is doubtful. When read in full, it is clear that Duff and Dan-Cohen would deploy their arguments for interventions overriding consent sparingly. Yet differences emerge between them: Dan-Cohen is, for instance, more receptive than is Duff to respecting the choices of sado-masochists.[271] If we turn from differences between liberally minded philosophers to the state of public opinion, there will be a signal lack of consensus over what freely chosen activities dehumanise, degrade, or disrespect the moral worth of the participants. If we opt for liberalism all the way down, we have a clear-cut basis for intervention but are likely to end up with more "free floating evils" than public opinion is prepared to tolerate. If we allow intervention on the back of such culturally contestable criteria as degradation and disrespect, we may give too much elbow room to pressures for conformity and intolerance.

The radically different cultural, social, and religious groups present within the jurisdiction of England and Wales renders impossible any large and stable consensus on the limits of consent. Indeed, because of the lack of any consensus emerging from its consultation exercise and the absence of any political enthusiasm to liberalise the current law to any degree, the Law Commission discontinued its consent project,[272] although it has announced a new project to review the law of consent.[273] However realistic, this is a matter for regret for anyone wishing to move on from the chaotic and overly punitive condition of the current law. Allowing effective consent to any harm falling short of serious harm would have significantly advanced tolerance and freedom. Considerable scope would still have been left for paternalism or, if you will, authoritarian communitarianism, a political necessity it seems. If scope is to be allowed to paternalism, it is important that the ground of intervention should be a genuine concern for the interests of the harmed agent and not mere moralism.[274] For that to be the case, only the person inflicting the harm should be subject to penal sanctions. The person harmed should not also be liable as a joint principal or accomplice. Currently, outside the narrow scope of the *Tyrrell* principle,[275] no distinction is drawn in terms of exposure to criminal liability between the person harmed and the person causing the harm. This is difficult to square with a paternalistic concern for the interests of the harmed agent. Apologists for the current legal position, under which those who harm and those who submit to harm are eligible for punishment, will invoke deterrence to defend the status quo in terms of paternalism. But the degree of deterrence added by punishing both camps is entirely conjectural: needing to be set against such conjectured gains is the palpable damage that convictions and punishments do to those who endure them. The present dispensation sits best with legal moralism. And legal moralism is not a proper basis for the deployment of criminal law in a modern, plural democracy.

[270] "Basic Values and the Victim's State of Mind" (2000) 88 *California LR* 759.

[271] Duff subsequently changed his position on sado-masochistic sex in *Answering for Crime* (2007) 131: "we should realise that this way of finding sexual gratification is, within that sub-culture, a way in which the participants express their love and respect for each other".

[272] Law Commission, *Eighth Programme (2001–02)* HC 227, para. 44.

[273] https://lawcom.gov.uk/project/consent-in-the-criminal-law/.

[274] For an argument in favour of a limited range of coercive measures to advance the best interests of those coerced, see Sullivan, "Liberalism and Constraining Choice: The Cases of Death and Serious Bodily Harm" in Smith and Deazley (eds.), *The Legal Medical and Cultural Regulation of the Body* (2009) 205, 225–33.

[275] [1894] 1 QB 710; above, § 7.6(iv)(a).

## § 11.10 Harassment

The Protection from Harassment Act 1997[276] provides, *inter alia*:[277]

> 1(1) A person must not pursue a course of conduct—
> (a) which amounts to the harassment of another, and
> (b) which he knows or ought to know amounts to harassment of the other.
> (1A) A person must not pursue a course of conduct—
> (a) which involves harassment of two or more persons, and
> (b) which he knows or ought to know involves harassment of those persons, and
> (c) by which he intends to persuade any person (whether or not one of those persons mentioned above)—
> (i) not to do something that he is entitled or required to do, or
> (ii) to do something that he is not under any obligation to do.
> (2) For the purposes of this section . . ., the person whose course of conduct is in question ought to know that it amounts to or involves harassment of another if a reasonable person in possession of the same information would think the course of conduct amounted to or involved harassment of the other.
> (3) Subsection (1) or (1A) does not apply to a course of conduct if the person who pursued it shows—
> (a) that it was pursued for the purpose of preventing or detecting crime,
> (b) that it was pursued under any enactment or rule of law or to comply with any condition or requirement imposed by any person under any enactment, or
> (c) that in the particular circumstances the pursuit of the course of conduct was reasonable.
> 2(1) A person who pursues a course of conduct in breach of section 1(1) or (1A) is guilty of an offence.
> . . .
> 4(1) A person whose course of conduct causes another to fear, on at least two occasions, that violence will be used against him is guilty of an offence if he knows or ought to know that his course of conduct will cause the other so to fear on each of these occasions.
> (2) For the purposes of this section, the person whose course of conduct is in question ought to know that it will cause another to fear that violence will be used against him on any occasion if a reasonable person in possession of the same information would think the course of conduct would cause the other so to fear on the occasion.

The expression "violence" in section 4 evokes some kind of physical attack. As we have seen in this chapter, in *Ireland and Burstow*,[278] the House of Lords brought non-contact acts that cause psychological injury into the mainstream of the criminal law in terms of offences and punishment. While the reasoning and ultimate implications of this decision has been questioned, these courses of conduct aimed at destabilising and diminishing the quality of the victim's life are properly regarded as serious offences against the person, notwithstanding the lack of any blow or physical attack. The activities known as stalking and harassment are now widely regarded as serious wrongs in our culture and cause considerable suffering.[279]

[276] Wells, "Stalking: The Criminal Law Response" [1997] *Crim LR* 463; Finch, *The Criminalisation of Stalking* (2001); Finch "The Perfect Stalking Law: An Evaluation of the Efficacy of the Protection from Harassment Act 1997" [2002] *Crim LR* 702.

[277] Subsection (1A) was inserted by s. 125 of the Serious Organised Crime and Police Act 2005. See also the new stalking offences inserted by the Protection of Freedoms Act 2012: below, § 11.10(iv).

[278] [1998] AC 147.

[279] In 2024 the Office for National Statistics reported that, after the age of 16, stalking affects 1 in 5 women (20.2%) and around 1 in 11 men (8.7%).

The Protection from Harassment Act 1997 is a legislative attempt directly to confront these wrongs, although it impinges on other conduct too, such as protests, demonstrations, and intrusive press activity. In its criminal law part, the Act creates the three offences set out above: two harassment offences in section 1 and a fear of violence offence in section 4. Offences have also been created within the Act relating specifically to stalking. We consider these offences in turn.

### *(i) Harassment of another*

In *Hilson v Crown Prosecution Service*,[280] the Administrative Court usefully summarised five elements of the first, and primary, harassment offence set out in section 1 of the Act:

(i) conduct which occurs on at least two occasions;
(ii) which is targeted at an individual who is foreseeably likely to be harmed by it;
(iii) which is calculated objectively to cause alarm or distress;
(iv) which is objectively oppressive and unacceptable, which will depend on the social or working context in which the conduct occurs;
(v) a line should be drawn between conduct which is unattractive and unreasonable (which is not criminal) and conduct which is of an order which will sustain criminal liability. The former may be irritating, unwelcome and provocative, but will fall on the side of the line of legitimate self-expression.

In *Hilson*, the defendants were convicted of harassing a judge by, amongst other things, contacting her using her personal email address, sending her a birthday card to her home address, and making various comments to court staff and in court identifying the judge's movements.

The most striking feature of the harassment offence is the absence of any definition of "harassment", the very activity to be proscribed, save that harassment includes alarming a person or causing them distress.[281] In *Hayes v Willoughby*,[282] Lord Sumption described "harassment" as being "an ordinary English word with a well understood meaning". In *Thomas v News Group Newspapers Ltd*,[283] Lord Phillips MR defined harassment as "a persistent and deliberate course of unreasonable and oppressive conduct, targeted at another person, which is calculated to and does cause that person alarm, fear or distress". For the purposes of the criminal law, in *Curtis*[284] "harassment" was unhelpfully defined as conduct which "must be unacceptable to a degree which would sustain criminal liability and also must be oppressive". However, in *Musharraf*[285] harassment was equated with a course of conduct that caused distress.

Section 1(2), in effect, provides that if a reasonable person would interpret D's course of conduct as amounting to harassment, then that course of conduct is harassment. Since the offence may be tried only summarily, the "reasonable person" in effect will be the stipendiary magistrate or the lay justices trying the case.

280 [2019] EWHC 1110 (Admin).
281 Protection from Harassment Act 1997, s. 7(2).
282 [2013] UKSC 17, [2013] 1 WLR 935, [1].
283 [2001] EWCA Civ 1233, [2002] EMLR 78, [30].
284 [2010] EWCA Crim 123, [2010] 1 WLR 2770, [29].
285 [2022] EWCA Crim 1482, [2023] 4 WLR 4, [26].

The scope of the primary offence is enormous. A university admissions tutor may understandably consider herself harassed after the fifth telephone call from an importunate applicant. But, even in her blackest mood, the tutor is unlikely to regard herself as the victim of an offence. Nevertheless, in *James*,[286] D was abusive in a number of phone calls whilst making a complaint to V, who managed the provision of social services. D was convicted of the offence, notwithstanding that some of the calls were return calls initiated by V.

To constitute the offence of harassment, there must, at least, be a "course of conduct". This requires the harassment of V on at least two occasions[287] and must involve some degree of connection between the two occasions.[288] The Act provides that if D aids, abets, counsels, or procures P's conduct on one occasion and, should P's conduct on a subsequent occasion, taken with the first occasion, make for a course of conduct by P, there is also a course of conduct on D's part, whether or not D was present on the second occasion.[289] However, two self-contained incidents involving interactions between the same persons will not constitute a course of conduct, as where D is unpleasant to V after some disagreement, is then reconciled to V, but on some future occasion is unpleasant again. But, provided there is the necessary degree of connection between the two episodes of harassment, it will not matter if there is a considerable time elapsing between them—annual demonstrations outside, say, a synagogue on a particular anniversary might well constitute an offence of harassment.

Although the offence requires the harassment of another by way of at least two episodes of conduct (to make for a course of conduct), it is not necessary that V be present to experience the harassment. In *Dunn*,[290] the Court of Appeal ruled that V had been harassed by D's conduct at V's home. D had intended to frighten all members of the household (including V) and it was immaterial that she was not present at the time.

To be guilty of the primary harassment offence, contrary to section 1(1), D must know, or at least ought to know, that his conduct is harassment. One might think that a negligence requirement is rather low culpability for a serious offence, but in fact the requirement falls short even of true negligence, especially in the context of group activity. If D aids, abets, counsels, or procures P's conduct on one occasion, D will be taken to know any matter that P knew or ought to have known on a subsequent occasion—whether or not D was present on that subsequent occasion.[291] This can be compared with general liability for complicity which requires actual knowledge of such matters.[292] Moreover, in determining what D ought to have known (even when acting alone), no account is to be taken of a cognitive disability such as schizophrenia.[293] In *Thomas v News Group Newspapers*,[294] in a preliminary ruling in civil proceedings,[295] the Court of Appeal held that there was no reason in principle why articles in a newspaper showing V in an unfavourable light should not constitute

286 [2009] EWHC 2925 (Admin).

287 Protection from Harassment Act 1997, s. 7(3), as inserted by the Serious Organised Crime and Police Act 2005, s. 125(7).

288 *Lau v DPP* [2000] Crim LR 580; (DC); *Hills* [2001] Crim LR 318 (CA).

289 Section 7(3A), as inserted by the Criminal Justice and Police Act 2001, s. 44.

290 [2001] Crim LR 130 (DC).

291 Protection from Harassment Act 1997, s. 7(3A)(b), as inserted by the Criminal Justice and Police Act 2001, s. 44.

292 See above, § 7.4(iv)(b).

293 *Colohan* [2001] EWCA Crim 1251.

294 [2001] EWCA Civ 1233, [2002] EMLR 78.

295 The 1997 Act also provides civil remedies for harassment.

harassment of V. The decision in *Thomas* confirms that the parameters of this offence are very broad indeed, and it may well be that prosecutions on particular facts will be open to objections under Articles 7 (non-retroactivity), 10 (freedom of expression), and 11 (freedom of peaceful assembly and association) of the ECHR.

The scope of the offence is curbed to a degree by section 1(3), which provides a defence, with the burden of proof on D, of acting for the purpose of preventing or detecting crime, complying with a statutory enactment, or acting reasonably.[296] It has been recognised that appropriate complaints to an employer or regulator would typically fall within the defence of reasonableness.[297] The interpretation of the first limb of this defence was considered by the Supreme Court in *Hayes v Willoughby*,[298] a case concerning civil liability for harassment. Since this limb of the defence is not curtailed by "reasonableness" and the focus is on D's purpose of preventing or detecting a crime, this appears to embody a subjective test; but that was not considered to be appropriate without some control mechanism, because, to use the words of Lord Sumption, a large proportion of those participating in conduct involving harassment will be "obsessives and cranks, who will commonly believe themselves to be entitled to act as they do".[299] Consequently, a hybrid interpretation was adopted. First, D's state of mind needed to be considered, to determine whether he did have the purpose to prevent or detect crime. Secondly, D's purpose needed to be a rational one, which imports a requirement of good faith, so that "there should be some logical connection between the evidence and ostensible reasons for the decision . . . an absence of arbitrariness, of capriciousness or of reasoning so outrageous in its defiance of logic as to be perverse".[300] This is a radical interpretation of the defence, which limits its ambit. It means that D will not be able to rely on the defence unless he can prove that he had applied his mind to the matter and concluded that his conduct was an appropriate method of preventing or detecting crime. This is not a test of whether a reasonable person would have reached the same decision; it is simply a matter of whether D's decision can be characterised as rational in the light of the evidence available to him. Significantly, Lord Reed dissented, preferring to interpret the first limb of the defence in purely subjective terms, both because Parliament did not qualify the defence by reference to rationality, and because the defence operates in both the civil and the criminal context, and in the latter it is not appropriate to restrict the defence artificially. In our view, Lord Reed is correct. Whilst the interpretation of the defence by the majority may be appropriate in the context of civil law claims, it is inappropriate artificially to restrict the defence for the criminal law by reference to vague notions of rationality.

### *(ii) "Persuasive" harassment of others*

The second, subsidiary, harassment offence, contrary to section 1(1A), has many features in common with the primary offence, contrary to section 1(1), but also points of difference. First, at least two persons must be subjected to conduct which *involved* harassment. For the primary offence, one or more persons must be subjected to conduct which

[296] The insanity defence is also available: *Loake v DPP* [2017] EWHC 2855 (Admin), [2018] QB 998.
[297] *Musharraf* [2022] EWCA Crim 1482, [2023] 4 WLR 4.
[298] [2013] UKSC 17, [2013] 1 WLR 935.
[299] *Ibid.*, [12].
[300] *Ibid.*, [14] (Lord Sumption).

*amounted* to harassment. The difference between involving and amounting is far from obvious: if conduct does not amount to harassment it can hardly involve harassment. Perhaps different terms are used because, for the primary offence, D need not have any particular objective, it being enough that his conduct amounts to harassment. By contrast, for the subsidiary offence, D must intend to persuade at least two persons not to engage in some form of lawful conduct. The different phraseology is perhaps to emphasise that conduct which is part of a bigger scheme than harassment for harassment's sake is within the subsidiary offence. (And yet the same is true of the primary offence!) Be that as it may, this form of the harassment offence seems designed to cover a situation where, say, D, an animal rights activist, seeks to persuade employees not to continue working for a company that tests its products on animals. If her persuasive efforts constitute harassment in the opinion of a reasonable person, and if she should have known this, she will be guilty of the subsidiary offence.

### *(iii) Causing fear of violence*

The offence created by section 4 of the 1997 Act has been interpreted as an alternative version of the offence of harassing another. Consequently, it must be established that D has put V in fear of violence on at least two occasions by a course of conduct which amounts to harassment.[301] It should be noted that, unlike assault, the fear need not be of immediate violence. Yet a blatant threat, say, to kneecap V next Wednesday will not of itself fall within section 4 because V's fear of violence must be caused by D on at least two occasions. Moreover, V must fear that violence *will* be used against her.[302] A well-founded apprehension even of the probability of violence will not suffice.[303] In the light of these factors, Lord Steyn in *Ireland and Burstow* considered that the Act offered deficient protection to recipients of telephone calls or messages redolent with threatened violence but short on the specifics of intended action.[304] Lord Steyn was right.

Moreover, it is necessary to show that there was a course of conduct which amounted to harassment and that there must be some nexus between the two or more occasions when V was caused to fear violence. In *Curtis*,[305] the Court of Appeal held that six incidents involving the use or threats of violence by one partner against the other did not constitute a "course of conduct" when this occurred over a nine-month period, particularly when the aggressive behaviour was interspersed with affection.

The offence under section 4 does not require any intent or recklessness on the part of D in causing V to fear violence. It is enough that a reasonable person would have foreseen

301 *Curtis* [2010] EWCA Crim 123, [2010] 1 WLR 2770, [20]; *Widdows* [2011] EWCA Crim 1500. Concern about the interpretation of the offence requiring proof of harassment was expressed by the same court in *Haque* [2011] EWCA Crim 1871, [2012] 1 Cr App R 5, [69]. The court recognised that the need to establish harassment meant that the prosecution had to establish that the conduct was targeted at an individual; that it was calculated to alarm, or cause distress to, that person; and that it was oppressive. The emphasis on "calculation" can be considered to contradict the objective test of fault, namely that a reasonable person would have foreseen that V would fear violence.

302 Fear that D will be violent to someone other than V does not suffice: *Caurti v DPP* [2002] Crim LR 131 (DC).

303 In *Henley* [2000] Crim LR 582 (CA), it was held to be an error to rule that it sufficed that V was "seriously frightened as to what *might* happen".

304 [1998] AC 147, 153. This might now be covered by the new offence of stalking which causes serious alarm or distress. See below § 11.10(iv).

305 [2010] EWCA Crim 123, [2010] 1 WLR 2770. See also *Widdows* [2011] EWCA Crim 1500.

that result. It might be thought that an offence which can be committed negligently should not have a maximum sentence of imprisonment for five years. Lord Steyn in *Ireland and Burstow*, on the other hand, considered five years too low a sentence for the worst kind of offending within section 4. That may well be true for cases where D has intentionally subjected V to a reign of terror with devastating effect. It would have been far better had there been gradations of offence in terms of a hierarchy of intention, recklessness and, if need be, negligence, with differential penalties attached.

### *(iv) Stalking*

The Protection of Freedoms Act 2012 created two new offences specifically relating to stalking.[306] The first of these is a summary offence of stalking, contrary to section 2A of the Protection from Harassment Act 1997. This involves a course of conduct which is in breach of section 1(1) of the Act and which amounts to the stalking of another person; namely, that the conduct amounts to harassment of another person, the acts or omission are associated with stalking, and D knows or ought to know that conduct amounts to harassment.[307] This definition involves a degree of circularity, but particular examples are given of acts or omissions which are associated with stalking,[308] such as following a person, contacting them, monitoring their use of electronic communication, watching or spying on them, or interfering with their property. Another example would be making complaints to another, such as an employer or regulator, about V. The maximum period of custody for this offence is 51 weeks.[309]

In addition, a new offence was created of perpetrating acts or omissions associated with stalking which either (i) cause another to fear violence would be used against them on at least two occasions, when D knew or ought to have known that the course of conduct would create such fear;[310] or (ii) cause serious alarm or distress which has a substantial effect on another's usual day-to-day activities.[311] The fear-of-violence version of the offence includes creating fear of a violent incident occurring in the future rather than immediately. This is wider than assault and, moreover, it does not require proof of a specific threat of violence.[312] The maximum sentence for this offence is 10 years' imprisonment.

For the most part, these new offences add nothing to the existing offences of harassment, save to label criminal conduct specifically as stalking, although liability is expanded to cover causing serious alarm or distress. The intention behind the creation of the new offences is to label criminal conduct specifically as stalking; even though a stalker may still be charged with one of the original harassment offences, if their course of conduct can be described as stalking then it is more likely and more appropriate that they will be prosecuted under the new offences.

[306] See MacEwan, "The New Stalking Offences in English Law: Will They Provide Effective Protection from Cyberstalking?" [2012] *Crim LR* 767.

[307] Protection from Harassment Act 1997, s. 2A(2).

[308] *Ibid*., s. 2A(3).

[309] Stalking Protection Orders can be made under the Stalking Protection Act 2019 to protect from the risks of stalking.

[310] Protection from Harassment Act 1997, s. 4A(b)(i).

[311] *Ibid*., s. 4A(b)(ii).

[312] *Qosja* [2016] EWCA Crim 1543, [2017] 1 WLR 311.

### *(v) Conclusion*

The Protection from Harassment Act 1997 is an unimpressive measure; a hasty product driven by political exigencies with legislative revisions and extensions made in the same vein, the most recent largely being of cosmetic effect to ensure that the language of stalking is now used. The legislation uses undefined terms and takes objective liability to the extent of deeming D to know of matters which were the thoughts and motivations of others at occasions where he was not present. A better solution to the genuine problem of threats, harassment, and stalking is required.

## § 11.11 Offences aggravated by hostility

There is considerable evidence that a significant number of violent attacks which take place in public are racially motivated and that the number of such attacks is on the increase.[313] Part II of the Crime and Disorder Act 1998 sought to strengthen the law's response to such attacks by providing that a racist motivation for violent and some cognate offences will constitute a racially aggravated form of the offence (a separate offence) subject to higher penalties.[314] Religious hostility was folded into this legislation on the same terms. The law on hate crime was criticised as being overly complex, confusing, and of unequal application as between different characteristics.[315] Following a review of the law on hate crime, the Law Commission[316] recommended significant reform of the law. The Government adopted a number of these recommendations. For instance, section 145 of the Crime and Policing Act 2026 substitutes a new section 28 of the Crime and Disorder Act 1998. This makes provision for the aggravation of offences by reference to hostility related to race, religion, disability, sexual orientation, transgender identity, and sex. An offence is aggravated by hostility relating to any of these characteristics if, at the time of committing a relevant offence, or immediately before or after the offence is committed, D demonstrates towards V hostility based on membership or presumed membership of a racial or religious group, or disability or presumed disability, sexual orientation or presumed sexual orientation, being or presumed to be transgender, or based on the sex or presumed sex of the victim.[317] Here, the hostility is something extraneous to the offence itself. It is something that accompanies offences, not something to be inferred from an offence *per se*, even if D is aware of V's membership of a particular racial or religious group or their disability, sexual orientation, transgender identity, or sex. So, something like a racial or religious insult aimed at V immediately before,

[313] In 1988 there were 4,383 race hate crimes reported to the police. In 2024/25 there were 82,940 race hate crimes recorded by the police, excluding the Metropolitan Police Service: *Hate Crime, England and Wales, year ending March 2025* (Home Office). This was 71% of the 115, 990 hate crimes recorded. There were 7,164 religious hate crimes, 18,702 sexual orientation hate crimes; 10,224 disability hate crimes; and 3,809 were transgender hate crimes (some of the crimes had more than one motivating factor, which is why the total percentage is more than 100%).

[314] Crime and Disorder Act 1998, s. 28. Note also the Public Order Act 1986, ss. 18–23 of which create offences of stirring up hatred by reference to race, religion, or sexual orientation, for example by the dissemination of inflammatory racist material.

[315] Walters, Owusu-Bempah, and Wiedlitzka, "Hate Crime and the Justice Gap: The Case for Law Reform" [2018] *Crim LR* 961. See also Demetriou and Partington. "Criminalising Hate: The Need for Rationalisation and Reform" [2022] *Crim LR* 448.

[316] Law Com. No. 402, *Hate Crime Laws: Final Report* (2021).

[317] Crime and Disorder Act 1998, s. 28(3)(a) and (4)(a).

during, or after the attack is required.[318] It is not necessary to show that hostility is part of the explanation for the attack: it suffices that hostility is manifested in some way.

Alternatively, a relevant offence will be aggravated by hostility if it is wholly or partly motivated by hostility towards members of a racial or religious group based on their membership of that group, or by hostility towards people who have a disability or a particular disability, or towards people of a sexual orientation, or who are transgender, or of a particular sex.[319]

For the purposes of section 28 references to a "racial group" means "a group of persons defined by reference to race, colour, nationality (including citizenship) or ethnic or national origins.[320] What constitutes membership of a racial group has been widely construed. In *White*,[321] D referred to V as an "African". This was held sufficiently specific to indicate hostility to V because of her membership of a racial group. Similarly in *M (A minor)*,[322] "bloody foreigner" sufficed, as did "immigrant doctor" in *A-G's Reference (No. 4 of 2004)*.[323] These are undeniably broad interpretations of what constitutes membership of a racial group; but any other approach would lead to some unedifying distinctions and benefit those who express their racial hostility in a coarse-grained way. References to "a religious group" means "a group of persons defined by reference to religious belief or lack of religious belief".[324] So, a cult where V claims some special relationship with the supernatural, and persuades D and other followers that the best guarantee of the afterlife is to follow his precepts, may well constitute a religious group. Should D lose his faith in V and physically attack him on the ground that he is a false prophet, his attack may be considered aggravated by religious hostility. References to "disability" means "any physical or mental impairment".[325] References to "transgender" include "references to being transexual, or undergoing, proposing to undergo or having undergone a process or part of a process of gender reassignment".[326]

Of the offences we have examined in this chapter, the maximum term of imprisonment for assault which is aggravated by hostility is two years' imprisonment; for assault occasioning ABH aggravated by hostility, seven years; for malicious wounding or GBH aggravated by hostility, seven years; for harassment aggravated by hostility, two years; for strangulation or suffocation aggravated by hostility, seven years; and for putting people in fear of violence aggravated by hostility, seven years.[327] As the aggravated version of these offences are separate offences in their own right, the element of D's hostility to V is something that has to be proved at trial or conceded by the defence. There is no provision for aggravation by hostility in respect of wounding or causing GBH with intent––as the maximum penalty for that offence is life imprisonment there is no scope for further aggravation. However, section 66

318 In *Parry* [2004] EWHC 3112 (Admin), an admission to the police 20 minutes after D's attack that his attack on V was racially motivated was held to be a demonstration of racial hostility immediately after the attack.

319 Crime and Disorder Act 1998, s. 28(3)(b) and (4)(b).

320 *Ibid*, s. 28(6)(a).

321 [2001] 1 WLR 1352 (CA).

322 [2004] EWHC 1453 (Admin); similarly *Rogers* [2005] EWCA Crim 2863.

323 [2005] EWCA Crim 889.

324 Crime and Disorder Act 1998, s. 28(6)(b).

325 *Ibid*, s. 28(6)(d).

326 *Ibid.*, s. 28(6)(e).

327 See ss. 29 and 32 of the Crime and Disorder Act 1998.

of the Sentencing Act 2020 provides that hostility relating to race, religion, disability, sexual orientation, or transgender identity is an aggravating factor in sentencing for all offences, save for those covered by the Crime and Disorder Act 1998, and if such hostility is proved there must be an announcement by the trial judge to that effect in open court. This provision does not, however, increase the maximum sentence for the crime, unlike the Crime and Disorder Act. The trial judge can have regard to hostility as an aggravating factor in sentencing even though D could have been but was not charged with the aggravated offence contrary to the Crime and Disorder Act 1998.[328]

What makes for hostility is undefined.[329] In *DPP v Pal*,[330] D and V were both described as being of Asian appearance. D had referred to V as a "brown Englishman" and a "white man's arse licker". Racial aggravation was held not to be present: D had taken exception to V's conduct, not to his race. D's hostility to V was based on his conception of how members of their shared racial group should interact with members of another racial group. The decision is understandable as an interpretation of the provisions but is uncomfortable in terms of social policy.[331] Suppose that V marries outside her religious group, an act of apostasy according to the group's religious norms, for which the sanction is a severe beating. The beating would not be religiously aggravated on the logic of *Pal*.[332] Perhaps the most disturbing feature of *Pal* is that it is consistent with the language of the statutory provisions. But protection can also be needed from the strictures of religion and claims of dominion or containment based on ethnic loyalties.[333]

Proof of an attack by D on a member, for example, of a different racial or religious group will not, of itself, establish racial or religious hostility. That fact will not even be prima facie proof of hostility if there is evidence of some non-racial or non-religious explanation for the attack. On the other hand, as a matter of evidence, if the prosecution can prove that D knew or presumed that V was a member of a different racial or religious group and there is no overt explanation for D's aggression (such as a non-religious or non-racial quarrel), D may legitimately be expected to raise some credible evidence of non-racial or non-religious motivation. If he does not do so, the prosecution's allegation of racial or religious hostility is likely to be sustained. In the absence of a credible explanation, actions may be allowed to speak loudly and clearly.[334]

328 *O'Leary* [2015] EWCA Crim 1306.

329 Walters, "Conceptualizing Hostility for Hate Crime Law: Minding 'the Minutiae' when Interpreting Section 28(1)(a) of the Crime and Disorder Act 1998" (2014) 34 *OJLS* 47 argues that D should be considered to have demonstrated hostility where she is aware that her behaviour is likely to be received as indicating hostility towards V's identity.

330 [2000] EWHC 1575 (QB).

331 In *Mcfarlane* [2002] EWHC Admin 485, *Pal* was said to be heavily dependent on its facts and that normally, where a racialist epithet was used during an attack, racial hostility would be made out.

332 In *Pal*, the court claimed that its reasoning would not extend, in the Court's own example, to a white man attacking another white man because of the latter's association with a black woman; but it is hard to see the difference in principle between this example and the facts of the case.

333 Section 28(6)(b) of the Crime and Disorder Act 1998 makes some movement in this direction by defining religious group to mean a group defined either by religious belief or lack of religious belief. Hence an attack on atheists, where hostility to atheism is demonstrated as part of the motivation for the attack, will constitute religious aggravation.

334 Inferences against D may be drawn from a failure to give evidence: Criminal Justice and Public Order Act 1994, s. 35. But note Owusu-Bempah, Walters, and Wiedlitzka, "Racially and Religiously Aggravated Offences: 'God's Gift to Defence'?" [2019] *Crim LR* 463, who identify difficulties in practice with demonstrating hostility.

## § 11.12 Reforming the non-fatal offences against the person

Judges and commentators have expressed a great deal of dissatisfaction with the law relating to non-fatal offences. The main focus of discontent has been on sections 47, 20, and 18 of the OAPA 1861, by far the most important sections of that Act in terms of the number of prosecutions. On one view, these offences may be viewed as an escalating ladder of gravity, in terms of the harm caused to the victim. From that perspective, the coverage provided is quirky and not easily rationalised. Section 47 requires an assault or battery which must occasion actual bodily harm. No mental element is required in respect of that bodily harm. What degree of directness is required for a battery is unclear. The maximum penalty for section 47 is five years' imprisonment, the same as for malicious wounding or infliction of grievous bodily harm under section 20, which does not reflect the fact that section 20 is regarded as a more serious offence.

In turn, section 20 concerns two different forms of harm—wounds and grievous bodily harm—which may well involve very different orders of magnitude. Whereas grievous bodily harm is by definition serious, a wound may be very minor. There seems no obvious reason, in modern times, to bracket wounds and serious bodily harm within the actus reus of one offence. Further, under section 20 a minimum mens rea of recklessness is required, but not as to a wound or grievous bodily harm; foresight of the risk of some, minor, bodily harm suffices if taking that risk is unreasonable in the circumstances.

Section 18 has given less ground for criticism. Although wounds and grievous bodily harm are again bracketed together, there must always be proof of an intent to cause grievous bodily harm or to resist lawful arrest or detention. This ensures that some measure of serious wrongdoing is involved for this very serious offence with its maximum term of life imprisonment. Nonetheless, it remains an offence that draws together things not obviously connected. Questions relating to arrest and detention are best dealt with in the family of offences relating to assaults on the police and other criminal justice officials. The term grievous bodily harm covers a wide range of injury, from, say, a broken arm to horrendous life-threatening injuries. Moreover, the offence takes two very different forms: as either an offence where a serious harm was intentionally caused or an offence where a serious harm was intended but not brought about.

In 1998, the Home Office proposed replacement offences that would constitute a simpler and more coherent pattern of offences,[335] largely reflecting recommendations made in 1993 by the Law Commission.[336] Subsequently, the Law Commission[337] reconsidered these proposals and, whilst broadly endorsing them, made some significant modifications. The Law Commission identified various criticisms of the existing offences: these include the thought that there are too many offences in the OAPA 1861 which are narrowly defined and differentiated by highly particularised factual scenarios; conversely, other offences, such as section 18, tend to assimilate morally different albeit related situations; the order and grading of the offences is unclear; and the language used is archaic and words are used without a clear meaning. At the heart of the Law Commission's recommendations was the

[335] Home Office, *Violence: Reforming the Offences Against the Person Act 1861* (1998).
[336] Law Com. No. 218, *Legislating the Criminal Code: Offences Against the Person and General Principles* (1993).
[337] Law Com. No, 361, *Reform of Offences Against the Person* (2015).

need for a logical hierarchy of offences and recognition of the principle of correspondence between mens rea and actus reus, such that the harm which needs to be intended or foreseen matches the harm done.

The Law Commission proposed, amongst other recommendations, the replacement of sections 18, 20, and 47 with three new offences:

(i) Intentionally causing serious injury to another, for which the maximum sentence would be life imprisonment.
(ii) Recklessly causing serious injury to another, for which the maximum sentence would be seven years.
(iii) Intentionally or recklessly causing injury to another, for which the maximum sentence would be five years.

Although the Home Office had recommended that intention (including oblique intention) and recklessness should be defined, the Law Commission considered that this is not necessary, since such terms should be understood in accordance with the general law. It is noteworthy that the language of injury is used, without distinguishing between bodily harm and wounding. It would follow that, for the most serious offences, wounding as presently defined will only constitute relevant harm if it can be characterised as serious. Further, injury would be defined to include both the transmission of disease (pending a wider review of the law on transmission of disease to determine whether specialised offences are required), and recognised psychological conditions, but not, as the Home Office Bill originally stated, all mental harm, which would have gone far beyond the existing law and beyond the domain of offences of violence.

For many criminal lawyers, the enactment of these proposals in place of sections 18, 20, and 47 would constitute a significant advance. The most obvious feature of the proposed offences is the absence of clutter; the expression is simple and direct, with actus reus linked to mens rea through nothing more than a causal connection. The mens rea terms are unexceptionable from the perspective of subjectivism and the correspondence principle. It is difficult to imagine that this scheme of offences would give rise to the same number of appeals, confusions, and complexities as does the current order.

If simplicity and economy of means are taken to be virtues (and this has been contested), there are nonetheless some criticisms of the revised scheme that may be offered. The proposals draw a distinction between injuries and serious injuries, yet provide no guidance on seriousness. As under the current law, what constitutes a serious injury will be a question of fact. Potentially, this brings an unduly large swathe of injury into the gravest offence—intentionally causing serious injury—which, like the present section 18, carries a maximum term of life imprisonment. There is something to be said in favour of a greater particularity here, with a tripartite division of physical harm offences into cases of (i) injury, (ii) serious injury, and (iii) grievous injury. These terms should have some degree of definition, with grievous injury confined to physical or mental harm that causes extreme pain and suffering, significant disfigurement, or significant disability.

In the sphere of serious injury, the proposals sharply demarcate causing serious injury with intent (maximum penalty life imprisonment) from recklessly causing serious injury (seven years maximum). For cases of causing injury, however, there is but one offence which can be committed either intentionally or recklessly. It is difficult to appreciate why the distinction between intent and recklessness loses its moral significance for cases involving lesser injury.[338]

The conditional welcome given here for these proposals was by no means universally shared among reactions to the Law Commission's original proposals in 1993, and much of the criticism expressed then remains applicable to the Law Commission's new recommendations. Horder complained that such reforms would strip the law of too much moral substance.[339] He emphasised the importance of "representative" or "fair" labelling,[340] which is achieved only if the definition of an offence conveys an accurate moral picture of what the defendant has done. To that end, he favoured the use of such graphic terms as "castrates, disables, disfigures, or dismembers . . . or removes an internal body part" in the definition of offences.[341] One may question, however, whether the awful details of the worst forms of violence need to feature in the *definition* of offences. Such cases receive close attention from the media and the factual details are widely disseminated in the press. The moral resonance of an offence need not require details of the *modus operandi*. For example, the term "murder" has great evocative power. Murder may extend over a vast range of particulars from, say, a painless lethal injection to agonising and protracted forms of death; but there is no need to identify gruesome ways of killing in order to convey the gravity of murder. Besides, if charges were to contain the amount of particularity recommended by Horder, there arises the risk of unmeritorious arguments on the applicability of the charge brought. Arguments concerning whether D's act was a disablement or disfigurement would be thoroughly unattractive. That said, we have commented already on the fact that the term "serious injury" is too broad and that a greater degree of subdivision and definition is required. To this extent Horder is clearly right.

Another critical voice was that of Gardner.[342] For him, each of sections 18, 20 and 47 of the OAPA 1861 has a distinctive value and ambit, which would be swept away by the proposals. Gardner argues that the central point about section 47 is the law's view that liability is appropriately triggered by an assault or battery: "By committing an assault one changes one's own normative position, so that certain adverse consequences and circumstances which would not have counted against one but for one's original assault now count against one automatically, and add to one's crime".[343] On this view, it is no surprise that section 47 has the same maximum penalty as section 20, that no mental element is required for the occasioning of actual bodily harm, and that (according to Gardner) "occasion" is a broader term than cause.

In Gardner's scheme, section 20 concerns the *infliction* of violence, which can take in a broader field of conduct than assault but keeps the offence away from such things as transmitting diseases. Here some degree of foresight should be required about the possible infliction of physical harm. Section 18, in dealing with *intended* consequences, appropriately moves to a broader *causal* standard when determining the presence of actus reus.

338 If, as we believe, the distinction between intention and recklessness retains moral purchase at this lower level of offending, the provision of separate offences of intentionally causing injury and recklessly causing injury would provide the further advantage that the former offence, being a crime where the culpability is confined to intent, would not come within the *Majewski* principle: see further below, § 18.4.

339 "Rethinking Non-fatal Offences Against the Person" (1994) 14 *OJLS* 335.

340 See above, § 2.4.

341 Horder, "Rethinking Non-fatal Offences Against the Person" (1994) 14 *OJLS* 335, 345.

342 "Rationality and the Rule of Law in Offences Against the Person" (1994) 53 *CLJ* 502.

343 *Ibid.*, 509.

Whilst this schema might be considered to be persuasive in normative terms, it has never been firmly established as part of English law. In actus reus terms, there was for many years a close association between sections 47 and 20, as it was considered that "inflict" required proof of an assault or battery. Although that connection was relaxed in *Wilson*,[344] there remains considerable doubt about the extent to which battery itself can accommodate forms of indirectly caused injury, rendering problematic the degree of disassociation between sections 47 and 20 when physical injury is in issue. Moreover, there is no authority that "occasion" in section 47 is a broader term than cause, although there is authority that it is synonymous with cause.[345] Indeed when psychiatric injury is an issue, "inflict" itself has been interpreted as "cause",[346] making for points of contact between sections 20 and 18 as well as section 47. Gardner seems to be seeking a preservation order on a house never built. The degrees of difference and similarity between the three offences follow no overarching pattern, a fact which by itself makes a case for reform.

Finally, something should be said about the proposals to reform assault and battery. The Law Commission envisages that the existing offences of assault and battery should be replicated in legislation by two renamed offences, with "battery" being called "physical assault" and what is presently called "assault" being called "threatened assault". This would have the virtue of fairly labelling the offences by reference to the distinction between contact and threat. The language of "physical assault" might be criticised, however, because it suggests direct physical contact between D and V; whereas under the existing law of battery, force can be applied indirectly to establish the offence.[347] This would be reflected in the definition of "physical assault" which would be committed if D intentionally or recklessly applies force to, or causes an impact on, the body of another. "Threatened assault" would be committed where D intentionally or recklessly causes the other to believe that any such force or impact is imminent.

The Law Commission also recommends the creation of a new offence of aggravated assault, which would be a summary offence with a maximum sentence of 12 months. This offence would be committed where D committed a physical or threatened assault that causes injury, regardless of whether D intended or was reckless about causing the injury. The Law Commission's reasons for recommending this offence are unconvincing: namely, to bridge the gap between the lowest level offence of assault, for which the maximum sentence is six months, and of causing injury, for which the maximum sentence is five years, by creating an offence to provide for cases where relatively low levels of injury are caused. The Law Commission considers that such an offence would provide an appropriate label for the person who causes injury but who does not deserve a sentence of more than 12 months, and would also allow for considerable cost-saving by confining this offence to Magistrates' Courts. But liability for this aggravated assault would be constructive, since no mens rea is required regarding the injury caused; undermining one of the Law Commission's core principles for reform of the offences against the person, namely the correspondence principle. Further, injury is undefined, so it will be unclear where the lines should be drawn between "physical assault" and "aggravated assault", and between that offence and the offence of causing injury.

[344] [1984] AC 242.
[345] *Roberts* (1971) 56 Cr App R 95 (CA).
[346] *Burstow* [1998] AC 147.
[347] *K* (1990) 91 Cr App R 23 (CA). See above, § 11.3(i).

It would have been preferable for the Law Commission to recommend that the maximum sentence for both physical and threatened assault be increased from 6 to 12 months, in order to enable the judge to reflect the aggravating effect of injury in the sentence imposed.

Although the Law Commission's proposals for reform are not perfect, they are workable and generally build sensibly on the current law with useful simplification and clarification: a striking contrast to more recent legislation. It is regrettable that Parliament has rejected multiple opportunities to implement them.

# 12

# THE PRINCIPAL SEXUAL OFFENCES

The regulation of sexual activity by the criminal law is not easy.[1] The law must respond to wrongful and harmful sexual misconduct, and ensure that sexual autonomy—a core part of personal identity[2]—is respected. These demands will not push uniformly in the direction of ever-more-expansive criminalisation. Sometimes the concept of sexual autonomy will tell against criminalisation. Although the majority of citizens might view a certain sexual activity as distasteful, this is not necessarily reason (or reason enough) for the criminal law to become involved. There are some aspects of sexual behaviour that are simply "not the criminal law's [and thus the public's] business", and which must remain part of the private sphere of sexual morality.[3] Even if this tension between reacting to conduct warranting punishment and respecting personal choice is recognised, resolving it is extremely difficult. Compounding the problem is the need for certainty and clarity in the criminal law.[4] Drawing clear lines in a complex and sensitive area such as sexual relations is fraught with challenges.

Over the years, English law has struggled to mediate these competing concerns.[5] Its main current effort to do so is contained in the Sexual Offences Act 2003 (SOA 2003), which came into force on 1 May 2004.[6] The SOA 2003 was intended to "to provide a clear, coherent and effective set of laws that increase protection, enable the appropriate punishment of abusers and ensure that the law is fair and non-discriminatory".[7] It also aimed to address the low prosecution and conviction rates in sexual offences. These

[1] See, generally, Green, *Criminalizing Sex* (2020).

[2] See Kennedy, "Criminalising Deceptive Sex: Sex, Identity and Recognition" (2021) 41 *LS* 91. Kennedy's thesis is expanded in Kennedy, *Inducing Intimacy* (2024).

[3] *Committee on Homosexual Offences and Prostitution: Report* (CM 247, 1957) 62.

[4] Above, § 2.3.

[5] For an interesting historical account, see Farmer, *Making the Modern Criminal Law* (2016) chap. 9.

[6] The SOA 2003 has been updated periodically—for instance, by the Voyeurism (Offences) Act 2019 to add in provisions to deal with "upskirting" (see SOA 2003, s. 67A). Some sexual offences are dealt with in other legislation. See, for instance, the offence of "disclosing, or threatening to disclose, private sexual photographs and films with intent to distress"—a response to "revenge pornography"—in s. 33 of the Criminal Justice and Courts Act 2015 (itself amended by the Domestic Abuse Act 2021, s. 69).

[7] From a Home Office press release, quoted by Arabella Thorp in Parliamentary Research Paper 03/62 (10 July 2003). On the genesis of the SOA 2003, see: Home Office, *Setting the Boundaries—Reforming the Law on Sex Offences* (2000); Lacey, "Beset by Boundaries: The Home Office Review of Sex Offences" [2001] *Crim LR* 3; Rumney, "The Review of Sex Offences and Rape Law Reform: Another False Dawn?" (2001) 64 *MLR* 890; *Protecting the Public: Strengthening Protection against Sex Offenders and Reforming the Law on Sexual Offences* (CM 5668, 2002); Home Affairs Committee, *Sexual Offences Bill* (Fifth Report of Session 2002–03, HC 639, 2003); *The Government Reply to the Fifth Report from the Home Affairs Committee Session 2002–2003* (HC 639); *Sexual Offences Bill* (CM 5986, 2003).

aims are laudable and, to the extent that it achieves them,[8] the SOA 2003 is an improvement on the previous law. As will be seen in this chapter, however, many aspects of the SOA 2003 are unsatisfactory. Some parts of the legislation are vague or insufficiently nuanced, leaving the courts to ensure the effective working of its provisions—a task that the Court of Appeal has performed, at best, inconsistently. There is also a tendency towards verbosity and overlapping offence definitions within the statute,[9] which leaves much in the hands of prosecutorial discretion. Formally, the SOA 2003 criminalises conduct that, in practice, was never intended to be prosecuted.[10]

Before elaborating on these points, a caveat is necessary. Although the focus of this chapter (given the nature of this book) is on the substantive criminal law, the effectiveness of the criminal justice system's response to sexual offending depends to a very large extent on rules of criminal procedure and evidence. For instance, the rules regulating the admissibility of "sexual history evidence"[11] and the collection of electronic communication data from suspects and complainants[12] play a key role in determining whether sexual offences are reported, and whether and how they are prosecuted.[13] The ability of wider society—particularly the ability of citizens called to act as jurors (and, indeed the abilities of lawyers and judges) to respond to cases without recourse to stereotypes, biases, and myths is also highly pertinent.[14] There is only so much that changes to the substantive definition of sexual offences can do without significant progress on these other fronts.

This chapter begins by outlining the law regarding the main non-consensual sexual offences. It then considers offences relating to children, which do not require proof that the complainant was not consenting, before considering certain familial sexual offences.[15]

[8] The number of successful convictions for rape remains a topic of serious concern. See Ministry of Justice, *The End-to-End Rape Review Report on Findings and Actions* (CP 437, 2021). It has been argued that such concerns often misapprehend the empirical reality concerning cases that do make it to trial: see Thomas, "Juries, Rape and Sexual Offences in the Crown Court 2007–2021" [2023] *Crim LR* 200; Saunders, "Myths and Realities: An Empirical Challenge to False Beliefs about Courtroom Practice in Rape and Serious Sexual Offence Cases" [2025] *Crim LR* 396.

[9] By way of contrast, to modernise the "core" areas of non-consensual sex, plus the sexual abuse of minors, in 1996 the Italian legislature inserted new provisions into the Italian Penal Code that consisted of nine articles, creating four criminal offences. The SOA 2003 includes 29 sections creating no less than 21 separate offences, many of which overlap with one another.

[10] An approach criticised trenchantly in Edwards, "Coming Clean about the Criminal Law" (2011) 5 *Crim Law and Philosophy* 315.

[11] For a recent overview of research in this area, see Hoyano, "Cross-examination of Sexual Complainants on Previous Sexual Behaviour: Views from the Barristers' Row" [2019] *Crim LR* 77. The Law Commission has recently proposed reforms of the relevant provisions (and various other rules of evidence and procedure), but at the time of writing these have not been legislated on: Law Com. No. 420, *Evidence in Sexual Offences Prosecutions* (2025).

[12] See Rumney and McPhee, "The Evidential Value of Electronic Communications Data in Rape and Sexual Offences Cases" [2021] *Crim LR* 20; Police, Crime, Sentencing and Courts Act 2022, Part 2, ch. 3.

[13] See, generally, King, Munro and Young Andrade, *Operation Soteria: Improving CPS Responses to Rape Complaints and Complainants* (Final Findings Report, University of Warwick, 2023), available at https://wrap.warwick.ac.uk/id/eprint/183258/7/Operataion%20Soteria_Full%20Report%202024.pdf.

[14] For discussion of the prevalence of such biases and myths amongst jurors, see: Thomas, "The 21st Century Jury: Contempt, Bias and the Impact of Jury Service" [2020] *Crim LR* 987, 998–1004; Chalmers, Leverick, and Munro, "Why the Jury Is, and Should Still Be, Out on Rape Deliberation" [2021] *Crim LR* 753; Leverick, "What Do We Know About Rape Myths and Jury Decision Making?" (2020) 24 *E&P* 255; Waiton, "What Do We Know About 'Rape Myth' Research and the Claim That There is 'Overwhelming' Evidence that Juries are Prejudiced in Rape Trials?" (2024) 28 *E&P* 154.

[15] For an account of various other sexual offences, see Rook and Ward, *Sexual Offences* (7th ed., 2025).

## § 12.1 Non-consensual sexual offences: common elements

The SOA 2003 contains four major offences that criminalise non-consensual sexual acts: rape (section 1); assault by penetration (section 2); sexual assault (section 3); and causing a person to engage in sexual activity without consent (section 4). These offences replace the former version of rape and the offence of indecent assault.[16] They also alter the law's reach, and the labelling and punishment of certain conduct that was already criminal. For instance, non-consensual digital penetration of V's vagina or anus would previously have been an indecent assault (maximum penalty: 10 years' imprisonment), but is now assault by penetration (with a maximum penalty in such cases of life imprisonment). Some conduct that would previously have fallen under (now abolished) offences relating to obtaining sexual activity by threat or deception now falls under the main non-consensual offences, such as rape, or is not criminal at all.

Before getting further into the specific elements of the SOA 2003's non-consensual offences, it is useful to consider the general elements that they have (by and large) in common. First, D's conduct or (in relation to section 4) the activity caused by D, must be intended. This typically straightforward element is dealt with in § 12.2. Secondly, each of the non-consensual offences involves "sexual" conduct. This requirement is implicitly satisfied in every case of rape; it is an explicit offence requirement that (if disputed) the Crown will have to prove beyond reasonable doubt in sections 2–4. The SOA 2003 makes provision for determining when conduct is sexual,[17] and we consider the relevant statutory wording in § 12.3. Thirdly, all four offences involve the absence of V's consent.[18] The absence of consent is crucial to identifying the wrong that D has perpetrated against V.[19] Consent is defined in the SOA 2003, but in such a vague manner that a significant, and problematic, body of case law has built up around that statutory definition. Moreover, the SOA 2003 creates various evidential[20] and conclusive[21] presumptions about V's non consent (an aspect of the actus reus) and about the lack of D's reasonable belief in V's consent (an aspect of mens rea). These matters are covered in § 12.4. Finally, in relation to that part of the mens

[16] Formerly found in the Sexual Offences Act 1956, ss. 1 (rape), 14–15 (indecent assault).
[17] SOA 2003, s. 78.
[18] Following the approach adopted in the other chapters, the text will refer to the defendant as D and the complainant as V. Note, however, that the SOA 2003 refers to "A" (the person performing/causing the activity) and "B" (another person engaging in, or being subjected to, the activity). Note, further, that efforts have been taken, where possible, to avoid language that suggests D is necessarily male and V is necessarily female.
[19] Some authors view at least some instances of penile penetration as being prima facie wrongful, with consent providing a defence: Dempsey and Herring, "Why Sexual Penetration Requires Justification" (2007) 27 *OJLS* 467; Wall, "Sexual Offences and General Reasons Not to Have Sex" (2015) 35 *OJLS* 777; Wall, "Justifying and Excusing Sex" (2019) 13 *Crim Law and Philosophy* 283; McCormack and Herring, "The Duties of the Penetrator and the Limits of Consent" [2024] *Crim LR* 94. The orthodox view remains that penile penetration is wrongful (even on a prima facie level) only if there is an absence of consent. For discussion, see: Dsouza, "Undermining Prima Facie Consent in the Criminal Law" (2014) 33 *Law and Philosophy* 489, 494–6; Greasley, "Sex, Reasons, Pro Tanto Wrongdoing, and the Structure of Rape Liability" (2021) 15 *Crim Law and Philosophy* 159. Furthermore, some authors have doubted the centrality of consent to debates about the "essence" of rape. See, e.g., Gardner, "The Opposite of Rape" (2018) 38 *OJLS* 48. Cf. Conaghan, "The Essence of Rape" (2019) 39 *OJLS* 151; Chadha, "Sexual Consent and Having Sex Together" (2020) 40 *OJLS* 619.
[20] SOA 2003, s. 75.
[21] *Ibid.*, s. 76.

rea concerning V's lack of consent, the prosecution must prove that D had no reasonable belief that V consented.[22] This form of mens rea is explored in § 12.5.

After these general matters have been covered, we will consider the specific definitions of each of the non-consensual offences.

## § 12.2 Common element 1: intentional performance or causing of conduct

The first three non-consensual offences considered in this chapter include a requirement that D intended the behavioural element of the actus reus: an intentional penetration with the penis in section 1 (rape);[23] an intentional penetration in section 2 (assault by penetration); an intentional touching of another person in section 3 (sexual assault). The fourth non-consensual offence considered in this chapter requires the intentional causing of a consequence (that another person engages in an activity).

In practice, if an act of penetration is proved, almost invariably the inference will be that it was intended. This will not, however, always be the case. For instance, in *Gabbai*,[24] D argued that he had intended to penetrate V's vagina—to which V had consented—and any penetration of her anus was accidental. The trial judge did not make it sufficiently clear to the jury that the Crown had to prove that D intended to penetrate V's anus before D could be convicted of rape. D's conviction was quashed.

Other acts might be more difficult to interpret. It is easy to envisage circumstances where the touching of a fully clothed person in a "sexual" manner may be completely accidental or inadvertent. For instance, the sudden stopping of a tube carriage might jolt D, with the consequence that D's hand touches V's breast. D should not be convicted of sexual assault (or any other form of assault), because the touching was not intended. Similarly, if D may have been in a state of automatism at the time of the physical contact, the case against him must fail.[25]

Can D deny the behaviour was intentional by pointing at D's extreme state of voluntary intoxication? The criminal law doctrines governing voluntary intoxication are set out below, in § 18.4. In general, where D lacks the requisite mens rea in respect of one or more elements of the actus reus, the doctrines allow a legal inference to be made that D actually has mens rea (in effect, deeming D to have mens rea), for any "basic intent" offence—but not where the offence requires proof of a "specific intent". In turn, this raises the question whether the offences in sections 1–4 are crimes of basic or specific intent.[26]

This question was considered in *Heard*.[27] D, who was extremely drunk, had to be taken to hospital by the police. Whilst he was waiting to be seen by a doctor, D became angry and punched one of the police officers accompanying him. D then undid his trousers, took his

[22] This is a fundamental shift from the subjective mens rea requirements contained in the former offences of indecent assault and rape. For an account of the previous law, see chapter 12 of the first edition of this book.

[23] Contrast the Sexual Offences (Scotland) Act 2009, s. 1(1) (rape), which covers intentional *and* reckless penetration.

[24] [2019] EWCA Crim 2287, [2020] 4 WLR 65.

[25] See *Abdulahi* [2022] EWCA Crim 412, discussed further below in § 12.3(i).

[26] Under its previous definition, rape was construed as a crime of basic intent. See *Woods* (1982) 74 Cr App R 312 (CA) (on recklessness as to consent) and *Fotheringham* (1989) 88 Cr App R 206 (CA) (on recklessness as to mistaken identity).

[27] [2007] EWCA Crim 125, [2008] QB 43; below, § 18.4(v).

penis in his hand, and rubbed it against the (trousered) thigh of the officer.[28] D was charged with sexual assault.

On the facts, the Court of Appeal concluded that D was not intoxicated *enough* to raise a reasonable doubt over whether he had deliberately touched the officer with his penis. None the less, the Court went on to express the view that the intention at issue in section 3 was a "basic" intention, on the ground that no purposive element was involved in the section: a deliberate touching that was in fact sexual sufficed, and it was not necessary to show that the touching was done for any ulterior purpose.[29] The Court explained that, had D been sufficiently intoxicated to raise a reasonable doubt over his intention, evidence of his intoxication would nevertheless have been inadmissible to deflect a finding that the touching was intended.

A similar analysis should apply to a charge of rape and assault by penetration where D achieves penetration despite his extreme voluntary intoxication. The situation regarding the section 4 offence (causing a person to engage in sexual activity without consent) is less clear, because D must intend a *consequence*, rather than his own behaviour. The point of whether the section 4 offence is one of basic or specific intent awaits decision.

The court's judgment in *Heard* also recognised an important further distinction. According to *Heard*, the voluntary intoxication rules apply if D's touching of V looks plausibly deliberate. But where D bumps into V while in a drugged or drunken state, the crucial requirement of intentional touching (or penetration, as the case may be) is not supplied by the standard intoxication doctrines. As recognised in *Heard* itself, even in a case of basic intent, a finding of such intent will not be made if "the mind did not go with the physical act".[30] It seems that "a drunken accident is still an accident":[31] where, viewed objectively, the physical conduct that caused the actus reus was patently non-intentional, the law of voluntary intoxication will not convert accidents into intentional sexual conduct.

## § 12.3 Common element 2: sexual conduct

The offences of assault by penetration, sexual assault, and causing a person to engage in sexual activity without consent explicitly require proof of "sexual" penetration, touching or other activity. This requirement is not included explicitly in the definition of rape. The reason for this, presumably, is that the sexuality of penile penetration is self-evident. If so, then every case of penile penetration is, inherently, a case of sexual conduct under the SOA 2003. Were this not so, it could be argued that the definition of rape excludes "non-sexual" penile penetrations, as where D penetrates V with his penis not for sexual gratification but to cause distress and humiliation.[32] We think, however, that any argument that penetrations

[28] D subsequently explained that "The only way I can make money is by moving my hips in a sexual way in Soho and I thought I would get away with doing it to you but I obviously didn't": *Heard* [2007] EWCA Crim 125, [2008] QB 43, [2].

[29] A proposition later confirmed in *A-G's Reference (No. 1 of 2020)* [2020] EWCA Crim 1665, [2021] QB 441, discussed below, § 12.3(iii).

[30] *Heard* [2007] EWCA Crim 125, [2008] QB 43, [19]–[23]. See, too, the decision in *Brady* [2006] EWCA Crim 2413 (discussed below, § 18.4(vi)).

[31] *Heard* [2007] EWCA Crim 125, [2008] QB 43, [23].

[32] Under the old law of indecent assault, acts intended to humiliate could still be, by their nature, inherently indecent. See *Lemmon* [2005] EWCA Crim 994.

so motivated are not sexual should be rejected. The humiliation and distress arises *from* non-consensual connection of this particularly intimate, sexual sort, regardless of whether D seeks sexual gratification.[33]

Moving beyond the context of penile penetration, section 78 of the SOA 2003 provides that "penetration, touching or any other activity is sexual if a reasonable person would consider that":

(a) whatever its circumstances or any person's purpose in relation to it, it is because of its nature sexual, or
(b) because of its nature it may be sexual and because of its circumstances or the purpose of any person in relation to it (or both) it is sexual.

The definition of "sexual" in section 78 is circular—it includes within its terms the very word that it sets out to define.[34] Section 78 effectively leaves open the basic question: what, exactly, is meant by the word "sexual"? Interpretational work is left for the courts, and—as explained below—they have largely devolved that task to juries.

It is clear from its bifurcated structure that section 78 was intended to preserve the type of approach the courts had taken to the meaning of the word "indecent" in the (now abolished) offence of indecent assault.[35] Thus, although there is an obvious distinction between the words "indecent" (which implies wrongfulness) and "sexual" (which does not), some instructive illustrations can be drawn from the previous law on indecency.[36]

### *(i) Penetrations, touchings, and other activities that are "because of [their] nature" sexual*

Obvious examples of activities that the reasonable person would consider to be, because of *their nature*, sexual are penile penetration of the vagina, anus, or mouth. As noted above, these penetrations need not be proved to be sexual if the charge is rape; their sexual element has been assumed by the legislature.

Oral–genital contact may also be thought of as an activity that is reasonably seen, because of its nature, as sexual. In most situations, that will be a safe assumption. The Maine case of *State v Kargar*[37] nevertheless provides a possible reason for avoiding generalisation. D was observed, and photographs were found by police of him, kissing his infant son's penis. The Maine legislature, finding it impossible to imagine non-sexual instances of oral–genital contact, had explicitly removed any element of sexual gratification from the offence definition. The same result would follow if oral–genital contact is considered "because of its nature" sexual under section 78(a). Kargar nevertheless had a non-sexual explanation for

[33] It is noteworthy that, in *Court* [1989] AC 28, Lord Ackner considered that intimate touching not motivated by sexual gratification would fall within the (former) offence of indecent assault. The relationship between indecency and sexual activity is considered below.

[34] See, further, Bennion, "The Meaning of 'Sexual' in the Sexual Offences Bill" (2003) 167 *Justice of the Peace* 784. The meaning of the word "sexual" is, it should be noted, also contested in philosophy. See Webber, "Sex" (2009) 84 *Philosophy* 233; Morgan, "What Makes an Attack Sexual?" (2021) 38 *J Appl Philosophy* 518.

[35] On which, see *Court* [1989] AC 28.

[36] Furthermore, the courts sometimes used to interpret the word "indecent" to mean "conduct that right-thinking people will consider an affront to the sexual modesty of [V]": *Court* [1989] AC 28, 34–35 (Lord Griffiths), 42 (Lord Ackner).

[37] 679 A2d 81 (1996).

his conduct. He was an Afghan refugee, and gave testimony (supported by the evidence of expert witnesses) that kissing one's son's penis (and even placing it inside one's mouth) is a sign of love for the child in Afghan culture. Kargar's conviction was quashed by the Maine Supreme Judicial Court, using the *de minimis* doctrine (in essence, a recognition that, although technically Kargar had committed the offence, the legislature did not intend his conviction).[38] Views will, presumably, differ over whether this cultural explanation should be enough to render similar activity non-sexual if carried out in England and Wales.[39] The point is that even apparently "obvious" examples of activities that are because of their nature sexual can be problematised.

Another complicated example was discussed in *Court*,[40] a decision concerning the former offence of indecent assault. There, it was said (*obiter*) that touching another person's vagina was *inherently* indecent even if done for a non-sexual reason.[41] Lord Ackner proposed a case where D, a doctor, takes a vaginal sample from V ostensibly for diagnosis but, in reality, for the purposes of some general research D is undertaking. Assuming no valid consent to the touching has been given in such circumstances, and that D had no belief in such consent, the offence of indecent assault would have been committed because D's act is (according to Lord Ackner) inherently indecent. A similar approach was employed in *Tabassum*,[42] where D examined V's breasts for a non-sexual reason (namely, to build up a data set for a computer program he was developing for sale to doctors).[43] Tabassum's conviction for indecent assault was upheld on appeal on the basis that touching others' breasts is inherently indecent. Should the same approach be taken under the SOA 2003?

The Court of Appeal's decision in *Abdulahi*[44] suggests that the answer is "yes". There, the Court was prepared to accept that the touching of a V's breast with the back of D's hand was "obviously and inevitably" sexual and, accordingly, the trial judge had been correct to direct the jury in terms of section 78(a).[45]

There are, however, convincing reasons why such activities should not be held to be, *because of their nature*, sexual.[46] Deeming all such touchings as sexual pushes the boundaries of the criminal law too far.[47] Firstly, it seems wrong to conceive of the physical examination of a breast, legitimately performed (as a procedure to see if further investigation of a suspected cancer is warranted), as an inherently "sexual" activity, even though it involves an intimate

[38] For critical discussion, see Duff, "'De Minimis' and the Structure of the Criminal Trial" (2023) 42 *Law and Philosophy* 57, 62–3, 73.

[39] See, further, Wanderer and Connors, "Culture and Crime: *Kargar* and the Existing Framework for a Cultural Defense" (1999) 47 *Buffalo LR* 829.

[40] [1989] AC 28.

[41] *Court* [1989] AC 28, 44 (Lord Ackner); cf. at 35 (Lord Griffiths).

[42] [2000] 2 Cr App R 328 (CA).

[43] D carried out what may have been genuine research into breast cancer, aware that women whom he examined mistakenly assumed he was a medical doctor. The Court of Appeal held that their mistake vitiated the women's consent.

[44] [2022] EWCA Crim 412.

[45] *Ibid.*, [35].

[46] Of course, some arguments about the non-sexual nature of such touchings will not be credible. For instance, in *Harris v GMC* [2020] EWHC 2518 (Admin), a tribunal was found to have fallen into error when it decided that clinically unnecessary vaginal examinations performed without gloves and informed consent were not sexual.

[47] See, further, Sullivan, "The Need for a Crime of Sexual Assault" [1989] *Crim LR* 331, where it is argued that the term "indecent assault", now superseded by "sexual assault", was both over-inclusive (in that the touching of intimate bodily parts was taken to be inherently indecent whatever D's reasons for touching V's body) and under-inclusive (in that certain acts, even if done in pursuit of sexual arousal, would remain inherently decent).

touching. The medical professional performing the examination is not engaged in prima facie "sexual" conduct, which she must *justify* as preventive medicine. She is simply performing preventive medicine. It might be wondered whether the Court of Appeal in *Abdulahi* was in fact illegitimately considering the context of the relevant touching (V was a nurse examining D when he, on V's account, suddenly placed his hand on V's breast) when it accepted that the trial judge had correctly analysed the case as one falling under section 78(a).[48] If so, the case ought to be have been considered under section 78(b) (analysed below).

Secondly, consider the case of a medically appropriate vaginal examination of a patient in circumstances where the patient cannot validly consent to sexual activity. Baby girls, still in nappies, often get thrush. A vaginal swab may be taken by a medical professional to confirm the diagnosis. Where the patient is a child, consent by a parent or someone *in loco parentis* may suffice.[49] If such consent is unavailable, however, resort to the defence of best-interests medical necessity will presumably be required in order to legitimate any such examination.[50] But necessity is a defence against prima facie wrongdoing, and it is tenuous at best to suggest that the medical professional has done anything even prima facie wrongful in the circumstances.

There is nothing remotely sexual about a typical colonoscopy. If the foregoing arguments are persuasive, then touching a person's penis, vagina, anus, or breasts should not, *pace Abdulahi*, be recognised as an activity that the reasonable person will automatically and always consider—because of its nature—to be sexual. These activities certainly *can* (and often *will*) be so viewed, even when the defendant claims an apparently non-sexual motivation. For example, in *Hill*,[51] D admitted inserting his fingers into V's vagina. The Court of Appeal thought that this was "some form of aggressive humiliation rather than a sexual act".[52] But D's attack on V was humiliating *because* it was sexual. D was properly convicted of sexual assault.[53]

The consequence of our analysis is that the category of conduct falling within paragraph (a) of section 78 should be very small indeed, since that category is, as the Court of Appeal ostensibly recognised in *Abdulahi*,[54] utterly blind to the context. Indeed, a worthwhile legislative reform of the SOA 2003 would be the removal of paragraph (a). The vast majority of penetrations, touchings, and other activities will fall within category (b), and paragraph (b) can cover all cases that might properly fall under paragraph (a).

### *(ii) Penetrations, touchings, and other activities that are ambiguous by nature*

Where a penetration, touching, or activity is not because of its nature sexual, but "because of its nature it *may* be sexual", paragraph (b) of section 78 requires us to consider whether it *is* sexual, from the reasonable person's perspective, "because of its circumstances or the purpose of any person in relation to it (or both)". The facts of *Court* provide an illustration

[48] For instance, the Court referred opaquely to "the deliberate touching of a woman's breast *in the manner described*": *Abdulahi* [2022] EWCA Crim 412, [35] (emphasis added).
[49] But can even a parent consent to something deemed to be "sexual" activity, on behalf of his or her child?
[50] See below, § 21.4(ii)(b).
[51] [2006] EWCA Crim 2575.
[52] *Ibid.*, [4].
[53] A more difficult case is where, e.g., D grabs V's penis in order to hurt V (see *V (KB)* [1993] 2 SCR 857).
[54] [2022] EWCA Crim 412, [36].

of this type of case.[55] D put V, a 12-year-old girl, over his knee and smacked her fully clothed bottom. If this was an act of unauthorised discipline for misbehaviour by V, it was a case of simple battery. D revealed to the police that he had smacked V's bottom because of his "buttock fetish". Accordingly, D was guilty of indecent assault. He would nowadays be guilty of sexual assault.

The structure of section 78, distinguishing penetrations, touchings, and other activities that (a) simply *are* sexual from those that merely (b) *may* be sexual, might be taken to imply that certain acts, because of their nature, *cannot* be regarded as sexual under section 78, even if they are done for sexual gratification. That was the position under the old law of indecent assault. For example, it was held in *George*[56] that when, for fetishistic reasons, D touched the shoes that V was wearing, D's sexual motive could not turn an inherently decent act into an indecent one. The law of indecency was, as a matter of authority, swept away by the reforms introduced by section 78. The approach in *George* seems, however, to have survived via the decision in *H*.[57]

In *H*, the Court of Appeal distinguished between two questions in the context of section 78(b): first, whether the penetration (touching, etc.) *could*, because of its nature, be sexual; and secondly, whether the penetration (touching, etc.) *was* sexual, because of its circumstances or any person's purpose (or both). The adoption of this distinction, which follows the wording of section 78(b), means that the Court of Appeal envisaged a category of conduct that can *never* be sexual. Perhaps tellingly, no concrete examples of absolutely non-sexual activities were provided. It was considered doubtful whether a sexual assault would occur on facts such as *George*, although the Court of Appeal acknowledged that the ultimate decision might be for the jury within the terms of section 78(b).[58] In other words, *George* might or might not involve a sexual assault. This uncertainty over whether the jury *should* be asked to decide whether D's conduct *was* sexual, from the reasonable person's perspective, is problematic. In our view, the first question posed in *H* is an unnecessary distraction. The practical answer is *always* going to be yes: the nature of *any* penetration, touching or other activity can potentially, from the reasonable person's perspective, be changed into a sexual act if done in pursuit of sexual gratification. This is particularly true of penetrations and touchings. If D touches V in any manner to attain a state of arousal, it is submitted that a sexual assault should be recognised to have occurred (assuming the touching is non-consensual, and D has the relevant mens rea). Such a touching is qualitatively different from, not to mention more threatening than, where D, say, takes hold of V's foot in order to ascertain V's shoe size.[59] Although the sphere of "other activities" is broad, the question whether, from the reasonable person's perspective, D's activity *was* sexual should also be open to the jury whenever there is evidence that the activity was carried out for the purpose of obtaining sexual gratification.[60]

[55] Though not for the majority of the Irish Supreme Court in *The People v FN* [2022] IESC 22, [22]: "Grabbing a young girl, putting her across a man's lap and repeatedly striking her buttocks is an affront to that child's sexual integrity and is objectively an indecent assault."

[56] [1956] Crim LR 52 (Assizes (Lincoln)).

[57] [2005] EWCA Crim 732, [2005] 1 WLR 2005.

[58] *Ibid.*, [11].

[59] See, further, Sullivan, "The Need for a Crime of Sexual Assault" [1989] *Crim LR* 331.

[60] In principle, this position holds where D performs a medically appropriate examination of V's breasts, but has a secret sexual motive for performing it. Cf. Rook and Ward, *Sexual Offences* (7th ed., 2025) para. 2.71; *Kumar* [2006] EWCA Crim 1946, [26] (a case on the old law of indecent assault).

Section 78(b) could be interpreted consistently with our position. Section 78(a) explains that some penetrations, touchings, and other activities are because of their nature *always* sexual from the reasonable person's perspective. Section 78(b) explains that there is a category of activities that are not by their nature *always* sexual but are *capable* of being so, again from the reasonable person's perspective. This does not imply, in terms of logic, a category of penetrations, touchings, and other activities that can *never* be sexual. All it implies is a category of penetrations, touchings, and other activities that *can* be rendered sexual, from the reasonable person's perspective, in the light of the circumstances and/or any person's purpose. On the view taken here, then, where D's conduct was not because of its nature sexual, the sole question for the jury should be whether the circumstances and/or any person's purpose rendered D's conduct sexual from the perspective of the reasonable person. In our view, there is no practical need for a category of inherently non-sexual penetration, touching, or other activity, and the statutory wording does not necessitate the recognition of one.

### *(iii) Mens rea and section 78*

One question left unanswered by section 78 is whether D must have a form of mens rea with regard to the sexual nature of the touching, penetration, or other activity: must D, for instance, intend it to be sexual, or know it to be sexual, or lack a reasonable belief that it is not sexual? In *A-G's Reference (No. 1 of 2020)*,[61] it was held that there is no requirement to prove that D intended that the relevant conduct be sexual.

This does not mean that such a sexual purpose is always *irrelevant*; the prosecution might be arguing, after all, that what *made* D's conduct sexual was D's possessing a sexual purpose. Such a purpose is simply not a *necessary* requirement for finding that D's conduct was sexual. That said, presumably D has to be at least aware of the circumstances that render his conduct sexual,[62] or that he is engaging in the conduct that is adjudged to be, because of its nature, sexual.[63] This is not to require that D recognises that these features of D's conduct rendered (or might render) the conduct *sexual*: that is an evaluative judgement for the finder of fact, not D. This approach is consistent with *A-G's Reference (No. 1 of 2020)*, and with the approach taken in other areas of the law, such as the law on dishonesty.[64]

Presumably, D will be prohibited from arguing that he was blind to the circumstances that rendered his conduct sexual due to his acute state of voluntary intoxication, but the point has yet to arise for decision.

## § 12.4 Common element 3: the absence of consent

For each of the non-consensual offences, it must be proved that V did not consent to the relevant activity. Consent has a specific meaning within the SOA 2003, which differs from the

[61] [2020] EWCA Crim 1665, [2021] QB 441.

[62] Additionally, if it is another person's purpose(s) that renders D's conduct sexual, then D will at least need to be aware of that other person's purpose(s).

[63] See the *obiter* comments in *Heard* [2007] EWCA Crim 125, [2008] QB 43, [15]. Admittedly, this subjective requirement of awareness runs counter to the more general objective approach to fault adopted in the SOA 2003. It could be that, consistent with that objective focus, the courts could impose liability where D *ought* to have been aware of engaging in the relevant conduct.

[64] Discussed below at § 13.8(iv).

understanding of consent in other areas of the law, such as in non-sexual offences against the person.[65]

Section 74 of the SOA 2003 provides that a person consents "if he agrees by choice, and has the freedom and capacity to make that choice". This definition is meant to offer more clarity than the previous law's distinction between consent, however reluctant, and mere "submission" falling short of consent.[66]

Even if section 74 says more than the previous understanding of consent, it raises difficult questions. The matters of when a person has the "capacity" and "freedom" to consent are difficult to resolve. This has meant that a substantial body of case law on the statutory definition of consent has built up—not all of it satisfactory. It is thus useful to consider the factors that have been identified by the courts as going to the question of capacity and freedom to choose under section 74.

To understand the type of situation that will fall under section 74, it is necessary first to explore sections 75 and 76 of the SOA 2003. These contain presumptions regarding the absence of consent and reasonable beliefs about consent. One objective of the SOA 2003 was to make it easier to convict people of sexual offences. Amongst the reasons why it was said to be difficult to secure their conviction under the old law were the problems of proving that V did not consent (especially when the only evidence of this was V's word),[67] and of proving that D knew or was reckless about V's non-consent. As will be seen below, it is no longer necessary to prove that D had such knowledge or was reckless about the matter of consent: the absence of a reasonable belief in consent is the relevant mens rea element employed in relation to the absence of consent under the SOA 2003. Proving the absence of such a belief might still, however, be difficult. In the hope of alleviating these remaining evidential difficulties, the SOA 2003 sets out a range of situations where it will be presumed both that V did not consent *and* that D did not reasonably believe that V consented.

### *(i) "Conclusive presumptions" about non-consent: section 76*

Section 76 of the SOA 2003 provides that it is to be *conclusively* presumed that V did not consent, and—equally importantly—that D did not reasonably believe V consented, where it is proved that D did the "relevant act"[68] (e.g. in sexual assault, that D intentionally touched V sexually) and either:

> (a) [D] intentionally deceived [V] as to the nature or purpose of the relevant act; [or]
> (b) [D] intentionally induced [V] to consent to the relevant act by impersonating a person known personally to [V].

These provisions "have their roots in the late nineteenth century".[69] It will, accordingly, be necessary to consider some pre-SOA 2003 authorities in the sections below.

[65] See above, § 11.9. For cogent criticism of this differentiated approach, see Elliott and de Than, "The Case for a Rational Reconstruction of Consent in the Criminal Law" (2007) 70 *MLR* 225.

[66] See: *Olugboja* [1982] QB 320 (CA); Gardner, "Appreciating *Olugboja*" (1996) 16 *LS* 275. As will be seen below, the distinction in *Olugboja* has been treated inconsistently under the SOA 2003.

[67] Furthermore, until 1994, juries were warned to be very careful before convicting D on the basis of V's uncorroborated testimony in sexual cases. See now Criminal Justice and Public Order Act 1994, s. 32.

[68] See Sexual Offences Act 2003, s. 77. Proof of the "relevant act" will involve proof of the other elements of the relevant offence: meaning that the conclusive presumptions, if operative, will remove all defence arguments from D.

[69] *R (Monica) v DPP, ex parte Boyling* [2018] EWHC 3508 (Admin), [2019] QB 1019, [31].

Although expressed in terms of a rule of *evidence*, these "conclusive presumptions" are in truth rules of substantive law. The same notion could have been expressed more simply by saying "a person does not in law consent to a sexual act in the following circumstances".[70] If the presence of these circumstances meant that V in law did not consent, and D was aware—or should have been aware—of those circumstances, D would then be deemed to have mens rea.

Section 76(2)(a) envisages intentional deceptions as to two elements of a sexual activity: nature and purpose. It is useful to consider these matters separately.

### (a) Deceptions regarding the nature of the activity

Implicit in the concept of the *nature* of an act is a distinction between the essence of the act and its non-essential attributes. Provided V understands the essence of the act, V's consent to that act will not be undermined (at least in terms of section 76), even if V is mistaken or ignorant regarding one or more non-essential attributes.

An example of a deception as to an *essential* attribute is the old case of *Williams*,[71] where D passed off his act of intercourse as *only* a medically approved method of improving V's singing voice.[72] Such a case would now be dealt with under section 76: if D was proved to have intentionally penetrated V's vagina with his penis, having *intentionally* deceived V by representing the activity as a medical (or some other therapeutic) procedure rather than a sexual activity, V would be presumed conclusively not to have consented, and D would be presumed conclusively not to have reasonably believed that V consented.

What, then, is a *non-essential* attribute of a sexual act? In *B*, it was held that, where D does not disclose that he may pass on a sexually transmitted infection to V, this does not vitiate V's consent to the *sexual* act.[73] (At the same time, because V does not consent to the risk of infection, D may commit a non-sexual offence against the person if V is infected.)[74] Similarly, V's consent was not vitiated by applying section 76 in *Jheeta*, where V agreed to have sex with D in the mistaken belief, induced by D, that D was suicidal and likely to kill himself unless V agreed.[75] (D was nevertheless convicted using the general definition of consent in section 74, as explained below.) In the same spirit, it was held in *Assange*[76] that the wearing or not wearing of a condom does not alter the "nature" of the

[70] Cp. Sexual Offences (Scotland) Act 2009, ss. 12, 14. See, further, Tadros, "Rape without Consent" (2006) 26 *OJLS* 515.

[71] [1923] 1 KB 340 (CA). See, too, *Flattery* (1877) 2 QBD 410.

[72] Importantly, the complainant in *Williams* did not know that the defendant was going to penetrate her with his penis. If she had known that, a difficult question would then have arisen over whether she was, in fact, deceived as to the "nature" of the activity—see below.

[73] [2006] EWCA Crim 2945, [2007] 1 WLR 1567, confirming *dicta* in *Dica* [2004] EWCA Crim 1103, [2004] QB 1257, [39] and *Konzani* [2005] EWCA Crim 706, [2005] 2 Cr App R 14, [41].

[74] See above, § 11.7.

[75] *Jheeta* [2007] EWCA Crim 1699, [2008] 1 WLR 2582. Additionally, V believed (as a result of D's deceptions) that she was liable to be fined if D committed suicide.

[76] *Assange v Swedish Prosecution Authority* [2011] EWHC 2849 (Admin). The issue arose in context of a European Arrest Warrant, for which Assange's liability to surrender depended on whether the acts in question would have amounted to criminal offences in England. The Divisional Court concluded that they would. Assange appealed unsuccessfully to the Supreme Court, but on grounds unrelated to this aspect of the Divisional Court's decision. In 2019, the Swedish authorities ended their investigation into the relevant allegations.

sexual activity under section 76.[77] V's consent is thus not vitiated under section 76 where D tells V that he will use a condom but in fact does not. (The Divisional Court then went on to say that, if V had made it clear that she would only consent if D used a condom, D's intentional and deceptive failure to respect the condition would vitiate her consent in the light of section 74, a matter to which we return below.) Finally, D's deception regarding his or her gender does not alter the (sexual) "nature" of the act, for the purposes of section 76 (though, again, it may be relevant under section 74).[78] These cases demonstrate that the courts have been extremely restrained when considering what will alter the "nature" of the act under section 76, because of the severe consequences, for D, of its application.[79]

*(b) Deceptions regarding the purpose of the activity*

Similar restraint has been visible in cases under section 76 concerning deceptions about the *purpose* of the act. From the statutory wording, one might think that the courts should investigate the purpose of *actions* (if such things can be determined), rather than the purpose of *actors*. The courts have, however, focused on D's purposes in engaging in the relevant activity.

For example, in *Devonald*,[80] D, a man of 37, wishing to humiliate V, a boy of 16 who had jilted D's daughter, assumed the identity of a non-existent 20-year-old girl ("Cassey"). Using this persona, D persuaded V to masturbate in front of a webcam. The Court of Appeal upheld D's conviction for causing a sexual activity without consent on the ground that he had deceived V as to the "nature or purpose of the act".

It appears that section 76's purpose limb applies only to cases where V fails *entirely* to appreciate D's purposes in engaging, or having V engage, in the relevant activity. For example, in *Bingham*,[81] D (V's boyfriend) created a fake online persona ("Grant"). "Grant" persuaded V to take intimate photographs of herself and send them to him. "Grant" then threatened to send the photos to V's employer unless she continued to take intimate photographs for him. V complained to D, who in turn purported (valiantly) to kill "Grant". Next, however, D created a second persona ("Chad"). "Chad" claimed to know both about the photos and the murder of "Grant". When V eventually contacted the police, D was found to be behind all of this, and was charged with causing a person to engage in sexual activity without consent. D explained initially that he was trying to make V stand up for herself. He eventually admitted that he also had the purpose of achieving sexual gratification. The Court of Appeal distinguished *Devonald* on the basis that, in that case, V had not appreciated D's purpose (humiliation) at all. V would, if asked, presumably have said that

77 Cf. the opinion of Abella, Moldaver, and Karakatsanis JJ in *Hutchinson* 2014 SCC 19, [2014] 1 SCR 346 and the ultimate decision in *Kirkpatrick* [2022] 2 SCR 480. As noted above, for the presumptions in s. 76 to be triggered, D must deceive V regarding the nature of the "relevant act". "Relevant act" is defined in s. 77 to mean, in the context of rape, "[D] intentionally penetrating, with his penis, the vagina, anus or mouth of [C]". This suggests a focus on the type of penetration, not its associated risks.

78 In *McNally* [2013] EWCA Crim 1051, [2014] QB 593, the Court of Appeal held that, as a matter of "common sense", the "nature" of D's act had been altered by D's "deception" regarding her gender: [26]. The case was, however, decided under section 74's general definition of consent, the view being taken that section 76 was beside the point: [18]. This treatment of the issue suggests that gender is not relevant to section 76, but *McNally* is by no means determinative. *McNally* is discussed further below, in § 12.4(iii)(c).

79 *Jheeta* [2007] EWCA Crim 1699, [2008] 1 WLR 2582, [23].

80 [2008] EWCA Crim 527.

81 [2013] EWCA Crim 823, [2013] 2 Cr App R 29.

Devonald's purpose was to obtain sexual gratification, which it was not. In *Bingham*, by contrast, V would, if asked, have said that D's purpose was to obtain sexual gratification, and *at least in part* it was.[82] This was enough to take *Bingham* out of section 76's conclusive presumptions. The conclusive nature of the presumptions under section 76 evidently weighed heavily with the Court.[83]

The same analysis can be applied to distinguish *Bingham* from the case of *Matt*.[84] There, D, a plumber, tricked V into believing that he was a casting agent for a television remake of the film *Basic Instinct*. D and V engaged in sexual activity, and D was subsequently charged with sexual assault, to which he pleaded guilty. He did so only after attempting to persuade the trial judge that section 76's conclusive presumptions could not apply in such a situation, because V must have appreciated that *part of* the purpose of engaging in the relevant activity was D's sexual arousal or gratification, even if V had been deceived as to another aspect of the activity's purpose (i.e. that it would lead to her being considered for an acting role). If this was right, then, on our reading of the law following *Bingham* (presented above), section 76's conclusive presumptions should have been inapplicable. In upholding D's conviction on the basis that the conclusive presumptions would indeed have applied at trial, the Court of Appeal concluded that "[t]he ostensible purpose of the activity, on the facts as presented by the Crown and accepted by the defence, was not sexual pleasure but simulated sexual pleasure for commercial reasons".[85] This must mean that the *sole* purpose of the activity, as far as V was aware, was *simulated* sexual arousal/gratification, and *actual* sexual arousal/gratification on D's part was in no way something that V envisaged as being part of the purpose of the sexual activity engaged in. A questionable distinction, perhaps,[86] but one that allows the case law on section 76's purpose limb to be read coherently.

Finally, consider the pre-SOA 2003 case of *Linekar*,[87] where V agreed to have sex with D on the basis that D would then pay V money. After they had had sex, D left without paying. The Court of Appeal concluded that V had not been raped.[88] Here, V was not deceived at all regarding D's purpose in engaging in sexual activity with her: she was deceived about D's intentions regarding what would happen afterwards. That would take the facts of *Linekar* outside section 76's sphere of application.[89]

### *(c) Impersonation of a person known personally to V*

Conclusive presumptions of non-consent, and of no reasonable belief in consent, will arise under section 76 if D intentionally impersonates someone known to V, and V is induced by the impersonation to consent to the sexual activity. The requirement for *personal*

[82] See, too, *Jheeta* [2007] EWCA Crim 1699, [2008] 1 WLR 2582.
[83] *Bingham* [2013] EWCA Crim 823, [2013] 2 Cr App R 29, [20].
[84] [2015] EWCA Crim 162.
[85] *Ibid*., [12].
[86] Does this mean that any actor simulating sex deceives the other party as to the purpose of the activity when they also (secretly) seek to derive "real" sexual pleasure from it?
[87] [1995] QB 250 (CA).
[88] The prosecution may have been wiser to charge D with obtaining sexual intercourse through false pretences under the Sexual Offences Act 1956, s. 3. This offence was abolished without replacement by the SOA 2003.
[89] As confirmed in *Jheeta* [2007] EWCA Crim 1699, [2008] 1 WLR 2582, [27]. The question of V's consent would have to be resolved under s. 74: see below, § 12.4(iii). It is likely that the Court of Appeal would find that V had consented under that section: *Lawrance* [2020] EWCA Crim 971, [2020] 1 WLR 5025, [34]. For an argument that *Linekar* would be dealt with better via a focus on conditional consent, rather than deception, see Chadha, "Conditional Consent" (2021) 40 *Law & Philosophy* 335.

acquaintance will exculpate someone who exploits a strong resemblance to, say, a celebrity (assuming, of course, that the celebrity is not a personal acquaintance of V's). It would also create an obstacle to using this limb of section 76 in a case like *Devonald*—"Cassey" was fictitious; D was not claiming that V had ever met "Cassey". That said, it is not unimaginable that the idea of personal acquaintance might well be stretched beyond persons who have met physically. Suppose that A (a real person) creates a genuine online profile and interacts with V. D logs on to A's online account and arranges to meet with V. V thinks D to be A, and willingly has sex with D under that misapprehension. Has D intentionally induced V's consent by impersonating someone "known personally" to V? No case raising this point has come before the courts, but there is no good reason to restrict impersonation to *physical* acquaintances, particularly given the prevalence of online relationships in contemporary society. There is no stretch of language here. A may not have met V "in person", but the range of meanings covered by "personally" includes reference to A "as an individual person (as distinct from others)".[90] That is the sense in issue here.

An important limitation on the impersonation limb of section 76 is that the impersonation must *induce* consent. Suppose that D's impersonation—of, say, a school friend whom V has not seen in 15 years—did not play any part in V's decision to engage in sexual activity with D. No conclusive presumptions of non-consent, or of no reasonable belief in consent, apply.

### *(ii) Section 75 and the "evidential presumptions"*

Section 75 of the SOA 2003 lists a set of circumstances in which an "evidential presumption" arises against D that V did not consent and—again, equally importantly—that D had no reasonable belief in V's consent.[91] V's lack of consent, and D's lack of a reasonable belief in V's consent, can be presumed if the prosecution proves that:

(i) D did the "relevant act" (e.g. in rape, intentionally penetrated V's vagina, anus or mouth with D's penis);
(ii) one of the circumstances listed in section 75(2) existed; and
(iii) D *knew* that the relevant circumstance(s) existed.

In contrast to the *conclusive* presumptions in section 76 (discussed above), the evidential presumptions in section 75 are *rebuttable*. D can overcome the presumptions in section 75 by leading evidence that suggests that V did in fact consent and/or that D reasonably believed V consented.

#### *(a) The evidential position*

In terms of the law of evidence, D has an "evidential burden" to satisfy if wishing to combat the section 75 presumption(s). To satisfy this evidential burden and rebut the relevant

[90] *Oxford English Dictionary* (3rd ed., 2008).

[91] The government's original idea was to go further and place a reverse legal burden on D. This would have meant that, if the prosecution could prove the existence of one of the set of circumstances, D would then have the burden of proving on the balance of probabilities that V consented, and/or that D reasonably believed V did. If D failed to offer such proof, the court would be obliged to presume that V had not consented, and that D had not reasonably believed V was consenting: *Protecting the Public—Strengthening Protection against Sex Offenders and Reforming the Law on Sexual Offences* (CM 5668, 2002) 16. This proposal was retracted because of concerns about the compatibility of a reverse legal burden with Art. 6(2) of the ECHR, which guarantees the presumption of innocence: see above, § 3.2.

presumption(s), D must point to evidence that is capable of raising a reasonable doubt, in the mind of a reasonable jury, regarding V's lack of consent and/or the absence of a reasonable belief in consent on D's part. Once such evidence is before the court, both sides are, in legal terms, "back to square one"—the prosecution has the full burden of persuading the court that V did not consent, and that D had no reasonable belief in consent. D will have the benefit of any reasonable doubt concerning those matters.

The evidence suggesting that V consented (and/or that D reasonably believed that V did) may, in theory, consist of nothing more than D's oral evidence. At first sight, this could mean that, in order to nullify the effect of section 75, all D needs to do is to go into the witness box and aver that V consented and/or that D reasonably believed V consented.[92] Section 75 would then have added a new complication to the law of sexual offences but to little effect. In *Ciccarelli*,[93] however, the Court of Appeal held that D did not discharge the evidential burden by merely asserting in the witness box that he reasonably believed V was consenting. In order to discharge the evidential burden, "some evidence *beyond the fanciful or speculative* had to be adduced to support the reasonableness of his belief".[94] In other words, the evidence called by D must be such that it could raise, in the mind of a reasonable jury, a *reasonable* doubt about the prosecution's claim that D lacked a reasonable belief in V's consent. Although it sets a relatively low bar, the decision in *Ciccarelli* helps to avoid the complete neutering of section 75.

### *(b) Circumstances giving rise to the evidential presumptions*

The circumstances that give rise to the evidential presumptions are set out in section 75(2). The first three circumstances are as follows:

> (a) any person was, at the time of the relevant act or immediately before it began, using violence against [V] or causing [V] to fear that immediate violence would be used against [V];
> (b) any person was, at the time of the relevant act or immediately before it began, causing [V] to fear that violence was being used, or that immediate violence would be used, against another person;
> (c) [V] was, and [D] was not, unlawfully detained at the time of the relevant act;

One may wonder why conditions (a)–(c) required specific provisions. Under the general test set down in section 74, one would have thought that, in such circumstances, a lack of freedom and capacity to consent would readily be found. D would have to produce some exceptional evidence to avoid a finding of non-consent.[95] That is, effectively, the position under section 75(2)(a)–(c); the use or threat of immediate violence or unlawful detention must ordinarily be incompatible with V's consent.

The inclusion of circumstances (a)–(c) is no easier to understand when regard is had to the presumption that D had no reasonable belief in V's consent. It will be remembered that

[92] Cf. McEwan, "'I Thought She Consented': Defeat of the Rape Shield or the Defence that Will Not Run?" [2006] *Crim LR* 969.

[93] [2011] EWCA Crim 2665, [2012] 1 Cr App R 15.

[94] *Ibid.*, [18] (emphasis added). A vaguely similar approach has been taken in respect of weak defence evidence in sexual cases in Canada: see, e.g., *Pappajohn* [1980] 2 SCR 120.

[95] It is conceivable that some sadomasochistic practices could fall under condition (a). D might then be able to raise the issue of consent. Similarly, subject to questions about V's freedom and capacity, it *may* be that V could validly consent to sexual intercourse with a kidnapper or guard.

D must *know* about the relevant circumstance, for instance that someone had threatened V with violence. In such circumstances, the absence of D's reasonable belief in consent is (again absent exceptional circumstances) readily found.

The next circumstance in which an evidential presumption will arise is where:

(d) [V] was asleep or otherwise unconscious at the time of the relevant act;

Again, it might be wondered why this provision is necessary. Under the previous law, the fact that V was asleep or otherwise unconscious would normally constitute incapacity to consent.[96] By contrast, condition (d) seems to allow for a possibility that V can validly consent to D's touching V sexually while V is unconscious.[97] In such a case, while V's non-consent (and D's lack of reasonable belief in consent) is to be presumed, D still has an opportunity to raise a reasonable doubt about these matters, making them a contested issue in the proceedings, and overcoming the evidential presumptions under section 75.

Admittedly, unless the arrangement between the parties is very precise ("Wake me up tomorrow . . ."), this conclusion is difficult to square with Lady Hale's oft-cited statement that "One does not consent to sex in general. One consents to this act of sex with this person at this time and in this place."[98] It also means that English law is now on a different path from Canadian law and Scots law. In *JA*,[99] a majority of the Supreme Court of Canada decided that "an individual must be conscious throughout the sexual activity in order to provide the requisite consent".[100] The majority's reasoning focused to a large extent on the statutory provisions regarding consent in the Canadian Criminal Code (which are very different from the provisions of the SOA 2003).[101] But the majority was additionally wary of the risk of spurious defences based on alleged prior consent, and the fact that an unconscious person—if held to be consenting to sexual activity whilst in that state—would be unable to withdraw that consent until conscious again. This latter concern has also proved important in Scotland,[102] where it was additionally noted that it was "axiomatic" that, where D is aware that V is unconscious, D will lack a reasonable belief in consent.[103]

Fish J, for the minority in *JA*, was particularly concerned with the following type of example:[104]

> "Adopting the Crown's position would also require us to find that cohabiting partners across Canada, including spouses, commit a sexual assault when either of them, *even with express prior consent*, kisses or caresses the other while the latter is asleep. The absurdity of this consequence makes plain that it is the product of an unintended and unacceptable extension of the [criminal law] upon which the Crown would cause this appeal to rest."

96 *Mayers* (1872) 12 Cox CC 311; *Larter* [1995] Crim LR 75 (CA).
97 See *BVA* [2025] EWCA Crim 1359, discussed further below in § 12.4(iii)(c).
98 *Cooper* [2009] UKHL 42, [2009] 1 WLR 1786, [27].
99 [2011] 2 SCR 440.
100 *Ibid.*, [3] (McLachlin CJ).
101 The provisions in the Canadian Code have also been interpreted in striking ways. For a critical analysis, see Plaxton, *Implied Consent and Sexual Assault* (2015).
102 *GW v HM Advocate* [2019] HCJ 23, 2019 JC 109.
103 *Ibid.*, [27].
104 *JA* [2011] 2 SCR 440, [74] (emphasis in original).

The existence of prosecutorial discretion (and the possible deployment of a *de minimis* defence) in such cases did not placate the dissentients.

For better or worse, it appears that, as a result of section 75(2)(d), English law presently sides with Fish J.[105] Unless and until that provision is amended or repealed,[106] prior consent to unconscious sexual activity (and correlatively a reasonable belief in consent to unconscious sexual activity)[107] is legally possible.

Similar issues in the context of existing sexual relationships might arise in relation to the next circumstance:

(e) because of [V]'s physical disability, [V] would not have been able at the time of the relevant act to communicate to [D] whether [V] consented;

In general, however, where a person performs a sexual act on a person who cannot at the time communicate consent because of disability, a very serious wrong is perpetrated.[108]

The final circumstance in which a presumption of no consent, and no reasonable belief in consent, can arise is as follows:

(f) any person had administered to or caused to be taken by [V], without [V]'s consent, a substance which, having regard to when it was administered or taken, was capable of causing or enabling [V] to be stupefied or overpowered at the time of the relevant act.

Where V *is* overpowered or stupefied by the relevant substance, the finding of non-consent within the terms of section 74 would normally be straightforward, even without the benefit of condition (f).[109] Condition (f) is, however, necessary for cases where the substance, although *capable* of causing (or enabling) V to be overpowered or stupefied at the time of the "relevant act", fails to do so. In such circumstances, section 75 requires D to raise evidence suggesting that V had not succumbed to (or even been significantly affected by) the substance and was in fact consenting to the relevant sexual activity, or that D reasonably believed this to be the case.

[105] See, further, the *obiter* comment in *Jheeta* [2007] EWCA Crim 1699, [2008] 1 WLR 2582, [22]. For a defence of the apparent English position, and an overview of the Canadian commentary following *JA*, see Jarvis, "The Timing of Consent" [2019] *Crim LR* 394.

[106] For an argument that this provision should have appeared in section 76, not section 75, see Temkin and Ashworth, "The Sexual Offences Act 2003: Rape, Sexual Assaults and the Problems of Consent" [2004] *Crim LR* 328, 337.

[107] Cp. *Hepburn* [2020] EWCA Crim 820, where the trial judge correctly directed the jury that no reasonable belief in such consent could arise where D had engaged in sexual activity with unconscious V, whom he barely knew.

[108] The exception comprises a case where V *is* consenting, but cannot communicate that at the time. Difficulties of proof abound in such cases. Additionally, *pace* the definition in the SOA 2003, some authors contend that sexual consent is *essentially* communicative—e.g. Dougherty, "Yes Means Yes: Consent as Communication" (2015) 43 *Philosophy and Public Affairs* 224. Cf. Ferzan, "Consent, Culpability and Rape" (2016) 13 *Ohio State J Crim Law* 397; Alexander, Hurd and Westen, "Consent Does Not Require Communication: A Reply to Dougherty" (2016) 35 *Law and Philosophy* 655; Tadros, *Wrongs and Crimes* (2016) chap. 10.

[109] To raise an issue of consent in such circumstances, D would presumably have to adduce evidence that V agreed in advance that D could make covert attempts to stupify or overpower V and could be allowed intercourse (or whatever sexual touching is at issue) if V were reduced to that condition. In *R (T) v DPP* [2003] EWHC 226 (Admin), it was held that even a momentary loss of consciousness constituted actual bodily harm for the purposes of s. 47 of the OAPA 1861. In the light of the decision in *Brown* [1994] 1 AC 212, which precludes the validity of any consent to the infliction of actual bodily harm save in limited circumstances (below, § 11.9(iii)), D may well commit an offence against s. 47 or s. 23 of the OAPA 1861 in such situations.

*(c) The scope of the presumptions in sections 75 and 76*

Sections 75 and 76 require proof that D "did the relevant act" before the relevant presumptions arise.[110] Section 77 provides more detail on such "relevant acts". For example, in relation to rape, the "relevant act" is intentionally penetrating V in one of the ways described in section 1. This appears to mean that the presumptions in sections 75 and 76 do not generally apply when D is charged with an inchoate offence, because D will typically not have completed the "relevant act".[111] This could mean, in turn, that a jury is directed on section 75 in relation to an allegation that D fondled V's breasts whilst V was asleep (the "relevant act" for sexual assault having occurred), but not on the more serious allegation that D then attempted to have sexual intercourse with still-unconscious V.

Despite the potential for juror confusion in such cases, the limitation on sections 75 and 76 is unlikely to have a significant practical impact on the breadth of D's liability. Inchoate liability tends to rely much more on the defendant's or defendants' mental state(s) than the "objective" facts, as the absence of a defence of factual impossibility demonstrates.[112] Accordingly, a presumption of non-consent would not be tremendously helpful in establishing, for example, whether the defendants had formed a conspiracy to commit rape.[113] Similarly, the presumptions in section 75 and 76 regarding the absence of a reasonable belief in consent would be of little assistance to the prosecution in relation to the inchoate offences: in assisting or encouraging crime, D must at least be reckless regarding V's non-consent;[114] in conspiracy, the defendants must intend or know that V will not consent;[115] and for attempts there remains controversy over whether the absence of a reasonable belief in V's consent is sufficient for liability.[116] Of course, the jury will benefit from direction on what *the law* considers consent to be in these contexts, and the trial judge could repurpose any relevant parts of sections 75 and 76 in this regard, but they do not strictly apply, and their presumptions will not formally operate.

### (iii) Beyond the evidential and conclusive presumptions

If a prosecution is brought on facts not covered by any evidential or conclusive presumption (or, indeed, if an evidential presumption is rebutted by D), the normal rules of proof will apply: the prosecution must establish that V did not consent, and that D lacked a reasonable belief that V consented. The definition of consent will be that given in section 74: that V "agrees by choice, and has the freedom and capacity to make that choice".

This definition is broad, which reflects the fact that whether valid consent has been given to sexual activity frequently involves normative as well as analytical questions, and the

[110] SOA 2003, ss. 75(1)(a), 76(1).

[111] Rodwell, "Problems with the Sexual Offences Act 2003" [2005] *Crim LR* 290. The presumptions would apply in the exceptional (perhaps entirely hypothetical) case where D completed the "relevant act" but did not commit the substantive offence in virtue of V's having consented. D could (depending on mens rea) be guilty of an attempt in such circumstances.

[112] See above, § 9.5.

[113] Such a presumption would be more meaningful in relation to attempts liability, but the mens rea issues mentioned below would still arise.

[114] See above, § 9.1(iii)(d).

[115] See above, § 9.2(v)(e).

[116] See above, § 9.3(iii)(b).

normative issues may change according to context.[117] Although "there is no defined list of circumstances which, for the purposes of section 74, are capable [of] vitiating consent",[118] the Court of Appeal has nevertheless identified various situations in which there will be an absence of freedom and capacity to make a choice. We consider those now.

*(a) Incapacity*

V's capacity to consent is a necessary, but not a sufficient, condition of V's consenting.[119] For consent to exist, that capacity must be accompanied by an actual choice by V to engage in sexual activity with D.

In assessing V's capacity, the focus of attention is on V's ability to understand the meaning and implications of V's decisions.[120] Those questions, at least, involve consideration of matters of objective fact, albeit of a psychological rather than physical kind. The prosecution must prove the absence of V's ability beyond reasonable doubt before an absence of consent is proved under section 74.[121]

Of particular difficulty are cases where V's incapacity arises from a state of voluntary intoxication. In what circumstances is the consent of a voluntarily intoxicated person valid?[122] If V was so drunk or drugged as to be unconscious, then, except perhaps in the unlikely (but possible) situation where V had intimated consent in advance,[123] there would be no question of V's having consented. At the other end of the scale, there is equally no doubt that where V is disinhibited by alcohol or drugs to the point of engaging willingly in sexual activity that would have been refused had V been sober, V's consent is valid: just as a drunken intent is still an intent,[124] the Court of Appeal has indicated that, albeit with indelicate phrasing, "drunken consent is still consent".[125] Between those two extremes there is a point where the "freedom and capacity" to choose that section 74

[117] Wertheimer, *Coercion* (1987); Dripps, "For a Negative, Normative Model of Consent, with a Comment on Preference Skepticism" (1996) 2 *Legal Theory* 113.

[118] *R (Monica) v DPP, ex parte Boyling* [2018] EWHC 3508 (Admin), [2019] QB 1019, [78].

[119] See, similarly, *GF* 2021 SCC 20, [24] (Karakatsanis J).

[120] In *D Borough Council v B* [2011] EWHC 101 (Fam), [2012] Fam 36, a civil case, Mostyn J held (at [42]) that capacity for these purposes requires an understanding and awareness of "the mechanics of the act; that there are health risks involved, particularly the acquisition of sexually transmitted and sexually transmissible infection; [and] that sex between a man and a woman may result in the woman becoming pregnant". See further *A* [2014] EWCA Crim 299, [2014] 1 WLR 2469, where the guidance on mental capacity found in the Mental Capacity Act 2005, ss. 2–3 was relied upon in the context of establishing capacity to consent under the SOA 2003. This approach was endorsed cautiously by the Supreme Court, with certain caveats, in *A Local Authority v JB* [2021] UKSC 52, [2021] 3 WLR 1381, [110] (Lord Stephens). In practice, a person who has sex with an adult whose mental capacity to consent is doubtful will probably be prosecuted for one of the specific offences relating to mentally disordered persons created by SOA 2003, ss. 30–42. On the issue of capacity in relation to those offences, see *Cooper* [2009] UKHL 42, [2009] 1 WLR 1786.

[121] *A* [2014] EWCA Crim 299, [2014] 1 WLR 2469.

[122] For an account of the difficult issues that arise in estimating the effect on consent of drink, drugs, and mind-altering substances, see Finch and Munro, "Intoxicated Consent and the Boundaries of Drug Assisted Rape" [2003] *Crim LR* 773. See, also, Clough, "Sober Regrets and Shared Risk Taking: Navigating Intoxicated Consent and Rape in the Courtroom" (2018) 82 *J Crim Law* 482.

[123] For example, if V (a sex worker) agrees to be rendered unconscious to gratify the desire of D, who enjoys intercourse with unconscious people: cf. the facts of *Pike* [1961] Crim LR 114 and 547 (CA).

[124] Below, § 18.4(ii).

[125] *Bree* [2007] EWCA Crim 804, [2008] QB 131, [32].

requires is lost. The difficulty is identifying this point.[126] In *Bree*,[127] the Court of Appeal remarked that:

> "We should perhaps underline that, as a matter of practical reality, capacity to consent may evaporate well before a complainant becomes unconscious. Whether this is so or not, however, is fact-specific, or more accurately, depends on the actual state of mind of the individuals involved on the particular occasion."

The vague guidance in *Bree* clearly leaves a lot of discretion to jurors,[128] and can be particularly problematic in cases where V cannot remember what happened[129] (which is not necessarily proof of V's earlier incapacity).[130] It should be stressed, however, that the remarks in *Bree* were made in the context of complainants who were voluntarily intoxicated. The courts can be expected to take a stricter line with defendants in cases where the complainant's intoxication is involuntary.[131] Judgements about consent, or the lack of consent, can be affected by the disapproval of D's conduct quite as much as estimates of V's state of mind.[132] Thus, where D has administered or caused V to take a substance without V's consent, it may be said that V's consent was not valid where V does something *only because of* the substance's disinhibiting effects.[133]

The preceding discussion concerned *capacity* to make a choice. The next sections present overviews of the case law on *freedom* to make a choice.[134]

[126] See Wallerstein, "'A Drunken Consent Is Still Consent'—Or Is It? A Critical Analysis of a Drunken Consent Following *Bree*" (2009) 73 *J Crim L* 318; Cowan, "The Trouble with Drink: Intoxication, (In)capacity and the Evaporation of Consent to Sex" (2008) 41 *Akron L Rev* 899.

[127] [2007] EWCA Crim 804, [2008] QB 131, [34]. The matter of directing the jury on matters of voluntary intoxication and consent was also considered in *Kamki* [2013] EWCA Crim 2335.

[128] Indeed, it has been queried whether the extent of remaining discretion invites biases and stereotypical assumptions about voluntary intoxication and openness to sexual activity into trials: see, further, Finch and Munro, "The Demon Drink and the Demonized Woman: Socio-sexual Stereotypes and Responsibility Attribution in Rape Trials Involving Intoxicants" (2007) 16 *Social & Legal Studies* 591; Rumney and Fenton, "Intoxicated Consent in Rape: *Bree* and Juror Decision-Making" (2008) 71 *MLR* 279; Gunby et al., "Alcohol-related Rape Cases: Barristers' Perspectives on the Sexual Offences Act 2003 and its Impact on Practice" (2010) 74 *J Crim L* 579.

[129] See, e.g., *Evans* [2016] EWCA Crim 452, [2016] 4 WLR 169; *Costanzo* [2021] EWCA Crim 615.

[130] *Seedy Tambedou* [2014] EWCA Crim 954. V's lack of memory might, of course, bear on the weight placed upon V's evidence: *Bree* [2007] EWCA Crim 804, [2008] QB 131, [26].

[131] Cf. *Lang* (1976) 62 Cr App R 50, 52 (CA). If D spikes V's drink in order to get V into this condition D will commit an offence under s. 61 of the SOA 2003 of "administering a substance with intent", an offence that the courts view particularly seriously—see *A-G's Reference (No. 31 of 2006)* [2007] EWCA Crim 1623, [2008] 1 Cr App R (S) 46, where the Court of Appeal increased a sentence of two years' imprisonment to three and a half.

[132] See, for instance, *Kirk* [2008] EWCA Crim 434, discussed in the next section. For proposals to define rape more in terms of the conduct of D rather than the state of mind of V, see Dripps, "For a Negative, Normative Model of Consent, with a Comment on Preference-skepticism" (1996) 2 *Legal Theory* 113 and West, "A Comment on Consent, Sex and Rape" (1996) 2 *Legal Theory* 233. Contrast Bogart, "Commodification and Phenomenology: Evading Consent in Theory Regarding Rape" (1996) 2 *Legal Theory* 253.

[133] This supports the case for having the evidential presumptions in s. 75(2)(f).

[134] No attempt has been made by the courts (or most commentators) to compare the severity of the following factors, because the effect of all of them is the same: either there is consent, or there is not. For an argument, however, that non-consensual sexual activity resulting from pressure/coercion is wrongful in a distinct, and more serious, way than sexual activity that is obtained through deception, see Pundik, "Coercion and Deception in Sexual Relations" (2015) 28 *Canadian J Law and Jurisprudence* 97. Those who coerce/pressurise others into sexual activity are confronted by actual non-consent and show a disregard for the reactions of their victims that is absent, Pundik contends, in cases of sexual activity obtained by deception. Pundik argues that different offences should, accordingly, cover these different wrongs. See also Chiesa, "Solving the Riddle of Rape by Deception" (2017) 35 *Yale Law & Policy Review* 407.

*(b) Coercion or pressure upon V*

The first factor that can remove V's freedom to choose is coercion or pressure arising from another person or the surrounding circumstances.[135] For instance, as we saw in § 12.4(ii)(b), an evidential presumption that V did not consent arises if D makes a threat of *immediate* violence to V or another person.[136] What, however, if D threatens to disfigure V in a few days' time unless V has sex with D now? As such a threat does not give rise to an evidential presumption of non-consent, might one infer that such threats are of a lesser order of magnitude and are necessarily compatible with V's consenting to sex with D? Such an inference should be resisted: the issue is, simply, whether V had the freedom to choose. Given the nature of D's threat, the jury may readily find a lack of consent under the general definition in section 74.

Less direct coercion or pressure may also vitiate consent under section 74. In *Kirk*,[137] V, a 13-year-old girl, had run away from home. V went to the workplace of D, who had previously sexually abused her, and, after waiting until everyone else had left, had sex with him for money. V's evidence, as summarised by the trial judge in his direction to the jury, was: "I was very hungry and needed to eat so I went to [D's place of work] . . . All I can say is that I ended up having sex with [D] for £3.25. I used the money to buy food." The Court of Appeal rightly upheld D's conviction for rape.

A similar problem can arise when an adult, with apparent willingness but inward revulsion, complies with a request for sex made by a person in a dominant position—a step-parent, for example—who has been sexually abusing V since childhood. In *C*,[138] the Court of Appeal held that it was open to the jury in such a case "to conclude that the evidence of . . . consent when the complainant was no longer a child was indeed apparent, not real, and that the appellant was well aware that in reality she was not consenting".

It is even possible that victims of alleged sexual offences might think they *were* consenting, when, due to the circumstances in which that choice was made, they lacked the freedom to consent in legal terms. In *Ali*,[139] the Court of Appeal noted that:

> "One of the consequences of grooming is that it has a tendency to limit or subvert the alleged victim's capacity to make free decisions, and it creates the risk that he or she simply submitted because of the environment of dependency created by those responsible for treating the alleged victim in this way. Indeed the individual may have been manipulated to the extent that he or she is unaware of, or confused about, the distinction between acquiescence and genuine agreement at the time the incident occurred."

In such cases, the jury must ultimately be directed to decide "whether the prosecution had made them sure that [V] did not genuinely consent to the sexual intercourse".[140] Reaching such a determination cannot always be easy.

[135] For an argument that coercion should not be assessed monolithically in this context, see Ferzan, "Consent and Coercion" (2020) 50 *Arizona State LJ* 951.
[136] SOA 2003, s. 75(2)(a)–(b).
[137] [2008] EWCA Crim 434. It has been suggested that *Kirk* and *Jheeta* (discussed below) are cases of undue influence by D, rather than pressure on V: Dsouza, "Undermining Prima Facie Consent in the Criminal Law" (2014) 33 *Law and Philosophy* 489, 516. Although this argument is interesting in theory, it is clear that the courts understood these cases to be ones of pressure, rather than influence.
[138] [2012] EWCA Crim 2034, [16].
[139] [2015] EWCA Crim 1279, [2015] 2 Cr App R 33, [58].
[140] *Gray* [2025] EWCA Crim 1042, [23].

The comment in *Ali* about the distinction between "acquiescence and genuine agreement" harks back to the pre-SOA 2003 distinction between consent and submission.[141] Indeed, it had been thought that the traditional line between consent and submission remained relevant to the definition of consent in section 74.[142] However, room for doubt on this point was introduced by the following *obiter* comment in *W*:[143]

> "the dichotomy set up by the judge (free consent/submitting to a demand that [V] felt unable to resist) . . . does not reflect the law. It is possible for a person to submit to a demand which he or she feels unable to resist, but without lacking the capacity or freedom to make a choice. This is an example of reluctant consent."

In saying this, the Court of Appeal is best understood as attempting to draw a vague line between two broad scenarios. In the first, D pesters V for sex, until V eventually agrees. This is perhaps "reluctant consent", as the Court puts it. One might argue that it is a form of "submission", but the Court would then say that it is not the *type* of submission that denies consent. In the second scenario, V agrees because of fears that, if V refuses to have sex with D, V's violent partner, T, will attack V.[144] This is pure submission to the circumstances, and no consent at all.

Mere submission is also plausibly demonstrated in *Jheeta*.[145] D persuaded his girlfriend, V, to continue a sexual relationship with him by sending her messages, purporting to come from the police, warning her that if she ended the relationship he was likely to commit suicide and, in this event, V could be fined. D's deceptive conduct began before, and continued after, the SOA 2003 came into force. On counts in the indictment charging the former offence of procuring sex by false representations[146] (relating to the pre-SOA 2003 period), D was unquestionably guilty. In relation to the post-SOA 2003 counts, the Court of Appeal held that V's consent had been vitiated. Although it is possible to read *Jheeta* as a case of deception, we think that it should be recognised principally as a case of *pressure* that vitiated consent.[147] The nature of the defendant's deceptions meant that V lacked the freedom to choose to engage in the relevant sexual activities.

It is sometimes suggested that a distinction should be drawn in this context between threats and offers.[148] Suppose that D offers V extremely preferential rates of rent, but makes this conditional on V's engaging in sexual activity with D (so-called sex-for-rent arrangements). On one view, however tempting the offer, D has arguably not done anything wrong in making it. Contrast threats: as when employer D explains to model employee V that, unless V engages in sexual activity with D, D will fire V.[149] Here, D is wrong to even make the threat.

On a more nuanced view, offers *can* overwhelm V's freedom in a similar way to threats, at least occasionally. Some "offers" will come with explicit,[150] implied, or at least reasonably

[141] *Olugboja* [1982] QB 320 (CA).
[142] See, e.g., *Robinson* [2011] EWCA Crim 916.
[143] [2015] EWCA Crim 559, [34].
[144] See *Ivor* [2021] EWCA Crim 923.
[145] [2007] EWCA Crim 1699, [2008] 1 WLR 2582.
[146] Sexual Offences Act 1956, s. 3.
[147] As it was in *R (Monica) v DPP, ex parte Boyling* [2018] EWHC 3508 (Admin), [2019] QB 1019, [69].
[148] See Green, *Criminalizing Sex* (2020) 129–32.
[149] Cp. *Latter v Braddell* (1881) 50 LJQB 166; *McCoy* 1953 (2) SA 4.
[150] Cp. *Wellard* (1978) 67 Cr App R 364, where D had been convicted of rape on the basis that he had offered to overlook V's wrongdoing if V engaged in sexual activity with him. He had explained that, if V did not accept, D would have to report her. The Court of Appeal took no issue with this conviction.

apprehended threats. Imagine D, a police officer, offers to let V off with a minor traffic offence if V engages in sexual activity. V might justifiably fear that, if D's offer is not accepted, D might invent a more serious offence.[151] Even without associated threats, offers do not always seem compatible with V's consent. Suppose that D offers V work in D's brothel, fully aware that V, an asylum seeker who has not applied for asylum at the port of entry, is without means of support. There is no threat here, but did V make a choice whilst possessing "the freedom . . . to make that choice"? If D does no more than offer V work in the brothel, D may seek to argue that V's choice was a free one. D may firmly believe this, but that of itself will not determine the question. Whether, on the facts, V's consent is vitiated is not for D (or indeed V) to decide; that is a question for the jury. It is far from easy to determine whether the brothel keeper would be found guilty of the offence of causing V to engage in sexual activity without consent.[152] It is certainly plausible that a jury would be entitled to convict D.

### *(c) Deceptions (and failures to disclose) "so closely connected to the nature of purpose of sexual [activity]" that they vitiate consent*

The second factor that has the potential to negate V's freedom to choose under section 74 is deception regarding, and/or failure to disclose, certain information. The courts have produced an unsatisfactory line of case law concerning *which* deceptions and failures to disclose can, and which cannot, vitiate consent under section 74. Initially, the courts declined to give a principled answer to that question, and seemed content to allow "broad common sense" to determine matters.[153] Following the decisions of the Divisional Court in *R (Monica) v DPP, ex p Boyling*[154] and the Court of Appeal in *Lawrance*,[155] a deception or a withholding of information will not vitiate consent under section 74 unless it is "so closely connected to the nature or purpose of sexual intercourse rather than the broad circumstances surrounding it that it is capable of negating consent".[156] It must also be proved that V would not have consented to the sexual activity with D had V known the truth about the subject matter of the deception or failure to inform.[157]

The "close connection" test offers a little more guidance than the previous "broad common sense" approach, but still leaves a lot of detail to be worked out. It is also vital to note that, under the "close connection" test, as understood in *Lawrance*, no distinction is to be drawn between lying about matter *x* and omitting to tell V about matter *x*. As the law currently stands, if matter *x* is capable of vitiating consent under section 74, either an "active"

[151] In an unreported decision referred to in *Olugboja* [1982] QB 320 (CA), Winn J ruled that a policeman charged with rape, on the basis of obtaining sexual intercourse with V by threatening to make false reports against her, had no case to answer. This result might not follow under the SOA 2003.

[152] In practice, the Crown would probably avoid this area of difficulty (and difficult questions of causation) by prosecuting the brothel keeper for causing or inciting prostitution for gain (SOA 2003, s. 52) or for controlling prostitution for gain (SOA 2003, s. 53), both of which carry a maximum sentence of seven years' imprisonment.

[153] *R (F) v DPP* [2013] EWHC 945 (Admin), [2014] QB 581, [26]; *McNally* [2013] EWCA Crim 1051, [2014] QB 593, [25].

[154] [2018] EWHC 3508 (Admin), [2019] QB 1019.

[155] [2020] EWCA Crim 971, [2020] 1 WLR 5025.

[156] *Lawrance* [2020] EWCA Crim 971, [2020] 1 WLR 5025, [35]; *R (Monica) v DPP, ex p Boyling* [2018] EWHC 3508 (Admin), [2019] QB 1019, [72].

[157] The discussion here centres on V's consent. D must, of course, *also* lack a reasonable belief in consent before D can be guilty of rape.

deception *or* a failure to disclose will negate V's consent. The merits and demerits of this identical treatment of deceptions and failures to inform are returned to below (*Deceptions versus failures to inform*).

It might be hoped that an examination of the case law on deceptions, failures to inform, and sexual consent would assist in fleshing out the "close connection" test and discovering its limits. Unfortunately, the case law is at best difficult to interpret, and at points inconsistent.[158] In order to traverse this difficult terrain, it is sensible to begin with cases where the courts have held that consent has indeed been vitiated under section 74 owing to deception, or an omission to inform V, about a particular matter.

*Deceptions (and failures to disclose) that satisfy the "close connection" test.*
In *Assange* (an extradition case),[159] it was suggested that, if V agrees to have sex with D on the condition that he wears a condom, and D intentionally breaches this condition, there is no consent under section 74. The matter of condom use thus satisfies the "close connection" test; it changes *how* the physical act was performed.

*Assange* was applied in *R (F) v DPP*,[160] where the Divisional Court ruled that, where V had made it clear to D that she consented on condition that D would not ejaculate inside her vagina, V's consent was vitiated if D then deliberately did so, or if he penetrated her with that intent. Again, this decision seems easy enough to explain utilising the "close connection" test, given the impact of D's deception (or at least D's failure to disclose his intentions) on what occurred, physically.

It is much more difficult, however, to explain the decision in *McNally*.[161] D was born with female genitalia but identified as male at the time of the alleged offences.[162] D presented as a young man ("Scott") and entered into a relationship with V, a young cisgender woman. D and V engaged in oral sex and digital penetration of V's vagina, with V thinking throughout that D was male. V indicated that she would not have engaged in those activities had she known the "truth", which both the courts and the complainant understood to be that D was female. The Court of Appeal held that, in the circumstances, D's deception[163] had vitiated V's consent—V did not have the freedom to make the relevant choice (i.e. to engage in this sexual activity with a man or a woman). This outcome was endorsed in both *Boyling* and *Lawrance*.

Why was the alleged deception in *McNally* "so closely connected to the nature or purpose of sexual [activity] rather than the broad circumstances surrounding it that it is capable of negating consent"?[164] In *Boyling*, it was explained that "as a matter of common sense, there was all the difference in the world between sexual activity with a boy and similar activity with a girl".[165] There is indeed a difference, but it needs to be related to the "close

[158] See Murray and Beattie, "Conditional Consent and Sexual Offences: Revisiting the Sexual Offences Act 2003 after *Lawrance*" [2021] *Crim LR* 556.
[159] [2011] EWHC 2849 (Admin).
[160] [2013] EWHC 945 (Admin), [2014] QB 581.
[161] [2013] EWCA Crim 1051, [2014] QB 593.
[162] Alex Sharpe is a prominent critic of the approach in these "gender fraud" cases. For the fullest account of her views, see Sharpe, *Sexual Intimacy and Gender "Fraud"* (2018).
[163] One criticism of *McNally* when it was decided is that it is arguable that D "deceived" nobody, and rather omitted to reveal information to V. As noted above, any distinction between deceptions and omissions to disclose appears subsequently to have been abolished in *Lawrance*.
[164] *Lawrance* [2020] EWCA Crim 971, [2020] 1 WLR 5025, [35].
[165] *R (Monica) v DPP, ex p Boyling* [2018] EWHC 3508 (Admin), [2019] QB 1019, [81].

connection" test. Even if one's gender history/biological sex is a "circumstance" surrounding sexual activity, the test requires that circumstance to be particularly closely related to that activity; deceptions regarding the "broad circumstances surrounding" the activity will not vitiate consent. The relevant link was explained in *Boyling* in terms of impersonation "given the centrality of an individual's sexuality to his or her identity".[166] The limits of this impersonation aspect of the "close connection" test will need to be tested in further litigation, and it remains a live question whether D, who identified as Scott (a male) at the relevant time, was "impersonating" anyone.

In *Lawrance*, no effort was made to explain why *McNally* was correctly decided. The explanations in *Lawrance* of why *Assange* and *R (F)* satisfy the "close connection" test centred on whether V had agreed to what physically occurred. But in *McNally*, V did agree to what physically occurred,[167] concerning what was used to penetrate and where. V's misapprehension[168] was best conceived of as regarding a surrounding circumstance: the gender history and transgender identity of V's partner. A contrast might be drawn here with the count that McNally declined to plead guilty to, and which was not pursued by the prosecution. That allegation was that D had penetrated V with a dildo, pretending that it was D's penis. In *that* situation, one could understand why the "close connection" test would be satisfied (but this test would be beside the point: section 76's presumptions would apply, due to D's deception about the "nature" of the relevant activity). *McNally* is a highly questionable decision, and more needs to be done to explain its compatibility with the "close connection" test in future judgments.[169]

A similar worry arises about the Court of Appeal's decision in *BVA*.[170] To simplify the facts,[171] V had consented to D's touching her in a sexual manner whilst she was asleep. What D had not told V was that he intended to produce a video recording of the encounter using his mobile phone. The Court of Appeal held that D's omission to tell V about the recording satisfied the "close connection" test, negating V's freedom to choose and vitiating V's consent under section 74. D was, in consequence, liable for sexual assault. The Court's strained reasoning in support of this conclusion is worth reproducing at length:[172]

> The filming was temporally and proximally connected to the touching: the filming started and stopped alongside the touching; the phone on which the film was being recorded was held right up close to [V]'s face and breasts; the appellant was holding the phone in one hand and touching [V]'s breasts with the other . . . If not the sole purpose, then a central purpose of the sexual touching was to film the sexual activity. The appellant used the phone's camera to record (and illuminate) [V] before, during and after the touching, with the camera shots sweeping across

[166] *Ibid.*, [77].

[167] For an argument that such activities are sufficiently close to what has been consented to, even in the case of deception by D, that they should not be viewed as criminal, see Sharpe, "Deceptive Sex: Rethinking Consent from the Gender Margins" (2025) 88 *MLR* 689, 703–5.

[168] Although the court conceived of *McNally* as involving deception, it is better analysed as a case of mistake: Gibson, "Deceptive Sexual Relations: A Theory of Criminal Liability" (2020) 40 *OJLS* 82, 90–91.

[169] In 2024, the Crown Prosecution Service updated its guidance on prosecuting cases involving "deception as to gender". For critical analysis of the preceding consultation exercise, see Sharpe, "'Deception as to Gender': A Review of Proposed Revisions to CPS Legal Guidance on Rape and Serious Offences" (2025) 89 *J Crim L* 29.

[170] [2025] EWCA Crim 1359, [2026] 1 WLR 621.

[171] D claimed that V was merely *pretending* to be asleep; V denied that she had consented to sexual activity whilst she was unconscious (but may have).

[172] [2025] EWCA Crim 1359, [2026] 1 WLR 621, [48]–[49].

> from [V]'s face, her breasts, over to the appellant's penis and back to [V]'s breasts. What was being created was a pornographic video for the appellant's immediate and potentially future sexual gratification (and potentially the gratification of others). As the Judge commented, it transformed what might otherwise have been a transient sexual touching into a permanent medium which could be watched in the future.

The Court's judgment invites speculation about which of these facts were determinative. If D had set up the camera on a tripod before touching V, would this have made a difference to whether V had consented? Similarly, if D had started the recording some time before the touching, and left the camera running afterwards, would this have made a difference? In both scenarios, there would still have been a transformation from "a transient sexual touching into a permanent medium which could be watched in the future". If one suspects that it is, above all, the recording itself that made the relevant difference, one is liable to be confused by the Court's concluding note that: "we have reached these conclusions on the specific facts before us. There may be cases when a failure to disclose filming of sexual activity will not vitiate consent, for example when the filming is no more than a background circumstance".[173] It is not clear how one is meant to discern on which side of the line a particular case falls.

It would have been preferable if the Court had held in *BVA* that, in relation to the relevant sexual touching, nothing *physically* different to what V had agreed to occurred. D had, to be sure, perpetrated a grave wrong against V by making the explicit recording without V's permission, but that grave wrong is reflected in the offence of voyeurism.[174] The Court in *BVA* noted this point, but dismissed it on the bases that overlap between criminal offences is not uncommon, and that certain sexual touchings would not constitute the offence of voyeurism (where V remains fully clothed, for instance).[175] It is true that overlap between offences is common, but the Court *created* the overlap in *BVA*; it was not plainly pre-existing. Furthermore, that some cases of sexual touching will not be captured by the voyeurism offence begs the relevant question: if there was no consent to *the sexual touching*, then D is liable for sexual assault; if V consented to the sexual touching, and remained fully clothed, it is not clear that any distinctive wrong has occurred even where D clandestinely records the encounter.

*BVA* shows that the law still has not reached a point where one can predict with real confidence which deceptions and omissions to disclose information will satisfy the "close connection" test and vitiate consent under section 74. The case law is similarly uncertain regarding which deceptions and failures to inform that *fail* to satisfy that test.

*Deceptions that fail to satisfy the "close connection" test.*

In *Boyling*, V challenged a decision not to prosecute D, a police officer, for (amongst other things) rape. D had, on the instructions of his superiors, pretended to be an activist ("Jim") in order to infiltrate a campaign group.[176] D had (without explicit authorisation, but arguably with implicit authorisation) formed a sexual relationship with V. After a subsequent, judge-led inquiry into the undercover operation, V discovered the truth about "Jim" via media reports. She explained that she would never have engaged in sexual activity with D

[173] *Ibid.*, [54].
[174] Sexual Offences Act 2003, s. 67.
[175] [2025] EWCA Crim 1359, [2026] 1 WLR 621, [51].
[176] D in fact formed relationships with three separate women whilst undercover.

had she known that "Jim" was in fact a police officer, and complained of rape.[177] Although the alleged offence took place before the SOA 2003 came into force, V's submission was that, on a "broad, common sense" view of the matter (such as that recommended in the earlier case law regarding consent under the SOA 2003), she had been deceived in a way that vitiated her consent under section 74, and that this understanding of consent existed even before the SOA 2003.

The Divisional Court rejected the contention that the post-SOA 2003 understanding of consent could be applied retrospectively in this manner. It further decided that, even if such a transposition of the law on consent had been possible, the CPS would still have been justified in not charging D with rape. His deceptions did not, in the Court's opinion, vitiate consent under the law as it stands today.[178] They lacked sufficient connection with the nature and purpose of sexual intercourse. But if *Boyling* involved a deception regarding extraneous circumstances pertaining to the identity of the person performing sexual activity, rather than to matters closely connected to the nature and purpose of the sexual activity, a question again arises concerning why *McNally* is different *enough* to sustain a conviction.

The facts of *Lawrance* are also difficult to reconcile with the "close connection" test endorsed by the Court of Appeal. D lied to V about having had a vasectomy, with the consequence that V agreed to have unprotected sex when otherwise she would have insisted on D's wearing a condom.[179] This deception apparently "related not to the physical performance of the sexual act but to risks or consequences associated with it".[180] But the physical act of sexual intercourse with a fertile man can be described as physically different from the act of sexual intercourse with one who is infertile: D's fertile semen is a physical substance, deposited in V's body. In *Assange* and *F*, the complainants had not consented to the presence of a physical substance within their bodies, and in *Lawrance* the complainant had not consented to the presence of a physical substance within hers. The Court of Appeal's view was that the *quality* of the relevant physical substance was at issue in *Assange* and *F*, whereas *Lawrance* concerned the possible consequences of the relevant physical substance's being inside V's vagina. It may be doubted whether that is a distinction significant enough to make the difference between rape and consensual sex.[181] Similarly, if the physical quality of D's sperm is not sufficiently "closely connected" to the relevant sexual act, and so does not vitiate consent to that act, one may wonder why the fact that D is recording the activity is.

The reference in *Lawrance* to the risks and consequences associated with sexual activity raises the question of deceptions regarding sexually transmitted infections. As noted above, prior to *Boyling* and *Lawrance*, it was sometimes thought that there was a distinction to be drawn in this area between "actively" lying about one's status (potentially vitiating consent) and omitting to reveal one's status (not capable of vitiating consent).[182] This distinction appeared to flow from comments in *B*, to the effect that "the fact that the defendant may

[177] Cp. the Australian case of *Michael* [2008] WASCA 66, where the victims (sex workers) indicated that they would never have discounted their fees, or provided sex *gratis*, had they not believed D's lie about *being* a police officer. This case was further complicated by the at least implicit threat of what might happen if they refused to have sex with D. By a majority, D's convictions for sexual penetration without consent were upheld on appeal.

[178] *R (Monica) v DPP, ex p Boyling* [2018] EWHC 3508 (Admin), [2019] QB 1019, [72].

[179] V subsequently discovered that she was pregnant, and underwent a termination.

[180] *Lawrance* [2020] EWCA Crim 971, [2020] 1 WLR 5025, [37].

[181] See Williams, "A Further Case on Obtaining Sex by Deception" (2021) 137 *LQR* 183.

[182] See the 7th edition of this book, § 12.3(iii)(c).

not have disclosed his HIV status is not a matter which could in any way be relevant to the issue of consent under section 74",[183] and in *McNally* that "[*B*] was not saying that HIV status could not vitiate consent if, for example, the complainant had been positively assured that the defendant was not HIV-positive: it left the issue open".[184] Any distinction between "active" deceptions and omissions to disclose is, however, now unsustainable. In *Lawrance*, it was indicated that the non-disclosure of one's HIV status cannot vitiate consent to sexual intercourse, and that "it makes no difference to the issue of consent whether . . . there was an express deception or . . . a failure to disclose".[185] Any liability in such situations thus appears now to be limited to the non-fatal, non-sexual offences against the person.[186]

Once again, this position is debatable. Above, it was noted that viewing the presence or absence of live sperm as a matter of the "quality" of a physical substance may be too quick. The same point can be made about the presence of HIV (or other transmissible infections) in D's semen. V may have consented to all *other* physical components of D's semen being deposited during unprotected sexual intercourse but has not consented to the live virus being deposited. That is not to say that such activity *must* be criminalised (competing considerations including privacy apply in this context),[187] or that it *must* be criminalised as a sexual offence,[188] but it is to doubt the coherence of the courts' approach to deception, omissions to inform, and consent.

In *Lawrance*, further hypothetical examples of deceptions and failures to inform that would not satisfy the "close connection" test were given by the Court of Appeal, including: "lies concerning marital status or being in a committed relationship; lies about political or religious views; lies about status, employment or wealth".[189] Furthermore, bigamists do not vitiate the consent of their deceived (or uninformed) spouses, and sex workers consent validly to sexual activity even if their clients never intend to pay.[190] Again, these examples all seem to draw a distinction between the physical aspects of sexual activity and its surrounding circumstances, a distinction that is particularly difficult to reconcile with decisions such as *McNally* and *BVA*.

*The current state of law on consent, deceptions, and omissions to inform under section 74.* Following *Lawrance*, and especially in the light of *BVA*, it cannot be pretended that this area of the law is satisfactory. The courts have produced lists of qualifying and non-qualifying deceptions and omissions to inform, but these lists appear inconsistent. What is clear is that the courts are anxious to avoid allowing too many deceptions or failures to disclose to be relevant under section 74. Indeed, there is a detectable unease in *Boyling* and *Lawrance* with navigating these choppy waters via case law rulings and without adequate legislative guidance. This may explain the assertion in *Lawrance* that Parliament did not intend section 74 to represent a change in approach from the common law on

[183] [2006] EWCA Crim 2945, [2007] 1 WLR 1567, [21].
[184] [2013] EWCA Crim 1051, [2014] QB 593, [24].
[185] *Lawrance* [2020] EWCA Crim 971, [2020] 1 WLR 5025, [41].
[186] See above, § 11.7.
[187] See Weait, *Intimacy and Responsibility* (2007); Chalmers, *Legal Responses to HIV and AIDS* (2008) chap. 6.
[188] See Cowan, "Offences of Sex or Violence? Consent, Fraud, and HIV Transmission" (2014) 17 *New Criminal LR* 135.
[189] *Lawrance* [2020] EWCA Crim 971, [2020] 1 WLR 5025, [34]. On wealth, see *McNally* [2013] EWCA Crim 1051, [2014] QB 593, [25].
[190] *Lawrance* [2020] EWCA Crim 971, [2020] 1 WLR 5025, [34], mirroring *Linekar* [1995] QB 250 (CA).

deceptions (and failures to disclose) and consent.[191] Having concluded that D was not liable for rape, for instance, the Court of Appeal in *Lawrance* noted that the issues around deception, failures to inform and sexual consent "require debate as a matter of social and public policy".[192] That is surely true, but the courts will undoubtedly be faced with more, difficult cases on deception, omissions to inform, and sexual consent before any such debate—which will not be straightforward[193]—takes place. Unfortunately, the outcome in *BVA* suggests that consistency between the stated "close connection" test and actual case outcomes remains elusive.

*Alternative approaches to deception and failures to inform.*
The previous sections illustrated the difficulties that the courts have encountered in dealing with deceptions, failures to inform, and consent. Part of the problem here surrounds the attempt to draw distinctions between different types of deception and failures to disclose.

Some theoretical accounts draw fewer lines than others. One account is premised on the view that respect for sexual autonomy demands that *any* deception, omission to inform, or indeed mistake that made or would have made a difference to V's decision to engage in sexual activity should be recognised as having vitiated V's (apparent) consent. This position has most prominently been advocated in the criminal law by Herring.[194] In philosophy, Dougherty has captured a similar idea through discussing deception relating to "deal breakers" regarding V's consent.[195]

Such approaches are logically sound.[196] But, if deployed in the criminal law (and not simply the moral realm), they risk making the concept of consent in sexual offences unduly stringent.[197] A finding of rape is in no sense outlandish where the matter that D deceived V, or failed to inform V about, was of vital importance to V and tightly bound to the act of sexual intercourse. But, on Herring's view, a conviction for rape would also follow if say, D, has sexual intercourse with his partner after deceitfully agreeing to her proposal to visit relatives at the weekend, without disclosing his plans instead to be travelling in the opposite direction to watch a rugby match. He may have told his lie not with sex in mind but to postpone the inevitable row they will have when he reveals that his plans for the weekend are different from hers. Yet later that evening, when they have fully mutual and enjoyable sex, under a Herring dispensation, D will be in the process of raping V if he knows or ought to know that she would not have agreed to sex on that occasion had she known the truth about

[191] *Lawrance* [2020] EWCA Crim 971, [2020] 1 WLR 5025, [42].

[192] *Ibid.* See, also, *Monica R (Monica) v DPP, ex p Boyling* [2018] EWHC 3508 (Admin), [2019] QB 1019, [83], [85].

[193] For instance, the Criminal Law Reform Now Network (a group of legal academics and practitioners) published 10 separate proposals for addressing the issue of sexual consent and deception: *Reforming the Relationship between Sexual Consent, Deception and Consent* (2021). Ultimately, the Network endorsed none of them, and proposed its own new offence of "inducing a person to engage in sexual activity by deception": *Reforming the Relationship between Sexual Consent, Deception and Mistake* (2023).

[194] See Herring, "Mistaken Sex" [2005] *Crim LR* 511.

[195] Dougherty, "Sex, Lies and Consent" (2013) 123 *Ethics* 717. Cf. Manson, "How Not to Think About the Ethics of Deceiving into Sex" (2017) 127 *Ethics* 717. Dougherty's position has now changed—see Dougherty, *The Scope of Consent* (2021).

[196] It can be doubted, however, how often such "deal breakers" tend to factor in V's reflective or unreflective assessment of the object of V's consent (i.e. what V is consenting *to*). See Dsouza, "False Beliefs and Consent to Sex" (2022) 85 *MLR* 1191.

[197] There are further objections to using a counterfactual test in this context. See Tadros, *Wrongs and Crimes* (2016) 244–6.

his plans for the weekend. Added to this point about the breadth of Herring's proposal is the fact that, as Bergelson has explained, there are competing considerations at issue—such as privacy, fair warning, etc.—when criminalisation is being contemplated.[198]

More nuanced accounts of deception (extended, where appropriate, to omissions to inform) are likely to be preferable. However, it is difficult to explicate that nuance in a sufficiently concrete manner. For instance, Kennedy starts from the premises that sexual relationships form an important part of one's self-identity, and that one's self-identity deserves respect due to its social and personal importance.[199] She contends that the topic of sex and deception might accordingly be analysed profitably through the lens of "identity non-recognition": "a failure on the part of the deceiver to respect the identity-formation of the person deceived".[200] For Kennedy, only *some* deceptions regarding sexual activity exhibit such disrespect, such as those that relate to explicit preconditions that V places on consent, or those that bear on "roles, statuses and group memberships that are commonly experienced or described as identities in any given time or place", even if they did not matter to V.[201] Of course, as Kennedy recognises, there will be difficult borderline cases. For instance, although Kennedy is correct that one's partner's infidelity can have a "devastating impact on the identity of the person deceived when it is discovered", and thus obtaining consent through lying about one's fidelity is on her account a *candidate* for criminalisation, a live question remains whether it should in fact be made criminal.[202] Kennedy's proposal nevertheless avoids the pitfalls of "too many" deceptions being candidates for criminalisation, and poses a more meaningful question than the "close connection" test. This is the kind of approach required to avoid *ad hoc*, and unsatisfactory, line drawing. It is plausible that it could also be applied to omissions to inform.

At the other extreme, it could be argued that criminal liability should be excluded altogether if D's deception does not fall within section 76 (and that omissions to inform V regarding the same matters would also not vitiate consent under section 74). However, that option seems implausible, in as much as it would arbitrarily downgrade deceptions falling outside section 76, and underplay D's wrongdoing in other cases where, but for the deception, the activity would not have occurred.[203]

A more moderate legal response would be to turn back the clock: to restrict the type of deceptions that can vitiate consent to those listed in section 76, and reinstate (and expand, to cover other genders) a distinct offence such as procuring a person to have sexual intercourse by "false pretences or false representations".[204] A similar offence was abolished when the SOA 2003 came into force—possibly because the view was taken that the section 4 offence of causing a person to engage in sexual activity without consent would cover such situations.[205] It is noteworthy, however, that such proposals have tended to draw the

[198] Bergelson, "Sex, Lies and Law: Rethinking Rape by Fraud" in Ashford, Reed, and Wake (eds.), *Consent and Control* (2016).

[199] Kennedy, "Criminalising Deceptive Sex: Sex, Identity and Recognition" (2021) 41 *LS* 91, 97. See, too, Kennedy, *Inducing Intimacy* (2024).

[200] Kennedy, "Criminalising Deceptive Sex: Sex, Identity and Recognition" (2021) 41 LS 91, 92.

[201] *Ibid.*, 99.

[202] *Ibid.*, 107.

[203] See, further, Rubenfeld, "The Riddle of Rape-by-Deception and the Myth of Sexual Autonomy" (2013) 122 *Yale LJ* 1372.

[204] Sexual Offences Act 1956, s. 3.

[205] Spencer, "Sex by Deception" [2013] 9 *Archbold Review* 6, 7.

distinction between deceptions and omissions to disclose that has, since *Lawrance*, been rejected by the Court of Appeal when interpreting section 74.

It might be thought that having an offence, or various offences, premised explicitly on deception would represent an improvement over the present law in terms of the labelling of offenders. For instance, Gibson contends that the law ought to distinguish between what he terms the *negative* and *positive* dimensions of sexual autonomy: "The former is the ability to refuse to have sexual relations with anyone at any time and place, for any reason or for no reason . . . the latter is the ability to choose the sexual activity one wishes to pursue, with any consenting person(s) at any time and place, for any reason."[206] Where V does not consent to sexual activity at all, the focus ought to be on the violation of V's negative sexual autonomy. But where D deceives V, this implicates both negative *and* positive aspects of sexual autonomy: V wants to engage in sexual activity—subject to conditions—but also wants to avoid sexual activity contrary to those conditions. Gibson contends that fair labelling requires these different wrongs to be distinguished, and that the best way to do this would be to have offences regarding deception that mirror the main non-consensual offences in sections 1–4 of the SOA 2003.

A difficulty with this approach, however, is that Gibson contends that the violation of V's positive sexual autonomy in cases of deception is relatively minor compared to the violation of V's negative sexual autonomy; "it is simply disappointment".[207] If this is the case, however, one wonders whether there really is a case for creating distinct deception offences. If, ultimately, the violation of negative sexual autonomy explains the core wrongdoing perpetrated by D in deception *and* non-deception cases, then the labelling concern is less pressing than Gibson suggests.

Furthermore, creating deception offences does not solve the problem of deciding which deceptions warrant criminalisation and which do not. It simply moves the problem. To an extent, this concern can be met by insisting that D must be aware (or, if that is too narrow an approach, that D ought to be aware) that the deception is material to V's consent, and not something to which V is indifferent.[208] Even so, the core issue remains: is it really the case that *any* deception impacting on V's consent should be the stuff of criminal liability? Or should there be a requirement that the concern would be considered material by a reasonable person?[209] If such a requirement were insisted upon, the lack of clarity encountered earlier raises its head once again. This is why a proposal for new offences premised on deception must be twinned with a more nuanced and principled view of which deceptions are, and which deceptions are not, apt candidates for criminalisation.

An additional concern relates to the public's viewing any reinstated procurement offence as a less serious form of rape. There is tremendous pressure to secure convictions in sexual offences cases, and concern has been expressed at the risk that borderline cases would be charged as the new offence, rather than as—say—rape, simply to encourage a jury to

[206] Gibson, "Deceptive Sexual Relations: A Theory of Criminal Liability" (2020) 40 *OJLS* 82, 94–5.
[207] *Ibid.*, 103.
[208] See, e.g., Criminal Law Reform Now Network, *Reforming the Relationship between Sexual Consent, Deception and Mistake* (2023), pp. 111–12. Note, however, that the Network proposes a "reasonable excuse" defence, which once again raises the question of whether some deceptions are an insufficient basis for criminal liability in this context.
[209] There was uncertainty on this point under the old offence: Smith, *Smith and Hogan: Criminal Law* (10th ed., 2002) 475.

convict more readily, or D to plead guilty.[210] These difficulties are not insurmountable, but they are real.[211]

As this section has demonstrated, it is not easy to reach a settled conclusion on what the law *ought* to be in this area. On the one hand, accounts that privilege sexual autonomy—and thus would allow all or many material deceptions to vitiate consent—adhere most closely to the justification for the existence of non-consensual sexual offences. On the other hand, it seems unlikely that the problem of sexual offending can be resolved if juries are unlikely to convict defendants, based on their conception of what offences such as rape "really" involve.[212] The law can do only so much to educate. The courts' seemingly narrower approach to deceptions post-*Lawrance* is, to this limited extent, defensible. But the law cannot *ignore* all other deceptions (and, once again, related omissions to inform) on this basis, which is the result of the present approach. Accordingly, the creation of distinct offences premised on deception, applied in a principled manner (perhaps that provided by Kennedy; perhaps one based on a "reasonable person" test), for which juries may be more ready to convict defendants, is to be supported. It is a compromise; and like all compromises, it is not ideal. But, if the details of such offences could be worked out in Parliament, they would represent an improvement over the present law.

*Deceptions versus failures to inform.*

As remarked upon in the previous subsection, much of the literature on this area of the law has focussed on deceptions, and not engaged to the same extent with failures to inform one's sexual partner about related matters. Accordingly, a final issue to be debated in any reform exercise is the role of omissions to inform a sexual partner of a certain fact, by contrast with "active" deception regarding that fact. As noted earlier, the courts at one time seemed to distinguish between these two matters, viewing only "active" deception as capable of vitiating consent under section 74. One possible explanation for such a distinction is that, by lying to V, D cuts off the option of V seeking the truth by asking, whereas in omissions to tell, V could seek further clarification regarding the truth from D.[213] Another explanation is that, in criminalising both deceptions and omissions to tell, the law imposes duties of disclosure on those engaging in sexual behaviour, and—as demonstrated by the limits placed on omissions liability generally[214]—the situations where such duties arise need to be spelled out particularly carefully.

Since *Lawrance*, the courts are clear that what matters is merely the *subject matter* of the deception or the omission to tell. One advantage of such a model is that it avoids difficult questions of working out whether there was an "active" deception, or a mere omission to correct V's misapprehension—a conceivably fine line. For instance, the Court of Appeal in *McNally* clearly viewed D as actively deceiving V about the matter of D's gender history, when another view is that D merely omitted to tell V the "truth" or correct V's

210 Sjolin, "Ten Years On: Consent under the Sexual Offences Act 2003" (2015) 79 *J Crim L* 20, 32.

211 See, further: *ibid.*; Spencer, "Sex by Deception" [2013] 9 *Archbold Review* 6; Williams, "*R v Flattery* (1877)" in Handler, Mares, and Williams (eds.), *Landmark Cases in Criminal Law* (2017) 147, 167–9.

212 Rightly or wrongly, at least some juries will be unwilling to convict D *of rape* because of a preconceived notion of what rape "really" involves, which differs from the law's conception of that wrong. See, further, Temkin and Ashworth, "The Sexual Offences Act 2003: Rape, Sexual Assaults and the Problems of Consent" [2004] *Crim LR* 328, 345–6.

213 Tolley, "Harmfulness and Wrongfulness in Sex-by-Deception" (2025) 19 *Crim L and Philosophy* 137, 148.

214 See above, § 4.1.

misapprehension. It is not inconceivable that real cases of sexual activity involve a mixture of both the "active" and the "passive" in this regard. Assuming, for the moment, that the matter of one's gender history ought to be relevant to the legal definition of consent to sexual offences, should the distinction between "active" deception and omission be relevant to D's liability? There is a plausible case, based on respect for V's sexual autonomy, for concluding that the answer is "no". The pitfall of the current approach is, as adverted to above, that the limits of D's duty to inform V are unclear, as is the extent to which D's competing rights to privacy, physical safety, etc., ought to be taken into account when crafting a criminal law response to omissions to provide V with information. These questions are no easier than those associated with working out *which* "active" deceptions ought to have legal salience, but await compelling judicial answers.[215]

The complications arising from the criminalisation of omissions to inform appear to have been raised somewhat inadvertently in *Lawrance*, a case that was very plainly about "active" deception regarding D's fertility. They were ignored in *BVA*, a case firmly premised on D's omission to inform V about his plans to record the encounter, presumably because any claim to have a "right" to record such interactions without both parties' knowing consent is implausible, and a duty on D to make the relevant disclosure to V is not onerous. In future cases, however, the Court of Appeal must either revert to its distinction between deceptions and non-disclosures or do far more to delimit the boundaries of the latter category.

*Summary.*

It is helpful to summarise the general conclusions above. First, the Court of Appeal has approached the conclusive presumptions in section 76 very narrowly, limiting their practical significance. Secondly, the evidential presumptions in section 75 offer some helpful clarifications, but arguably the general definition of consent under section 74 was already adequate to deal with many such scenarios. Thirdly, the Court of Appeal has produced a complex case law on a range of factors that will vitiate consent under section 74, and has regularly struggled to delineate them clearly and apply them consistently. This is, to a degree, inevitable: consent is a complex matter, and it does virtually all of the normative heavy lifting in defining the offences in sections 1–4 of the SOA 2003. What must be borne in mind, however, is that vagueness is generally undesirable in the context of the criminal law.[216] There are far too many areas of the law under section 74 where even experts on the law are forced to guess about the likely outcome of not-unrealistic hypothetical cases. For instance, the decision in *BVA* does not seem to have been predictable, given the case law preceding it. If even legal experts cannot predict accurately whether liability for some of the most serious offences available under English criminal law will be imposed, there is little hope for the lay citizen. This objection is not merely relevant to potential defendants. It is equally unclear to those considering reporting a potential sexual offence to the police, and to prosecutors considering whether there is a case to proceed with.

As indicated above, the issue of what to do with this area of the law is deeply contested. The general topic of consent in the criminal law is due to be examined soon by the Law Commission,[217] so any legislative reform is likely to lie some years in the future. In the

[215] For brief thoughts, see Tolley, "Harmfulness and Wrongfulness in Sex-by-Deception" (2025) 19 *Crim L and Philosophy* 137, 147–9.

[216] See the discussion above in §§ 2.2–2.3.

[217] At the time of writing, the Law Commission has announced this project, but not published any substantive work on it. See https://lawcom.gov.uk/project/consent-in-the-criminal-law/.

meantime, it would be desirable, given the confusion that the Court of Appeal's decisions to date have created, and the limited avenues for that Court to disown its own precedents, for the Supreme Court to be asked to pass judgment on at least the following questions: (i) which deceptions can vitiate consent under section 74?; and (ii) are omissions to inform properly dealt with in a manner identical to that applying to such deceptions? If the Supreme Court were to endorse the "close connection" test, it would be incumbent upon it to provide compelling explanations for the outcomes in cases decided to date, and to disavow decisions where no such explanations can be given.

## § 12.5 Common element 4: the absence of a reasonable belief in consent

The non-consensual offences include a mens rea element in relation to the absence of V's consent: D must lack a reasonable belief that V is consenting. This formulation means that the following situations will satisfy the fault requirement with regard to the absence of consent: D hopes that V will not consent; D knows that V is not consenting; D believes that V is not consenting; D is (subjectively) reckless whether V is consenting; D does not think about whether V is consenting; and D believes that V is consenting, but that belief is not based on reasonable grounds (in essence, a form of negligence with regard to belief-formation).[218]

This approach to fault marks a notable change from the previous law, by introducing an objective test in cases where D claims to have believed that V was consenting. For the purposes of the pre-SOA 2003 law, in *Morgan*,[219] the House of Lords had ruled that, in principle, a man who had sexual intercourse with a woman without her consent was not guilty of rape if he had honestly believed that she was consenting, however unreasonable his belief might have been. Although there was little evidence that in practice juries acquitted defendants who claimed that they honestly, but unreasonably, believed the complainant had consented, the decision in *Morgan* was widely thought to send an undesirable message about what was permissible in sexual relations.[220] The government that promoted the reforms in the SOA 2003 made the reversal of *Morgan* one of the key elements in its revision of the law on sexual offences.

Whether the absence of a reasonable belief formula has the desired effect is questionable, and depends on how the courts interpret it. Regrettably, there are at least two ways in which the legislation might have missed its mark. The first concerns the nature of "reasonableness" itself—the SOA 2003 does not make clear *to whom* D's belief must be reasonable, and this opens up the possibility (once again) that harmful stereotypes about the nature of sexual offending and victimhood will influence judgements about D's mens rea.[221]

[218] See Stark, *Culpable Carelessness* (2016) chap. 8.

[219] [1976] AC 182; discussed further in § 18.1.

[220] The Sexual Offences (Amendment) Act 1976 was passed after *Morgan*. Section 1(2) provided that the jury was to consider the grounds for D's belief in ascertaining whether it thought he might have actually held it. The substantive law remained unchanged, however. If the jury concluded it was reasonably possible that D honestly believed that V had consented, D was still to be acquitted.

[221] Cowan, "'Freedom and the Capacity to Make a Choice': A Feminist Analysis of Consent in the Criminal Law of Rape" in Munro and Stychin (eds.), *Sexuality and the Law* (2007) 51, 60. See, further, Finch and Munro, "Breaking Boundaries? Sexual Consent in the Jury Room" (2006) 26 *LS* 303; Larcombe *et al.*, "'I Think It's Rape and I Think He Would be Found Not Guilty': Focus Group Perceptions of (Unreasonable) Belief in Consent in Rape Law" (2016) 25 *Social & Legal Studies* 611.

Secondly, the legislation provides that:

> Whether a belief is reasonable is to be determined having regard to all the circumstances, including any steps [D] has taken to ascertain whether [V] consents.[222]

An obvious question is what "all the circumstances" include. In other situations where the courts are called upon to decide whether behaviour was reasonable—for example, in the tort of negligence—it goes without saying that they make the decision taking account of "all the circumstances"; but by "all the circumstances" they normally mean those that are *external* to D. If a driver is sued for negligence she is barred from arguing that, though her driving fell short of the objective standard of the reasonable person, by the standards of a person with her (in)ability she was doing rather well.[223] The courts tend to take an equally hard-nosed line when dealing with prosecutions for offences of negligence.[224] Thus, in the context of the offence of dangerous driving, they have said that the question is whether his driving was objectively dangerous, and it is irrelevant that he was "doing his incompetent best".[225] This might suggest that, in the context of sections 1–4 of the SOA 2003,[226] no allowance would be made for D who, as a result of learning disabilities, believed V had consented when a non-disabled person would have realised V did not.

In its original form, the Sexual Offences Bill provided a test that was purely objective: D would have been guilty if "a reasonable person would in all the circumstances doubt whether [the complainant] consents". But in Parliament this evoked opposition on the ground that it potentially bore too heavily on those with learning disabilities, who might in consequence be judged by standards they could not attain.[227] This is why the "all the circumstances" provision was added. The general idea behind this formulation is that, in the case of a defendant with learning disabilities, these would form part of the "circumstances", and hence be taken into account in establishing whether the belief was reasonable.[228]

If "all the circumstances" were taken to include *all* those that are internal to D, this could have the effect of defeating the intended reform. Taken to the limit, it would mean making allowance not only for the fact that D had learning disabilities, but also that D's judgement was clouded by mental disorder—and indeed that D was by nature arrogant, impetuous, or stupid.[229] The practical effect of this might be to make the test of mens rea essentially subjective, effectively restoring the position as it was under *Morgan*.

[222] This formula is repeated four times in the Act, once in relation to each of the offences: see SOA 2003, ss. 1(2), 2(2), 3(2), and 4(2). If D has a reasonable belief that X is consenting, and then (reasonably) mistakes V for X, D still has a reasonable belief in consent and should not be guilty. See the bizarre facts at issue in *A-G's Reference (No. 79 of 2006)* [2006] EWCA Crim 2626, [2007] 1 Cr App R (S) 122.

[223] *Nettleship v Weston* [1971] 2 QB 691 (CA).

[224] See the discussion of personal characteristics in negligence, above, § 5.5(ii).

[225] *Evans* [1963] 1 QB 412, 418 (CA).

[226] There is a possible distinction: it could be said that in driving offences this is a "behavioural" element of the actus reus rather than, as here, a "circumstances or consequences issue". See above, § 5.5(iii).

[227] See Temkin and Ashworth, "The Sexual Offences Act 2003: Rape, Sexual Assaults and the Problems of Consent" [2004] *Crim LR* 328, 340–1.

[228] *Ibid.*, 341.

[229] Presumably, the fact that D is voluntarily intoxicated will not be taken into account, in keeping with the law's general rejection of such arguments in offences of "basic intent" (see below, § 18.3) and rejection of beliefs stemming from voluntary intoxication in the context of self-defence (see below, § 21.2(iv)(a)). There is, as yet, no case law on this point.

Moved by considerations of this sort, in *B*—a case involving a schizophrenic defendant—the Court of Appeal said:[230]

> "We conclude that unless and until the state of mind amounts to insanity in law, then under the rule enacted in the Sexual Offences Act beliefs in consent arising from conditions such as delusional psychotic illness or personality disorders must be judged by objective standards of reasonableness and not by taking into account a mental disorder which induced a belief which could not reasonably arise without it."

In so ruling, however, the Court was prepared to accept that, despite this, "cases could arise in which the reasonableness [of D's belief] depends on the reading by [D] of subtle social signals, and in which his impaired ability to do so is relevant to the reasonableness of his belief".[231] The fact that D has been diagnosed with autism can, then, in theory be relevant to the assessment of the reasonableness of D's belief in consent.[232]

Further litigation on this point seems inevitable. The approach outlined in *B* fails to separate the truly culpable from those in need of treatment, no doubt a result of the limits placed upon the insanity defence by English law.[233] Conditions such as schizophrenia should be taken into account when assessing the reasonableness of D's beliefs about consent.

Despite these criticisable features of the legislation, the law has allowed the conviction of defendants who apparently believed, albeit on spurious grounds, that V was consenting. For instance, in *Ivor*,[234] the defendants had sex with V—the girlfriend a violent man, T—well aware of: the coercive control that T exercised over V; V's fear of T becoming violent if she refused his commands; and the fact that V had had to take copious amounts of drink and take drugs before she could bring herself to have sex with the defendants. The defendants argued that V appeared to be consenting, and nothing put them on notice that they should inquire further. Given the "mosaic" of evidence from various sources about the state of the defendants' awareness of the circumstances surrounding the relevant sexual activity, the Court of Appeal upheld their convictions without hesitation.[235]

## § 12.6 Rape

Having explored the general concepts underlying the non-consensual sexual offences, we turn now to consider the more specific components of the offences contained in sections 1–4 of the SOA 2003. We start with rape. Section 1 of the Act provides:

> (1) [D] commits an offence if—
> (a) he intentionally penetrates the vagina, anus or mouth of [V] with his penis,
> (b) [V] does not consent to the penetration, and
> (c) [D] does not reasonably believe that [V] consents.

The maximum sentence is life imprisonment.[236]

230 [2013] EWCA Crim 3, [2013] 1 Cr App R 36, [40].

231 *Ibid.*, [41]. Cf. *TS* [2008] EWCA Crim 6.

232 *Jacobs* [2023] EWCA Crim 1503, [2024] 4 WLR 8, [76]–[81]. The Court of Appeal emphasised that the relevance of D's autism will depend on the precise facts at issue in the trial: in *Jacobs*, D's diagnosis was relevant to explaining his reaction in the aftermath of the alleged offence, *not* D's beliefs about V's consent.

233 See below, § 19.2.

234 [2021] EWCA Crim 923.

235 *Ibid.*, [37].

236 SOA 2003, s. 1(4).

Rape is the only one of the offences to be considered here that requires a male perpetrator,[237] someone who intentionally penetrates the vagina, anus, or mouth of another non-consenting person *with his penis*. There was some controversial authority that the former offence of rape could be committed by a woman through an innocent agent.[238] Such a verdict now seems precluded by the wording of the SOA 2003.[239]

D must penetrate V's vagina, anus or mouth, and penetration continues from entry to withdrawal.[240] Accordingly, D may rape V if he continues to penetrate V when an initial consent is revoked prior to withdrawal.[241] Vaginal penetration occurs as soon as there is entry of the vulva;[242] the occurrence or absence of ejaculation is irrelevant. It is also immaterial if the vagina penetrated is surgically constructed, for example through gender reassignment surgery.[243] As noted above, anal and oral penetrations also constitute rape. Non-consensual penile penetration of V's anus has been rape since 1994.[244] Prior to the SOA 2003, non-consensual penile penetration of V's mouth would not have been rape (it would instead have been indecent assault).

## § 12.7 Assault by penetration

Section 2 of the SOA 2003 provides:

(1) [D] commits an offence if—

(a) he intentionally penetrates the vagina or anus of another person [V] with a part of his body or anything else,

(b) the penetration is sexual,

(c) [V] does not consent to the penetration, and

(d) [D] does not reasonably believe that [V] consents.

A striking feature of this offence is its potential breadth, particularly considering the maximum penalty of life imprisonment.[245] Although the intentional, non-consensual, penetration must be of the anus or vagina, it may be done with any part of the body or with anything else.[246]

237 Although, as explained in SOA 2003, s. 79(3): "References to a part of the body include references to a part surgically constructed (in particular, through gender reassignment surgery)."

238 *Cogan and Leak* [1976] QB 217 (CA). See above, § 7.6(ii)(b).

239 Secondary liability remains possible. If D1 assists or encourages D2 to penetrate V's vagina, mouth, or anus with D2's penis, D1 will (assuming she possesses the relevant mens rea) be an accomplice to any rape that D2 perpetrates. Further, should D1 procure D2 so to act while D2 reasonably believes that V consents, D2 would nonetheless have committed the actus reus of rape, apparently a sufficient basis with which to find complicity by D1: *DPP v K and B* [1997] 1 Cr App R 36 (CA); above, § 7.6(ii)(b). Furthermore, a defendant who caused a person to engage in sexual activity without consent might be liable for the offence under s. 4 of the SOA 2003.

240 SOA 2003, s. 79(2).

241 As was the position under the previous law: *Kaitamaki* [1985] AC 147 (PC); *Cooper* [1994] Crim LR 531 (CA).

242 SOA 2003, s. 79(9).

243 *Ibid*., s. 79(3).

244 As a result of Criminal Justice and Public Order Act 1994, s. 142.

245 SOA 2003, s. 2(4).

246 Herein lies another reason why routine medical procedures involving a speculum, swabs, and the like should not be considered *because of their nature* to be sexual (above, § 12.3(i)). If they were, D, a doctor, who takes a vaginal swab from a patient, V, ostensibly for the sake of a treatment required by V but, covertly, to collect data for a study unconnected with V's medical needs, could be liable for the s. 2 offence (if D's deception is significant enough to vitiate consent and assuming that D has no reasonable belief in V's consent).

It will be noted that there is an overlap with the offence of rape whenever the vagina or anus of V is penetrated by D's penis. This was a deliberate act by the legislature, to allow for cases where it can be proved that D was responsible for an act of penetration by some bodily part or object but it cannot be proved beyond reasonable doubt that D used his penis.[247] It would be an injustice if D could escape conviction by trading on this lack of clarity to evade conviction for *both* rape and assault by penetration. The compromise position is that D will be acquitted of rape and convicted of assault by penetration.

One may of course question whether rape should be limited to penile penetration.[248] Why not expand the boundaries of rape to include what is covered by the section 2 offence? The answer to this question turns, ultimately, on what one takes the "wrong of rape" to be,[249] but the legislature has (for better or worse) taken the view that there is something *special* about penile penetration. Such penetration may be thought to be the ultimate kind of forced intimacy, as well as being the form most redolent of risk of disease and (in terms of vaginal penetration) unwanted pregnancy.[250] This point is, in any event, of limited practical import in terms of sentencing. Both rape and assault by penetration attract maximum sentences of life imprisonment. There is nevertheless an important point concerning labelling: whether D, who penetrates V's anus with a sex toy, without V's consent, should be identified by the law as a "rapist". Perhaps not, but the point is debatable.[251] (Similar points arise in relation to the section 4 offence of causing a person to engage in sexual activity without consent: below, § 12.9.)

## § 12.8 Sexual assault

Section 3 of the SOA 2003 provides:

> (1) [D] commits an offence if—
> (a) he intentionally touches another person [V],
> (b) the touching is sexual,
> (c) [V] does not consent to the touching, and
> (d) [D] does not reasonably believe that [V] consents.

[247] Cp. the Scottish case of *Garvock v HM Advocate* 1991 SCCR 593.

[248] Much depends, of course, on what rape is taken to mean and whether it has an "essence". For searching discussion, see Conaghan, "The Essence of Rape" (2019) 39 *OJLS* 151.

[249] See Gardner and Shute, "The Wrongness of Rape" in Horder (ed.), *Oxford Essays in Jurisprudence* (4th series, 2000) 193. For a convincing reply, see Stanton-Ife, "Horrific Crime" in Duff *et al.* (eds.), *The Boundaries of the Criminal Law* (2011) 138.

[250] It has been argued that the core of the wrong of rape is disrespect for V's autonomy, the use of her body in a purely instrumental manner which disregards her personhood. As such, rape in its "pure" form would take place where D, using a condom, penetrates an insensate V who never becomes aware of what D has done and suffers no adverse physical or psychological effects: Gardner and Shute, "The Wrongness of Rape" in Horder (ed.), *Oxford Essays in Jurisprudence* (4th series, 2000) 193; cf. Plaxton, "Nussbaum on Sexual Instrumentalization" (2016) 10 *Crim Law and Philosophy* 1. On Gardner and Shute's view, the "core" wrong would have occurred whenever D uses the body of an insensate V for sexual gratification and whatever form his conduct takes, implying no difference in the basic wrong of the offences of rape, assault by penetration, and sexual assault. But, of course, a typical instance of rape will be fully experienced by the victim and will inflict serious psychological trauma, as well as risking physical injury, infection, and—in the case of vaginal penetration—unwanted pregnancy. Although such effects are not within the formal definition of rape (and will often accompany other non-consensual sexual offences), they are very much part of our conception of rape and explain why rape is appropriately characterised as a form of violence (although it need not involve *physical* violence) against V, as well as a wrong of disregard for V's sexual autonomy.

[251] See: McKeever, "Can a Woman Rape a Man and Does It Matter?" (2019) 13 *Crim Law and Philosophy* 599; Weare, "'Oh You're a Guy, How Could You be Raped by a Woman, That Makes No Sense': Towards a Case for Legally Recognising and Labelling 'Forced to Penetrate' Cases as Rape" (2018) 14 *International J Law in Context* 110.

The maximum penalty is 10 years' imprisonment if tried on indictment, or 6 months' imprisonment if tried summarily.[252]

Sexual assault covers non-consensual, non-penetrative, sexual acts, requiring proof that D touched V. V's person includes reference to a body part surgically constructed, in particular through gender reassignment surgery.[253] A "touching" includes a touching amounting to penetration,[254] another aspect of overlap within sections 1–4 of the SOA 2003. The term "touching" covers much else besides, including touching made with any part of the body, or using anything else, and *through* anything.[255] It was confirmed in *H*[256] that V's body includes V's clothes and it seems that V need feel no pressure on V's body. Accordingly, D may "touch" V through ejaculating onto V's clothing.[257] Should D intentionally brush V's fully clothed crotch without V's consent, D may well also commit sexual assault.

One point of restriction, however, is that the offence is confined to *touching*; which, in the pedantic terms of English law, is strictly speaking a battery. Accordingly, to continue our example, if D attempts but fails to touch V's crotch, yet puts V in fear of an imminent touching, D may well perpetrate a simple assault but not a sexual assault.[258]

More difficult scenarios have arisen. For instance, in a case from 2019, D pleaded guilty to sexual assault, apparently on the basis that he had ejaculated into V's tea before giving it to her to drink.[259] If one assumes that this activity is sexual,[260] did D "touch" V? The point was not argued; D pleaded guilty. It nevertheless seems to stretch the boundaries of the English language too far to conceive of D's conduct as involving even an indirect "touching" of V.[261] Liability under section 24 of the Offences Against the Person Act 1861 (malicious application of a "noxious" thing) more naturally captures the wrongdoing at issue in such cases.[262]

## § 12.9 Causing a person to engage in sexual activity without consent

Section 4 of the SOA 2003 provides:

> (1) [D] commits an offence if—
> (a) he intentionally causes [V] to engage in an activity,
> (b) the activity is sexual,

[252] SOA 2003, s. 3(4).
[253] *Ibid.*, s. 79(3).
[254] *Ibid.*, s. 79(8).
[255] *Ibid.*
[256] [2005] EWCA Crim 732, [2005] 1 WLR 2005.
[257] The defendant in *Bounekhla* [2006] EWCA Crim 1217 pleaded guilty to sexual assault in such circumstances.
[258] There may, of course, be an attempted sexual assault on such facts. Concerning the mens rea of criminal attempts in this area, see below, § 9.3(iii)(b).
[259] See https://www.bbc.co.uk/news/uk-england-stoke-staffordshire-47002405.
[260] The presence of semen is plausibly enough to make this conduct that is, "because of its nature", sexual, and it appears that D wished by his conduct to "humiliate" V, a "respectable" woman. Presumably this conduct was thought by D to be humiliating *because* it was sexual.
[261] Compare a scenario where D, a chef, spits (clandestinely) in V's burger before handing it over to the waiter to be served to V. Spitting *on* someone is sufficient "contact" for battery (*Smith* (1866) F & F 1066, 176 ER 910). D's conduct here is nevertheless inappositely described as "contact", and thus the actus reus of battery.
[262] Suppose, however, that D did not intend for V to learn what he had done, but interfered with V's tea simply for his own sexual gratification. In the absence of an intention to "injure, aggrieve, or annoy" V (which is required for the s. 24 OAPA 1861 offence), it would appear—assuming this is not a sexual assault, because of the absence of "touching"—that D has committed no offence whatsoever.

(c) [V] does not consent to engaging in the activity, and
(d) [D] does not reasonably believe that [V] consents.

The maximum penalty is life imprisonment in certain circumstances.[263] Otherwise, it is 10 years' imprisonment if tried on indictment, or 6 months' imprisonment if tried summarily.[264]

Where the interchange is between D and V, and no one else, much of the conduct covered in sections 1–3 will fall also within this offence. With the exception of sexual violations of overwhelmed or passive victims (who could not be said to be "engaged in an activity"), the overlap of section 4 with the other three offences is considerable.

What, then, is the distinctive coverage of this offence? For the moment, confining ourselves to interactions between D and V, situations where D causes V to touch D (or indeed V) sexually seem to be included.[265] Consider also a case where D compels V to have intercourse with her. This means that what might loosely be described as "female rape" is an offence potentially carrying with it a maximum penalty of life imprisonment.[266]

Moving beyond two-party interactions, D commits the section 4 offence if D causes V to engage in non-consensual sexual activity with T: T may be innocent of D's machinations, an accomplice of D, or even a co-complainant with V.

D must cause V to engage in an activity to which V does not consent. If V acts because of something violent or coercive that D does, or threatens to do, it is inevitable that D will be found to have caused V to do it. Significant deceptions by D could also lead to a finding that D caused V to engage in a sexual activity without consent. As we saw in § 12.4, these very facts can establish V's lack of consent. But the two elements may not coincide. On some approaches to causation, for example, D might be said to have "caused" V to have sex with D by overcoming V's reluctance with a very large sum of money.[267] It does not follow that the ensuing sexual act was non-consensual, even in cases where D has exploited the economic circumstances of V.[268]

It is worth dwelling briefly on the last point. A real difficulty in this area is that extreme economic hardship can, in our view, be highly coercive. In the example of the brothel keeper (§ 12.4(iii)(b) above), it is no great stretch of the English language to say that––through offering V work in his brothel––D has caused V (a desperate asylum seeker) to engage in sexual activity (and, on the same basis, without V's consent). Finding D liable in such cases would have significant implications not merely for the scope of section 4, but also for the other non-consensual offences in the SOA 2003. No doubt those responsible for formulating and implementing a draconian asylum policy are effectively beyond the purview of this offence and, if they are exempt, D should be too. Yet it is remarkable that modern drafting of serious offences can give rise to such conjectures about their scope.[269]

263 These circumstances are where the activity involves "penetration of [V]'s anus or vagina . . . penetration of [V]'s mouth with a person's penis . . . penetration of a person's anus or vagina with a part of [V]'s body or by [V] with anything else, or . . . penetration of a person's mouth with [V]'s penis": SOA 2003, s. 4(4).

264 Ibid., s. 4(5).

265 See, e.g., *Devonald* [2008] EWCA Crim 527.

266 Assuming penile penetration of D's vagina, anus or mouth is involved: SOA 2003, s. 4(4).

267 A broad view of causation, one that would plot a causal pathway connecting the conduct of D and the voluntary actions of V, has occasionally been taken by the courts. But see the critical analysis above at § 4.2(iii)(e).

268 See, however, the discussion of *Kirk* [2008] EWCA Crim 434, above, § 12.4(iii)(b).

269 Research into the application of s. 4 has been sparse to date, but see Weare, "The Penetrative Offence in Section 4 of the Sexual Offences Act 2003" (2020) 60 *Brit J Criminol* 930.

## § 12.10 Consensual sexual offences

The SOA 2003 creates five groups of what might be called "consensual sex offences"—that is, cases where a form of sexual behaviour constitutes a criminal offence, even if the other person involved consents to it. (The presence of consent is not, of course, a legal ingredient in these offences, and defendants can be prosecuted for them in cases where consent was absent and their behaviour therefore constituted one of the non-consensual offences discussed earlier.)

The first two groups involve sexual acts with persons who are under the age of legal consent (16). The third penalises sexual acts with persons under the age of 18 when done by those whom the law deems to be, at the relevant time, in a "position of trust". The fourth penalises sexual acts with persons under 18 when done by any of a wide range of family members. The fifth penalises "sex with an adult relative": sexual acts when performed by persons over the age of consent who are closely related to one another.

## § 12.11 Child sex offences[270]

### *(i) Offences involving children under 13*

Sections 5–8 of the SOA 2003 create four criminal offences of sexual behaviour with children who are under 13. The first is called "rape of a child under 13",[271] the second is "assault of a child under 13 by penetration",[272] and the third is "sexual assault of a child under 13".[273] In each case, the actus reus is the same as for the similarly named non-consensual offence set out earlier in the SOA 2003, except that the words "[V] does not consent" are replaced by the words "the other person is under 13". The fourth offence is "causing or inciting a child under 13 to engage in sexual activity".[274] This offence is similar to the offence in section 4 of "causing a person to engage in sexual activity without consent", except that the presence of consent is irrelevant and the offence extends beyond "causing" sexual activity to include "inciting" it.[275]

These four offences are constructed on the basis that, because a child under 13 is unable, legally, to consent, to engage them in consensual sexual activity is morally equivalent to forcing it upon an older person who does not consent. In many situations—for example, where D is 50 and performs a sexual act with a child of 5—this will obviously be so. However, where the participants are of a similar age, or where (as is possible) D is even younger

[270] See, generally, Spencer, "Child and Family Offences" [2004] *Crim LR* 347.

[271] SOA 2003, s. 5. The maximum penalty for this offence is life imprisonment: s. 5(2).

[272] *Ibid.*, s. 6. The maximum penalty for this offence is life imprisonment: s. 6(2).

[273] *Ibid.*, s. 7. The maximum penalty for this offence is 14 years' imprisonment on indictment and 6 months' imprisonment if tried summarily: s. 7(2).

[274] *Ibid.*, s. 8. The maximum sentence is dependent on the activity engaged in. If it involves "penetration of [V]'s anus or vagina . . . penetration of [V]'s mouth with a person's penis . . . penetration of a person's anus or vagina with a part of [V]'s body or by [V] with anything else, or . . . penetration of a person's mouth with [V]'s penis", the maximum penalty is life imprisonment: s. 8(2). In other cases, the maximum penalty is 14 years' imprisonment on indictment, and 6 months' imprisonment when tried summarily: s. 8(3).

[275] Indeed, it has been held that s. 8 creates two offences, one involving causation and the other involving incitement: *Walker* [2006] EWCA Crim 1907. This drafting avoids issues of causation arising in cases where V (factually, if not legally) consents to the relevant activity.

than the other participant, an issue of fair labelling arises.[276] If, at her suggestion, a boy of 12 has sexual intercourse with a girl of the same age, or allows her to fellate him, it is surely questionable whether it is appropriate to label him a "rapist" (or, indeed, her as having committed a "sexual assault"). Furthermore, these offences, unlike their equivalents under the old law,[277] carry strict liability as to the age of the other participant. Although the drafting of the provisions does not make this explicit, Parliament plainly intended strict liability to apply.[278] So it follows that, in the previous example, the boy of 12 would be in law a "rapist", even if the girl told him she was 13—or 16—and he honestly and reasonably believed her. (Equally, she would be liable for sexual assault of a child under 13.)

### *(ii) Offences involving children under 16*

Sections 9–15 of the SOA 2003 create a further six offences penalising various forms of sexual behaviour with a person under the age of 16. Although mainly directed against sexual acts with older children, they apply no less to sexual acts with younger ones, and where the child is under 13 they overlap with the offences discussed in the previous section.[279] Although less severely punishable than those created by sections 5–8, all of these offences are potentially triable on indictment and punishable with imprisonment.[280]

Section 9 creates an offence of "sexual activity with a child", which is committed by any intentional touching of a person under 16 that is "sexual" in the sense given to that word by section 78, which was discussed in § 12.3, above. The defendant must be aged over 18 to commit the offence. The maximum penalty (depending on the activity engaged in) is either life imprisonment, or 14 years' imprisonment when tried on indictment (6 months' imprisonment when tried summarily).[281]

Section 10 creates the offence of "causing or inciting a child to engage in sexual activity". The defendant must be over 18 to commit this offence, and the maximum penalties are the same as for the section 9 offence.[282] Section 11 creates a third offence of "engaging in sexual activity in the presence of a child",[283] and section 12 a fourth offence of causing a child to watch a sexual act, or showing a child a pornographic picture. Again, the defendant must be over 18 to commit this offence. The maximum sentences for both offences are 10 years' imprisonment if tried on indictment, or six months' imprisonment if tried summarily.[284]

[276] Above, § 2.4.

[277] See: *B (A Minor) v DPP* [2000] 2 AC 428; *K* [2001] UKHL 41, [2002] 1 AC 462; *Kumar* [2004] EWCA Crim 3207, [2005] 1 WLR 1352.

[278] Confirmed in *G* [2008] UKHL 37, [2009] 1 AC 92.

[279] This is a deviation from the original plan, which was that the second group of offences should be entirely separate from the first. For the history of the matter, see Spencer, "Child and Family Offences" [2004] *Crim LR* 347, 353.

[280] Maximum penalties range from 6 months to 14 years, depending on the nature of the sexual act and the court before which the offence is tried.

[281] Life imprisonment applies if the activity involves "penetration of [V]'s anus or vagina . . . penetration of [V]'s mouth with a person's penis . . . penetration of a person's anus or vagina with a part of [V]'s body or by [V] with anything else, or . . . penetration of a person's mouth with [V]'s penis": SOA 2003, s. 9(2). For other activities, see s. 9(3).

[282] SOA 2003, ss. 10(2)–(3).

[283] There must be a link between the child's presence and the obtaining of sexual gratification. It is not sufficient to prove merely that D engaged in sexual activity and that a child was coincidentally present: *B* [2018] EWCA Crim 1439, [2019] 1 WLR 3177.

[284] SOA 2003, ss. 11(2), 12(2).

These (and the "under 13" offences) are supplemented by two specific preliminary offences: "arranging or facilitating the commission of a child sex offence"[285] and the offence usually called "grooming"—having communicated with a child on at least two earlier occasions, meeting them, or travelling to meet them, with the intention of committing a sexual offence.[286]

Unlike the "under 13" offences, the "under 16" offences are drafted so as to provide some protection for defendants who engage in sexual acts with a child or young person whom they reasonably believe to be over the age of consent. To be convicted of any of the offences in sections 9–12, D must be proved to have had no reasonable belief that the child was aged 16 or over. If the child was under 13, however, strict liability is imposed with regard to the child's age.[287]

Once again, although both groups of child sex offences discussed thus far were aimed at adult paedophiles who prey upon the young and vulnerable, they are not so limited, and also punish all forms of sexual behaviour between consenting children. By section 13, persons under 18 who commit what would otherwise be one of the "under 16" offences set out in sections 9–12 incur a lower range of penalties: 5 years' imprisonment if tried on indictment, and 6 months' imprisonment if tried summarily. But even this limited concession does not apply to the "under 13" offences, however young the defendant who commits them. In this regard, it must be noted that English law sets an age of consent that it is among the highest in Western Europe, and an age of criminal responsibility which, at 10, is among the lowest. The bite of the low age of criminal responsibility has been strengthened by the abolition of the *doli incapax* rule, which until 1998 prevented children between the age of 10 and 14 incurring criminal liability except where they realised that their conduct was morally wrong.[288]

The result of all of this is to bring within the criminal law a range of sexual acts, some of which are usually thought to be normal and not improper, and others at least not seriously wrong. They include, for example, mouth-to-mouth kissing,[289] or minor acts of sexual exploration between consenting 14- or 15-year-olds. Data consistently demonstrates that it is relatively common for those under 16 to engage in sexual activity, including sexual intercourse.[290] This means that the SOA 2003's provisions are so out of line with the normal sexual behaviour of young people that their practical effect must be to make indictable offenders out of all but a minority of the population. This was a feature of the old law as well, and one for which it was forcefully criticised.[291] It seems paradoxical that in a law intended

[285] *Ibid.*, s. 14. The maximum penalty for this offence is 14 years' imprisonment on indictment, and 6 months' imprisonment if tried summarily: s. 14(4).

[286] *Ibid.*, s. 15. The maximum penalty for this offence is 10 years' imprisonment on indictment, and 6 months' imprisonment if tried summarily: s. 15(4).

[287] *Ibid.*, ss. 9(1)(c), 10(1)(c), 11(1)(d), 12(1)(c).

[288] See below, § 19.3(ii).

[289] Mouth-to-mouth kissing, if done for erotic pleasure, is unquestionably "sexual behaviour", and prosecutions are sometimes brought where matters go no further than this. For an example, see *Lamb* [2007] EWCA Crim 1766.

[290] Wellings et al., *Sexual Behaviour in Britain* (1994) 40; Erens, McManus, Prescott, Field et al., *National Survey of Sexual Attitudes and Lifestyles II* (2003) 5; Mercer et al, "Changes in Sexual Attitudes and Lifestyles in Britain Through the Life Course and Over Time" (2013) 382 *The Lancet* 1781, 1786; Palmer et al., "Prevalence and Correlates of 'Sexual Competence' at First Heterosexual Intercourse among Young People in Britain" (2019) 45 *British Medical Journal Sexual and Reproductive Health* 127.

[291] Hogan, "Modernising the Law of Sexual Offences" in Glazebrook (ed.), *Reshaping the Criminal Law* (1978) 174.

to "modernise Victorian laws on sex offences" this blemish should have been not cured, but reinforced and, through the use of strict liability in some offences, exacerbated.

This point concerning overcriminalisation was made when the Sexual Offences Bill was before Parliament, but all moves to restrict the scope of the child sex offences were resisted by the government on the ground that they might provide unwanted loopholes for paedophiles. The resulting breadth of the offences did not matter, it was said, because the police and the Crown Prosecution Service have a discretion to prosecute which they can be expected to exercise intelligently.[292] One wonders, however, if it is appropriate to leave this much up to prosecutors, however diligently they perform their role. It is noteworthy in this regard that reliance on prosecutorial discretion has been avoided in other jurisdictions by drafting criminal offences of sex with minors so as to exclude certain consensual acts between minors who are close in age.[293] Alas, this step was not taken when the SOA 2003 was passed.

This part of English law is, as a result, inconsistent, in that it permits persons under 16 who understand their implications to consent to medical procedures, however serious—and indeed to the prescription of contraceptive medication[294]—whilst at the same time forbidding them to consent to sexual acts, however trivial. It is also oppressive because, despite the government's assurances at the time the SOA 2003 was passed and the formal guidance issued by the Crown Prosecution Service stressing that "the overriding purpose of the legislation is to protect children and it was not Parliament's intention to punish children unnecessarily or for the criminal law to intervene where it was wholly inappropriate", and adding that "[c]onsensual sexual activity would not normally require criminal proceedings in the absence of aggravating features",[295] heavy-handed prosecutions do indeed take place.[296] In

[292] "We should create the offence and leave it to the prosecutor to decide": Paul Goggins, Under-Secretary of State, Standing Committee B, 11 September 2003, 135. At the second reading of the Bill, the Home Secretary, David Blunkett, offered to "buy a flagon of champagne for anyone who comes up with a satisfactory answer" as to how the law could be framed without leaving undesirable loopholes: Hansard (HC), vol. 429, no. 129, col. 195 (15 July 2003).

[293] In France, for example, the criminal offence of consensual sex with minors is defined so as to exclude defendants who are themselves under the age of 18 (Code pénal Art. 227–25); and in Italy the equivalent offence does not apply to sexual acts with minors provided (i) the minor is over 13 and (ii) there is no more than three years' difference in age between them (Codice penale Art. 609 quater, para. 5). Under Scots law, the fact that the difference in age between the parties does not exceed two years can constitute a defence to some consensual offences: Sexual Offences (Scotland) Act 2009, s. 39(3).

[294] See, further, SOA 2003, s. 73, which provides a limited defence for those who would otherwise be aiding, abetting, or counselling an offence under certain sections of the Act. This defence would be available to a doctor prescribing contraception to V, a 13-year-old girl, to limit the risk of V becoming pregnant, well aware that this would encourage V to engage in sexual activity.

[295] Crown Prosecution Service, *Rape and Sexual Offences: Updated Guidance* (2021), chap. 13: https://www.cps.gov.uk/prosecution-guidance/rape-and-sexual-offences-chapter-13-sexual-offences-and-youths .

[296] For one example out of many, see *C* (2009) 173 CL & JW 303 (CA). D, a boy of 14, had consensual sex with his girlfriend, A, aged 14. After they broke up, D started going out with A's friend B, aged 13, and these two also had consensual sex. B's mother found out and told the police, when by chance she read on B's mobile phone a text conversation between A and B comparing notes. For this, D, a "good student" from a "respectable family", was prosecuted for "sexual activity with a child" contrary to s. 13, pleaded guilty, and initially received an eight-month custodial sentence—reduced to a supervision order on appeal. The girls were equally guilty, yet were not prosecuted. For other examples of proceedings that seem heavy-handed, see: *R (S) v DPP* [2006] EWHC 2231 (Admin); *D* [2006] EWCA Crim 111, [2006] Cr App R (S) 330 (52). Cf. *R (BH) v Llandundo Youth Court* [2014] EWHC 1833 (Admin), where the decision to commit two boys (who were 11 at the time of the alleged offence) to trial in the Crown Court for causing or inciting a child under 13 to engage in sexual activity was quashed, and the case was referred to the Youth Court. In that case, V was *not* consenting.

theory, a prosecution brought in breach of the prosecutor's publicly stated policy can be attacked either by inviting the court of trial to stay the proceedings as an abuse of process or by seeking judicial review of the decision to institute it. In practice, however, such attacks are usually unsuccessful.[297]

Article 8 of the ECHR obliges contracting states to respect, within limits, the right of its citizens to a private life. In the case of a prosecution for under-age sex that was particularly oppressive, could this guarantee be invoked? An attempt to do so was made, unsuccessfully, in *G*.[298] A boy aged 15 had sexual intercourse with a girl of 12 and later pleaded guilty to the offence of "rape of a child under 13", contrary to section 5 of the SOA 2003, on the basis that she had consented and that she had told him that she too was 15. G later sought to argue that a conviction on these facts for such a grave and stigmatic offence was disproportionate and violated his rights under Article 8. If criminal proceedings were appropriate, he contended, he should have been prosecuted for the less serious offence under section 13 ("child sexual offences committed by children or young persons"). This argument was accepted by two members of the House of Lords, but the majority gave it short shrift. Lord Hoffmann contemptuously dismissed the proceedings as "another example of the regrettable tendency to try to convert the whole system of justice into questions of human rights".[299] Using more moderate language, Lady Hale said "the prosecution, conviction and sentence were both rational and proportionate in the pursuit of the legitimate aims of the protection of the health and morals and rights and freedoms of others",[300] while Lord Mance said that the statutory scheme was justified by "the strong protective needs of children under 13"—protective needs which, it seems, are sufficiently strong to justify making criminals out of both parties where two children engage in consensual sexual activity.[301]

## § 12.12 "Abuse of trust"

Sections 16–24 of the SOA 2003 create four offences of sexual behaviour with children by persons who are in a position of trust. For the purposes of these provisions, "children" are those aged under 18; hence some persons over the age of consent are included. The sexual acts that are so prohibited are the same as those set out in the "under 16" offences: "sexual activity" (meaning any sexual touching), causing or inciting a "child" to engage in sexual activity", engaging in sexual activity when a "child" is present, and causing a "child" to watch a sexual act or see a pornographic image. What amounts to a "position of trust" is set out in sections 21 and 22; the persons listed include schoolteachers, staff in hospitals and care homes, and any other categories of person designated by the Secretary of State. The Police, Crime, Sentencing and Courts Act 2022 added section 22A to the SOA 2003, expanding the

[297] As in *S v DPP* [2006] EWHC 2231 (Admin). A judicial review did succeed in *R (E, S and R) v DPP* [2011] EWHC 1465 (Admin), [2012] 1 Cr App R 6, but on highly unusual facts. Cf. *R (CM) v CPS* [2014] EWHC 4457 (Admin).

[298] [2008] UKHL 37, [2009] 1 AC 92.

[299] *Ibid.*, [10].

[300] *Ibid.*, [55].

[301] *Ibid.*, [72]. D later raised the Art. 8 issue again an application to the ECtHR, but his application was ruled inadmissible: *G v United Kingdom* (2011) 53 EHRR SE 25.

list of positions of trust to include a person who knowingly "coaches, trains, supervises or instructs [a person under 18], on a regular basis, in sport or religion".[302]

Given their overlap with the "under 16" offences, it is questionable whether there is any need for these "abuse of trust" offences. No such offence was known to English law until 2000, when the precursor to these provisions was hastily created,[303] not in response to any public pressure but as a gesture needed to persuade Parliament to agree to lower the age of consent for homosexual acts from 18 to 16. Opposition focused on the risk that a change in the law would leave homosexual teachers free to form sexual relationships with their older pupils. In practice, the main impact of these offences is to criminalise all forms of sexual contact—however minor—between teachers and their pupils aged 16 and 17. For teachers to form consensual sexual relationships with their older pupils may be misbehaviour that fully justifies dismissal, but does it follow that it ought to be a criminal offence?[304] The wording of the relevant offences also renders criminal any sexual contact between persons who, according to the civil law, are legally competent to marry or form civil partnerships: a point that is recognised by section 23, which provides a defence for sexual acts performed in the context of a marriage or a civil partnership.

## § 12.13 "Familial child sex offences"

Sections 25–9 of the SOA 2003 create four offences of sexual acts when performed with persons under the age of 18 by those whom the Act defines as "family members". The range of sexual acts prohibited is slightly narrower than is covered by the "under 16" and "abuse of trust" offences. It is limited to "sexual activity" in the sense of any form of sexual touching,[305] and D's inciting another family member to touch D sexually.[306] The "family relationships" to which these offences apply are set out in some detail in section 27. There are three groups. The first consists of parents, grandparents, brothers, sisters, half-brothers, half-sisters, aunts, uncles, and foster-parents; these count as "family members" whether or not the "victim" of the offence has ever lived with them. The second comprises step-parents, step-brothers, step-sisters, cousins, and people who have shared a common foster-parent. These count as family members if they have ever lived in the same household as the "victim", or at some point have been involved in caring for him or her. The third group includes all

[302] Police, Crime, Sentencing and Courts Act 2022, s. 47.

[303] Sexual Offences (Amendment) Act 2000, s. 3.

[304] In *Lamb* [2007] EWCA Crim 1766, a 31-year-old teacher was prosecuted for allegedly kissing, on two occasions, 17-year-old sixth-form girls, with their consent, at balls celebrating the end of the school year. The proceedings involved a six-day trial in the Crown Court, at the end of which he was convicted and given a suspended sentence, and then a further hearing in the Court of Appeal, which ultimately quashed his conviction because of a misdirection on the evidence. Was this, one wonders, an appropriate use of scarce resources?

[305] SOA 2003, s. 25. The maximum sentence varies with the age of the defendant and the activity engaged in. If the defendant is over 18 years of age, and the activity involved "penetration of [V]'s anus or vagina . . . penetration of [V]'s mouth with a person's penis . . . penetration of a person's anus or vagina with a part of [V]'s body or by [V] with anything else, or . . . penetration of a person's mouth with [V]'s penis", the maximum penalty is 14 years' imprisonment and summary trial is unavailable: s. 25(4)(a). In other cases where the defendant is over 18, the maximum penalty is 14 years' imprisonment on indictment, or 6 months' imprisonment if tried summarily: s. 25(4)(b). If the defendant is under 18, the maximum penalty is 5 years' imprisonment on indictment, or 6 months' imprisonment if tried summarily: s. 25(5).

[306] *Ibid.*, s. 26. The maximum penalties are the same as under s. 25.

persons whatsoever who are currently living with the "victim" and are currently involved in providing care.

These offences were completely new: the previous law contained an offence of incest, but this was limited to vaginal intercourse between a small number of close relatives; the new law, by contrast, penalises a much wider range of sexual activity.[307] As with the "abuse of trust" offences, these offences overlap with the "under 16" offences, and their practical impact is limited to sexual acts with persons aged 16 and 17. As with the "abuse of trust" offences, this group of offences also potentially criminalises sexual conduct between persons whom the civil law permits to marry or form a civil partnership. Section 28 creates a defence for those who have done so.

## § 12.14 Sex with an adult relative

The offences discussed in the previous section are complemented by two further new offences concerning "sex with an adult relative". Section 64 makes it an offence for a person over 16 to perform an act of penetrative sex with another person who is a parent, grandparent, child, grandchild, brother, sister, half-brother, half-sister, uncle, aunt, nephew, or niece, and who is over the age of 18,[308] while section 65 creates a "passive" version of the same behaviour. The previous law contained a precursor to these offences in the crime of incest, which criminalised consensual sex between close relatives irrespective of their age, but these replacement offences go much further. First, whereas incest was limited to acts of vaginal intercourse, the new offences cover any form of penetrative sex (including oral sex). Secondly, whereas incest was limited to sexual intercourse between a narrow range of close relatives, the new offences extend to a wider list, including uncles and aunts and nephews and nieces, and—true to the policy of making the new law on sexual offences gender neutral—to sex between consenting males as well as to sex between consenting men and women.

It is a controversial issue whether sexual activity between consenting family members over the age of consent should be criminalised in its own right.[309] The arguments in favour of criminalisation often rest on questionable foundations.[310] One might think, for example, that the maintenance of a religious prohibition on certain relationships is a dubious basis for criminalisation in a modern liberal democracy such as ours. Similar issues arise in relation to a second argument: that such criminal offences protect the stability of the nuclear family. Is this end necessarily worth pursuit through the law and, if so, is a *criminal* prohibition necessary to pursue it? This second argument also proves too much: why not, on the same basis, criminalise familial misdeeds such as adultery, persistent drunkenness, and the like?

[307] For example, the behaviour in *F* [2008] EWCA Crim 2842, [2009] 2 Cr App R (S) 184 (24), where a 19-year-old received a three-year custodial sentence for putting his finger into the vagina of his 17-year-old sister, with her consent. Prior to the SOA 2003, no criminal offence would have been committed.

[308] A bizarre consequence of the offences being limited in this way appears to be that D could mount a defence along the lines that the Crown cannot prove the other person was over the age of 18 at the time.

[309] See: Bowsher, "Incest—Should Incest between Consenting Adults be a Crime?" [2015] *Crim LR* 208; Green, *Criminalizing Sex* (2020) chap. 14.

[310] See, further, Spencer, "Child and Family Offences" [2004] *Crim LR* 347, 356–8. For a critique of the reasons given by the Home Office for continuing to criminalise consensual sexual activity between adult relatives via the SOA 2003, see Roffee, "The Synthetic Necessary Truth behind New Labour's Criminalisation of Incest" (2014) 23 *Social & Legal Studies* 113.

Thirdly, the avoidance of genetic abnormalities in children (a justification for the previous offence of incest[311]) cannot justify the sweeping nature of the provisions described above. The provisions would cover mouth-to-mouth kissing between first cousins aged 17 who at some point in their life lived under the same roof, as well as homosexual sexual activity. Neither activity carries with it a risk of pregnancy, let alone genetic abnormality. Furthermore, this argument again proves too much: other significant risk factors for genetic abnormality in children (such as advanced maternal age) do not form the basis of criminal prohibitions on consensual sexual activity between adults.

At first glance, the fourth argument for criminalisation is stronger: that such relationships are *often* abusive (at least in terms of abuse of trust, if not physically), even if they are not *necessarily* so.[312] Crafting a criminal offence that would target only abusive relationships would, it may be argued, be too difficult. But such offences already exist—including offences of violence and the sexual offences mentioned above.[313] True, a prohibition of sexual activity between certain adult relatives (which avoids questions about abuse, injury, consent, etc.) makes successful prosecution simpler. But that is not a strong argument for *having* the crimes under sections 64–65 of the SOA 2003, unless the alternative offences gestured to above would be ineffective (an empirical matter that cannot be resolved here).

As Bergelson argues persuasively, what appears to do most of the work in justifying offences of incest (and similar offences such as those found in the SOA 2003) is a fifth "argument": that there is a societal taboo around such sexual activities—the "yuck" factor, as she evocatively describes it.[314] Connected with this taboo is the apparent social unacceptability of "legitimating" such sexual relationships through decriminalisation. The real question is whether these are, after all, justifications for (rather than explanations for the existence of) criminal offences that capture much activity that would, were the parties not related to one another, be recognised as consensual and legally unproblematic.[315] It is not clear that the answer is "Yes".

In *Stübing v Germany*,[316] a German law criminalising incest between consenting adults was challenged by a man who had been convicted after having consensual sexual intercourse with his adult sister. Though accepting that Article 8 of the Convention (the right to respect for a private life) was engaged, the European Court of Human Rights held that the German offence could be justified under Article 8(2), which permits the state to interfere with private lives where this is "necessary in a democratic society . . . for the protection of health or morals, or for the protection of the rights and freedoms of others". In so holding, the Court

[311] See Bailey and Blackburn, "The Punishment of Incest Act 1908: A Case Study in Law Creation" [1979] *Crim LR* 708, 715–7; Wolfram, "Eugenics and the Punishment of Incest Act 1908" [1983] *Crim LR* 308. By contrast, the Home Office described this argument as insignificant: *Setting the Boundaries—Reforming the Law on Sex Offences* (2000) para. 5.1.9.

[312] An argument emphasised in Temkin, "Do We Need a Crime of Incest?" (1991) 44 *CLP* 185. See, also, the versions of this argument presented throughout *Setting the Boundaries—Reforming the Law on Sex Offences* (2000) Part 5.

[313] In *Setting the Boundaries—Reforming the Law on Sex Offences* (2000) paras. 5.8.1–8, the Home Office argued that the offences under discussion here were necessary to provide "redress" for those who in later life realise that "the relationship they have been involved in has not been appropriate": which overlooks the fact that if the course of conduct began during the complainant's early life the defendant would be guilty of a range of other offences.

[314] Bergelson, "Vice Is Nice but Incest Is Best: The Problem of a Moral Taboo" (2013) 7 *Crim Law and Philosophy* 43.

[315] See, further, Hörnle, "Consensual Adult Incest: A Sex Offense?" (2014) 17 *New Crim LR* 76.

[316] (2012) 55 EHRR 24.

took into account, among other things, the risk of genetic abnormalities when children are born as a result of incestuous relationships. As noted above, the English offences, unlike the German one, extend to cover sexual acts from which the birth of children could not possibly result. Their justification under Article 8(2) would be less easily established.[317] In doctrine and in theory, then, there are strong reasons to doubt the place of offences such as those found in sections 64–65 of the SOA 2003 in contemporary English criminal law.

## § 12.15 Jurisdiction

Traditionally, the basic rule of English criminal law was *territoriality*.[318] To be punishable as a criminal offence in England and Wales, the act in question had to have taken place there. As Viscount Simonds put it in one case, "apart from those exceptional cases in which specific provision is made in regard to acts committed abroad, the whole body of the criminal law of England deals only with acts committed in England".[319] With the increasing ease of foreign travel in modern times has come a number of statutory exceptions. One important exception concerns sexual offences. Section 72 of the SOA 2003[320] gives the courts in England and Wales jurisdiction over a range of sexual offences involving children or young persons where these are committed outside the United Kingdom by a "United Kingdom national"[321] or by a person who is resident within the UK, provided that the behaviour also constitutes a criminal offence in country where it occurred.[322]

[317] See, further, Roffee, "No Consensus on Incest? Criminalisation and Compatibility with the European Convention on Human Rights" (2014) 14 *Human Rights LR* 541. Roffee concludes that ss. 64 and 65 of the SOA 2003 plausibly breach Art. 8 when read with the prohibition against discriminatory enjoyment of rights in Art. 14, but that the "application of the concept of margin of appreciation [in the ECtHR's jurisprudence] prevents this discussion from being heard" (572).

[318] See, generally, Hirst, *Jurisdiction and the Ambit of the Criminal Law* (2003).

[319] *Cox v Army Council* [1963] AC 48, 67.

[320] Re-enacting a rule first introduced by the Sex Offenders Act 1997.

[321] A term which s. 72(9) defines as British citizens, plus certain other stated groups.

[322] Where a limitation period on prosecution has expired in the other jurisdiction, this does not prevent a prosecution in England and Wales under s. 72: *DA* [2023] EWCA Crim 1428, [2024] 4 WLR 78.

# 13

# THEFT

## § 13.1 The criminalisation of theft and the recasting of the law in the 1960s

That theft is a crime is hardly controversial. Theft, or larceny (as it was formerly called in England and Wales and is still so-called in some jurisdictions), is a paradigmatic criminal offence the world over. Perhaps the issue ought to be more controversial than it is. For to argue that theft ought not to be a crime is not tantamount to a claim that there should be no *legal* regulation of stealing. Victims, a theft abolitionist might say, should be compensated of course, but that is a role for the civil law. So why not leave the matter to the civil law, by means of the torts of conversion or trespass to goods, etc.? Doing so would have the attractive consequence of removing the vast costs of prosecuting and punishing thieves—often with imprisonment—and doing so without depriving victims of a remedy.[1] Certainly, there is no shortage of arguments of various kinds against any such abolition of the crime of theft. One form of legal moralist would object that abolition of a criminal law of theft would mark a serious failure of the function of the criminal law, i.e., to achieve justice by punishing all and only those who are morally culpable for engaging in a culpable act.[2] Those who insist that criminalisation can only be legitimate if the terms of the harm principle are met, will argue that theft is, in the relevant sense, harmful and hence aptly criminalised.[3] A classical utilitarian,[4] or a proponent of a mixed theory of punishment,[5] might object that leaving the legal regulation of stealing to the civil law alone would weaken the deterrent effect of the law as a whole. Many more arguments could be brought to bear on the issue.[6] Even those who agree that compensation of victims should be the essential legal response to stealing might doubt, for practical reasons, that the civil law has sufficient resources for the task without the backing of the criminal law. Civil justice for many can be prohibitively expensive, and while some victims of theft will be in a position to pursue civil remedies—they may, for example, know the identity of the perpetrator and can afford to pay lawyers—others will lack the necessary financial resources and/or knowledge. To such victims of theft, compounding the practical unavailability of civil remedies with the absence of any criminal law response would appear a double injustice.

[1] Cp. below, § 16.5, on regulatory alternatives to criminalization.
[2] Moore, *Placing Blame* (1997) chs. 2–3.
[3] Simester and Sullivan, "On the Nature and Rationale of Property Offences" in Duff and Green (eds.), *Defining Crimes* (2005) 168, 170–3. Cp. Stanton-Ife, "Where is the Harm in Theft?" in Simester (ed.), *Modern Criminal Law* (2024) 123.
[4] Such as that found in Bentham, *An Introduction to the Principles of Morals and Legislation* (1789).
[5] Such as that contained in Hart, *Punishment and Responsibility* (2nd ed., 2008).
[6] See below, Chapter 16.

Whether or not the case for decriminalisation of theft ought to be taken more seriously, or is rightly discounted, there seems no foreseeable prospect of such a step being taken. If the criminalisation of theft is largely uncontroversial, however, the same is not true of the questions why, to what extent, and in what form theft should be criminalised. One influential understanding is that theft is legitimately criminalised to protect property rights.[7] This view is sometimes combined with scepticism about the role of dishonesty in theft: the dishonesty of a perpetrator's conduct should be relevant only in the technical sense of "claim of right", which evinces no disrespect to property rights. Accordingly, mistakes on the part of a defendant about the owner's consent or as to the content of civil law property rights ought to exculpate, but beyond that any moral notion of dishonesty should have no role. Another view stresses the morally dishonest nature of theft. In large measure what makes a thief's action criminally wrongful, the argument goes, *is* its dishonesty; hence the law should define theft in terms of dishonesty in order to recognise, build into, and uphold "a standard of character" in the property dealings of a society.[8] A third view is that theft is legitimately criminalised because it wrongfully interferes with the "sovereignty" of others.[9] Again, historically, the concern of larceny and theft lay in the threat posed to the King's peace by stealing, insofar as it raised the risk of retributive violence or public fear, a view that remains applicable today.[10] While these arguments are presented as rivals, an interesting question is how far a pluralist account of theft's legitimate criminalisation may be plausible.

Turning to the law of theft in England and Wales, a watershed moment came in the late 1960s. The old offence of larceny was abandoned and in its place the offence of theft was created. Theft is defined in section 1(1) of the Theft Act 1968, which radically recast this area of the law along lines proposed by the Criminal Law Revision Committee.[11] A prominent part in the preparation of this report was played by two of the most respected legal writers of the day: Professors Glanville Williams and J.C. Smith.[12] It is fascinating to read the (mostly negative) responses of both authors to the law as it developed through the interpretations of the courts in the decades immediately following the passing of the 1968 Act. In a nutshell, the complaint of both is that the actus reus of theft, in the hands of the highest courts, has been rendered too weak and insufficiently tethered to the civil law, while the mens rea of theft has been rendered too prominent, and in particular the element of dishonesty has become too moralised. In one of his last pronouncements, Williams speaks of "the danger

[7] Simester and Sullivan, "On the Nature and Rationale of Property Offences" in Duff and Green (eds.), *Defining Crimes* (2005) 168. Cp. *Smith, Hogan, and Ormerod* 896: "it is submitted that . . . the underlying purpose of theft . . . [is] to protect property, a civil law concept". This is in apparent tension with another claim made elsewhere in the same source—that "the criminal law is concerned with keeping the King's peace, not vindicating individual property rights" (*ibid.*, 915). Presumably, the two statements can be reconciled by holding that both protection of property and maintenance of the King's peace are legitimate concerns or purposes of the criminal law.

[8] Gardner, *Offences and Defences* (2007) 121. Duff argues that, while we can say that a defendant's action counts as theft because of the dishonesty it displays, the vice of dishonesty should here be understood only in an "etiolated" sense: Duff, "Virtue, Vice, and Criminal Liability: Do We Want an Aristotelian Criminal Law?" (2002) 6 *Buffalo Crim LR* 147, 172.

[9] Ripstein, "Beyond the Harm Principle" (2006) 34 *Philosophy and Public Affairs* 214, 231.

[10] Emphasised in Steel, "The Harms and Wrongs of Stealing" (2008) 31 *University of South Wales LJ* 712. Cp. *Lakeman* [2026] EWCA Crim 4, [2026] 2 WLR 696, [42].

[11] Criminal Law Revision Committee, Eighth Report, *Theft and Related Offences*, Cmnd. 2977 (1966).

[12] J.C. Smith (1922–2003) was the original author of *Smith's Law of Theft*, now in its ninth edition. Glanville Williams (1911–1997) reacted to the first decade and a half of judicial interpretation of the Theft Act 1968 in Part V of Williams, *TBCL*, and had a strong influence on A.T.H. Smith's major work, *Property Offences* (1994). For an account of the earlier law in its final stages, see Smith and Hogan, *Criminal Law* (1965).

of supposing that all difficulties can be resolved by invoking the idea of dishonesty", a supposition he plainly did not think the senior judiciary innocent of.[13] Smith's verdict on the first 30 years of the 1968 Act is contained in the title of his essay "The Sad Fate of the Theft Act 1968".[14] Why sad? Smith argued that the appellate courts had failed to interpret the Act in accordance with the intentions of its authors. Reluctant "to allow a manifestly dishonest person go free", the judges have recreated the muddle of the old law of larceny in the new law of theft. Smith bleakly concluded:[15]

> "It was said that under the law of larceny the judges interpreted the concept of possession in such a way as to allow the conviction of the dishonest person in the particular case before the court. This inevitably led to conflicting decisions and the muddle which cried out for reform. Much the same happened in relation to the notion of appropriation in the Theft Act."

As will be seen below, subsequent decades have provided further examples of such judicial missteps. Against this, might it be argued that the judiciary has made of the Theft Act 1968 a pragmatic, workable law of theft that discriminates appropriately between those deserving of criminal censure for stealing and those who do not, and which has stood the test of time? This appears to be the view of Lord Steyn in *Hinks*,[16] one of the landmark—and most controversial cases—that we consider below.

In the following sections, each of the elements of theft will be examined and critically engaged with in detail.

## § 13.2 The definition of theft

Theft is defined in section 1(1) of the Theft Act 1968. Section 1(1) provides:

> A person is guilty of theft if he dishonestly appropriates property belonging to another with the intention of permanently depriving the other of it; and "thief" and "steal" shall be construed accordingly.

The offence contains five elements, each of which must be proved by the prosecution. The first three elements comprise the actus reus:

(i) there must be *property* (i.e. something capable of being stolen);
(ii) that property must *belong* to another; and
(iii) D must *appropriate* the property.

The final two elements constitute the mens rea:

(iv) D must intend permanently to deprive another person of the property; and
(v) D must act dishonestly.

Each of these elements will be considered below.[17]

[13] "Note by Glanville Williams" in A.T.H. Smith, *Property Offences* (1994), x.
[14] J.C. Smith, "The Sad Fate of the Theft Act 1968" in Swadling and Jones (eds.), *The Search for Principle: Essays in Honour of Lord Goff of Chievely* (1999) 97.
[15] *Ibid.*, 113.
[16] [2001] 2 AC 241.
[17] For more detailed treatment, albeit now showing its age, see Ormerod and Williams, *Smith's Law of Theft* (9th ed., 2007).

## § 13.3 Property

A vast range of things can be stolen. Section 4(1) of the 1968 Act enacts a general rule that:

> "Property" includes any money and all other property, real or personal, including things in action and other intangible property.

This is an "inclusive not an exhaustive definition" of "the widest ambit"[18] and "should not be constrained to any greater extent than principle or policy requires".[19] Section 4 lists examples of what counts as property, while leaving it open that other examples may be recognised. The major change from the pre-1968 law relates to intangible property and land. Prior to 1968, at common law and under the Larceny Act 1916, land and intangible property had been excluded from the ambit of a larceny. The central element of the actus reus of larceny was "taking and carrying away" —something it is impossible to do to intangible property, and very difficult to do with land. This limitation is undone by section 4(1) of the 1968 Act. "Real property"—that is land, buildings and things forming part of the land—is explicitly included, albeit subject to strong qualification as will be seen below. Also included are "things in action"—that is rights that can be enforced by means of legal action—and "other intangible property." The most obvious inclusions to the eyes of the non-lawyer are undoubtedly "money", in the form of notes and coins in physical form, and "personal property" —such as tangible items like mobile phones and bicycles, but personal property is not necessarily restricted to tangible items. It can be understood simply as "all the property that is left once land—that is real property—has been subtracted."[20] If these terms are not already wide enough, section 4(1) also includes the residual term "all other property" placing beyond doubt the non-exhaustive nature of the kinds of property listed in the definition. Subject to certain exceptions in section 4(2)–(4), any type of property can be stolen. But it remains necessary to show (a) that the thing stolen is, in law, an item of property; and (b) that none of the exceptions apply.

### *(i) What counts as property?*

Most instances of theft are straightforward: D absconds with a flat screen television or some other chattel—a piece of tangible personal property. Other cases, however, may be less obvious. Suppose D usurps V's right of way, or takes a train ride without first buying a ticket. Are these cases of theft? In order to answer that question, we need first to know whether the thing taken is, in law, "property". That term itself is not defined by the Theft Act, and its definition will in large measure be a matter for the civil law, although the courts insist that the law of theft is ultimately free to come to its own understanding of what property is.[21] In what follows we will survey the main areas of difficulty.

#### *(a) Things in action and other intangible property*

A thing in action, also called a chose in action, is something in which the law acknowledges property rights but which has no physical existence. The rights cannot be asserted

[18] *Lakeman* [2026] EWCA Crim 4, [2026] 2 WLR 696, [55].
[19] *Ibid.*, [4].
[20] Bridge, *Personal Property Law* (4th ed., 2015), 10.
[21] *Lakeman* [2026] EWCA Crim 4, [2026] 2 WLR 696, [10]. See, further, below, § 13.3(i)(d).

physically and can be vindicated only by legal action (hence a thing "in action"). Examples of choses in action are a debt, shares in a company,[22] and a trade mark or copyright. Under section 4(1), all these things are capable of being stolen.

However, mere information, even a trade secret, does not qualify for protection as intangible property under the law of theft. In *Oxford v Moss*,[23] a university student took an examination paper before the examination and copied it before returning the paper to its original location. He was held not to have committed theft. Even though the information on the examination paper was no longer confidential, in the eyes of the law the university had not been deprived of any property. It would have been different if the student had not intended to return the examination paper itself, since he could then have been convicted of stealing the paper on which the examination was typed. The Court of Appeal in *Lakeman*[24] interpreted "pure information" in *Oxford v Moss* as meaning "simply knowledge" while giving two reasons why knowledge cannot qualify as property that can be stolen: first because it "exists simply in a person's head and independently of anything representing or recording it on any form of medium," and, secondly, because "the transfer of knowledge from A to B does not deprive A of that knowledge or A's ability to use it." Certainly, the passage of knowledge from A to B does not deprive A of the knowledge and probably not *some* ability on A's part to use it either, but it can severely curtail A's ability to use the knowledge. The facts of *Oxford v Moss* themselves illustrate this: an entire new examination paper had to be set. Can it not accurately be said that the student's conduct rendered the relevant information or knowledge effectively *useless* to the university?

Even where the right being interfered with is property for the purposes of the Act, the interference may not always count as theft. Breach of copyright, for instance, violates a chose in action. But photocopying a textbook does not deprive the copyright owner of the book. Neither does it deprive her of copyright in that book.[25]

There are hard questions of policy at issue here. Industrial espionage is a serious matter. Information can be worth an enormous amount of money. It may be the subject of contract, and its acquisition often involves the expenditure of considerable human and financial resources. We take it for granted that the recipe for Coca Cola is secret, both from us and from the manufacturer's competitors. Certainly it receives protection under the civil law, albeit not from the law of property.[26] Why not from the law of theft? In modern times, a nation's economic activity depends upon owners being able to protect the intangible rewards of their labours just as much as the tangible chattels they produce. The knowledge generated by research and development activities is vital to economic growth, and the case for criminalising theft of that knowledge is at least arguable.[27]

On the other hand, extending the law of theft to include the appropriation of information raises difficult questions concerning the proper scope of protection. Should all confidential

[22] Cp. *Grubb* [1915] 2 KB 683 (CA).

[23] (1979) 68 Cr App R 183 (DC).

[24] *Lakeman* [2026] EWCA Crim 4, [2026] 2 WLR 696, [52]–[53].

[25] Cp. *Lloyd* [1985] QB 829 (CA); *Rank Film Distributors Ltd v Video Information Centre* [1982] AC 380, 445; *Storrow and Poole* [1983] Crim LR 332 (Central Criminal Court).

[26] *Fraser v Thames Television* [1984] QB 44 (DC); *A-G v Observer Ltd* [1992] 1 AC 191. See, further, Stuckey, "The Equitable Action for Breach of Confidence: Is Information Ever Property?" (1981) 9 *Sydney LR* 402.

[27] See Cross, "Protecting Confidential Information under the Criminal Law of Theft and Fraud" (1991) 11 *OJLS* 264; Davies, "Protection of Intellectual Property—A Myth?" (2004) 68 *J Crim Law* 398. Compare the Model Penal Code, § 223.0(6): "'Property' means anything of value".

information be protected, or just trade secrets? When is information sufficiently confidential? What if the information is a matter of public interest?[28] An ingredient in theft is "intention permanently to deprive" (§ 13.7 below); how would that concept apply to theft of information? A number of statutes already criminalise certain types of "theft" of information;[29] further change, if needed, should come by legislation rather than judicial innovation.

*(b) Services*

A service is not property.[30] So, for example, a ride on a train cannot be stolen,[31] though D's activity may comprise some other offence such as obtaining services dishonestly;[32] and one may steal the piece of paper on which the ticket is printed.

*(c) Bank accounts*

The relationship between banker and customer is one of debtor and creditor[33] or, if the account is in overdraft, vice versa. Since debts are a type of chose in action, it follows that the customer's right to draw on a credit balance is property within the scope of section 4(1), and can be stolen. Additionally, an agreed overdraft facility, which has not been fully drawn down, gives the customer a legal right against the bank and so also constitutes a chose in action.[34]

The case of *Kohn*[35] provides a useful example. D was a director of company C, which had an account with bank B. D had signing authority on the company's account. He dishonestly drew cheques on that account for personal purposes, thereby causing C's account with B to be debited. D was convicted of theft: he had stolen C's right of action, against B, for the amount by which C's account was debited.

D was not, however, convicted of theft in respect of every cheque. Most of the cheques had been drawn when C's account was in credit or within the authorised overdraft limit. In these cases D appropriated C's chose in action. One cheque, however, was drawn when the account was in overdraft beyond the authorised limit. The Court of Appeal held that in the last situation there was no theft. If an account is overdrawn beyond its agreed limit, the bank has no legal obligation to meet the cheque. Hence, C had no chose in action against B, and there was nothing for D to steal.[36]

[28] Cp. Cripps, "The Public Interest Defence to the Action for Breach of Confidence and the Law Commission's Proposals on Disclosure in the Public Interest" (1984) 4 *OJLS* 361.
[29] See Spencer, "Blagging and the Criminal Law" [2018] 3 *Archbold Review* 4.
[30] *Bagley* (1924) 17 Cr App R 162 (CA).
[31] Cp. *Boulton* (1849) 1 Den 508, 169 ER 349; *Beecham* (1851) 5 Cox 181.
[32] Contrary to s. 11 of the Fraud Act 2006 – see below, § 15.7. Under s. 5(3) of the Railway Regulation Act 1889 it is a criminal offence to travel or attempt to travel without a ticket, or to intentionally travel beyond the point covered by a valid ticket, with intent to avoid payment of the fare; an offence now ferociously reinforced by ss. 17 and 18 of the Railway Byelaws 2005, which make it a criminal offence to travel without a valid ticket, even without fraudulent intent. Under Art. 143 of the Air Navigation Order 2009/3015 it is a criminal offence to be a stowaway upon an aircraft.
[33] *Foley v Hill* (1848) 2 HLC 28, 9 ER 1002.
[34] *Kohn* (1979) 69 Cr App R 395 (CA).
[35] *Ibid*. Cp. *Williams (Roy)* [2001] 1 Cr App R 362 (CT), in which D, a builder, dishonestly overcharged customers for work done. D's conviction for theft was upheld on the basis that, by presenting a customer's cheque for payment, he appropriated that customer's bank account (i.e. the chose in action held by that customer against the bank): but see now § 13.6(vi) below.
[36] Cp. *Navvabi* [1986] 3 All ER 102. D might, however, have been guilty of stealing the proceeds of the cheque, following the decision in *Gomez* (below, § 13.6(ii)).

In addition to the question of identifying what property is stolen, theft from a bank account also presents problems concerning the act of appropriation and the intention to deprive permanently. We consider these issues below, in § 13.6(vi) and § 13.7.

*(d) Digital assets*

The law of theft has shown itself able to adapt its understanding of property to changing historical circumstances. As bank accounts proliferated in the twentieth century, what is colloquially known as "money in the bank" was, as just seen, accommodated under the banner of "things in action" in addition to coins and notes, recognised in the 1968 Act simply as "money".[37] In the twenty-first century, as the proportion of life lived online increases, the question arises how far new forms of virtual asset should be recognised as property for the purposes of the law of theft. Digital assets[38] in the form of cryptocurrencies such as Bitcoin (that is, units of electronic data which those who hold them and those wishing to acquire them are prepared to treat as having monetary value), have been treated by the civil courts as property, at least for certain legal purposes. In *AA v Persons Unknown*,[39] for example, Bryan J decided that, although they were not choses in action, Bitcoins could still be the subject of proprietary injunctions, a decision since endorsed by the Court of Appeal in *Tulip Trading Ltd v Bitcoin Association BSV and Others.*[40] In Australia, in *Yeates (a pseudonym)*,[41] the Supreme Court of Appeal of Victoria held that Bitcoin is intangible property under the Crimes Act, whose definition of property is couched in identical terms to section 4 of the Theft Act. As well as Bitcoin and other cryptocurrencies, digital assets take many other forms such as in-game digital assets, digital carbon credits, cryptotokens, and so on.[42] Are these "property" for the purposes of the Theft Act?

The Court of Appeal, in *Lakeman*,[43] reflected in detail on the status as property of digital assets for the purposes of theft. D gained access to 68 accounts of players of the video game *Old School Runescape* and stripped those accounts of billions of "gold pieces". D then sold the "gold pieces" online to other players for both Bitcoin and regular "fiat" currency—the estimated real world trading value of the gold pieces standing at £543,123. The trial judge initially ruled that the "gold pieces" could not qualify as property and therefore could not be stolen. The starting point and central focus of the reasoning on which this initial ruling was based was the status of the "gold pieces" as property under *the civil law*, as it had been in the Australian case of *Yeates* (mentioned above in relation to Bitcoin). On a prosecution appeal against the trial judge's ruling, the Court of Appeal emphasized that, while the civil law position may provide "helpful indicia in the criminal context", it is not determinative.[44] The "starting point and the central focus" of any inquiry into the property status of digital assets for the purposes of theft ought, the Court held, to be the criminal law, specifically "the words of s. 4 of the Theft Act in the context of a statute seeking to criminalise the dishonest

[37] Theft Act 1968, s. 4(1).
[38] On which, see Haynes and Yeoh (eds.), *Law and Regulation of Cryptocurrencies and Cryptoassets* (2nd ed., 2025).
[39] [2019] EWHC 3556 (Comm). See, further, the note by Low at (2020) 136 *LQR* 345.
[40] [2023] EWCA Civ 83, [2023] 4 WLR 16.
[41] [2025] VSCA 288.
[42] Law Com. No. 412, *Digital Assets: Final Report* (2023).
[43] [2026] EWCA Crim 4, [2026] 2 WLR 696.
[44] *Ibid.*, [84].

taking of things".[45] Section 4(1) must be given the widest ambit possible, subject to considerations of principle or policy. The words that section contains are "apt to catch anything which can as a matter of normal use of language be described as capable of being stolen, unless there are good reasons why such a thing should be excepted".[46] The "gold pieces" could be so described, there being no good reason why they should be excepted. In support of this conclusion, the Court drew on the language used by the Privy Council in *A-G of Hong Kong v Nai-Keung*,[47] finding that the "gold pieces" were both "freely bought and sold" and were "clearly . . . the subject of dishonest dealing which deprive[d] the game player of the benefit they confer".[48]

By contrast, the trial judge's initial ruling in *Lakeman* had assumed the inquiry was largely into the civil law. The trial judge had applied the *Ainsworth* criteria[49] for determining when a thing counts as a property right in the civil law. These criteria—the thing must be definable, identifiable by third parties, capable in its nature of assumption by third parties, and have some degree of permanence or stability—were all said to apply to the "gold coins". So far, so good for the property status of the "gold coins". However, in order to count as a property right or interest, the trial judge thought that it was also necessary under the civil law that the thing be "rivalrous".[50] A thing is rivalrous "if the use or consumption of the thing by a person . . . necessarily prejudices the use or consumption of that thing by one or more other persons",[51] and the initial ruling that the "gold coins" were not property was in part based on its putative failure to meet this criterion—because "one gold piece is the same as any other, and their supply is infinite".[52] It was here that the Court of Appeal disagreed. Whatever the position under civil law, the civil law is not "determinative" of what is "property for the purposes of the definitions in the Theft Act."[53]

Before returning briefly to the implications of the Court's stance on the civil–criminal divide in this context, another issue of potential general importance to the status of digital assets as property was considered in *Lakeman*. The trial judge's initial ruling that the "gold pieces" were not property was based not only on the putative failure to satisfy the rivalrous criterion, but also on the basis that they were akin to pure information under *Oxford v Moss*.[54] The argument, as stated (but not endorsed) by the Law Commission, is that "all digital things are nothing more than strings of (alphanumerical) data, represented in code by a stored sequence of bytes. On this analysis, those digital things could be said to be nothing more than pure information",[55] and therefore not property. The Court of Appeal rejected this form of argument in *Lakeman*, by drawing a distinction between a digital asset "as a visual and functional thing" and "the code which gives rise to its visual manifestation and functionality".[56] It is the former that the prosecution was arguing constituted property

[45] *Ibid.*, [39].
[46] *Ibid.*, [84]. Exceptions include those already contained in section 4, the pure information principle (above, §13.3(i)(a)) and corpses and body parts (below, §13.3(i)(e)).
[47] [1987] 1 WLR 1339 (PC).
[48] [2026] EWCA Crim 4, [2026] 2 WLR 696, [56].
[49] *National Provincial Bank v Ainsworth* [1965] AC 1175, 1247–1248.
[50] In *Tulip Trading* [2023] EWCA Civ 83, [2023] 4 WLR 16, the Court held that a cryptocurrency like Bitcoin is property specifically because it is rivalrous and capable of assumption by a third party.
[51] Law Com. No. 412, *Digital Assets: Final Report* (2023), para. 4.28.
[52] [2026] EWCA Crim 4, [2026] 2 WLR 696, [20].
[53] *Ibid.*, [46].
[54] *Ibid.*, [21].
[55] Law Com. No. 416, *Digital Assets as Personal Property. Supplemental Report and Draft Bill* (2024), para. 2.28.
[56] [2026] EWCA Crim 4, [2026] 2 WLR 696, [35].

for the purposes of theft: "Although the gold pieces exist in a virtual world they have a real world existence which manifests itself not only in their appearance and use on the screen but in real world trading. They are real functional things distinct from the code which creates them."[57] This argument can be applied generally to digital assets as and when their status as property comes to be considered.

Returning to the question of the place of the civil law in determining what is property for the purposes of theft, the Court firmly rejected a defence argument that the "gold pieces" could not in the relevant sense be "freely bought and sold" because out-of-game purchasing and selling of them was contractually forbidden. The defendant had sold these assets, as observed above, for fiat currency and Bitcoin, but on the black market, which could not be classed as "free" sale. Countering this argument, the Court pointed out that Class A drugs are property within the meaning of the Theft Act, notwithstanding the fact that they cannot lawfully be bought and sold (with limited exceptions).[58] In *Smith*,[59] for example, D had been convicted of robbing another person of some heroin, the robbery requiring proof of a theft. The Court of Appeal rejected there the argument that the law of theft did not apply to property that it was illegal to possess. The Court in *Lakeman* concluded that the "principle to be applied in the present appeal" is that "the criminal law is concerned with keeping the [King's] peace, not vindicating individual property rights".[60]

The property status of other in-game assets and digital assets in general will need to be examined on a case-by-case basis, along the lines spelled out in *Lakeman*.[61] The case joins other well-known decisions on the Theft Act—such as *Turner (No. 2)* and *Hinks*—in asserting the ultimate independence of the criminal law from the civil law while interpreting the actus reus of theft. Is seems doubtful that this distinction will lead to discord. It is notable that, for all of its stress on the right of the criminal law to come to its own understanding of "property", the Court in *Lakeman* put no little energy into examining the civil law in order to argue, *pace* the trial judge's initial ruling, that the civil law criteria *were* in fact met so that the "gold coins" *were* property in civil law terms.[62] While, on the Court's view, the civil law gives no more than "helpful *indicia* in the criminal context", if their own example is to be followed, considering such *indicia* in the future will be a task that needs to be taken very seriously by the courts in determining which digital assets count as property for the purposes of theft.

### (e) Body parts

Some things, though corporeal, cannot be owned at all. At common law this included wild animals (*ferae naturae*) when at large,[63] and the human body, even when deceased;[64]

[57] *Ibid.*, [30].
[58] *Ibid.*, [56].
[59] [2011] EWCA Crim 66; [2011] 1 Cr App R 30.
[60] A quotation from Ormerod and Williams, *Smith's Law of Theft* (9th ed., 2007) 80, cited by Lord Judge CJ in *Smith* [2011] EWCA Crim 66, [2011] 1 Cr App R 30, [10].
[61] [2026] EWCA Crim 4, [2026] 2 WLR 696, [79].
[62] Parliament, in passing the Property (Digital Assets etc.) Act 2025, has decided against setting any authoritative list of digital assets that count as property under the civil law, in favour of legislation designed to facilitate the flexible development of the law by the courts.
[63] Even a landowner does not own or possess the wild animals on his land. Cp. *Howlett and Howlett* [1968] Crim LR 222 (CA).
[64] *Williams v Williams* (1880) 20 Ch D 659, 662 (extending to a corpse the logic of the proposition that a live human body cannot be subject to ownership).

so a human corpse could not be stolen, by contrast with the corpse of a farm animal.[65] The position with regard to animals is now covered by section 4(4) (see below, § 13.3(ii)(c)). However, the question of the human body or body parts is not covered in the Theft Act, and remains somewhat uncertain. There is an interim right to possession (not ownership) of a corpse which vests in those charged with its burial.[66] Apart from this, the courts have recognised a limited possessory right in a corpse or body part if being used as a medical specimen or as an exhibit in a museum, at least where the item has acquired different attributes by undergoing a lawful application of skill (e.g. dissection or embalming).[67]

The fact that there may be certain limited rights to a corpse or parts thereof does not resolve the question whether that corpse or its parts can be stolen. The problem can be summarised as follows. First, although there may be possessory rights in some circumstances, it appears those rights do not amount to full ownership. And if parts of dead bodies are incapable of being owned, then it is arguable that they are not *property* within section 4(1), and therefore cannot be stolen.[68]

The contrary position is that since possession is one of the rights of ownership, such limited rights as may be had in body parts or a corpse nonetheless amount to *property* rights, enforceable by proprietary remedies, which fall short of ownership.[69] They are rights *in rem*,[70] enforceable against third parties. And since limited property rights are available, this suggests that, arguably, a corpse *is* property, albeit property that is incapable of being owned. That this second analysis may now represent the law was accepted by the Court of Appeal in *Kelly* when upholding the defendants' convictions on the narrower basis that the parts in question were medical specimens.[71] In our view, the second analysis is to be preferred generally: a taking of a corpse or body part in contravention of any property right suffices. Adopting such analysis has the practical advantage of allowing a conviction for theft when, say, a corpse is stolen from the executors. Even if this is accepted, however, a second problem for the law is to identify *when* such rights can arise. For example, it remains unclear under present law whether anyone has a property right to a human embryo or to a body part designated for transplant surgery;[72] and thus whether such items can be stolen. It is certainly arguable that such items deserve the protection of the criminal law.[73]

[65] *Edwards* (1877) 13 Cox CC 384.

[66] *Calma v Sesar* (1992) 106 FLR 446; *Dobson v North Tyneside HA* [1996] 4 All ER 474, 478 (CA).

[67] *Kelly* [1999] QB 621 (CA); applying *Doodeward v Spence* (1908) 6 CLR 406. In the latter case, Griffith CJ was careful not to say that a corpse could be owned, but rather that it could be in the lawful possession of someone, and that the law would protect that lawful possession. Note that preserving a brain in paraffin prior to a post-mortem examination was held not to turn it into an item in which others could have a right of possession or property in *Dobson v North Tyneside HA* [1996] 4 All ER 474 (CA). See Maclean, "Resurrection of the Body Snatchers" (2000) 150 *NLJ* 174.

[68] Even though s. 5(1) of the Theft Act 1968 provides that for the purposes of theft, "property shall be regarded as belonging to any person having possession or control of it, or having in it any proprietary right or interest", this does not dispense with the separate requirement in ss. 1 and 4 that the thing stolen be property.

[69] Cp. de Stoop, "The Law in Australia Relating to the Transplantation of Organs from Cadavers" (1974) 48 *ALJ* 21, 22.

[70] I.e. a right that held *in respect of* a particular thing and which is enforceable against others generally (e.g. ownership of a car); by contrast with a right *in personam*, which is enforceable only against particular persons (e.g. a debt).

[71] [1999] QB 621 (CA).

[72] See, e.g., Andrews, "The Legal Status of the Embryo" (1986) 32 *Loyola LR* 257.

[73] Lavoie, "Ownership of Human Tissue: Life after *Moore v Regents of the University of California*" (1989) 75 *Virginia LR* 1363. See also Wall, "The Legal Status of Body Parts: a Framework" (2011) 31 *OJLS* 783; and Singh, "The Body as Me and Mine: The Case for Property Rights in (Attached) Body Parts" (2021) 66 *McGill LJ* 565.

In *Yearworth v North Bristol NHS Trust*,[74] the Court of Appeal were faced, in the context of a civil action for negligence, with the related question whether property rights exist in products of a living body: in this case, frozen sperm stored in a sperm bank, which negligent storage by the defendant's employees had allowed to perish. A powerful court consisting of the Lord Chief Justice, the Master of the Rolls, and a Lord Justice of Appeal decided the question in the affirmative, and ruled that the men's claim was therefore entitled to succeed. In this case they might have reached their decision by applying the reasoning in *Kelly* and related cases—namely that in principle there is no property in sperm, but an exception applies where it has undergone treatment (in this case, freezing)—but they declined to do so. Instead, they decided the case on the broader basis that "for the purposes of their claims in negligence, the men had ownership of the sperm which they ejaculated". As well as deciding the point in relation to products of the living body, and presumably amputated parts of living bodies too,[75] this case casts further doubt on the correctness of the traditional reasoning in respect of ownership of dead bodies and their parts, suggesting the possibility that the courts in future might discard it altogether.

With that said interference with such things as body parts is arguably not the sort of wrongdoing for which property offences are the suitable means of control, and warrants criminalisation by means of separate, more specific legislation: as already exists with the Human Tissue Act 2004, which allows certain persons a right to possess body parts in particular circumstances (while making it a criminal offence for them to do so when the procedures laid down by the Act have not been followed).[76]

### *(f) Electricity, gas, and water*

Electricity, like other forms of energy such as heat,[77] is not property. In *Low v Blease*,[78] D broke into a house and sought to warm himself by switching on the electric fire. He was held not guilty of burglary; he had not entered with intent to steal because the electricity consumed by the fire could not be stolen. Section 13 of the 1968 Act accordingly enacts a separate offence of dishonestly abstracting electricity.

Gas, on the other hand, is property and can be stolen.[79] The same is true for water that has been placed in a container such as a pipe.[80] Water in a lake or pond is a severable part of the land on which it stands,[81] and is therefore subject to the rules governing theft of land (below).

### *(g) Identity*

Although "identity theft" is a phrase in common usage, a person's identity is not considered to be their property for the purpose of the law of theft. Neither need it be, because "identity

[74] [2009] EWCA Civ 37, [2010] 2 QB 1; Quigley, "Property: The Future of Human Tissue?" (2009) 17 *Medical LR* 457.

[75] At [45(d)], the Court of Appeal suggested that a surgeon presented with a finger amputated in a factory accident who then negligently damaged it before starting the medical procedure to reattach it would be liable, whether or not the finger had been the subject of any preliminary work that had "changed its attributes".

[76] And with the Sexual Offences Act 2003, s. 70 (creating a specific offence of necrophilia); and see also Spencer, "Criminal Liability for the Desecration of a Corpse" [2004] 6 *Archbold News* 7.

[77] *Clinton v Cahill* [1998] NI 200.

[78] [1975] Crim LR 513 (DC).

[79] *White* (1853) Dears 203, 169 ER 696; *Firth* (1869) LR 1 CCR 172.

[80] *Ferens v O'Brien* (1883) 11 QBD 21.

[81] Burn, *Cheshire and Burn's Modern Law of Real Property* (18th ed., 2011) 163.

thieves" usually impersonate others with a view to gain, which makes them guilty of the crime of fraud (discussed in Chapter 15 below). In addition, by statute there exists a range of specific offences of "personation", of which the impersonator is guilty even if his motive is not financial.[82]

### *(ii) The exceptions in section 4(2)–(4)*

Notwithstanding the general rule in section 4(1) that any type of property can be stolen, section 4 contains provisions applicable where the subject matter of the theft is real property, a plant growing wild, or a wild animal.

#### *(a) Land*

The ruling in section 4(1) that real property can be stolen is significantly qualified by section 4(2), which provides:

A person cannot steal land, or things forming part of land and severed from it by him or by his directions, except in the following cases, that is to say—

(a) when he is a trustee or personal representative, or is authorised by power of attorney, or as a liquidator of a company, or otherwise, to sell or dispose of land belonging to another, and he appropriates the land or anything forming part of it by dealing with it in breach of the confidence reposed in him; or

(b) when he is not in possession of the land and appropriates anything forming part of the land by severing it or causing it to be severed, or after it has been severed; or

(c) when, being in possession of the land under a tenancy, he appropriates the whole or part of any fixture or structure let to be used with the land.

Section 4(2)(a) covers trustees and the like[83] who fraudulently convert land in breach of the terms under which the land is entrusted to them.[84] Section 4(2)(b) makes it possible for anyone to steal part of the land—including fixtures, plants, trees, and soil—by severing the item from the land, or by appropriating it after severance.[85] Under section 4(2)(c), a tenant is capable of stealing fixtures and structures which he removes from the property.[86]

The exceptions leave intact the general rule, which is that a person, however dishonest, does not commit theft by entering upon another person's land with a view to making it his own. At the date when the Theft Act was passed it was widely felt that such behaviour should not fall within the ambit of the criminal law. This was largely because a squatter who succeeds in staying put for 12 years can thereby acquire legal title and it was thought that, if the conduct was capable of transferring ownership it could not properly be treated as a

[82] For a list, see *Archbold* (2026) § 22-76–22-82.
[83] Cp. *Daniels v Daniels* [1978] Ch 406 (company directors).
[84] In *Gimbert* [2018] EWCA Crim 2190, [2019] 2 WLR 72, a prosecution for theft of land relying on this provision failed (paradoxically) because the power of attorney turned out to be invalid. On the facts, D was clearly guilty of fraud by abuse of position: see § 15.5 below.
[85] Cp. *Foley* (1889) 17 Cox CC 142 (grass); *Skujins* [1956] Crim LR 266 (Oxford County Quarter Sessions) (farm gate); *Carver v Pierce* (1648) Style 66, 82 ER 534 (dung).
[86] For discussion of some of the difficulties and anomalies associated with s. 4(2) see A.T.H. Smith, *Property Offences* (1994) § 3.34ff.

theft: a once scrupulous attitude towards the need for compatibility between the civil and the criminal law which, as we shall see later in this chapter, is nowadays very much dissipated.[87] Meanwhile, although the general rule is still that land cannot be stolen, in the years since 1968 Parliament has repeatedly intervened to render criminal various different forms of civil trespass: as in 2012, with an offence of squatting in a residential building, and again in 2022, with a new offence of squatting on land in a vehicle.[88]

*(b) Things growing wild*

At common law, things growing wild are part of the land on which they grow. Prima facie, therefore, under section 4(2)(b) anything growing wild on land can be stolen through being severed from the land or, once severed, through being then appropriated by D. However, section 4(3) creates a further restriction:

> A person who picks mushrooms growing wild on any land, or who picks flowers, fruit or foliage from a plant growing wild on any land, does not (although not in possession of the land) steal what he picks, unless he does it for reward or for sale or other commercial purpose.
>
> For purposes of this subsection "mushroom" includes any fungus, and "plant" includes any shrub or tree.

In essence, this means that D is exempt from liability provided:

(i) he removes *part* of the plant (not the whole, unless it is a mushroom);
(ii) the plant is growing *wild* (not cultivated);
(iii) he *picks* it (rather than, say, chops it down); and
(iv) he does so for a non-commercial purpose (for example, to make jam for personal consumption).

*(c) Wild creatures*

At common law a wild creature is owned by no one, and so cannot be stolen.[89] However, if such an animal is captured or killed, the person on whose land the capture or killing occurs thereupon acquires ownership of the creature.[90] Consequently, any subsequent appropriation of the animal or its carcass would prima facie be a theft. Section 4(4) abrogates this result for the purposes of the 1968 Act:

> Wild creatures, tamed or untamed, shall be regarded as property; but a person cannot steal a wild creature not tamed nor ordinarily kept in captivity, or the carcase or any such wild creature, unless either it has been reduced into possession by or on behalf of another person and possession of it has not since been lost or abandoned, or another person is in course of reducing it into possession.

[87] Below, § 13.6.

[88] Legal Aid, Sentencing and Punishment of Offenders Act 2012, s. 144. See Cobb, "Property's Outlaws: Squatting, Land Use and Criminal Trespass" [2012] *Crim LR* 114. The current list of offences of criminal trespass are summarised in a document on the Crown Prosecution Service website entitled "Trespass and Nuisance on Land": (see https://www.cps.gov.uk/legal-guidance/trespass-and-nuisance-land).

[89] Cp. *Cresswell v DPP* [2006] EWHC 3379 (Admin), [2007] Env LR D8: badgers not reduced into possession are not property (either at common law or in the context of s. 10 of the Criminal Damage Act 1971). There are, however, a number of specific offences of poaching: see *Blackstone's Criminal Practice* (2026), § B.13.96.

[90] *Blades v Higgs* (1865) 11 HL Cas 621, 11 ER 1474.

It follows that a wild creature may be stolen only if: (i) it is tamed or ordinarily kept in captivity; or (ii) it has been reduced into and remains in another person's possession; or (iii) it is in the process of being reduced into possession by another person. By way of example, domestic pets or the animals in a zoo are capable of being stolen, since they are (i) tamed or ordinarily kept in captivity. Bees that return to a hive can also be stolen, not because they are tamed or kept but because (ii) they have been reduced into possession (and possession has not since been lost). A poacher, on the other hand, does not steal the rabbit he captures. But if a second person, D, takes the rabbit from the poacher when the latter is (iii) in the process of capturing it, D then steals the rabbit.[91]

To count as property, the thing in question must be something capable of being owned. The fact that the victim of the alleged theft herself committed a criminal offence by owning or possessing it is, of course, irrelevant. So where three villains attacked a drug dealer and forcibly took his heroin, they committed robbery[92] (that is, theft accompanied by violence).[93]

## § 13.4 Belonging to another (I)—the basics

It is impossible to steal property from oneself.[94] Some other person must have an interest in the subject matter of the theft before that item can be stolen. This is not to deny that D can steal something she owns. While D may be the owner, other persons may have an immediate right to possession or control, or some proprietary interest that can be asserted against the owner: V, say, may have a lien,[95] or some other interest in the property. In such a case the property can be stolen by D (or by anyone else). But if D is the absolute owner of the property, so that no one else is joint owner or has any lesser proprietary right or a right to possession or control, she cannot steal it. It does not "belong to another" for the purposes of section 1 of the Act.

The meaning of "belonging to another" is elaborated in section 5. The key provision is section 5(1):

> Property is to be regarded as belonging to any person having possession or control of it, or having in it any proprietary right or interest (not being an equitable interest arising only from an agreement to transfer or grant an interest).

In general, this means that for the purposes of theft an item "belongs" to everyone with any form of proprietary interest in the item, whatever the nature of that interest—i.e. whether it be a right of ownership or possession, or a proprietary interest existing only at equity. Generally speaking, therefore, D commits the actus reus of a theft whenever he appropriates property in which someone else has a proprietary interest.

It may seem natural to assume that a proprietary interest must always mean a proprietary interest *under the civil law*. Doubt has been cast on this proposition by the Court of

[91] This extends the common law, which formerly required that the reduction into possession be completed before the animal or carcass could be stolen. See *Roe* (1870) 11 Cox 554.

[92] *Smith* [2011] EWCA Crim 66, [2011] 1 Cr App R 30.

[93] As is explained below, § 14.3.

[94] Although, remarkably, one can steal property by the very act of acquiring absolute ownership of it: *Hinks* [2001] 2 AC 241. See further below, § 13.6(ii)(c).

[95] See below, § 13.4(ii).

Appeal in *Lakeman*,[96] where it is asserted that not all aspects of the definition of "belonging to another" depend on the civil law as to proprietary interests in property. While the Court acknowledged that "some aspects of that definition undoubtedly depend upon the civil law as to proprietary interests in property" the judgment firmly asserted the ultimate independence of the criminal law: "In particular property can belong to another when it is in the control of that other, and control need not connote any private law proprietary interest." Possession and control are said by the Court to be "factual concepts", which are "not qualified by or dependent upon any legal right to possess or control. They do not depend upon such possession or control being lawful as a matter of civil law."[97] Arguably the comments are *obiter* since the ruling in *Lakeman*—that "gold coins" in the video game *Old School Runescape* are property for the purposes of the law of theft—does not depend on them. However they are a robust statement of the thinking of the Court on the matter.[98] While for the most part the question of when property "belongs to another" is a matter of civil law definition, the criminal law of theft, it appears, is free to depart from any such definition for its own purposes. If that is correct, is this a desirable state of affairs, or another symptom of what JC Smith decried as judicial reluctance "to allow a manifestly dishonest person go free" even at the cost of inconsistency and conflict in the law?[99] The issue mirrors the controversy over the interpretation of appropriation under section 3 and indeed the Court of Appeal *in Lakeman* adapted the arguments of the majority of the House of Lords in *Hinks* in favour of the analogous position as regards the term "belonging to another".[100]

The rule stated here gives rise to a number of special cases, which benefit by further discussion here and in § 13.5.

### *(i) What interests are protected by section 5?*

We have noted that section 5(1) protects virtually any form of proprietary interest, whether of ownership or possession, and whether at common law or equity and possibly as a "factual concept" that does not depend on the civil law.[101] Although the section mentions "possession *or* control", it is not clear that the latter term adds much. Physical control would in any event also constitute a possessory interest, and, at least where proprietary interests are taken to be civil law interests, any other right of control would presumably only qualify if it were enforceable *in rem*, i.e. if it were a proprietary interest.

On the other hand, equitable proprietary interests should be distinguished from interests that may arise when D enters into an agreement to sell goods to V on some future date. The provision in section 5(1) makes it clear that the latter sort of interest is not protected, by contrast with contracts of sale that transfer ownership immediately. Hence if, before the agreed date of the future transfer to V, D were to resell the goods to T, D would not commit theft from V.

The inclusion of equitable proprietary interests has opened the way for a significant expansion of the scope of theft in recent years, given the important role of the constructive

[96] [2026] EWCA Crim 4, [2026] 2 WLR 696, [55].
[97] *Ibid.*, [43].
[98] Cp. *Woodman* [1974] QB 754, 758 (CA); *Turner (No 2)* [1971] 1 WLR 901, 904 (CA); *Kelly* [1999] QB 621, 631 (CA).
[99] Above, § 13.1.
[100] On which see below, § 13.6.
[101] *Lakeman* [2026] EWCA Crim 4, [2026] 2 WLR 696, [43].

trust in modern civil law. Because of the complexity of the law of constructive trusts, we will deal with this topic separately, in § 13.5.

### *(ii) Theft by an owner under section 5(1)*

As we have mentioned, one implication of section 5(1) is that even an owner may commit theft, provided the victim of the theft is deprived of an interest recognised under section 5. This might occur in a case where someone else has a lien[102] over the goods. In the New Zealand case of *Cox*,[103] a garage repairing a car had a lien over it. D dishonestly retrieved the car and was convicted of theft, as the lien had conferred a possessory interest. Similarly, in *Slowly*[104] V sold onions to D, for which he had not yet been paid. Until paid, V (being a seller in possession) was entitled to assert a lien over the goods.[105] Accordingly, D's dishonest taking of the goods was theft. Similarly in *Rose v Matt*,[106] the owner of a travelling clock deposited it as security for the price of unpaid goods but then later removed it from the shop when nobody was looking. He had stolen the clock.

Another standard case in which an owner may commit theft is if there is more than one owner. If D and V are co-owners of a chattel and D dishonestly sells the chattel, D is guilty of theft. Similarly, it has been ruled that a partner may be convicted of theft of property belonging to the partnership.[107]

### *(iii) Theft by an absolute owner? When D's interest is better than V's*

In principle, there should be one important exception to the general proposition that property may be stolen from anyone having a proprietary interest therein. Consider the following, fairly straightforward, case:

> Suppose that V is a thief who has stolen a television set from D. D remains absolute owner of the television, but while in possession V has a lesser proprietary (possessory) interest in the television, which he may maintain against anyone save D. V's interest is sufficient for the property to belong to V under section 5(1). Consequently, if T dishonestly removes the television from V's house, T is himself guilty of stealing from V (and D).[108]

Now the exception. In a case of this sort, D—the owner—should not be held to have stolen the television by retaking it from V. This is because V has no property right in the television maintainable against D. *Vis-à-vis* D, the television belongs to no one else. By contrast, *vis-à-vis* T, the television belongs to both D and V; hence T can steal it from V and from D.[109]

[102] That is, a right to retain possession that is enforceable even against the owner until some condition is met: *Hammonds v Barclay* (1802) 2 East 227, 235, 102 ER 356, 359.

[103] [1923] NZLR 596.

[104] (1873) 12 Cox 269.

[105] Sale of Goods Act 1979, s. 39; *Dennant v Skinner* [1948] 2 KB 164 (DC).

[106] [1951] 1 KB 810 (DC).

[107] *Bonner* [1970] 1 WLR 838 (CA).

[108] *Buckley v Gross* (1863) 3 B & S 566, 122 ER 213; *Daniel v Rogers* [1918] 2 KB 228, 234 (CA); *Parker v British Airways Board* [1982] QB 1004, 1009 (Donaldson LJ) (CA).

[109] A helpful illustration of the priority of interests is *Costello v Chief Constable of Derbyshire* [2001] All ER 150 (CA). D was in possession of a stolen car that was seized by the police. The owner, however, could not be traced. In those circumstances, the Court held that D was entitled to recover the car from the police, because he had better title to the car than anyone apart from the original owner.

One illustration of this exception is the Crown Court decision in *Meredith*.[110] D's car had been impounded by the police and removed to a police station. Without consent, D then recovered his car from the police station. D was acquitted of theft, after the trial judge ruled that the police had no right to retain possession of the car against the owner.

Obvious as all this may seem, there is appellate authority to the contrary. In *Turner (No. 2)*,[111] D had taken his car to a garage for repair. Subsequently and dishonestly, he recovered the car without paying for the repairs. D was convicted of theft. Prima facie, this looks right: the car surely "belonged to" the garage for the purpose of section 5(1), since the garage would have been entitled to assert a lien over the car until the repairs were paid for.[112] Unfortunately, the trial judge directed the jury to disregard the issue of liens. Consequently, the Court of Appeal was obliged to consider D's appeal on the footing that there was no lien. The Court nonetheless upheld the conviction, reasoning that even as a mere bailee at will, the garage had a possessory interest in the car (maintainable against anyone except D) sufficient to qualify for section 5(1). According to the Court of Appeal, "there is no ground for qualifying the words 'possession or control' in any way", i.e. by excluding from section 5(1) any proprietary interests inferior to those of the defendant.

The decision is absurd.[113] If no lien existed, the car belonged to D and D alone. The gist of theft is interference with someone else's property rights. D did no such thing. He merely exercised proprietary rights to which he was entitled (albeit in order to evade a debt).

### *(iv) Has D become an absolute owner?*

Assuming that an absolute owner cannot steal her own goods, and subject to section 5(2)–(4),[114] cases will often arise when D acquires possession or control of property innocently enough but subsequently, and dishonestly, decides to keep it from the person from whom the property was acquired. For example:

> D enters into a hire-purchase contract with V Ltd. to acquire a television set. She takes the television set home, intending to honour the agreement. However, a few months later, she finds herself in financial difficulties. She stops paying V Ltd., sells the television, and pockets the proceeds.

In this case, D steals the television set when she offers it for sale.[115] In a hire-purchase agreement, possession passes but the property in the goods remains with the seller until all instalments have been paid. Thus an on-sale by the hirer–possessor is theft. Likewise, borrowing something, and then keeping it having decided not to return it, may amount to theft—on the basis of the keeping rather than the borrowing—since the borrower legitimately acquires possession but does not acquire ownership.

110 [1973] Crim LR 253 (CA). Cp. Model Penal Code, § 223.0(7): "'property of another' includes property in which any person other than the actor has an interest *which the actor is not privileged to infringe*" (emphasis added).

111 [1971] 2 All ER 441 (CA).

112 Cp. *Cox* [1923] NZLR 596; above, § 13.4(ii).

113 The same adjective is used in A.T.H. Smith, *Property Offences* (1994) § 4–43. A factor underlying the decision may have been that, as the rules of criminal procedure then stood, the result of quashing the defendant's conviction would have been that a man who was almost certainly guilty was acquitted; since 1988, however, the Court of Appeal has had a general power when quashing a conviction to order a retrial.

114 Below, § 13.5(ii)–(iv).

115 Below, § 13.6(i).

However, other cases may be more difficult:

> D purchases a table from V on one month's credit. When he takes delivery of the table, D intends to honour his obligation to V. Later, however, D decides not to pay. He sells the table to T, an innocent third party, and absconds with the cash.

Does D steal the table? The general rule is that if V—the person from whom the property is acquired—retains ownership or some other interest in the property, D will be guilty of theft by his later dishonest appropriation of the goods. Otherwise, if V delivers the goods and transfers property in them to D, who subsequently forms the intent not to pay for them, D does not commit theft. It is therefore crucial to determine whether, and at what point in time, D has become the owner of property that formerly belonged to V. Apart from some specific provisions in section 5(2)–(4) of the Theft Act 1968, to be considered in due course, the criminal law provides no answer to this question, which must be decided by reference to civil law rules.

This point is of central importance. In principle, consistency of criminal law and civil law concepts is essential in theft, which after all is concerned with the protection of property rights.[116] It would be unsatisfactory if D could be convicted of theft when she had not in fact interfered with V's property rights. As Williams writes, "the object of the law of theft is to attach a penal sanction to certain violations of property rights; so (it may be urged) if there is no violation of property rights under the general (civil) law, there should be no theft".[117] It was said in this text, as far back as Chapter 1, that there ought to be no criminalisation without harm.[118] In theft, the relevant harm is infringement of another's property rights. Protection against that harm *is the very purpose* of criminalising theft. The rights (specifically, ownership and possession) which are protected are creatures of civil law. Therefore, unless those civil law rights are in fact infringed, the harm does not occur and theft should not lie.

In deciding whether ownership has passed already to D for the purposes of section 5(1), there are two principal issues. One is to ascertain whether title has prima facie passed, or whether D merely has possession. Here one needs to look at the terms of the agreement between V and D, in particular whether V has reserved some property right in the goods.

The second issue is that, even where a prima facie transfer of title has been identified, the transfer may be vitiated. In general, there are three ways in which this may occur. First, the transaction may be induced by D's wrongful duress, fraud, false pretences, etc. In such cases, any title acquired by D will be at least voidable, if not void, and the transaction can constitute theft.[119] Secondly, even though D has not induced the transaction by any wrongdoing,

[116] Cp. J.C. Smith, "Civil Law Concepts in the Criminal Law" (1972B) 31 *CLJ* 197. Although see *Morris* [1984] AC 320, 334, for the dubious (and unnecessary) claim that the criminal law should not be concerned with the niceties of the civil law. The approach taken in *Walker* [1984] Crim LR 112 (CA) and in *Tillings v Tillings* [1985] Crim LR 393 (CA) is to be preferred; cp. *Nabina* [2000] Crim LR 481 (CA). Compare too *Dobson v General Accident Fire and Life Assurance Corp* [1989] 3 All ER 927, 937 (CA): whether property belongs to another "is a question to which the criminal law offers no answer and which can only be answered by reference to civil law principles".

[117] Glanville Williams, "Theft, Consent and Illegality" [1977] *Crim LR* 127, 138. *Per* A.T.H. Smith, *Property Offences* (1994) § 5–49, "if the civil law sees no reason to permit the owner to complain of an interference with his property why should the criminal law do so?"

[118] Above, § 1.2.

[119] The leading case is *Gomez*: below, § 13.6(ii)(a)–(b).

V may have made a fundamental mistake. In that case, the transaction is void.[120] V retains title to the goods and they can be stolen by D. Finally, V, acting on behalf of the true owner, may not have authority to pass title. In that case, again, the transaction is void and D cannot become owner of the property.

In the following sections, we discuss aspects of these problems in more detail. (A third issue, to be discussed later, arises where D does become the legal owner of the property but is subject either to a constructive trust or to one of the extensional provisions in section 5(2)–(4), in which case theft may still be possible. These cases will be explored in § 13.5.)

*(a) Has ownership passed, prima facie?*

The general rule, which is subject to a number of statutory and common law provisos, is that title passes if and when the transferor so intends it to pass. It is not possible here to give a comprehensive account of the civil law regarding transfer of property. Rather, we propose briefly to mention some well-known situations, and to illustrate the relationship between the relevant civil law rules and the criminal law of theft.

*Case 1: Contracts for sale of goods.*

Where ascertained goods are sold, the rules on passing of title are to be found in the Sale of Goods Act 1979. The basic rule, stated in section 17, is that where there is a contract for the sale of specific or ascertained goods, property in them passes when the buyer and seller so intend. In the case of sale of unascertained goods, section 16 provides that no property in them can be transferred to the buyer unless and until the goods are ascertained.[121] Section 18 provides that if there is no agreement regarding the passing of title, then property passes at the time the contract is made.[122]

One consequence of section 17 is that a seller may pass possession but reserve ownership. This is standard, for example, in hire-purchase contracts, where property remains in the seller until the buyer has paid for the goods. Although the buyer has lawful possession, a charge of theft would lie where the buyer then usurps the seller's rights of ownership over those goods, e.g. by dishonestly selling them.

*Case 2: Rescission.*

In *Walker*,[123] D sold V a defective video recorder which V returned for repair. After some time, V then issued a summons claiming the price of the video recorder as the "return of money paid for defective goods". D thereafter sold the video recorder. His conviction for theft was quashed. Arguably, the summons had the effect of rescinding the original contract of sale; revesting ownership of the machine once again in D.

[120] Voidability is not an option in the case of a unilateral mistake. A transaction can be voidable, as opposed to void, only when D has acted in some way wrongfully. If P's mistake is fundamental, the transaction is void; if not, the transaction is entirely valid and unimpeachable.

[121] See, e.g., *Re Goldcorp Exchange* [1995] 1 AC 74 (PC): buyers had no legal or equitable interest in an undifferentiated bulk of gold bullion. This rule is subject to certain exceptions for sales of undivided shares in an ascertained bulk (see, in particular, the Sale of Goods (Amendment) Act 1995).

[122] Provided the goods are specific and deliverable, and the contract is unconditional. Other rules in s. 18 apply where these criteria are not met.

[123] [1984] Crim LR 112 (CA).

*Case 3: Receptacles.*
The owner of a vending or similar machine, such as a coin-operated telephone, becomes the owner of any money as soon as it is inserted.[124] This is explicable on the general rule: the depositor intends to pass ownership when he inserts a coin in prepayment. Even if the machine malfunctions and he does not get what he pays for, his remedy is a refund, not a retrieval of the particular coin inserted. It is thus the actus reus of theft to retake money from such a machine, except by authorised means (e.g. pressing the refund button).

Similarly, when petrol is sold at a service station, ownership passes when the petrol is pumped into the tank of the vehicle. Thus a motorist who fills his tank intending to pay for the petrol, but then decides not to pay for it and drives off, commits no theft.[125] He already owns and has possession of the petrol before he forms the mens rea of theft, and instead commits the offence of making off without payment.[126]

*Case 4: Contents.*
If a person puts a valuable ring in a desk drawer, and after death her executor sells the desk, the buyer may not keep the ring on finding it, since it was not included in the sale.[127] A dishonest failure to return it would constitute theft. Ownership of the ring remains in the executor since he does not intend to pass title to it when he sells the desk.

### *(b) Is the passing of title voidable for duress, misrepresentation, etc?*

It is clear that transfers, even those pursuant to a contract, are voidable at common law if they are induced by the recipient's wrongdoing, e.g. by duress or misrepresentation.[128] Similarly, transfers affected by undue influence are voidable in equity.[129] In light of the House of Lords decision in *Gomez*,[130] the dishonest receipt of goods pursuant to such a voidable transfer can now be theft. This, strictly speaking, puts the criminal law at odds with the civil law, as a voidable title is a "perfect title"[131] until the transaction conferring ownership on D is set aside. Such conflicts are returned to below.

### *(c) Is the passing of title void for mistake?*

O's consent to the transfer of title may be negated by a "fundamental" mistake, whether or not induced by fraud or misrepresentation. A mistake is fundamental if and only if its existence makes it reasonable to say that there is no intention on O's part to transfer *this* property

[124] *Martin v Marsh* [1955] Crim LR 781 (DC); *Hollings* (1940) 4 J Cr L 370; cp. *Jean* [1968] 2 CCC 204.
[125] *Greenberg* [1972] Crim LR 331 (Quarter Sessions); *Edwards v Ddin* [1976] 3 All ER 705 (DC). This assumes that the controversial decision in *Hinks* [2000] UKHL 53, [2001] 2 AC 241 (below, § 13.6(ii)(c)) applies only to circumstances where the act of appropriation is coincident with, and not subsequent to, the obtaining of ownership.
[126] Theft Act 1978, s. 3.
[127] *Thomas v Greenslade* [1954] CLY 3421; *Moffatt v Kazana* [1969] 2 QB 152 (Assizes (Nottingham)); *Merry v Green* (1841) 7 M & W 623, 151 ER 916.
[128] See, e.g., Furmston, *Cheshire, Fifoot and Furmston's Law of Contract* (17th ed., 2017) ch. 9; Winfield, "Quasi-Contract Arising from Compulsion" (1944) 60 *LQR* 341; *Cooper v Joel* (1859) 1 De GF & J 240, 45 ER 350; *Wauton v Coppard* [1899] 1 Ch 92. Indeed, in cases of grave physical duress or fundamental misrepresentation the transfer may even be void: Lanham, "Duress and Void Contracts" (1966) 29 *MLR* 615.
[129] *Gomez* [1993] AC 442. This should have been the approach taken by the Court of Appeal in *Hinks* [2001] 2 AC 241; below, § 13.6(ii)(c).
[130] Below, § 13.6(ii)(a).
[131] A legal term of art, meaning that the person with such title is able to pass valid title to another; it is not, of course, a "perfect title" in the literal sense of the word because it is liable to be set aside.

to *this* person.[132] As the High Court of Australia put it, what this means is that a mistake is sufficiently fundamental if it is "as to the identity of the transferee or as to the identity of the thing delivered, or as to the quantity of the thing delivered".[133] Applying this test is not always clear-cut. Moreover, even where O's mistake is not sufficiently fundamental, it may well generate liability for theft under section 5(4), which we will consider below (§ 13.5(iv)).

*Case 1: Mistake regarding property.*
Mistake as to the identity of the property will always defeat consent. In *Davies*,[134] the proprietor of a nursing home induced two old ladies to endorse cheques made out to them by signing on the back, and then paid the cheques into his own account. The victims had not known that they were endorsing cheques, but merely thought that they were signing pieces of paper. For this reason property in the cheques never passed to D, who was thus rightly convicted of theft. Here the mistake was obviously fundamental: in each case V believed the property to be a valueless piece of paper, whereas in reality it was a bill of exchange—a different type of thing altogether.

*Case 2: Mistake regarding quantity.*
If the owner intends to deal only with a specific number of goods handed over, then there is no consent as to the excess. But if O's intention is to hand over a group of things, a mistake as to the number of items in the group does *not* negate the intention to hand them all over.

An example of the former variety is *Russell v Smith*:[135]

> D was a driver for a haulage company. He was instructed to collect a one-ton load of pig meal from P. P, when loading the meal, inadvertently loaded an additional eight sacks. When D discovered the error, he sold the eight sacks to T.

P intended to give D the number of sacks corresponding to one ton of meal; there was no intention to put the additional sacks on the lorry. Thus P remained owner of the eight extra sacks, which D stole when he appropriated them by offering to sell (and selling) them to T. Contrast this decision with an example where P offers to sell D all the pig meal then stored at his warehouse; which P mistakenly thinks amounts to one ton's worth, when in fact it is eight sacks more than that weight. In the latter case, D acquires ownership of the entirety of the property.

The distinction at work here is between a mistake which simply motivates or underlies P's intention to pass title to certain goods, and one which negates P's intention to pass title in those very goods which were in fact delivered. It is, in short, the difference between a mistake as to *what* P is passing to D, and a mistake as to *why* he is doing so.[136]

*Case 3: Mistake regarding transferee.*
Mistake as to the identity of the other party may vitiate consent, but only if the identity was crucial to O's decision to give consent to the transfer.[137] In *Hudson*, D received and

[132] Williams, "Mistake in the Law of Theft" (1977) 36 *CLJ* 62, 64.
[133] *Ilich* (1986) 162 CLR 110, 126.
[134] [1982] 1 All ER 513 (CA).
[135] [1958] 1 QB 27 (DC).
[136] Analogous to the distinction in contract law between a mistake "in the motive or reason for making the offer", and a mistake in the terms of the offer itself: *Imperial Glass v Consolidated Supplies* (1960) 22 DLR (2d) 759.
[137] Thus *Cundy v Lindsay* (1878) 3 App Cas 459 may be distinguished from *King's Norton Metal Co v Edridge* (1897) 14 TLR 98, where the rogue's assumed name was of no particular significance.

paid into his bank account a cheque which was inadvertently made out to him, but obviously intended for someone else with the same surname. He was convicted of stealing the cheque.[138]

It seems that a mistake about the transferee's identity supplies the best explanation of another well-known case, *Middleton*.[139] In that case, D went to withdraw 10 shillings from his Post Office savings account, which had at that time a balance of 11 shillings. The Post Office practice was to pay out withdrawals pursuant to a warrant obtained by D and a letter of advice from the Postmaster General sent direct to the relevant branch. Unfortunately the clerk consulted the wrong letter of advice, which related to a different account holder, and paid out £8 16s 10d. The Court of Criminal Appeal held that D was properly convicted of larceny, as the clerk's intention to pass title to the money was vitiated by his mistake. Since the clerk clearly did intend to give D £8 16s 10d, and not 10 shillings, he made no mistake about the nature or quantity of the property transferred.[140] Rather, his mistake is best seen as being about D's identity, which he had mistaken for that of the person named in the letter of advice.[141]

In 1972, the Court of Appeal purported to follow *Middleton* in *Gilks*.[142] G placed various bets at a betting shop, including one on "Fighting Taffy", which was unplaced in a race won by "Fighting Scot". When he went to collect his winnings on the various bets he had placed, the bookmaker mistakenly thought G had backed the winner, and calculated and paid out an amount well in excess of G's true winnings. G, realising the mistake, decided to pocket the entirety. His conviction for theft was upheld on the footing that *Middleton*[143] had established, in such cases, that property in money paid by mistake does not pass. It is submitted, however, that the Court of Appeal's reasoning was flawed. The bookmaker's error was an antecedent one of calculation[144] and not of the sort found in *Middleton*, where the clerk had paid the right amount to the wrong person. The bookmaker paid G (the right person) exactly the amount he intended. Therefore ownership of the money had passed to G.[145]

[138] [1943] KB 458. But this is not an absolute rule, at least where the parties deal face to face. In *Ingram v Little* [1961] 1 QB 31 a contract for sale of a car to a rogue under a false name (whose cheque bounced) was held void, but in *Lewis v Averay* [1972] 1 QB 198 a similar sale to a rogue believing him to be a certain TV actor was held valid. Possibly the only explanation for this anomaly is that in the latter case there was no actual misrepresentation by the buyer. Even before these cases, the considerable difficulties in this area of law had been pointed out by Williams, "Mistake as to Party in the Law of Contract" (1945) 23 *Can Bar Rev* 271.

[139] (1873) 12 Cox CC 417.

[140] *Per* Bramwell B (dissenting): "No doubt the clerk did not intend to do an act of the sort described, and give to Middleton what did not belong to him. Yet he intended to do the act he did. What he did he did not do involuntarily, nor accidentally, but on purpose": (1873) 12 Cox CC 417, 428.

[141] (1873) 12 Cox CC 417, 419: the clerk "certainly meant that the prisoner should take up that money, though he only meant this because of a mistake as to the identity of the prisoner with the person really entitled to that money." Cp. Smith and Hogan, *Criminal Law* (1965) 354. On whether the facts really support such a finding, *contra* the dissent by Cleasby B (1873) 12 Cox CC 417, 441–2. Cp. Turner, "Two Cases of Larceny" in Turner and Radzinowicz (eds.), *The Modern Approach to Criminal Law* (1948) 356, 359.

[142] [1972] 3 All ER 280 (CA). See the criticism by J.C. Smith in [1972] Crim LR 586. Compare *Prince* (1868) LR 1 CCR 150.

[143] (1873) 12 Cox CC 417.

[144] Of the sort found in *Moynes v Coopper* [1956] 1 QB 439 (DC); below, § 13.5(iv).

[145] There is some authority (*Chase Manhatten Bank v Israel British Bank* [1981] 1 Ch 105 and *Shadrokh-Cigari* [1988] Crim LR 465 (CA)) to the effect that, when making a mistake of this sort, V may retain equitable title in the money. These cases, which are controversial, are discussed in § 13.5(i)(a).

However, even assuming that ownership did pass to G, as the law now stands this may not matter; because, as we shall explain in § 13.6 when discussing appropriation, a line of cases decided after *Gilks* suggests—surprisingly—that it is now possible to commit theft by a dishonest act notwithstanding that the act has the legal effect of passing ownership.[146]

*(d) Other mistakes—and the possibilities of constructive trusts or section 5(4)*

The general rule is that, failing a "fundamental" mistake of the kinds identified in the foregoing paragraphs, the transaction is effective to pass title in the relevant property from O to D; thereafter, prima facie, that property cannot be stolen by D. In such cases, a charge of theft may still be available if the property still belongs to O in equity or by virtue of section 5(1)–(4). These extensions to section 5(1) are discussed in detail below (§ 13.5); but, in the context of mistakes, it is worth drawing particular attention to the role of section 5(4) and to developments in equity. Suppose that O mistakenly imagines she owes D £100 when, in fact, she owes £70. If she then pays him £100, D normally acquires absolute title to all of the money (O makes no fundamental mistake about what she is paying him), but he becomes liable under civil law to repay the excess £30. In those circumstances, section 5(4) operates to deem that excess as belonging to O for the purposes of theft. If D dishonestly keeps the £30, he then commits theft. Section 5(4) is the subject of § 13.5(iv) below. Additionally, there is authority that, under certain conditions, O retains equitable title to the excess and D holds the excess as a constructive trustee; in which case the property still belongs to O within the core terms of section 5(1). This possibility is considered in § 13.5(i)(a).

*(e) Was the transferor authorised to pass title?*

Property will not pass if the transferor does not have the owner's authority to pass title. In *Bhachu*, a dishonest cashier acted in collusion with D by "selling" the goods to her at a price below the authorised price.[147] In such a case, the cashier does not have the authority to pass title on O's behalf, and the goods are converted by D when she takes them out of the shop.[148] Similarly, D steals those items assuming the other elements of theft are made out. By contrast, an unintentional error on the part of an agent does not mean that the agent's conduct is unauthorised, even if the recipient is dishonest.[149]

### (v) Abandonment and loss: is finding theft?

If an owner intentionally abandons goods, they become ownerless, and therefore cannot be stolen.[150] Abandonment of ownership requires a giving up of the owner's physical control of an item, accompanied by the cessation of any intention to possess that item and of any intention to exclude other persons from its possession—i.e. a deliberate relinquishing of

[146] Note also that, quite apart from subsequent legal developments, s. 5(4) would ordinarily apply to such overpayments, but did not do so in this case because it arose out of a wager: below, § 13.4(iv)(d), 13.5(iv).
[147] (1977) 65 Cr App R 261 (CA). Cp. *Tideswell* [1905] 2 KB 273.
[148] In such circumstances, it seems that the cashier herself steals the goods when she offers to sell them at an undervalue: see *Pitham and Hehl* (1977) 65 Cr App R 45 (CA), below, § 13.6(i).
[149] *Jackson* (1826) 1 Mod 119, 168 ER 1208; *Prince* (1868) LR 1 CCR 150.
[150] Cp. *Ellerman Wilson Line v Webster* [1952] 1 Lloyd's Rep 179, 180 (DC).

all rights over the item.[151] Merely lost, rather than abandoned, property can still be stolen. Consider the following example:

> David finds a wallet in a busy street, and picks it up. He looks in the wallet for evidence of the owner's identity and finds none, but does find some money. He puts the wallet in his pocket. Does David commit the actus reus of theft?

Typically, in "finding" cases, it is important to resolve whether the thing found belongs to another: whether, in this scenario, there is another person with a right of property in the wallet and its contents. In turn, this is likely to depend on whether the wallet is abandoned or merely lost. If lost, then the person who originally lost the wallet remains its owner. By contrast, if abandoned, the wallet is unowned when David picks it up and puts it in his pocket.

Generally speaking, the courts are reluctant to find that goods have been "abandoned" rather than merely lost.[152] It will not suffice, for example, merely to put rubbish out for collection,[153] or to bury a dead animal.[154] Normally, as in these examples, some right in the subject matter (such as the right of exclusion of others from the subject matter) will be preserved.

Let us assume, since it contains money, that in David's case the wallet was not abandoned. It is worth noting that, if David had formed an honest belief that the goods were abandoned rather than lost, he would not commit theft.[155] However, this is because of the lack of mens rea (dishonesty), rather than the absence of an actus reus.

### (a) *When does a finder acquire ownership?*

Once abandoned, ownership of items vests in the first person to take possession of them. Possession, in turn, is normally taken by intentionally exercising control over the items. This may be done physically, for example by picking the thing up. Where chattels are abandoned on occupied land, however, the occupier will often acquire possession even before the chattel is found. In general, there are three types of cases in which the occupier acquires a better title than the finder.[156]

First, if the thing found is embedded in,[157] under,[158] or otherwise attached[159] to the land, it belongs to the occupier or owner (as the case may be)[160] of the land regardless of who finds it.[161]

[151] Cp. Hudson, "Abandonment" in Palmer and McKendrick, *Interests in Goods* (1993); *The Crystal* [1894] AC 508.

[152] Cp. Hudson, "Is Divesting Abandonment Possible at Common Law?" (1984) 100 *LQR* 110.

[153] *Williams v Phillips* (1957) 41 Cr App R 5 (DC). As long as the rubbish remained on the owner's premises it was not abandoned; property in it passed when collected by the local authority. In *Ricketts v Basildon Magistrates* [2010] EWHC 2358 (Admin) the defendant had helped himself to items left outside a charity shop when it was closed. It was held that the would-be donors, by attempting in this way to give them to the charity shop, had not abandoned them.

[154] *Edwards* (1877) 13 Cox CC 384.

[155] *Small* [1987] Crim LR 777 (CA); *White* (1912) 7 Cr App R 266 (CA).

[156] See Reisman, "Possession and the Law of Finders" (1939) 52 *Harv LR* 1105; Tay, "Problems in the Law of Finding" (1964) 37 *ALJ* 350; Harris, "The Concept of Possession in English Law" in Guest (ed.), *Oxford Essays in Jurisprudence* (1961) 69, 80ff.

[157] *Elwes v Brigg Gas Company* (1886) 33 Ch D 562.

[158] *Rowe* (1859) Bell 93, 169 ER 1180; *South Staffordshire Water Co v Sharman* [1896] 2 QB 44 (items lying under water; though in the latter case the defendant was also an employee).

[159] E.g., sealed inside a fixture: *City of London Corporation v Appleyard* [1963] 2 All ER 834 (DC); *Moffatt v Kazana* [1969] 2 QB 152 (Assizes (Nottingham)).

[160] Itself a matter of potential controversy: see, e.g., *Elwes v Brigg Gas Company* (1886) 33 Ch D 562.

[161] *Waverley* [1995] 4 All ER 756 (CA).

Secondly, if something is found loose by an employee on the employer's property, the employer has a superior right to possession of that thing, in priority to the employee-finder.[162]

Finally, where the item is found lying loose on the land, the occupier can acquire a prior title either by: (a) restricting public access to the land upon which the items lie;[163] or (where the land is open to public access) by (b) manifesting an intention to exercise control over the land and the things thereon.[164] Obviously if the item is found by a visitor inside D's private home, D has a superior title since the public does not have general access to the home. The following two cases are less straightforward illustrations of possibility (a):

> In *Woodman*,[165] D took scrap metal from a factory site. E, the occupier of the site, had no knowledge of the existence of the scrap, as it had sold all the scrap on the site to B for removal. In fact, B had removed the bulk of the scrap but left some pieces behind, which B deemed too inaccessible to be worth the cost of removing. The site had been wound down and was now disused, although a barbed-wire fence had been erected around the site to exclude trespassers.

D's conviction was upheld by the Court of Appeal. When B abandoned the scrap, ownership would have reverted to E as the occupier of the land, since E had manifested an intention to exclude trespassers by fencing off the site.

> In *Hibbert v McKiernan*,[166] D trespassed on a private golf course and dishonestly took eight golf balls which had been lost—and, it was found, subsequently abandoned—by their former owners.

The Divisional Court held that D was rightly convicted of theft from the golf club. Even if the balls had truly been abandoned (a doubtful conclusion, since clearly they had been lost unintentionally),[167] the golf club, as occupier of the land, had a better possessory title than D. D was a trespasser whose presence on the course was excluded.

On the other hand, where the premises are open to the public, the occupier's position is weaker, and she gains prior title only if she has manifested an intention to exercise control over the things that are or might be on the premises. In *Parker v British Airways Board*,[168] Parker found a gold bracelet in an executive lounge (in which he was entitled to be) at Heathrow airport. He handed the bracelet in to British Airways (who, as lessees, occupied the lounge), asking that the bracelet be returned to him if unclaimed. British Airways sold the bracelet. Parker succeeded in a tortious action for conversion of the bracelet. The Court of Appeal held that Parker's rights as finder could be displaced only if British Airways could show as occupiers an obvious intention to exercise such control over the lounge and things

[162] *The Title of the Finder* (1899) 33 ILT 225; *Willey v Synan* (1937) 57 CLR 200; *Grafstein v Holme* [1958] 12 DLR (2d) 727.

[163] *Parker v British Airways Board* [1982] QB 1004, 1013, 1019 (Donaldson LJ), 1020 (Eveleigh LJ), 1021 (Sir David Cairns) (CA).

[164] *Waverley* [1995] 4 All ER 756 (CA); cp. *Parker v British Airways Board* [1982] QB 1004, 1018 (CA).

[165] [1974] QB 754 (CA).

[166] [1948] 2 KB 142 (DC).

[167] A finding made by the justices at first instance (who seem to have confused abandonment of the search with abandonment of the balls themselves) and accepted, without being approved (cp. *ibid.*, 151), by the Divisional Court for purposes of the appeal. If lost rather than abandoned, a charge of theft from the original owners of the balls would have been straightforward. A slightly different case with identical result is *Rostron* [2003] EWCA Crim 2206 where, under the rules of the club by which players were bound, lost balls were deemed to be "surrendered" to the club. Thus title passed to the club by contractual assignment rather than by the law governing possession of abandoned property; and the defendants were rightly convicted of stealing from the club.

[168] [1982] 1 All ER 834 (CA); discussed by Roberts, "More Lost Than Found" (1982) 45 *MLR* 683.

in it that the bracelet was in their possession before the plaintiff found it.[169] On the evidence, there was no manifestation of such an intention as would give the defendants a right superior to that of the plaintiff; the airline's instructions to staff for dealing with lost articles were not published to users of the lounge, and it did not carry out searches for lost articles.

A special exception is "treasure", as defined in section 1 of the Treasure Act 1996. Any items falling within that definition (such as articles over 300 years old when found that are composed of at least 10 per cent gold or silver) are, by virtue of the Act, the property of the Crown.

## § 13.5 Belonging to another (II): extensions in the Act and in equity

There is a variety of ways in which the reach of the criminal law has been extended to protect interests in property rights beyond those falling within section 5(1).[170] Much of the variety is added by sections 5(2),[171] 5(3),[172] and 5(4).[173] These subsections are intended to cover specific *lacunae* in the scope of section 5(1). In at least one other area, however, liability under section 5(1) itself has been enlarged as a result of changes in the civil law, notably the expansion of the constructive trust since the passing of the 1968 Act.

### *(i) The growth of the constructive trust*[174]

In § 13.4, we saw that section 5(1) includes almost any form of proprietary right or interest within the range of what may be stolen, including, in particular, equitable proprietary interests. This covers, first and foremost, the case where property is held on an express trust (i.e. a legal arrangement deliberately set up for one person to manage property for the benefit of another person).[175] However, a consequence of embracing any proprietary interest within the terms of section 5(1) is that, in recent years, developments in the law governing constructive trusts have brought a variety of new situations potentially within the net of criminal liability.

A constructive trust is a type of trust that arises by operation of law, rather than pursuant to the intention of the parties.[176] If D holds property in circumstances where, in equity and good conscience, the property ought to be owned or enjoyed by V, a constructive trust may be imposed upon D. This has the consequence that, although D is the legal owner of the

[169] It was also suggested that D's rights might be displaced had he acted dishonestly. However, unless D's dishonesty were such as to make him a trespasser *ab initio*, it is hard to see how this qualification can be justified. See A.T.H. Smith, *Property Offences* (1994) § 4–20, 4–21.

[170] This section is intended for advanced students of criminal law and practitioners; those interested merely in an introduction to the law of theft can proceed to § 13.6.

[171] Below, § 13.5(ii).

[172] Below, § 13.5(iii).

[173] Below, § 13.5(iv).

[174] See generally Virgo, *Principles of Equity and Trusts* (5th ed., 2023) chap. 9.

[175] For an introduction, see *ibid*, chaps. 3 and 4.

[176] Trust lawyers are divided as to whether constructive trusts are "institutional", meaning that they arise automatically, or "remedial", meaning that they are (in effect) a fiction employed by the courts, in their discretion, to secure a just result. In *FHR European Ventures LLP v Cedar Capital Partners LLC* [2014] UKSC 45, [2015] AC 250, the Supreme Court opted for the first of these two views. See also *Crown Prosecution Service v Aquila Advisory Ltd* [2021] UKSC 49, [2021] 1 WLR 5666, [88] (Lord Stephens). For discussion, see Virgo, *Principles of Equity and Trusts* (5th ed., 2023) chap. 9.

property, he holds that property for the benefit of V—the equitable owner. Such equitable ownership is sufficient for the purposes of section 5(1), so that the relevant property can be stolen from V (including by D).

The law of constructive trusts is too complex to be treated in depth here. We will simply introduce and briefly discuss some of the paradigm cases. What will be said in the following paragraphs assumes—unavoidably—some familiarity with the relevant civil law concepts.

*(a) Property obtained by mistake*

In § 13.4(iv)(c) and (d), we considered the situation where D obtains property pursuant to another's mistake. Where D has induced the mistake we saw that title to the property normally passes but is voidable, so that D may still be convicted of theft.[177] Otherwise, if the mistake is not fundamental, title passes. In such circumstances, since D becomes absolute owner, section 5(1) does not apply and he cannot be convicted of theft (unless, as will be discussed in § 13.5(iv), the case falls exceptionally within section 5(4)).

Such was the settled law against which the Theft Act 1968 was enacted. But there is now authority that, while title passes to D at law, the law may recognise an equitable interest of V's in the property—which would be a sufficient property interest to qualify within section 5(1). In *Chase Manhattan Bank v Israel British Bank*,[178] the plaintiff bank paid $2 million by mistake into another bank for the account of the defendant, which then went bankrupt. The plaintiff sought to recover the overpayment. Goulding J ruled in favour of the plaintiff, holding that a person who pays money to another under a mistake of fact retains an equitable proprietary right or interest in the money. This reasoning was later doubted by Lord Browne-Wilkinson in his speech in *Westdeutsche Landesbank Girozentrale v Islington LBC*.[179] The basis for a constructive trust, he said, was "unconscionabilty"; and it was not unconscionable conduct, as such, to receive a mistaken payment. However, if a person who had received such a payment, having discovered the mistake, then used the money, or failed to pay it back, his conduct would be unconscionable, and a constructive trust could then arise. "Although the mere receipt of the moneys, in ignorance of the mistake, gives rise to no trust, the retention of the moneys after the recipient bank learned of the mistake may well have given rise to a constructive trust."[180]

In *Shadrokh-Cigari*,[181] a child's bank account was mistakenly credited with £286,000. D, the child's guardian, procured the child to authorise the issue of four banker's drafts in D's favour. Applying *Chase Manhattan*, the Court of Appeal held that D stole the drafts from the bank. Since the drafts had been drawn by the bank in error, the bank retained an equitable interest in them. Hence, for the purposes of section 5(1), they belonged to the bank. As D was aware of the mistake and consciously took advantage of it, even under Lord Browne-Wilkinson's narrower formulation of the law a constructive trust presumably arose at the point when D appropriated the property, even if it did not arise before.

[177] Above, § 13.4(iv)(b).
[178] [1981] Ch 105, 119.
[179] [1996] AC 669, 714.
[180] *Ibid.*, 715. A further complication was added when the Supreme Court suggested in *Bailey v Angove Pty Ltd* [2016] UKSC 47, [2016] 1 WLR 3179 that, to give rise to a constructive trust, the transfer's mistake must be "fundamental". For criticism, see Virgo, *Principles of Equity and Trusts* (5th ed., 2023) chap. 9.
[181] [1988] Crim LR 465 (CA).

In the light of this, it seems that the right result was reached in *Shadrokh-Cigari*, if not for exactly the right reason.[182] In *Shadrokh-Cigari* the Court of Appeal also upheld the conviction on a second basis: namely that, because the property was received under a mistake, the situation was covered by section 5(4) (discussed in § 13.5(iv) below). D's conviction can be justified on this basis too, irrespective of the existence (or non-existence) of a constructive trust.[183]

*Shadrokh-Cigari* was later applied by the Court of Appeal in *Webster.*[184] Here an army officer who had won a medal was later sent a second duplicate medal by mistake. He passed it over to D, his administrative officer, to deal with, intending him to return it, but instead of doing so D sold it on eBay. His theft conviction was affirmed on the basis, inter alia, that the Secretary of State retained an equitable interest in the duplicate medal that had been given to the officer in error.

*(b) Property obtained by fraud*

In *Re Holmes*,[185] an extradition case, D was alleged to be a dishonest employee of the X bank in Germany who had abused his position to cause the X bank to make a direct transfer of 15.5 million US dollars from its own funds, using the SWIFT[186] system of inter-bank transfers, to the Y bank in Holland. Y bank credited the funds an account which D controlled, from which D spirited them away to the Bahamas, Switzerland, Australia, Austria, and Indonesia. Under the law of extradition as it then stood,[187] D was liable to be extradited to Germany only if his behaviour constituted an offence under English law as well, which he claimed it was not. The Divisional Court held that, in England, D would have committed an offence of fraud.[188] For good measure it added, obiter, that he would also be guilty of theft in relation to the funds received by the Y bank, in respect of which there existed a constructive trust in favour of the X bank. In so holding, the Court quoted the following passage from Lord Browne-Wilkinson's speech in the *Westdeutsche* case:[189]

> "Although it is difficult to find clear authority for the proposition, when property is obtained by fraud equity imposes a constructive trust on the fraudulent recipient: the property is recoverable and traceable in equity."

It also added that, if the money had been transferred by the X bank from an account at that bank that could be identified, D would also have been guilty of theft of the chose in action represented by that bank account.[190]

[182] See Ormerod and Williams, *Smith's Law of Theft* (9th ed., 2007) §§ 2.257–2.258.

[183] Though this basis was also doubted by J.C. Smith in his comment on the decision in [1988] Crim LR 465, 467.

[184] [2006] EWCA Crim 2894.

[185] [2004] EWHC 2020 (Admin), [2005] 1 WLR 1857.

[186] SWIFT stands for Society for Worldwide Interbank Financial Telecommunication.

[187] Under Part I of the Extradition Act 2003, which was not yet in force, this "double criminality" requirement has been curtailed in the context of extradition between the UK and EU Member States. See Spencer, "The European Arrest Warrant" (2003–4) 6 *Cambridge Yearbook of European Legal Studies* 201.

[188] The offence, now abolished, of obtaining a money transfer by deception, contrary to the Theft Act 1968, s. 15A; today he would be guilty of fraud, under ss. 1 and 4 of the Fraud Act 2006 (fraud by abuse of position). See Chapter 15 below.

[189] Followed and applied in *Armstrong DLW GmbH v Winnington Networks Ltd* [2012] EWHC 10 (Ch), [2013] Ch 156; and see further Virgo, *Principles of Equity and Trusts* (5th ed., 2023) 290-291.

[190] *Williams* [2001] 1 Cr App R 362 (§ 13.3(c) above) and *Chan Man-sin*, § 13.6(vi) below.

*(c) Making a profit from abuse of fiduciary position*

If D "occupies a position in which he is expected to safeguard, or not to act against, the financial interests of another person", and dishonestly abuses that position with a view to financial gain, he will be guilty of the offence of fraud by abuse of position, as will be explained later (§ 15.5 below). If such a person does make a financial gain, the civil law will make him personally liable to account for it to the person, V, whose interests he was expected to protect. And in some situations the civil law goes even further in protecting V by treating D as holding the profit he has made on a constructive trust in V's favour. In this situation, V has, once again, a proprietary right over the property; and in consequence, section 5(1) of the Theft Act potentially applies to make D guilty of the offence of theft, as well as fraud by abuse of position.

Whether a constructive trust arises in this situation depends on whether D occupied, in law, the position of "fiduciary". This term lacks a precise legal definition, but:[191]

> "A 'fiduciary' is essentially somebody, person A, who is in a relationship with another person, B, in which B is entitled to expect that A will act either in B's best interests or in their joint interests, to the exclusion of A's own interest. In determining whether a person is a fiduciary, it is first necessary to consider whether that person is in a relationship with another that falls within one of the recognized categories of fiduciary relationships. If it does not, it is then necessary to examine the factual circumstances of the relationship to determine whether there are sufficient hallmarks of a fiduciary relationship to enable the court to conclude that the relationship is indeed fiduciary."

Recognised categories of fiduciary relationship include those involving agents, solicitors, company directors, and partners.[192] Beyond that, whether a given person counts as a fiduciary will depend on the facts of the case, and this is a question that it is sometimes difficult to answer.

Until recently, there was a further difficulty, this time in relation to the types of gain to which a constructive trust might possibly attach. It would certainly attach to profits made from interference with the principal's property, or improperly exploiting an opportunity that should have been available to him; but according to some of the authorities it would not attach to profits derived from a third party, such as bribes or unauthorised commissions.[193] Forty years ago, these decisions were relied on by the Court of Appeal to endorse an acquittal in *A-G's Reference (No. 1 of 1985)*.[194] D was the manager of a public house and an employee of the brewers to whom the house was tied. In contravention of the terms of his employment, he sought to sell beer purchased privately from a wholesaler to supplement his profits. The Court thought that such circumstances would not give rise to a trust and, even if it did, that it would not be a trust falling within the ambit of section 5(1).[195] But in 2014 the Supreme Court, in *FHR European Ventures LLP v Cedar Capital Partners LLC*,[196] overruled this line of cases, together with *A-G's Reference (No. 1 of 1985)* insofar as it

[191] Virgo, *Principles of Equity and Trusts* (5th ed., 2023) 468.
[192] *Ibid.*, 468.
[193] In particular, *Lister v Stubbs* (1890) 45 Ch D 1.
[194] [1986] QB 491 (CA). An earlier decision to similar effect is *Powell v MacRae* [1977] Crim LR 571 (DC).
[195] We will consider the policy merits of this view below, in § 13.5(i)(d).
[196] [2014] UKSC 45, [2015] AC 250. See also *Crown Prosecution Service v Aquila Advisory Ltd* [2021] UKSC 49, [2021] 1 WLR 5666.

depended on them. It now follows that a constructive trust can indeed attach to bribes and other improper benefits deriving from third parties.

Another difficulty remains. A widely accepted view is that a person who falls outside the recognised categories may be a fiduciary if: (i) he or she has expressly or impliedly undertaken to act in the best interests of the other; and (ii) he or she has a discretionary power to affect the principal's legal or practical interests.[197] On this basis, an ordinary employee is unlikely to be a constructive trustee for his employer's benefit, and hence unlikely to be guilty of theft by virtue of section 5(1) if he accepts a bribe or makes an unauthorised profit on the side. So for example where, as in the old case of *Cullum*,[198] the captain of a barge carries cargo contrary to his instructions and appropriates the resulting profits, he is probably not guilty of stealing the profits; nor, likewise, the manager of the public house in *A-G's Reference (No. 1 of 1985)*. As previously mentioned, they would nevertheless now commit the offence of fraud by abuse of position.

*(d) The merits of criminalising theft as a constructive trustee*

We noted above that in *A-G's Reference (No. 1 of 1985)*,[199] the Court of Appeal refused to accept that constructive trusts fell within the scope of section 5(1). Albeit that decision has since been overruled in law, in terms of policy its position was understandable. Constructive trusts were developed by the civil law with aims in mind that are characteristically irrelevant to the criminal law,[200] and often in the context of litigation to determine whether V should have a prior claim in insolvency over a third party, T. It is not obvious that the question whether D steals from V should be determined by the unrelated issue of priority between V and T.

Moreover, in this area the label "theft" does not always accurately capture the nature of D's wrongdoing. Consider the example where D, a fiduciary, accepts a bribe. In such a case the obvious charge to bring is one for the offence of bribery,[201] in respect of his initial acceptance of the bribe, or fraud by abuse of position, and not for subsequent theft of the proceeds. And issues of fair labelling aside,[202] extending theft liability to constructive trusts has the further disadvantage of decreasing certainty in the law, and reducing the level of fair warning available to citizens.[203] As Lord Lane pointed out in *A-G's Reference* itself, "if something is so abstruse and so far from the understanding of ordinary people as to what constitutes stealing, it should not amount to stealing".[204] If conduct of this sort should be punishable as a property offence, the proper place for it is in the law of fraud. As we shall see in Chapter 15, the Fraud Act 2006 created a tripartite offence of fraud, one form of which is "fraud by abuse of position". This offence unquestionably covers dishonest employees who

[197] Virgo, *Principles of Equity and Trusts* (5th ed., 2023) 471; quoting the Canadian case of *Galambos v Perez* 2009 SCC 48, [2009] 3 SCR 247.

[198] (1873) LR 2 CCR 28.

[199] [1986] QB 491 (CA); above, § 13.5(i)(c).

[200] *Per* A.T.H. Smith, "Constructive Trusts in the Law of Theft" [1977] *Crim LR* 395, 400: "the civil law imposes constructive trusts in situations, and for multifarious reasons, which may have nothing to do with the purposes of the criminal law".

[201] Contrary to the Bribery Act 2010.

[202] Cp. the discussion of fair labelling in § 2.4.

[203] Above, § 2.3.

[204] [1986] QB 491, 507 (CA); adding the telling comment that "There are topics of conversation more popular in public houses than the finer points of the equitable doctrine of the constructive trust."

abuse their position to make money on the side. For this offence, as we shall later see, it is not a legal requirement that D should be a "fiduciary". It is for this offence, and not theft, that dishonest employees should now be prosecuted.[205]

### *(ii) Theft of an interest protected by section 5(2): trust property*

As we have seen, a trustee can typically be convicted of theft of trust property under section 5(1), since any beneficiary of the trust would normally have an equitable interest in the trust property, which would qualify for protection as a proprietary interest under section 5(1). However, particularly in the case of charitable trusts, or discretionary trusts for a very large class (for instance, students of a particular educational institution),[206] sometimes there may be no individual beneficiary with an equitable interest in the trust. Such cases are covered by section 5(2):

> Where property is subject to a trust, the persons to whom it belongs shall be regarded as including any person having a right to enforce the trust, and an intention to defeat the trust shall be regarded accordingly as an intention to deprive of the property any person having that right.

A charitable trust is enforceable by the Attorney General. For the purposes of theft, therefore, its property belongs to the Attorney General, and may be stolen by the trustee.[207]

### *(iii) Theft of an interest protected by section 5(3): property received on account*

What if a person such as stockbroker, solicitor, or estate agent, having received property from a client, fraudulently misuses it for his own benefit? One way of dealing with such persons is under section 5(3):

> Where a person receives property from or on account of another, and is under an obligation to the other to retain and deal with that property or its proceeds in a particular way, the property or proceeds shall be regarded (as against him) as belonging to the other.

The section overlaps to a considerable extent with section 5(1), since persons receiving property on account will generally be fiduciaries who have legal but not equitable title to that property. In such cases, for purposes of theft the property can be stolen from the equitable owner (*per* section 5(1)) and from the person on whose account it is received (*per* section 5(3)). Section 5(3) comes into its own, however, when no one apart from D has any legal or equitable interest in the property stolen.[208] Suppose T gives D money for a specific purpose, e.g. to pay the gas bill. There would normally be no expectation that D will pay the bill using the exact banknotes, cheque, etc., that T gives him. T intends, rather, that D should pay out either the money T gives him, its proceeds, or (if D has it) an equivalent sum; in effect, that D should maintain a sufficient fund to make the payment. In this situation D is the owner of the money, but may have a duty to account falling within section

[205] Making secret profits had previously been held indictable as conspiracy to defraud: *Button* (1848) 3 Cox CC 229; *Rashid* [1977] 2 All ER 237 (CA); *Doukas* [1978] 1 All ER 1061 (CA).

[206] Cp. *Vestey v IRC* [1980] AC 1148.

[207] The analysis was missed by the Court of Appeal in *Dyke and Munro* [2002] 1 Cr App R 404.

[208] Cp. *Klineberg* [1999] 1 Cr App R 427 (CA), 432: s. 5(3) "is essentially a deeming provision by which property or its proceeds 'shall be regarded' as belonging to another, even though, on a strict civil law analysis, it does not".

5(3).[209] If he fails to do so, he can be convicted of theft of the money received from T or its proceeds.

Section 5(3) would also capture situations in which we would hold D to be under a fiduciary obligation notwithstanding that he has legal and equitable ownership of a thing. There is authority for the proposition that the residuary legatees of an estate have no proprietary interest before the estate is administered,[210] but we would think the executor guilty of theft were he dishonestly to appropriate the estate property to his own use. Another example is provided by the *Quistclose*[211] line of cases, where the transferees of money were obliged to keep it separate and to use it for specific purposes, even though there was no beneficial interest vesting in the intended recipients, nor, initially, in the transferors.

On the other hand, it is not always easy to determine when a person receives money on account. The obligation must be a *legal* obligation. A moral or social obligation is not sufficient.[212] When does this legal obligation arise?

*(a) The receipt on account distinguished from mere personal liability*

A duty to account does *not* exist where the relationship between D and the transferor of the property is that of debtor and creditor, such that the transferor's remedy against D is merely *in personam*. In theory, the difference between a duty to account and a liability *in personam* is clear enough. There is no duty to account when the recipient is entitled to the property both legally and beneficially, without any particular obligations attaching to her use of that property or its proceeds, so that she may deal with it as her own. In that case, the recipient's obligations operate as collateral, independent liabilities (e.g. a contractual debt). By contrast, where there is a receipt on account, D does not have untrammelled ownership of the property, and is entitled to dispose of and deal with the property or its proceeds only subject to the terms on which it was received.

However, it is not always a simple matter to distinguish them in practice. J.C. Smith, discussing the (former) offence of fraudulent conversion, has suggested the following test where money is transferred:[213]

> "Was the transferee permitted, under the terms of the contract, to use the money as he thought fit; or was he obliged to apply it in a particular way or to retain an equivalent sum, either in his possession or in a bank? Only in the latter event can the transferee commit fraudulent conversion."

The distinction is often relevant in a civil law context, especially in an insolvency, where it may be important to decide whether the money forms part of a debtor's general assets to be distributed among creditors, or whether it may be recovered intact by the transferor.[214]

209 As the court held in *Davidge v Bunnett* [1984] Crim LR 297 (DC).

210 *Commr of Stamp Duties (Queensland) v Livingstone* [1965] AC 694 (PC).

211 *Quistclose Investments Ltd v Rolls Razor Ltd* [1968] 1 All ER 613 (CA).

212 Cp. *Huskinson* [1988] Crim LR 620 (DC); *Meech* [1974] QB 549, 554 (CA); *Hall* [1973] QB 126 (CA); J.C. Smith, "The Scope of Fraudulent Conversion" [1961] *Crim LR* 741 and 797, 799ff.

213 J.C. Smith, "The Scope of Fraudulent Conversion" [1961] *Crim LR* 741 and 797, 800. This test was adopted in *Stephens v R.* (1978) 52 ALJR 662, 669. For a useful illustration, compare *Hotine* (1904) 68 JP 143 with *Donald Smith* [1924] 2 KB 194 (CA).

214 For example in the *Quistclose* line of cases: *Quistclose Investments Ltd v Rolls Razor Ltd* [1968] 1 All ER 613 (CA).

In the criminal context, a simple example may be found in the travel agency business. A travel agent generally receives money from customers in return for an obligation to provide the ticket, and may use the money received from customers as he chooses. It was held in *Hall*[215] that this creates a debtor–creditor relationship. In that case, D had received deposits for air tickets and paid the money into a general trading account; he then failed to supply tickets to the clients. Although his conduct was "condemned as scandalous",[216] in the absence of special arrangements imposing on him an obligation to deal with clients' money in a particular way, he had no duty to account and therefore did not commit theft.[217] By contrast, in *Re Kumar*,[218] D, also a travel agent, had specifically agreed a trustee relationship in respect of moneys received from airline ticket sales. After deducting commission, D was required each month to remit the proceeds to IATA; which he failed to do. In these circumstances D had a duty to account and was ruled to have committed a theft.

One standard application of section 5(3) is to charity collectors.[219] In *Wain*,[220] D raised money from the public by conducting charitable discotheques and other events. Subsequently, he failed to hand the money over and instead spent it. D's conviction was upheld by the Court of Appeal on the basis that he was obliged to retain the proceeds of his fundraising for the benefit of the charity; hence, under section 5(3), the money belonged to the charity for the purposes of theft.

### *(iv) Theft of an interest protected by section 5(4): where there is an obligation to make restitution*

Suppose that C is a wages clerk. When making up the pay packets one week, he accidentally puts a £50 note, which has stuck to another note, into D's packet, so that it now contains £200 instead of £150. Upon discovering the error, D resolves to say nothing and spends the money. He is guilty of stealing the £50 note. C's mistake was a fundamental one of quantity (above, § 13.4(iv)(c)), and the £50 note still belongs to the employer. Section 5(1) applies straightforwardly.

Contrast, under pre-1968 law, *Moynes v Coopper*,[221] where a wages clerk miscalculated the amount due to D. Although the employee was thus overpaid, the clerk intended to pay the amount of money actually paid. Hence title in the whole amount paid passed to D, and D could not be convicted of larceny. The employer had no proprietary claim to the money in D's hands, merely a personal claim in restitution against D for "money had and

[215] [1973] QB 126 (CA). Cp. *Robertson* [1977] Crim LR 629 (Crown Court (Kingston upon Thames))—but contrast *Brewster* (1979) 69 Cr App R 375 (CA) (insurance brokers).

[216] [1973] QB 126, 131 (CA).

[217] Nowadays, D would likely have committed fraud in such circumstances.

[218] [2000] Crim LR 504 (DC).

[219] *Quaere* whether such cases in any event give rise to a constructive trust, falling within the scope of s. 5(1)–(2).

[220] [1995] 2 Cr App R 660 (CA); rightly disapproving *Lewis v Lethbridge* [1987] Crim LR 59 (DC). In the latter case, D had obtained sponsorships for the benefit of a charity, but then kept the money. D's conviction was quashed because the magistrates had made no finding of fact that the charity expected D to maintain a separate fund with the money; but, as the Court in *Wain* pointed out, an obligation to account for the moneys or their proceeds need not come from the beneficiary. It can originate from the donors.

[221] [1956] 1 QB 439 (DC). Cp. *Davis* (1989) 88 Cr App R 347 (CA).

received".[222] However, since the passing of the Theft Act 1968 mistakes of the latter variety are now covered by the special provisions of section 5(4):

> Where a person gets property by another's mistake, and is under an obligation to make restoration (in whole or in part) of the property or its proceeds or the value thereof, then to the extent of that obligation the property shall be regarded (as against him) as belonging to the person entitled to restoration, and an intention not to make restoration shall be regarded accordingly as an intention to deprive that person of the property or its proceeds.

Moynes would now be guilty of theft, notwithstanding that he in no way infringed his employer's property rights. The effect of section 5(4) can be seen in *A-G's Reference (No. 1 of 1983)*.[223] D, a police constable, had her salary paid by direct debit. By mistake, she was overpaid on one occasion by £74.74. On the assumption that she subsequently decided, dishonestly, not to repay the sum, the Court of Appeal ruled that she would be guilty of theft. Notwithstanding that she owned outright the content of her bank account, and was entitled to draw upon it as she wished, there was a legal obligation upon D to repay to her employer a sum equivalent to the overpayment once she discovered the mistake. By virtue of section 5(4), that sum (of £74.74) was *deemed* for the purposes of theft to belong to the employer, and so could be stolen by D.

The obligation must be a legal and not a moral obligation to make repayment.[224] Recall the betting case of *Gilks*,[225] discussed in § 13.4(iv)(c). While the mistake in that case was of the same type as that in *Moynes v Cooper*, as the law then stood no legal obligation to make repayment arose in *Gilks* because the overpayment was in virtue of a wager.[226] Thus *Gilks* did not fall within the ambit of section 5(4).

Although the decision in *Moynes* was much criticised at the time,[227] its undoing by section 5(4) could be seen as an overreaction. The defendant in *Moynes* was a mere debtor; section 5(4) effectively makes personal liability the stuff of theft: arguably a misuse of the concept of theft. In practical terms, furthermore, there is the practical point that some people who are basically law-abiding and who would never go out and steal might well be tempted to keep an accidental overpayment, which suggests that section 5(4) stretches the reach of the criminal law too wide.

If these arguments look strong in the context of overpayments that are relatively small, they look less convincing where the sums are large. In a case such as *Shadrokh-Cigari*,[228] discussed above in § 13.5(i)(a), where the defendant dishonestly spirited away an accidental overpayment of £286,000, it is harder to argue that the criminal law should not be involved; and even harder to feel sympathy for the defendant in *Sandeep Singh*,[229] where the sum accidentally overpaid was £766,098.

[222] There is, however, controversial authority to the effect that even though title passes at law, the unilaterally mistaken payer may sometimes retain an equitable interest in the goods—which would be a sufficient property interest to qualify within s. 5(1). Because of its complexity, we consider this possibility separately, in § 13.5(i)(a) above.

[223] [1985] QB 182 (CA).

[224] *Gilks* [1972] 3 All ER 280, 283 (CA). Cp. the discussion of s. 5(3) above, § 13.5(iii).

[225] [1972] 3 All ER 280 (CA); above, § 13.4(iv)(c) (Case 3).

[226] Gaming Act 1845, s. 18; Gaming Act 1892, s. 1. Since then, the Gambling Act 2005 has repealed the legislation which formerly rendered all gaming debts legally unenforceable.

[227] See, e.g., [1956] Crim LR 516.

[228] [1988] Crim LR 465 (CA).

[229] Leicester Crown Court, October 2017. The defendant pleaded guilty and was sentenced to a year's imprisonment: *Leicester Mercury*, 9 October 2017.

## § 13.6 Appropriation

So far, we have considered what can be stolen: what sort of *property*, and what sort of *interest* in that property, is susceptible of theft. The third issue for the actus reus of theft is what sort of *action*, in connection with that property, is prohibited? Under section 1, D must "appropriate" the stolen property, a term elaborated upon by section 3(1):

> Any assumption by a person of the rights of an owner amounts to an appropriation, and this includes, where he has come by the property (innocently or not) without stealing it, any later assumption of a right to it by keeping or dealing with it as owner.

Although this definition is not intended to be exhaustive,[230] it appears to be at least as wide as any ordinary language concept of appropriation, and for practical purposes it is comprehensive. The history of the interpretation of section 3(1) is the sorry story of a statutory provision being construed so loosely as to deprive it of solid content. We shall try to avoid its retelling here, save in so far as necessary. As things stand, the gist of appropriation is as follows:

> D appropriates an item when he does anything in connection with it that only an owner (or someone having rights derived from ownership) has the right to do, or that an owner has the right to exclude others from doing.

For instance, D appropriates something when he touches it, destroys it, gives it to another person, sells it, or even offers it for sale. The right to do each of these things is a right of ownership, and D assumes one of those rights when he does any of these actions. Note that D need only assume any *one* of the rights of ownership, not *all* of them, by his action.[231] Thus touching something is an appropriation even though one may do so without assuming all the facets of ownership.

Any act of appropriation is sufficient. There is no need for it to be the very act by which D intends to deprive V of the item stolen. It is sufficient that D appropriates the item while intending that the owner should be deprived, even if that deprivation will be accomplished only by some later act of D's.[232] Suppose, for example, that D changes the labels on two products (say, product A and product B) in a supermarket, intending to buy the more expensive item, product A, at an undervalue. He steals product A as soon as he touches it, as a mere touch is now to be regarded as an appropriation; even though this act is only preliminary to the further act(s) of appropriation by which the owner will be deprived.[233]

Before we elaborate upon this analysis in the following pages, it is worth commenting that, although this interpretation of section 3(1) must now be accepted, it seems at variance with the plain words of the statute: any assumption of "the rights of an owner" seemingly indicates an assumption of the *entirety* of the owner's rights. As we shall see, because of

[230] Cp. Report of the Criminal Law Revision Committee, *Theft and Related Offences* Cmnd. 2977 (1966) para. 34.

[231] *Morris* [1984] AC 320, where the House of Lords rejected the appellant's argument to the contrary.

[232] *Ibid.*

[233] That said, it is arguably the case that in order to amount to an appropriation the act must be done with the intention of assuming the rights of an owner. If that is right, a person who picks up a purse in the street intending to hand it in to the police does not "appropriate" it, and would not be guilty of theft for that reason, quite apart from that he acts without dishonesty or the intent permanently to deprive. See Melissaris, "The Concept of Appropriation and the Offence of Theft" (2007) 70 *MLR* 581.

questionable interpretations, acts which previously would have been merely preparatory to theft—and which are not part of the gravamen of theft—are now treated as the theft itself.[234]

### *(i) Some examples of appropriation*

It is helpful to illustrate the variety of forms of conduct that can constitute theft. In *Pitham and Hehl*,[235] M offered to sell P and H some furniture, which all concerned knew did not belong to M. Convictions for handling by P and H were upheld on appeal, on the footing that M committed theft when he offered to sell the goods; hence P and H were guilty of handling goods that were stolen when they received them. The decision may be doubted on the facts,[236] but is clear authority that offering to sell goods assumes a right of the owner and is therefore an appropriation.

In *Chan Nai-Keung*,[237] D, a director of a company which exported textiles, dishonestly sold a large quantity of the company's export quotas (a form of intangible property). D's conviction for theft was upheld by the Privy Council.

The framers of the Theft Act 1968 envisaged that the term "appropriation" would cover the same ground as the civil law concept of conversion,[238] and it seems clear that any form of conversion will also be an appropriation. This includes conversion by a person who legitimately has possession of the goods in a bailment ("a bailment involves one person taking custody of another person's goods":[239] a dry cleaner, say, who takes in a customer's clothing, or a holiday maker who hires a car from a garage). It is a theftuous conversion where a bailee had the loan of a boat, which he pledged as security for a financial transaction,[240] or where a bailee obliterates the identifying marks of certain property by painting it.[241]

### *(ii) Restrictions on the scope of appropriation?*

Prima facie, the scope of appropriation is astoundingly wide, with the consequence that the actus reus of theft is usually a simple matter for the prosecution to establish. Provided D does anything whatsoever in connection with property belonging to another person, the

[234] In *Morris, ibid.*, Lord Roskill conceded that there was force in the view that the expression, "the rights of an owner", means all rights, not one or some. For his Lordship, however, it was decisive that s. 3(1) goes on to speak of "any later assumption of *a right*". Remarkably, he omitted the subsequent words, "by keeping or dealing with it as an owner", which make it clear that D must keep or deal with the property by assuming the entirety of the rights to it.

[235] (1977) 65 Cr App R 45 (CA). Cp. *Rogers v Arnott* [1960] 2 QB 244 (DC).

[236] Since all three knew that M had no authority to sell the furniture, M's "offer" seems to have been a mere sham rather than an appropriation. As Smith wrote, "D did not purport to be the owner or to be acting with his authority. It was not really an offer to sell at all but a proposal for a joint theft of the goods": Ormerod and Williams, *Smith's Law of Theft* (9th ed., 2007) § 2.79.

[237] *A-G of Hong Kong v Chan Nai-Keung* (1988) 86 Cr App R 174 (PC).

[238] See below, § 13.6(ii)(b).

[239] Goudkamp and Nolan, *Winfield and Jolowicz on Tort* (21st ed., 2025), para. 1-029 (cp. § 17.3 on conversion in general).

[240] In other words, where he granted a chattel security over the property lent to him: Cp. *Dunbar* [1963] NZLR 253.

[241] As in *Russell* [1977] 2 NZLR 20.

actus reus is made out; if he is dishonest and has an intention permanently to deprive, he steals it. Consider the following situation:

> Walter decides to steal a car. He walks down the street until he finds a Ford Mondeo with its doors unlocked. He opens the door and gets into the car. Unfortunately for him, he finds that his skeleton ignition key does not work. He gives up and goes home.

This looks like an attempted theft, subject to the question whether Walter had passed the stage of mere preparation and had in fact commenced the attempt. But it is not. It is a consummated theft, complete as soon as Walter touched the door. That was an appropriation: since all the other elements of theft were present, the offence was committed at that point.

The result is worrying as well as surprising. In Chapter 1 of this book, we discussed the proposition that criminal offences should require both harm and culpability before imposing the sanctions of conviction and punishment. Unfortunately, the modern law of theft appears virtually to have dispensed with harm. Conceptually, and at the level of ordinary language, the gist of theft is depriving another person of his property rights. Legally, theft is no such thing. Looked at objectively, D's behaviour may be ordinary and harmless, yet be the actus reus of theft. Consider the case of *Dip Kaur v Chief Constable for Hampshire*:[242]

> D was in a shop where she found a pair of shoes, one of which was marked for sale at £6.99, the other at £4.99. She took the shoes to the cashier, hoping that the cashier would see the lower (incorrect) price. She was charged £4.99. Her conviction for theft was quashed, for the reason that the cashier's mistake (in thinking £4.99 was the correct price) did not negate her intention to sell the goods to D for £4.99; thus, when D left the shop, she owned the shoes and could not steal them.

As things stand, the case would now be decided differently. D, if dishonest, stole the shoes as soon as she picked them off the sale rack—notwithstanding that the subsequent transaction was valid and she became their owner.

### *(a) Possible qualification 1: unauthorised or wrongful appropriations?*

It might be thought that one way out of this difficulty is to read an implicit qualification into section 3(1): rather than simply "any assumption" of the rights of the owner, section 3(1) may be interpreted as requiring "any unauthorised assumption", or perhaps any "usurpation" of the owner's rights. This approach would better reflect the core idea that theft involves some form of harmful interference with another person's property rights, and that appropriation lacks a theftuous character unless it conflicts with the victim's rights.[243]

At one point, the House of Lords appeared to favour such a qualification. In *Morris*,[244] D took goods from the shelves of a supermarket. He replaced the price labels attached to them with labels showing a lesser price than the originals. He was arrested after buying the goods at the lesser price and was subsequently convicted of theft. The House upheld the conviction, on the basis that D appropriated the goods and committed theft when he switched the

[242] [1981] 2 All ER 430 (DC).

[243] Cp. Model Penal Code, § 223.2 (the interference must be "unlawful").

[244] [1984] AC 320; discussed by Leigh, "Some Remarks on Appropriation in the Law of Theft after *Morris*" (1985) 48 *MLR* 167. Cases exhibiting similar reasoning include *Meech* [1974] QB 549 (CA); *Hircock* (1978) 67 Cr App R 278 (CA); *Morgan* [1991] RTR 365 (CA); *Fritschy* [1985] Crim LR 745 (CA).

price labels. The decision is clearly right, since D's act was an unauthorised appropriation of the goods. However, in the course of his judgment Lord Roskill dealt specifically with a point raised by counsel for the Crown:[245]

> "My Lords, Mr. Jeffreys sought to argue that any removal from the shelves of the supermarket, even if unaccompanied by label switching, was without more an appropriation. In one passage in his judgment in Morris's case, the learned Lord Chief Justice appears to have accepted the submission, for he said [1983] QB 587, 596 [CA]: 'it seems to us that in taking the article from the shelf the customer is indeed assuming one of the rights of the owner—the right to move the article from its position on the shelf to carry it to the check-out.' With the utmost respect, I cannot accept this statement as correct. If one postulates an honest customer taking goods from a shelf to put in his or her trolley to take to the checkpoint there to pay the proper price, I am unable to see that any of these actions involves any assumption by the shopper of the rights of the supermarket. *In the context of section 3(1), the concept of appropriation in my view involves not an act expressly or impliedly authorised by the owner but an act by way of adverse interference with or usurpation of those rights.* When the honest shopper acts as I have just described, he or she is acting with the implied authority of the owner of the supermarket to take the goods from the shelf, put them in the trolley, take them to the checkpoint and there pay the correct price, at which moment the property in the goods will pass to the shopper for the first time. . . . I do not think that section 3(1) envisages any such act as an 'appropriation,' whatever may be the meaning of that word in other fields such as contract or sale of goods law."

We have italicised the key proposition asserted by Lord Roskill, but the example he discusses is also helpful. It is this reasoning that justifies the quashing of D's conviction in *Dip Kaur* (above) where, by contrast with the defendant in *Morris*, D's handling of the shoes involved no unauthorised action. She simply picked them up and took them to the counter, something any shopper has an implied licence to do.[246]

Unfortunately, Lord Roskill's analysis was inconsistent with the earlier House of Lords decision in *Lawrence v Metropolitan Police Commissioner*.[247] In that case D, a taxi-driver, drove a newly arrived foreign student with little English from Victoria Station to an address in London. The student had offered a £1 note for the fare, which D said was not enough before extracting a further £6 from the student's open wallet. In truth, the legally authorised fare for the journey was approximately 50 pence. Although the student had permitted D to take the excess money, the House upheld D's conviction for theft. The student's consent was irrelevant:[248]

> "I see no ground for concluding that the omission [from section 1(1) of the Theft Act 1968] of the words 'without the consent of the owner' was inadvertent and not deliberate, and to read the subsection as if they were included is, in my opinion, wholly unwarranted. Parliament by the omission of these words has relieved the prosecution of the burden of establishing that the taking was without the owner's consent. That is no longer an ingredient of the offence.

245 [1984] AC 320, 332.

246 Admittedly, it could be argued that such a licence (to carry goods within the shop) extends only to honest shoppers; a similar restriction has been allowed in the context of burglarious trespass (criticised below, § 14.4(ii)(a)). Besides being an artificial construction, however, such a move could be said to make proof of the actus reus dependent on proving an element of mens rea, which would be to put the cart before the horse; though see note 228 above.

247 [1972] AC 626.

248 *Ibid.*, 632. Cp. *Dobson v General Accident Fire and Life Assurance Corporation plc* [1990] 1 QB 274 (CA).

> . . . That there was appropriation in this case is clear. Section 3 (1) states that any assumption by a person of the rights of an owner amounts to an appropriation. Here there was clearly such an assumption. . . . [An appropriation] may occur even though the owner has permitted or consented to the property being taken."

The conflict in approach between *Lawrence* and *Morris* was resolved in *Gomez*,[249] in which their Lordships affirmed *Lawrence*. D, the assistant manager of a shop, had formed a plan with R, a customer, to acquire goods in exchange for two stolen cheques. Knowing that the cheques were stolen, D deceived the shop manager into authorising the sale of the goods to R in exchange for the cheques. Instead of charging him with obtaining property by deception[250] (as should have occurred), the prosecution charged D with theft. The Court of Appeal quashed his conviction, on the ground that ownership of the goods had passed; since the manager had consented to the transaction, possession of the goods was authorised and therefore there was no appropriation. The House of Lords, by a majority, restored the conviction:

> "The decision in *Lawrence* was a clear decision of this House upon the construction of the word 'appropriate' in section 1(1) of the Act, which had stood for 12 years when doubt was thrown upon it by obiter dicta in *Morris*. *Lawrence* must be regarded as authoritative and correct, and there is no question of it now being right to depart from it."[251]

The upshot of *Gomez* is that the scope of "appropriation" in theft is not limited to unauthorised or wrongful appropriations but includes even appropriations made with consent of the owner.[252]

### (b) *What was wrong with* Gomez?

Quite apart from the fact that it virtually demolished any distinction between theft and the (then) offence of obtaining by deception,[253] the decision in *Gomez* was questionable for other reasons. The majority judgments by Lord Keith and Lord Browne-Wilkinson treated the matter largely as an issue of precedent: the analysis of appropriation in *Lawrence* was part of the *ratio decidendi* of that case, whereas it was merely *obiter dicta* in *Morris*. They barely mentioned the issues of principle at stake, and were unswayed by the evidence that the legislature could not have intended such a broad interpretation of appropriation. The majority judgments are also profoundly disappointing because they contain no recognition, anywhere, that the interpretation of criminal statutes is a matter that should be governed by

249 [1993] AC 442.

250 Contrary to s. 15 of the Theft Act 1968; an offence later abolished and replaced by a new and broader offence of fraud: below, § 15.1.

251 *Gomez* [1993] AC 442, 464.

252 See, e.g., *Williams (Roy)* [2001] 1 Cr App R 362. D dishonestly overcharged a number of clients for building work. He was convicted of stealing from his clients' bank accounts, notwithstanding that each appropriation from those accounts was with the consent of the customer who wrote the cheque. See § 13.6(vi) below.

253 See Shute and Horder, "Thieving and Deceiving—What Is the Difference?" (1993) 56 *MLR* 548; Clarkson, "Theft and Fair Labelling" (1993) 56 *MLR* 554. A few instances of non-overlap are identified in Heaton, "Deceiving without Thieving" [2001] *Crim LR* 712. Earlier writing prior to *Gomez* includes Koffman, "The Nature of Appropriation" [1982] *Crim LR* 331; Leigh, "Some Remarks on Appropriation" (1985) 48 *MLR* 167; Gardner, "Is Theft a Rip-off?" (1990) 10 *OJLS* 441; Halpin, "The Appropriate Appropriation" [1991] *Crim LR* 426. Glazebrook, however, approves of *Lawrence* for pragmatic reasons: "Thief or Swindler: Who Cares?" (1991) 50 *CLJ* 389. For discussion of the former offence of obtaining by deception and its successor under the Fraud Act 2006, see Chapter 15 below.

general principles, which include the principle that, in the absence of any compelling policy reason suggesting Parliament really intended the wider meaning, statutes creating criminal liability should not be extensively construed.[254]

The better view is that if V transfers ownership of the goods to D, D as owner should be incapable of stealing those goods. As Lord Lowry pointed out in his minority judgment,[255] this was the view of the Criminal Law Revision Committee (CLRC), upon whose report the Theft Act 1968 was based.[256] When framing the Act, the CLRC equated appropriation with conversion[257]—a term that certainly requires unauthorised usurpation of another's property rights—and preferred the former word only because the latter was regarded as unduly technical terminology.

At the level of principle, the reasons a defendant who acquires ownership should not be convicted of theft are also compelling. The difficulty with *Gomez* is not the particular outcome, but the wider implications. The actus reus of theft was so broadened that in practice it has no boundaries. Every transaction between two parties that pertains to property, whether corporate or private, whether consensual or involuntary, is now, apparently, the actus reus of a theft. This result has two effects. The first is to make a nonsense of the relationship between theft and the civil law of property. On the face of it, *Gomez* means that a defendant who acquires ownership by a transaction can also, by that very transaction, commit a crime. In principle these two results cannot stand together. It is a long-standing rule of equity "that the Courts will not recognize a benefit accruing to a criminal from his crime":[258] no one may benefit by his wrong.[259] If so, either there should be no crime, or the civil law must change (so that D does not get title). The purpose of an offence such as theft is to protect property rights. Unlike crimes such as assault, the rights being protected are necessarily rooted in the civil law. The decision in *Gomez* ignores that constraint.

The other effect of *Gomez* is to extend the offence of theft backwards in time, violating the harm principle in a second way. Earlier, we discussed the case of *Dip Kaur v Chief Constable for Hampshire*,[260] and noted that this case could now be theft as soon as D picked the shoes off the sale rack—well before she approached the cashier. Previously, picking the shoes up would have been mere preparation, and not even an attempt to steal. Now (if accompanied by mens rea) it is not merely an attempt, but a full-blown theft. This result contravenes all the principles guiding the parsimonious criminalisation of harmless, preparatory activity.[261] Touching a pair of shoes inside a shop is hardly theftuous behaviour. There is no harm. Sometimes, where there is no harm and the behaviour is by itself innocent, liability for an attempt may be appropriate. But merely touching the shoes, a precursor to approaching the cashier with them, should surely be regarded as mere preparation

[254] As explained in § 3.1 above. In some Continental criminal codes, the rule against the extensive construction of criminal statutes is laid down explicitly. Article 111-4 of the French *Code pénal* provides, "*La loi pénale est d'interprétation stricte*"—"criminal statutes are to be strictly construed".

[255] *Gomez* [1993] AC 442, 470ff.

[256] *Theft and Related Offences*, Cmnd. 2977 (1966).

[257] *Ibid.*, para. 34.

[258] *Beresford v Royal Insurance Co Ltd* [1938] AC 586, 599 (Lord Atkin).

[259] See, e.g., *Cleaver v Mutual Reserve Fund Ass.* [1892] 1 QB 147; *Re Giles, decd.* [1972] 1 Ch 546.

[260] [1981] 2 All ER 430 (DC). Above, § 13.6(ii).

[261] Above, § 1.2(i). Cp. Giles and Uglow, "Appropriation and Manifest Criminality in Theft" (1992) 56 *J Crim L* 179.

for theft. Yet on the authority of *Gomez*, and assuming all of the elements of theft could be established, it could be the full-blown offence.

*(c) Possible qualification 2: voidable appropriations?*

At first it was thought that *Gomez* was subject to an important limitation. In that case, D had induced the manager to part with the goods by deception. Thus, although title passed to D and his accomplice, at common law that title was voidable—like any transaction induced by deception, fraud, undue influence, or misrepresentation.[262] Arguably, therefore, *Gomez* could be distinguished from cases where D acquires full, unimpeachable ownership of the goods. *Gomez* rules that the acquisition of a voidable title is the actus reus of theft. But it does not decide that D appropriates goods when she acquires a fully valid title to them.

For good or ill, the House of Lords then rejected this distinction in the subsequent case of *Hinks*.[263] The facts were as follows:

> D had become friendly with V, a 53-year-old man described as naïve, gullible and of limited intelligence but with a considerable sum in his building society account. She successfully encouraged him to make a series of gifts totalling £60,000 and a TV set. The transfers were, it seems, valid gifts; though unintelligent, V clearly had the necessary capacity, in civil law terms, to dispose of his property if he chose. Gifts made by vulnerable persons to those who make abusive use of their moral hold over them, like transactions brought about by fraud, are potentially voidable, and V's gifts to D might well have been voidable on this ground.[264] However, this point was not explored at trial, and the judge did not direct the jury's attention to it, treating D's improper use of her influence over V merely as a matter relating to the issue of dishonesty.

Notwithstanding this omission, the House of Lords (by a majority of three to two) upheld D's conviction. Concurring in a speech delivered by Lord Steyn, the majority rejected D's argument that a finding of theft under the Act is subject to an exception where the relevant appropriation was an acquisition of fully valid title, holding that the language of the 1968 Act stipulates no such exception. Any appropriation, with or without the consent of the owner, falls within the Act. Even the *very acquisition* of indefeasible ownership, in accordance with the transferor's intentions, is an appropriation from V and the actus reus of theft. Provided D is dishonest, and intends not to return the property, she steals it. In so holding, the majority accepted that this created a potential conflict between the criminal and the civil law, but were undeterred by this. "In a practical world," said Lord Steyn, "there will sometimes be some disharmony between the two systems. In any event, it would be wrong to assume on a priori grounds that the criminal law rather than the civil law is defective."[265]

Although, in many respects, it takes only one small step beyond *Gomez*, this is an extraordinary decision.[266] No doubt exploitation of the vulnerable warrants redress. The exploitation of those who are weak minded, especially the old, by unscrupulous and grasping

[262] Cp. *Wheatley and Penn v The Commissioner of Police of the British Virgin Islands* [2006] UKPC 24, noted below.

[263] [2001] 2 AC 241. Cp. *Hopkins and Kendrick* [1997] Crim LR 359 (CA); *contra Mazo* [1997] 2 Cr App R 518 (CA). The earlier cases are usefully discussed by J.C. Smith, *The Law of Theft* (8th ed., 1997) §§ 2–21, 2–22.

[264] For a discussion of the authorities, see *Cresswell v Potter* [1978] 1 WLR 255 (Ch).

[265] [2001] 2 AC 241, 252.

[266] A decision not, however, without defenders: see Shute, "Appropriation and the Law of Theft" [2002] *Crim LR* 445; Bogg and Stanton-Ife, "Protecting the Vulnerable: Legality, Harm and Theft" (2003) 23 *Legal Studies* 402. The law established in *Hinks* had also been advocated by Gardner, "Property and Theft" [1998] *Crim LR* 35.

persons is a real and recurrent problem, one that is likely to get worse as the number of old people in the population increases, and it is right in principle that such conduct should be a criminal offence. All this is no doubt what the majority had in mind when they upheld the defendant's conviction for theft in this case. However, the law of theft is fundamentally unsuited to that task. Such behaviour is surely a form of fraud, not a form of theft. (Indeed, as we see in Chapter 15, some such cases can now be prosecuted under the Fraud Act 2006 as "fraud by abuse of position"—an offence that did not exist when *Hinks* was decided.)

The main problem with *Hinks* is that it turns the very rationale of property offences on its head. Theft is designed to protect and reinforce property rights.[267] But the effect of *Hinks* is to cut property offences adrift from the law of property rights: the cart is now before the horse.[268] Consider the law of contract. It is standard law that if D stays silent in the face of a mistake by P, which is not reflected in the terms of the transaction, P is bound to that transaction and has no remedy.[269] Adapting the facts of *Leaf v International Galleries*,[270] the purchase of a painting in the mistaken belief that it was a Constable from a gallery owner, D, who knows of the mistake but says nothing is, in the law of contract, valid; and D could sue for the unpaid purchase price. Yet if *Hinks* is right, the price paid by the buyer is stolen by D should a jury be persuaded that D is dishonest. But this would be absurd.[271]

In the later case of *Wheatley and Penn v The Commissioner of Police of the British Virgin Islands*,[272] the defendants were convicted of theft after D1 corruptly allocated government construction contracts to D2, notwithstanding that the contracts were at an appropriate price. The Privy Council, after noting that considerations of gain or loss were now irrelevant to the question of appropriation,[273] went on to emphasise that, in the present instance, "there is no dissonance between the criminal and the civil law, since the contracts made by the first appellant, contrary to his authority and with the connivance of the second appellant, were plainly voidable at the suit of the Government".[274] If *Hinks* is right, voidability is now irrelevant. Yet it is no surprise that the courts still find the point significant. *Hinks* is a troubling decision.

Given the potential expansiveness of the decision, a point of limitation should be stressed. *Hinks* deals with the scenario where the act of acquiring title is charged as theft; where the acquisition of title by D is coincident with the transfer from V. From that perspective D, in the extended sense that the law allows, has appropriated property belonging

[267] Cp. Simester and Sullivan, "On the Nature and Rationale of Property Offences" in Duff and Green (eds.), *Defining Crimes* (2005) 168, § 2.

[268] Lord Hobhouse (dissenting) sees this when he observes that "[t]here is no law against appropriating your own property" (at 856; see generally 854–6; also 865).

[269] *Smith v Hughes* (1871) LR 6 QB 597; *Bell v Lever Brothers Ltd* [1932] AC 161.

[270] [1950] 2 KB 86 (CA).

[271] That the problems of the conflict between the civil and the criminal law that result from *Hinks* are not imaginary is illustrated by a first-instance case in which a couple, who had become the care-givers of a vulnerable man, persuaded him to give to them most of his property *inter vivos* and to leave the rest of it to them in his will. For this, they were prosecuted and convicted of conspiracy to steal; and two-and-a-half years after their victim's death his body remained unburied because the defendants—whom his will made his executors—were in prison, and in no position to organise a funeral. "Anger as Swindled Farmer Lies Unburied", *Western Gazette*, 23 April 2009. The facts of the case were truly shocking because the couple also physically neglected the man—to the point where they were seemingly fortunate to avoid a prosecution for manslaughter.

[272] [2006] UKPC 24, [2006] 1 WLR 1683.

[273] *Ibid.*, [9]–[10].

[274] *Ibid.*, [11].

to V if the deprivation and acquisition of the property are regarded as two aspects of the one transaction. The case does not decide that once D has acquired valid title to property, any *subsequent* dishonest appropriation of that property by D, *after* absolute ownership is transferred, will amount to theft. (Such cases can only be theft if section 5(3)–(4) applies.)

One other point of qualification is made by Lord Hutton in his dissent in *Hinks*. His Lordship observed that section 2(1)(a) of the Theft Act 1968 provides that a person's appropriation is not to be regarded as dishonest if he appropriates property in the belief that he has, in law, the right to deprive the other of it.[275] Typically, a person who acquires ownership of goods will also (correctly!) *believe* that she has a right to them. Where this is so, a charge of theft will fail for lack of dishonesty.[276] Hence, in the example based on *Leaf v International Galleries* above, the gallery owner may say: "I know it was sharp practice, but I also knew it was permissible within the (civil) law, otherwise I would not have done it. I sought throughout to abide by the law and made all the disclosures that the law required of me in order for the transaction to be valid." In such a scenario it is arguable that, by virtue of section 2(1)(a), D may not in law be considered dishonest. Furthermore, even if D does not reason with himself in that fashion and is merely keen to make the contract at that price, he will be aware of the facts which in law make the contract valid. From the perspective of the civil law, he does not have to believe in a claim of right to the money that V pays; he simply *has* the right to the money at civil law. It is quite remarkable that persons who unreflectingly enter valid contracts could in theory find themselves facing a charge of theft, a matter with clear implications for the fair notice protection guaranteed by Article 7 of the ECHR.[277]

### *(iii) Theft by keeping or omission*

The mere decision to steal is not sufficient for theft.[278] There must be conduct as well, amounting to an appropriation. We have noted that this is not a very stringent restriction: picking a tin of beans off the shelves of a supermarket is theft if D does so with intent to steal. Thus, although a decision to thieve is not enough, some very preliminary conduct is.

Moreover, the conduct may be an omission, as distinct from a fresh positive act. It is sufficient for theft that D keeps property lawfully obtained: indeed, section 3(1) expressly states that a person may steal something by "keeping . . . it as owner". In the New Zealand case of *Subritzky*,[279] failing to return a toy taken innocently by D's child was held to be theft by conversion and, it is submitted, would be theft by appropriation also. Likewise borrowing

[275] Below, § 13.8(i).

[276] As it happens, Lord Hutton's dissent goes further: it advocates a general rule that there can never be a finding of dishonesty where the transfer of ownership is fully valid. But such a rule was implicitly rejected by the majority decision. The exploitative conduct by Karen Hinks was dishonest: everyone, and most importantly the jury, agreed on this. Nonetheless, on the particular facts of a different case, there may be room to invoke s. 2(1)(a).

[277] Whilst accepting the need for the civil law of property and the law of theft to sing in unison, Green argues that it is the civil law, not the criminal law, that is out of tune with the needs of modern society—and that the civil law which should therefore be reformed: "Theft and Conversion" (2012) 128 *LQR* 564.

[278] Cp. *Eddy v Niman* (1981) 73 Cr App R 237 (DC); though the decision must now be read in light of *Gomez* [1993] AC 442 (above, § 13.6(ii)(a)).

[279] [1990] 2 NZLR 717. Similar facts occurred in the English case of *Walters v Lunt* [1951] 2 All ER 645 (DC), a decision based on the old law of larceny. See also *Thomas* (1953) 37 Cr App R 169 (CA).

a thing, and then keeping it having decided not to return it, may amount to theft—on the basis of the keeping rather than the borrowing.

The possibility of theft by keeping must, however, be approached with some caution. Generally, there is no liability for omissions in the criminal law and it seems that theft by keeping may be subject to special restrictions. In *Broom v Crowther*,[280] D purchased a stolen theodolite (a surveying instrument). Subsequently, he discovered that the device was stolen. D kept the theodolite for a further week until it was seized by the police. On appeal, D claimed that, after learning the truth of the matter, he had merely left the theodolite sitting in his bedroom while he pondered what to do; and that this was not an appropriation within the terms of the Theft Act 1968. The Divisional Court quashed his conviction for theft.

Usually, such a defendant may escape conviction by denying mens rea, since it will be difficult to prove dishonesty is these circumstances. It seems, however, that not all omissions to return something ("keepings") will count as appropriations. The qualifications are twofold. First, section 3(1) states that a person may steal something by "keeping . . . it *as owner*". This suggests, as *Broom v Crowther* seems to emphasise, that a mere "keeping" which does not manifest any decision to treat the property as D's own will not count as an appropriation. The keeping must amount, in effect, to a conversion: D's conduct must amount to a *usurpation* or denial of O's rights. This may depend upon the intention with which D acts: thus merely leaving the item in a drawer for safekeeping, as opposed to keeping the thing for oneself, is not a conversion[281] and, if *Broom v Crowther* is right, neither is it an appropriation for the purposes of theft. If the found item is placed in the drawer to be sold later, it has been appropriated.

Secondly, the essence of keepings is that they are omissions. As we saw in Chapter 4, the law is rightly reluctant to impose criminal liability for mere omissions, unless the circumstances give rise to a specific duty obligating D to act. It is submitted that this general principle applies also to theft. In other words, an omission cannot be an appropriation unless it is in contravention of D's duty to return the goods to V. Suppose the following three cases:

(1) D1 has hired a car from V. The period of hire has not expired. D1 decides to keep the car once the period of hire expires. He leaves it sitting on the driveway.
(2) D2 has hired a car from V. The period of hire has not expired. D2 decides to sell the car, which he then drives to Ireland, intending to trade it in there for a new vehicle.[282]
(3) D3 has hired a car from V. The period of hire has since expired. D3 decides to keep the car, which he leaves parked on his driveway.

Case (2) is straightforwardly one of theft: D2 appropriates the car by his positive act of driving it to Ireland. Equally, however, it is submitted that case (1) is not theft. Since the period of hire has not expired, D1 is under no duty to do return the car, and his omission to do so should not be regarded as an actus reus of theft.

[280] (1984) 148 JP 592 (DC). The case is also notable on a point concerning bona fide purchasers: below, § 13.6(v).
[281] Cp. *Police v Moodley* [1974] 1 NZLR 644.
[282] *Morgan* [1991] RTR 365 (CA).

Case (3) is more complex. D3's omission to return the car is in breach of the duty he owes to V, so prima facie is a "keeping" for the purposes of section 3(1). It is necessary, therefore, also to determine whether he has kept the car "as owner", or whether the *Broom v Crowther* exception is available. In our view, this is a case of theft.

### *(iv) Multiple and continuing appropriations*

Consider the following scenario, which is based on an example discussed in § 13.4(v):

> David finds a wallet in a busy street, and picks it up. He looks in the wallet for evidence of the owner's identity and finds none. The wallet contains no money. David puts the wallet in his pocket, concluding that it is lost rather than abandoned but that the true owner cannot be found. He then takes the wallet home and, on looking more carefully inside, finds the owner's name and address. Deciding to keep the wallet anyway because of its attractive appearance, he puts the wallet in a drawer. A month later, he takes the wallet out of the drawer and starts to use it.

How many times does David appropriate the wallet? When does he steal it? Section 3(1) states that *any* assumption of the rights of an owner is an appropriation, "and this includes, where he has come by the property (innocently or not) *without stealing it*, any later assumption of a right to it by keeping or dealing with it as owner". The specific inclusion of later appropriations, subject to the qualification "without stealing it", means that David appropriates the wallet *every* time he does anything with it, *until* he steals it. Once there is a moment in time when all the elements of theft are present, the wallet is stolen and he does not keep re-stealing it thereafter.[283] Let us conclude, in the above example, that David is not dishonest and lacks the mens rea for theft until he gets home and discovers the owner's name.[284] It follows that David appropriates the wallet (*inter alia*) when he picks it up, when he looks through it, when he puts it in his pocket, when he carries it with him, and when he puts it in the drawer. But not when he starts to use it a month later: by then, it is already stolen.

Sometimes the location or timing of a theft matters. In *Atakpu and Abrahams*,[285] the defendants used false documents to hire cars in Germany and Belgium. They drove the cars to England, intending to sell them, but were arrested by customs officials on arrival at Dover. The convictions for conspiracy to steal the vehicles were quashed, on the ground that the thefts were not committed in England and therefore English courts lacked jurisdiction. On the authority of *Gomez*,[286] the cars were first appropriated in Germany and Belgium. Given that the defendants had the mens rea for theft at that time, the cars were therefore

283 Williams, "Appropriation: A Single or Continuous Act?" [1978] *Crim LR* 69, 69: "A man steals a watch, and two weeks later sells it. In common sense and ordinary language he is not guilty of a second theft when he sells it. Otherwise it would be possible, in theory, to convict a thief of theft of a silver teapot every time he uses it to make the tea."

284 *Per* s. 2(1)(c): below, § 13.8(iii).

285 [1994] QB 69 (CA). See also *Morgan* [1991] RTR 365 (CA), where D took a leased car to Ireland and traded it in for a new car; he was convicted of theft in England.

286 Above, § 13.6(ii)(a). If *Gomez* had adopted the analysis in *Morris*, the problem would not have arisen since the first theftuous (in the sense of unauthorised) appropriation would have been when the cars were offered for sale in England.

already stolen before being brought into this country.[287] Hence, there could be no conspiracy to steal them in England.[288] As Ward J put it:[289]

> "Endeavouring to summarise it would seem that (1) theft can occur in an instant by a single appropriation but it can also involve a course of dealing with property lasting longer and involving several appropriations before the transaction is complete; (2) theft is a finite act—it has a beginning and it has an end; (3) at what point the transaction is complete is a matter for the jury to decide upon the facts of each case; (4) though there may be several appropriations in the course of a single theft or several appropriations of different goods each constituting a separate theft as in *Reg. v Skipp* [1975] Crim LR 114, no case suggests that there can be successive thefts of the same property. . . ."

Similarly, D can be convicted of robbery only if the use or threat of force occurs immediately before or at the time of the theft.[290] Thus if D steals goods from a supermarket, and after leaving the shop threatens the driver of the taxi carrying him, D commits no robbery since the theft is already complete.

It seems that an appropriation can also be a *continuing* act,[291] as opposed to one which is always completed instantaneously. Suppose the following variation:

> D picks goods off the shelf at a supermarket and puts them inside her jacket, intending to leave without paying for them. On the authority of *Gomez*, she has already stolen the goods. While approaching the cashier, however, she is accosted by the store's security guard. D strikes the guard violently, and runs from the store with the goods.

Does D commit robbery? The common-sense answer seems to be yes—even though, if the goods are already stolen, it is hard to see how that answer can be justified in law. The answer is justified by holding that D's appropriation of the goods was a single continuing act, lasting (say) for the period during which she puts the goods in her jacket and carries them out of the supermarket. While such an analysis sits somewhat uneasily with *Gomez*,[292] a number of decisions appear to recognise the possibility.[293] (An alternative approach, in the specific context of robbery, might be to construe liberally the requirement in section 8(1) that the force be used "at the time of" the stealing; thereby embracing force used in the proximate aftermath of D's theftuous act.[294])

[287] Contrast *Ashcroft* [2003] EWCA Crim 2365, where D, a haulier, was convicted of conspiring to steal goods in England which were first loaded onto his lorries in Scotland before being diverted in England. The Court of Appeal—it is submitted wrongly—dismissed D's claim that the theft occurred in Scotland, describing that analysis (at [43], [45]) as "some way removed from reality and we do not believe that *Gomez* was ever intended to apply to the sort of situation that obtains in this case. . . . In our judgment there never was in any ordinary sense of the word an 'appropriation' of the stolen goods until the conspirators removed them from the containers." But it is an ineluctable implication of *Gomez* that the goods were first appropriated in Scotland.

[288] For criticism of the jurisdictional aspects of *Atakpu* see Sullivan and Warbrick, "Territoriality, Theft and *Atakpu*" [1994] *Crim LR* 650, who argue that since the Theft Act 1968 does not have extra-territorial effect, the defendants' actions in Germany and Belgium were not appropriations within the Act. See also below, § 13.9.

[289] [1994] QB 69, 79 (CA).

[290] Theft Act 1968, s. 8(1). See below, § 14.3; and *Vinall* [2011] EWCA Crim 2652, [2012] 1 Cr App R 29.

[291] Cp. *Fagan v Metropolitan Police Commissioner* [1969] 1 QB 439 (DC); above, § 4.1(i)(b) (Case 4).

[292] Cp. *Atakpu and Abraham* [1994] QB 69, 80 (CA); but contrast *Lockley* [1995] Crim LR 656 (CA).

[293] E.g. *Bowden* [2002] EWCA Crim 1279; *Donaghy v Marshall* [1981] Crim LR 644 (Crown Court (Snaresbrook)); *Hale* (1979) 68 Cr App R 415 (CA); *Pitham and Hehl* (1977) 65 Cr App R 45, 49 (CA) (while denying it in the instant case). See Williams, "Appropriation: A Single or Continuous Act?" [1973] *Crim LR* 69.

[294] Cp. *Hale* (1979) 68 Cr App R 415 (CA); below, § 14.2(iii).

### (v) Bona fide purchasers

What is known as the *nemo dat* rule[295] means that if R steals a book from O, O retains ownership of the book even when R then sells the book to D, a purchaser who acts in good faith. Prima facie, if D were then to discover that the book was stolen, she would herself become liable to be convicted for theft. This possibility is avoided by section 3(2), which provides:

> Where property or a right or interest in property is or purports to be transferred for value to a person acting in good faith, no later assumption by him of rights which he believed himself to be acquiring shall, by reason of any defect in the transferor's title, amount to theft of the property.

In *Wheeler*,[296] a dealer purchased a variety of military antiques. He then sold one of the items, a medal. Subsequently, before delivering the medal and receiving payment, he discovered that the medal was stolen. His conviction was quashed: the application of section 3(2) meant that D committed no theft by completing the transaction. Neither was D guilty of handling.[297] (He might, however, be guilty of the offence of fraud if the purchaser had been induced to make payment by D's representation, implied or express, that D was their owner.)[298]

It appears that a purchaser will not be regarded as "in good faith" for the purposes of section 3(2) if she suspects that the goods are stolen. It is not necessary for her to be convinced of the matter. In *Broom v Crowther*,[299] D purchased a theodolite (a piece of surveying equipment) from R for £5. The instrument was worth about £200. After later discovering that it was in fact stolen, D kept the theodolite for a further week until it was seized by the police. In convicting him for theft, the magistrates ruled that the exception in section 3(2) was inapplicable, since D had not acted in good faith: at the time when he made the purchase, D had suspected the device was stolen and had accepted R's denial without pursuing the matter because the bargain was so advantageous. (The conviction was quashed on other grounds: see § 13.6(iii) above.)

### (vi) Bank accounts

Suppose D, a company director of V Ltd., forges a cheque on V's account with bank B. Does D commit theft? The answer, it appears, is yes. V's account with B is a chose in action that can be stolen[300] and, according to the Privy Council in *Chan Man-sin*,[301] V appropriates that account when he assumes V's right, as owner, to draw cheques on the account.

[295] The principle *nemo dat quod non habet* means that nobody can pass on a title to property that they do not themselves possess.
[296] (1991) 92 Cr App R 279 (CA).
[297] *Bloxham* [1983] 1 AC 109.
[298] Surprisingly, the Court in *Wheeler* also quashed D's conviction for obtaining by deception (as the offence then was), apparently reasoning that there was no deception: because the sale was in market overt, D's implied representation that the buyer would get good title to the medal was true. But D had *expressly* stated that the medal was not stolen, which was a deception.
[299] (1984) 148 JP 592 (DC). See Spencer, "Handling, Theft and the *Mala Fide* Purchaser" [1985] *Crim LR* 92; Williams, "Handling, Theft and the Purchaser who takes a Chance" [1985] *Crim LR* 432; Spencer, "Handling and Taking Risks—A Reply to Professor Williams" [1985] *Crim LR* 440. The case is discussed earlier, in § 13.6(iii), in respect of a different point taken by D in his successful appeal.
[300] Above, § 13.3(i)(c).
[301] *Chan Man-sin v A-G of Hong Kong* [1988] 1 All ER 1 (PC). The same analysis appears in *Burke* [2000] Crim LR 413 (CA). See also below, § 13.7(ii).

It must be said that this reasoning is debatable. Prima facie, D obtained by deception; he stole nothing—at least, nothing from V.[302] In particular, although the bank account was clearly property belonging to V, it is arguable that nothing done by D affected or was even relevant to that account. The bank only *purported* to debit V's account—in law it still owed V the full account balance—because the forged cheque was a nullity, nothing more.[303] Although D *pretended* to deal with V's bank account, in law he no more dealt with V's chose in action against B than he dealt with any of the accounts held by anyone else at the bank. The real wrong was obtaining by deception the *proceeds* of the cheque[304]—but the victim of that crime was bank B, not V. No property right of V's was harmed by D. If that is right, why should V be treated as the victim of a theft?

On the other hand, and in defence of the current law, it may be argued that by pretending to deal with V's bank account, D "assumed" the right of an owner over the account and therefore appropriated it within the meaning of section 3(1).[305] Moreover, V *will* normally suffer the disadvantage of a wrongful debit against its account, which will remain in place, and cause an effective loss to V, until the forgery is discovered (if ever). So, although the law on this point is problematic, it is not without justification.

The analysis is different where the cheque is not a nullity. *Chan Man-sin* may be contrasted with the case of *Kohn*,[306] where D had authority to draw cheques.[307] He abused that authority by withdrawing money for personal gain. In that case, the cheques were valid and not mere forgeries, so that the company's bank account was rightfully debited. Thus D was properly convicted of theft, from the company, by appropriating its bank account.

Another difficult case is where D, by dishonest conduct, induces V to debit her bank account in D's favour. In *Williams*,[308] as we saw earlier, the Court of Appeal decided this could be an appropriation, and so upheld the conviction of D, a dishonest builder, who had presented V with a dishonestly inflated bill, which V had paid by writing a cheque that D presented to V's bank, which duly debited V's account in D's favour. This result is hard to square, however, with the later case of *Darroux*:[309]

> The defendant was the manager employed by a charity to run a sheltered housing project which it owned. Her duties included keeping records of the hours that she and the other employees worked and passing them to X Ltd, which provided the charity with payroll services, and which would then calculate the employees' earnings and issue instructions to the charity's bank to pay

[302] Unless, perhaps, he stole the paper on which the cheque was written. Given that D obtained by deception—pursuant, therefore, to a voidable transfer—the decision in *Gomez* (above, § 13.6(ii)(a)) means that he may also have stolen whatever he obtained in return for the forged cheque.

[303] *Tai Hing Cotton Mill Ltd v Liu Chong Hing Bank Ltd* [1986] AC 80 (PC).

[304] This proposition is subject to further complication where the "proceeds" take the form of a money transfer (cp. *Preddy* [1996] AC 815, swiftly remedied by s. 15A of the Theft Act 1968). See below, § 15.1.

[305] That was also the conclusion of the Court of Appeal in *Re Osman* [1990] 1 WLR 277, 294–5, where D, a company chairman, sent a telex instructing the company's bank to transfer money from the company's account. The Court ruled that purporting to deal with the bank account qua owner was, in itself, an appropriation regardless of the effect on the account itself and even if the account was never debited. For approving comment, see [1988] Crim LR 611.

[306] (1979) 69 Cr App R 395 (CA); discussed above, § 13.3(i)(c).

[307] To similar effect is *Hilton* [1997] 2 Cr App R 445 (CA), where D controlled a charity's bank account and had authority to instruct the bank to make transfers.

[308] [2001] 1 Cr App R 362 (CA).

[309] [2018] EWCA Crim 1009, [2019] QB 33.

them by direct debit. By dishonestly exaggerating the hours that she had worked, she caused herself to be significantly overpaid.

On these facts the Court quashed the conviction, on the ground that there was no appropriation. In so holding it followed *Briggs*,[310] the facts of which were slightly more complicated, but were in principle the same: D, by fraud, induced X, who held funds in a bank account for V, to apply the balance of the account to the benefit of D.[311] But *Briggs* is a problematical decision because, surprisingly, it was decided with no reference to the trilogy of House of Lords decisions on appropriation: *Lawrence v Metropolitan Police Commissioner*, *Gomez*, and *Hinks*. In the first of these, *Lawrence*, the House of Lords accepted the proposition that it is an appropriation, and hence potentially a theft, to use deceptive conduct to cause the victim to make a payment—and in *Gomez* and *Hinks* the decision in *Lawrence* was then followed and approved. If the use of deceptive conduct to cause V to make a payment is an appropriation of the funds transferred, it is hard to see why it cannot also be an appropriation to deceive a person who controls V's bank account to achieve the same result.

In *Darroux*, the Court of Appeal noticed that these key decisions were not discussed in *Briggs*, but was untroubled by the omission. It ought to have been troubled, though, because the omission means that *Briggs* was decided *per incuriam*. At the same time, the Court in *Darroux* distinguished *Williams* by holding that the builder's inducing V to write a cheque was proximate enough to securing a payment from V's bank account to count as an appropriation, whereas Darroux's submitting a false claim to X Ltd "was too far removed to be an act of appropriation with regard to the bank account".[312] The distinction is a fine one, but it means that, for now at least, the decision in *Williams* represents the law.

In practice, there is now no need to stretch the boundaries of the crime of theft by prosecuting dishonest people such as Williams, Briggs, and Darroux for *theft* because their behaviour now falls squarely within the crime of fraud created by the Fraud Act 2006, described in Chapter 15 below. As the Court of Appeal observed in *Darroux* itself, that is the offence with which they should be charged.

### (vii) Law reform?

The overcriminalisation resulting from the decisions in *Gomez* and *Hinks* should make us consider whether the time has come to recast the law of theft again, as was done with the Theft Act in 1968.[313] But such a reform seems unlikely, unless and until the potential overbreadth of the law produces actual prosecutions that strike the public as visibly unjust.

310 [2004] EWCA Crim 3662, [2004] 1 Cr App R 34.

311 D, a relative of V1 and V2, "helped" the elderly Vs to sell their big house and buy a small one more suited to their current needs. The big house was sold, and the proceeds of sale held by a firm of conveyancers, Bentons. D then arranged for the Vs to get Bentons to transfer the necessary slice of the proceeds to the vendors of the small house and, against the wishes of the Vs, induced the vendors of the small house to convey it to D instead of to the Vs. The Court of Appeal quashed D's conviction for theft on the ground that D's conduct did not amount to an appropriation of the fund, belonging to the Vs and currently in the hands of Bentons. The case is criticised by Heaton, "Cheques and Balances" [2005] *Crim LR* 747, and by Ormerod at [2004] *Crim LR* 409.

312 [2018] EWCA Crim 1009, [2019] QB 33, [61].

313 For one suggestion, see Tamblyn, "Reforming Theft: Taking without Consent" [2020] *Crim LR* 597.

## § 13.7 Intention permanently to deprive

### *(i) The core definition*

Dishonest borrowing is not theft, no matter how much inconvenience it causes the owner. If D, a law student, dishonestly takes a book from the law library by concealing it in his bag, he commits theft if he intends not to return the book, but not if he means to keep the book only until the end of term.[314] It is not theft even if D realises there is a chance he will be unable to return the book (e.g. because he has a habit of losing books in his possession).[315] To fulfil the requirements of theft, D must have the *intention* permanently to deprive V of her property. This requirement, stated in section 1(1), is not defined in the Theft Act 1968, although there are some complex supplementary provisions in section 6 (see § 13.7(ii)). For the most part, however, the core meaning of "intention permanently to deprive" has presented few problems. Generally, it is sufficient that D has an intention indefinitely to exclude V from exercising her right to the property.

#### *(a) Dishonest borrowing*

Some writers have questioned the rule that borrowing is not theft,[316] and its wisdom is certainly arguable. The owner may well have a civil action against D for use and enjoyment, and in many cases the very point of her ownership is to monopolise the use and enjoyment of which she is deprived by D. Suppose that O, a law student, owns a textbook on criminal law. D dishonestly takes the book, intending to keep it until the criminal law exam has been sat by both D and O. As things stand, D has not stolen the book.[317] Yet O has been frustrated in the very reason she bought the book. She is likely to have to buy another copy in the meantime. Provided D is dishonest, there is a good case for treating such behaviour as criminal, and at least an arguable case for treating it as theft.

Additionally, criminalisation of dishonest borrowing may assist in resolving an evidential difficulty. Sometimes where D claims that he intended to return the thing "borrowed" (e.g. where D takes a book from the library), it may be hard to prove that he intended to keep the thing permanently.

Against these arguments, it may be thought harsh to equate a mere borrowing with theft. Although the inconvenience to O may sometimes be comparable, as a *general* proposition the wrong of permanently taking O's property is far more substantial than the wrong of temporarily interfering with her use and enjoyment. In practice, evidential difficulties with the present law have not been overwhelming, and are surely insufficient to justify a radical change in the substantive law. Moreover, enacting an offence of dishonest borrowing would place even greater pressure on the issue of dishonesty, itself (as we shall see) a judgement call by the jury. To do so would leave the law of theft both extraordinarily wide and extremely vague, thereby undermining the principle of fair warning and the rule of law, and potentially giving rise to incompatibility with Article 7 of the European Convention.

314 Cp. *Neal v Gribble* [1978] RTR 409 (DC).

315 Cp. *Crump* (1825) 1 C & P 658, 171 ER 1357. This would be a case of recklessness whether the owner is deprived, rather than of intention: above, §§ 5.1(iii), 5.2.

316 Williams, "Temporary Appropriation should be Theft" [1981] *Crim LR* 129; Bein, "The Theft of Use and the Element of 'Intent to Deprive Permanently' in Larceny" (1968) 3 *Israel LR* 368.

317 Neither does s. 6(1) apply: below, § 13.7(ii)(b).

While not enacting a general offence, the 1968 Act does criminalise specific forms of borrowing. Certain cases are treated as theft by virtue of section 6, which is considered in § 13.7(ii) below. There are also some specific offences. Section 12 creates an offence of taking a motor vehicle or other conveyance without authority; section 12A enacts a related offence of aggravated vehicle-taking; while section 11 criminalises the removal (with or without an intention permanently to deprive) of items from public buildings.[318]

*(b) Deprivation*

The essence of theft is deprivation, not gain. Thus, what must be intended is that the owner be deprived (permanently), not that any benefit endure to D or anyone else. Thus it is theft for D to appropriate O's goods intending to destroy them,[319] to hide them so that they are never found,[320] or to give them away. This point, which was also true under the pre-Act law of larceny,[321] is now made explicit in section 1(2) of the 1968 Act:

> It is immaterial whether the appropriation is made with a view to gain, or is made for the thief's own benefit.

*(c) Change of mind*

If D steals something, intending to keep it, then later changes his mind and decides to return the thing, this is theft.[322] It is too late. At the time the actus reus occurs, D has the mens rea for theft.

*(d) An ulterior intention*

The intent to deprive is an ulterior intention,[323] accompanying the actus reus rather than directed toward the actus reus itself. Thus the requirement is not merely that D intend the appropriation *per se*, but that the act of appropriation be done with the *further* intent that the owner be deprived permanently, either by that act or by some other act.

The importance of this point is that there is no requirement that D should intend to deprive V by *that very* act of appropriation. As was noted in § 13.6, it is sufficient that D appropriates the goods while intending that the owner should be deprived, even if the deprivation will be accomplished only by some later act of D's.[324] Suppose, for example, that D changes the labels on two products (product A and product B) in a supermarket, intending to buy the more expensive item, product A, at the lower price of product B. D steals product

[318] And students should note the Highways Act 1980, s. 174(4), under which a person commits an offence if he "takes down, alters or removes any barrier, traffic sign, support or light erected or placed in pursuance of subsection (1) above or any fence, barrier, traffic sign or light erected or placed on or near a street in pursuance of any other enactment for the purpose of warning users of the street of any obstruction, whether caused by the execution of works in or near the street or otherwise, or of protecting them from danger arising out of such an obstruction".

[319] *Welsh* [1974] RTR 478 (CA) (D, a motorist stopped on suspicion of drink-driving, destroyed a urine sample that he had given for analysis); cp. *Cabbage* (1815) R & R 292, 168 ER 809 (D backed a horse down a mineshaft in order to destroy evidence of the horse's theft).

[320] Cp. *Wynn* (1848) 1 Den 365, 169 ER 283 (D, a postal worker, flushed letters down a lavatory in order to conceal the fact that he had sorted them incorrectly).

[321] Turner, "Larceny and Lucrum" (1941) 4 *Toronto LJ* 296.

[322] Cp. *Easom* [1971] 2 QB 315, 320 (CA).

[323] Above, § 5.1(vii).

[324] *Morris* [1984] AC 320.

A as soon as he touches it, even though this is not the act of appropriation by which the owner will be deprived.

*(e) Paying for or returning similar goods*

In *Velumyl*,[325] D dishonestly borrowed £1,050 from his employer's safe, without authority and in breach of company rules. D apparently intended to repay the amount borrowed. He was nonetheless convicted of theft. Although D intended to return an equivalent sum of money, it would not be the identical notes and coins that he had taken, merely substitute money to the same value. Hence, the Court concluded, D intended to deprive V permanently of the particular notes and coins that he appropriated.

Similarly, if D were to take a bag of sugar from V's kitchen, intending to buy another bag and replace it, D would still intend to deprive V permanently of the particular bag taken. *A fortiori*, a case where D intends to give V some money to pay for the sugar.[326] (Of course, an issue may arise in such cases whether D has acted dishonestly.)

*(f) Conditional intention*

In *Easom*,[327] D picked up a handbag in a cinema. He searched through the handbag in order to ascertain its contents, then put the handbag back having decided that none of the contents were worth stealing. D was charged with theft of "one handbag, one purse, one notebook, a quantity of tissues, a quantity of cosmetics and one pen", and at first instance was convicted. However, the Court of Appeal quashed his conviction, ruling that:[328]

> "In every case of theft the appropriation must be accompanied by the intention of permanently depriving the owner of his property. What may be loosely described as a 'conditional' appropriation will not do. If the appropriator has it in mind merely to deprive the owner of such of his property as, on examination, proves worth taking and then, finding that the booty is valueless to the appropriator, leaves it ready . . . to be repossessed by the owner, the appropriator has not stolen. If a dishonest postal sorter picks up a pile of letters, intending to steal any which are registered, but, on finding that none of them are, replaces them, he has stolen nothing."

The decision is probably right, but only in terms of the precise charge that was brought. D certainly appropriated the purse, notebook, tissues, etc., inside the handbag. However, at no time did D intend to deprive the owner of such things. He was looking for something else.

Suppose, however, that D had been charged with stealing "the contents" of the handbag. In that case, D should have been convicted.[329] Again, he certainly appropriated the contents.[330] Thus the actus reus element of theft is satisfied. This time, however, the mens

[325] [1989] Crim LR 299 (CA). Cp. *McCall* (1971) 55 Cr App R 175 (CA); *Duru* [1973] 3 All ER 715 (CA); *Williams* [1953] 1 All ER 1068, 1070 (CA).

[326] Cp. Theft Act 1968, s. 2(2).

[327] [1971] 2 QB 315 (CA).

[328] *Ibid.*, 319.

[329] *A-G's Reference (Nos. 1 and 2 of 1979)* [1980] QB 180 (CA).

[330] Note that the terminology of a "conditional appropriation", coined in the quotation from *Easom* in the text, must be regarded as outmoded in the wake of *Gomez* (above, § 13.6(ii)(a)). If even an authorised touching of goods is now regarded as an appropriation, D's conduct in *Easom* is surely also an appropriation.

rea requirement is also satisfied—by a conditional intention.[331] Not yet knowing what they were, D intended to steal any of "the contents" of the handbag should they prove desirable. Thus, it is submitted, he appropriated the contents with intent (conditionally) to deprive the owner of them. Since conditional intention is treated in law as intention,[332] that looks like theft. The fact that he subsequently returned the bag and its contents is irrelevant. They were already stolen.[333]

At the level of policy, there seems little merit in acquitting the defendant in such circumstances. Pre-*Gomez*, it may have been appropriate to treat such cases either as mere preparatory action or as an attempted theft, but that possibility is now gone. D plans to steal the contents, subject only to a condition outside his control (i.e. that they are valuable); he executes the plan; he appropriates the contents. The actus reus of theft has already occurred. Certainly, D's conduct can no longer be regarded as merely preparatory. Given his moral culpability, D ought to be convicted of theft.

A different type of case is where D intends to steal valuable contents, if any, from a handbag which he has no intent to take but puts the handbag back because it is empty. That is a case of attempted theft;[334] because there is no actus reus. Although, in such a case, D has a (conditional) intent to steal the contents, he does not appropriate them since they do not exist.

There is a third type of case. Consider the following variation:

> D takes V's handbag, intending to keep the diamond ring that (he thinks) is in the bag. Later, he discovers that the handbag contains no ring, merely some credit cards (for which D has no use). He returns the bag with the credit cards inside.

D does not steal the handbag, since he has no intention to keep the bag itself. He does not steal a ring, since there is none; though he could be charged with attempted theft of the ring.[335] Neither does he steal the credit cards *per se*, since he has no intention to deprive the owner of them. Moreover, this is not a case of conditional intention to steal anything valuable. Rather, it involves a specific, frustrated, intention to steal a diamond ring. Should D be convicted of theft of "the contents" of the handbag, or only of attempted theft of the ring?

As the law stands, it appears that D can be convicted of theft of the contents.[336] This description may seem rather vague, but it should be recalled that the Theft Act criminalises theft of any "property belonging to another". Even though it matters to D, from the point of view of the law the difference between a ring and credit cards is an immaterial variation.[337]

331 A fine distinction exists between the case of a defendant who investigates the contents with a view to later deciding whether to steal (i.e. one who has not yet made any decision to steal) and that of one who has decided to steal the contents should they prove upon investigation to be valuable. Arguably, the close psychological relationship between decisions and intentions suggests that in the former case (and perhaps in *Easom* itself) the defendant has not yet formed an intention to steal, provided D's conduct is more than preparatory. However, such a fine distinction arguably is out of place here, since the condition upon which the decision depends is merely a matter of circumstances external to the defendant. It certainly would not operate to exculpate the postal sorter in the example cited by the court.

332 Above, § 5.1(viii). See Campbell, "Conditional Intention" (1982) 2 *LS* 77; also Child, "Understanding Ulterior Mens Rea" (2017) 76 *CLJ* 311.

333 Cp. above, § 13.6(ii)(b).

334 Cp. *Smith and Smith* [1986] Crim LR 166 (CA).

335 Contrast *Husseyn* (1978) 67 Cr App R 131, a case decided before the law on impossible attempts was altered by the Criminal Attempts Act 1981 (see above, § 9.5).

336 Cp. *A-G's Reference (Nos. 1 and 2 of 1979)* [1980] QB 180 (CA).

337 See above, § 5.7.

D had the actus reus for theft of the cards and the mens rea for theft of a ring. Both are forms of property, which is all the Act requires.

If doubts exist as to how far a conditional intent will do for the completed offence of theft, there is no doubt that such an intent will usually satisfy the mens rea requirement for a number of other related offences: in particular, conspiracy,[338] attempted theft,[339] and burglary.[340]

### *(ii) Section 6: extensions and special cases*

Often, a thief has no particular agenda regarding the fate of the property he steals. If D means to pawn stolen goods, or to use them before discarding them, he may not intend that the original owner be permanently deprived. He may be indifferent to their ultimate destiny. While many of these cases can be treated as intention on the basis that it is virtually certain the owner will be deprived permanently,[341] sometimes it may be quite likely that the owner will recover the property. In order to make it explicit that the Act extends to such cases, Parliament enacted section 6:

> (1) A person appropriating property belonging to another without meaning the other permanently to lose the thing itself is nevertheless to be regarded as having the intention of permanently depriving the other of it if his intention is to treat the thing as his own to dispose of regardless of the other's rights; and a borrowing or lending of it may amount to so treating it if, but only if, the borrowing or lending is for a period and in circumstances making it equivalent to an outright taking or disposal.
>
> (2) Without prejudice to the generality of subsection (1) above, where a person, having possession or control (lawfully or not) of property belonging to another, parts with the property under a condition as to its return which he may not be able to perform, this (if done for purposes of his own and without the other's authority) amounts to treating the property as his own to dispose of regardless of the other's rights.

Section 6 is not clearly worded and the drafting makes a straightforward interpretation of this section impossible. The history of the provision suggests that the idea was simply to codify the case law that had interpreted the phrase "intention permanently to deprive" when it appeared in the definition of larceny, the precursor offence to theft. According to this earlier case law, an intention to deprive (i.e. not mere recklessness) was normally required, but there were three cases in which recklessness, or something akin to it, was sufficient. The first was the "ransom principle", whereby it counted as an intention to deprive if the defendant's idea was to return the property only if the owner was prepared to pay for it.[342] The second was the "essential quality" principle, whereby it counted as an intention permanently to deprive if the defendant meant the owner to get his property back only after it had undergone a fundamental change; for example, a live horse taken and a dead horse returned.[343] The third was the "pawning principle", whereby it counted as an intention permanently to deprive if the defendant pawned another person's property without his

[338] § 9.2(ii) above.
[339] § 9.4(iii) above.
[340] § 14.3(iv) below; this was the point at issue in *A-G's Reference (Nos. 1 and 2 of 1979)* [1980] QB 180 (CA).
[341] Above, § 5.1(iv).
[342] *Hall* (1849) 3 Cox 245; *Peters* (1843) 1 Car and Kir 246, 174 ER 795.
[343] Cp. *Cabbage* (1815) Russ & Ry 292, 168 ER 809; *Richards* (1844) 1 Car & Kir 532, 174 ER 925.

consent, hoping to be able to redeem the pledge but realising he might be unable to do so.[344] However, the wording of the section does not make it clear that codification of such rules was the intended aim, and the purpose can only be detected by reading the parliamentary debates.[345] As the language of section 6(1) is singularly opaque, it is possible to give it a wide meaning, or a narrow one—so some cases interpret it in the narrow sense, others in the wider one.

One of the earlier decisions on section 6 is *Lloyd*.[346] D, a film projectionist, borrowed films and passed them to E, who made and sold pirate copies of the films. The Court of Appeal ruled this was not theft.[347] In reaching this decision the court referred to pre-1968 case law, and (in essence) took the position that section 6 merely confirmed it. Although section 6 makes it clear that some "borrowings" involve an intention permanently to deprive, the court said:

> "Borrowing is *ex hypothesi* not something which is done with intention permanently to deprive. This half of the subsection, we believe, is intended to make it clear that a mere borrowing is never enough to constitute the necessary guilty mind unless the intention is to return the 'thing' in such a changed state that it can truly be said that all its goodness or virtue is gone."

More recently, a similar approach was taken in *Mitchell*.[348] Here D was one of a gang of thieves who, having crashed their getaway car, violently hijacked V's BMW, eventually abandoning it a few miles away on the road with its hazard lights flashing. For this D was convicted of robbery—a crime which, as we explain in Chapter 14, is theft aggravated by violence. Having referred to *Lloyd*, the Court of Appeal quashed D's robbery conviction on the ground that there was no underlying theft. In this case, D did not intend V to lose her car permanently, and his intention to take it temporarily could not be converted into an intention permanently to deprive by invoking section 6(1).

However, section 6(1) does say, *inter alia*, that a defendant is "to be regarded as having the intention of permanently depriving the other of it if his intention is to treat the thing as his own to dispose of regardless of the other's rights". Although the phrase "dispose of" can be read in a narrow sense, as meaning "to get rid of once and for all", it can also be read in a wide sense, to mean "to deal with". And there are cases in which the courts have taken it in the wider sense, thereby converting into theft acts by defendants who did not really mean the owner to lose his property. One such case is *DPP v Lavender*,[349] where D dishonestly removed two doors from a house and hung them in another house. Both houses were owned by the council. The Divisional Court ruled that D had committed theft. Although the council had not in fact been deprived of the doors, D had nonetheless "disposed" of them within the meaning of section 6(1). With respect, this result seems odd. There was no disposal of the doors in the narrow sense—they were not thrown out, destroyed, or sold.[350] They were merely moved, and there was no suggestion by his conduct that D intended to treat them as his own, since they continued to be affixed to council property. Another

344 *Beecham* (1851) 5 Cox 181.
345 See Spencer, "The Metamorphosis of Section 6 of the Theft Act" [1977] *Crim LR* 653.
346 [1985] QB 829 (CA).
347 *Ibid.*, 836 (Lord Lane CJ). Cp. *Bagshaw* [1988] Crim LR 321 (CA).
348 [2008] EWCA Crim 850.
349 [1994] Crim LR 297 (DC). Cp. *Cahill* [1993] Crim LR 141 (CA).
350 For discussion, see A.T.H. Smith, *Property Offences* (1994) §§ 6-33, 6-34.

case to take this line is *Marshall*.[351] In this case, D had been making money in the London underground by begging unexpired day tickets from passengers who had completed their last journeys of the day and reselling them to other passengers. For this D was convicted of theft of the tickets from London Transport, which had issued them. On appeal, he sought to argue that, as he knew the tickets would eventually find their way back to London Transport at the end of the day, he had no intention permanently to deprive. Rejecting the narrow construction that was put on section 6 in *Lloyd*, the Court of Appeal upheld the conviction.

The courts have also taken a broad view of section 6 when dealing with those who have improperly interfered with other people's bank accounts. In *Chan Man-sin*,[352] discussed earlier, D dishonestly drew cheques on his employer's bank account. The Privy Council ruled that D had dealt with the company's property (i.e. its chose in action against the bank) as if it were his to dispose of without regard to the company's rights. But if, as we saw in § 13.6(vi), unauthorised drawings of this sort are a nullity, then arguably D did not dispose of the account at all. At law, nothing done by D in any way affected the relationship between the company and the bank. D merely tricked the bank into crediting D's own account (and wrongly posting a debit to V's account). The Privy Council appears to have equated "purporting or pretending to dispose of the thing as one's own" with "disposing of the thing as one's own". The decision is debatable. Nonetheless, as things stand, this is the law: the intent to make an apparent or pretended disposal is sufficient for section 6(1).

What can be said with some degree of certainty is that section 6(1) covers both the "ransom principle" and the "essential quality principle", by which the courts extended the concept of intention permanently to deprive before 1968. An example of the first is *Raphael*,[353] where D's conviction for theft was affirmed where he had taken V's car away from him by force, and then attempted to sell it back to him. And an example of the second is *DPP v J*,[354] in which the defendants forcibly took V's headphones, snapped them, and returned them to V. On appeal, it was held that the magistrates had been wrong to accept a submission of no case to answer: a person who took something and dealt with it for the purpose of rendering it useless demonstrated the intention of treating that article as his own to dispose of. But a definitive answer to the question of how much other ground (if any) the section covers is obscure, and destined to remain so until the day—if it comes—that the matter is finally resolved by the Supreme Court.[355]

### *(a) Parting with property under a condition as to its return*

If D dishonestly takes goods and pawns or pledges them, intending to redeem and return the goods but aware there is a risk he may be unable to do so, the operation of section 6(2) means that he commits theft. It is difficult to see why pledging goods should not count as a disposition within the scope of section 6(1), in which case section 6(2) is unnecessary.

351 [1998] 2 Cr App R 282 (CA).

352 [1988] 1 All ER 1 (PC); also *Burke* [2000] Crim LR 413 (CA); *Re Osman* [1990] 1 WLR 277, 294–5 (DC). See above, §§ 13.3(i)(c), 13.6(vi).

353 [2008] EWCA Crim 1014.

354 [2002] EWHC 291 (Admin).

355 The Court of Appeal reviewed a long list of authorities on s. 6 in *Vinall* [2011] EWCA Crim 2652, [2012] 1 Cr App R 29, concluding that, uncertain as its outer limits may be, the section does extend the concept of intention permanently to deprive beyond the limits of the pre-existing common law. The case is further discussed in relation to robbery: below, § 14.3.

## § 13.8 Dishonesty

In addition to the other elements required for theft, D must appropriate the property dishonestly. Unfortunately, the 1968 Act gives no definition of dishonesty. This is not to say that the Act is silent on the matter. According to section 2:

(1) A person's appropriation of property belonging to another is not to be regarded as dishonest—
(a) if he appropriates the property in the belief that he has in law the right to deprive the other of it, on behalf of himself or of a third person; or
(b) if he appropriates the property in the belief that he would have the other's consent if the other knew of the appropriation and the circumstances of it; or
(c) (except where the property came to him as trustee or personal representative) if he appropriates the property in the belief that the person to whom the property belongs cannot be discovered by taking reasonable steps.
(2) A person's appropriation of property belonging to another may be dishonest notwithstanding that he is willing to pay for the property.

The operation of these provisions is, however, purely negative. If D falls within section 2(1), he is not dishonest. But if he falls outside the section, it does not follow that he *is* dishonest. The question whether he is dishonest must then be asked and answered independently. Similarly, section 2(2) merely excludes one defence from operating as a matter of law. If D was willing to pay for the property, he may or may not be dishonest—that question must be asked, and answered, separately—when account may be taken of the fact that she was willing to pay.

In deciding the issue of dishonesty, therefore, it is necessary to begin with section 2(1). It is only if those provisions do not apply that we must investigate the issue more generally.

### *(i) Belief that he has the right to deprive: section 2(1)(a)*

Section 2(1)(a) codifies the old common law defence of colour of right: D's belief that he is legally entitled to act as he does forecloses any finding of dishonesty. This means that D does not commit theft if she may have honestly believed her appropriation of the thing was *legally* entitled, even where her belief was based on ignorance, mistake of fact, or even mistake of law.[356] Examples of colour of right defences abound in the common law. In *Bernhard*,[357] for example, a woman who blackmailed her former lover thought she had a right to the money claimed; she was acquitted of demanding money with menaces. Similarly, in *Skivington*,[358] D held up a wages clerk and demanded his wife's wages: though this was an assault, it was held there was no theft and therefore no robbery, since he believed he had a lawful claim to the money.

*Skivington* demonstrates that since colour of right is a defence to theft, it is also a defence to other crimes in which theft or an intent to steal is an ingredient, such as

[356] *Bernhard* [1938] 2 KB 264 (CA).

[357] *Ibid.* V agreed to pay his mistress (D) a sum of money, which he did not; she then threatened to expose him to his wife and the public unless he paid up. D was acquitted of demanding money with menaces with intent to steal, as she—mistakenly—thought she had a valid claim to the money.

[358] [1968] 1 QB 166 (CA); cp. *Robinson* [1977] Crim LR 173 (CA).

robbery and burglary. In such cases, if D believes he is entitled to the money, the charge fails for lack of the theftuous element; it is irrelevant whether D believes he had a right to use force.

It may seem odd that such acquittals can be based on a mistake of law. But, as we have said, the moral wrong of theft can at least in part be thought of as the deliberate assumption of, or interference with, another's property rights. It is D's mental state that marks out that interference as deserving the attention of the criminal law, and more than a mere tortious conversion. It follows that someone who thinks she is not violating another person's property rights lacks the guilty mind that makes her actions worth criminalising.

For similar reasons, it is clear that an honest mistake is sufficient even if it be unreasonable. In *Holden*,[359] D, who worked for a tyre company, was charged with theft of scrap tyres from his employer. He claimed that he had seen others take tyres and had been permitted to do so by a supervisor. It was company policy that taking tyres, or permitting others to do so, was sackable conduct. D was convicted of theft after the judge directed the jury that the test of dishonesty was whether D reasonably believed he had a right to take the tyres. The Court of Appeal quashed the conviction. D's conduct was certainly a civil wrong. But, if the defendant was to be believed, he did not mean to act wrongfully. A mistake may be honest even when unreasonable, and negligent violation of another's property rights is not, and should not be, the stuff of theft.

A distinction should be drawn between the defence that D believes she has a *legal* right to the thing allegedly stolen, which operates through section 2(1)(a), and a belief that she has a *moral* justification for her act. Belief in moral justification may, but will not necessarily, include a belief that D is legally entitled to the thing taken. Where D knows she has no legal right to the thing, her belief in a moral right alone is not sufficient for the colour of right defence in section 2(1)(a).[360] It may, however, lead to her being found not dishonest on the general test (below, § 13.8(iv)).

### *(ii) Belief that the other would consent: section 2(1)(b)*

Social life is unavoidably a co-operative enterprise. Frequently, we anticipate the generosity of our family and friends by taking and using property in their absence. When we do so, we assume that the owner will not object. For example, in a prosecution for larceny prior to the Theft Act 1968, a farmer borrowed a bale of his neighbour's hay expecting to replace it with a bale of his own.[361] Although he had an intention permanently to deprive his neighbour of the particular bale he "borrowed",[362] his behaviour was accounted not dishonest and he was acquitted of larceny. This type of case is now covered by section 2(1)(b).

[359] [1991] Crim LR 478 (CA).

[360] Cp. *Harris v Harrison* [1963] Crim LR 497 (DC) (at common law). In *Hemmerly* (1976) 30 CCC (2d) 141, D, a drug dealer, was convicted of robbery. In his defence he argued that he was entitled to the money taken, as the victim owed it to him. However, it was clear that D did not believe he had a legal claim to the money; although belief in a moral right might negative dishonesty, it was held not to do so in this case.

[361] Case noted [1956] Crim LR 360.

[362] Above, § 13.7(i)(e).

### *(iii) Belief that the owner cannot be found: section 2(1)(c)*

Section 2(1)(c) encapsulates the finder's defence.[363] Recall the example stated earlier in this chapter:[364]

> David finds a wallet in a busy street, and picks it up. He looks in the wallet for evidence of the owner's identity and finds none, but does find some money. He puts the wallet in his pocket.

Does David commit theft? Assuming the wallet is indeed lost rather than abandoned, the question turns on whether David is dishonest. If he believes the owner cannot be found by taking reasonable steps, section 2(1)(c) will operate to absolve him.

Three points about this defence should be emphasised. First, David need not consider whether the owner can be found if *all possible* steps are taken. Only reasonable steps need be considered. What is reasonable will depend on the circumstances. If the wallet is inexpensive and contains very little money, David will probably not be required to make any great effort (even so, were an open police station close by, it may be adjudged unreasonable not to hand in the wallet). If the wallet contains hundreds of pounds, rather more may be expected.

The second point is that the question of what D *believes* is subjective. Consider the following variation:

> Joan finds a wallet in a busy street, and picks it up. She looks in the wallet for evidence of the owner's identity and finds none, but does find a few pound coins. (In fact, there is a name and address label in the wallet, but Joan's examination of the wallet is a careless one and she does not see it.) Joan puts the wallet in her pocket, concluding that it is lost rather than abandoned but that the true owner cannot be found. She then spends the money and takes the wallet home. On reaching home and looking more carefully inside the wallet, she finds the owner's name and address. Deciding to keep the wallet anyway, she puts it in a drawer.

Joan's initial mistake about the impossibility of tracing the owner need not be a reasonable one to take her outside the realm of dishonesty. Since she genuinely believes that the owner cannot be found, she is entitled to be regarded as not dishonest by virtue of section 2(1)(c). Hence, when she spends the money, she commits no theft. However, facts may change, and the defence may cease to be available—as in the example here. Joan is guilty of stealing the *wallet* when she puts it in the drawer.[365]

The foregoing points intersect at the requirement of "reasonable steps". In principle, while it is a subjective enquiry into what D's beliefs are about the circumstances, the assessment whether the steps (she believes to be) required to locate the owner are *reasonable* is an objective matter, which it is for the court to determine rather than D.[366] Suppose that

[363] Though its application is not restricted to finders, and would exculpate bailees where the bailor was now untraceable. See A.T.H. Smith, *Property Offences* (1994) § 7–42.

[364] Above, § 13.4(v).

[365] Cp. *Minigall v McCammon* [1970] SASR 82.

[366] This is generally true of reasonableness requirements: cp. the justificatory defences, discussed below, § 21.2(ii), (iv). Contrast, unusually, the defence of lawful excuse under s. 5 of the Criminal Damage Act 1971: below, § 14.5(vi)(b) (a reasonable means of protection). The emphatic role of s. 5(3) in that Act finds no correspondent here.

D finds a wallet containing £1,000 in notes, but has little sense of obligation and genuinely believes it is unreasonable to expect her to be inconvenienced by walking some 600 yards to the nearby police station in order to notify them of her discovery (which, she recognises, may help to locate the owner). Section 2(1)(c) would not be available.

### *(iv) The general test for dishonesty*

Assuming the defendant cannot avail herself of the defences contained in section 2(1), dishonesty falls to be resolved under the general test. This gives rise to two issues. The first relates to decision-making authority: who decides if a defendant is dishonest under the general test—judge or jury? The second issue concerns the content of the test: how is the applicable test to be worded or formulated? As for the first issue, whether the defendant was dishonest is a question of fact for the jury in much the same way as the evaluation whether force used was "reasonable" in the context of self-defence.[367] This point requires some explanation. The Supreme Court in *Hayes and Palombo* has confirmed that "[q]uestions of law are for the judge to decide", while the role of the jury "is to find the facts and apply the law as explained by the judge to those facts to arrive at a verdict".[368] The Court approvingly cited the words of Lord Reid in *Cozens v Brutus*,[369] to the effect that "the meaning of an ordinary word of the English language is not a question of law". Not long after the Theft Act 1968 came into force, the Court of Appeal in *Feely*[370] identified "dishonesty" as one such ordinary word of the English language to be treated as a question of fact, to be determined by the finder of fact, not the judge. "Fact" here is not contrasted with "value" as it often is in commonsense discourse; a judgment that someone was dishonest is an evaluative one, but as confirmed by the Supreme Court in *Hayes and Palombo*, it is a question of fact nevertheless. Thus it is useful to describe dishonesty as a question of "secondary or evaluative fact", to distinguish it from what may be called "primary fact", the commonsensical idea of fact as in "there is a cat in the garden" or "she intends to go to Scotland tomorrow". This is a departure from the position as it was before 1968. In the old crime of larceny (which theft has replaced), the defendant's guilt or innocence depended on whether he had acted "fraudulently". This was treated as a question of *law* and was narrowly interpreted by the judges. Hence the substitution in the 1968 Act of the old larceny term, "fraudulently", for the theft term, "dishonestly," was no mere change in terminology, but also marked a shift in decision-making authority away from the judge and to the jury. It has always been a controversial development. Williams thought such an evaluative question an unsuitable one for juries to decide. It invited, he believed, "lax notions about the right of property" into the law,[371] and he acidly commented that the "rot commenced with ... *Feely*",[372] a view strongly contested by Tur among others.[373] Nevertheless, as noted

[367] Below, § 21.2.
[368] [2025] UKSC 29, [2025] 1 WLR 3553, [106].
[369] [1973] AC 854, 861.
[370] [1973] QB 530, 537–8 (CA).
[371] *TBCL* 726.
[372] *Ibid.*, 725.
[373] Tur, "Dishonesty and the Jury: A Case Study in the Moral Content of Law" (1984) 18 *Royal Institute of Philosophy Supplements* 75.

above, that dishonesty is a question of fact for the jury has received strong recent support from the Supreme Court.[374]

Turning to the second question—the content of the test—initially there was uncertainty about exactly what it was that the tribunal of fact should be called upon to decide here. Some of the earlier cases took the position that the test of dishonesty was purely objective ("Was D dishonest according to generally accepted standards of behaviour"?),[375] while others took the view that it was subjective ("Did D believe that his behaviour was dishonest?").[376] In the 1982 case of *Ghosh*,[377] the Court of Appeal set out a two-part test for the jury or magistrates to apply, incorporating elements of both approaches:[378]

(i) Was what was done dishonest according to the ordinary standards of reasonable and honest people?
(ii) Did the defendant realise that reasonable and honest people would regard what he did as dishonest?

If the answer to both questions is yes, the jury should conclude that the defendant was dishonest.[379]

Although *Ghosh*, and the case law leading up to it, attracted an extensive critical literature,[380] the decision stood until 2017 when the Supreme Court condemned the second limb of the test in *Ivey v Genting Casinos (UK) Ltd*.[381] The facts of *Ivey v Genting* were as follows:

> Ivey was a professional gambler who sued for £7.7 million which he claimed he had won at punto banco (a kind of baccarat) in a casino run by Genting. Genting resisted Ivey's claim

[374] *Hayes* [2025] UKSC 29, [2025] 1 WLR 3553, [106]. For all that, it could be that the status of dishonesty as a question of fact for the jury is not as secure as this backing implies. At the time of writing, The Courts and Tribunals Bill (HC Bill (2024-26) [389]) is wending its way through the parliamentary process. Among much else, the government plans to cut back on jury trials for either-way offences such as theft, with the possible result that a significant proportion of thefts currently tried by jury will come to be tried by judge alone. Should the relevant provisions pass into legislation, so that significantly more theft cases are tried not by jury but by judge alone, this is likely to put strain on the current legal position that dishonesty is a question of fact for the jury, not a question of law for the judge. The sole judge would in such cases need to be both the trier of law and of fact, making a nonsense of the distinction. It is true that currently a significant number of theft cases are not tried by jury, but by magistrates. However, unlike judges, and like juries, the presence of (lay) magistrates in the criminal process is aimed at injecting community and non-professional norms and standards into the criminal justice system. Magistrates, moreover, deal with the relatively less serious cases of theft.

[375] *Feely* [1973] QB 530, 537–8 (CA).

[376] *Boggeln v Williams* [1978] 2 All ER 1061 (DC). To similar effect is *Gilks* [1972] 3 All ER 280, 283, where the Court of Appeal approved the trial judge's direction that the jury should "try and place yourselves in [the appellant's] position at that time and answer the question whether in your view he thought he was acting honestly or dishonestly". See also *Landy* [1981] 1 All ER 1172 (CA) (conspiracy to defraud); contrast *Greenstein* [1976] 1 All ER 1 (CA) (obtaining by deception).

[377] [1982] QB 1053 (CA).

[378] *Ibid.*, 1064.

[379] The *Ghosh* direction on dishonesty did not need not be given in every case, only when there was evidence of a divergence between the defendant's standards of honesty and those of "reasonable and honest people". See, among other cases, *Roberts* (1987) 84 Cr App R 117 (CA).

[380] See, e.g., Elliott, "Dishonesty under the Theft Act" [1972] *Crim LR* 625; Wasik, "Mens Rea, Motive and the Problem of 'Dishonesty' in the Law of Theft" [1977] *Crim LR* 543; Campbell, "The Test of Dishonesty in *R* v *Ghosh*" (1984) 43 *CLJ* 349; Griew, "Dishonesty: The Objections to *Feely* and *Ghosh*" [1985] *Crim LR* 341; Halpin, "The Test for Dishonesty" [1996] *Crim LR* 283; Halpin, *Definition in the Criminal Law* (2004) chap. 4.

[381] [2017] UKSC 67, [2018] AC 391.

> on the ground that he had cheated. Denying cheating, Ivey said that an ingredient in cheating is dishonesty as defined in *Ghosh*, which—as we have seen—then required both conduct in breach of accepted standards of behaviour and awareness by the actor that this is so. Ivey admitted raising his chances of winning by using a covert stratagem to which the casino owners would have objected if they had known of it; but said he thought it was legitimate to do so, which meant that he had not cheated.

Dismissing his appeal, the Supreme Court held that dishonesty in the sense required under the Theft Act is not a necessary element in cheating at cards. This holding was enough to dispose of the case. But the Court then went on to reject the second limb of the *Ghosh* test. The proper test, the Court said, was:

(a) what was the defendant's actual state of knowledge or belief as to the facts; and
(b) was his conduct dishonest by the standards of ordinary decent people?

The new first limb of the test, unlike the second limb of the original test in *Ghosh*, is a question of primary fact, involving no assessment of the *quality* of the defendant's behaviour; and for determining whether a given piece of behaviour is honest or dishonest we are now left with what was formerly the first limb of the *Ghosh* test, standing on its own. The Supreme Court's opinion was *obiter dicta* in a civil case, and according to the normal rules of precedent did not mean that the decision in *Ghosh* was partly overruled. But three years later a strong Court of Appeal in *Barton*,[382] sitting with five judges instead of the usual three, accepted the Supreme Court's criticisms, thereby affirming that the general test of dishonesty now consists of the application of the first limb of *Ghosh* test alone: "was what was done dishonest according to the ordinary standards of reasonable and honest people?"

Although this first limb of the Ghosh test has survived, the objective test that it contains is open to the criticism that it is rather open-ended to ask the jury to apply a standard of "reasonable and honest people" (in *Ghosh*) or of "ordinary decent people" (the phrase used in the earlier case of *Feely*[383]). Even though this is done with the intention of imposing an objective standard for dishonesty, it assumes juries and magistrates are heterogeneous and have consistent values, which is surely not the case.[384] Values in this country vary widely, both across and within socio-economic and cultural divides, and there is no reason to suppose that such variation does not extend to judgements of dishonesty. Do we really all concur, *pace* Lord Lane in *Ghosh*, that Robin Hood was dishonest—or that openly using force to release battery hens or destroy genetically modified crops is dishonest? Obviously, if different persons can reasonably hold different views about these questions, there is a risk of different verdicts, on the same set of facts, from different courts. Even an informed defendant may be unable to predict whether his

382 [2020] EWCA Crim 575, [2021] QB 685.

383 [1973] QB 530, 538 (CA).

384 It may be countered, so far as juries at least are concerned, that this assumption is not made by the test. What is required of juries, it may be said, is that they come to collective verdicts, not that they necessarily reach these verdicts *for the same reasons* as each other. If a unanimous or majority verdict, as the case may be, cannot be obtained, there must be an acquittal. Perhaps what the law seeks of a jury is something akin to what Rawls calls an "overlapping consensus": Rawls, "The Idea of an Overlapping Consensus" (1987) 7 *OJLS* 1. This counterargument works less well where it falls to a magistrate to decide the question of dishonesty, rather than a collective body such as a jury.

behaviour will contravene the law. Arguably, such uncertainty contravenes Article 7 of the ECHR.[385]

Dealing further with the first limb of the *Ghosh* test (which the decision in *Ivey* leaves untouched), an important point of principle arises where D belongs to a particular group. In such a case, who are the "reasonable and honest people" by whose standards the issue of honesty is determined? Is it "reasonable and honest" members of D's specialist group, or "reasonable and honest" members of society in general? The point arose in *Hayes*.[386] D, a banker, had been accused of conspiring with others to rig the LIBOR rate[387] in favour of the bank for which he worked and thereby, indirectly, in favour of himself. For this he was prosecuted for conspiracy to defraud (another crime in which dishonesty is an ingredient)[388] and convicted at a trial conducted on the basis that the appropriate standard was that of reasonable and honest members of society in general, rather than reasonable and honest bankers. Affirming his conviction, the Court of Appeal held that the trial judge's approach had been correct.[389]

Finally, after Hayes had served five and a half years in prison, his conviction was overturned by the Supreme Court,[390] because—as explained above—a question of fact, for the jury, had been treated erroneously as one of law, for the judge. The Supreme Court did not, however, suggest that the Court of Appeal had misunderstood the relevant test to be applied: the standard is that of reasonable honest members of society, not reasonable and honest bankers, or other sub-group.

### *(a) Criticisms of the second limb of the* Ghosh *test, and reasons for its amputation*

The second, subjective limb of the *Ghosh* test was widely criticised on the basis that it is vital to the authority of a legal system that its laws set an objective touchstone, and defendants, it might be thought, should not be permitted to supplant their own values (or even their own views of what society's values are) for those of the law.[391] Where defendants are

[385] See, in particular, the discussion of this point in LCCP No. 155, *Fraud and Deception* (1999) para. 5.33ff. A prescient early note is McKenna, "The Undefined Adverb in Criminal Statutes" [1966] *Crim LR* 548, 552–3. In this connection it is worth noting that, in 2003, the legislature in New Zealand reformed the law to give dishonesty a more concrete meaning, whereby "dishonestly, in relation to an act or omission, means done or omitted without a belief that there was express or implied consent to, or authority for, the act or omission from a person entitled to give such consent or authority". See s. 217 of the Crimes Act 1961, as amended; *Hayes* [2008] 2 NZSC 3, 2 NZLR 321.

[386] [2015] EWCA Crim 1944. In so holding, the Court of Appeal seems to have accepted—albeit without argument—that the standards of the specialist group to which D belongs might be relevant to the second, subjective limb of the test. This is surprising, because the issue in the second limb of the test is whether D believed that "reasonable and honest" people would approve of what he did: which seems to be a reference to the same group as in the first limb. See the note by Rogers at [2016] 3 *Archbold Review* 7.

[387] LIBOR is an acronym for the London Interbank Offered Rate. This is the interest rate which banks can charge each other on commercial loans in the London market.

[388] See § 15.9 below.

[389] An earlier decision to similar effect was *Lockwood* [1986] Crim LR 244 (CA). So it seems that even in corporate frauds we apply the standards of ordinary decent people—not "current notions of fair trading among commercial men", as was suggested in *re Patrick Lyon* [1933] Ch 786, 790 and *Landy* [1981] 1 All ER 1172, 1181 (CA) ("a man of his intelligence and experience"). For discussion, see Levi, "Fraud Trials in Perspective" [1984] *Crim LR* 384; Elliott, "Directors' Thefts and Dishonesty" [1991] *Crim LR* 732.

[390] [2025] UKSC 29, [2025] 1 WLR 3553.

[391] "To permit one who knows but does not accede to the community valuation of interests to have an individual standard would at once destroy the law": Seavey, "Negligence—Subjective or Objective?" (1927) 41 *Harvard LR* 1, 11.

prosecuted for groping their secretarial staff, for possession of cocaine, or for persuading family members to "take" the penalty points they have incurred for speeding, we do not expect them to be acquitted if they say, however truthfully, "But I thought everybody does it". One would have thought the law should equally refuse to listen to excuses of this sort when they are put forward by those accused of thieving by dipping into tills or of fraud by fiddling their expenses. "For the courts to take their criminal law from the man on the Clapham omnibus is one thing; to take it from the man accused of stealing it is quite another."[392]

Despite these criticisms it seems that for some 30 years the two-limbed *Ghosh* test was popular with judges and also with the legislature. The courts themselves decided that dishonesty, as interpreted in *Ghosh*, is an element of the common law offence of conspiracy to defraud,[393] and, it has been suggested, of the common law offence of misconduct in public office.[394] And Parliament, presumably aware of the way in which the term was then interpreted, repeatedly used the word "dishonestly" when enacting new legislation in relation to fraud;[395] indeed, as will be seen in Chapter 15, in 2006 it reformed the law of fraud in such a way as to make dishonesty the central element in a new general offence of fraud. Contrary to what might have been expected, it does not seem to have been suggested that, in practice, the dishonesty requirement produced unexpected acquittals, or made this part of the law otherwise difficult to enforce.[396]

More recently, however, there was a shift of opinion in both the legislature and the courts.[397] In 2013, Parliament amended the "cartel" offence created by section 188 of the Enterprise Act 2002 so as to remove dishonesty as an ingredient in the offence, on the ground that it made the offence unworkable. Four years later came the Supreme Court's condemnation of the second limb of the *Ghosh* test in *Ivey v Genting*.[398]

The central ground for the Supreme Court's condemnation was that this limb of the test allowed the defendant to be judged by his own standards of behaviour—which had the "unintended effect that the more warped the defendant's standards of honesty are, the less likely it is that he will be convicted of dishonest behaviour".[399] A subsidiary reason was that the test of honesty in civil law is purely objective, and the second limb of the *Ghosh* test "has led to an unprincipled divergence between the test for dishonesty in criminal proceedings and the test of the same concept when it arises in the context of civil justice".[400]

[392] Spencer, commenting on *Ghosh* (1982) 41 *CLJ* 222.
[393] Below, § 15.9.
[394] *W* [2010] EWCA Crim 372, [2010] QB 787.
[395] See, e.g., s. 111A of the Social Security Administration Act 1992.
[396] Admittedly, it has been suggested that uncertainty resulting from the *Ghosh* test was one of the reasons why the police failed to bring theft charges against any of the large number of people who, in 2007, helped themselves to the cargo of a ship wrecked in Branscombe Bay: Glover, "Can Dishonesty be Salvaged? Theft and the Grounding of the *MSC Napoli*" (2010) 74 *J Crim Law* 53.
[397] Possibly connected with the "expenses scandal" in Parliament, and the unedifying spectacle of Members of the Upper House, on trial for frauds in relation to their official expenses, trying to persuade juries to acquit them because they believed fraudulent expenses claims to be part of the "office culture": Lord Taylor of Warwick (BBC News, 25 January 2011) and Lord Hanningfield (BBC News, 26 May 2011).
[398] [2017] UKSC 67, [2018] AC 391.
[399] *Ibid.*, [57(1)].
[400] *Ibid.*, [57(4)].

If the second limb of the *Ghosh* test had attracted criticism from legal writers, so too did the Supreme Court's attempt to dispose of it in *Ivey v Genting*.[401] One criticism concerned the confusion caused by the Supreme Court's purporting to do so via *obiter dicta* in a civil case, thereby casting doubt upon *Ghosh*, yet leaving it as an authority still in theory binding on first-instance courts. But another and more important reason was that there were answers to the Supreme Court's objections to the second limb of the *Ghosh* test: answers that the Supreme Court did not address.

Given that an unsuccessful defendant in criminal proceedings faces far graver consequences than the losing party to a civil action, there were surely valid reasons for interpreting the dishonesty requirement in criminal proceedings more generously; and so the divergent treatment of the concept in civil and in criminal law can hardly be described as "unprincipled". Neither was the second limb of the *Ghosh* test the only instance where the criminal law allows a defendant to be judged by her own views of what is right and wrong.[402] And more importantly, a strong reason in favour of the second limb of the *Ghosh* test was that, in a crime of theft—which, since *Gomez* and *Hinks*, potentially extends to cover any acquisition of another's property—the second limb of the *Ghosh* test set an important limitation to the offence, by ensuring the acquittal of anyone who genuinely believed that his conduct was proper according to ordinary standards of honest and reasonable people. By rejecting this limitation, the Supreme Court, like the House of Lords in *Gomez* and *Hinks*, was extending the offence of theft yet further.[403] If the decisions in *Gomez* and *Hinks* were thought defensible because of the subjectivity of the *Ghosh* test's second limb, that argument has now disappeared.

Surprisingly, when the Court of Appeal in *Barton* followed the Supreme Court in *Ivey*, it did so without any serious consideration of the arguments of principle that pointed the other way:[404]

> "We are satisfied that the decision in *Ivey* is correct, is to be preferred, and that there is no obstacle in the doctrine of stare decisis to its being applied as the law of England and Wales."

Which means, regrettably, that the second limb of *Ghosh* was amputated without any principled discussion of its merits, or of the implications of its removal for the further widening of the law of theft and of the extensive range of other property offences of which "dishonesty" is one of the ingredients.[405]

[401] The various commentaries and essays include Richardson, [2017] 39 *Crim L Week* 4; Dyson and Jarvis, "Poison Ivey or Herbal Tea Leaf?" [2018] *LQR* 198; Virgo, "Cheating and Dishonesty" (2018) 77 *CLJ* 18; Laird [2018] *Crim LR* 395; Dsouza, "Why *Ivey* was a Mistake (aka Two Times I Flirted with Theft)" in Simester (ed.), *Modern Criminal Law* (2024) 71.

[402] Another example is s. 5 of the Criminal Damage Act 1971: see § 14.5 (vi) below. A further example is blackmail, contrary to s. 21 of the Theft Act 1968, in which the defendant is not guilty if he makes the demand with menaces "in the belief that . . . the use of the menaces is a proper means of reinforcing the demand".

[403] A point made by Virgo, "Cheating and Dishonesty" (2018) 77 *CLJ* 18.

[404] *Barton* [2020] EWCA Crim 575, [2021] QB 685, [1].

[405] For criticism of the decision in the legal press, see the notes by Campbell-Tiech [2020] 17 *Criminal Law Week* 10, Sullivan and Simester (2020) 136 *LQR* 523, and Thomas and Pegg (2020) 84 *J Criminal Law* 385. *Ivey* and *Barton* are criticised in detail in relation to the doctrine of precedent in Lamond., "Precedent in English Criminal Law" in Simester (ed.), *Modern Criminal Law* (2024) 287. But research by Finch suggests that the change may make little difference in practice: "The Elephant in the (Jury) Room: Exploring Mock Jurors' Understanding of Different Approaches to Dishonesty" [2021] *Crim LR* 513.

## § 13.9 Jurisdiction over Theft Act offences

### *(i) National cases*

For criminal procedure purposes, theft is an "either-way offence". This means that, in principle, a case of theft can be dealt with either by summary proceedings in a Magistrates' Court, or on indictment in a Crown Court, with a trial by jury if D elects to plead not guilty.[406] The general idea is that petty thefts are dealt with summarily,[407] and the Crown Court is reserved for cases of importance; but as defendants charged with either-way offences have a right to insist on jury trial,[408] a number of trivial cases of theft have regularly found their way into the Crown Court. As Crown Court proceedings are much more expensive than summary proceedings, this has led to repeated moves to make petty theft a purely summary offence. To date, all such moves have failed. The most recent attempt was section 176 of the Antisocial Behaviour, Crime and Policing Act 2014,[409] which has now made low-value shoplifting[410] a purely summary offence; but as the new provision then goes on to preserve the defendant's right to jury trial, its practical impact is likely to be very small.[411]

### *(ii) International cases*

Nowadays, theftuous and fraudulent conduct frequently has a transnational dimension. For example, D, from London, may obtain access by electronic means to V's New York bank account and dishonestly transfer funds from that account to an account he has opened for himself in a Swiss bank. Or D may send a deceptive telex from London to Hong Kong, causing V to transfer for D's benefit funds held in a Hong Kong bank. It may well be that the conduct just described merits trial and punishment before an English court, since there may be damage to interests which fall properly within the purview of English criminal law.[412]

At common law, any claim to jurisdiction now requires proof that either (i) the last constituent element, *or* (ii) a "substantial" component, of the actus reus of the offence took place in England or Wales; *and* that there is no reason of comity with foreign legal systems

[406] This position may change, should the Courts and Tribunals Bill 2025–26 pass in its current form into law. The right of an adult defendant charged with either-way offences such as theft to elect trial by jury will be removed. It will be a judicial decision whether such offences are to be tried in the magistrates' court or the Crown Court.

[407] Again this may change, should the Courts and Tribunals Bill pass into law. The government's existing power to increase (by regulation) the maximum custodial sentence a magistrates' court can impose for a single either-way offence like theft will be increased from the current maximum of 12 months, to 18 or 24 months. Should the magistrates' courts come to deal with theft offences where the sentence may stretch to that length, they will certainly be responsible for *serious* cases of theft, not only what may be described as "petty theft".

[408] Most controversially, should the Courts and Tribunals Bill pass into law, the right of jury trial will be removed from serious (if not quite *the most* serious) cases of theft. Judge-only trials are, under the proposed legislation, to be permitted where a custodial sentence of up to three years is likely to be imposed.

[409] By adding a new s. 22A to the Magistrates' Courts Act 1980.

[410] Meaning goods the value of which does not exceed £200.

[411] Redesignating low-value shoplifting as a summary offence does deprive the magistrates and the Crown Prosecution Service of their previous right to insist that the case should be dealt with in the Crown Court; but unlike the defendant's equivalent right, it was very rarely exercised.

[412] UK nationals, including companies, may suffer loss of property owned overseas. Moreover, the City of London and other financial centres may suffer loss of reputation and confidence if perceived as havens for international fraud: see further Law Com. No. 180, *Jurisdiction over Offences of Fraud and Dishonesty with a Foreign Element* (1989).

not to try the offence here.[413] Frequently, asserting jurisdiction will be possible notwithstanding a substantial transnational element on the facts.[414] In *Re Osman*,[415] acts were done in Hong Kong (where the law of theft was the same as in England) which took effect on property situated in other countries. It was held that the property had been appropriated in Hong Kong, without prejudice to the possibility that appropriation also occurred where the property was located. Similarly, a blackmailing demand is made when a letter is posted in England, even if the addressee will receive the letter in Germany.[416]

The modern common law has fallen broadly into line with Part I of the Criminal Justice Act 1993,[417] which attempts to achieve consistency between theft and offences of fraud and dishonesty regarding jurisdiction over offences with transnational elements. If an offence is listed in Part I of the Criminal Justice Act 1993,[418] under section 2 of that Act an assumption of jurisdiction will be permitted notwithstanding that elements of the offence have taken place overseas provided a "relevant event"—i.e. any definitional element of the offence—occurs in England and Wales.[419]

413 *Smith (Wallace Duncan) (No. 4)* [2004] EWCA Crim 631, [2004] QB 1418; not following *Manning* [1999] QB 980 (CA).

414 Save for specific statutory exceptions, English courts do not accept jurisdiction over conduct perpetrated entirely outside England and Wales, even in respect of a British subject. For common law crimes, constraints of venue and ambit ensured that "all crime is local". For statutory crimes, there is a very strong presumption that criminal statutes are concerned and only concerned with prescribing acts or omissions perpetrated in the United Kingdom: *Cox v Army Council* [1963] AC 48.

415 [1990] 1 WLR 277 (DC).

416 *Treacy* [1971] AC 537.

417 Part I came into effect in August 1999: SI 1999, No. 1189 (32); SI 1999, No. 1499 (42).

418 The listed offences in s. 1 of the Criminal Justice Act 1993 include: theft; false accounting; false statements by company directors; blackmail; handling stolen goods; fraud and related offences; forgery and allied offences; conspiracy to defraud; and the common law offence of cheating in relation to the public revenue.

419 "For the purposes of this Part, 'relevant event' . . . means . . . any act or omission or other event (including any result of one or more acts or omissions) proof of which is required for the commission of the offence": Criminal Justice Act 1993, s. 2(1).

# 14

# RELATED OFFENCES

It is impossible, in a work of this nature, to analyse all the offences besides theft which concern themselves with harms to property.[1] In Chapter 15, fraud offences will be considered. Those are offences which, unlike theft and the offences considered in this chapter, often involve the wrongful manipulation of other persons, so that invasion of a victim's property interests is, at least prima facie, consensual: "whereas the thief makes war on a social practice from the outside, the deceiver is the traitor within".[2] Besides theft, however, there are many other property offences which are external to, and attack rather than insidiously use, the law's established processes for allocating and transferring property rights. In this chapter, we consider five such offences.

## § 14.1 Handling stolen goods

"There would not be so many thieves if there were no receivers."[3] The crime of handling is in many ways a special case of being an accessory to theft,[4] one which deserves independent criminalisation because of the important role that "fences"—and indeed end-purchasers—of stolen goods play in the economics of the offence. Logically and temporally, theft is prior to handling: the latter presupposes the former.[5] Historically, too, theft was originally a far more significant crime than handling. Prior to the Industrial Revolution, chattels were relatively few and there was little mobility between population centres.[6] Hence, stolen property

[1] For detailed treatments, see further Ormerod and Williams, *Smith's Law of Theft* (9th ed., 2007).

[2] Shute and Horder, "Thieving and Deceiving: What Is the Difference?" (1993) 56 *MLR* 548, 553.

[3] *Battams* (1979) 1 Cr App R (S) 15, 16 (CA). According to Klockars, *The Professional Fence* (1974) 165–6, "the observation itself is better understood as an hyperbolic plea for attention to the criminal receiver than as an accurate statement of his relationship to theft. . . . In brief, if there were no receivers, there would still be all sorts of thieves, and possibly more thieves of sorts we don't like than we have now."

[4] Indeed, this was how it was first criminalised, in s. 4 of An Act to take away Clergy from some Offenders and to bring other to Justice, 1691, 3 W & M c. 9 (receivers deemed to be accessories). Earlier law disclosed an offence only if D actually received or abetted the thief himself: *Dawson's Case* (1602) 2 Bracton 337, 339, 80 ER 4. For a brief history, see Hall, *Theft, Law and Society* (2nd ed., 1952) 52–8. The old position is now reversed, and receiving the thief does not constitute receiving the goods stolen: *Wiley* (1850) 4 Cox CC 412, 169 ER 408.

[5] Although receiving is normally associated with theft, the modern offence can also be committed in respect of blackmail, fraud, and by withdrawing a wrongful credit. Thus, one who launders the proceeds of blackmail may be guilty of handling under the Theft Act 1968. It is unclear why handling should be restricted to these specific crimes and not apply to the proceeds of crime more generally, as it does in some other jurisdictions. (Cp. Howarth, "Handling Stolen Goods and Handling Salmon" [1987] *Crim LR* 460.) Contrast, e.g., s. 246 of the Crimes Act 1961 (NZ), which makes it an offence to receive anything "stolen or obtained by any other crime". However, as will be noted in § 14.2, the expanded scope of modern laundering legislation compasses the proceeds of any criminal conduct—potentially swallowing the traditional offence of handling.

[6] Chappell and Walsh, "'No Questions Asked', A Consideration of the Crime of Criminal Receiving" (1974) 20 *Crime and Delinquency* 157, 160.

could be traced fairly easily and there were few commercial opportunities for redistribution of such property. Theft, in turn, tended to be committed to satisfy personal needs rather than for profit.

In modern society, the explosion of property offences is a simple matter of economics: in the market for stolen goods, supply has increased to meet demand. Professional fences are the brokers who make that market: handling is the channel through which commercial forces drive theft.[7] Reflecting this, the maximum penalty for handling is imprisonment for 14 years, by contrast with a maximum of seven years for theft.

In addition, those who deal in stolen goods also provide the means by which merchandise can be "laundered", so that the tangible evidence of theft effectively disappears.[8] Mass-produced items, once sold on, cannot normally be traced. By providing an outlet for the efficient disposal of such items, handlers reduce the risk that theft will be detected. Thus one, largely unrecognised, role that professional fences perform is the obstruction of justice.

Yet these considerations are somewhat abstract, and their victims are not harmed so immediately as they are by the theft itself. Consequently, the wrongness of handling—unlike that of another offence of profiting from others' crimes, the possession of child pornography—has never caught the popular imagination. Indeed, in practice it sometimes happens that those accused of theft or burglary are prepared to plead guilty to handling if the charge of theft or burglary is dropped, even though the offence of handling carries a higher penalty.[9] This may be in part because the Theft Act draws no distinction between the lay receiver, who may once in his lifetime buy stolen goods for his own consumption, and the criminal businessman who maintains an organisation and thus supports the theft industry. With this in mind, in previous editions of this book we suggested that that the law was at fault in failing to deal strongly enough with professional handling. In 2002, Parliament, mindful of this problem, created the new and broadly based offence of "laundering", which was designed to strike hard at professional money launderers. But, as we shall see later, this new offence, like handling, is as apt to catch the little fish as it is the big one: to the point where, if exploited to the limit, it would make the offence of handling stolen goods redundant.[10]

Section 22(1) of the Theft Act 1968 defines handling as follows:

> A person handles stolen goods if (otherwise than in the course of the stealing) knowing or believing them to be stolen goods he dishonestly receives the goods, or dishonestly undertakes or assists in their retention, removal, disposal or realisation by or for the benefit of another person, or if he arranges to do so.

The section stipulates four main elements. The actus reus is:

(i) that D handles goods; and
(ii) the goods were stolen.

[7] Cp. Klockars, *The Professional Fence* (1974); Blakey and Goldsmith, "Criminal Redistribution of Stolen Property: The Need for Reform" (1976) 74 *Mich LR* 1512; Sutton, Schneider and Hetherington, *Tackling Theft with the Market Reduction Approach* (2001); *Shelton* (1986) 83 Cr App R 379, 385 (CA).

[8] Chappell and Walsh, "Receiving Stolen Property: The Need for a Systematic Inquiry into the Fencing Process" (1974) 11 *Criminology* 484, 494.

[9] An instructive example is *Sainthouse* [1980] Crim LR 506 (CA), where a casual (i.e. non-professional) receiver was prepared to plead guilty to handling but not to theft.

[10] See below, § 14.2.

The mens rea components are:

(iii) D knows or believes the goods were stolen or dishonestly obtained; and
(iv) dishonesty.

### *(i) Handling*

Prior to the passing of the Theft Act 1968, the only mode of handling goods was receiving them, something that required the defendant to take possession of or control over the goods. This limitation made it difficult to convict those professional fences who facilitated dispositions of goods without themselves ever coming into physical contact with or acquiring the goods. Under section 22(1), the behavioural element of the offence can now be done in the following ways:[11]

(i) through receiving, or arranging to receive, the goods;
(ii) through assisting in their retention, removal, disposal, or realisation by another person, or through arranging to do so; or
(iii) through assisting in their retention, removal, disposal, or realisation for the benefit of another person, or through arranging to do so.

In each of these cases, the handling must occur otherwise than in the course of the original stealing. It must be observed, at the outset of this discussion, that the drafting of section 22(1) is inelegant and does not lend itself to clear elucidation. In particular, the actus reus of handling is specified in terms both wide and uncertain.[12]

#### *(a) Receiving*

The law on receiving pre dates the Act.[13] The actus reus requirement in receiving is that H acquires (joint or sole) possession or control over the goods from another person.[14] The acquisition of possession or control is a single finite act: once possession or control is acquired, the receiving is complete and later dealing with the goods cannot be treated as a continuing or further act of receiving.

H need not take personal physical custody of the goods. Possession *or* control is sufficient. Regarding the first of these, "possession" is established by showing: (i) that the goods are either in H's immediate physical custody or located at a place over which H has control (e.g. in H's house); and (ii) a mental element, the intent by H to possess the goods.

The mental element is essential. H cannot be in possession of property that he does not know exists.[15] Suppose, for instance, that T, having stolen a wallet, disposes of it by slipping

[11] *Bloxham* [1983] 1 AC 109, 113–14; below, § 14.1(i)(c).

[12] Spencer, "The Mishandling of Handling" [1981] *Crim LR* 682, 683–4; Blake, "The Innocent Purchaser and Section 22 of the Theft Act" [1972] *Crim LR* 494.

[13] Cp. *Smythe* (1981) 72 Cr App R 8, 11 (CA) ("receiving, or handling as it has now become").

[14] In *Seymour* [1954] 1 All ER 1006 (CA) the Court sought to correct a tendency to find people guilty of receiving, rather than theft, whenever they were found in possession of stolen goods. Lord Goddard CJ emphasised that to find someone guilty of receiving, the jury must be satisfied that D received from *someone else*: "[i]f he is the thief, he cannot be guilty of receiving because a man cannot receive from himself, but must receive the property from somebody else". Thus, where the evidence is as consistent with theft as it is with handling, the indictment ought to contain a count for theft and a count for handling. See below, § 14.1(vi).

[15] See also above, § 5.6 (iv).

the wallet into H's bag without H's knowledge. In such a case, for the purposes of receiving H does not take possession of the wallet, at least until she knows she has it. Similarly, if goods stolen by another are found in H's house, it must be shown either that H had arranged for them to be delivered there[16] or, alternatively, that H had realised the goods were present and intentionally exercised control over them. In *Cavendish*,[17] Lord Parker CJ put the test in the following way:

> "It is quite clear, without referring to authority, that for a man to be found to have possession, actual or constructive, of goods, something more must be proved than that the goods have been found on his premises. It must be shown either, if he was absent, that on his return he became aware of them and exercised some control over them or . . . that the goods had come, albeit in his absence, at his invitation or by arrangement."

The importance of the mental ingredient involved in acquiring possession or control can be seen in *Healey*.[18] In that case, the defendant was hired to assist in melting down some stolen tin. The defendant's conviction for receiving was quashed by the Court of Criminal Appeal, because the trial judge had not drawn the jury's attention to the difference between a person who was merely assisting, even if dishonestly, and a person who by his assistance had become a joint possessor with the principal whom he was assisting. The Court cited a passage from *Hobson v Impett*:[19]

> "It is not the law that, if a man knows goods are stolen and puts his hands on them, that in itself makes him guilty of receiving, because it does not follow that he is taking them into his control. The control may still be in the thief or the man whom he is assisting, and the alleged receiver may be only picking the goods up without taking them into his possession, the goods all the time remaining in the possession of the person whom he is helping."

As this passage makes clear, physical possession, e.g. in the sense of touching something, is insufficient without the accompanying intent thereby to possess or control the thing. To similar effect is the decision in *Hawes v Edwards*.[20] A parcel containing stolen goods was delivered to D's address. After the delivery, police officers entered the premises and found D together with the opened parcel. One of the officers asked D whether he had signed for the parcel, to which he responded, "No, I am examining the contents before I sign for it". D's conviction for receiving was quashed. Although he had opened the parcel, he had not yet decided whether to acquire possession from the thieves. In effect, the thieves had offered to transfer the goods to him, and D had yet to accept their offer.

Conversely, physical possession is not always *required*. If the defendant lacks actual custody of the stolen goods, she may nonetheless be found to have "control" over them. This occurs when custody is in the hands of an agent or servant acting under the defendant's direction, through whom the defendant exercises control over the goods.[21] Again, the exercise of control imports a mental element, and one cannot unknowingly exercise control over something. Hence, according to Lord Parker CJ, "a man cannot be convicted of

[16] *Lloyd* [1992] Crim LR 361 (CA); *Cavendish* [1961] 2 All ER 856 (CA).
[17] [1961] 2 All ER 856, 858 (CA).
[18] [1965] 1 All ER 365 (CA).
[19] (1957) 41 Cr App R 138, 141 (DC). See *Healey* [1965] 1 All ER 365, 369 (CA).
[20] (1949) 113 JP 303 (DC); cp. *Freedman* (1931) 22 Cr App R 133 (CA).
[21] *Smith* (1855) Dears 494, 169 ER 818; *Miller* (1854) 6 Cox 353.

receiving goods of which delivery has been taken by his servant unless there is evidence that he, the employer, had given the servant authority or instructions to take the goods".[22]

*(b) Arranging to receive*

Handling can also be committed in inchoate form. Under section 22(1) what, prior to 1968, would have been (at most) an attempt or a conspiracy to receive is now a full offence. If the prosecution can prove that H made an arrangement to receive the goods, she is guilty of handling them; there is no need to prove that she actually received the goods. However, the arrangement must be made after the goods are stolen, since it is necessary that H should know or believe the goods are stolen property at the time of making the arrangement.[23]

*(c) Undertaking or assisting in the retention, removal, disposal, or realisation*

Section 22(1) makes H guilty of handling if he undertakes or assists to retain, remove, dispose of, or realise the goods, by or for the benefit of another person. According to Lord Bridge:[24]

> "First, the offender may himself undertake the activity for the benefit of another person. Secondly, the activity may be undertaken by another person and the offender may assist him. Of course, if the thief or an original receiver and his friend act together in, say, removing the stolen goods, the friend may be committing the offence in both ways."

Typically, this encompasses cases where H organises the on-sale of stolen goods without herself ever taking possession of them,[25] or where H assists the thief to fence or realise the value of the goods. The formula would also capture situations where H promises to destroy or assists in destroying (or otherwise "disposing" of) stolen property; as well as cases where H undertakes or assists to store ("retain") the stolen items.[26] Merely using the goods, however, is not sufficient. In *Sanders*,[27] D used a stolen heater in his father's garage, where D was employed. Although the father was guilty of handling, D was not.

Neither is passive acquiescence sufficient. In *Coleman*,[28] H's wife used money she had stolen to pay for legal fees which had been incurred jointly by H and his wife. H was charged with assisting his wife to dispose of the money. The Court of Appeal quashed his conviction after the trial judge misdirected the jury that it was sufficient for handling that H was dishonest and was getting the benefit of the disposal. Knowingly standing by while a benefit is conferred is not in itself assistance, though it may be circumstantial evidence supporting a wider case that H encouraged or assisted his wife in the disposal. The decision seems right, on the principle that there is generally no criminal liability for omissions. Thus, in *Brown*,[29] H's failure to tell the police that stolen goods were in his flat when instructing them to "get

22 *Cavendish* [1961] 2 All ER 856, 858 (CA); a continuation of the remarks quoted earlier in this section.
23 *Park* (1988) 87 Cr App R 164 (CA). If an agreement to handle stolen goods is made prior to the theft, the proper charge is conspiracy (*ibid.*, 173). It may also be appropriate to charge the would-be handler as an accessory to the contemplated theft, or with an inchoate offence of encouraging or assisting it.
24 *Bloxham* [1983] AC 109, 113–14.
25 Cp. the facts of *Watson* [1916] 2 KB 385 (CA).
26 *Pitchley* (1973) 57 Cr App R 30, 37 (CA): retain means "keep possession of".
27 (1982) 75 Cr App R 84 (CA). Cp. the law governing the taking of possession by employees who find goods: above, § 13.4(v)(a).
28 (1985) 150 JP 175 (CA).
29 [1970] 1 QB 105 (CA).

lost" was held not to be assisting in their retention. In the absence of a duty to disclose, H's omission was an insufficient basis for criminal liability.[30]

By contrast, in *Kanwar*,[31] H actively lied by telling the police that she had purchased articles which her husband had stolen. The effect of these lies, had they been believed by the police, would have been to assist her husband to retain the stolen articles. On that basis, H's appeal against conviction for handling stolen goods was dismissed by the Court of Appeal.

In *Kanwar*, the finding that positive representations by H could be assistance seems right. Nonetheless, the decision itself is problematic for a different reason: H's "assistance" was ineffective because her lies were not believed. The Court met this difficulty with the bald assertion that "[t]he requisite assistance need not be successful in its object".[32] With respect, this proposition must be qualified. It is possible to assist in a project which, ultimately, is unsuccessful. If H's lies had been temporarily believed but, later, the police had discovered the truth, it might then be reasonable to say that H provided assistance towards the retention of the stolen articles. But on the facts of the case, her lies were wholly ineffectual. She merely attempted to assist. As such, her conviction should have been for attempted handling rather than the full offence.

*(d) Arranging to undertake or assist in the retention, removal, disposal, or realisation*

One might think that "arranging to assist" in disposing of stolen goods has the hallmarks of an inchoate offence. But under section 22(1), it constitutes the full offence of handling. Thus if, in *Kanwar*, H had promised the thief (i.e. "undertaken") to tell lies, or had made a plan ("arrangement") with someone else to conceal the stolen goods, no difficulty would have arisen: she would be guilty of handling even before the undertaking or arrangement was implemented.

Potentially, this extends the substantive law of handling far into the realm of inchoate offences. Indeed, in extreme cases it would take handling through inchoate wrongs and out the other side, into the field of mere preparation. Given that an undertaking to retain is itself inchoate in nature, making arrangements in advance of giving such an undertaking must be preparatory even to the inchoate wrong. Yet, under section 22(1), both of these constitute the full offence of handling. To some extent, the apparent width of this provision is narrowed in practice by the requirement that there be in existence, at the time, stolen goods to which H's arrangement relates. Nonetheless, it may be questioned whether the mere making of an arrangement to undertake to dispose of those goods comprises a crystallised harm sufficient to warrant criminalisation.

*(e) By or for the benefit of another*

The requirement that the arranging, assisting, or undertaking be "by or for the benefit of another person" is awkwardly expressed. What it seems to mean is that, apart from traditional receiving, there are two types of handling by dealing:

(i) where H acts as a principal, by arranging or undertaking to deal with (i.e. retain, dispose of, etc.) the property *for the benefit of someone else*; and

[30] Above, § 4.1(i).
[31] [1982] 2 All ER 528 (CA).
[32] *Ibid.*, 529.

(ii) where H has a secondary role, by arranging or assisting *someone else to* deal with the property (i.e. "by another person").

What this means is that if H deals with the property on his own, solely for his own benefit, he does not handle.[33] (That is, unless he receives the property.) In *Bloxham*,[34] H purchased a car in good faith. Later he realised the car was stolen, whereupon he sold it at an undervalue to T, an innocent party. H's conviction for handling was quashed by the House of Lords. Although he had disposed of the car, and T had benefited thereby, H had not dealt with the car *for the benefit* of T or anyone else. Rather, H had acted on his own behalf. Moreover, because H also acted by himself, neither could he be convicted on the alternative basis that he had arranged or assisted in the disposal *by another person*.[35]

### *(f) Otherwise than in the course of stealing*

The original theft cannot also be a handling: the goods must be stolen before they can be handled. Section 22 re-enacts this rule, which was part of the common law of receiving,[36] by the proviso that the handling must occur "otherwise than in the course of the stealing". In so doing, it helps to preserve the functional distinctiveness of handling, which involves wrongdoing by receiving or dealing with goods *after* they are stolen.

The converse does not hold. Virtually every handling is also a theft, since both receiving and dealing with property will count as an "appropriation" for the purposes of theft.[37] This overlap is less problematic, however, since theft carries a lesser maximum penalty than handling.[38] We consider the issue of overlaps further in § 14.1(vi).

It is unclear how long a period is included within "the course of the stealing". Suppose the following example:

> D picks goods off the shelf at a supermarket and puts them inside her jacket, intending to leave without paying for them. On the authority of *Gomez*, she has already stolen the goods. As part of the plan, however, D then meets H, her accomplice, in another aisle and passes over some of the goods. H conceals them and leaves separately.

Does H handle the goods? Common sense suggests not (and that it is a joint theft), but the law has yet to answer this question unequivocally. In principle, once there is an appropriation by the thief, the offence of "theft" is complete and committed. This suggests that, in law, the theft is finished—which would make H guilty of handling.[39]

There are two possible ways round this conclusion. One is to rule that D's appropriation of the goods was a single continuing act, lasting (say) until she left the supermarket. While there is no case post-*Gomez* wholeheartedly adopting such an analysis—and it is

[33] Cp. *Sloggett* [1972] 1 QB 430, 434 (CA); also the commentary on *Slater and Suddens* [1996] Crim LR 494.
[34] [1983] 1 AC 109 (HL); reversing [1981] 2 All ER 647 (CA). The decision by the Court of Appeal was strongly criticised by Spencer, "The Mishandling of Handling" [1981] *Crim LR* 682.
[35] As occurred in *Tokeley-Parry* [1999] Crim LR 578 (CA), where D arranged for T to smuggle (i.e. "remove", within the terms of s. 22(1)) stolen antiques from Egypt into England.
[36] *Seymour* [1954] 1 All ER 1006 (CA); *Thompson* [1965] Crim LR 553 (CA).
[37] Cp. *Stapylton v O'Callaghan* [1973] 2 All ER 782 (DC); Smith, "Theft and/or Handling" [1977] *Crim LR* 517.
[38] Seven years' imprisonment, by contrast with 14 for handling. See ss. 7 (as amended by the Criminal Justice Act 1991, s. 26) and 22(2).
[39] Cp. *Pitham and Hehl* (1977) 65 Cr App R 45, 49 (CA), where D's offer dishonestly to "sell" V's goods to H was held to constitute theft, such that H's purporting to buy the goods and carry them away was handling. For criticism of the decision, see § 13.6(i); also the text below, § 14.3(iii).

not easy to reconcile with *Gomez*[40]—the balance of the decisions appears to favour this analysis.[41]

Alternatively, and perhaps equally plausibly, it is open to the courts to rule that the phrase "the course of the stealing" covers a period extending beyond the duration of the theftuous act of appropriation.[42] As a matter of ordinary language, the term "theft" legitimately describes the whole transaction by D and H in the supermarket; moreover, it seems an appropriate word to capture the moral significance of their course of activity, when viewed as a whole. For the purposes of section 22(1), there seems no reason to restrict interpretation of "the course of the stealing" to the technical instant of appropriation required to be proved under section 1.

Even granted the analysis suggested here, however, the boundaries of theft will be vague. In the example set out above, when is the course of the theft by D (and H) completed, so that the goods can thereafter be handled? Is it after D moves past the cashier's counter, when she is outside the premises, when she is some metres down the road, or at some other moment? To some extent, the answer will involve drawing lines intuitively, depending on such factors as whether the thief is still at the scene of the crime.[43]

### *(ii) Stolen goods*

The things handled must be "stolen", and they must be "goods", within the meaning of the Act. Both these terms require discussion.

#### *(a) Goods*

The definition of "goods" is set out in section 34(2)(b):

> "goods", except in so far as the context otherwise requires, includes money and every other description of property except land, and includes things severed from the land by stealing.

This definition is almost coextensive with the definition of "property" for the purposes of theft (above, § 13.3), with the main exception that D cannot be guilty of handling land unless severed.[44] In *A-G's Reference (No. 4 of 1979)*,[45] the Court of Appeal confirmed that things in action can be handled. Although they cannot be "received" (which requires a physical taking of possession or control over the goods), following the enactment of the 1968 Act intangible property can now be handled by retention, removal, disposal, or

[40] Cp. *Atakpu and Abraham* [1994] QB 69, 80 (CA). Contrast, however, *Lockley* [1995] Crim LR 656 (CA).

[41] E.g. *Hale* (1979) 68 Cr App R 415 (CA); *Donaghy v Marshall* [1981] Crim LR 644 (Crown Court (Snaresbrook)); *Lockley* [1995] Crim LR 656 (CA); *Bowden* [2002] EWCA Crim 1279. See Williams, "Appropriation: A Single or Continuous Act?" [1973] *Crim LR* 69.

[42] Cp. *Hale* (1979) 68 Cr App R 415 (CA), regarding the requirement in robbery, *per* s. 8(1), that force be used "at the time of" the stealing. See below, § 14.3(iii).

[43] Contrast *Pitham and Hehl* (1977) 65 Cr App R 45 (CA) (theft of furniture complete as soon as D offered to sell it to H) with *Gregory* (1983) 77 Cr App R 41 (CA) (during a burglary, theft might continue before property is removed from the building).

[44] The possible theft of land is subject to different restrictions, set out in s. 4(2) of the Theft Act 1968. See above, § 13.3(ii).

[45] [1981] 1 All ER 1193 (CA). The decision must now be doubted on other grounds, in light of *Preddy* [1996] AC 815. (See generally below, § 15.1.) However, there seems no reason to doubt its authority on this point.

realisation. Thus, if H assists D to negotiate a cheque obtained by fraud, she becomes guilty of handling.[46]

*(b) Stolen*

It is not sufficient that the goods have been obtained by crime. They must have been obtained pursuant to certain particular crimes. *Per* section 24(4), the three main offences are theft contrary to section 1, blackmail contrary to section 21, and fraud contrary to section 1 of the Fraud Act 2006.[47] In light of *Gomez*,[48] cases of obtaining by blackmail or fraud generally also constitute theft, and theft is the most important principal offence lying behind convictions for handling. Goods which are obtained through offences of which theft is an element—e.g. burglary and robbery—can also be handled.[49]

It is not necessary to prove the identity of either the person who actually committed the crime or the owner of the property.[50] Provided the evidence discloses that the property was obtained by theft or another crime, even the acquittal of the particular person charged with committing that theft is irrelevant to the charge of receiving.[51] However, it *is* essential to prove that the property was stolen,[52] or obtained by blackmail or fraud that constitutes a *crime*. So, for example, where the person charged with originally stealing a thing is acquitted (or cannot be charged at all) on the ground of legal incapacity such as minority or insanity,[53] the handler cannot be convicted in the absence of other evidence showing the property was obtained by theft. An illustration of this is the pre-Act case of *Walters v Lunt*,[54] in which the defendants took possession of a tricycle that their child, aged seven years, had wrongfully brought home. The Court ruled they could not be convicted of receiving since the child, being under the age of criminal responsibility, could not be guilty of larceny.

In cases of this sort, the defendants may still be convicted of an attempt to handle stolen goods,[55] at least where they are unaware of the circumstances exculpating the original "thief". More straightforwardly, as the Court pointed out in *Walters v Lunt*, their subsequent dealing with the tricycle would itself have been larceny, and would now be theft under section 1.

[46] Cp. *Pitchley* (1973) 57 Cr App R 30 (CA) (money in a bank account).

[47] Section 24A(8) adds obtaining by withdrawal of a wrongful credit. Thus, whereas it is now a separate criminal offence merely to retain a wrongful credit (s. 24A(1)), it is handling to withdraw the proceeds.

[48] Above, § 13.6(ii)(a).

[49] *Pitham and Hehl* (1977) 65 Cr App R 45 (CA); *Smythe* (1981) 72 Cr App R 8 (CA); *Gregory* (1983) 77 Cr App R 41 (CA).

[50] *Carr & Wilson* (1882) 10 QBD 76 (bonds stolen from an English ship moored in Holland, thief and circumstances of the theft unknown). In *Fuschillo* [1940] 2 All ER 489 (CA), D was charged with receiving a vast quantity of sugar, although it was not proven who had stolen it or from whom it was stolen. The Court of Criminal Appeal applied *dicta* in *Sbarra* (1919) 13 Cr App R 118, 120 (CA) to the effect that "the circumstances in which a defendant receives goods may of themselves prove that the goods were stolen, and further may prove that he knew it at the time when he received them. It is not a rule of law that there must be other evidence of the theft."

[51] *Close* [1977] Crim LR 107 (CA). For criticism of that decision on its particular facts, see Smith, *Property Offences* (1994) §§ 30–08, 30–09.

[52] *Cording* [1983] Crim LR 175 (Crown Court (Snaresbrook)); cp. *Creamer* [1919] 1 KB 564 (CA).

[53] Cp. *Farrell* [1975] 2 NZLR 753, in which the person from whom H received a stolen cheque was acquitted of theft on the ground of insanity. Consequently, the Court held, the evidence against H lacked an essential ingredient of the receiving charge, namely that the cheque was "stolen" within the meaning of the criminal law.

[54] [1951] 2 All ER 645 (DC).

[55] Cp. *Toye* [1984] Crim LR 555 (Crown Court (Southwark)).

*(c) Proceeds*

The handler need not handle the whole of the thing stolen. It is sufficient, for example, that D receives parts of a car which has been stolen (e.g. the wheels or the sound system), or parts of a stolen computer, such as the processor or graphics card. Furthermore, the property need not be in the same state or condition as it was when stolen. A stolen car can be received even though substantially damaged in an accident before it arrives in D's hands. Similarly, section 22 would apply to the handling of mutton from a sheep that was alive when stolen.[56]

The above are examples where the identity of the stolen property is unchanged in the hands of the handler, even though its character may have partially altered. What about changes of identity? At common law, the thing received had to be the actual thing that was first stolen, not its proceeds or a substitute.[57] In this form, the law was rather too generous to those involved in laundering the proceeds of theft, since it conferred an immunity from prosecution upon subsequent participants in the laundering "chain", once the original item was exchanged.[58] That immunity is now overridden by section 24(2), which extends the scope of stolen goods to include:

(a) any other goods which directly or indirectly represent or have at any time represented the stolen goods in the hands of the thief as being the proceeds of any disposal or realisation of the whole or part of the goods stolen or of goods so representing the stolen goods; and
(b) any other goods which directly or indirectly represent or have at any time represented the stolen goods in the hands of a handler of the stolen goods or any part of them as being the proceeds of any disposal or realisation of the whole or part of the stolen goods handled by him or of goods so representing them.

This rather tortuous prose means that if a thief or handler exchanges stolen goods for other goods, the other goods are deemed also to be stolen.[59] But if an innocent person, into whose hands stolen goods fall, exchanges those stolen goods for other goods, the other goods she receives are not deemed stolen. For example:

> D steals a television set. She fences it to H in exchange for a bicycle. H knows the set is stolen. In turn, H sells it at a car boot sale to T for £30. T is an innocent buyer. Later, T swaps the television with his neighbour for a lawnmower.

The television is stolen property throughout this example. The bicycle becomes stolen property when D receives it in exchange for the television. The £30 also becomes stolen when H receives it from T. The lawnmower, however, never becomes stolen property, since it was received only by T, who was innocent and neither a thief nor a handler.

[56] Cp. *Cowell and Green* (1796) 2 East PC 617.

[57] *Walkley* (1829) 4 C & P 133, 172 ER 640.

[58] It appears that the civil law is in the process of filling this lacuna. Common law tracing now allows P to claim the proceeds of an unauthorised exchange-transaction: see *Trustee of the Property of FC Jones and Sons v Jones* [1997] Ch 159 (CA); *Foskett v McKeown* [2001] AC 102. On this analysis, the victim of a theft may acquire title in the exchange proceeds, and subsequent handlers may be guilty of theft.

[59] *Forsyth* [1997] 2 Cr App R 299 (CA). See especially the commentaries at [1997] Crim LR 589 and 755.

*(d) Goods which are no longer stolen*

Goods are no longer stolen, and cannot be handled, once they re-enter into the possession of the legal owner or a person authorised by the owner to possess them. By section 24(3), this may occur in two ways:

> . . . [N]o goods shall be regarded as having continued to be stolen goods after they have been restored to the person from whom they were stolen or to other lawful possession or custody, or after that person and any other person claiming through him have otherwise ceased as regards those goods to have any right to restitution in respect of the theft.

The first way in which goods become not stolen, then, is if they are restored to the original owner or to an authorised possessor. Suppose, for example, that the police recover stolen goods but then, with the consent of the owner, return them to the location where they were discovered in order to trap a would-be receiver. In that case, the subsequent purchaser cannot be convicted of handling.[60] However, she would remain guilty of attempting to handle the goods,[61] and would normally also commit a fresh theft.[62]

Whether goods have been reduced into possession is a question of fact, and turns on the intention of the possessor. In *A-G's Reference (No. 1 of 1974)*,[63] a police officer spotted a van containing packages of new clothing which he (rightly) suspected were stolen. He immobilised the vehicle by removing its rotor arm, and kept watch. The defendant later got into the van and attempted to start it, whereupon he was questioned by the police officer. After offering an implausible explanation for the packages, the defendant was arrested. At issue both during trial and on appeal was whether the police officer had taken possession of the clothing or whether he was merely watching it with a view to catching the handler. In the judgment of the Court of Appeal:[64]

> "it depended primarily on the intentions of the police officer. If the police officer seeing these goods in the back of the car had made up his mind that he would take them into custody, that he would reduce them into his possession or control, take charge of them so that they could not be removed and so that he would have the disposal of them, then it would be a perfectly proper conclusion to say that he had taken possession of the goods. On the other hand, if the truth of the matter is that he was of an entirely open mind at that stage as to whether the goods were to be seized or not and was of an entirely open mind as to whether he should take possession of them or not, but merely stood by so that when the driver of the car appeared he could ask certain questions of that driver as to the nature of the goods and why they were there, then there is no reason whatever to suggest that he had taken the goods into his possession or control."

The rule, then, is analogous to that governing the possession of abandoned goods:[65] a person takes possession if he intentionally exercises control over the goods. In principle,

60 *A-G's Reference (No. 1 of 1974)* [1974] QB 744 (CA). Cp. *Dolan* (1855) Dears 436, 169 ER 794; *Schmidt* (1866) LR 1 CCR 15; *Hancock* (1878) 14 Cox CC 119. For discussion, see Blakey and Goldsmith, "Criminal Redistribution of Stolen Property: The Need for Reform" (1976) 74 *Mich LR* 1512, 1552ff.

61 Cp. Criminal Attempts Act 1981, s. 1(2)(3); above, § 9.5(iii).

62 *Greater London Metropolitan Police Commissioner v Streeter* (1980) 71 Cr App R 113, 119.

63 [1974] QB 744 (CA).

64 *Ibid.*, 753.

65 Above, § 13.4(v)(a).

merely standing by is not sufficient. However, the decision is one for the jury on the facts of each case. Consequently, the Court concluded:[66]

> "that the trial judge was wrong in withdrawing the issue from the jury. As a matter of law he was not entitled to conclude from the facts . . . that these goods were reduced into the possession of the police officer. What he should have done in our opinion would have been to have left that issue to the jury for decision, directing the jury that they should find that the prosecution case was without substance if they thought that the police officer had assumed control of the goods as such and reduced them into his possession. Whereas on the other hand, they should have found the case proved, assuming that they were satisfied about its other elements, if they were of the opinion that the police officer in removing the rotor arm and standing by and watching was doing no more than ensure that the driver should not get away without interrogation and was not at that stage seeking to assume possession of the goods as such at all."

Secondly, goods may cease to be stolen if a third party acquires indefeasible legal ownership of them, usually by purchasing them in good faith. Normally in such cases the rule *nemo dat quod non habet* will prevent other persons from acquiring ownership, since at law a person cannot transfer to another any better title to goods than she has herself.[67] However, there are some exceptions to this, enacted by statutes such as the Sale of Goods Act 1979.[68] Alternatively, where the goods are obtained by blackmail or fraud, the transaction is likely to be voidable rather than void, in which case they will cease to be stolen should the original owner elect to affirm the transaction (e.g. through ratifying the contract by which the goods were obtained), even without the intervention of a *bona fide* purchaser for value.

### *(iii) Knowledge or belief*

At the time the goods are received or otherwise handled, the defendant must *know or believe that the goods are stolen.* It is not necessary that the defendant should know the particular way in which the goods were obtained,[69] or their owner,[70] or even the specific nature of the goods,[71] provided she knows they were obtained by theft, fraud, or blackmail.

The meaning of "knowledge" was considered in § 5.4, where it was said that knowing means "knowing, or correctly believing".[72] In essence, this requires that the defendant must accept, or assume, and have no serious doubt, that the goods he handles were obtained by crime. In particular, it is not enough that the defendant thinks the goods are "probably" stolen.[73] Neither is it sufficient that D *suspects* the goods are stolen: " 'Knowing' is not the

[66] [1974] QB 744, 754 (CA).
[67] Sale of Goods Act 1979, s. 21.
[68] E.g., if the rogue has obtained a voidable title to the goods that has not been avoided at time of on-sale (Sale of Goods Act 1979, s. 23), or is a mercantile agent with authorised possession (Factors Act 1889, s. 2).
[69] Cp. *DPP v Nieser* [1959] 1 QB 254 (DC).
[70] *Fuschillo* [1940] 2 All ER 489 (CA).
[71] *McCullum* (1973) 57 Cr App R 645 (CA).
[72] See also Griew, "Consistency, Communication and Codification" in Glazebrook (ed.), *Reshaping the Criminal Law* (1978) 57. On the role of knowledge in handling and criminal law more generally, cp. Stark, "Against Knowledge (in the Criminal Law)" in Simester (ed.), *Modern Criminal Law* (2024), 25, 37-40.
[73] *Reader* (1978) 66 Cr App R 33, 36 (CA).

equivalent of 'having a pretty good idea'".[74] In *Griffiths*,[75] the trial judge instructed the jury that it would be sufficient if the defendant "suspects that goods are stolen and then deliberately shuts his eyes to the circumstances". The Court of Appeal held that this was a misdirection.[76] (However, as we shall note in § 14.2(ii)(b), suspicion may warrant a conviction for a laundering offence.)

For practical purposes, knowledge and belief are coextensive.[77] The case law has sometimes sought to draw minor distinctions between these two cognitive states. According to the 1859 case of *White*:[78]

> "The knowledge charged in this indictment need not be such *knowledge* as would be acquired if the prisoner had actually seen the [item being] stolen; it is sufficient if you think the circumstances were such, accompanying the transaction, as to make the prisoner *believe* that it had been stolen."

Similarly, in *Hall*, it was observed that:[79]

> "A man may be said to know that goods are stolen when he is told by someone with first-hand knowledge (someone such as the thief or the burglar) that such is the case. Belief, of course, is something short of knowledge. It may be said to be the state of mind of a person who says to himself: 'I cannot say I know for certain that these goods are stolen but there can be no other reasonable conclusion in the light of all the circumstances, in the light of all that I have heard and seen.'"

But these distinctions, which merely concern the *basis* of one's knowledge or belief, are without great value. It is generally impossible to know anything with utter certainty: even the evidence of one's own eyes may occasionally be doubted. What counts is whether the defendant has a settled belief, with no serious doubt, that the goods are stolen. Consistent with this view, the better guidance is that set out by the Court of Appeal in *Moys*:[80]

> "The question is a subjective one and it must be proved that the defendant was aware of the theft or that he believed the goods to be stolen. Suspicion that they were stolen, even coupled with the fact that he shut his eyes to the circumstances, is not enough, although those matters may be taken into account by a jury when deciding whether or not the necessary knowledge or belief existed."

### (a) Wilful blindness

What, however, if H suspects the goods are stolen and deliberately refrains from enquiring any further into the question? In this situation H's mental state may be described as one of *wilful blindness*. Does H's failure to make that further enquiry itself establish the requisite

[74] *Woods* [1969] 1 QB 447, 452 (CA). Although a pre-Act decision, this still represents the law: *Grainge* [1974] 1 All ER 928 (CA); *Reader* (1978) 66 Cr App R 33 (CA). A helpful review of the law is found in *Forsyth* [1997] 2 Cr App R 299, 317–21 (CA). More recently, the distinction between suspicion and knowledge or belief has been affirmed by the House of Lords in the context of conspiracy: *Saik* [2006] UKHL 18, [2007] 1 AC 18, [32] (Lord Nicholls), [78] (Lord Hope), [120] (Lord Brown).

[75] (1974) 60 Cr App R 14, 16 (CA). Taken as a whole, however, the judge's direction was thought to be adequate, and the defendant's appeal was dismissed.

[76] Cp. The discussion of willful blindness, below § 14.1(iii)(a).

[77] Subject to the point that "knowledge" implies a *correct* belief: above, § 5.1(v).

[78] (1859) 1 F&F 665, 175 ER 898 (Bramwell B, emphasis added).

[79] (1985) 81 Cr App R 260, 264 (CA).

[80] (1984) 79 Cr App R 72, 76 (CA); preferred in *Forsyth* [1997] 2 Cr App R 299, 321 (CA) as guidance that is "clear and more readily understandable by a jury and avoids the potential for confusion inherent in a *Hall* direction".

knowledge or belief? As was stated in § 5.4(i), generally the answer is no. That wilful blindness is not automatically deemed to be knowledge[81] for the purposes of handling was made clear by the Court of Appeal in *Griffiths*:[82]

> "To direct the jury that the offence is committed if the defendant, suspecting that the goods were stolen, deliberately shut his eyes to the circumstances as an alternative to knowing or believing the goods were stolen is a misdirection. To direct the jury that, in common sense and in law, they may find that the defendant knew or believed the goods to be stolen because he deliberately closed his eyes to the circumstances is a perfectly proper direction."

Knowledge and belief are subjective phenomena. They cannot be established by showing that the defendant *ought* to have realised the goods were stolen.[83] However, as the closing sentence of the quotation makes clear, the obviousness of the truth may be an *evidential* factor, supporting the inference that in fact H knew he was handling stolen property. A failure by H to make some enquiry may, in certain circumstances, be taken into account in considering whether the prosecution has proved beyond reasonable doubt the existence of knowledge or belief. A jury may legitimately come to the conclusion that the defendant abstained from enquiry because he knew already what the answer was going to be, and then infer that his omission to enquire stemmed not from mere suspicion, but from his positive belief that the goods were stolen.[84]

Nonetheless, there is still room for the wilful blindness doctrine, as the basis for deeming in law a belief that goods were stolen. It operates where H believes the goods are almost certainly stolen, and where any slight doubt on the matter could easily be resolved by his further enquiry. If H deliberately refrains from making that enquiry, especially if he does so in order later to be able to deny knowledge, he is to be attributed with knowledge. However, the scope of the doctrine is very narrow.[85]

*(b) Recklessness: a case for law reform?*

The approach of the courts to wilful blindness is arguably contrary to the intention of those who drafted the Act. According to the Criminal Law Revision Committee, commenting on the law prior to the 1968 Act:[86]

> "The man who buys the goods at a ridiculously low price from an unknown seller whom he meets in a public house may not *know* that the goods were stolen, and he may take the precaution of asking no questions. Yet it may be clear on the evidence that he *believes* that the goods were stolen. In such cases the prosecution may fail (rightly, as the [pre-Act] law now stands) for want . . . of guilty knowledge."

[81] As might be suggested by somewhat ambiguous *dicta* in *Atwal v Massey* [1971] 3 All ER 881 (DC).
[82] (1974) 60 Cr App R 14, 18 (CA); cp. *Saik* [2006] UKHL 18, [2007] 1 AC 18, [62] (Lord Hope). Similarly, in *Smith* (1977) 64 Cr App R 217 (CA), 220, Lawton LJ stated: "We are satisfied that except in most unusual cases juries are capable of understanding what is meant by the word 'believing'. . . . Phrases such as 'suspecting that the goods were stolen and then wilfully shutting one's eyes to the obvious' should not be used as a definition of 'believing'."
[83] *Atwal v Massey* [1971] 3 All ER 881, 882 (DC); *Bellenie* [1980] Crim LR 437 (CA); *Havard* (1916) 11 Cr App R 2 (CA).
[84] Cp. *Crooks* [1981] 2 NZLR 53, 59, which contains a useful discussion of knowledge and belief.
[85] Wilful blindness is discussed further in § 5.4(i).
[86] *Theft and Related Offences* Cmnd. 2977 (1966) para. 134. But see the important gloss by Williams, "Handling, Theft and the Purchaser Who Takes a Chance" [1985] *Crim LR* 432, 433–4.

By inserting "or believing" into the mens rea requirement for handling, the Committee seemingly sought to extend the law to capture such cases. As it turns out, they failed. That should not surprise, because the meaning of "believe" is too close to that of "know" to mark a meaningful extension. It certainly does *not* mean "suspect". What the Committee might have been better to do was to signal its intention more clearly by expressly widening the mens rea requirement into the realm of recklessness: e.g. by stipulating "believing the goods are probably stolen" or "believing the goods may be stolen" to be sufficient mens rea.[87]

It is a difficult question whether the law ought to have been extended into recklessness, or whether it is right to insist on knowledge or belief. On the one hand, it is difficult to prove the mens rea of handling, hence the perceived need for a recent possession doctrine and statutory evidential aids (discussed in the next subsections);[88] fewer dishonest handlers would escape conviction if recklessness were sufficient. The concern about convicting for mere suspicion could be allayed by requiring that H believe the goods are *probably* stolen (i.e. more probably stolen than not).[89] Moreover, dishonestly buying goods which are (correctly) thought by H to be probably stolen satisfies the twin criteria of harm and culpability. It is harmful to the original owner and helpful to the thief, and it is culpable. Hence, it may be thought, there are strong reasons in favour of criminalisation.

Against this argument, it is improbable that the change would much affect the position of professional fences, who are likely to know rather than suspect the provenance of the goods. Thus its greatest value would be against the casual or occasional receiver—the purchaser at a car boot sale, or the pawnbroker, who suspects but is uncertain whether the goods are stolen, and would not buy or accept the goods if she knew the truth. These forms of legitimate commercial activity might be stifled if the purchaser or broker were required consciously to risk criminal conviction by her activity.[90]

On balance, we incline toward the former argument. The risk of over-extending the criminal law is safeguarded against by the further mens rea requirement that the defendant must not only be reckless but also *dishonest*.[91] The pawnbroker who suspects goods are stolen but has no way of knowing the truth should not (and probably would not, by a jury) be accounted dishonest, especially if his acceptance of the goods is consistent with standard practice in the industry.[92] By insisting on knowledge or a firm belief, the law condones rather than stigmatises the "fallen off the back of a lorry" culture in our society—a culture, it must be said, that is overdue for eradication. (But as we shall explain below in § 14.2, some of those who escape criminal liability for handling because they merely suspect the goods are stolen will now commit one of the offences of money-laundering.)

[87] There is, of course, an "objective" element to recklessness: the foreseen risk must be taken unreasonably.

[88] Below, § 14.1(iii)(c), (d).

[89] Spencer, "Handling, Theft and the *Mala Fide* Purchaser" [1985] *Crim LR* 92, 95–6. Blakey and Goldsmith, "Criminal Redistribution of Stolen Property: The Need for Reform" (1976) 74 *Mich LR* 1512, 1560 advocate a standard of awareness of "a substantial risk" that the property was stolen.

[90] See Williams, "Handling, Theft and the Purchaser Who Takes a Chance" [1985] *Crim LR* 432, 435–6.

[91] Spencer, "Handling and Taking Risks—A Reply to Professor Williams" [1985] *Crim LR* 440. See below, § 14.1(iv).

[92] On the relevance of standard practices, see Smith, *Property Offences* (1994) § 7–84. Cp. the argument rejected in *Hayes* [2015] EWCA Crim 1944, [2018] 1 Cr App R 10 (overruled on distinct grounds in *Hayes* [2025] UKSC 29, [2025] 1 WLR 3553).

*(c) Evidence of mens rea: the doctrine of recent possession*

Proof of mens rea in handling can be difficult. The prosecution may be able to establish that H had possession of stolen goods, but unless it can give some account of how those goods were acquired, or of what H intended to do with the goods, it may be very difficult to prove that H knew or believed the goods were stolen. To meet this challenge, judges have evolved a device of prima facie inference, from which proof of possession can, under certain circumstances, support an inference of criminality. This is known as the doctrine of recent possession.

The "doctrine" of recent possession, which originates in the common law, means that where the prosecution can prove possession by D of property recently stolen, the jury can presume that D is either the thief or a dishonest receiver, in the absence of a credible explanation of how D otherwise came by the property.[93] It has been described as:[94]

> "a convenient way of referring compendiously to the inferences of fact which, in the absence of any satisfactory explanation by the accused, may be drawn as a matter of common sense from other facts, including, in particular, the fact that the accused has in his possession property which it is proved had been unlawfully obtained shortly before he was found to be in possession of it."

Before the inference from recent possession can be invoked, the prosecution must prove the relevant property was stolen, and that it was stolen recently. How recent is "recent"? It depends on the facts, and in particular on the nature of the property. Possession of a stolen £20 pound note would ordinarily be unlikely to support an inference of theft or handling after more than a few days; 11 months was too long for stereo equipment in *Simmons*;[95] but the doctrine was applicable after four months in the case of a corporate bond.[96]

The classic direction is found in *Aves*:[97]

> "Where the only evidence is that an accused person is in possession of property recently stolen, a jury may infer guilty knowledge (a) if he offers no explanation to account for his possession, or (b) if the jury are satisfied that the explanation he does offer is untrue. If, however, the explanation offered is one which leaves the jury in doubt whether he knew the property was stolen, they should be told that the case has not been proved, and, therefore, the verdict should be Not Guilty."

Thus stated, it is clear that recent possession is simply a matter of ordinary evidential inference from circumstances, and gives rise at most to an "evidential" burden on the part of D.[98] The onus of proving both actus reus and mens rea remains on the prosecution, and if D does give a non-incredible explanation for his innocent possession of the property, the

[93] Cp. *Smythe* (1981) 72 Cr App R 8, 11 (CA).

[94] *DPP v Nieser* [1959] 1 QB 254, 266 (DC). See also *Raviraj* (1987) 85 Cr App R 93 (CA): the doctrine is only an extension of a general proposition that guilt may be inferred from unreasonable behaviour by the accused in response to his being confronted with facts which prima facie suggest his guilt. Although in some jurisdictions it has been held that the rule is limited to theft, its application to receiving may be justified on the pragmatic ground that criminal receivers can rarely be detected in the act of receiving, so that direct evidence is rarely available. Cp. Hall, *Theft, Law and Society* (2nd ed., 1952) 175.

[95] [1986] Crim LR 397 (CA).

[96] *Livock* (1914) 10 Cr App R 264 (CA).

[97] [1950] 2 All ER 330 (CA). See also *Ketteringham* (1927) 19 Cr App R 159 (CA); *Hepworth* [1955] 2 QB 600 (CA); *Cash* [1985] QB 801, 804 (CA).

[98] See above, § 3.2.

jury may not infer knowledge or belief from the bare fact of possession. The presumption's dependence upon the fact of possession makes the evidential inference of limited value against sophisticated professional fences, who are unlikely to take actual possession of the goods for themselves; or who, if they do take possession, are likely to take the precaution of ensuring they can offer a plausible explanation, e.g. by integrating possession of stolen goods with their other, legitimate, business activities.[99]

*(d) Proof of guilty knowledge under section 27(3)*

In addition to the doctrine of recent possession, the prosecutor has long-standing statutory aid. Section 27(3) provides that, in proving knowledge or belief on a charge of handling, the prosecution may give as evidence: (a) the fact that other stolen property was handled by D or in D's possession at some time during the 12 months preceding the current offence charged (i.e. prior possession); or (b) the fact that D was convicted of theft or handling within the period of five years before being charged with the current offence (i.e. previous convictions).[100]

Formerly these provisions stood out as an uncomfortable exception to the general rule that rendered inadmissible a defendant's previous misdeeds as evidence of his present guilt, and the provisions were criticised on that account. The general rule was radically amended by the Criminal Justice Act 2003, which now makes such evidence admissible in any case where it is relevant to an important matter in dispute between the prosecution and the defence.[101] In the light of this, section 27(3) is now practically redundant.[102]

### *(iv) Dishonesty*

It is an essential element of the section 22 offence that the goods have been handled dishonestly. Suppose, for instance, that H knowingly takes possession of stolen goods and passes them to someone else. H may well have performed the actus reus of handling (a disposal for the benefit of another person). But if H is a police officer, recovering the goods on behalf of the owner, he is not guilty of an offence—because his actions are most unlikely to be regarded by the jury as dishonest. This analysis is illustrated by the pre-Act case of *Matthews*,[103] in which the Court of Criminal Appeal held that a person who had received stolen property intending to hand it over at once to the police or the true owner could not be guilty of receiving stolen property.

The test of dishonesty in handling is the same as that in theft, and the leading case in both contexts is *Ghosh*, as now curtailed by *Ivey v Genting* and *Barton*.[104] Note, however, that the specific defences provided by section 2 of the Theft Act 1968 apply only in the

[99] See Klockars, *The Professional Fence* (1974) 80–93; Hall, *Theft, Law and Society* (2nd ed., 1952) 189–90.

[100] These rules date from the Prevention of Crimes Act 1871, which replaced even more stringent provisions enacted two years earlier by s. 11 of the Habitual Criminals Act 1869.

[101] Criminal Justice Act 2003, s. 101(1)(d). On the 2003 reform, see Spencer, *Evidence of Bad Character* (3rd ed., 2016).

[102] Indeed, in the Report from which the 2003 reform derives, the Law Commission recommended their repeal: Law Com. No. 273, *Evidence of Bad Character in Criminal Proceedings* (2001) para. 11.55.

[103] [1950] 1 All ER 137, 138 (CA).

[104] *Ghosh* [1982] QB 1053 (CA); *Ivey v Genting* [2017] UKSC 67, [2018] AC 391; *Barton* [2020] EWCA Crim 575, [2021] QB 685. These cases are discussed above in § 13.8(iv).

context of theft and not to handling. Where such exculpatory circumstances exist on a handling charge, they operate simply as factors to be considered when determining dishonesty on general principles.[105] The issue is one of fact, and is for the jury to decide.

### *(v) Concurrence of actus reus and mens rea*

As we saw in § 5.8, it is a fundamental principle of criminal law that the actus reus and mens rea must coincide: there must be a moment in time at which all the elements of the offence are simultaneously made out. In the context of handling, this means that knowledge acquired, or dishonesty formed, after the actus reus is insufficient.

Suppose D takes possession of goods innocently and then learns they are stolen, or receives them intending to hand the goods over to the police (so without dishonesty) and later changes her mind. At this point she cannot commit handling by receiving. Once possession is taken, it cannot be retaken; the actus reus of receiving is completed and is not a continuing act.[106] Other forms of handling, however, can be repeated or continuing.[107] Thus D would become guilty of handling if, having become dishonest, she then disposed of the goods for the benefit of another person. But if D merely retains the goods for her own benefit she does not handle. The proper charge would be theft of the goods by D.[108]

### *(vi) Handling versus theft*

Even though handling must occur after the original theft is completed,[109] virtually all handlings are themselves thefts.[110] Hence, in proving handling, the prosecution generally proves two different offences constituted by the same action. In principle, there is no objection to this, since not all thefts are handlings and the two offences have different maximum penalties. Moreover, they capture quite different modes of wrongdoing concerning another person's property interests. Where the facts establish that D received from a thief, therefore, the prosecution should charge handling rather than theft.

However, sometimes the facts may be uncertain, so that it is unclear which of the two offences has been committed by D. This often arises when D is found in possession of stolen goods and the prosecution cannot establish how D acquired possession of the goods (e.g. whether D stole them herself, or received them from the original thief). The doctrine of recent possession,[111] which often applies to such cases, supports a conviction for either theft or handling, without preference. Consequently, the jury or magistrates may be sure beyond reasonable doubt that D is either thief or handler, without knowing which of the two.

In such cases, it is permissible for the prosecution to charge D with alternative counts of theft[112] and handling. In *Stapylton v O'Callaghan*,[113] the Divisional Court, dealing with an appeal by way of case stated from a magistrates' court, said that as D's handling (if that

[105] See above, § 13.8.
[106] *Johnson* (1911) 6 Cr App R 218; *Matthews* [1950] 1 All ER 137, 138 (CA); *Smythe* (1981) 72 Cr App R 8, 13 (CA).
[107] Cp. *Pitchley* (1973) 57 Cr App R 30 (CA); *Smythe* (1981) 72 Cr App R 8, 13 (CA).
[108] *Matthews* [1950] 1 All ER 137, 138 (CA).
[109] Cp. s. 22(1): "otherwise than in the course of stealing".
[110] See above, § 14.1(i)(f).
[111] Above, § 14.1(iii)(c).
[112] Or robbery or burglary, as the case may be, depending on the circumstances of the original theft.
[113] [1973] 2 All ER 782 (DC).

is what he had really done) would also have amounted to a theft, the bench should have convicted D of theft. In *Shelton*,[114] where a similar situation had arisen in the Crown Court, the Court of Appeal approved a direction by the judge which encouraged the jury to take a similar approach.[115] Given that, of the two possible offences, it is theft that carries the lower maximum penalty, the result is not unjust to the defendant.

## § 14.2 Laundering

Sections 327, 328, and 329 of the Proceeds of Crime Act (POCA) 2002 create three related offences of laundering "criminal property".[116] By section 327 it is an offence to conceal, disguise, convert, transfer or remove criminal property. By section 328 a person "commits an offence if he enters into or becomes concerned in an arrangement which he knows or suspects facilitates (by whatever means) the acquisition, retention, use or control of criminal property by or on behalf of another person". And by section 329 a person commits an offence if he acquires criminal property, uses it, or has it in possession.

These offences are aimed at those who help major criminals disguise the proceeds of large-scale criminal activities: for example, the property developer whose activities are financed by a drug baron; or the people trafficker who is rewarded for his contribution by shares in the property company, on which large dividends are later paid. Generally the "criminal property" everyone had in mind in these cases is money, in large quantities. As such, these offences form one part of a much bigger legislative scheme, which also imposes obligations on a range of financial businesses to inform the authorities if they suspect that those with whom they deal are involved in money-laundering,[117] and does much else besides.[118] However, the offences created by sections 327, 328, and 329 are themselves not limited to large-scale transactions, and in consequence they duplicate to a very large extent the offence of handling stolen goods—and indeed some other criminal offences too.

### *(i) Criminal property*

A central requirement in all three of these offences is that D's behaviour should relate to "criminal property". This is defined, in a back-to-front way, by section 340(2), which provides as follows:

> Criminal conduct is conduct which—
> (a) constitutes an offence in any part of the United Kingdom, or
> (b) would constitute an offence in any part of the United Kingdom if it occurred there.

114 (1986) 83 Cr App R 379 (CA).

115 The Court provided that, "in the unlikely event of the jury not agreeing amongst themselves whether theft or handling has been proved, they should be discharged".

116 These offences replace with one single set of offences a messy situation under the previous law, which deployed two sets of offences, one under the Criminal Justice Act 1988 and another under the Drug Trafficking Act 1994.

117 These offences are not covered in this book; for the details, see *Archbold* (2026) chap. 26.

118 A range of extra legislative weapons were created by the Criminal Finances Act 2017. Foremost among these are "unexplained wealth orders", whereby certain persons who appear to be suspiciously wealthy can be required to explain the origins of their wealth; but it seems that despite the publicity given to them they have so far been little used: see Moiseienko, "The Limitations of Unexplained Wealth Orders" [2022] *Crim LR* 230.

(3) Property is criminal property if—

(a) it constitutes a person's benefit from criminal conduct or it represents such a benefit (in whole or part and whether directly or indirectly), and

(b) the alleged offender knows or suspects that it constitutes or represents such a benefit.

(4) It is immaterial—

(a) who carried out the conduct;

(b) who benefited from it;

(c) whether the conduct occurred before or after the passing of this Act.

(5) A person benefits from conduct if he obtains property as a result of or in connection with the conduct.[119]

This definition is extremely wide. If taken at face value, it would make D potentially guilty of money-laundering by reason of the simple fact of committing a crime from which he derived a financial benefit: including theft, or fraud, obviously—and less obviously, tax evasion, drug dealing, and a range of other acquisitive offences. Plainly, such duplication would be undesirable and fortunately the courts have avoided it (at least to some extent) by interpreting section 340 as requiring the benefit to arise from some crime *other* than any crime which D incidentally commits when he carries out the act(s) in relation to the property that constitute the offence under sections 327, 328, or 329.

In *Geary*,[120] D was prosecuted under section 328 in respect of an "arrangement" to facilitate another person to acquire, retain, or control criminal property. The prosecution case was that D had received a large sum of money which X had earlier obtained by fraud. As such, the money was "criminal property" and if D had known this he would have been guilty of the offence charged. D's story, however, was that X had given him the money to look after in order to hide it from X's wife, whom X was divorcing in proceedings in which he wanted to present himself to the court as poorer than he really was. If this account were true, then D and X were guilty of a conspiracy to pervert the course of justice. But this, said the Court of Appeal, was not enough to make D guilty of the section 328 offence because even if, on D's account, the money acquired the status of "criminal property" when it was handed over in pursuit of the conspiracy, it did not have that status before it was handed over. In so holding, the Court followed the same line as had been taken, in the context of a prosecution under section 327, in the earlier case of *Loizou*.[121] And in *Akhtar*,[122] the Court of Appeal later said, as might be expected, that the same limitation applied to "criminal property" in the context of all three of the laundering offences.

This limit on the scope of criminal property is sometimes expressed by saying that the subject-matter of the laundering offence must represent the benefit of a crime committed *before* the conduct by D in respect of which he stands accused of money-laundering. But although the crime which turns the subject-matter of the offence into "criminal property" will usually take place before the acts alleged as laundering, it need not do so, and in some cases it will be committed at the same time. Believing that the "predicate offence" (as it is usually called) must be committed earlier in time, in *GH*[123] the Court of Appeal held that

[119] The definition is continued in subsections (6)–(10); subsection (9) provides that "property" includes all property, real or personal, tangible or intangible.

[120] [2010] EWCA Crim 1925, [2011] 1 WLR 1634.

[121] [2004] EWCA Crim 1579, [2005] 2 Cr App R 37.

[122] [2011] EWCA Crim 146, [2011] 1 Cr App R 37.

[123] [2015] UKSC 24, [2015] 1 WLR 2126; on appeal from [2013] EWCA Crim 2237.

D was not guilty of money-laundering by "arranging" (under section 328) when he made his bank account available to B, who made a dishonest living by selling non-existent motor-insurance to credulous motorists, as a receptacle into which the victims of B's frauds could be directed to pay their premiums. But in the Supreme Court this ruling was reversed. Distinguishing *Geary*, it said the issue was not whether the subject-matter of the laundering offence was somebody's benefit from a crime committed earlier in time, but whether it was somebody's benefit from a crime committed *independently* of the acts in respect of which D now stood accused of money-laundering. Here, D was accused of money-laundering by reason of the arrangement he had made with B to enable B to receive and store the money which B extracted from the victims of his frauds. And this money "became criminal property in the hands of B, not by reason of the arrangement made between B and [D] but by reason of the fact that it was obtained through fraud perpetrated on the victims."[124]

If "criminal property" presupposes the existence of a separate "predicate offence", it does not presuppose the existence of a separate offender who committed it. Indeed, when defining "criminal property" section 340 expressly provides that it is immaterial "who carried out the [criminal] conduct" and "who benefited from it". It follows that, in principle, the criminal who committed the offences which gave rise to the existence of "criminal property" can then commit offences of money-laundering by reason of what he or she does with it thereafter. Thus a drug-dealer who by his illicit trade builds up a fortune commits an offence under section 327 if he hides it away somewhere, or uses it to buy a luxury apartment, or spirits it off to South America. Equally, a person who steals a BMW commits a further offence under section 329 if he "uses" it by driving it around, or even if he merely keeps it to gloat over in the privacy of his garage.[125] In this respect, these two money-laundering offences differ significantly from the offence of handling, which, as we saw earlier, is carefully constructed to make it impossible for the original thief to commit an offence of handling by reason of what she does with the property afterwards. But if a second person is not required for the section 327 and 329 offences, a second person *is* required for the commission of an offence under section 328—the "arranging" offence—because this section specifically states that the arrangement must be one which facilitates "the acquisition, retention, use or control of criminal property *by or on behalf of another person*."

Additionally, if "criminal property" presupposes the existence of a separate "predicate offence", there is no need, according to the case law, for the prosecution to identify it, or to show who committed it. In *Craig*,[126] the Court of Appeal held, in the context of a prosecution under section 329, that D's guilt can be established by circumstantial evidence suggesting that he has acquired or possessed "criminal property" the nature and source of which are not identified. In this case the prosecution produced evidence that D had "used quantities of cash, expensive motor vehicles and jet skis, which could not be justified on the wages that he had earned", and at a time when "his income was declared as nil". Taken with D's

[124] Crucially, as explained below in § 15.1, the frauds were complete when B made relevant false representations, and *not* when the victims transferred the money into D's account. The need for a distinct "predicate offence" appears to have been overlooked in *Ogden*: below, § 14.2(ii)(c).

[125] Conduct which would seem to be an offence under s. 329(1)(c). For an example from real life, see *Miller*: a dishonest builder who was sentenced to four years' imprisonment for fraudulent trading (by systematically cheating his customers) and for money-laundering (by spending the proceeds on holidays in Las Vegas, New York, Greece and Tenerife and a deposit on a luxury car): *Eastern Daily Press*, 2 March 2019.

[126] [2007] EWCA Crim 2913.

failure to provide any convincing explanation of where the money came from, this, said the prosecution, showed that he had been profiting from crime; but neither the prosecution nor the judge in his direction to the jury sought to identify the crimes or types of crime from which the profit came. On such evidence, said the Court of Appeal, the jury was entitled to convict D of money-laundering.[127] In *Anwoir*, the Court of Appeal took the view that it was rightly decided:[128]

> "there are two ways in which the Crown can prove the property derives from crime, (a) by showing that it derives from conduct of a specific kind or kinds and that conduct of that kind or those kinds is unlawful, or (b) by evidence of the circumstances in which the property is handled which are such as to give rise to the irresistible inference that it can only be derived from crime."

So, to borrow the title of a chapter from Thackeray's *Vanity Fair*, a defendant is liable to be convicted of money-laundering on evidence that shows no more than that he is a person who apparently knows "how to live well on nothing a year". This is contentious, as the Court of Appeal itself recognised in *Anwoir*, where it certified a point public importance for the purpose of an appeal to the House of Lords; but leave to appeal was refused, and for now that is where the matter rests.[129]

### *(ii) The three offences: further details*

#### *(a) Actus reus*

By section 327, an offence is committed where a person "(a) conceals criminal property, (b) disguises criminal property, (c) converts criminal property, (d) transfers criminal property", or "(e) removes criminal property from England and Wales or from Scotland or from Northern Ireland". The range of behaviour covered by these expressions, which are largely self-explanatory, is clearly very wide; and the case-law shows no inclination to narrow it. In *Fazal*,[130] the Court of Appeal held that a person is guilty of "converting" criminal property where he allowed another person the use of his bank account as a depositary for the proceeds of his crimes, even though he himself took no positive action in relation to the money. This conduct was, of course, more obviously covered by the section 328 offence of making an arrangement that facilitates another person's acquisition, retention, use, or control. But the Court said that the statutory provisions are not mutually exclusive.

By section 328, an offence is committed where a person "enters into or becomes concerned in an arrangement which he knows or suspects facilitates (by whatever means) the acquisition, retention, use or control of criminal property by or on behalf of another person". The key phrase here is "an arrangement". Though wide, its breadth is not infinite. Thus in *Dare v CPS*,[131] the Administrative Court held that, although the offence would be

[127] But the conviction was quashed on another ground—the judge's failure to put D's defence to the jury adequately. For a critique of the decision: Richardson, [2008] 7 *Criminal Law Week*, No. 5.

[128] [2008] EWCA Crim 1354, [2009] 1 WLR 980; Walters, "Prosecuting Money Launderers: Do the Prosecution Have to Prove the Predicate Offence?" [2009] *Crim LR* 571.

[129] See *Kuchadia* [2015] EWCA Crim 1252, [2015] 1 WLR 4895, and the vigorous criticism by Richardson, [2015] 34 *Criminal Law Week*, No. 6.

[130] [2009] EWCA Crim 1697, [2010] 1 WLR 694.

[131] [2012] EWHC 2074 (Admin).

committed by a potential purchaser who made an agreement with another person to buy a stolen car, it was not committed where the buyer and seller had only got as far as the preliminary discussions. However, if there is a firm agreement, there is no reason why the section 328 offence should not be committed where the arrangement relates to something which, though not yet "criminal property", will have become so by the time the arrangement is carried out: as where D makes a definite arrangement with X to buy a car (or a series of cars) which X has not yet stolen, but plans to steal to order; or where D agrees to allow X to use his bank account to store the proceeds of crimes yet to be committed.[132]

By section 329, an offence is committed where a person "(a) acquires criminal property, (b) uses criminal property", or "(c) has possession of criminal property".[133] These phrases, which once again are largely self-explanatory, also cover a wide range of behaviour. However, the section 329 offence differs from the previous two offences in one important respect, because it is subject to a specific defence which does not apply to the others. By section 329(2)(c), D avoids criminal liability under section 329 if "he acquired or used or had possession of the property for adequate consideration". In *Hogan v DPP*,[134] the Court of Appeal held that what amounts to "adequate consideration" is ultimately a question of fact, and an issue on which D is entitled to the benefit of the doubt; and further, if D did acquire the property for adequate consideration, he is not guilty of the section 329 offence[135] even if he knew full well the property was stolen, and whether or not the court thinks he was dishonest.

For all three of these offences, however, D incurs no liability if any one of a list of other conditions is met. Thus D is exempt if, before he did the act, he made a "disclosure" to "a constable, an officer of Revenue and Customs or a nominated officer",[136] or intended to do so and had a reasonable excuse for leaving it until afterwards, and in certain other more specific circumstances.[137]

### (b) *Mens rea*

In the offence of handling, as we saw, the mens rea requirements are exacting; D must "know or believe" that the goods were stolen, and in addition his conduct must be "dishonest". For the money-laundering offences the mens rea requirement is much less exacting. For all three offences it is sufficient that D "knows or suspects" that the property is "criminal property".[138]

### (c) *The relationship between money-laundering and other property offences*

The money-laundering offences are aimed at those who help major criminals disguise the proceeds of large-scale criminal activities. As was noted earlier, the "criminal property"

[132] On this, see *Smith, Hogan, and Ormerod* § 33.1.3.1.

[133] In 1996, as part of the hurried legislative response to *Preddy* (see § 15.1 below), s. 24A was added to the Theft Act 1968 to create a new offence of "dishonestly retaining a wrongful credit". A "wrongful credit" is defined in s. 24(2A) to mean a credit which derives from theft, blackmail, fraud, or stolen goods. Although the offence is now largely duplicated by POCA s. 329, it remains in force.

[134] [2007] EWHC 978 (Admin), [2007] 1 WLR 2944.

[135] Although possibly to charges under ss. 327 or 328.

[136] Section 338.

[137] Other conditions include the fact that the property was obtained abroad by conduct which was legal there and, where the person who received or otherwise dealt with the property was a bank or similar, that the property was a sum of money less than £250.

[138] By virtue of s. 340(2)(b), which (rather oddly) incorporates this requirement into the definition of "criminal property", and again, and more specifically, by virtue of s. 328(1) in relation to that offence.

which the lawmakers had in mind was money, in large quantities. However, the offences themselves are much broader than that. Most obviously, the "acquisition" offence created by section 329 clearly covers handling by receiving. Stolen goods fall within the definition of "criminal property" set out in section 340(3), and having received them D will "have possession" of them, and may have "acquired" them too. This will be so not only if the property in question is the proceeds of a major bank robbery, but equally if it is (say) a stolen games console that D bought from a shady character at a car boot sale or in the local pub.

From the prosecutor's point of view, a charge of laundering under section 329 of POCA 2002 has a number of practical advantages over a charge of handling under section 22 of the Theft Act 1968. First, whereas handling only applies where the goods were obtained by theft, blackmail, or fraud,[139] "criminal property" for the purpose of the laundering offences means property obtained through any crime at all. Secondly, as we saw in § 14.1(iii), the mens rea requirement for handling is exacting, because D is guilty of handling only where he acted "knowing or believing" that the goods were stolen. For the section 329 offence, by contrast, it is enough that D merely *suspected* that the goods were "criminal property".[140] Thirdly, an ingredient in the offence of handling is "dishonesty", which means that D is not guilty if the tribunal of fact accepts that his behaviour was in accordance with accepted standards in society.[141] There is no such let-out for D where he is charged under section 329. Lastly, the section 329 offence can be established by evidence that is more general and less specific than the evidence needed to support a charge of handling. To convict D of handling, the prosecution must produce evidence to show that, acting with the necessary mens rea, D received or otherwise dealt with an item of stolen property that is identified—which, as we have seen, is not necessary for money-laundering.

As against this, the section 329 offence has two disadvantages for prosecutors compared with handling: D is exempt from liability if, first, D acquired, used or had possession of the property for adequate consideration;[142] and secondly, and much less plausibly, if D had notified the relevant authorities as to what was going on. Despite this, prosecutors are understandably tempted to use section 329 in cases where, on the face of it, handling would be the obvious charge. In *Wilkinson v DPP*,[143] for example, a defendant was found riding a stolen mini motorcycle in circumstances suggesting he had either stolen it himself or acquired it from the person who had done so. For this he was prosecuted under section 329 rather than for theft, burglary, or handling. He sought to challenge the decision of the Crown Prosecution Service to prosecute him for this offence by way of judicial review. The Divisional Court expressed disquiet about the choice of charge, but the application for judicial review was rejected. Similar disquiet was expressed by the Court of Appeal in the later

[139] Theft Act 1968, s. 24(4). The scope of handling is also expanded, to a small extent, by s. 24A(8): See note 47 above.
[140] POCA 2002, s. 340(3)(b). On an expansive reading of s. 328 (though not ss. 327 or 329), D could commit an offence of money laundering by "arranging" if he wrongly *suspects* that the property which is the subject-matter of the arrangement is "criminal property" (where in fact it is not). But it seems unlikely that the courts would so construe it—both on grounds of principle, and in the light of the decision in *Montila* [2004] UKHL 50, [2004] 1 WLR 3141, where the House of Lords refused to give such an interpretation to a similar offence under the previous law.
[141] Above, § 14.1(iv).
[142] Section 329(2)(c).
[143] [2006] EWHC 3012 (Admin); noted by Rule, [2007] 1 *Archbold News*, 5.

and almost identical case of *Rose*;[144] and also by the Supreme Court in *GH*.[145] But expressions of judicial disquiet such as these do not, of course, curtail the scope of the offence. At present the only thing that keeps section 329 of POCA 2002 in check is the sense of proportion and fair play within the CPS,[146] which, as cases such as *Rose* and *ex parte Wilkinson* show, occasionally deserts them.[147] This overlap would not exist if "criminal property" in section 340(2) were read in a restrictive sense, so that the phrase "constitutes a person's benefit from criminal conduct" means "constitutes a person's benefit from *another person's* criminal conduct"—but this is impossible, given that section 340(3) expressly says "it is immaterial . . . who carried out the conduct". In 2005, Parliament amended POCA 2002[148] to limit the offences in various ways, among other things by providing that where a bank is the potential defendant and the conduct alleged to constitute laundering is a transaction with an existing bank account, the transaction must involve more than £250. A further and more general threshold limit is surely called for, to avoid the obvious problems of fair labelling that can otherwise arise.[149]

Nor is this the only possible overlap. In *Ogden*,[150] members of a family of drug-dealers were prosecuted for a range of offences, among them conspiracy to convert criminal property contrary to section 327. The Court of Appeal upheld the convictions for this offence. Dealing in goods, it said, is one method of converting them; and as "illegal drugs by their nature always represent 'criminal property'",[151] any person who sells illegal drugs is automatically guilty of the additional offence of money-laundering. Disputing this analysis, the defence argued that if it were correct, a person who bought illegal drugs, or merely possessed them for his own personal use, would automatically commit an offence of money-laundering under section 329 (acquisition, or possession). The Court of Appeal accepted this but brushed the point aside, saying "We have no doubt that good sense will prevail . . .". The mistake the Court made here, surely, was to forget that, as a result of section 340, "criminal property" means (in essence) the profit generated by another crime, and to interpret it as meaning any property that it is a criminal offence to possess. If "criminal property" is read in this extended sense, then money-laundering duplicates an even wider range of other criminal offences: to name but a few, downloading, storing, or distributing child pornography,[152] unlawfully possessing a prohibited weapon,[153] and taking eggs from a wild bird's nest.[154] In the face of such overlap, a prosecutor's "good sense" is little comfort to

144 [2008] EWCA Crim 239, [2008] 1 WLR 2113.

145 [2015] UKSC 24, [2015] 1 WLR 2126; [48]–[49].

146 The CPS's official Legal Guidance in respect of money-laundering contains the following: "Prosecutors should identify the most appropriate charge to reflect the suspect's criminality, rather than consider the provisions of sections 327 to 329 of POCA as providing an alternative to offences of handling stolen goods in all cases." This document is published on the CPS website at https://www.cps.gov.uk/legal-guidance/money-laundering-offences.

147 In *Rose* [2008] EWCA Crim 239, [2008] 1 WLR 2113, [18], the Court of Appeal quoted statistics furnished by the CPS to rebut the claim that they were routinely using s. 329 as a substitute for handling; in 2007 there were 1,856 charges under s. 329, as against 19,931 of handling.

148 By the Serious Organised Crime and Police Act 2005, amending ss. 327, 328, and 329 of POCA 2002.

149 Above, § 2.4.

150 [2016] EWCA Crim 6, [2017] 1 WLR 1224.

151 *Ibid.*, [52].

152 Protection of Children Act 1978, s. 1.

153 Firearms Act 1968, s. 5

154 Wildlife and Countryside Act 1981, s. 1.

potential defendants, or indeed those concerned with the coherence of the criminal law and the principle of fair labelling.

## § 14.3 Robbery

Robbery was originally an offence at common law, later defined by statute.[155] In its current form the offence is criminalised by section 8 of the Theft Act 1968:

> (1) A person is guilty of robbery if he steals, and immediately before or at the time of doing so, and in order to do so, he uses force on any person or puts or seeks to put any person in fear of being then and there subjected to force.
>
> (2) A person guilty of robbery, or of an assault with intent to rob, shall on conviction on indictment be liable to imprisonment for life.

Simply put, robbery is a species of theft which is aggravated by assault and/or battery. Thus it is to some extent unusual, in that it combines a property offence with an offence of violence against the person, with penalties more severe than the punishments for those individual offences. Partly, this is because the introduction of force makes theft more likely to succeed and, conversely, the object of theft makes the assault more highly motivated, arguably exposing the victim to a greater risk of injury.[156] More importantly, however, the use of force to complete a theft changes the moral character of D's action, such that it is legitimate to criminalise D's wrong specifically by the "combined" offence of robbery. What is significant about robbery is not merely that D usurps V's property rights, but how she does so. The expectations of personal and property security are preconditions of a stable, meaningful life; for both individuals and society. Robbery undermines *both* of these expectations. Unlike theft, the victim of a robbery cannot resort to any reassuring knowledge that at least her interest in personal integrity was not attacked. Thus it is perhaps misleading to suggest that robbery is a species of aggravated theft. The difference is one of kind, not merely one of degree.[157]

Nonetheless, characterising robbery as a species of "theft" does reflect the law, in that the offence of robbery presupposes the existence of a theft. The elements of robbery are as follows:

(i) theft;
(ii) accompanied by the use or threat of force;
(iii) which occurs immediately before or at the time of the theft; and
(iv) where the force is used or threatened in order to commit theft.

### *(i) Theft*

The offence of theft must be proved before there can be any question of robbery.[158]

Hence, if the defendant is not dishonest in appropriating the relevant property, no robbery is committed. The case of *Skivington*,[159] discussed in § 13.8(i), is instructive. D threat-

[155] Larceny Act 1916, s. 23 (re-enacting a provision of the Larceny Act 1861).
[156] Note, "A Rationale of the Law of Aggravated Theft" (1954) 54 *Columbia LR* 84, 102.
[157] Simester and Sullivan, "On the Nature and Rationale of Property Offences" in Duff and Green (eds.), *Defining Crimes* (2005) 168, 194–5.
[158] *Guy* (1991) 93 Cr App R 108 (CA). The uncertainty expressed on this point in *Forrester* [1992] Crim LR 792 (CA) was, it is submitted, unwarranted—as the note on the case observes: [1992] Crim LR 792, 794–5.
[159] [1968] 1 QB 166 (CA) (decided prior to the Theft Act 1968); cp. *Robinson* [1977] Crim LR 173 (CA); *Hemmings* (1864) 4 F & F 50, 176 ER 462.

ened a wages clerk with a knife and demanded his wife's wages: though this was an assault, it was held there was no larceny (and would now be no theft) and therefore no robbery, since D believed he had a lawful claim to the wages. This amounted to a belief that he had a right to deprive the clerk of the money; therefore D would not now be dishonest within the meaning of section 2(1)(a).

Note that the claim of right asserted by D in *Skivington* will operate solely in respect of the theft element. Where theft of the property cannot be proved, it is irrelevant—for the purposes of robbery—whether D believes he has a right to use force.[160] However, the absence of justification in respect of the force used will mean that D is independently guilty of an offence against the person.[161]

Similarly, no robbery is committed if D took the property with no intent permanently to deprive. Thus in *Mitchell*,[162] D violently hijacked V's BMW, abandoning it a few miles away on the road with its hazard lights flashing. The Court of Appeal quashed D's robbery conviction on the ground that there was no underlying theft because it was clear from the evidence that D did not intend V to lose her car permanently. The same result was reached in *Vinall*,[163] where the subject-matter of the hijack was a cycle rather than a luxury car.

### *(ii) Use or threat of force*

Whether or not force is used is a question of fact for the jury to decide.[164] The main difficulty that may arise is where D exerts only a slight and non-violent pressure. In *Dawson*, D1 jostled V, causing V to lose his balance and giving D2 an opportunity to relieve V of his wallet. The Court of Appeal held this was sufficient evidence of force for the offence of robbery to go to the jury.

The trial judge in *Dawson* had directed that the force used had to be "substantial". However, the Court of Appeal refused to endorse that qualification, preferring to leave the question open. There are difficult issues here, and they remain unresolved. A mere touching, involving very slight pressure that in no way interferes with V's freedom of movement, should in our view not count as force for the purposes of robbery:[165] but it is, from the perspective of physics, an application of force. What seems to be required is that the force be *significant* (rather than substantial), in that it in some way modifies V's movement or freedom of movement. A test along these lines would adequately explain *Dawson* (which was in our view rightly decided). It would also explain the decision in *Hale*,[166] where D put

[160] Cp. *Langham* (1984) 36 SASR 48. Contrast, in the United States, *People v Reid* 508 NE (2d) 661 (1987); Model Penal Code, § 222.1; ruling that a claim of right that would negate a simple theft would not *ipso facto* negate robbery. Arguably, the American approach is to be preferred. In theft, the claim of right under s. 2(1)(a) implies that D did not realise he was wrongly usurping V's property rights. In *Skivington*, the claim of right was invoked by D for a more complex purpose: effectively, to justify D's forcible self-help by extra-judicial means. Arguably, where excessive force is used, a mere claim of right should not automatically exculpate D from a charge of robbery. See Note, "A Rationale of the Law of Aggravated Theft" (1954) 54 *Columbia LR* 84, 98.

[161] Cp. *Wilson* [1984] AC 242, where D was convicted of assault occasioning actual bodily harm as an alternative to burglary.

[162] [2008] EWCA Crim 850; discussed above, § 13.7(ii).

[163] [2011] EWCA Crim 2652, [2012] 1 Cr App R 29.

[164] *Dawson and James* (1977) 64 Cr App R 170 (CA).

[165] Analogously, opening an unlocked door in the normal way does not count as a forcible entry: cp. *Ryan v Shilcock* (1851) 7 Exch 72, 75, 155 ER 861, 862.

[166] (1979) 68 Cr App R 415 (CA).

his hand over V's mouth in order to stop V from shouting for help. The Court of Appeal affirmed D's conviction for robbery.

One upshot of the wide interpretation of force is that the crime of robbery has a very broad range, encompassing within the same label both a theft accompanied by a minor push and a theft committed using weapons and serious violence.[167] As such, the crime appears to violate the principle of fair labelling, since a conviction for "robbery" does not clearly indicate the seriousness of D's wrongdoing.[168] There is a case here for law reform; in particular, for dividing the existing single crime of robbery into two or three more narrowly defined categories, according to whether the theft was accompanied merely by significant force, by the use of weapons, or by serious violence.[169]

*(a) Force against the person or against the property?*

Suppose D violently snatches V's bag, without touching V herself. Is this robbery? In other words, must force be applied directly to the person, or is it sufficient that the appropriation be "by force", directed at the stolen property but impacting indirectly on V? At common law, the rule was that the force had to be directed at the person.[170] A snatching was not enough, unless the victim was thereby injured.[171]

It appears, however, that this distinction is not preserved in section 8(1)—contrary to the intentions of those who framed the Act.[172] In *Clouden*,[173] D tore a basket from V's grasp and ran off with it. Because D approached her from behind, V had no opportunity to resist and D offered no force directly to her person. At common law this was not robbery but, said the Court of Appeal, "the old distinctions have gone".[174] D's appeal against conviction was dismissed. Force against property, which causes force to be applied to the person, is sufficient, even if V is uninjured.

The decision in *Clouden* has been criticised for muddying the clear waters distinguishing robbery from theft. As Sir John Smith commented, the case looks more akin to that of the pickpocket than the bank robber.[175] In *P and Others*,[176] the Divisional Court, having considered *Clouden*, stressed that a *substantial* degree of force is a necessary ingredient in the offence of robbery, whether applied to V's body or to the property. In so holding,

[167] For a sense of the variety, compare O'Donnell and Morrison, "Armed and Dangerous? The Use of Firearms in Robbery" (1997) 36 *Howard J Crim Justice* 305; Gill, *Commercial Robbery* (2000); and Smith, *The Nature of Personal Robbery* (2003).

[168] See above, § 2.4; Ashworth, "Robbery Re-assessed" [2002] *Crim LR* 851.

[169] Compare in this context the crime of burglary, discussed below in § 14.4.

[170] *Gnosil* (1824) 1 C & P 304, 171 ER 1206: "The mere act of taking, being forcible, will not make this offence a highway robbery: to constitute the crime of highway robbery, the force must be . . . of such a nature, as to shew that it was intended to overpower the party robbed, and prevent his resisting, and not merely to get possession of the property stolen. Thus, if a man walking after a woman in the street, were by violence to pull her shawl from her shoulders, though he might use considerable violence, it would not, in my opinion, be highway robbery." See also *Baker* (1783) 1 Leach 290, 168 ER 247; *Steward* 2 East PC 702.

[171] As in *Moore* (1784) 1 Leach 335, 168 ER 270, where D snatched a diamond pin fastened to V's hair, tearing away part of her hair in the process.

[172] Report of the Criminal Law Revision Committee, *Theft and Related Offences* Cmnd. 2977 (1966) para. 65.

[173] [1987] Crim LR 56 (CA).

[174] Citing *Dawson and James* (1977) 64 Cr App R 170 (CA).

[175] [1987] Crim LR 56, 57 (CA).

[176] *P and Others v Director of Public Prosecutions* [2012] EWHC 1657 (Admin), [2013] 1 WLR 2337; noted by Ormerod in [2013] Crim LR 151.

it quashed convictions for robbery imposed for snatching a cigarette out of another person's hand. In such a case the force used, they suggested, must be a degree of force which would potentially have been painful if V had sought to resist it.[177] Despite this, however, in *Martins*,[178] where the victim said the defendant had "snatched" or "grabbed" the property he was holding, the Court of Appeal upheld the robbery conviction, on the basis that this meant the victim "would inevitably have been gripping his items of property sufficiently tightly that his grip had to be overcome by the use of force in order for the appellant to take them from him".

*(b) Threats of force*

The actual application of force is not required. Under section 8(1), it is sufficient if D "puts or seeks to put any person in fear of being then and there subjected to force". This is consistent with the law of assault, which includes threats to apply force as well as its actual application.[179] The victim must apprehend being subjected "there and then" to force: threatening to disclose embarrassing details about someone's past, or to apply force at a later date, unless she hands over property may be blackmail,[180] but not robbery.

Although by section 8(1) part of the definition of the offence is that D "puts or seeks to put [V] in fear of being . . . subjected to force", this means only that D must cause or try to cause V to anticipate the use of force upon him. It does not mean that the prosecution have to prove that V was frightened, or that D sought to frighten him. So, where a gang of youths surrounded V, who submitted to their emptying his pockets because he foresaw that force would be used on him if he resisted, they were rightly convicted of robbery even though in evidence V denied feeling "scared" or "particularly threatened".[181]

*(c) Third persons*

The force need not be used or threatened against the victim of the theft.[182] If D points a gun at V's colleague, T, in order to obtain money from V, D commits robbery (of V). Note, however, that if force is merely threatened rather than applied, it is the person against whom force is threatened who must be "put in fear of being then and there subjected to force". Suppose, for example, that D threatens V that she will shoot V's friend, T, unless V hands money over to D. T is out of earshot, or hears but fails to understand the threat. Somewhat surprisingly, on these facts, D does not commit robbery.[183] V is not put in fear of being subjected to force, since the force is threatened against T. T is not put in fear of being subjected

[177] A observation that Ormerod (*ibid.*) suggests ought to be read with caution: "There need not be 'pain', merely use of force on any person. Wrenching a shoe from a prosthetic leg would surely be robbery from the wearer even if no pain was felt by him."

[178] [2021] EWCA Crim 223.

[179] Above, Chapter 11.

[180] Theft Act 1968, s. 21. Blackmail is not covered in this book; for details of the offence, see *Smith, Hogan, and Ormerod* chap. 24.

[181] *R v DPP* [2007] EWHC 739 (Admin).

[182] See Andrews, "Robbery" [1966] *Crim LR* 524, 524–6.

[183] Section 8(1) appears in this respect to be slightly narrower than the common law. Previously, it was robbery if D took property by threatening immediately to kill the victim's child: *Donally* (1799) 2 East PC 715, 718; *Reane* (1794) 2 Leach 616, 619, 168 ER 410, 412 n. 1.

to force, since the threat is directed to V and T does not hear it. This could only be a case of blackmail.[184]

### *(iii) Immediately before or at the time of the theft*

Suppose the following example:

> D picks V's pocket, extracting V's wallet. V realises what D has done and immediately accosts her. D violently strikes V and runs off.

Has D committed robbery, or is she guilty of separate offences of theft and battery?[185] The answer depends on whether the battery occurs "at the time of the theft". If the theft is completed and D's use of force is merely in order to escape, she is not guilty of robbery.[186] This analysis is reinforced by the requirement, to be discussed in § 14.3(iv), that the force be used or threatened in order to *commit* theft, rather than (say) to escape after having committed it.

What timeframe does "at the time of the theft" import? This question arises elsewhere in the Theft Act, and was considered in §§ 13.6(iv) and 14.1(i)(f). Prima facie, robbery cannot be committed if the force is used or threatened after the offence of theft is completed. The difficulty with this restriction is that, under the interpretation of appropriation established in *Morris* and *Gomez*,[187] the wallet is stolen by D as soon as it is touched. Thereafter, D cannot become guilty of robbery. One example of this analysis is the decision by the Court of Appeal in *Pitham and Hehl*,[188] a handling case. M had offered to sell P and H some furniture that did not belong to him. P and H were convicted of handling and appealed on the ground that the handling occurred "in the course of" the theft by M, and so was excluded by the proviso in section 22.[189] However, the Court upheld the convictions, diagnosing that M, the thief:[190]

> "took the two appellants to 20 Parry Road, showed them the property and invited them to buy what they wanted. He was then, in the words of [s. 3(1)], 'assuming the rights of the owner.' The moment he did that he appropriated [the owner's] goods to himself. The appropriation was complete. After this appropriation had been completed there was no question of these two appellants taking part, in the words of section 22, in dealing with the goods 'in the course of stealing.'"

As a general rule, this is too extreme.[191] It would mean that, were V to accost D—and be met with violence—while D was still extracting the wallet from V's pocket, D could not commit robbery.

The obvious solution to this difficulty is to accept that robbery cannot be committed after the theft is complete, but to describe D's appropriation of the wallet as a "continuing

[184] Theft Act 1968, s. 21.
[185] Above, Chapter 11.
[186] As was intended: see the Report of the Criminal Law Revision Committee, *Theft and Related Offences* Cmnd. 2977 (1966) para. 66.
[187] Above, § 13.6, 13.6(ii).
[188] (1977) 65 Cr App R 45 (CA). Cp. *Corcoran v Anderton* (1980) 71 Cr App R 104 (CA).
[189] See above, § 14.1(i)(f).
[190] (1977) 65 Cr App R 45, 49 (CA).
[191] Indeed, the Court in *Pitham and Hehl* was careful not to foreclose the possibility of an alternative conclusion in different fact situations.

act", i.e. to regard the act of appropriation as continuing after D has touched the wallet. The balance of the case law supports this analysis. In *Hale*, for example, the Court of Appeal stated that:[192]

> "the act of appropriation does not suddenly cease. It is a continuous act and it is a matter for the jury to decide whether or not the act of appropriation has finished."

If, as seems most likely, the continuing act analysis ultimately prevails, robbery will be possible after D's act of appropriation begins but not after it ends; the determination of when the appropriation ends will depend on the facts of each case. (In the example given, it would no doubt be after D has withdrawn her hand from V's pocket, and perhaps when she begins to walk away.)

An alternative solution would be to disengage the phrase "at the time of the theft" from the technical question when the theft is committed, and interpret that phrase as referring to D's theftuous activity or escapade, viewed in its wider context. Hence, one might say "the offence of theft is established" for the purposes of section 1 as soon as D's hand touches the wallet; but that it was still "at the time of the theft" for the purposes of section 8 until D began, say, to escape.[193] One advantage of this interpretation is that it requires no manipulating of the definition of theft in order to satisfy the demands of robbery—it avoids having the cart drive the horse.

### *(iv) In order to commit theft*

The mere coincidence of theft and force is insufficient for robbery. Force must be used, or threatened, *in order* to steal.[194] The motive counts. If D assaults V and then, while V is unconscious, decides to take V's watch, D commits assault and theft but not robbery.

Implicitly, the element of motive imports an associated requirement that D's use of force must itself be intentional. If D accidentally knocks V over while trying to pick his pocket, she cannot be guilty of robbery since she does not mean to use force in order to relieve V of his wallet.[195] Similarly, suppose that D inadvertently frightens V who, in fear, offers her money. D may commit theft should she dishonestly take advantage of V's fear and accept the money, but she does not rob.[196]

### *(v) Assault with intent to rob*

Section 8(2) creates a supplementary offence of assault with intent to rob, which is punishable to the same extent as the completed offence. In practice, the existence of this offence means that it will rarely be necessary to charge D with attempted robbery, as most attempted robberies will also constitute assault with intent to rob. An attempted robbery

192 (1979) 68 Cr App R 415, 418 (CA). Note that this case was decided before *Gomez*; see also *Donaghy v Marshall* [1981] Crim LR 644 (Crown Court (Snaresbrook)). In *Lockley* [1995] Crim LR 656 (CA), the Court of Appeal endorsed a continuing act analysis and thought that *Hale* was unaffected by *Gomez*; but *Hale* and *Gomez* were said by the same court to be difficult to reconcile in *Atakpu and Abraham* [1994] QB 69, 80 (CA). More recently, the possibility of a continuing act has been acknowledged in *Bowden* [2002] EWCA Crim 1279.

193 Cp. the suggestion in *Atakpu and Abraham* [1994] QB 69, 80 (CA): was D still "on the job"?

194 Cp. *Shendley* [1970] Crim LR 49 (CA); *James* [1997] Crim LR 598 (CA).

195 Cp. *Edwards* (1843) 1 Cox CC 32.

196 *Bruce* [1975] 3 All ER 277, 279 (CA).

would, however, exist where, although D assaults V in order to steal, V in fact has no property for D to steal.

## § 14.4 Burglary

Burglary has been a serious offence since the earliest days of the common law. By the second half of the twentieth century the law relating to burglary, and the related offence of housebreaking, had become technical and complicated, and it was thought that simplification and rationalisation was needed. With that in mind, the Theft Act rolled the two offences into one to create a single new offence of burglary. As we shall see, however, the new law is neither entirely simple nor completely rational.

The offence of burglary is now to be found in section 9 of the Theft Act 1968. So far as is immediately relevant, the section provides:

> (1) A person is guilty of burglary if—
> (a) he enters any building or part of a building as a trespasser and with intent to commit any such offence as is mentioned in subsection (2) below; or
> (b) having entered any building or part of a building as a trespasser he steals or attempts to steal anything in the building or that part of it or inflicts or attempts to inflict on any person therein any grievous bodily harm.
>
> (2) The offences referred to in subsection (1)(a) above are offences of stealing anything in the building or part of a building in question, of inflicting on any person therein any grievous bodily harm, and of doing unlawful damage to the building or anything therein.

The offence carries a maximum penalty of 10 years, or 14 years if the building is a dwelling.[197] Section 10 goes on to create a further offence of "aggravated burglary", which is burglary when in possession of "any firearm or imitation firearm, any weapon of offence or any explosive". For aggravated burglary the maximum penalty is imprisonment for life.[198]

In distinguishing between paragraphs (a) and (b) of section 9(1), the section creates two types of offence of simple burglary, one committed at the time of entry and one that is committed inside the building. The elements of the offence under section 9(1)(a) are as follows:

(a) entry by D;
(b) as a knowing or reckless trespasser;
(c) into a building or part of a building;
(d1) with intent, at the time of entry, to commit one of the following ("ulterior") crimes: stealing, inflicting grievous bodily harm, or doing unlawful damage.

[197] The case law on what constitutes a "dwelling" was reviewed in *Chipunza* [2021] EWCA Crim 597. There, the Court of Appeal, whilst stressing that it is a question of fact in every case, said that hotel rooms will usually fall outside the definition, unless (as sometimes happens) they are occupied by long-stay guests.

[198] The Court of Appeal has held that aggravated offence is not committed by an armed accessory to a burglary who waits outside while his unarmed colleague is at work within: *Klass* [1998] 1 Cr App R 453 (CA); affirmed in *Wiggins* [2012] EWCA Crim 885. The reason for this seeming generosity is that the aggravated offence exists to discourage burglars from entering property when bearing arms—rather than to discourage them from setting out to burgle when "tooled up".

Under section 9(1)(b), the required elements are:

(a) entry by D;
(b) as a knowing or reckless trespasser;
(c) into a building or part of a building; and
(d2) while in the building, D commits one of the following (ulterior) crimes: stealing, attempting to steal, inflicting grievous bodily harm, or attempting to inflict grievous bodily harm.

In either case, by virtue of section 9(3), for the purposes of sentencing for (non-aggravated) burglary the court must also determine whether the building is a dwelling.[199] Technically, by enacting different maximum penalties for dwellings as opposed to other buildings,[200] the effect of section 9(3) is to create different offences, corresponding to the different maximum penalties.[201] There are, therefore, four types of offence in all: two for section 9(1)(a)[202] and two for section 9(1)(b).

The resulting offence is peculiarly lop-sided, in that the lists of other offences which turn a trespassory entry into a burglary differ as between the section 9(1)(a) offence and the offence created by section 9(1)(b).[203] As originally designed by the Criminal Law Revision Committee, the lists would have been the same, which would have made the offence much simpler; but the original plan was modified as the legislation passed through Parliament. Originally, the list of intended crimes in section 9(1)(a) included one additional crime. It was also burglary to enter as a trespasser with intent to commit rape (as will be seen when discussing the notorious case of *Collins*,[204] below). However, that version of burglary was deleted by the Sexual Offences Act 2003, which introduced a separate and wider offence of trespass with intent to commit a sexual offence.[205]

### *(i) Entry*

Entry is a physical activity rather than an instantaneous event.[206] Consequently, it can be difficult to draw the line between a completed entry, for the purposes of burglary, and an incomplete attempt. At common law, it was sufficient if any part whatsoever of the body protruded inside the building. Thus, for example, inserting a fingertip beyond the line of

[199] At common law, a dwelling is a place that is regularly slept in: *Lyons* (1778) 1 Leach 185, 168 ER 195; *Thompson* (1796) 2 Leach 771, 168 ER 485. In *Hudson v CPS* [2017] EWHC 841 (Admin), [2017] 2 Cr App R 21, the defendants burgled a furnished flat which was temporarily empty after the tenant had left. The Divisional Court held that, in principle, a building normally inhabited could still be a "dwelling" for the purposes of s. 9(3) of the Theft Act even though it was temporarily unoccupied. If uninhabited for a long time it would cease to be a dwelling; whether it had become so is a question of fact and degree.

[200] See too s. 111 of the Powers of Criminal Courts (Sentencing) Act 2000 (prescribing a minimum sentence of three years' imprisonment for a third domestic burglary conviction).

[201] See *Courtie* [1984] AC 463, 471 (Lord Diplock).

[202] That is, trespassory entry of a dwelling with intent to commit, etc.; and trespassory entry of a building not being a dwelling with intent to commit, etc.

[203] Under the earlier law, the offences of burglary and housebreaking depended on the commission of, or intention to commit, a *felony*. See further below, § 14.4(iv).

[204] § 14.4(ii).

[205] Contrary to s. 63 of the Sexual Offences Act 2003.

[206] Smith, *Property Offences* (1994) § 28–27.

the window frame,[207] or grasping the inner sill of a window,[208] would amount to an entry. This test had the advantage of at least being reasonably straightforward to apply, even if it turned "entry" into rather a technical concept. The Theft Act 1968, which was enacted against the background of this law, makes no reference itself to what constitutes an entry, and it seems to have been assumed during the passage of the Act that the common law rules would continue to apply.[209]

Since enactment of the Act, however, modern cases have sought to qualify the common law test. In *Collins*,[210] Edmund Davies LJ stated that the entry must be "effective and substantial" to satisfy section 9. In *Brown*,[211] however, the Court of Appeal rejected "substantial" as a requirement and said that the entry need only be "effective". D had been seen standing outside, but with the top half of his body inside, a shop's display window. He was apparently rummaging inside the window for goods. While, ultimately, entry is a question of fact for the jury, the Court ruled there was no need for D's whole body to be inside the building and that, on these facts, there had clearly been an entry.

Notwithstanding *Brown*, it is unclear how important is the requirement for "effective" entry. In *Ryan*,[212] only D's head and arm entered the building before D became stuck, so that he was never in a position to steal. The Court of Appeal held that it was irrelevant whether his entry had been sufficiently effective to put D in a position to steal. This seems right, but it raises the question: can "effective" or "substantial" be given any meaningful role in qualifying the requirement for entry? If an arm and head suffice, where is the line to be drawn? How can *Ryan* be distinguished from the fingertip entry?

It is submitted that no useful line can be drawn, and that the "effective" (or "substantial") test advanced in these cases should be either disregarded or understood as a *de minimis* rule: a trivial or practically negligible entry, e.g. by the tip of a finger, is insufficient for section 9; but any significant intrusion inside the space of the building qualifies as an entry, even if it does not put D in a position to commit one of the ulterior offences mentioned in section 9.

### *(a) Instruments*

At common law, entry could be done by an instrument, unless the instrument was intruded solely to enable D to enter in person. For example, casting hooks through a window in order to drag carpets out of the building was sufficient for burglary,[213] but inserting a jemmy in order to lever open a door (and thereby enter oneself) was not.[214] Presumably, the rule that entry by instrument is sufficient will continue to apply under section 9. It is less clear, however, that the exception should be preserved for jemmies and the like which are used to secure entry. The exception arose out of the requirement at common law that there be both

[207] *Davis* (1823) Russ & Ry 499, 168 ER 917. Cp. *Bailey* (1818) Russ & Ry 341, 168 ER 835, and cases cited there; *Perkes* (1824) 1 C & P 300, 171 ER 1204.
[208] *Parkin* [1950] 1 KB 155 (CA).
[209] HL Debs., vol. 290, cols. 85–6.
[210] [1973] 1 QB 100, 106 (CA). The facts of the case are set out below, in § 14.4(ii).
[211] [1985] Crim LR 212 (CA).
[212] (1995) 160 JP 610 (CA).
[213] *Anon* (1583) 1 Anderson 114, 123 ER 383. Cp. *Richardson and Brown* [1998] 2 Cr App R (S) 87 (CA) (using a JCB digger to ram the wall of a bank and to scoop out the cash dispenser installed there).
[214] Cp. *Hughes* (1785) 1 Leach 406, 168 ER 305.

a "breaking" and an "entry"; it was thought that where an instrument entered the building in the activity of breaking, that could not by itself also constitute the entry.[215] Since the 1968 Act removes the element of "breaking" from burglary, this rationale no longer applies.

### *(ii) As a trespasser*

The actus reus of the earlier law was "breaking and entering". The concept of breaking, like entering, had collected a body of case law around it, and it was in the hope of simplifying matters that the new law replaced the requirement of "breaking" with a requirement that D should be a trespasser when he enters the building. But the concept of entry *as a trespasser* has not proved to be an easy one, as we shall see.

Trespass is a tort, and whether D is a trespasser is a question purely of civil law, of which only a summary can be given here. Apart from situations where entry is specifically authorised by law,[216] the main criterion is whether D has received consent to enter from someone authorised to give that consent. The most striking case on trespassory entry under the 1968 Act is *Collins*.[217] The facts of the case were as follows:

> D, naked in all material respects,[218] had climbed up to a bedroom window with intent to commit rape when he was seen by the occupier's daughter, who was in bed at the time. Mistaking D for her boyfriend, the daughter invited D to climb through the window for the purpose of having sexual intercourse. This he did, and it was only while they were in the throes of intercourse that the daughter realised her mistake; whereupon she slapped him in the face, bit him, and retired to the bathroom.

The facts disclose two possible moments at which D might have become guilty of burglary. The first possibility turned on whether D had already effected an entry through the window, onto the inner sill, when he was invited in. If so, a conviction for burglary would be straightforward and the later invitation irrelevant, since the offence under section 9(1)(a) was by then complete (recall that, until the reforms of the Sexual Offences Act 2003, an intention to commit rape was sufficient for the offence in section 9(1)(a)).

On the first question there was insufficient evidence to support D's conviction. Alternatively, therefore, assuming D entered only after he was invited in, it was necessary to decide whether he was a trespasser at that later moment. The Court of Appeal ruled that D committed no burglary. Prima facie, D had received permission to enter from a person authorised to give it. As we shall see below, although the mistake vitiated that permission and D was in law a trespasser,[219] the apparent invitation prevented his entry from being a knowing or reckless trespass.[220]

[215] This is the best explanation of *Tucker* (1844) 1 Cox CC 73, where insertion of a knife in order to lever open a window latch was held to be an entry. D had already committed a breaking by first smashing the window pane (cp. 2 East PC, chap. xv § 3).

[216] E.g. where police officers act in execution of a search warrant, or where a landlord distrains for rent.

[217] [1973] 1 QB 100. As was noted earlier, rape is no longer a qualifying offence within s. 9(1)(a).

[218] According to the Court of Appeal (*per* Edmund Davies LJ at 102–3), D had "stripped off all his clothes, with the exception of his socks, because apparently he took the view that if the girl's mother entered the bedroom it would be easier to effect a rapid escape if he had his socks on than if he was in his bare feet. That is a matter about which we are not called upon to express any view, and would in any event find ourselves unable to express one."

[219] Below, § 14.4(ii)(b).

[220] Below, § 14.4(ii)(c).

*(a) Authority to enter*

The person who permits D's entry must be authorised to do so. Apart from the occupier of the property (usually the owner or leaseholder), any other member of the household has a general authority to invite persons on to the premises for lawful purposes,[221] although this invitation can be revoked or overridden by the occupier.[222]

D will also be a trespasser if the terms of his authority to enter are exceeded. In *Jones and Smith*,[223] D had a general licence to enter his father's house. One night, he went to the house and stole two television sets. His conviction for burglary was upheld by the Court of Appeal. D's licence did not extend so far as to permit entry for an unlawful purpose such as theft.[224]

Glanville Williams has criticised the decision in *Jones and Smith*,[225] suggesting that it forces the issue of trespass to depend on D's mental state (i.e. his criminal purpose) rather than upon any objective facts, such as the express terms of D's licence. Apart from causing burglary to look like a thoughtcrime, the possibility that D's mental state may make his entry unauthorised requires, in turn, that the courts draw lines which are not at all obvious in advance. This is contrary to the aspiration that the law should give fair warning to defendants of their potential crimes. Additionally, if it is the intent to commit theft that makes D a trespasser, the range of burglary is considerably expanded—on this view, if D enters a shop intending to shoplift, D is a burglar. It is to be hoped that the rule in *Jones and Smith* will not be extended to buildings that are open generally to the public. Otherwise, a person who writes a graffito on the wall of a public lavatory would appear to be a burglar.

Notwithstanding these criticisms of *Jones and Smith*, the current law appears to be that D is a trespasser if he enters with an intention to exceed the terms of his licence while on the property.[226] Those terms may be explicit: in *Taylor v Jackson*,[227] for example, V gave D permission to enter his land and hunt for rabbits. Instead, D went onto the land in order to hunt for hares. This was held to be evidence of trespass.

Alternatively, the terms of the licence may be implicit. Typically, there will be implicit restrictions which (i) exclude entry in order to commit a tort or a criminal offence.[228] They probably (ii) also exclude other activities which are wrongful or dangerous:[229] "When you invite a person into your house to use the staircase you do not invite him to slide down the banisters".[230] Similarly, (iii) entry with an intention which is contrary to or undermines the

221 E.g. *Robson v Hallett* [1967] 2 QB 939 (DC) (police officers were not trespassers when invited onto the premises by the occupier's son); *Collins* [1973] QB 100, 107 (CA).

222 As it was in *Robson v Hallett* [1967] 2 QB 939 (DC).

223 [1976] 3 All ER 54 (CA).

224 Arguably, the decision is better justified on the ground that D came with an accomplice, who had no authority to enter at all, and whom D abetted. For discussion, see Smith, *Property Offences* (1994) § 28–12f.

225 *TBCL* 847ff. See Pace, "Burglarious Trespass" [1985] *Crim LR* 716.

226 Of course, D may become a trespasser after entering, if his subsequent actions exceed the terms of his licence. But this does not help us here, since for burglary D must be a trespasser at the moment when he enters. The civil law doctrine of trespass *ab initio* has no application to the criminal law: *Collins* [1973] QB 100, 107 (CA).

227 (1898) 78 LT 555.

228 Cp. *Jones and Smith* [1976] 3 All ER 54 (CA).

229 *Hillen and Pettigrew v ICI (Alkali) Ltd* [1936] AC 65, 69.

230 *The Calgarth, the Otarama* [1927] P 93, 110. Cited by Lord Atkin in *Hillen and Pettigrew v vICI (Alkali) Ltd* [1936] AC 65, 69.

purpose for which the licence was granted is likely also to be trespass.[231] These categories may well overlap; as in *Barker*,[232] an Australian case, where D had been asked by V, his neighbour, to keep an eye on V's house while V was away. Instead, D entered and stole some furniture. D's conviction for burglary was upheld by the High Court.

*(b) Mistaken authorisation*

In *Collins* (above), the daughter's invitation to enter was invalidated by a fundamental mistake regarding D's identity.[233] Hence, D did not have a genuine authorisation to enter, and did so as a trespasser. (The case turned therefore on whether D knew of the mistake, and so entered knowing he was or might be trespassing.) Where the occupier's mistake is not fundamental, authorisation to enter will nonetheless be invalid if it is obtained by deception or fraud. Presumably, by analogy with pre-Act law,[234] D's entry under these circumstances would be as a trespasser.

*(c) Mental element in criminal trespass*

Under civil law, an action for trespass to land lay even though the defendant had no idea that he was not entitled to enter the property. If D enters a neighbour's house, thinking by mistake it is his own, D commits a tort.[235] This rule of strict liability does not apply in the criminal law. To be guilty of burglary, D must know or be subjectively reckless about the facts that make his entry a trespass. As Edmund-Davies LJ stated in *Collins*:[236]

> "there cannot be a conviction for entering premises 'as a trespasser' within the meaning of section 9 of the Theft Act unless the person entering does so knowing that he is a trespasser and nevertheless deliberately enters, or, at the very least, is reckless as to whether or not he is entering the premises of another without the other party's consent."

This is not to require that D knows he is, *in law*, a trespasser; rather that he knows or recognises the possible existence of the *facts*, i.e. those facts which make him a trespasser. Thus in *Collins* (above), where D entered through the window at the mistaken invitation of the lady inside, D's appeal against conviction was allowed "on the basis that the jury were never invited to consider the vital question whether this young man did enter the premises as a trespasser, that is to say knowing perfectly well that he had no invitation to enter or reckless of whether or not his entry was with permission". Thus, had D been aware of the woman's mistake about D's identity, he would have been guilty of burglary.

[231] "So far as he sets foot on so much as the premises as lie outside the invitation or uses them for purposes which are alien to the invitation he is not an invitee but a trespasser": *Hillen and Pettigrew v vICI (Alkali) Ltd* [1936] AC 65, 69. Cp. *Savoy Hotel v BBC* (1983) 133 NLJ 105, though contrast *Byrne v Kinematograph Renters Society Ltd* [1958] 2 All ER 579 (Ch) for a different result on analogous facts.

[232] (1983) 153 CLR 338.

[233] Cp. the discussion of mistakes, above, § 13.4(iv)(c).

[234] In *Boyle* [1954] 2 QB 292 (CA), D tricked V into permitting D to enter by pretending he was an employee of the BBC sent to investigate problems with local radio transmissions. On these facts, D was held guilty of house breaking.

[235] *Basely v Clarkson* (1682) 3 Lev 37, 83 ER 565; *Conway v Wimpey & Co (No 2)* [1951] 2 KB 266, 273–4 (CA).

[236] [1973] QB 100, 105 (CA).

### *(iii) A building or part of a building*

What counts as a building cannot be stated with precision. According to Byles J, it is "a structure of considerable size and intended to be permanent or at least to endure for a considerable time";[237] although these words were intended to be elucidatory rather than definitive. Byles J's test would exclude a tent[238] or a Portaloo, and probably a telephone box. On the other hand, it seems the building need not be affixed to the soil. In *B and S v Leathley*,[239] the Carlisle Crown Court, applying the statement of Byles J, ruled that a large freezer container, which was sitting on railway sleepers and could be moved by crane, was a building. The Court took into account that the container had lockable doors, was connected to an independent electricity supply, and was intended by its owner to remain *in situ* for the foreseeable future. Implicit in *B and S v Leathley* is that detached outbuildings are also buildings for the purposes of burglary. Hence, a trespassory entry into a garage would be capable of constituting burglary.[240]

Prima facie, the definition of a building excludes vehicles.[241] However, where vehicles or vessels are inhabited, the scope of burglary is specifically extended by section 9(4), which provides:

> References in subsection (1) and (2) above to a building and the reference in subsection (3) above to a building which is also a dwelling, shall apply also to an inhabited vehicle or vessel, and shall apply to any such vehicle or vessel at times when the person having a habitation in it is not there as well as at times when he is.

Thus breaking into a caravan or houseboat would be burglary while the vehicle or boat is being used as a residence, even if the resident is away at the time. A caravan that is used only for holidays, however, would be "inhabited" only during the holiday and probably, therefore, could not be burgled at other times.[242]

#### *(a) Part of a building*

The phrase "part of a building" is included because of the possibility that D may have permission to enter a building, without being allowed access to the whole of the interior. In such cases, D can commit burglary by intruding into that part of the building where her entry is disallowed. A hotel guest, for example, commits burglary by entering another guest's room with intent to steal, even though she has permission to be in the hotel. Similarly, in *Walkington*,[243] D's general permission to enter a shop did not save her from conviction for burglary when she went behind the counter in order to plunder the till. The counter effectively bounded an area from which customers were excluded.

[237] *Stevens v Gourlay* (1859) 7 CBNS 99, 112, 141 ER 752, 757.

[238] Cp. Criminal Law Revision Committee, *Theft and Related Offences* Cmnd. 2977 (1966) para. 78.

[239] [1979] Crim LR 314 (Crown Court (Carlisle)).

[240] Cp. *Whitmore v Bedford* (1843) 5 Man & G 9, 134 ER 460.

[241] E.g. an articulated lorry trailer: *Norfolk Constabulary v Seekings and Gould* [1986] Crim LR 167 (Crown Court (Norwich)), differing from *B and S v Leathley* [1979] Crim LR 314 (Crown Court (Carlisle)) in that the trailer still rested on its own wheels. Compare s. 292(4) of the Canadian Criminal Code, which specifically includes railway stock, trailers, and aircraft.

[242] Cp. the common law definition of a dwelling as a place that is regularly slept in: *Lyons* (1778) 1 Leach 185, 168 ER 195; *Thompson* (1796) 2 Leach 771, 168 ER 485.

[243] [1979] 2 All ER 716 (CA).

It is not clear whether a building can be severed into "parts" without some sort of physical division, such as the barrier that was created by the sales counter in *Walkington*. Certainly, any physical division need not be permanent, since in *Walkington* itself the counter was a movable one. In principle, it ought to be sufficient for the purposes of establishing a trespassory entry that the area is clearly demarcated, even if this is done merely by drawing lines on the floor. However, the point remains undecided.

### *(iv) With intent to commit, or committing, the ulterior offence*

Burglary, whether under section 9(1)(a) or under 9(1)(b), presupposes an "ulterior offence". In the first variety of the offence D must enter with intent to commit a listed crime, and in the second he must actually do so.

Under section 9(1)(a), the offence of burglarious entry, the prosecution must prove that *at the time he entered* D intended[244] therein to commit one of the following offences: stealing, inflicting grievous bodily harm, or doing unlawful damage. The offence is committed at point of entry; if, having entered, D then changes his mind and leaves without committing the offence, it is too late. The offence is committed and cannot be undone.

As with all future-intent offences, difficult questions sometimes arise if D's intent is conditional. Suppose that D enters a building intending to steal only if he finds something worth stealing. In principle, cases of conditional intention should be treated as ones of intention, so that D is guilty of burglary in this example.[245] Conditional intention is discussed further in the context of theft, above, in § 13.7(i)(f).[246] In the context of the difficulties there discussed, however, notice that whereas one cannot *steal* something that does not exist, one can *intend* to do so; hence D can be guilty of burglary when he enters V's house with conditional intent to steal a diamond (should it be there), even though there is no diamond.

Under section 9(1)(b), burglary is constituted by committing, or attempting, the offences either of theft or of inflicting grievous bodily harm, *after* D has entered the building as a trespasser. Thus the time at which burglary is committed is when D commits, or attempts to commit, the ulterior offence once inside the building.

Note that, under both paragraphs of section 9(1), the intended, committed or attempted offence must be within the building (or part-building) that D has entered as a trespasser. Hence if D enters V's flat without permission, solely in order to access his own adjacent flat where, for insurance purposes, he intends to stage a "theft" of electronic equipment, he does not commit burglary. His trespassory entry into V's flat was without intent to steal "therein".

#### *(a) Stealing*

For the purposes of burglary, "stealing" connotes theft, contrary to section 1, and does not refer to obtaining by fraud or blackmail.[247] Wherever "steal" carries a wider meaning than

[244] As the terms of s. 9(1)(a) make clear, recklessness is insufficient: *A v DPP* [2003] All ER (D) 393 (Jun) (DC). For the purposes of the intoxication rules (below, § 18.4), the offence is one of specific intent: *Durante* [1972] 1 WLR 1612 (CA).

[245] *A-G's References (Nos. 1 and 2 of 1979)* [1980] QB 180 (CA).

[246] See also the general discussion above, § 5.1(viii).

[247] Cp. *Low v Blease* [1975] Crim LR 513 (DC) (entry with intent dishonestly to use electricity, although contrary to s. 13, was not burglary, since using electricity was not theft within s. 1).

"theft", the Act makes this clear by express provision,[248] and no such provision is made for burglary. Note, however, that in the wake of *Gomez*[249] any obtaining by fraud is likely anyway to be theft; thus the apparently narrow meaning of "stealing" in section 9(1) imposes few practical restrictions.[250]

*(b) Inflicting grievous bodily harm*

Section 9 refers to the infliction of grievous bodily harm, which is—as noted above in chapter 11—a term found in section 20 of the Offences against the Person Act 1861, but not section 18 (which refers to *causing* grievous bodily harm). It is nevertheless clear, from the requirement that D *intends* to "inflict" grievous bodily harm, that the statute refers to the section 18 offence, not the section 20 offence.

For section 9(1)(b), the relevant offences are sections 18, 20, and 23 of the OAPA 1861. Those offences are discussed in Chapter 11 and will not be traversed here. One rather odd decision must, however, be mentioned. In *Wilson*,[251] the defendants entered a house and committed a serious assault on the occupants. They were charged with burglary under section 9(1)(b). On appeal, the Court of Appeal stated that there was no requirement in section 9(1)(b) that D's action actually be an *offence*:[252]

> "It seems unlikely that in this context Parliament intended to restrict the expression 'inflict grievous bodily harm' to the narrow area of assault. To test this proposition it may be helpful to consider a set of circumstance that could not be described as fanciful. An intruder gains access to the house without breaking in (where there is an open window, for instance). He is on the premises as a trespasser, and his intrusion is observed by someone in the house of whom he may not even be aware, and as a result that person suffers severe shock, with a resulting stroke. In such a case it is difficult to see how an assault could be alleged; but nevertheless his presence would have been a direct cause of the stroke,[253] which must amount to grievous bodily harm. Should such an event fall outside the provisions of s 9, when causing some damage to the property falls fairly within it?"

Thus, the Court concluded, whatever the proper interpretation of the words "to inflict grievous bodily harm" in the OAPA 1861, "we would be of the opinion that they have the wider meaning in section 9(1)(b) of the 1968 Act".[254]

With respect to the Court of Appeal, this conclusion—and the example given by the Court—is bizarre. While it is true that section 9(1)(a) includes, and section 9(1)(b) omits, the word "offence", in fact that omission was a mere error of drafting.[255] The Court's interpretation of section 9(1)(b) makes it possible to commit burglary by accident—turning the

[248] E.g. in the case of handling: above, § 14.1(ii)(a).

[249] [1993] AC 442. See above, § 13.6(ii).

[250] Bearing in mind the discussion of *Jones and Smith* [1976] 3 All ER 54 (CA) above, in § 14.4(ii)(a), this appears to suggest that someone entering a social security office intending fraudulently to claim an unemployment benefit would commit burglary. It is to be hoped that such a case would not be treated as involving a trespass.

[251] [1984] AC 242 (HL); *sub nom. Jenkins and Jenkins* [1983] 1 All ER 1000 (CA).

[252] [1983] 1 All ER 1000, 1004 (CA). No comment was made on this point by the House of Lords, which reversed the Court of Appeal's decision on other grounds.

[253] But surely not an infliction: see Gardner, "Rationality and the Rule of Law in Offences Against the Person" (1994) 53 *CLJ* 502, 504–6.

[254] [1983] 1 All ER 1000, 1005 (CA).

[255] Smith, "Burglary under the Theft Bill" [1968] *Crim LR* 367.

offence into one of strict liability.[256] There is no question but that this was not the intention of Parliament.[257] Burglary is a very serious offence which carries a substantial penalty, and it is extraordinary that it may be committed without mens rea (save to enter as a trespasser, which is a wholly different type of wrongdoing). It is to be hoped that, in the future, the Court's view will not be followed.

*(c) Unlawful damage*

Damage is unlawful when it is contrary to the Criminal Damage Act 1971 (below, § 14.5–6). In particular, it is an offence under section 1 of that Act intentionally or recklessly to destroy or damage any property belonging to another. Note that unlawful damage is a relevant offence only for the purposes of burglarious *entry*, contrary to section 9(1)(a). Thus a trespasser who vandalises the interior of a building does not commit burglary unless she entered the building intending to do so.

### *(v) The rationale of burglary*

Some writers have expressed scepticism as to whether burglary deserves its status as a separate and serious offence. Robinson asks:[258]

> "One may wonder, then, why burglary is retained as an offense in modern codes. Conviction for criminal intrusion and for attempt to commit the intended offense would seem adequately and properly to punish the conduct constituting burglary."

On this view, it is all the more puzzling, one may add, that burglary carries a maximum sentence greater than theft itself. The crime is, in Robinson's view, explicable only by historical tradition.

In our view, however, a separate and serious offence of burglary is in principle justified. In the first place, it involves a separate and distinct evil from the "ulterior offences" upon which it in a sense depends: the violation of personal space. As such, it is a wrong in its own right. The trespassory entry by D not only exposes V to risk of a serious ulterior crime; in so doing, it also violates V's right to respect for private life—an important protected interest under Article 8 of the ECHR.

The strongest case of this—subject under section 9(3) to distinctive sentencing provisions—is where the premises are a dwelling-house.[259] Interaction with and exposure to other members of society is integral to public life; conversely, our sense of identity and well-being as individuals depends upon our being able to reserve private space, from which other persons can be excluded. It is through controlling our private environment that we are able to have 'breathing space' from interactions with other people. Burglary compromises that space. It is hardly surprising that house burglary, in particular, causes victims great distress even if they were absent at the material time. The victim of such a burglary cannot be

[256] Strict, rather than constructive, liability, because the further element of the offence is not a mere consequence but a *novus actus* by D. See above, Chapter 6.

[257] See the commentary on *Jenkins and Jenkins* at [1983] Crim LR 386.

[258] *Criminal Law* (1997) 778.

[259] Indeed, this was originally the only variety of burglary known to the common law. See 3 Coke Inst. 63.

sure of the peaceable and secure enjoyment even of her own home. For most people, when the integrity of their private space cannot be taken for granted, one of the foundations of their well-being is destroyed.

An analogous if less powerful claim can be made for burglary of other buildings. One of the main functions of structures such as warehouses, offices, and the like is to help safeguard people and property by establishing a physical separation from the public environment. Within that secured space, people can relax at least some of the precautions they may take when in public, by putting down their handbags, remaining late to work, and the like. Conversely, if that space is not perceived to be fully secure, such practices become disrupted. Even in these non-domestic contexts, the existence and control of a realm of quasi-private space affects the manner in which we live.

The existence of secured private space also influences how we organise our property. Just as at home, goods in warehouses and offices can be arrayed or stocked without securing each individually. Thus a related harm of burglary is that it gives D unparalleled access to take (or damage) a whole range of V's goods, whether domestic or commercial, in a way that, say, pickpocketing does not. Here too, the case of a domestic burglary is an aggravated one: the goods to which D has access tend to include our highly personal things (underclothes, private letters, and the like) as well as things with high sentimental value—something that reinforces the sense of violation experienced by burglary victims.

The "personal space" argument is supplemented by consequentialist considerations. Entry into a building is a significant physical step by which D commits herself to carrying out the ulterior crime. In effect, it ups the stakes, making it more likely that the ulterior offence will be committed. Moreover, because the activity occurs inside a building, it increases the probability that incidental violence will ensue should D be chanced upon by someone else:[260]

> "Frequently a person discovered in the course of committing a crime [in public] is in a position where he realizes that resistance is useless and that he must flee or surrender. Again, the person who discovers the criminal does not always have a sufficient interest to offer forcible intervention. Both of these factual situations are conducive to the non-occurrence of incidental crimes. Neither is likely to result when a trespasser is discovered while committing a crime in a dwelling;[261] rather, resistance to the criminal and consequent injury to occupants, seems probable."

To these two arguments there is a third and practical one that can be added. Burglary in its section 9(1)(a) version is a convenient offence for prosecuting those who have, in a literal and non-legal sense, attempted to commit a crime, in circumstances where a charge of attempt might run into difficulties because, as the law stands, an attempt must involve behaviour that is "more than merely preparatory to the commission of the offence".[262]

### *(vi) A case for reform*

However, if there are good reasons for the existence of a crime of burglary in general, the particular offence that is created by section 9 of the Theft Act is open to the criticism that it is doubly inept. If the rationale for the offence is as we have described it, the section 9 offence is

[260] Note, "A Rationale of the Law of Burglary" (1951) 51 *Col LR* 1009, 1026.
[261] It is submitted that this is true, to a lesser extent, of any other building.
[262] For a graphic illustration of the problem see *Geddes* [1996] Crim LR 894 (CA); discussed above, § 9.4(i)(c).

too wide in some respects, and other respects too narrow. It is too wide because it covers any building, including a public one. Whose personal space is violated, one wonders, if D enters a railway station with a view to picking pockets? It is also too wide because the concept of "entry as a trespasser", as interpreted in *Jones and Smith*, potentially extends the offence of burglary to behaviour that can only with difficulty be seen as a "violation" of a private area: for example, entering a supermarket during opening hours with the intention not of purchasing but of shoplifting. And the offence is too narrow because it fails to cover a range of violations of personal space which are extremely serious: for example, breaking into a person's home in order to seek private information or to plant bugging devices; or bursting into a neighbour's house in order to verbally abuse him in the presence of his wife and family.[263]

In the codes of continental Europe the equivalent of burglary commonly consists of two offences. First, theft when committed in an inhabited building is an aggravated form of theft, to which a higher penalty attaches.[264] Secondly, there is a general offence of trespassing into other people's homes.[265] Yet oddly, UK governments, though prepared to create limited offences of aggravated trespass[266] and ever-ready to back the creation of new offences of trespassing upon state property,[267] have been resistant to the idea of making it a criminal offence to trespass into people's homes. When in 1991 the Calcutt Committee[268] proposed criminal offences of trespass into private property to obtain information, the Government eventually rejected the idea as likely to "prevent responsible journalism",[269] and the unsuccessful prosecution of the Buckingham Palace intruder who woke the Queen at 7 a.m. led only, after some delay, to a new offence of breaking into royal palaces.[270] Regrettably, it seems probable that the real reason for the Government's resistance to general legislation in this area is a fear that it would inhibit covert policing and the activities of the secret service. About the time this public discussion was taking place, it came to light that the Home Secretary had issued a circular to the police, encouraging them to use Watergate-style break-ins to plant listening devices, even though to do so amounted to a civil trespass.[271]

## § 14.5 Criminal damage

This area of the law has a tangled history. Originally, arson was a felony at common law, and to this specific form of criminal damage other crimes of damage were added piecemeal over

[263] Though this sort of behaviour may sometimes constitute a distinct criminal offence; as in *Qosja* [2016] EWCA Crim 1543, [2017] 1 WLR 311.

[264] *Code pénal*, art. 311–4 para. 6 (France); *Codice penale*, art. 625 (Italy); StGB § 243 (Germany).

[265] *Code pénal*, art. 226–4 (France); *Codice penale*, art. 633 (Italy); StGB §§ 123–4 (Germany).

[266] Criminal Justice and Public Order Act 1994, Part V; and now a further offence of squatting in residential property, created by s. 144 of the Legal Aid, Sentencing and Punishment of Offenders Act 2012.

[267] For a lengthy list, see Williams, *TBCL*, 916–17, who concludes "One day, no doubt, we shall have some more sensible and general provision for criminal trespass".

[268] *Report of the Committee on Privacy and Related Matters* Cm. 1102 (1990).

[269] *Privacy and Media Intrusion—The Government's Response* Cm. 2918 (1995), para. 3.26.

[270] See Spencer, "Another Royal anniversary" [2017] 8 *Archbold Review* 8. Section 128 of the Serious Organised Crime and Police Act 2005 empowers the Secretary of State to designate the premises to which the offence applies. The current list includes not only the Royal palaces but also No. 10 Downing Street and Chequers.

[271] *Khan* [1997] AC 558. The sequel to this case was *Khan v UK* (2001) 31 EHRR 45, in which the United Kingdom was condemned for failure to respect Article 8 of the ECHR, and the enactment of Part II of the Police Act 1997, giving the police the legal right to do this sort of thing in certain circumstances, and provided the procedure laid down by the Act is followed.

the years. In 1861 this muddle was consolidated by an Act of Parliament,[272] a statute similar in style and spirit to the Offences Against the Person Act.[273] But unlike offences against the person, the law relating to criminal damage was later recast in a simpler and more rational form by a major reforming statute, the Criminal Damage Act, in 1971.[274]

The offence of criminal damage is contained in section 1(1) of the Criminal Damage Act:

> A person who without lawful excuse destroys or damages property belonging to another intending to destroy or damage any such property or being reckless whether any such property would be destroyed or damaged shall be guilty of an offence.

The offence, which is punishable by imprisonment for a maximum of 10 years, contains six main elements. The actus reus is:

(i) that D destroys or damages
(ii) property; and
(iii) the property belongs to another.

The mens rea components are:

(iv) D intends or is reckless about destroying or damaging the property; and
(v) D intends or is reckless about whether the property belongs to another.

Finally, the section provides for a defence:

(vi) D's conduct is without lawful excuse.

We shall consider these elements in turn.

### *(i) Destroys or damages*

There must be some physical damage to the property. We will focus here on the meaning of "damages" rather than "destroys", since the latter term seems to add nothing to the former, save in that it is apt to comprehend many of the more extreme or comprehensive instances of damage.

What counts as damage is a question of fact and degree for the jury, and requires evaluation of the particular circumstances of the case.[275] There is no requirement that the damage be severe. One who walks across another's lawn may damage it by flattening the grass.[276] Neither is there any requirement that the damage be permanent or irreparable. Smearing mud graffiti on the wall of a police cell, which cost £7 to clean off, has been ruled capable of being criminal damage.[277] Similarly, it has been held that erasing a computer program can be criminal damage. In *Cox v Riley*,[278] D intentionally deleted the program from a printed circuit card that operated a computerised saw, rendering the saw inoperable. He was

[272] The Malicious Damage Act 1861.
[273] See Chapter 11.
[274] The 1971 Act was based on a Report from the Law Commission: Law Com. No. 29, *Criminal Law: Offences of Damage to Property* (1970).
[275] *Roe v Kingerlee* [1986] Crim LR 735 (DC); *Samuels v Stubbs* [1972] 4 SASR 200, 203; *Hardman v Chief Constable of Avon and Somerset* [1986] Crim LR 330 (Crown Court (Bristol)).
[276] *Gayford v Chouler* [1898] 1 QB 316 (DC).
[277] *Roe v Kingerlee* [1986] Crim LR 735 (DC).
[278] (1986) 83 Cr App R 54 (DC).

convicted of criminal damage, a conviction upheld on appeal on the ground that deletion of the program constituted damage to the circuit card, since it necessitated expending time, labour and money to reprogram the card. The Divisional Court cited a helpful discussion from the unreported case of *Henderson v Battley*, in which D was charged with damaging a development land site in the Isle of Dogs. The site, which had been cleared, was flat except for one pile of crushed concrete kept for use in the laying of temporary roads during the development. Without authority, D dumped 30 lorry loads of soil and rubble and mud on the site, effectively using it as a tip. The Court of Appeal held that, even though the underlying land was not itself altered, dumping rubbish could constitute criminal damage:[279]

> "if as here there is evidence that the owner of the land reasonably found it necessary to spend about £2,000 to remove the results of the appellant's operations it is not irrelevant to the question of whether this land, as a building site, was damaged. Ultimately whether damage was done to this land was a question of fact and degree for the jury. Damage can be of various kinds. In the Concise Oxford Dictionary 'damage' is defined as 'injury impairing value or usefulness.' That is a definition which would fit in very well with doing something to a cleared building site which at any rate for the time being impairs its usefulness as such. In addition, as it necessitates work and the expenditure of a large sum of money to restore it to its former state, it reduces its present value as a building site. This land was a perfectly good building site which did not need £2,000 spending on it in order to sell or use it as such until the appellants began their operations."

The Court also relied upon *Fisher*,[280] where D inserted an object into a machine and made other alterations that temporarily rendered the machine useless. This was held capable of constituting damage, on the basis that it took two hours' labour (albeit no additional materials) to restore the machine to proper working order.[281]

Overall, what emerges from the cases is a two-part test: any significant alteration to property can count as damage, provided it requires more than a trivial expenditure of time, effort, or money to undo. In respect of undoing the alteration, we may contrast the smearing of mud on a wall with a scenario in which D affixes a "Post-it" note to V's door. The note can simply be lifted off, and it is submitted that D's act does not damage the door. In similar vein, spitting on a policeman's raincoat was ruled not to be damage in so far as the spittle could be removed simply by wiping it with a damp cloth.[282] Painting silhouettes on a pavement using soluble paint, on the other hand, was rightly held to be criminal damage after the local authority washed the markings away with high-pressure jets, even though they would eventually have been dissolved by rain.[283] Rainwater would not have removed the damage forthwith. But that still leaves the question of when there is a significant alteration. Standard *indicia* are if the property is rendered either less usable[284] or less valuable.[285]

A recurrent case of difficulty is where some act falling short of physical injury is done to a vehicle, or to some other piece of machinery, in order to detain it or temporarily immobilise

[279] Court of Appeal, Criminal Division, 29/11/84, at 3B; quoted in *Cox v Riley* (1986) 83 Cr App R 54, 57 (DC).
[280] (1865) LR 1 CCR 7.
[281] Where a part of a piece of equipment is disabled by the removal of a part or parts, the appropriate charge is damage to the *equipment*, not to part or parts of it which were removed: *Morphitis v Salmon* [1990] Crim LR 48 (DC).
[282] *A (A Juvenile) v R* [1978] Crim LR 689 (CC).
[283] *Hardman v Chief Constable of Avon and Somerset* [1986] Crim LR 330 (Crown Court (Bristol)).
[284] *Roper v Knott* [1898] 1 QB 868 (DC) (spoiling milk by adulterating it with water).
[285] *Foster* (1852) 6 Cox CC 25.

it. In *Drake v DPP*, it was held not to constitute criminal damage to attach a wheel-clamp to a car; a ruling which was criticised by Professor J. C. Smith who said that if a car can be damaged by removing something, "it seems logical that it can be damaged by adding something".[286] In *Grajewski v DPP (NSW)*,[287] the High Court of Australia dealt with the appeal of a climate change protestor who had chained himself to a machine used for loading coal onto a ship for export. The Court held (by a majority of four to one) that the protestor had not committed criminal damage under Australian legislation that is closely modelled on the Criminal Damage 1971. In so holding it rejected the prosecution argument that mere "temporary functional derangement" constituted criminal damage. For criminal damage, the Court held, some infringement of the physical integrity of the property is required:[288]

> "Inoperability may be the product of damage done to property but it does not, of itself, constitute damage to property. Nothing in the authorities justifies an interpretation of the expression 'destroys or damages' as extending to conduct which does not in any respect alter the physical integrity of the thing said to be damaged."

If conduct of this sort does not usually amount to criminal damage, it may of course still constitute some other criminal offence. The clamping (or otherwise immobilising) of motor vehicles without lawful authority has been made a criminal offence by section 54 of the Protection of Freedoms Act 2012. Letting someone else's tyres down will be an offence under section 25 of the Road Traffic Act 1988 if the vehicle is on a road or in a parking place provided by a local authority. And in *Brown*,[289] a climate change protestor who glued himself to an aircraft, thereby disrupting air traffic at London City Airport, was convicted of the more serious common law offence of public nuisance[290] and received a prison sentence.

### *(ii) Property*

Most tangible things can be damaged. According to section 10(1) of the 1971 Act:

> In this Act "property" means property of a tangible nature, whether real or personal, including money and—
>
> (a) including wild creatures which have been tamed or are ordinarily kept in captivity, and any other wild creatures or their carcasses if, but only if, they have been reduced into possession which has not been lost or abandoned or are in the course of being reduced into possession; but
>
> (b) not including mushrooms growing wild on any land or flowers, fruit or foliage of a plant growing wild on any land.

For the purposes of this subsection "mushroom" includes any fungus and "plant" includes any shrub or tree.

As with the law of theft, the scope of the offence is wide-ranging and includes most forms of tangible property known to the common law. Indeed, like the definition in section

[286] [1994] RTR 411 (DC).

[287] [2019] HCA 8.

[288] *Ibid.*, [49]. For a discussion of the *Grajewski* case, with approval of the test proposed, see Grevling, "Damaging Property" [2020] *Crim LR* 497.

[289] [2022] EWCA Crim 6.

[290] Note that s. 78 of the Police, Crime, Sentencing and Courts Act 2022 has since replaced the common law offence of public nuisance with a statutory version of the offence.

4(1) of the Theft Act 1968, "property" is not here statutorily defined; we must begin with that concept as it is understood in the civil law,[291] and section 10(1) simply operates to modify the underlying civil law concept.

The most important difference from theft is that criminal damage requires the property to be *tangible*, something that reflects the physical nature of the concept of damage within the 1971 Act. Hence extinguishing a debt (owed to V) by appropriating V's bank account cannot be criminal damage, even though it might be said to "destroy" V's chose in action, because choses in action are intangible property and fall outwith the scope of section 10(1). The appropriate charge in such circumstances is theft.

A second point of difference is that land can be damaged, without being subject to the restrictions applicable in the context of theft.[292] Additionally, things growing wild cannot be damaged, whereas they can be stolen if picked for a commercial purpose.[293]

### *(iii) Belonging to another*

Under section 1(1), criminal damage can be committed only when the property damaged "belongs" to someone other than V.[294] This means that some other person must have an interest in the subject matter of the damage. As with theft, this does not preclude D's being the owner of the item, so long as her ownership is not absolute; as when V, say, has a lien over the property, or is a joint owner, or has some other interest in the property. In such a case the property can be criminally damaged by D (or by anyone else, including V). But if D is absolute owner of the property, she cannot commit the offence under section 1(1). It does not "belong to another" for the purposes of the Act.

The meaning of "belonging to another" is elaborated in section 10:

> (2) Property shall be treated for the purposes of this Act as belonging to any person
> (a) having the custody or control of it;
> (b) having in it any proprietary right or interest (not being an equitable interest arising only from an agreement to transfer or grant an interest); or
> (c) having a charge on it.
>
> (3) Where property is subject to a trust, the persons to whom it belongs shall be so treated as including any person having a right to enforce the trust.
> (4) Property of a corporation sole shall be so treated as belonging to the corporation notwithstanding a vacancy in the corporation.

As with the corresponding provisions in section 5 of the Theft Act, the scope of the section is effective to protect virtually any form of proprietary interest, whether of ownership or possession, and whether at common law or equity. Although the section mentions "custody *or* control", it is not clear that the latter term adds anything. Physical control would in any event constitute a form of custody, and any other right of control would presumably only qualify if it were enforceable *in rem*, i.e. if it were a proprietary interest. Similarly, the inclusion of a "charge" in section 10(2)(c) is arguably superfluous, since charges are normally a form of proprietary interest.

[291] For general discussion, see above, § 13.3.
[292] Theft Act 1968, s. 4(2); above, § 13.3(ii)(a).
[293] Theft Act 1968, s. 4(3); above, § 13.3(ii)(b).
[294] The aggravated criminal damage offence does not require this: see below, § 14.6.

On the other hand, where there is no custody or control there *must* be a proprietary interest. Thus the section does not protect interests that may arise when D enters into an agreement to sell goods to V on some future date. Section 10(2)(b) makes it clear that the latter sort of interest is not protected, by contrast with contracts of sale that transfer ownership immediately. Hence if, before the agreed date of the future transfer, D were to destroy the goods, D would not commit criminal damage. Similarly, neither is D guilty of an offence under section 1(1) if he sets fire to his car intending to claim the insurance, because an insurer has no proprietary interest in the subject matter of the policy.[295]

### *(iv) Intentional or reckless damage*

The *damage* (or destruction) must be done either intentionally or (subjectively) recklessly. If D throws a stone at V and misses, he does not become guilty of criminal damage when the stone misses V but goes on to break V's window, unless the risk of its doing so was foreseen by D at the time of the throwing.[296] The subjective nature of this recklessness requirement was authoritatively reasserted by the House of Lords in *G*,[297] overruling the decision in *Caldwell*[298] which was for a time authority that failing to foresee an obvious and serious risk of the actus reus could also constitute recklessness. These decisions are discussed in detail in § 5.2(i) above. In gist, the law now requires that D either intends to damage the property,[299] or actually foresees a risk that the property will be damaged by her conduct.

As with recklessness generally, in the latter case the risk D foresees must also be an unreasonable one to run.[300] No doubt, for example, by hitting a six at the village cricket ground D creates a slight risk of causing damage to a neighbouring house. Suppose that, although he does not intend such damage, he is aware of the risk. Typically, nonetheless, the risk he creates is a reasonable one and, if a window should be broken, D will not be accounted reckless.[301]

### *(v) Intention or recklessness whether the property belongs to another*

In respect of the offence in section 1(1), the general requirement of intention or recklessness extends to the actus reus element that the property *belongs to another*. To count as "intention" when applied to circumstances,[302] D would need either to hope, know, or believe that the property belongs to someone else.[303] But this is not especially important, since it is anyway sufficient that D is (subjectively) reckless about the ownership of the property. Given the meaning of the latter term in the context of circumstances,[304] D will be reckless whether the property belongs to another if she either recognises a risk that the property

[295] Cp. *Denton* [1981] 1 WLR 1446, 1448–9 (CA).
[296] Cp. *Pembliton* (1874) LR 2 CCC 119.
[297] [2003] UKHL 50, [2004] AC 1034.
[298] [1982] AC 341.
[299] Above, § 5.1.
[300] This proviso is noted above, § 5.2.
[301] Famously, neither is he negligent in tort law: *Miller v Jackson* [1977] QB 966 (CA); *Bolton v Stone* [1951] AC 850.
[302] Above, § 5.1(v).
[303] In the wider sense of belonging to another defined by s. 10; above, § 14.5(iii).
[304] Above, § 5.2(iii).

is not absolutely hers; or if, in the extensional case allowed for by the House of Lords in *B (a minor) v DPP*,[305] she acts without believing that the property belongs to her (i.e. if she has no belief either way).

The importance of this mens rea element is emphasised in *Smith (David)*.[306] D, a tenant, with permission installed stereo wiring in his flat which he covered by mounting covering panels and other materials. Upon termination of the tenancy, D damaged the panels in order to remove the wiring. By operation of law, the panels had become part of the flat when installed and so belonged to the owner. Nonetheless, although D was certainly civilly liable for the damage, his conviction of criminal damage was quashed, since D honestly believed that the panels were his. In the Court's analysis:[307]

> "Construing the language of section 1(1) we have no doubt that the actus reus is 'destroying or damaging any property belonging to another.' It is not possible to exclude the words 'belonging to another' which describes the 'property'. Applying the ordinary principles of mens rea, the intention and recklessness and the absence of lawful excuse required to constitute the offence have reference to property belonging to another. It follows that in our judgment no offence is committed under this section if a person destroys or causes damage to property belonging to another if he does so in the honest though mistaken belief that the property is his own, and provided that the belief is honestly held it is irrelevant to consider whether or not it is a justifiable belief."

### *(vi) Without lawful excuse*

As with other offences, the offence of criminal damage is only prima facie established by proof of the foregoing actus reus and mens rea elements. D may still have a defence; for example, if he acted in self-defence or in circumstances of necessity. Unusually, however, the Act offers its own lengthy supplementary definition of "lawful excuse" in section 5:

> (1) This section applies to any offence under section 1(1) above and any offence under section 2 or 3 above other than one involving a threat by the person charged to destroy or damage property in a way which he knows is likely to endanger the life of another or involving an intent by the person charged to use or cause or permit the use of something in his custody or under his control so to destroy or damage property.
>
> (2) A person charged with an offence to which this section applies shall, whether or not he would be treated for the purposes of this Act as having a lawful excuse apart from this subsection, be treated for those purposes as having a lawful excuse—
>
> (a) if at the time of the act or acts alleged to constitute the offence he believed that the person or persons whom he believed to be entitled to consent to the destruction of or damage to the property in question had so consented, or would have so consented to it if he or they had known of the destruction or damage and its circumstances; or
>
> (b) if he destroyed or damaged or threatened to destroy or damage the property in question or, in the case of a charge of an offence under section 3 above, intended to use or cause or permit the use of something to destroy or damage it, in order to protect property belonging to himself or another or a right or interest in property which was or which he believed to be

305 [2000] 2 AC 428, 459 (Lord Mackay), 466 (Lord Nicholls).
306 [1974] QB 354 (CA).
307 *Ibid.*, 360.

vested in himself or another, and at the time of the act or acts alleged to constitute the offence he believed—

(i) that the property, right or interest was in immediate need of protection; and

(ii) that the means of protection adopted or proposed to be adopted were or would be reasonable having regard to all the circumstances.

(3) For the purposes of this section it is immaterial whether a belief is justified or not if it is honestly held.

(4) For the purposes of subsection (2) above a right or interest in property includes any right or privilege in or over land, whether created by grant, licence or otherwise.

(5) This section shall not be construed as casting doubt on any defence recognised by law as a defence to criminal charges.

Section 5(2) lays down two statutory grounds of lawful excuse: consent and defence of property. For both versions, section 5(3) makes clear that the test is subjective: the availability of the defence depends on what D *believed*, rather than the actual fact of the matter or whether D's belief was reasonable. Unusually, this is so even if D makes a mistake due to voluntary intoxication.[308] We consider the two versions of the defence in turn.

### *(a) Consent*

Section 5(2)(a) establishes a defence of lawful excuse if D believes that the owner (or other person entitled to consent, such as the owner's representative) has consented to the damage's being inflicted, or would have done so had she known about it.[309] A striking illustration is *Denton*,[310] in which D set fire to his employer's cotton mill, causing some £40,000 worth of damage. He acted purportedly in the belief that his employer had encouraged him to do so, since the business was in difficulty and a fire would "help its financial circumstances". On these facts, the Court of Appeal quashed D's conviction. The underlying fraudulent motive was irrelevant, at least to a charge of criminal damage: D's belief that he had consent, from someone he thought entitled to give such consent,[311] was sufficient to establish a lawful excuse.

In *A-G's Reference (No. 1 of 2023)*,[312] D threw large quantities of pink paint on the buildings of political parties, charities, and trade unions. She did so in order to protest the climate emergency and what she saw as those institutions' culpable inaction. She sought to rely not on any belief in the *actual* consent of the owners,[313] but instead on her belief that they "would have consented" had they known of the damage and its circumstances. She stated that if the owners were "emotionally engaged, they would have consented to a bit of pink paint being thrown", adding "it has got to be a shock impact, so they wake up".[314] She also said she believed those entitled to give consent would do so if aware that they were

[308] *Jaggard v Dickinson* [1981] QB 527 (DC). D had been given permission to treat her friend's house as her own. She broke into the wrong house one evening, drunkenly thinking it was her friend's. D's conviction was quashed on the footing that she genuinely believed she had consent to break in; and s. 5(3) stipulates a subjective rather than objective test. See below, § 18.3(vi).

[309] Compare s. 2(1)(b) of the Theft Act 1968; above, § 13.8(ii).

[310] [1981] 1 WLR 1446 (CA).

[311] Not including God: *Blake v DPP* [1993] Crim LR 586 (DC).

[312] *A-G's Reference (No. 1 of 2023)* [2024] EWCA Crim 243, [2024] 1 WLR 3205.

[313] The Court used the term "owner" as shorthand for the actual term used in section 5(2)(a), "the person or persons whom [s]he believed to be entitled to consent".

[314] *A-G's Reference (No. 1 of 2023)* [2024] EWCA Crim 243, [2024] 1 WLR 3205, [14].

being alerted to the nature and extent of man-made climate change. The main question referred to the Court of Appeal regarded the correct interpretation of the words "known of the destruction or the damage and its circumstances" in section 5(2)(a). The Court also took the opportunity to review section 5(2)(a) more generally in the light of "the dearth of authority" on it.[315]

The Court confirmed that the relevant belief that the owner would have consented must be "genuine".[316] Further, D's belief that V consented must not be "formed to explain the conduct after the event . . . Nor can it be a belief founded on the actual or potential effect of efforts that might be deployed after the event to persuade the owner to consent".[317] Moreover, D's belief must be that the relevant person *would* have consented, not *might* have, nor that they *should* have. The inclusion of the phrase "would have" in section 5(2)(a) involves a certainty in the belief in the owner's consent—D must be *sure* the relevant person would consent.[318] The belief also must be evidence-based.

The requirement that D must be "certain" or "sure" that the owner would consent seems too strong. The Court gave the example of D damaging a car window, having discovered a child locked alone in a car on a hot day. If D, believing the child to be at risk of harm unless freed, says they believed at the time that the owner of the car would have consented to the damage, the defence in section 5(2)(a) may be available. However, what if D states on the same facts that they believed *most* car owners would consent in the circumstances, though it occurred to him that *some* possibly might not because they would think he is exaggerating the risk or ought instead to call the fire brigade? In this variation of the Court's example, D thinks consent would be *very likely* received from the car's owner, and certainly *should* be forthcoming. D's mindset here is not one of being *sure* that the absent car owner would consent. Yet, in our view, the defence ought still to be available. It seems undoubtedly right to conclude that "might have consented" is too weak to capture the meaning of "would have consented", and also that "should have consented" is the wrong kind of belief (normative, rather than cognitive). Nonetheless, a cognitive belief falling short of certainty ought not to be categorically excluded from the scope of a belief that V "would have consented". For instance, we think that a belief that the owner would *very likely* have consented ought to be sufficient.

D's reliance in *A-G's Reference (No. 1 of 2023)* on the "impact" of the damage and the need to "wake up" the owners did not relate to the owner's belief at the time of the act(s) alleged to constitute the offence. Further, if the owners had to become "emotionally engaged" before they would consent, that suggests no genuine belief on D's part that they already would do so. In other words, there appears to be no genuine evidence-based, time-relative, belief that the owner[319] *would* consent in this case.[320] Turning to the meaning of the term "circumstances" in subsection 5(2)(a), the Court stated that:[321]

> "The possessive pronoun 'its' is central. It delimits the 'circumstances'. It is only the circumstances of the damage which are relevant. The circumstances must relate to the destruction of,

[315] *Ibid.*, [19].
[316] *Ibid.*, [41].
[317] *Ibid.*, [40].
[318] *Ibid.*, [42].
[319] Or those believed to be entitled to consent.
[320] *A-G's Reference (No. 1 of 2023)* [2024] EWCA Crim 243, [2024] 1 WLR 3205, [14].
[321] *Ibid.*, [44].

> or damage to, the property. Thus, the relevant circumstances may include matters such as the time, place and the extent of the damage caused. These factors would be linked to the damage and directly relevant to the owner's hypothetical decision as to consent. They do not include the political or philosophical beliefs of the person causing the damage."

This analysis of the role of "circumstances" in "knowledge of the damage and its circumstances" is not easy to follow. The examples given by the Court of what count as "circumstances" that "relate" to the damage appear to add nothing that is not already implicit in the requirement to prove "damage" itself—in the present context the "circumstances" of the damage would include the "amount X of pink paint ('extent') at 3pm ('time') at Building B ('place')", matters that would need to be stated when identifying "damage", even if the "circumstances" were not mentioned in the subsection. The contrast drawn with D's political or philosophical beliefs--apparently not relevant "circumstances"--is also puzzling. It is possible that such beliefs *could* be relevant to the question whether D honestly believed that V would consent to the damage. Consider the following hypothetical case: a wealthy performing artist is known for her support for environmental causes. The artist owns many properties, two of which have undergone damage in recent years. Property 1 underwent damage when squatters broke in, leading the artist to complain publicly about the infringement of her rights. Property 2, by contrast, was damaged with graffiti supporting environmental causes. This time, the artist commented publicly that she did not object because she shared the beliefs expressed in the graffiti. What if D decides to damage the artist's Property 3 in manner identical to what was done to Property 2? Could D not argue that he believed the artist would consent to *that* damage, given what he knows about her views on the damage to Property 2, and given that she had expressed shared political and philosophical beliefs? "I'm a fellow believer", he might say, "not a squatter". No doubt D's political or philosophical beliefs will be irrelevant in most cases, but that is because there will rarely be any reason to believe that V knows about them--and thus crucially that D could not plausibly have *believed* V *would* consent because of them. The case of the artist is different.

A final relevant "circumstance" for the purposes of section 5(2)(a) concerns D's "reason for the damage" or "the foundation of the alleged belief for the putative consent".[322] The defendant in question in the *Reference* case had as her "reason for the damage . . . that it was an act of protest against climate change" and another defendant might have as a "reason" for damaging property "to rescue [a] child".[323] Hence D's reason for damaging property appears to count as a "circumstance", a conclusion that does give independent content to the term "circumstances". An owner might consent to D's damage if D is acting to avert an emergency, but not to the same damage where, say, D acts to remove the owner's property for his own leisure purposes.

Unfortunately, the Court goes on to hold that there must also be "an objective element" to the defence in section 5(2)(a):[324]

> "The need for a direct nexus between the circumstances of the damage and the anticipated giving of consent is implicit in the statutory language. The circumstances must belong to the

[322] *Ibid.*, [47]–[48].

[323] Though despite this and confusingly it is also said "The circumstances must belong to the damage, not to the defendant" (*ibid.*, [46]), though if D's intentions belong to anyone or anything they surely belong to D?

[324] *Ibid.*, [46]

damage, not to the defendant. To this extent there is an objective element to the defence. . . . [T] he circumstances cannot be so remote from the damage as no longer to be part of the damage. There must be a sufficient connection between the damage and its circumstances."

Quite apart from the fact that "circumstances", as seen above, are said to include D's reason(s) for damaging property, which must "belong" to D, not to "the damage", it is hard to see how the "need for a direct nexus between the circumstances of the damage and the anticipated giving of consent" is implicit in the statutory language, given its thoroughly subjective nature. This "direct nexus" requirement draws on a similar requirement in section 5(2)(b),which is discussed and criticised below.[325]

That's D's belief must be genuine, evidence-based, time-relative, and specifically directed at the consent of the person believed to be entitled to consent, are factors implicit in the wording of 5(2)(a); they impose real constraints upon the defence. Beyond these factors, it is unlikely that Parliament intended to open a space for judicially added "objective elements", or content-based exclusions on what can count as "the circumstances" of the damage (such as D's "political or philosophical beliefs").

*(b) Defence of property*

Frequently this defence will overlap with the defence of prevention of crime in section 3 of the Criminal Law Act 1967 (discussed in § 21.2). However, it is available even when the threat to property is not itself criminal.[326] In *Chamberlain v Lindon*,[327] for example, following a dispute about the extent of D's right of way over part of V's land, V built a wall restricting D's vehicular access. D demolished the wall. The Divisional Court affirmed his acquittal of criminal damage, because D had acted in order to protect his right of way, which was a "right or interest in property" falling within section 5(2)(b).

In order to qualify for the defence, D must believe: (i) that the property (or interest therein) belonged to himself or another; (ii) that it was in *immediate* need of protection; and (iii) that conduct was a *reasonable* means of protecting the property. D's conduct must also be undertaken (iv) *in order to* protect the property. These elements deserve separate consideration.

*Belonging to himself or another.*

Interestingly, there is nothing in the section to suggest that "another" cannot be the very owner of the damaged property, as when D breaks into V's house in order to put out a fire there. Section 5(2)(b) seems to require only that the property or interest being protected was thought by D to belong to *someone*, and not to be abandoned or otherwise ownerless. The point was important in *Cresswell v DPP*,[328] where the defendants went onto farmland and destroyed badger traps in order to protect wild badgers. Because the badgers had not been reduced into possession they were ownerless and not property, so fell outside the scope of section 5. The defendants' convictions were upheld.

[325] See below, § 14.5 vi (b).

[326] But, unlike the defence of prevention of crime, there must be a threat to *property*: cp. *Cresswell v DPP* [2006] EWHC 3379 (Admin), [2007] Env LR D8; *Kelleher* [2003] EWCA Crim 3525, (2003) 147 SJLB 1395; *Baker* [1997] Crim LR 497 (CA).

[327] [1998] 1 WLR 1252 (DC).

[328] [2006] EWHC 3379 (Admin), [2007] Env LR D8.

*Immediate need of protection.*
Whether D believes the property is in need of protection is a subjective question. But the courts have held that whether the perceived need counts as "immediate" is an *objective* question to be determined by the jury (or judge, as the case may be), in light of the facts and circumstances that D believes to exist. This point was decisive in *Hill*,[329] where D was charged with possessing articles (namely hacksaw blades) with intent to damage the perimeter fence of a naval base.[330] She claimed that her purpose was to bring about the abandonment of the base which, in the event of international hostilities breaking out, she believed would be the target of a nuclear strike with consequential damage to surrounding property, including hers. Even accepting her view of the facts, however, the Court of Appeal ruled that the perceived threat was not immediate. The defence requires "that she believed that immediate action had to be taken to do something which would otherwise be a crime in order to prevent the immediate risk of something worse happening".[331] On D's own account, there was no "immediate" risk at hand. It seems that this will turn, in part, on whether the perceived threat has crystallised or remains as yet conjectural. *Hill* was distinguished on this basis in *Chamberlain v Lindon* (above), where D had demolished V's wall to preserve a right of way:[332]

> "The appellants in [Hill] had professed to be concerned as to the potential consequences of a possible nuclear attack in the future. Here, on the facts, as believed by the defendant, his right of way was actually being obstructed. . . . [I]t was not a case of there being a risk of an obstruction at some future speculative date—there was a present need to remove the obstruction. The defendant was not destroying or damaging property as some sort of pre-emptive strike to prevent some future obstruction."

*A reasonable means of protection.*
Somewhat surprisingly, the statute makes it clear that what counts is D's own belief that her response is reasonable; the matter is not one for objective assessment by the court:[333]

> "[T]he question is not whether the means of protection adopted by the defendant were objectively reasonable having regard to all the circumstances, but whether the defendant believed them to be so. By virtue of section 5(3) it is immaterial whether his belief was justified, provided it was honestly held."

In this respect, the section 5 defence is more generous than other, more general, justificatory defences found in the criminal law, where the courts have—rightly—held that the defendant's response must be *objectively* reasonable or proportionate, regardless of D's own views on the question.[334] As we shall see in the next paragraph, the generosity of section 5 to defendants makes the courts uneasy, and in some cases they have sought to limit it.

[329] *Hill and Hall* (1989) 89 Cr App R 74 (CA).
[330] Contrary to s. 3 of the Criminal Damage Act 1971.
[331] (1989) 89 Cr App R 74, 79–80 (CA).
[332] [1998] 1 WLR 1252, 1260 (CA). The Court also pointed to the defendant's viewpoint that, the longer the wall remained, the more urgent the need to remove it, to avoid any suggestion of acquiescence in the obstruction.
[333] *Chamberlain v Lindon* [1998] 1 WLR 1252, 1262 (DC).
[334] Below, § 21.2(iii).

*In order to protect the property.*
D must actually have the purpose of protecting property, although that need not be her only reason for acting.[335] Purpose is a subjective concept—it turns on *why* D acted, on what she was trying to achieve. However, the courts have bent the wording by purporting to add an objective gloss to the interpretation of "in order to protect property" in section 5(2)(b). In *Hunt*,[336] D was assisting his wife who was deputy warden in a block of old persons' flats. He discovered that the fire alarm was not working; apparently the Council had been informed but had not repaired the alarm. D subsequently set fire to some bedding in a relatively isolated part of the block of flats in order to (i) draw attention to the defective alarm and thereby (ii) protect the block of flats from the risks posed by the defective alarm. Affirming his conviction, the Court of Appeal accepted the first purpose but rejected the second:[337]

> "The question whether or not a particular act of destruction or damage or threat of destruction or damage was done or made in order to protect property belonging to another must be, on the true construction of the statute, an objective test. Therefore we have to ask ourselves whether, whatever the state of this man's mind and assuming an honest belief, that which he admittedly did was done in order to protect this particular property, namely the old people's home in Hertfordshire?
>
> If one formulates the question in that way, in the view of each member of this Court, for the reason Slynn J gave during the argument, it admits of only one answer: this was not done in order to protect property; it was done in order to draw attention to the defective state of the fire alarm. It was not an act which *in itself* did protect or was capable of protecting property."

But purpose is a subjective, not objective, concept. What this gloss amounts to is a new requirement, not found in the statute: that D's immediate action must "in itself" be capable of protecting property. But this requirement is simply not part of section 5(2), which requires that D's purpose in acting be to protect property, and that D actually believe his immediate action is a reasonable way of seeking to achieve that purpose. There is no requirement that his action should achieve the purpose *directly*.[338] Suppose that D breaks into V's house in order to telephone the fire brigade because T's house, next door, is ablaze. Breaking into the house is not "in itself" capable of protecting T's property. Yet no-one would or should deny that D has a lawful excuse under section 5(2)(b).

It is submitted that the better explanation of *Hunt* is that, notwithstanding his genuine purpose to bolster the protection mechanisms in the block of flats, the lawful excuse within section 5 was unavailable because the threat was not immediate.

Undeterred by *Hunt*, protestors often seek to invoke section 5 in situations which that decision would probably exclude—and in practice juries are often sympathetic. Thus in 2000 a jury famously acquitted 27 protesters accused of destroying genetically modified maize, whose defence was that they believed their act was necessary to protect other crops and plants in the surrounding area.[339] Similarly, in 2008 another jury acquitted a group of Greenpeace activists who had painted the name of the Prime Minister on the chimney of

[335] *Chamberlain v Lindon* [1998] 1 WLR 1252, 1259 (DC).
[336] (1978) 66 Cr App R 105 (CA).
[337] *Ibid.*, 108 (emphasis added).
[338] A similar requirement of proximity is suggested in *Hill* (1989) 89 Cr App R 74, 79 (CA).
[339] "GM Chaos as Melchett is Freed", *The Times*, 21 September 2000.

Kingsnorth power station: their defence was that they believed their act was necessary to prevent climate change from damaging property all over the world.[340] But less successful with his jury was the man who decapitated a statue of Baroness Thatcher, allegedly causing £150,000 of damage, who sought to invoke section 5 on the ground that he believed his act was necessary to prevent the destruction of the world by globalisation and the spread of materialistic values.[341]

*(c) A doubtful case: the reasonable exercise of Convention rights?*

As we saw in Chapter 2, section 3(1) of the Human Rights Act 1998 requires the courts to interpret legislation "so far as possible . . . in a way which is compatible with the Convention Rights". These rights include the right to freedom of thought, conscience, and religion (Article 9), to freedom of expression (Article 10), and to freedom of assembly and association (Article 11). As we also saw, these protected rights impose some broad limits on the state's use of the criminal law to punish those who demonstrate their views on public issues by holding peaceful demonstrations in public places. In *Ziegler v DPP*,[342] for example, the Supreme Court took Articles 10 and 11 into account in deciding that a demonstration against the arms trade involving the partial blockage of a public road leading to an arms fair could be viewed as a reasonable use of the highway, and hence not the criminal offence of unlawfully obstructing the highway contrary to section 137 of the Highways Act 1980.

Demonstrators sometimes seek to make their point by acts which damage property: by painting slogans on walls, for example, or by daubing or destroying monuments erected to commemorate persons of whom they disapprove. To what extent, if any, is it a defence to a charge of criminal damage brought in such a case that the damage was a reasonable exercise of the defendant's Convention rights—either as a matter of substantive law by rendering legal what would otherwise be a criminal offence, or as a matter of criminal procedure, by rendering the decision to prosecute an abuse of process?

The case law suggests that a defence along either of these lines, with very limited exceptions, should fail. When such a defence was attempted at the start of the century by an anti-nuclear protestor who was prosecuted for criminal damage in cutting the perimeter fence at the Atomic Weapons Establishment at Aldermaston, the Divisional Court rejected it. Lord Justice Buxton said:[343]

> "Article 10 requires that there should be a proportionate response to expressions of opinion; that is to say, proportionate in the context of the actual expression of opinion involved. There are plenty of other ways of expressing disapproval of nuclear weapons and Aldermaston's activities, other than committing a crime. . . . She has no right, and Article 10 gives her no right, to express herself in whatever mode she chooses, whatever the damage or inconvenience to others. . . . In my judgement . . . there is no prospect of the Strasbourg Court finding that this conviction involved any breach of Article 10, nor would I do so."

340 "Protesters Cleared over Damage to Power Plant", *The Times*, 11 September 2008.

341 *Kelleher* [2003] EWCA Crim 3525. The trial judge directed the jury in accordance with *Hunt*, and the Court of Appeal upheld the conviction, reaffirming the objective test set out in that decision. The defendant in this case was sentenced to three months' imprisonment.

342 [2021] UKSC 23, [2021] 3 WLR 179.

343 *Hutchinson v Newbury Magistrates' Court* [2000] EWHC 61 (Admin), [64], [66].

In *Brown*,[344] the case of the climate change protestor who glued himself to an aircraft, the Court of Appeal asserted that the Convention rights in Articles 10 and 11 provided no defence to the crime of public nuisance, and that—if they could not be raised as a substantive defence—they should not be allowed to "come in by the back door as part of an application to stay a case on the ground of abuse of process".[345] In the Court's view, the earlier decision in *Ziegler* (above) "appears to have been misunderstood by some as immunising peaceful protesters from arrest and from the operation of the criminal law in broad circumstances, which on any view it does not".[346] This was said in the context of the common law offence of public nuisance, rather than the statutory offence of criminal damage, but it is suggested that the Court's reasoning is equally applicable in that context too. Articles 9, 10, and 11 of the Convention provide for limits on the exercise of these rights where these are "necessary in a democratic society"; and a prohibition on their exercise by damaging or destroying property that belongs to someone or something else is surely a necessary limitation.[347]

In essence, this position was confirmed by the Court of Appeal in *A-G's Reference (No. 1 of 2022)*.[348] In the words of Lord Burnett CJ:[349]

> "The [ECHR] does not provide protection to those who cause criminal damage during protest which is violent or not peaceful. Neither does it provide protection when the damage is inflicted violently or not peacefully. Articles 9, 10 and 11 are not engaged in those circumstances and no question of proportionality arises. Moreover, prosecution and conviction for causing significant damage to property, even if inflicted in a way which is "peaceful" could not, in our view, be disproportionate in [ECHR] terms. Given the nature of cases that are heard in the Crown Court it is inevitable that, for one or both of these reasons, the issue should not be left to the jury. That will be because the conduct in question was on any view not peaceful, alternatively the damage was significant, or both."

Lord Burnett CJ alluded to a category of offences whereby "proof of the relevant ingredients of the offence is sufficient to justify *any* conviction as a proportionate interference with *any* rights engaged under articles 9, 10 and 11, without the need for a fact-specific proportionality assessment in individual cases".[350] Aggravated trespass is an example,[351] and it was argued on behalf of the Attorney General that criminal damage should also fall into that category.[352] Rejecting the submission, his Lordship stated that criminal damage does not "automatically" fall in that category.[353] However, he emphasised that, as regards criminal damage, "the circumstances in which such [an] assessment would be needed are very limited".[354] In particular, a fact-specific proportionality assessment was not needed

344 [2022] EWCA Crim 6, [2022] WLR (D) 56.
345 Ibid., [37]
346 Ibid., [29]. Subsequently, the Divisional Court has aligned itself with the Court of Appeal in heavily restricting the impact of *Ziegler*: e.g. *DPP v Cuciurean* [2022] EWHC 736 (Admin), [2022] 2 Cr App R 8.
347 See further below, § 21.4(iii).
348 [2022] EWCA Crim 1259, [2023] KB 37.
349 *Ibid.*, [120].
350 *Ibid.*, [116] (emphasis added).
351 *Cuciurean* [2022] EWHC 736 (Admin); *James v DPP* [2015] EWHC 3296 (Admin), [2016] 1 WLR 2118.
352 *A-G's Reference (No. 1 of 2022)* [2022] EWCA Crim 1259, [2023] KB 37, [114].
353 *Ibid.*, [116].
354 *Ibid.*

on the facts that had prompted the reference. The statue of Sir Edward Colston—an early eighteenth century Bristol merchant and philanthropist with strong links to the slave trade—was first toppled by protesters and then thrown into Bristol harbour, damaging it. The defendants raised various defences to criminal damage based on Articles 9, 10 and 11 of the ECHR, suggesting the use of the criminal law was disproportionate to their exercise of these rights. In the event, the Court found that the toppling of the statue was "violent" and that the damage to the statue was "significant", hence no case-specific proportionality assessment was needed.[355]

On the other hand, a case-specific assessment of the proportionality of a conviction for criminal damage with ECHR rights may be needed where the damage concerned is "minor or temporary". For example, in *Hardman v Chief Constable of Avon and Somerset*,[356] it was held that the use of water-soluble whitewash used for paintings on a pavement constituted "damage" under section 1(1) of the Criminal Damage Act 1971, even though it would have been washed away naturally by rain over time. In *A-G's Reference (No. 1 of 2022)*, the Court considered what the position would be if the painting in *Hardman* had been part of a political protest, concluding that a prosecution or conviction of the painter might well amount to a disproportionate interference with their ECHR rights.[357] In such a case, a case-specific proportionality assessment would be required.

### *(vii) Criminal damage—a distinctive wrong*

Similarly to offences such as robbery and burglary, criminal damage resembles theft in that it is intrinsically bound up with the violation of another person's property rights. Indeed, to deprive the owner of a chattel by destroying it can be the actus reus of a theft.[358] Like those other offences, however, criminal damage merits separate criminalisation because of the distinctive manner in which V's rights are violated. Many typical instances of vandalism involve the infliction of damage using percussive force, fire, or explosions, conduct that may well endanger others, or cause alarm and concern even to bystanders lacking any proprietary interest in the property being damaged. (Hence, as we will see in § 14.6, the enactment of aggravated criminal damage offences.) To that extent, the offence becomes part of the family of offences concerned with restraining violence and disorder—concerns generally outside the ambit of theft *simpliciter*, save for lootings in circumstances of civil tumult. And, to the extent that it is associated with these different forms of wrongful conduct, criminal damage is a proprietary wrong different in kind from theft. Vandalism frequently has an expressive dimension, communicating a contempt for society, and for the victim, which goes beyond a mere appropriation of property rights; that further wrong, in turn, warrants a label distinct from theft.

Not all types of vandalism involve violence. But all cases of vandalism share a second, intrinsic feature: criminal damage is concerned with the item of property *per se*, and not just with another's rights over that item. When D steals V's book, she does not attack the item itself but, rather, pre-empts V's rights to use and exchange the book. The book itself remains usable and exchangeable; indeed, it is simply the subject of an involuntary exchange. By

[355] *Ibid.*, [123].
[356] [1986] Crim LR 330 (Crown Court (Bristol)).
[357] *A-G's Reference (No. 1 of 2022)* [2022] EWCA Crim 1259, [2023] KB 37, [29], [116].
[358] *Cabbage* (1815) Russ & Ry 292, 168 ER 809.

contrast, when E destroys V's book he attacks the use- and exchange-value of the item in anyone's hands and not merely V's. Its value is lost *tout court*, not just to V; society's store of wealth is diminished. In this respect, the harm of criminal damage differs from that of theft.

## § 14.6 Aggravated criminal damage and arson

Section 1(2) of the Criminal Damage Act 1971 creates an aggravated offence of intentionally or recklessly destroying or damaging property and thereby endangering life:

> A person who without lawful excuse destroys or damages any property, whether belonging to himself or another—
> (a) intending to destroy or damage any property or being reckless as to whether any property would be destroyed or damaged; and
> (b) intending by the destruction or damage to endanger the life of another or being reckless as to whether the life of another would be thereby endangered;
> shall be guilty of an offence.

There are three main elements to the offence, which is punishable by life imprisonment.[359] The actus reus is:

(i) that D destroys or damages property belonging to *someone*.

The law on this is the same as for the section 1(1) offence, and is discussed above in § 14.5(i)–(iii); except that there is no requirement in section 1(2) that the property belong to someone other than D.[360] This reflects the fact that the aggravated offence is not truly a property offence at all, but rather an endangerment-based offence against the person.[361] For the same reason, the lawful excuse defence in section 5 is unavailable to a charge under section 1(2).[362] However, other general defences, such as self-defence, are available in the normal way.[363]

The mens rea components of the aggravated offence are:

(i) D intends or is reckless about destroying or damaging the property (as above, § 14.5(iv); and
(ii) D intends thereby to endanger the life of another, or is (at least) reckless whether the life of another will thereby be endangered.

Section 1(2) might be termed an ulterior mens rea offence.[364] There is no actus reus requirement that anyone's life in fact be endangered; all that is required is that property is damaged

[359] *Per* s. 4.
[360] Cp. *A-G's Reference (No. 98 of 2001)* [2001] EWCA Crim 3068, [2002] 2 Cr App R(S) 25; *Parker* [1993] Crim LR 856 (CA).
[361] Cp. *Merrick* [1996] 1 Cr App R 130 (CA), and the critical discussion in Elliott, "Endangering Life by Destroying or Damaging Property" [1997] *Crim LR* 382, 388–9. An extreme example of endangerment is *Cox* [2017] EWCA 1356, [2018] 1 Cr App R (S) 3. In that case, a drunken passenger deliberately started a fire in a waste-bin in the toilet of an aircraft when flying at 33,000 feet: a reckless act for which the Court of Appeal, on an Attorney General's Reference, increased the original sentence from four and half years to nine and a half years.
[362] *Per* s. 5(1), set out above in § 14.5(vi).
[363] This is made clear by the express retention of the phrase, "without lawful excuse" in the opening line of s. 1(2) notwithstanding that the supplementary definition in s. 5 is inapplicable to s. 1(2).
[364] Cp. Horder, "Crimes of Ulterior Intent" in Simester and Smith (eds.), *Harm and Culpability* (1996) 153.

with the intent or in the (subjective)[365] belief that life may be endangered thereby. This point is illustrated in *Parker*,[366] where D set fire to his semi-detached house, realising that his neighbours' lives may be endangered. His conviction was upheld notwithstanding that the neighbours turned out to be away.

The language of section 1(2)(b) stipulates that the endangerment must be *by* (or "thereby") the damage or destruction. It is not enough that D's act happens to cause both property damage and personal danger: the former must be (foreseen or intended as) a route to the latter. In *Steer*, D fired a rifle at the windows of V's house, both intending to cause damage and being reckless whether life would be endangered. His conviction under section 1(2) was nonetheless quashed. He was reckless whether life would be endangered *by the bullets*, not by the damage to the house. The crucial nexus, "thereby", was missing:[367]

> "To be guilty under subsection (2) he must additionally have intended to endanger life or been reckless as to whether life would be endangered 'by the damage' to property which he caused. This is the context in which the words must be construed and it seems to me impossible to read the words 'by the damage' as meaning 'by the damage or by the act which caused the damage.'"

On the other hand, D would have been guilty of the offence had he foreseen danger to life caused by the spray of glass from the broken windows.

Relatedly, there is no requirement that the damage caused must be the same as that which was contemplated by D. It is enough that D intends or foresees endangering life by the property damage that he contemplates will follow from his actions; and that, by acting as he does, D causes *some* property damage:[368]

> "Thus, if a defendant throws a brick at the windscreen of a moving vehicle, given that he causes some damage to the vehicle, whether he is guilty under section 1(2) does not depend on whether the brick hits or misses the windscreen, but whether he intended to hit it and intended that the damage therefrom should endanger life or whether he was reckless as to that outcome."

Implicitly, it is not necessary that the property damage that ultimately results from D's actions should itself endanger life.

### *(i) Arson*

By virtue of section 1(3),[369] in cases where the criminal damage in section 1(1) or 1(2) is caused by fire, the offence is called *arson* (or arson with intent to endanger life, etc., as the case may be) and is punishable by life imprisonment.[370] The mens rea requirement

[365] *Cooper* [2004] EWCA Crim 1382; following *G* [2003] UKHL 50, above, § 5.2(i). The Court in *Cooper* opined at [12] that "[i]t is now, in the light of *G*, incumbent on a trial judge to direct a jury, in a case of this kind, that the risk of danger to life was obvious and significant to the defendant. In other words, a subjective element is essential before the jury can convict of this offence." *Quaere* however whether the risk now need even be obvious, as opposed to foreseen (and, as foreseen, an unreasonable risk to run).

[366] [1993] Crim LR 856 (CA). Note that Parker was decided prior to *G* and *Cooper* (see preceding footnote) and applied an objective standard of recklessness.

[367] [1988] AC 111, 117 (Lord Bridge). Cp. *Webster* [1995] 2 All ER 168 (CA).

[368] *Webster, ibid.*, 497; approving *Dudley* [1989] Crim LR 57 (CA).

[369] "An offence committed under this section by destroying or damaging property by fire shall be charged as arson." Section 1(3) effectively rejects the Law Commission's recommendation that there should be no separate offence of arson (although criminal damage should incur a greater maximum penalty when caused by fire): Law Com. No. 29, *Report on Offences of Damage to Property* (1970) paras. 28–33.

[370] *Per* s. 4.

is correspondingly modified: D must intend, or foresee, causing damage *by fire*. It is not enough that the contemplated damage happens unexpectedly to cause a fire, even if that fire then endangers the lives of others.[371]

## § 14.7 Preliminary offences

As with sexual offences[372] and with fraud,[373] criminal damage and arson are backed up by a range of preliminary offences defined in "inchoate mode". Section 2 of the Criminal Damage Act creates an offence of uttering threats to damage or destroy property, and section 3 an offence of possessing anything with intent to do so. This policy is taken further by the Explosive Substances Act 1883. In addition to an offence of "unlawfully and maliciously" causing an explosion likely to endanger life or cause serious damage to property,[374] the 1883 Act creates an offence of making or possessing an explosive substance with intent to do this.[375] And to make doubly sure, it creates a further offence of making or possessing an explosive substance "under such circumstances as to give rise to a reasonable suspicion that he is not making it or does not have it in his possession or under his control for a lawful object".[376] Where such circumstances are shown, the defendant is guilty "unless he can show that he made it or had it in his possession or under his control for a lawful object".[377] The first two of these three offences are punishable with life imprisonment, the third with 14 years' imprisonment.

371 Cp. *Cooper (G) and Cooper (Y)* [1991] Crim LR 524 (CA).
372 See Chapter 12.
373 See below, § 15.6.
374 Explosive Substances Act 1883, s. 2.
375 *Ibid*., s. 3(1)(a).
376 *Ibid*., s. 4.
377 The case law to date assumes that the burden so placed on the defendant is a legal one: see *A-G's Reference (No. 2 of 1983)* [1984] QB 456; *Berry* [1985] AC 246. But in the light of Art. 6(2) of the ECHR and the decision *Sheldrake and A-G's Reference (No. 4 of 2002)* [2004] UKHL 43, [2005] 1 AC 264, the courts may in future reconsider the matter and interpret it as imposing an evidential burden only. See above, § 3.2.

# 15

# FRAUD

Theft is not the only way of usurping another's property rights. Sometimes, the wrongfulness of the defendant's behaviour may be more subtle. It may, for example, lie in the fact that D duped V into transferring ownership consensually[1] or into performing services for D, or in the fact that she fraudulently gained from the use of V's assets even though V suffered no loss. In common with theftuous offences, wrongdoing of this sort involves dishonest behaviour by D regarding the property of another. However, its prevention often requires the enactment of offences which differ substantially from traditional forms of theft.

The extent to which such offences are necessary has sometimes been questioned.[2] For example, although acquisition by deception may not give rise to tortious claims in trespass or conversion,[3] other civil law remedies, such as deceit, are usually available to the aggrieved party. In addition, much commercial wrongdoing is controlled by administrative regulation of the marketplace, buttressed by the civil sanctions available to professional bodies. Given such existing sanctions, and the commitment in this country to a broadly liberal economic philosophy, is it really essential to fence in the marketplace with criminal law?

The answer is yes. Our rights to private property are part of the very fabric of the modern United Kingdom.[4] Property relations are shared elements which help to structure our interpersonal relations within the community. As such, they are integral to our membership of society, and to the understanding we have of our own lives. In particular, one feature of our participation in a broadly liberal society is the autonomy we have in respect of our property—the freedom to use, control, and dispose of that property as we wish.

As was noted above, in Chapter 13, there are limitations to our autonomy as proprietors. Even the freedoms of contract and testament are substantially constrained by law. Neither may we use our assets to fund criminal activities, and we are compelled by the State to contribute through taxation to certain communal goals which may not be of direct personal benefit to us. Nonetheless, the importance of individualism to the UK polity means that personal property rights have attracted better protection from the criminal law than many more abstract social or community values, such as an unpolluted environment or a well-educated populace. By contrast with these examples, the occurrence of harms is more readily criminalised and prosecuted when there is an identifiable victim whose concrete individual rights have been transgressed.

[1] Although, following *Gomez* and *Hinks*, this case would now also be theft. See above, § 13.6(ii).

[2] See, e.g., *Jones* (1703) 2 Ld Raymond 1013, 92 ER 174; *Goodhall* (1821) Russ & Ry 461, 168 ER 898.

[3] Since possession and/or title will normally have passed, at least prima facie.

[4] Cf. Waldron, *The Right to Private Property* (1988); Ryan, *Property and Political Theory* (1986); Nozick, *Anarchy, State and Utopia* (1974); Epstein, "Property as a Fundamental Civil Right" (1992) 29 *Cal West LR* 187; Harris, *Property and Justice* (1996); Penner, *Property Rights* (2020); Dagan, *A Liberal Theory of Property* (2021).

This imbalance may be reason for complaint, but not on the basis that property rights deserve reduced protection. Indeed, the harms involved in property offences shade into those addressed by offences against the person, and any suggestion that offences against property are concerned solely with material loss would be misleading. The violation of our homes by a burglary, for example, may cause psychological injury and distress quite independent of the quantum of loss. Offences such as theft, fraud, and blackmail are generally categorised as property offences, and understandably so, for they involve wrongful acquisition of property. But they are also, in a very real sense, offences against the person. In each case, the conduct prohibited can be seen as an attack upon the victim's entitlement to dispose of his property by his own full and informed choice. Thus, the conduct represents an attack upon the victim's rights of free will and autonomy, and upon his freedom to exercise control over his own situation. Blackmail, for instance, involves D infringing V's legitimate control over his own affairs by imposing her free will in place of his.[5] This subjugation of V resembles an assault as much as it does a "property" wrong. Fraud by false representation, understood in this sense, is a crime partly because it entails the manipulation or exploitation of another. Unlike the corresponding civil law remedies, property offences, in differing ways, protect the individual's entitlement to respect as an autonomous member of our society.

Although fraud has been with us always, recent years have witnessed its enormous growth.[6] Email, the Internet, and social media have made it possible for people to deal with one another at a distance in a way that was never before possible, which has led (among other things) to an explosion of high-volume, relatively low-value fraud that has become one of the uglier defining features of our times. Almost half of all estimated frauds are online-enabled.[7] Generative artificial intelligence "(GenAI)" has vastly increased the volume of fraud, while voice cloning, deepfakes, and large language models enhance the credibility and sophistication of fraudulent conduct.[8] Large scale phishing operations no longer require specialized computer skills, due to the emergence of marketplaces on the dark and grey web that sell phishing kits and "fraud as a service" subscriptions.[9] About these phenomena, and indeed the crime of fraud in general, there is a widespread sense that worryingly little is being done either by way of prevention or of catching and punishing those responsible when it occurs.[10] The problem is compounded by a longstanding and growing backlog in the caseload of the Crown Court,[11] with fraud—as the "number 1 offence"[12]—especially affected.

[5] The crime of blackmail is not dealt with in this book. For detailed discussion, see *Smith, Hogan, and Ormerod*, chap. 24; *Archbold* (2026) § 21-207ff.

[6] There were an estimated 4.4 million incidents of fraud in year ending December 2025 in England and Wales, a 30% increase since 2017. Office for National Statistics (2026), *Crime in England and Wales: year ending December 2025*, https://www.ons.gov.uk/peoplepopulationandcommunity/crimeandjustice/bulletins/crimeinenglandandwales/latest#fraud (23 April 2026).

[7] Home Office *Fraud Strategy 2026 to 2029, Disrupting Crime, Supporting Economic Resilience and Delivering Justice*. CP 1523 (2026) 11.

[8] *Ibid.*, 12. See, further, Collins, "The Industrialisation of Fraud: Understanding Fraud in a Digital Era" (2026) 46 *LS* 46.

[9] Home Office *Fraud Strategy 2026 to 2029, Disrupting Crime, Supporting Economic Resilience and Delivering Justice*. CP 1523 (2026) 12.

[10] According to the Home Office: "In the year ending September 2025, only 3,631 individuals ultimately received a sentence [for fraud]". *Ibid.*, 50.

[11] In December 2024, the Crown Court backlog stood at 75,000: Leveson, *Independent Review of the Criminal Courts: Part 1* (Ministry of Justice, July 2025) 4.

[12] The estimated number of fraud offences in the year ending September 2025 was a startling 45% of all crime in the Crime Survey of England and Wales: "Around 1 in 14 adults were victims of fraud in this period": Home Office, *Fraud Strategy 2026 to 2029*: CP 1523 (2026) 7.

Multi-million-pound economic crime is investigated and prosecuted by a specialist agency, the Serious Fraud Office,[13] but the responsibility for dealing with smaller frauds usually rests with local police forces, many of which are ill-equipped to deal with it and give it low priority.[14] One consequence of this is the increasing use, against fraud, of private prosecutions by those who can afford to bring them—and the emergence of specialist law firms prepared to undertake such prosecutions.[15] The Government has sought to allay the sense that little is being done, expressing its determination to "turn the tide", by publishing its *Fraud Strategy 2026–2029*. Much that is there planned is constructive and will, it can be hoped, make a positive difference in time, including better information-gathering, better collaboration between law enforcement agencies, more use of preventive strategies, educational campaigns, and the civil law. Unfortunately, the modest scale of the earmarked financial investment suggests only limited progress is likely.[16] As far as the substantive law itself is concerned, there is no suggestion that the main fraud offences—the focus of this chapter—are themselves in need of modification or are otherwise any part of the problem. The problem, as the government appears to see it, is not that the wrong fraud offences are in place, but that they are under-prosecuted, prosecuted too slowly, and in need of strong supplementation by the strategies mentioned above, on which the *Fraud Strategy* document focuses.[17]

It should additionally be noted that large companies can nowadays be guilty of the offence of "failure to prevent fraud".[18] Where, with intent to benefit the relevant large organisation, an employee, agent or associate of the organisation commits a fraud offence—for example,

[13] In *Hayes* [2025] UKSC 29, [2025] 1 WLR 3553, the Supreme Court sharply criticised the role played by the Serious Fraud Office (SFO) as prosecutor in a 13-year investigation into benchmark interest rate manipulation. The investigation led to a number of convictions, including those of Tom Hayes and Carlo Palombo, whose convictions the Supreme Court quashed only after both had served significant prison sentences. In a number of cases including those that led to Hayes' and Palombo's convictions, the SFO had, the Court found, sowed the seeds of confusion (*ibid.*, [54]), by means of its "hopelessly vague" drafting (*ibid.*, [55]), meaning neither the defence nor the trial judges could understand clearly what case was being alleged against the defendants, raising "concerns about the effectiveness of the criminal appeal system in England and Wales in confronting legal error" (*ibid.*, [1]) Cp. below § 15.9 (ii).

[14] In 2022 a Parliamentary enquiry was told that "fraud is a third of all reported crime but accounts for 1% of police resources": House of Commons Treasury Committee, *Economic Crime*, 11th Report of 2021–22, HC 145, 2 February 2022, para. 53.

[15] A prominent example was the private prosecution, by the insurance company DAS, of a group of its former executives, the earlier stages of which reached the Court of Appeal in *D Ltd v A and others* [2017] EWCA Crim 1172, and the unsuccessful attempt of one of the convicted defendants to appeal against her sentence in Jones (Sally) [2021] EWCA Crim 1195.

[16] Home Office, *Fraud Strategy 2026 to 2029* (2026) 3. The government undertakes to invest over £250 million between 2026 and 2029 to deliver the strategy (*ibid.*, 4). To put this level of investment in perspective, the government itself estimates that fraud against businesses and individuals cost the economy £14.4 billion in 2023–2024 alone (*ibid.*). See, further, Collins, "Why Fraud Prevention is Relevant to Criminal Law Theorists" in Simester (ed.), *Modern Criminal Law* (2024) 265.

[17] Controversially, the *Fraud Strategy* states that "Government will introduce judge-only trials for the most complex of fraud cases (by the end of Parliament)" (paras. 6.5, 128). This follows on from Recommendation 44 in Leveson, *Independent Review of the Criminal Courts: Part 1* (Ministry of Justice, 2025) 318. Remarkably, legislation to remove jury trials from serious fraud cases was introduced over two decades ago by s. 43 Criminal Justice Act 2003. This section was never brought into force, and was repealed by s. 113 of the Protection of Freedoms Act 2012. At the time of writing, the Courts and Tribunals Bill is wending its way through the legislative process. For a compelling critique of the relevant Leveson proposal, see Vickers, Baloch, Clifford and Bacon, "Leveson Part 1: Abolishing Jury Trial in Complex Fraud", *Red Lion Chambers, Fraud Newsletter*, 16 July 2025: https://redlionchambers.substack.com/p/focus-e8f.

[18] Economic Crime and Corporate Transparency Act 2023, s. 199.

under sections 1–4[19] or 11[20] of the Fraud Act 2006—the organisation will itself be guilty of failure to prevent fraud, unless it had reasonable prevention measures in place at the relevant time (or, if it did not have such measures, it was not reasonable for it to have them). This offence aims to shift the culture in large companies against fraud by spreading responsibility for fraud beyond individual perpetrators to large companies that profit from it.[21]

## § 15.1 Statutory fraud—general

The major measure for criminalising fraudulent conduct is the Fraud Act 2006.[22] It is with the offences created by this legislation that this chapter is mainly concerned. For the details of the law of fraud as it stood before that date, readers should refer to earlier editions. A thumbnail account of it is given here, however, to put the 2006 Act into context and explain the thinking behind its introduction.

The recent history[23] of the law of fraud is that, together with the law of theft, it was recast in the Theft Act 1968 through the principal offence of obtaining property by deception,[24] flanked by subsidiary offences that included procuring the execution of a valuable security by deception,[25] and an opaquely drafted offence called "obtaining a pecuniary advantage by deception".[26] The 1968 makeover of fraud was less successful than the reform of theft,[27] and in 1978 it was necessary to pass a further Theft Act, creating three further fraud offences: obtaining services by deception,[28] evading liability by deception,[29] and making off without payment.[30] In 1996, the House of Lords, in a spirit completely opposite to the one which three years earlier had animated their decision on the scope of theft in *Gomez*,[31] gave the offence of obtaining property by deception a narrow and technical interpretation, holding that it did not cover the person who by deception caused a bank or building society to transfer money to his bank account.[32] In response, it was necessary to create a further new offence of obtaining a money transfer by deception.[33] In the background to this clut-

[19] Below, §§ 15.2–15.5.

[20] Below, § 15.7.

[21] There is no offence where the relevant organisation itself "was, or was intended to be, a victim of the fraud offence": Economic Crime and Corporate Transparency Act 2023, s. 3.

[22] For helpful analysis of the key provisions, see Ormerod, "The Fraud Act 2006: Criminalising Lying?" [2007] *Crim LR* 193. See also Ormerod and Williams, *Smith's Law of Theft* (9th ed., 2007).

[23] The early history of the matter is that from the Middle Ages there was a general common law offence of cheating, which was supplemented from an early date by a range of specific statutory offences. For a list, see Blackstone, *Commentaries* (1765–9), Book IV, chap. 12, § 9. The usual penalty for the various forms of cheating was the pillory, the rationale, in the days before newspapers and easy travel, in part being the need to warn the public of a fellow citizen who was not to be trusted to do business with.

[24] Theft Act 1968, s. 15.

[25] *Ibid.*, s. 20; the typical example was telling lies to persuade someone to write a cheque.

[26] *Ibid.*, s. 16.

[27] This was not entirely the fault of the Criminal Law Revision Committee, whose proposals were in this case departed from when the Bill that became the Theft Act 1968 was prepared and enacted.

[28] Theft Act 1978, s. 1.

[29] *Ibid.*, s. 2.

[30] *Ibid.*, s. 3.

[31] [1993] AC 442; above, § 13.6(ii)(a).

[32] *Preddy* [1996] AC 815; surprisingly, the panel contained two of the judges who formed part of the majority in *Gomez*.

[33] Theft Act 1968, ss. 15A and 15B, hastily added by the Theft (Amendment) Act 1996.

ter of narrowly drawn offences lurked the protean common law offence of conspiracy to defraud, ready to be invoked by prosecutors against any customers who proved particularly difficult. The resulting law was complicated and its fragmented state provided ample means for defendants to wrong-foot prosecutors by arguing that, dishonest though they were, they had been charged with the wrong offence. In the light of this, the government referred the law of fraud to the Law Commission, whose proposals were largely accepted in the Fraud Act 2006.[34]

The Fraud Act 2006 abolished a swathe of specific fraud offences[35] and replaced them with a general fraud offence that can be committed in one of three ways, namely (i) by false representation, (ii) by failing to disclose information, and (iii) by abuse of position. As there is but one offence, as a matter of substantive law it would not matter if the evidence establishes that fraud was committed in another fashion to that initially alleged by the prosecution. The prosecution may base their case on a false representation which they fail to prove, yet nonetheless establish that a fraud was perpetrated by D's failure to disclose information to V that he was under a legal duty to divulge. As a matter of practice, however, the prosecution should set out the case against D as clearly as possible,[36] and any trial must be fair within the terms of Article 6 of the ECHR.[37] A further innovation is that, unlike the previous offences, the actus reus of the 2006 Act's fraud offence is "minimalist". An essential ingredient in the 2006 Act offence, like the old ones, is dishonesty. But whereas the predecessor offences required D by his dishonesty to have obtained something, or to have caused something to happen, under the 2006 Act it is enough that D behaved dishonestly with this aim in mind. Each form of the offence of fraud is a conduct crime, not a result crime.[38] In effect, fraud is nowadays an inchoate offence, although, since technically it is a substantive crime in its own right, a further layer of inchoate liability will attach.[39] Much conduct that would formerly be regarded as preliminary to fraudulent conduct—and even beyond the scope of inchoate offences—will now constitute completed criminal offences. The general effect of this, of course, is to move the stage at which D incurs criminal liability to an earlier point in time. A practical illustration is the case of *Jeevarajah*:[40]

> D1 and D2 ran a corner shop, at which lottery tickets were sold. V would regularly buy tickets there, and each time he bought new tickets he would ask D1 and D2 if any of his last tickets had won. When one day he did have a winning ticket, they falsely told him that he had as usual lost, and then sought unsuccessfully to claim the money for themselves.

34 LCCP No. 155, *Legislating the Criminal Code: Fraud and Deception* (1989); Law Com. No. 276, *Fraud* (2002), on which see Sullivan, "Fraud: The Latest Law Commission Proposals" (2003) 52 *J Crim Law* 139; Home Office, *Fraud Law Reform: Consultation on Proposals for Legislation* (2004).

35 Obtaining property by deception (Theft Act 1968, s.15); obtaining a money transfer by deception (*ibid.*, s. 15A); obtaining a pecuniary advantage by deception (*ibid.*, s. 16); procuring the execution of a valuable security by deception (*ibid.*, s. 20); obtaining services by deception (Theft Act 1978, s. 1); evading liability by deception (*ibid.*, s. 2).

36 *Maxwell* [1978] 3 All ER 1140, 1142 (HL).

37 It is an important principle of criminal procedure that, where the prosecution has advanced the case against a defendant on one basis, the court may not be invited to convict him on a different basis which he has had no chance to contest. For an example of this principle in action see *Falconer-Attlee* (1974) 58 Cr App R 348 (CA).

38 An exception is dishonestly obtaining services; below, § 15.7.

39 As is the case for the statutory offence of aiding and abetting suicide: *McCann* (1971) 56 Cr App R 359 (CA).

40 [2012] EWCA Crim 1299.

For this, D1 and D2 were prosecuted for fraud under the Fraud Act, to which they pleaded guilty.[41] Under the earlier law, this would have been at most an attempt—with room for argument about proximity, as is always a possibility with attempt.[42] Under the new law the defendants committed the full offence of fraud at the point when they told their lie to V, let alone when they subsequently tried to claim the money.

The turn towards redefining fraud offences in the "inchoate mode" was noted above. This effect is accentuated by the Act's also creating two offences of possession of articles for use in fraud, and making or supplying articles for use in frauds. Elsewhere, the common-law offence of incitement has been replaced by a statutory regime the reach of which is considerably wider,[43] and other parts of the law have been similarly widened.[44] Helpful as this is to prosecutors, it raises serious questions in relation to the legitimate scope and intrusiveness of criminalisation, which we discuss in the next chapter.

Before analysing the ingredients of the offence of fraud, a word should be said about legislative technique. Whatever one may think about the way in which the Fraud Act 2006 extends the reach of criminal liability beyond its former limits, this law does have the merit of being clearly drafted, and the resulting law is much simpler and more accessible than it was before. Six complicated offences have been replaced by one single main offence, plus three supplementary offences; together with the parts of the earlier law that remain in force, the general law of criminal fraud now consists of some eight offences.[45] This is in sharp contrast to the law on sexual offences: as we saw in Chapter 12, to cover the central ground of sexual violence and the sexual abuse of children, the Sexual Offences Act 2003 created no fewer than 21 separate offences, and the total number of sexual offences it contains is some 50. Moreover, whereas the provisions of the Fraud Act are short and simple, many of those of Sexual Offences Act are long and complicated. It is possible to envisage the provisions of the Fraud Act forming part of an eventual criminal code, but not those of the Sexual Offences Act.

Mention should be made of a provision that the Fraud Act 2006 does not contain. Despite the consistent view of the Law Commission that any legislation subsequent to its report abolish the offence of conspiracy to defraud,[46] the Government refused to remove this "indefensible anomaly".[47] The refusal was based exclusively on pragmatism: the risk of gaps in the coverage of fraudulent conduct.[48] In the decades since the Fraud Act passed into law it has seemed a safe bet that any future editions of this work will continue to have a section on conspiracy to defraud.[49] Perhaps confidence in the prediction may be a little less warranted after the Supreme Court's criticism of the offence in *Hayes*.[50] In an attempt to prevent the over-use of this offence, the Attorney General has issued official guidance to

[41] They were sentenced to 14 months' imprisonment, against which they unsuccessfully appealed.

[42] The possibility arises because whether D's behaviour was sufficiently proximate to the completed crime is ultimately a question of fact, not law; see above, § 9.4

[43] Serious Crime Act 2007, Part 2 (offences of assisting or encouraging crime); above, § 9.1.

[44] Another example is the law on terrorism, which has been widely expanded by the creation of new preliminary offences, e.g. by s. 5 of the Terrorism Act 2006.

[45] Fraud; possession of articles for use in frauds; making or supplying articles for use in frauds; obtaining services dishonestly; making off without payment; forgery; false accounting; conspiracy to defraud.

[46] Most recently Law Com. No. 276, *Fraud* (2002) para. 1.4.

[47] *Ibid.*

[48] HL Debate, cols. 1113–16, 14 March 2006: Lord Goldsmith, Attorney General.

[49] In this edition it is treated below in § 15.9.

[50] [2025] UKSC 29, [2025] 1 WLR 3553. Below, § 15.9.

prosecutors concerning when conspiracy to defraud should be charged instead of a substantive offence.[51] Despite this official move to restrict its use and the rather dim view recently taken of the offence by the Supreme Court, however, conspiracy to defraud remains for the time being very much alive.[52]

Below we analyse the three forms of the fraud offence. Before we descend to detail the different ways of committing fraud, we shall first examine the features that are common to all three forms of the offence. There must be proof of dishonesty, and there must be an intent to gain or to cause loss or risk of loss in money or property. We shall deal with those elements in full before examining in further detail the three branches of the offence: (i) fraud by false representation; (ii) fraud by failing to disclose information; and (iii) fraud by abuse of position.

## § 15.2 Common elements: "intent to make a gain or cause a loss" and "dishonesty"

### *(i) Intent to make a gain or cause a loss*

In each of the three forms of fraud under the 2006 Act, intention must be proved: the required intent must be to make a gain for oneself or another, or to cause loss to another, or to expose another to a risk of loss.[53] There are, then, alternative forms the intent can take. In *Ames*[54] it was, however, held that intention is a "single ingredient" of the offence.[55] D appealed against his conviction for fraud on the basis that more than one of these forms of intent had been alleged against him, and the jury had not been directed that they needed to be unanimous on the presence of at least one of them before they could find him guilty.[56] Refusing D's appeal, the Court of Appeal held that "[w]hether the financial impact intended is gain, loss, or both, does not matter"; there is no requirement that the jury all agree which alternative is established, when more than one is alleged.[57] It is sufficient that they are all sure that D had one of the relevant forms of intention alleged.

Section 5 of the Fraud Act is as follows:

**5 "Gain" and "loss"**

(1) The references to gain and loss in sections 2 to 4 are to be read in accordance with this section.

(2) "Gain" and "loss"—

(a) extend only to gain or loss in money or other property;

(b) include any such gain or loss whether temporary or permanent;

and "property" means any property whether real or personal (including things in action and other intangible property).

(3) "Gain" includes a gain by keeping what one has, as well as a gain by getting what one does not have.

(4) "Loss" includes a loss by not getting what one might get, as well as a loss by parting with what one has.

[51] Available online at https://www.gov.uk/guidance/use-of-the-common-law-offence-of-conspiracy-to-defraud--6.
[52] Some examples of its recent use are given in § 15.9(v) below.
[53] Fraud Act 2006, s. 2(1)(b), 3(1)(b) and 4(1)(c).
[54] [2023] EWCA Crim 1463, [2024] 1 WLR 1860.
[55] *Ibid.*, [56].
[56] *Ibid.*, [5].
[57] *Ibid.*, [56].

Confining gains and losses to money and property reins in, modestly, what remains a very wide offence. To make a false representation to obtain confidential information about a forthcoming takeover bid may fall foul of insider trading legislation, but it will not be fraud by false representation: confidential information without more is not a form of intangible property.[58] Some very important gains that are not directly economic are thereby excluded from the scope of fraud, as when D gains entry to a prestigious university by inflating his grades on his application form (and causes the loss of a vital opportunity to the better-qualified candidate he displaces)—or when, having got there, he cheats in his exams to improve the quality of his degree. Or consider a journalist in salaried employment, who tells lies to gain access to the subject of an important interview.[59] The journalist would not commit fraud by false representation, although the position would perhaps be different if he were a freelance writer (or photographer) who was hoping to sell the interview or the picture to the press.

That said, the fact that the offence covers frauds intended to cause loss as well as gains, and that "loss" includes a loss by not getting what one might get as well as a loss by parting with what one has, means that frauds committed to obtain something that does not count as "property" will fall within the offence if they enable D to get a free benefit for which he would otherwise have had to pay. Thus, in principle, telling lies to obtain sexual favours falls outside the scope of the offence of fraud because sexual favours are not property; thus, it would not catch someone like the defendant in *Jheeta*,[60] who persuaded his over-trusting girlfriend to continue their relationship by producing false evidence that he was suicidal. However, if V had been a sex worker and D had persuaded her to have sex with him on the basis of a promise to pay, which D did not intend to keep, his fraud would have been intended to cause V a loss, and an offence under the Fraud Act would have been committed.

In the usual case where D makes a false representation in order to make a gain, the intent involved will almost invariably be the natural, core sense of the term,[61] as when D tells a deliberate lie in order dishonestly to obtain money from V. However, it is also possible to envisage circumstances where D's intent to make a gain will be of the non-core, foresight-of-moral-certainty variety.[62] Suppose that D goes to Lord's cricket ground wearing a Marylebone Cricket Club tie. His principal objective in doing so is to pass himself off as a member of the MCC among his friends and acquaintances, but he knows that, as on previous occasions, he will be charged the lower admission price payable by members. He commits fraud by false representation.

Where the allegation is that D intended to cause loss to another, the intent will typically be of the non-core variety, unless V is motivated by malice. So, if D borrows £50 from V, assuring her that he will pay her on Sunday but knowing that in his foreseeable financial circumstances he has no chance of doing so, he commits fraud. That still holds even if he

58 See the discussion above, § 13.3(i)(a).

59 For a real example, see the Report of Lord Dyson's investigation into the way in which the journalist Martin Bashir obtained the famous BBC interview with Princess Diana in 1995: online at http://downloads.bbc.co.uk/aboutthebbc/reports/reports/dyson-report-20-may-21.pdf; see, also, Size, "R v Bashir? The Case for Charging Martin Bashir with Fraud" [2021] *Crim LR* 774.

60 [2007] EWCA Crim 1699, [2008] 1 WLR 2582; above, § 12.3(iii)(b).

61 Above, § 5.1(i)–(iii).

62 Above, § 5.1(iv).

intends to buy a lottery ticket with part of the money and fervently hopes he will be a millionaire following the draw on Saturday night. He knows it is virtually certain that V will not be paid on Sunday, and the intention to cause V loss can be found.

Note that it is enough to expose another to a *risk* of loss.[63] In other words, D is potentially guilty of the offence where he is reckless whether V will lose out (although he must still, at base, intend to expose V to that risk), as well as where he believes that V's losing out is virtually certain to occur. This is a considerable extension of the reach of fraud, applying to each of the three ways of committing the offence contained in the Fraud Act. Suppose that, in a variant of the £50 loan example, D expects to be able to repay V on Sunday because he anticipates payment of a debt he is owed on Friday. However, he is aware of a risk that repayment may not happen until some time later. D knows that he has exposed V to the risk of loss which, the Act stipulates,[64] includes temporary losses. Many times each day, individuals and organisations will enter time-bounded repayment commitments aware that contingencies of various kinds may preclude the timely meeting of their obligation to repay. If D is aware of a non-minimal risk of time default in repaying V, he intends to expose V to the risk of loss. Making a binding commitment to pay on time will be a false representation if D is aware of the possibility of default unless V has been made aware of and accepts the risk of untimely payment. It is submitted that much, if not most, conduct of this kind should be responded to by the renegotiation of credit terms against a backdrop of civil law enforcement of bad debts, and not remedied by the criminal law. However, whether particular incidents of this sort constitute fraud will depend now upon the vagaries of dishonesty.[65]

*(a) Intending to generate a gain or loss by means of the fraud*

The intent must go together with the fraud. So, for an offence of fraud by false representation, D must intend to make the gain *by making the representation*.[66] Suppose that D enters a conversation with V and at some point falsely claims to own a house abroad, merely intending to raise his status in the eyes of V. At some later point in the conversation D, having forgotten his earlier lie, successfully asks V for a loan of £300. Even if V would not have made this loan but for his assumption about the financial means of homeowners, D commits no offence. At the time he made his false representation, he did not intend to make money by lying. It would be different if, when asking for money, D decided to exploit his earlier lie about his "house abroad" to extract some money from V. The false representation still has effect and now it is being deployed by D to make a gain for himself.

Under the previous law of fraud, the main offences required not only that D acted fraudulently, but that he obtained something by doing so. This gave rise to problems of causation and remoteness. On the whole, the case law took the line that the fraudulent act must be the direct and immediate cause of the obtaining, and not merely create the setting in which a more immediate cause could operate. Thus, where a man told lies that enabled him to place a bet on credit, and the horse he had backed then won, he was held not guilty of obtaining the winnings by false pretences, because the immediate cause of his gain was the fact that

[63] Sections 2(1)(b)(ii), 3(b)(ii), and 4(1)(c)(ii). Such an intention also suffices for conspiracy to defraud: *Allsop* (1976) 64 Cr App R 29; below, § 15.9(iii)(a), (iv).

[64] Section 5(2)(b).

[65] See above, § 13.8(iv).

[66] Section 2(1)(b).

the horse had won;[67] and in another case it was held (at first instance) that a woman who obtained a teaching post by means of a forged certificate was not guilty of obtaining her salary by false pretences, because the immediate cause was her doing her job.[68] In other cases, however, a more robust line was taken. In *Button*,[69] a conviction was upheld for obtaining a prize by false pretences where a runner had lied to obtain a handicap advantage, the Court rejecting the argument that the immediate cause of the obtaining was that he had won the race. Similarly, in *King*,[70] a conviction for attempting to obtain money by deception was upheld where fraudulent contractors had lied to persuade a householder to allow them to cut down her trees, in the hope of getting her to pay for the work, the Court rejecting the argument that the deception merely provided the opportunity to earn the money by cutting down the trees. Comparable reasoning was applied in *Miller*,[71] where a dishonest motorist extracted exorbitant fares for driving foreigners from airports, whom he had persuaded to enter his vehicle by pretending to be a licensed taxi driver. In order to circumvent this problem, section 16 of the Theft Act 1968—now repealed—created specific offences of using deception in order to obtain insurance, to obtain the opportunity to earn money in employment, or to win money by betting.

Although the 2006 Act's offence of fraud is defined in the "inchoate mode" and it is no longer necessary to prove that as a result of the fraud D actually obtained anything, the problem discussed in the previous paragraph has not completely gone away. Although D is guilty even where nothing was obtained, the prosecution must still show that D *intended* to make a gain or cause a loss *by means of* the fraud he has practised. Under section 2, D is guilty of fraud where he "intends, by making the representation" to make a gain or cause a loss; under section 3, D is guilty of fraud where he "intends, by failing to disclose the information" to make a gain or cause a loss; and by section 4, D is guilty of fraud where he "intends, by means of the abuse of that position" to make a gain or cause a loss. In consequence, causal speculation may still be necessary. If a gain has been made (or loss caused, etc.), it will provide a useful focus for determining whether the gain was made by making the representation. If no gain is actually made, the question must be along the lines of asking whether the gain that D intended would, if realised, have been made *by* making the representation.

A case of particular difficulty is where D lies to get a job. Clearly any salary that is to be paid to D would constitute a gain—but would that gain have been made *by way of* the false representation? Formerly, D could be charged with the specific offence under the then section 16 of the Theft Act 1968, but that is no longer an option. As this point is one of some practical importance, it is surprising that the Fraud Act fails to deal with it explicitly.[72]

[67] *Clucas* [1949] 2 KB 226 (CA).
[68] *Lewis* (1922) Russell (12th ed.) Vol. II, 1186 n. 66, discussed in *King* [1987] QB 547 (CA).
[69] [1900] 2 QB 597.
[70] [1987] QB 547 (CA).
[71] (1992) 95 Cr App R 421 (CA). This case is criticised by A.T.H. Smith, *Property Offences* (1994) § 17.125.
[72] Prosecutions under the Fraud Act have been brought for doing this, but the point remains open because all those prosecuted seem to have pleaded guilty. In *Andrewes* [2020] EWCA Crim 1055, a defendant who had pleaded guilty later sought to argue that the causal link between the lies he told to get the jobs and the money that he later earned for doing them was too remote for the earnings to be treated as the proceeds of his crimes for the purpose of confiscation proceedings—an argument that was resoundingly rejected. This suggests, by implication if not expressly, that a person who lies in order to obtain employment commits the crime of fraud. Those who tell lies to obtain jobs will often commit other offences. Fortunately for their potential patients, it is a criminal offence for unqualified persons to practice as doctors (Medical Act 1983, s. 49) or as dentists (Dentists Act 1984, s. 38). For the possible application of the offence of forgery, see below, § 15.11.

In *Razoq*,[73] D was a hospital doctor who joined a *locum* agency, after having been suspended from his hospital job, and carried out several *locum* jobs for payment. He failed to disclose the disciplinary proceedings against him to the *locum* agency, and also claimed to have certain qualifications that he did not in fact possess. D was convicted of fraud on the bases that his lies about his qualifications were made with the intention of making a gain (section 2), and that his failure to disclose the disciplinary proceedings against him had a similar aim (section 3).

(A similar and topical example is "phishing": sending fraudulent electronic communications, purporting to come from legitimate sources, designed to persuade the recipients to reveal their personal details—which the sender hopes to use later to extract money by practising identity fraud.[74])

The point of principle at issue here arose in *Gilbert*,[75] in which D had told lies to a bank in order to persuade it to open an account, which she and others planned to use in connection with property deals out of which they were hoping to make money. The Court of Appeal quashed D's conviction for fraud, apparently[76] because it thought the profits of the eventual deals, if they materialised, would be too remote from the lies by which D persuaded the bank to open the account. The boundaries of remoteness have yet to be clarified.

In a number of recurrent situations, possible difficulties of this sort are circumvented by the existence of specific offences: for example, section 42 of the Gambling Act 2005, whereby a person commits a criminal offence if she cheats at gambling "or does anything to enable another person to cheat at gambling"—cheating including, for these purposes, improper improvement of the chance of winning.[77]

### *(ii) Dishonesty*

Following in the footsteps of the legislation it replaced, the Fraud Act 2006 contains no definition of the key element of dishonesty. Of course, in run-of-the-mill cases this will cause no difficulty, as when D tells V he is collecting a debt that V owes to E, D lacking any intention to pass the money to E. If the prosecution proves these facts, they will normally also have proved D's dishonesty. But suppose that E owes D money to the same value as V's debt to E, and D thinks the only way he will ever be paid is to intercept the payment that V is due to make to E? Imagine further that, after receiving the money from V by claiming he is collecting it for E, D then informs V why he did so and advises V not to make any further payment to E. If D were to be charged with *theft* of the money received from V, the issue of dishonesty would be resolved with the aid of the claim of right provision to be found in

[73] [2012] EWCA Crim 674 [2012].

[74] If it does not amount to fraud, "phishing" will sometimes involve the commission of a different offence: e.g., the unauthorised obtaining of personal data contrary to s. 170 of the Data Protection Act 2018. (But this offence only applies where the personal information was stored in a filing system managed by a "data-controller".)

[75] [2012] EWCA Crim 2392.

[76] The judgment was unreserved and it is not entirely clear whether the conviction was quashed because of this, or simply because the Court of Appeal thought the judge had not explained the issue with sufficient clarity to the jury.

[77] By s. 42(2), "it is immaterial whether a person who cheats improves his chances of winning anything, or wins anything". This offence, among others, featured in the high-profile prosecution of members of the Pakistani cricket team for match-fixing: see *Majeed* [2012] EWCA Crim 1186, [2012] 2 Cr App R 18.

section 2(1)(a) of the Theft Act 1968.[78] As there is no similar provision in the Fraud Act 2006, the judge or magistrates at D's trial for fraud by false representation can only have recourse to the test for dishonesty in disputable cases set down in *Ghosh*,[79] as now truncated in *Ivey v Genting Casinos*,[80] and in *Barton*:[81] was what was done dishonest according to the ordinary standards of reasonable and honest people?

This failure in the 2006 Act to make special provision for recurring cases is in principle regrettable. The case of the D–V–E debt triangle is not straightforward in terms of moral evaluation—what, for juror X, may be an example of legitimate self-help may be, for juror Y, a disreputable machination—and the law needs to set a standard for such divisive cases. The fact that the Fraud Act 2006 neglects to set any standard leaves the matter at large, with the *Ivey* test the only, and a rather uncertain, guide.[82] We will return to this lack of clarity that the absence of even a partial definition of dishonesty engenders when examining the other mens rea elements.

## § 15.3 Fraud by false representation: section 2

### *(i) The actus reus*

This form of the fraud offence is defined by section 2 of the Fraud Act 2006, which is as follows:

> **2 Fraud by false representation**
> (1) A person is in breach of this section if he—
> (a) dishonestly makes a false representation, and
> (b) intends, by making the representation—
> (i) to make a gain for himself or another, or
> (ii) to cause loss to another or to expose another to a risk of loss.
> (2) A representation is false if—
> (a) it is untrue or misleading, and
> (b) the person making it knows that it is, or might be, untrue or misleading.
> (3) "Representation" means any representation as to fact or law, including a representation as to the state of mind of—
> (a) the person making the representation, or
> (b) any other person.
> (4) A representation may be express or implied.
> (5) For the purposes of this section a representation may be regarded as made if it (or anything implying it) is submitted in any form to any system or device designed to receive, convey or respond to communications (with or without human intervention).

The conduct element of this form of fraud is the making of a false representation. This generates three points of inquiry: (a) what counts as a representation; (b) when is the

[78] See the discussion above, § 13(8)(i).
[79] [1982] QB 1053, 1064 (CA).
[80] [2017] UKSC 67, [2018] AC 391.
[81] [2020] EWCA Crim 575, [2021] QB 685; for discussion, see § 13.8(iv) above.
[82] Although there is no control over perverse applications of the test of dishonesty by juries, the Divisional Court is willing to intervene when it disapproves of the way in which magistrates have applied it. For an example see *Gohill v DPP* [2007] EWHC 239 (Admin).

representation false; and (c) when is the representation "made"? We consider each of these points in turn.

*(a) A representation*

As under the previous law,[83] this may be a representation as to fact or law, and it may be as to a person's state of mind—typically, D's intention to pay for something, but potentially it could be about anybody's intention to do anything. Also as under the previous law, the representation may be express, or implied. In *Sharma*,[84] it was stressed that, where fraud by false representation is charged, the representation on which the case depends must be precisely formulated in the information or indictment. A statement about what will happen in the future, be that a promise or a prediction, is not a representation of "fact or law", and so does not qualify. However, such a statement may contain an implied representation that D intends to act accordingly, but—if that is a prosecutor's case—that must be clearly formulated as an implied representation in the charge. Under the old law the courts had decided, in relation to various recurrent situations in everyday life, that certain implied representations are made, and the same approach is likely to be taken with the new. Thus writing a cheque implies a representation that it will be honoured when presented for payment.[85] As Robert Goff LJ said in *Gilmartin*,[86]

> "by the simple giving of a cheque, whether postdated or not, the drawer impliedly represents that the state of facts existing at the date of delivery of the cheque is such that in the ordinary course the cheque will on presentation for payment on or after the date specified in the cheque, be met."

As noted above in relation to *Sharma*, since this is a prediction of future events, a further representation must be implied from it that the drawer of the cheque presently intends and expects that it will be honoured when presented. Another common situation is the use of a credit card or bank card, which involves a representation that the person using it has authority to do so.[87] When a person fills in a withdrawal form at a bank, she makes an implied representation that the bank is indebted to her in that amount[88]—unless, presumably, overdraft facilities have been arranged. Where D purports to sell goods to V, there is usually an implied representation that D has the capacity to pass ownership of the goods,[89]

[83] Theft Act 1968 s. 15(4): "For the purposes of this section 'deception' means any deception (whether deliberate or reckless) by words or conduct as to fact or as to law, including a deception as to the present intentions of the person using the deception or any other person".

[84] [2025] EWCA Crim 1122.

[85] *DPP v Turner* [1974] AC 357, 367 (Lord Reid). (Note that this representation encompasses the implied representations stated in the old case of *Hazelton* (1874) LR 2 CCR 134. It is submitted that the earlier case may now be disregarded.) See also the discussion in Smith, *Property Offences* (1994) § 17.52.

[86] [1983] QB 953, 962 (CA).

[87] *MPC v Charles* [1977] AC 177; *Lambie* [1982] AC 449. These decisions, however, fail to address the causation point—that the vendor accepting the card may rely only upon the minimum representation required to validate the charge transaction, i.e. that the customer is the person named on the face of the card (itself an implied representation: *Abdullah* [1982] Crim LR 122 (Crown Court (Croydon)). See Smith, "The Idea of Criminal Deception" [1982] *Crim LR* 721.

[88] *Hamilton* (1991) 92 Cr App R 54 (CA).

[89] *Sampson* (1885) 52 LT (NS) 772. Cf. *Eichholz v Bannister* (1864) 17 CB (NS) 708, 723, 144 ER 284, 290: "in almost all the transactions of sale in common life the seller by the very act of selling holds out to the buyer that he is the owner of the article he offers for sale".

and that the goods are genuine.[90] Conversely, where D buys or orders goods, she impliedly represents her present intention to pay for them;[91] and where payment on the spot is expected (e.g. at a restaurant or service station), she impliedly represents also that she has the ability to pay.[92] So, for instance, where D takes a taxi, she implies by her conduct that she has money for the fare.[93] Furthermore, D is also sometimes treated as making an implied representation when, having made a statement that was true at the time, it is later falsified by events, and D thereafter acquiesces in V's continuing to act on the basis that the situation is still as it was. Thus in *Rai*,[94] D obtained a grant from the Birmingham City Council to install a bathroom in his house for the use of his aged and infirm mother. Before work was commenced, D's mother died. D refrained from notifying the council of his mother's death, and the council subsequently commissioned builders to install the bathroom. D's conviction for obtaining the building services by deception was upheld by the Court of Appeal, on the ground that allowing the works to be done in his house without explaining the change of circumstances amounted to deception. He could nowadays be found to be making an implied false representation when he acquiesced to the work's being conducted.

A different result eventuated on the facts in *United Arab Emirates v Allen*.[95] In that case, the Divisional Court held that, where a person gave a lender an undated cheque as security for a loan, she was not required to seek the lending institution out and warn it when her bank balance dwindled to the point that the cheque would no longer be honoured if presented. The result might have been different, one suspects, if instead of handing all the money over at the outset, the loan was handed over in instalments—and by accepting an instalment the borrower, like the defendant in *Rai*, had allowed the alleged victim of the fraud to confer a benefit on her after she knew that the situation had materially changed.

A false representation will normally be made by words, but it can equally be made by conduct: as in the celebrated nineteenth-century case in which a person who was not a member of the university obtained credit from a tradesman by entering his shop dressed in an Oxford cap and gown.[96]

*(b) False*

By section 2(2)(b) a representation is false "if it is untrue *or misleading*". Clearly some representations may be literally true but are nonetheless to be regarded as false because, although

90 *Jean Jacques Williams* [1980] Crim LR 589 (CA).

91 *DPP v Ray* [1974] AC 370.

92 *Ibid.*, 379, 382.

93 *Waterfall* [1970] 1 QB 148, 150 (CA).

94 [2000] 1 Cr App R 242 (CA). Contrast, in Australia, *Nelson v R* [1987] WAR 57, 60 (Burt CJ), where it was said that the rule of equity, that a person has a duty to disclose in a pre-contractual situation where a statement inducing a contract becomes false prior to conclusion of the contract, "is not a rule which has anything to do with the criminal offence of obtaining something by a false pretence". The application of the equitable rule was also rejected by Lord Hodson in *DPP v Ray* [1974] AC 370, 389. However, his Lordship was in the minority and the point was not taken up by the majority.

95 [2012] EWHC 1712 (Admin), [2012] 1 WLR 3419. In this case the lender's extradition was sought by the United Arab Emirates, where the transaction had taken place and where her behaviour apparently did constitute a criminal offence. The issue arose because the UK only extradites to that country where the behaviour in question would also have constituted a crime in the UK.

96 *Barnard* (1837) 7 C & P 784, 173 ER 342; cf. *Parker and Bulteel* (1916) 25 Cox CC 145: a banker who keeps his doors open and continues to trade may thereby represent that he is solvent.

true, they are misleading. When will this be? Take a hypothetical case discussed in *Hinks*:[97] a situation where D and V are negotiating the sale of D's garage. V asks D what the turnover of the business was, as per the latest set of accounts, and receives in response the true figures. V's subsequent offer price reflects a valuation based on the assumption that the figures were a useful guide to future profitability. D knows this, but is also aware that a bypass road to be constructed in the near future will take away practically all the passing trade. Just as the House of Lords did not entirely rule out that D's accepting V's purchase price could be theft of V's money, we must take seriously the prospect that D might also be guilty of fraud by false representation when he gives V the accurate figures: the offence does not require the actual making of the gain or loss. Were the figures misleading? In the context of V's query, it is submitted that the answer is yes. One problem with this answer is that it takes the criminal law beyond what constitutes a misrepresentation for the purposes of the law of contract, where the boundaries of the concept are mediated by the principle of *caveat emptor* (the basic rule of English civil law that when a person sells something he is under no obligation to disclose its defects, and it is the buyer's business to discover them). A related issue is the dishonest trader who, sensing that his customer is gullible, quotes an excessive price for goods to be supplied or work to be done, which the customer foolishly accepts. In some cases (e.g. clauses imposing penalties for late payment), the excessive charge may be legally invalid.[98] Such cases aside, however, and absent any positive misrepresentation, the resulting contract would normally be binding; but could his statement be misleading, in the sense that his figures falsely implied that he was quoting the going rate?[99] Extending the notion of falsity to representations that are misleading yet true could lead to further incoherence at the interface of criminal and civil law.

### *(c) Made*

A final point about fraud by false representation is a basic one about the actus reus. Although the offence of fraud is now inchoate in the sense that the defendant who makes a false representation commits an offence of fraud whether or not any gain or loss results, it is still necessary for the representation to be "made". When, as a matter of law, does this happen? If D writes a begging letter that contains a false representation, it could be made when he writes it, when he sends it, or when it actually comes to the attention of the sender. Although in a sense the representation was "made" when the letter was written, we suggest this interpretation is too wide; apart from any other consideration, sections 6 and 7 of the Fraud Act create specific offences of possessing and making articles for use in frauds, which this interpretation of the main offence would make redundant. At the other end of the scale, if the false representation has been uttered, there seems no particularly good reason to require the prosecutor to prove that it came to anyone's attention. It is therefore suggested that a false representation is made when it is uttered.[100] In the case of an oral representation,

[97] [2001] 2 AC 241, 251–2 (Lord Steyn).

[98] As in *Whatcott* [2019] EWCA Crim 1889, where the Court of Appeal held that in such case the validity or otherwise of the charge is a matter of law to be determined by the judge.

[99] Overcharging gullible customers in this way can in principle be theft: as in *Williams* [2001] 1 Cr App R 362 (CA); see above, § 13.6 (vi). If the trader is someone with whom the gullible customer deals regularly and has come to trust, he could possibly be guilty of fraud by abuse of position: see below, § 15.5.

[100] This view is also taken by *Smith, Hogan, and Ormerod*, § 22.3.2.1 and by the editors of *Archbold* (2026), § 21-327.

this means when the maker spoke it, whether or not it was heard; in the case of a letter, it would be when it was posted; and in the case of an email, it would be "made" when it was sent. Although a representation, by its nature, must be intended to reach someone, there seems to be no reason why in law a "false representation" must be made to an identified individual, and we suggest that the offence potentially covers acquisitive lies uttered to the world in general: for example, by a fraudulent advertisement in a newspaper,[101] or in the following situation with which most readers are likely to be familiar.

> David, having acquired a list of 20,000 email addresses, sends them all an email falsely informing them that they have won a lottery, and that they can claim their prize by sending an "administrative fee", by Western Union, to D's address in Tobleronia.

*(d) False representations made to systems and devices*

Under the former law of deception, only persons could be deceived.[102] This left some serious gaps in the control of fraudulent conduct. For instance, in *Re Holmes*,[103] where D's extradition was sought for a multi-million dollar bank fraud committed in Germany, the Court of Appeal pointed out, with regret, that D would have committed no deception offences in England if, without telling any lies, he had dishonestly secured a bank transfer by using wholly automated processes. To plug this gap, section 2(5) provides:

> For the purposes of this section a representation may be regarded as made if it (or anything implying it) is submitted in any form to any system or device designed to receive, convey or respond to communications (with or without human intervention).The language seems well adapted to its purposes and will help to ensure justice in a case such as *Re Holmes.*

### *(ii) Mens rea*

There are three elements to the mens rea: the false representation must be made dishonestly;[104] it must be made with intent to gain or cause loss, or to expose another to the risk of loss;[105] and it must be made with knowledge that the representation either is untrue or misleading, or that it might be untrue or misleading.[106] We considered the first two of these elements above, in § 15.2.

*(a) Knowledge that the representation is or might be untrue or misleading*

This mens rea element is imported into the definition of a "false representation" by section 2(2)(b). The plainest and least problematic case will be where D knows that his representation is untrue. If D says he is just about to come into a considerable inheritance when he knows that he will receive just £100 from the deceased, he is camped in the territory of

[101] As in the old case of *Silverlock* [1894] 2 QB 766.

[102] See further, 3rd edition, § 15.4(iii)(c).

[103] [2004] EWHC 2020, [2005] 1 WLR 1857; the Court of Appeal also discussed the issue of whether D was guilty here of theft: see above, § 13.5(i)(b).

[104] Section 2(1)(a); above, § 15.2(ii).

[105] Section 2(1)(b); above, § 15.2(i).

[106] Section 2(2). To be guilty, D must of course be subjectively aware that the statement was untrue or misleading. So it is a serious misdirection to tell a jury that D is guilty if he ought to have been aware of this: *Augunas* [2013] EWCA Crim 2046, [2014] 1 Cr App R 241.

fraud when he tells this lie to induce a large loan from V. Also well within the notion of fraudulent behaviour is when D says to V, "I am sure this painting is a genuine Constable", when in reality he is not sure, because he is aware of the distinct possibility that it might be an expert copy.

Yet one soon reaches territory where there is genuine doubt about the propriety of criminalising aspects of D's conduct. It is well known, for instance, that the attribution of paintings to artists long departed can be a matter of fine judgement on which experts of equal standing may disagree. Go back to the assurance that D gives to V about the attribution of a painting to Constable. After claiming that he is so convinced, D adds, "Professor Jones, perhaps our leading Constable scholar, is of that view too". All manner of nuances may be in play here. Professor Jones may well be a leading Constable scholar, but he may be notorious within his scholarly community for his willingness to make positive attributions, particularly when used as a consultant to a leading dealer with a painting of contested provenance to sell. And what if D knows that Professor Jones's positive attribution was a probabilistic, "on the balance of evidence" conclusion and he also knows that Professor Smith, regarded by his peers as *the* Constable scholar, was dismissive of the painting, convinced that it was a copy. As V dithers about spending what for him is a vast sum of money, D remarks that there has been great interest from the United States, a statement based on a tentative email from a US client. And what of V? Is it in point that he is an experienced purchaser of high-value art who will essentially make his own judgement about the value of the painting? Does the analysis change if he is a first-time buyer of high-value art, trusting of and guided by D? Does the fact that fraud by false representation may be proved without proof that anyone was deceived, or that any gain or loss occurred, have any relevance to what constitutes a false representation? Must D's representation be misleading in some general, objective sense or is it enough that D knew it might mislead *V*? If the painting is subsequently shown to be a copy, bought by V at a price well in excess of its true value, a potential prosecutor of D for the offence of fraud by false representation will have much to ponder. (The answer to these problems may be that the representation must be known by its maker to be capable of misleading the person to whom it is made.)[107]

## § 15.4 Fraud by failing to disclose information: section 3

Section 3 of the Fraud Act 2006 makes D liable for fraud if he dishonestly fails to disclose information that he is under a legal duty to disclose, intending by failing to disclose the information to gain for himself or cause loss to another, or to expose another to the risk of loss. The section provides as follows:

**3 Fraud by failing to disclose information**

A person is in breach of this section if he—

(a) dishonestly fails to disclose to another person information which he is under a legal duty to disclose, and

(b) intends, by failing to disclose the information—

  (i) to make a gain for himself or another, or

  (ii) to cause loss to another or to expose another to a risk of loss.

[107] We are grateful to the late Mr Peter Glazebrook for this suggestion.

The core element of this variant of fraud is the breach of a *legal* duty to disclose information. The Law Commission, and at first the government, initially envisaged this limb of the new fraud offence as going wider, and covering not only failure to disclose information that the civil law requires to be disclosed, but also any failure to disclose information which D knows V is trusting him to disclose.[108] This proposed second limb was criticised as liable to bring the criminal law into collision with the civil law, and in particular the *caveat emptor* rule (introduced above). Thus, when a person sells a house, for example, he need not tell the buyer that it is full of woodworm or dry rot, or that the house next door is occupied by the "neighbour from Hell", whose presence is the reason for the sale. This rule comes as a surprise to many people who think that honest sellers would reveal such things; and the proposed second limb could easily have resulted in sellers being successfully prosecuted for fraud for sales the completion of which, in civil law, they would be entitled to enforce.[109] In the light of this objection the government changed its mind, and introduced a Fraud Bill in which the "failure to disclose" limb of the offence was limited to cases where D was under a legal duty to disclose. Thus, where the prosecutor is unable to identify a legal duty, a prosecution for this type of fraud must fail; as, for example where the alleged non-disclosure was the defendant's failure to inform the local council of her residence at a property in respect of which the occupier was obliged to pay council tax, and the relevant legislation imposed no duty on occupiers to volunteer information in the absence of a request.[110] We must therefore ask: to what sort of legal duties does section 3 apply? The following passage from the Law Commission's report is a useful guide:[111]

> "Such a duty may derive from statute (such as provisions governing company prospectuses), from the fact that the transaction in question is one of the utmost good faith (such as a contract for insurance), from the express or implied terms of a contract, from the customs of a particular trade or market, or from the existence of a fiduciary relationship between the parties (such as agent and principal). For this purpose [the fraud offence] there is a legal duty to disclose information not only if the defendant's failure to disclose it gives the victim a cause of action for damages, but also if the law gives the victim the right to set aside any change in his or her legal position to which he or she may consent as a result of non-disclosure. For example, a person in a fiduciary position has a duty to disclose material information when entering into a contract with his or her beneficiary, in the sense that a failure to make such disclosure will entitle the beneficiary to rescind the contract and to reclaim any property transferred under it."

Statutory duties to disclose are very common; but where a duty to disclose is imposed by a statute, that statute usually makes it a criminal offence to fail to comply with it.[112] So, in

[108] Law Com No. 276, *Fraud* (2002); Home Office, *Fraud Law Reform: Consultation on Proposals for Legislation* (2004) § 20.

[109] The *caveat emptor* rule is subject to certain important exceptions—particularly in respect of chattels, when sold in the course of trade or business. In such a sale the seller impliedly guarantees that they are of "satisfactory quality" and, where the buyer's purpose is known to the seller, that they are "fit for purpose": Sale of Goods Act 1979, s. 14, and for consumer sales, Consumer Rights Act 2015, ss. 9 and 10.

[110] *D* [2019] EWCA Crim 209.

[111] Law Com. No. 276, *Fraud* (2002) para. 7.28.

[112] For example, Regulations made under the Public Health (Control of Disease) Act 1984 impose duties on various people to notify the public authorities about a range of dangerous diseases; and by s. 15 of the Act a failure to notify as required is made a criminal offence; and s. 94 of the Road Traffic Act 1988 requires holders of driving licences to inform the Secretary of State (DVLA) if they are aware that they suffer from certain medical conditions.

practice, a failure to fulfil a statutory duty to disclose is likely to be prosecuted as an offence under the legislation that created it, rather than as an offence of fraud, even where it is done with intent to make a gain or cause a loss (or a risk of loss). In practice, most failures to disclose that result in prosecutions for the offence of fraud are likely to arise from contracts. A legal duty to disclose can arise from a contract in a number of different ways.

First, and most obviously, D may be bound by a contract to V which imposes on him an ongoing obligation to disclose certain matters as and when they happen. For example, a supervisor in a supermarket might be required by his contract of employment to report thefts or other pieces of grave misconduct by the other staff. If D noticed an assistant commit a theft, and because she was his girlfriend deliberately failed to report it, his failure to disclose might make him guilty of an offence of fraud.[113]

Secondly, some contracts are entered into on the basis that one party has disclosed all material matters to the other. With certain types of contract, notably contracts of insurance, this is the rule unless the parties have agreed otherwise; such contracts are known as contracts of "utmost good faith" or, to lawyers who like Latin, contracts *uberrimae fidei*.[114] Even outside these specific types of contract, it is open to the parties to make any kind of contract on this basis. An employer, for example, could make it a condition of an employment contract that the person appointed must reveal his criminal convictions (if any). In either of these situations there would clearly be a legal duty to disclose, and a non-disclosure could potentially result in criminal liability for fraud if the other elements of the offence—in particular, dishonesty and a sufficient causal link between the failure to disclose and the intended gain, loss or risk of loss[115]—were present.[116]

Another case of "legal duty to disclose" arising in the field of contract is where a person induces a contract by making a representation that is true at the time, but which, by the time the contract is carried out, has been falsified by events. In this situation the law treats the original representation as "continuing"; the deliberate failure to correct it then constitutes a misrepresentation, which—like any other misrepresentation—gives the innocent party the right to rescind the contract.[117] Here a fraudulent failure to point out the true position could presumably also ground a prosecution for fraud under section 3 of the Fraud Act; and in a case like *Rai*[118] (where D omitted to reveal the death of his mother to the Council) there is a possible overlap with fraud by false representation contrary to section 2.

A "legal duty" to disclose could also arise by operation of the law of tort. If D hired V a piece of equipment, intentionally failing to point out that it is electrically unsafe, and V accidentally electrocuted himself when using it, V's tortious claim against D would involve the argument that D owed V, in general terms, a "duty of care", and, in specific terms, a "duty to warn"—which would presumably count as a "legal duty to disclose" for the purpose of triggering criminal liability under section 3, if the other ingredients of the offence were

113 Though probably not done with the intention to cause loss in the sense of a *desire* to do so, D would presumably have "oblique intention", which would be sufficient; see above, § 15.2(i); also § 5.1(iv).

114 Although insurance contracts fall into this category, contracts with mortgage suppliers do not: as was recognised in *White* [2014] EWCA Crim 714, (2014) 2 Cr App R 14 where the Court quashed D's conviction under s. 3 of the Fraud Act for failing to disclose, when obtaining a mortgage, that he was unemployed.

115 See above, § 15.2(a).

116 An example is *Razoq* [2012] EWCA Crim 674, where a doctor seeking a post as a locum was required by his potential employer to disclose any disciplinary proceedings to which he was subject, and failed to do so.

117 *With v O'Flanagan* [1936] Ch 575.

118 [2000] 1 Cr App R 242 (CA); see above, § 15.3(i)(a).

present.[119] Some other cases are less clear-cut. One is the situation where, under an exception to the *caveat emptor* rule, a seller impliedly guarantees the quality of the goods she sells. In this situation the seller is civilly liable to the buyer if, unknown to the buyer, the goods contain a hidden defect. But does that mean that the seller is under a "legal duty" to disclose it? A defendant prosecuted for fraud in such a case would presumably argue that she was under a legal duty to deliver goods of satisfactory quality, but that is not the same thing as being under a legal duty to disclose defects. In response, the prosecutor might try to argue that the seller in such a situation impliedly represents that the goods are of satisfactory quality, so making the seller criminally liability for fraud by false representation under section 2. Undeniably, the full enforcement of this form of fraud will involve in-depth consideration of civil law issues. This is entirely appropriate in the context of a modern law of fraud. Here criminal courts will have to address the civil law and the criminal law from a perspective of unity[120] and set aside their reluctance to investigate difficult civil law questions.[121]

From the fact that it is an ingredient in section 3 that D's failure to disclose should be committed with the aim of making a gain or causing a loss it necessarily follows that the failure must be an intentional one. However, section 3 does not tell us whether, in addition to knowing that he has kept quiet about something, D must also be aware that the information was something which the law required him to reveal. Here two well-known principles pull in opposite directions. One is the principle that, where a statute creating an offence consisting of an actus reus is silent on whether mens rea is required, the existence of a mens rea requirement is presumed.[122] The other is that "ignorance of the law is no defence".[123] How this conflict is to be resolved here is not easy. In general, the "ignorance of law is no defence" rule is limited to mistakes about the criminal law—that is, whether a given type of act is a criminal offence—and it does not apply to a mistake of civil law "at one remove" upon which the existence of criminal liability depends. As those legal duties to disclose which trigger criminal liability under section 3 of the Fraud Act are likely to be predominantly imposed by civil law, this would suggest that in this case the mens rea principle prevails. On the other hand, the courts might reason that, as D is protected by a requirement that his behaviour be "dishonest", he does not need the further protection of being guilty only where he knew the law required him to disclose. "OK, I knew it was dishonest not to mention it, but I thought it was legal" is not, after all, a line of defence that is likely to engage much judicial sympathy.

## § 15.5 Fraud by abuse of position

Section 4 of the Fraud Act is as follows:

**4 Fraud by abuse of position**

(1) A person is in breach of this section if he—

(a) occupies a position in which he is expected to safeguard, or not to act against, the financial interests of another person,

(b) dishonestly abuses that position, and

[119] If the defect in the equipment makes it dangerous to the user and D provides it in the course of business, it is more likely that he would be prosecuted for an offence under s. 3 of the Health and Safety at Work etc. Act 1974.

[120] Avoiding the incoherence exemplified by the decision in *Hinks* [2001] 2 AC 241; see above, § 13.6(ii)(c).

[121] As in *Morris* [1984] AC 320, 334; above, § 13.6(ii).

[122] *Sweet v Parsley* [1970] AC 132; above, § 6.1.

[123] Below, § 18.2.

(c) intends, by means of the abuse of that position—
(i) to make a gain for himself or another, or
(ii) to cause loss to another or to expose another to a risk of loss.

(2) A person may be regarded as having abused his position even though his conduct consisted of an omission rather than an act.

According to the Law Commission, this offence is intended for the situation in which D is in a position in which she "is expected" to act in a certain kind of way, and abuses it by acting otherwise. Unlike the offence of fraud by failure to disclose, there is no requirement here that the "expectation" that D behave in a particular kind of way should have any legal teeth attached to it. The offence applies, obviously, where the obligation D is under to safeguard V's financial interests is one imposed by the civil law, but in principle it equally applies where his obligation is a purely moral one. It is enough that D, in the position that he occupies, "is expected" to safeguard V's financial interests.

The Act does not identify the person who should do the expecting. The Law Commission clearly envisaged that this person was V. Thus in their report they said that

> "The essence of the kind of relationship which in our view should be a prerequisite of this form of the offence is that *the victim* has voluntarily put the defendant in a privileged position, by virtue of which the defendant is expected to safeguard the victim's financial interests or given power to damage those interests."[124]

However, the requirement that the relationship be one that V has voluntarily created is not reflected in the way that section 4 is drafted; in consequence, the offence is also committed where D is placed in the position that he abuses not by V, but by operation of the law. Thus it potentially applies not only where (for example) V has chosen to empower D to act on his behalf by a lasting power of attorney, but also where X has died nominating D as executor of a will of which V is a beneficiary, and in the situation where V is mentally incapable and a civil court, without V being aware of this, has made an order authorising D to manage V's affairs. This, we believe, is right, because, although a person who abuses either of these positions will often in the process commit fraud by failure to disclose, or even theft, situations could arise in which D's dishonest abuse of one of these positions would otherwise fall outside the reach of the criminal law.[125]

In these two cases, and in many others, D's obligation to safeguard V's financial position will be a legal one. Indeed, very often D will owe V what the law calls a "fiduciary duty",[126] though a fiduciary relationship, at least in its traditional forms, will not be necessary. In a passage from its report later reprinted in the government's Explanatory Notes, the Law Commission gave the following thumbnail sketch of the range of relationships it had in mind when devising the offence.

> "The necessary relationship will be present between trustee and beneficiary, director and company, professional person and client, agent and principal, employee and employer, or between partners. It may arise otherwise, for example within a family, or in the context of voluntary work, or in any context where the parties are not at arm's length. In nearly all cases where it arises, it will be recognised by the civil law as importing fiduciary duties, and any relationship that is so recognised will suffice. We see no reason, however, why the existence of such

124 Law Com. No. 276, *Fraud* (2002) para. 7.37 (emphasis added).

125 For example, if under s. 18 of the Mental Capacity Act 2005 the court made an order authorising D to run V's business, and D then deliberately ran V's business down by diverting V's customers to his own.

126 See above, § 13.5.

duties should be essential. This does not of course mean that it would be entirely a matter for the fact-finders whether the necessary relationship exists. The question whether the particular facts alleged can properly be described as giving rise to that relationship will be an issue capable of being ruled upon by the judge and, if the case goes to the jury, of being the subject of directions."[127]

It will be clear from this that the offence of fraud by abuse of position provides a relatively straightforward means of deterring and punishing a number of forms of dishonesty that are worthy of the attention of the criminal law, but which can be brought within the scope of other offences of dishonesty only with difficulty, if at all. One such group comprises acquisitive family members, neighbours, or acquaintances who batten on vulnerable people and relieve them of their money or other property by inducing them to make them gifts or exorbitant payments for minor services, or otherwise financially abuse them. As we saw earlier, the House of Lords contrived to bring one example of this behaviour within the ambit of the crime of theft—albeit at the cost of tension between the criminal and civil law—in *Hinks*;[128] but other cases, similar in principle, can be imagined which could not be brought within the scope of theft—for example, if instead of persuading a vulnerable person to give him money, D induced him to allow D to use or occupy his property without payment, thereby avoiding the need to pay rent somewhere else. Another unscrupulous person who would seem to be caught by section 4 is the tradesman who regularly supplies V with goods or services, building up over the course of time a relationship in which V comes to trust him, but then abuses V's trust by charging him prices that are far above the going rate. In *Silverman*,[129] the Court of Appeal said that a defendant who had grossly overcharged two elderly women for rewiring and redecorating a house could be guilty of the (now abolished) offence of obtaining property by deception:[130] given the situation of mutual trust, which had built up over a number of years, D had impliedly represented that his firm would derive no more than a modest profit from the work. We suggest that, should these facts occur again, such a defendant would now be guilty of the offence of fraud by abuse of position.

Another previously troublesome group for which this offence provides a straightforward solution are dishonest employees who take bribes, make secret profits, or otherwise enrich themselves at the expense of their employers.[131] As a well-established feature of contracts of employment is a "duty of trust and confidence" which is mutual, and hence applies to employers as well as to employees,[132] it follows that dishonest employers who cheat their employees fall within the potential reach of the offence as well. So it was no surprise when, in *Col v DPP*,[133] the Divisional Court ruled that an employer who exploited a vulnerable Filipino domestic servant by paying her less than her contracted wages and making her work longer hours could be prosecuted for fraud by abuse of position.[134]

[127] Law Com. No. 276, *Fraud* (2002) para. 738.
[128] [2001] 2 AC 241; see above, § 13.6(ii)(c).
[129] (1988) 86 Cr App R 213 (CA); also *Stevens* (1844) 1 Cox CC 83.
[130] Theft Act 1968, s. 15.
[131] See above, 13.5(i)(b) and (c).
[132] *Malik v Bank of Credit and Commerce International SA* [1998] AC 20; and see Freedland *et al.* (eds.), *The Contract of Employment* (2016).
[133] [2022] EWHC 601 (Admin).
[134] Another possible application could be to the directors of a company who neglect to maintain payments to the employees' pension fund in order to spend on dividends to shareholders: see Spencer, "The Criminal Liability of Directors Whose Companies Collapse" [2016] 10 *Archbold Review* 5.

The outer limits of the section 4 offence were explored in *Valujevs*.[135] In that case, D was an unlicensed[136] gangmaster whose business was providing labourers for Fenland farmers. He was accused, among other things, of fraud by abuse of position, on the basis of his having undertaken the payment of the labourers' wages, from which he had been making exorbitant deductions. In interlocutory proceedings, the Court of Appeal ruled that the proceedings on this count could properly proceed. The key ingredient in section 4 is an "expectation" that D would safeguard and not act against the financial interests of another. Such an expectation exists, the Court said, if a reasonable third person, viewing the arrangement from outside, would expect D so to behave: "It would be untenable to suggest that the expectation should be that of either the potential victim (the test would, in all likelihood, be too low) or the defendant (the test is likely to be set too high)."[137] In a jury trial, it added, the judge should first decide whether the defendant's position could potentially satisfy this test; if so, it was then for the jury to decide if it does.

The Court further qualified its remarks by saying that, although the section 4 offence does not require a "fiduciary duty" in the strict legal sense,[138] it does require "an obligation that is akin" to one. So section 4 "does not apply to those who simply supply accommodation, goods, services or labour, whether on favourable or unfavourable terms and whether or not they have a stronger bargaining position."[139]

If fraud by abuse of position has the advantage of flexibility, it also has the corresponding disadvantage of being distinctly vague. As put forward by the Law Commission, the offence would have been limited to an abuse of position that was carried out covertly: in the Draft Bill attached to Law Commission's Report, an ingredient in the proposed offence was that the defendant "dishonestly *and secretly* abuses that position". But even this modest limitation did not appeal to the government,[140] and it is not reflected in the drafting of the Act. Apart from those discussed above, the only limiting requirement in the definition of the offence appears to be that D must have entered into, or been placed in, a relationship with V that is more than merely transitory. The result is that, as so often with the Fraud Act 2006, the only real limit to the offence is dishonesty, which as we saw earlier means the *Ghosh* test, as truncated by *Ivey v Genting* and *Barton*.[141] This variety of the offence of fraud has the potential to catch a range of unscrupulously acquisitive people who in moral terms deserve the attention of the criminal law. It could also, however, potentially catch a range of people whom there is no pressing need to bring within the criminal law at all—and even some whose behaviour, if improper, falls far outside the scope of what most people would regard as fraud: for example, the employee who is persistently late for work, or persistently

[135] [2014] EWCA Crim 2888, [2015] QB 745.

[136] The Gangmasters (Licensing) Act 2004 imposes a compulsory licensing regime, with the aim of controlling abuses of the type seen here.

[137] [2014] EWCA Crim 2888, [2015] QB 745, [41].

[138] For an explanation, see § 13.5(i)(c) above.

[139] [2014] EWCA Crim 2888, [2015] QB 745, [43].

[140] Having floated the idea of including this requirement in *Fraud Law Reform—Consultation on Proposals for Legislation* (May 2004), the government eventually rejected it lest it "lead to technical arguments in court", concluding that "the value-laden concepts of 'dishonesty' and 'abuse' were sufficient in themselves to set the parameters for the offence". *Fraud Law Reform, Government Response to Consultations* (2004) §§ 28–9.

[141] *Ghosh* [1982] QB 1053 (CA); *Ivey v Genting* [2017] UKSC 67, [2018] AC 391; *Barton* [2020] EWCA Crim 575, [2021] QB 685. These cases are discussed above in § 13.8(iv); see also § 15.2 above and, further, Ormerod, "The Fraud Act 2006: Criminalising Lying?" [2007] *Crim LR* 193, 209.

shirks when he gets there.[142] It is therefore reassuring, at least to some limited extent, that the official guidance issued to the CPS on the exercise of the discretion to prosecute under the Fraud Act 2006[143] says that "Prosecutors should guard against the criminal law being used as a debt collection agency or to protect the commercial interests of companies and organisations".

## § 15.6 Possessing, making and supplying articles for use in frauds

By turning the main offence of fraud into a "conduct offence" instead of a "result offence", the Fraud Act 2006 widened the net of criminal liability, in particular by pushing backwards the point in time at which a move in the direction of a crime turns into a completed criminal offence. This effect is accentuated by the fact that the Act also creates two backup offences: possessing articles for use in frauds and making or supplying articles for use in frauds. These two offences were the brainchild not of the Law Commission, which devised the new tripartite offence of fraud, but of the Home Office. It justified them by referring to the existing offence of "going equipped"—that is to say, being out and about carrying the necessary equipment—to commit various offences under the Theft Act,[144] which it said "merits reconsideration".[145] By "reconsideration" it meant "major extension", and a major extension of this form of inchoate liability is what these two new offences have achieved.

The possession offence is created by section 6(1):

> A person is guilty of an offence if he has in his possession or under his control any article for use in the course of or in connection with any fraud.

This offence goes far beyond the "going equipped" provision in section 25 of the Theft Act from which it supposedly derived, because it applies where D possesses or controls the article anywhere, including in the privacy of his home. It is also very broad, because it covers the possession of "any article for use in the course of or in connection with any fraud". So it includes not only articles that have been made or adapted for this purpose, but also, potentially, articles whose normal use is innocent (e.g. a jerrycan for storing petrol).[146] Taken to the limit, it would seem to cover the possession (or control) of a pencil or a pen, which D—or even someone else—intends to use to complete a form making a fraudulent insurance claim, or to write a begging letter with a lie in it. In the light of this, it was a welcome development when the Court of Appeal in *Sakalauskas*[147] made it clear that a person is only

[142] An employee "occupies a position in which he is expected to safeguard, or not act against, the financial interests" of his employer, and there is therefore a strong argument under section 4 that by behaving in this way he is acting against them. If prosecuted for fraud, he might argue that he acted without the necessary intention to make a gain or cause a loss; though this argument might fail, because, as we saw in § 15.2, an oblique intention appears to be enough.

[143] Published on the website of the Crown Prosecution Service; online at http://www.cps.gov.uk/legal/d_to_g/fraud_act/#a10.

[144] Theft Act 1968, s. 25. In its original form the offence was going equipped for any "burglary, theft or cheat"; as amended by the Fraud Act 2006, it is now limited to going equipped for any "burglary or theft".

[145] Home Office, *Fraud Law Reform—Consultation on Proposals for Legislation* (2004).

[146] As in *Sakalauskas* [2013] EWCA Crim 2278, [2014] 1 WLR 1204, discussed below in the text.

[147] *Ibid.*

guilty of the possession offence when the article is intended for use in the commission of an offence and he is actually aware of this.

In *Sakalauskas*, the narrow point before the Court was whether the section 6 offence is limited to the possession of articles meant for future use in fraud, or covers the possession of articles used to commit frauds in the past. The Court decided that it is limited to articles intended for future use.[148] Subsequently in *Smith*,[149] however, the Court of Appeal held that the offence is committed by the defendant's possessing an article that he intended to use to conceal a fraud that he had previously committed. This interpretation seems to follow from the way that section 6 is phrased. As we saw, it covers the possession of articles intended for "use in the course of fraud", and also those intended for use "in connection" with them.

Less worrying on grounds of possible overbreadth is the new offence of making or supplying articles for use in frauds. So far as is relevant, section 7 of the Fraud Act 2006 is as follows:

> (1) A person is guilty of an offence if he makes, adapts, supplies or offers to supply any article—
> (a) knowing that it is designed or adapted for use in the course of or in connection with fraud, or
> (b) intending it to be used to commit, or assist in the commission of, fraud.

As an example of the sort of behaviour this offence is aimed at, the official Explanatory Notes mention the person who makes and markets "black boxes" which dishonest householders can fit to electricity meters, causing them to run slow or backwards.[150] This is conduct which the House of Lords in *Hollinshead*[151] managed, with some difficulty, to squeeze into the offence of conspiracy to defraud, but it obviously extends to catch those who produce equipment that is capable of causing damage that is much more extensive. Section 8(1) makes it clear that "article" includes "any program or data held in electronic form". So it would cover, for example, computer equipment for cloning credit cards.

Unlike the possession offence, section 7 is drafted so as to impose clear limits upon its scope. The actus reus requires positive conduct in the form of "making, adapting, supplying or offering", and there is a strong mens rea requirement too: to be guilty, D must either know that the equipment is designed or adapted for use in fraud, or intend that it be so used. Knowing that the equipment *may* or even *probably will* be these things is not sufficient.

## § 15.7 Dishonestly obtaining services

The Theft Act 1968 gave ample protection to owners against dishonest invasions or acquisitions of their property rights, but provided little, if any, protection against dishonesty for those who provided services. In 1978 this problem was addressed by the creation of a new offence of obtaining services by deception.[152] However, that offence was limited to obtaining

[148] Applying *Ellames* [1974] 1 WLR 1391 (CA), a decision on the Theft Act 1968, s. 25(1) offence of "going equipped".
[149] [2020] EWCA Crim 38, [2020] 1 Cr App R 23.
[150] Explanatory Notes, § 28.
[151] [1985] AC 975.
[152] Theft Act 1978, s. 1, enacted in response to the Thirteenth Report of the Criminal Law Revision Committee: *Section 16 of the Theft Act 1968* Cmnd. 6733 (1977).

services by telling lies and did not cover the situation where, without deception, a dishonest person simply helped himself to them. Though this difficulty was partly met by various specific offences, like the offence under the Railway Regulation Act 1889 of travelling on trains without payment of the fare,[153] this was thought to be an undesirable gap in the law. Therefore, the Fraud Act 2006 abolished the offence of obtaining services by deception, and section 11 created in its place a wider offence of obtaining services dishonestly.

The section 11 offence is committed where a person "obtains services for himself or another by a dishonest act".[154] Hence an obtaining *is* required. The offence is not defined in the inchoate mode, bucking the trend of recent fraud offences noted above.[155] It is limited, however, to services which are provided in the expectation that they will be paid for or have been paid for, and the person who obtains them knows that they are (or might be) provided on this basis and intends to get them without payment, or without paying the full price.[156] Unlike the offence of making off without payment, which is discussed in the next section, the offence is not restricted to services the payment for which is legally enforceable. Thus it is an offence under section 11 of the Fraud Act to obtain the sexual services of a sex worker dishonestly, although it is not the offence of making off without payment if, having obtained them without dishonesty, the customer runs off without paying.

The offence of dishonestly obtaining services is not committed, however, by dishonestly obtaining services which are rendered, and meant to be rendered, free of charge. Thus a dishonest householder who, by falsely claiming to have injured his back, persuades his trusting neighbour to carry his furniture downstairs as a good turn would not be guilty of the offence; and it would make no difference if the neighbour were by trade a furniture remover, who normally charged for his work.[157] *A fortiori* there would be no criminal liability under section 11 in a case like *Jheeta*,[158] where, by an elaborate fraud, D persuaded his girlfriend V to continue having sexual intercourse with him.

By section 11(2)(b), it is an ingredient in the offence that the defendant obtains the services "without any payment having been made for or in respect of them or without payment having been made in full". Rather surprisingly, section 11 does not state that this means payment by or on behalf of the defendant. From this omission, it seemingly follows that the offence would not be committed if the service the defendant dishonestly obtained was paid for, but by someone else—as might happen if the defendant obtained the service by making unauthorised use of a credit card or debit card, in circumstances where the credit company or bank then paid the bill.[159] Nonetheless, in this situation, the defendant would usually be guilty of some other fraud offence, such as fraud by false representation.

[153] Railway Regulation Act 1889, s. 5(3); cf. art. 143 of the Air Navigation Order 2009/3015, which makes it a criminal offence to stow oneself away upon an aircraft.

[154] Fraud Act 2006, s. 11(1).

[155] Above § 15.1.

[156] Fraud Act 2006, s. 11(2).

[157] Though in such a case D would commit the offence of fraud by false representation; under s. 5(4), a "loss" includes a loss "by not getting what one might get"; so the false representation causes the neighbour a loss if he would otherwise have charged for what he did.

[158] [2007] EWCA Crim 1699, [2008] 1 WLR 2582; see above, § 12.3(iii)(b).

[159] On this possibility, see also *Smith, Hogan, and Ormerod*, § 22.6.2.4.

## § 15.8 Making off without payment

Section 3 of the Theft Act 1978 is as follows:

**Making off without payment.**
(1) Subject to subsection (3) below, a person who, knowing that payment on the spot for any goods supplied or service done is required or expected from him, dishonestly makes off without having paid as required or expected and with intent to avoid payment of the amount due shall be guilty of an offence.
(2) For purposes of this section "payment on the spot" includes payment at the time of collecting goods on which work has been done or in respect of which service has been provided.
(3) Subsection (1) above shall not apply where the supply of the goods or the doing of the service is contrary to law, or where the service done is such that payment is not legally enforceable.

This offence was created to deal with the specific problem of the person who runs off without paying. If she was dishonest from the outset and obtained the goods or services when she never had any intention of paying for them, she is likely to be guilty of a range of other offences, including fraud by false representation; if she actually obtains property or services, then the offences she is guilty of are theft or dishonestly obtaining services. However, there is a problem if D was initially honest but changed her mind only after the property or services had been obtained. If, for example, D intends to pay for a meal in a restaurant at the time she orders it, she does not commit an offence of fraud by false representation when she places the order. If she still intends to pay for it when it is served and she eats it, she is not then dishonest and she commits no offence of theft. Furthermore, when she eats the food it becomes her property, and if she later decides to run away without paying she commits no theft because, although she is now dishonest, she does not appropriate "property belonging to another". If it is property at all, the half-digested meal now in her stomach belongs in law to her and her alone. Unlike the case where V gives D money which D pays into her bank account, there is no room for argument here that the restaurateur retains some form of residual ownership, in respect of which he can be regarded as the victim of a theft. Unlike dishonest savers, dishonest diners cannot be made to disgorge *in specie* their ill-gotten gains. It was to fill this gap in the law that this offence was created.[160]

Though this provision is clearly drafted, it leaves open two points of doubt, both of which have been answered in the case law. The first is whether the phrase "with intent to avoid payment" means with the intention of avoiding it permanently or whether—subject to the requirement of dishonesty—D is also guilty if she intends to pay later. In *Allen*,[161] the House of Lords held that D is guilty only where she intends to avoid payment permanently. The second is the scope of the phrase "makes off". This clearly covers sneaking away or running away (and, indeed, strolling away, eye-balling the restaurateur as she goes, where D is bigger and more muscular than V). But does it cover the case where D tells V a lie that persuades V to consent to her leaving? In *Vincent*,[162] the Court of Appeal held that it does not. Unlike

[160] Criminal Law Revision Committee, Thirteenth Report, *Section 16 of the Theft Act 1968* Cmnd. 6733 (1977). Spencer, "The Theft Act 1978" [1979] *Crim LR* 24. Other legal systems have also found it necessary to create a special offence to deal with this form of dishonesty; see art. 313-5 of the French *Code pénal* ("*filouterie*").
[161] [1985] AC 1029.
[162] [2001] 2 Cr App R 150 (CA).

in the case of theft, the courts have declined to interpret this offence extensively, and have resolved its ambiguities in favour of the defendant.

As is the case in fraud, "dishonestly" is determined according to the test in *Ivey* and *Barton* and the standards of ordinary and decent people. Also, as noted above in relation to fraud,[163] there is here no equivalent of the "claim of right" provisions in theft.[164] Consider an incident reported in the local press, of a woman who, on discovering her bicycle had been stolen and then brazenly advertised for sale, posed as a purchaser to secure a "test ride", whereupon she rode the bicycle off without returning to pay.[165] If charged with theft, she would have a good defence by virtue of claim of right under section 2 of the Theft Act. If charged with fraud by false representation, her dishonesty or otherwise would turn on the *Ivey/Barton* standards of ordinary decent people. So far as the dishonesty element is concerned, the same would be true if she were charged with making off without payment. Interestingly, however, section 3(3) of the 1978 Act would play a role here to provide a defence, given the supply of the goods would be "contrary to law".

## § 15.9 Conspiracy to defraud

Prior to the Fraud Act 2006, there was no general criminal offence of fraud. The defrauding of one individual by another did not *per se* constitute a crime.[166] For the most part, fraud was criminalised historically through more specific offences, which addressed particular forms of economic activity when done with a fraudulent intent.[167]

However, the common law does recognise an offence of *conspiracy* to defraud, operative where the fraud involves two or more persons acting together.[168] The essence of the offence is an agreement to practise a fraud on somebody.[169] In *Scott*,[170] the House of Lords thought it "clearly the law" that:

> "an agreement by two or more by dishonesty to deprive a person of something which is his or to which he is or would be or might be entitled and an agreement by two or more by dishonesty to injure some proprietary right of his, suffices to constitute the offence of conspiracy to defraud."

Although its importance has diminished with the enactment of various statutory offences, especially the Fraud Act 2006, conspiracy to defraud remains a catch-all offence covering conduct that does not fall under other substantive fraud offences. The scope of the crime is extremely wide, because of the broad definition of fraud; especially the fact that the

[163] Above § 15.2 (ii).

[164] Above § 13.8 (i)–(iii).

[165] Reported in *Bristol Live*, 15 July 2017. https://www.bristolpost.co.uk/news/bristol-news/woman-tells-dramatic-moment-stole-203259

[166] *Wheatly* (1761) 2 Burr 1125, 97 ER 746. An exception was the old offence of cheat, which was confined to fraud "in a subject concerning the public, which, as between subject and subject, would only be actionable by a civil action": *Bembridge* (1783) 22 St Tr 1, 99 ER 679 (Lord Mansfield).

[167] See Smith, *Property Offences* (1994), esp. chap. 22.

[168] *Hevey* (1782) 1 Leach 232, 168 ER 218. See Hadden, "Conspiracy to Defraud" (1966) 24 *CLJ* 248; Gillies, "The Offence of Conspiracy to Defraud" (1977) 51 *ALJ* 247.

[169] *Wai Yu-tsang v R* [1991] 4 All ER 664 (PC).

[170] *Scott v Metropolitan Police Commissioner* [1975] AC 819, 840 (Viscount Dilhorne).

conspiracy need not be to commit an offence, but may also be to commit a civil wrong;[171] and according to some old authorities, perhaps certain kinds of moral wrongs.[172] For these reasons, the offence might be thought prima facie objectionable and one to be used sparingly. Its broad language offers little guidance to prospective offenders—by contrast, a series of offences each of which specifies an actus reus more narrowly offers better guidance to citizens, by warning clearly that proposed conduct falls within the reach of the criminal law.[173]

Furthermore, the offence makes illegal conduct by two defendants that may not be criminal when done by only one.[174] It is hard to see how that distinction between individual and group, and its very serious consequences, are justified. Why does the moral character of an ordinary civil or moral wrong change, *so much so that it becomes a crime*, simply because it is perpetrated by two rather than one?[175] The anomaly created by conspiracy to defraud is, moreover, difficult to reconcile with the ordinary crime of conspiracy *per se*,[176] which requires that the conduct conspired at should itself be an offence.

Aggravating these problems is the difficulty of drawing a boundary between mere sharp practice in the commercial sphere and criminal dishonesty. The two shade into each other,[177] and in practice it may be the element of conspiracy that redesignates a transaction from unscrupulous to illegal. Perhaps as a consequence of this, in the public mind fraud has tended to lack the graphic moral character of theft or handling, and there is a continuing debate whether commercial malpractice is a proper subject for "public law", or whether it should primarily be dealt with by civil law mechanisms; particularly since such wrongdoing is often perceived to be victimless, in that there may be no identifiable individual who is directly and immediately out of pocket as a result of the defendant's activities.[178] Even where the activities are regulated by criminal law, the law's control mechanisms are different from those for street crime, in terms of the social standing of the suspects, and in terms

[171] *Warburton* (1870) LR 1 CCR 274; *Weaver* (1931) 45 CLR 321, 334. In *Potter* [1953] 1 All ER 296 (Assizes (Leeds)), a recalcitrant debenture-holder entered into an agreement whereby he was guaranteed an additional 7 shillings in the pound on his debentures from an outside source, in return for his agreement to a scheme whereby all debenture holders were to agree to a composition of 8 shillings in the pound. D's counsel argued that the private agreement was merely unenforceable or void as a fraudulent preference, and did not constitute an indictable offence. Cassells J disagreed, holding that there was an indictable offence of conspiracy, although at trial both defendants were acquitted.

[172] *Timothy* (1858) 1 F & F 39, 175 ER 616; *Heymann v R.* (1873) LR 8 QB 102, 105; cf. *Weaver* (1931) 45 CLR 321, 346–7 (but see at 349). These authorities might not be followed after *Norris* v *US* [2008] UKHL 16, [2008] AC 920 and *Goldshield plc* [2008] UKHL 17, [2009] 1 WLR 458; see below. Moreover, in recent years it has been repeatedly stated that the agreement needed for a conspiracy to defraud must include an element of unlawfulness in its object or means. It cannot comprise an agreement to achieve a lawful object by lawful means: *Evans* [2014] 1 WLR 2817, [138]–[160]; *Barton* [2020] EWCA Crim 575, [2021] QB 685; *Hayes* [2025] UKSC 29, [2025] 1 WLR 3553, [49]. Some *obiter* comments of Lord Leggatt in the Supreme Court in *Hayes* (e.g. [216]) appear to go further. See below § 15.9 (ii).

[173] See the discussion of fair warning, above, § 2.3.

[174] This too is disapproved of in obiter comments by Lord Leggatt in *Hayes* [2025] UKSC 29, [2025] 1 WLR 3553. See below, § 15.9 (ii).

[175] For an argument that the moral character of the wrong changes when there is conspiracy, see Dennis, "The Rationale of Criminal Conspiracy" (1977) 93 *LQR* 39. But Dennis does not suggest that the moral character of the defendants' activities changes so drastically that a conspiracy to do a mere civil wrong (let alone lawful acts) should be criminalised.

[176] Contrary to s. 1(1) of the Criminal Law Act 1977. See above, § 9.3.

[177] According to the Law Commission, Law Com. No. 276, *Fraud* (2002) para. 1.6, "the common law offence of conspiracy is so wide that it offers little guidance on the difference between fraudulent and lawful conduct".

[178] See the general discussion at the beginning of this chapter.

of the comparative immunity of "white-collar crimes" from police surveillance or normal criminal prosecution.[179] Nonetheless, serious commercial fraud has increased considerably, and is extremely costly to society in economic terms. No doubt this is attributable to the evolution of commercial practices.[180] Modern credit economies enable fraudsters to manipulate wealth in large denominations, without being constrained by having to deal with its physical manifestation. The techniques of wrongdoing multiply as the variety and complexity of financial transactions increases, requiring specialist knowledge to initiate, process, and, above all, monitor. This changing nature of commercial and financial life presents at least one reason for retention of a fall-back crime such as conspiracy to defraud, since it may be impossible for specific legislation constantly to keep up with the mutating ways in which fraud may be committed, especially given modern communications and computing innovations, and the globalisation of securities and other markets.[181]

The elements of conspiracy to defraud are:

(i) an agreement between two or more persons;
(ii) that contemplates using fraudulent means;
(iii) to prejudice the rights of another person, or to induce another to act contrary to her public duty;
(iv) dishonesty and an intention to carry out the agreement.

We consider these elements in turn.

### *(i) Agreement with another person*

The law on this point is the same as for ordinary conspiracy.[182] There must be an act of agreement, constituting a joint decision to commit the fraud (even if not all parties will actually perform the agreed offence). Preliminary negotiations or discussions regarding the possibility of doing something fraudulent, which do not crystallise into any firm decision, are insufficient.[183] Neither is there a conspiracy where the parties each have the same thought or intention, but have not communicated this to each other: a concurrence between two people of "mere wicked thoughts not intended to be acted upon"[184] will not do. The joint decision required for conspiracy exists only if there is a genuine agreement to defraud between the parties.

In general, there are three kinds of conspiratorial agreement. The simplest variety is where each conspirator is aware of the existence of all the others and knows that they are

[179] Levi, *Regulating Fraud* (1987) 15. See also Hadden, "Fraud in the City: The Role of the Criminal Law" [1983] *Crim LR* 500.

[180] Cf. Hall, *Theft, Law and Society* (2nd ed., 1952) 300.

[181] See Sullivan, "Fraud and the Efficacy of the Criminal Law: A Proposal for a Wide Residual Offence" [1985] *Crim LR* 616; McBarnet and Whelan, "The Elusive Spirit of the Law: Formalism and the Struggle for Legal Control" (1991) 54 *MLR* 848; Smith, "Conspiracy to Defraud: Some Comments on the Law Commission's Report" [1995] *Crim LR* 209.

[182] See the more detailed discussion above, in § 9.3(ii); also Orchard, "'Agreement' in Criminal Conspiracy" [1974] *Crim LR* 297 and 335.

[183] This is the explanation of *Walker* [1962] Crim LR 458 (CA). D had participated in discussions about a planned payroll robbery, but later withdrew. His conviction was quashed as it was not proven that the discussions had progressed beyond the stage of negotiation before his withdrawal. See above, § 9.3(ii)(c); also *Barnard* (1980) 70 Cr App R 28 (CA).

[184] *Banks* (1873) 12 Cox CC 393, 399.

parties to the agreement. The second, more complex, case is the "wheel" (or "cartwheel") conspiracy, where A, B, and C (the spokes) are all individually in contact with D (the hub), but have never met each other.[185] The third variant is the "chain" conspiracy, where A contacts B, who contacts C, who contacts D, and so on.[186] However, it is important not to roll up a number of separate transactions in one conspiracy charge. This point is made in *Griffiths*,[187] where a lime supplier (Griffiths), his accountant, and seven farmers whom Griffiths supplied were charged with conspiracy to defraud the government of subsidies. Their convictions were quashed on appeal, as there was no evidence of any collusion between the farmers, either directly or through the intermediation of Griffiths, but only of separate conspiracies between the supplier and individual farmers.[188]

Like statutory conspiracy, a conspiracy to defraud, once formed, does not admit of withdrawal. After an agreement is reached, and the other elements are established, the crime of conspiracy to defraud is complete and it is irrelevant that subsequently one party decides, or all of the parties decide, to abandon the agreement.[189]

### *(ii) By fraudulent means*

The conspiracy must involve the use of fraudulent or dishonest means.[190] To illustrate the importance of this requirement, suppose that a solicitor acting in her professional capacity agrees to perform services for her client which will cause loss to another party. These facts disclose no conspiracy to defraud unless the services go beyond her ordinary duties as a solicitor.[191] Similarly, many business decisions do—and are meant to—prejudice the economic interests of rivals, yet one is entitled to neglect those rival interests provided the decision involves a legitimate course of action. Thus, in *Zemmel*,[192] the defendants' agreement to delay paying a creditor was held by the Court of Appeal not to be a conspiracy to defraud. To the extent that the decision is based on the premise that stalling on one's payment obligations, even dishonestly, is not a criminal offence, the example may now be doubted. The case predates the Fraud Act 2006 and if all the elements of fraud can be made out, this conduct might be caught. In particular fraud, unlike theft, does not require an

[185] Cf. *Ex p Coffey, Re Evans* [1971] NSWLR 434.

[186] *Ardalan* [1972] 2 All ER 257 (CA). Note, however, the cautionary words of Roskill LJ (at 262) that "words or phrases such as 'wheels', 'cartwheels', 'chain', 'sub-conspiracies' and so on are used only to illustrate and clarify the principle and for no other purpose".

[187] [1966] 1 QB 589 (CA).

[188] *Ibid.*, 599: "It is right and proper to say that the judge correctly pointed out the principle, saying that the Crown had to prove that the conspirators put their heads together to defraud the Ministry. The trouble is that it never seems to have been considered . . . whether or not in this case each farmer put his head together with Griffiths' head without any thought of a general conspiracy." Hence, although each defendant may have conspired separately with Griffiths, the convictions were unsafe since the defendants should not have been joined in a conglomerate charge.

[189] Above, § 9.3(ii)(d). Cf. *O'Brien* (1955) 2 DLR 311, 314 (Taschereau J): "If a person, with one or several others, agrees to commit an unlawful act, and later, after having had the intention to carry it through, refuses to put the plan into effect, that person is nevertheless guilty".

[190] In *Scott* [1975] AC 819, 840, this criterion is encapsulated in the phrase "by dishonesty", operating as an actus reus element; see the passage quoted above in the text at § 15.9. In order clearly to distinguish it from the mens rea component of dishonesty (below, § 15.9(iv)), we refer to this element as "by fraudulent means". Early cases express it in the requirement that a common law conspiracy be either to do an unlawful act or to do a lawful act *by unlawful means*: *Jones* (1832) 4 B & Ad 345, 349, 110 ER 485, 487.

[191] *Tighe and Maher* (1926) 26 SR (NSW) 94.

[192] (1985) 81 Cr App R 279 (CA).

intention to permanently deprive, its scope stretching to "gain or loss, whether temporary or permanent".[193] However, whether it is a good example or not, it stands for the idea that permissible conduct cannot count as the relevant fraudulent or dishonest means for conspiracy to defraud. Impermissible conduct would plainly include criminal conduct, but does it include mere civil wrongs? This is the normal assumption.[194]

The Supreme Court in *Hayes*,[195] while not citing *Zemmel*, appeared to allude to the case in saying:

> given that refusing to pay a debt, even if known to be due, is not a criminal offence, it would make no sense for the common law to treat agreeing with someone else not to pay a debt (knowing that this will cause loss to the creditor) as a criminal offence.

"Unless", Lord Leggett concluded, "the intended means involves criminal conduct, I see no reason why an agreement to use that means to achieve a lawful object should be a crime".[196] This remark was *obiter* and Ormerod points out that "if the conduct agreed upon by the conspirators must amount to a criminal offence, a charge of statutory conspiracy under section 1 of the Criminal Law Act 1977 will be available in any event".[197] This *obiter* comment could nevertheless potentially be significant: should Lord Leggatt's remarks come to be accepted as the legal position, Ormerod suggests, it may even "signal [the] death knell" of conspiracy to defraud, although the offence "has withstood seemingly mortal wounds before".[198] Until an authoritative judgment, the assumption must be that fraudulent or dishonest means can include civilly wrongful conduct.[199]

On the other hand, the requirement of fraudulent *modus operandi* is quite easily satisfied. Obviously, the use of deceit or falsehood is sufficient (although it would nowadays anyway fall within the scope of section 1 of the Fraud Act 2006). In *Lewis*,[200] for example, it was held that an arrangement made for mock bidding at an auction could be a conspiracy to defraud, since the scheme was intended, through a deception, to induce innocent buyers to bid more than necessary. Similarly, in *A-G's Reference (No. 1 of 1982)*,[201] manufacturing fake whisky was held to be a conspiracy to defraud unknowing purchasers. These are cases where the agreement involved a false representation, express or implied. But conspiracy to defraud has a much wider scope than this. In *Weaver*,[202] the High Court of Australia said that the offence embraces "every kind and description of fraudulent statement, conduct, trick, or device", including "false accounts, fabricated shares, false representations or conduct".[203] Even if there is no representation, many cases will involve deceit; as in *Hollinshead*,[204] where

[193] Above, § 15.2(i). cp. A.T.H. Smith, *Property Offences* (1994) para. 19.23, J.C. Smith, *The Law of Theft* (2nd ed., 1972) paras. 5.57–5.60; Fisher and Arlidge, *Arlidge and Parry on Fraud* (6th ed., 2020) para. 20.028.
[194] See above § 15.9.
[195] [2025] UKSC 29, [2025] 1 WLR 3553, [216].
[196] *Ibid.*
[197] Ormerod "Focus: *Hayes & Palombo* – a 'watershed' judgment", Red Lion Chambers, August 19, 2025. See-https://redlionchambers.co.uk/focus-hayes-palombo-a-watershed-judgment/.
[198] *Ibid.*
[199] See above, § 15.9.
[200] (1869) 11 Cox CC 404.
[201] [1983] QB 751 (CA).
[202] (1931) 45 CLR 321.
[203] *Ibid.*, 334.
[204] [1985] AC 975.

the defendants agreed to manufacture and sell "black box" devices whose only purpose was to cause electricity meters to produce erroneous readings.

Moreover, there is no *requirement* that there be either a falsehood or that anyone must be deceived.[205] In *Scott*,[206] for example, the defendants bribed cinema employees to let them borrow films, which were then copied in breach of copyright. Their behaviour was certainly fraudulent, even though it involved neither falsehood nor deceit.

### *(iii) The object of the conspiracy*

Conspiracy to defraud may be committed in either of two general forms: by conspiring to prejudice the rights of another person, or to induce another to act contrary to her public duty.

#### *(a) To prejudice the rights of another*

The paradigm case of conspiracy to defraud is where D conspires to obtain a benefit at the expense of another's assets. In many cases this can, and should, be charged as a statutory conspiracy; as either conspiracy to steal, or conspiracy to commit the (statutory) offence of fraud under section 1 of the Fraud Act 2006. However, conspiracy to defraud, unlike theft, is not limited to the case where D's plan is to obtain something that is recognised as "property" for the purposes of that offence: thus it encompasses depriving someone of land, or exploiting another's confidential information.

It is possible that the offence may even extend to dishonest plans to interfere with "interests" of a kind that the civil law would not recognise as "property" at all. It has been suggested, for example, that it might cover using dishonest means to persuade a testatrix to change her will in favour of the defendants.[207] This would not be theft even of an equitable interest, since the (erstwhile) potential beneficiaries under a will have merely a *spes successionis*—an expectation or chance of succession—and are not deprived of any proprietary right. However, such an extensive interpretation of interests was rejected by Hickinbottom J in *Evans*.[208] In that case, D and others were directors of a company formed to carry out open-cast coal-mining in South Wales. This operation required licences from various public authorities, which were granted on condition that the land be restored after the coal had been extracted. Hoping to evade this obligation, they allegedly concocted a scheme to transfer the freehold of the sites—together, they hoped, with the obligation to restore the sites—to dummy companies in the British Virgin Islands against whom the public authorities would find it impossible to enforce the conditions of the licences. Hickinbottom J ruled that this conduct did not constitute a conspiracy to

[205] Contrast the definition by Buckley J in *Re London & Globe Finance Corp Ltd* [1903] 1 Ch 728, 732, which (wrongly) suggests that deceit is necessary for fraud: "To deceive is, I apprehend, to induce a man to believe that a thing is true which is false, and which the person practising the deceit knows or believes to be false. To defraud is to deprive by deceit: it is by deceit to induce a man to act to his injury. More tersely it may be put, that to deceive is by falsehood to induce a state of mind; to defraud is by deceit to induce a course of action."

[206] [1975] AC 819. See also *Sinclair* [1968] 1 WLR 1246 (CA); *Hollinshead* [1985] AC 975.

[207] See the commentary by J.C. Smith on *Tillings and Tillings* [1985] Crim LR 393 (CA).

[208] [2014] 1 WLR 2817 (Crown Court (Cardiff)); discussed by Jarvis, "Conspiracy to Defraud: A Siren to Lure Unwary Prosecutors" [2014] *Crim LR* 738.

defraud the public authorities, because their statutory powers to enforce the conditions of the licence did not count as a proprietary interest. *Evans* was a ruling at first instance, which for procedural reasons the Crown was unable to appeal,[209] and it was doubted, *obiter*, by the Court of Appeal.[210] But like the *Norris* case, which is discussed below, it demonstrates a growing unwillingness in the courts to extend the boundaries of conspiracy to defraud.[211]

The core of defrauding is disadvantage to others: usually, deprivation of or prejudice to a victim's interests. So it is not necessary that the purpose of the conspiracy should be to benefit anyone.[212] In *Welham v DPP*, Lord Radcliffe pointed out that:[213]

> "Although in the nature of things [defrauding] is almost invariably associated with the obtaining of an advantage for the person who commits the fraud, it is the effect upon the person who is the object of the fraud that ultimately determines its meaning."

The law thus looks at the effect of the fraud on the victim, irrespective of whether the defendants sought thereby to make a gain.

Further, if we concentrate upon the victim, we find that she may be defrauded even if she suffers no loss. It is sufficient that the conspiracy *puts at risk* the economic, or property, interests or rights of the victim.[214] In *Scott* (above, § 15.9(ii)), a conspiracy to defraud was established notwithstanding that the breach of copyright caused no direct pecuniary loss to the cinema owners, and simply had the potential to deprive them of profits. Similarly, in *Adams v R* it was said by the Privy Council that there may be a conspiracy to defraud based upon an agreement dishonestly to conceal information, where the conspirator is under a duty to disclose it, or upon an agreement dishonestly to withhold information from persons entitled to require its disclosure.[215] This is the case whether or not those persons suffer financial harm as a result.

[209] The judge's ruling was made in response to a defence application, under the Crime and Disorder Act 1998, to dismiss the charges on the ground that the evidence the Crown proposed to call would not justify a conviction. As the law currently stands there is no right of appeal against such a ruling—anomalously, given that a judge's ruling of "no case to answer" when made after the evidence has been called is subject to appeal. The only step open to the Crown in *Evans* was to try to relaunch the proceedings by persuading a High Court Judge to issue a voluntary bill of indictment. This the Crown attempted to do, but without success: see [2015] EWHC 263 (QB), [2015] 1 WLR 3595, and further comment by Jarvis, [2015] *Crim LR* 704.

[210] *H* [2015] EWCA Crim 46, an interlocutory appeal in the prosecution that resulted in *Hayes* [2015] EWCA Crim 1944 (above, § 13.8(iv)).

[211] As part of its case, the Crown alleged that the defendants had, by fraud, induced the company's auditors to release funds which the company had set aside to pay for the restoration—some of which then found its way, via other shell companies, into their own pockets. If proved, these allegations would have supported convictions for a number of other offences, including conspiracy to defraud the company. The growing unwillingness in the courts to extend conspiracy to defraud is also evident on the part of the Supreme Court in *Hayes* [2025] UKSC 29, [2025] 1 WLR 3553.

[212] Cf. *Cope* (1719) 1 Str 144, 93 ER 438.

[213] [1961] AC 103, 123. (D was charged with uttering forged documents with intent to defraud, contrary to s. 6 of the Forgery Act 1912.) Cf. Viscount Dilhorne in *Scott v MPC* [1975] AC 819, 839: "'to defraud' ordinarily means, in my opinion, to deprive a person dishonestly of something which is his or of something to which he is or would or might but for the perpetration of the fraud be entitled".

[214] *Allsop* (1976) 64 Cr App R 29 (CA); *Wai Yu-tsang v R* [1992] 1 AC 269 (PC).

[215] [1995] 1 WLR 52, 65 (PC). The Privy Council held that a conspiracy to defraud existed where company directors dishonestly agreed to conceal information relating to secret profits, so as to impede action by the company to recover those profits. However, there must still be an intention to act to the prejudice of some extant right: "A person is not prejudiced if he is hindered in inquiring into the source of moneys in which he has no interest. He can only suffer prejudice in relation to some right or interest which he possesses."

The victim need not be a particular person, and in the past the offence has been applied to conspiracies to rig markets.[216] In *Norris v Government of the United States of America*,[217] however, the House of Lords held that conspiracy to defraud should not cover this ground. A cartel agreement, it said, does not amount to a conspiracy to defraud in the absence of some aggravating factor, such as "fraud, misrepresentation, violence, intimidation or inducement of a breach of contract".[218] In reaching this decision it was influenced by the notion that, in order to comply with Article 7 of the ECHR, a prohibition imposed by the criminal law must be sufficiently clear and certain, and in this connection it referred to its previous decisions in *Rimmington*[219] and *Jones*.[220] No previous cartel agreement, said the Law Lords, had been held to amount to a conspiracy to defraud where no such aggravating factor was present, and they did not think it right to extend the boundaries of the offence to cover such a situation. In the past, conspiracy to defraud has been a protean offence, often extended by the courts to cover new situations, but from *Norris v USA* (and from *Goldshield Group plc*,[221] which followed and applied it) it seems that its expansive days are past. In 2002, Parliament created a statutory offence of price-fixing, punishable with up to five years' imprisonment,[222] and it is for that offence that those who conspire to rig the market should now be prosecuted. Similarly, Parliament created a statutory offence of "making misleading statements in relation to benchmarks" under section 91(1) of the Financial Services Act 2012. That came too late to lay as the charge against Tom Hayes (and others),[223] since his alleged wrongful interference with the Japanese yen LIBOR rate that led to the charge of conspiracy to defraud occurred between 2006 and 2010. But in future those suspected of conspiring to interfere with benchmarks should be prosecuted under the 2012 Act.

### *(b) To induce another to act contrary to her public duty*

In addition to defrauding particular persons and unascertained persons through the marketplace, the fraud may also be on the "public" at large, where no individual's particular interests (actual or potential) are jeopardised. "Where the intended victim of a 'conspiracy to defraud' is a person performing public duties as distinct from a private individual it is sufficient if the purpose is to cause him to act contrary to his duty."[224] Consequently, there may be a conspiracy fraudulently to obtain a driving licence,[225] National Insurance number,[226] confidential information,[227] or membership of a society.[228] But for this head of

[216] Early authorities include *De Berenger* (1814) 3 M & S 67, 105 ER 536; *Burch* (1865) 4 F & F 407, 176 ER 622; *Aspinall* (1876) 1 QBD 730, affirmed 35 LT 738, 741n; *Scott v Brown, Doering, McNab & Co* (1892) 2 QB 724.

[217] [2008] UKHL 16, [2008] AC 920.

[218] Per Lord Bingham at para. 17.

[219] [2005] UKHL 63, [2006] 2 AC 459; and see above, § 2.2.

[220] [2006] UKHL 16, [2007] 1 AC 136.

[221] [2008] UKHL 17, [2009] 1 WLR 458.

[222] Enterprise Act 2002, Part 6. For an account of the first prosecution under the Act (*Whittle and others* [2008] EWCA Crim 2560), see Lucraft, Payne, and Rawlings, "The Dunlop Three: The Cartel Offence Makes its Debut" [2006] 1 *Archbold News* 7. In order to make it easier to secure convictions, in 2013 Parliament amended s. 188 of the Enterprise Act 2002 to remove "dishonesty" as an element.

[223] Cp. *Hayes* [2025] UKSC 29, [2025] 1 WLR 3553.

[224] *Scott v MPC* [1975] AC 819, 841 (Lord Diplock).

[225] *Potter* [1958] 2 All ER 51 (Assizes (Leicester)).

[226] *Moses & Ansbro* [1991] Crim LR 617 (CA).

[227] *DPP v Withers* [1975] AC 842.

[228] Cf. *Bassey* (1931) 22 Cr App R 160 (CA), where an unqualified student acting alone, who attempted to gain admission to the Inner Temple by the use of forged references and degree certificates, was held to have defrauded the Benchers of that Inn.

conspiracy to defraud it seems that the public official must be caused to *act*, rather than prevented from doing so. In *Evans* (discussed in § 15.9(iii)(a) above), the Crown also failed in an attempt to argue that the defendants were guilty of this alternative form of conspiracy to defraud: their scheme, if intended to prevent the authorities from enforcing the planning conditions, was not intended to cause them to *act* contrary to their duties.

There is some authority that cases involving public officials are not distinctive, but rather illustrations of a more general proposition that conspiracy to defraud does not require an intention to cause loss, so that cases of "public duty" fraud might extend to victims not occupying a public office: "the expression 'intent to defraud' is not to be given a narrow meaning, involving an intention to cause economic loss to another. In broad terms, it means simply an intention to practise a fraud on another, or an intention to act to the prejudice of another man's right."[229] However, that authority should be understood as establishing no more than the proposition set out in the foregoing subsection (§ 15.9(iii)(a)), that it is ordinarily sufficient in conspiracy to defraud that the victim's rights or interests are deliberately put at risk and that there is no need for the conspirators to aim at causing loss.[230] Any wider interpretation should be doubted, since it would further extend an already vague and overbroad offence. Moreover, it would be contrary to House of Lords authority that the public duty cases are a "special line of cases",[231] a separate category,[232] and perhaps a surviving variety of the now-rejected generic wrong of conspiracy to effect a public mischief.[233] Lord Kilbrandon asserts, and defends, the distinctiveness of defrauding a public official most clearly in *Withers v DPP*:[234]

> "Moreover, as regards the first count, I am not prepared to accept that 'officials of banks and building societies' are public officers within the meaning of *Welham v Director of Public Prosecutions* [1961] AC 103. The fact that very many people have bank accounts and some deal with building societies does not change the relationship between institution and customer from a private to a public one. It would be dangerous to use analogy for the purpose of extending a meaning of fraud which has already, for the purposes of the law of conspiracy, gone beyond its common content of prejudice to proprietary rights."

Quite so.

[229] *Wai Yu-tsang v R* [1992] 1 AC 269, 276 (PC); citing Lord Denning's judgment in *Welham v DPP* [1961] AC 103, 133.

[230] This analysis would explain the rejection of Lord Diplock's separate categorisation in *Scott v Metropolitan Police Commissioner* [1975] AC 819, 841 by the Privy Council in *Wai Yu-tsang v R* [1992] 1 AC 269 (PC).

[231] *Welham v DPP* [1961] AC 103, 124 (Lord Radcliffe); cf. also *Withers v DPP* [1975] AC 842, 873 (Lord Simon).

[232] *Scott v MPC* [1975] AC 819, 841, *per* Lord Diplock: "(2) Where the intended victim of a 'conspiracy to defraud' is a private individual the purpose of the conspirators must be to cause the victim economic loss by depriving him of some property or right, corporeal or incorporeal, to which he is or would or might become entitled. The intended means by which the purpose is to be achieved must be dishonest. They need not involve fraudulent misrepresentation such as is needed to constitute the civil tort of deceit. Dishonesty of any kind is enough. (3) Where the intended victim of a 'conspiracy to defraud' is a person performing public duties as distinct from a private individual it is sufficient if the purpose is to cause him to act contrary to his public duty, and the intended means of achieving this purpose are dishonest. The purpose need not involve causing economic loss to anyone." Although Lord Diplock's categorisation was disapproved in *Wai Yu-tsang v R* [1992] 1 AC 269, 277 (PC), the disagreement was motivated by rejection of his Lordship's analysis of category (2), in particular of the requirement that actual loss be intended.

[233] Held to disclose no offence known to law in *Withers v DPP* [1975] AC 842.

[234] [1975] AC 842, 877. Unfortunately, the decision was not considered in *Wai Yu-tsang v R* [1992] 1 AC 269 (PC).

### (c) Illegality of object?

As was pointed out earlier (§ 15.9), and unlike ordinary conspiracy,[235] the object of a conspiracy to defraud need not itself constitute an offence when done. This, perhaps, is an inevitable consequence of finding a conspiracy to defraud where V's interests are merely put at risk—in the absence of a crystallised loss or gain, the contemplated activities may well be insufficiently harmful to attract the wrath of criminalisation. Nonetheless, it is submitted that the scope of conspiracy to defraud should be confined to conspiracies at least to commit a legal wrong, and that conspiracy to commit a moral wrong, *simpliciter*, should not fall within the criminal law.[236]

### (d) Impossibility

What happens where the means chosen by the conspirators fail to work, e.g. because the intended victims were already aware of the facts and could not be deceived? By contrast with the modern statutory offence of conspiracy, impossibility is a defence to conspiracies at common law,[237] and therefore remains a defence to the charge of conspiracy to defraud. Thus, in general, no offence is committed when the conspiracy necessarily cannot achieve its objective because of legal or physical impossibility.[238] The defence of impossibility is discussed in more detail above, in § 9.4.

## (iv) Mens rea: dishonesty and an intention to carry out the agreement

The mens rea of conspiracy to defraud is sometimes described as an "intent to defraud". In fact, the mens rea components are more specific than this:

(i) dishonesty; and
(ii) intention to carry out the agreement.

The first element, dishonesty, bears the same meaning as it does for the general test of dishonesty in theft.[239] Although, at one time, it was suggested that the meanings were different,[240] this possibility was expressly negated by the Court of Appeal in *Ghosh*.[241] So *Ghosh*, as narrowed in *Ivey v Genting Casinos Ltd* and *Barton*,[242] is currently the leading case on the meaning of dishonesty for both offences.[243]

235 See above, § 9.3.
236 Cf. Williams, *CLGP* §§ 222, 226.
237 *DPP v Nock* [1978] AC 979.
238 Cf. *Bennett* (1979) 68 Cr App R 168 (CA), distinguishing cases where the means employed were physically incapable of achieving the purpose from an agreement which might have worked, but which failed because of the behaviour of some person external to the agreement.
239 See above, § 13.8. There is, however, no equivalent in conspiracy to defraud of "claim of right" dishonesty in theft under section 2 of the Theft Act 1968.
240 In that the test of dishonesty was subjective for conspiracy to defraud, but objective for theft: *McIvor* [1982] 1 All ER 491, 497 (CA); *Landy* [1981] 1 All ER 1172, 1181 (CA).
241 [1982] QB 1053, 1059–61 (CA).
242 *Ghosh* [1982] QB 1053 (CA); *Ivey v Genting* [2017] UKSC 67, [2018] AC 391; *Barton* [2020] EWCA Crim 575, [2021] QB 685: above, § 13.8(iv).
243 Note that no equivalent of Theft Act 1968, s. 2, exists in relation to conspiracy to defraud.

Secondly, there must be an intention on the part of the alleged conspirator to carry out her part of the agreement.[244] Thus there is no conspiracy by D if he appears to agree, but secretly intends to frustrate the execution of the plan;[245] nor if D has no intention of playing his allocated role.[246] As with all crimes where motive is not part of the mens rea, a benign motive or purpose will not of itself foreclose an agreement to defraud from constituting a conspiracy. It is sufficient that the agreement exists and that D intends to carry it out.[247]

It might be thought that conspiracy to defraud requires, perhaps in addition to the above two elements, a separate intent to defraud. Not so. Proof of an intention to carry out the agreement to defraud is, of itself, sufficient to establish an intent to defraud; thus, in the context of conspiracy, the requirement of an intent to defraud adds nothing to the two elements identified here. In particular, since fraud may be committed simply by placing another's rights or interests in jeopardy, an "intent to defraud" means simply a (dishonest) intention to act to the potential prejudice of another person's rights[248]—i.e. to carry out the agreement. This includes deliberately putting V's rights at risk, whether or not actual loss is intended. As the Court of Appeal stated in *Sinclair*:[249]

> "To cheat and defraud is to act with deliberate dishonesty to the prejudice of another person's proprietary right. In the context of this case the alleged conspiracy to cheat and defraud is an agreement by a director of a company and others dishonestly to take a risk with the assets of the company by using them in a manner which was known to be not in the best interests of the company and to be prejudicial to the minority shareholders."

Similarly, in *Allsop*, the Court of Appeal remarked:[250]

> "If the deceit which is employed imperils the economic interest of the person deceived, this is sufficient to constitute fraud even though in the event no actual loss is suffered and notwithstanding that the deceiver did not desire to bring about an actual loss. . . . Interests which are imperilled are less valuable in terms of money than those same interests when they are secure and protected. Where a person intends by deceit to induce a course of conduct in another which puts that other's economic interests in jeopardy he is guilty of fraud even though he does not intend or desire that actual loss should ultimately be suffered by that other in this context."

### *(v) Conspiracy to defraud, statutory fraud, and clarity of law*

In its protean form, as it existed before the House of Lords decided in *Norris v USA*[251] that it was not to be further extended, it was questionable whether conspiracy to defraud met the standards of clarity required for a system of criminal law fit for a liberal democracy. The offence had an enormous, non-particularised scope, with its crucial reliance on the notion of dishonesty. In the *Fourteenth Report* of the Joint Parliamentary Committee on Human

[244] Cf. *Gemmell* [1985] 2 NZLR 740; *O'Brien* [1955] 2 DLR 311.
[245] *Anderson* [1986] AC 27, 38ff.
[246] Cf. *Thomson* (1965) 50 Cr App R 1 (CA).
[247] *Wai Yu-tsang* [1992] 1 AC 269 (PC); *Hagan* [1985] Crim LR 598 (CA). See also the discussion of *Smith* [1960] 2 QB 423 (CA), above, § 5. However, as Smith notes in his commentary on *Hagan* [1985] Crim LR 598, 599 (CA), D's motive may sometimes raise issues relevant to the question of dishonesty, e.g. when D believes he has a claim of right.
[248] *Wai Yu-tsang* [1992] 1 AC 269, 276 (Lord Goff) (PC).
[249] [1968] 1 WLR 1246, 1250 (CA). See also *Olan, Hudsson & Hartnett* (1978) 41 CCC (2d) 145.
[250] (1976) 64 Cr App R 29, 31–2 (CA).
[251] [2008] UKHL 16, [2008] AC 920; see above, § 15.9(iii)(a).

Rights,[252] the compatibility of conspiracy to defraud with Article 7 of the ECHR was doubted,[253] because of its over-reliance on jury findings of dishonesty. It was widely anticipated that the Fraud Act 2006 would abolish conspiracy to defraud but, as we have seen, it did not. Furthermore, in *Barton*,[254] and again in *Bermingham*,[255] the Court of Appeal gave short shrift to the argument that the offence is incompatible with Article 7 of the Convention.[256] Conspiracy to defraud continues to operate in tandem with statutory fraud and in recent years there have been some high-profile prosecutions for the offence.[257] And notwithstanding the issue of Guidelines by the Attorney-General, which aim to limit prosecutions for conspiracy to defraud to frauds committed on a grand scale,[258] and to forms of fraudulent behaviour that cannot otherwise be prosecuted, it seems that prosecutions for conspiracy to defraud are still sometimes brought in cases which do not fall within these narrow categories.[259] The offence of statutory fraud proposed in the Bill was taken to have a more substantial conduct element than conspiracy to defraud, making less objectionable the recourse to dishonesty.[260] But, as we have seen in our discussion of fraud by false representation[261] and, particularly, fraud by abuse of position,[262] reliance on a judgment of dishonesty is pervasive. Recall too the hollowing-out of the actus reus in theft by the decisions in *Gomez*[263] and *Hinks*,[264] which considerably increases the role of dishonesty in that offence.[265] It was once said that you could communicate the substance of property offences and offences against the person with the precept, "be honest and refrain from violence".[266] Certainly the first part of that advice is the best that can be offered by way of advance guidance about the content of large parts of the modern law of fraud and theft.

252 Session 2004–05, para. 2.12.

253 Art. 7, which proscribes retroactive criminal law, has been interpreted as requiring minimum standards of clarity for criminal offences: above, § 2.2.

254 [2020] EWCA Crim 575, [2021] QB 685.

255 [2020] EWCA Crim 1662.

256 On this see Collins, "Testing Conspiracy to Defraud's Resilience" [2021] *Crim LR* 902. A different tone, perhaps, is sounded by the Supreme Court in *Hayes* [2025] UKSC 29, [2025] 1 WLR 3553 on this point. The court noted that the offence "has been criticised as excessively broad and vague and incompatible with the principle that the law should be sufficiently certain to enable a person to know what conduct will amount to a crime" ([48]). While the criticism is not explicitly endorsed by the Supreme Court, it is nevertheless viewed as essential that, where the offence is charged in future, a prosecutor specify the content of the alleged agreement with particularity ([50]).

257 Among them the LIBOR rate-fixing prosecutions on which a number of books have been written, including Verity, *Rigged* (2023). These prosecutions led to *Hayes* [2015] EWCA Crim 1944 and *Hayes* [2025] UKSC 29, [2025] 1 WLR 3553, discussed in § 13.8(iv), above. Other high profile prosecutions include that in relation to open-cast mining in South Wales which produced *Evans* [2014] 1 WLR 2817 (Crown Court (Cardiff)), discussed in § 15.9.(iii)(a) above; and a prosecution for conspiracy to defraud brought in respect of a large-scale motor-insurance fraud in County Durham, part of which later reached the Court of Appeal as *McKenzie* [2013] EWCA Crim 1544, [2014] 1 Cr App R (S) 68. It was also the offence at the head of the multi-count indictment in *Barton* [2020] EWCA Crim 575, [2021] QB 685, where over the space of 20 years Barton and his associates had extracted millions of pounds from vulnerable elderly residents in a private care home; offences for which lengthy sentences of imprisonment were imposed.

258 Available online at https://www.gov.uk/guidance/use-of-the-common-law-offence-of-conspiracy-to-defraud--6.

259 See, e.g., *W* [2017] EWCA Crim 1758, [2018] 1 Cr App R (S) 20, where the defendant, hoping to avoid being identified as the father of a child and consequentially liable for maintenance payments, got a friend to supply a DNA sample, which he then pretended to be his. Having pleaded guilty he then appealed against the sentence, which was reduced from two years to 18 months.

260 *Ibid.*, para. 2.14.

261 Above, § 15.3.

262 Above, § 15.5.

263 [1993] AC 442.

264 [2001] 2 AC 241.

265 See above, § 13.6(ii)(a)–(c).

266 Quoted by Glanville Williams, in the preface to his *Textbook of Criminal Law* (1st ed., 1978).

## § 15.10 Specific offences of fraud

The general offences of fraud described in this chapter are supplemented by a great many specific statutory ones. Thus it is, for example, a specific statutory offence to cheat at gambling,[267] to make a false statement to obtain a driving licence (or to prevent someone from obtaining one),[268] to make a false statement to obtain a passport,[269] and to make a false statement when registering an offshore company.[270] A battery of highly specific offences criminalises the making of false statements in connection with applications for various types of grant.[271] At the head of these in terms of practical importance is the offence of making a false statement or representation with a view to obtaining a social security benefit.[272] It is also a statutory offence to fraudulently evade income tax[273] and VAT,[274] and here the statutory offences are backed up by an ancient and far-reaching common law offence of "cheating the public revenue", for which life imprisonment could in theory be imposed.[275] For those who run fraudulent businesses there is a more general offence of fraudulent trading.[276] Many (though not all) of these offences cover misbehaviour that could equally be prosecuted as fraud under section 1 of the Fraud Act 2006, but the investigation and prosecution of these offences is usually in the hands of the government departments responsible for the area of public business to which they relate, whose officials are familiar with the specific offences and prefer to use them. On the one hand, this patchwork of fraud-based offences does not aid the cohesion of the law, but on the other hand, they make for a series of offences each of which specifies an actus reus more narrowly than the catch all conspiracy to defraud, offering better guidance to citizens, fairer warning that the conduct in question falls within the reach of the criminal law.[277]

## § 15.11 Forgery and false accounting

The law of fraud is also buttressed by two other general offences: forgery and false accounting. Though both are practically important, here they will be described in outline only.[278]

[267] Gambling Act 2005, s. 42.
[268] Road Traffic Act 1988, s. 174.
[269] Criminal Justice Act 1925, s. 36.
[270] Economic Crime (Transparency and Enforcement) Act 2022, s. 32.
[271] See, e.g., s. 51 of the Agriculture Act 1993.
[272] Social Security Administration Act 1992, s. 111A.
[273] Taxes Management Act 1970, s. 106A.
[274] Value Added Tax Act 1994, s. 72.
[275] For the details, see *Archbold* (2026), § 30–134ff. The offence covers, inter alia, defrauding the revenue by omission: *Redford* (1989) 89 Cr App R 1 (CA); and in *Hunt* [1994] Crim LR 747 (CA) the Court interpreted it as a "conduct crime", of which a person can be guilty even though no loss to the Revenue has actually occurred. Cheating the Revenue was originally just one aspect of an even broader common law offence of cheating, which was abolished except as regards frauds on the revenue by the Theft Act 1968, s. 32(1). In *Dosanjh* [2013] EWCA Crim 2366, [2014] 1 WLR 1780, the Court of Appeal said that, for a serious instance of VAT fraud, it was appropriate to prosecute the defendant for the common law offence and for him then to be sentenced more severely than would have been possible under the statutory regime.
[276] Companies Act 2006, s. 993. See *Archbold* (2026), § 30–1.
[277] See above, § 15.9.
[278] For a fuller account of forgery see *Archbold* (2026), chap. 22 and *Smith, Hogan, and Ormerod*, chap. 29; for false accounting, see *Archbold* (2026), § 21–177ff and *Smith, Hogan, and Ormerod*, § 23.1.

In its present form Forgery derives from the Forgery and Counterfeiting Act 1981, a reforming and codifying statute based on a report by the Law Commission.[279] The basic definition of the offence is set out in section 1 of this Act, which is as follows:

> A person is guilty of forgery if he makes a false instrument, with the intention that he or another shall use it to induce somebody to accept it as genuine, and by reason of so accepting it to do or not to do some act to his own or any other person's prejudice.

As with previous versions of the offence, the essential element of the offence of forgery is the making of an "instrument" which purports to be something it is not. Thus, as is often said, "a forgery is a document which not only tells a lie, but tells a lie about itself".[280] Although most forgeries comprise false documents, the offence can be committed in relation to anything that counts as an "instrument" within the definition set out in section 8, which includes not only documents of all types, but also postage stamps and Inland Revenue stamps, and "any disc, tape, sound track or other device on or in which information is recorded or stored by mechanical, electronic or other means". Banknotes are specifically excluded from this definition; the creation of false money, whether in coin or paper form, and of whatever country, is specifically covered by separate provisions of the Act.[281]

The concept of "falsity" is elaborated in some detail by section 9 of the Act, and section 10 provides an extensive (and exhaustive) definition of intending to induce a person to act to his "prejudice". Among the cases listed is enabling a person to "earn remuneration or greater remuneration" from that person. So, if doubt exists as to whether a person who tells lies to get a job commits an offence under the Fraud Act,[282] he is clearly guilty of forgery if, to support his lie, he fabricates a bogus reference or degree certificate. The basic offence of forgery is flanked by back-up offences of knowingly possessing forgeries[283] and knowingly making use of them.[284] So the fraudulent job-seeker is also guilty if he obtains these documents from a friend whose literary or artistic skills are superior to his own. Unlike most of the other offences of fraud, it is not an ingredient in the offence of forgery that D's behaviour be "dishonest". So although the Fraud Act 2006 contemplates the possibility of the "honest liar", the Forgery and Counterfeiting Act 1981 gives no quarter to his friend the "honest forger".

The requirement that a forgery purport to be something it is not means that the crooked accountant who "cooks the books" does not commit a forgery; even if the firm's books as cooked contain entries that are false, the books are still their books. To meet this and other difficulties, section 17 of the Theft Act 1968 creates an offence of false accounting.[285] It is as follows:

> (1) Where a person dishonestly, with a view to gain for himself or another or with intent to cause loss to another,—

[279] Law Com. No. 55, *Report on Forgery and Counterfeit Currency* (1973).
[280] Kenny, *Outlines of Criminal Law* (14th ed., 1932) 264.
[281] In particular, Forgery and Counterfeiting Act 1981, s. 27.
[282] See above, § 15.2(i)(a).
[283] Forgery and Counterfeiting Act 1981, s. 5.
[284] *Ibid.*, ss. 3 and 4.
[285] There were precursor offences, dating from the nineteenth century, of falsification of accounts. See the Criminal Law Revision Committee, Eighth Report, *Theft and Related Offences* (Cmnd. 2977, 1966), paras. 102ff.

(a) destroys, defaces, conceals or falsifies any account or any record or document made or required for any accounting purpose; or
(b) in furnishing information for any purpose produces or makes use of any account, or any such record or document as aforesaid, which to his knowledge is or may be misleading, false or deceptive in a material particular;

he shall, on conviction on indictment, be liable to imprisonment for a term not exceeding seven years.

(2) For purposes of this section a person who makes or concurs in making in an account or other document an entry which is or may be misleading, false or deceptive in a material particular, or who omits or concurs in omitting a material particular from an account or other document, is to be treated as falsifying the account or document.

This offence is more generous to defendants than forgery, because here an essential ingredient is dishonesty, as understood in *Ghosh* (and as truncated by *Ivey v Genting* and *Barton*).[286] However, although a defendant whose actions were in accordance with accepted standards in society has a defence, it seems that he has no defence if he was unaware that the document he falsified or destroyed was required for accounting purposes. Surprisingly, the Court of Appeal in *Graham*[287] suggested that in this respect section 17 is an offence of strict liability.

[286] *Ghosh* [1982] QB 1053 (CA); *Ivey v Genting* [2017] UKSC 67, [2018] AC 391; *Barton* [2020] EWCA Crim 575, [2021] QB 685. See §§ 13.8(iv) and 15.2(ii) above.
[287] [1997] 1 Cr App R 302, 314 (CA).

# 16

# THE MORAL LIMITS OF CRIMINALISATION

Over the past few chapters we have investigated some of the better-known common law and statutory offences. There are, of course, many other offences, both minor and serious, known to the law. Beyond that, however, there are many forms of wrongdoing that are rightly not offences at all. As a regulatory device, the criminal law is a bluntly coercive and morally loaded tool, something to be used sparingly and with care. The process known as *criminalisation* is problematic: although it may frequently be appropriate, indeed necessary, to have criminal prohibitions, we should always be careful of overextending the reach of the criminal law, and of infringing too far upon citizens' rights of free choice and individual liberty. We *should* use the criminal law to prohibit conduct—but not too much.

The question becomes, therefore, *when* should the state extend the criminal law to regulate conduct? Notice that this is not a question about whether the state *can* criminalise something: in constitutional terms, Parliament has wide-ranging legal powers to regulate the conduct of its citizens, including by the criminal law. Rather, the question is a normative one. Suppose that a responsible legislature seeks to enact an appropriate, morally justifiable, range of criminal prohibitions. What criteria should it apply when deciding whether to proscribe something? The decision whether conduct is sufficiently serious to warrant criminalisation always involves difficult judgements, and will be affected by the political values, state of development, and social structure(s) of a society. There is no sphere of industrial, commercial, or administrative activity untouched by the criminal law. As criminal lawyers, however, we must ask whether conduct made criminal merits that designation.

A useful starting point is that there should be parsimony in criminalisation: offences "should be created only when absolutely necessary".[1] The criminal sanction is the most drastic of the state's standard tools for regulating the conduct of individuals. It represents the most severe infringement of a person's liberty and, as such, should be available only where there is a clear social justification.

Broadly speaking, we can identify two types of criteria that must be met if the creation of an offence is to be morally legitimate. There must, first, be a prima facie *positive* case for state regulation, in that the activity at issue must be not only wrongful but sufficiently serious to warrant intervention. In general, as we shall argue, this requires that the conduct leads directly or (under certain conditions) indirectly to significant levels of harm or offence being suffered by others.

Secondly, certain *negative* constraints must also be met. In particular, it must be shown that the *criminal* law offers the best method of regulation, being preferable to alternative methods of legal control that are available to the state; and the practicalities must be considered of

[1] *Per* Lord Williams of Mostyn, HL Deb., vol. 602, col. WA 58; June 18, 1999.

drawing up an offence in terms that are effective, enforceable, and meet rule of law and other concerns. If these negative constraints cannot be met, then the state ought not to criminalise certain types of conduct, notwithstanding that there is a prima facie positive case for doing so.

In this chapter, we will focus mainly on the competing *positive* grounds for state intervention: the main types of reasons why the state might validly choose to intervene and criminalise some action. Later, we will briefly discuss some of the negative constraints that might nonetheless make the criminal law an inappropriate response.

When is behaviour, prima facie, sufficiently serious to warrant criminalisation? This question is highly controversial, because it raises squarely the issue of the limits of the state's moral authority over individuals. Joel Feinberg's classic discussion of the problem identifies four possible grounds of justifiable intervention: harm to others, offence to others, immorality, and harm to self.[2] As we shall see, liberal philosophers (including Feinberg himself) tend to endorse only the first two of those grounds, rejecting the case for criminalising conduct on purely moralistic or paternalistic grounds.[3] Below we offer a short introduction to these four grounds of state intervention.

## § 16.1 The harm principle

At the core of liberalism is the proposition that the state is justified in intervening to regulate conduct only when that conduct causes or risks *harm to others*. Conduct that merely harms oneself, or which is thought to be immoral but otherwise harmless, is on this account ineligible for prohibition. Famously, the harm principle was first articulated by John Stuart Mill:[4]

> "The principle is, that the sole end for which mankind are warranted, individually or collectively, in interfering with the liberty of action of any of their number is self-protection. That the only purpose for which power can rightfully be exercised over any member of a civilised community against his will is to prevent harm to others. His own good, either physical or moral, is not a sufficient warrant."

Expressed in this way, the harm principle is a negative constraint: in the absence of harm or a risk of harm, the state is not morally entitled to intervene. It does not follow that, conversely, the state *is* justified in intervening whenever D's conduct causes or risks harm to others. That conclusion can only be reached after further factors are considered, such as those to be discussed below. Perhaps more importantly, Mill offers no definition of what counts as a *harm*, which leaves much to be done by way of interpretation before the harm principle can be put to use.

Liberal philosophers have built on Mill's analysis in an attempt to eradicate these problems. The most extensive exposition is offered by Feinberg, who summarises the principle as follows:[5]

> "It is always a good reason in support of penal legislation that it would be effective in preventing (eliminating, reducing) harm to persons other than the actor (the one prohibited from acting) and there is no other means that is equally effective at no greater cost to other values."

[2] *The Moral Limits of the Criminal Law* (1984–87): vol. 1, *Harm to Others* (1984); vol. 2, *Offense to Others* (1985); vol. 3, *Harm to Self* (1986); vol. 4, *Harmless Wrongdoing* (1988).

[3] A more thoroughgoing scepticism about the possibility of general moral constraints upon criminalisation is found in Tadros, *Wrongs and Crimes* (2016); but see, in reply, Husak, "Wrongs, Crimes and Criminalization" (2019) 13 *Crim Law and Philosophy* 393, 397–400.

[4] *On Liberty* chap. 1, para. 9.

[5] *Harm to Others* (1984) 26. See also Simester and von Hirsch, *Crimes, Harms, and Wrongs* (2011) chap. 3.

Notice that this is formulated as a positive claim. On Feinberg's account, if creating a criminal offence would prevent harm to others, there is a positive reason in favour of criminalisation. By contrast with Mill's negative formulation, Feinberg articulates the harm principle in a way that leaves it possible for him, and us, to accept the legitimacy of other, supplementary, grounds for criminalisation (such as offence) where the conduct is not likely to be harmful.

A second feature of Feinberg's version of the harm principle is that it is *instrumental* rather than *act*-centred. There is nothing in his principle that requires the prohibited act *itself* to be harmful, or even that it risks causing harm. Gardner and Shute embrace this instrumental version:[6]

> "It is no objection under the harm principle that a harmless action was criminalized, nor even that an action with no tendency to cause harm was criminalized. It is enough to meet the demands of the harm principle that, if the action were not criminalized, *that* would be harmful."

What matters for Gardner and Shute, in other words, is not the question, "is this act (potentially) harmful?" but, rather, "would harm (potentially) follow if this act were permitted?" For example, the *prospect* that I might be burgled may lead me to avoid taking lengthy holidays, to take out insurance, to install an alarm in my house, and so forth—all plausibly harms insofar as they set back my interests. Suppose it were made an offence for postal workers to inform third parties that a householder was away from home. The offence could be justified under this version of the harm principle if there were reason to think that it would be at least partially effective in reducing such precautionary costs.

Hence there are multiple versions of the harm principle to choose from.[7] On instrumental versions of the harm principle, it need not be objectionable that certain *per se* harmless acts are criminalised.[8] And one might prefer a version of the principle (whether instrumental or act-centred) in which harm is an *essential* condition of criminalising conduct, or prefer a version in which it is merely one ground for doing so. In the latter case, for example, one might subscribe to Feinberg's articulation of the harm principle and at the same time consistently accept that the state is also justified in criminalising some conduct on the grounds that it is immoral (albeit not harmful). That last option would, however, be inconsistent with Mill's version of the harm principle. Especially for political liberal theory, part of the point of the Millian harm principle is that it forces an enquiry into the consequences of conduct and its prohibition—does it lead to harm to anyone other than the actor? According to the harm principle, proponents of a particular criminal offence cannot simply allege that the relevant conduct is immoral. Rather, they must identify what are the particular effects both of that conduct,[9] and of its prohibition: the distinct ways in which both the conduct and its prohibition involve damage to the lives of other persons. Such claims can then be subjected to public and legislative debate. Empirical evidence, for example, of a link between the relevant conduct and the alleged harm can be demanded and scrutinised.

Consider, for example, the decision by the House of Lords in *Brown*[10] that, in the context of sadomasochistic sexual activity, it is an offence to inflict actual bodily harm on another person notwithstanding that the "victim" consents. One justification offered for this act

[6] "The Wrongness of Rape" in Horder (ed.), *Oxford Essays in Jurisprudence* (4th series, 2000) 193, 216.

[7] This point is helpfully brought out by Edwards, "Harm Principles" (2014) 20 *Legal Theory* 253. Indirect harm of the sort Gardner and Shute contemplate is, however, subject to remoteness constraints: see below, § 16.1(v).

[8] Contra, e.g., Ripstein, "Beyond the Harm Principle" (2006) 34 *Philosophy and Public Affairs* 216; Duff, *Answering for Crime* (2007) chap. 6.

[9] Packer, *The Limits of the Criminal Sanction* (1968) 262.

[10] [1994] 1 AC 212. See also §§ 11.9(iii).

of judicial criminalisation was that the legalisation of such activities might encourage the seduction and "corruption of young men" and therefore harm them.[11] But would it? It is a cheap claim to make when no supporting evidence is offered. Given the presumption against criminalisation, the onus is on its proponents to bring clear evidence that creating a new offence *will* prevent the relevant harm from occurring, or at least significantly reduce the instances of such harm.

This onus is too often ignored. A particularly bad example is the enactment of an offence of possessing "non-photographic pornographic images of children", i.e. pornographic cartoons and the like. No children need be involved in the making of such images. Nonetheless, claimed the Home Office, such images were potentially harmful, both because they might be used to "groom" children and because they might "fuel abuse of real children by reinforcing potential abusers' inappropriate feelings toward children", and presumably tend to increase the incidences of actual abuse.[12] Not only was no evidence offered to support these claimed effects, but such evidence was expressly disclaimed:[13]

> "We are unaware of any specific research into whether there is a link between accessing these fantasy images of child sex abuse and the commission of offences against children, but it is *felt* by police and children's welfare organisations that the possession and circulation of these images serves to legitimize and reinforce highly inappropriate views about children."

So, notwithstanding the seriousness of any decision to criminalise, the government was willing to legislate on the basis of no more than a bare assertion, made by those to whom it listens most. This is a straightforward abandonment of the obligation to justify any prohibition in terms of the harm principle.

In the following paragraphs we consider aspects of the harm principle in more detail.

### *(i) What counts as a harm?*

A harm, on Feinberg's account, is a "thwarting, setting back, or defeating of an interest".[14] When we are harmed, one or more of our interests is left in a worse state than it was beforehand. In turn, a person's *interests* comprise the things that help make his life go well:[15] thus, when we are harmed, our lives tend to be changed for the worse. Harm involves the impairment of a person's opportunities to engage in worthwhile activities and relationships, and to pursue valuable, self-chosen, goals. In this sense, harm is prospective rather than

[11] *Ibid.*, 246 (Lord Jauncey).

[12] Home Office, *Consultation on the Possession of Non-photographic Visual Depictions of Child Sexual Abuse* (2007) 5. See the sensitive discussion by Ost, "Criminalising Fabricated Images of Child Pornography: A Matter of Harm or Morality?" (2010) 30 *Legal Studies* 230. The upshot was s. 62 of the Coroners and Justice Act 2009.

[13] Home Office, *ibid.*, 1 (emphasis added).

[14] *Harm to Others* (1984) 33.

[15] In Feinberg's account, "One's interests . . . consist of all those things in which one has a stake. . . . These interests, or perhaps more accurately, the things these interests are *in*, are distinguishable components of a person's well-being: he flourishes or languishes as they flourish or languish. What promotes them is to his advantage or *in his interest*; what thwarts them is to his detriment or *against his interest*" (*Harm to Others* (1984) 34). See, too, his "Harm to Others: a Rejoinder" (1986) *Criminal Justice Ethics* 16, 26, where Feinberg recapitulates: "I argued that to harm a person was to set back his interest and violate his right. To have an interest, in turn, is to have a stake in some outcome, just as if one had 'invested' some of one's own good in it, thus assuming the risk of personal harm or setback."

backward-looking: it involves a diminution of one's opportunities, going forwards, to enjoy or pursue a good life.

Characteristically, harm is brought about through the impairment of V's personal or proprietary resources. However, as Feinberg observes, what makes such impairment harmful is not the impairment *per se* but its implication for V's well-being:[16]

> "A broken arm is an impaired arm, one which has (temporarily) lost its capacity to serve a person's needs effectively, and in virtue of that impairment, its possessor's welfare interest is harmed."

Similarly, in the context of property crimes, one can say that "any harm to a person by denying him the use or the value of his property is a harm to him precisely because it diminishes his opportunities".[17]

Clearly, people have interests in their property and personal integrity. But we have other interests that are capable of being harmed. Hyman Gross suggests that, before it can be said that a person has an interest in something (X), the thing must "be of sufficient value to [the person] that the assertion of a claim by or on behalf of [that person] based on the loss or significant impairment of X is not unreasonable".[18] He offers a four-part categorisation of the types of cases where one's interests are harmed: (i) "violations of interest in retaining or maintaining what one is entitled to have" (e.g. theft); (ii) "offences to sensibility" (e.g. obscenity); (iii) "impairment of collective welfare" (e.g. counterfeiting, which undermines the economy); and (iv) "violations of governmental interests" (e.g. contempt of court).[19]

We consider offences to sensibility in § 16.2 below, under the rubric of the offence principle. But categories (iii) and (iv) show that we can be harmed without directly being a victim; and, indeed, when there is no victim at all. Hence, on occasion, it may be appropriate to enact "victimless" crimes. Tax evasion is rightly a crime notwithstanding that there is no individual victim who is deprived of assets directly. Perhaps it is not the same sort of harm (or wrong) as that involved in theft. But if T illegitimately reduces his tax burden, T effectively takes from, and harms (and wrongs), her fellow taxpayers. The money must come from somewhere: if not from T, then from others. The obligation to pay tax is a collective duty, one that each person owes to her fellow citizens and not merely to the state.

Similarly, attacks on the integrity of the currency (e.g. large-scale counterfeiting) or on the operation of the judicial systems (e.g. perjury) matter in part because they tend to undermine state-implemented regimes that exist for the benefit of us all. State intervention is warranted because the community as a whole would also suffer harm were these general regimes to be undermined. Undermining the currency, for instance, would lead to losses of value stored as currency and tend to destabilise the systems that co-ordinate a nation's

[16] *Harm to Others* (1984) 53. Cp. Kleinig's claim that, in the case of a temporary hurt or an abduction that has no lasting effects upon its victim, there may be interference with a welfare interest but no harm: Kleinig, "Crime and the Concept of Harm" (1978) 15 *Am Phil Q* 27, 32; Feinberg, *Harm to Others* (1984) 52–3.

[17] Raz, "Autonomy, Toleration, and the Harm Principle" in Gavison (ed.), *Issues in Contemporary Legal Philosophy* (1987) 313, 327. Cp. Perry, "Corrective v. Distributive Justice" in Horder (ed.), *Oxford Essays in Jurisprudence* (4th series, 2000) 237, 256: "The main reason that personal injury constitutes harm is that it interferes with personal autonomy. It interferes, that is to say, with the set of opportunities and options from which one is able to choose what to do in one's life."

[18] *A Theory of Criminal Justice* (1979) 116.

[19] *Ibid.*, 119–21.

economic activity;[20] which, in turn, would deprive people of many opportunities for personal and social advancement. Minimising or preventing that sort of indirect, prospective harm to our interests is rightly the concern of the criminal law.

### *(ii) Seriousness*

Indeed, once the nature of the harm is identified, we can see why some apparently victimless crimes, such as counterfeiting, are regarded as very serious indeed. This is one of the payoffs of the harm principle: in forcing us to consider *why* we are concerned about the activity that is to be criminalised, it gives us tools with which to determine whether it merits criminalisation.

Von Hirsch and Jareborg have developed this point in the context of victim-oriented crimes.[21] In their seminal paper, the authors identify four generic interests that we all have directly: (i) physical integrity (health, safety, avoidance of physical pain); (ii) material support and amenity (nutrition, shelter, basic amenities); (iii) freedom from humiliation or degrading treatment; and (iv) privacy and autonomy. The justification of any existing or prospective crime can then be assessed in two steps, as follows.

First, one should identify which category of interest the crime is designed to protect. Secondly, it is necessary to assess the degree to which standard instances of that crime will adversely affect the living standard—the opportunities for V to live a good life—of a typical victim. Von Hirsch and Jareborg divide the severity of these effects into four bands: (a) subsistence (simple survival with only basic human functions); (b) minimal well-being (maintaining minimal levels of comfort and dignity); (c) adequate well-being (maintaining adequate levels of comfort and dignity); and (d) significant enhancement (above-adequate quality of life).

On this approach, we can see that homicide attacks physical integrity in such a way as to undermine even subsistence; it is, thus, more serious than a typical robbery and much more serious than petty theft or a minor assault. On the other hand, road traffic regulations become extremely important, since they too are concerned with avoiding deaths and thus protect our fundamental interests. It may be that, because it is less culpable, dangerous driving should be punished less severely than murder. But, like murder, the existence of an offence of dangerous driving is justified within the harm principle by the desirability of avoiding deaths on the roads.

### *(iii) Harms and wrongs*

In Feinberg's words,[22]

> "One person wrongs another when his indefensible (unjustifiable and inexcusable) conduct violates the other's right, and in all but certain very special cases such conduct will also invade the other's interest and thus be harmful in the sense [of a setback to interests]."

In order to be a prima facie candidate for criminalisation, the causing of harm must also involve a wrong.[23] Suppose, for example, that a judge sentences P to imprisonment for life

[20] See *St Margaret's Trust Ltd* [1958] 1 WLR 522, 527 (CA).

[21] "Gauging Criminal Harm: A Living-Standard Analysis" (1991) 11 *OJLS* 1.

[22] *Harm to Others* (1984) 34.

[23] See Raz, "Autonomy, Toleration, and the Harm Principle" in Gavison (ed.), *Issues in Contemporary Legal Philosophy* (1987) 313, 328: "Since 'causing harm' by its very meaning demands that the action is prima facie wrong

following P's conviction of murder. P's interests will be set back by such a sentence. He will lose his freedom and many opportunities to advance his life and prospects. Nonetheless, the judge does no wrong in depriving P of his freedom in this way. Even though P's situation is worsened when he is deprived of his liberty, P has lost nothing to which he had a right.

The example illustrates that, just as we can be wronged without being harmed, we can be harmed (our interests can be set back) without being wronged. Indeed, the latter is something that often occurs in economic transactions. In a broadly free market, individuals are entitled to pursue their own interests. In so doing, they wrong no one even if their self-advancing conduct has deleterious side-effects for others. Side-effects are a natural feature of competitive interaction: if D tenders successfully for a contract, D may know that in so doing she will deprive others of that contract and, in turn, weaken their commercial viability, cause employees to be laid off, and so forth. Yet D does no wrong and the case falls outside the scope of the harm principle.[24]

### *(iv) Balancing requirements*

Even if a harmful action *is* wrongful, it should not necessarily be criminalised. The harm principle provides for a balancing of interests, one that considers the extent and likelihood of the harm involved and weighs that against the implications of criminalisation. Feinberg's account presents a number of factors to be taken into account at this stage:[25]

(a) "the greater the gravity of a possible harm, the less probable its occurrence need be to justify prohibition of the conduct that threatens to produce it;
(b) the greater the probability of harm, the less grave the harm need be to justify coercion;
(c) the greater the magnitude of the risk of harm, itself compounded out of gravity and probability, the less reasonable it is to accept the risk;
(d) the more valuable (useful) the dangerous conduct, both to the actor and to others, the more reasonable it is to take the risk of harmful consequences, and for extremely valuable conduct it is reasonable run risks up to the point of clear and present danger;
(e) the more reasonable a risk of harm (the danger), the weaker is the case for prohibiting the conduct that creates it."

A responsible legislator should, therefore, consider the gravity and likelihood of the wrongful harm and weigh that against the social value of the conduct to be prohibited and the degree

it is a normative concept acquiring its specific meaning from the moral theory within which it is embedded". The requirement for a wrong is particularly important in the special case where the harm is "reactive": Simester and von Hirsch, *Crimes, Harms, and Wrongs* (2011) § 3.2(c).

[24] Admittedly, that view assumes there is value in having free markets, perhaps subject to exceptions for cases of obvious market failure. Others, not only Marxists, think very differently and see the damaging implications of free competition as a good reason to limit or even abolish free competition. There are deep waters here, waters that a treatise on criminal law cannot chart. Whether something is a wrong is a moral question, and much of the more detailed content of morality is affected by conventions that vary across societies. (A good example is the age of consent to sexual activity, which differs amongst nations even within Europe.) For present purposes, it suffices to acknowledge that our discussion of criminalisation principles assumes a broadly liberal philosophy that may be appropriate in England and Wales, but which cannot seamlessly be applied across the world.

[25] *Harm to Others* (1984) 216.

of intrusion upon citizens' lives that criminalisation would involve. The greater the gravity and likelihood of the harm, the stronger the case for criminalisation; conversely, the more valuable the conduct is, or the more the prohibition would limit liberty, the stronger the case against criminalisation. In addition, other rights that a citizen may have, for example to free speech or privacy, should be respected.[26] These rights may militate against creating certain types of crimes,[27] especially (as we shall see below) in the context of offensive behaviour.

It is a calculation of this sort that justifies the setting of speed limits. In the United Kingdom, for example, it is prohibited to drive on the motorway at speeds in excess of 70 miles per hour. Is this a legitimate criminal law? Yes: driving at 75 miles per hour may not be inherently immoral or wrong, and might bring about no harm whatsoever. But the faster one drives, the higher the probability that if something goes wrong, serious injury and property damage will result. Hence the case for setting speed limits can fall within the harm principle, and is, *prima facie*, amenable to criminal regulation. On the other hand, even though setting the motorway speed limit at (say) 10 miles per hour would save more lives, the social costs, in terms of inefficient transportation systems, would be too great. Decisions of this sort require a balancing of factors, such as the effect on public mobility of setting the limit too low, against the costs, in terms of scale and likelihood of injuries, of setting the limit too high.

Resolution of that balancing process will depend on reference to standard cases. The harm principle is in play here because speeding *standardly* causes or creates a risk of harm, even if not in every instance. Inevitably, the criminal law is a blunt instrument, regulating in terms of average cases and incapable of reflecting the myriad variations upon those cases that real life delivers.

To a large extent, this constraint is a matter of resources, and of their efficient use—it is simply uneconomic to frame and administer laws that take into account the particularities of every person's situation. Hence, criminal law tends to prohibit actions on the basis of their typical risks and consequences, leaving further refinement, if any, to the realm of exceptions. It is an offence, we have said, to drive faster than 70 miles per hour on the motorway. This is so notwithstanding that there is no intrinsic significance to that speed. Depending on the circumstances (perhaps all lanes of the motorway ahead are empty) and on the particular driver (perhaps he is Lewis Hamilton), there may on occasion be no significant risk when a driver travels on the motorway at a faster clip than 70 miles per hour.[28] Nonetheless, specifying a precise limit is a convenient and enforceable means by which to regulate dangerous driving; and the limit itself is determined by reference to risks in standard cases (hence, near a school, the limit is usually 20 miles per hour, whereas on other urban roads it is often 30 miles per hour, and so on).

### *(v) Remote harms*

Many actions are not immediately harmful but may lead to harm *remotely*.[29] My selling you a handgun, for example, does not in itself harm you but rather puts you in a position where

[26] This general approach may be termed the "standard harms analysis": Simester and von Hirsch, *Crimes, Harms, and Wrongs* (2011) § 4.2.

[27] Horder, for example, argues persuasively that criminalisation is not the appropriate way to regulate lying during election campaigns: "Criminal Law at the Limit: Countering False Claims in Elections and Referendums" (2021) 84 *MLR* 429.

[28] For an argument that such conduct may legitimately be criminalised despite not being wrongful, see Cornford, "Rethinking the Wrongfulness Constraint on Criminalization" (2017) 36 *Law and Philosophy* 615.

[29] Simester and von Hirsch, *Crimes, Harms, and Wrongs* (2011) chap. 4.

subsequently you may harm another person. This possibility is an implicit feature of inchoate offences, such as encouraging or assisting murder; and of what are sometimes called "substantive inchoate" offences, such as the offence of "going equipped". It is a crime to be on the street at night when in possession of an article, such as a jemmy (or "crowbar"), for use in connection with a burglary.[30] The justification for this offence is not that I have the jemmy, but rather that I may use it.

Remote harms present a particular challenge for the harm principle, a challenge additional to the kinds of evidential issues noted earlier, in the context of *Brown*.[31] While it may sometimes be appropriate, very often there are difficulties involved in basing criminalisation on remote harms, especially those predicated on the eventual criminal choices of third persons. Suppose that, as Murray has argued, there is evidence that unregulated premarital sex yields higher rates of illegitimate births, leading to more children growing up in impoverished households with weakened parental control; and that, in turn, this generates higher crime rates amongst these offspring.[32] If we concede the empirical links, we can conclude that unregulated premarital sex leads to harm. But it does not follow that there is even a prima facie case for criminalising premarital sex. The harm is produced not by D's own conduct but by the subsequent choices of third parties (in this case, offspring) whom D does not control. That being so, it is not clear why the harm should be D's lookout: why should D be accountable, through the criminal law, for the freely chosen subsequent actions of others?[33] Why, in other words, should D lose an otherwise harmless option just because of the subsequent independent choices that others may make?

On occasion it is apt to prohibit an activity because of a remote harm. This may occur where D's act in some way underwrites or facilitates the later wrongdoing by others. For example, it may be appropriate to prohibit D from publishing a book detailing various ways of killing one's enemies, because the link between D's activity and murders by others influenced or helped by D's book is sufficiently close that the remote harm can fairly be imputed back to D. But in the absence of special reasons for imputing remote harms to D, the mere existence of such harms supplies no reason for criminalising D's otherwise innocent conduct.

To invoke the harm principle, we have noted, an action must not only lead to harm; it must also be a wrong. This constraint is particularly apposite to remote harm. The criminal law embodies, by its nature, an element of blame or censure. But in remote harm cases, it still needs to be shown why D should be condemned for her non-harmful action, just because that action happens to be linked, through chains of complex social interaction, to the subsequent injurious behaviour of some separate and autonomous person, E. Prima facie, it seems unjust to impose penal censure on D, at least where D has no power to control the harmful choices of E, and where D has not sought to assist or encourage those choices. This challenge is especially pertinent with the increasing deployment of pre-emptive or

[30] Theft Act 1968, s. 25.

[31] Above, § 16.1.

[32] See Murray, *The Emerging British Underclass* (London 1990); also Murray, *Underclass* (London 1994). Cf. Simester and von Hirsch, *Crimes, Harms, and Wrongs* (2011) § 4.4(a).

[33] *Ibid.*, 61: "An actor may properly be held responsible if he brings about a harmful result himself, or if he brings it about through another person, e.g. by inducement or persuasion. But to hold him liable merely because (say) another person chooses voluntarily to follow his example, in a manner that causes or risks harm, infringes basic notions of the separateness of persons as choosing agents. It is that other person who has made the culpable choice of bringing about harm, not the original actor."

"prophylactic" crimes designed to safeguard against terrorist and other threats to collective security.[34]

## § 16.2 The offence principle

Suppose that, one day, D and E catch a bus into town. While riding on the bus, they decide to have sexual intercourse, notwithstanding the presence of the other passengers. Their conduct may not harm anyone else, and plausibly falls outside the scope of the harm principle. Yet it will cause great offence, no doubt, to many others on the bus who are forced to witness their activity. Should conduct of that sort be criminalised?

Feinberg certainly thinks so:[35]

> "It is always a good reason in support of a proposed criminal prohibition that it would probably be an effective way of preventing serious offense (as opposed to injury or harm) to persons other than the actor, and that it is probably a necessary means to that end."

Many, probably most, liberals agree that actions may sometimes be prohibited on the grounds of their offensiveness, and there is widespread acceptance of the offence principle as a second principle of criminalisation, one that supplements the harm principle.

Merely showing that D's conduct is disgusting or unpleasant will not invoke the offence principle. For Feinberg, conduct is offensive when it affronts other people's sensibilities, i.e. when it causes them involuntarily to undergo an unpleasant and disliked psychological experience, by way of reaction to the conduct. Causing any such affront, in his view, constitutes prima facie grounds for invoking the criminal law, provided the matter is sufficiently serious.

There must, however, be widespread and serious affront caused to others. Moreover, on Feinberg's account, the case for criminalisation must satisfy a sophisticated balancing test that is designed to criminalise offence more sparingly than harm. First, a responsible legislator should consider the impact of the conduct on its audience, by examining the magnitude of the affront to see how pervasively and intensely it is felt. As part of that examination, a standard of "reasonable avoidability" is imposed: the easier it is for members of the public to avoid settings where the conduct occurs, the less serious the offence is. Pornography may cause affront to many when viewed involuntarily or unexpectedly, but V cannot reasonably complain if he has specifically visited an adult cinema to see it.

Secondly, the importance of the offending conduct should be examined from the actor's perspective. The more central the conduct is to an actor's way of life, the greater is the claim not to have the conduct prohibited. As part of this examination, a standard of "alternative opportunities" is applied: restrictions on the conduct become more acceptable if there are satisfactory alternative times and places at which the actor could perform the conduct with less offence (say by showing pornography only at home or in adult cinemas and not more generally).

The broader social impact of the conduct needs also to be considered. The more independent general usefulness the supposedly offending conduct has, the less the claim to

[34] For discussion, see Horder, "Harmless Wrongdoing and the Anticipatory Perspective on Criminalisation" in Sullivan and Dennis (eds.), *Seeking Security* (2012) 79; also, in the same volume, Simester, "Prophylactic Crimes", 59.

[35] *Offense to Others* (1985) 1. See also the collection of essays in von Hirsch and Simester (eds.), *Incivilities* (2006).

prohibition. For this purpose, free expression of opinion is, following Mill, deemed to have its own social value, "in virtue of the great social utility of free expression and discussion generally, as well as the vital personal interest most people have in being able to speak their minds fearlessly".[36] I may cause considerable and widespread offence when I advocate the legalisation of, say, necrophilia; but the importance of preserving free political debate is such as to outweigh any case for criminalisation that the offence may generate.

### *(i) Offensive conduct as a wrong*

The application of these considerations means that, on Feinberg's account, some conduct that widely offends should still be legally permissible, e.g. when committed in settings readily avoidable by others. Thus, although nudity may legitimately be criminalised when practised on city streets, similar exposure might nonetheless be permitted at designated beaches, which those not so inclined need not visit.

Even so, however, Feinberg underplays a further consideration: the need for the affront to be wrongful. It is not affront *per se* to the sensibilities of others—even widespread affront—that should justify possible state intervention, but affront *plus* valid reasons for objecting to the conduct.[37] Suppose, for example, that the sight of an interracial couple holding hands causes enormous affront in a particular community. It seems to us that, regardless of the scale of the reaction, there is no case for invoking the offence principle here, because there is nothing wrong with that couple's behaviour.[38]

This point is particularly important in the criminal law, which *punishes*, and censures, the offender for having done wrong. That being the case, the criminalisation of conduct should require a plausible claim of wrongdoing. With conduct that supposedly is offensive, one must therefore ask: why does the actor deserve censure? If the essence of offence is merely that the conduct displeases many people, then it is not clear that wrongdoing has occurred at all. "I don't like it" should never suffice as a basis for criminalisation, regardless of the numbers who say it. Better reasons need to be provided why there is something reprehensible about the behaviour that deserves a censuring response.

What makes offensive conduct wrong, generally speaking, is the manner in which it treats other persons. Racial insults are a paradigm of this class of case: they tend both to cause affront in the audience and to do so by communicating contempt for that audience. Another variety of offence is exhibitionism. Suppose that D is sitting peaceably in the park, but cannot concentrate on his newspaper because E and F are copulating noisily on the grass nearby. D may rightly complain. He has a legitimate claim not to have the intimate facts of E and F's relationship forced upon him. This may be singularly in point in locations like parks, which we value, *inter alia*, as places to interact with other persons who are not intimates, and where, consequently, such offensive activities are likely to cause much greater discomfort than they would in more private contexts.

[36] Feinberg, *Offense to Others* (1985) 44.

[37] Simester and von Hirsch, *Crimes, Harms, and Wrongs* (2011) chap. 6.

[38] Admittedly, as might be suggested by the example of the interracial couple, perceptions of morality can change over time. Societies as a whole can suffer from moral ignorance—many did exactly that regarding slavery. That is one of the worries about legal moralism, discussed in § 16.3 below.

***(ii) A communicative and conventional wrong***

In so far as offensive conduct is something that communicates to V, the person experiencing the conduct, a lack of respect and consideration, it is characteristically a form of expressive action. As such, even if one accepts the offence principle as a legitimate ground of criminalisation, such cases should be criminalised sparingly because of the importance of allowing free expression in a society. The need to accommodate diverse and sometimes inconsistent styles of life, which may depend for their success on being publicly manifested, militates in favour of a "thick skin" approach to the regulation of expressive acts, even when those acts are offensive to others. Friction is a characteristic of social interaction, at least in a pluralistic society. Such societies require of their members a certain robustness of sensibility, so that incivility may be tolerated for the sake of personal and cultural diversity.

A second reason for caution with the offence principle is how close its application can resemble that of the next principle we shall discuss, Legal Moralism.[39] Some of the most uncontroversial examples of offence involve sexual activity in public places. The examples are uncontroversial because there remains a strong moral consensus disapproving of such conduct, a consensus which underpins the convention that it should not be done. What counts for the offence principle may be the convention, but what generates the convention is the widespread moral view.

At the same time, the convention is not *merely* the articulation of a moral view. Legal Moralism is concerned with regulating actions that are morally wrong: the offence principle, by contrast, is concerned with how we treat each other. Conventions such as those governing acceptable conduct in public places thus serve an important instrumental purpose, by helping to delineate the boundaries between personal and public, and setting the terms of our interaction with strangers. D's respect for V implies respect for the terms under which they (usually, by convention) interact. This holds independently of the particular terms of the convention. When D exposes himself, uninvited, to V, he both violates the applicable social convention and, further, wrongs V by failing to respect the socially agreed terms under which she interacts with others.

## § 16.3 Legal Moralism

According to legal moralism, it is legitimate to use the criminal law to prohibit immorality *per se*—conduct that is wrong independently of any adverse effect it may have on other people. As Feinberg puts it, legal moralists hold that it "can be morally legitimate to prohibit conduct on the ground that it is inherently immoral, even though it causes neither harm nor offense to the actor or to others".[40] Legal moralism finds it justifiable to criminalise acts

[39] The potential for overlap may be seen in *DPP v Collins* [2006] UKHL 40, [2006] 1 WLR 2223; noted [2007] Crim LR 98, (2006) 17 Ent LR 236: in the context of sending a grossly offensive message by means of a public electronic communications network, contrary to s. 127(1)(a) of the Communications Act 2003, what counts as "grossly offensive" is an objective question, based on the standards of an "open and just" society (at [9]). As the commentators observe, even a private, adult chat-line call might therefore be illegal.

[40] *Harm to Others* (1984) 27. By the time he wrote *Harmless Wrongdoing* (1988), Feinberg himself had come to think that the state has *some* reason to regulate wrongs which float free of human interests; although he maintained that such reasons were likely to be insufficient to justify criminalisation. See *ibid.*, 321–3.

that may be termed free-floating evils, in that they neither infringe the rights of, nor harm, any other person.

Most obviously, such acts might include private, self-regarding, or consensual immorality, and the violation of religious norms.[41] A good example is *Brown*, mentioned earlier,[42] where the House of Lords held that, in the context of sadomasochistic sexual activity, the infliction of actual bodily harm upon a consenting adult "victim" was an offence. From the perspective of the harm principle, there is no wrong to V since the activity occurs with V's consent. But from the perspective of legal moralism, D's conduct may be regarded as inherently wrong—and therefore legitimately proscribed. (Indeed, V's consent simply makes V, too, a participant in the offence.) Another illustration is *Shaw v DPP*,[43] in which the defendant was charged with an offence of conspiring to corrupt public morals.[44] On appeal, the count in the indictment charging this offence was upheld by the House of Lords. According to Lord Simonds, "there remains in the courts of law a residual power to enforce the supreme and fundamental purpose of the law, to conserve not only the safety and order but also the moral welfare of the state".[45]

At one time, Lord Devlin controversially argued for legal moralism on the ground that a society's moral values are an indispensable part of its structural framework.[46] In turn, if harmless immoralities were permitted, this would tend to undermine the social fabric, dissolving the moral consensus underpinning society and leading, ultimately, to social disintegration and anarchy. Strictly speaking, Devlin's argument is not an argument in favour of pure legal moralism. Rather, it rests implicitly on the harm principle. Social disintegration, if it occurred, would certainly be a bad thing for the lives and interests of citizens. Further, if permitting some immoral act would lead to social disintegration then, subject to the problem of remote harms noted in § 16.1(i)(e), the state has prima facie reason to criminalise the act. To do so would not violate the liberal precepts of the harm principle.

The main problem with Devlin's social harm argument is the need to establish an empirical link between mere immorality and social disintegration. It may be that certain specific, immoral acts will tend to threaten the continuance of the social structure, but that possibility needs to be investigated for *each* specific act, and cannot simply be asserted as a general truth for *all* immoral acts, however minor.

More generally, pure legal moralism shares with Lord Devlin's version the characteristic of entrenching the *status quo ante*. By its nature, legal moralism is conservative, in that immorality is measured against the prevailing social mores of the time: difference in moral value is, by that standard, immoral and may therefore be suppressed. One objection to this approach, therefore, is that not all change is bad. The abolition of slavery was a good thing; so, too, it is desirable that mixed-race couples may now publicise their association, even in communities where segregation formerly was enforced. Especially in a heterogeneous society containing a wide variety of subcultures, moral stagnation enforced by the criminal law

[41] See, e.g., Feinberg, *Harmless Wrongdoing* (1988) 20–5. Cp. *R (on the application of Stephen Green) v The City of Westminster Magistrates' Court* [2007] EWHC 2785 (Admin), (2008) 19 Ent LR 54 (blasphemy, an offence since repealed).

[42] [1994] 1 AC 212; above, § 16.1; also § 11.9(iii).

[43] [1962] AC 220.

[44] Until then unknown: see above, §§ 2.2–3.

[45] [1962] AC 220, 267.

[46] Devlin, *The Enforcement of Morals* (1965) 8–14.

seems unattractive. Difference, even conflict, between the lives and values of citizens can be a dynamic force for the evolution of a vigorous, thriving, and valuable culture.

A related difficulty with legal moralism is the problem of identifying a stable classification of immoral acts. Are homosexual acts immoral in a manner that means they may permissibly be criminalised? It depends who, when, and where one asks. Criminalisation merely on the basis of immorality leaves a great deal to the whims and fashions of the times (and, indeed, of the prevailing location or culture: adultery, not proscribed at all in many countries, is a capital offence in others). The nature of modern secularism is such that it is increasingly unclear what moral frameworks are available, or agreed upon, by which to gauge whether an act is immoral and therefore eligible for proscription. As Alldridge has pointed out, some activities that once were regarded as *malum in se* are now entirely permissible, whereas some commercial activities that formerly were permitted are now regarded as very serious wrongs.[47] Thus a private, consenting homosexual act used to be a serious crime and now is (rightly) none whatsoever[48]—yet the essential nature of the conduct has not changed in the interim.

Perhaps surprisingly, this *ad hoc* view of morality was celebrated as a virtue by Lord Devlin: "*Shaw's* case settles for the purpose of the law that morality in England means what twelve men and women think it means—in other words it is to be ascertained as a question of fact".[49] Yet many areas of morality are open to honest and reasoned disagreement. The regulation of obscenity, for example, governs situations where different juries may reach opposite conclusions over what is moral and what is immoral. And criminal lawyers know all too well the difficulty of applying a homogeneous standard of "dishonesty" in theft.[50] This suggests that it will not do to criminalise conduct merely on the assumption that there is for each moral dispute an "objective" resolution.[51]

Were England and Wales a uniform society comprised of citizens with identical values, Lord Devlin's approach might present few problems. But that is not the case. Ours is a multicultural environment, incorporating diverse ethnic, religious, moral and philosophical perspectives. The law regulates in order to assist in the smooth functioning of our society, yet a multicultural society also needs tolerance. The guidance provided by the harm and offence principles are important aids in ensuring that tolerance, by ruling out criminal censure for mere immorality.[52] Prohibition on grounds of immorality exposes even legislators to the charge that, in truth, they are simply imposing their own moral values upon the nation.

There are better versions of legal moralism in subsequent literature.[53] Those versions tend to invoke critical ("objective") morality, rather than conventional morality, as the ground for criminalisation; and to claim that preventing immorality gives us *some* reason in favour of criminalising, a reason that need not be decisive—so it does not follow on such versions that we should *always* criminalise immoral conduct.[54]

47 Alldridge, "Making Criminal Law Known" in Shute and Simester (eds.), *Criminal Law Theory* (2002) 103, 107–11.

48 Cp. amendment of s. 12 of the Sexual Offences Act 1956 by s. 1 of the Sexual Offences Act 1967.

49 "Law, Democracy and Morality" (1962) 110 U Penn LR 635, 648.

50 Above, § 13.8(iv)(a).

51 For this reason, it is to be welcomed that acting *contra bonos mores* has been ruled too vague to count as criminal: *Hashman and Harrup v United Kingdom* (1999) 30 EHRR 241.

52 See generally Feinberg, *Harmless Wrongdoing* (1988).

53 See, e.g., Moore, *Placing Blame* (1997) chap. 16; Duff, "Towards a Modest Legal Moralism" (2014) 8 *Crim Law and Philosophy* 217; Duff, *The Realm of Criminal Law* (2018); also the essays in Renzo (ed.), *Symposium on Law, Liberty and Morality* (2013) 7 *Crim Law and Philosophy* 417–548.

54 As Edwards points out, however, those more recent versions tend to share, along with their earlier counterparts, a focus upon the immorality *of the conduct that is being considered for prohibition*. This makes those versions

It seems plausible that immorality is at least a condition of criminalisation. In Chapter 1 we emphasised the condemnatory nature of the criminal law. Criminal convictions articulate public judgements of wrongful behaviour by the defendant: that she has acted reprehensibly.[55] She is labelled as a wrongdoer who is eligible for punishment. When the state makes such pronouncements, it ought to tell the truth. In turn, this means that the prohibited act should actually *be* morally wrongful.[56]

Legal moralism, however, goes beyond that. It claims that immorality supplies a positive reason to criminalise. Indeed, for most legal moralists, immorality can in principle justify criminalisation without appeal to considerations such as harm or offence. At this point, the argument becomes more controversial. The difficulty lies in the potential for legal moralism to clash with the liberal ideal of autonomy. Criminalisation takes options away from people. It is an intrusive and condemnatory form of coercion. Accepting the general case for criminalising mere immorality will, inevitably, lead to restrictions of autonomy, especially because the criminal law is very coarse grained, so that its prohibitions are typically framed in broad rather than narrow terms. Given the diversity of human needs and preferences, criminal prohibitions will inevitably deprive some individuals of freedoms that are valuable to them: such persons will, in effect, be harmed by the prohibitions.

The strongest cases for depriving people of opportunities in this way arise where D's activity is likely to diminish the opportunities for others to live good lives. In these cases, a condition of D's well-being (her autonomy) is weighed against a condition of V's well-being: like is compared with like. But in these very cases, D's conduct is by definition harmful. Where, by contrast, the conduct is merely immoral, the interests of persons (such as D) are being weighed only against abstract judgements of morality. There is no well-being or autonomy-based reason *for* criminalisation, only against: like is not being compared with like. In a liberal society, the interests of persons should take priority at this point. Thus it is arguable that mere immorality is, by itself, insufficient for criminalisation.

## § 16.4 Paternalism

Feinberg summarises the Paternalistic justification of criminalisation as follows:[57]

> "It is always a good reason in support of a prohibition that it is probably necessary to prevent harm (physical, psychological, or economic) to the actor himself and there is probably no other means that is equally effective at no greater cost to other values."

Like the harm principle, paternalism demands harm. But it goes beyond the harm principle in that it warrants the criminalisation of self-harm: D may be prohibited, *for her own sake*, from performing certain acts. A standard legal example of such prohibitions is the criminal

of legal moralism act-centred rather than instrumental (by contrast, say, with Feinberg's formulations of the harm and offence principles: above, § 16.1). See Edwards, "An Instrumental Legal Moralism" (2018) 3 *Oxford Studies in Philosophy of Law* 153; Duff, *The Realm of Criminal Law* (Oxford: Oxford University Press, 2018) 243–9.

[55] Above, § 1.1(iii).

[56] Often, especially in crimes *mala prohibita*, the conduct is wrongful only *in light of the law*. For accounts of how this can be legitimate, see, e.g., Duff and Marshall, "'Remote Harms' and the Two Harm Principles" in Simester, du Bois-Pedain, and Neumann (eds.), *Liberal Criminal Theory: Essays for Andreas von Hirsch* (2014) 205, 214–22; Simester and von Hirsch, *Crimes, Harms, and Wrongs* (2011) 24–9.

[57] *Harm to Others* (1984) 26–7.

law duty to wear seat belts when driving a car.[58] The duty is imposed for D's own benefit, on the grounds that persons who fail to wear a seat belt are likely to suffer much more severe injuries in an accident than are those who wear one.[59]

Prima facie, there seems little that is objectionable about a law requiring persons to wear seat belts when in a car. But this is one of the strongest cases for paternalistic intervention. The obligation is a minor one, which does not hinder the activity of driving. It is a burden easily discharged, while the harm at risk and the costs of treatment are substantial. The state's insistence that D wear a seat belt is not destructive of her style of life. Thus the case is one where the disvalue attached to the infringement of D's autonomy is minor, and arguably outweighed by the interest in D's welfare that is advanced.

Paternalistic intervention may be appropriate more generally in cases where D's choice to harm herself cannot be said to be considered or responsible. Children and those lacking mental capacity have extensive restrictions imposed upon their ability to engage in sexual intercourse, on the grounds that the character and consequences of their choice to do so may not be fully understood.

But even if this argument be accepted in respect of seat belts and non-responsible actors, it cannot be generalised very far. In *Harm to Self*, Feinberg considers the theory of a broadly based paternalism in detail—and rejects it:[60]

> "The cases for and against legal paternalism then can be summed up as follows. In favor of the principle is the fact that there are many laws now on the books that *seem* to have had paternalism as an essential part of their implicit rationales, and that some of these at least, seem to most of us to be sensible and legitimate restrictions. It is also a consideration in favor of paternalism that preventable personal harm (set-back interest) is universally thought to be a great evil, and that such harm is no less harmful when self-caused than when caused by others. If society can substantially diminish the net amount of harm to interests caused from *all* sources, that would be a great social gain. If that prospect provides the moral basis underlying the harm to others principle, why should it not have application as well to self-caused harm and thus support equally the principle of legal paternalism?
>
> On the other side, it is argued that a consistent application of legal paternalism would lead to the creation of new crimes that would be odious and offensive to common sense, leading to the general punishment of risk-takers, the enforcement of prudence, and the interference with saints and heroes. Moreover, hard paternalistic justification of any restriction of personal liberty is especially offensive morally, because it invades the realm of personal autonomy where each competent, responsible, adult human being should reign supreme."

The obligation is on the legal paternalist to show why it is justified to coerce D and promote her welfare at the expense of her autonomy.

One way of approaching that challenge is by arguing that autonomy is only of instrumental value: having options is valuable only in so far as the options themselves are valuable. On this view, there is no value in permitting self-maiming, say by cutting one's arm

[58] We concentrate here on the driver on the ground that back-seat passengers who fail to wear seat belts may harm not only themselves but also those seated in front of them.

[59] It is sometimes argued that there is harm to others in such cases, since the state is likely to incur greater costs in providing healthcare to drivers who are more seriously injured after failing to wear a seat belt. This argument is not straightforward, however, since the state's intervention is voluntary; it is open to the state to refuse to treat such persons, or to require them to take out private insurance.

[60] *Harm to Self* (1986) 25.

off, because there is no value in the activity that is being permitted. However, this argument establishes only that there is no obligation on the state positively to foster or support such activities. It does not follow that the state has the right to *prohibit* valueless activities. Justified proscription through the criminal law requires something stronger: positive reasons why we should coerce, threaten, and impose sanctions upon a wrongdoer. The paternalistic legislative assertion, "We are sending you to jail for your own good", makes very little sense when addressed to responsible, autonomous, citizens in a mature liberal democracy. It amounts to saying, "we shall harm you lest you harm yourself". And punishing the choices of one autonomous agent as a deterrent to others is equally objectionable.

A moment's reflection, moreover, reveals that the potential for invasive paternalism is enormous. So many features of modern life are not especially good for us—getting drunk, playing dangerous sports, smoking, eating fatty foods, failing to take regular exercise. A consistent paternalist should seek to eliminate them all. But freedom includes the freedom to go wrong. Respect for persons as autonomous agents involves respect for individuals as deliberating agents who have the capacity independently to pursue goals and values which they have themselves adopted. If we are not allowed to choose badly then, in effect, our choices are no longer determined by our own goals and values. A paternalistic legal system which made people's choices for them may well end up alienating people from their own conduct:[61]

> "Why not interfere with someone else's shaping of his own life? . . . I conjecture that the answer is connected with that elusive and difficult notion: the meaning of life. A person's shaping his life in accordance with some overall plan is his way of giving meaning to his life; only a being with the capacity to so shape his life can have or strive for a meaningful life."

Our well-being does not just require the successful pursuit of valuable goals; it requires also that we identify and engage with those goals—that they be *our* goals. Paternalism, by contrast, imposes the state's goals and values upon us. In the criminal law, moreover, it does so coercively. When a person's choices are pre-empted by the law, she does not shape her own life.[62] And to live a meaningful life, one must shape it oneself.[63]

## § 16.5 Negative grounds for intervention: regulatory alternatives

Perhaps we can establish a positive case for regulating some candidate activity through the criminal law. But we need also to consider whether, nonetheless, there are reasons *not* to criminalise. The next stage of the enquiry involves considering whether the criminal law is the most appropriate tool for regulating the activity. In particular, the advantages and disadvantages of using the criminal law should be measured against those accruing to alternative regulatory mechanisms. As a general rule, if some other form of state intervention falling short of criminalisation would effectively regulate the conduct at issue, that alternative should be preferred. The criminal prohibition should be deployed only as a last resort.

[61] Nozick, *Anarchy, State and Utopia* (1974) 50.

[62] Raz, *The Morality of Freedom* (1986) 382.

[63] For a more confined defence of paternalism, advocating the continuing use and development of civil law methods to prevent (in particular) teenage and young adult suicides and serious self-harm, see Sullivan, "Liberalism and Constraining Choice: the Cases of Death and Serious Bodily Harm" in Smith and Deazley (eds.), *The Legal, Medical and Cultural Regulation of the Body* (2009) 205.

### *(i) Tax*

On occasions in the past, Western governments have attempted to regulate alcohol by criminal prohibition. The results were disastrous: sales and consumption simply went underground, creating a black market ripe for extortion and racketeering. Nowadays, control is exercised via licensing arrangements and tax. One of the standard modern functions of the tax system is to regulate behaviour by manipulating the cost of products in order to reduce (or sometimes, increase[64]) demand. The mechanism of tax is one means by which the state can influence, without prohibiting outright, the behaviour of citizens. Part of the overt rationale for tobacco and alcohol duties is to deter consumers from smoking and drinking and, at least in part, to help ensure that the price of cigarettes and alcohol reflects the true cost to society (including healthcare costs) of these products.

Consumption taxes of this sort do, of course, affect options. If the price of his cigarettes is increased, D will have less money left for other activities. In the absence of offsetting income tax rebates, such measures tend to have a regressive effect on the poor. As such, tax measures are both an improvement on criminalisation in so far as they are less coercive and preserve more options for citizens and, at the same time, less equitable than criminalisation in so far as they are likely to affect different socio-economic classes asymmetrically.

### *(ii) Tort law*

A second option is for the state to regulate an activity by means of a statutory or common law tort. Intervention through the civil law involves significant burdens in terms of time and money associated with the civil legal process, but remains less coercive than the criminal justice process: there is no arrest, no imprisonment, and no record of a criminal conviction. In some situations, therefore, the creation of a statutory tort may be an excellent alternative to criminal sanctions. This is especially so when considering compliance incentives for large corporations. An industrial accident costing many lives might lead to a company facing fines without limits if the accident was caused by gross failures of senior management;[65] yet that same company may be far more concerned by the millions of pounds it might incur in tort damages on account of simple negligence.

Civil liability is not a complete alternative to its criminal counterpart. Tort law effectively prices rather than prohibits; it lacks the mandatory character of the criminal law, and requires a claimant with adequate resources to bring a legal action. Moreover, in many instances tortfeasers may be able to defray the costs of liability by means of insurance.

### *(iii) Other mechanisms*

There is a variety of other methods for addressing harmful or odious behaviour, including advertising and licensing. A classic example of the former is the campaign against drink-driving, which has been instrumental in bringing about a sea-change in public attitudes toward the wrongfulness of driving after consuming alcohol. Although not appropriate to

[64] For example, in the case of children. One reason for providing benefits and/or tax credits to parents is that children are, *inter alia*, public goods; hence the state has reason to subsidise part of the cost of their upbringing.

[65] Corporate Manslaughter and Homicide Act 2007, s. 1.

all varieties of wrong (for example, there is normally no need to polemicise against performing acts that are already widely perceived as *mala in se*), education and advertising can in some instances raise awareness of the potential harmfulness of an activity where that harmfulness had previously gone unremarked.

Licensing is also a familiar form of modern regulation. The performance of many activities—e.g. running a public house, possessing a firearm, and even driving—requires a licence. All of these activities import risks of harm, either direct or remote. But each is valuable, and it may be inappropriate, because of the social costs, to criminalise the activity altogether. So the activities are permitted, but only under conditions that are regulated by means of licensing systems. The criminal law, in turn, sits in the background to prohibit persons from carrying out each activity without, or in breach of, the licence. Licensing systems represent a significant limitation of individual liberty, but fall a long way short of outright prohibition. Moreover, they offer a more flexible tool than do generalised criminal laws, since the terms of each licence can be adapted to specific cases by the magistrates or authority responsible for administering that licence.

Another modern-day mechanism for monitoring specialist commercial activities is the establishment of activity-specific regulatory agencies equipped with powers to impose sanctions, including disqualifications and financial penalties, for norm-violating behaviour. According to the Law Commission, "There are now over 60 national regulators with the power, subject to certain limitations or checks, to make (criminal) law".[66] These kinds of agencies are particularly familiar in the financial services industry and the delivery of public utilities. There are certainly dangers in these kinds of regulation,[67] not least of which is the risk of having a punitive system without the protections embedded in the criminal law. As a means of administering standards of conduct for commercial actors, however, they can offer a useful alternative to the use of strict-liability criminal offences, while not displacing the role of the criminal law in more serious forms of wrongdoing.[68]

### *(iv) Contra: some advantages of using the criminal law*

Even though alternative methods of regulation, if practical, should normally be preferred to the criminal law, it is worth noting that there are sometimes advantages in resorting to criminalisation. Unlike any other area of law, the criminal law systematically stigmatises activities (through prohibition) and persons (though conviction and punishment). But sometimes that stigmatisation is appropriate. Murder should be criminalised, not taxed. The symbolic significance of enacting that some activity is a criminal offence can be a reason *in favour* of criminalisation, at least where stigmatisation of the activity is desirable. If used selectively, the creation of a criminal law can be a tool for communicating to the public that the prohibited activity is a serious wrong that *must* not be done.

[66] LCCP No. 195, *Criminal Liability in Regulatory Contexts* (2010) para. 1.21.

[67] See, e.g., Braithwaite, *Regulatory Capitalism* (2008) 4: "the reciprocal relationship between corporatization and regulation creates a world in which there is more governance of all kinds. *1984* did arrive."

[68] See Macrory, *Regulatory Justice* (2006). See also LCCP No. 195, *Criminal Liability in Regulatory Contexts* (2010). The Macrory Review recommended introducing into English law a civil-law regime of non-fault monetary administrative penalties. The difficulty any regulatory system of this kind faces, of course, is to avoid issuing judgments involving censorious hard treatment—in which case, the process becomes in-substance criminal: cp. *Öztürk v Germany* (1984) 6 EHRR 409.

There are also some practical considerations. Given that the state pays the costs of investigating, prosecuting, and punishing criminal conduct, it may be better placed to regulate wrongs than are, say, private individuals through the law of tort. Suppose that V's neighbour, D, throws a stone through one of the panes in V's greenhouse, which it will cost some £20 to replace. It is likely to be impractical for V to pursue D through the law of tort. But a criminal prosecution will cost V only my time. In this respect, despite the formidable nature of our criminal justice system, and of being subjected to its processes, criminal regulation by the state may yet augment the rule of law, through increasing the consistency with which legal rights are enforced in like cases, rather than leaving the matter to irregular administration by individual claimants.

## § 16.6 Negative grounds for intervention: the rule of law

If the criminal law *is* to be used, its deployment should comply with a variety of constraints, both rule of law and pragmatic. The former, which we outline here, were discussed more fully in chapter 2.

### *(i) Rule of law constraints on criminalisation*

First, it is desirable that the form of the criminal law proposed meets rule of law constraints, which were considered in §§ 2.1–4. In particular, the law should be prospective not retrospective (§ 2.2).[69] Secondly, the law should give fair warning, by defining the prohibited activity with sufficient certainty (§ 2.3). It needs to be understandable, predictable, and not vague. The more clearly defined the offence, the less potential there is for injustice with respect to those whose conduct falls close to its limits. Further, the more certainty there is in the drafting, the more confident society can be that an individual convicted under that offence is fairly labelled (§ 2.4). The law must make clear what sort of criminal each offender is—what the conviction is for. The criminal law speaks to society as well as wrongdoers when it convicts them, and it should communicate its judgment with precision, by accurately naming and describing the crime of which they are convicted.

Specificity of drafting has an additional dimension, in that more narrowly defined crimes are less likely to lead to discretionary enforcement. If an offence is too broadly drafted, so that it requires selective prosecution, the liability of defendants is, in effect, remaindered to the decisions of officials—creating the risk of unfair, inappropriate, or potentially even discriminatory prosecutions.[70] It is not unknown for defendants to be found guilty of offences even though, in the view of the court, a prosecution should not have been brought.[71] This possibility should be minimised.

[69] Cp. Art. 7(1) of the ECHR: "no one shall be held guilty of any criminal offence on account of any act or omission which did not constitute a criminal offence under national or international law at the time when it was committed. Nor shall a heavier penalty be imposed than the one that was applicable at the time the criminal offence was committed." This rule is also a common law principle of statutory interpretation: "in the absence of express words or a truly necessary implication, Parliament must be presumed to legislate on the assumption that the principle of legality will supplement the text." *B (a minor) v DPP* [2000] AC 428, 470 (Lord Steyn).

[70] Compare the use, not intended by the legislature, of Anti-Social Behaviour Orders (now replaced by a variety of other legal measures) against prostitutes and beggars: Burney, "'No Spitting': Regulation of Offensive Behaviour in England and Wales" in von Hirsch and Simester (eds.), *Incivilities* (2006) 195, 206.

[71] E.g. *Smedleys Ltd v Breed* [1974] AC 839; *Hart v Bex* [1957] Crim LR 622 (DC); *James & Son v Smee* [1955] 1 QB 78 (DC).

### *(ii) The individuation of offences*

How many offences do we need? Do we really need to distinguish theft from deception, rape from sexual assault, and sections 18 from 20 in the OAPA 1861? Or would it be enough just to have instead a few generic crimes including, say, violation of another's property right; violation of another's person; damaging the environment; and so on? The answer to the last question is no. While the law may sometimes draw unnecessary distinctions, broad category offences would be inappropriate. Enacting only generic crimes would tend to suppress the fact that, within each field of harmful wrongdoing, each of our existing offences may involve a different wrong, a different harm, or both. It is for this reason that they are rightly separate offences.

In looking to explain and justify the existence of any offence, it is necessary to identify what harm, and what wrong, is addressed by that crime. Obtaining by deception may, for example, lead to much the same immediate harm as does theft—a straightforward diminution of V's resources—but the wrong is different. The thief bypasses ordinary mechanisms for allocating and transferring property. The deceiver exploits them, and induces V to make the transfer herself. Thus deception is not inconsistent with V's proprietary rights in the same manner as is theft. As such, the two are rightly distinguished by criminal law.[72]

This claim, about the importance of drawing distinctions, is an extension of the principles of fair warning (§ 2.3) and fair labelling (§ 2.4). *Ex ante*, citizens need to know where they stand. They need advance warning concerning their actions; in particular, about whether what they are going to do is a crime and, if so, what sort of crime it is. *Ex post*, offenders ought to be labelled with an adequate degree of precision, in order that the criminal record sufficiently identifies the gist of D's criminal wrongdoing. Both principles require that each offence is labelled and defined in such a way that it conveys to citizens an accurate moral picture of the prohibited conduct, one that is neither misleading nor unduly vague or overgeneralised. Offences should, so far as is practical, reflect meaningful distinctions in the public mind between different types of culpable wrongdoing. This mandates that they are drawn up in such a way that they capture, and differentiate, significant differences in the harmfulness, wrongfulness, and/or culpability of various types of action.

By way of illustration, the distinctions between murder, maiming, and criminal damage are significant because the harms (and indeed the wrongs) at stake are quite different. Their differences are sufficient to warrant enacting separate offences, since the meaning and moral significance of each action is clearly distinguished in the public mind. Attempted murder, too, is rightly distinguished from murder because of the difference in resulting harm. And even if the harm is identical in murder and manslaughter, distinguishing the two is justifiable because they constitute significantly different wrongs. Likewise, although the harms of theft and of criminal damage are similar, the manners in which they are inflicted involve two different forms of wrongdoing; forms that are sufficiently distinct in the public mind to warrant independent recognition by the criminal law.

Occasionally, too, there may be a case for distinguishing between two harmful activities on the grounds of culpability. An assault being negligent with regard to any consequential risks to life would typically lack the same culpability as an assault being reckless

[72] Simester and Sullivan, "On the Nature and Rationale of Property Offences" in Duff and Green (eds.), *Defining Crimes* (2005) 168, 188–90; Chalmers and Leverick, "Fair Labelling in Criminal Law" (2008) 71 *MLR* 217, 239–40.

about those same risks—and, if ever worthy of being criminalised as form of a homicide (which we doubt), ought surely to be a separate offence and not lumped in with murder or manslaughter.

Not every difference is worthy of capture. Even though many US states follow the old common law in drawing a rudimentary distinction between petty and grand larceny, nobody would suggest that there should be a much more refined series of theft offences, graded in minute detail (say, theft of less than £50 value; theft of less than £100 value; theft of less than £200 value; and so on). Excessively specific offences risk clogging the trial process with unmeritorious technical argument, and obfuscating the moral clarity of the law's communications. At least in the context of non-specialist activities such as property offences, people (both *ex ante* and *ex post*) need to know the law's requirements in gist and not precisely. As such, meaning is better conveyed through publicly shared moral distinctions that are broadly rather than narrowly significant, provided those broader distinctions communicate an adequately nuanced statement of the prohibited wrongdoing. The degree of specificity that the law should adopt when distinguishing various harms and wrongs is, therefore, a trade-off that depends in part on the range of moral differentiations informing the public imagination. The fragmentation of the particular must be balanced against the vagueness of the general.

## § 16.7 Negative grounds for intervention: practical constraints

Finally, in addition to rule of law constraints, a variety of other considerations must be taken into account before concluding that criminalisation through the proposed offence is the right response.

### *(i) What side-effects will criminalisation have?*

Suppose a clearly drafted law is proposed that criminalises the failure to disclose one's HIV-positive status to a sexual partner. One thing to consider before enacting such a law is whether it will have the effect of deterring those persons who are most at risk of contracting HIV from being tested. By not knowing their status, they keep themselves outside the scope of the offence—but without advancing the underlying aim of the offence, which is to protect their partners. In these sorts of cases, the legislator should consider whether, in effect, enacting the proposed law will do more harm than good.

It has not escaped judicial notice that one of the concerns about the use of drugs is consequential criminality: the prospect that drug users will steal, deal in drugs, enter into prostitution, or commit other crimes in order to finance their habit.[73] But a responsible legislator might also think that these considerations argue for *de*criminalisation. The price of illegal drugs is high because the drugs are illegal—if not illegal, no doubt users will need less money to pay for their habits, leading (it may be thought) to a significant reduction in consequential crime. Compare, too, the eras of alcohol prohibition, which led to an upsurge in violent conflict between gangs involved in the black market that arose to replace the licit

[73] E.g. *R v Aramah* (1982) 4 Cr App R (S) 407, 408–9 (Lord Lane CJ). See more generally Alldridge, "Dealing with Drug Dealing" in Simester and Smith (eds.), *Harm and Culpability* (1996) 239.

trade. If criminalisation of an activity is likely to produce such undesirable consequences as these, that is a powerful reason not to prohibit.

### *(ii) Pragmatics of the criminal justice system*

A proposed offence might also be rejected for reasons of implementation. In particular, the offence needs to be capable of being administered, by enforcement authorities and prosecutors. Ideally, it will be specified in clear and unambiguous terms, so that (as well as giving fair warning to citizens) those responsible for its administration will be confident of their ability to use the new law with predictable outcomes. Further, the terms it uses will cohere with and not reinvent existing legal concepts, facilitating understanding by professionals within the criminal justice system and avoiding the need for costly retraining exercises.

Another consideration is policing. The detection of some proposed crimes may be too difficult: this is one reason not to criminalise, say, unmarried sexual intercourse that takes place in private. Alternatively, crimes may be detectable only by invasive methods of surveillance; it needs to be considered to what extent the power to use such methods is desirable. There is also the question of cost: how expensive are the means of investigation? Will enforcement agencies be able to afford to monitor the new offence? Will effective policing of the offence require additional resources and legal powers?

There are many other issues that must be resolved when a new offence is created (mode of trial, evidential requirements, sentencing options, etc.). We cannot do justice to them all here. The key point is that, even though a prima facie case can be made in favour of criminalising an activity, e.g. because it is harmful to others, it does not follow that criminal legislation is the best response. Other forms of intervention need to be considered; sometimes, it may be best not to legislate at all. The criminal law is a powerful, expensive, and invasive tool. It should not be used lightly.

# 17

# DEFENCES: AN OVERVIEW

In Chapters 10–15 we have outlined a number of different offences in English criminal law, discussing the elements (actus reus and mens rea) as they are defined and applied. In Chapters 18–21 we discuss a range of (complete[1]) defences that a defendant may invoke when charged with those offences.

If D brings about the actus reus of an offence with the requisite mens rea, then, prima facie, she has committed that offence. But these are not the only components of criminal liability. Conduct which is prima facie an offence will not lead to a conviction if the defendant has a recognised defence:

> "[A]s a matter of analysis we can think of a crime as being made up of three ingredients, actus reus, mens rea and (a negative element) absence of a valid defence."[2]

To illustrate this distinction, consider the following scenario:

> Imagine that you are watching a video showing D striking V in the face with his fist. From the clip, it seems that D's conduct was deliberate. There is no indication that D was in a state of automatism[3] or that the blow was in any way accidental. You are instructed to give an account of what, if any, criminal offences D may have committed.

It appears that D has committed a battery. The elements of that offence, set out above in § 11.3, look to be satisfied. Indeed, if V has suffered more than transient and trifling injury, other more serious offences may also come into play.[4]

Before we attribute any criminal liability, however, we need to know more about *why* D struck V. This enquiry is not open ended. When analysing offences, we did not engage with the full complexity of D's intentions or beliefs within any single event, but rather we focused only on those mental states relevant to the mens rea of the offence charged. Similarly, for defences, our enquiry into *why* D struck V is qualified: we are only looking for reasons that have the potential to engage a recognised criminal defence, to block D's path to liability. Many of these (legally relevant) reasons will be discussed in the chapters that follow. For example: despite the appearance of a deliberate strike, D may not have understood his actions due to an involuntarily intoxicated mistake (Chapter 18); D may have been delusional, perhaps not recognising V as a person at all (Chapter 19); D's attack may have been

[1] The successful application of a complete defence results in D's acquittal. Partial defences, in contrast, merely reduce liability from a more serious to a less serious criminal conviction. The only partial defences currently are those that apply to murder, by way of voluntary manslaughter, discussed above, §§ 10.5, 10.6.

[2] Lanham, "Larsonneur Revisited" [1976] *Crim LR* 276, 276. On the distinction between "offence elements" and "defence elements" see generally Campbell, "Offence and Defence" in Dennis (ed.), *Criminal Law and Criminal Justice* (1987) 73; Williams, "Offences and Defences" (1982) 2 *LS* 233; above, § 1.3.

[3] Above, § 4.3.

[4] OAPA 1861, ss. 47, 20, 18.

deliberate, but done on the coercive instruction of another (Chapter 20); or D may have been defending against an imminent attack from V (Chapter 21). D's deliberate punching of V confronts us with evidence of a prima facie crime unless there is some *explanation* why, despite appearances, D should not be convicted for that crime. All of these explanations, and various others like them, can be described, in the broadest of terms, as "defences".

Our focus here, and in the following chapters, is on the "general" defences. These are defences that apply to (i.e. have the potential to refute D's liability for) a wide range of offences, and across offence types. For example, the defence of insanity will apply with equal effect regardless of the offence charged.[5] This is why, despite engaging with several offence-specific defences in earlier chapters,[6] discussion of the general defences is reserved to these final chapters and will be analysed in relation to the full range of offences.

In the present chapter, we provide some essential introductory material that is relevant across the general defences. First, we unpack two important distinctions used to categorise the general defences, focusing on their structure (failure of proof versus substantive defences[7]) and their exculpatory claims (justification and excuse[8]). Following this, we discuss burdens of proof,[9] before finally providing a brief schematic of the defences we will be analysing.[10]

## § 17.1 "Failure of proof" versus "supervening" defences

Defences may take very different forms but generally fall into one of two groups. First, the explanation D offers may suggest that the prosecution has failed to prove the definitional elements of the crime charged (i.e. the actus reus and the mens rea). Alternatively, D's explanation may concede that the definitional elements of the crime charged are present but contend that, nonetheless, liability should not be imposed because D's conduct was justified or excused.[11]

Strictly speaking, "defences" falling within the first group are not defences at all: they are denials that the prosecution has satisfied its burden of proof. D is not appealing to a set of rules to exculpate herself from an offence prima facie committed, but denying that she committed the prima facie offence itself; D "didn't do it", so there is no need for a defence. It remains common for failure of proof claims to be called, loosely, defences. For example, we might describe as a "defence" D's claim that she was wrongly identified as the perpetrator (i.e. a denial of responsibility for any offence elements), or that she caused the harm accidentally (a denial of mens rea, save for strict liability offences, and possibly of voluntariness), and so on. Beyond this, there are several examples where failures of proof

[5] Below, § 19.2.

[6] Such as the defence of acting reasonably when assisting or encouraging crimes (above, § 9.1(iv)(b)) and the defence of consent for the offences against the person (above, § 11.9).

[7] Below, § 17.1.

[8] Below, § 17.2.

[9] Below, § 17.3.

[10] Below, § 17.4.

[11] Statutory exemptions or diplomatic immunity could be described as a third structure of "defence", ousting D's conduct from the realm of the court. Such defences are procedural, however, rather than substantive, and are outside the sphere of this text. Cf. Dsouza, "Justifications and Rights-Displacements" (2024) 18 *Crim Law and Philosophy* 519.

are explicitly described as defences within the common law. Perhaps the most prominent examples relate to automatism[12] and intoxication.[13] To illustrate the latter:

> Suppose, in our example above, that D's punch broke V's jaw. D has been charged with causing grievous bodily harm with intent to cause grievous bodily harm.[14] In a case of direct attack, a finding that D intended seriously to hurt V may be inferred from the primary facts unless D can cast doubt on the reliability of that inference.[15] He may seek to do this, for example, by adducing evidence that he was intoxicated and thus did not form the intent the crime requires.[16]

If D succeeds in raising a reasonable doubt as to his intent, he will not be liable for the section 18 offence; his intoxication "defence" will have been successful. But, notwithstanding that courts and commentators often use the language of defences to characterise such cases, they are, in substance, failure of proof claims. It is important to recognise the structural differences between these claims and those within the second group.

By contrast with failure of proof "defences", the second group comprises what may be termed supervening or true defences. In this second group, proof of the elements of the prima facie offence *is not* denied. Rather, D claims that a conviction would be unjust because justificatory or excusatory circumstances were present.[17] For instance:

> Assume that D struck V in order to defend himself, because V was about to attack him with a knife. D's response to the danger here is not unreasonable; and so what would otherwise be unlawful becomes lawful. There was an intentional infliction of force on another, but a finding of battery is deflected by the justifiable nature of D's actions.

On these facts, D is entitled to an acquittal.

The structural differences between these two types of grounds for acquittal are conceptually clear. But since the outcome is the same—D's acquittal—we might question whether the distinction matters in practice. Indeed, within the common law, it remains unclear whether certain liability elements should be interpreted as offence elements (where denial becomes a failure of proof) or supervening defences (appealed to for exculpation); and judges have adopted different conventions. Consent, in the context of non-fatal offending, provides a prominent example. In *Brown*,[18] the House of Lords had to decide, *inter alia*, whether consent by V to the force applied by D was compatible with proof of *assault* occasioning actual bodily harm.[19] For the minority,[20] lack of consent was analysed as an integral element of the actus reus of assault; so the presence of consent would imply a failure of proof of the prima facie offence. For the majority,[21] the application of force constituted the actus reus of the offence and consent was something to be raised by way of supervening defence. Yet in practice, the dynamics of the trial often look the same, whichever perspective is adopted. If the prosecution adduces convincing evidence that D deliberately struck V, a conviction for

[12] See § 4.3 and § 18.5; and Child and Reed, "Automatism Is Never a Defence" (2014) 65 *NILQ* 167.
[13] Below, § 18.4. Simester, "Intoxication Is Never a Defence" [2009] *Crim LR* 3.
[14] OAPA 1861, s. 18.
[15] *Moloney* [1985] AC 905; *Beeson* [1994] Crim LR 190 (CA).
[16] *Beard* [1920] AC 479; *Sheehan* [1975] 2 All ER 960 (CA).
[17] *Per* Smith, "On Actus Reus and Mens Rea" in Glazebrook (ed.), *Reshaping the Criminal Law* (1978) 95, 98: "they do not negative either traditional mens rea *or* actus reus, but operate in some way independently".
[18] [1994] AC 212. See above, § 11.9 and below, § 21.1.
[19] The term "assault" in s. 47 of the OAPA 1861 comprehends battery as well as "pure" assault; see above, § 11.4.
[20] Lord Mustill and Lord Slynn.
[21] Lords Templeman, Jauncey, and Lowry.

battery will normally follow unless D offers some explanation to avoid conviction. Whether his explanation (V consented) is conceptualised as throwing doubt on the prosecution's prima facie case or as raising a supervening defence in response to the prima facie case, an evidential onus effectively (and in the case of defences, formally) rests on D to raise the issue. If D's evidence raises the possibility of V's consent, the prosecution then has the legal burden of disproving the reality of V's consent.[22]

To answer this pragmatic scepticism: there are at least two reasons why distinguishing between failures of proof and supervening defences matters, and why courts *should* avoid the language of defences entirely in relation to the former. The first is conceptual, recognising that using the language of defences to describe the absence of offence elements has the potential to confuse and distort debate.[23] We see this in the analysis and application of automatism, for example, where the language of defences has been employed to understand the basic *offence requirement* of voluntary action. If one analyses voluntariness as an essential offence element, threshold questions tend to become focused on what level of capacity and/or control is required to establish a responsible agent eligible for blame.[24] However, once the same issue is recast as a defence enquiry, employing the term automatism, a quite different and more restrictive question emerges, asking what level of incapacity and/or lack of control D must demonstrate to remove himself from criminal blame. Arguably, the current threshold established in *Coley*,[25] placing irrational and unaware conduct *within* the scope of voluntariness, was only made possible by focusing on the defence enquiry alone.[26] This is problematic not simply because we disagree with the Draconian approach adopted in *Coley*, but also because it is premised on an implicit mischaracterisation: D is not seeking to exculpate himself from established criminal blame, we are questioning whether such blame should be attributed to start with; we are questioning whether D is even *eligible* for blaming judgements in respect of his behaviour: in a sense, whether he has "acted" at all.

The second reason why it is important to distinguish the two groups relates to the application of prior fault rules. Prior fault rules apply where, as Robinson puts it, D is culpable for "causing the conditions of his own defence".[27] Take the following example:

> Let us imagine that D wants to harm V, but does not want to get into trouble for doing so. Contriving to make use of a criminal defence, D intentionally provokes V into attacking him with a knife, and then strikes V in a manner that prevents the knife attack.

If we take the final part of this account alone—D's striking V to prevent a knife attack—D's conduct may well satisfy the terms of self-defence as a supervening defence. However, it is far from clear that D should be allowed to rely on the defence. We may want to exclude its availability because of D's *prior* conduct.[28] A variety of prior fault rules exist within the current law, qualifying or excluding the application of supervening defences. Prior fault rules

[22] Below, § 17.3.
[23] Simester, *Fundamentals*, chap. 17.
[24] This is how we discuss voluntariness above, § 4.3.
[25] [2013] EWCA Crim 223, [2013] MHLR 171.
[26] Child, "Defence of a Basic Voluntary Act Requirement in Criminal Law from Philosophies of Action" (2020) 23 *New Crim LR* 437.
[27] Robinson, "Causing the Conditions of One's Own Defense" (1985) 71 *Virg LR* 1.
[28] Below, § 21.2(i)(b); *Rashford* [2005] EWCA Crim 3377.

also apply to certain failure of proof defences as well. But herein lies the crucial point: prior fault rules perform a very different role in the context of failures of proof. For example:

> D voluntarily consumes a cocktail of alcohol and various drugs, prompting a cluster of auditory and visual hallucinations. Believing he is hitting a punching bag, D hits V.

Taking the final part of this account alone—D's striking what he believes to be a punching bag—D may correctly claim to lack mens rea for an offence against the person (i.e. raising a failure of proof). Again, however, given D's *prior* drug taking, there is a strong intuition that D should not escape liability on this basis; and, as we discuss in Chapter 18, the common law has developed prior fault rules to prevent this outcome. There is an important difference here from D provoking attack for the purpose of self-defence however; one easily lost where failures of proof are conflated with supervening defences. Prior fault in the context of a failure of proof is not simply preventing the application of an exculpatory defence. Rather, prior fault rules are effectively substituting for missing mens rea and/or voluntariness elements to establish criminal blame. As such, the use of prior fault in this context requires particular scrutiny, asking whether D's prior fault is capable of establishing culpability of equivalence with those missing offence elements.[29]

## § 17.2 Justifications, excuses, and exemptions

As a further sub-division, within the group of *supervening defences*, it is common for academics in particular to distinguish between "justificatory" and "excusatory" defences, as well as (though less often) a category of "exemptions" from liability.[30] D may be acquitted in circumstances where his putatively criminal conduct may be said to be *justified* (e.g. reasonable force used to repel a deadly threat). Or he may be acquitted in circumstances where he is *excused* because his conduct was insufficiently culpable for a conviction, but where his actions remain a legal wrong (e.g. where D punched V because he mistakenly—and unreasonably—assumed that V was about to attack him).[31] The language of *exemption* may be used to describe defences that apply to remove D from the realms of criminal judgement altogether, such as legal infancy (e.g. D punches V, but D is five years old).[32]

Suggestions have been made that a formal legal distinction should be drawn between justified conduct and excused conduct, a distinction to be reflected by different forms of

[29] Williams, "Voluntary Intoxication—A Lost Cause" (2013) 129 *LQR* 264; Child, "Prior-Fault: Blocking Defences or Constructing Crimes" in Reed and Bohlander (eds.) *General Defences* (2014) 37.

[30] Simester, *Fundamentals*, chaps. 17–19; Dsousa, *Rationale-Based Defences in Criminal Law* (2017); Dressler, "Reflections on *Dudley and Stephens* and Killing the Innocent: Taking the Wrong Conceptual Path" in Baker and Horder (eds.), *The Sanctity of Life and the Criminal Law* (2013) 126; Horder, *Excusing Crime* (2004); Corrado (ed.), *Justification and Excuse in the Criminal Law* (1994); Smith, *Justification and Excuse in the Criminal Law* (1989); Greenawalt, "The Perplexing Borders of Justification and Excuse" (1984) 84 *Col LR* 1897; Dressler, "New Thoughts about the Concept of Justification in the Criminal Law: A Critique of Fletcher's Thinking and Rethinking" (1984) 32 *UCLA LR* 61; Williams, "The Theory of Excuses" [1982] *Crim LR* 732; Fletcher, *Rethinking Criminal Law* (1978) chap. 10.

[31] As in *Ashley v Chief Constable for Sussex* [2008] UKHL 25, [2008] 1 AC 962, where the House of Lords accepted that D did not commit any crime when he used force on V because he believed, albeit unreasonably, that force was necessary to prevent crime, yet held that D's conduct was tortious.

[32] Below, § 19.3.

acquittal and in the taxonomy of criminal defences.[33] We do not use the distinction as an organising principle in the following chapters (save for the special case of necessity). Nonetheless, in light of the frequent arguments that have been made in favour of using the distinction to classify defences, it is necessary to explain why we have not deployed it here.

At one time, English law distinguished justifiable homicide from excusable homicide. A justified killer could retain his possessions whereas a merely excused killer had to forfeit his possessions to the Crown. In 1828, forfeiture was abolished, and since then this jurisdiction has not distinguished between justification and excuse on the formal plane. Paul Robinson, for one, would reinstitute a formal distinction between cases of justification and cases of excuse. For Robinson, if D is merely excused, he should receive a verdict in the form "not guilty by reason of excuse". Although D would be acquitted, civil coercive measures may be taken to further the goals of special deterrence and rehabilitation. If D's conduct is found to be justified, then, according to Robinson, the verdict should be "justified" and D would be free from any form of coercive measures.[34]

Clearly, if the distinction between justification and excuse is to be as salient as Robinson proposes, a clear and usable differentiation is required between cases of justification and cases of excuse. How does Robinson mark the difference? For him, the justification of conduct does *not* require investigating the motivation and practical reasoning of the actor. Justification arises, in a utilitarian fashion, from the consequences that D's conduct brings about. If those consequences are beneficial for society, the conduct is justified. For excuses, on the other hand, the consequences of D's conduct may violate legally protected interests, but D may nonetheless be excused provided that, in all the circumstances, he is insufficiently blameworthy to merit conviction. As Robinson succinctly puts it, "an actor's *conduct* is justified; *an actor* is excused".[35]

Robinson's position is vividly illustrated by his view of the case of Motti Ashkenazi, an Israeli who, with dishonest intent, took a backpack he saw lying on a crowded beach. Unbeknown to Ashkenazi, the bag contained a bomb: inadvertently, he saved many lives. Because of this, Robinson would deny that Ashkenazi committed theft.[36] He argues that such conduct would not fall within the prohibitory norm of theft, because the criminal law is not concerned to punish beneficent outcomes. This principle, which exempts a person such as Ashkenazi, provides a derogation from the prohibitory norm of the offence in question. Following his acquittal, a law-making precedent would be established to the effect that property belonging to others may lawfully be removed if lives are thereby saved. This is a general norm about legally justified conduct, not specific to any particular actor. On Robinson's view, to be within the derogation, D need not be aware that his conduct will achieve a good outcome; indeed, as in Ashkenazi's case, his motive may be reprehensible.

Contrast a situation where D is merely excused: a case, say, where D misconstrues V's peaceable intention and strikes a pre-emptive blow because he erroneously assumes that V is about to attack. D's striking V violates V's right not to be unlawfully harmed, something

[33] Robinson, "Criminal Law Defenses: A Systematic Analysis" (1982) 82 *Col LR* 199; Schopp, *Justification Defences and Just Convictions* (1988).

[34] Robinson, "Criminal Law Defenses: A Systematic Analysis" (1982) 82 *Col LR* 199, 245–7.

[35] Robinson, *Fundamentals of Criminal Law* (1988) 664.

[36] Indeed, according to Robinson, Ashkenazi had a "right" to take the bag, in that anyone who knew the true facts would not be allowed to interfere with Ashkenazi's taking of the bag.

that remains a cause for concern even if we excuse D from criminal liability. In this case, when we assess D's responsibility for that harm, the focus is on his state of mind and disposition. It is because D *thought* he was under attack and therefore was not acting in an aggressive or predatory manner that we may excuse him.[37] Whether an excuse is granted requires an estimate of blameworthiness. If the mistake was an unreasonable one, arguably he should still be punished for the intrusion on V's rights; although, currently, English law merely requires that D's mistake be genuine.[38] According to Robinson, when D is excused, we make a finding that in *these* circumstances it would be unjust to convict D. The court's judgment is personal to D and generates no law-making precedent to guide the conduct of others in the future.[39]

Robinson's theorisation of the excuse/justification distinction has been highly influential and, if correct, it should be deployed as a central organising principle in any account of defences. Ultimately, however, his theorisation is unconvincing.[40] Robinson's contention that questions going to D's motivation and practical reasoning should be excluded from findings of justification is not a necessary truth, merely a position that Robinson adopts. English law, for instance, does not take the view that good outcomes, *by themselves*, entail justification. In the famous case of *Dadson*,[41] D shot and wounded V, an escaping felon. The court accepted that (at that time) a person was justified in shooting to prevent the escape of fleeing felons. But D did not know V was a felon and, because of that, he was convicted of unlawful wounding with intent to do grievous bodily harm. As one would expect, Robinson has argued that *Dadson* is wrongly decided,[42] yet even he concedes that a conviction for *attempted* unlawful wounding would have been in order in the case.[43]

Moreover, once we allow, as English law does, evaluations of personal motivation and blameworthiness to enter into the question of justification, it is even possible for a bad outcome to be the result of *justified* conduct:

> Suppose, for instance, that D, an armed police officer, receives an order to kill V instantly. He has been informed by his superiors (and has no reason to doubt the information) that V is a terrorist on the point of detonating a bomb in a crowded street. D follows his orders and shoots V dead. Unfortunately, those instructing D had made a tragic error. V was going about her lawful business.

We know that according to Robinson, D should receive a verdict of "not guilty by reason of excuse" and should potentially also be subject to civil deterrent or remedial measures.

[37] Which is why, according to Robinson, someone apprised of the true facts would commit an offence against V if she assists D's attack.

[38] See below, § 18.1(v).

[39] See also Fletcher, "The Individualisation of Excusing Conditions" (1974) 47 *So Cal LR* 1269; Katz, "On What Underlies Excuse" (2023) 18 *Crim Law and Philosophy* 537.

[40] For penetrating critique of an "objectivist" view of justification, see Greenawalt, "The Perplexing Boundaries of Justification and Excuse" (1984) 84 *Col LR* 1897.

[41] (1850) 2 Den 35.

[42] "Competing Theories of Justification: Deeds v. Reasons" in Simester and Smith (eds.), *Harm and Culpability* (1996) 45. On this point, see further, from *Harm and Culpability*, Gardner, "Justifications and Reasons", 103; Simester, *Fundamentals*, chap 16; Edwards, "Justification and Motivation" (2023) 18 *Crim Law and Philosophy* 1.

[43] This is a considerable concession by Robinson to the objectivist rigour of his position since, if attempt liability remains possible, the beneficent outcome does not preclude criminal liability. Robinson's theory, in allowing this concession, effectively takes a particular view on what constitutes "harm" in the context of substantive offences. The harm, in Robinson's account, is not "wounding" but "unjustified wounding"; in turn, Dadson attempted but failed to inflict an unjustified wound.

But why merely excused? One might plausibly argue the other way: that D's motivation was impeccable—to prevent widespread loss of life. There was no flaw in his practical reasoning—he shot the person identified as an immediate threat, and had no reason to think the information he was given was false. Should he receive the same order in like circumstances in the future, he should carry out the order. He would be justified in doing so and in breach of his duty as a police officer should he decline, *irrespective of whether V was a terrorist* (provided D had no reason to think that the order received was based on an erroneous risk assessment). Moreover, just as in the case of Ashkenazi, we can generalise the grounds of D's acquittal into a law-making precedent. The case would inform us that a person intending to use proportionate means to save lives will commit no offence, notwithstanding that he causes the death of an innocent person, if he had good reason to believe that the means he employed were necessary and proportionate.[44]

Of course, from *V's* perspective, everything depends on V's status. If V is a terrorist, any resort to force to pre-empt D's lawful use of force upon him would be an offence against D. But if V is innocent, he should be allowed to defend himself even when he knows that D has made a reasonable mistake and is doing his duty as a law enforcement official. As an innocent person, V is in full possession of his right to life.[45] Admittedly, the fact that in such circumstances D and V are both entitled to use force against the other is not tidy. Indeed, for policy reasons, there is something to be said for denying V any right to use force against D, if D is a policeman or other official acting in the legitimate execution of his duty.[46] Yet such a restriction would effectively sacrifice V's right to life in favour of greater safety for law enforcers.[47] Irrespective of the soundness or otherwise of such a policy, there is no logical or moral *imperative* requiring self-sacrifice.[48] This analysis is consonant with the decision of the High Court in *Oraki*.[49] Police officers (correctly) suspected that D was driving a car, owned by his mother, E, without adequate insurance. When the police pulled the car over and confirmed that D lacked insurance, they explained that they

[44] Even if Robinson insists, as he would, that the bad outcome makes this a case of excuse, it is an excuse very different in structure from, say, that afforded by duress. The reasons for affording the excuse can be formulated as a guide for future conduct.

[45] Contrast, for example, the situation where V launches an unlawful and deadly attack on D which D can only repel by using deadly force on V.

[46] The issue is inconclusively discussed in *Kenlin v Gardiner* [1967] 2 QB 510 (DC). There is a lengthy discussion of this matter in *Lawson and Forsythe* [1986] VR 515, with a majority favouring the view that the fact that D is acting lawfully in the execution of his duty should not categorically deny the right of V to defend himself against the officers. In *Oraki* [2018] EWHC 115 (Admin), [2018] QB 1086, the Divisional Court carefully analysed *Kenlin v Gardner* and found that, properly understood, the case does not support the proposition that force may not be used against a police officer acting lawfully in the execution of her duty.

[47] See further Sullivan, "The Hard Treatment of Innocent Persons in State Responses to the Threat of Large Scale and Imminent Terrorist Violence: Examining the Legal Constraints" in Sullivan and Dennis (eds.), *Seeking Security* (2012) 293, 300–5.

[48] The conclusion that in these circumstances both D and V may be said to be justified in using force against each other has been criticised as a logical contradiction. It is true that a reasons rather than deeds account of justification may entail that circumstances arise where the criminal law cannot give priority to one right-holder over another when each lawfully resorts to the use of force. However, this is not contradiction. It merely illustrates that if the focus is on grounds for blame and punishment we may encounter persons who in moral terms are in the same case. Of course, the fact that D is justified in killing the innocent V does not qualify or limit V's innocent status—something that should be reflected in compensatory entitlements at civil law. See further Husak, "Conflicts of Justifications" (1999) 18 *Law and Philosophy* 41; Husak, "On the Supposed Priority of Justification to Excuse" (2005) 24 *Law and Philosophy* 557.

[49] [2018] EWHC 115 (Admin), [2018] QB 1086.

would be (lawfully) seizing E's car. E took loud verbal exception to the police's intervention, jumped into the driver's seat, and was then lawfully restrained by an officer, V, from driving away. E took even greater exception to this restriction, and released a succession of screams. Concerned for the safety of his mother, D pulled V away from E. The High Court held that D was entitled to raise the defence of self-defence (on behalf of another) and quashed his conviction for obstructing a police officer in the lawful execution of his duty. The police officer, V, was found to be acting lawfully when he restrained E. As it was assumed at trial that D's belief that his mother was under attack was reasonable,[50] his actions too were lawful, despite his mistake. Clearly, the police actions were reasonable on any view, as the restraint was proportionate and their suspicions of unlawful driving well-founded. So, there can be occasions when lawful force can be met with lawful force, a conclusion that may be considered untidy in terms of who is entitled to do what to whom, but which is unavoidable when resolving the rights of contending individuals who are acting reasonably.[51]

We need not employ Robinson's version of the justification/excuse divide, of course. We could adopt a model which would consider not merely outcomes but also the nature and quality of D's motivation and practical reasoning.[52] But we will not follow that course here, for several reasons. First, there may be situations where a finding of no liability is clearly warranted but where neither the head of justification nor that of excuse seems adequately to capture D's non-liability. Suppose, for example, that D has paranoid schizophrenia and believes that V is an agent of the Devil and must be killed at all costs. It would be conventional to say that his killing V is excusable on the grounds of his insanity. (Clearly, it is not justified by his insanity.) But should we really *excuse* people such as D? When we excuse, we tolerate. Perhaps the excused defendant should have done better. Yet, in all the circumstances, our judgement of why she acted as she did is not sufficiently adverse to warrant sanctions. But in D's case, his conduct in killing V does not constitute a condonable lapse from the standards of self-control we might reasonably expect of him. It is not that D's action is understandable and insufficiently culpable. Rather, D is not responsible, as a deliberative agent, for his action at all. We *exempt* D because his mental condition places him outside that scheme of reference whereby moral judgements—distinctions between justification and excuse—derive their meaning.[53] It is here that the third category of "exemption defences" may be applied (albeit this further distinction imports, as we shall see, further definitional issues for the law).

Secondly, particular defences may straddle the boundaries of justification, excuse, and exemption, however those terms are defined. For instance, duress is typically characterised as an excuse. Frequently, it is. In *Hudson and Taylor*,[54] D and E, aged 17 and 19, committed perjury when failing to identify a suspect at a wounding trial, having been threatened by a

[50] *Ibid.*, [6].

[51] For unreasonable mistakes and exculpation, see below, § 18.1(v). For discussion of whether law enforcement officials should be absolved from criminal liability on the basis of unreasonable mistakes, see below, § 21.2(v); see also Simester, "On Justifications and Excuses" in Zedner and Roberts (eds.), *Principles and Values in Criminal Law and Criminal Justice* (2012) 95, 108–10.

[52] For instance, Uniacke uses the term "agent-perspectivally justified" for this approach: *Permissible Killing* (1994) 48–9.

[53] Moore, *Law and Psychiatry* (1984) 197–8, 244–5.

[54] [1971] 2 QB 202 (CA); below, § 20.1(ii)(b).

third party to be "cut up" if they did so. D was able to rely on the defence of duress:[55] we may have preferred D to withstand the threat and comply with her legal duties, but in the realm of excuse, the focus was on the fear she must have experienced and how difficult it must have been in the circumstances to do her duty. By contrast, there have been a series of cases where the defence of "duress of circumstances" has been successfully invoked as something more akin to a justification in answer to motoring offences. For example, in *Willer*,[56] D drove his car in a pedestrianised precinct in order to avoid a threat of death or serious bodily harm from a crowd. Now, understandably, D was in very great fear and that fear, of itself, would have allowed him exemption within the terms of the defence of duress. But to focus on the fear alone is to distort D's story. If driving through the precinct was without risk to others, then it was far better that D did so rather than be killed or badly hurt. His action was justified.[57] And even if not experiencing any of the pressures of fear—he may be icily calm—his justification is sufficient of itself.

Finally, there may be situations where there is agreement that D should not be convicted but disagreement whether, on the same facts, his conduct was justifiable or excusable (or whether D was exempted). Take a case where D is charged with the battery of his son, V. D claims the defence of reasonable chastisement.[58] One strand of opinion holds that certain forms of physical punishment are fully justifiable in response to the serious misbehaviour of children. Alternatively, one may hold the view that chastisement of children is never appropriate, however serious the child's misconduct, but, given the diversity and strength of the differing views of reasonable people on this topic, think that persons of a different persuasion should not be convicted for beating their children (provided the chastisement does not exceed certain limits). Accordingly, there may be consensus among a group of individuals that a defence of reasonable chastisement should be available but a diversity of views about the nature of this defence, whether justification or excuse.

In the chapters that follow, although we refer to the justifying, excusing, and/or exempting effects of certain defences, we do not employ the distinction as a formal or organising rubric. Although the categories can be useful as a lens through which to view and evaluate defences, their definition and application remain insufficiently certain.[59] The only exception is what may be termed non-coerced necessity. Non-coerced necessity comprises situations where D decides to contravene the letter of the law in order to achieve an outcome

[55] In the light of *Hasan* [2005] UKHL 22, [2005] 2 AC 467, as applied in *Batchelor* [2013] EWCA Crim 2638, duress is now unavailable on similar facts, but this is due to the separate issue of whether D should have (when giving evidence in court) recognised that she was safe to report the threats she had received. For further discussion, see below, § 20.1(ii)(b).

[56] (1986) 83 Cr App R 225 (CA).

[57] And see *Pipe* [2012] EWHC 1821 (Admin), where the Divisional Court ruled that D should have been allowed to argue that driving in excess of the speed limit was justified when driving to hospital with his injured son (who had a suspected broken leg), following the failure of an ambulance to arrive. The case cited in support of that view was *Conway* [1989] QB 290 (CA), a case resolved under the rubric of duress of circumstances. In *Pipe*, however, the injury had already occurred and there was no risk of death. Given that duress is confined to immediate threats of death, serious bodily injury, or rape, the applicable defence would seem to be necessity.

[58] Above, § 11.8.

[59] For the argument that dividing the territory of defences under a binary system of justification and excuse leads to oversimplification, see Duff, *Answering for Crime* (2007) 264–84; for the view that preoccupation with whether conduct is justified or excused can distract from the central question of whether conduct is sufficiently culpable to be punished, see Alexander and Ferzan, *Crime and Culpability* (2009) 88–93; for some general scepticism about the utility of the distinction between justification and excuse, see Dennis, "On Necessity as a Defence to Crime: Possibilities, Problems and the Limits of Justification and Excuse" (2009) 3 *Crim Law and Philosophy* 29.

of greater social benefit than would accrue through compliance with law. We may speak of such a decision as "non-coerced" if D's personal interests are not at stake: for example, where D, a doctor, decides that the mentally incompetent V's best interests would be served by a sterilisation operation. A defence of necessity may be allowed in such circumstances.[60] It is a claim of justification, not of excuse or exemption. For such a defence to be afforded, D's calculation must be right; if her cost–benefit analysis is found wanting, her defence of necessity will fail.[61]

## § 17.3 Burden of proof for defences

We have already discussed burdens of proof in some detail at § 3.2 above. However, as we move to analyse defences, a headline from that discussion bares repetition. Although it is typically the role of the defendant to *raise* potential defences, this does not equate with a reversal in the burden of proof. D must provide some evidential basis for the defence she is seeking to introduce (i.e. satisfy an evidential burden), but having done so it is for the prosecution to disprove one or more elements of that defence to the criminal standard (i.e. beyond reasonable doubt).[62]

Notable exceptions to this rule, in the realm of defences, are the irresponsibility defences of insanity[63] and diminished responsibility.[64] In both cases, the legal burden of proof is placed upon D to establish the elements of the defence on the civil standard (i.e. on the balance of probabilities). Despite the lower standard of proof, any reversal of this kind must be carefully scrutinised for its compatibility with the presumption of innocence.

## § 17.4 The defences to be considered—an outline scheme

The present state of English law does not permit a logically derived scheme for presenting defences. In the following chapters, we thus organise our account of defences under broad and to some extent overlapping categories.

First, in Chapter 18, we will consider *failure of proof defences*, such as intoxication and mistake. In each case, D's appeal is not to a supervening defence—not to a defence properly so called—but to a denial of offence elements. It is important to understand how such denials can undermine liability. However, of perhaps greater interest in this chapter, we also explore how prior fault rules (for voluntary intoxication in particular) may be used to create liability in circumstances where (due to a successful denial of elements) it would not otherwise exist. In the flowchart below, we illustrate the process of analysing a denial of proof defence ("AR" and "MR" are used as abbreviations for actus reus and mens rea respectively).

60 Below, § 21.4.

61 It would be possible for D's conduct to remain within the realm of necessity (on a non-Robinsonian account) if she has made a *reasonable* mistake of fact, provided the cost–benefit analysis was appropriate to the facts she reasonably assumed.

62 This is a necessary corollary of the presumption of innocence, enshrined within Article 6(2) ECHR.

63 Below, § 19.2.

64 Above, § 10.6.

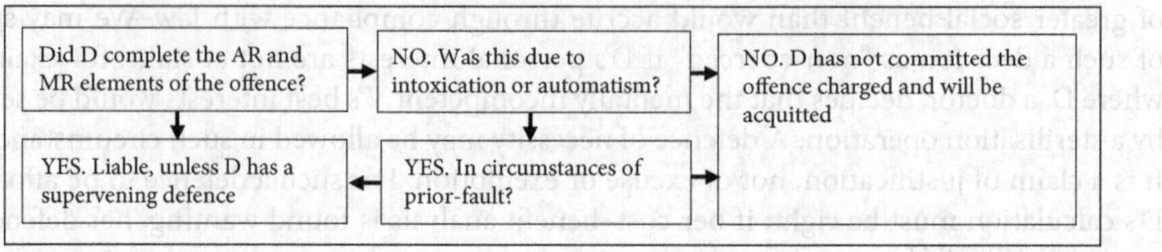


Secondly, we will turn in Chapter 19 to *irresponsibility defences*. These defences concern circumstances where, in the light of some mental health condition of D, or other internal disorder, or as a result of infancy, it would be unjust to convict D for any crime. Such defences apply to excuse D from liability; or perhaps more accurately, in most cases at least, to exempt D from liability as an insufficiently responsible agent.

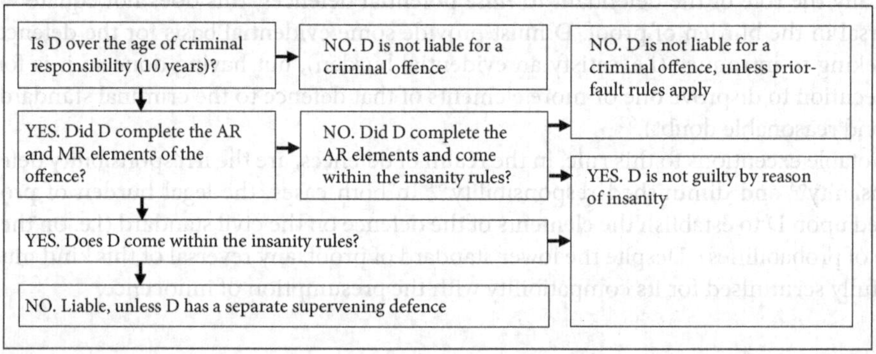


Finally in Chapters 20 and 21, we turn to supervening defences that apply to excuse or justify D's otherwise criminal conduct. Chapter 20 is concerned with *defences of circumstantial pressure*. These defences are available to persons who have the capacity to obey the law but are exculpated by virtue of the pressure imposed by particular contexts. The defence of duress is the core member of this class of defence. We will also consider here the defences of duress of circumstances, modern slavery or trafficking, and superior orders. Chapter 21 then considers *defences of permissible conduct*. These are defences which permit contravention of the letter of the law provided D has acted for a qualifying reason. Unlike, say, insanity, these defences incorporate reasons in favour of acting in a particular way and, to an extent, allow a measure of planning and prediction: "I hope he will not attack but, if he does, I can defend myself." They include the defence of self and others, prevention of crime and unlawful escapes, and necessity.

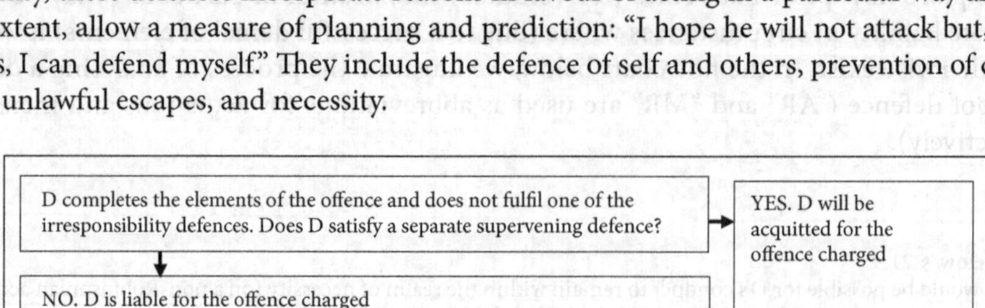

# 18

# FAILURE OF PROOF

"Failure of proof" arguments operate to defeat liability, but they do *not* do so as supervening defences.[1] Supervening defences (defences properly-so-called) arise where D's conduct has satisfied the definitional elements of an offence and D appeals to a separate legal rule to defeat liability. Supervening defences are discussed in Chapters 19–21. Failure of proof arguments are different: rather than appealing to a separate set of legal rules, D's claim is simply that the prosecution has failed to discharge their legal burden to prove the elements of the offence charged, or failed to disprove an otherwise available defence. It is useful to keep the following simple equation in mind.

| |
|---|
| Offence Definitional Elements (Actus Reus + Mens Rea) +<br>Absence of a Defence = Liability |

As noted in the previous chapter, we can think of the actus reus and mens rea elements as together constituting a *prima facie offence*. D's denial of a prima facie offence can take many forms. D may offer an alibi claim, such as being "out of town" when the offence was committed locally, effectively denying responsibility for all of the offence elements (complete denial); or D may admit certain actus reus elements, but claim to have acted involuntarily and/or without mens rea (partial denial). In the context of defences, a failure of proof argument does not challenge the existence of the prima facie offence, but the ability of the prosecution to disprove elements of a supervening defence. Thus, where the prosecution claims that a certain defence element was absent, a failure of proof argument seeks to challenge that claim. In both cases, whether the prosecution has failed to prove the definitional elements of an offence, or has failed to disprove a supervening defence, liability cannot be established. D is not under an obligation to prove her innocence, of course, but challenges of this kind to the prosecution account may prevent the criminal standard of proof—guilt beyond reasonable doubt—from being met.

In this chapter, we discuss three different types of "failure of proof" argument, and how they have been received by the courts. We begin with ignorance and mistake of fact (§ 18.1), where D's mistake gives rise to a plausible denial of an offence element, and/or gives rise to a potential defence. Secondly, we explore ignorance and mistake of law (§ 18.2), where D contravenes rules that were not apparent to him at the time of offending. And thirdly, we discuss so-called impossibility arguments (§ 18.3), where, despite D's awareness of a legal duty to act in a particular manner, it is impossible (and/or D believes that it is impossible) for him to do so.

[1] Discussed above, § 17.1.

In the final two sections (§ 18.4 and § 18.5), we discuss legal rules that have developed to push back against failure of proof arguments in certain circumstances. Referred to as "prior fault" rules, these can apply where D's previous conduct has contributed to her later mistakes and/or ignorance. The logic here is that, where D's failure of proof argument originates from her own previous fault, it should not be permitted to undermine the prosecution's case against her. The paradigm example of this arises in cases of voluntary intoxication, where D's intoxicated mistakes give rise to a prima facie denial of offence elements, or to a putative mistaken defence. In cases of this kind, the criminal law has developed rules that provide a route to liability, although such rules remain deeply contested in both form and substance. Recognising special rules in the context of voluntary intoxication also gives rise to issues of consistency (our focus in § 18.5), including in the treatment of rules discussed elsewhere in this textbook (e.g. automatism and insanity).

## § 18.1 Ignorance and mistake of fact

Many instances of ignorance or mistake of fact will have no impact on a defendant's liability. For example, D may take valuable property believing that it belongs to X, a wealthy person against whom he has a grudge. In fact the property belongs to V, D's best friend. But for that mistake, D would not have appropriated the property. D's mistake therefore explains his conduct, but is nevertheless irrelevant to his liability. All the elements of theft are present when D takes the property and D lacks any legally recognised excuse.

Ignorance and mistake of fact will *only* be relevant to D's liability where they engage with an element of the potential offence in such a way that they amount to a denial of mens rea, or where they relate to a supervening defence. With one exception,[2] where mistakes are legally relevant, they are relevant only to questions of exculpation: mistakes may explain D's conduct in committing an offence, as in our theft example above, but mistakes cannot produce liability that would not otherwise be found. This is the case even should D's mistake reveal a propensity to commit criminal acts. For example, in *Taaffe*,[3] D concealed a packet when entering the United Kingdom. The packet was found to contain drugs. The prosecution accepted D's claim that he thought the sealed packet contained foreign currency. He concealed the packet because he thought it was an offence to import money from overseas. His conduct was, in fact, perfectly legal.[4] The prosecution argued that D's belief that he was acting illegally, together with the fact that he was in possession of drugs, entailed liability for the offence of knowingly importing goods subject to import control. The House of Lords quashed his conviction. His mere belief that he was committing a crime did not suffice to constitute the mens rea for the offence charged.

[2] The one exception to the general principle that mistakes are relevant only to exculpation applies in the law of attempts. Facts may exist which render a particular crime impossible to commit. For example, X sells a cheap video recorder to D. Because the price is so low, D is sure that she is acquiring a stolen item. Were that assumption correct, she would commit the offence of handling stolen goods. If her assumption turns out to be incorrect, liability for that offence is precluded. However, since the Criminal Attempts Act 1981, she is guilty of attempting to handle stolen goods. The impossibility of committing the full offence affords no defence to a charge of attempt. See above, § 9.4.

[3] *Taaffe* [1984] AC 539.

[4] Though larger amounts must be declared.

### *(i) Historical context*

The functional relevance of mistake has changed markedly over the last century, particularly with the rise of subjective elements of mens rea and (to a lesser extent) within defences. For much of the last century, where D's mistake was relevant to the offence charged, it was relevant as a form of (what we might now call) due diligence defence: as long as D's mistake was an objectively *reasonable* one to have made on the facts, he would be afforded a defence.[5] In *Tolson*,[6] the Court of Crown Cases Reserved resolved, by a majority, that there would be a defence to a charge of bigamy if D had reasonable grounds to believe that she was free to enter into marriage. Accordingly, on the facts of *Tolson*, a reasonable belief that one's husband had drowned at sea would suffice for an acquittal, but a similar belief, however strongly held, based on inadequate grounds would not.

The passing of section 8 of the Criminal Justice Act 1967 represented a major turning point: proof of the mens rea elements of intention or foresight in an offence had to be proof of the subjective intention or foresight *possessed by the defendant*. Section 8 disallowed a jury from drawing an inference of intent or foresight of a particular result solely on the basis that such a result was the natural and probable consequence of D's conduct.[7] As such, if D did not apprehend that his conduct would bring about a likely consequence, he could not be taken to have intended or foreseen that consequence, however foolish or indifferent his lack of awareness showed him to be. A wholly unreasonable mistake of fact may well, then, negate intention or foresight. This requirement gave rise to a contradiction. How could there be an insistence, *post* section 8, that a mistake, to provide a defence, must be based on reasonable grounds if D's mistake precluded either intent or foresight with respect to a definitional element of the offence?

The question was addressed by the House of Lords in *Morgan*,[8] which now provides the starting point for contemporary analysis of mistake of fact in English law.

### *(ii) Subjective mens rea and mistake*

*Morgan* provides clear precedent that even unreasonable mistakes are capable of negating subjective mens rea.[9] In that case, a military officer told his subordinates that they should have sex with his wife; she would feign non-consent, but this was because of a sexual preference of hers. The subordinates had sex with V, who was very clearly not consenting. They claimed, however, to have honestly believed that her communication of non-consent was insincere. At the time *Morgan* was decided, the offence of rape required D to be at least reckless as to V's non-consent.[10] At trial, and in the Court of Appeal,[11] it was ruled that to defeat a finding of mens rea, D's purported belief in V's consent had to be based on reasonable grounds. In the Court of Appeal, Bridge LJ finessed the contradiction between this reasonableness requirement and the terms of section 8 of the Criminal Justice Act 1967 (disallowing

[5] *Rose* (1884) 15 Cox CC 540; *Chisham* (1963) 47 Cr App R 130 (CA).
[6] (1889) 23 QBD 168.
[7] Above, § 5.1(ix).
[8] [1976] AC 182 (HL).
[9] *Ibid.*
[10] Since the Sexual Offences Act 2003, D must have reasonable grounds for his belief that V is consenting before it will be inconsistent with D's having the relevant form of mens rea. See above, § 12.5.
[11] [1975] 1 All ER 8 (CA).

mens rea inferences from objective probabilities alone) by asserting that unless a mistake was based on reasonable grounds, there would be an insufficient basis, as a matter of evidence, on which to raise mistake.[12] The House of Lords rejected this evidential analysis. Their Lordships accepted that where there were *reasonable* grounds for D's mistaken belief, then the jury is more likely to accept that the mistake was genuine and honestly made, but ruled that evidence of an honest belief remained relevant to findings of (subjective) mens rea even if the belief was unreasonably held. Even an unreasonable mistake might negate liability for an offence because, as Lord Hailsham explained, in the context of rape:[13]

> "Once one has accepted, what seems to me abundantly clear, that the prohibited act in rape is non-consensual sexual intercourse, and that the guilty state of mind is an intention to commit it, it seems to me to follow as a matter of inexorable logic that there is no room either for a 'defence' of honest belief or mistake, or of a defence of honest and reasonable belief or mistake. Either the prosecution proves that the accused had the requisite intent, or it does not. In the former case it succeeds, and in the latter it fails."

This passage makes clear that where the issue is proof of a subjective form of mens rea it is, strictly, a misnomer to speak of a "defence" of mistake of fact. The issue is whether mens rea has been established. Where D's mistake of fact is incompatible with the mental element of the offence charged (e.g. where D is mistaken as to a fact that he must intend or know for the purposes of liability), he does not claim a "defence" of mistaken belief—rather, he denies mens rea on the basis of a failure of proof.

The approach to mistake elucidated in *Morgan* is now consistently applied to all offences requiring subjective mens rea. However, not all offences are drafted with equal precision, and particular care is required when applying the rule where the mens rea of an offence does not precisely correspond to the actus reus elements.[14] If the mens rea required for a particular offence does not relate to the entirety of the actus reus, what would otherwise be a mistake germane to liability may turn out to be immaterial. In *Ellis*,[15] for example, D was charged with knowingly evading a restriction on the importation of a Class A drug—an offence in its own right and not a mere instance of a more general offence concerned with the importation of controlled items.[16] D claimed to believe that he was bringing controlled pornography rather than heroin into the country. The Court of Appeal ruled that the mens rea required was knowledge that the item in possession was an item subject to import control.[17] It was unnecessary that D should know the nature of the item in question. Accordingly, his conviction for evading the restriction of Class A drugs was confirmed. The logic of *Morgan* does not apply in such a case, save in circumstances where D genuinely believed,

[12] *Ibid*., 14.

[13] [1976] AC 182, 214. Cf. *Smith* [1974] QB 354, 360 (CA).

[14] We discuss the correspondence principle, above, § 6.5.

[15] (1987) 84 Cr App_R 235 (CA). See too *Forbes* [2001] UKHL 40, [2002] 2 AC 512.

[16] Following the decision of the House of Lords in *Courtie* [1984] AC 463, if a statute provides that particular facts or circumstances increase the maximum penalty for an offence, a discrete offence is created incorporating those facts or circumstances as defining elements. This rule applies in the case of drugs, since greater penalties are provided for Class A drugs than for non-Class A drugs.

[17] D was charged under s. 170(2) of the Customs and Excise Management Act 1979 which requires, *inter alia*, that D be "knowingly concerned" in the importation of a controlled drug. The requirement of knowledge relates to the item in possession. D could not have known he was in possession of pornography because he had no pornographic items in his possession. At most, he believed that he did. Whereas *true* beliefs may be accounted in law as knowledge (above, § 5.4), it strains credulity to breaking-point to classify a false belief as a form of knowledge.

however unreasonably, that he was not carrying any form of contraband (or, as in *Taafe*, he was mistaken regarding the legal status of the thing possessed).

### *(iii) Objective mens rea and mistake*

Despite the prominence of subjective mens rea within the definition of most serious offences—and certainly a majority of the offences discussed in this textbook—objective mens rea elements continue to play an important role within the criminal law. The legislature has continued to adopt objective standards for definitional features of serious crimes in measures such as the Modern Slavery Act 2015, the Sexual Offences Act 2003, the Proceeds of Crime Act 2002, and the Terrorism Act 2000. English law lacks a general theory to guide decision-making on the appropriate use of subjective and objective elements. The resulting inconsistency is only likely to be settled by way of a criminal code, a remote prospect indeed.[18]

Inconsistency in the deployment of subjective and objective mens rea elements is important here because it has a direct impact on the relevance of factual mistakes. The principal non-consensual sexual offences (sections 1–4 of the Sexual Offences Act 2003), for example, no longer require D to be reckless as to an absence of consent; rather, D satisfies the mens rea when he lacks a *reasonable belief* in consent. Under the old law pre-2003, which required subjective recklessness, any mistaken belief that V was consenting, however unreasonable, would preclude a finding of mens rea: the principle from *Morgan* applied. However, for the section 1–4 offences, which are satisfied by the absence of a reasonable belief, D's mistaken belief will only undermine a finding of mens rea if it is objectively reasonable.

The case of *B* provides a useful illustration,[19] as well as clarification of the relationship between mental delusions and claims of reasonable mistake. D, a person with schizophrenia, believed he had sexual healing powers. V, his wife, submitted but did not consent to intercourse with him. D was later with rape. It was argued for D at his trial that, in assessing whether D's belief in V's consent was reasonable,[20] the question should be whether it was reasonable in the particular circumstances of D, circumstances that should include his disorder which gave rise to the false belief. Hughes LJ curtly dismissed the submission: "A delusional belief in consent, if entertained, would be by definition irrational and thus unreasonable."[21] His Lordship went on to suggest a possible distinction between delusional beliefs and beliefs which were not necessarily irrational but which, nonetheless, were beliefs that ordinary people would not hold. He referenced, in particular, persons of "less than ordinary intelligence" or with an "inability to recognise behavioural cues". His Lordship considered that beliefs attributable to those conditions were not necessarily irrational and hence unreasonable.[22] Drawing lines between delusional beliefs on the one hand and obtuse yet reasonable beliefs on the other will not be easy.

[18] The Law Commission for England and Wales announced the abandonment of the criminal law codification project in 2008: Law Com. No. 311, *Tenth Programme of Law Reform* (2008).

[19] [2013] EWCA Crim 3, [2013] 1 Cr App R 36; above, § 5.5(ii).

[20] As is required by s. 1(2) of the Sexual Offences Act 2003.

[21] [2013] EWCA Crim 3, [2013] 1 Cr App R 36, [35].

[22] *Ibid.*, [41].

### *(iv) Strict liability and mistake*

Evidence of ignorance or mistake of fact is irrelevant to the application of strict liability offence elements.[23] Strict liability elements essentially sideline D's mental state as an issue of relevance, and this includes D's mistaken beliefs about these elements (whether reasonably held or not). Evidence about mistakes remains potentially relevant, of course, where an offence combines strict liability elements with other elements that require mens rea, since mistakes will remain potentially relevant to those requiring mens rea, and in the application of defences (including defences of "due diligence").

### *(v) Ignorance, mistake of fact, and defences*

Just as ignorance and mistake of fact can be incompatible with D's having mens rea, making them relevant as a potential failure of proof in offending, so too can they qualify the application of a supervening defence. For example, let us imagine that D wrongly (and perhaps unreasonably) believes that V is about to launch a deadly attack, and so D hits V with a bat (causing serious injury) to make his escape. D has intentionally caused serious harm to V, and so has committed an offence against the person. D will only avoid liability if his acts come within the terms of self-defence.[24] It is quite possible, within the current law, that D's claim of defence will be successful, but this is only true because self-defence is defined to allow D to rely upon his mistaken beliefs about the dangerousness of the situation, even if they are unreasonably held.[25] Other defences, as we will discuss, operate differently.

The primary focus in this chapter is on ignorance and mistake as denials of offending, and so we defer much of the more detailed discussion of mistaken defences to Chapters 19–21. The rules for mistaken defences can also be complex, and so they are better discussed after we have introduced the standard terms upon which each of the supervening defences applies. However, two more general points are usefully introduced here, relating to (a) reasonable mistake as a supervening defence, and (b) the inconsistent treatment of mistake across certain supervening defences.

#### *(a) Reasonable mistake as a supervening defence*

We have mentioned already the well-known and long-standing decision in *Tolson*,[26] which recognised an independent defence of "reasonable mistake" for the offence of bigamy. Bigamy is a common law offence committed when "whosoever, being married, shall marry another person during the life of the former husband or wife". As a strict liability offence, D's honest but mistaken belief in the dissolution or nullity of the previous marriage, or the death of the previous spouse, will not negate the offence—there is no subjective mens rea requirement to be undermined.[27] However, following *Tolson*, a supervening defence was acknowledged, excusing D who reasonably believed that he had capacity to enter into a valid form of marriage.

[23] We discuss strict liability above, in Chapter 6.
[24] Given statutory footing, at least in part, within the Criminal Justice and Immigration Act 2008, s. 76.
[25] *Gladstone Williams* [1987] 3 All ER 411 (CA).
[26] (1889) 23 QBD 168; noted above in § 18.1(i).
[27] Above, § 18.1(iv).

In *Morgan*, the House of Lords indicated that its decision should not be read as overruling *Tolson*.[28] Rather, *Tolson* was distinguished because it related to a strict liability offence. For Lord Cross, this was crucial:[29]

> "If the words defining an offence provide either expressly or impliedly that a man is not to be guilty of it if he believes something to be true, then he cannot be found guilty if the jury think that he may have believed it to be true, however inadequate were his reasons for doing so. But, if the definition of the offence is on the face of it 'absolute' and the defendant is seeking to escape his prima facie liability by a defence of mistaken belief, I can see no hardship to him in requiring the mistake—if it is to afford him a defence—to be based on reasonable grounds."

Lord Cross's account provides a cogent distinction between rape (the offence at issue in *Morgan*), which at the time had an explicit, subjective mental element regarding the absence of consent, and the crime of bigamy, which is strict liability regarding the fact of being married already. Indeed, there are many offences that make no reference to a mental element. As a matter of judicial interpretation, however, the approach outlined by Lord Cross has rarely been taken. More typically, courts have either found an implication of subjective mens rea from the statutory context or determined that the offence is one of strict liability. Strict liability tempered by a defence of reasonable mistake is an option not considered.[30] Such an approach has taken hold only in bigamy,[31] and in the former offence of taking a girl under the age of 16 from the possession of her parents or guardian.[32] As the House of Lords has now confirmed,[33] despite the *potential* for the rule in *Tolson* to be applied more widely, particularly within the class of strict liability offences, the rule lacks any generality.

*(b) The inconsistent treatment of mistake across supervening defences*

D's ignorance or mistake may be relevant to the terms of a supervening defence. We provided an illustration of this already, where D seriously harms V in the mistaken belief that such force is necessary to avoid attack. The rules here have become complex, and so we defer much of the discussion to the following chapters where we analyse mistakes in the context of each specific defence. However, it is useful to highlight here that the treatment of mistake, across supervening defences, has been applied inconsistently and without a clear theoretical underpinning. A comparison between self-defence and duress illustrates this point well.

In the context of self-defence,[34] there is an obvious potential for force to be used by someone mistaken as to the threat faced. Historically, a line of authority had required that any mistake about the need to use defensive force had to be reasonable if it were to have an exculpatory effect.[35] Even after *Morgan*, that objective test was reaffirmed in *Albert v Lavin*,[36] where the Divisional Court distinguished *Morgan* on grounds that *Morgan* was concerned with the denial of offence elements rather than the application of a supervening

[28] [1976] AC 182, 201–2 (Lord Cross), 214–15 (Lord Hailsham).
[29] [1976] AC 182, 202–3.
[30] We discuss the merits of this middle ground approach above, § 6.4.
[31] *King* [1964] 1 QB 285 (CA); *Gould* [1968] 2 QB 65 (CA).
[32] *Hibbert* (1869) LR 1 CCR 184.
[33] *B (a minor) v DPP* [2000] 2 AC 428. The decision in *Tolson* was given no salience in the review of approaches to mens rea by the House of Lords in *G* [2003] UKHL 50, [2004] 1 AC 1034.
[34] Discussed below, § 21.2.
[35] *Rose* (1884) 15 Cox CC 540; *Chisham* (1963) 47 Cr App R 130 (CA).
[36] [1981] 1 All ER 628 (DC); affirmed on other grounds [1982] AC 546 (HL).

defence.[37] This view, however, was eventually overturned in *Gladstone Williams*.[38] Rejecting the terms of the offence/defence distinction relied upon in *Albert v Lavin*, the Court of Appeal instead applied a subjective test regarding the necessity of using force in self-defence: D is entitled to rely upon his belief in the existence of a threat that renders D's use of force necessary, even where that belief is unreasonable.[39] This subjectivist approach was subsequently endorsed by the Privy Council in *Beckford*,[40] and has been given statutory expression within section 76(4) of the Criminal Justice and Immigration Act 2008. However, even now, areas of uncertainty remain, and we see the re-emergence of hybrid objective tests in relation to various subsets of defendants (e.g. in circumstances of intoxication, of insanity, and even non-insane delusions).[41]

Moving to the defence of duress, similar issues arise regarding mistakes about the presence or seriousness of the threat that motivates D's actions. In contrast to self-defence, however, in cases of mistaken duress a wholly objective approach is taken. In *Graham*,[42] the Court of Appeal held that a mistaken belief in the existence of circumstances constituting legally adequate duress must be based on reasonable grounds if it is to constitute a defence, an approach endorsed by the House of Lords in *Howe*;[43] and again in *Hasan*.[44] The latter case in particular bases its refusal to endorse a subjective approach on a concern to tighten the conditions of a defence easily fabricated and abused.[45]

Clarkson and Keating have offered one explanation for the current divergence of approach between cases of duress and cases of self-defence. For them, the difference may be explained on the basis that a belief in the need to use preventive force is a belief that one's conduct is justified, whereas a belief that one may be subjected to duress amounts to a claim merely to be excused.[46] They rationalised this divergence on the grounds that, in the former case, a defendant believes he is acting in a lawful and justified—i.e. blameless—manner; by contrast with the latter case, where even if D were right his conduct would be neither lawful nor justified. This view implies the claim that if D1 attacks V because he unreasonably assumes that V is about to attack him, D1 is in better moral standing than, say, D2, who drives his car through a pedestrianised area to escape V whom he unreasonably assumed

[37] [1981] 1 All ER 628, 639 (Hodgson J) (DC).

[38] [1987] 3 All ER 411 (CA).

[39] Of course, D cannot use any *degree* of force. He must use force proportionate to the danger he mistakenly apprehended. That is a question to be assessed objectively.

[40] [1988] AC 130. For critical commentary, see Simester, "Mistakes in Defence" (1992) 12 *OJLS* 295.

[41] Below, § 21.2(iv).

[42] [1982] 1 All ER 801.

[43] [1987] AC 417.

[44] [2005] 2 AC 467.

[45] *Ibid.*, [20]–[22]. That kind of policy-based reasoning could be applied to self-defence, of course, when such claims are unsupported by objective fact. Indeed, some cases have attempted to move duress into line with self-defence. For example, in *Martin (David)* [2000] 2 Cr App R 42, the Court of Appeal ruled that it was a misdirection for the trial judge to direct that D should have had reasonable grounds to believe that his mother's life was in danger before excusing on the ground of mistaken duress. Instead, the jury should have been directed that a genuine belief, reasonable or otherwise, would suffice. In the light of the endorsement of a reasonable mistake requirement in duress by the House of Lords in *Hasan*, we can put *Martin (David)* to one side as an aberration in the case law on mistaken duress, albeit one indicative of the general instability of the law's approach to mistake.

[46] *Criminal Law* (6th ed., 2007) 197–8. It is of some interest to note that, writing alone, Clarkson has proposed that duress, self-defence, and necessity should be integrated within a unified defence—a proposal that contradicts the division jointly argued for. See Clarkson, "Necessary Action: A New Defence" [2004] *Crim LR* 81; contra, Chan and Simester, "Duress, Necessity: How Many Defences?" (2005) 16 *King's College LJ* 121.

was about to kill him. D1's mistake relates to self-defence (justification) and D2's to duress of circumstances (excuse). But it is far from obvious that they are in different moral case.[47]

The reason for the different approaches appears rather to be the happenstance that typifies our uncodified criminal law. The element of unlawfulness that must, axiomatically, accompany the commission of any offence may, as in *Gladstone Williams*, be treated as something integral to the definition of the offence. Where that analysis is employed, the wholly subjective approach taken in *Morgan* will prevail and any genuine belief in facts which would have rendered D's conduct lawful will provide an excuse. However, if the matter is not covered by authority, a court minded not to follow the subjectivism of *Morgan* may, as in *Graham*, treat the defence in question as something extraneous to the defining elements of the offence. If that analysis is employed, a court may then require that mistakes must be based on reasonable grounds to afford a defence—as in *Graham*. It has been persuasively argued that resolving such issues by reference to the categories of defining elements or defence elements is to elevate legalism over substantive moral assessment.[48] For instance, lack of consent is clearly a defining element of rape. Yet there are good reasons why a belief in V's consent to sex should be based on reasonable grounds, a position now achieved under the Sexual Offences Act 2003 for rape and other non-consensual sexual offences.[49]

### *(vi) Mistake of fact and mistake about an applicable standard*

It is customary to draw a distinction between mistakes of fact on the one hand and mistakes of law on the other, with only the former kind of mistake providing for a failure of proof. We shall address the fact/law divide in the next section. Before we do, it is necessary to consider another distinction which is more easily confused: the distinction between facts and standards.

Not all applicable standards are reduced to specific rules of law. For instance, section 3 of the Criminal Law Act 1967 allows force to be used in the prevention of crime provided it is "reasonable in the circumstances". What constitutes reasonable force in the particular circumstances is a question of fact. By the very nature of the reasonableness standard, it is a matter for objective appraisal. But if the matter is one of fact rather than law, arguably a person who has used unreasonable force may claim to have made a mistake of fact if she believed the force employed was appropriate to the circumstances. Such an argument was accepted by the Court of Appeal in *Scarlett*,[50] where D, a pub landlord, was found guilty of constructive manslaughter at trial on the basis of having committed battery against V, a customer, whom he used excessive force to eject. On appeal, his conviction was quashed on the ground that, if D believed the circumstances called for the degree of force he used, his mistake entitled him to the defence even if his belief was unreasonable.[51]

*Scarlett* was wrongly decided and should not be followed. The judgment of the Court of Appeal confuses the category of facts (data concerning surrounding circumstances) with

[47] As argued earlier, assigning defences to the categories of either justification or excuse will run up against the difficulty that defences may operate over the two categories: § 17.2.

[48] Tur, "Subjectivism and Objectivism: Towards Synthesis" in Shute, Gardner, and Horder (eds.), *Action and Value in Criminal Law* (1993) 213.

[49] Above, §§ 12.6–9.

[50] [1993] 4 All ER 629 (CA).

[51] *Ibid.*, 636 (Beldam LJ).

the category of standards (evaluations) which, juridically, are likened to questions of fact only because the matter is left to the jury rather than the judge to adjudicate upon. Despite their classification as matters of fact, such standards are normative, requiring an objective assessment which may well be at variance with D's own evaluation of her conduct. In *Scarlett*, the Court took itself to be applying the decision in *Gladstone Williams*.[52] That decision, as we have noted, merely decides that if a person mistakenly assumes that she or another is about to be attacked, her actions are to be judged as if that assumed fact were true. There is nothing in the case that obliges subsequent courts to accept a defendant's own view of what constitutes *a reasonable* response to the situation that she perceived herself to be in. The approach in *Scarlett* undermines section 3 of the Criminal Law Act 1967, which *mandates* that any force deployed to prevent crime be reasonable. A police officer, for instance, acting excessively but with a genuine zeal in the cause of crime prevention may, if *Scarlett* were correct, claim a defence of mistake of fact. Fortunately, in *Owino*,[53] where there was a gross disproportion between D's violent response and the danger he claimed to be facing from V, the Court of Appeal confirmed D's conviction for malicious wounding and stated that, should there be any conflict between its previous decisions in *Gladstone Williams* and *Scarlett*, it was the former decision that should prevail. A similar view was expressed in subsequent cases.[54] The matter is now put beyond doubt by the Criminal Justice and Immigration Act 2008 for cases involving force used by way of self-defence, defence of property, or the prevention of crime. Section 76(6) of that Act specifies that the degree of force used by D is not to be regarded as having been reasonable in the circumstances as D believed them to be if it was a disproportionate response to those circumstances.

Accordingly, the relevance of mistake of fact as a failure of proof is confined to facts in the sense of data about the world: it concerns misperceptions on the part of D regarding the circumstances in which she acted. Examples would be mistakes about the intentions of another; or mistakenly assuming that certain property was D's own. Misperceptions of normative standards (is driving in a certain way "dangerous", for instance) fall outside its scope.

## § 18.2 Ignorance and mistake of law

"Ignorance of law is no excuse" is a saying widely disseminated in our culture and, as generalisations go, it has a large core of truth.[55] In *Esop*,[56] D, a subject of the Ottoman Empire, was accused of committing buggery while aboard a ship docked in an English port. Such conduct was not an offence in the Ottoman Empire and the court accepted that D, as a complete stranger to England and its ways, had no reason to think that he was breaking the law.

[52] [1987] 3 All ER 411 (CA).

[53] [1996] 2 Cr App R 128 (CA).

[54] E.g., *DPP v Armstrong-Braun* [1999] Crim LR 416 (DC); *Shaw v R* [2001] 1 WLR 1519 (PC); *Martin (David)* [2000] 2 Cr App R 42 (CA); *Forrester v Leckey* [2005] NICA 26; and *Rashford* [2005] EWCA Crim 3377.

[55] Ashworth, "Excusable Mistake of Law" [1974] *Crim LR* 652; Husak and von Hirsch, "Culpability and Mistake of Law" in Shute, Gardner, and Horder (eds.), *Action and Value in Criminal Law* (1993) 157; Smith, "Error and Mistake of Law in Anglo-American Criminal Law" (1984) 14 *Anglo-American LR* 3. Cf. Husak, *Ignorance of Law* (2016), taking a novel and expanded view of ignorance of law.

[56] (1836) 7 C & P 456, 173 ER 203.

These factors were held irrelevant to his liability.[57] From *Bailey*,[58] it appears that ignorance of law will not afford an excuse even if D was in a situation where it was impossible for him to learn that the relevant law applied to him: accordingly, it did not avail D to demonstrate that the statutory provision in question had been extended to British vessels while his ship was at sea and beyond communication with England. Neither will a positive belief, based on legal advice, that one's conduct is lawful give grounds for excuse.[59] In *Cooper v Simmons*,[60] D, an apprentice, received misleading legal advice that he was no longer bound by his indentures following the death of his master. Nevertheless, he was convicted of unlawfully absenting himself from his apprenticeship.

It may seem perfectly reasonable that D's legal position should be determined by the law as it actually is and not how he has assumed it to be (or been assured that it is). However, that holds true only provided the law is readily ascertainable—which may be far from the case, particularly for areas of activity extensively and frequently regulated. Typically, the regulatory scheme is a patchwork of primary and secondary legislation of considerable volume.[61] Even experienced lawyers practising in a particular regulatory domain may be unaware of significant changes in the law within that domain. In *Chambers*,[62] changes in the law relating to confiscation of the proceeds of crime which were favourable to defendants were known neither to the Customs and Excise prosecutors nor, seemingly, to defence lawyers, despite those changes having occurred some five years before the confiscation proceedings. In fairness to the lawyers involved, the public and private sector databases used by the profession did not register the changes. There arose the disturbing possibility that prison sentences were being served by persons who had failed to comply with the terms of a confiscation order lacking any valid legal basis.[63] To date, this lamentable state of affairs has not prompted the courts to modify the maxim that ignorance of law is no excuse.

However, it would be a mistake to assert that D's state of legal knowledge is *invariably* irrelevant to the question whether she has committed an offence. Such knowledge will, of course, be relevant where a statutory offence expressly provides that particular forms of knowledge or beliefs about legal questions are germane. Further, courts occasionally construe statutory offences as requiring, by implication, knowledge or beliefs concerning questions of law. Additionally, the discretionary jurisdiction to stay criminal proceedings as an abuse of process may well require consideration of the defendant's legal knowledge or beliefs, for instance if D has been misled regarding the content of the law by a State official.[64] Below, we look in more detail at some of these possibilities.

[57] In *Christian v R* [2006] UKPC 47, [2007] 2 AC 400, the Privy Council confirmed that it was irrelevant to liability for various sexual offences, including rape, that the defendants (Pitcairn Islanders) were unaware that they were subject to English criminal law. See further Power, "Pitcairn Island: Sexual Offending, Cultural Difference, and Ignorance of the Law" [2007] *Crim LR* 609.

[58] (1800) Russ & Ry 1, 168 ER 651.

[59] Discussed in Babb and Emmerich, "Official Misrepresentations of the Law and Fairness" (2023) 17 *Crim Law and Philosophy* 83.

[60] (1862) 26 JP 486.

[61] Discussed in Ashworth, "Ignorance of the Criminal Law, and Duties to Avoid it" (2011) 74 *MLR* 1.

[62] [2008] EWCA Crim 2467.

[63] Customs and Excise gave an undertaking to the Court of Appeal to review past cases in the light of the newly discovered change in the law.

[64] Choo, *Abuse of Process and Judicial Stays of Criminal Proceedings* (2nd ed., 2008).

### *(i) Mistake or ignorance of law: construing offences*

Statutes may make explicit reference to the defendant's legal knowledge or beliefs. For instance, section 2(1)(a) of the Theft Act 1968 provides that D's appropriation of property belonging to another is not to be regarded as dishonest if she believes she has, in law, the right to deprive the other of it. Alternatively, even if the statute is not explicit, a court may conclude that the mens rea for a particular offence is negated by a mistake of law made by D. In *Smith*,[65] D damaged V's speakers when detaching them from the wall of D's rented flat. D had installed the speakers himself. He naturally assumed that he was removing his own speakers but, unawares, by affixing them to the wall he had made the items, in legal terms, fixtures and, hence, the property of the landlord (V). On one view, D's conviction at trial for criminal damage is uncontroversial. He was reckless about damaging the speakers, as he anticipated that the manner of removal which he employed might damage them. He was aware of the facts that made the speakers V's property—he himself had fixed them to the wall. That D was unaware of the property-transferring effect of his conduct was regarded by the trial judge as a mistake of law, relevant to mitigation but not to liability for the offence.

The Court of Appeal quashed D's conviction. It took the gravamen of criminal damage to be the destruction or damage of property that *D knew belonged*, or *had* foreseen *may* belong, to another. The Court discussed the matter in terms of mens rea, which is entirely appropriate. The point is that mens rea in this context required a degree of awareness by D of the actual or possible legal status of the speakers.

Another way of categorising the appellate ruling in *Smith* is to say that a mistake of civil law was in issue and questions of civil law are equivalent to questions of fact. But while it is true that courts are far readier to allow mistakes of civil law to exempt than they are to exculpate for mistakes of substantive criminal law, there is no hard and fast rule. The effect of the master's death on the legal relationship of master and apprentice is clearly a matter of civil law. Yet, as we saw in *Cooper v Simmons*,[66] D's mistaken belief that the death of his master had freed him from his obligations of service did not provide a defence to a criminal charge of unlawfully absenting himself from his apprenticeship. Conversely, there are cases, albeit rare, where courts have inferred that Parliament intended that ignorance of a rule of criminal law should excuse. For instance, in *Secretary of State for Trade and Industry v Hart*,[67] D acted as auditor of a company of which he was a director. In so doing, he appeared to be in breach of the terms of section 13(5) of the Companies Act 1976, which prohibits any person from acting as auditor of a company if "he knows that he is disqualified for appointment to that office". D knew all the facts (i.e. that he was a director of the company) that made for his disqualification:[68] for fairly obvious reasons, one cannot be both director and auditor of the same company. Yet the Divisional Court held that something further was required to satisfy the requirement of knowledge: knowledge of the statutory disqualification rules was a prerequisite of liability. D's mistake was clearly a mistake of criminal law. Nonetheless, Ormrod LJ stated:[69]

> "If that means that he is entitled to rely on ignorance of the law as a defence, in contrast to the usual practice and the usual rule, the answer is that the section gives him that right."

65 [1974] QB 354 (CA).
66 (1862) 26 JP 486; above, § 18.2.
67 [1982] 1 WLR 481 (DC).
68 By virtue of s. 161(2) of the Companies Act 1948.
69 [1982] 1 WLR 481, 822 (DC).

There is no settled jurisprudence to guide us regarding when the approach taken in *Hart* will be adopted. Contrast the decision in *Johnson v Youden*,[70] where P built a house under the authority of a building licence that was subject to a condition limiting the price for which the house might subsequently be sold. P sold the house for a net price in excess of the limit, thereby contravening section 7 of the Building Materials and Housing Act 1945. D, P's solicitor, was charged as an accomplice to P's offence. It was accepted that, to be an accomplice, D would have to possess knowledge of the essential elements of P's offence at the time he gave P encouragement or assistance. Despite the fact that D had read the Act and had formed the opinion that the transaction, as structured, was lawful, the Divisional Court directed the justices to convict. Knowledge was satisfied on the basis of D's awareness of the terms of the licence and of the terms of the sale. The Court held it was not necessary to know that the transaction was in breach of the Act, since to require such knowledge would be to excuse D on the basis of ignorance of law.

It may seem perfectly reasonable to expect solicitors to apprise themselves of law applicable to their area of practice. Equally, however, one would suppose that a company director should appreciate that the essence of a company audit is independent scrutiny of the financial situation of the company. All that can be said with any measure of confidence is that the line taken in *Johnson* v *Youden* is more typical than that adopted in *Hart*. It can also be said that, generally, courts will be more receptive to acquit D where his mistake or ignorance is of the civil law rather than of the criminal law (e.g., mistakes regarding property ownership or parental responsibility). What is signally lacking in English law is any discussion of what general principles should be invoked when determining whether, if at all, mistake or ignorance of law should excuse.

### *(ii) Mistake or ignorance of law: abuse of process, and the right to fair trial*

In *Arrowsmith*,[71] D distributed leaflets to soldiers eligible to serve in Northern Ireland, urging them to desist from serving in that province. She was prosecuted under the Incitement to Disaffection Act 1934. *Inter alia*, she defended herself on the basis that a letter she received from the Director of Public Prosecutions would have led any reasonable person, including the defendant, to believe that distribution of the leaflets did not contravene the Act. Accordingly, she claimed a defence of excusable mistake of law, a claim rejected both at trial and on appeal.[72]

The case raises some difficult questions. Clearly, prosecuting authorities should not be disadvantaged by offering *bona fide* advice to persons seeking to stay on the right side of the law. Such advice may be optimistically interpreted or disingenuously construed, and the prosecutorial task should not be stymied through such contingencies. Indeed, it is clearly right that advice, even advice reasonably relied upon, should not pre-empt a court's right, and duty, to determine the law. Not infrequently, persons will receive legal advice to the

[70] [1950] 1 KB 544 (DC).
[71] [1975] QB 678 (CA).
[72] The facts of *Arrowsmith* were not conducive to recognition of an excusable mistake of law defence arising from official advice. D had received a letter from the Director of Public Prosecutions (whose consent was required) indicating that he would not be consenting to a prosecution in respect of earlier distributions of the pamphlet, a weak basis from which to infer that the DPP took D's conduct to be lawful. The Court of Appeal gave no indication of what the position would have been on stronger facts.

effect, say, that premises which they own meet requirements of the Health and Safety at Work Act 1974 or that their factory emissions comply with environmental legislation. It may well be in the public interest that such advice should be judicially scrutinised and appropriate standards imposed. Civil servants should not have the power to issue dispensations from the law.

Even so, a strong ethical case remains for allowing a defence of reasonable or excusable mistake of law, at least in certain circumstances. We see this, for example, in specific cases where official assurance is provided by prosecution agencies themselves (as opposed to agents further detached from proceedings, such as civil servants);[73] and where assurances are provided regarding very specific forms of conduct.

In the absence of a recognised substantive defence, however, such arguments will typically take the form of procedural claims for an abuse of process. In *Croydon Justices, ex parte Dean*,[74] it was found to be an abuse of process to instigate criminal proceedings against a person who had agreed to give evidence in return for an assurance that he would not be prosecuted. Similarly, in *Postermobile Plc v Brent LBC*,[75] D's appeal was allowed—establishing an abuse of process—where D sought advice regarding the legality of temporary advertisements, only to be prosecuted by the same Council Authority that provided the assurance that posting such advertisements was permitted. These cases demonstrate the potential for an abuse of process argument, but it should be emphasised that both involve assurances from those closely linked to the prosecution agencies. As stated in *Postermobile*, D did not "ask the Council's gardener or porter for advice on planning law"/. Where the source of an assurance is further detached from prosecutors, abuse of process arguments have been less successful. For example, in *AJ*,[76] there was no abuse of process regarding the prosecution of D for going to fight in Syria, despite D's fighting for a group aligned with UK interests, and despite assurances and encouragement from a police officer.[77]

### *(a) A right to receive guidance in ECHR-protected activities; and a right to rely on guidance received generally?*

The argument that an assurance, by an appropriate public official, that conduct will not be prosecuted should preclude a subsequent prosecution for an offence which is based on that conduct was boosted by the decision of the House of Lords in *Purdy*.[78] This was not a case where a relevant official had given an assurance to D that he would not be prosecuted. The applicants were seeking information from the Director of Prosecutions concerning the circumstances in which the Director would be likely to authorise a prosecution should D assist V's suicide by acts done in England enabling V to travel to a country where suicide was lawful.[79] There was public knowledge of over 150 previous cases of facilitating travel abroad for

[73] For discussion of how such defences may be justified, see Babb and Emmerich, "Official Misrepresentations of the Law and Fairness" (2023) 17 *Crim Law and Philosophy* 83.

[74] (1994) 98 Cr App R 76 (DC).

[75] Times, December 8, 1997.

[76] [2019] EWCA Crim 647.

[77] Any trial that constitutes an abuse of process is, further, likely to contravene Article 6 of the ECHR, which secures the defendant's right to a fair trial. The appropriate remedy, in such circumstances, is to permanently stay the proceedings against the defendant.

[78] [2009] UKHL 45, [2010] 1 AC 345.

[79] Under s. 2(4) of the Suicide Act 1961, the DPP must give consent for any prosecution brought for assisting suicide contrary to s. 1(2).

the purpose of suicide and none of those cases had resulted in a prosecution. The Director's legal and policy analysis of such cases was unclear; all that he had said officially was that it should not be assumed that assistance of the kind D had in mind would not be prosecuted.

The House of Lords ruled unanimously that the state of uncertainty regarding any possible prosecution engaged the right of V to respect for private and family life as guaranteed by Article 8(1) of the ECHR. If the State is to interfere with the right to respect for a private life, then, among other things, it must do so in "accordance with the law", as is required by Article 8(2). In giving the leading opinion of the Appellate Committee, Lord Rodger held that in the context of Article 8(2) the term "law" embraced the decision-making of the Director of Public Prosecutions regarding consent to prosecutions for the offence of assisting suicide.[80] Lord Rodger concluded that the Director's decision-making concerning assisted suicide lacked the foreseeability and accessibility that the European Convention requires. To remedy those deficiencies, the Director was obliged to draft and publicly disseminate a sufficiently informative policy document regarding the giving of consent to prosecutions for assisting suicide.[81]

To be sure, *Purdy* is a very particular and poignant case, but it is not devoid of significance for our discussion. By no means will every case engage Article 8 where there is uncertainty about future prosecution. However, Lord Rodger's analysis of the requirements of legality in the context of the ECHR has clear relevance for Article 7. As has already been seen,[82] and will consider further below, Article 7, as interpreted, goes further than proscribing retroactive penal law. The criminal law must achieve minimum standards of clarity and consistency. It is clear from *Purdy* that the DPP would be in breach of Article 8 in the (very unlikely) future event of consenting to a prosecution for assisting suicide in circumstances where the published policy indicated that no such prosecution would be brought.[83] It should also follow that the Director would breach Article 7. A similar conclusion should also hold for any case where a prosecutor, acting within the terms of her office, has given an assurance that a prosecution will not be brought—whether or not that assurance is conveyed in a public policy document or by way of a verifiable undertaking to a specific individual, and whether or not there was an ECHR-based right to receive such guidance.

### *(iii) Ignorance of law and Article 7 of the ECHR*

As well as affecting prosecution decisions, Article 7-type arguments may also be relevant during the trial itself.[84] Consider the facts of *Lim Chin Aik*,[85] where D was prosecuted for being an unregistered alien present in Singapore. A registration requirement had been imposed on aliens present in Singapore by an unpublished ordinance about which persons affected by its terms had not been notified. The Privy Council construed the offence as

[80] [2009] UKHL 45, [44].

[81] *Ibid.*, [54–59].

[82] For the earlier discussion, see § 2.3.

[83] Cf. Rogers "Prosecutorial Policies, Prosecutorial Systems, and the *Purdy* Litigation" [2010] *Crim LR* 543. The guidance is to be found at https://www.cps.gov.uk/legal-guidance/suicide-policy-prosecutors-respect-cases-encouraging-or-assisting-suicide (last updated October 2014).

[84] The impact of Article 7 remains uncertain and contested. Usefully discussed in Boucht and Emberland, "'Mental Link' as a Condition for Punishment Under Article 7 of the European Convention on Human Rights" (2026, online) *European Journal of Crime, Criminal Law and Criminal Justice*.

[85] [1963] AC 160. See too *Chambers* [2008] EWCA Crim 2467.

requiring mens rea and advised that D lacked mens rea because he was unaware of any duty to register.

In its own terms, the decision is entirely satisfactory. Yet by characterising the matter as one of mens rea, the broader question of when ignorance of law may excuse is not addressed. Neither is the tension with earlier authority such as *Bailey*.[86] Broader considerations may nowadays be encouraged by Article 7 of the ECHR, which proscribes retroactive penal law. Of course, the mischief at work in cases such as *Lim Chin Aik* and *Bailey* is not, strictly, retroactivity: the laws under which the respective defendants were prosecuted existed at the time of their conduct. Yet from the perspective of fairness to the defendant, no distinction can be drawn between retroactive law and unpublished law which cannot be known to the defendant or anyone else at the time of her conduct.[87] Article 7 protection should be extended to such cases.

It is doubtful whether Article 7 protection will be extended to laws that may not be widely known by the public yet which are passed directly by Parliament (rather than regulation by statutory instrument) and are published and accessible online. But as Ashworth observes,[88] such is the volume of recent criminal law that the substance of serious criminal offences in core areas of the criminal law, such as sexual offences, may be completely unknown to those who breach their terms. He instances *Thomas*,[89] where D contravened section 25 of the Sexual Offences Act 2003 ("sexual activity with a child family member") by having sexual intercourse with V, aged 17, who had been fostered by D and his wife. Fostering had ended two years before the intercourse, when V left D's care to live in other accommodation. Had V been 18 years of age there would have been no offence. It was accepted that D was wholly unaware that his conduct was criminal, yet he was sentenced to imprisonment for four years, reduced on appeal to two years in the light of D's unawareness that he was committing an offence.

Ashworth argues strongly that English law should provide a defence of excusable ignorance of criminal law in cases such as *Thomas*. He accepts that adult citizens are under a duty to obtain a reasonable knowledge of the criminal law, but insists that the duty should be pitched at a reasonable level of expectation. He argues for far more proactivity from the government in disseminating knowledge of the criminal law. The moral sentiment behind Ashworth's proposals is powerful,[90] but the detail of any such new defence is likely to be difficult to resolve.[91] Even with will and commitment, there will be limits to the state's capacity to inculcate knowledge of the criminal law. Obedience to the strictures imposed upon conduct is highly dependent on cultural norms and values rather than the letter of the law, even for serious offences. Consider section 25 of the Sexual Offences Act 2003: the idea

[86] (1800) Russ and Ry 1, 168 ER 651 (CCR).

[87] See above, §§ 2.2–3.

[88] "Ignorance of the Criminal Law, and Duties to Avoid it" (2011) 74 *MLR* 1; see further Ashworth, *Positive Obligations in Criminal Law* (2013) chap. 3.

[89] [2006] 1 Cr App R (S) 602 (CA).

[90] Such a defence is available in France. Article 122-3 of the Code pénal provides: "N'est pas pénalement responsable la personne qui justifie avoir cru, par une erreur sur le droit qu'elle n'était pas en mesure d'éviter, pouvoir légitimement accomplir l'acte."

[91] For arguments against a mistake of law defence, see Azmat, "What Mistake of Law Just Might Be: Legal Moralism, Liberal Positivism, and the Mistake of Law Doctrine" (2015) 18 *New Criminal LR* 369. Azmat's chief concern is that a mistake of law defence will provide a "safe harbour" for those who should have made a greater effort to ascertain the applicable law, thereby undermining the duty to know the law and creating inefficiencies by shifting the burden of rebuttal onto prosecutors and courts.

informing the variant of the offence at issue in *Thomas* appears to be that a sexual relationship between a carer and a formerly cared-for child is not lawful until the child has reached 18. Is that restriction aligned with reasonable expectations? Such questions may be very difficult to adjudicate.

## § 18.3 Impossibility

Where the law imposes a duty to complete certain conduct, no liability should be found where it is impossible for D (through no fault of her own) to complete the conduct required.[92] A common law rule to this effect is identifiable, for example, in cases where D's "failure" to leave the country is owing to her advanced pregnancy and restrictions on travel,[93] where "failure" to provide paperwork is owing to its non-existence,[94] and so on.

In terms of the structure of the criminal law, we submit that the impossibility rule is best analysed as a "failure of proof", not as a supervening defence. Rather than being a matter of defence, such as duress, impossibility raises an issue going to the very suppositions of criminal liability. If D is not responsible for the impossibility, then he may properly claim that the omission he is charged with, or the status he is blamed for acquiring, is not something which is linked to any voluntary conduct ascribable to him. That is to say: impossibility is a species of *involuntariness*. For this reason, the cases on impossibility are discussed above, in § 4.3(ii).

Criminal liability, properly understood, must always be associated with some voluntary act or omission on the part of D.[95] Such voluntary acts or omissions may be identified some time before the relevant duty is actually breached: for example, if D is unable to discharge some legal obligation because he chose to go to bed and was asleep at the time the duty fell to be done, he may properly be convicted in respect of his failure of duty.[96] However, if there are no voluntary acts or omissions, there is nothing on which any form of *criminal* liability can properly be based: for example, where D cannot perform his duty because, through no fault of his own, someone has unforeseeably tied him to a bed. It is remarkable that this simple and fundamental restraint on criminal liability is not consistently respected.[97]

Remarkable or otherwise, however, English law appears impervious to the injustice of liability in such cases. In *Hampshire County Council v E*,[98] D was charged with being the parent of a child of compulsory school age, a child who "fails to attend school regularly".[99] The Divisional Court was adamant that liability could be imposed on an utterly blameless parent who could not have ensured attendance by any means, whenever a literal reading of this statutory provision covered the facts at hand. By contrast, in *Robinson-Pierre*,[100] we find a rare instance of reading the plain terms of a statutory provision in light of a principle

[92] Smart, "Criminal Responsibility for Failing to Do the Impossible" (1987) 103 *LQR* 532; Williams, *CLGP*, 746–8.
[93] *Finau* [1984] 2 NZLR 396.
[94] *Stockdale v Coulson* [1974] 3 All ER 154 (DC).
[95] Above, § 4.3(ii).
[96] Prior fault is discussed above, § 4.3(iii).
[97] Although recognition of this principle would prevent certain forms of injustice, the principle is still compatible with the existence of very bad laws. For instance, respect for the principle would disallow, say, criminal liability for the mere fact of having curly hair; yet it would not forestall a law which required those with curly hair to shave their heads. See above, § 4.1(ii)(a).
[98] [2007] EWHC 2584 (Admin).
[99] Contrary to the Education Act 1996 s. 441.
[100] [2013] EWCA Crim 2396, [2014] 1 WLR 2638.

that it ought to comport with the minimal requirements necessary for any coherent finding of criminal liability. It is an offence for D to be an owner of a dog that is out of control in a public place, and the offence is aggravated if the dog should injure somebody while out of control.[101] D's dog did attack and injure V in public, but only because police officers had, without warning, battered his front door down, allowing the animal to run out of the house. D was convicted at first instance: he was the owner of the dog, a dog that had attacked and injured V in public, while out of control; there was nothing more to prove in terms of the explicit elements of the offence. The Court of Appeal held otherwise. It saw no sense in convicting D for an incident which was the product of a third-party intervention that D could not prevent, and held that Parliament could not have intended that the offence could be committed in such circumstances. It would be pleasant to think that *Robinson-Pierre* might presage a less literal approach than has prevailed in so many other cases, but the possibility that it will be confined to the particular offence at issue cannot be discounted.[102] A principled and consistent recognition that voluntary conduct is a prerequisite of any form of criminal liability would obviate the need for any defence of impossibility.[103]

## § 18.4 Prior fault and intoxication

In the sections above, we have (for the most part) assumed that D is blameless in her ignorance and/or when making mistakes of fact or law. In this context, it should be uncontroversial for D to raise her ignorance and/or mistake to demonstrate a failure of proof on the part of the prosecution, exposing the absence of offence elements (or the availability of a supervening defence). However, what of cases where D's ignorance or mistake may be traced back to her previous blameworthy choices? Suppose, for example, that D becomes voluntarily intoxicated with alcohol and causes damage to another's property, claiming afterwards – plausibly – that she lacked any intention or foresight regarding the damage because of her intoxicated state. The fact of D's intoxication provides evidence in support of D's claim to have lacked mens rea on a charge of criminal damage (i.e. denying essential elements of the offence),[104] but it also exposes her prior fault in bringing about the circumstances in which the damage was mistakenly caused.

In cases of this kind, the courts have understandably been reluctant to allow failure of proof arguments to succeed, and have developed a number of discreet rules that empower the prosecution to push back against them.[105] These are referred to collectively as "prior

[101] Dangerous Dogs Act 1991, s. 3.

[102] Even in the context of the s. 3 offence, the impact of this approach has since been neutered by a legislative amendment making the offence applicable in relation to "any location in England or Wales (whether or not a public place)". The offence is aggravated if the out-of-control dog attacks anyone.

[103] Above, § 4.3. See Sullivan, "Conduct and Proof of Conduct: Minimum Conditions for Criminal Liability" in Kaikobad and Bohlander (eds.), *International Law and Power, Perspectives on Legal Order and Justice: Essays in Honour of Colin Warbrick* (2009) 235; Child, "Defence of a Basic Voluntary Act Requirement in Criminal Law from Philosophies of Action" (2020) 23(4) *New Crim LR* 437. If preferred, this could be expressed as an insistence on confining criminal punishment to events within D's *control*: cf. Simester, *Fundamentals* chap. 8; Husak, "Does Criminal Liability Require an Act" in Duff (ed.), *Philosophy and Criminal Law* (1998) 60; Duff, *Answering for Crime* (2007) § 5.5.

[104] Criminal Damage Act 1971, s. 1.

[105] We have already discussed a sub-set of prior fault cases above, § 5.8(i)(d).

fault rules".[106] The most developed prior fault rule applies to cases of voluntary intoxication, such as our example, where D's intoxication results in mistake making relevant to her offence or defence, and/or to a denial of voluntariness. In such cases, where it is proved that D was voluntarily intoxicated with a dangerous drug, and this resulted in the relevant mistake and/or involuntariness, the prior fault intoxication rule will allow liability to be found, at least in relation to a sub-set of so-called "basic intent" offences.[107]

We explore the detail of this rule in the sub-sections below. First, however, it is important to emphasis its unique and controversial nature. Despite D's being able to evidence an apparent failure of proof claim, the prior fault intoxication rule permits liability to be established on the basis of blameworthy conduct (i.e., voluntary intoxication) quite distinct from the elements of the offence or defence at issue. It is no doubt because of this that the framing of the prior fault intoxication rule continues to provoke debate; and it is here that we begin.

### *(i) Framing prior fault intoxication rules*

There are at least three accounts that compete for the legal framing of prior fault intoxication: intoxication as a defence; intoxication as a form of excluded evidence; and intoxication as a mechanism for inculpation. Each one can be identified within the courts and academic literature, though only the third option provides a potentially coherent explanation for the current law; and it is that framing that will be employed in our discussion of the intoxication rule that follows. It is useful to provide a brief account of each however, not least to aid the understanding of older case law and other sources.

The most longstanding description of the intoxication rule is that it represents an intoxication *defence*. Essentially, where D denies certain offence elements on the basis of his intoxicated state (i.e., denies mens rea and/or voluntariness), such denials are recast as if D were raising a supervening defence. From here, in circumstances where intoxication rules apply, the preferred description is simply that D's liability ensues because "D is not permitted to raise the intoxication defence". This is the dominant framing of intoxication within the leading case of *Majewski*,[108] and internationally.[109] Describing intoxication as a defence, however, has always been (and remains) a misleading mischaracterisation.[110] Supervening defences apply to exculpate prima facie offences; they engage only after all *the actus reus and mens rea* elements of an offence have been satisfied. Where D satisfies those elements (commits a prima facie offence), however, intoxication is irrelevant. There is no basis upon which D, satisfying the elements of a prima facie offence, can draw upon her intoxicated state as any form of substantive excuse.[111]

[106] Child, Hunt and Crombag, *Prior Fault Criminalization* (2026); Child, "Prior Fault: Blocking Defences or Constructing Crimes" in Reed and Bohlander (eds.), *General Defences* (2014) 37; Robinson, "Causing the Conditions of One's Own Defence" (1985) 71 *Virginia Law Review* 1.

[107] Child, Hunt and Crombag, *Prior Fault Criminalization* (2026) chap. 2; Law Com. No. 314, *Intoxication and Criminal Liability* (2009).

[108] *DPP v Majewski* [1977] AC 443. E.g. at 476: "it is no excuse in law that, because of drink or drugs which the accused himself had taken knowingly and willingly, he had deprived himself of the ability to exercise self-control, to realise the possible consequences of what he was doing, or even to be conscious that he was doing it. As in the instant case, the jury may be properly instructed that they 'can ignore the subject of drink or drugs as being in any way a defence' to charges of this character".

[109] Discussed in Simester, "Getting drunk in Singapore and Malaysia" [2012] *Singapore Journal of Legal Studies* 1.

[110] Simester, "Intoxication is Never a Defence" [2009] *Crim LR* 3.

[111] *Kingston* [1995] 2 AC 355, discussed further below.

As an alternative to presenting the intoxication rule as a "defence", it has at times been framed instead as a rule of *evidence*. Here, rather than presenting the intoxication rule as a substantive mechanism, we are simply told that D may not raise evidence of intoxication. The logic provides that, where D's conduct appears voluntary and intentional, excluding evidence of intoxication (that might otherwise establish doubt) will allow the prosecution to prove that the offence was committed. As stated in *Richardson and Irwin*, "in considering what the defendant actually foresaw the jury must disregard the fact that the appellants had been drinking".[112] However, this approach produces an absurdity: it is an oxymoron to talk of *actual* foresight if the evidential rule at issue is designed to produce a counterfactual picture of what D's foresight would have been if sober. The rule is not (as sometimes claimed) seeking to exclude "irrelevant" evidence, at least within any standard legal definition of that term. Evidence of D's intoxication will often be relevant to his foresight of contested facts, perhaps irresistibly so where it demonstrates an extreme lack of capacity. In this way, describing the intoxication rule in evidential terms involves excluding evidence which is potentially highly relevant to demonstrating D's innocence, and conceives of "proving" factual guilt on the basis of a counterfactual fiction.

Our preferred framing of the intoxication rule recognises it as a inculpatory mechanism, allowing the prosecution to establish an alternative route to liability despite what would otherwise amount to a failure of proof. Intoxication rules apply to *construct* liability, taking D's objective fault in becoming intoxicated and using that fault to substitute for certain missing offence elements and/or to deny certain defence elements.[113] This mechanism is simple enough to state, but it poses considerable challenges within a system of law that would not typically allow objective fault exhibited at one point in time to satisfy subjective mens rea and/or voluntariness requirements at another. We return to such challenges when discussing reform options below.

### *(ii) Applying prior fault intoxication rules: offences*

When discussing the application of intoxication rules, it is useful to distinguish "offences" (i.e. where D denies offending) and "defences" (i.e. where D claims a supervening defence). We begin with a denial of offending: cases where evidence of D's intoxication raises doubt concerning essential elements of mens rea and/or voluntariness as a failure of proof.[114] The question is how and when prior fault intoxication rules operate to construct an alternative route to liability.

The recognition of a prior fault rule is not inevitable, and there remain several jurisdictions that do not do so.[115] In such jurisdictions, intoxication becomes largely unremarkable. It provides an explanation for D's claim to have lacked mens rea and/or voluntariness alongside any number of others. English law has not, however, adopted this approach. Voluntary intoxication is notable in this jurisdiction for its ability—through common law intoxication

[112] [1999] 1 Cr App R 392, 395 (CA). See also the Criminal Code Act 1995 (Commonwealth), s 8(1): "Evidence of self-induced intoxication cannot be considered in determining whether a fault element of basic intent existed."

[113] See Yaffe, "Intoxication, Recklessness and Negligence" (2012) 9 *Ohio State Journal of Criminal Law* 545.

[114] Where there is *no* potential failure of proof (i.e. where D has committed the offence) the intoxication rules do not apply, even if D is intoxicated at the time of the offence. "A drunken intent is nevertheless an intent": *Sheehan and Moore* (1974) 60 Cr App R 308, 312 (CA). We discuss cases of this kind further below.

[115] Discussed in Orchard, "Surviving without *Majewski* Down Under" [1993] *Crim LR* 426.

rules—to manufacture liability that could not otherwise be found. The common intuition that an intoxicated harm should be punishable in criminal law has given rise to a wide-ranging inculpatory tool for the prosecution.[116]

The leading case on the intoxication rules is *Majewski*.[117] D was charged with assault, an offence that can be committed where D intends to make V apprehend immediate unlawful violence, or is reckless regarding that outcome. D had consumed large quantities of drink and drugs. He attacked V in circumstances that, from an external perspective, indicated a deliberate assault. D claimed neither to have intended nor foreseen an assault or battery; at the time of the incident, he claimed, he was "a drunken automaton", not conscious of what he was doing. It was argued for D that section 8 of the Criminal Justice Act 1967 required that proof of D's intention or foresight must be established by reference "to all the evidence", including evidence of his intoxicated condition. Lord Elwyn-Jones, for a unanimous House of Lords, rejected this argument. He presented the intoxication rules in the following terms:[118]

> "If a man of his own volition takes a substance which causes him to cast off the restraints of reason and conscience, no wrong is done to him by holding him answerable criminally for any injury he may do while in that condition. His course of conduct in reducing himself by drugs and drink to that condition in my view supplies the evidence of mens rea, of guilty mind certainly sufficient for crimes of basic intent. It is a reckless course of conduct and recklessness is enough to constitute the necessary mens rea in assault cases."

Under this approach, although D may in fact have lacked mens rea, his prior fault is highlighted as legal justification for convicting and punishing D *as if* all offence elements were established. It will readily be appreciated that the "recklessness" referenced by his Lordship is not the recklessness that would otherwise be required to establish assault. There is no need to prove that D foresaw, when becoming intoxicated, any threat of force inflicted on V. The essence of this form of prior fault appears to be that D, by taking drugs or alcohol, has "cast off thc constraints of reason and conscience".

The intoxication rules are best understood as a combination of four elements, all of which must be satisfied for liability to follow. The first two elements focus on D's prior fault (establishing a blameworthy choice). The third and fourth elements translate that prior fault into liability for a particular category of offences. We take the following elements in turn:

| | |
|---|---|
| *Element 1*: | D must be voluntarily intoxicated. |
| *Element 2*: | D must have taken a dangerous drug. |
| *Element 3*: | D must be charged with a basic intent offence (or act with "Dutch courage"). |
| *Element 4*: | D's intoxication must have caused his involuntariness and/or lack of mens rea. |

### *(iii) Element 1: voluntary intoxication*

In order to establish an element of prior choice upon which blame may be constructed, the first step is to establish that D was voluntarily intoxicated.

[116] Another alternative is to allow prior fault intoxication to substitute for missing mens rea, but not for involuntariness. We see this approach debated in Canada, for example. Healy, "Legislative Revision of Extreme Intoxication Cases in Canada" [2022] *Crim LR* 957.
[117] [1977] AC 443.
[118] [1977] AC 443, 474–5.

*(a) Intoxication*

No legal definition of intoxication exists. There is no statement concerning what level of disinhibition or confusion induced by drink or drugs is sufficient for legal purposes. We might posit that no such definition is required: on basic principles, the question ought to be whether the impact of any drink or drugs taken by D makes it reasonably possible that he did not form the mens rea and/or voluntariness that the offence requires. This, after all, is the basis of D's failure of proof claim.

However, where D's intoxication becomes relevant to the prior fault intoxication rule, its legal role goes well beyond the denial of offence elements. Rather, it becomes an integral part of the culpability required for the crime itself.[119] Where this is so, some minimum threshold of intoxication is necessary: for a crime of basic intent, the prosecution should not be relieved from its burden of proof by establishing that D had taken *some* quantity of drink or drugs prior to the conduct alleged.[120] Unfortunately, no such threshold is currently acknowledged; and so any level of intoxication is potentially sufficient, provided that it caused D's lack of mens rea and/or voluntariness.[121]

The lack of a definition also makes it difficult to distinguish intoxication from other causes of involuntariness and mistake of fact. We discuss this further below in § 18.5, but it is useful here to note some headline distinctions recognised at common law. On the one hand, the intoxication rule clearly engages cases where drugs are active in D's system at the time of causing harm. On the other hand, it has been consistently held that states of drug withdrawal,[122] and/or brain effects caused by historic drug use,[123] are not covered by the intoxication rules. This used to be the end of the story, focused on the presence or absence of drugs in D's system at the relevant time.[124] However, the case of *Taj* has introduced significant new uncertainty.[125] In that case, a five-member Court of Appeal found that the prior fault intoxication rules could be applied where D's psychosis (resulting in a relevant mistake of fact) was attributable to D's *previous* state of intoxication, regardless of whether D was in a drug-on-board state at the time of his offence. The full impact of *Taj* remains difficult to predict. Moving the temporal threshold for intoxication in this way is certainly problematic: it forces courts to make fine-grained distinctions between alternative causes of psychosis in a manner that is not scientifically credible.[126] It is possible that *Taj* will be confined to its particular context, an intoxicated mistake in self-defence,[127] and will not be

119 *Ibid.*

120 There is an *obiter* remark in *Stubbs* (1989) 88 Cr App R 53, 54 (CA) that the intoxication needed to be "very extreme".

121 This causal requirement is discussed within Element 4 below.

122 *Harris* [2013] EWCA Crim 223, [2013] MHLR 171.

123 *Beard* [1920] AC 479, 501.

124 Crombag, Child, and Fortson, "Understanding the 'Fault' in Prior-Fault Intoxication" in Reed and Bohlander (eds.), *Fault* (2022) 86.

125 [2018] EWCA Crim 1743, [2019] QB 655. See Dsouza, 'Intoxication, Psychoses, and Self-defence: Evaluating *Taj*' [2018] *Arch Rev* 6.

126 It is notable that even within *Taj*, a subsequent diagnosis of bipolar disorder presented an *alternative* explanation for D's psychosis, requiring the Court of Appeal to engage with the possibility that intoxication was not a relevant factor. [2018] EWCA Crim 1743, [2019] QB 655 [61]–[64]. Discussed in Child, Crombag, and Sullivan, "Defending the Delusional, the Irrational, and the Dangerous" [2020] *Crim LR* 306; Crombag, Child, and Sullivan, "Drunk, Dangerous and Delusional: How Legal Concept Creep Risks Overcriminalisation" (2020) 115(12) *Addiction* 2200, and debate responses in the same volume.

127 Below, §§ 18.4(vii) and 21.2(iv).

applied to cases in the *Majewski* category where mens rea is being constructed. Confining *Taj* in this way has some merit, but it is not supported by anything said in the case itself.[128] It would also be anomalous to maintain two separate definitions of intoxication. The better route, we believe, is to reverse the decision in *Taj*, and make the scope of intoxication rules depend once again on the presence of drugs in D's system at the time of the actus reus.[129]

### *(b) Voluntary*

An "involuntary" state of intoxication does not come within the *Majewski* regime. "Voluntary" here means *advertently chosen*: D's intoxication is involuntary when she has not *chosen* to take a relevant risk of impaired capacity with her future conduct, and so there is no prior fault intoxication with which to manufacture liability. Clear cases of involuntary intoxication arise where, without his knowledge, D is slipped a destabilising drug;[130] or where a medically prescribed drug is taken for therapeutic reasons, if no warning is given about any destabilising properties of the drug.[131] However, outside of this, a narrow view of "involuntary" has been maintained. If, for example, D is aware that she is taking intoxicating substances, any subsequent inebriation will be taken to be voluntary even if a mistake has been made about the strength of the item taken.[132]

Potentially, the largest group of persons who may claim that their intoxication is involuntary comprises those addicted to alcohol or other intoxicants.[133] However, the threshold for involuntariness has been maintained strictly by the courts, requiring a condition in which D had no choice about when to take her first drink of the day and was unable to refrain from drinking thereafter.[134] If D's dependency on alcohol reaches these extremes, it is clear that D should not be treated as voluntarily intoxicated. But these restrictions are so stringent that few, if any, alcoholics could satisfy them. In the narrow context of diminished responsibility as a partial defence to murder, a more accommodating approach has been adopted, allowing the effects of intoxication to be taken into account as part of D's alcoholism (i.e. , as part of D's relevant mental health disorder).[135] But outside of this narrow context, it seems that addiction alone will not be sufficient to deny voluntary intoxication.[136]

[128] E.g., at [56]: "*DPP v. Majewski* focused on crime committed while specifically under the influence of drugs or alcohol. Having said that, however, it is difficult to see why the language (and the policy identified) is not equally apposite to the immediate and proximate consequences of such misuse."

[129] Child, Crombag, and Sullivan, "Defending the Delusional, the Irrational, and the Dangerous" [2020] *Crim LR* 306.

[130] *Ross v HM Advocate* 1991 SLT 564.

[131] In principle this should apply to the condition known as "pathological intoxication", where relatively small quantities of alcohol may activate a form of latent epilepsy or other conditions. However, such a phenomenon may be regarded as a form of insanity: Mackay, *Mental Condition Defences in the Criminal Law* (1995) 165–9; and see below, Chapter 19.

[132] *Allen* [1988] Crim LR 698 (CA). A more difficult case would involve D voluntarily taking one intoxicant (e.g. alcohol), which is then involuntarily laced with further drugs. In such cases, a court is likely to look for the predominant cause of D's intoxication, finding involuntary intoxication where D's initial voluntary drug taking is effectively overridden. Law Com. No. 314, *Intoxication and Criminal Liability* (2009) paras. 3.126–3.127.

[133] Discussed across the chapters in Goldberg and Manguele (eds.), *Criminal Law and Prior Fault* (2025).

[134] *Tandy* [1989] 1 All ER 267 (CA).

[135] *Wood* [2008] EWCA Crim 1305, [2009] 1 WLR 496; *Stewart* [2009] EWCA Crim 593, [2009] 1 WLR 2507.

[136] For Robinson, where D's addiction arose from historic voluntary consumption, this may be sufficient to justify treating V as voluntarily intoxicated. Robinson, "A Brief Summary and Critique of Criminal Liability Rules for Intoxicated Conduct" (2018) 82 *J Crim L* 381, part V.

### *(iv) Element 2: dangerous drug*

In order to establish that D's prior choice (voluntary consumption) was a *blameworthy* choice, the drug taken must be classified as "dangerous". The test for dangerousness here is a legal one, based on an objective common-sense view of which drugs D should have known could lead to impaired control and decision-making. No distinction is drawn between alcohol and drugs such as heroin, cocaine, cannabis, and LSD; dangerousness is about the potential effects of the drug rather than its legal status.[137] Where the drug is *not* commonly understood to cause relevant impairment, it will be classified as non-dangerous, and the intoxication rules will not apply. The only exception here is where D has special knowledge or experience that a typically non-dangerous drug may nevertheless have a relevant destabilising effect on him, in which case subjective awareness will be sufficient to establish the drug (for D) as a dangerous drug.[138]

Librium and Valium, and compounds such as insulin, when taken for therapeutic reasons, are examples of typically non-dangerous drugs. If drugs are taken to treat the symptoms of some underlying condition of D, normal mens rea principles will apply and the special rules relating to voluntary intoxication will not be relevant. In *Bailey*,[139] D, a diabetic, took insulin for his condition, but neglected to follow the dietary regime his doctor prescribed. D became hypoglycaemic, lost control of his actions (a condition regarded as one of sane automatism), and attacked V. In *Hardie*,[140] D, upset and agitated, took an excessive quantity of Librium belonging to someone else in an attempt to pacify himself. D set fire to V's flat. He claimed that the drugs disorientated him, rendering him incapable of appreciating the destructive nature of his conduct. In both cases, the Court of Appeal ruled that the trial judges had erred in directing the jury that *Majewski* applied. Instead, because they were non-dangerous drugs, the normal principles of mens rea were taken to be the applicable standard; as such, the prosecution had to prove D *in fact* had mens rea at the time of the actus reus in order to secure a conviction.

The key to both decisions is a commendable reluctance to subject persons taking drugs for therapeutic benefit to the regime of social protection endorsed by the House of Lords in *Majewski*. *Bailey*, in particular, is instructive on this point. In *Bailey*, D was not immune from criticism; his hypoglycaemic condition would have been avoided had he followed his doctor's instructions. Yet the Court took appropriate and compassionate cognisance of the fact that, for a diabetic, the taking of insulin and the management of its destabilising effects is a lifetime burden. In *Hardie*, there are some distracting *dicta* to the effect that tranquillising drugs such as Librium and Valium differ in their pharmacological properties from alcohol: the former drugs are of "soporific effect" whereas the latter gives rise to "aggression and violence".[141] But this is a false distinction. The physiological properties of tranquilising drugs and alcohol are similar; their effects ensue from depressing the central nervous system. The essential point about *Hardie* is that D was taking the drug to calm his nerves, and he did not anticipate the drug's destabilising effects that followed.

[137] *Lipman* [1970] 1 QB 152 (CA).
[138] *Bailey* [1983] 2 All ER 503 (CA).
[139] *Ibid.*
[140] [1984] 3 All ER 848 (CA).
[141] *Ibid.*, 853 (Parker LJ).

### (v) *Element 3: basic intent offence (or "Dutch courage")*

Having established the basis for D's prior fault (i.e. voluntary intoxication with a dangerous drug), the next question is how that prior fault can be used to substitute for missing mens rea and/or voluntariness at the point of D's potential offence. In answering this question, a distinction is drawn between (i) so-called *basic intent* offences, where D's prior fault will substitute for any missing mens rea and/or voluntariness element, resulting in liability, and (ii) so-called *specific intent* offences, where D's prior fault will not (typically[142]) substitute for any missing mens rea and/or voluntariness, resulting in acquittal. The labels "basic" and "specific" intent are terms of art, distinguishing the two categories, and tell us little about how that distinction should be drawn.[143]

#### (a) *Distinguishing basic and specific intent offences*

Separating crimes into categories of basic and specific intent is essential for the operation of the intoxication rules. However, the doctrinal and theoretical underpinning for this distinction remains opaque despite a century of jurisprudence. The leading case on this issue is, once again, the House of Lords decision in *Majewski*.[144] The case offers two accounts of the distinction, neither of which is by itself complete.

The first account is given by Lord Elwyn-Jones.[145] His Lordship considered that a crime of specific intent was a crime where the mens rea extends beyond the actus reus; that is, a crime of *ulterior* intent.[146] The idea certainly has appeal. Burglary, for instance, can be considered a crime of specific intent because all that is required by way of an actus reus is an entry as a trespasser into a building. The offence is complete on entry if it can be proved that D had the *further* intention to steal.[147] Consider, too, the intentional or reckless causing of criminal damage being reckless as to whether life was endangered:[148] according to the Court of Appeal in *Heard*,[149] this is a crime of specific intent. That is because, even though recklessness is sufficient fault regarding the endangerment of life, "endangerment of life" goes beyond the actus reus requirements of the offence. Since the offence of aggravated criminal damage does not require that life actually be endangered, but merely an act of criminal damage which is believed to carry that risk, this is an offence of ulterior mens rea. On the analysis in *Heard* the crime is one of specific intent.[150]

Despite the plausibility of this definition of specific intent, it does not explain all of the case law. It is well established that murder is a crime of specific intent.[151] Yet in murder, the mens rea need not extend to the entirety of the actus reus, let alone go beyond it, because an

[142] We discuss "Dutch courage" as the exception to this rule below.

[143] On the origin of these terms, as well as a more general critique, see Gough, "Intoxication and Criminal Liability: The Law Commission's Proposed Reforms" (1996) 112 *LQR* 335, 342.

[144] [1977] AC 443.

[145] *Ibid.*, 471, citing Lord Simon's speech in *Morgan* [1976] AC 182, 216.

[146] See above, § 5.1(vii).

[147] Theft Act 1968, s. 9(1)(a); above, § 14.4.

[148] Criminal Damage Act 1971, s. 1(2)(b).

[149] [2007] EWCA Crim 125, [2008] QB 43; above, § 12.2.

[150] [2007] EWCA Crim 125, [2008] QB 43, [31]; endorsing the view of Lord Edmund Davies in *Caldwell* [1982] AC 341. Cf. *Coley* [2013] EWCA Crim 223, [2013] MHLR 171, [57], where the Court acknowledged *Heard* but noted that the decision was *obiter* on this point and suggested that the matter may need to be revisited on a future occasion.

[151] *Beard* [1920] AC 479; *Gallagher* [1963] AC 349; *Sheehan* (1974) 60 Cr App R 308 (CA).

intent to cause grievous bodily harm will suffice.[152] Further, on Lord Elwyn-Jones's definition, the same crime could be of either specific intent or basic intent, depending on how it is committed. Section 18 of the OAPA 1861 penalises wounding with intent to cause grievous bodily harm and, additionally, causing grievous bodily harm with intent to cause grievous bodily harm.[153] Where the actus reus of the offence takes the form of a wound insufficiently serious to constitute grievous bodily harm, the intent to be provided is a specific intent of the form indicated by Lord Elwyn-Jones. But where the actus reus has taken the form of grievous bodily harm, the intent to be proved need only correspond to the actus reus and does not go beyond it. It is no longer a specific intent crime in his Lordship's terms. Yet it is accepted that section 18 is a crime of specific intent whatever form its takes.[154]

An alternative account was given by Lord Simon, who considered that an offence of specific intent was a crime where the mens rea required proof of a "purposive element".[155] The most straightforward interpretation of this test would translate "purpose" (a term that is not typically used within English criminal law) into an "intention" standard. Thus, specific intent offences would be identifiable though their requirement of intention as mens rea, including within paradigms specific intent offences such as murder; and D's prior fault would not be able to substitute for missing mens rea and/or voluntariness for such offences, because it would not be capable of establishing an equivalent culpability. In contrast, basic intent offences would be those requiring a mens rea of recklessness, including paradigm basic intent offences such as assault; and D's prior fault would be able to substitute for missing mens rea and/or voluntariness for such offences because, as expressed in *Majewski* and *Heard*,[156] D's prior fault is widely understood to provide fault equivalent to a recklessness standard. The basic terms of this distinction is capable of explaining much of the case law, and its key assumption—of equivalence between prior fault intoxication and recklessness – can support several of the more sophisticated attempts to clarify (and justify) the operation of prior fault rules.[157]

However, again, this account does not provide a complete explanation for the basic/specific intent distinction within the current law. On one hand, not all recklessness offences have identified as basic intent offences, including the earlier example of aggravated criminal damage where D is reckless as to the endangerment of life. And on the other hand, several offences requiring intention have been categorised as ones of basic intent. In *Heard*,[158] for example, the Court of Appeal considered the offence of sexual assault.[159] One element of that offence that must be proved is an intentional touching, although intention is not required for the other elements of the offence (such as V's lack of consent). For the Court, a distinction could be drawn such that the "intentional" touching need not be "purposive", and so the offence was concluded to be a crime of basic intent. But this will not do. If purpose is not to be translated into intention (as we have suggested it should be), then it is

[152] Above, § 10.3(i)(a).
[153] There are other variations of mens rea for the section 18 offence as well. Above, § 11.6(ii).
[154] *Bratty v A-G for Northern Ireland* [1973] AC 386; *Pordage* [1975] Crim LR 575 (CA); *Davies* [1991] Crim LR 469 (CA).
[155] [1977] AC 443, 480.
[156] *Majewski* [1977] AC 443 and *Heard* [2007] EWCA Crim 125, [2008] QB 43.
[157] See Yaffe, "Intoxication, Recklessness and Negligence" (2012) 9(2) *Ohio State Journal of Criminal Law* 545; and discussion of Law Com. No. 314, *Intoxication and Criminal Liability* (2009) below.
[158] [2007] EWCA Crim 125, [2008] QB 43, [31].
[159] Contrary to s. 3 of the Sexual Offences Act 2003; above, § 12.8.

incumbent upon the Court to define their use of that term; and to explain how paradigm examples of specific intent offences such as murder may be understood as purposive crimes (i.e., not merely intentional crimes).

In the light of this confusion, the only safe course is to follow relevant precedents. On that basis, a list of established specific intent crimes can be drawn up. Murder, wounding, or causing grievous bodily harm with intent to cause grievous bodily harm are crimes of specific intent, as are theft,[160] burglary,[161] and handling stolen goods.[162] Most other crimes requiring proof of mens rea are crimes of basic intent. Examples of basic intent offences include manslaughter,[163] assault occasioning actual bodily harm,[164] assault and battery,[165] rape,[166] sexual assault,[167] and criminal damage (where recklessness is alleged).[168] The distinction can be identified—broadly—as tracing a separation of intention based offences and recklessness based offences, but this is a division, as we have discussed, that is far from consistent in its application.

*(b) Basic intent offences*

Where D is charged with a basic intent offence, D's prior fault intoxication may be used to substitute for any mens rea and/or voluntariness element that cannot otherwise be proved as a result of her intoxication. D will be labelled and punished *as if* she committed that offence. Thus, for example, where D causes grievous bodily harm to V, plausibly lacking any mens rea and/or voluntariness, she will not be liable for a section 18 GBH offence (specific intent),[169] but she may nevertheless be convicted of a section 20 offence (basic intent).[170]

*(c) Specific intent offences and "Dutch courage"*

For crimes of specific intent, the position is straightforward. In *Beard*,[171] the House of Lords ruled that on a charge of murder (a crime of specific intent), evidence of D's drunkenness was relevant to the finding of whether D had intended to kill or seriously hurt V. So, intoxication is recognised as a simple failure of proof argument, with no space for prior fault substitution. Lord Birkenhead's leading judgment caused some confusion for later courts by stating that evidence of drunkenness would be relevant in crimes of specific intent if it "showed that [D] was *incapable* of forming a specific intent".[172] In *Sheehan*,[173] however, the Court of Appeal affirmed that language of Lord Birkenhead should be read in the light of the decision in *Woolmington* regarding the burden of proof in criminal cases.[174] Accordingly,

[160] *Ruse v Read* [1949] 1 KB 377 (DC).
[161] *Durante* [1972] 1 WLR 1612 (CA); *Hutchins* [1988] Crim LR 379 (CA).
[162] *Ibid.*
[163] *Beard* [1920] AC 479.
[164] *Bolton v Crawley* [1972] Crim LR 222 (DC).
[165] *Majewski* [1977] AC 443.
[166] *Grout* [2011] EWCA Crim 299, [2011] 1 Cr App R 38.
[167] *Heard* [2007] EWCA Crim 125, [2008] QB 43.
[168] *Caldwell* [1981] 1 All ER 961.
[169] OAPA 1861, s. 18; above, § 11.6.
[170] OAPA 1861, s. 20; above, § 11.5.
[171] [1920] AC 479. See Handler, "Intoxication and Criminal Responsibility in England, 1819–1920" (2013) 33 *OJLS* 243.
[172] *Ibid.*, 501–2 (emphasis added).
[173] [1975] 2 All ER 960.
[174] [1935] AC 462; above, § 3.2.

the question in specific intent cases is not whether D was capable of forming the required specific intent but *whether D in fact formed the intent*. Evidence of intoxication may throw a reasonable doubt on the prosecution's case as a failure of proof just like any other evidence germane to the issue of intent.[175]

There is—in theory at least—one exception to this position for specific intent offences. This relates to a defendant who becomes intoxicated *in order to* commit the specific intent offence (so-called "Dutch courage" cases). This possibility was discussed in *AG for Northern Ireland v Gallagher*,[176] where D drank most of a bottle of whisky before killing his wife. D was found guilty of murder, on the basis that he intended to kill at the relevant point in time (in other words, this was a simple case of an intoxicated intention, and thus of intention[177]). However, Lord Denning considered, *obiter*, that even if D lacked intention at the point of killing his wife due to extreme intoxication, it would still be possible to find liability for murder (a specific intent offence). In his Lordship's analysis, D could be treated as satisfying the mens rea requirement in murder on the basis of his prior intention.[178] The logic of the outcome here is compelling, but it should be noted that no special application of the intoxication rules is required to achieve it. Where D becomes intoxicated in order to kill another, it should be open for the jury to find that his act of getting drunk, done with intent to kill, was causally related to the killing of V.[179]

### *(vi) Element 4: causal relationship*

Where D lacked mens rea for a basic intent offence, the fact that D was intoxicated is relevant only if the prosecution can establish that, *but for* D's intoxicated condition, she would have been aware of the relevant risk.[180] In this manner, it must be proved that D's intoxication made a difference.[181]

But what if the intoxication was part of the explanation of the actus reus? Consider *Brady*,[182] where D climbed a balcony above a dance floor, stood on the balcony rail, and fell onto V, a dancer, below, causing permanent disabling injury to V. Because of the way the matter was argued at trial, the Court of Appeal was limited to considering whether D's fall could be regarded as a "malicious" act in the context of maliciously inflicting grievous bodily harm under section 20 of the OAPA 1861. It was ruled that the fall did not come within

[175] For recent discussion of when and how this direction should be given to a jury, see *Aidid* [2021] EWCA Crim 581, [2021] 1 WLR 4939 (CA).

[176] [1963] AC 349.

[177] *Sheehan and Moore* (1974) 60 Cr App R 308 (CA).

[178] *Ibid*., 382: "I think the law on this point should take a clear stand. If a man, whilst sane and sober, forms an intention to kill and makes preparation for it . . . and then gets himself drunk so as to give himself Dutch courage to do the killing, and whilst drunk carries out his intention, he cannot rely on this self-induced drunkenness as a defence to a charge of murder, nor even as reducing it to manslaughter. . . . The wickedness of his mind before he got drunk is enough to condemn him, coupled with the act which he intended to do and did do. A psychopath who goes out intending to kill, knowing it is wrong, and does kill, cannot escape the consequences by making himself drunk before doing it."

[179] Discussed in Child, "Prior Fault: Blocking Defences or Constructing Crimes" in Reed and Bohlander (eds), *General Defences* (2014) 37.

[180] That is the position under section 6(5) of the Public Order Act 1986 for offences under that Act. The principle should be regarded as of general application. A provision to apply this principle to non-fatal offences against the person is made in the Home Office Bill: see further below, § 18.4(viii).

[181] *Richardson and Irwin* [1999] 1 Cr App R 392 (CA); *Aitken, Bennett and Barson* [1992] 1 WLR 1066 (CA).

[182] [2006] EWCA Crim 2413, [2007] Crim LR 564.

the ruling in *Majewski*:[183] it was an accident, not an attack. The outcome might have been different had the court been able to consider the precursor to the fall, the non-accidental climb, which was considered, entirely reasonably, to be a cause of D's injury. Then the issue would have been whether D would have foreseen the risk of falling and injuring someone had he made the climb sober. If that were the case, he would be liable for maliciously inflicting grievous bodily harm. The key question is: what D would have foreseen if he had done the activity whilst sober, *not* whether D would have done the activity if sober.

That accidents, even if attributable to a state of intoxication, fall outside the scope of *Majewski* receives strong, if *obiter*, support from *Heard*,[184] where the view was taken that any accidental touching would not be treated as a deliberate touching even if D would not have made the contact with V but for his inebriated state. Even in such circumstances, "the mind must go with the body" if the touching is to be regarded as deliberate.[185] Intriguingly, the Court of Appeal felt that the element of deliberateness would be lacking in a case such as *Lipman*,[186] where D, in an LSD-induced trance, took himself to be grappling with a snake whereas in reality he was strangling V. But the killing in *Lipman* was not an accident; it was the product of conduct actively performed by D, albeit in a state of hallucination. The relevant question should be, post-*Brady*, whether, had he been sober, D would have recognised the risk of harming V. There is no reason to doubt that the verdict of manslaughter reached in that case would be repeated on similar facts under that test.

#### *(vii) Applying prior fault intoxication rules: defences*

We saw in § 18.1 that mistakes of fact can be relevant both to the proof of offence elements (i.e. when they give rise to a potential denial of mens rea) and to supervening defences. So far, in our analysis of the intoxication rules, we have focused on intoxication as a denial of the offence elements: D may successfully deny mens rea and/or voluntariness, but in basic intent offences the intoxication rules may apply nonetheless to manufacture liability. In this section, we consider intoxicated mistakes in the context of a supervening defence. Take, for example, an intoxicated defendant who mistakenly believes that defensive force is required, and then relies on self-defence to avoid liability. In such a case, the prior fault intoxication rules operate to prevent D from relying on her intoxicated mistake to secure an acquittal.

*Majewski* was not a case that involved any form of defensive mistake. D claimed that his mind was blank, not that he had formed any false view of his circumstances. Accordingly, it would have been possible to read *Majewski* as inapplicable to mistaken defence cases, an approach adopted by Mustill J (as he then was) in *Jaggard v Dickinson*.[187] D had caused damage to a house in order to gain entry. In her intoxicated state she entered a house believing it to be the house of a friend, and that the owner would have consented, had she been aware of the circumstances, to D's unusual method of gaining access. Section 5(2) of the Criminal Damage Act 1971 provides a defence to a charge of criminal damage if D "believes" the owner of the property would have consented to her actions. In allowing D's appeal, Mustill J denied that quashing her conviction was to allow voluntary intoxication

[183] [1977] AC 443.
[184] [2007] EWCA Crim 125, [2008] QB 43.
[185] *Ibid.*, [17].
[186] [1970] 1 QB 152 (CA).
[187] [1981] QB 527 (DC).

to preclude mens rea in crimes of basic intent. Her conviction was quashed because she *believed* she had (or would have had) the owner's consent and not because she was drunk. As such, she fell within the literal terms of the section 5(2) defence. However, Mustill J's approach has not been generally accepted.[188] Working against it has been a concern over the propensity of intoxicated persons to make mistakes leading to violent or forceful conduct. That concern has led the courts to treat cases of intoxicated mistakes as being within the mischief addressed by the House of Lords in *Majewski*. Doing so accords with the view, expressed by Lord Elwyn-Jones in that case, that intoxication is a form of culpability. The defence in section 5(2) of the Criminal Damage Act 1971 is now, therefore, anomalous.

We analyse the treatment of intoxicated mistakes for supervening defences in the context of our discussion of each of the defences in Chapters 19–21. In broad terms, as we shall see, the law has developed to prevent D from relying on intoxicated mistakes to establish a defence, based on a similar policy-focused rationale that we see in *Majewski*. Where defences are defined in objective terms, the objective reasonable person is not intoxicated; and even where defences are defined in subjective terms, D's intoxicated mistakes are (often singularly) discounted when applying the defence.

### *(viii) Reforming the intoxication rules*

The law relating to intoxication is complex and replete with uncertainties of conception and ambit; it is striking to note the critical attention that equivalent rules are receiving in other common law jurisdictions.[189] Looking forward, there are two credible routes to reform, although neither appears likely to be implemented in England and Wales in the near future.

The first route amounts to a codification and—at least partially—a rationalisation of the current law. This approach was endorsed by the Law Commission in its most recent intoxication project, which reported in 2009.[190] In its report, the Commission broadly accepted the idea of formally equating, in culpability terms, voluntary intoxication with a state of subjective recklessness.[191] Similarly, the Commission would codify a provision to prevent D from relying on intoxicated mistakes in the application of criminal defences.[192] The result would be a consistent position, and one (in stark contrast to the current common law) that clarifies the inculpatory function of the intoxication rules. Unfortunately, the Commission's approach falls down in three key areas, and was rejected by the then-government as a viable route to reform. First is a problem of theory: beyond recognising the equivalence of intoxication and recklessness within the current law, the Commission did very little to explain or justify that equivalence as the basis for its recommendations.[193] Second is a problem of

[188] See the authorities discussed in § 21.2(iv) below, which disallow intoxicated mistaken beliefs as to self-defence; also *Woods* (1982) 74 Cr App R 312 (CA) and *Fotheringham* (1989) 88 Cr App R 206 (CA), which disfavour intoxicated beliefs in consent as valid defences. *Jaggard* is thus anomalous.

[189] See, for example, the Canadian Supreme Court judgment in *Brown* [2022] SCC 18: contrary to s. 33.1 of the Criminal Code (self-induced intoxication), which was found to violate s. 7 of the Canadian Charter of Rights and Freedoms (right to life, liberty, and security), voluntary intoxication is not capable of substituting for a lack of voluntary action. Healy, "Legislative Revision of Extreme Intoxication Cases in Canada" [2022] *Crim LR* 957.

[190] Law Com. No. 314, *Intoxication and Criminal Liability* (2009). For a discussion of earlier proposals, see Home Office, *Violence: Reforming the Offences against the Person Act 1861* (1998) Draft Bill, cl. 19.

[191] *Ibid.*, Recommendation 1, para. 3.35.

[192] *Ibid.*, Recommendation 4, para. 3.80.

[193] For the best attempt at this, see Horder, "Sobering Up? The Law Commission on Criminal Intoxication" (1995) 58 *MLR* 534.

complexity: in making an equation between intoxication and recklessness, the Commission's approach focused upon the potential for intoxication to substitute for specific missing mens rea elements within individual offences. This allowed the Commission to move away from the broad-brush and imprecise categorisation of crimes into basic and specific intent: in doing so, however, the recommendation would have required juries to be directed differently on the effects of intoxication for different elements within a single offence.[194] Third is a problem of consistency: despite firm (if problematic) positions in the first two key areas, the Commission defaulted to offence-based (as opposed to element-based) analysis when applying intoxication to inchoate and accomplice liability, making those forms of liability anomalous.[195]

The second route to reform begins with a rejection of the current law, and a rejection of arguments equating intoxication with a state of subjective recklessness. Nothing further is *required* from this point. Rather, as we see in a small number of common law jurisdictions, standard principles of criminal law can be applied to intoxicated and non-intoxicated defendants alike, recognising that intoxication as a genuine denial of mens rea will be extremely rare.[196] Alternatively, whilst rejecting the equivalence of intoxication and recklessness, we might nevertheless conclude that voluntarily intoxicated defendants are in a special class, and deserving of criminal blame even when causing harms inadvertently or involuntarily. If this latter position is accepted, the challenge becomes to create a new intoxication offence, an offence that accurately captures, labels, and punishes D for what he has done (i.e. for becoming *that* voluntarily intoxicated, leading to harm).[197] Although we do not find offences of this kind (yet) within the common law world, the German offence of "dangerous intoxication" provides a relatively simple model for consideration.[198]

### *(ix) Intoxication as a supervening defence?*

The voluntary consumption of alcohol is closely associated with the subsequent commission of crimes—particularly crimes of violence and property damage.[199] Various drugs may have a disinhibiting impact on D, and it may be quite accurate for D to claim that he would not have committed an offence if it were not for the drugs in his system. However, despite

[194] See also *Heard* [2007] EWCA Crim 125, [2008] QB 43, where Hughes LJ's analysis and application of the intoxication rules also involves the separation of offence elements.

[195] For this and further criticisms, see Child, "Drink, Drugs and Law Reform: A Review of Law Commission Report No. 314" [2009] *Crim LR* 488.

[196] This approach is taken in the Australian state of Victoria, for example.

[197] This route was once favoured by the Law Commission: LCCP No. 127, *Intoxication and Criminal Liability* (1992); a position changed following consultation in Law Com. No. 229 (1995). See also Williams, "Voluntary Intoxication—A Lost Cause?" (2013) 129 *LQR* 264. Most recently, a prior fault offence model is set out in Child, Hunt and Crombag, *Prior Fault Criminalization* (2026).

[198] German Criminal Code, § 323a. See Goldberg et al., "Prior-Fault blame in England and Wales, Germany and the Netherlands" (2021) 8(1) *Journal of International and Comparative Law* 53.

[199] "Alcohol is a cortical depressant. Since it is the higher and most recently evolved brain functions which are first affected by depressants, the immediate effect of a dose of alcohol is to inhibit those cerebral functions which are associated with orderly community behaviour and with finer critical judgments": Mason, *Forensic Medicine for Lawyers* (6th ed., 2015). Numerous studies have indicated that many violent offenders have taken significant amounts of drink or drugs at the time of the offence. There is, of course, no straightforward causal link: personal, gender, and cultural factors will strongly influence how intoxicated persons behave. See further Hodge, "Alcohol and Violence" in Taylor (ed.), *Violence in Society* (1993) 127; Dingwall, *Alcohol and Crime* (2005).

the explanatory role of intoxication within such cases, voluntary intoxication does not provide a route to any form of excusatory defence.

This position seems eminently sensible; but what of exceptional cases where D's intoxication is involuntary? In *Kingston*,[200] D took himself to be drinking a normal cup of coffee, but in fact it had been laced with destabilising drugs by a malevolent third party. D, a person with paedophilic inclinations, became disinhibited and performed non-penetrative sexual acts on an unconscious (and also drugged) teenage boy. The House of Lords confirmed D's conviction for indecent assault. At trial, it was found that, notwithstanding the disinhibiting effects of the drugs, D intended his sexual actions. Therefore, said their Lordships, he was guilty of the offence. The term mens rea was treated as a technical expression denoting nothing more than the mental element specified for the offence in question, a mental element which was present on the facts;[201] intoxication, even involuntary intoxication, provided no defence.

A more expansive view of the exculpatory effect of a state of involuntary intoxication had been taken by the Court of Appeal in *Kingston*.[202] That Court was prepared to allow a defence to any crime for a person involuntarily intoxicated, provided D would not have done what he did had he not been intoxicated. The breadth of this newly created, and short-lived, defence was alarmingly wide. Nonetheless, there is something to be said for the underlying rationale. A person who commits a crime arguably should be allowed a defence if a state of involuntary intoxication induced conduct on his part that otherwise would not have occurred and which was not characteristic of him.[203] Be that as it may, however, the House of Lords in *Kingston* took the view that any development along those lines was a matter for the legislature and not for the courts. The Law Commission has recommended, in this respect, that the current position should remain: involuntary intoxication may be adduced as evidence to raise reasonable doubt over mens rea or support a claim of mistake for all crimes of mens rea, but it should not constitute any form of substantive defence.[204]

A related issue arises where D is involuntarily intoxicated and subsequently charged with a crime of negligence. Involuntary intoxication *may* qualify the test for negligence. In principle, the fact that D's state was involuntary may deflect the grounds of criticism inherent in negligence. The standard applied in such cases should be that of the reasonable person who is involuntarily intoxicated. However, the law on this matter is uncertain, and awaits definitive resolution.[205]

For crimes of strict liability, there is no elbow room even for a plea of involuntary intoxication; liability is imposed on the basis of commission of the actus reus. Should involuntary intoxication lead to a condition of automatism, however, an actus reus should not be attributed to D because her conduct would not have been a voluntary act or omission.[206]

200 [1995] 2 AC 355.

201 *Ibid.*, 366–7.

202 [1994] QB 81 (CA).

203 Sullivan, "Making Excuses" in Simester and Smith (eds.), *Harm and Culpability* (1996) 131; Sullivan, "Involuntary Intoxication and Beyond" [1994] *Crim LR* 272.

204 Law Com. No. 314, *Intoxication and Criminal Liability* (2009) part 4.

205 In *Hardie* [1984] 3 All ER 848, the Court of Appeal quashed D's conviction for criminal damage as the trial judge had ruled inadmissible evidence that D had not foreseen the consequences of his conduct because of medication he had taken in order to calm himself. However, the Court of Appeal's decision could alternatively be explained on the basis of an oversight that *Caldwell* recklessness was the applicable standard.

206 Above, § 4.3(iii)(d). See also the recommendation to this effect in Law Com. No. 229, *Intoxication and Criminal Liability* (1995) para. 8.36.

## § 18.5 Overlapping explanations: intoxication, automatism, and insanity

Although *any* failure of proof will be sufficient in principle to negate an offence element, the factual circumstances of that denial may still be crucial to establishing D's guilt, if any, in respect of that offence. We focused on intoxication in § 18.4 as a special case, not least because of the broad application for prior fault rules that work to create liability where D's denial of an offence element arises from voluntary intoxication. But intoxication is not the only failure of proof argument that warrants special consideration, and two others are discussed in this book.

The first—discussed in § 4.3—is automatism: D denies that she acted or omitted to act *voluntarily*, and thereby denies the offence charged. Where D's involuntariness at the time of the actus reus is caused by her prior voluntary consumption of a dangerous drug, the intoxication rules will apply.[207] However, different rules will apply where D's automatic state is caused by a prior external factor *other than* a dangerous drug. There is limited case law on this point,[208] which has focused on the consumption of non-dangerous drugs, but the better view is that prior fault in these circumstances will require D to have subjectively foreseen that her conduct risked causing a lack of voluntary control yet continued unreasonably to run that risk.[209] Should this foresight condition be satisfied, and where D goes on to cause harms when in an involuntary state, her prior fault will be sufficient to substitute for missing voluntariness and mens rea elements when charged with a basic intent offence.[210]

The second failure of proof defence deserving of special mention—discussed in § 19.2—is insanity: insanity rules operate as a failure of proof where D denies offence elements on the basis that she was operating under a defect of reason, caused by a disease of the mind, that led her not to understand the nature or quality of her action, or not to understand that it was wrong.[211] Where the insanity rules apply, D should be found "not guilty by reason of insanity" and various disposal options (including compulsory treatment and/or supervision) become available to the court.[212] The potential for prior fault based inculpation continues to be mooted in the context of insanity,[213] but this has been consistently resisted at common law.[214]

207 *Lipman* [1970] 1 QB 152 (CA).

208 The case law also lacks consistency: e.g. *Quick* [1973] QB 910 (CA); *Bailey* [1983] 2 All ER 503 (CA); *Hardie* [1984] 3 All ER 848 (CA).

209 This interpretation of the current law is preferred by the Law Commission: Law Com. Discussion Paper, *Insanity and Automatism* (2013) paras. 6.12–28. Discussed in Child and Reed, "Automatism Is Never a Defence" (2014) 65 *NILQ* 167.

210 This is an example of a prior fault rule because D's foresight of involuntariness is being used to substitute for subsequent missing elements of mens rea that are of a different kind. Where D not only foresees the risk of involuntariness, but also foresees that such involuntariness might result in the specific harms that later come about in fact, liability may be established through standard legal principles. See the discussion of antecedent fault above, § 5.8(i)(d).

211 Illustrated by the leading case of *Sullivan* [1984] AC 156 (HL).

212 Criminal Procedure (Insanity) Act 1964, s. 5.

213 Mitchell, *Self-Made Madness* (2003); Law Com. Discussion Paper, *Insanity and Automatism* (2013) chap. 6; Mackay and Hughes, "Insanity and Blaming the Mentally Ill [2022] *Criminal LR* 21; Wondemaghen, "Evaluating Predominant Causes of Insanity in Cases of Drug-induced Psychoses" [2015] *Int J Forensic Ment Health* 76.

214 *Beard* [1920] AC 479 (HL), 500–01: "The law takes no note of the cause of the insanity . . . drunkenness is one thing and the diseases to which drunkenness leads are different things; and if a man by drunkenness brings on a state of disease which causes such a degree of madness, . . . then he would not be criminally responsible." Reiterated in *Taj* [2018] EWCA Crim 1743, [2019] QB 655 (CA); *Harris* [2013] EWCA Crim 223, [2013] MHLR 171 (CA). There are several potential explanations for the absence of a prior fault doctrine here, including the availability of compulsory supervision and other disposals within the special verdict (i.e. reducing public policy concerns about the unqualified acquittal of potentially dangerous defendants). Another difficulty is establishing causal links from D's prior conduct to the manifestation of disordered behaviour. Even in jurisdictions that recognise something akin to prior fault insanity, it is this causal concern that is often used to explain its lack of use in practice. Goldberg et al., "Prior-Fault Blame in England and Wales, Germany and the Netherlands" (2021) 8 *Journal of International and Comparative* Law 53, part IV.

The current law, therefore, requires courts to separate cases depending upon D's explanation for the event that gave rise to a failure of proof. We illustrate this in the table below:

| | |
|---|---|
| Failure of proof due to prior fault intoxication | D may still be liable for a basic intent offence (or, in "Dutch courage" cases, even for a specific intent offence) |
| Failure of proof due to prior fault automatism (from the voluntary consumption of a non-dangerous drug[215]) | D may still be liable for a basic intent offence; but proving prior fault will require D's subjective foresight of the risk of destabilisation |
| Failure of proof due to insanity | D will be not guilty by reason of insanity (special verdict) |
| Failure of proof due to any other reason | D will receive an unqualified acquittal |

Despite the importance of being able to distinguish between these sets of rules in practice, in order to know which rules to apply to a given case, the law has become increasingly uncertain and problematic.[216] Where there are multiple potential explanations for a failure of proof, concurrent or consecutive, particular care must be taken.

In *Stripp*,[217] D, while intoxicated, fell over and sustained a concussion. It was held that if the dominant cause of his automatous state was concussion rather than alcohol, he would be able to raise a plea of automatism and would not be subject to the *Majewski* principles. A similar approach was taken in *Burns*,[218] where the cumulative effects of brain damage, alcohol, and medication rendered D an automaton. He was permitted to defend himself on the basis of automatism because his condition was primarily due to the effects of his medication. By contrast, in *Lipman*,[219] D's state of automatism was entirely attributable to the drug LSD. Consequently, the mens rea and voluntariness elements of manslaughter were attributed to him on the basis that he was voluntarily intoxicated at the material time.

D's condition in *Lipman* was far from the slurred speech and unsteady gait long associated with too much alcohol. The LSD produced a trance-like condition with hallucinations. Yet, since that condition came about directly from the voluntary consumption of a dangerous drug, no plea of sane automatism will be entertained. A similar approach is seen in *Coley*.[220] D, aged 17, had spent the day playing combat video games and smoking cannabis. He went to bed, but arose in the early hours. Arming himself with a knife and dressed in combat gear, D then entered the house next door using a key (he was allowed free access to the house), where he stabbed V. D denied recollection of this incident at his trial for attempted murder. The Court of Appeal, confirming D's conviction for this

215 The current case law is limited to non-dangerous drug cases. However, there is no reason in principle why it should not apply in relation to other causes of automatism. This is recognised in the Law Commission's discussion of "loss of capacity by non-dangerous drugs *or other conduct*" (emphasis added): Law Com. Discussion Paper, *Insanity and Automatism* (2013) paras. 6.12–28. See also Child and Reed, "Automatism Is Never a Defence" (2014) 65 *NILQ* 167.

216 Child, Crombag, and Sullivan, "Defending the Delusional, the Irrational, and the Dangerous" [2020] Crim LR 306; Loughnan and Wake, "Of Blurred Boundaries and Prior Fault: Insanity, Automatism and Intoxication" in Reed and Bohlander (eds.), *General Defences in Criminal Law* (2014) 113.

217 (1979) 69 Cr App R 318 (CA).

218 (1974) 58 Cr App R 364 (CA).

219 [1970] 1 QB 152 (CA).

220 [2013] EWCA Crim 223, [2013] MHLR 171.

offence, regarded claims about D's condition as claims of voluntary intoxication rather than of insanity or sane automatism. There was expert evidence to the effect that the cannabis consumption might have caused a "brief psychotic episode";[221] yet since this condition was attributable to a drug still active in his system, there was no disease of the mind. Accordingly, there could be no defence of insanity. Moreover, even if D had in fact been in an automatic state, that would not have generated any basis for a plea of sane automatism: it is long established "that a self-induced incapacity will not excuse".[222] Finally, it was held that there was, in the event, no reasonable doubt raised over D's mens rea. D's conviction for attempted murder was upheld accordingly.

The content of D's drug-induced delusion can also matter. In *Lipman*, it was not contested that D took V to be a snake. That ruled out any finding that D intended to kill or cause serious harm to a person, limiting his liability to manslaughter. In *Coley*, one of the psychiatric expert witnesses was of the view that D's delusion may have been to the effect that he was a character in a combat video game.[223] If that view had been accepted, D would have been found to have lacked any intent to kill or hurt a human being and, since V survived the stabbing, D's liability would have been limited to offences against the person that merely require proof of basic intent. The other two psychiatrists testified that, although D was in a delusional state, he was capable of organised complex behaviour, suggesting awareness that his victim was a live person.[224] The jury accepted the latter view, finding that D acted with intent to kill and convicting him of attempted murder, a verdict upheld on appeal.

The analysis changes if D's state of mind comes about from the withdrawal symptoms which arise from *abstinence* from a drug. In *Davis*,[225] Stephen J considered delirium tremens (hallucinosis), a condition arising from the reaction of the brain and nerve receptors to the withdrawal of alcohol, to be a disease of the mind. *Davis* was endorsed by Lord Birkenhead in *Beard*:[226]

> "But drunkenness is one thing and the diseases to which drunkenness leads are different things, and if a man by drunkenness brings on a state of disease which causes such a degree of madness, even for a time, which would have relieved him from responsibility if it had been caused in any other way, then he would not be criminally responsible."

This comports with the ordinary understanding of what it means to be intoxicated or drugged. If the alcohol or drug is no longer chemically active in D's brain and bodily systems, then any mental disorder that D may currently have is a form of internal disorder which in legal terms is regarded as a defect of reason arising from a disease of the mind, notwithstanding that the condition would not have arisen but for previous drinking. As Hughes LJ put it in *Coley*, hallucinosis arising from desistance from drugs or alcohol after previous indulgence, "is a condition brought about from the protest of the brain and nerve receptors against the removal of intoxicants to which the body has become accustomed".[227]

221 *Ibid.*, [9].
222 *Ibid.*, [19], quoting from the decision of the Court of Appeal in *Quick* [1973] QB 910. Strictly speaking, the possibility of non-insane automatism did not arise in *Coley* because the jury found that D had a specific intent to kill.
223 *Ibid.*, [23].
224 *Ibid.*
225 (1881) 14 Cox CC 563.
226 [1920] AC 479, 501.
227 [2013] EWCA Crim 223, [2013] MHLR 171, [15].

In *Harris*,[228] the voices and hallucinations experienced by D, resulting in very odd behaviour, were found to be withdrawal symptoms following sudden abstinence from heavy drinking. Six days after his last alcoholic drink, those voices instructed him to burn down his own house. D complied, potentially endangering the lives of his neighbours. The trial judge was of the view that because D's hallucinosis would not have occurred but for his prior drinking, his condition was one of intoxication. Convincingly, the Court of Appeal disagreed. His hallucinosis was a defect of reason arising from a disease of the mind because his disordered state arose from the *absence* of alcohol rather than its presence. This conclusion led to the quashing of his conviction for aggravated arson, an offence that comprises setting a fire with intent to endanger the lives of others or being reckless whether others' lives would be endangered. The Court held that it was reasonably possible that, in his disordered state of mind, D did not intend or foresee a risk to others' lives. Perhaps surprisingly, however, the Court was of the opinion that he fell outside the *M'Naghten* Rules because he was aware of the nature and quality of his act in that he knew he was setting a fire. But as he failed to apprehend that the fire might spread next door from his semi-detached property, it seems that D failed to understand the nature and quality of his act; specifically, the kind of wrong (endangering lives by arson) with which he was charged.[229] A special verdict of not guilty by reason of insanity would have avoided a conviction but allowed supervision in the interests of public safety.

A verdict of not guilty by reason of insanity would also seem the right outcome on the facts of *Taj*.[230] D drank very heavily from Friday until the early hours of Saturday morning. On Sunday afternoon, he made a vicious attack on V (an electrician), mistakenly assuming that the equipment and wires in the boot of V's car were the components of a bomb that V was assembling, shortly to explode. D was arrested almost immediately after this attack. In the police interview that followed D's arrest, he showed no signs of intoxication. No blood tests were taken to ascertain alcohol levels. At his trial for attempted murder, it was conceded by the prosecution that alcohol was not chemically present in D's system at the time of his attack on V. It was also accepted, by both prosecution and defence, that D intended to kill V. In the light of *Davis*, *Beard*, and *Harris*, it would seem that intoxication could be ruled out as explaining D's condition at the time of his attack. Seemingly, the explanation was an internal condition in the nature of a defect of reason arising from a disease of the mind. Further, as will be discussed in § 19.2(ii)(e), these facts fit perfectly with the neglected third limb of the *M'Naghten* Rules, which deals with delusions:[231]

> "[D] must be considered in the same situation as to responsibility as to the facts to which his delusion exists were real. For example, if under the influence of his delusion, he supposes another man to be in the act of attempting to take away his life, and he kills that man, as he supposes, in self-defence, he would be exempt from punishment."

That seems to fit the bill for *Taj*. Given his condition, D lacked culpability. If his delusional belief had been true, he would have been praised, not blamed, for his actions.

Yet that is not how *Taj* went. The respective expert witnesses for the prosecution and defence were agreed that D was not insane. They also concurred that his delusion arose

228 *Ibid.* (decided together with *Coley*).
229 We discuss the "nature and quality" limb of the *M'Naghten* rules below, § 19.2(ii)(c).
230 [2018] EWCA Crim 1743, [2019] QB 655.
231 *M'Naghten* (1843) 10 Cl & F 200, 8 ER 718, 211.

from "alcohol-induced psychosis". The defence did not seek a verdict of insanity at trial. (An unsuccessful attempt was later made to raise the issue of D's sanity on appeal.) Instead, it sought an outright acquittal on the grounds of mistaken self-defence and prevention of crime. As we see in § 21.2(ii), this plea is assessed on the basis of D's subjective beliefs about the danger he was facing, except where D's mistaken belief is "attributable to intoxication that was voluntarily induced".[232] The reference to "intoxication" would seem to be a reference to a condition that D was in when he attacked V. However, in the light of the expert evidence that D's psychotic condition would not have arisen but for his previous drinking, the trial judge ruled that D's delusion was attributable to intoxication that was voluntarily induced. D was found guilty of attempted murder.

That verdict was upheld by the Court of Appeal. "In our view," the Court ruled, "the words, 'attributable to intoxication' . . . are broad enough to encompass . . . a mistaken state of mind immediately and proximately consequent upon earlier drink or drug-taking."[233] It must be said that considerable work is being done here by the phrase "immediately and proximately". Its implication is that the hallucinoses experienced by the defendants in *Davis* and *Harris* were, contrary to the findings in those cases, states of voluntary intoxication. The judgments of the Court of Appeal can be searched in vain for any biochemical explanation of why the mental disorder of the defendant in *Harris* arose from the absence of alcohol, whereas in *Taj* the defendant was still legally intoxicated, despite the accepted absence of alcohol from D's system.[234] The distinction seemingly comes down to semantics: the expert witnesses in *Taj* described D's condition as alcohol-*induced* psychosis; in *Harris*, D's condition was described as alcohol-*withdrawal* psychosis. What both cases have in common, of course, is that, but for prior drinking, a post-intoxication state of psychosis would not have arisen. In *Harris*, Hughes LJ rejected the trial judge's ruling that any state of mental disorder attributable to prior drinking was a condition of voluntary intoxication in legal terms. For Hughes LJ, that would have led to a significant extension of what was regarded as voluntary intoxication in terms of *Majewski*.[235] The extension was willingly embraced in *Taj*.

The different outcomes across the two cases reflect the determination of the Court of Appeal in *Taj* to uphold the conviction of D.[236] As to the future, it might prove significant for findings of voluntary intoxication that in *Harris*, when D set the fire, he had not taken alcohol for six days, whereas in *Taj*, D had drunk a great deal of alcohol approximately two days prior to his attack on V. Doubtless, the longer is the gap between the last drink (or drug-taking) and D's destructive or violent conduct, the less plausible is the claim that he was in a state of intoxication at the time; even when expert witnesses are certain that but for

232 Criminal Justice and Immigration Act 2008, s. 76(5).

233 [2018] EWCA Crim 1743, [2019] QB 655, [60].

234 In *Taj* it was accepted that when D attacked V he was not intoxicated in the literal sense but could be regarded as intoxicated in a legal sense because, "[D's] episode of paranoia which led him to mistake the innocent [V] as a terrorist was a direct result of his earlier drink and drug taking in the previous days and weeks" [57]. The same was true in *Harris*: no previous drinking, no hallucinosis.

235 [2013] EWCA Crim 223, [2013] MHLR 171, [59].

236 In this context, it is also worth noting that Sir Brian Levenson, giving the judgment of the Court, was open to the possibility that the finding that D was legally intoxicated might be contested. In his view, D's conviction could also be upheld by reference to the finding in *Oye* [2013] EWCA Crim 1725, [2014] 1WLR 3354, that a defence of mistaken self-defence could not be founded on an insane delusion. (See below, § 21.2(iv).) Yet *Oye* is cited in *Taj* not to find the appellant insane and therefore exempt from punishment but to uphold a verdict of guilty and to impose a sentence of 19 years' imprisonment. This is a borrowing from the law on insanity to confirm a verdict of guilty on a person assumed to be sane.

the drinking or the drug-taking D would not have acted as he did. But what should count for a finding of intoxication is whether the drink or drugs were chemically active in D's system at the time. Taj's trial proceeded on the basis that the alcohol he had drunk was not chemically active at the time he attacked V. In *Lindo*,[237] a case not cited in *Taj*, the Court of Appeal—in the context of the partial defence of diminished responsibility—drew a clear distinction between a state of mind produced by drugs which were chemically active and a subsequent drug-induced psychosis (a condition that may last for days, even months). The latter state is to be regarded as a recognised medical condition rather than a state of voluntary intoxication.[238] That distinction could, and should, have been made on the facts of *Taj*.

[237] [2016] EWCA Crim 1940.
[238] *Ibid.*, [17].

# 19

# IRRESPONSIBILITY DEFENCES

Irresponsibility defences, as we refer to them here, present as denials of mental capacity: claims that D lacked the means for sufficient moral reasoning and rationality to be (fully) accountable for his conduct.[1] We have already encountered *partial* defensive claims of this kind when discussing the defences of diminished responsibility and infanticide, which apply to reduce D's liability from murder to manslaughter or (for infanticide) to an outcome equivalent to manslaughter.[2] In this chapter, we focus on *complete* denials of responsibility, arising in the contexts of insanity at trial, insanity as a defence, and legal infancy.

That fully irresponsible agents should be exempted from liability is clear, but the terms of (and thresholds for) such exemption remain uncertain and contested. This includes fundamental questions about whether irresponsibility should be judged in terms of simple status (e.g. age or mental disorder), or combined with subjective awareness tests or other criteria at the point when D acts.[3] In this manner, it is possible to present irresponsibility as an *exempting* mechanism, excluding D's conduct from criminal adjudication (most obviously in cases of legal infancy and insanity at trial); as a *failure of proof*, challenging evidence of mens rea and/or voluntariness (we see this, in certain cases, where insanity presents as a "defence"); or as a form of *excuse*, where D has committed an offence, but does so in circumstances that suggest a lack of culpability (we see, again, in certain cases where insanity presents as a "defence").[4]

## § 19.1 Insanity at trial

Insanity rules arise at two distinct points in the criminal process, depending on when D's alleged insanity[5] manifests:

(1) *Insanity at trial.* The question here is whether it is fair to commence or continue trial proceedings. The focus is on D's capacity at the time of the trial, and not D's capacity at the time of the alleged offence.

[1] Simester, *Fundamentals*, chap. 17. See also, more generally, Mackay, *Mental Condition Defences in the Criminal Law* (1995).

[2] Above, §§ 10.6 and 10.9.

[3] See, e.g., Moore, *Law and Psychiatry* (1984) chap. 6; Morse, "Excusing the Crazy: The Insanity Defence Reconsidered" (1985) 58 *So Cal LR* 777; Moore, "The Quest for a Responsible Responsibility Test: Norwegian Insanity Law After Breivik" (2015) 9 *Crim Law and Philosophy* 645; Gröning, "Has Norway Abandoned its Medical Model?" [2021] *Crim LR* 191.

[4] In such cases, the label "defence" is problematic (discussed above, § 17.1).

[5] The term "insanity" is problematic for various reasons, including its potential to insult those to whom it is applied. However, it remains as a legal (non-medical) term of art. For criticism, including recommendations for the redefinition and renaming of insanity rules, see Law Commission Discussion Paper, *Insanity and Automatism* (2013).

(2) *Insanity defence.* The question here is whether D has a defence of insanity, due to a lack of relevant capacity at the time of the alleged offence.

In this section, we focus on insanity at trial. Here—rather than being a defence—insanity is operating as a procedural rule, focused on whether and in what form a trial should proceed. It is a "plea in bar of trial".

### *(i) Removal to a mental hospital by order of the Home Secretary*

Where D is in custody awaiting trial, and his mental condition warrants, he may be transferred to a hospital. Under the provisions of the Mental Health Act 1983, the Home Secretary, if satisfied on the basis of reports from at least two medical practitioners that D is suffering from mental illness or severe mental impairment, may order that D be detained in a hospital if the minister is of the opinion that this is in the public interest.[6]

On the face of it, this is an extremely wide power, but it appears to be exercised with restraint. It is, in practice, reserved for cases of profound disability; situations where it is obvious that any trial would serve no useful purpose given the current condition of D. Should D make a sufficient recovery, the practice is for D then to be brought to trial.[7]

### *(ii) Unfitness to plead*

Under sections 4 and 4A of the Criminal Procedure (Insanity) Act 1964,[8] a finding may be made, on the initiative of the defence, prosecution, or trial judge, that D is unfit to plead.[9] Normally the matter will be dealt with on arraignment, before the trial begins.[10] The question of fitness is one for the judge to determine.[11] If the judge makes a finding at this stage that D is fit to stand trial, and D then pleads not guilty, a jury is empanelled for the trial itself. However, the judge may consider that the strength of the prosecution case should be tested before the issue of fitness is resolved: should that be the case, the judge may postpone the issue until the opening of the defence case.[12] If, at that later stage, the judge finds that D has no case to answer, D is acquitted. Should there be a case to answer, however, the court will then determine whether D is fit to plead before hearing the defence.

#### *(a) Determining unfitness*

Criteria of unfitness are left unspecified in the Criminal Procedure (Insanity) Act 1964, which leaves the test of unfitness to the determination of the courts. From the early nineteenth century, the test has been narrowly cognitive, and focused on D's capacity to

[6] Mental Health Act 1983, s. 48.

[7] See Law Com. No. 364, *Unfitness to Plead* (2016) chap. 2.

[8] As amended by the Criminal Procedure (Insanity and Unfitness to Plead) Act 1991 and the Domestic Violence, Crimes and Victims Act 2004.

[9] See generally Mackay, *Mental Condition Defences in the Criminal Law* (1995) chap. 5; Mackay, "The Development of Fitness to Plead in English Law" in Mackay and Brookbanks (eds.), *Fitness to Plead* (2018); Law Com. No. 364, *Unfitness to Plead* (2016); Bevan, "Making it Work? The Case of *Roberts* and Uneven Progress in the Reform of Unfitness to Plead Procedures" [2020] *Crim LR* 215.

[10] On the potential for unfitness to be found retrospectively, see *Ismael* [2024] EWCA Crim 301, [2025] MHLR 51.

[11] Domestic Violence, Crime and Victims Act 2004, s. 22.

[12] Criminal Procedure (Insanity and Unfitness to Plead) Act 1991, s. 4(2).

"plead to the indictment" and to be "of sufficient intellect to comprehend the course of the proceedings in the trial so as to make a proper defence, to challenge a juror to whom he may wish to object and comprehend the details of the evidence".[13] What this test, still approved in the twenty-first century,[14] does not do is ask whether D has genuine "decisional competence"—the wherewithal to reflect with a degree of insight where his best interests lie.[15] For instance, the test will not assist a defendant who, because of his affliction, irrationally refuses to instruct that a relevant line of defence be presented.

Does a person who is found fit to plead but is otherwise lacking in decisional competence receive a fair trial as guaranteed by Article 6 of the ECHR?[16] Although much will depend on the impact of the disability at the trial itself, there is, it is suggested, one useful general principle that *should* be (but is not currently) applied. If, as a result of the impact of D's disability on the course of the trial, there may be reason to think that a verdict of guilty would not have been returned had D been possessed of adequate decisional competence, the trial should be adjudged unfair. Better still would be for English law to adopt the test propounded by the US Supreme Court when determining fitness to plead: whether D has "sufficient present ability to consult his lawyer with a reasonable degree of rational understanding—and whether he has a rational as well as factual understanding of the proceedings against him".[17] Such hopes seem ill-founded in the light of decisions such as *Moyle*.[18] D suffered from paranoid delusions and as a consequence believed that the court and even his own lawyers were united in a conspiracy against him. The Court of Appeal accepted that his circumstances were far from ideal, in terms of seeking his own best interests on a rational basis, but it refused to budge from the narrow cognitive test hitherto applied; and on that basis confirmed that D was fit to plead.

The unfitness to plead procedures were reviewed by the Law Commission in 2016.[19] Drawing upon ECHR Article 6 jurisprudence,[20] the Commission's overarching principle was that D "should be able to participate effectively in the proceedings on the offence or offences charged".[21] When addressing that principle, the following matters should be considered: the assistance available to D in the proceedings;[22] D's understanding of what the charges mean and their nature, and D's understanding of the evidence, the trial process, and the consequences of conviction;[23] D's ability to give instructions to a legal representative, follow the proceedings, and give evidence; D's abilities to decide how to plead, whether to give evidence, and whether to elect a Crown Court trial;[24] and, finally, D's "ability to make any other decision that may need to be made in connection with the trial".[25]

[13] *Pritchard* (1836) 7 C & P 303.

[14] *Marcantonio* [2016] EWCA Crim 14, [2016] 2 Cr App R 9; *M* [2003] EWCA Crim 3452.

[15] For very persuasive advocacy of a test of decisional competence, see Mackay, "On Being Insane in Jersey Part 3: The Case of the *Attorney General v O'Driscoll*" [2004] *Crim LR* 219.

[16] Discussed in LCCP No. 197, *Unfitness to Plead* (2010) paras. 2.88–2.106.

[17] *Dusky v US*, 362 US 402 (1960).

[18] [2008] EWCA Crim 3059, [2009] MHLR 91.

[19] Law Com. No. 364, *Unfitness to Plead* (2016).

[20] *Ibid.*, paras. 1.42 and 3.19–3.21.

[21] *Ibid.*, para. 3.53.

[22] *Ibid.*, para. 3.61.

[23] *Ibid.*, paras. 3.85–3.86.

[24] *Ibid.*, paras. 3.107–3.116.

[25] *Ibid.*, para. 3.117.

The Law Commission's recommendations have been accepted (in large part) by the government, but have not —as yet—been taken forward into legislation.[26] However, the language of "effective participation", and recognition of the various elements contained within that requirement, have already begun to influence the Court of Appeal.[27] A consistent reformulation, along these lines, of the criteria that should be used when deciding whether D is fit to plead would be very welcome. The matter addressed goes deeper than the current law, probing the question whether D has any mental grasp on how his interests might be served. For instance, it seems likely that in the circumstances obtaining in *Moyle* (above), D would not be found fit to plead under the Law Commission's proposed model.

Even where the test for unfitness is expanded from simple cognition to matters of effective participation, it is still solely (and properly) confined to D's capacity to understand the trial process. Disadvantages stemming from circumstance outside the trial process, which have no bearing on his understanding of that process, will not prevent a trial, even if they place D in a difficult position at the trial itself. To illustrate: in *Podola*,[28] D claimed he had no recollection of the circumstances or the reasons for his killing of V because of his "hysterical amnesia" concerning the incident. Because D was otherwise healthy at the time of his trial, he was judged fit to plead. It is considered that *Podola* was correctly decided. Of course, D might be under a disadvantage at his trial.[29] It may be that he killed in self-defence and could explain why that was necessary if only he could remember. But his lack of recall does not affect his decisional competence. Once decisional competence is established, it is appropriate that a trial should be held, where such matters as the nature and causes of hysterical amnesia can be tested properly before a jury.

*(b) Where D is unfit to plead*

Prior to 1991, a person found unfit to plead was held at the disposal of the Home Secretary without any determination of the evidence against them. Consequently, there were cases of persons being detained for substantial periods of time despite considerable doubt over the basis of the allegations made against them. A significant and welcome reform introduced by the Criminal Procedure (Insanity and Unfitness to Plead) Act 1991 provides that, upon there being a finding of unfitness to plead, a jury shall then decide on such evidence already given (if any) and such evidence introduced by the prosecution or defence whether D "did the act or made the omission" charged against him as the offence.[30] This is known as a "trial of the facts". If the jury is not satisfied that D did the act or omission constituting the actus reus of the offence, D is acquitted and therefore not subject to any coercive disposal measures or future prosecution.[31]

[26] *Government response to the Law Commission report on 'Unfitness to Plead'* (Policy Paper, 25 Oct. 2023).

[27] See, e.g., *Marcantonio and Chitolie* [2016] EWCA Crim 14, [7]; *Ehi-Palmer* [2016] EWCA Crim 1844, [55].

[28] [1960] 1 QB 325 (CA).

[29] He may be under a particular disadvantage since, should D choose not to give evidence at trial (on account of his lack of memory), the court or jury may draw adverse inferences: Criminal Justice and Public Order Act 1994, s. 35; *Barry* [2010] EWCA Crim 195, [2010] 2 All ER 1004. See Owusu-Bempah, *Defendant Participation in the Criminal Process* (2017) chap. 4.

[30] Criminal Procedure Insanity Act 1964, s. 4A.

[31] *Ibid*., s. 4A(4). As with any other acquittal, the barring of future prosecution (double jeopardy) is subject to the exception in the Criminal Justice Act 2003, Part 10.

Although clearly an advance on the previous position, the current law is not without its drawbacks. Inevitably, a person unfit to plead will experience difficulty in effectively participating in the trial of the facts. As the proceedings are not a criminal trial, the full protection of Article 6 of the ECHR is not engaged,[32] and a finding that D did the act or made the omission will not be disturbed despite D's difficulties in comprehending (and refuting) the evidence called against him.

There are also drawbacks to the substantive legal test. Narrowing the trial focus to a single issue (whether D "did the act or made the omission" required) may be superficially attractive, but in order to isolate the acts or omissions at issue, the test requires a form of element analysis (i.e. identifying and separating offence elements) to be applied to offences that were not designed with this form of division in mind. The result has been considerable unclarity and inconsistency, particularly where offence terms appear to combine physical and mental requirements. In *B (M)*,[33] for example, the Court of Appeal found that for the offence of voyeurism the "act" (of "voyeurism") imported the purpose of obtaining sexual gratification. The Court accepted that such purpose went to D's state of mind, but found that it was so integral to the type of action relevant to the offence (i.e. distinguishing voyeurism from mere observation) that action and purpose could not sensibly be separated. On the other hand, it was decided that a further requirement of the offence, D's awareness regarding V's non-consent to being watched, was sufficiently distinct from D's act to be irrelevant to the trial of the facts.[34] Similarly in *Young*,[35] in the context of an offence requiring proof of the dishonest concealment of a material fact,[36] the intention to conceal was found to be an integral part of the act of concealment but the purpose of the concealment and any related dishonesty were not.[37]

Looking beyond D's offence, we might assume that a focus on acts or omissions alone would rule out any consideration of defences that might have been available to D. However, in *Antoine*,[38] despite confirming that evidence of diminished responsibility should be inadmissible because it goes beyond D's acts or omissions to his mental state, the House of Lords drew a distinction between defences that can be established by "objective evidence" rather than by reference to D's "state of mind".[39] Lord Hutton, with whom all their Lordships agreed, considered that defences such as mistake, accident, or self-defence could be established by reference to "objective evidence". But this is problematic. Whilst certain evidence may be assessed objectively, with examples from *Wells and Others* including CCTV, cell site evidence of location (i.e. mobile phone location), scene-of-crime, and expert forensic evidence,[40] it is far from clear that such evidence alone would be sufficient to establish the defences highlighted by Lord Hutton. In particular, where mistake of fact is typically relevant to a denial of mens rea,[41] and self-defence requires subjective belief in the necessity

[32] *Kerr* [2001] EWCA Crim 2024, [2002] 1 WLR 824; affirmed in *H* [2003] UKHL 1, [2003] 1 WLR 411.
[33] [2012] EWCA Crim 770, [2013] 1 WLR 499.
[34] *Ibid.*, [63]–[66].
[35] *R (Young) v Central Criminal Court* [2002] EWHC 548 (Admin).
[36] An offence under what is now the Financial Services Act 2012, s. 89.
[37] See also *Goldsmith* [2024] EWCA Crim 780, discussing the absence of a "bright line" separating actus reus and mens rea elements.
[38] [2001] 1 AC 340.
[39] *Ibid.*, 376.
[40] [2015] EWCA Crim 2, [2015] 1 WLR 2797.
[41] Discussed above, § 18.1.

of force,[42] it is difficult to see how these requirements can be satisfied without reference to D's state of mind.

Obviously, the current position is not ideal. The Law Commission has recommended that the prosecution be required to prove *all* the elements of the offence beyond a reasonable doubt against a defendant found unfit to stand trial. If the prosecution can do this, D will be subject to the orders of the court; otherwise, D will be given an unqualified acquittal.[43] So far, however, the Law Commission's proposals have not been implemented.

### (c) Disposal orders

Upon a finding of unfitness to plead, together with a finding that D did the act or omission alleged, D becomes subject to the disposal of the court. The court has a range of disposal options geared to the needs of the defendant and the protection of the public. These include: a hospital order (with or without a restriction order); a supervision order; or an order for absolute discharge.[44] Where D is found *not* to have completed the act or omission, he will simply be released.

Historically, murder was a special case. Where the charge was murder, the 1991 Act permitted only one outcome: indefinite detention in a special hospital until released with the permission of the Home Secretary or by order of a Mental Health Review Tribunal.[45] Sensibly, this discrepancy was addressed following the case of *Grant*,[46] in which the Court of Appeal expressed doubt whether the 1991 regime for persons charged with murder was compatible with Article 5 of the ECHR (the right to liberty and security) and associated jurisprudence, which allows the detention of those with a mental disorder only if necessary for treatment or protection of the patient and/or others. Those criteria are not addressed in the determination of whether D did the act or made the omission. As a consequence of subsequent amending legislation,[47] section 5 of the Criminal Procedure (Insanity) Act 1964 now provides the full range of disposal options for murder cases but also provides that if the grounds for a hospital order with restriction are present in such a case, then such an order must be made.

## § 19.2 Insanity defence

The defence of insanity is a long-established feature of English law, and one of considerable symbolic importance.[48] It signals that the rules of the criminal law are addressed to rational persons who have the capacity to understand and comply with rules. Persons lacking such capacity when causing potential criminal harms may need to be restrained, but there is a long-held sentiment that they should not be designated criminals.[49]

[42] Discussed below, § 21.2.

[43] Law Com. No. 364, *Unfitness to Plead* (2016) para. 5.85. See, further, Loughnan, "Between Fairness and 'Dangerousness': Reforming the Law on Unfitness to Plead" [2016] *Crim LR* 451.

[44] Set out in Criminal Procedure (Insanity) Act 1964, s. 5 (as amended by the Domestic Violence, Crime and Victims Act 2004).

[45] Pursuant to the underlying Act: Criminal Procedure (Insanity) Act 1964, s. 5(2).

[46] [2001] EWCA Crim 2611, [2002] QB 1030.

[47] Domestic Violence, Crime and Victims Act 2004, s. 24.

[48] The first recorded case of outright acquittal by reason of insanity in England was in 1505: Walker, *Crime and Insanity in England* (1968) 26. It seems the defendant was set free.

[49] See Mackay, *Mental Condition Defences in Criminal Law* (1995) chap. 2; Loughnan, *Manifest Madness* (2012).

The state of the current insanity defence, however, is lamentable. As we discuss below, insanity remains a common law defence, based upon the *M'Naghten* Rules articulated in 1843.[50] It retains several features unsuited to a modern legal system, including the label "insanity" which remains profoundly unattractive to defendants, and which does not track (and does not attempt to track) any medical/psychiatric understanding of mental health disorder. Incremental reforms have been possible, including most importantly to the outcome for those availing themselves of the defence: moving from compulsory and indefinite hospital detention to a selection of more appropriate (and humane) disposal options.[51] However, despite changes of this kind, the insanity defence is rarely used in practice;[52] and that remains true despite the high number of persons with mental health disorders within the criminal justice system.[53] Indeed, many defendants whose mental condition may undercut culpability for the offence charged nonetheless choose to plead guilty or defend themselves on other grounds.

Yet the marginalisation of the insanity defence does not mean that it can be ignored or considered only cursorily. The minimum standard of rationality demanded by law to warrant inclusion in the class of persons who are subject to punishment is a topic of intrinsic importance for the legitimacy of state punishment. Further, even the most practically minded criminal lawyer needs to be aware of what constitutes an insanity plea. This is because not only the defendant but also the judge and even the prosecution may raise the issue of insanity if the facts of the case indicate that grounds for the defence are present. Accordingly, a defendant seeking to plead automatism or a lack of mens rea may find that her plea is treated, even against her wishes, as a plea of insanity.[54] Theoretically, the same switch may occur if she pleads diminished responsibility to a charge of murder.[55]

### (i) Preliminary points on structure and process

We discuss the elements of the insanity defence below at § 19.2(ii). But first it is useful to understand some of its particular features.

#### (a) Failure of proof and supervening defence

Uniquely, the *M'Naghten* Rules can apply *either* in the context of a failure of proof claim (i.e. when they explain why D does not satisfy the definitional elements of the offence charged), or as a supervening defence (i.e. as a defence where D has satisfied the definitional elements of the relevant offence). In both cases, if D has completed the physical elements specified in the actus reus of an offence, and where D is proved to have been within the insanity rules, she will be diverted to the special insanity verdict (discussed below).[56]

[50] (1843) 10 C & F 200, 8 ER 718. See, Mackay, "The M'Naghten Rules—A Brief Historical Note" [2019] *Crim LR* 966.

[51] Discussed below, § 19.2(i)(b).

[52] Mackay and Kearns, "More Facts about the Insanity Defence" [1999] *Crim LR* 714; Mackay, "Ten More Years of the Insanity Defence" [2012] *Crim LR* 946.

[53] See Justice Committee, *Mental Health in Prisons* (5th Report, 2021). Bradley, *The Bradley Report* (2009).

[54] *Kemp* [1957] 1 QB 399 (Assizes Bristol); *Sullivan* [1984] AC 156.

[55] Criminal Procedure (Insanity) Act 1964, s. 6. It seems the provision is not used.

[56] Discussed in Child and Sullivan, "When Does the Insanity Defence Apply? Some Recent Cases" [2014] *Crim LR* 788.

There are well-established rationales for insanity to maintain both roles, but it is questionable whether they are entirely compatible within a single set of rules. Where circumstances of insanity are raised as part of a failure of proof argument, the insanity rules do not operate as a defence at all: if the elements of an offence cannot be proven, then there is no logical space for a defence. Rather, although such rules are still standardly referred to as part of the "insanity defence", the court is actually diverting D from an unqualified acquittal (otherwise available where D is not proven to have acted with the required mens rea) in order to maintain the court's control over the disposal of D.[57] In this manner, we can readily understand why defendants may want to resist the application of the "defence"; and why courts rationalise its application on forward-looking grounds of public policy and social protection. As Lord Denning said in *Bratty*:[58]

> "Suppose a crime is committed by a man in a state of automatism or clouded consciousness due to a recurrent disease of the mind. Such an act is no doubt involuntary, but it does not give rise to an unqualified acquittal, for that would mean that he would be let at large to do it again. The only proper verdict is one which ensures that the person who suffers from the disease is kept secure in a hospital so as not to be a danger to himself or others."

Where insanity is applied as a supervening defence, in contrast, its role is much more clearly exculpatory. Here D has committed an offence and would otherwise be liable to conviction, with insanity offering a route to a qualified acquittal. The narrow terms of the current defence—discussed below—may restrict its availability to D in practice, but (in this function) a verdict of not guilty by reason of insanity is likely to represent D's preferred outcome.

The two roles of the insanity defence are not explicitly distinguished in the elements of the defence itself,[59] and we do not separate our analysis in this way below. However, they are usefully borne in mind, particularly when evaluating the current law and reform options. For example, any argument for interpreting the exculpatory function of the insanity defence more expansively, or reforming it in a similar manner, must bear in mind that more defendants who lack mens rea will also be caught within the expanded "defence" (i.e. where insanity functions as part of a failure of proof argument) and will be denied unqualified acquittals as a result. The most recent Law Commission proposals make a good case study for this concern: the Commission's formulated defence of "not guilty by reason of medical condition" would expand the catchment of insanity (across both roles) considerably.[60]

### (b) *The special verdict*

Failure of proof arguments and complete defences will typically result in D's unqualified acquittal, certainly in the absence of prior fault.[61] Not so for insanity. The acquittal conferred as a result of a successful plea is the special verdict of "not guilty by reason of insanity",[62] which leaves the defendant under the control of the court.

[57] Diversion should not be confused with prior fault inculpation, discussed below, § 19.2(iv).

[58] *Bratty v Attorney General for Northern Ireland* [1963] AC 386, 410.

[59] It is possible to draw a rough distinction between cases where D does not understand the nature or quality of her action (usually insanity as a denial of offending) and those where D does not understand what they were doing was wrong (usually insanity as a defence), but this is not true for all cases. See below, § 19.2(ii).

[60] Law Com. Discussion Paper, *Insanity and Automatism* (2013). The Commission will return to the topic of insanity as part of its 14th Programme, announced in 2025.

[61] Notably, prior fault rules do not currently apply to the insanity defence. Discussed below, § 19.2(iv).

[62] Trial of Lunatics Act 1883, s. 2(1).

Prior to the Criminal Procedure (Insanity and Unfitness to Plead) Act 1991, the sole disposal outcome was a period of indefinite detention in a hospital unless and until the Home Secretary ordered release. This inflexibility has now been changed by legislation: a range of non-penal measures is available to the judge at her discretion, ranging from a supervision order to a hospital order with or without restriction of time.[63]

### (c) *Burden of proof*

The law establishes a presumption of sanity and so, raising the defence requires D to prove her insanity (i.e. the burden of proof is reversed).[64] This burden of proof is discharged on the balance of probabilities.[65]

Reversing the burden of proof in cases where insanity is raised as a supervening defence is not unproblematic, particularly given the potential for D's continued mental impairment at trial. As we noted in § 3.2, reverse burdens of proof are vulnerable to scrutiny under the terms of Article 6(2) of the ECHR (which guarantees the presumption of innocence) and may, on occasion, be "read down" as imposing merely an evidential burden. In *Lambert*,[66] and subsequent cases,[67] however, the Court of Appeal ruled that there was no contravention of Article 6(2) in placing the onus of proof on D to establish his diminished responsibility in response to a charge of murder. Influential on the Court's findings has been the fact that the prosecution has to prove the elements of murder before the burden is imposed on D (i.e. the reversal applies to a supervening defence).

Reversing the burden of proof for insanity will not always satisfy this condition however, where the defence is engaged within a failure of proof argument. Where insanity relates to a failure of proof argument, it is explaining an *absence* of mens rea and/or voluntary action. In such cases, the prosecution is in effect relieved of its burden of proof on vital elements of the offence charged, and in those cases it seems appropriate in principle that D's burden should be reduced to an evidential one. This would have the effect of requiring D only to make insanity a "live" issue in proceedings, whereupon the prosecution would be required to disprove insanity beyond reasonable doubt if it wished to secure D's conviction. It is worth noting that, in its discussion paper on the law of insanity, the Law Commission considered that to impose a persuasive burden on D on matters which go to core elements of the offence contravenes the presumption of innocence guaranteed by Article 6(2).[68]

As things stand, however, no English court has addressed the tension between the burden of proof in insanity and the usual requirement for the prosecution to prove a voluntary act and mens rea attributable to D. Under section 2(1) of the Trial of Lunatics Act 1883, where insanity is proved, the special verdict follows provided the jury is satisfied that D "did the act or made the omission charged, but was insane". This confirms that, if D is found to be insane, the prosecution need only prove beyond reasonable doubt the physical movements or absence of movement which, if done voluntarily by a sane person, would establish the

63 Criminal Procedure (Insanity) Act 1964 as amended by the Criminal Procedure (Insanity and Unfitness to Plead) Act 1991 and Domestic Violence, Crimes and Victims Act 2004.

64 *Bratty v A-G for Northern Ireland* [1963] AC 386.

65 *Carr-Briant* [1943] KB 607 (CA).

66 [2002] QB 1112 (CA).

67 See, for example, *Foye* [2013] EWCA Crim 475, (2013) 177 JP 449.

68 Law Com. Discussion Paper, *Insanity and Automatism* (2013) paras. 8.9–8.59.

actus reus of the offence. The special verdict requires no proof of any mens rea for the crime with which D is charged.[69]

D may not wish to claim a defence of insanity. Following the decision in *Kemp*,[70] however, the prosecution or the judge may insist (in a case where D, for example, claims lack of mens rea because of an epileptic seizure) that D's explanation for his lack of mens rea rests upon a defect of reason arising from a disease of the mind and amounts to a plea of insanity. Frequently, the defence will reject that route to acquittal and plead guilty to the offence charged, in order to avoid potential detention in a secure hospital. It seems just that, if D does insist on contesting the case, the prosecution should be required to prove beyond reasonable doubt that D is legally insane or alternatively guilty. There is indirect support for this view from section 12 of the Criminal Appeal Act 1968 which provides for an appeal from a verdict of insanity. Effectively, section 12 recognises that insanity, with its special verdict, is not a defence in the ordinary sense. It is one thing to insist that D prove his insanity on the balance of probabilities if he seeks a *defence* of insanity; quite another thing to lessen the normal burden of proof on the prosecution to a balance of probabilities when D contests a verdict of insanity.[71]

### (d) *Findings of insanity: the role of judge and jury*

Any finding of insanity must be supported by evidence provided by two medical practitioners.[72] They will testify to what they consider to have been D's mental condition at the time of the crime he is alleged to have committed. Whether their evidence proves D's insanity is a matter for the jury who will be directed by the judge about what makes for insanity in the eye of the law. As will be seen below, what is regarded as a state of insanity at law may differ considerably from clinical understandings of mental disorder. "Insanity" is not itself a medical term. It will be for the jury to consider the expert testimony and any other evidence that may bear on D's state of mind at the time of his alleged offence. The expert witnesses, even if on opposing sides, may be in agreement that D was mentally disordered in a clinical sense and they may, as they sometimes do, opine that he was insane in the legal sense too. It is up to the jury to find whether the expert testimony and other relevant evidence has persuaded them that D was legally insane at the time of his alleged offence.

If the trial was fair, and the jury was properly directed, an appellate court will be reluctant to disturb a jury's dismissal of an insanity plea on the ground that it is at odds with the expert testimony. But a jury verdict may, exceptionally, be considered unsafe if the discord between unchallenged expert testimony and the jury verdict is pronounced. In *Oye*,[73] the two medical witnesses were agreed that D was undergoing "a florid psychotic episode" caused by some internal disorder (undiagnosed) inducing a delusion that the police officers he attacked were possessed by evil spirits intent on harming him. Nothing in the course of the trial threw doubt on that testimony. The Court of Appeal accepted that the evidence given by the experts proved D's insanity at the time of his attack. D's conviction was

[69] *A-G's Reference (No. 3 of 1998)* [2000] QB 401 (CA).

[70] [1957] 1 QB 399 (Assizes Bristol).

[71] For an excellent critique of the current position, see Jones, "Insanity, Automatism and the Burden of Proof on the Accused" (1995) 111 *LQR* 475.

[72] Criminal Procedure (Insanity and Fitness to Plead) Act 1991, s. 1(1).

[73] [2013] EWCA Crim 1725, [2014] 1 WLR 3354.

accordingly unsafe and, in its place, a finding of insanity was made. In *Golds*,[74] the Supreme Court took the same approach in the context of the partial defence of diminished responsibility. In formal terms, expert testimony is not legally required to support a plea of diminished responsibility, but in practical terms it is a necessity. The Supreme Court considered the expert witnesses had clearly established that D's mental condition at the time he killed V satisfied the statutory terms of the partial defence. Nothing emerged in the course of the trial to cast doubt on this evidence. D's murder conviction was accordingly quashed, and a verdict of manslaughter substituted.

### *(ii) The M'Naghten Rules*

In England and Wales, the insanity defence is based on the *M'Naghten* Rules.[75] These rules comprise a series of answers given by judges of the Queen's Bench in 1843 to questions put by members of the House of Lords. The occasion was prompted by the public outcry that followed the acquittal, on grounds of insanity, of Daniel M'Naghten, who had killed Sir Edmund Drummond in an attempt to murder the then Prime Minister, Sir Robert Peel.[76]

Strictly speaking, at the time the answers were given, in terms of precedent, they were of no binding effect. However, they are regarded as an authoritative and comprehensive statement of the law, and their status as binding precedent was later assured by the House of Lords' decision in *Sullivan*.[77] For the defence of insanity to apply, the Rules provide that D must prove on the balance of probabilities that:

*Element 1*: There was a defect of reason.
*Element 2*: The defect of reason emanated from a disease of the mind.
*Element 3*: The defect of reason either:
(a) caused D to be unaware of the nature and quality of his act; or
(b) caused D not to know that his act was wrong.

We consider these elements in turn.[78]

#### *(a) Element 1: defect of reason*

It is appropriate to define insanity in terms of failures of rationality. We do not regard persons whose foundational beliefs or practical reasoning are radically defective as accountable moral agents if their bizarre beliefs or reasoning appear to arise from some internal pathology. If, under the influence of drink or drugs, D believes she can execute some dangerous manoeuvre, we may, other things being equal, hold her morally responsible for any harm that follows her attempt to do so. Should the same belief arise from schizophrenic delusions, talk of moral responsibility would seem to miss the mark.

[74] [2016] UKSC 61, [2016] 1 WLR 5231, endorsing *Brennan* [2014] EWCA Crim 2387, [2015] 1 WLR 2060.
[75] (1843) 10 C & F 200, 8 ER 718.
[76] West and Walk, *Daniel McNaughton* (1977); Loughnan, "M'Naghten's Case" in Handler, Mares, and Williams (eds.), *Landmark Cases in Criminal Law* (2017) 125. There is uncertainty over the correct spelling of the defendant's name: "M'Naghten" is the most common version.
[77] [1984] AC 156, 171.
[78] The Rules also contain a provision relating to insane delusions. In summary, it provides that, when considering D's criminal liability, the court should assess the situation as if the delusion were true. It is generally agreed that the provision adds little of substance to the main body of the Rules, but there are cases which fit neatly within the provision: see below, § 19.1(ii)(e).

For the purposes of the insanity defence, the defect of reason may arise for a brief period of time and need not constitute an aspect of D's character. A temporary blackout is sufficient.[79] In *Clarke*,[80] "defect of reason" was taken to imply the cessation of a relevant deliberative faculty for however brief a period of time. The details of the case were as follows:

> D, in a depressed state, had inadvertently taken an item from a supermarket shelf and placed it in her shopping bag. In response to a charge of theft, she claimed an absence of dishonesty on the basis that she had absent-mindedly put the item in her bag, due to depression. The trial judge held her to be raising a plea of insanity, whereupon she changed her plea to guilty and appealed the ruling. The Court of Appeal ruled that she had not put her sanity in issue. She was not asserting a defect of reason arising from a disease of the mind. She had failed to exercise a faculty (attention) she still possessed.

The reasoning in *Clarke* is unconvincing. It would have been entirely apt to say that D's mental processes were defective. Nonetheless, the disapplication of the insanity defence in *Clarke* is appropriate. An alternative way of achieving that outcome would have been to accept that D was suffering from a cognitive defect, but to deny that it arose from a "disease of the mind". This would require defining the latter phrase in terms which exclude conditions such as depression. We turn now to the definition of that phrase.

*(b) Element 2: disease of the mind*

It needs to be stressed again that what constitutes a disease of the mind within the scope of the *M'Naghten* Rules is a legal, not a medical, question. Although section 1 of the Criminal Procedure (Insanity and Unfitness to Plead) Act 1991 requires evidence to be given by two or more medical practitioners before the special verdict of not guilty by reason of insanity may be returned, the medical witnesses will be giving evidence in response to criteria set down by law. What matters is whether the evidence demonstrates that D was within the legal conception of insanity at the time the actus reus occurred.

"Disease of the mind" therefore should not be conflated with "mental disorder", a point usefully illustrated in the judgment of Devlin J in *Kemp*.[81] D, by all accounts a loving husband, suddenly and violently attacked V, his wife. He claimed to have acted in a state of automatism: evidence was given that he was suffering from arteriosclerosis, a condition that could produce an automatous state by cutting off the blood supply to the brain. Devlin J ruled that a plea of non-insane automatism was unavailable. A disease of the mind, for the purpose of the *M'Naghten* Rules, was any *internal* disorder which affected the faculties of memory, reason, or understanding. Accordingly, the evidence raised on D's behalf was evidence of insanity. It was irrelevant that such a notion of insanity might be greeted with incredulity outside a courtroom; neither did it matter that the actual episode of insanity was of brief duration. Devlin J's approach has been consistently followed by appellate courts and received conclusive endorsement by the House of Lords in *Sullivan*,[82] where a state of automatism arising from an epileptic fit was ruled to be a disease of the mind.

The cardinal limiting factor on what constitutes a disease of the mind is that, to be classified as a form of insanity, the condition must arise from some psychosis, organic or

[79] Provided, of course, that it arises from a disease of the mind: see below, § 19.1(ii)(b).

[80] [1972] 1 All ER 219 (CA).

[81] [1957] 1 QB 399 (Assizes (Bristol)).

[82] [1984] AC 156.

functional disorder, injury, or other inherent condition; or, to employ the summary expression used by the courts, from some factor "internal" to the defendant. Conversely, a state of destabilisation engendered by "external" factors is not, legally, a disease of the mind. Accordingly, in *Quick*,[83] where D became *hypo*glycaemic as a consequence of the insulin he had taken for his diabetic condition, triggering an automatic state, the Court of Appeal ruled that he was entitled to raise a claim of non-insane automatism. The direct cause of D's condition was the insulin, an external factor. By contrast, in *Hennessy*,[84] D, a diabetic, became automatic having *failed* to take his insulin. Consequently, he was *hyper*glycaemic. Hennessy was denied a claim of non-insane automatism because his condition was a symptom of his diabetes (i.e. an internal cause). Each defendant had in common mismanagement of his illness and dangerousness after entering into an automatic condition. What is remarkable is their differing treatment at the hands of the law. In a case such as *Quick*, if D raises the possibility that he was an automaton at the time of the conduct alleged to constitute an offence, the burden of proof (to prove his actions were voluntary) is on the prosecution and D will receive an unqualified acquittal should that burden not be discharged. In a case such as *Hennessy*, D must prove the elements of insane automatism, and will only receive a special verdict of acquittal by reason of insanity if he does.[85]

If the court is satisfied that D's claim to have been an automaton or to have lacked mens rea stems from some form of internal disorder, he will be taken to have raised a plea of insanity even if the form of disorder afflicting D has not been identified. In *Burgess*,[86] D performed a violent act, apparently while asleep. The medical evidence failed to identify any underlying cause of the incident, but testimony was given that violent somnambulism was abnormal and must, in the absence of any evidence of an external cause, arise from some internal condition.[87] Accordingly, the explanation—whatever it was—constituted a disease of the mind.[88]

The approach in *Burgess* mirrors that taken by the Supreme Court of Canada in *Rabey*,[89] where D claimed that the shock of his would-be girlfriend V's rejection of his advances had induced a state of disassociation at the time of his attack upon her, rendering him incapable of forming mens rea. D claimed that this condition was induced by an external factor—V's rejection of him—and should be regarded as a state of non-insane automatism. The Supreme Court held that because D's reaction was so abnormal and extreme, it must have been the product of some internal predisposing factor which was merely *triggered*, not *caused*, by V's rejection. Accordingly, insanity was the only defence available on such facts.

[83] [1973] QB 910 (CA).

[84] [1989] 1 WLR 287 (CA).

[85] See the remarks above, § 19.2(i)(c).

[86] [1991] 2 QB 92 (CA).

[87] For a very useful account of the aetiology of sleep disorders and the appropriate legal responses to sleep disordered behaviours, see Wilson *et al.*, "Violence, Sleepwalking and the Criminal Law" [2005] *Crim LR* 624.

[88] Mackay has criticised the decision on the ground that the somnambulism did not lead to the cessation of the faculties of memory, reason, and understanding; that was caused by the preceding condition of sleep, a normal condition: *Mental Condition Defences* (1995) 45–51, citing the Supreme Court of Canada's decision in *Parks* [1992] 2 SCR 871. Perhaps, in defence of *Burgess*, D's bodily movements may be said to combine with the condition of sleep, producing a discrete, disordered state, a compound of sleep and the internal disorder which leads to the ambulatory activity. Such an answer is not an argument of principle for classifying sleepwalking as a form of insanity, merely acknowledgement that it is somewhat forced to maintain a separation between somnambulism and sleep when the states are, as they must be, coincident. However, for criticism of this rationalisation of the decision in *Burgess*, see Mackay, "Sleepwalking, Automatism and Insanity" [2006] *Crim LR* 901.

[89] [1980] 2 SCR 513.

In *Rabey*, it was suggested, *obiter*, that if an external event is so traumatic in its impact as to cause a state of disassociation in persons of normal sensibility, a defence of non-insane automatism might be available.[90] This suggestion was followed in the English Crown Court case of *T*,[91] where D, acting in a state of disassociation induced by the effects of being raped three days earlier, was held entitled to plead non-insane automatism to a charge of robbery.

To summarise this section: under English law, the source of a defect of reasoning will generally be regarded as a disease of the mind if either: (i) it is "internal" to the defendant (*Kemp*, *Sullivan*, *Hennessy*, *Burgess*); or (ii) it is an "external" trigger that would not normally produce such a result in ordinary persons (as in *Rabey*), so that by inference it discloses an internal cause. Where the source is external *and* the sort of event likely to cause a defect of reasoning even in normal persons (*Quick*, *T*), the case is not one of insanity, but instead non-insane automatism or lack of mens rea.

The explicit policy that has driven this capacious definition of a disease of the mind is the legitimate concern that certain persons likely to be involved in repeated episodes of dangerous behaviour should be subject to restraint, rather than be given an unqualified acquittal on the basis of automatism or lack of mens rea. Lord Denning forcefully expressed the view that any mental disorder which had manifested itself in violence and which was prone to recur should be classified as a disease of the mind.[92] It is submitted, however, that the legitimate concern for public safety should be resolved through civil rather than criminal procedures.[93] As things stand, persons of good character, such as the defendants in *Kemp* and *Sullivan*, may prefer to plead guilty to offences they did not commit rather than pursue an insanity plea with all its forensic uncertainties, pejorative overtones and uncertain disposals. Even on its own terms, it seems that the criteria employed do not provide a reliable measure for future dangerousness: just as internal causes (caught by insanity) may be temporary or non-dangerous,[94] so external causes (excluded from insanity) may entail significant risks of recurrence.[95]

Within the terms of this (flawed) public protection rationale, the insanity plea has an exclusionary character: its application prevents D relying on alternative routes to an (unqualified) acquittal. In the typical case such as *Sullivan*, D provides evidence suggestive of a lack of mens rea or of automatism. If the explanation for this state of affairs rests on some internal disorder, however, D is disallowed access to these simple denials of offending and must plead and prove insanity to avoid conviction. Whatever the merits or otherwise of this "trumping" effect of the insanity plea,[96] in terms of equality of treatment it should

[90] *Ibid.*, 20, quoting from the decision by the Ontario Court of Appeal (1977) 79 DLR (3d) 414, 435. It is of interest that the High Court of Australia in *Falconer* (1990) 65 ALJR 20, another "psychic blow" case, has rejected the internal/external factor analysis favoured in England and Canada. A state of disassociation caused by the shock of an event is to be regarded as a form of non-insane automatism unless there is identification of some underlying disability afflicting D which is suggestive of future dangerousness.

[91] [1990] Crim LR 256 (Crown Court). See *Huckerby* [2004] EWCA Crim 3251, on the relevance of PTSD and dissociation more generally.

[92] *Bratty v A-G for Northern Ireland* [1963] AC 386, 410.

[93] The Mental Health Act 1983 provides for the civil commitment of persons suffering from mental disorder, severe mental impairment, mental impairment, and psychopathic disorder if such persons constitute a danger to themselves or to others.

[94] E.g., an operable congestion of blood on the brain (*Kemp* [1957] 1 QB 399 (Assizes (Bristol))).

[95] E.g., external events leading to post-traumatic stress disorder.

[96] What may be the unwelcome intrusion of this defence into D's case is recognised by provision for an appeal against a ruling that insanity is the applicable defence: Criminal Appeal Act 1968, s. 12.

be consistently applied. Yet, in practice, it is inconsistently applied. So, in *Harris*,[97] D was acquitted of aggravated arson on the basis of a reasonable doubt over whether, in setting fire to his own flat, he foresaw that it might spread to the semi-detached house next door and endanger the lives of any occupants, even though his failure to consider this risk stemmed from an internal disorder.[98] In *Oye*,[99] because of an internal disorder, D thought he was under attack by evil spirits, taking the form of police officers. He was allowed at trial to raise the defence of mistaken self-defence (which, if successful, would have resulted in an unqualified acquittal), as well as insanity.[100] Whether or not one agrees with the nature and consequences of the insanity plea, while it remains in play it should be applied predictably to defendants in like cases.[101]

Inconsistent application of this kind becomes even more problematic in mixed cause cases, of the kind we discussed at the end of Chapter 18.[102] The established approach here, where there are both internal and external causes of D's condition, is to focus on the "predominant cause". That was the case in *Roach*,[103] for example, where personality disorder, prescription drugs, alcohol, and fatigue all seemingly played a part in bringing about D's automatic state, but D's conduct was classified as non-insane automatism because the external causes were dominant. These conclusions appeared until recently to be firmly settled, but the Court of Appeal decision in *Taj* has caused some disruption.[104] Prior to *Taj*, a clear-cut distinction was drawn between intoxicants that were still chemically active in D's system and affecting his mental capacities (external factor) and circumstances where the intoxicants were no longer chemically active. In the latter case, any mental instability was taken to arise from an internal disorder even if it was the case that the instability would not have arisen had the intoxicants not been taken. In other words, a distinction was drawn between the direct effects on the brain from drinking or drug-taking (external) and the withdrawal effects on the brain from ceasing drinking and drug-taking (internal). Contrary to previous authority,[105] the Court of Appeal ruled in *Taj* that D can remain intoxicated in the eye of the law, even when the drink or drugs are no longer chemically active, if his state of instability

97 [2013] EWCA Crim 223, [2013] MHLR 171.

98 See too *Stephenson* [1979] QB 695 (CA), where D's acquittal of arson was upheld on the basis of lack of recklessness because his schizophrenia may have prevented him from realising that the fire he set would spread. The leading case of *Sullivan* [1984] AC 156 makes no separation between the act and its consequences when determining whether D was aware of the nature and quality of his act. For criticism of *Harris* and other cases to like effect, see Child and Sullivan, "When Does the Insanity Defence Apply? Some Recent Cases" [2014] *Crim LR* 788.

99 [2013] EWCA Crim 1725, [2014] 1 WLR 3354.

100 At trial, the jury were first directed on mistaken self-defence and then insanity. If the jury had found in favour of mistaken self-defence it would have lacked any jurisdiction to consider insanity as D was entitled to an unqualified acquittal, a matter not considered by the presiding judge when giving his directions. The jury found him guilty: the Court of Appeal substituted a verdict of insanity on the ground that the expert evidence that D was experiencing a "florid psychotic episode" went unchallenged at the trial. The Court of Appeal made no criticism of the trial judge for allowing the defence of mistaken self-defence to go to the jury but did say (at [63]) that "An insane person cannot set the standards as to the degree of force used by reference to his own insanity." If that is correct, the reason is not to be found in the legislative provisions relating to mistaken self-defence (Criminal Justice and Immigration Act 2008, s. 76), which do not exclude insane beliefs but what can be called the exclusionary effect of the insanity defence, a defence which for reasons of public safety supervenes over other mental state defences such as mistaken self-defence and lack of mens rea.

101 Discussed below, § 21.2(iv)(b).

102 Above, § 18.5.

103 [2001] EWCA Crim 2698.

104 *Taj* [2018] EWCA Crim 1743, [2019] QB 655.

105 See § 18.5.

or delusion would not have arisen but for his prior taking of intoxicants. The former view should prevail, but it may take a decision of the Supreme Court to resolve this matter.[106]

*(c) Element 3a: the nature and quality of D's act*

The third element of the *M'Naghten* Rules can be satisfied in one of two ways, often referred to as the two "limbs". The first limb arises where D's defect of reason induced by a disease of the mind causes D not to appreciate the nature and quality of her act. Where this limb applies, the insanity "defence" is likely to apply as a failure of proof argument and so, if satisfied, D will be diverted from the unqualified acquittal that would otherwise be available to those lacking mens rea or acting involuntarily. A person such as the defendant in *Sullivan* does not apprehend the nature and quality of his conduct if he is in a state of automatism induced by an epileptic seizure. Neither, to take Stephen's example, would a person who cut off a sleeping man's head because it would be great fun to see him look for it when he woke up.[107]

The expression "nature and quality" has been construed narrowly to mean nothing more than the *physical* nature of D's conduct.[108] Many persons who are radically psychotic will still appreciate the nature and quality of their acts in the limited sense adopted by English law. Suppose that, because of her schizophrenic delusions, D thinks she has been ordered by some higher authority to kill V. If she is aware that V is a person, she will fall outside this limb of the *M'Naghten* Rules. This narrow approach seems at odds with the meaning of the phrase "nature *and* quality" of the act. "Quality" would seem to include matters reaching beyond a bare-bones appreciation of what one is physically doing. Yet modern cases continue with this narrow approach. D may be held to understand the nature and quality of his act if aware that he is setting a fire, even if taken to be unaware of the propensity of fires to spread.[109] D may be found to know the nature and quality of his act if aware that he is attacking V, even if his psychosis leads him to believe that V is a terrorist about to explode a bomb.[110] And D may be found to know the nature and quality of his act even if he believes that he is controlled by another, in the context of a command delusion.[111]

Encouragingly, some courts have taken a broader approach. In *Loake v CPS*,[112] D sent a large number of text messages to her estranged husband. She was charged with harassment: a course of conduct amounting to harassment of another, which D knows or ought to know amounts to harassment.[113] D claimed that her mental condition precluded any awareness on her part that her incessant texting made for harassment. The magistrates ruled that what made for harassment was an objective matter, untethered from any state of mind of D's. The Divisional Court ruled that D's insanity defence should have been heard: "If a person suffering from severe dementia such as they cannot recall events beyond a few minutes,

[106] Child, Crombag, and Sullivan, "Defending the Delusional, the Irrational, and the Dangerous" [2020] *Crim LR* 306.

[107] *History of the Criminal Law* (1883) vol. II, 166.

[108] *Codère* (1917) 12 Cr App R 21 (CCA).

[109] *Harris* [2013] EWCA Crim 223, [2013] MHLR 171, [54].

[110] *Taj* [2018] EWCA Crim 1743, [2019] QB 655.

[111] *Keal* [2022] EWCA Crim 341, [2022] 4 WLR 41. See Grainger, "Insanity and Command Delusions" (2022) 81 *CLJ* 467.

[112] [2017] EWHC 2855 (Admin), [2018] QB 998.

[113] Protection from Harassment Act 1997, s. 2. See above, § 11.10.

repeatedly telephoned or texted the same individual, on each occasion believing they are doing so for the first time, they would not know the nature and quality of their act."[114]

Only time will tell whether this more rounded approach will take root, but it is hoped that it will. Persons with significant mental disorders fall outside the *M'Naghten* Rules because of the narrow interpretation of this first limb. A less superficial reading of what makes for a true understanding of the nature and quality of one's acts offers a wider protection of those with mental disorders from criminal sanctions.[115]

*(d) Element 3b: knowledge that D's act is wrong*

Should D appreciate the nature and quality of his acts, he may still receive a verdict of insanity should it be the case that he did not know that his act was wrong (the second limb of the third element of the *M'Naghten* Rules). D will not know that his conduct is "wrong", and satisfy this limb of the insanity test, if:

(i) D does not know that his conduct contravenes the law;[116] and
(ii) D does not know that his conduct transgresses "the ordinary standards adopted by reasonable men".[117]

By requiring a lack of knowledge regarding legal wrongfulness (i), *and* a lack of knowledge regarding moral wrongfulness (ii), English law has adopted a particularly narrow interpretation of this limb of *M'Naghten*.[118] As a result, even defendants with severe mental health disorders and detachments will regularly fall outside of the Rules. In *Sutcliffe*,[119] for example, D took it as his divinely endorsed mission to kill sex workers. He doubtless knew his conduct was contrary to law (and that it would be disapproved of by persons of his acquaintance). He was, in fact, schizophrenic to a severe degree, but still quite sane within the terms of the English law of insanity.[120]

The requirement for D to lack knowledge of *legal* wrongfulness in order to qualify for this limb of the insanity rules was established in the leading case of *Windle*;[121] and later confirmed by the Court of Appeal in *Johnson*.[122] Within the latter judgment, there was some sympathy for the view that the interpretation of the insanity test is too confined. Nonetheless, the Court refused the invitation to adopt any wider conception of the meaning

[114] [2017] EWHC 2855 (Admin), [2018] QB 998, [56].
[115] Mackay, "'Nature', 'Quality' and Mens Rea—Some Observations on 'Defect of Reason' and the First Limb of the M'Naghten Rules" [2020] *Crim LR* 588.
[116] *Windle* [1952] 2 QB 826 (CA); *M'Naghten* (1843) 10 Cl & F 200, 209, 8 ER 718, 722.
[117] *Keal* [2022] EWCA Crim 341, [2022] 4 WLR 41, [41]; *Codère* (1917) 12 Cr App R 21, 27 (CA); *M'Naghten* (1843) 10 Cl & F 200, 210, 8 ER 718, 723.
[118] In *Stapleton v R* (1952) 86 CLR 358, the High Court of Australia was of the view that the *M'Naghten* Rules were too narrowly construed in English law, and that a defence of insanity should be available to D if he believes that his act was right by the standards of reasonable men notwithstanding his awareness of the illegality of his conduct. For contrasting views of the decision, see Morris (1953) 16 *MLR* 435 and Montrose (1954) 17 *MLR* 383.
[119] *The Times*, 30 April 1981.
[120] The defence of insanity is narrower in 2000 than in 1800. In *Hadfield* (1800) 27 St Tr 1281, D shot at the king in order that he, D, should hang and thereby escape the imminent destruction of the world by God. He was found insane. As Williams observes, D clearly knew his act was contrary to law, thereby establishing his sanity: *CLGP* 493–4.
[121] [1952] 2 QB 826 (CA).
[122] [2007] EWCA Crim 1978.

of wrong.[123] It has been argued that *Windle* is based on an inaccurate reading of the *M'Naghten* Rules and the state of the law prior to the Rules.[124] Technically, however, *Windle* and *Johnson* remain intact as precedents; no relevant, binding authority was overlooked in those cases.

Far from broadening the wrongness limb, more recent authorities have confirmed that—to qualify within the *M'Naghten* Rules—D must be unaware of both legal *and* moral wrongfulness. This was the position adopted in *Keal*,[125] in the context of command delusions that caused D, seemingly without any ability to stop himself, to attack his family. The need for unawareness of both legal *and* moral wrongfulness has since been confirmed in *Jan Usman*.[126]

*(e) Insane delusions*

There is a passage in the *M'Naghten* Rules (a third limb) that deals specifically with persons who labour under a "partial delusion only" but who are not in other respects insane.[127] This will arise, for example, where D understands that she is attacking a person, but does so because of a mistaken delusional belief in the need to defend herself. According to *M'Naghten*, the responsibility of such a person is to be considered as if the facts with respect to which the delusion exists were real: if D's conduct would have been justified or excused if her delusional belief had been a true belief, she should be exempted from punishment by receiving the special verdict. As their Lordships opined,[128]

> "if under the influence of his delusion he supposes another man to be in the act of attempting to take away his life, and he kills that man, as he supposes, in self-defence, he would be exempt from punishment."

Traditionally, it has been thought that this express provision for partial delusions did not add anything to the substance of the *M'Naghten* Rules. It is possible to interpret examples of this kind as coming within the first two limbs of the Rules: as examples of a defendant's acting without knowledge of the nature and quality of their actions, and/or without knowledge that those actions are wrong. The apparent superfluity of this aspect of the *M'Naghten* Rules was borne out by the lack of case law arising thereunder.

However, with the progressively narrower interpretation of limbs one and two, the third limb may become more prominent. In *Oye*,[129] where a deluded D believed that police officers were evil spirits who were set on killing him, the third limb of the rules was explicitly referenced by the Court of Appeal when substituting D's conviction for a verdict of not guilty by reason of insanity. The reference may have been unnecessary: D probably would not have known that his conduct was wrong; moreover, if he believed that the officers were non-earthly beings (albeit adopting human form) he would not have been aware of the nature and quality of his acts. That said, there was an exact fit between the facts of the case

[123] For an argument that it was open to the Court of Appeal to adopt a wider test, see Mackay, "Righting the Wrong?—Some Observations on the Second Limb of the M'Naghten Rules" [2009] *Crim LR* 80.
[124] Manwaring, "*Windle* Revisited" [2018] *Crim LR* 987.
[125] [2022] EWCA Crim 341, [2022] 4 WLR 41, [41].
[126] [2023] EWCA Crim 313.
[127] (1843) 10 Cl & Fin 200, 211.
[128] *Ibid.*
[129] [2013] EWCA Crim 1725, [2014] 1 WLR 3354.

and the self-defence example posited in the part of the *M'Naghten* Rules dealing with partial delusion. Moreover, apart from the very violent conduct that led to criminal proceedings, there was no evidence of mental disturbance before or shortly after the incident.[130] Apart from his delusional episode, D was in other respects sane. It is understandable why the little-cited portion of *M'Naghten* was invoked.

Indeed, the third (delusional) limb may offer more than might appear at first sight. In *Taj*,[131] D was taken to know the nature and quality of his act when attacking V, despite his psychotic mistaken belief that V was a terrorist about to explode a bomb; and the court did not address whether his delusional belief meant that he did not know he was doing something wrong. The third limb of the *M'Naghten* Rules was not considered in *Taj*, and D was found liable for attempted murder.[132] In our view, this was a mistake. The third limb frames the question of insanity in a stark and clear-cut manner: had his delusional belief been true, D would have received praise, not blame, for his actions. As with *Oye*, the fit between the facts and the third limb seems exact. It is hoped that the courts make more recourse to the third limb of *M'Naghten* in the future.

*(f) The scope of the M'Naghten Rules*

The *M'Naghten* Rules lay down criteria for a general defence of insanity applicable to all offences. At one point, however, that was not the view of the Divisional Court, that ruled *DPP v H*[133] that a defence of insanity had no application to an offence of strict liability. The ruling was based on an error, namely the view that a successful plea of insanity established a lack of mens rea. But as we have seen, this is true only of the "nature and quality" limb of the Rules; and the "knowledge that the act is wrong" limb may provide for a defence applicable in circumstances where D has mens rea. An important rationale of the insanity defence is to protect mentally disordered persons from punishment. This concern is engaged for all criminal offences.

Happily, this rationale was given full recognition by the Divisional Court in *Loake v CPS*.[134] D was charged before magistrates with harassment contrary to section 2 of the Protection from Harassment Act 1997. Applying *DPP v H*, the magistrates dismissed D's plea of insanity on the basis that the offence of harassment imposed liability on an objective basis. What D considered to be the nature of her conduct was irrelevant; what mattered was whether her conduct amounted to harassment from an objective perspective. On appeal, the Divisional Court fully appreciated that the *M'Naghten* Rules stretched beyond questions of mens rea and protected persons charged with strict or objective liability offences if their internal disorder prevented them appreciating the wrongfulness of their conduct. Given

[130] There was some speculation among the expert witnesses that the delusional episode was induced by smoking strong cannabis; later, however, there was agreement between them that it was a psychotic episode caused by some unspecified internal condition.

[131] [2018] EWCA Crim 1743, [2019] QB 655.

[132] As discussed in § 18.4(iii)(a), although the drink that D had taken some 30 hours ago was no longer chemically active in his system, his condition was (controversially) ruled to be a state of intoxication. An attempt by D to raise the issue of his sanity at the appellate stage was dismissed, on the basis that insanity did not arise on the facts, because at the trial the expert witnesses were agreed that D understood the nature and quality of his act.

[133] [1997] 1 WLR 1406 (DC); above, § 6.2.

[134] [2017] EWHC 2855 (Admin), [2018] QB 998; above, § 19.2(ii)(c).

the clarity of the analysis in *Loake*, which is so clearly correct, *DPP v H* may safely be set to one side.[135]

### *(iii) Insanity and the ECHR*

In our earlier discussion of the burden of proof in insanity, it was noted that imposing a legal (i.e. persuasive) burden on D to show that her conduct was involuntary or done without mens rea is arguably in breach of Article 6(2) of the ECHR.[136] The problems of aligning the English law of insanity with the minimum standards required by the ECHR do not end there, however.

Article 5(1) of the ECHR allows, "in accordance with a procedure prescribed by law", "the lawful detention of persons of unsound mind". Under the jurisprudence interpreting Article 5, there is a requirement that the question of unsoundness of mind must be resolved by reference to "objective medical expertise".[137] Thus the detention on grounds of insanity of anyone who, by good-practice standards of the medical profession,[138] is not considered to be of unsound mind will contravene Article 5. While section 1 of the Criminal Procedure (Insanity and Unfitness to Plead) Act 1991 requires evidence from two medical practitioners before a special verdict can be returned by a jury, this provision does not address the point that the category of insanity in English law allows detention of persons who are not of unsound mind in any acceptable medical sense.[139] If a medical expert witness were to testify that D's automatism stems from, say, his underlying diabetes, the common law will designate the condition as internal, and thus D's defence will be one of insanity.[140] The presentation of persons with conditions such as diabetes as being of "unsound mind" would be rejected by any reputable body of "objective medical expertise".

Decisions such as *Sullivan* and *Kemp*, where defendants who were in no sense mentally ill faced a choice between pleading guilty to crimes they did not commit or pleading insanity, therefore involve fundamental contraventions of human rights. Such persons should be allowed to contest their guilt without risk of detention under a classification of insanity.[141]

These arguments can be put directly in domestic law.[142] By virtue of section 6 of the Human Rights Act 1998, a court is obliged to apply what is required under the Convention even if that requires departing from previous decisions of the highest authority such as the

[135] As stated in *ibid.*, [54]: "We have come to the conclusion that the quoted remarks of McCowan LJ in *Director of Public Prosecutions v H* [regarding the inapplicability of insanity to strict liability offences] should be regarded as misleading, and should not be followed."
[136] § 19.2(i)(c).
[137] Harris et al, *Law of the European Convention on Human Rights* (5th ed., 2023).
[138] *Winterwerp v Netherlands* (1979) 2 EHRR 387. The European Court of Human Rights laid down three conditions: (i) the individual detained must be reliably shown by objective medical expertise to be of unsound mind; (ii) the individual's mental disorder must be of a kind or degree warranting compulsory confinement; and (iii) the disorder must persist throughout the period of detention.
[139] As Sutherland and Gearty have noted: "Insanity and the European Court of Human Rights" [1992] *Crim LR* 418, 420–1; see too Baker, "Human Rights, *M'Naghten* and the 1991 Act" [1994] *Crim LR* 84; Mackay and Gearty, "On Being Insane in Jersey" [2001] *Crim LR* 560; Mackay, "On Being Insane in Jersey Part Two" [2002] *Crim LR* 728.
[140] *Hennessy* [1989] 1 WLR 287 (CA).
[141] It may be that, if a particular person can reliably be predicted to be a danger to others, a form of non-punitive civil commitment may be permissible. On the difficulty of reliable prediction, see Floud and Young, *Dangerousness and Criminal Justice* (1981); Palmstierna, "Only About One in Thirty Predictions of Assault by Discharged Psychiatric Patients will be Correct" [1999] *BMJ* 1270.
[142] See above, § 2.5.

House of Lords' decision in *Sullivan*. In criminal law contexts, findings of insanity which are compatible with objective medical expertise would be greatly facilitated if courts were to use, as a benchmark, those mental conditions which permit compulsory civil commitment.[143]

### *(iv) Insanity and prior fault*

We have discussed the potential for prior fault rules to apply where D's failure of proof argument relies on evidence of his voluntary intoxication or an otherwise culpable incapacity.[144] In such cases, where prior fault is found, it will be possible for the prosecution to establish D's liability for a basic intent offence even where D lacked mens rea and/or voluntariness when causing the relevant harms. In the context of insanity, one might anticipate that similar prior-fault rules might apply where D's previous conduct has caused or exacerbated his mental health disorder (e.g. where D chooses not to take medication, or, more controversially, perhaps in circumstances of addiction).

Crucially, however, prior fault rules of this kind do *not* apply to insanity, whether insanity is argued as a failure of proof or as a supervening defence. The exclusion of prior fault from insanity cases was clearly articulated in the case of *Davies* in 1881,[145] quoted with approval by the House of Lords in the seminal case of *Beard* in 1920:[146]

> "drunkenness is one thing and the diseases to which drunkenness leads are different things; and if a man by drunkenness brings on a state of disease which causes such a degree of madness, even for a time, which would have relieved him from responsibility if it had been caused in any other way, then he will not be criminally responsible".

Indeed, speaking categorically, the Lords stated that "the law takes no notice of the cause of insanity."[147]

Notwithstanding the clarity of the law on this point, dismissing the (potentially blameworthy) causal route of insanity, whilst continuing to examine the causal route of *externally* caused incapacities, creates a very strict internal/external cause distinction. Essentially, there may be no consideration of prior fault for internal cause conditions, but there is potential for prior fault for many external cause conditions. This is a causal distinction that can be extremely difficult to draw, in both scientific and legal terms, particularly in cases of concurrent or overlapping causes (e.g. where D is experiencing the effects of mental health disorder and drug- or alcohol-induced intoxication).[148] However, despite such difficulties, and even in cases where such difficulties arise, the courts have treated the exclusion of prior fault from insanity cases as the subject of clear and binding authority.[149]

The continued appropriateness of that exclusion remains contested. The contestation is motivated in part by the practical difficulties of separating internal and external cause conditions. Beyond that, though, and more fundamentally, internal-cause cases can evoke the same policy and culpability considerations that underpin the application of prior fault

143 Mental Health Act 1983.
144 See above, § 18.4 (prior fault intoxication) and § 5.8(i)(d) (prior fault automatism).
145 *Davies* (1881) 14 Cox CC 563.
146 *Beard* [1990] AC 479, 500.
147 *Ibid.*
148 See above, § 18.5.
149 E.g. *Taj* [2018] EWCA Crim 1743, [2019] QB 655.

rules elsewhere. If D chooses to not take medication for example, and then—in a resulting state of psychological confusion—causes harm without mens rea and/or voluntariness, an acquittal on that basis may strike us as inappropriate. D may not be fully responsible when causing harm, but her previous choices provide a form of meta-responsibility that—arguably—should extend as a route to criminalisation.[150] Indeed, outside of English law, several jurisdictions are already willing to engage with prior fault rules in cases of this kind.[151]

### (v) *Reform of insanity law*

In normative and conceptual terms, the English law of insanity is open to significant criticism. Yet the law of insanity has remained essentially unchanged since the mid-nineteenth century.[152] The Law Commission has produced a scoping paper followed by a discussion paper in 2013, focused on identifying the ways in which the law of insanity and its perceived difficulties impact on the day-to-day operation of the criminal justice system.[153] That is a very relevant question. Legislative reforms relating to the disposal options that a judge has following a verdict of not guilty by reason of insanity have removed a lot of the sting from the criticisms of the current law. Nowadays, even following a special verdict on a charge of murder, D does not face the prospect of mandatory indefinite detention until a government minister decides it is safe for him to be released. Yet even the most practically minded and cost-conscious reform initiative must also address fundamental questions. And for the insanity defence the most fundamental question is: when does D's mental condition remove him from blame and censure?

The current narrow interpretation of the two principal limbs of the *M'Naghten* Rules is one of the main reasons why the insanity defence is not more frequently employed. Despite the increased range of disposal outcomes following a special verdict,[154] there are relatively few insanity pleas each year.[155] Arguably a more expansive mental disorder defence is required to address the needs of mentally ill persons who become defendants in criminal trials. Following a pause of some 12 years since its discussion paper was published, the Law Commission has confirmed that it will be completing its review of insanity as part of its 14th Programme of Law Reform.[156] Such a review is to be welcomed, as will be the Commission's engagement with critiques of its 2013 proposals. We highlight three principal options for reform,[157] beginning with the Commission's previous approach.

[150] On a conception of meta-responsibility, and on prior fault insanity in general, see Mitchell, *Self-Made Madness* (2003). The intuition is shared by the Law Commission, *Insanity and Automatism* (Discussion Paper, 2013). Cf. Mackay and Hughes, "Insanity and Blaming the Mentally Ill: A Critique of the Prior Fault Principle in the Law Commission's Discussion Paper" [2022] *Crim LR* 21.

[151] Within many civil law jurisdictions (including, e.g. Germany and the Netherlands) the insanity rules are the *primary* vehicle for the application of prior fault rules, though these remain principally focused on the role of voluntary intoxication.

[152] As the insanity defence was most important in the context of capital murder, the introduction of the defence of diminished responsibility in 1957 reduced the practical importance of insanity and in that sense can be regarded as a significant reform in the provision of mental disorder defences.

[153] *Insanity and Automatism* (2012); Peay, "Insanity and Automatism: Questions From and About the Law Commission Scoping Paper" [2012] *Crim LR* 927; Law Commission, Discussion Paper, *Insanity and Automatism* (2013).

[154] Criminal Procedure (Insanity and Unfitness to Plead) Act 1991: including a hospital order (with or without restriction), a guardianship order, supervision and treatment order, and an absolute discharge.

[155] Mackay and Kearns, "More Fact(s) about the Insanity Defence" [1999] *Crim LR* 714

[156] Announced in 2025.

[157] For further comparative discussion, see Mackay and Brookbanks (eds.), *The Insanity Defence: International and Comparative Perspectives* (2022).

### (a) The Law Commission

The approach of the Commission back in 2013 may in some ways appear radical, proposing the abolition of common law insanity and its replacement with a new statutory defence of "not criminally responsible by reason of a recognised medical condition".[158] The recognised medical condition here could be physical and/or mental in nature, qualifying as long as it caused D to lack capacity: (1) rationally to form a judgement about his conduct or circumstances; (2) to understand the wrongfulness of what he was charged with, not isolated to legal wrongfulness; or (3) to control his conduct in the relevant circumstances. D would not be required to prove the elements of the new defence, though a lesser evidential burden would remain.[159]

Below the headlines, however, the Commission's proposals do not signal a significant theoretical shift from the current law. The reformed tests remain cognitive in nature, focused on D's awareness and control, rather than the broader status of his condition. This may be appropriate, but a purely cognitive focus may become problematic where—as the Commission clearly signals—the aim is to expand the potential application of insanity. The risk is that insanity may apply too widely as a defence, applicable to those who lack a complete understanding of their conduct, but who may nevertheless be deserving of liability.[160] Similarly, but to converse effect, where insanity is triggered within a failure of proof argument, broadening the terms of insanity will result in greater diversion to insanity from an otherwise unqualified acquittal.[161]

### (b) Insanity as exemption

An alternative approach to insanity eschews cognitive tests in favour of a focus on diagnosis-type and disorder, typically referred to as the "medical model" for insanity. Essentially, under this view, insanity rules should be perceived as a form of criminal exclusion, removing categories of defendant from potential liability based on a mental disorder diagnosis, akin to the removal from potential liability of those under the age of criminal responsibility. A form of the medical model has been applicable in states such as Norway,[162] and has—at one time at least—been proposed for adoption within English law.[163] The medical model is perhaps most forcefully advocated in writings by Moore.[164]

158 In this context, it is worth noting that Scotland abolished the language of "insanity" in 2010: see the Criminal Procedure (Scotland) Act 1995, s. 51A.

159 Law Commission, Discussion Paper, *Insanity and Automatism* (2013). See paras. 4.123–4.130 for the terms of the defence. Discussed in Livings et al. (eds), *Mental Condition Defences and the Criminal Justice System* (2015).

160 The case of Breivik, discussed in (b) below, may be relevant here.

161 Discussed in Hogg and Child, "Not Guilty by Reasons Other than Insanity" in Simester (ed.), *Modern Criminal Law* (2024) 155.

162 Under the Norwegian Criminal Code, s. 44, any person who was psychotic or unconscious at the time of his or her otherwise criminal act is deemed irresponsible.

163 Report of the Committee on Mentally Abnormal Offenders (Cmnd. 6244, 1975), which recommended allowing a defence of mental disorder if D suffered from severe mental illness or severe subnormality. Persons in that class would receive a special verdict and remain within the jurisdiction of the court if the elements of the offence are proved and any defence such as a genuine belief in the need for self-defence disproved. Note, however, the further constraint in the Law Com. No. 177, *Draft Criminal Code* (1989), cl. 35(2), which refuses a defence to persons in that category if it is proved beyond reasonable doubt "that the offence was not attributable to the disorder".

164 "The Quest for a Responsible Responsibility Test: Norwegian Insanity Law after Breivik" (2015) 9 *Crim Law and Philosophy* 645, 680–1; see too Moore, *Law and Psychiatry* (1984) chap. 6.

Medical models can offer an attractive alternative to cognitive approaches, not least because of their potential for greater legal certainty in application (in particular, their identifying excluded groups through medical diagnosis). However, it remains questionable whether greater certainty through diagnosis can produce a threshold for insanity that *fairly* separates the responsible from the non-responsible in relation to specific events. A case in point is that of Anders Breivik, following which the Norwegian law has come under considerable scrutiny.[165] Breivik displayed considerable planning when exploding a car bomb, causing eight deaths, and then killing a further sixty-nine persons with an automatic weapon.[166] He was found guilty of murder, but not before two court-appointed psychiatrists reported that he was psychotic because of his schizophrenia and therefore not criminally responsible under Norwegian law. That report was superseded by a second psychiatric report which found the Breivik was not psychotic, clearing the path to a criminal trial.[167] What is not in dispute is that Breivik was a fervent admirer of Adolf Hitler and believed that his violent acts and the promulgation of his racist views would prove inspirational and, as in the case of Hitler, culminate in an authoritarian regime that would replace effete democracy. In the first psychiatric report his world view and the atrocity it led to were the product of schizophrenia : in the second report,[168] he was a political extremist responsible for his thoughts and deeds. Breivik is serving the maximum penalties available for mass murder under Norwegian law and may be held in preventive detention for the remainder of his life.

### *(c) The abolition of insanity*

Another response would be to abolish the insanity defence entirely. Abolitionists may be sceptics such as Thomas Szasz, who refers to mental illness as a convenient myth exploited by the "ill" and their carers.[169] However, the Szasz viewpoint founders against the advances made in the reliable identification of mental disorders.[170] More telling is the abolitionist proposal made by Norval Morris.[171] He asserts that a cohort of mentally disordered persons comprising a statistically significant number of individuals and representative of the main kinds of mental disorder will contain no greater incidence of persons with offending behaviour than an equivalent sized cohort made up of randomly selected persons. Moreover, if

[165] Moore, "The Quest for a Responsible Responsibility Test: Norwegian Insanity Law after Breivik" (2015) 9 *Crim Law and Philosophy* 645.

[166] When setting his car bomb adjacent to a government building, Breivik placed a sign ("Sewer cleaning in progress") to explain the smell of sulphur. Later, he dressed in police uniform to gain access to the summer camp where he killed his further victims. For a brief yet informative account of Breivik's crimes and his mental condition at the time they were committed, see Wessely, "Anders Breivik, the Public and Psychiatry" (2012) 379 *The Lancet* 1563.

[167] If an insanity plea is raised in Norway, D is examined by two psychiatrists who report to the Commission of Forensic Medicine. If that report is passed on to the trial court, the matter of D's mental condition is almost invariably determined according to the findings in the report. It is unusual for the Commission to order a second report: see further Moore, "The Quest for a Responsible Responsibility Test: Norwegian Insanity Law after Breivik" (2015) 9 *Crim Law and Philosophy* 645, 646–7.

[168] This was accepted by the trial court, which found that his beliefs were intelligible in the context of an extremist political culture. The court also took into account that, although a paranoid loner, Breivik could function efficiently in a range of areas: Oslo District Court Judgment, TOSLO-2011–188627-24E (24 August 2012) 59–66.

[169] *The Manufacture of Madness* (1970); *The Myth of Mental Illness* (1961).

[170] American Medical Association, *DSM-5* (2022).

[171] "The Criminal Responsibility of the Mentally Ill" (1982) 33 *Syracuse LR* 477.

we were to compare both those groups with an equivalent cohort of males between the ages of 14 and 22, living in socially deprived circumstances in inner-city areas, we would find a much greater incidence of offenders in the last group.[172]

The abolitionist (or "integrationist") position would remove the defence of insanity, amending the remaining law where necessary (e.g. general mens rea definitions and other defences) to allow the conduct of defendants with mental disorders to be appraised without recourse to a distinct set of specialist rules or processes.[173] Accordingly, if a mentally disordered person's condition precluded mens rea, she should receive an unqualified acquittal like anyone else. If she is considered dangerous, then civil commitment should be considered; but that job should not be done through the insanity defence.[174] If D has mens rea, she should be convicted and her disorder considered when determining what sentence or treatment she should receive.

The case for abolition has considerable merit, but it typically underplays the fact that there *are* persons so disordered or so deficient in cognitive capacities that the presence, in formal terms, of mens rea would not entail any measure of culpability.[175] For those persons, any form of conviction is wrong: an injustice is done to persons severely psychotic if thereby deprived of any capacity for sequential thought and practical reasoning, and the same holds for profoundly learning-disabled persons or those with advanced dementia. These extreme conditions are capable of satisfactory definition; persons with such conditions should not be found guilty of crimes because they are so irrational or mentally disabled as to be beyond any moral scheme of reference. It is for this reason that the case for partial abolition may be more attractive: removing the diversion to insanity from a failure of proof argument, but maintaining the potential for insanity as a supervening defence.[176]

## § 19.3 Legal infancy

During childhood, and for some time afterwards, our brains are still undergoing stages of development. However, even from a very young age, it is possible to cause harms and form basic mental states as defined within the criminal law. The challenge for the law is to identify suitable thresholds, protecting underdeveloped and irresponsible minors from potential criminal conviction, whilst capturing those who (despite ongoing stages of development)

[172] Significant research carried out after Morris's article indicates that certain diagnoses, notably schizophrenia, are predictive of violence but not strongly predictive: Bowden, "Violence and Mental Disorder" in Walker (ed.), *Dangerous People* (1996) 13. However, the point remains that age, gender, and social circumstances are more highly correlated with crime, including violent crime.

[173] See, more recently, Hogg, "The Insanity Defence: An Argument for Abolition" (2015) 79 *J Crim L* 250; Slobogin, "An End to Insanity" (2000) 86 *Va LR* 1199; Minkowitz, "Rethinking Criminal Responsibility from a Critical Disability Perspective" 23 (2014) *Griffith LR* 434.

[174] Institutional arrangements would have to be made to ensure that the civil process should be initiated immediately for persons acquitted but reasonably taken to be dangerous to others or themselves. The important thing is that if an offence has not been proved, any confinement should satisfy the terms of mental health legislation concerned with therapy and personal and public safety.

[175] Perlin, "God Said to Abraham/Kill Me a Son" (2017) 54 *Am Crim LR* 477; Bonnie, "The Moral Basis of the Insanity Defense" (1983) 69 *ABAJ* 194; Brady, "Abolish the Insanity Defense? No!" (1971) 8 *Houston LR* 629.

[176] Hogg and Child, "Not Guilty by Reasons Other than Insanity" in Simester (ed.), *Modern Criminal Law* (2024) 155.

are deemed sufficiently responsible to be answerable to the criminal law.[177] We discuss three categories of defendant below.

### (i) Children below the age of 10 years

At common law, any child under the age of 7 was *doli incapax* (i.e. deemed legally incapable of committing a crime).[178] The qualifying age was raised by statute to 10 years in 1963.[179] This remains low in comparison with other jurisdictions, and continues to receive cogent criticism.[180] More recently, it is notable that Scotland has raised the minimum age of criminal responsibility in that jurisdiction to 12.[181] Although provision was made at one time to raise the age in England and Wales to 14,[182] it was never put into effect. In fact, legislative policy has often gone into reverse, with greater emphasis on punitive responses to wrongdoing by children and young people.[183] The reform debate is therefore ongoing. One recent twist arises from a report commissioned by the Welsh Government, recommending that the age of criminal responsibility should be raised independently in Wales to 12 years.[184]

As noted above, the current law in England and Wales sets the age of criminal responsibility at 10 years old. Whatever a child under the age of 10 does, with whatever state of mind, it cannot constitute a crime; although it may lead to the imposition of a civil care order.[185] The incapacity of the child may well affect the legal position of persons associated with the conduct perpetrated by the legal infant. If D, a person above the age of criminal responsibility, were to instruct C, an infant under the age of 10, to take property from V, this, all other things being equal, would constitute a theft by D through the innocent agency of C.[186] If C were to take V's property on his own initiative and hand it on to D, D's dishonest acceptance of the property would constitute theft rather than a handling offence.[187]

Given the very low age of criminal responsibility in England and Wales, it is worth noting that, in recent history, latitude was shown to those under the age of 14.

[177] See Keating, "How Should the Criminal Law Respond to the 'Special Status' of Children?" in Child and Duff (eds.) *Criminal Law Reform Now* (2019) 165, and the response from Yaffe (*ibid.*, 184). For a fuller articulation of Yaffe's alternative analysis, refocusing the question away from cognitive development towards issues of political enfranchisement, see Yaffe, *The Age of Culpability* (2018). For Yaffe, adolescents "are owed leniency not because of their psychological or behavioural immaturity but because they are denied for good reasons as much say over the law as adults; in particular, they are denied the vote so the law is not theirs to the same degree that it is ours" (184). Yaffe provides a compelling critique of purely cognitive rationales for leniency. Ultimately, however, Yaffe's focus on voting rights is unconvincing as an explanation for (legal) infancy-based exculpation.

[178] Kean, "The History of the Criminal Liability of Children" (1937) 53 *LQR* 364.

[179] Children and Young Persons Act 1933, s. 50, as amended by the Children and Young Persons Act 1963, s. 16.

[180] The age of criminal responsibility is low compared, for instance, to France (13), Germany (14), and Spain (16); it has been criticised as too low by the UN Committee on the Rights of the Child, *Concluding Observations: Great Britain and Northern Ireland* (2008). See further, Ashworth, *Positive Obligations in Criminal Law* (2013) 177.

[181] The Age of Criminal Responsibility (Scotland) Act 2019, amending the Criminal Procedure (Scotland) Act 1995, s. 41.

[182] Children and Young Persons Act 1969, ss. 4, 70(1).

[183] Criminal Justice and Public Order Act 1994; Crime and Disorder Act 1998.

[184] Welsh Justice Commission, *Justice in Wales for the People of Wales* (2019). See Hodgetts, "An Evolution in Devolution? Welsh Criminal Justice and the Commission on Justice in Wales" [2021] *Crim LR* 34.

[185] Children Act 1989, s. 25.

[186] The innocent agency doctrine is discussed above, § 7.3(i).

[187] *Walters v Lunt* [1951] 2 All ER 645 (CA).

### *(ii) Children between the age of 10 and 13 years (inclusive)*

At common law, there was a presumption that a child aged above 9 years and below 14 was *doli incapax* (i.e. deemed legally incapable of committing a crime), a presumption rebutted if the prosecution could prove a "mischievous discretion" on the part of D—the capacity to differentiate between right and wrong.[188] The need to establish mischievous discretion was something additional to the mens rea required for the offence with which the legal infant was charged. This presumption of *doli incapax* came under attack predominantly on the ground that it excused those legal infants most in need of reformative or corrective measures.[189] It was abolished by section 34 of the Crime and Disorder Act 1998, which provides:

> The rebuttable presumption of criminal law that a child aged 10 or over is incapable of committing an offence is hereby abolished.

On the face of it, the meaning of this provision seems clear. It abolishes a presumption. Accordingly, it might be thought to remain open for a child under 14 to raise the defence of *doli incapax*.[190] On general principles of proof, the child would present evidence suggestive of an incapacity to make judgements of right and wrong and then the onus would be on the prosecution to prove beyond reasonable doubt that the child possessed a sufficient sense of right and wrong to warrant a criminal conviction.[191] That was the view of the Solicitor General on the second reading of the Bill. He envisaged a child raising the defence if he has "genuine learning difficulties and . . . is genuinely at sea on the question of right and wrong".[192]

Yet, despite the seeming clarity of section 34, a view was taken that the abolition of the presumption entails the abolition of the defence of *doli incapax* altogether for children aged 10 years and over, an interpretation endorsed in a Home Office circular on the Act.[193] This view accords with the attitude expressed by judges and politicians before the 1994 Act, that the defence of *doli incapax* was an indulgence incompatible with an effective response to juvenile offending. The case law on *doli incapax* is confined to situations where the prosecution sought to demonstrate the presence of mischievous discretion; there was no jurisprudence, before the coming into force of section 34, on raising *doli incapax* as a distinct defence. Conditioned by that background, it is understandable, perhaps, that the abolition of the presumption could be taken to mean the abolition of the legal infancy defence altogether in the case of children between the ages of 10 and 14. And that was the view taken by the House of Lords in *JTB*.[194] The Appellate Committee accepted that the presumption of *doli incapax* and the defence of *doli incapax* were two different things, and that to hold that section 34 abolished the presumption while leaving intact the defence was a tenable reading of the section. But, questionably invoking the interpretive latitude permitted by *Pepper v Hart*,[195] Lord Phillips, in his majority judgment, perused the parliamentary debates on section 34 and was satisfied that ministers used the term *doli incapax* to include both the defence and

188 *Owen* (1830) 4 C & P 236; *Manley* (1844) 1 Cox CC 104; *Gorrie* (1919) 83 JP 136.
189 See, especially, *C* [1996] AC 1.
190 As is cogently argued in Walker, "The End of an Old Song?" (1999) 149 *NLJ* 64.
191 *Woolmington v DPP* [1935] AC 462.
192 *Hansard*, Lords, 16 December 1997, col. 596.
193 As cited in *Walker*, "The End of an Old Song" (1999) 149 *NLJ* 64, the circular reads: "children who are over the age of criminal responsibility (10- to 13-year-olds) will be treated in the same way as other juveniles (14- to 17-year-olds) when deciding whether or not prosecution is appropriate".
194 [2009] UKHL 20, [2009] 1 AC 1310.
195 [1993] AC 593.

the presumption, and that they intended the measure to abolish *doli incapax* in both dimensions.[196] On that basis, the defence was taken to have been abolished by section 34.

England and Wales does make certain other allowances for defendants of a young age. Typically, any trial will be held in the Youth Court rather than the Crown Court. However, if the offending is serious (most notably murder) the venue may still be the Crown Court albeit Article 6 (fair trial) of the ECHR requires special measures to allow effective participation in the proceedings for children and young people.[197] The defences of duress and self-defence, as interpreted, can take into account the age of D and so too can the partial defences to murder of diminished responsibility and loss of self-control. In 2013, the Law Commission proposed a defence for persons who cannot "understand that the conduct was something he or she ought not to do".[198] However, if enacted in its current form it will only apply if the failure of understanding is based on a "recognised medical condition"; so it would not assist, say, a developmentally immature 13-year-old. There would still be cases such as *Wilson*,[199] where the 13-year-old D participated in a murder instigated and predominantly carried out by his father, but under duress. That defence is not, of course, available in murder and, although "swept along" by his father, D was found to have the requisite intent and was therefore guilty of murder. In the words of Ashworth, "A child of 13 would only have a hazy and under-developed understanding of the social meaning of serious injury and death . . . a child of that age cannot really understand the significance of such acts and their consequences."[200] But under the current law: no matter.

From a children's welfare perspective, the position of child and adolescent offenders in England and Wales is far from satisfactory.[201] Imposing full criminal responsibility from the age of 10 contrasts sharply with the European average of 14 and with the requirement imposed on contracting parties to the United Nations Convention on the Rights of the Child that the age of criminal responsibility be no lower than 12. UK governments have repeatedly confirmed that there is no prospect of raising the age of criminal responsibility for England and Wales. This is unfortunate. Raising the age to 14, without restoring the presumption of *doli incapax*, and thereby unequivocally excluding convictions for children under 14, would be an advance.[202]

[196] *JTB* was a very questionable application of this already controversial decision. On the face of it, the terms of s. 34 are not ambiguous. It abolishes the presumption but not the defence itself. *Pepper v Hart* is used by Lord Phillips to go behind the text and subvert its meaning; and, moreover, to do so against the interests of D. In its original conception, *Pepper v Hart* conferred an exceptional and rare permission to consult *Hansard* for ministerial statements in support of an interpretation of an otherwise ambiguous provision in a manner which would not disturb settled and reasonable expectations. See further Bennion, "Mens Rea and Defendants below the Age of Discretion" [2009] *Crim LR* 757; Bailey, "Interpreting Parliamentary Inaction" (2020) 79 *CLJ* 245, 247.

[197] *T v United Kingdom* (2000) 30 EHRR 121; *V v United Kingdom* (1999) ECHR 171; *SC v United Kingdom* (2005) 40 EHRR 10. Special measures are provided in the Youth Justice and Criminal Evidence Act 1999, Part 2. Although the explicit provision of special measures for vulnerable defendants is limited within the statute, courts have been willing to extend the use of other special measures to defendants (particularly youths). See Fairclough, "Speaking up for Injustice" [2018] *Crim LR* 4.

[198] Law Commission, Discussion Paper, *Insanity and Automatism* (2013) para. 4.126.

[199] [2007] EWCA Crim 1251, [2007] 2 Cr App R 31.

[200] Ashworth, *Positive Obligations in Criminal Law* (2013) 177.

[201] Brown, "Reviewing the Age of Criminal Responsibility" [2018] *Crim LR* 904; Keating "How Should the Criminal Law Respond to the 'Special Status' of Children?" in Child and Duff (eds.), *Criminal Law Reform Now* (2019) 165.

[202] Cf. For a more individualised approach to capacity, Hamer and Crofts, "The Logic and Value of the Presumption of Doli Incapax (Failing That, an Incapacity Defence)" (2023) 43 *OJLS* 546.

### *(iii) Adolescents between the age of 14 and 18 years*

The brains of adolescents differ from those of adults in that adolescent brains are still at the developmental stage. With adolescents, there is typically more impulsivity, a disregard for long-term consequences, and a lack of perspective and judgement.[203] The influence of peers and the desire for status and security within the peer group can be potent.[204] Older members of the peer group and associated adults can manipulate adolescents for their own ends (frequently profits from drug dealing) and introduce and facilitate seriously criminal behaviour of a kind that would otherwise not have been contemplated.[205] Of course, the same fallibilities may be present in some adults, even of an advanced age. (No fool like an old fool.) There comes a point where we say of a person, "well, that is how she or he is". For adolescents, it is best to defer that judgement for as long as practicable. It is not suggested that deferment should take the form of categorical exemption from conviction and punishment. If D, a 14-year-old, has harmed V in a serious way, convicting him for the relevant crime may be the most effective way of underscoring the wrong that he has done. And D may have done something truly dreadful, requiring a highly punitive outcome.[206] But wherever possible, there should be diversion from the criminal justice system with appropriate interventions within the framework of the Children Act 1989 of a social, educational, and psychological kind, aimed at reducing the risk of future offending. Even where criminal punishment is warranted, it should be lesser punishment than would be imposed on an adult offender in a like case. And punishment of an adolescent should be conjoined with reformative measures to deliver on the legislative requirement to consider the welfare of the child even when a punitive response is also appropriate.

There are two reasons for this special treatment. First, the impulsivity, suggestibility, and lack of prudence associated with the brain states of adolescents are mitigating factors. Secondly, adolescents are at a developmental stage and may develop for the better or the worse. If the better path remains a feasible option, it should be pursued to enhance D's welfare, with associated societal gains.

203 Blakemore and Choudhury, "Development of the Adolescent Brain: Implications for Executive Function and Social Cognition (2006) 47 *J Child Psychiatry and Psychology* 296.

204 Wolf *et al.*, "The Audience Effect in Adolescence Depends on Who's Looking Over your Shoulder" (2015) 43 *J Adolescence* 5.

205 Children's Commissioner for England, *Keeping Kids Safe* (2019).

206 As, for instance, in the case of Aaron Campbell, a 16-year-old who abducted V, aged 6, from her home, raped her and then strangled her. He received a life sentence for murder with a minimum term of 27 years: *The Guardian*, 21 March 2019.

# 20

# DEFENCES OF CIRCUMSTANTIAL PRESSURE

The defences explored in this chapter are linked by the common feature of circumstantial pressure: D may have satisfied the definitional elements of an offence, but we recognise that D was faced with a (morally) impossible choice. These defences are not marking a concession to *individual* frailty; we do not excuse D because of his unique response to the pressures faced. Rather, and explicitly, these are concessions to *human* frailty in general, we are excusing D because we concede that any reasonable person in D's position might have acted similarly. As the adage goes, "there but for the grace of God, go I". It should be no surprise, therefore, that defences in this chapter are marked by their reliance on objective criteria, measuring D's conduct against reasonable standards of steadfastness under pressure. Perhaps more surprising though, as we will discuss, has been the progressive narrowing of the potential application of these defences across several appellate court decisions.[1]

Each defence is marked by a particular source and/or degree of circumstantial pressure. In what follows, we discuss: (1) duress by threats; (2) duress of circumstances; (3) slavery or trafficking; (4) superior orders; and (5) entrapment.

## § 20.1 Duress by threat

The common law has long conceded that if prima facie crimes (excluding murder, attempted murder, and probably treason) are committed under threat of immediate or almost immediate death, serious bodily harm, or (more recently) rape, D may warrant an acquittal. The rationale for this concession is debated. One argument has been that the deterrent force of the criminal law is ineffective when competing with countervailing threats of this kind. It is sound utilitarian theory to confine the imposition of sanctions to circumstances where they will secure likely compliance. Why make an uncertain threat of future imprisonment or fine in the face of an unyielding and certain threat of death, serious bodily harm, or rape?[2] The point is well made in respect of individual deterrence. In terms of general deterrence, however, it may be thought particularly appropriate for the criminal law to be at its most unyielding when privately organised violence undermines its official sanctions, an

[1] On compulsion and the criminal law more generally, see Edwards, "Coercion and Compulsion—Re-imagining Crimes and Defences" [2016] *Crim LR* 876.

[2] For this reason, Bentham approved the provision of a defence of duress: *Introduction to the Principles of Morals and Legislation* (1789) chap. xiv, para. 11.

argument not without force in a time of terrorist organisations and violent gangs.[3] Alternatively, it is possible to subscribe to general deterrence as a justifying principle for state punishment, while insisting that the infliction of a sanction upon a particular individual should satisfy the demands of justice.[4] From the perspective of just deserts, it would be unacceptably Draconian to punish persons who have acted to avoid catastrophic harm to themselves, or to those to whom they are attached or feel responsible.[5] For the most part, this last sentiment reflects the current state of English law.

Duress is commonly regarded as the quintessential excuse, a concession to human frailty: a conception of the defence endorsed by the House of Lords in *Hasan*.[6] On most occasions, it does indeed operate as an excuse. D might be worthy of praise were he to resist the coercion, and his failure to do that may be wrongful; but we excuse him because he *understandably* did the wrong thing by submitting to the pressure. Yet this analysis is not always appropriate. Suppose that D, a taxi-driver, is carrying X, an armed man, in his cab. X instructs D to park the vehicle outside a tobacconist's so that he may purchase cigarettes. D observes that parking is prohibited on the road adjacent to the shop; but X responds that he will blow D's brains out unless he does as he is told. It would be perverse to say that we *excuse* D for parking in the wrong place. He would have acted permissibly, such is the disparity of the respective harms.[7] Where the balance of harms is finer, the pressure exerted on D is largely why we exonerate him. But where the discrepancy between the cost of complying with the letter of the law and the value of yielding to the threat is of the magnitude of our taxi-driver example, his act is surely justifiable. Whether excused or justified, however, he qualifies for the defence of duress.

Regardless of whether, in particular cases, the emphasis is on excusatory pressure or on justifiable choice, duress operates as a "pure" supervening defence. A plea of duress leaves intact the definitional elements of the offence charged. It is only when those elements have been proved against D that we need turn to duress as a way of avoiding the conviction that would otherwise follow. While, on occasion, attempts have been made to explain the defence of duress on the ground that, to be successful, it must negate actus reus or mens rea, we concur with the observation by Lord Bingham in *Hasan* that "where duress is established it does not ordinarily operate to negative any legal ingredient of the crime".[8]

For centuries, duress has involved situations where D committed a crime nominated by X, the person issuing the threat. More recently, the boundaries of the defence were significantly enlarged, accommodating situations now known as "duress of circumstances". These

[3] "Criminal law is itself a system of compulsion on the widest scale. It is a collection of threats of injury to life, liberty, and property if people do commit crimes. Are such threats to be withdrawn as soon as they are encountered by opposing threats?": Stephen, *History of the Criminal Law of England* (1883) vol. II, 107–8.

[4] Hart, *Punishment and Responsibility* (1968) chap. 7.

[5] Some theorists, such as Schopp, believe that a conviction should be recorded against D; but not even he requires D to be punished. Schopp's views are discussed below, § 20.1(iv).

[6] [2005] UKHL 22, [2005] 2 AC 467, [18] (Lord Bingham).

[7] Under the rubric of duress (unlike that of necessity) we do not acquit D *for* doing the right thing: we acquit because he was under threat of death and acted in response to that threat. But where the disparity between what the duressor requires and what the duressor threatens is great, it seems right to conclude that D was justified in acting as he did unless we accord some transcendental value to compliance with the letter of the law. See Simester, *Fundamentals*, chap. 17.

[8] [2005] UKHL 22, [2005] 2 AC 467, [18]. However, his Lordship took the view that duress always operates in the realm of excuse; contrasting with the view expressed here that, according to circumstances, duress may be variously excusatory or justificatory. We discuss the nature and rationale of duress further below, § 20.1(iv).

are cases where the threat and demand need not be identified in another person: D (or another) is under threat of death, serious harm or rape and, in order to avoid the harm, D, on his own initiative, commits what ordinarily would be a crime. Duress of circumstances is now established as a discrete subdivision of the defence, and we discuss it below at § 20.2.[9] In this section we will examine duress in its traditional sense: a threat of death, serious injury, or rape by X which will be lifted only if D commits a crime nominated by X.

As we set out below, the two core elements of duress focus on X's threat and demand, and then on D's response to that threat. However, before applying the elements of duress, we must first ensure that the offence type and/or circumstances do not exclude its potential application.

| | |
|---|---|
| *Exclusions*: | Duress will not apply to (a) certain offences, and (b) in circumstances of prior fault. |
| *Element 1*: | X's threat and demand: X causes D to reasonably believe that D, or another he is responsible for, will immediately suffer death, serious injury, or rape from X unless D commits an offence. |
| *Element 2*: | D's response: D commits the offence demanded by X because his will is overborne, having shown reasonable steadfastness. |

### *(i) Exclusions*

We explore two types of exclusion in this section: the first relates to the type of offence D has committed; the second to D's conduct preceding the threat from X. If either exclusion applies then duress is not available, regardless of whether the elements of the defence are otherwise satisfied.

#### *(a) Excluded offences*

The defence of duress will *not* apply where D has committed murder, attempted murder, and at least certain forms of treason.[10] Beyond this, duress is a general defence, applying to all offences, including those of strict liability.[11]

For murder or attempted murder, then, D's resistance to a threat of death, serious injury, or rape must be unwavering. In *Howe*,[12] the House of Lords ruled that duress could not be

[9] The recognition of "duress by circumstances" has helped prepare the way for an unequivocal recognition of a defence of necessity in English law. In this chapter we will examine the borderland between duress of circumstances and necessity, but we will defer a full consideration of the defence of necessity to § 21.4.

[10] We discuss the exclusion of murder and attempted murder immediately below. On duress and treason, see *Purdy* (1946) 10 JCL 182 (duress applicable to a British prisoner of war forced to assist German propaganda in the Second World War) and *Steane* [1947] KB 997, 1005 (CA).

[11] But note the decision of the Divisional Court in *Hampshire County Council v E* [2007] EWHC 2584 (Admin), where the defence of duress was considered to be inapplicable to the strict liability/status offence based on child truancy from school. Yet there are decisions, such as *Martin* [1989] 1 All ER 652 (CA), where duress has been found applicable to a strict liability offence (driving without a valid licence). In *E*, the particular nature of the offence charged was stressed: namely, to be a parent of a child of compulsory school age failing to attend school regularly contrary to s. 444(1) of the Education Act 1996. According to the Court, liability did not require any voluntary act or omission on the part of a defendant parent; the fact of non-attendance sufficed for liability. On that impoverished view of the sufficient conditions for criminal liability there is a certain logic in excluding duress as a defence for absolute (as interpreted) status offences. For further criticism of this Draconian style of interpretation, see above, § 18.3.

[12] [1987] AC 417.

invoked as a defence to murder, whether D's involvement was as a principal or an accomplice.[13] In *Gotts*,[14] the House of Lords held that the rule in *Howe* extended to cases of attempted murder. On the other hand, in *Ness*,[15] there was a ruling at trial that duress could be raised as a defence to conspiracy to murder.[16] The position is even more anomalous for a person who intentionally causes grievous bodily harm (that is to say, acts with a sufficient mens rea for murder), who may raise a defence of duress if his victim should survive the attack. The anomaly, of course, arises from the constructive nature of murder, which introduces a significant element of luck into liability for such crimes.[17]

The exclusion of murder and attempted murder from the defence of duress is too rigid. Lord Hailsham, arguing in favour of the current law, stated that to allow the defence in such cases would be to vindicate "the coward and the poltroon".[18] Heroism is a quality to be praised, but it does not follow that its absence is reason for censure. There will be occasions where we would expect even a person of reasonable firmness to be coerced into participating in murder, for example if a taxi-driver were to find his cab commandeered by armed terrorists and himself ordered at gunpoint to be the driver for a terrorist operation. It cannot be right that the taxi-driver will receive the same mandatory sentence as those who threatened him and who carried out the killings. And the same inflexibility applies to youngsters. In *Wilson*,[19] a boy of 13 was pressurised by his father to assist in the killing of V. The exclusion of the defence was confirmed by the Court of Appeal despite its recognition that D was unable to resist his violent and overbearing father. It is noteworthy that in the context of a case where he was seeking to narrow the defence of duress, Lord Bingham stated that the argument for the extension of the defence to murder was, in logic, "irresistible".[20] The Law Commission has also recommended extension of the defence to murder,[21] but no related legislation has been brought forward.

### (b) *Prior-fault exclusion: Voluntary exposure to threats*

Duress may not be available as a defence if D voluntarily associates with persons who resort to violence when committing offences, or joins an organisation aware that the infliction of violence is one of its organising principles. So, if D joins a terrorist organisation or an organised criminal gang, it will not excuse him that he was later faced with a choice

[13] *Howe* overruled *Lynch* [1975] AC 653, where the House of Lords had permitted duress to be raised to *complicity* in murder, and confirmed *Abbott* [1976] 3 All ER 140, where the Privy Council had denied a defence of duress to murder as a principal.

[14] [1992] 2 AC 412.

[15] [2011] Crim LR 645 (CA).

[16] See also *Moss (Caryn)* [2023] UKPC 28. The Privy Council was prepared (*obiter*) to accept that duress could be a defence to conspiracy to murder.

[17] See above, § 6.5 (moral luck and constructive liability), and § 10.3 (constructive liability in murder).

[18] *Howe* [1987] AC 417, 432. For more on *Howe* and the reasons duress was excluded as a potential defence to murder, see Stark, "*R v Howe*" in Handler et al (eds.), *Landmark Cases in Criminal Law* (2017) 309; Elkington, "The Historical Development of Duress and the Unfounded Result of Denying Duress as a Defence to Murder" (2023) 87 *J Crim L* 207.

[19] [2007] EWCA Crim 1251, [2007] 2 Cr App R 31.

[20] *Hasan* [2005] UKHL 22, [2005] 2 AC 467, [21].

[21] Law Com. No. 304, *Murder, Manslaughter and Infanticide* (2006) Part 6. The Law Commission's proposal placed the burden of proof on D and required that there must be an immediate threat of fatal harm.

between offending and suffering "discipline" involving serious physical harm.[22] This is a salutary principle, an important limitation on the capacity of an intrinsically violent organisation to provide its membership with immunity from wrongdoing. Nonetheless, it should be open to D to contend that he has left the organisation, or dissociated himself from his acquaintances, of his own volition; thereafter, he should not be precluded from raising the defence.[23] Additionally, D should not lose the defence if he was made to join the gang by a threat of imminent violence which continued thereafter and culminated in the commission of an offence.

The exclusionary doctrine was bolstered by the decision of the House of Lords in *Hasan*.[24] D had worked as driver and minder for E, who ran an escort agency. After X, a violent drug dealer, became E's boyfriend, D was ousted from his role. Nonetheless, D and X remained in contact. Subsequently, X ordered D to carry out a burglary in the company of another person, F, informing D that F would kill him unless the crime was carried out. On these facts, the House of Lords ruled that any claim of duress must fail.[25]

> "The policy of the law must be to discourage association with known criminals, and it should be slow to excuse the criminal conduct of those who do so. If a person voluntarily becomes or remains associated with others engaged in criminal activity in a situation where he knows or ought reasonably to know that he may be the subject of compulsion by them or their associates, he cannot rely on the defence of duress to excuse any act which he is thereafter compelled to do by them."

The width of this statement should be emphasised. The fact of association is enough: D's association with X need not involve any joint criminal activity. Presumably D must know that X is a criminal, although Lord Bingham does not explicitly state this. Once the fact of association is proved, D will be denied access to the defence of duress if he ought reasonably to have known that X might subject him to compulsion, or that X might threaten him or be violent to him. It is not necessary that D should have reasonably anticipated that X might coerce him into the commission of a crime.

In *Hasan*, Baroness Hale expressed an understandable fear that women in relationships with violent men might be denied the defence merely on the basis that they should have foreseen that X might coerce and/or threaten them in the course of the relationship. She would insist that D should be proved to have foreseen that X would coerce them into committing a crime. Lady Hale thought that this test would have been satisfied on the facts of *Hasan*. The majority disavowed that limitation, confirming an earlier decision, *Harmer*.[26] There, D was coerced by E into smuggling Class A drugs. D was a drug addict and was aware of the risk that E might be violent to him should he fail to pay on time for drugs supplied. D had not anticipated that E would coerce him into committing criminal acts to clear his indebtedness. Nonetheless, the Court of Appeal upheld the ruling of the trial judge in refusing D a defence of duress. The fact that D was aware of the risk of violence from E

[22] *Sharp* [1987] QB 853 (CA). (An organised criminal gang: D was threatened with being shot when seeking to withdraw from a robbery; a defence of duress was denied.)

[23] An analogy might be drawn with the defence of withdrawal, which allows D to extricate herself from liability as a secondary party if she has acted sufficiently to extinguish her previous assistance or encouragement of P. See above, § 7.6(vi).

[24] [2005] UKHL 22, [2005] 2 AC 467.

[25] *Ibid*., [38].

[26] [2001] EWCA Crim 2930.

should he form an association with him precluded any reliance on E's threats as a form of duress. The exclusion of duress does not require foresight of coercion by X to commit an offence.

### *(ii) Element 1: X's threat and demand*

Duress is not a simple "balance of evils" defence, applicable whenever the harm avoided is greater than the harm perpetrated. Rather, X's threat must meet particular thresholds of seriousness; it must constitute an "immediate" threat, and X must "nominate" a particular offence for D to commit.

#### *(a) The seriousness of the threat*

The threat must be to inflict immediate, or almost immediate, death, serious bodily harm,[27] or rape.[28] No other threats are regarded, in law, as having sufficient coercive effect.[29] It is easy to envisage how other kinds of threat, e.g. to destroy a thriving business, or to expose details of a person's personal life, might be extremely effective in undermining resistance. Nonetheless, as a matter of policy, a threat of at least serious bodily harm is insisted upon. Whether threats of serious psychiatric harm will be sufficient remains unclear. Despite Court of Appeal authority in 1997 indicating that only *physical* harms would suffice for duress,[30] the long recognition of serious psychiatric injury as a form of grievous bodily harm (in the context of non-fatal offences against the person)[31] makes its exclusion from duress increasingly anomalous.[32]

Beyond this, there seems little immediate prospect of a more liberal approach. In *Quayle*,[33] the Court of Appeal refused to enlarge the notion of bodily harm to accommodate physical *pain*, even extreme physical pain.[34] Moreover, in *Hasan*, the House of Lords took judicial notice of the increasing recourse to duress as a defence, especially in relation to drug dealing and associated offences, and of the difficulty experienced by prosecutors in disproving the elements of the defence (particularly when it is raised late in the day). These considerations have prompted an overt policy to confine the defence within narrow limits.[35] In this climate, we may assume that a rigid requirement for threats of death, serious harm, or rape will remain an essential condition of duress for the foreseeable future.

[27] There are many authorities which insist that only death or serious harm will suffice; they are confirmed in an authoritative review of the defence by *Hasan* [2005] UKHL 22, [2005] 2 AC 467.

[28] The Court of Appeal accepted in *A(RJ)* [2012] EWCA Crim 434, [2012] 2 Cr App R 8, and *CS* [2012] EWCA Crim 389, [2012] 1 WLR 3081, that in principle a threat of rape could lead to duress being raised as a defence.

[29] In *Steane* [1947] KB 997, 1005 (CA), Goddard LCJ spoke, *obiter*, in terms of false imprisonment constituting adequate duress but in *Dao* [2012] EWCA Crim 1717, false imprisonment was not considered sufficient to raise duress. In *Valderrama-Vega* [1985] Crim LR 220 (CA), financial pressures and sexual blackmail were thought not to constitute legally adequate duress.

[30] *Baker* [1997] Crim LR 497 (CA).

[31] *Burstow* [1998] AC 147; above, § 11.5(i)(a).

[32] The expansion of the current list to include rape in 2012 demonstrates that there is some potential for the list to grow, at least to reflect developments in the law elsewhere.

[33] [2005] EWCA Crim 1415, [2005] 1 WLR 3642.

[34] The Court of Appeal required "extraneous circumstances capable of objective scrutiny by judge and jury" (*ibid.*, [75]).

[35] [2005] UKHL 22, [2005] 2 AC 467, [21].

*(b) The threat must be immediate or almost immediate and unavoidable*

The immediacy of the threatened harm is an important requirement. At one time, the courts showed a degree of sensitivity and realism in applying this criterion. In *Hudson*,[36] D gave false testimony when she observed X staring at her intently as she was about to give evidence in a criminal trial involving defendants with a well-founded reputation for serious violence. D knew X was associated with the defendants: the previous evening, X had visited D's house and threatened to "cut her up" if she testified against them. D accordingly gave false testimony. On appeal against D's conviction for perjury, the Court of Appeal ruled that a defence of duress should have been left to the jury. The Court took the view that a threat may be "present" or operative despite a delay in its implementation. Whereas the trial judge had been of the view that the defence must fail as D was safe in court when giving her perjured testimony, for the Court of Appeal it was enough that the threats could have been implemented later that day on the streets of Salford.[37]

In *Abdul-Hussain*,[38] the Court of Appeal suggested that "imminent" was a more appropriate term than immediate and, certainly, an imminent rather than an immediate harm was at issue in *Hudson*. At the same time, "imminence" must still be understood as referring to something due to happen in the very near future. In *Cole*,[39] the Court of Appeal was, it is submitted, right to reject a defence of duress to robbery when D robbed building societies in order to pay debts on a due date, hoping thereby to avoid violence on a later date. Indeed, the decision in *Abdul-Hussain* itself was questionable on its facts. D and others hijacked a plane in order to travel to England from Sudan. They had good reason to fear that the Sudanese authorities might deport them to Iraq (where they were likely to be tortured and killed) at some time yet to be resolved. The Court of Appeal ruled that the trial judge was wrong to remove the issue of duress from the jury on the grounds of a lack of immediately threatened harm, characterising the threat as present and ongoing. Arguably, a stricter view of imminence should be taken if the defence is to be kept within manageable bounds. That concern was very much in the mind of the House of Lords in *Hasan*. Although the matter did not fall for decision, Lord Bingham in his majority judgment specifically approved of the approach in *Cole* and disapproved of what he felt was a lax approach to the immediacy requirement in *Hudson* and, particularly, *Abdul-Hussain*,[40] where the risk would crystallise only at some future date. In the view of the majority, the implementation of the threat must follow "immediately or almost immediately".[41]

So it seems that "imminence" is not enough. It is possible, even in the light of Lord Bingham's stricter approach in *Hasan*, to distinguish between *Hudson* and *Abdul-Hussain*. In *Abdul-Hussain*, the prospect of return to Iraq at the time of the hijack in Sudan was real but subject to contingencies and an uncertain timeline. In *Hudson*, by contrast, X was present

[36] [1971] 2 QB 202 (CA).

[37] By way of corollary, the Court of Appeal insisted that a realistic view should be taken of the degree of police protection available to D.

[38] [1999] Crim LR 570 (CA).

[39] [1994] Crim LR 582 (CA); below, § 20.1(ii)(c).

[40] Baroness Hale was the only other member of the House of Lords who gave a judgment on the duress aspect of *Hasan* and she favoured a rather less strict attitude to the defining conditions of the defence than did the other members of the bench (who concurred with Lord Bingham). The matter was *obiter* since, as discussed above at § 20.1(i)(b), the House concurred unanimously that duress should be unavailable because D had voluntarily exposed himself to the risk of being coerced to commit offences.

[41] [2005] UKHL 22, [2005] 2 AC 467, [28].

in court looking intently at D as she gave evidence; and it was accepted that there was a real possibility that X and others would inflict serious violence on D later that same day. It is noteworthy that Baroness Hale, in a separate judgment in *Hasan*, considered that the other members of the House were overly concerned with denying the defence to criminals and their associates and insufficiently sensitive to the awful dilemmas that may confront vulnerable and innocent people caught up in the violence of others and beyond effective protection from the police and other agencies. Unfortunately, the more sympathetic attitude of Baroness Hale has not attracted judicial support. In *Batchelor*,[42] Lord Bingham's reservations concerning the decision in *Hudson* were adopted and reinforced: "The teenaged girls were no doubt in genuine and real fear of their safety in *Hudson* but that was not a justification for applying the defence of duress, because they had the opportunity to avoid the threat."[43] In *Batchelor*, D had not reported his difficulties to the police, because he had been told that his children would be tortured should he do so. His failure to contact the authorities precluded any reliance on the defence of duress.[44]

In addition to being immediate or almost immediate, the threat must also be unavoidable.[45] The exculpatory force of duress is based on the lack of viable alternatives: commit the offence or be killed (or seriously hurt, or raped). If there is a "safe avenue of escape", that should be taken.[46] Similarly, if effective protection is available to D, her defence of duress is likely to fail.[47] This was the case in *Johnson*,[48] where D provided false testimony on the instruction of her abusive partner. In rejecting D's plea of duress, the Court of Appeal made specific reference to a series of opportunities available for D to escape, including offers of alternative housing or admission to a refuge facility.

In practice, immediacy will in most circumstances be strongly linked with unavoidability. But they are separable: as when X points a knife at D and threatens to stab her forthwith unless she hands over the keys to the bank's safe, but D makes her escape through a side door. If the threat is not of almost immediate application, then, as Lord Bingham put it in *Hasan*, "there may be little if any room for doubt that [D] could have taken evasive action, whether by going to the police or in some other way".[49] But on particular facts, a less than completely immediate threat may nonetheless be in substance unavoidable: as the Court of Appeal recognised on the facts of *Hudson*.[50] Yet, from the negative attitude to that decision on the part of the majority in *Hasan*, it seems that a threat must be unavoidable *and* almost immediate. The fact that D acted as she did because she believed, entirely reasonably, that

[42] [2013] EWCA Crim 2638.

[43] *Ibid.*, [15].

[44] It seems that any physical opportunity to contact the police must be taken, regardless of the consequences. In the Australian case of *Taiapa* [2009] HCA 53, D drove to collect drugs on the order of X after D, his pregnant wife, and his mother had been threatened at gunpoint by X. Despite the fact that D's wife and mother were placed in great and immediate danger, his failure to drive to the police rather than collect the drugs entailed the failure of his plea of duress: "an unparticularised concern that police protection may not be a guarantee of safety cannot without more supply reasonable grounds for a belief that there is no option other than to break the law in order to escape the execution of a threat" (at [40]).

[45] "No one could question that if a person can avoid the effects of duress by escaping from the threats, without damage to himself, he must do so": *Sharp* [1987] QB 853, 857 (Lord Lane CJ) (CA).

[46] *Gill* [1963] 2 All ER 688 (CA); *Hurley and Murray* [1967] VR 526; *N* [2007] EWCA Crim 3479.

[47] *Hudson* [1971] 2 QB 202 (CA); *Baker* [1999] 2 Cr App R 335 (CA).

[48] [2022] EWCA Crim 832.

[49] [2005] UKHL 22, [2005] 2 AC 467, [28]. Cf., in Australia, *Taiapa v R* [2009] HCA 53, [31ff].

[50] [1971] 2 QB 202 (CA).

she would die or be very seriously hurt if she did not is insufficient. It is difficult to see how such an unyielding approach will not lead to convictions of some defendants who are entirely blameless. It is also unfortunate that such a central requirement of the defence of duress exists in this state of doctrinal uncertainty.

### (c) *Nomination of the crime*

Duress by threats includes an explicit requirement that the threatener must specify D's crime. By contrast, in *Cole*,[51] D was ordered by X to make timely repayment of a debt or suffer serious harm. Consequently, he robbed a branch of a building society in order to obtain money to repay X. D was refused a defence of duress, *inter alia* because X had not *nominated*, expressly or impliedly, the crime D should commit. Robbing a building society was, rather, D's response to the predicament posed by X.

Historically, *Cole* is in line with the common law on duress by threats.[52] Yet it is hard to discern what normative significance nomination has. Moreover, any requirement of nomination would appear now to be superseded by the evolution of the new subcategory of duress known as duress of circumstances (below, § 20.2). Under that head of duress, it is enough that D commits the offence (short of murder or attempted murder) as a response to an imminent threat of death, serious injury, or rape.[53] From D's perspective, the moral and legal issues at stake in duress by threats and duress of circumstances are essentially the same. Arguably, the nomination requirement should be abandoned for duress more broadly. *Cole* itself can be explained on the basis of the finding that, in any event, the threat was insufficiently immediate.

### (d) *Indirect threats*

Typically, the threat will be made directly by X to D. But what matters is whether it was reasonable for D to believe that she, her immediate family, or someone she felt responsible for was under imminent threat of death, serious bodily harm, or rape from X, by whatever route the threat was communicated. In *Brandford*,[54] D was told by her boyfriend, E, that, unless E dealt in Class A drugs for X, E would shortly be killed by X. D agreed to help E supply drugs to buyers. The prosecution argued that what was required to defend herself from a charge of conspiracy to deal drugs was evidence of some direct communication of the threat from X himself. The Court of Appeal disagreed: depending upon the circumstances a threat may be (or reasonably seem to be) very real even if indirectly relayed.[55]

Just as the paradigm of duress involves direct threats from X, so the recipient of those threats will invariably be D herself. Indeed, the essence of the defence is the pressure that the threat exerts on D herself, a threat sufficient to sway a person of reasonable firmness. But the pressure on D may be equally or even more intense should the threat be targeted against E, the husband, or child or any other person closely connected with D. The defence

[51] [1994] Crim LR 582 (CA).

[52] *Hudson* [1971] 2 QB 202 (CA); *DPP for NI v Lynch* [1975] AC 653.

[53] The Court of Appeal discussed some duress of circumstance cases but considered that the offences which fell to be excused under that head were, unlike the robberies in *Cole*, "spontaneous" reactions to the threats. The adjective is unhelpful. In every case they were *chosen* reactions, offences committed under the volition of the defendants and unnominated by anyone else.

[54] [2016] EWCA Crim 1794, [2017] 4 WLR 17.

[55] *Ibid.*, [39].

of duress accommodates such situations,[56] and there is every reason in principle why it should. D may be able to resist a threat to herself yet be unable to resist where the threat of death, serious harm, or rape is directed at a loved one. Indeed, the defence of duress should not be constrained by any closed list of relationships. Suppose that X, a bank robber, threatens to shoot a customer unless D, a bank employee, hands over the key to the safe. It is easy to imagine how D may feel constrained to comply.[57] In *Hasan*, Lord Bingham stated that the threat could be to D, his immediate family, and to any "person for whose safety the defendant would reasonably regard himself as responsible".[58] "Responsibility" here is not restricted to those whom the law would regard as dependents; in *Brandford*, the Court of Appeal accepted that D's fear that her boyfriend might be killed by X was a sufficiently compelling threat to place her under duress.[59]

### (e) *What if D's belief in the threat is mistaken?*

Sometimes, D may believe that a threat of death, serious injury, or rape exists when that is not in fact the case. Here, duress will remain available as long as D's belief was *reasonably* held.

In *Graham*,[60] the Court of Appeal considered that if D reasonably believed in the existence of circumstances that would have given a sober person of reasonable firmness good cause to fear death or serious injury, then he was entitled to raise the defence. Confusingly, in a later case, *Martin (David)*,[61] the Court of Appeal endorsed a subjective approach to mistaken duress, and seemed to take the same view in *Safi*.[62] In *Hasan*, however, the requirement for a reasonable mistake was reaffirmed by the House of Lords.[63] Although the affirmation was *obiter*, it was in the course of a wide-ranging review of the defence and should be regarded as settling the issue.

Note the inconsistent approaches taken between duress and self-defence. Beliefs relating to the need to use force in self-defence or the prevention of crime need only be genuine and need not be based on reasonable grounds,[64] whereas belief in the existence of the threat in duress must be based on reasonable grounds. It may well be that these differences are appropriate in their respective fields of application, but these discrepancies have not been addressed in the case law.[65] For cases of self-defence and force used in the prevention of crime, the matter is now clarified by statute: a genuine if unreasonable belief in the need to

[56] *Hurley and Murray* [1967] VR 526 (threats to *de facto* wife); *Ortiz* (1986) 83 Cr App R 173 (CA) (assumption that threats to wife and daughter would suffice); *Martin* [1989] 1 All ER 652 (CA) (offending to ward off a threat of suicide by wife). In *CS* [2012] EWCA Crim 389, [2012] 1 WLR 3081, a threat of sexual abuse to a daughter was considered capable of raising a defence of duress provided the abuse would constitute rape. The defence failed for other reasons.

[57] It is noteworthy that in *Conway* [1989] QB 290 (CA), the threat constituting duress of circumstances was to D's passenger rather than D. The Court did not investigate the nature of the relationship between D and the passenger. Law Com. No. 177, *Draft Criminal Code* (1989), cl. 42, refers to threats "to cause death or serious personal harm to himself *or another*" (emphasis added).

[58] [2005] UKHL 22, [2005] 2 AC 467, [21]–[23].

[59] [2016] EWCA Crim 1794, [2017] 4 WLR 17, [46].

[60] [1982] 1 All ER 801, 806 (CA); see too *Cairns* [1999] 2 Cr App R 137 (CA).

[61] *Martin* [2000] 2 Cr App R 42 (CA). The favouring of an objective approach in *Graham* had been approved, *obiter*, by the House of Lords in *Howe* [1987] AC 417.

[62] [2003] Crim LR 721 (CA).

[63] [2005] UKHL 22, [2005] 2 AC 467, [23].

[64] Below, § 21.2(ii).

[65] See Alldridge, "Developing the Defence of Duress" [1986] *Crim LR* 433.

use force may form the basis of a defence provided the force used was proportionate to the circumstances that D believed to exist.[66]

What of duress cases where D's mistaken belief is caused, at least in part, by a mental or physical disorder? Suppose that D, a person with paranoid schizophrenia, misconstrues an impatient remark by X about D's delay in repaying a loan as a threat to kill him unless the debt is repaid by stealing from V. As a result, D steals from V. If D wished to raise mistaken duress as a defence to theft, there would seem little scope for D to bring his condition into play when evaluating whether his belief in a death threat was reasonable. The fact that the belief is attributable to his mental disorder undermines any claim that it was reasonable.

### (iii) Element 2: D's response

Duress is only available where D is genuinely coerced into committing an offence, having demonstrated (at least) reasonable levels of resistance.

#### (a) Resistance to the threat

In *Graham*, the Court of Appeal ruled that the threat made by X must, in all the circumstances, have been enough to overcome the resistance of a "sober person of reasonable firmness".[67] Recall that the threat must be a threat of imminent death, serious bodily harm, or rape. One might consider that most persons of reasonable firmness would succumb to pressure of that extreme kind. However, the decision in *Graham*, which was approved by the House of Lords in *Howe*,[68] makes clear that a balancing exercise must be done on each occasion between the threat and the crime that X requires D to commit. The more serious the offence and the greater its impact on innocent third parties, the more that is to be expected of D by way of resistance. As Lords Wilberforce and Edmund-Davies remarked in *Abbott*, "the more dreadful the circumstances of the [crime], . . . the stronger and more irresistible the duress needed before it could be regarded as affording any defence".[69]

#### (b) A sober person of reasonable firmness

What characteristics constitute the sober person of reasonable firmness? This notional person may be attributed the age and sex of the defendant and must be assumed to be sober.[70] If the defendant is pregnant, so too is the notional person.[71] Unsurprisingly, timidity and pliancy were held in *Graham* to be irrelevant: to attribute them to the reasonable person would have been to contradict the objective yardstick of reasonable firmness.[72]

[66] Criminal Justice and Immigration Act, s. 76(4), (6); below, § 21.2.
[67] [1982] 1 All ER 801, 806 (CA).
[68] [1987] AC 417.
[69] [1976] 3 All ER 140, 152 (PC) (dissenting). The comments are made in the context of murder (and, as we shall see, are no longer applicable to that offence), but remain in point for other offences.
[70] In *Graham* [1982] 1 All ER 801, 806 (CA), Lane LCJ drew a direct (and questionable) analogy with provocation (now loss of control) and aligned the "characteristics" applicable to pleas of provocation with characteristics allowed when applying the defence of duress.
[71] *Bowen* [1996] 4 All ER 837, 844 (CA), where there is added fear for the unborn child.
[72] Confirmed in *Bowen*, *ibid.*: "The mere fact that the accused is more pliable, vulnerable, timid, or susceptible to threats than a normal person are not characteristics [*sic*] with which it is legitimate to invest the reasonable/ordinary person for the purpose of considering the objective test".

In *Emery*,[73] the Court of Appeal stated *obiter* that a recognised psychiatric condition or mental illness could be attributed to the person of reasonable firmness. The Court envisaged that a jury could properly be asked what degree of resistance should have been shown by a woman suffering from post-traumatic stress disorder which had resulted in a condition of learned helplessness. Yet, even if D's condition is a product of psychiatric disorder, there seems to be an element of contradiction in attributing learned helplessness to "a woman of reasonable firmness". A possible way of reconciling this position with an objective test is to allow such a condition to be attributed if a woman of reasonable firmness would have been afflicted with learned helplessness had she been subjected to the same experiences as D. However, this rationalisation, which is not made explicit in *Emery*, leads to singularly unattractive distinctions. It is not clear why a state of learned helplessness generated by life's vicissitudes should be treated more favourably than a similar condition which arises from a person's genetic endowment.[74] Arguably, such cases should be dealt with within a liberally drafted defence of diminished responsibility unconfined to cases of murder,[75] rather than by undermining the coherence of the reasonable firmness standard.[76]

What *is* clear, at least, is that any condition which does not amount to a mental illness or psychiatric disorder will not be attributed. The case law excludes, for example, personal characteristics such as "grossly elevated neurotic state",[77] unusual vulnerability to pressure,[78] and lack of firmness arising from sexual abuse.[79]

### *(c) Impact of the threat*

Even if a threat of death, serious harm, or rape has been made, and it would have moved to action a person of reasonable firmness, it does not follow that D will automatically be allowed a defence of duress. She *herself* must be influenced by that threat to commit the crime. If the crime is something she in fact perpetrated for other reasons, the defence is not available. On the other hand, provided the threat was *a* material reason why D committed the crime, it need not have been the sole or even the dominant reason. In *Valderrama-Vega*,[80] D was confronted with threats of financial loss, exposure of his homosexuality, and physical violence. Only the last, of course, qualifies as legal duress. The Court of Appeal held that D was entitled to raise a defence of duress if it was realistically possible that he would not have committed the crime but for threats of violence. If so, it was immaterial that other pressures were operating at the same time. Likewise, in *Brandford*,[81] D became party to a conspiracy to deal drugs with E because of fear for E's life if she did not help him deal

[73] (1993) 14 Cr App R (S) 394 (CA).

[74] For a telling critique of applying an objective standard in duress, see Smith, "Duress and Steadfastness: In Pursuit of the Unintelligible" [1999] *Crim LR* 363.

[75] See Horder, "Pleading Involuntary Lack of Capacity" (1993) 52 *CLJ* 298; Horder, *Excusing Crime* (2004) 183–5.

[76] Recall the similar difficulties which undermined the reasonable person standard in (what was then) provocation, later resolved by reverting to an objective standard tempered only by the sex and age of D: *A-G for Jersey v Holley* [2005] UKPC 23, [2005] 2 AC 580; and adopted within the reformed defence of loss of control, Coroners and Justice Act 2009, s. 54.

[77] *Hegarty* [1994] Crim LR 353 (CA).

[78] *Horne* [1994] Crim LR 584 (CA).

[79] *Hirst* [1995] 1 Cr App R 82 (CA).

[80] [1985] Crim LR 220 (CA).

[81] [2016] EWCA Crim 1794, [2017] 4 WLR 17.

drugs and because she was in love with him. The Court of Appeal accepted that because her offending was due at least in part to her fear that X, who controlled E's drug dealing, might kill E should E not reach his sales targets, duress was available to D, even though maintaining her relationship with E was also a powerful factor.[82]

### *(iv) A rationale of duress*

There has been considerable doctrinal uncertainty concerning why duress should provide a defence. The claim has been made that threats as extreme as death, serious bodily harm, or rape induce conduct which is involuntary and, consequently, not fairly attributable to the person coerced.[83] On this view, duress may even negate the actus reus of the offence. Yet this explanation does not convince. The involuntariness in question in cases of duress is of a less fundamental kind than the physical involuntariness of conduct occurring in a state of automatism or as a consequence of a reflex response.[84] When D commits a crime rather than be killed, she is making a choice, albeit in circumstances not of her own making.[85] Of course, a person choosing between death or committing a crime is making a choice of a different order from that involved in choosing, say, between a winter or summer holiday. Yet the decision to commit the crime is a product of deliberation. It is, in that sense, *her* choice, albeit a constrained one. Even the most coercive of threats is compatible with proof of voluntariness, as English law implicitly recognises when denying the defence of duress to anyone charged with murder.

Alternatively, it has been asserted that duress of sufficient potency is incompatible with a finding of mens rea.[86] This is equally unconvincing. In English law, the term mens rea is a technical expression, a reference to the mental element required for the offence in question.[87] Sometimes the presence of duress may negate particular forms of mens rea: a manner of driving that would otherwise be accounted "careless" may not deserve that description if, for example, driving as D did was the only way of escaping a threat of death.[88] Yet most often the presence of duress is compatible with proof of mens rea. If D commits crime Z rather than be killed, she does so deliberately. D intends the wrong she commits, even if she regrets having to do so. The exclusion of duress as a defence to murder again underscores this point. Findings that D possessed the mens rea for murder, despite the psychological impact on D of an immediate threat of death, have been made in several cases.[89]

[82] *Ibid.*, [40]. (D's defence failed for other reasons.)

[83] *Per* Widgery LJ in *Hudson* [1971] 2 QB 202, 206 (CA), "It is clearly established that duress provides a defence . . . if the will of the accused has been overborne by threats of death or serious personal injury so that the commission of the alleged offence was no longer the voluntary act of the accused."

[84] Discussed above, § 4.3(i).

[85] "A criminal walking to execution is under compulsion if any man can be said to be so, but his motions are just as much voluntary as if he [were] going to leave his place of confinement and regain his liberty. He walks to his death because he prefers it to being carried": Stephen, *History of the Criminal Law of England* (1883) vol. II, 102.

[86] *Paquette* (1997) 70 DLR (3d) 129.

[87] *Yip Chiu-cheung* [1995] AC 111 (PC); *Kingston* [1995] 2 AC 355.

[88] *Harris* [1995] 1 Cr App R 170 (CA). But see *Backshall* [1999] 1 Cr App R 35, where the Court of Appeal held, on a charge of driving without due care and attention, that the issue of necessity or duress of circumstances would be more clearly resolved by invoking those defences, rather than by assessing whether the driving was done with due care and attention.

[89] See, e.g., *Abbott* [1977] AC 755 (PC).

We conclude, therefore, that duress is generally compatible with proof of the definitional elements of the offence with which the defendant is charged. Schopp has argued that the presence of those definitional elements should entail a conviction because duress does not provide any plausible ground of excuse or justification.[90] Contrasting duress with mistake-based and disability defences, Schopp observes that defendants pleading duress possess the capacities of responsible agents and possess the knowledge with which to exercise these capacities. As he puts it, defendants raising duress "act on action plans that include the acts exemplifying the objective offence elements as intended components".[91] The choice to offend is theirs. Schopp acknowledges that duress may have considerable mitigating force and concedes that in many cases no punishment whatever would be warranted. In order to allow for such cases, he proposes a special verdict to be available, "a purely vindicating conviction" from which no penal consequences would flow. For him, recording a conviction of this special kind would reflect the general community condemnation of conduct which breaches the rules of the criminal law by an agent free from disability and lacking any deficiencies in knowledge or perception.[92] But Schopp radically underestimates the stigmatic impact of a conviction for a serious offence. Allowing duress, in appropriate circumstances, to provide complete exculpation signals that the criminal law, which is a system of *blame* as well as punishment,[93] withholds its censure from conduct that at most demonstrates a failure of virtue. The criminal law does not demand supererogation, let alone perfection. The essence of duress is a pressure to conform to the will of the duressor which not even a person of reasonable firmness could have resisted. When that condition is met, it is defamatory to impose a conviction.

Properly understood, the defence of duress is based on a moral evaluation of D's conduct. It asks whether we can be sure that an ordinary person of reasonable firmness would have done better than D. It is not a disability defence; in principle, it is available to D even though she may have been calm and entirely rational when responding to a threat of death. Sometimes, the jury's task will be easy. Surely, they may conclude, it is better that D gives a burglar the keys to V's house rather than be instantly shot. At other times, intractable decisions may arise: it must be a dreadful thing to be under threat of death at the hands of an oppressive political regime, but it is also dreadful to hijack an aeroplane, spreading insecurity and terror.[94] Either way, in resolving such questions, we can only employ the normative standard of an ordinary person of reasonable firmness with reference to the values and interests at stake in the instant case. It should not be enough to establish duress for a defendant to claim that she failed to resist a threat because of weakness of will or timidity. It *should* be enough for her to answer that only persons of special virtue could have done better.[95]

It has also been argued that the key to the defence of duress is that D must act out of necessity and that duress, along with self-defence and necessity, should be conjoined into a single defence of "necessary action".[96] But there are salient differences between these

[90] Schopp, *Justification Defenses and Just Convictions* (1998) chap. 5.
[91] *Ibid.*, 141.
[92] *Ibid.*, 142–6.
[93] Above, § 1.1(iii).
[94] *Abdul-Hussain* [1999] Crim LR 570 (CA).
[95] Rather than focusing on steadfastness and virtue, it has been argued that the defence would be better understood and constructed as a response to fear: Williams, "Duress and Loss of Control: Fear and Anger in Excusatory Defences" (2020) 71 *Northern Ireland Legal Quarterly* 401.
[96] Clarkson, "Necessary Action: A New Defence" [2004] *Crim LR* 81; contrast Chan and Simester, "Duress, Necessity: How Many Defences?" (2005) 16 *King's College LJ* 121.

currently separated defences. In its pure form, a plea of necessity is a claim that D has done more good than harm by non-compliance with the law. A plausible claim that the world was left a better place is not required, and not the point, in duress. It is neither a necessary nor sufficient condition. Duress differs from self-defence in that the victim of any harmful act done by D will not be the duressor, whereas self-defence is directed at the source of the danger (or a person who, inadvertently or otherwise, is assisting or impeding an effective response to the danger).[97] These differences underscore the distinctiveness of duress as a defence. The threshold is set very high: an immediate threat of death, serious bodily harm, or rape. To insist on steadfast compliance with the letter of the law in the face of such immediate and grave peril is to ask for too much, even in the case of a person of reasonable firmness. Duress is a concession allowed on a more limited basis than the permissions that may be granted within the terms of self-defence and necessity.

## § 20.2 Duress of circumstances

Duress of circumstances has emerged from duress by threats as an alternative defence, mirroring each of the elements of duress by threats discussed in § 20.1 apart from one crucial point of distinction. Whereas duress by threats requires the specific communication of a threat and demand from X, duress of circumstances provides a defence where the threat arises from D's surroundings, including circumstances where it does not originate from another person at all. For example, where D sees a tidal wave approaching, there may be no person telling her to break into a nearby car to make her escape, but the circumstantial duress upon her to do so (i.e. reasonably fearing for her life) is rightly understood as no less excusing.[98]

Again, there are two central elements to the defence, focused on "threat-demand" and "response". The same exclusions of the defence apply.[99]

| | |
|---|---|
| *Exclusions:* | Duress will not apply to (a) certain offences, and (b) in circumstances of prior fault. |
| *Element 1:* | Circumstantial threat and demand: the circumstances cause D to reasonably believe that D, or another he is responsible for, will immediately suffer death, serious injury, or rape unless D commits an offence. |
| *Element 2:* | D's response: D commits the offence because of the threat, having shown reasonable steadfastness. |

### *(i) Duress of circumstances distinguished from duress by threats*

In a sequence of cases—*Willer*,[100] *Conway*,[101] and *Martin*[102]—the Court of Appeal laid the foundation for a "duress of circumstances" defence. The first two cases involved driving

[97] *Richens* [2011] EWCA Crim 1626, [2011] 2 Cr App R 26.
[98] Gardner, "Necessity's Newest Invention" (1991) 11 *OJLS* 125.
[99] The application of prior fault exclusion (on grounds of prior association) is usefully discussed and confirmed in *Phair* [2022] NICA 66. See, further, Taggart, "Duress of Circumstances and Voluntary Association" (2023) 74 *Northern Ireland Legal Quarterly* 388.
[100] (1986) 83 Cr App R 225 (CA).
[101] [1989] QB 290 (CA).
[102] [1989] 1 All ER 652 (CA).

offences; it was ruled on both occasions that a defence of duress should have been left to the jury in the light of evidence that the vehicles had been driven as they had in order to escape X threatening serious violence. These rulings were confirmed in *Martin*, where the Court of Appeal ruled that D should have been allowed to raise a defence of duress in answer to a charge of driving while disqualified. D's wife had threatened to kill herself unless D drove their son to his place of work, and D reluctantly complied.

*Martin* itself can be explained in terms of duress by threats. It is true that the threat was not directed at D, but it was (self-)directed to his wife and there is authority that a threat to one's wife will suffice.[103] Furthermore, the crime that D had to commit was implicit in the terms of the threat. *Conway* and *Willer*, however, clearly entered new territory. In these cases, D responded to the threat by committing a crime of his own choosing. It was certainly not a case of X's directing D to do something. X, on the account offered by D, would have preferred D to do nothing; to stay where he was so that X could inflict violence on him.

Interestingly, there was no suggestion by the Court of Appeal in either decision that any extension of the law had occurred. Prior to these cases, the predominant view was that committing a crime of one's own initiative in order to avoid harm founded, if anything, a plea of necessity rather than duress (unless the circumstances fell within self-defence).[104] Further, it is thought that conduct covered by necessity must be justified conduct; conduct that is merely excused cannot be said to have been necessary. Accordingly, *Willer* and *Conway* advanced the law of excuse-based defences. Properly so. A threat of death or serious bodily harm was present in each case, and the crimes were committed under the pressure of such threats. It is clearly established that if X tells D to drive his car on the pavement or be shot, D would have a defence of duress were he to do as he was told. There seems little justification for treating the circumstances that arose in *Willer* differently merely because D drove of his own initiative onto the pavement to escape being shot. By analogy with duress by threats, it will be sufficient that a person of reasonable firmness would have responded to the pressure in a manner similar to D, provided D's response did not take the form of committing or attempting murder (or certain forms of treason).

One important limitation on the range of threats that D can invoke by way of defence is that the threat must emanate from an external source. D cannot, for example, raise duress of circumstance in answer to a charge of prison escape by reference to the suicidal urges to which his confinement gave rise.[105]

### *(ii) Duress of circumstances distinguished from necessity*

The duress of circumstance cases discussed above were found relevant on the facts of *Pommell*.[106] D was arrested late at night in his bed and in possession of a sub-machine gun. On his account, he came to have the gun because he had persuaded X, who was planning "to shoot some geezer with it", to hand it over to him. D, so his story went, had taken it into his custody in order to hand it to his brother who would turn it over to the police; D would, he said, have done so in the morning but for the inconvenience of his arrest. The trial judge

[103] *Hurley and Murray* [1967] VR 526; *Ortiz* (1986) 83 Cr App R 173 (CA).
[104] See Elliot, "Necessity, Duress and Self-defence" [1989] *Crim LR* 611; Horder, "Self-defence, Necessity and Duress: Understanding the Relationship" (1998) 1 *Canadian J Law & Jurisprudence* 143.
[105] *Rogers and Rose* (1998) 1 Cr App R 143 (CA).
[106] [1995] 2 Cr App R 607 (CA).

had ruled that no defence issue arose on these facts, even assuming them to be true.[107] The Court of Appeal disagreed. Authorities such as *Willer* required his story, if supported by any evidence, to be put to the jury. The prosecution would therefore have to prove that the defence was not made out.

It should be noted that *Pommell* is a different kind of case from any of those discussed in § 20.2(i) above. According to his version of events, D himself was never under any immediate threat or pressure from X. The "geezer" whom X intended to kill was not nearby when D persuaded X to hand over the weapon. What D was doing (on his account) amounted to a responsible exercise in citizenship, unconstrained by any danger or pressure. Here we are dealing with a case of necessity rather than duress. This is indirectly acknowledged by the Court, which uses the expressions "duress" and "necessity" indifferently in its judgment. D seems clearly to have been justified in taking possession of the gun. It is surely better to be in possession of a firearm without a licence than to permit X to follow his murderous path. But where D acts in such a fashion, not under coercion himself, he *must* be justified; whereas duress may be allowed to excuse. Accordingly, *Pommell* may be regarded, at least *sub silentio*, as a case of necessity, a defence to be discussed more fully below.[108]

The same vacillation between necessity and duress occurred in *CS*.[109] In that case, D was charged with the abduction of a child contrary to section 1 of the Child Abduction Act 1984. D claimed that it was necessary to take the child (V) to Spain as she reasonably believed that, in the UK, V was in imminent danger of serious harm arising from sexual abuse by V's father. At the pre-trial hearing and on appeal, reference was made predominantly to the defence of necessity but also to duress of circumstances: the Court of Appeal found it unnecessary to determine whether there was any difference between the two defences.[110]

But differentiation was desirable. Both defences were rejected, firstly on the ground that D lacked any reasonable belief that V was immediately or even imminently threatened with serious bodily harm. A second ground of rejection was that, even if there was a well-founded belief that V was imminently threatened with serious harm, the 1984 Act provided defences of consent and reasonable belief in consent by the parties entitled to access to the child.[111] In the eyes of the Court, the existence of the statutory defences, together with D's right to bring her concerns to a child protection hearing, removed any need for V to resort to self-help. This conflation of duress and necessity obscures recognition of matters which relate to one defence rather than the other.[112] The availability of other solutions to D (besides taking the law into her own hands) was clearly relevant to a plea of necessity,[113]

[107] Remarkably, Mr Pommell subsequently came into possession of a gun for a second time and again was frustrated from handing it into police custody by premature arrest. This time he successfully raised an interesting point in the law of evidence: *Pommell* [1999] Crim LR 576 (CA).

[108] Below, § 21.4.

[109] [2012] EWCA Crim 389, [2012] 1 WLR 3081. And see too *S and L* [2009] EWCA Crim 85, [2009] 2 Cr App R 11, for the treatment of necessity and duress as interchangeable terms and the insistence on an immediate threat of death or serious harm.

[110] *CS* [2012] EWCA Crim 389, [2012] 1 WLR 3081, [15]. Reference could more appropriately have been made to duress by threats because, as discussed above, that form of the defence extends to threats made against persons to whom D feels a sense of responsibility.

[111] Ss. 1(4), 1(5). These defences were hardly in point for D given the state of her relationship with V's father.

[112] Chan and Simester, "Duress, Necessity: How Many Defences?" (2005) 16 *King's College LJ* 121; Stark, "Necessity and Nicklinson" [2013] *Crim LR* 949; cf. Clarkson, "Necessary Action: A New Defence" [2004] *Crim LR* 81.

[113] The Court of Appeal cited *Quayle* [2005] EWCA Crim 1415, [2005] 1 WLR 3642 on this further ground of rejection, a necessity not a duress case. See further below, § 21.4(iii).

a defence which can be raised not only for immediate emergencies but also for ongoing states of affairs and less immediate dangers. But in cases where there is a genuine and reasonable belief in a threat of immediate death, serious harm, or rape there may be no realistic recourse to anything other than self-help.

The lack of understanding of the differences between necessity and duress in *CS* is evident from the Court's opinion that for either defence to apply there must be an immediate threat of death or serious bodily harm. To be sure, there may well arise circumstances of dire emergency where both defences will be in play. But their respective rationales differ. For duress, essentially one is asking whether a person of reasonable firmness and stability would have succumbed to the threat. For necessity, there is a broader question: in the circumstances that D was in (or reasonably believed herself to be in), was departing from the letter of the law a legitimate option? That last question does not always require an emergency involving an immediate threat.[114] Moreover, it can properly be put in cases such as where D acted to save a person with a learning disability from becoming pregnant,[115] or to protect a vulnerable V from the dangers that would arise if V were free to come and go as he pleased.[116] Its availability thus goes beyond the avoidance of death, serious bodily harm, or rape.[117]

Unfortunately, courts continue to conflate duress of circumstance and necessity (and other defences). This is evident in the "Stansted 15" case *Thacker and Ors*,[118] a case involving 15 direct-action protesters who breached the security perimeter fence at London Stansted Airport, erected a scaffolding structure and chained themselves in place to disrupt and prevent a deportation flight chartered by the Home Office. The defendants raised various defences, including duress of circumstance and necessity, but having set them out the Court of Appeal continued with an analysis that conflated both defences.[119] Doing so creates a damaging unclarity in the terms of such defences; here concerning their availability in the context of "political" actions, and where D's motivations may be split between protecting identified individuals from perceived harms and advancing a more general political ideology.[120] As the duress of circumstance defence continues to mature in the common law, recognising and accounting for its distinct terms and distinct excusatory rational remains an essential, if sometimes neglected, task.

## § 20.3 Defence for slavery or trafficking victims

Duress, either by threats or circumstances, provides a certain level of protection for those threatened or compelled to commit crimes, but (as we have discussed) duress is constructed in restrictive terms, and the interpretation of those terms has (progressively) narrowed.[121]

[114] Cf. *Re A (Children)* [2001] Fam 147; below, § 21.4(ii)(e).
[115] *Re F (Mental Patient: Sterilisation)* [1990] 2 AC 1.
[116] *Re L, R v Bournewood Community and NHS Trust, ex parte L* [1999] 1 AC 458.
[117] In *Pipe v DPP* [2012] EWHC 1821 (Admin), the Court ruled that the magistrates should have allowed D to raise the defence of necessity when speeding to take his partner's son to hospital following the failure of the ambulance service to respond to an emergency call. The boy was in great pain following a broken leg but was not in danger of any other serious harm.
[118] [2021] EWCA Crim 97, [2021] QB 644.
[119] *Ibid.*, [90]–[103].
[120] Discussed in Cammiss, Hayes, and Doherty, "Necessity, Non-violent Direct Activism, and the Stansted 15: Reasserting 'Hoffmann's Bargain'" (2022) 86 MLR 1515.
[121] Above, § 20.1-2.

In particular, the threshold requirement of threats of death, serious injury, or rape, and the objective requirement of reasonable fortitude in the face of such threats, means that many defendants—especially defendants from vulnerable groups, unable to meet the standards of the reasonable person—will fall outside of its terms. This has resulted in criticism of duress and calls for it to be interpreted more liberally, either in general or as it applies to certain groups such as abused women.[122] An alternative approach is to maintain a basic level of protection through duress, but to supplement this with more broadly defined, bespoke defences of a similar kind applicable to particular groups of vulnerable defendants. An example of this is the defence for slavery or trafficking victims set out in section 45 of the Modern Slavery Act 2015.[123]

The problems associated with modern-day slavery and people trafficking are well known, with vulnerable people exploited by traffickers and gangs across a number of criminal industries including drug cultivation, sex work, and beyond. Where victims of gangs and traffickers commit offences themselves, as will often be the case in such illegal enterprises, and where their offending has resulted from their exploitation as victims of slavery and/or trafficking (i.e. from their circumstantial pressures), an exculpatory defence is appropriate. Indeed, the provision of a defence in such circumstances is mandated by Article 26 of the Council of Europe Convention on Action Against Trafficking Human Beings.[124] Prior to 2015, defendants in this position would have to rely on duress, if applicable on the facts; or rely on the CPS not to bring a prosecution.[125] The section 45 defence does not replace these options, but it does provide a bespoke supervening defence designed to protect these vulnerable groups.[126]

It is clear from the terms of the defence that it is intended to apply more broadly than the common law duress defence. However, its drafters were equally concerned not to allow the defence to be "abused" by serious criminals. The final construction of the defence represents an uneasy compromise between these two aims.[127]

45. Defence for slavery or trafficking victims who commit an offence

(1) A person is not guilty of an offence if—
- (a) the person is aged 18 or over when the person does the act which constitutes the offence,
- (b) the person does that act because the person is compelled to do it,
- (c) the compulsion is attributable to slavery or to relevant exploitation, and
- (d) a reasonable person in the same situation as the person and having the person's relevant characteristics would have no realistic alternative to doing that act.

[122] See, e.g., Loveless, "Domestic Violence, Coercion and Duress" [2010] *Crim LR* 93.

[123] An earlier example was the defence of marital coercion, which was abolished by s. 177 of the Anti-Social Behaviour, Crime and Policing Act 2014. That defence, which was in any event rarely raised, is discussed in § 20.2 of the fifth edition of this work.

[124] "Each Party shall, in accordance with the basic principles of its legal system, provide for the possibility of not imposing penalties on victims for their involvement in unlawful activities, to the extent that they have been compelled to do so." See also Directive 2011/36/EU, Art. 8.

[125] Informed by DPP guidance, discussed in *CS* [2021] EWCA Crim 134; *DS* [2020] EWCA Crim 285, [2021] 1 WLR 303. Cf. Gregory, "The Modern Slavery Defence" (2022) 81 *CLJ* 470.

[126] In force from 31 July 2015. It has been confirmed in *CS* [2021] EWCA Crim 134 that s. 45 does not apply retrospectively before this date.

[127] Gerry, Pagano, and Hodgetts, "Disorganised Crime: Legal and Evidential Challenges of Raising a Modern Slavery Act 2015 Defence" [2022] Crim LR 961; Muraszkiewicz, "Protecting Victims of Human Trafficking from Liability: An Evaluation of Section 45 of the Modern Slavery Act" (2019) 93 *J Crim L* 10; Laird, "Evaluating the Relationship between Section 45 of the Modern Slavery Act 2015 and the Defence of Duress" [2016] *Crim LR* 395.

(2) A person may be compelled to do something by another person or by the person's circumstances.

(3) Compulsion is attributable to slavery or to relevant exploitation only if—

(a) it is, or is part of, conduct which constitutes an offence under section 1 or conduct which constitutes relevant exploitation, or

(b) it is a direct consequence of a person being, or having been, a victim of slavery or a victim of relevant exploitation.

As with duress, there are three main parts to this defence:

| | |
|---|---|
| *Exclusions:* | Section 45 does not apply to a number of listed offences. |
| *Element 1:* | D must be compelled to offend as a result of his slavery or relevant exploitation. |
| *Element 2:* | A reasonable person (sharing D's characteristics) would have had no realistic alternative but to have acted in the same way. |

An alternative version of the defence is also provided for defendants under the age of 18,[128] allowing causation short of compulsion within element 1, and removing the "no realistic alternative" requirement from element 2.[129]

### *(i) Exclusions*

A striking feature of the section 45 defence is the extent of the offences explicitly excluded from its ambit. Section 45(7) excludes all offences in schedule 4, which provides a list of well over 100 offences, including homicide, non-fatal offences, certain sexual offences, certain property offences, as well as offences related to trafficking. The list reflects the concern, highlighted above, that the section 45 defence should not be available to those committing serious offences: where such offences are committed D will only escape liability where she satisfies all the criteria of a defence such as duress or self-defence.

### *(ii) Defence elements*

There are several progressive features within the section 45 defence, expanding beyond the terms of duress, although much of it remains untested in the courts. Most importantly, the threshold threat required for duress (i.e. death, serious harm, or rape) is not replicated in section 45. Rather, it is sufficient for D to raise evidence of compulsion linked to his slavery or relevant exploitation, which the prosecution carries the burden of disproving.[130] Causal links of this kind may still be difficult to raise in practice,[131] but the broad terms of the defence will allow some flexibility in presenting the full extent and implications of D's circumstances.

[128] Modern Slavery Act 2015, s. 45(4).

[129] On which, see *ADG* [2023] EWCA Crim 1309, [2024] 1 WLR 2027: appeal allowed where the trial judge misdirected the jury having referred to the need for "compulsion" several times in a case where D was under 18 years.

[130] *K(M)* [2018] EWCA Crim 667, [2019] QB 86.

[131] See, e.g., *AGM* [2022] EWCA Crim 920: where a causal link to D's offending was doubted, but her appeal was allowed on other grounds.

Element 2 in the list above is more familiar to the common law defence of duress, requiring D to demonstrate a reasonable level of fortitude in response to compulsion, and denying the defence in circumstances where D could and should have avoided offending (i.e. the "no realistic alternative" test). As with duress, objective requirements of this kind are intended to keep the defence within bounds, providing a concession to general human frailties (as opposed to those of the individual defendant) frailty. D's "relevant circumstances" may be taken into account, but these are explicitly limited in section 45(5) to "age, sex and any physical or mental illness or disability". The danger here, highlighted by various commentators,[132] is that a vulnerable person in D's position, having been trafficked and/or exploited over a period of time, may not demonstrate the same fortitude as the hypothetical reasonable person; and a form of learned helplessness may lead them not to take advantage of reasonable opportunities to escape.

This last possibility was discussed in the case of *N*,[133] in which a Vietnamese national (trafficked into the UK to work in a cannabis factory) appealed against his conviction for cultivation offences *inter alia* on the basis that proceedings should have been stayed (ceased permanently) when his trafficked status became clear. The case centred on the potential for a section 45 defence to have been raised. Responding to the appeal, prosecutors maintained that section 45 was not available on the facts, highlighting D's various opportunities to escape his captors and/or seek protection from the police.[134] As discussed above,[135] it is likely that arguments of this kind would have been sufficient to undermine a claim of duress. However, allowing the appeal, the Court of Appeal criticised the prosecution for "failing to appreciate the reality of the applicant's situation, and his circumstances", and clarified that such circumstances should "include his history at the hands of the traffickers in other countries and resultant fears".[136] This interpretation of section 45 is to be welcomed. If section 45 is to provide protection for the victims of slavery and trafficking, its objective tests must be capable of engaging with the particular circumstances and vulnerabilities of that group.

## § 20.4 Superior orders

Criminal conduct cannot be justified or excused on the basis of the order of a superior, be that superior a public or private official. This is an important constitutional principle, founded on the lack of any dispensing power in English law: officials should not generally have the power to authorise or excuse unlawful acts.[137] A superior order may preclude liability on another ground, however. For example, if D is ordered to destroy property and is instructed that it is the property of his employer, he will lack mens rea for the crime of criminal damage.[138] In general, however, in the absence of a defence of reasonable mistake

[132] See, e.g., Laird, "Evaluating the Relationship between Section 45 of the Modern Slavery Act 2015 and the Defence of Duress" [2016] *Crim LR* 395.

[133] [2019] EWCA Crim 984.

[134] *Ibid.*, [31]–[32]. These included, for example, D being "left apparently unsupervised for days at a time", and having "the necessary characteristics to take opportunities to escape his traffickers".

[135] In § 20.1(ii)(b).

[136] *N* [2019] EWCA Crim 984, [43].

[137] *Entick v Carrington* (1765) 19 St Tr 1029, 95 ER 807.

[138] *James* (1837) 8 C & P 131, 173 ER 429.

of law,[139] a belief that conduct is lawful merely because of the order of a superior will not avail if the mens rea of the offence is present. Accordingly, an undercover police officer committed the offence of drug-trafficking when he took drugs from Hong Kong to Sydney because he knew the item transported to be drugs—the fact that he was part of a police operation to expose and convict drug-traffickers was held to be irrelevant.[140]

The lack of any power on the part of officials to suspend the operation of law is an admirable constitutional principle. However, in the context of criminal trials, it may produce harsh results. To illustrate this, consider a similar scenario to that in *Kelly v Minister of Defence*,[141] a civil action arising from a soldier shooting and killing V, a person whom he took to be a terrorist. V in fact was a joy-rider.[142] Envisage a parallel situation where, in circumstances such as those in *Kelly*, D receives an order from E, his commanding officer, to shoot to kill V. D's options in such circumstances are unenviable: if he refuses the order he might well be court-martialled for disobeying a lawful order, whereas obedience to an unlawful order may lead to a mandatory life sentence. Under the current, uncertain, state of the law it is not clear whether the order would be lawful, so either outcome is possible. A junior soldier is surely in no position to decide these issues. Resolving the important and competing principles at stake in such cases is not easy, particularly as cases such as *Kelly* tend to arise in highly charged political contexts.

## § 20.5 Entrapment

Not infrequently, police and other law enforcement officials resort to forms of encouragement, pressure, or persuasion in order to obtain evidence of criminal activity.[143] For instance, E, a plain-clothes police officer, may present himself as a person anxious to acquire illegal drugs. D may be an unsuspecting drug dealer and supply drugs in response to a first request by E. Alternatively, D may not be a drug dealer but may nonetheless obtain drugs to supply E because E has offered a large sum of money for this service, or because E has frightened him into doing so by some form of threat. There may well arise situations where we can be sure that D would not have committed the offence with which he was charged but for the machinations of E.

In line with the primary theme of this chapter, we have a form of what might (loosely) be thought of as circumstantial pressure—encouragement from E—that provides a potential basis for exculpation. But encouragement alone, short of threats of serious violence (i.e. of the kind giving rise to a defence of duress), provides a weak basis for potential criminal excuse: D may not have committed the offence without E's encouragement, but we

[139] Above, § 18.2.

[140] *Yip Chiu-cheung* [1995] 1 AC 111 (PC). The House of Lords in *Clegg* [1995] 1 AC 482 confirmed, *obiter*, that military orders would not afford a defence.

[141] [1989] NI 341.

[142] *Inter alia*, the soldier was seeking to prevent V from committing terrorist crimes in the future, a permissible justification according to the Court of Appeal of Northern Ireland. The open-ended nature of the contemplated timeframe may be thought problematic on rule of law grounds.

[143] Katz, "Entrapment through the Lens of the Actio Libera in Causa" (2013) 7 *Crim Law and Phil* 587; Kim, "Entrapment, Culpability, and Legitimacy" (2020) 39 *Law & Phil* 67; Hill et al., "The Concept of Entrapment" (2018) 12(4) *Crim Law and Phil* 539; Redmayne, "Exploring Entrapment" in Zedner and Roberts (eds.), *Principles and Values in Criminal Law and Criminal Justice* (2012) 157; Ho, "State Entrapment" (2010) 31 *LS* 71; Squires, "The Problem with Entrapment" (2006) 26 *OJLS* 351.

still expect her to resist such temptations. Entrapment, when it is recognised as a *form of* defence, is singled out because of the special source of that encouragement. The question is whether the state, having caused D to offend, is acting legitimately in then prosecuting her for that crime?

The answer to this question is not straightforward. English law recognises no supervening defence of entrapment.[144] However, where E entraps D through encouragement or threat, if sufficiently egregious, this may give rise to the permanent cessation of proceedings on the basis that the prosecution is an abuse of process (drawing upon D's fair trial rights guaranteed by Article 6(1) of the ECHR and its associated jurisprudence), or the exclusion at the trial of evidence obtained by such means. These are procedural and evidential remedies.

The House of Lords provided some useful guidance on what count as sufficiently egregious methods in the important conjoined appeals of *Loosely* and *A-G's Reference (No. 3 of 2000)*,[145] albeit, unsurprisingly, nothing approaching an exact formula is provided. Much will depend on the nature of the offence, the propensities of the offender, and the difficulties of enforcement. In the broadest of terms, a distinction is drawn between providing D with an unexceptional opportunity to offend—a standard opportunity freely taken—and conduct that provides D with an exceptional opportunity to offend, placing unconscionable pressure on D, such that he commits an offence he would not otherwise have committed. In the latter scenario, the trial court will typically stay the proceedings as an abuse of process.

144 Hence entrapment is only discussed briefly. For a lengthier discussion, see § 20.6 of the 8th edition of this work.

145 [2001] UKHL 53, [2001] 1 WLR 2060. See, further, Ashworth, "Redrawing the Boundaries of Entrapment" [2002] *Crim LR* 161.

# 21

# PERMISSIBLE CONDUCT

In this chapter we explore defences that are linked by a claim of permissible conduct: D has satisfied the definitional elements of an offence, but maintains that her choice to commit the offence was justified in the circumstances. Typically, this involves *both* a claim about the balance of harms (i.e. that the harm avoided by D's offence was greater than the harm inflicted) as well as a claim about reasons or motive (i.e. that D acted for known good reasons).[1] Where both claims are true, far from blaming D, she may well be deserving of praise. For example, where D thwarts a would-be bank robbery by forcibly restraining the robber until the police arrive, she may well commit a prima facie offence against the person—satisfying both the actus reus and mens rea elements—but she has also done the right thing. D's conduct is not simply excused: it is justified.

There is a clear and compelling moral case for defences where D has acted in a permissible way, avoiding many of the uncertain excusatory or exempting thresholds discussed in relation to defences of irresponsibility (Chapter 19) and defences of circumstantial pressure (Chapter 20). But other uncertainties arise. For example, on the distinction between offence and defence elements, there is debate whether "permissible conduct" should require a defence at all. Where D has done the right thing for the right reasons, as with the restraint of the would-be bank robber above, should we provide D with a *defence*, or should we reinterpret or reform the scope of the *offence* elements to ensure such conduct is outwith them?[2]

The application of these rules as "defences" is less controversial, however, where D's ostensibly "good reasons" for offending are based on mistakes, or are contrived. In such cases, it may be that no defence should be available at all, but even where it is, that defence will be excusatory rather than justificatory in nature. D has not done the right thing.

In earlier chapters, we discussed some offence-specific defences that recognise permissible conduct, including the defence of "acting reasonably" when assisting or encouraging crime,[3] and the "lawful excuse" defence that applies to the destroying or damaging of the property of another.[4] This chapter focuses on permissible conduct defences with a general application: (1) consent; (2) self-defence and the prevention of crime; (3) the defence of property; and (4) necessity.

[1] See Dsousa, *Rationale-Based Defences in Criminal Law* (2017); Simester, *Fundamentals*, chap. 18. The position is different where potentially justifying reasons are unknown to D: above, § 17.2.

[2] See, e.g., debates about the status of consent (below, §§ 11.9, 21.1), and "unlawfulness" in the context of self-defence (below, § 21.2).

[3] Serious Crime Act 2007, s. 50. See above, § 9.1(iv)(b).

[4] Criminal Damage Act 1971, s. 5. See above, § 14.5(vi).

## § 21.1 Consent

Consent to basic physical interaction provides an essential ingredient for social life. We may not much like jostling onto a busy train, for example, or brushing past others on the pavement, but a deemed consent here is necessarily implicit if we are to travel around busy cities.[5] Justification in these circumstances is uncontroversial. However, the defensive potential for consent goes well beyond such quotidian scenarios. Exhibiting what has been described as a legal and moral "magic",[6] consent has the potential to transform serious offences against the person into permissible events (e.g. in the context of surgery and sport), and would-be sexual offences into positive encounters of mutual benefit. It is in these contexts that the precise definitions of consent are most important. Unfortunately, however, it is also in these contexts where legal understandings of consent are most problematic.[7]

Because of the current conceptual and doctrinal uncertainty about the scope of consent in different areas of law, we do not offer a general account of the elements of consent in this chapter. Rather, we provide in-depth analysis of consent as it relates separately to non-fatal offences against the person in Chapter 11, and sexual offences in Chapter 12. This reflects the divergent manner in which consent has been interpreted and applied between these two areas: with consent *generally* viewed as a supervening defence in the context of non-fatal offences,[8] but with non-consent required as part of the actus reus of several sexual offences.[9]

The Law Commission has committed to a review of consent as part of its 14th Programme of Law Reform, launched in 2025. In doing so, the Commission are re-starting a project that has been stalled since 1995.[10] Interestingly, it seems that the Commission will be reviewing consent in general, as it applies to both non-fatal and sexual offences.

## § 21.2 Self-defence and the prevention of crime

Self-defence and the prevention of crime defence are discussed together in this section, reflecting their considerable overlap in both scope and substance.[11] In the broadest terms, self-defence (sometimes referred to as "private defence") applies where D uses reasonable force to protect herself or others from imminent harm from another; and the prevention of crime defence (sometimes referred to as "public defence") applies where D uses reasonable force to prevent the imminent commission of a criminal act by another. Thus, where D is attacked by V with a knife, and D hits V to escape the attack, it is likely that both self-defence and the prevention of crime defence will apply: D has acted in the interests of self-preservation, as well as to prevent V's criminal attack. However, despite considerable

[5] *Collins v Wilcock* [1984] 3 All ER 374 (DC).

[6] Hurd, "The Moral Magic of Consent" (1996) 2 *Legal Theory* 168.

[7] There is a vast literature on the meaning of consent. See, e.g., LCCP No. 139, *Consent in the Criminal Law* (1995); Roberts, "The Philosophical Foundations of Consent in the Criminal Law" (1997) 17 *OJLS* 389; Reed et al. (eds.) *Consent* (2017).

[8] In Chapter 11 we discuss consent as a defence to such offences, reflecting the preponderance of authority, but this classification is not uncontroversial. See, e.g., Williams, "Consent and Public Policy" [1962] *Crim LR* 74; Shute, "Something Old, Something New, Something Borrowed" [1996] *Crim LR* 684; Law Com. No. 361, *Reform of Offences Against the Person* (2015) paras. 5.20–5.26.

[9] The Sexual Offences Act 2003, ss. 1–4. See above, § 12.4.

[10] Law Com. No 139, *Consent in the Criminal Law* (1995).

[11] Leverick, *Killing in Self-Defence* (2006).

overlap between the two, sometimes only one or the other defence will apply. For example, if V in our previous example were below the age of criminal responsibility, D's defensive force may still be justified as legitimate self-defence,[12] but it is not force deployed in the prevention of crime because V's acts cannot constitute an offence. Conversely, the range of force that may be used in the prevention of crime defence is wider than self-defence in that crimes may be prevented by recourse to reasonable force even where no threat to life or limb is present. Where, for example, V is about to break into an unoccupied building to commit theft, she can lawfully be prevented from doing so by forcible means if that is reasonable.

Self-defence is a common law defence. The prevention of crime defence, by contrast, is defined in section 3 of the Criminal Law Act 1967:

> 3. Use of force in making arrest, etc.
>
> (1) A person may use such force as is reasonable in the circumstances in the prevention of crime, or in effecting or assisting in the lawful arrest of offenders or suspected offenders or of persons unlawfully at large.

Section 3 provides a broad defence that applies regardless of D's personal connection to the offence being committed. However, it has been held that the crime to be prevented must at least be a crime triable in England or Wales. In *Jones*,[13] the defendants claimed that various forms of damage inflicted on RAF property were instances of reasonable force used to prevent crimes of aggression set to be committed by Her Majesty's Government in Iraq. It was ruled that section 3 was not engaged because its application is restricted to crimes triable in England and Wales, whereas crimes of aggression are crimes contrary to international law and not crimes contrary to English law. The Court of Appeal noted that there is nothing in the legislative history of section 3 suggestive of an extra-territorial reach.

In an effort to clarify the application of both self-defence and prevention of crime,[14] section 76 of the Criminal Justice and Immigration Act 2008 sets out various criteria for resolving whether the use of force by D is to be considered reasonable. This provision is worth quoting at length, given its length and complexity:

> 76. Reasonable force for purposes of self-defence etc.
>
> (1) This section applies where in proceedings for an offence—
>
> (a) an issue arises as to whether a person charged with the offence ("D") is entitled to rely on a defence within subsection (2), and
>
> (b) the question arises whether the degree of force used by D against a person ("V") was reasonable in the circumstances.
>
> (2) The defences are—
>
> (a) the common law defence of self-defence; and
>
> (aa) the common law defence of defence of property; and
>
> (b) the defence . . . provided by section 3(1) of the Criminal Law Act 1967 . . .
>
> (3) The question whether the degree of force used by D was reasonable in the circumstances is to be decided by reference to the circumstances as D believed them to be . . .

[12] D's conduct must still satisfy the terms of self-defence, discussed below; and the fact V was a minor will be relevant to that analysis.

[13] [2004] EWCA Crim 1981, [2005] QB 259.

[14] Section 76 also applies to defence of property.

(4) If D claims to have held a particular belief as regards the existence of any circumstances—
(a) the reasonableness or otherwise of that belief is relevant to the question whether D genuinely held it; but
(b) if it is determined that D did genuinely hold it, D is entitled to rely on it for the purposes of subsection (3), whether or not—
(i) it was mistaken, or
(ii) (if it was mistaken) the mistake was a reasonable one to have made . . .

(6) In a case other than a householder case, the degree of force used by D is not to be regarded as having been reasonable in the circumstances as D believed them to be if it was disproportionate in those circumstances.

(6A) In deciding the question mentioned in subsection (3), a possibility that D could have retreated is to be considered (so far as relevant) as a factor to be taken into account, rather than as giving rise to a duty to retreat.

(7) In deciding the question mentioned in subsection (3) the following considerations are to be taken into account (so far as relevant in the circumstances of the case)—
(a) that a person acting for a legitimate purpose may not be able to weigh to a nicety the exact measure of any necessary action; and
(b) that evidence of a person's having only done what the person honestly and instinctively thought was necessary for a legitimate purpose constitutes strong evidence that only reasonable action was taken by that person for that purpose.

(8) Subsections (6A) and (7) are not to be read as preventing other matters from being taken into account where they are relevant to deciding the question mentioned in subsection (3) . . .

(9) This section, except so far as making different provision for householder cases, is intended to clarify the operation of the existing defences mentioned in subsection (2).

(10) In this section—
(a) "legitimate purpose" means—
(i) the purpose of self-defence under the common law,
(ia) the purpose of defence of property under the common law, or
(ii) the prevention of crime or effecting or assisting in the lawful arrest of persons mentioned in the provisions referred to in subsection (2)(b);
(b) references to self-defence include acting in defence of another person; and
(c) references to the degree of force used are to the type and amount of force used.

Despite the apparently modest aim of the provision, i.e. "clarifying the operation of existing defences",[15] section 76 provides a detailed confirmation and entrenchment of common law principles, and now represents the starting point for much of the analysis in this area. This is reflected in our discussion, which combines both defences across the following four areas:

*Exclusions*: Self-defence and the prevention of crime defence will not apply to (a) certain types of offending, and (b) in circumstances of prior fault.

*Element 1*: Necessity of force: it must have been subjectively necessary for D to use some force against V to protect himself or another, or in the prevention of crime.

*Element 2*: Reasonableness of force: the force used by D must have been objectively reasonable, on the facts as he subjectively believed them to be.

[15] Section 76(9). Note the exception of "householder cases" (i.e. those where D uses force against a trespasser within a dwelling) where s. 76 creates bespoke terms of defence. We do not quote these subsections here, but discuss them separately below, § 21.2(iv)(d).

*Exceptional categories*: The standard terms of the defences are modified in certain categories of mistaken defence, and where D is a householder using force against a trespasser.

In order to raise either defence, D is obliged to provide some evidence of self-defence or the prevention of crime; it is then for the prosecution to prove beyond reasonable doubt that the defence is not applicable.[16] If the prosecution fails in this task, D is entitled to be acquitted.

### (i) Exclusions

The principal elements of self-defence and the prevention of crime defence require that D acted with belief that defensive force was necessary, and that the actual force used by D was reasonable in those circumstances. We examine those elements further below. First, however, it is useful to begin with an issue of context, highlighting circumstances where the defences will be categorically excluded. Specifically, the defences will not apply to certain types of offending by D, and will not apply in certain circumstances of prior fault.[17]

#### (a) Excluded offences

Self-defence and the prevention of crime defence apply to justify the use of "*force*" by D, as confirmed by both section 3(1) of the 1967 Act and section 76(1) of the 2008 Act. Thus, where D's offence does *not* involve an element of force, neither defence is engaged.

Clearly, "force" comprehends any violence to which D has resorted and, additionally, covers such forceful conduct as the breaking of a window or the battering down of a door.[18] The term, as a matter of ordinary language, will not cover any acts that lack a violent or percussive character. In *Blake*,[19] for example, D was charged with criminal damage after he wrote a biblical quotation on a concrete pillar at the perimeter of the Houses of Parliament, protesting military action in Iraq and Kuwait. D relied, *inter alia*, on the section 3 defence, but this was rejected on the basis that his conduct—writing with a marker pen—did not amount to a use of force.[20] Likewise, in *Hutchinson v Newbury Magistrates' Court*,[21] it was held that wire-cutting a perimeter fence did not constitute "force".

These decisions are unexceptionable in terms of the literal meaning of the word "force", but may have unfortunate consequences. It appears anomalous, for example, that the defendant in *Blake* was excluded from the prevention of crime defence because of the restraint he showed in the use of a marker pen; the implication being that D would have been better placed to raise section 3 if he brought a hammer and chisel to the task. On the principle that the "greater includes the lesser", if D can justify an act of force as a response to particular circumstances, *a fortiori* justification should be accorded to a lesser, non-forceful

[16] *Cunningham* [2025] EWCA Crim 662; *O'Brian* [2004] EWCA Crim 2900. See above, § 3.2.

[17] These are distinct from (what we term) exceptional categories, discussed below, § 21.2(iv). Exceptional categories relate to particular groups of cases where the defences *will* apply, but where the doctrinal construction of the defences varies from standard cases.

[18] *Swales v Cox* [1981] 1 QB 849 (DC).

[19] [1993] Crim LR 586 (DC). See also the discussion of force in the context of robbery: above, § 14.3(ii).

[20] Neither is a defence for this kind of conduct provided for by the Criminal Damage Act 1971.

[21] *The Independent*, 20 November 2000 (DC).

response to the same situation.[22] Yet the decision in *Blake* indicates the contrary, and it is notable that in the cases of *Conway*[23] and *Willer*,[24] where, in each case, D escaped unlawful serious violence by committing a driving offence, the Court of Appeal chose to extend the defence of duress (to accommodate circumstances where the crime was not nominated by the duressor) rather than gloss the term "force" in order to bring the cases within self-defence or the prevention of crime. It will be recalled, however, that a defence of duress is available only if the harm threatened is death, serious bodily harm, or rape, and cannot be raised to a charge of murder, attempted murder, and certain treason offences. Further, a mistaken belief in the relevant threat must, if it is to support a duress defence, be based on reasonable grounds.[25] These restrictions do not apply to the use of defensive force or to a mistaken belief in the need for such force.[26] To have a stricter regime for non-violent responses seems insupportable.

In *DPP v Bayer*,[27] the Divisional Court expressed sympathy for the view that all forms of conduct directed at preventing crime should be appraised within the terms of section 3 of the 1967 Act, and that conduct otherwise criminal but not involving force should not lead to liability if it is a reasonable measure to prevent the commission of a crime. But the case law remains mixed. In Bayer, it was accepted that D tying himself to V's tractor would qualify as the use of "force" within section 3.[28] Similarly, in *Jones*,[29] Lord Bingham and Lord Hoffmann were prepared to assume without deciding that non-violent forms of obstruction of vehicles and persons could fall within section 3 in response to charges of obstruction. Against this liberalising trend, in *Riddell*, the Court of Appeal insisted that force in the natural meaning of the word must have been used in order to bring section 3 into play. Self-defence would be denied if D had driven in an unlawful manner to escape violence from V unless, in some sense, D had used his vehicle as a weapon.[30] By contrast, Singh LJ in *Oraki* was of the opinion, *obiter*, that section 3 was not confined to the use of force: he thought, for example, that D's conduct would fall within section 3 should he use his car as a stationary barrier against V's car, if that was a proportionate response to the danger he apprehended from V.[31] Singh LJ's approach is the correct one, on the principle that the greater includes the lesser. Rather than stretching the meaning of "force" beyond its natural meaning, if D would have been justified within the terms of section 3 in using force against V, any lesser defensive response (such as obstructing the highway) should be similarly justified.

A clearer position has been adopted for acts "immediately preparatory" to the use of force, with clarification that the defences of self-defence and prevention of crime will not be excluded.[32] Thus, for example, if D picks up a weapon to use in legitimate self-defence, her

[22] Perhaps such a case could now be defended on the basis of necessity: below, § 21.4.

[23] [1989] QB 290 (CA).

[24] (1986) 83 Cr App R 225 (CA).

[25] Above, § 20.1(ii)(e).

[26] Below, § 21.2(ii).

[27] [2004] Crim LR 663 (DC).

[28] *Ibid.* D argued that he was trying to prevent the causing of harm to property resulting from the sowing and harvesting of genetically modified crops.

[29] [2006] UKHL 16, [2007] 1 AC 136.

[30] [2017] EWCA Crim 413, [2017] 1 WLR 3593, [42]. On the facts, the Court found that D had used her car as a weapon.

[31] [2018] EWHC 115 (Admin), [2018] QB 1086, [28].

[32] *AG's Reference (No. 2 of 1983)* [1984] QB 546 (CA). See also *McAuley* [2009] EWCA Crim 2130, [2010] 1 Cr App R 11. Discussed further below, § 21.2(ii)(b).

defence will apply both to the use of the weapon (forceful conduct) and to the potentially unlawful possession of the weapon before its use (immediately preparatory conduct). The temporal borderline of immediately preparatory conduct is not entirely clear, and may usefully be clarified, but extending the reach of the defences beyond acts of force *simpliciter* is defensible.

### *(b) Prior-fault exclusion: contrived defence*

Self-defence and the prevention of crime defence are not subject to the same broad prior fault exclusions that apply in duress, particularly that based on voluntary association with violent individuals.[33] Indeed, the defences discussed here will not necessarily be excluded where D provokes V in a situation that gives rise to D's needing to use defensive force against V; D's defences will not be excluded simply because she was initially the aggressor in an altercation with V.[34] However, the defences will be excluded where D has contrived to create the circumstances where defensive force becomes necessary *in order* to use such force against V: where D consciously manipulates V into an attack against D so that (D intends) she will have a defence in place for the force she uses against V in any "defensive" response.[35]

The potential for prior fault exclusion was reviewed in *Keane* by Hughes LJ,[36] who advised that merely because V "turns the tables" on the initial aggressor, D, does not mean that D becomes a defender at that turning point.[37] The key consideration is whether V's response to D's attack took a disproportionate form.[38] There will be easy cases, as when V immediately responds with a knife to D's unarmed aggression. In less clear-cut cases, there may be fine lines for the jury to draw between D's unlawfully participating in a fight that he started and the moment it became justifiable for him to use force in defending himself from V. Because of these difficulties, it may be tempting to disqualify from self-defence anyone who is the initial antagonist, particularly anyone seeking a fight. Yet even the most disagreeable of persons may legitimately defend themselves. Imagine that D, who is unarmed, pushes V and abuses him in racist terms. V, furious, then rushes at D with a knife. D is entitled to defend himself, provided he uses proportionate means, however disreputable his provoking conduct and character. D has not forfeited his right to life or bodily integrity.

### ***(ii) Element 1: was it subjectively necessary to use any force?***

Force used in self-defence or in the prevention of crime must be "such force as is reasonable in the circumstances" if it is to be lawful. Difficult issues may arise when appraising a particular incident involving force. Broadly, they will involve questions concerning the necessity to use force at all and whether the amount of force used was a proportionate response

33 Above, § 20.1(i)(b).
34 *Rashford* [2005] EWCA Crim 3377; *Burns v HM Advocate* 1995 SLT 1090; *Harvey* [2009] EWCA Crim 469.
35 *Mason* (1756) 1 East PC 239; *Browne* [1973] NI 96, 107. See Child, Hunt and Crombag, *Prior Fault Criminalization* (2026) chap. 10; Robinson, "Causing the Conditions of One's Own Defence: A Study of the Limits of Theory in Criminal Law Doctrine" (1985) 71 *Va LR* 1; Alexander, "Causing the Conditions of One's Own Defense: A Theoretical Non-problem" (2013) 7 *Crim Law and Philosophy* 623; Hecht, "Provocateurs and their Rights to Self-defence" (2019) 13 *Crim Law and Philosophy* 165.
36 [2010] EWCA Crim 2514.
37 *Ibid.*, [6].
38 *Ibid.*, [17].

to the circumstances. We begin with the requirement that D must subjectively believe that the use of defensive force is necessary, to protect private or public interests.[39]

The focus on *defensive* force is key here, and the defences will only be available where D uses force in order to defend against attack or prevent crime, which excludes force used in revenge against previous attacks from V. In *Williams (Demario)*,[40] V was among a group of youths who gate-crashed a house party, stabbed D in the arm, and stole his necklace. D and others subsequently caught and stabbed V, killing him. For the Court of Appeal, D's use of force against V was not defensive, but rather amounted to an act of retaliation or revenge.

Probably the most important aspect of the necessity test, however, is that it is based on D's *subjective* beliefs (i.e. it is not set against an objective reasonable person standard). This subjective focus is entrenched in section 76(3) of the 2008 Act, and marks an important point of distinction from duress (above, § 20.1.) that requires D's belief in the need for force to be *reasonably* held.[41] Indeed, at one time, an objective standard for D's beliefs was also required for self-defence. In *Albert v Lavin*,[42] D assumed that he was under restraint by a passer-by, whom he hit; in fact, V was a plain-clothes police officer attempting to restrain D from queue-jumping at a bus stop. V had intervened because he feared that D's conduct would lead to a breach of the peace in the light of the irate responses of fellow passengers. It was argued on D's behalf that, although D's belief that V was not a police officer may have been unreasonable, he was entitled to a defence of mistaken self-defence.[43] The Divisional Court confirmed the magistrates' ruling that such a belief, to afford a defence, had to be reasonable. The preference for a subjective belief test in *Morgan*,[44] it was explained, concerned the *definitional* elements of offences (for instance, the absence of consent in rape). In the case at hand, by contrast, the definitional elements were present—D had intentionally inflicted force on V. The question for the Court was not whether there had been an assault but whether the assault was an *unlawful* assault.[45] The Divisional Court approved previous authority which ruled that force based on an unreasonable belief in justificatory facts was unlawful force.[46]

The analysis in *Albert v Lavin* was successfully challenged in *Gladstone Williams*.[47] The Court of Appeal rejected the notion that the requirement of unlawfulness was something that stood apart from the offence itself. The unlawfulness was integral to the offence and, on that view, the mens rea for assault was an intent to apply *unlawful* violence. Consequently, a person who believed that force was necessary to protect another from violence would lack

[39] Cf. Manwaring, "Unnecessary Self-Defence" (2025) 46 *OJLS* 87, contending that "necessity" should not be considered as a separate element of self-defence, and should instead be seen as a factor bearing upon the broader question of "reasonableness" in self-defence.

[40] [2020] EWCA Crim 193. Cp. *Thain* [1985] NI 457.

[41] *Graham* [1982] 1 All ER 801 (CA); *Howe* [1987] AC 417; *Hasan* [2005] UKHL 22, [2005] 2 AC 467. The latter case in particular bases its refusal to endorse a subjective approach on a concern to tighten the conditions of a defence easily fabricated and abused. That kind of policy-based reasoning could be applied to claims to have acted in self-defence, when such claims are unsupported by objective fact.

[42] [1981] 2 WLR 1070 (DC); affirmed on other grounds in [1982] AC 546 (HL).

[43] The Divisional Court assumed that only police officers could physically restrain persons to prevent a breach of the peace. The House of Lords subsequently held that all subjects have this right. On that view, D's mistake, unreasonable or otherwise, was immaterial.

[44] [1976] AC 182. Discussed above, § 18.1.

[45] [1981] 1 All ER 628, 639 (Hodgson J) (DC).

[46] *Weston* (1879) 14 Cox CC 346; *Rose* (1884) 15 Cox CC 540; *Owens v HM Advocate* 1946 JC 119; *Chisham* (1963) 47 Cr App R 130.

[47] [1987] 3 All ER 411 (CA).

an intent to inflict unlawful force. The approach in *Gladstone Williams* was endorsed by the Privy Council in *Beckford*,[48] and may be regarded as authoritative for cases involving beliefs in the need for preventive or defensive force. (Of course, D cannot use *any* degree of force. He must use force proportionate to the danger he mistakenly apprehended. That was and remains a question to be assessed objectively, as will be explained shortly.)

The approach adopted in *Gladstone Williams* is now endorsed by section 76(3) of the 2008 Act. A useful case, demonstrating the broad application of the rule, is *Oraki*.[49] There, the Divisional Court concluded that force could lawfully be used even against police officers and other officials acting lawfully, provided D genuinely believed the officers were acting unlawfully. That conclusion was implicit in the decisions in *Gladstone Williams* and *Beckford*: however, the ruling in *Oraki* is a helpful clarification, in as much as there were *dicta* in earlier cases which doubted whether it could ever be lawful to use force against officials acting lawfully.[50]

*(a) Does necessary force entail a duty to retreat?*

It is clear that D's use of defensive force may remain sufficiently necessary even where he has had an opportunity to retreat (i.e. to avoid the confrontation with V) and chooses not to do so. Section 76(6A) of the 2008 Act rules out any "duty to retreat" within the current law, although it states that the jury may take such circumstances into account when assessing the reasonableness of the force D used.

Historically, D was required to take any safe avenue of retreat.[51] On one view, this is a sensible rule entailed by any requirement that use of force be necessary. A deliberate failure to retreat rendered the subsequent use of force something that was avoidable. Ashworth is a firm advocate of a rule of retreat, particularly for cases where in order to stand his ground, D would have to use fatal force against V. Ashworth contends that, if D is obliged to retreat to a place of safety in such cases, then there is full compliance with the right to life guaranteed by Article 2 of the ECHR: D lives and V lives.[52] However, even before the explicit rejection of any duty to retreat in the 2008 Act, the unqualified requirement of reasonableness in section 3 of the Criminal Law Act 1967 had already prompted the Court of Appeal to interpret an opportunity for retreat as simply a factor (among others) for the jury to consider.[53]

The current position, rejecting a duty to retreat, is welcome in that it allows due weight to be given to D's right to autonomy. If D is behaving in a non-threatening, law-abiding manner in a place where she has a right to be, she should be under no duty to exert herself at the unlawful behest of V. The question of sufficient necessity to use force should normally take, as its baseline, D's right to the peaceful enjoyment of her autonomous choices. This is supported in the important case of *Field*,[54] which ruled that D may remain at a place of lawful resort notwithstanding his knowledge that V may attack him should he stay there.

[48] [1988] AC 130 (PC). For critical commentary, see Simester, "Mistakes in Defence" (1992) 12 *OJLS* 295.

[49] [2018] EWHC 115 (Admin), [2018] QB 1086.

[50] *Kenlin v Gardner* [1967] 2 QB 510 (DC) was the authority most usually cited to support the protection of officers from any degree of force but was found in *Oraki* not to be decisive on this matter.

[51] Turner, *Kenny's Outlines of Criminal Law* (16th ed., 1952) 113–14.

[52] Ashworth, *Principles* of Criminal Law (6th ed., 2009) 120–4.

[53] That is, an opportunity to retreat would not be definitive on the questions of necessary or reasonableness of force. *Julien* [1969] 1 WLR 839 (CA).

[54] [1972] Crim LR 435 (CA).

By electing to visit a place of known danger, D does not forfeit his right to defend himself should he elect to stay where he is despite the threat of imminent violence. The right to maintain a lawful presence would be particularly in point where D's presence is objected to by V on racist or other disreputable grounds. To maintain for such cases that the preservation of V's life should always trump the enjoyment of D's civil rights is too rigid a stance.

The case is even more compelling where V's life is not threatened. In *Redmond-Bate*,[55] for example, the Divisional Court had to decide whether D and others had legitimately been arrested for breach of the peace. D had been preaching, quite lawfully, on cathedral steps. A crowd of about 100 gathered, some of whom showed hostility to D. D was arrested when she refused to desist from preaching. In finding the arrest unlawful, the Court held that citizens could not be called upon to desist from lawful conduct. Only when lawful conduct gives rise to a reasonable apprehension that it will, *by interfering with the rights or liberties of others*, provoke violence, is a police officer empowered to take steps to prevent it.

The absence of a duty to retreat does not, of course, make the potential for retreat irrelevant in all cases, and section 76(6A) retains reference to it as a factor that the jury may properly take into account. A different set of considerations might apply for a case where, say, V is infuriated because D is sitting in V's favourite chair in the pub, and D knows he could restore V to calm simply by sitting in another chair. Here it may well be thought unreasonable for D to resort to fatal force in order to remain *in situ* even if that was the only way he could do so.

### *(b) Does necessary force exclude pre-emption?*

The effective prevention of a crime or an attack may require pre-emptive force. There is no requirement within the terms of section 76 of the 2008 Act, or from appellate authority, that D must wait until V actually attacks him before making a defensive response. It suffices that V's attack was imminent.

The two defences are not entirely consistent on this issue, however. There is authority that the timeframe for preventive responses is more generous in prevention of crime cases than in self-defence cases. If D, a police officer, is sure that V will commit a serious offence in the future, arguably it is reasonable to use force to prevent that crime even though its commission is not yet imminent. Such a view was endorsed by the Court of Appeal of Northern Ireland in *Kelly*,[56] where D, a soldier, shot and killed V, the driver of a car. There was reason to think that V and his fellow passengers were terrorists and that, if allowed to escape, they would commit terrorist offences in the future. It was held that this (mistaken[57]) belief justified the use of force, even though D was not firing to prevent V from committing some imminent, identified, offence; he was preventing non-specific crimes at some future time.

It is submitted that the approach in *Kelly* is unsustainable.[58] The criminal law contains significant restrictions on the use of force and restraint which are at odds with this decision.

[55] [1999] Crim LR 998 (DC).

[56] [1989] NI 341.

[57] In fact, V and his passengers were joyriders and not terrorists.

[58] Surprisingly, the decision was upheld by the European Commission of Human Rights (*Kelly v UK* (1993) 74 DR 139), who found no contravention of Art. 2 of the ECHR on the basis that the force was used to effect a lawful arrest within the terms of Art. 2. As Professor Sir John Smith observes, how can a shooting carried out with an intent to kill be spoken of as an "arrest"? See Smith, "The Right to Life and the Right to Kill in Law Enforcement" (1994) 144 *NLJ* 354.

If we turn to the law of arrest, a pre-emptive arrest is not possible until V is "about to" commit a crime.[59] The law of criminal attempts requires an act which is sufficiently proximate to the commission of a completed offence.[60] It is paradoxical that on facts such as those in *Kelly*, D could not have used the slightest degree of restraint to make an arrest to prevent a crime yet to be committed but, nonetheless, was entitled to use fatal force for that end. This inconsistency cannot be sustained. The laws of arrest and criminal attempt set parameters for the deployment of preventative force under section 3 of the Criminal Law Act 1967, parameters which were overlooked in *Kelly*.

However, without resiling from these points of criticism, it should be noted that the United Kingdom government does seem to take a view of the boundaries of legitimate, preventative force that is aligned with *Kelly*. It has used drones, controlled and directed by persons in the United Kingdom, to kill persons located abroad who are taken to be members of terrorist organisations hostile to the United Kingdom and its citizens.[61] These killings seek to prevent and deter terrorists from perpetrating acts of terror at some future time and place. The UK government has confidently asserted that these killings are lawful in terms of international and domestic law.[62]

Although the use of force should be subjected to strict time restraints, more latitude may be allowed for pre-emptive measures falling short of actual violence. In *Cousins*,[63] D showed a shotgun to V and threatened that he would use it at some future time unless X, a close relative of V, withdrew his threat to kill D. On appeal, D's conviction for making threats to kill was quashed because, contrary to the ruling of the trial judge, D was entitled to raise a section 3 defence despite the fact that his life was not in imminent danger. The Court of Appeal emphasised that the case involved the threat of violence and not the use of force. In *A-G's Reference (No. 2 of 1983)*,[64] the Court of Appeal ruled that D's possession of petrol bombs was possession for a lawful purpose, the purpose being to defend his shop premises from ransack at a time of urban riots. The Court assumed that D would have been entitled to use petrol bombs to defend his premises should these come under attack. It followed that he was entitled to put himself in a position to use such means.[65]

In both *Cousins* and *A-G's Reference*, the Court of Appeal considered that offences other than the offences charged *had* been committed: in the former case, unlawful possession of a firearm because of a lack of licence; in the latter, the unlawful manufacture and storing of explosives.[66] These *obiter dicta* need to be treated with some caution. If the firearm and explosives, respectively, were obtained prior to the existence of the relevant threats, then liability for those offences ensues. Yet if the items were obtained by way of response to the

[59] Police and Criminal Evidence Act 1984, s. 24(7)(a).

[60] Above, § 9.3(i).

[61] As these killings are planned and initiated within the territory of the United Kingdom, they would be subject to the English law of homicide: see above, § 10.2(v).

[62] *Hansard*, HC cols. 25–7 (7 September 2015). For a useful discussion of the claim that these killings are lawful under domestic law, see Gardner, "The Domestic Criminal Legality of the RAF Drone Strike in Syria in August 2015" [2016] *Crim LR* 35.

[63] [1982] QB 526 (CA).

[64] [1984] QB 456 (CA).

[65] Cf. *Wills (Vivian Barrington)* [2024] EWCA Crim 1351, where D's conviction was upheld for possessing a firearm with intent to cause fear of violence. There is no requirement for a jury to be directed on pre-emption where D is obviously the aggressor.

[66] See too *Fegan* [1972] NI 80, where it was held that possession of a firearm to protect oneself against violence would be possession for a lawful object even though the possession was in itself unlawful for being unlicenced.

threats, liability should not arise. If the use of a firearm as a threat is lawful in particular circumstances, it would be inconsistent to hold that acquiring a firearm to use lawfully in particular *identified* circumstances is unlawful. As we are dealing with conduct preliminary to the threat or use of force, prima facie it should not matter how items such as guns or explosives are acquired, provided they are acquired in order to respond to identified circumstances where the use or threatened use of such items would be lawful. (Contrast a scenario where D acquires a gun "just in case".) Of course, the longer D has possessed the gun, explosives, etc., the more difficult it will be to associate the acquisition of the item with a particular identifiable threat.

The imminence requirement may work harshly for D when she is subjected to episodes of violence by V, a more powerful person than D. D's only defensive option may be to take advantage of some moment of calm where D is unawares and vulnerable.[67] The worry is that allowing a full defence, particularly for fatal violence inflicted pre-emptively, would be very difficult to confine to deserving circumstances. For instance, one would not want to legitimate anticipatory gangland killings, however real the "kill or be killed" dilemma that prompted them.[68] Some accommodation to what may be called the dilemma of powerlessness is provided for by section 54 of the Coroners and Justice Act 2009. In the context of a charge of murder, if D has killed in response to a fear of serious violence (which need not be a fear of imminent violence) from V or another, she will be convicted of manslaughter rather than murder provided her fear of serious violence induced a lack of self-control at the time of the killing.[69]

*(c) Can force against innocents be necessary?*

In paradigm cases where D uses force in self-defence or the prevention of crime, the object of that force (V) will not be an innocent party. Indeed, D's defensive force is justified in part *because* V is not innocent, and D does the right thing in restraining V from perpetrating imminent or ongoing harms. Where V is an innocent party, using force against her will typically not be necessary and so the defences will fail. However, this is not universally true, and exceptional cases will allow the defences to apply even where V is innocent.[70] We have already discussed one example of this, where D acts in mistaken self-defence or prevention of crime: D honestly believes that using force against V is necessary to prevent attack or criminality, but D is wrong, and V may be entirely innocent.[71] Two further examples are discussed here. First, where V does attack D (or perhaps endangers D) and yet V is an innocent party; and second, where D uses force against V (an innocent party) in order to restrain the attack or criminal offence of a third party (P).

It is generally accepted that D may defend herself against unjustified force even if she knows that the force in question does not constitute a criminal act. Suppose that D, a nurse

[67] Howes, "Women who Kill: Why Self-defence Rarely Works for Women who Kill their Abuser" [2021] *Crim LR* 945.

[68] A useful comparison may be drawn with Lord Bingham's restatement of the law of duress in *Hasan* [2005] UKHL 22, [2005] 2 AC 467, where he was very concerned to exclude from the defence threats made by D's criminal associates.

[69] Sections 54, 55(1)–(4).

[70] In such circumstances, even where the defences apply, there is a separate question as to whether D's conduct is justified or excused. Above, § 17.2.

[71] Above, § 21.2(ii).

in a mental health hospital, is attacked by V, a patient she knows to be legally insane. It is submitted that D can take all reasonable steps to defend herself including, should it be necessary, the use of fatal force. Were this incident assessed from the perspective of the right to life, it could be argued that V, satisfying the terms of the defence of insanity, has not forfeited any of his rights by making this attack. From a right-to-life perspective, there is no obvious reason why it should be V rather than D who dies. Yet, even though D and V have rights to life of equal standing, it is V, albeit blamelessly, who has violated D's right to autonomy. D is under no obligation to surrender her life for the benefit of V's life. Her right to autonomy allows self-preference, the sustaining of her own life with its responsibilities to those close to her, provided she does not actively violate the right to autonomy of others.[72]

The logic of this analysis flows to any situation where V's conduct constitutes an encroachment of D's autonomy and a threat to the security of her person. It is not necessary that V's conduct should take the form of an attack on D. Consider a situation that arose in the course of the Zeebrugge ferry disaster.[73] D and others were seeking to climb a rope ladder in order to leave the hold of a ship that was filling with seawater. The way was barred by V who, immobilised by fear, clung to the ladder despite urgent requests to climb it. D, in order to save himself and others from drowning, tore V from the ladder. Consequently, V died from drowning; D and others climbed to safety. It may be objected that D's act was not done in self-defence or in defence of others because V was not attacking anyone. Yet V's behaviour constituted an immediate threat of death to others and encroached on their autonomy by restricting, without justification, their freedom of movement. There seems no difference of principle between this situation and being attacked or endangered by someone who lacks responsibility due to a mental disorder. It may be said that the ferry disaster situation is a case of duress of circumstances and, possibly, of necessity. Conceptually, such a classification is possible (though not exhaustive). The drawback of rejecting the characterisation of D's conduct as (also) self-defence is that duress and (generally) necessity are not available defences to a charge of murder.[74]

It is important to repeat that the right to self-defence will arise only if V's conduct is a threat to D's security of person *and* an encroachment on her autonomy. To take a famous example, suppose that in open seas V is first to a wooden plank, sufficient to support her but nobody else. D will drown unless he is able to take sole occupancy of it.[75] In a sense, V's possession of the plank is an immediate threat to D's life. Yet D should not be permitted to remove her from it. By taking possession of the plank, V exercised her own autonomy without violating D's.

A more recent example of this line of reasoning is provided in *Re A (Children)*.[76] Ward LJ justified a separation operation that entailed the survival of one conjoined twin J, and the certain death of the other twin, M. M's own heart and lungs were inadequate to sustain M's life. While joined to J, M survived only by relying on J's heart to pump the blood oxygenated by J. It was estimated that J's heart would fail under the strain within three to six months, with the inevitable consequence that both J and M would die. If a successful separation operation were to be carried out, J's prospects for a healthy life were good. M would

[72] See further Uniacke, *Permissible Killing* (1994) 158–93.
[73] Discussed in Smith, *Justification and Excuse in the Criminal Law* (1989) 73–4.
[74] See §§ 20.1(i)(a), 21.4(ii).
[75] Cicero, *De Officiis* iii, 23.
[76] [2001] Fam 147 (CA).

necessarily die as a result. Ward LJ equated M's life-sapping dependence on J's heart and lungs as tantamount to an attack upon J, an attack from which J was entitled to be defended. In resolving that the killing of M would be lawful self-defence, he stressed J's prospects for a normal life, by contrast with M who was "self-designated" for death. On first impression this reference to "self-designation" sits oddly with a right of self-defence.[77] If V launches an unlawful attack on D that, of itself, gives D an entitlement to defend himself, even if D is an old man with a terminal illness and V a healthy young man. Yet in the context of *Re A*, the drawing of a contrast between the life prospects of M, on the one hand, and J, on the other, is understandable. It was the fact that M's dependence radically cut down J's life expectancy that made their coexistence a threat to J; things would have been otherwise had J's outlook been as dire as M's. It would be unwise to hazard any generalisation concerning the scope of self-defence from facts so specific as those in *Re A (Children)*, particularly as only Ward LJ based his judgment on this ground. Moreover, there is a considerable technical difficulty in subsuming the facts of the case under self-defence, particularly the imminence requirement. J, at the time of the operation, was estimated to have three to six months to live, yet it would have been grotesque to delay the intervention until she was at death's door. Nonetheless, the case gives support for the view that facts such as those discussed above arising in the course of Zeebrugge tragedy can fall within the purview of self-defence.

Next, we consider circumstances where D aims to use force against P (a third party) for defensive or crime prevention reasons, but harms V (an innocent party) in so doing. *Hichens*[78] endorses the view that proportionate force can be used against innocent, non-threatening persons if that is the only way to prevent a crime by P. The examples given in that case are untroubling: no one can object to D, a policeman, "bundling" V out of his path in order to engage P, who is carrying a live explosive. More troubling examples, however, abound. Imagine a scenario where D (a police officer) is confronted with a violent and armed assailant (P). P clasps V to his body as a human shield and breaks cover while firing at the surrounding police. The fire is returned by the officers and V is killed by a police bullet. It is very likely that the police response would be found justifiable.[79]

One limitation on using preventative force against innocent persons in this manner would be that serious injury or death cannot be intentionally inflicted as a means to prevent P's crime. Suppose that P and his fellow hostage-takers threaten to kill the hostages unless V is handed over to them. D, who is supervising the police response, is aware that the threat to the hostages is very serious but is also aware that P wishes to get his hands on V in order to kill him. The better view is that V cannot lawfully be handed over to P.

What, then, of the much discussed case of the passenger plane, hijacked by terrorists, flying towards the high, densely populated building? The dilemma facing D, the Ministry of Defence decision-taker, is that, although the building and the persons present inside can only be saved by destroying the plane while in flight, ordering the destruction of the plane is to order the intentional killing of its passengers. That is why the German Supreme Court, addressing this situation as a scenario rather than an *ex post* reality, ruled that legislation

[77] Quite apart from the difficulty of characterising M as an innocent attacker, since she was not *acting* at all: cf. Chan and Simester, "Duress, Necessity: How Many Defences?" (2005) 16 *King's College LJ* 121, 128–9.

[78] [2011] EWCA Crim 1626, [2011] 2 Cr App R 26.

[79] The shooting scenario in the text is based on the facts of *Pagett* (1983) 76 Cr App R 279 (CA), where P was found to have caused V's death in that he created a situation where the police were duty bound to use force to prevent his escape. See above, § 4.2(iii)(c) (case 1).

authorising the destruction of the plane in such cases was unconstitutional.[80] For the Court, the taking of innocent life could not be condoned by legislation because it would violate the right to dignity (Article 1 of the German Constitution) and the right to life (Article 2 of the German Constitution). The UK Select Committee on Defence has taken a different view, and advises destruction of the plane.[81] The latter position takes a hard but in many ways attractive line. On the facts available to D, the passengers will die in any event. Better then that the people in the building should live.[82]

But what if D acted on a miscalculation with terrible consequences? Let us say that the plane destroyed on the orders of D had strayed from its flight path and was flying low over London, doing so to avoid severe turbulence. Because of a fault in air-to-ground communications, no messages were exchanged between the pilot and air traffic control. D assumed a terrorist hijack and the imminent destruction of a high-rise building. When discussing mistakes concerning circumstances giving rise to defences, we saw that, as things stand, an unreasonable mistake as to the need to use force in the prevention of crime could yet be an excusing mistake.[83] There is much to be said for a reasonableness standard where the intentional taking of innocent lives is involved; particularly, as with our hypothetical, where D is a public official.

### *(iii) Element 2: was the force used reasonable?*

Beyond the threshold requirement that D's force be subjectively *necessary*, self-defence and prevention of crime also require that the degree of force employed by D be *reasonable*. The reasonableness test, set out in section 76 of the 2008 Act, takes the facts as D subjectively believed them to be (even if D was unreasonably mistaken), and asks whether the force used by D was objectively reasonable on the basis of those facts. Crucially, the test here focuses on the force used by D and not its consequences.[84] Thus, where V attacks D with her fists, it is highly unlikely that an intentionally lethal response from D in defence would be reasonable. However, if D's response was to push V away to avoid the attack, this is likely to be reasonable even if (unforeseen by D) V falls and hits her head on a disguised object resulting in her death.

Whether the force used by D was reasonable in the circumstances is a question of fact to be determined by the jury. As with any question of fact, guidance, including strong guidance, may be given by the trial judge. The jury should be advised that the judgment of reasonableness should be on broad and liberal grounds, eschewing the benefits of

[80] Judgment of the German Federal Constitutional Court of 15 February 2006, 1 BvR 357/05; invalidating § 114 III of the Air-Transport Security Act (2005). For discussion of this case, see Bohlander, "*In Extremis?* Hijacked Airplanes, 'Collateral Damage' and the Limits of the Criminal Law" [2006] *Crim LR* 579.

[81] House of Commons Defence Committee, *Defence and Security in the UK: Sixth Report of Session 2001–02* (Vol. I: Report and Proceedings of the Committee) HC 518-I (2002) paras. 8–9. The general legal justification here is necessity. More straightforwardly, justification can be found within the statutory authority under s. 3 of the Criminal Law Act 1967 to use reasonable force in the prevention of crime. Clearly the destruction of the building will be a crime, and it is well established that fatal force can be used to prevent crime if proportionate to the occasion, whereas doubts remain whether innocent life can be taken under the rubric of necessity.

[82] For further discussion, see Hörnle, "Hijacked Planes: May they Be Shot Down?" (2007) 10 *New Criminal LR* 582; Sullivan, "The Hard Treatment of Innocent Persons in State Responses to the Threat of Large Scale and Imminent Terrorist Violence: Examining the Legal Restraints" in Sullivan and Dennis (eds.), *Seeking Security* (2012) 293, 305–9.

[83] Above, § 21.2(ii).

[84] *Keane* [2010] EWCA Crim 2514; *Noye* [2011] EWCA Crim 650, [9], [55].

hindsight—jewellers' scales are not required.[85] Or, as it is put in the Criminal Justice and Immigration Act 2008, "a person acting for a legitimate purpose may not be able to weigh to a nicety the exact measure of any necessary action".[86] In a similar vein, it should be made clear to the jury that "evidence of a person having only done what the person honestly and instinctively thought was necessary for a legitimate purpose constitutes strong evidence that only reasonable action was taken by that person for that purpose".[87] If there is cogent evidence that D, through excessive fear and anxiety, clearly went "over the top", the trial judge would be entitled to rule out any claim of reasonable force. The 2008 Act clearly states that (excepting "householder" cases, returned to below) the force used by D is not to be regarded as having been reasonable in the circumstances as D believed them to be if it was disproportionate in those circumstances.[88] But there is a strong presumption that the jury rather than the judge should resolve the issue. Only in the plainest case should a judge, after finding that some force was necessary, remove a defence from the jury on the grounds of disproportionality (where, for instance, no jury could reasonably find that D's response was proportionate).

It is appropriate that the law should employ a broad and liberal approach here, taking account of D's perception of the event. However, the test retains an important objective dimension: D's perception of the appropriateness of her response is not determinative on the question of reasonable force. In *Scarlett*,[89] for example, D caused the death of V, a trespasser, by using what the jury found to be excessive force when ejecting V from the premises. On appeal, D's conviction for manslaughter was quashed on the basis that, if D thought the force he employed was reasonable (even though it was found to be excessive), he was entitled to a defence of mistaken self-defence. The decision in *Scarlett* is based on a misreading of *Gladstone Williams*,[90] where it was decided that, if D makes a mistake of fact concerning the need for force, his conduct is to be evaluated as if his mistaken assumption were a true assumption. *Williams*, however, does not require D to be given the benefit of his mistaken view about what constitutes reasonable force. *Williams* involved a mistake of circumstantial fact, a mistaken assumption that V was an aggressor whereas in truth he was a police officer making an arrest; *Scarlett* involves a mistake of normative evaluation.[91] This distinction was clearly perceived in two subsequent decisions of the Court of Appeal, namely *Owino*[92] and *Armstrong-Braun*.[93] In neither case was *Scarlett* said to be wrong, but the "correct" reading of *Gladstone Williams* was emphasised. The clarification provided for by section 76(6) of the Criminal Justice and Immigration Act 2008 is helpful: "In a case other than a householder case, the degree of force used by D is not to be regarded as having been reasonable in the circumstances as D believed them to be if it was disproportionate

[85] *Reed v Wastie* [1972] Crim LR 221 (DC).
[86] Section 76(7)(a).
[87] Section 76(7)(b). Drawn from *Palmer* [1971] 1 AC 814 (PC) (Lord Morris).
[88] Section 76(6).
[89] [1993] 4 All ER 629 (CA).
[90] [1987] 3 All ER 411 (CA).
[91] Although the reasonableness of D's force is a question of "fact" in the sense that it is for the jury rather than the judge to resolve, it is not the same type of fact as the circumstantial facts mistaken by the defendant in *Williams*. For further discussion of the distinction, see above, § 18.1.
[92] (1996) 2 Cr App R 128 (CA).
[93] [1999] Crim LR 416 (DC).

in those circumstances." This is clearly an objective test.[94] It seems safe to conclude that *Scarlett* will not be followed.

Questions of proportionality may require difficult judgements by juries. The only guidance they have is their own sense of what is reasonable. A particular jury may find it reasonably possible that killing to avoid serious bodily harm was permissible (securing D's acquittal), whereas another jury in a similar case may be sure that such means were excessive when compared to the threat (securing D's conviction). There is something to be said for giving more explicit guidance on commonly recurring situations, as is done, for example, in the US Model Penal Code: the Code has a number of provisions, occupying several pages of close print, that deal separately with self-protection; protection of other persons; protection of property; law enforcement; and persons with special responsibilities for care and safety of others.[95] Judgements may be particularly difficult to make when incommensurable values are in play. It is often said that it can never be justified to kill in order to protect property. Yet it is not obviously a categorical truth that any individual's life is of more intrinsic worth than any item of property. Is it necessarily unreasonable to kill a terrorist if such is the only means of preventing the destruction of priceless historic artefacts? The answer depends, in part, on one's core values. The lack of consensus on such issues suggests that the law should provide specific rules rather than leave such matters to *ad hoc* evaluations. To some extent that is now the case where the force used by D was fatal force. Article 2 of the ECHR allows certain derogations from V's right to life, but makes no provision for the protection of property.

The lack of precision and guidance within the reasonableness test is particularly problematic because of the binary nature of the outcome. If a jury should find that the force was excessive, the defences of self-defence and prevention of crime will fail *in toto*. If there was an entitlement to use *some* force, this may be thought to attenuate culpability to an extent. Where the sentence is subject to the discretion of the judge, any diminution of culpability can be reflected in the sentence passed. That is, of course, not possible where the sentence is fixed by law, as it is for the crime of murder. In certain states of Australia, a form of manslaughter was judicially created to allow for such a verdict where D had killed with the mens rea for murder but in circumstances where he was entitled to use a degree of force, albeit a lesser degree than the force he used.[96] A similar judicial initiative has been consistently rejected in England and Wales, most recently by the House of Lords in *Clegg*.[97] Indeed, the idea has been dropped in the land of its origin, on the ground that directions to juries required an excessive degree of complexity.[98] This seems unfortunate. As a matter of principle, a right to use a degree of violence towards the victim must surely, on occasion, diminish the culpability of D. A suitable direction to juries would appear no more intractable than for the cognate issues of loss of control and diminished responsibility.[99]

[94] Even in householder cases, the ultimate question is whether the householder used such force as was reasonable in the circumstances: below, § 21.2(iv)(d).

[95] See §§ 3.04–08. Compare too Law Com. No. 177, *A Criminal Code for England and Wales* (1989) cl. 44.

[96] *McKay* [1957] ALR 648; *Howe* (1958) 100 CLR 448.

[97] [1995] 1 AC 482; see *Palmer* [1971] 1 All ER 1077 (PC).

[98] *Zecevic* (1987) 61 ALJR 375.

[99] The Law Commission has recommended that a proposed offence of first-degree murder should be reduced to second-degree murder if D killed V because he was in fear of serious violence and a person of ordinary stability might have done the same or something similar in the circumstances: Law Com. No. 304, *Murder, Manslaughter and Infanticide* (2006).

### *(iv) Exceptional categories*

The standard terms of self-defence and the prevention of crime defence, set out above, will be modified for certain exceptional categories of defendant. Chiefly, this relates to mistaken self-defence or prevention of crime defences, where D's mistake is attributable to intoxication, insanity, and/or a psychiatric presentation outside the terms of legal insanity. A further exceptional category has been recognised in statute where D is a "householder"[100] who uses force against a trespasser.

#### *(a) Intoxicated mistakes*

Section 76(5) of the 2008 Act confirms the previous common law position that D may not "rely on any mistaken belief attributable to intoxication that was voluntarily induced". Thus, whereas a non-intoxicated defendant can rely on their mistaken beliefs (even unreasonable mistaken beliefs) to claim that the force they used was sufficiently necessary and reasonable on the facts as they believed them to be, a voluntarily intoxicated defendant cannot rely on a mistaken belief (however honestly held) induced or attributable to that state. Rather, in circumstances of voluntary intoxication, D will only be permitted to rely on mistakes that would have been made by a reasonable sober person in their position (i.e. the subjective test becomes an objective test). The legal treatment of voluntary intoxication here mirrors its position elsewhere in the context of supervening defences.[101]

It should be remembered, however, that the treatment of intoxicated mistakes is not identical between offences and defences. In the context of intoxicated mistakes and mens rea, an important distinction is maintained between specific intent offences (where an intoxicated lack of mens rea may negate liability) and basic intent offences (where intoxication rules may apply to substitute for missing mens rea elements).[102] In contrast, where D wishes to rely on an intoxicated mistake in self-defence or the prevention of crime, he will be prevented from doing so regardless of whether the force he used is alleged to be a basic or specific intent offence. This view was adopted in two cases, *O'Grady*[103] and *O'Connor*.[104] In *O'Grady*, D's conviction for manslaughter was confirmed on the basis that his drunken belief that he was being attacked by V would not found a defence of mistaken self-defence. As manslaughter is a crime of basic intent, the ruling is unexceptionable. However, the court stated, *obiter*, that D's drunken belief would be disregarded even on a charge of murder. In *O'Connor*, this view was taken to be binding.[105] The approach was later approved and applied in *Hatton*,[106] where D was not permitted to raise a drink-induced belief that he was under attack by way of defence to murder. The lack of consistency between offences and defences has been criticised,[107] but should not trouble us. As the Law Commission has

[100] As will be seen below, D need not be a "householder" in any sense beyond being in the relevant property as a non-trespasser.

[101] Above, § 18.4.

[102] *Ibid.*

[103] [1987] QB 995 (CA); see the note by Milgate at (1987) 46 *CLJ* 381.

[104] [1991] Crim LR 135 (CA).

[105] *O'Connor* involved an appeal against murder: in the event, the appeal succeeded on the ground that evidence of his intoxicated state was relevant to the question of whether D intended to kill or cause grievous bodily harm. So, again, remarks about the irrelevance of drunken mistakes relating to elements of defences were *obiter*.

[106] [2005] EWCA Crim 2951, [2006] 1 Cr App R 16.

[107] E.g., Dingwall, "Intoxicated Mistakes about the Need for Self-defence" (2007) 70 *MLR* 127.

observed, the equating of voluntary intoxication with a certain degree of culpability (i.e., providing the basis for mens rea substitution in crimes of basic intent) provides little guidance on the quite separate question of when and how such intoxication should amend the terms of a supervening defence.[108]

The boundaries of this exceptional category—"attributable to intoxication"—were explored in the 2018 case *Taj*.[109] The category includes those with drugs active in their system at the time of the offence,[110] but it was not previously thought to extend beyond that.[111] In *Taj*, however, the Court of Appeal accepted that a mistake may be attributable to intoxication even where D does not have drugs active in his system, on the basis (in this case) that D's mistake was connected to a form of drug-induced psychosis that was itself caused by previous drug-taking. Drawing on the terms of the 2008 Act, it was asserted that "the words 'attributable to intoxication' in s. 76(5) are broad enough to encompass . . . a mistaken state of mind immediately and proximately consequent upon earlier drink or drug-taking".[112] This approach has the potential to significantly expand the application of intoxication rules in circumstances of self-defence, and potentially beyond.[113] The merits of such expansion are not clear. What is clear, however, is that by expanding the interpretation of "attributable to intoxication" beyond a drug-active state, the boundaries of the legal category will rely on precise causal distinctions in an area of scientific and clinical uncertainty.[114] In cases of comorbidity—such as *Taj*—these distinctions will be almost impossible to draw.[115] Further legal clarification is required here; such clarification should return the boundary of this category to cases where drugs are active in D's system at the time of the actus reus.

### (b) *Insane mistakes*

For the purposes of self-defence and the prevention of crime, section 76 of the 2008 Act makes no explicit distinction for defendants who may alternatively satisfy the terms of legal insanity or diminished responsibility. However, it is a distinction that has emerged in the common law; albeit in a form that requires further clarification to provide consistent and principled guidance.[116]

In *Martin (Anthony)*,[117] a case of self-defence, the Court of Appeal confirmed that the belief in a need to use force to defend oneself need not be based on reasonable grounds: a genuine belief sufficed. However, the Court of Appeal introduced a distinction between

[108] Law Com. No. 314. *Intoxication and Criminal Liability* (2009) paras 3.53–3.83. See Child, Hunt and Crombag, *Prior Fault Criminalization* (2026) chap. 9.

[109] [2018] EWCA Crim 1743, [2019] QB 655.

[110] *DPP v Majewski* [1977] AC 443.

[111] See, e.g., *Beard* [1920] AC 479, 496–501 on the distinction between intoxication and mental illness resulting from chronic drug use; and *Davis* (1881) 14 Cox CC 563 on the distinction between intoxication and post-intoxication withdrawal.

[112] *Taj* [2018] EWCA Crim 1743, [2019] QB 655, [60].

[113] The Court of Appeal makes clear, *obiter*, that the same interpretation could be applied for intoxication as it relates to a denial of mens rea, presented as "an application of *Majewski*, rather than an extension of that decision or, at the highest, a most incremental extension" [57].

[114] Child, Crombag and Sullivan, "Defending the Delusional, the Irrational, and the Dangerous" [2020] *Crim LR* 306; Child, Crombag and Sullivan, "Drunk, Dangerous and Delusional: How Legal Concept Creep Risks Overcriminalisation" (2020) 115(12) *Addiction* 2200, and debate responses in the same volume.

[115] Discussed further above, § 18.5.

[116] Child and Sullivan, "When Does the Insanity Defence Apply? Some Recent Cases" [2014] *Crim LR* 788.

[117] [2001] EWCA Crim 2245, [2003] QB 1.

(i) the facts on which D's perception that he was under attack was based and (ii) the danger presented by those facts. In relation to the latter, D had claimed that his personality disorder, exacerbated by depression, induced him to perceive a greater threat to his safety arising from a burglary at his isolated farmhouse than would have been perceived by someone without depression. The Court held that, whereas the facts must be taken to be as D saw them, the danger presented by those facts must be evaluated *objectively*. D's plea of mistaken self-defence therefore failed, because his response to the objectively ascertained danger (rather than his imagined danger) was excessive.

The distinction drawn by the Court of Appeal between the facts *per se* and the danger arising from the facts is spurious. Suppose that V reaches into the inside of his jacket to extract a cigarette lighter; D assumes he is reaching for a gun. According to *Martin (Anthony)*, we are to allow D the benefit of his belief that V was reaching for a gun, however unreasonable D's belief, but must make an objective appraisal of the danger arising from these presumed facts. The potential for unfairness was perceived clearly by the Privy Council in *Shaw v R*,[118] a case decided shortly before *Martin (Anthony)* and not cited in the latter case. In *Shaw*, the appellants were appealing against a direction which invited the jury to assess the reasonableness of D's self-defence on the basis of the facts as they were, rather than the facts as D believed them to be. The Privy Council expressed the proper test for self-defence as follows:[119]

> "In the opinion of the Board it was necessary for the trial judge to ask two essential questions (however expressed) for the jury's consideration. (1) Did the appellant honestly believe or may he honestly have believed that it was necessary to defend himself? (2) If so, and taking the circumstances *and the danger* as the appellant honestly believed them to be, was the amount of force which he used reasonable?"

Much the better view, then, is that D must be assessed on the basis of the danger he took to be present—a fully subjective test of D's beliefs. As we discussed above at § 21.2(ii), the statutory clarification of defensive and preventive force reaffirms this subjective approach to D's state of belief and assesses the reasonableness of his response relative to his beliefs.[120]

However, the strength of the policy consideration that led to the forced distinction between belief in the need to defend oneself (subjective test) and the danger presented by the supposed attack (objective test) should be acknowledged. In *Martin (Anthony)*, it ensured the failure of D's defence of mistaken self-defence, whereas D's plea of diminished responsibility succeeded. That may be seen as a more balanced result than unqualified acquittal for a man who was psychologically disposed to overreact. The difficulty in achieving that outcome is that the common law of mistaken self-defence, as well as its statutory restatement in the 2008 Act, stipulate that (except in cases of voluntary intoxication) D's response is to be judged according to (i) his genuine belief in the need for self-defence,[121] and (ii) whether that response was disproportionate to the subjectively perceived danger.[122] In the interests of public protection, there is much to be said for a statutory change in the law, to disallow pleas of mistaken self-defence based on delusional beliefs caused by a

[118] [2001] 1 WLR 1519 (PC).
[119] *Ibid.*, 1527 (emphasis added).
[120] Criminal Justice and Immigration Act 2008, s. 76.
[121] Section 76(3).
[122] Section 76(6).

mental disorder whenever the partial defence of diminished responsibility,[123] or the special verdict of insanity,[124] are available alternatives. On a constructive interpretation of the case, it could be said that *Martin (Anthony)* has brought about this change without statutory intervention for charges of murder where diminished responsibility is proved: diminished responsibility will supervene over any claim to have acted in mistaken self-defence.

In the interests of public protection, there is also a strong case for ruling that insanity should be the sole defence, and mistaken self-defence be made unavailable to D, should it be proved that D was insane at the time of his offence. In *Oye*,[125] D, while in a psychotic state, attacked police whom he took to be evil spirits wishing him harm. Both mistaken self-defence and insanity were put to the jury—and rejected. On appeal, the Court of Appeal, in the light of uncontested expert opinion that D was legally insane, substituted D's convictions for affray and grievous bodily harm with a verdict of not guilty by reason of insanity notwithstanding the jury's rejection of this defence. No place was found for mistaken self-defence: "An insane person cannot set the standards of reasonableness as to the degree of force used by reference to his own insanity."[126]

Because D was ultimately found by the Court of Appeal to be insane, the dismissal of mistaken self-defence could have been justified on the ground that, in the interest of protecting the public from dangerous persons, the insanity plea supervenes over any other defence otherwise available: so that, once D is found to be insane,[127] all other lines of defence are closed.[128] But that was not the basis of the decision. The Court of Appeal made no criticism of the trial judge for directing the jury on both mistaken self-defence and insanity. The Court's criticism was confined to his directing the jury on mistaken self-defence *first*, rather than insanity.[129] But the two defences are not compatible. Although the jury rejected both defences, suppose they had *accepted* both of them: there would be one route to a verdict entitling D to an unqualified acquittal and another leaving D acquitted yet still under the jurisdiction of the court. One of these defences must have priority over the other.

The Court of Appeal did not tackle this problem. Instead, the rejection of mistaken self-defence based on an insane delusion was explained in *Oye* on the basis that section 76(6) of the 2008 Act brings an objective element to mistaken self-defence.[130] But that provision deals only with the reasonableness of D's *response* to the perceived circumstances; it does not encroach upon section 76(3), which allows mistaken self-defence to be raised according to the circumstances that D genuinely believed to exist. The dismissal of mistaken self-defence

[123] Section 2 of the Homicide Act 1957 (as amended) provides a partial defence of diminished responsibility, reducing the verdict to manslaughter for a person charged with murder if, according to the criteria set out in the section, he can prove (on a balance of probabilities) that his responsibility for his actions was substantially impaired. See above, § 10.6.

[124] Above, § 19.2.

[125] [2013] EWCA Crim 1725, [2014] 1 WLR 3354.

[126] *Ibid.*, [47].

[127] If D raises insanity as a defence, he must prove his insanity on a balance of probabilities. Insanity can also be raised by the prosecution or the trial judge; the better view is that in those cases insanity must be established beyond reasonable doubt: see above, § 19.2(i)(c). The verdict of insanity is known as a *special verdict*, a verdict that excludes blame and punishment but leaves D open to court orders which include confinement. See Chapter 19 for a full account of the defence.

[128] D would, of course, be able to raise such matters as alibi, mistaken identity, or diplomatic immunity.

[129] [2013] EWCA Crim 1725, [2014] 1 WLR 3354, [58]. The trial judge first gave a direction on self-defence, a direction which did not exclude insane delusions from the scope of that defence. He then gave a direction on insanity.

[130] *Ibid.*, [47].

would have been better explained by reference to the proposition that, once established, a defence of insanity displaces all other defences.

The reasoning in *Oye*, then, is opaque, but one can clearly discern the Court's unwillingness to allow self-defence to be predicated on genuine but insane delusions.[131] Reading the case holistically, it is submitted that the best view of the current law is the following: if D subjectively but mistakenly believes that facts exist such that his use of force in self-defence would be reasonable, then if that mistake arises either because of a condition satisfying the *M'Naghten* definition of insanity, or because of a condition amounting to diminished responsibility within section 2 of the Homicide Act 1957, the proper verdicts are not guilty by reason of insanity or manslaughter, respectively. Otherwise, D is entitled to rely on those subjective beliefs and claim self-defence (or prevention of crime) in the normal way, conditional as always upon the reasonableness of D's response to the facts as he perceived them.[132]

*(c) Non-insane but delusional mistakes*

In cases where D's mental condition falls short of insanity and (in murder cases) of diminished responsibility, any arguments about prioritization and/or diversion to irresponsibility defences fall away. But what of D's potential claim of mistaken self-defence or the defence of property?

In *Press*,[133] D was allowed to raise mistaken self-defence by claiming that his condition of post-traumatic stress disorder led him to believe that it was necessary to use force of the gravity he applied. The Court of Appeal found that his mental condition could be referenced to support his belief that such force was necessary, and when considering whether his response was proportionate to the facts as he supposed them to be. *Oye* was distinguished on the basis that the expert evidence in the instant case fell short of establishing an insane delusion. On the (contestable[134]) assumption that the dismissal of insanity in *Press* was correct, *Oye* was distinguishable in the light of the exclusionary effect of proven insanity, even though that point was not addressed in *Oye* itself.

However, subsequently, and without reference to *Press*, the Court of Appeal in *Taj* ruled that D's mistaken psychotic belief that a violent intervention was necessary to stop V from exploding a bomb could not give rise to mistaken self-defence/prevention of crime.[135] Much of the appeal in *Taj*, discussed above, focused on intoxication as the likely cause of this mistake, preventing him from relying (for the purposes of self-defence) on his subjective mistaken beliefs.[136] However, crucially for present purposes, at the time of Taj's appeal hearing a distinct mental condition (bipolar disorder) was recognised as an *alternative* cause of his delusion-inducing psychosis.[137] Since this alternative cause was not "attributable to intoxication" and was not held to come within the insanity rules,[138] the possibility

[131] *Ibid.*, [44]–[46].

[132] Above, § 21.2(iii).

[133] [2013] EWCA Crim 1849.

[134] It is not obvious why D's PTSD was not a disease of the mind for the purposes of an insanity defence, if it led to his belief that the force used was justified and therefore not "wrong" within the meaning of the *M'Naghten* Rules: above, §19.2(ii)(d).

[135] [2018] EWCA Crim 1743, [2019] QB 655.

[136] Above, § 21.2(iv)(a).

[137] *Taj* [2018] EWCA Crim 1743, [2019] QB 655, [61]–[65].

[138] Expert evidence that D was not insane was accepted by both defence and prosecution. However, it is difficult to see why his diagnosis did not, in legal terms, give rise to a condition of insanity. As an internal condition it would be designated a defect of reason arising from a disease of the mind, precluding any recognition by D that his

of self-defence would appear to have been open. But this possibility was quickly dismissed by the Court of Appeal. For the Court, dictum from Oye that insane persons cannot set standards of reasonableness was equally apposite to the facts of Taj, despite Taj's mental condition falling short of insanity.

We separate the discussion of this exceptional "category" from the one above, where D is diverted to insanity or diminished responsibility, because in a case such as *Taj* no such diversion is available. Rather, by modifying the second element of self-defence and prevention of crime in these cases, not allowing the reasonableness of force to be judged on the facts that D mistakenly believed them to be, the result is liability. The current position is difficult to justify, and should be reconsidered: whilst there may be policy reasons for modifying the defences in circumstances of prior fault intoxication, and diverting defendants to the special verdict in circumstances of insanity, diverting a further group of blameless delusional defendants should only be permissible if there is an alternative defence to which that diversion is aimed.[139] In short, the analysis in *Press* should be preferred to that in *Taj*.

### *(d) Householders*

It will sometimes be necessary for a householder[140] (D) to use force against a trespasser (V) who invades her property; and where she does so, self-defence and the prevention of crime defence will generally apply.[141] At one time, that was the end of the story. However, following several cases that received wide press coverage, in which householder defendants were prosecuted or under the threat of prosecution for harms caused to a trespasser,[142] section 76 of the 2008 Act was amended with a view to allowing householders a greater degree of latitude when acting in self-defence.[143] The amendments, set out below, apply only to a householder defendant acting in self-defence; householder defendants have no special status in the context of a section 3 prevention of crime defence.

76. Reasonable force for purposes of self-defence etc.

(5A) In a householder case, the degree of force used by D is not to be regarded as having been reasonable in the circumstances as D believed them to be if it was grossly disproportionate in those circumstances.

(8A) For the purposes of this section "*a householder case*" is a case where—

(a) the defence concerned is the common law defence of self-defence,

(b) the force concerned is force used by D while in or partly in a building, or part of a building, that is a dwelling or is forces accommodation (or is both),

(c) D is not a trespasser at the time the force is used, and

(d) at that time D believed V to be in, or entering, the building or part as a trespasser.

conduct was wrong. Moreover, the facts neatly fit the little-used limb of the *M'Naghten* Rules dealing with insane delusions: see below, § 19.2(ii)(e).

[139] Child, Crombag, and Sullivan, "Defending the Delusional, the Irrational, and the Dangerous" [2020] *Crim LR* 306.

[140] Again, D need not be a "householder" in any sense beyond being in the relevant property as a non-trespasser.

[141] See also the defence of property, below § 21.3.

[142] Perhaps the best-known of these cases is that of Tony Martin, who was charged with murder as a consequence of fatally shooting a burglar who was on the point of entering his isolated farmhouse: *Martin (Anthony)* [2001] EWCA Crim 2245, [2003] QB 1; above, § 21.2(iv)(b). Despite the concerns raised by cases such as Martin's, such prosecutions are rare. E.g., a survey by the Crime Prosecution Service of cases between 1990 and 2005 found only 11 prosecutions. Almost without exception these cases involved disproportionate force often inflicted past the point of danger: Lipscombe, *Householders and the Criminal Law of Self-defence* (2013).

[143] Crime and Courts Act 2013, s. 43.

(8B) Where—
(a) a part of a building is a dwelling where D dwells,
(b) another part of the building is a place of work for D or another person who dwells in the first part, and
(c) that other part is internally accessible from the first part, that other part, and any internal means of access between the two parts, are each treated for the purposes of subsection (8A) as a part of a building that is a dwelling.
(8C) Where—
(a) a part of a building is forces accommodation that is living or sleeping accommodation for D,
(b) another part of the building is a place of work for D or another person for whom the first part is living or sleeping accommodation, and
(c) that other part is internally accessible from the first part, that other part, and any internal means of access between the two parts, are each treated for the purposes of subsection (8A) as a part of a building that is forces accommodation.
(8D) Subsections (4) and (5) apply for the purposes of subsection (8A)(d) as they apply for the purposes of subsection (3).
(8E) The fact that a person derives title from a trespasser, or has the permission of a trespasser, does not prevent the person from being a trespasser for the purposes of subsection (8A).
(8F) In subsections (8A) to (8C)—
"*building*" includes a vehicle or vessel, and
"*forces accommodation*" means service living accommodation for the purposes of Part 3 of the Armed Forces Act 2006 by virtue of section 96(1)(a) or (b) of that Act.

To be within the zone of latitude, D must not be a trespasser himself and must use force in self-defence while in or partly within a building that is his dwelling or armed forces accommodation that he occupies. D must also believe that V is a trespasser.[144] In *Cheeseman*,[145] the question arose whether what made for trespass in this context should be confined to intruders—that is, persons who enter the dwelling as trespassers. D had invited V into his dwelling for a drink: V's status changed from invitee to trespasser when he started trashing D's dwelling. For the Court of Appeal this sufficed to make V a trespasser within the scope of the householder provisions. What really mattered was whether D believed V to be a trespasser at the time he was defending himself against V.[146] Similarly to the law of self-defence, the legislation merely requires D to *believe* that V is a trespasser; it does not require that V must *be* a trespasser or that D's belief be a reasonable one.[147] However, unless V's status as a trespasser is self-evident in the circumstances, *Magson* suggests that some evidential basis for D's belief will be required, particularly when the issue is raised for the first time on appeal.[148]

When evaluating D's response in a "householder case", the degree of force used by D in self-defence "is not to be regarded as reasonable in the circumstances as D believed them to be if it was grossly disproportionate to those circumstances".[149] Thus, whilst it remains the case that "disproportionate" force is not to be regarded as reasonable force in non-householder cases, the position is on the face of it different in householder cases.[150]

[144] Criminal Justice and Immigration Act, s. 76(8A).
[145] [2019] EWCA Crim 149, [2019] 1 WLR 3621.
[146] *Ibid.*, [12].
[147] Section 76(8A)(d). Note that in *Cheeseman*, V was a trespasser within the understanding of the law when force was used against him.
[148] [2022] EWCA Crim 1064.
[149] Section 76(5A).
[150] Section 76(6).

The implication of this legislative development appeared to be that disproportionate force (falling short of *grossly* disproportionate force) in self-defence by householders in dwellings was to be condoned. Such a reading was borne out by a Ministry of Justice circular stating that the objective of the revision is "to strengthen the law in favour of householders who use force in self-defence", providing "greater latitude in extreme cases".[151] Yet the same publication also advised that the householder provisions must be read in conjunction with the rest of section 76 of the 2008 Act, which requires any force used to be reasonable in the circumstances as the defendant believed them to be.[152]

This conundrum was addressed in *Collins*.[153] In that case, D had restrained V, a trespasser in D's home, with a headlock for some six minutes before the police arrived. V suffered severe brain damage. The Crown Prosecution Service (CPS) decided not to prosecute D, taking the view that disproportionate force on the part of householders was condonable and therefore a conviction was not a realistic prospect on the facts of the case. V, the claimant, argued that a law of self-defence in those terms contravened Article 2 of the ECHR, which restricted lethal or life-threatening force in self-defence to force that was absolutely necessary.

However, Leveson LJ ruled that the CPS had misunderstood the applicable law. The householder provisions do not authorise the use of disproportionate (falling short of *grossly* disproportionate) force by householders *tout court*. Force of that degree might or might not be considered reasonable force by a jury. The test to be applied at common law, and under the terms of section 76(3), was whether the force used by D was reasonable in the circumstances as D believed them to be. Properly understood in this way, the householder provisions were held to be compliant with the Convention: the jurisprudence firmly established that restricting defensive force to force that was reasonable in the circumstances was an acceptable standard to employ.[154]

Many will welcome this minimalist reading by the Divisional Court of the controversial householder provisions. Yet there is an undeniable tension here. As we have seen, when a jury is deciding whether D used reasonable force, it must give careful attention to whether D acted in a manner that he honestly and instinctively thought was necessary.[155] A finding that force, despite this latitude allowed to D, was nevertheless disproportionate rather argues against any finding that the force was reasonable. Leveson LJ gives one situation where such a finding might occur. He instances a case where a householder declines an opportunity for safe retreat. Leveson LJ considered that while such a failure to retreat might undermine a plea of self-defence in a non-householder case, in a householder case the jury might allow the defence even though they considered that a failure to retreat rendered the force used disproportionate.

[151] Ministry of Justice Circular 2013/02, paras. 8 and 11. The circular gives one factual example of the kind of case where s. 43 might be decisive at para. 20. The ordeal described would be terrifying for a householder, but the response of the householder seems far from extreme (one blow to the back of the violent intruder's head as he departs through the shattered door of the premises that he has forcefully entered) and something one would expect to be within the law of self-defence in any event in terms of sending the intruder on his way.

[152] Section 76(3).

[153] *R (Denby Collins) v Secretary of State for Justice* [2016] EWHC 33 (Admin). See Dsouza, "Understanding the 'House-holder Defence': Proportionality and Reasonableness in Defensive Force" (2016) 75 *CLJ* 192.

[154] A matter considered very fully in the case: *R (Denby Collins) v Secretary of State for Justice* [2016] EWHC 33 (Admin), [35]–[64].

[155] Section 76(7)(b).

This is very puzzling. The question of retreat is normally considered to go to the question of the necessity to use any force at all rather than to an evaluation of the degree of force used.[156]

The reasoning in *Collins* was scrutinised by a five-member panel of the Court of Appeal in *Ray*.[157] D had formed a relationship with E, much to the annoyance of V, who arrived at D's house one night, threatening violence. D tried to make V leave the house and in the course of a violent struggle stabbed and killed V, resulting in D's conviction for murder. On appeal it was argued, on behalf of D, that the judgment in *Collins* undermined the latitude the legislature intended householders to have, namely the right to use any degree of force against intruders provided the force used was not grossly disproportionate. The Court of Appeal, while confirming D's murder conviction, accepted that householders were in a privileged position to this extent: in a non-householder case, a finding that force was disproportionate would entail the conclusion that the force was unreasonable. That would not be the case for a householder, unless grossly disproportionate force had been used. Yet the jury must still evaluate, in a case of disproportionate force falling short of grossly disproportionate force, whether the degree of force used by the householder was reasonable in all the circumstances. That is to say: in a householder case, a jury may be instructed that it is open to them to find that disproportionate force was none the less reasonable force, but it is also open to them to find that it was not reasonable force.[158]

It is worth emphasising that the qualifying circumstances, where a householder may claim whatever latitude these ill-advised changes permit, are limited to self-defence and the defence of others.[159] Any act that focuses exclusively on the defence or recovery of property, or on detaining the intruder (as when D uses force to prevent the trespasser V from leaving the house), is subject to the normal proportionality requirement. Should V, in such circumstances, manage to escape from the house and hide in D's garden, then once outside the household[160] any force that D may use against V in self-defence must not be disproportionate force. All other aspects of self-defence and defence of property will also apply, including the requirement that D's offence involves force, and the exclusion of the defences in circumstances of prior fault.[161] On the latter, the question was raised in *Gill* whether a householder (D) would lose the additional protections from section 76(5A) where D is engaged in a criminal enterprise.[162] The case involved mistaken self-defence, where D stabbed a police officer (V) executing a legal drugs-related raid of his property. It was accepted that D stabbed V not knowing that V was a police officer, but rather in belief that V was from a rival drug gang intent on causing serious injury or death to D and others inside. It was on this basis that D raised mistaken self-defence, including the additional protections afforded for those acting to ward off trespassers in certain buildings. However,

[156] "In a householder case the failure [to retreat] and thus the use of force may be disproportionate but still reasonable": [2016] EWHC 33 (Admin), [23]. The idea seems to be that because recourse to force was avoidable, its use was a disproportionate yet possibly reasonable response. But it is perfectly sensible to say that force was proportionate to the attack faced but nonetheless unreasonable because the attack could have been safely avoided. It does not make the same kind of sense to say that because an attack could have been but was not avoided, any force used to repel it is disproportionate.

[157] [2017] EWCA Crim 1391, [2018] QB 948.

[158] This interpretation has been confirmed in *Nethercott* [2023] EWCA Crim 248.

[159] Section 76(8A)(a).

[160] Sections 76(8A)(b)–(d) and 76(8B)(a)–(c).

[161] Above, § 21.2(i).

[162] *Gill* [2023] EWCA Crim 259.

for the trial judge, allowing these additional protections to apply in the context of someone committing offences of this kind (i.e. drug offences), thereby making themselves more susceptible to attack, was "a million miles away" from the intentions of Parliament.[163] Applying a prior fault logic similar to voluntary association in duress,[164] the trial judge declined to direct the jury on the householder test, and directed them instead to apply the standard test for mistaken self-defence. The Court of Appeal allowed D's appeal, however, holding that the householder rules should apply to everyone within the statutory criteria, and therefore treating them as not applying to D would be contrary to the rule of law.[165]

*(e) New "exceptional" categories*

In recognising certain defendant groups as exceptional and amending the terms of self-defence in relation to those groups, an obvious question emerges regarding the potential for recognising further such categories of defendant in the future. Indeed, in view of the householder reforms in particular, where the normative case for special treatment is questionable, the route to potential reform may appear relatively open. The reality of this, of course, will have as much to do with politics as with law, but it has given rise to a creative line of thinking within the literature.

Arguably, the best case for reform of this kind has centred on victims of abuse who kill their abuser. Self-defence and the prevention of crime defences are notoriously difficult defences to access for such defendants, both in terms of necessity (e.g., regarding potential for retreat/escape, and imminence) as well as broader issues of reasonableness (e.g., it can be difficult to demonstrate proportionality, particularly where D kills V outside of a specific physical confrontation). In view of this, various proposals have been explored in the academic literature for expanding self-defence, including through the recognition of abuse victims as a new special category of defendant.[166] The Law Commission began exploring potential reforms of this kind in its initial work on domestic homicide,[167] a project that has now transformed into a full review of homicide.[168]

### *(v) European Convention on Human Rights*

Article 2 of the ECHR provides that everyone's right to life shall be protected by law. Deprivation of life will not contravene Article 2 if, *inter alia*, it results from the use of force which is no more than *absolutely necessary*:

(a) in defence of any person from unlawful violence; or
(b) in order to effect a lawful arrest or to prevent the escape of a person lawfully detained.

[163] *Ibid.*, [23]–[24].
[164] Above, § 20.1(i)(b).
[165] *Gill* [2023] EWCA Crim 259, [33].
[166] Bettinson and Wake, "A New Self-Defence Framework for Domestic Abuse Survivors who Use Violent Resistance in Response" (2023) 87 *MLR* 141; Edwards, "'Demasculinising' the Defences of Self-Defence, the 'Householder Defence' and Duress" [2022] *Crim LR* 111; McPherson, "The Problem of Complex Defence Strategies" [2025] *Crim LR* 264.
[167] Law Com. Background Paper. *Defences for Victims of Domestic Abuse Who Kill Their Abusers* (2025).
[168] The Law Commission announced the new project and call for evidence in 2025.

Although the potential for lethal force in defence is consistent with Article 2, it is questionable whether current self-defence and prevention of crime defences are sufficiently restricted to "absolutely necessary" force alone. It will be remembered that mistakes about the facts justifying defensive force will not necessarily undermine D's defence in English law, even where such beliefs are unreasonably held.[169] This becomes relevant to the direct actions of the state (i.e., via state officials) regarding Article 2, as well as "framework obligation" under Article 2 which requires the state to set up its criminal law so as to adequately protect the lives of its citizens.

Should the action of a state official, such as a police officer or soldier, contravene Convention standards, that conduct will directly implicate the United Kingdom. Through its official, the state itself has breached the Convention. Accordingly, when concerned with acts by state officials the English courts should construe the broad terms of section 3 of the Criminal Law Act 1967 to conform with Article 2.[170] Although the Convention standard of "absolute necessity" contrasts with the reasonableness standard prescribed by section 3, the Convention jurisprudence does not take the phrase literally—certainly a *reasonable* belief in the need for force, even if mistaken, will comply with Article 2.[171] But what of an *unreasonable* belief in the need for force? Under the Convention, it has been suggested that a reasonable belief may be required for law enforcement officials;[172] and therefore a state law enforcement official who causes death while acting unreasonably may well incur a liability on the part of the United Kingdom to pay compensation under the provisions of the European Convention on Human Rights. Yet it does not follow from that that the United Kingdom is obliged to amend its law of homicide to create a special offence or defence-exclusion for its officials.[173] The question would be whether a state obligation to pay compensation if its officials negligently cause deaths,[174] coupled with homicide liability where a state official caused death and was unable to rely on self-defence or the prevention of crime defence, suffices for compliance with Article 2 of the ECHR.[175] In our view, it does.

Where a private individual uses force against another individual, the state is not directly implicated in any wrong that may have arisen. But here, to comply with the framework

[169] Above, § 21.2(ii).

[170] This includes taking into account any settled jurisprudence of the ECHR relating to Art. 2: Human Rights Act 1998, s. 2.

[171] *McCann and others v UK* (1996) 21 EHRR 97; *Andronicou v Cyprus* (1998) 25 EHRR 491. In *Juozaitene, Bikulius v Lithunia* (2008) 47 EHRR 55, it was strongly emphasised that state officials must act reasonably when resorting to fatal force. For a full and learned account of the Convention jurisprudence on force used in crime prevention and self-defence, and its compatibility with the law of England and Wales, see the judgment of Leveson LJ in *R (Denby Collins) v Secretary of State for Justice* [2016] EWHC 33 (Admin), [2016] QB 862, [35]–[71].

[172] See, e.g., Leverick, *Killing in Self-defence* (2006).

[173] After all, when a police officer, like anyone else, is tried for a crime, that person is tried in their capacity as an individual citizen, not *qua* state official. The conviction is personal, not official. There are, to be sure, some crimes that can only be committed by a state official such as misconduct in public office. In such cases the role is partly constitutive of the wrong. This does not apply in cases of self-defence. That is less obviously the case when the official is using force in the prevention of crime; but even in those cases, the official will be empowered under the terms of s. 3 of the Criminal Law Act 1967, which confers on *everyone* a power to use reasonable force in the prevention of crime.

[174] Confirmed in *Ashley v Chief Constable of Sussex* [2008] UKHL 25 (unreasonable mistake by police no answer in tort).

[175] Cf. Rogers, "Applying the Doctrine of Positive Obligations in the European Convention on Human Rights to Domestic Substantive Criminal Law in Domestic Proceedings" [2003] *Crim LR* 690.

obligation, adequate criminal laws must be in place to protect the Article 2 right to life.[176] If the criminal law were found to be too permissive in allowing the taking of life, this might result in the state contravening this obligation under Article 2.[177] The question then arises whether allowing private individuals a defence of unreasonable mistake, in cases involving death, insufficiently protects the right to life of persons overall. Here an issue of balance arises: the protection of the public may need to be reconciled with the degree of culpability required for just punishment. Empirical questions surface too: how much more dangerous is a society that allows a defence of unreasonable mistake in homicide contexts? One would need also to note that not all unreasonable mistakes excuse. A belief that force was proportionate will not avail if the force is found to be excessive, for example.[178] On balance, it is submitted that allowing some latitude to unreasonable mistakes for homicides perpetrated by private individuals does not bring the United Kingdom into breach of Article 2.[179]

Article 2 permits the use of fatal force to prevent unlawful violence. There is no reference to the defence of property and, because Article 2 is regarded as a fundamental provision to be construed strictly, use of fatal force to protect property is likely to contravene the Convention. It seems very likely that any law permitting force to prevent crime which allowed private citizens to take life in order to protect property will therefore be found wanting in terms of the state's framework obligation to ensure adequate protection of citizens' lives. Earlier in this chapter (§ 21.2(iii)), we questioned whether it would always be unreasonable to take life to defend property. Under the Convention, that appears to be the position. Force short of lethal force raises different issues, to which we now turn.

## § 21.3 Defence of property

There is a long-standing common law right to protect property by reasonable force;[180] also now recognised within section 76 of the 2008 Act.[181] Very frequently this defence will add no further element to issues arising from force used in the prevention of crime or in

[176] This includes associated procedural matters, such as decisions to prosecute. See discussion in *Da Silva v UK* (2016) 63 EHRR 12; Rogers, "A Human Rights Perspective on the Evidential Test for Bringing Prosecutions" [2017] *Crim LR* 678.

[177] Discussed in *R (Denby Collins) v Secretary of State for Justice* [2016] EWHC 33 (Admin), [2016] QB 862, where the Divisional Court found that the potential for disproportionate defensive force in householder cases did not result in breach of the UK's obligations under Article 2.

[178] *Clegg* [1995] 1 AC 482.

[179] For differing view of this question, see Leverick, "Is English Self-defence Law Incompatible with Art 2 of the ECHR?" [2002] *Crim LR* 347; Smith, "The Use of Force in Public or Private Defence and Article 2" [2002] *Crim LR* 958; Leverick, "The Use of Force in Public and Private Defence and Article 2: A Reply to Professor Smith" [2002] *Crim LR* 963. Notwithstanding the view expressed here in the text, the Joint Parliamentary Committee on Human Rights, in reviewing the retention of the subjective test in what became s. 76 of the Criminal Justice and Immigration Act 2008, considered that the retention of this test might put the UK in breach of Article 2, particularly in cases involving the use of force by public law enforcement officials: *Fifteenth Report of Session 2007/2008 Legislation* HL paper No. 81; HC paper No. 440, paras. 2.26–2.28.

[180] *Green v Goddard* (1704) 2 Salk 641. For more recent discussion of the defence, see *Williams (Demario)* [2020] EWCA Crim 193.

[181] Legal Aid, Sentencing and Punishment of Offenders Act 2012, s. 148 (amending s. 76 of the Criminal Justice and Immigration Act 2008).

self-defence; and can be understood using the same two elements of necessary and reasonable force.

*Element 1*: Necessity of force: it must have been subjectively necessary for D to use some force against V to protect his property rights.

*Element 2*: Reasonableness of force: the force used by D must have been objectively reasonable, on the facts as he subjectively believed them to be.

So, if V should break into D's home with intent to steal, D can use reasonable force to prevent V from appropriating his property, and the same applies to repelling any attack upon him that V might make. If V is merely a trespasser, and not a criminal,[182] D is still entitled to use force to eject him. However, D must start with peaceable means.[183] If V's trespass was non-forceful, D must, for instance, first tell V to leave and allow him time to do so before resorting to force to eject V.[184] A similar right to use force extends to moveable property as well as buildings and land: if V has taken D's moveable property by non-forceful means, D must give V the chance to hand back the property before using force to reclaim it.[185]

In *Hussey*,[186] the Court of Criminal Appeal gave forceful expression to D's right to defend his home. It was said that D could lawfully kill V if that was the only way that D could prevent V from unlawfully ejecting D from D's home. It must be rare indeed for D to face the immediate and unlawful loss of his home to V without the threat of bodily harm, abduction, or false imprisonment. But where loss of possession of his home is the only thing that is threatened, it seems unlikely, *pace Hussey*, that D can resort to fatal force, even if that is the only way to keep possession. There are legal means of redress for unlawful eviction. It is doubtful, as was discussed in § 21.2(v), whether the "framework obligation" under Article 2 of the ECHR allows states to craft their criminal laws to allow fatal force to protect property, even where D faces the permanent loss of the property without any realistic legal redress. Where there is legal redress, the proscription of fatal force is even more likely to be necessary.

Where defence of property is the only defence available, D should be cautious about using force. Suppose that D has invited V to dinner at his home. V has outstayed his welcome and ignored several heavy hints that it is time for him to go. While reasonable force can be used to eject a trespasser, and V would become a trespasser if D finally lost patience and ordered him to leave, it is doubtful whether he can enforce his order by force if V remains a bore rather than a threat. In *Burns*,[187] D picked up V, a sex worker, in his car and drove to a secluded spot. On reaching the destination, D decided that he did not want sex with her. He paid her the amount agreed and ordered her to leave the car. Not unreasonably, V refused to leave as it was her understanding that after sex she would be driven back to where D had picked her up. D forcibly ejected her. The Court of Appeal confirmed D's

[182] The scope of non-criminal trespass in residential property was considerably reduced by s. 144 of the Legal Aid, Sentencing and Punishment of Offenders Act 2012, which made squatting in residential premises, even if unoccupied, a criminal offence.

[183] Note that nothing in this requirement forecloses the possibility that an initially peaceable defence of property may be escalated, following a more violent response from V, into a situation requiring D to act in defence of her person.

[184] *Green v Goddard* (1704) 2 Salk 641.

[185] *Bird v Jones* (1845) 7 QB 742.

[186] (1924) 18 Cr App R 160 (CA).

[187] [2010] EWCA Crim 1023, [2010] 1 WLR 2694.

conviction for assault occasioning actual bodily harm. Force was not necessary. D could restore quiet possession of his car by driving back to the pickup point.[188]

## § 21.4 Necessity

The defence of necessity can be presented in beguilingly simple terms, applying to justify D's otherwise criminal conduct when that conduct is performed for a recognised greater good. Indeed, the defence is often described in terms of "lesser evils". Conduct of this kind should not typically be prosecuted at all,[189] but where it is, it is right that D should be availed with a substantive defence.

But, as a substantive legal rule, necessity remains something of an enigma:[190] despite references to the language of necessity as far back as the sixteenth century,[191] it continues to lack a specific definition;[192] despite its potential breadth as a simple balance of evils defence,[193] its application in practice remains restricted and piecemeal;[194] and even when recognised as a defence on certain facts, the evolution of other defences and legislation will often step in to remove any future reliance on necessity.[195] In marked contrast with other supervening defences, we characterise necessity as an imperfect safety net, existing to catch justified conduct that might otherwise fall between other defences and result in liability, but only doing so in the most compelling cases. In this section, then, we discuss how the defence has evolved, how it is applied in practice, and how it might best be rationalised. We do not—as we have done with other defences—provide an opening summary statement of the defence elements, because this defence, as we discuss below, continues to defy the identification of concrete defining elements.

At various points, concerns about the clarity and appropriate application for necessity have led to its rejection. English case law contains some vigorous rejections of any notion that necessity may be invoked as an excuse or justification for a crime. In *Kitson*, D,[196] who was asleep on the back seat of a car, awoke to find the car was moving down the hill on which it was parked. To avert catastrophe, he assumed control of the vehicle and steered it safely to a stationary position on the side of the road. The fact that he was responding to an

[188] Although the matter is not entirely clear from his judgment, it seems Lord Judge CJ considered that V became a trespasser in D's car upon being told to leave, but it was a trespass that could be terminated without resort to violence. A better view is that V was not a trespasser but was a passenger entitled to be taken back into town by D. On that view not even a presumptive right to use force against her would arise on the facts of the case.

[189] The Code for Crown Prosecutors requires consideration of the "public interest" (or otherwise) in prosecuting.

[190] Fletcher, *Rethinking Criminal Law* (1978) 759–97, 818–35, 855–75; Smith, *Justification and Excuse in the Criminal Law* (1989) chap. 3; Schopp, *Justification Defences and Just Convictions* (1998) chap. 6; Brudner, "A Theory of Necessity" (1987) 7 *OJLS* 338; Gardner, "Necessity's Newest Inventions" (1991) 11 *OJLS* 125; Dennis, "On Necessity as a Defence to Crime: Possibilities, Problems and the Limits of Justification and Excuse" (2009) 3 *Crim L and Philosophy* 29; Mares, "Emergencies, Necessity and the Prevention of Crime" in Simester (ed.), *Modern Criminal Law* (2024) 201.

[191] *Forgossa* (1552) 1 Plowd 1.

[192] The Law Commission, in its most recent treatment of the defence, concluded that it should be left undefined: Law Com. No. 218. *Offences Against the Person and General Principles* (1992) cl. 36(2).

[193] We discuss alternative rationales below, § 21.4(ii).

[194] Even where the defence is allowed, as we will see, it is common for courts to isolate such cases to their (typically unusual) facts. See, e.g., *Re A (Children)* [2000] 4 All ER 961 (CA).

[195] We see this, e.g., in the evolution of duress of circumstances discussed below (and above, § 20.2).

[196] (1955) 39 Cr App R 66 (CA).

emergency and refrained from driving any further once the situation was resolved did not exempt him from liability for driving a car when unfit due to drink. In *Buckoke v GLC*,[197] the Court of Appeal had to decide whether a driver of a fire engine on an emergency call could elect to drive through a red traffic light. The answer was a resounding no, an answer to be given even if the road was clear and a person some 50 yards from the now stationary vehicles required immediate life-saving rescue from the fire service. A final example is afforded by *Southwark LBC v Williams*,[198] where the Court of Appeal rejected an argument that homeless people could take temporary refuge in vacant council premises without committing acts of trespass. Indeed, even the Law Commission, at one time, recommended that, to whatever extent is *does* exist, necessity should be abolished.[199]

These are older examples. Yet the intransigent approach taken in them still surfaces. In *R (Nicklinson) v Ministry of Justice*, an ambitious argument that voluntary euthanasia and assisted suicide could be justified as a necessary and proportionate response to the suffering of the applicants was raised before the Court of Appeal.[200] One ground for rejection given by the Court was that English law knows no general defence of necessity.[201] It is notable that no attempt was made by the applicants to revive a necessity argument before the Supreme Court.[202]

As will be demonstrated below, the Court of Appeal was wrong to assert that English law does not recognise a general defence of necessity. But before we consider the relevant cases, we should recognise the central concerns which even now lead to claims that the defence is unknown and which will always and properly limit the defence to a modest and supplementary role. There is an understandable reluctance to allow individuals to be the judge of when to dispense with the letter of the law:[203]

> "The law regards with the deepest suspicion any remedies of self-help, and permits these remedies to be resorted to only in very special circumstances. The reason for such circumspection is clear—necessity can very easily become simply a mask for anarchy."

This is a rule of law argument; and an argument of democratic legitimacy.[204] The legal system will simply not work if its authority is optional. Derogation from its rules is not permitted save in specific, confined circumstances. It is clearly in the public interest that traffic signals be rigidly obeyed: general security would be much diminished if overriding discretions were allowed. The use of vacant council properties is best resolved by the local political decision-making processes, implemented by consistent administration rather than *ad hoc* self-help. And so on. The drawback produced by this unyielding stance is that it exposes to criminal liability persons whose conduct may have brought about significant benefit and whose motivation may have been impeccable. This is a powerful consideration

[197] [1971] 1 Ch 655 (CA).
[198] [1971] 1 Ch 734 (CA).
[199] Law Com. No. 83, *Defences of General Application* (1977).
[200] [2013] EWCA Civ 961, [2014] 2 All ER 32. See Stark, "Necessity and Nicklinson" [2013] *Crim LR* 949.
[201] *Ibid.*, [28].
[202] [2014] UKSC 38, [2015] AC 657. In the Supreme Court, the applicants made no argument for the permissibility of voluntary euthanasia but made some headway with the claim that the right to private life guaranteed under Art. 8 of the ECHR could permit assistance in suicide for persons in the dire circumstances of the applicants.
[203] *Southwark London Borough v Williams* [1971] Ch 734, 740 (Edmund Davies LJ) (CA). Cf. Brudner, "A Theory of Necessity" (1987) 7 *OJLS* 338, 342–4. See also Simester, *Fundamentals* chap. 18.
[204] Both are discussed below, § 21.4(ii).

and warrants the admissibility of a necessity plea. Yet it is a plea that imports considerable difficulties of definition and ambit.

### *(i) Recognition of a necessity defence*

In the latter part of the 1980s, the defence of necessity experienced something of a re-emergence in practice. However, in large part, this did not arise from any considered reflection but by way of extending the defence of duress to embrace duress of circumstances, removing the requirement of a crime nominated by the duressor. Cases such as *Conway*[205] and *Willer*[206] allowed the ground covered by duress to encroach on territory which, if within the realm of defences at all, could only previously have been accommodated by referencing necessity. Nonetheless, those cases adhere to the informing idea of duress, namely that the defendant's act was coerced by a fear of immediate death, serious bodily harm, or rape. Essentially, the content of the legal norm violated is not being challenged by claiming the priority of a competing value; rather, the argument is that compliance with law cannot reasonably be expected from a person under such pressure. This is, paradigmatically, the theory of an excuse, not a justification.[207] Further, the crime of murder remains outside the scope of the duress defence; so too do wrongs committed in response to any lesser threat than immediate death, serious harm, or rape.[208] By contrast, neither of those strictures apply on those rare occasions where a defence of necessity is permitted to address the ethical quality of D's intervention rather than the pressure that D was under when he acted.

Duress of circumstances was later extended to a very different situation in the case of *Pommel*.[209] D took possession of a sub-machine gun from a person who had it in mind "to kill some geezer". D himself was not that "geezer" and was under no threat. Essentially, his reasoning was that it was better to take possession of the gun, despite his lack of a licence, rather than to allow it to remain in the hands of a person intending to use it to kill. D was asserting the value of saving life over the letter of the gun-control laws while at the same time furthering the ultimate goals of gun laws, namely keeping weapons out of the wrong hands. If D was telling the truth,[210] this is a defence of necessity; as seems implicitly to have been recognised by the Court of Appeal, which used the terms necessity and duress interchangeably.[211]

A more considered recognition of a defence of necessity was given by the House of Lords in two cases involving incompetent patients. In the first, *Re F (Mental Patient:*

[205] [1989] QB 290 (CA).

[206] (1986) 83 Cr App R 225 (CA).

[207] Because such claims are so troubling to the coherence of the legal order, the Supreme Court of Canada (save for Wilson J) was of the opinion in *Perka* (1984) 13 DLR (4th) 1 that necessity claims must operate in the realm of excuse. But as we shall see, necessity pleas will be raised in circumstances where D herself is unpressurised; as, for example, where D, a surgeon, decides that V's best interests as someone with a severe learning disability who is sexually active will be served by a sterilisation operation. It should not be enough to excuse D for carrying out such a radical intervention without V's consent: the operation must be, all things considered, the right thing to do.

[208] See above, § 20.1(ii).

[209] [1995] 2 Cr App R 607 (CA); above, § 20.2(ii).

[210] D's account was dismissed by the trial judge as "utterly incredible", but it was held on appeal that it should nevertheless have been put to the jury to decide.

[211] In *Quayle* [2005] EWCA Crim 1415, [2005] 1 WLR 3642, [41]–[42], there is recognition that *Pommel* is a different category to the other duress by circumstances authorities.

*Sterilisation)*,[212] the legality of a sterilisation operation on a sexually active but learning-disabled patient was in issue. Pregnancy was judged to be something which it was in the interests of the patient to avoid at all costs; measures short of sterilisation were assessed as ineffective or impracticable. Lords Brandon and Goff premised the legality of the operation on ground of necessity. In *Bournewood Community and Mental Health NHS Trust*,[213] the legality of the detention and treatment of an informally admitted mentally incompetent patient whose detention fell outside the regime provided by the Mental Health Act 1983 was held, unanimously, to be justified by necessity. Cases of considerable antiquity were restored to memory,[214] grounding the ruling that a defence of necessity is known to English law.[215] What the decision (and previous decisions) lacks, however, is any considered discussion of the rationale and ambit of the defence.[216]

### *(ii) The rationale and ambit of necessity*

Discussion of necessity inevitably contains a large measure of conjecture. The idea behind the defence is simple and beguiling: achieve the greater good rather than slavishly follow the letter of the law. There will be occasions where following this injunction will produce incontrovertible gains in welfare and an absence of countervailing harms. Yet an absence of countervailing harms is not a necessary condition for raising the defence. A balance of harms test may be allowed in some circumstances. In other situations, vested legal rights take priority, and prevent D from justifying the harm done to V on a balance of harms test.

There is no unitary rationale of the necessity defence.[217] Rather, within the general rubric of "necessity", the defence cloaks a number of intertwined justificatory reasons. What they have in common is at least a degree of urgency, which may fall short of immediate emergency. Sometimes it may be possible to seek the assistance of the courts *ex ante* to determine the legality of a proposed course of action. In medical cases, the courts have shown a commendable degree of procedural flexibility in advising on the legality of proposed surgery, surgery that would constitute a criminal act unless warranted by necessity. Yet there will be occasions where immediate action is called for—E will die, say, unless D drives to hospital in excess of the speed limit. Nowadays, a court may rule, *ex post facto*, that D was entitled to drive in excess of the limit. As the threatened danger was death, a court minded to find D not guilty may prefer to achieve that result by way of excusatory duress rather than justificatory necessity. If D was speeding to hospital because E was in excruciating pain, the duress option would not be available, however,[218] and the difficulties that the necessity plea brings would have to be faced.

[212] [1990] 2 AC 1.
[213] [1998] 3 All ER 289 (HL).
[214] *Mouse's Case* (1608) 12 Co Rep 63.
[215] In *Hasan* [2005] UKHL 22, [2005] 2 AC 467 and *Quayle* [2005] EWCA Crim 1415, [2005] 1 WLR 3642, one can find *dicta* sceptical about whether talk of a general defence of necessity is grounded in legal reality but at the same time a recognition that cases such as *Re F* and *Bournewood* cannot really be placed under the rubric of duress of circumstances.
[216] St George's Healthcare NHS Trust v. S [1998] 3 All ER 673 (CA).
[217] Cp. Chan and Simester, "Duress, Necessity: How Many Defences?" (2005) 16 *King's College LJ* 121.
[218] *Quayle* [2005] EWCA Crim 1415, [2005] 1 WLR 3642 (pain, however severe, insufficient to raise duress). Cf. *Pipe v DPP* [2012] EWHC 1821 (Admin), [2012] All ER (D) 238 (May).

What must be present in every case if a defence of necessity is to succeed is an identifiable harm which can only be avoided if, in the near future, the letter of the law is breached. If the harm is more remote than that (particularly where the harm has a degree of conjecture and imprecision), D cannot take the law into her own hands and must address her concerns in some other fashion. In *Shayler*,[219] D, a civil servant employed in MI5, was concerned that the kind of covert actions supported by the service threatened rather than enhanced public security. He was held to be in breach of the Official Secrets Act 1989, consequent on sharing secret information with a newspaper. Even on the assumption that his concerns were warranted, he was not attempting to avert some imminent catastrophe by the only possible and proportionate means. There was no forthcoming event his actions were intended to avert, merely a fear that the covert operations of MI5 threatened public security generally.

Since necessity has such an uncertain scope, its frequent recognition could potentially undermine the authority of law. If defendants were permitted to break laws *whenever* there was, say, a lesser-evils justification (below), the generality of those laws would be undermined and their application would have to be reassessed on a case-by-case basis. It is for the legal system to determine when its prima facie laws may be broken. Ideally, in a democracy, the freedom of action that a perceived necessity requires should be afforded by legislative change. Yet constraints of time may preclude resort to legislation. In those circumstances, wherever possible, guidance from a court should be sought before the putatively illegal action is taken; as was done, for instance, in the conjoined twins separation case of *Re A (Children)*.[220] Where that is impossible and the only recourse is direct action by D, D may—exceptionally—be found to have been justified by necessity.

### *(a) A lesser-evils justification*

The most obvious rationale for allowing necessity is a recognition that, on occasion, more welfare may ensue from breaking than from keeping the law. The defence looks to the consequences of particular episodes of conduct rather than to the desert of the actor. To be sure, on many occasions where a necessity defence may be invoked, the defendant is meritorious or blameless. Yet if, say, a driver of a fire engine decides to pass through a red light with complete safety on a clear road in order to effect a life-saving rescue, it misses the point to say that a conviction for a road traffic offence is not merited on retributivist grounds. The gain in welfare arising from saving a life rather than opting for compliance with regulatory law is so salient that it eclipses any issues of culpability and blame typically associated with law-breaking.

The fire engine case is an easy example because the offence in question was a victimless offence; no one's rights or interests were overridden when making the rescue. Contrast the following case:

> D takes money from V to give to X so that X may have a life-saving operation only available to those who can travel abroad and pay for it. V is an elderly billionaire who lives alone in a large mansion full of cardboard boxes stuffed with money. He has no relatives, has made no will, and possesses no plans whatever for his money. Yet he resolutely refuses to give any of it away.

[219] [2001] 1 WLR 2206 (CA).
[220] [2000] 4 All ER 961 (CA).

To take any of V's money should surely be theft, even if D is able to take the money in circumstances causing V no distress whatever (e.g. D takes one box from hundreds and V remains wholly unaware that it has gone). Where breaching the law involves harming an innocent person, there is a strong presumption against any claim that the wrong can be made right by reference to necessity. A balance of evils analysis cannot ordinarily abrogate the legally protected interests of persons who do not waive their rights. Outside specific situations, there is no principle of appropriation licensing the violation of another's rights merely on grounds of necessity.[221] In all probability, this limitation is unyielding in cases where the right violated relates to V's person,[222] but it may be, as discussed below, that a balance of harms test may still be applicable in a case where V's proprietary right is infringed in circumstances where adequate compensation can normally be given.

*(b) Intervention in V's own interests where V is incompetent*

This rights-based limitation on what would otherwise be an essentially utilitarian balancing exercise is always in point where the right-holder is competent to enforce or waive her rights. Matters are different where the right-holder is incompetent. In *Re F*,[223] a compulsory sterilisation operation was lawfully carried out. In *Bournewood*,[224] a person with severe learning disabilities was detained for compulsory treatment even though his adoptive family was anxious to bring him home. The rights overridden were of the most fundamental nature. Was it to the point that the persons whose rights were overridden were deemed incompetent to know their best interests and the procedures were carried out for the presumed benefit of these subjects? Probably; particularly in light of the Court of Appeal's decision in *St George's Healthcare NHS Trust v S*,[225] which vindicated the right of a pregnant woman to refuse a caesarean section, notwithstanding that the operation was required to preserve the life of the mother and of the unborn child. The judgement of the best interests of incompetent persons is a sensitive and troubling matter, something recognised particularly by Lord Steyn in *Bournewood*.[226]

*(c) Violating rights of an autonomous innocent victim*

The most important constraint on the necessity plea is that it cannot be invoked in circumstances where D overrides a legal right of a non-consenting person whose conduct constitutes no threat to the person or property of others. That is why D cannot take any money from V, the misanthropic billionaire, in the example discussed in § 21.4(a). It is why a person in a rare blood group cannot be forced to donate blood, however urgent the need for

[221] For instance, the Criminal Damage Act 1971 allows V's property to be destroyed or damaged if that is the only way of avoiding imminent and greater damage to D's property; but there are no general legal provisions permitting the use of other persons' property in circumstances of emergency.

[222] On the inability of certain "lesser-evil" considerations to override the rights of victims, see Simester, "Necessity, Torture and the Rule of Law" in Ramraj (ed.), *Emergencies and the Limits of Legality* (2008) 289, §§ II, IV.

[223] [1990] 2 AC 1.

[224] [1998] 3 All ER 289 (HL).

[225] [1998] 3 All ER 673 (CA).

[226] [1998] 3 All ER 289, 307–9 (HL). In *HL v UK* (2004) EHRR 761, the European Court of Human Rights held that detaining persons in hospitals under the common law of necessity contravened the right to liberty and security of the person guaranteed by Art. 5(1) of the Convention. The Mental Capacity Act 2005 (as amended by s. 50 of the Mental Health Act 2007) now makes it unlawful to deprive persons of liberty in hospitals or care homes for safety or for treatment, unless an authorisation order is in place or under an order of the Court of Protection. For a review of the operational conditions for the making of these orders and their compliance with the Convention, see *P* [2014] UKSC 19.

blood from this group.[227] This fundamental limitation is not expressly stated in any English case. Yet its existence can be assumed with some assurance, particularly in the light to the decision in *St George's Healthcare NHS Trust* v *S*,[228] which, as we noted above, unequivocally upholds the right of a competent person to refuse any form of medical or surgical intervention however pressing the need for assistance. Furthermore, that case decides that a life-saving procedure cannot be forced upon an unwilling person even if, at one and the same time, another significant interest—here the safe delivery of a late-term foetus—would be secured. If a person's legal rights cannot be overridden in order to treat her own medical needs, they cannot be violated in order to further the treatment of someone else.

*(d) Violating property rights*

This important limitation is subject to some *de minimis* exceptions. On occasion, the infringement of a right may be transitory and inflict no lasting setback to the interests of the right-holder by comparison with the value being protected, for example, where the infringement is required to preserve life. As Devlin J remarked in *Esso Petroleum Co Ltd v Southport Corporation*, a tort case:[229]

> "The safety of human lives belongs to a different scale of values from the safety of property. The two are beyond comparison and the necessity for saving life has at all times been considered a proper ground for inflicting such damage as may be necessary upon another's property."

For example: it may be necessary for D to borrow V's car without permission to effect the rescue of X. Or it may be necessary to break into the absent V's house in order to telephone an ambulance required to take X to hospital for vital emergency treatment. In each of these cases, provided the situation is an emergency, such minor infringements of rights are compatible with allowing a necessity plea. Sufficient regard of V's interests will be offered if he is entitled to full compensation for any loss sustained.[230] Where the same conduct is both a tort and a crime, the courts have allowed compensation for the tort despite acquitting of the crime, as when a civil assault is committed because a reasonable belief in the need to use force was lacking but where D's genuine belief that the force was required to prevent a crime excused D from criminal liability.[231] Similarly, it would be possible to allow necessity in criminal proceedings for damaging or using property, but deny that defence when V demands compensation for any financial loss. In such circumstances necessity would operate as a form of excuse as D's conduct is not fully justified in all legal dimensions.

What if V refuses or resists the use of his property by D? It seems that D may, say, pick up V's mobile phone from the table to alert emergency services even should V have declined D's request to use the phone. It may well be that D is entitled to use a reasonable degree of force should V attempt to take back the phone until the emergency call is made. But could D use a degree of force on V to access the phone in the first place? When, if ever, can V's right to personal integrity be violated in order to secure a greater good? The law provides no answers to any of these questions.

[227] Discussed in Dennis, "On Necessity as a Defence to Crime: Possibilities, Problems and the Limits of Justification and Excuse" (2009) 3 *Crim L and Philosophy* 29, 44–5.
[228] [1998] 3 All ER 673 (CA).
[229] [1956] AC 218, 228 (first-instance judgment).
[230] Cf. the famous tort case of *Vincent v Lake Erie Transportation Co.* 124 NW 221 (1910).
[231] *Ashley v Chief Constable of Sussex Police* [2008] UKHL 25, [2008] AC 962.

*(e) Violating rights of personal integrity*

Given the paramount importance of personal autonomy in a liberal democracy, it is difficult to imagine circumstances where the *de minimis* exception would ever permit the violation of an innocent (and competent) victim's *person*. The view that the personal integrity of competent persons may never be violated is supported by the strong body of judicial opinion, such as that expressed by Lord McKay in *Howe*[232] (a duress by threats case) that the famous case of *Dudley and Stephens*[233] precludes the raising of necessity as a defence to murder. In *Dudley and Stephens*, D and others, survivors of a shipwreck, were adrift in an open boat in the South Atlantic. They killed and consumed, without his consent, the youngest and weakest member of their party. But for this act, D and his companions would probably have died prior to rescue.[234] The case clearly decides that there is no defence to murder in such circumstances. In so far as D was arguing that the threat of imminent death excused his act, the denial of a defence can be understood; he was raising what we now would call a defence of duress of circumstances and, for better or worse, it is well established that a defence of duress is not available for murder.[235] Alternatively, we can read D's defence as a claim that he did the right thing: had this drastic step not been taken, all would have died including the victim of the killing. An emphasis on the value of the act raises the defence of necessity, giving weight to an interpretation of *Dudley and Stephens* to the effect that necessity is not available as a defence to murder. Either way, it appears that current law refuses to countenance a defence to murder unless the circumstances can be brought within the rubrics of self-defence or the prevention of crime (above, § 21.2).

There *may* be one exception to this rule: where V is the source of the danger faced by D. It is important to notice that *Dudley and Stephens* was not concerned with that possibility. Coleridge LCJ referred to the victim as "a weak and unoffending boy". He was an autonomous individual and constituted no threat to anyone else. Because of this, he had a right to be left alone. But what of cases where V is a source of danger? Consider the following case:

> D and others have survived a shipwreck. They are in a lifeboat on the open seas, which is filled to capacity. V, who is in the water, is holding on to the side of the boat. D realises that the weight of all the passengers, combined with V's actions, is causing the lifeboat to ship water. If V is allowed to continue holding on, the boat will ultimately sink, entailing the death of everyone.

On these facts, D is presumably entitled to fend V off, even if that means V will drown more quickly. The case is similar to that which occurred during the Zeebrugge ferry disaster,

[232] [1987] AC 417.

[233] (1884) 14 QBD 273.

[234] A fascinating historical and sociolegal account of the case is given by Simpson, *Cannibalism and the Common Law* (1984). The jury, by special verdict, found that D and others would probably have died had they not killed and consumed V. The killing took place on the eighth day adrift and rescue came on the twentieth day. Legally speaking, therefore, D's act was necessary for survival, particularly in the light of the prosecution's burden of proof. Despite this, Coleridge LCJ queried the necessity of the act as an act of survival by noting that D might have been picked up next day or not picked up at all and, in either case, the killing would have been profitless. But D must be tried on the facts as they occurred and not on the basis of what might have been. To judge necessity on the basis of speculating on the range of possible worlds from a given baseline would be, effectively, to eliminate the defence.

[235] *Howe* [1987] AC 417. Joshua Dressler has argued that the failure in *Dudley* to focus exclusively on whether the defendants' conduct could be excused rather than justified has "misshaped the law of necessity and excuse" not merely in England but across the common law world: "Reflections on *Dudley and Stephens* and Killing the Innocent: Taking a Wrong Conceptual Path" in Baker and Horder (eds.), *The Sanctity of Life and the Criminal Law* (2013) 126, 129. A common reading of *Dudley* is that the killing of an innocent, non-threatening person can neither be justified nor excused: the judgment of Lord Coleridge uses the terms - "justification" and "excuse" as synonyms for raising a defence.

described above in § 21.2(ii)(c). Arguably, such situations should be accommodated within the defence of self-defence, which permits violence to the person extending even to murder. But if not self-defence,[236] then a defence of necessity should in principle be available.

The prospects for the availability of such a defence are enhanced to a degree by the judgment of Brooke LJ in *Re A (Children)*.[237] As already discussed, the Court of Appeal permitted a separation operation to be carried out to allow a normal span of life for J even though the surgery inevitably entailed the death of her conjoined twin M. One of the three appellate judges, Brooke LJ squarely based his decision on the grounds of necessity (although it should be noted that Ward LJ expressed his agreement with Brooke LJ's decision). Brooke LJ found the operation to be justified on a straightforward application of the following three criteria, endorsed originally by Stephen:

(i) the act is needed to avoid inevitable and irreparable evil;
(ii) no more should be done than is reasonably necessary for the purpose to be achieved; and
(iii) the evil inflicted must not be disproportionate to the evil avoided.

Taken at face value, these criteria are over-inclusive. They would allow extreme invasions of the personal integrity of autonomous, non-threatening persons whenever, on a consequentialist weighing of advantage, welfare overall would be increased. The facts of *Re A* should be stressed. Innocent though she indubitably was, M's demands on J's bodily resources were characterised as a direct threat to the life of J, a threat that would terminate an otherwise viable life within three to six months. From that perspective, the affinity with the emergency that arose in the context of the Zeebrugge ferry is reasonably close, M being the source of the threat. One factor informing these situations is that V's position is not significantly worsened by D's intervention. Either way, V will die. Even in *Re A*, the operation aside, M was "self-designated for a very early death". This consideration may well be crucial if personal injury is ever to be permitted under the guise of necessity. Suppose the following example:

> D, V, and others are speleologists. They are exploring a series of caves underground. Unfortunately, and through no one's fault, V becomes trapped in the mouth of one of the caves. The waters in the cave are rapidly rising, and the cave will soon be flooded. The trapped man is immovable. He is preventing the escape and survival not only of himself but also of his fellow speleologists. The only way of unblocking the exit is by cutting off his arm. Even though V objects, D performs the amputation and everyone survives.

Necessity ought, we contend, to be available here as a defence to a charge of inflicting grievous bodily harm. This is not a case in which D is protecting his life against a threat posed by V's behaviour, so this is unlikely to be a case of self-defence. Rather, the speleologists face a common danger. It matters here not only (i) that like cases of self-defence, D's response is addressed to the source of the peril (and not to a third party), but also (ii) that V's interests

[236] If self-defence is confined to repulsing attacks, then fending off V may not fall with its purview.

[237] [2000] 4 All ER 961 (CA). For discussion see Uniacke, "Was Mary's Death Murder?" (2001) 9 *Medical LR* 9; Huxtable, "Separation of the Conjoined Twins: Where Next for English Law?" [2002] *Crim LR* 549; Michalowski, "Sanctity of Life: Are Some Lives More Sacred than Others?" [2002] *LS* 377; Chan and Simester, "Duress, Necessity: How Many Defences?" (2005) 16 *King's College LJ* 121.

are served as well as D's—D has not simply preferred his own interests to those of V. The latter condition is not a requirement of the defence of self-defence.[238]

Considerable caution is in order when assessing whether these conditions apply to circumstances going beyond the precise facts of the very few cases to hand. In the speleologist scenario discussed above, nobody died. What if the only way of allowing the escape of D and the others would inevitably have caused the death of V? A starting point would be the decision in *Re A*, where the innocent yet life-threatening M was killed as a consequence of an operation intended to allow J a longer and better life. As we know, for Ward LJ it was a case of self-defence and for Brooke LJ a case of necessity. Although referencing these general defences, both judges were careful to say that nothing decided in the case had application beyond the particular circumstances of the case.[239] In *Nicklinson*, the Divisional Court,[240] and the Court of Appeal,[241] dismissed emphatically the notion that *Re A* had any bearing on the question of the permissibility of voluntary euthanasia. In terms of principle, one obvious point of difference between the facts of *Nicklinson* and *Re A* is that, in *Re A*, those responsible for the medical care of J and M owed competing duties of care to J and M and, in that sense, were in an unavoidable dilemma which only some authority set above them could resolve.[242] Could we say the same about D and his fellow, trapped speleologists? Although D's situation may not be as stringent in terms of the *duties* he owes to those immediately affected by his conduct, he too faces a scenario of vital competing interests. He too faces the dilemma of failing other(s) if he refuses to sacrifice the one. Thus, the reasoning behind *Re A* is in point here.[243] However, the possibility that the case would be rigidly confined to its medical context cannot be discounted.

### *(iii) Limiting necessity: legislative priority and direct-action protest*

Necessity is a common law principle. Accordingly, it should yield wherever statutory provision has been made for the emergency, crisis, or interest invoked to justify D's act. If, for example, as a consequence of the decision in *Re F (Mental Patient: Sterilisation)*,[244] Parliament had enacted that sterilisation operations could not be carried out without the consent of the patient, necessity could never again be invoked in the circumstances of the *Re F* case. In *Bournewood*, the Court of Appeal took the view that the Mental Health Act 1983 provided a comprehensive regime for the detention and treatment of mentally incompetent

[238] Condition (i) is also significant. Suppose that T, a terrorist, threatens to shoot D unless D, in turn, participates in a mission to murder V. If D does so, the case is neither self-defence nor necessity. It can only be argued as one of duress (and, as we saw, in § 20.1(i)(a), it would fail under the current law of duress). It would have been otherwise if D had responded by shooting T. Justification requires addressing the source of the danger, not deflecting it upon someone else.

[239] [2001] Fam 147, 204–5 (Ward LJ), 239 (Brooke LJ) (CA).

[240] *R (on the application of Nicklinson) v Ministry of Justice* [2012] EWHC 2381 (Admin).

[241] [2013] EWCA Civ 961, [2014] 2 All ER 32.

[242] No distinction was made between J and M in terms of their status as interest-bearing persons. On that basis, the unfortunate M had interests distinct from J's, interests not easy to specify and protect but which, none the less, were to some extent in tension with J's. As Stark argues, the Court in *Nicklinson* was therefore correct to rule that the necessity-based arguments in *Re A* had no relevance to the issues of euthanasia and suicide arising in that case: "Necessity and Nicklinson" [2013] *Crim LR* 949.

[243] It is noteworthy that both Brooke LJ and Ward LJ approved the life-saving though life-taking action of the corporal in the Zeebrugge tragedy.

[244] [1990] 2 AC 1.

patients.[245] V fell outside this scheme and, appropriately, on its view of the Act, the Court of Appeal ruled that necessity could not be invoked to authorise V's continuing detention. By contrast, the House of Lords held (convincingly, in the light of the legislative history) that the scheme of the 1983 Act was not comprehensive and had designedly made no provision for patients such as V who were compliant and did not object to detention but who essentially lacked any means of volition to accept or reject detention and treatment. Accordingly, the immediate best interests of that class of patient could be addressed under the head of common law necessity.

The same analysis was employed in *Quayle*,[246] where the relevant statutory scheme left no room for necessity to apply. One aspect of the case concerned persons who were involved in providing cannabis and various cannabis derivatives for other persons who, it appeared, could only find palliative relief for very painful symptoms by using these substances. Both possession and supply of these substances contravened provisions of the Misuse of Drugs Act 1971. That Act, as well as proscribing in general terms the possession, supply, etc., of controlled drugs, sets up an elaborate scheme for their lawful possession. The Court of Appeal took this scheme to be comprehensive and complete. It did not make general provision for doctors, let alone non-medically qualified persons, to supply cannabis for pain relief. Express provision was made for the medical use of opiates but no express provision was made for cannabis. Consequently, there was no space for a judicial ruling allowing the palliative use of cannabis on the ground of common law necessity. The area of concern was regulated by a statutory scheme.[247]

Of course, D may well object that the statutory scheme found to be incompatible with raising necessity failed to meet her needs. For instance, in *CS*,[248] D believed that her daughter V was in imminent danger of serious sexual abuse from D's ex-partner. To protect V, D took her to live in Spain, in breach of custody provisions regulating access to V by D's ex-partner, thereby committing the offence of child abduction. The Court of Appeal ruled that necessity could not be relied upon because D's belief that V was at risk of rape was unreasonable. The court went on to add that, even if the belief was well-founded, necessity would still not have been an available defence because there were statutory defences of consent or reasonable belief in consent by the other parties to the custody arrangements, as well as access to the family courts to raise her concerns about her ex-partner. Yet, if D had a well-founded fear that her daughter might be raped on the next visit to her father required under the custody arrangements, these defences and access to the court at some future point in time seem beside the point. Courts should not be too astute to clip the wings of necessity by finding that statutory schemes preclude its application.

As well as bowing out where the area of concern is already regulated, courts will be reluctant to intervene under the head of necessity where a claim of necessitous intervention is used to legitimate forms of direct action protest or opposition to government actions or policies which involve criminal acts on the part of the protestors. In *Jones*,[249] D and oth-

[245] [1998] All ER 634.

[246] [2005] EWCA Crim 1415; [2006] 1 All ER 988.

[247] This remains the case even where, post-2018, the medical use of cannabis products has expanded considerably. For those who continue to self-medicate illegally (i.e., outside of the legal schemes), necessity arguments are likely to fail.

[248] [2012] EWCA Crim 389, [2012] 1 WLR 3081.

[249] [2004] EWCA Crim 1981, [2005] QB 259.

ers perpetrated acts of criminal damage at RAF airbases and claimed vindication on the ground that their otherwise criminal acts were reasonable force in the prevention of crime within the terms of section 3 of the Criminal Law Act 1967, the crime in question being the international law crime of aggression, committed, it was alleged, by the United Kingdom against Iraq. Cautious about the application of the defence in these circumstances, Lord Hoffmann emphasised that "ordinary citizens who apprehend breaches of the law . . . are normally expected to call in the police and not take the law into their own hands";[250] further stating on direct-action protest cases that:[251]

> "In a case in which the defence requires that the acts of the defendant should in all the circumstances have been reasonable, his acts must be considered in the context of a functioning state in which legal disputes can be peacefully submitted to the courts and disputes over what should be law or government policy can be submitted to the arbitrament of the democratic process. In such circumstances, the apprehension, however honest or reasonable, of acts which are thought to be unlawful or contrary to the public interest, cannot justify the commission of criminal acts and the issue of justification should be withdrawn from the jury."

There is a perfectly sensible caution within these comments against non-state actors opting for criminal conduct where other legal and proportionate options are available. But line drawing of this kind, limiting the application of defences, inevitably raises difficult questions about the appropriateness and timeliness of alternative actions through the courts or ballot box; and through this, the precise obligations of the "functioning state". Further entanglement in this issue was avoided in *Jones*, however, by ruling that section 3 was only concerned with crimes justiciable within England and Wales. This took the international law crime of aggression outside of its scope,[252] and left the precedential value of Lord Hoffmann's broader comments somewhat in doubt.[253]

The case of *Thacker* provides useful clarification.[254] The case involved 15 direct-action protesters who breached the security perimeter fence at London Stansted Airport, erecting a scaffolding structure and chaining themselves in place to disrupt and prevent a deportation flight chartered by the Home Office. The defendants attempted to raise a section 3 prevention of crime defence, duress of circumstances, and necessity, highlighting evidence that the lives of those on board the flight would be in danger if they were successfully deported to West Africa. However, adopting the approach in *Jones*, the defences were withdrawn by the trial judge and the defendants eventually convicted. The defendants appealed on five grounds, including that the trial judge was wrong to withdraw the defences. The appeal was successful on the first ground, concerning the inappropriateness of the offences charged.[255] However, crucially for present proposes, the ground of appeal relating to the defences was not accepted. Rather, the Court of Appeal clarified that Lord Hoffmann's *dicta* in *Jones* (quoted above) should be

[250] *Ibid.*, [78].
[251] *Ibid.*, [99].
[252] One may wonder whether such a ruling would have been forthcoming against a person who used reasonable force in England against V, a French citizen, to prevent him from leaving England to carry out a murder in France.
[253] An analogous upshot occurred in *Shayler* [2001] 1 WLR 2206 (HL) (above, § 21.4(ii)) where D claimed it had been essential to breach official secrecy legislation to alert the public to the dangers they were in due to secret service incompetence. The Court of Appeal dismissed the necessity claim on the merits, as previously discussed: the House of Lords thought any discussion of necessity to be an irrelevancy.
[254] [2021] EWCA Crim 97, [2021] QB 644.
[255] The prosecution had chosen to charge the defendants with an extremely serious offence under s. 1(2)(b) of the Aviation and Maritime Security Act 1990, with consent from the Attorney General. As the Court of Appeal demonstrates, the elements of this offence were simply not made out on the facts.

considered as the binding *ratio* of that case. Just as importantly, that *dicta* applies beyond prevention of crime cases to duress of circumstances and necessity.[256] In this manner, akin to a specific statutory scheme, the legal and political mechanisms available within the "functioning state" must now be recognised as limits on the availability of such defences. There is much to be said for this position, emphasising that justified criminal conduct cannot be found in the face of adequate non-criminal alternatives. However, as with specific statutory regimes, courts should take care not to treat Lord Hoffmann's *dicta* as a categorical exclusion, clipping the wings of necessity where the state fails *in fact* to provide adequate alternatives.[257]

Simon Gardner has argued that necessity claims cannot be avoided, however politically embarrassing a particular claim may be, if they raise a matter of legality and principle against Her Majesty's Government and not a mere difference of policy.[258] He turns to the ECHR as the major constraint on what the government may legitimately do and advocates the legal protection of forms of direct action which attempt to secure government compliance with the Convention. For instance, he envisages the courts protecting persons who have forcibly released prisoners whose detention is found to have been in breach of Article 5 of the ECHR. We anticipate that courts will rule, *contra* Gardner, that the only avenue of redress for unlawful detention is by way of legal challenge and not through the *ex post* vindication of forms of criminal conduct.

Necessity is a doctrine to be used sparingly in order to cover crises and gaps in provision which lead to an urgent need for remedial action; it is not a force for major changes to the laws of modern legal systems. This is particularly the case for the divisive issue of to what extent, if at all, voluntary euthanasia or assistance in suicide should be made available at the request of competent adults.[259] In England and Wales, arguments based on necessity that in circumstances of acute suffering medical assistance in dying should be legally permissible have failed to gain any traction.[260]

Where a social problem is structural and continuous, it is best addressed through the legislative and political process.[261] A homeless person cannot occupy an empty property as a home.[262] But anyone may take temporary shelter in such a property to avoid an immediate catastrophe.

[256] [2021] EWCA Crim 97, [2021] QB 644, [98]–[100].

[257] Usefully discussed in Cammiss *et al.*, "Necessity, Non-violent Direct Activism, and the Stansted 15" (2021) 85 *MLR* 1515; Cammiss *et al.*, "Defending the Integrity Principle: Necessity, Remorse and Moral Consistency in the Protest Trial" (2025) 45 *OJLS* 329.

[258] "Direct Action and the Defence of Necessity" [2005] *Crim LR* 371.

[259] "In a system governed by the rule of law, any such dispensing power requires great caution. It should not be used as a means of introducing major and controversial policy change": *R (on the application of Nicklinson) v Ministry of Justice* [2012] EWHC 2381 (Admin), [74] (Toulson LJ).

[260] Where courts are performing their familiar task of interpreting cases and legislation, building on work already done, bold steps may be taken, even in controversial areas such as assistance in dying. As noted, in *Nicklinson*, necessity was considered to be an unsuitable basis for change; by contrast, arguments based on Art. 8 of the European Convention (right to private life) made in the Supreme Court persuaded Lady Hale and Lord Kerr that the denial of medical assistance in suicide to persons who found themselves in the circumstances of the applicants was a breach of Art. 8. Lord Neuberger, Lord Mance, and Lord Wilson accepted the force of the applicants' arguments but gave no rulings on the matter.

[261] This matter weighed heavily with the Court of Appeal in *Quayle*. The problem of pain relief was persistent and ongoing. See further, Lenckner, "The Principle of Interest Balancing as a General Basis of Justification" in Eser and Fletcher (eds.), *Justification and Excuse* (1987) vol. 1, 493. Arguably, the decision in *Bournewood* [1999] 1 AC 458 is at odds with this limitation since, although the courts were being faced with an emergency, the problem was systemic.

[262] *Southwark London Borough Council v Williams* [1971] 1 Ch 734 (CA).

### *(iv) Conclusion*

The defence of necessity must be carefully distinguished from the defence of duress of circumstances. Under the latter head, the primary focus is on the pressure that D was under, an excusatory claim premised on a threat of death, serious bodily harm, or rape. In the case of a necessity plea, attention is paid foremost to the value of D's act, the claim that by breaking the letter of the law more benefit was obtained than would have been the case with compliance. In principle, necessity should be available as a defence for all offences, including (sometimes) murder. Affording a necessity defence should not be at the expense of legal rights held by competent non-consenting persons. This principle is subject to a *de minimis* exception which will allow some infringements of rights by reason of necessity, albeit subject to full compensation to the right holder. Rarely, if ever, will this exception permit the violation of V's body. The bodies of non-competent persons may be violated on the ground of necessity but only where the necessitous intervention is for the benefit of the person violated.

It is inevitable that a defence with such a destabilising idea at its core should be ring-fenced by reference to legal rights which cannot be overridden in any circumstances or only in very exceptional cases. There is an understandable tendency for courts to resort to duress of circumstances rather than employ the idea of necessity even when the latter defence would seem more in point.[263] In practical terms, the coverage of the defence of necessity is extremely limited. The circumstances arising in *Re F* and *Bournewood* are now covered by legislation.[264] The most significant modern case is *Re A*, where what would otherwise be murder was legitimated. Perhaps the most significant feature of that case was what might be termed the doctors' dilemma. They owed duties to each of J and M, duties that were to some extent incompatible, in as much as fulfilling J's best interests entailed the death of M. The law must come to the aid of persons who find themselves in circumstances where, whatever path is chosen, criminal liability beckons. Persons striving to do the right thing in stressful circumstances where the law may pull in different directions should be protected from such liability unless their choices are egregious.[265] Indeed, it has been suggested that justificatory necessity is confined to these conflict of duty situations.[266] That would be unfortunate because there may arise circumstances where necessitous interventions should be permitted for persons with a liberty to intervene rather than a duty. Either way, however, successful recourse to the defence of necessity will be a rare event.

[263] In *Pommell* [1995] 2 Cr App R 607, D claimed to have taken possession of a gun to prevent P from shooting V. As D was not under threat at all and the threat to V was not immediate, the case would seem to be one of necessity rather than duress: the Court of Appeal referred to necessity and duress of circumstances interchangeably.

[264] See above, § 21.4(ii)(b). The Mental Capacity Act 2005 lays down procedures and guidance for deciding when incompetent persons over the age of 16 may be treated and/or detained in their best interests. Because persons detained under the Mental Health Act 1983 are not within the terms of the 2005 Act, a lacuna arises when a person detained under the 1983 Act requires medical treatment for reasons not relating to his or her mental health condition. In such circumstances the High Court can invoke its inherent jurisdiction to decide what course of action is in the best interests of the person within its protection: as in *Great Western Hospitals NHS Foundation Trust v AA and Others* [2014] EWHC 132 (Family).

[265] D should be judged on what risk assessment could be made in the circumstances, particularly where an immediate decision is necessary.

[266] "Justification must be premised on the need to fulfil a duty conflicting with the one which the accused is charged with having breached": *Perka* [1984] 2 SCR 232, 274 (Wilson J).

# 22

# DEFENCES AND BLAME: SOME OBSERVATIONS

In §§ 1.3 and 17.1, we discussed the structure of criminal liability. There, we noted that many questions of criminal liability can be resolved by deploying a threefold analysis along the following lines:

(i) Is there an actus reus?
(ii) Is there mens rea?
(iii) Is there any supervening defence?

Employing this procedure will frequently be straightforward and useful. A negative answer to (i) or (ii) will generally preclude liability and it is appropriate to ascertain whether the definitional elements of a crime are present before turning, if necessary, to such matters as justification and excuse. If English law were more precise and consistent in its terminology, we might expect the term "defence" to be confined to issues arising under (iii), whereas matters contested within the terms of (i) or (ii) should go to questions of "definition" rather than defence. As we have seen, however, English law does not follow this pattern of usage. What are termed defences in the case law may arise under any of these headings. An ascription of an actus reus may be contested by raising a "defence" of automatism. Mens rea may be denied by claiming a "defence" of mistake. If what otherwise would be a crime is committed in response to an immediate threat of death, a defence of duress may be raised. Only this last case is a case of defence, within the terms of the threefold analysis.[1]

It is important to understand the nature and role of what we term "true" or "supervening"[2] defences. These are defences which go to (iii), relating to pressures, exemptions, and permissions, rather than denials of actus reus or mens rea.[3] When defining or interpreting the ambit of offences, legislatures and courts seek to identify particular types of wrongs. Delineation of these wrongs requires specification of the defining elements—actus reus and

[1] It would be a mistake to become preoccupied with correct usage. After all, it is perfectly natural to say that D is defending herself when she contests an issue on which her liability depends. So, D may argue that to take V's new car without his permission and return it after driving 10,000 miles is not theft, because she lacked an intent to deprive V of his car permanently. Conceptually, whether she has an intent to deprive permanently is a question about the defining elements of theft but there is no vice in describing D's arguments as her defence to the charge of theft. However, when evaluating the substance of the law, it is important to understand the precise role that a legal rule is playing. See Chapter 18, discussing failure of proof arguments that are commonly (though inaccurately) labelled as defences.

[2] A term coined in Simester, "Mistakes in Defence" (1992) 12 *OJLS* 295.

[3] Exemptions, such as legal infancy, may be a special case. They supervene liability as a form of defence, but will typically be applied *before* detailed engagement with actus reus and mens rea; diverting D to a separate, non-criminal process.

mens rea. To collide with someone accidentally is not to assault that person: an assault is something done intentionally or recklessly. The wrong that is murder has intentionality at its core. When identifying and individuating wrongs, we should seek as much clarity and precision as is feasible. In so far as possible, we must capture the essence of the wrong *ex ante*, in order to afford fair warning[4] and to avoid unfair labelling.[5] Inevitably, however, circumstances will arise when the defining elements of a particular offence are made out but where blame and punishment are unwarranted because of the presence of culpability-eliminating factors at the time of the offence. Supervening defences serve to ensure justice is done to defendants who would otherwise be convicted because their conduct fits the definition of an offence. *Typically*, when that definition is met, blame and punishment are merited. But not always: it is for those times that supervening defences are needed, when proof of the defining elements of an offence does not demonstrate that D's conduct should be considered criminal. Supervening defences bar the rest of the path to conviction.

A conviction, especially for a stigmatic criminal offence, is detrimental *per se*: D suffers a significant setback to her interests if she is convicted of a serious offence, even if she receives an absolute discharge. A conviction is a public act of blame and it must be warranted. Unfortunately, the defences currently allowed under English law provide inadequate protection. As things stand, persons may be convicted of offences despite an absence of wrongdoing or a lack of sufficient—or indeed any—culpability. This is for two sorts of reason. First, there are systemic limitations to the kind of exoneration that any criminal law system can recognise (i.e. things defences cannot do, discussed below in § 22.1). These limitations are intrinsic to a system reliant on the application of rules. They entail the conviction of certain defendants who may be morally blameless. At least at the formal level of adjudication, even the fairest systems of criminal law will convict some people who do not deserve to be blamed or punished for their conduct. That melancholy fact provides no warrant for a second category of cases, however. There are situations where defences *could* be, but are not, made available to blameless persons despite the lack of any systemic need to exclude them. We discuss things that defences fail to do below in § 22.2.

## § 22.1 Some things defences cannot do

Under the conventions of our criminal law, only a limited range of conditions may be taken into account when assessing whether, despite the presence of the definitional elements of an offence, D may nonetheless be excluded from liability. Here we discuss the systemic constraints on defences.

### *(i) Justifications and divergent values*

Inevitably, any legal adjudication of blamelessness is constrained by the substantive values resident in the norms of the criminal law. What makes for a criminal wrong can vary enormously according to time and place. Within relatively recent times, conduct such as adultery and consensual anal sex has been the subject of serious criminal offences in various

[4] Above, § 2.3.
[5] Above, § 2.4.

Anglophone jurisdictions. Where such crimes remain in place, the conduct *must* be treated as wrongful in any criminal litigation. If D has an adulterous affair in a jurisdiction where adultery is criminal, he is blameworthy within the conventions of that legal system. Any assessment of criminal wrongdoing and culpability is made in the context of a particular criminal jurisdiction. One must accept as a *datum* the substantive morality contained in the criminal-law norms of that jurisdiction.

This constraint is bound up with the authority of a legal system. Law works, *inter alia*, by coercing people. It imposes a standard of legally acceptable behaviour and demands that people conform to that standard. If the norms that the law would have us observe were displaced, in each case, by those of the particular defendant, then the law would have no standard to impose.[6] Whatever one takes to be the purposes of law, their achievement requires the coordination of individuals' behaviour by ordering ("do not") rather than asking ("unless you want to"). Individuals cannot be legally justified in conducting themselves above or outside the compass of the law merely because they have different moral values—even if they are right. Any criminal legal system which aims to prevent wrongs must be able to determine wrongful behaviour by a standard independent of the defendant. It may be that D concedes the wrongfulness of her conduct in terms of her own beliefs. Or perhaps she does not. No matter.[7]

The claim to authority that legal norms exert has significant implications for the availability of particular defences.[8] Consider the rule *ignorantia juris non excusat*: ignorance of the law does not excuse.[9] Suppose D is unaware of a prima facie offence that mandates behaviour she would not otherwise choose. The most difficult cases of this type arise in offences *mala prohibita*—when the defendant's action is to be avoided only because proscribed. For example, the only "wrong" about driving slightly, but safely, in excess of the speed limit is that one does so in breach of the law, rather than of the reasons for which that law was made. From D's perspective, even if she desires to comply with the law, no reason to modify her behaviour is generated by such offences unless D is aware of them. As such, D's ignorance is analogous to mistakes of fact and blameless when reasonable.[10] Yet the law may have institutional reasons to disallow her defence. Sometimes, as in the driving example, D can be regarded as culpable for negligently failing to ascertain relevant law before embarking on a particular course of conduct. But the main arguments are instrumental and based, especially, upon the difficulty of proving the defendant ought to have known the law,

[6] "To permit one who knows but does not accede to the community valuation of interests to have an individual standard would at once destroy the law": Seavey, "Negligence—Subjective or Objective?" (1927) 41 *Harvard LR* 1, 11. It is, of course, a further question whether the law's claim to authority is itself justified. In an unjust society, persons who receive few material advantages may have little attachment or regard for the prevailing social order, particularly if unequal outcomes track systemic divisions of race and gender. In such societies, defiance of aspects of the criminal law may be a warranted moral and political stance. Yet even then the reasons that ground morally legitimate defiance do not form any basis for exculpation *within* the terms of the criminal law itself. Intrinsically, the criminal law protects the status quo and criminal law defences must fall within that framework.

[7] Cf. Husak, *Ignorance of Law* (2016), exploring the potential substantive relevance of ignorance where criminal law fails to track morality.

[8] On the importance of understanding criminal law in its institutional context, see Thorburn, "Justifications, Powers and Authority" (2008) 117 *Yale LJ* 1070.

[9] Above, § 18.2.

[10] For discussion of what wrong, if any, is perpetrated when D breaches regulatory law in circumstances that do not engage with any underlying regulatory rationale, see Husak, *Ignorance of Law* (2016) chap. 3; Duff, *Answering for Crime* (2007) 166–74; Schauer and Zeckhauser, "Regulation by Generalization", AEI-Brookings Joint Centre for Regulatory Studies Working Paper No. 05-16 (2005).

and upon the need to provide incentives for citizens to become acquainted with law.[11] The literature on ignorance of law is vast,[12] and we cannot conclude the debate here. The point is that these instrumental arguments depend on the need for the legal system to be effective even at some cost to countervailing moral constraints. Thus, they point toward a rule governing mistakes of law that is, at least partly, disconnected from judgments of culpability.

In § 21.4, we noted that similar concerns about the authoritative status of law have inhibited recognition of a defence of necessity. People are not permitted to choose for themselves whether some legal prohibition should be obeyed in particular circumstances; that, the courts have said, would be a recipe for anarchy.[13] This is a consideration that informs all justificatory defences. In general, individuals are not free to choose to break the law unless the situation is urgent, so that it cannot be resolved by recourse to the legal system. D cannot raze V's field to create a firebreak, thereby protecting the villagers against the realistic *prospect* of a forest fire, unless authorised by law. But she may do so if the fire is real and upon them.

### *(ii) Limiting excuses*

Implicit in the claim to authority for the criminal law are further limitations. It is important that the practical scope of excusatory defences does not undermine the capacity of criminal law to sustain a system of order through rules.[14] Consequently, many episodes of blameless conduct which fall within the defining elements of offences must be regarded as crimes, notwithstanding that they are products of the normal and countless vicissitudes of life. Consider, for example, D, a man devastated by the recent departure of his partner. He drinks alcohol by way of solace and, being unaccustomed to alcohol, he rapidly becomes intoxicated. While in that condition, he is taunted by V and, in his disinhibited state, D lashes out at V with his fists. Even if D's life was exemplary up to that point, he must still be held liable for assault. Were we to allow an excuse based on his current life situation, we would then be committed to entertaining many other narratives of how "normal" life had dealt harshly with an accused. Yet, if we change our example to a situation where D did not know he was drinking alcohol because his soft drinks were surreptitiously laced, arguably he should now have a supervening defence. An excuse based on the fact of involuntary intoxication is exceptional, bounded, and forensically manageable. Were it to choose to

[11] "The principle that ignorance of the law should not be a defence in criminal matters is not justified because it is fair, it is justified because it is necessary, even though it will sometimes produce an anomalous result": *Campbell* (1972) 21 CRNS 273, 280 (Kerans DCJ). Cp. *People v O'Brien* 31 Pac 45, 47 (1892). For an instrumental counter-argument, see *State v O'Neil* (1910) 126 NW 454, 456.

[12] In the criminal context, see, e.g., Husak, *Ignorance of Law* (2016); Azmat, "What Mistake of Law Just Might Be: Legal Moralism, Liberal Positivism, and the Mistake of Law Doctrine" (2015) 18 *New Criminal LR* 369; Ashworth, *Positive Obligations in Criminal Law* (2013) chap. 7; Ashworth, "Ignorance of the Criminal Law and Duties to Avoid It" (2011) 74 *MLR* 1. Brett, "Mistake of Law as a Criminal Defence" (1966) 5 *Melbourne U LR* 179; Hall and Seligman, "Mistake of Law and *Mens Rea*" (1941) 8 *U Chicago LR* 641; Keedy, "Ignorance and Mistake in the Criminal Law" (1908) 22 *Harvard LR* 75; Williams, *TBCL*, 451–63; Fletcher, *Rethinking Criminal Law* (1978) 736–58; Hall, *General Principles of Criminal Law* (2nd ed., 1947) 376–92.

[13] *Southwark London Borough v Williams* [1971] Ch 734, 740 (Edmund Davies LJ) (CA).

[14] For a thorough and nuanced discussion of the nature and limits of excusatory claims, see Horder, *Excusing Crime* (2004).

do so, English law could, within certain limits, afford a defence of involuntary intoxication without undermining a system of ordering by rule.[15]

No doubt this conclusion would be attacked by critical theorists, who may regard a distinction between agents who drink while in thrall to strong emotions and agents who drink unwittingly as yet another of the arbitrary distinctions that undermine any claim of the criminal law to be based on consistent principles.[16] Norrie, for instance, has made much of the fact that we allow a defence of duress based on violence but disallow, as any excuse, the impact of poverty deprivation on conduct.[17] In some situations, his critique has considerable force.[18] Assessed in terms of culpability, there may be little difference if D shoplifts because she has been threatened with violence by her husband or shoplifts because she cannot face the disappointment of her children at Christmas. The short explanation for the variance is that we can sustain a law of theft even if we allow an excuse on the basis of violent coercion but not if we excuse on the grounds of economic deprivation. Maintenance of a law of theft in an unequal society may well entail the conviction of persons who must be held blameworthy within the terms of the criminal law but whose conduct does not merit punishment when judged by a wider frame of reference. Such judgments in favour of waiving punishment will tend to lack force outside the sphere of drastic deprivations relating to such necessities as food, shelter, and medical treatment: resentment at economic exclusion from the many other good things that money can buy is understandable but not mitigating. This intransigence can be parodied as the hard-nosed legal maintenance of economic inequality. But there is also equality of dignity and respect to which all citizens are entitled. That entitlement does not sit well with any claim that a person's disadvantaged position derogates from the responsibilities of citizenship unless one rejects on impersonal grounds the social order itself.[19]

The fact that the criminal law must employ a conception of blame that will, on occasion, include persons of good character suggests that the criminal law has little concern with the quality of a defendant's character. Its concern is with particular episodes of conduct and whether a finding of blame, in the sense under discussion, can be made in respect of them.[20] The character of D is relevant to liability (as opposed to mitigation) only if it can be presented as afflicted by some form of pathology germane to a mental condition defence. D may be a firm believer in euthanasia and, moved by compassion for V, she may bring about his death. The fact that D has led an impeccable life of selfless public service will have no bearing on her liability for murder. If, however, her concern for V has caused her to

[15] See Sullivan, "Making Excuses" in Simester and Smith (eds.), *Harm and Culpability* (1996) 131, arguing that for some (but not all) crimes, a defence should be available if D would not have offended but for a state of disinhibition caused by involuntary intoxication. Contrast Moore, who would confine the defence to situations where involuntary intoxication "incapacitates to the point of insanity": "Stephen Morse on the Fundamental Psycho-legal Error" (2016) 10 *Crim Law and Philosophy* 45, 46.

[16] Kelman, "Interpretive Construction in the Substantive Criminal Law" (1981) 33 *Stanford LR* 591.

[17] See Norrie, *Punishment, Responsibility and Justice* (2000), discussed in Sullivan, "Is Criminal Law Possible?" (2001) 22 *OJLS* 424.

[18] See further Tadros, "Poverty and Criminal Responsibility" (2009) 43 *Journal of Value Inquiry* 391; Beade, "Who Can Blame Whom? Moral Standing to Blame and Punish Deprived Citizens" (2018) 13 *Crim Law and Philosophy* 271; Kennefick, *The Boundaries of Blame* (2025).

[19] For a lucid account on the basic conditions and capacities for responsibility and accountability before the criminal law, see Gardner, *Offences and Defences* (2007) chap. 9.

[20] Moore, "Choice, Character and Excuse" in Paul, Miller, and Paul (eds.), *Crime, Culpability and Remedy* (1990) 29; but see also, in the same volume, Arenella, "Character, Choice and Moral Agency" 59.

become extremely depressed, which has in turn led to her killing V, she may be able to raise a plea of diminished responsibility to a murder charge.[21]

### *(iii) Responsibility and free will: a deterministic universe*

Determinism represents a claim, both in science and philosophy, that all individual choices, like all other aspects of the universe, are essentially predetermined; that none of us experience what we might describe as free will, regardless of our mental capacities.[22] Suppose that, at time $t_1$, P wonders whether to continue the struggle to finish his overdue paper; to pour himself a glass of wine and watch the rugby match he has earlier recorded; or just to go to bed. If, at $t_2$, he opts for bed, for determinists he is not in fact opting but rather following the path that nature has set down for him. Sapolsky, for example, argues that the totality of the good or bad things that humans do is causally imposed by the laws of nature, even our social practices: "Our social world is as much a product of our determined materialist brain as are our simple motor movements."[23] The implications of this claim for the criminal law, if correct, are obvious and fundamental. If we do not act with free will, then we are not responsible for our choices; and if none of us are responsible for our choices, then the criminal law (at least any criminal law predicated on retributivist theory) has no legitimate basis for punishing those who commit crimes.[24] As Sapolsky states, "neuroscience shows [the criminal justice system] makes no sense and should be abolished".[25]

Despite the force of this challenge, however, the determinist critique has had little impact on the current criminal justice system. To some extent, this may be explained by simple non-engagement. Following Peter Westen,[26] there is an acceptance that academic criminal lawyers, even those with theoretical interests, can do their work without taking a position on whether to be a hard determinist, a compatibilist (i.e. a person who believes that what is known scientifically about human behaviour need not entail a commitment to not finding agents responsible for their conduct), or a person who believes that a criminal law based on Anglo-American principles must commit to free will irrespective of the state of scientific knowledge about the nature and influences on human behaviour. One widely cited paper on modern neuroscience is entitled "For the Law, Neuroscience Changes Nothing and Everything".[27] As yet, nothing has changed for criminal lawyers. Scientific work on the nature and influences of human conduct remains a work in progress. No stance is taken on determinism, compatibilism, or the reality (or otherwise) of free will. It continues to be assumed that D can be found responsible and culpable on the basis of her voluntary acts or omissions—voluntary in the sense of an absence of coercion, physical constraint, or mental disorder.

[21] Homicide Act 1957, s. 2. Above, § 10.6.

[22] For an accessible introduction to the implications of determinism, see Sapolsky, *Behave: The Biology of Humans at Our Best and Worst* (2017); Plomin, *Blueprint: How DNA Makes Us Who We Are* (2018).

[23] Sapolsky, *Behave* (2017) 592.

[24] Caruso, *Rejecting Retributivism: Free Will, Punishment, and Criminal Justice* (2021).

[25] Sapolsky, *Behave* (2017) 580. Sapolsky accepts that dangerous persons must be confined and allows that some degree of punishment may be needed by way of deterrence. He is adamantly dismissive of any conception of punishment in terms of something that the offender deserves.

[26] "Getting the Fly out of the Bottle: The False Problem of Free Will and Determinism" (2005) 8 *Buffalo Crim LR* 101.

[27] By Greene and Cohen (2004) 359 *Philosophical Transactions of the Royal Society, Biological Science* 1775.

But is Westen correct, or do those defending the current system need to adopt a position that clearly rejects the determinist critique? Michael Moore insists that any worthwhile account of criminal blame and punishment must take a position on the debate.[28] He argues that a sufficient degree of free agency is essential to validate morally the imposition of criminal sanctions and punishment. While Moore is cognisant of modern advances in neuroscience, his claim that criminal liability is in the main imposed on persons who have freely acted or omitted to act is essentially metaphysical. Contrast Stephen Morse's position.[29] For Morse, criminal law theory and neuroscience (or human biology more broadly) can stay in their respective silos. Anglophone societies cannot dispense with criminal law, either now or in any conceivable future; and Anglo-American criminal law must assume free will even if the assumption is no more than folk psychology. Morse is unconcerned by this, because the vast majority of persons in Western societies believe in free will on the basis of their lived experiences. That is enough to sustain the theory and practice of the criminal law. Michael Gazzaniga, one of the founders of modern neuroscience, concurs with Morse. For Gazzaniga, neuroscience is about investigating the working of individual brains under laboratory conditions. The social interaction of persons (or as he sometimes puts it, the interaction between different brains) is something apart: "Responsibility comes out of the agreement that humans have with each other to live in the social world. The participants have to be held accountable for their actions. Without that rule, nothing works."[30] Essentially Morse and Gazzaniga insist that, whatever the discoveries made by neuroscience, the social and moral concepts of agency and responsibility will remain indispensable to the functioning of Western societies.

The existence of free will may also be defended within the field of neuroscience. Even if the laws of physics are complete and causally closed at the particle and subparticle level of investigation, different natural properties may emerge when the totality of brain activity is addressed at the level of the brain as a neural system to which human agents make inputs—not from outside the neural system but within it. The physicist Sean Carrol considers that there can be "a reconciliation between impersonal underlying laws [of particle and subparticle physics] and a rich macroscopic world populated by human agents, with values, self-awareness and the ability to make decisions".[31] His crucial conjecture is that the brain, at the level of a neural system, operates in a probabilistic, quantum manner.[32] Recall P, who at $t_1$ was wondering whether to keep working, watch a recording, or go to bed. In Sapolsky's deterministic world, bed was the only place he was going. For Carroll, and others of like scientific persuasion,[33] at $t_1$ all three options were possible. The quantum brain processes that worked out in favour of bed at $t_2$ were not merely compatible with free will: they *were* free will.

[28] See Moore, *Mechanical Choices* (2020); Moore, "Stephen Morse on the Fundamental Psycho-legal Error" (2016) 10 *Crim Law and Philosophy* 45; Moore, "Responsible Choices, Desert-Based Legal Institutions and the Challenges of Contemporary Neuroscience" (2012) 29 *Social Philosophy and Policy* 233.

[29] See, e.g., Morse, "The Neuroscientific Non-challenge to Meaning, Morals and Purpose" in Caruso and Flanagan (eds.), *Neuroexistensialism* (2018) 333.

[30] Gazzinaga, "On Determinism and Human Responsibility" in Caruso and Flanagan (eds.), *Neuroexistensialism* (2018) 223, 232.

[31] Carroll, "Purpose, Freedom, and the Laws of Nature" in Caruso and Flanagan (eds.), *Neuroexistensialism* (2018) 298, 304; at much greater length, see Carroll, *The Big Picture* (2016).

[32] It should be noted here that much of Carroll's work is in the nature of informed scientific speculation and is, as such, controversial.

[33] See, e.g., Tse, *The Neural Basis of Free Will* (2013).

### *(iv) Responsibility and free will: character and capacity*

The determinist challenge to free will discussed above, that *all* choices are predetermined externally, has typically remained on the sidelines of substantive criminal law discussion. As we have explained, its essential claims jar with our perceptions and lived experience as autonomous choosing agents. However, perhaps curiously, similar challenges made on less abstracted terms—focusing on character and capacity—are much more common within legal debate. The question here is whether someone's character-based predisposition to certain types of offending, or their degree of capacity-based control, can and should feature within legal tests of responsibility and culpability?

There are clear echoes here of the broader free will debate, engaging issues that affect our conceptions of humanity and morality. In particular, there are unanswerable questions about when a person's character is "normal" and, as Bernard Williams noted, disputes about the degree to which that should count in matters of responsibility.[34] Law, morality, and society each works with a concept of the "voluntary" that informs judgements of wrongdoing. But that concept is not profound. Even if D's action is done with mens rea and in a normal state of mind, there are deeper questions about why D is someone who wants to act as she does; whether it is within her choice or control to be such a person; whether her character is itself "voluntarily" chosen. One might then ask: is it fair that D should be subject to state punishment because she is the sort of person she is (when, one might say, that is not something D is responsible for)? The concept of voluntariness offers no assistance with such questions. It shapes our analysis of physical conduct and casts no deeper light. Voluntariness may discern whether, given who and how she is, D deserves criminal sanctions within the rules and principles of a particular jurisdiction. But it cannot reveal whether D deserves to be the person that she is.

As we saw in § 4.3, the criminal law does not punish conduct that is physically involuntary. Otherwise, however, the law assumes that all adult citizens are capable of understanding and complying with its rules, an assumption displaced only if D's transgression is attributable to a condition falling within the *M'Naghten* insanity Rules. If D stabs and injures V while in thrall to a psychotic delusion that V was an evil spirit about to kill him, there may be an acceptance that D should be confined in a place of safety but not be punished.[35] It does not excuse D, however, to demonstrate that he was *psychologically* incapable of obeying the law on a particular occasion. D, a chronic alcoholic, is guilty of theft if he takes a bottle of spirits belonging to V, notwithstanding his craving for alcohol and his lack of funds.[36] In this manner, the law recognises a high waterline for judgements of irresponsibility, requiring those below the line to conform regardless of their dispositions.

As with our chronic alcoholic above, the legal expectation for compliance will often extend (outside the insanity defence) to those with serious mental disorders and impaired capacity. Peter Arenella,[37] for example, has argued forcefully but without success that persons with profoundly disordered personalities, who are incapable of any degree of identification or sympathy with the interests of others, should be dealt with outside the framework

[34] "Moral Responsibility and Political Freedom" (1997) 56 *CLJ* 96, 101–2. A reply by Duff and von Hirsch follows: "Responsibility, Retribution and the 'Voluntary': A Response to Williams" (1997) 56 *CLJ* 103.

[35] The facts of *Oye* [2013] EWCA Crim 1725, [2014] 1 WLR 3354. The jury convicted D of affray and offences against the person. Unusually, the Court of Appeal substituted a verdict of not guilty by reason of insanity.

[36] *Powell v Texas* 392 US 514 (1968).

[37] "Convicting the Morally Blameless: Reassessing the Relationship Between Legal and Moral Accountability" (1992) 39 *UCLA LR* 1511.

of the criminal law. A further vivid example is provided by the case of *Keal*.[38] D was found guilty of attempting to murder three members of his family, whom he attacked under the delusional belief that he was possessed and controlled by the devil and had no choice in his actions. D appealed his convictions, arguing *inter alia* that a correct interpretation of *M'Naghten* should allow the insanity defence to apply where a mental disorder creates the perception of external control and manipulation. D's appeal was dismissed, with the clear statement from Lord Burnett CJ that the "defence of insanity is not available to a defendant who, although he knew what he was doing was wrong, he believed that he had no choice but to commit the act in question".[39]

It is difficult to justify the legal position that has been maintained in *Keal*, particularly when we reflect on D's apparent absence of choice and culpability. However, it is important to recognise that cases of this kind present considerable challenges to the legal system. Criminal law legislation and adjudication cannot, on any long-term basis, stray too far from strong community sentiments concerning the immorality of particular forms of conduct.[40] This is what Strawson has famously called "reactive attitudes".[41] It is the "otherness" of a person afflicted with schizophrenia and other conditions inducing psychosis that attenuates the urge to blame and punish. But even in the case of persons with severe mental disorders such as schizophrenics, revulsion arising from extreme conduct on D's part may supervene over any sympathy his condition might otherwise arouse, particularly where the conduct was sustained, and involved forethought and planning.[42] Recall the earlier discussion of the case of Anders Breivik, a person with atrocious views and the perpetrator of horrendous deeds.[43] The Norwegian criminal justice system vacillated. At first, Breivik was found to be irresponsible on the basis of a diagnosis of schizophrenia; yet he was subsequently convicted of multiple murders on the basis of a finding of sanity. Plomin maintains that genetic research suggests there are no clear lines between what are regarded as mental disorders and non-disorders. For him, qualitative judgements cannot be made about mental conditions; there are only quantitative dimensions to be measured. More pithily, to borrow the title of the relevant chapter, "Abnormal Is Normal".[44] That line of thinking supports the conclusion that persons capable of planning and executing horrific acts should be held responsible for those acts, whatever the psychiatric diagnosis of their condition.

Should an exceptional category be recognised where D's character is consciously manipulated by another, in cases of so-called brainwashing?[45] Such was the claim of Patty Hearst, who was abducted and indoctrinated, as she claimed, by a cell of urban terrorists before she participated in bank robberies and other criminal acts. Yet, within the set of values that she had been induced to adopt, her acts were the product of her volition and comported with her practical reasoning.[46] If, in our present circumstances, we are capable of practical reasoning and are physically and psychologically unconstrained, we are judged accountable for what we do. The test is always whether we are capable of moral agency, as we are now, and

[38] [2022] EWCA Crim 341, [2022] 4 WLR 41.
[39] *Ibid.*, [48].
[40] Robinson and Darley, *Justice, Liability and Blame* (1995).
[41] "Freedom and Resentment" in *Freedom and Resentment* (1974) 1. See too Horder, "Criminal Law: Between Determinism, Liberalism, and Criminal Justice" (1996) 49 *Current Legal Problems* 159.
[42] As in *Sutcliffe*, *The Times*, 30 April, 1981.
[43] Above, § 19.2(v).
[44] Plomin, *Blueprint* (2018) chap. 5.
[45] See Alldridge, "Brainwashing as a Criminal Law Defence" [1984] *Crim LR* 726.
[46] Vuoso, "Background Responsibility and Excuse" (1987) 96 *Yale LJ* 1661.

regardless of how we came to be what we are. If we satisfy that test, we are responsible and cannot evade *conviction*. It does not follow, however, that someone in the position of Patty Hearst should be *punished*, especially if she has been restored to her former law-abiding character by the time of her trial. These unusual circumstances ask searching questions concerning the foundational core of retributivism. As we have argued, the grounds for liability are present in this case. Does it follow that some measure of deserved punishment follows from that conclusion? In our view, punishment can be withheld in such an exceptional case without threat to the foundations and practice of criminal liability.

## § 22.2 Some things the defences fail to do

Within its institutional limitations, one might reasonably anticipate that the defences afforded by the criminal law of England and Wales will, largely, ensure acquittals for the blameless. Broadly, supervening defences fall within two major categories. First, there are defences which focus on some aspect of D himself, an aspect which renders him morally irresponsible for the conduct forming the substance of the offence charged. Within that group are legal infancy, insanity, and, to an extent, diminished responsibility (which merely deems responsibility to be attenuated rather than absent). Secondly, rather than picking out a particular quality of D's that pre-empts her moral responsibility for the offence,[47] there are defences which arise on the basis that any person, placed in the same set of circumstances or making the same factual assumptions as D, could not fairly have been expected to comply with the letter of the law. This second category includes excuses and justifications:[48] indeed, falling within this latter group may be situations where, from a societal perspective, committing a prima facie offence is the preferred option.

Unfortunately, even where the constraints of institutional possibility do not apply, English law does not always exculpate the blameless.[49] We focus here on the definition of irresponsibility defences and circumstances where D cannot reasonably be expected to conform with the law.

### (i) *Irresponsibility defences*

We discussed defences of irresponsibility in Chapter 19. In this subsection we provide some further critique of their narrow construction in many areas, and their non-existence in others.

#### (a) *Legal infancy*

Certain mental conditions may be incompatible with justified blame. Young children afford an obvious example. From an early age, children are capable of aggressive and predatory conduct. Such conduct may need to be restrained but a degree of maturity, a capacity for

[47] This generalisation is subject to any allowances made, within the "reasonable man" standards that operate in excuses such as duress and loss of control, for weaknesses peculiar to the defendant: above, §§ 10.5(iii)(c), 20.1(iii)(b). Thus, the division we have made here is not clear-cut.

[48] Thus, as Gardner points out, excuses do not deny responsibility: "The Gist of Excuses" (1998) 1 *Buffalo Crim LR* 575, 588ff.

[49] Sullivan, "Avoiding Criminal Liability and Excessive Punishment for Persons Who Lack Culpability" in Reed and Bohlander (eds.), *General Defences in Criminal Law* (2014) 25.

self-criticism, is required before formal pronouncements of blame and punishment are apt. English law takes the age of 10 as the threshold for criminal guilt. There must be considerable doubt whether pre-teenage children have, as a class, sufficient insight and maturity to be full candidates for blame and punishment. Some recognition that children of that age may lack the insight and maturity that should be a condition for full criminal responsibility was afforded by the defence of *doli incapax* for persons between 10 and 14. But, as we have discussed, that defence was swept away by the House of Lords as a consequence of a very contestable piece of statutory interpretation.[50] Not long before that decision, the European Commissioner for Human Rights had called for a raising of the age of criminal responsibility in England and Wales to bring that jurisdiction's treatment of children within the European mainstream.[51] Now the situation is even worse than the circumstances that informed his report.[52]

Particular concern arises where young children receive long terms of incarceration for serious offences. In *R v Secretary of State for the Home Department, ex p Venables*, two 10-year-old boys were detained at Her Majesty's pleasure for murder.[53] Even if we assume a culpability commensurate with that gravest of crimes, the 15-year "tariff" (minimum term of imprisonment prior to consideration for release on parole) the pair received raises a major issue of principle. At the age of 18 they were to be transferred to young offender institutions and thereafter to prison. To what extent is a person of, say, 22 years the "same" person as he was at 10? Even if he is not in any perceptible sense a better person at 22, is there a sufficient link between his present self and his earlier conduct to justify a continuing expiation of that conduct? The trial and punishment of young children raises questions concerning not only a sufficiency of culpability at the time of the crime, but also the connection between past conduct and present punishment for that conduct during a period of continuous growth and change.

### (b) *Insanity*

In addition to legal infancy, insanity has long been accepted in many cultures as incompatible with moral agency. For those afflicted with psychotic disorders in particular, their profoundly disturbed sense of reality can place them beyond any community of blame constituted by a sufficient core of shared assumptions guiding practical reason. Alas, the *M'Naghten* Rules exclude many profoundly disturbed people.[54] The class of psychotic persons outside the Rules may be said to constitute a body who should *generally* be ineligible for blame and are victims of injustice when convicted and punished.[55] This approach has

[50] *R v JTB* [2009] UKHL 20, [2009] 1 AC 1310; discussed above, § 19.3(ii).

[51] *Report by Mr Alvaro Gil-Robles, Commissioner for Human Rights on his Visit to the United Kingdom* (Com DH (2005) 6) paras. 105–7.

[52] See Ashworth, *Positive Obligations in Criminal Law* (2013) chap. 7; Keating, "How Should the Criminal Law Respond to the 'Special Status' of Children?" in Child and Duff (eds.) *Criminal Law Reform Now* (2019) chap. 5.

[53] [1998] AC 407. Ultimately, the boys were released on parole after spending eight years in custody.

[54] Above, § 19.2.

[55] Moore, "The Quest for a Responsible Responsibility Test: Norwegian Insanity Law after Breivik" (2015) 9 *Crim Law and Philosophy* 645. There is force in the view that the insanity defence should be a pure status defence akin to infancy and confined to persons radically deficient in terms of their reasoning capacity: persons, in the words of Moore, akin to "Infants, animals [and] trees" (680).

been adopted in some jurisdictions, including, notably, in Norway, where it has come under considerable scrutiny following the case of Anders Breivik.[56]

Under current English law, "insanity" is confined to particular cognitive defects, which are defined and applied narrowly. Short of moving to a model of status-based exclusion from liability, the more likely route for progressive reform in English law is to expand the class of persons incrementally within the *M'Naghten* Rules by interpreting the key terms of the defence more expansively. Some movement has been made in this regard, and we commend the approaches adopted in cases such as *Loake*,[57] recognising the potential application of insanity when D is charged with a strict liability or negligence-based offence, and *Oye*,[58] where insanity was applied by the Court of Appeal despite some uncertainty relating to the comorbid causes of D's delusions.[59] However, such cases should be recognised as exceptions to the rule. Despite academic critique,[60] courts have consistently resisted opportunities to revise the restrictive terms of the common law insanity test. We see this, for example, in the interpretation of the much-criticised wrongfulness limb;[61] in the application of insanity where D is delusional;[62] and more recently, in the potential for insanity where D believes that his conduct is entirely beyond his control.[63] In 2025, the Law Commission announced that it will be continuing its project on insanity (paused since 2013), representing a vital new opportunity for reform.

*(c) Involuntary destabilisation?*

Persons who are not legally insane may nonetheless find themselves in a destabilised condition and, in such a state, may perpetrate the actus reus of a crime. Where the condition is not self-induced and is incompatible with proof of mens rea, no conviction for the crime is possible.[64] If, however, the definitional elements of a crime are present, liability will ensue: no supervening defence currently exists for this class of defendant, outside of the partial defences to murder. Recall *Kingston*,[65] where D was involuntarily drugged by a third party for the purposes of blackmail and then recorded committing an indecent assault (whilst disinhibited by the drugs). On the basis that D demonstrated sufficient capacity to form mens rea, and that "drunken intent is a criminal intent", the House of Lords were satisfied

[56] Gröning, "Has Norway Abandoned its Medical Model? Thoughts about the Criminal Insanity Law Reform Post 22 July" [2021] *Crim LR* 191; Gröning *et al.*, "Remodelling Criminal Insanity: Exploring Philosophical, Legal, and Medical Premises of the Medical Model Used in Norwegian Law" (2022) 81 *International Journal of Law and Psychiatry* 1.

[57] [2017] EWHC 2855 (Admin), [2018] QB 998. Cf. *DPP v H* [1997] 1 WLR 1406 (DC) and *Colohan* [2001] Crim LR 845 (CA) suggesting insanity would not apply to such offences.

[58] [2013] EWCA Crim 1725, [2014] 1 WLR 3354.

[59] It is also notable that insanity was applied to both of D's offences, the initial affray and the later attack on arresting officers. The Court of Appeal focused much of the discussion on the later attack, highlighting D's delusional belief that the police had demon faces (satisfying the first limb of the insanity rules, combined with the delusional limb). However, by applying insanity to the earlier affray, the Court also endorsed a more liberal approach: at the time of the affray, D acted in the belief that his victims were agents of evil spirits, but he was not experiencing visual delusions related to their physical form.

[60] For references, see the discussion of insanity above, § 19.2.

[61] *Johnson* [2007] EWCA Crim 1978; *Keal* [2022] EWCA Crim 341, [2022] 4 WLR 41.

[62] *Taj* [2018] EWCA Crim 1743, [2019] QB 655.

[63] *Keal* [2022] EWCA Crim 341, [2022] 4 WLR 41.

[64] On failure of proof, see above, § 18.1.

[65] [1995] 2 AC 355; above, § 18.4(ix).

that D was liable for the assault. This reversed the decision of the Court of Appeal,[66] which had allowed involuntary intoxication to serve as a defence to any crime provided the actus reus would not have been perpetrated but for the effects of the drink.

In correcting the generosity of the Court of Appeal, the House of Lords in our view took an unduly formal view of the nature of criminal guilt. Guilt, for their Lordships, consisted merely in the presence of the definitional elements of the crime and the absence of any legally recognised justification or excuse. Even if the defendant were blameless, he would still be guilty of the offence. This approach completely disregards the reputational consequences of a conviction for a stigmatic offence: the public judgement of blame that inheres in the fact of conviction alone. It is submitted that, if a court accepts D is blameless, the conditions that explain his blamelessness should provide, wherever systemically possible, the basis of a defence.

There are a number of personal conditions compatible with mens rea that may preclude a sufficient moral culpability for conviction. Non-exhaustively, these include involuntary intoxication, confused states of consciousness induced by medication, the destabilising effects of post-traumatic stress disorder, premenstrual tension, epilepsy, arteriosclerosis, cerebral tumours, and diabetes. Such conditions may trigger outbursts of motiveless violence from persons who are otherwise morally well-disposed. The way that English law deals with these conditions at the present time is manifestly unsatisfactory.[67] Sometimes, sympathy for a defendant may influence a court to find that the mental element for a crime is not made out—even though this may seem at variance with the facts of the case. If the mental element is held to be absent, either a straightforward acquittal or a qualified verdict of insanity will follow, depending on whether the court characterises the condition as arising from internal or external factors. If the mental element is found to be present, then an acquittal cannot follow, outside of the narrow terms of insanity. Arguably, a general defence *should* be available for those afflicted with any of these conditions, notwithstanding the presence of mens rea. Of course, the availability of such a defence should be subject to a number of restrictive conditions.[68] But, where those conditions are met, it is submitted that this class of blameless persons could be excluded from liability without undermining the structure and cohesion of the criminal law.

In our discussion of murder, we noted the terms of the partial defence of loss of control.[69] The defence allows the culpability-reducing factors of gross provocation and fear of serious violence to be taken into account at the trial stage. The introduction of such a partial defence is particularly in point for murder because of the mandatory penalty. There is nothing, in principle, however, against the introduction of forms of legal mitigation (as opposed to sentencing discretion) for other offences. Jeremy Horder, for instance, has advocated the extension of diminished responsibility to offences other than murder;[70] a line of thought that has also been pursued by others.[71] If diminished responsibility were to be established

[66] [1993] 4 All ER 373 (CA).

[67] Sullivan, "Making Excuses" in Simester and Smith (eds.), *Harm and Culpability* (1996) 131, 145–50.

[68] In particular, provided (i) D would not have committed the offence but for being in a state of disequilibrium occasioned by his diabetes, post-traumatic stress, etc.; (ii) the offence at issue is not amongst the most serious of crimes, such as murder, rape, etc.; and (iii) D has not previously been convicted for a similar offence.

[69] Above, § 10.5(iii).

[70] "Pleading Involuntary Lack of Capacity" (1993) 52 *CLJ* 298, 316.

[71] See Wasik, "Partial Excuses in the Criminal Law" (1982) 45 *MLR* 516, 522; Kennefick, *The Boundaries of Blame* (2025).

in a non-homicide context, perhaps one could "cap" the maximum penalty that could be imposed to, say, half the maximum sentence otherwise provided for the offence. This form of mitigation would thus become a matter of *entitlement*, to be won in argument at trial or by concession on the part of the prosecution. There is merit in acknowledging the diminution of guilt via law rather than judicial discretion; something that has been recognised in the creation of so-called hate crimes, where factors that would previously have aggravated D's sentence have been transposed into new forms of liability. Accordingly, forms of legal mitigation such as loss of control and diminished responsibility, which are currently confined to murder, arguably should be available for offences generally.

### *(ii) When conformity with law cannot reasonably be expected*

Beyond those who we might deem irresponsible, there remains a second category of defendants who (although not lacking capacity) cannot reasonably be expected to obey the law within certain circumstances of emergency and/or pressure. It is not that there is anything peculiar to D himself which precludes liability. *Anyone*—or at least, anyone like D—placed in similar circumstances could not reasonably have been expected to do differently. The emphasis is on the reasons or explanations why D acted as he did or found himself in the situation that he was, reasons or explanations potentially applicable to any actor.

Expectations of conformity with law may be pitched at unattainable levels. The most glaring situation of this kind is where, for reasons beyond the control of D and in circumstances that do not reveal any fault on her part, criminal liability is attached by way of an involuntarily acquired status, as in the notorious case of *Larsonneur*.[72] In principle, questions of involuntariness and control should be accommodated within the offence requirement of voluntary conduct.[73] Failing that, the blamelessness of defendants should be accommodated by way of a defence of impossibility.[74] But at present, English law tends to disregard principle in favour of *ad hoc* decisions, frequently tailored to the language of the particular offence.

Almost as fundamental in their unfairness are cases where liability will be incurred as an inevitable concomitant of carrying on a lawful trade or business. If peas are to be canned on an industrial scale, it is inevitable that some cans will contain foreign bodies, whatever reasonable checks and controls are put in place.[75] If "adult" videos, tobacco, or lottery tickets are allowed as items of commerce, then even careful shopkeepers and their assistants will sell or hire such items to persons who look older than they are, whatever precautions are taken.[76] To date, there seems no judicial inclination to mitigate the inherent unfairness of strict liability by way of a due diligence defence. Far from it. In *Chargot Ltd*,[77] the House of Lords considered the nature of the liability arising under the Health and Safety at Work etc. Act 1974, which requires employers "to ensure as far as is reasonably practicable, the health, safety and welfare at work". A fatal accident had occurred in the workplace. There was no evidence to suggest that the employer was in any way at fault for this. The Appellate

[72] (1934) 24 Cr App R 74 (CA); above, § 4.1(ii)(a).
[73] Above, § 4.3.
[74] Above, §§ 4.3(ii) and 18.3.
[75] *Smedleys Ltd v Breed* [1974] AC 839. See above, Chapter 6, on such offences more generally.
[76] *Harrow LBC v Shah* [1999] 3 All ER 302 (DC).
[77] [2008] UKHL 73, [2009] 1 WLR 1.

Committee ruled that a workplace fatal accident *of itself* established a failure to ensure the health and safety of the deceased employee. When such a finding is made, the 1974 Act requires the employer to prove that the avoidance of the accident was not reasonably practicable.[78] Unsurprisingly, that could not be done given the absence of any discernible explanation for the accident.[79] The effect of the decision is to impose serious criminal liability on employers and associated management for any unexplained or unexplainable accident. If one starts from the premise that to run a lawful business is not a dubious activity, the decision in *Chargot* is harsh in the extreme. When faced with incidents that cannot be explained by way of reasonable investigation, it should surely suffice to exculpate that the employer and associated management can demonstrate due diligence in matters of health and safety. Suitably adapted, such a defence would also be relevant to a plea of excusable ignorance or mistake of law.

Less frequently encountered, but potentially productive of grave injustice when it arises, is the failure of English law to recognise any defence of superior orders. Consider a situation where D, an armed soldier, is ordered by his commanding officer, E, to shoot V. The reason for the order is, let us suppose, the belief that if V were allowed to escape, he will commit terrorist offences at some future time. It is probably the case that the order is unlawful; force used in the prevention of crime is likely to be found lawful only when the crime is imminent.[80] The position of D is invidious. If he disobeys the order, adverse career and disciplinary consequences may well follow. Besides, D may believe, quite reasonably, that the order given by E is an order to do something which is lawful. Were he to be tried for murder consequent upon following the order, however, the prospect of a conviction on such facts would appear to be strong. Equally strong, it is submitted, is a plea for excuse on the part of D.

In respect of the other defences recognised by English law, claims that blameless people are insufficiently accommodated are more controversial. The scope of the defence of duress has been criticised on the grounds that it is unavailable to a charge of murder or attempted murder.[81] Yet it is not *obviously* wrong to deny impunity for killing (or trying to kill) an innocent person in order to escape death, serious harm, or rape oneself, and the counter-arguments should be acknowledged even if one favours, as we do, extending the defence to murder and attempted murder.[82] Similarly, whether the defences of mistaken self-defence or prevention of crime are under-inclusive of the blameless is a matter of controversy.[83] More consistently, a focus has been placed upon the masculine construction of certain defences, and upon the overly restrictive terms in which they apply to many female defendants.[84] Arguably, too, English law is unduly restrictive in denying any form of mitigation to a person

[78] Section 40.

[79] The deceased had been driving a dumper truck which overturned, burying the driver under the load of soil it was transporting across the worksite.

[80] Cf. the more expansive approach favoured in *Kelly* [1989] NI 341. See above, § 20.4.

[81] Smith, *Justification and Excuse in the Criminal Law* (1989) 92–5; above, § 20.1(i)(a). The Law Commission has previously proposed the extension of duress to murder: Law Com. No. 304, *Murder, Manslaughter and Infanticide* (2006) part 6.

[82] For some thoughtful points, see Horder, "Occupying the Moral High Ground? The Law Commission on Duress" [1994] *Crim LR* 334, 335–6, 339–40.

[83] Simester, "Mistakes in Defence" (1992) 12 *OJLS* 295; above, § 21.2(ii).

[84] See, e.g., Edwards, "'Demasculinising' the Defences of Self-defence, the 'Householder Defence' and Duress" [2022] *Crim LR* 111. See, further, above, § 21.2(iv)(e).

who was entitled to use some degree of force but who used force excessive for the occasion.[85] Certainly in the context of murder, the availability of a manslaughter verdict in such circumstances would be a welcome departure from the rigidity of the mandatory life sentence.

## § 22.3 Defence doctrine and judicial creativity

In principle, the previous section demonstrates that more could be done to exculpate blameless defendants. What chance is there of judicial innovation to meet these needs?[86] In *Lynch*,[87] the House of Lords decided, by a majority, to extend the defence of duress to the crime of murder (a decision later reversed in *Howe*[88]). In the judgments in *Lynch*, two very different attitudes to enlarging the coverage of defences were expressed. For the majority of the House, extending the defence of duress to acts of complicity in murder was an appropriate task for the highest appellate court, notwithstanding established institutional authority that the defence was not available in such circumstances. Lord Wilberforce said:[89]

> "I have no doubt that it is open to us, on normal judicial principles, to hold the defence admissible. We are here in the domain of the common law: our task is to fit what we can see as principle and authority to the facts before us, and it is no obstacle that these facts are new. The judges have always assumed responsibility for deciding questions of principle relating to criminal liability and guilt, and particularly for setting the standards by which the law expects normal men to act."

For the minority, this amounted to a usurpation of legislative authority. Lord Simon castigated the majority's approach:[90]

"I can hardly conceive of circumstances less suitable than the instant for five members of an appellate committee of your Lordships' House to arrogate to ourselves so momentous a law-making initiative."

In the context of *defence* doctrine, the more expansive approach of Lord Wilberforce is to be preferred. The judicial role is well suited to expanding defence doctrine and even, when circumstances require so, the creation of a novel defence.

In terms of the propriety of judicial law-making, one may distinguish between grounds of inculpation, on the one hand, and grounds of exculpation on the other.[91] In the former case, clarity and generality of application are important virtues when defining the prima facie offence. Further, any significant enlargement of a class of conduct which may be punished is a task for the legislature and not for an unelected judiciary. For exculpatory questions, however, it is possible to craft principled responses to the quiddity of a particular case without undermining the normative framework of the criminal law. The difference between questions of inculpation and exculpation was adverted to by Hughes LJ in *Dowds*, where his Lordship rejected the

[85] Above, § 21.2(iii).

[86] Sullivan, "Avoiding Criminal Liability and Excessive Punishment for Persons Who Lack Culpability" in Reed and Bohlander (eds.), *General Defences in Criminal Law* (2014) 25. On judicial development of the criminal law, see, Horder, "The Courts' Development of the Criminal Law and the Role of Declarations" (2020) 40 *LS* 42; Stark, "Judicial Development of the Criminal Law by the Supreme Court" (2021) 41 *OJLS* 1.

[87] [1975] AC 653.

[88] [1987] AC 417.

[89] [1975] AC 653, 684.

[90] *Ibid.*, 696.

[91] See, e.g., Smith, "Judicial Law Making in the Criminal Law" (1984) 100 *LQR* 46, esp. 63–7; cf. Stark, "*Howe* (1987)" in Handler, Mares and Williams (eds.), *Landmark Cases in Criminal Law* (2017) 309.

argument that the presumption of strict construction had any role when dealing with the availability of defences.[92] However, he had in mind the rejection or narrowing of defences rather than their expansion.[93] The late twentieth-century development of the defence of duress of circumstances, and the overdue recognition of a defence of necessity indicate the willingness of some contemporary judges to give practical effect to findings of blamelessness.

But there are also calls for judicial restraint, and legitimate concerns raised about the limits of undemocratic judicial law-making, even in the context of exculpatory rules.[94] In *C v DPP*,[95] the House of Lords, in reinstating the then presumption of *doli incapax* for 10- to 14-year-olds,[96] spoke in general terms of the propriety of judicial law-making in criminal law. Speaking for the Appellate Committee, Lord Lowry laid down what he termed "aids of navigation". They are:[97]

> "(1) If the solution is doubtful, the judges should beware of imposing their own remedy. (2) Caution should prevail if Parliament has rejected opportunities of clearing up a known difficulty or has legislated, while leaving the difficulty untouched. (3) Disputed matters of social policy are less suitable areas for judicial intervention than purely legal problems. (4) Fundamental legal doctrines should not be lightly set aside. (5) Judges should not make a change unless they can achieve finality and certainty."

These navigational aids are intended for general guidance. But, it is submitted, they are too restrictive when applied to the development of defence doctrine, by contrast with enlarging the scope of offences. At risk of repetition, what should drive the development of defence doctrine is a refusal to countenance the conviction of a blameless person for a serious criminal offence. We must accept that full expression of that principle is limited by the nature of the criminal law itself. But subject to that important proviso, what *can* be done by way of exempting blameless persons, should be done. This may require a disregard for some of Lord Lowry's navigational aids, particularly the matter of finality and certainty. For example, consider the decision in *Bournewood*,[98] which at long last recognised a defence of necessity. Beyond the facts of *Bournewood*, the limits of the defence are impossible to state with any assurance. That brings a degree of disvalue; but the disvalue is outweighed by the value of providing the defence. The primary norms of the criminal law remain intact as a guide to action. They are not unduly undermined by allowing departures from the letter of law in cases of obvious necessity.

On the matter of sensitivity to the condition of blamelessness, judicial creativity may be required. In an important extra-judicial lecture, for example, Mrs Justice Arden (as she then was) gave her views on the centrality of the Human Rights Act 1998 to the substantive criminal law and, in particular, her view of the likely impact of Article 3 of the ECHR which proscribes torture and "inhuman and degrading treatment or punishment". The hypothetical case that she posed is so resonant of possibilities that it may be quoted in full:[99]

[92] [2012] EWCA Crim 281, [2012] 1 WLR 2576, [38].

[93] Hughes LJ took the presumption to apply to the defining elements of offences, but it is equally in point where the ambit of criminal liability is expanded by limiting or rejecting defences.

[94] The House of Lords and Privy Council have each held that there may be a conviction for a serious stigmatic offence in circumstances where the defendant is blameless. E.g., in *Clegg* [1995] 1 AC 482, the House of Lords expressed a reserved attitude to the judicial creation and extension of defences.

[95] [1996] AC 1.

[96] Now abolished by the Crime and Disorder Act 1998, s. 34; above § 19.3(ii).

[97] [1996] AC 1, 28.

[98] [1999] 1 AC 458; above, § 21.4.

[99] "Criminal Law at the Crossroads: The Impact on Human Rights from the Law Commission's Perspective and the Need for a Code" [1999] *Crim LR* 439, 450; above, § 2.5(I).

> "Suppose as a result of an accident, which was not the result of any negligence or intention, a factory owner pollutes the environment around his factory. He admits that the damage was caused by his factory and he pays a large sum of money to clear up the mess with a view to limiting the damage to his reputation. Suppose that he is then prosecuted for an environmental offence involving strict liability which carries an unlimited fine and he resists conviction on the ground that the accident had occurred accidentally and without fault. He contends that a conviction would cause him great loss of reputation. Can he successfully contend that for the law to impose strict liability, so that a person can show that the damage was not due to any negligence on his part, and that he has taken all the steps required to rectify the damage caused, has no defence, infringes his rights under Article 3?"

Mrs Justice Arden, who was at the time Chair of the Law Commission, considered the likely answer to this question to be affirmative and envisaged a court creating a "due diligence and all reasonable steps to rectify" defence under the wide powers of construction provided by section 3 of the Human Rights Act 1998. She also adverted to Article 6(2), which provides that "everyone charged with a criminal offence shall be presumed innocent until proved guilty according to law", and queried the legitimacy of strict liability offences in the light of this presumption.

Strict liability has been judicially tolerated for a long time and confirmed at the appellate level.[100] Yet if other judges, in addition to Mrs Justice Arden, were to read the ECHR and the interpretative possibilities of the Human Rights Act 1998 as boldly as she has, the lot of blameless defendants could significantly improve. Unfortunately, such speculation seems more optimistic than predictive. In *Barnfather v London Borough of Islington and Secretary of State for Education and Skills*,[101] the Divisional Court had to consider whether D, a parent blameless in respect of her child's truanting from school, was guilty of an offence which in literal terms made parents guilty of an offence if the child "fails to attend regularly at the school".[102] In upholding D's conviction, the Court confirmed authority finding the only constituent of the offence to be the child's truanting. Article 6(2) was of no assistance to D: the presumption of innocence was found to have no bearing on the substantive content of criminal offences. The same offence was at issue in *Hampshire County Council v E*,[103] where the Divisional Court confirmed D's conviction even on the assumption that her drug-taking and drug-dealing 15-year-old son might have killed or seriously harmed her had she tried to ensure his school attendance. The Court rejected the defence of duress on the ground that her liability was not founded on her own conduct.[104] Too often, judges fail to explore the resources of theory and doctrine in cases where conviction of a blameless person might thereby be avoided.[105]

There are, however, some examples where the courts go beyond the all too literal interpretation of statutory provisions criticised here in order to avoid conviction of the blameless.

[100] The House of Lords has confirmed the ECHR-compatibility of strict liability even in serious offences such as rape: *G* [2008] UKHL 37, [2009] 1 AC 92.
[101] [2003] EWHC 418 (Admin).
[102] Education Act 1996, s. 444(1).
[103] [2007] EWHC 2584 (Admin).
[104] See further Sullivan, "Parents and Their Truanting Children: An English Lesson in Liability without Responsibility" (2010) 12 *Otago LR* 285.
[105] For a particularly egregious example, see *Rehman* [2005] EWCA Crim 2056, [2006] 1 Cr App R (S) 77. For other examples of imprisonment of persons lacking any form of fault, see Ashworth, *Positive Obligations in Criminal Law* (2013) chap. 4, esp. 123–8.

The *Hampshire* case can usefully be contrasted with *Robinson-Pierre*.[106] In the former case, the fact that D's liability was triggered by her unruly son's behaviour, rather than by any conduct of her own, was the pretext to neuter the defence of duress. In *Robinson-Pierre*, the fact that the escape of D's dog into a public place, uncontrolled and on the attack, was the result of its release by third parties led the Court of Appeal to reason that Parliament could not have intended to punish the owner in such circumstances, as no public interest would be served and an unfair conviction imposed. Even though, on a literal interpretation, the offence in question was seemingly committed by the owner,[107] the Court of Appeal was prepared to interpret its terms in the light of fairness and proportionality. So simple and commonsensical is the reasoning, the temptation arises to treat *Robinson-Pierre* as a case of general importance. However, the decision in *Hampshire* forms part of a long-standing set of cases rigidly enforcing the school truanting offence and refusing any form of exemption save for those specifically referred to in the applicable legislation.[108]

Another example of judicial creativity, in protection of the blameless, may be identified through the use of abuse of process to stay proceedings. In *L and others*,[109] three of the appellants had been convicted of offences of producing and supplying cannabis. It was accepted that all three had been trafficked into the United Kingdom. There was considerable obscurity about the details of the trafficking and the respective ages of the appellants.[110] Be that as it may, the Court of Appeal found that being subjected to trafficking and the associated isolation and vulnerability "extinguished" any culpability for these offences. The Court of Appeal ruled that this lack of culpability should have led to a successful challenge to the prosecution at trial as an abuse of the process of the court. Accordingly, all the convictions were quashed. The potential implications of this case are significant: the door was opened to the view that, whenever D can establish that he lacked any culpability in respect of any offence he has been charged with, he can claim that any further proceeding concerning that offence is an abuse of process. We should not be rash of course, and there were special features surrounding *L* that inclined the court to be particularly averse to confirming the convictions.[111] Yet, assuming that the abuse of process doctrine is more than "a wilderness of single instances",[112] there may be other successful challenges on that ground where the lack of culpability is particularly striking.[113]

[106] [2013] EWCA Crim 2396, [2014] 1 WLR 2638.

[107] Section 3 of the Dangerous Dogs Act 1991 on the face of it penalised any dog owner whose dog was in a public place and out of control. (Note that section 3 has since been amended, making it applicable in relation to "any location in England or Wales (whether or not a public place)".) The offence is aggravated if the out-of-control dog attacks anyone.

[108] See further above, §§ 4.3(ii)(b), 18.3.

[109] [2013] EWCA Crim 991, [2014] 1 All ER 113.

[110] *Ibid*., [45], [54], [67].

[111] It is possible to explain *L* on the more restrictive ground that it can be an abuse of process to prosecute defendants for conduct that the state was obliged under international law not to criminalise. The United Kingdom is party to the Council of Europe Convention on Action Against Trafficking in Human Beings. At the time of the appeal in *L*, the defendants had served their sentences; the appeals were consequent on interventions by the Child Protection Agency and the United Kingdom Borders Agency. Sullivan, "Avoiding Criminal Liability and Excessive Punishment for Persons Who Lack Culpability" in Reed and Bohlander (eds.), *General Defences in Criminal Law* (2014) 25, 26–9.

[112] Alfred, Lord Tennyson, *Aylmer's Field*.

[113] Cf. Rogers, "Reclaiming the Essence of 'Second Limb' Abuse of Process" [2022] *Crim LR* 665.

# BIBLIOGRAPHY


Adams, F., "Homicide and the Supposed Corpse" (1968) 1 *Otago LR* 278.

Advisory Council on the Penal System, *Sentences of Imprisonment: A Review of Maximum Penalties* (London: HMSO, 1978).

Advisory Group on the Law of Rape (Heilbron Committee), *Report of the Advisory Group on the Law of Rape* Cmnd. 6352 (London: HMSO, 1975).

Alexander, L., "Causing the Conditions of One's Own Defense: A Theoretical Non-Problem" (2013) 7 *Criminal Law and Philosophy* 623.

——, "Criminal Liability for Omissions: An Inventory of Issues" in S. Shute and A.P. Simester (eds.), *Criminal Law Theory: Doctrines of the General Part* (Oxford: Oxford University Press, 2000) 121.

——, "Is There a Case for Strict Liability?" (2018) 12 *Criminal Law and Philosophy* 531.

——, "The Moral Magic of Consent (II)" (1996) 2 *Legal Theory* 165.

Alexander, L. and Ferzan, K., *Crime and Culpability: A Theory of Criminal Law* (New York: Cambridge University Press, 2009).

——, *Reflections on Crime and Culpability: Problems and Puzzles* (Cambridge: Cambridge University Press, 2018).

Alexander, L., Hurd, H., and Westen, P., "Consent Does Not Require Communication: A Reply to Dougherty" (2016) 35 *Law and Philosophy* 655.

Alldridge, P., "Common Sense, Innocent Agency, and Causation" (1992) 3 *Criminal Law Forum* 299.

——, "Dealing with Drug Dealing" in A.P. Simester and A.T.H. Smith (eds.), *Harm and Culpability* (Oxford: Oxford University Press, 1996) 239.

——, "Developing the Defence of Duress" [1986] *Criminal LR* 433.

——, "Making Criminal Law Known" in S. Shute and A.P. Simester (eds.), *Criminal Law Theory: Doctrines of the General Part* (Oxford: Oxford University Press, 2002) 103.

——, "The Doctrine of Innocent Agency" (1990) 2 *Criminal Law Forum* 45.

——, "The Limits of Confiscation" [2011] *Criminal LR* 827.

——, *Money Laundering Law* (Oxford: Hart Publishing, 2003).

Allen, C., *Legal Duties and Other Essays in Jurisprudence* (Oxford: Oxford University Press, 1931).

Almond, P., "Public Perceptions of Work-related Fatality Cases: Reaching the Outer Limits of 'Populist Punitiveness'?" (2008) 48 *British Journal of Criminology* 448.

——, "The Health and Safety at Work Act at 50: A 'Long Revolution' in Workplace Criminal Liability" [2025] *Criminal LR* 377.

American Psychiatric Association, *Diagnostic and Statistical Manual of Mental Disorders* (Arlington: American Psychiatric Publishing, Inc., 4th ed., 2000).

Amirthalingam, K., "Caldwell Recklessness Is Dead, Long Live Mens Rea's Fecklessness" (2004) 67 *Modern LR* 491.

André, J., "Nagel, Williams and Moral Luck" (1983) 43 *Analysis* 202.

Andrews, L.B., "The Legal Status of the Embryo" (1986) 32 *Loyola LR* 257.

Andrews, J.A., "Robbery" [1966] *Criminal LR* 524.

——, "Wilfulness: A Lesson in Ambiguity" (1981) 1 *Legal Studies* 303.

Annas, J., "How Basic are Basic Actions?" (1977–78) 78 *Proceedings of the Aristotelian Society* 195.

Antrobus, S., "The Criminal Liability of Directors for Health and Safety Breaches and Manslaughter" [2013] *Criminal LR* 309.

Archibald, B.P., "The Constitutionalisation of the General Part of the Criminal Law" (1988) 67 *Canadian Bar Review* 403.

Arden, M., "Criminal Law at the Crossroads: The Impact on Human Rights from the Law Commission's Perspective and the Need for a Code" [1999] *Criminal LR* 439.

Arenella, P., "Character, Choice, and Moral Agency" in E.F. Paul, F.D. Miller, and J. Paul (eds.), *Crime, Culpability and Remedy* (Oxford: Blackwell, 1990) 59.

——, "Convicting the Morally Blameless: Reassessing the Relationship between Legal and Moral Accountability" (1992) 39 *UCLA LR* 1511.

Arlidge, A., "The Trial of Dr David Moor" [2000] *Criminal LR* 31.

Ashworth, A., "A Change of Normative Position: Determining the Contours of Culpability in Criminal Law" (2008) 11 *New Criminal LR* 232.

——, "A Decade of Human Rights in Criminal Justice" [2014] *Criminal LR* 325.

——, "A New Generation of Omissions Offences?" [2018] *Criminal LR* 354.

——, "Belief, Intent, and Criminal Liability" in J. Eekelaar and J. Bell (eds.), *Oxford Essays in Jurisprudence* (Oxford: Oxford University Press, 3rd Series, 1987) 1.

——, "Criminal Attempts and the Role of Resulting Harm under the Code and in the Common Law" (1988) 19 *Rutgers LJ* 725.

——, "Criminal Liability in a Medical Context: The Treatment of Good Intentions" in A.P. Simester and A.T.H. Smith (eds.), *Harm and Culpability* (Oxford: Oxford University Press, 1996) 173.

——, "Defining Criminal Offences without Harm" in P. Smith (ed.), *Criminal Law: Essays in Honour of J.C. Smith* (London: Butterworths, 1987) 7.

——, "Four Threats to the Presumption of Innocence" (2006) 10 *Evidence and Proof* 241.

——, "Ignorance of the Criminal Law, and Duties to Avoid it" (2011) 74 *Modern LR* 1.

——, "Interpreting Criminal Statutes: A Crisis of Legality?" (1991) 107 *Law Quarterly Review* 419.

——, "Is the Criminal Law a Lost Cause?" (2000) 116 *Law Quarterly Review* 225.

——, "Manslaughter by Omission and the Rule of Law" [2015] *Criminal LR* 563.

——, "Manslaughter: Generic or Nominate Offences?" in C. Clarkson and S. Cunningham (eds.), *Criminal Liability for Non-aggressive Deaths* (Aldershot: Ashgate, 2008).

——, "Positive Duties, Regulation and the Criminal Sanction" (2017) 133 *Law Quarterly Review* 606.

——, "Principles, Pragmatism and the Law Commission's Recommendations on Homicide Law Reform" [2007] *Criminal LR* 345.

——, "Public Duties and Criminal Omissions: Some Unresolved Questions" [2011] *J Commonwealth Criminal Law* 1.

——, "Reason, Logic and Criminal Liability" (1975) 91 *Law Quarterly Review* 102.

——, "Redrawing the Boundaries of Entrapment" [2002] *Criminal LR* 161.

——, "Robbery Re-assessed" [2002] *Criminal LR* 851.

——, "Self-defence and the Right to Life" (1975) 34 *Cambridge LJ* 272.

——, "Taking the Consequences" in S. Shute, J. Gardner and J. Horder (eds.), *Action and Value in Criminal Law* (Oxford: Oxford University Press, 1993) 107.

——, "Testing Fidelity to Legal Values: Official Involvement and Criminal Justice" in S. Shute and A.P. Simester (eds.), *Criminal Law: Doctrines of the General Part* (Oxford: Oxford University Press, 2002) 299.

——, "The Doctrine of Provocation" (1976) 32 *Cambridge LJ* 292.

——, "The Elasticity of Mens Rea" in C. Tapper (ed.), *Crime, Proof and Punishment: Essays in Memory of Sir Rupert Cross* (London: Butterworths, 1981) 45.

——, "The European Convention and Criminal Law" in Cambridge Centre for Public Law, *The Human Rights Act and the Criminal and Regulatory Process* (Oxford: Hart Publishing, 1999) 37.

——, "The Human Rights Act and the Substantive Criminal Law: A Non-minimalist View" [2000] *Criminal LR* 564.

——, "The Scope of Criminal Liability for Omissions" (1989) 105 *Law Quarterly Review* 424.

——, "Transferred Malice and Punishment for Unforeseen Consequences" in P. Glazebrook (ed.), *Reshaping the Criminal Law* (London: Sweet & Maxwell, 1978) 77.

——, *Positive Obligations in Criminal Law* (Oxford: Hart Publishing, 2013).
——, *Principles of Criminal Law* (Oxford: Oxford University Press, 2nd ed., 1995).
——, *Sentencing and Justice* (Cambridge: Cambridge University Press, 6th ed., 2015).
Ashworth, A. and Blake, M., "The Presumption of Innocence in English Criminal Law" [1996] *Criminal LR* 306.
Ashworth, A., Emmerson, B., and Macdonald, B., *Human Rights and Criminal Justice* (London: Sweet & Maxwell, 2nd ed., 2007).
Ashworth, A., Hirsch, A. von, and Roberts, J.V. (eds.), *Principled Sentencing: Readings on Theory and Policy* (Oxford: Hart Publishing, 3rd ed., 2009).
Atiyah, P.S., "Common Law and Statute Law" (1985) 48 *Modern LR* 1.
——, *Vicarious Liability in the Law of Torts* (London: Butterworths, 1969).
Azmat, A.T., "What Mistake Of Law Just Might Be: Legal Moralism, Liberal Positivism, And The Mistake Of Law Doctrine" (2015) 18 *New Criminal LR* 369.
Babb, M. and Emmerich, L., "Official Misrepresentations of the Law and Fairness" (2023) 17 *Criminal Law and Philosophy* 83.
Bakalis, C., "Legislating Against Hatred: The Law Commission's Report on Hate Crime" [2015] *Criminal LR* 192.
Baker, B.M., "Mens Rea, Negligence and Criminal Law Reform" (1987) 6 *Law and Philosophy* 53.
Baker, E., "Human Rights, McNaghten and the 1991 Act" [1994] *Criminal LR* 84.
——, "Taking European Criminal Law Seriously" [1998] *Criminal LR* 361.
Bailey, D., "Interpreting Parliamentary Inaction" (2020) 79 *Cambridge LJ* 245.
Bailey, V. and Blackburn, S., "The Punishment of Incest Act 1980: A Case Study in Law Creation" [1979] *Criminal LR* 708.
Bailin, A., "Criminalising Free Speech?" [2011] *Criminal LR* 705.
Bailin, A. and Craven, E., "Compensation for Miscarriages of Justice—Who Now Qualifies?" [2014] *Criminal LR* 511.
Baldwin, R., "Why Rules Don't Work" (1990) 53 *Modern LR* 321.
Bamforth, N., "Sado-masochism and Consent" [1994] *Criminal LR* 661.
——, "The Application of the Human Rights Act 1998 to Public Authorities and Private Bodies" (1999) 58 *Cambridge LJ* 159.
Barlow, N.L.A., "Drug Intoxication and the Principle of *Capacitas Rationalis*" (1984) 100 *Law Quarterly Review* 639.
Baron, M., "Negligence, *Mens Rea*, and What We Want the Element to *Mens Rea* to Provide (2020) 14 *Criminal Law and Philosophy* 69.
Bayles, M., "Character, Purpose and Criminal Responsibility" (1982) 1 *Law and Philosophy* 5.
Bayne, T. and Levy, N., "Amputees by Choice: Bodily Integrity Disorder and the Ethics of Amputation" (2005) 22 *Journal of Applied Philosophy* 75.
Beade, G., "Who Can Blame Whom? Moral Standing to Blame and Punish Deprived Citizens" (2018) 13 *Criminal Law and Philosophy* 271.
Becker, B.C., "Human Being: The Boundaries of the Concept" (1974) 4 *Philosophy and Public Affairs* 334.
Bein, D., "The Theft of Use and the Element of 'Intent to Deprive Permanently' in Larceny" (1968) 3 *Israel LR* 368.
Bell, J. and Engle, G., *Cross on Statutory Interpretation* (London: Butterworths, 3rd ed., 1995).
Benn, A., "Classism as Hate Crime: Proposing Class as a Protected Ground in Criminal Law" [2021] *Criminal LR* 809.
Bennion, F., "Mens Rea and Defendants below the Age of Discretion [2009] *Criminal LR* 757.
Bennett, J., "Morality and Consequences" in S. McMurrin (ed.), *The Tanner Lectures in Human Values* (Cambridge: Cambridge University Press, 1981) 47.
——, *The Act Itself* (Oxford: Oxford University Press, 1995).
Bennion, F., "The Meaning of 'Sexual' in the Sexual Offences Bill" (2003) 167 *Justice of the Peace* 764.

——, "Mens Rea and Defendants below the Age of Discretion" [2009] *Criminal LR* 757.
Bentham, J., *An Introduction to the Principles of Morals and Legislation* (1789).
Bergelson, V., "Sex, Lies and Law: Rethinking Rape by Fraud" in C. Ashford, A. Reed, and N. Wake (eds.), *Consent and Control* (Newcastle upon Tyne: Cambridge Scholars Publishing, 2016).
——, "The Right to Be Hurt. Testing the Boundaries of Consent" (2007) 75 *George Washington LR* 165.
——, "Vice Is Nice but Incest Is Best: The Problem of a Moral Taboo" (2013) 7 *Criminal Law and Philosophy* 43.
Bettinson, V. and Wake, N., "A New Self-Defence Framework for Domestic Abuse Survivors who Use Violent Resistance in Response" (2023) 87 *Modern LR* 141.
Bevan, M., "Making it Work? The Case of Roberts and Uneven Progress in the Reform of Unfitness to Plead Procedures" [2020] *Criminal LR* 215.
Beynon, H., "Causation, Omissions and Complicity" [1987] *Criminal LR* 539.
——, "Doctors as Murderers" [1982] *Criminal LR* 17.
Birch, D., "Suffering in Silence: A Cost-benefit Analysis of Section 34 of the Criminal Justice and Public Order Act 1994" [1999] *Criminal LR* 769.
Birks, P., "Misdirected Funds: Restitution from the Recipient" (1980) *Lloyds Maritime and Commercial Law Quarterly* 296.
——, *An Introduction to the Law of Restitution* (Oxford: Oxford University Press, 1989).
Blake, L.W., "The Innocent Purchaser and Section 22 of the Theft Act" [1972] *Criminal LR* 494.
Blake, M., "Physician-assisted Suicide: A Criminal Offence or a Patient's Right?" (1997) 5 *Medical LR* 294.
Blakemore, S.J. and Choudhury, S., "Development of the Adolescent Brain: Implications for Executive Function and Social Cognition (2006) 47 *Journal of Child Psychiatry and Psychology* 296.
Blakey, G.R. and Goldsmith, M., "Criminal Redistribution of Stolen Property: The Need for Reform" (1976) 74 *Mich LR* 1512.
Blom-Cooper, L. and Morris, T., *Fine Lines and Distinctions: Murder, Manslaughter and the Unlawful Taking of Human Life* (Hook: Waterside Press, 2011).
——, *With Malice Aforethought: A Study of the Crime and Punishment for Homicide* (Oxford: Hart Publishing, 2004).
Bluglass, R., "Infanticide" [1978] *Bulletin of the Royal College of Psychiatrists* 14.
Bogart, J.H., "Commodification and Phenomenology: Evading Consent in Theory Regarding Rape" (1996) 2 *Legal Theory* 253.
Bogg, A. and Stanton-Ife, J., "Protecting the Vulnerable: Legality, Harm and Theft" (2003) 23 *Legal Studies* 402.
Bohlander, M., "*In extremis?* Hijacked Airplanes, 'Collateral Damage' and the Limits of the Criminal Law" [2006] *Criminal LR* 579.
——, "Mistaken Sex, Political Correctness and Correct Policy" (2007) 71 *Journal of Criminal Law* 412.
——, "Transferred Malice and Transferred Defenses: A Critique of the Traditional Doctrine and Arguments for a Change in Paradigm" (2010) 13 *New Criminal LR* 555.
——, "The Sexual Offences Act 2003 and the *Tyrrell* Principle—Criminalising the Victims?" [2005] *Criminal LR* 701.
Bonnie, R.J., "The Moral Basis of the Insanity Defense" (1983) 69 *American Bar Assoc J* 194.
Boucht, P.J. and Emberland, M., "'Mental Link' as a Condition for Punishment Under Article 7 of the European Convention on Human Rights" [2026[ *European Journal of Crime, Criminal Law and Criminal Justice* (online).
Bowden, P., "Violence and Mental Disorder" in N. Walker (ed.), *Dangerous People* (London: Blackstone Press, 1996) 13.
Bowley, M., "Talking about Sex" (1999) 149 *New LJ* 1739.
Bows, H., "Violence and Abuse of Older People—A Review of Current Proposals for Criminalisation" [2020] *Criminal LR* 882.
Bowsher, P., "Incest—Should Incest between Consenting Adults Be a Crime?" [2015] *Criminal LR* 208.

Bracton, *De Legibus et Consuetudinibus Angliae* (c. 1235).
Bradley, K., *The Bradley Report: Lord Bradley's Review of People with Mental Health Problems or Learning Disabilities in the Criminal Justice System* (London: Department of Health, 2009).
Brady, J.B., "Abolish the Insanity Defense? No!" (1971) 8 *Houston LR* 629.
Braithwaite, J., *Regulatory Capitalism: How it Works, Ideas for Making it Work Better* (Cheltenham: Edward Elgar, 2008).
Brett, P., "Mistake of Law as a Criminal Defence" (1966) 5 *Melbourne ULR* 179.
——, "Strict Responsibility: Possible Solutions" (1974) 37 *Modern LR* 417.
——, "The Physiology of Provocation" [1970] *Criminal LR* 640.
——, *Inquiry into Criminal Guilt* (London: Sweet & Maxwell, 1960).
Brink, D., *Fair Opportunity and Responsibility* (Oxford: Oxford University Press, 2021).
Broderick, P.A., "Conditional Objectives of Conspiracies" (1985) 94 *Yale LJ* 895.
Bronitt, S., "Defending *Giorgianni*" (1993) 17 *Criminal LJ* 242 and 305.
——, "Spreading Disease and the Criminal Law" [1994] *Criminal LR* 21.
Brown, P., "Reviewing the Age of Criminal Responsibility" [2018] *Criminal LR* 904.
Brudner, A., "A Theory of Necessity" (1987) 7 *Oxford Journal of Legal Studies* 338.
——, "Guilt under the Charter: The Lure of Parliamentary Supremacy" (1998) 40 *Criminal Law Quarterly* 287.
Bruneau, D. and Taylor, A., "In Defence of *Pace and Rogers*" [2015] 8 *Archbold Review* 6.
Buard, J., "'Intent'" [1978] *Criminal LR* 5.
Burn, E.H., *Cheshire and Burn's Modern Law of Real Property* (London: Butterworths, 15th ed., 1994) 165.
Buxton, R., "Being an Accessory to One's Own Murder" [2012] *Criminal LR* 275.
——, "By any Unlawful Act" (1966) 82 *Law Quarterly Review* 174.
——, "Complicity in the Criminal Code" (1969) 85 *Law Quarterly Review* 252.
——, "Joint Enterprise" [2009] *Criminal LR* 233.
——, "Some Simple Thoughts on Intention" [1988] *Criminal LR* 484.
——, "The Human Rights Act and the Substantive Criminal Law" [2000] *Criminal LR* 331.
Cambridge Centre for Public Law, *Constitutional Reform in the United Kingdom. Practice and Principles.* (Oxford: Hart Publishing, 1998).
——, *The Human Rights Act and the Criminal Justice and Regulatory Process* (Oxford: Hart Publishing, 1999).
Cammiss, S., Hayes, G., and Doherty, B., "Defending the Integrity Principle : Necessity, Remorse and Moral Consistency in the Protest Trial" (2025) 45 *Oxford Journal of Legal Styudies* 329.
——, "Necessity, Non-violent Direct Activism, and the Stansted 15: Reasserting 'Hoffmann's Bargain'" (2022) 85 *Modern LR* 1515.
Camp, P., "Section 69 of the Army Act 1955" [1999] *New LJ* 1736.
Campbell, K., "Conditional Intention" (1982) 2 *Legal Studies* 77.
——, "Offence and Defence" in I. Dennis (ed.), *Criminal Law and Criminal Justice* (London: Sweet & Maxwell, 1987) 73.
——, "The Test of Dishonesty in *R* v. *Ghosh*" (1984) 43 *Cambridge LJ* 349.
Card, R. and Molloy, J., *Card, Cross & Jones: Criminal Law* (Oxford: Oxford University Press, 22nd ed., 2016).
Carlton, D.W. and Fischel, D.R., "The Regulation of Insider Trading" (1983) 35 *Stanford LR* 857.
Carroll, S.M., "Purpose, Freedom, and the Laws of Nature" in G. Caruso and O. Flanagan (eds.), *Neuroexistensialism: Meaning, Purpose and Morals in the Age of Neuroscience* (New York: Oxford University Press, 2018) 298.
——, *The Big Picture: On the Origins of Life, Meaning and the Universe Itself* (New York: Dutton, 2016).
Carson, W.G., "Symbolic and Instrumental Dimensions of Early Factory Legislation" in R. Hood (ed.), *Crime, Criminology and Public Policy: Essays in Honour of Sir Leon Radzinowicz* (London: Heinemann Educational, 1974).

——, "The Conventionalisation of Early Factory Crime" (1979) 7 *Int J Soc Law* 37.
Caruso, G. D., *Rejecting Retributivism: Free Will, Punishment, and Criminal Justice* (Cambridge: Cambridge University Press, 2021).
Chadha, K., "Conditional Consent" (2021) 40 *Law and Philosophy* 335.
——, "Sexual Consent and Having Sex Together" (2020) 40 *Oxford Journal of Legal Studies* 619.
Chalmers, J., "'Frenzied Law Making': Overcriminalization by Numbers" (2014) 67 *Current Legal Problems* 483.
——, *Legal Responses to HIV and Aids* (Oxford: Hart Publishing, 2008).
Chalmers, J. and Leverick, F., "Criminal Law in the Shadows: Creating Offences in Delegated Legislation" (2018) 38 *Legal Studies* 221.
——, "Fair Labelling in Criminal Law" (2008) 71 *Modern LR* 217.
——, "Quantifying Criminalization" in R.A. Duff *et al.* (eds.), *Criminalization: The Political Morality of the Criminal Law* (Oxford: Oxford University Press, 2015) 54.
——, "Tracking the Creation of Criminal Offences" [2013] *Criminal LR* 543.
Chalmers, J., Leverick, F., and Munro, V., "Why the Jury Is, and Should Still Be, Out on Rape Deliberation" [2021] *Criminal LR* 753.
Chalmers, J., Leverick, F., and Shaw, M., "Is Formal Criminalization Really on the Rise? Evidence from the 1950s" [2015] *Criminal LR* 177.
Chan, W. and Simester, A.P., "Duress, Necessity: How Many Defences?" (2005) 16 *King's College LJ* 121.
——, "Four Functions of Mens Rea" (2011) 70 *Cambridge LJ* 381.
Chappell, D. and Walsh, M., "'No Questions Asked,' A Consideration of the Crime of Criminal Receiving" (1974) 20 *Crime and Delinquency* 157.
——, "Receiving Stolen Property: The Need for a Systematic Inquiry into the Fencing Process" (1974) 11 *Criminology* 484.
Chiesa, L.E., "Solving the Riddle of Rape by Deception" (2017) 35 *Yale Law & Policy Review* 407.
——, "Drink, Drugs and Law Reform: A Review of Law Commission Report No. 314" [2009] *Criminal LR* 488.
Child, J.J, "Exploring the Mens Rea Requirements of the Serious Crime Act 2007 Assisting and Encouraging Offences" (2012) 76 *Journal of Criminal Law* 220.
——, "Prior-Fault: Blocking Defences or Constructing Crimes" in A. Reed and M. Bohlander (eds.), *General Defences in Criminal Law: Domestic and Comparative Perspectives* (Aldershot: Ashgate, 2014) 37.
——, "The Structure, Coherence and Limits of Inchoate Liability: The New *Ulterior* Element" (2014) 34 *Legal Studies* 537.
——, "Understanding Ulterior Mens Rea: Future Conduct Intention *Is* Conditional Intention" (2017) 76 *Cambridge LJ* 311.
——, "Wrong on Many Levels: Understanding Crimes Across and Between Events" [2024] *Criminal LR* 378.
Child, J.J., Crombag, H. S., and Sullivan, G.R., "Defending the Delusional, the Irrational, and the Dangerous" [2020] *Criminal LR* 206.
Child, J.J. and Hunt, A., "Beyond the Present-Fault Paradigm: Expanding *Mens rea* Definitions in the General Part" (2022) 42 *Oxford Journal of Legal Studies* 438.
Child, J.J., Hunt, A. and Crombag, H, *Prior Fault Criminalization* (Oxford: Oxford University Press, 2026).
Child, J.J. and Reed, A., "Automatism Is Never a Defence" (2014) 65 *Northern Ireland Law Quarterly* 167.
Child, J.J. and Sullivan, G.R., "The Current State of Murder in English Law" in A. Reed and M. Bohlander (eds.), *Homicide in Criminal Law: A Research Companion* (Abingdon: Routledge, 2019) 62.
——, "When Does the Insanity Defence Apply? Some Recent Cases" [2014] *Criminal LR* 788.
Chin, G.J., "Race, the War on Drugs, and the Collateral Consequences of Criminal Conviction" (2002) 6 *J Gender, Race & Justice* 255.
Choo, A.L-T., *Abuse of Process and Judicial Stays of Criminal Proceedings* (Oxford: Oxford University Press, 2nd ed., 2008).

Clarkson, C.M.V., "Attempt: The Conduct Requirement" (2009) 29 *Oxford Journal of Legal Studies* 25.
——, "Complicity, *Powell* and Manslaughter" [1998] *Criminal LR* 556.
——, "Corporate Manslaughter: Yet More Government Proposals" [2005] *Criminal LR* 677.
——, "Kicking Corporate Bodies and Damning Their Souls" (1996) 59 *Modern LR* 557.
——, "Necessary Action: A New Defence" [2004] *Criminal LR* 81.
——, "Theft and Fair Labelling" (1993) 56 *Modern LR* 554.
Clarkson, C.M.V., Cretney, S., Davis, G., and Shepherd, J., "Assaults: The Relationship between Seriousness, Criminalisation and Punishment" [1994] *Criminal LR* 4.
Clarkson, C.M.V. and Cunningham, S. (eds.), *Criminal Liability for Non-aggressive Deaths* (Aldershot: Ashgate, 2008).
—— and Keating, H., *Criminal Law: Text and Materials* (London: Sweet & Maxwell, 6th ed., 2007).
Clement, R., "Consent to Body Modification in Criminal Law" (2018) 77 *Cambridge LJ* 451.
Clifford, A. and Reurts, N., "Corporate Criminal Liability in the Supply Chain: A Coherent Divergence?" [2018] *Criminal LR* 633.
Clough, A., "Sober Regrets and Shared Risk Taking: Navigating Intoxicated Consent and Rape in the Courtroom" (2018) 82 *Journal of Criminal Law* 482.
Cobb, N., "Property's Outlaws: Squatting, Land Use and Criminal Trespass" [2012] *Criminal LR* 114.
Coffee, J., "Does 'Unlawful' Mean 'Criminal'?: Reflections on the Disappearing Tort/Crime Distinction in American Law" (1991) 71 *Boston ULR* 193.
——, "No Soul to Damn: No Body to Kick: An Unscandalized Inquiry into the Problem of Corporate Punishment" (1981) 79 *Michigan LR* 386.
Cohen, M.D., "The 'Actus Reus' and Offences of 'Situation'" (1972) 7 *Israel LR* 186.
Coke, E., *Third Institute* (1641).
Coleman, K., Hird, C., and Povey, D., *Violent Crime Overview, Homicide and Gun Crime 2004/05* Home Office Statistical Bulletin 02/06 (London: Home Office, 2006).
Collins, J., "Testing Conspiracy to Defraud's Resilience" [2021] *Criminal LR* 902.
——, "The Industrialisation of Fraud: Understanding Fraud in a Digital Era" (2026) 46 *Legal Studies* 46.
Colvin, E., "Criminal Law and the Rule of Law" in P. Fitzgerald (ed.), *Crime, Justice and Codification: Essays in Commemoration of Jacques Fortin* (Toronto: Carswell, 1986) 125.
Committee on Mentally Abnormal Offenders, *Report of the Committee on Mentally Abnormal Offenders* Cmnd. 6244 (London: HMSO, 1975).
Committee on the Penalties for Homicide, *Report on the Penalties for Homicide* Cmnd. 5137 (Edinburgh: HMSO, 1972).
Cooke, R., *Turning Points of the Common Law* (London: Sweet & Maxwell, 1997).
Corda, A., "The Transformational Function of the Criminal Law: In Search of Operational Boundaries" (2020) 23 *New Criminal LR* 584.
Cornford, A., "Beyond Fair Labelling" (2022) 42 *Oxford Journal of Legal Studies* 985.
——, "Resultant Luck and Criminal Liability" in R.A. Duff et al. (eds.), *The Structures of Criminal Law* (Oxford: Oxford University Press, 2011) 36.
——, "Rethinking the Wrongfulness Constraint on Criminalization" (2017) 36 *Law and Philosophy* 615.
Corrado, M. (ed.), *Justification and Excuse in the Criminal Law: An Anthology* (New York: Garland Publishing, 1994).
Council of Europe, *European Convention on Human Rights, Year: 1974* (Leiden: Martinus Nijhoff, 1976).
Cowan, S., "'Freedom and the Capacity to Make a Choice': A Feminist Analysis of Consent in the Criminal Law of Rape" in V. Munro and C. Stychin (eds.), *Sexuality and the Law: Feminist Engagements* (Abingdon: Routledge-Cavendish, 2007) 51.
——, "Offences of Sex or Violence? Consent, Fraud, and HIV Transmission" (2014) 17 *New Criminal LR* 135.
——, "The Trouble with Drink: Intoxication, (In)capacity and the Evaporation of Consent to Sex" (2008) 41 *Akron LR* 899.

Criminal Law Reform Now Network, *Reforming the Relationship between Sexual Consent, Deception and Consent* (2021), available at http://www.clrnn.co.uk/publications-reports.
Criminal Law Revision Committee, Eleventh Report, *Evidence (General)* Cmnd. 4991 (1971).
——, Fourteenth Report, *Offences Against the Person* Cmnd. 7844 (1980).
——, Fifteenth Report, *Sexual Offences* Cmnd. 9213 (1984).
——, Thirteenth Report, *Section 16 of the Theft Act 1968* Cmnd. 6733 (1977).
——, Eighth Report, *Theft and Related Offences* Cmnd. 2977 (1966).
——, *Working Paper on Section 16 of the Theft Act 1968* (1974).
Cripps, Y., "The Public Interest Defence to the Action for Breach of Confidence and the Law Commission's Proposals on Disclosure in the Public Interest" (1984) 4 *Oxford Journal of Legal Studies* 361.
Crombag, H., Child, J.J., and Fortson, R., "Understanding the 'Fault' in Prior-Fault Intoxication" in A. Reed and M. Bohlander (eds.), *Fault in Criminal Law: A Research Companion* (London: Routledge, 2022).
Crombag, H. S., Child, J.J., and Sullivan, G. R., "Drunk, Dangerous and Delusional: How Legal Concept Creep Risks Overcriminalisation" (2020) 115 *Addiction* 2200.
Cross, J.T., "Protecting Confidential Information under the Criminal Law of Theft and Fraud" (1991) 11 *Oxford Journal of Legal Studies* 264.
Cross, R., "Duress and Aiding and Abetting (A Reply)" (1953) 69 *Law Quarterly Review* 354.
Cross, R. and Jones, P.A., *An Introduction to Criminal Law* (London: Butterworths, 3rd ed., 1953).
Cunningham, S., "Complicating Complicity: Aiding and Abetting Causing Death by Dangerous Driving in *R* v *Martin*" (2011) 74 *Modern LR* 767.
——, "Has Law Reform Policy been Driven in the Right Direction? How the New Causing Death by Driving Offences are Operating in Practice" [2013] *Criminal LR* 711.
——, "Recklessness: Being Reckless and Acting Recklessly" (2010) 21 *King's College LJ* 445.
Dagan, H., *A Liberal Theory of Property* (Cambirdge: Cambridge University Press, 2021).
Dan-Cohen, M., "Basic Values and the Victim's State of Mind" (2000) 88 *California LR* 759.
——, *Rights, Persons and Organisations: A Legal Theory for Bureaucratic Society* (Berkeley: University of California Press, 1986).
Davidson, D., *Essays on Actions and Events* (Oxford: Oxford University Press, 1980).
Davies, C.R., "Protection of Intellectual Property—A Myth?" [2004] *Journal of Criminal Law* 398.
Davis, F.T., "Judicial Review of Deferred Prosecution Agreements: A Comparative Study" (2022) 60 *Columbia Journal of Transnational Law* 751.
Daw, R. and Solomon, A., "Assisted Suicide and Identifying the Public Interest in the Decision to Prosecute" [2010] *Criminal LR* 737.
Dell, S., *Murder into Manslaughter: The Diminished Responsibility Defence in Practice* (London: Institute of Psychiatry, 1984).
Demetriou, S. and N. Partington. "Criminalising Hate: The Need for Rationalisation and Reform" [2022] *Criminal LR* 448.
Dempsey, M., "Victimless Conduct and the Volenti Maxim: How Consent Works" (2013) 7 *Criminal Law and Philosophy* 11.
Dempsey, M. and Herring, J., "Why Sexual Penetration Requires Justification" (2007) 27 *Oxford Journal of Legal Studies* 467.
Denning, A.T., *Responsibility Before the Law: A Lecture* (Jerusalem: Magnes Press, 1961).
Dennis, I., "Intention and Complicity: A Reply" [1988] *Criminal LR* 649.
——, "On Necessity as a Defence to Crime: Possibilities, Problems and the Limits of Justification and Excuse" (2009) 3 *Criminal Law and Philosophy* 29.
——, "Reverse Onuses and the Presumption of Innocence: In Search of Principle" [2005] *Criminal LR* 901.
——, "Silence in the Police Station: The Marginalisation of Section 34" [2002] *Criminal LR* 25.
——, "The Criminal Justice and Public Order Act 1994: The Evidence Provisions" [1995] *Criminal LR* 4.

——, "The Law Commission and the Criminal Law: Reflections on the Codification Project" in M. Dyson, J. Lee and S. Stark (eds.), *Fifty Years of the Law Commissions: The Dynamics of Law Reform* (Oxford: Hart Publishing, 2016) 108.
——, "The Rationale of Criminal Conspiracy" (1977) 93 *Law Quarterly Review* 39.
——, "The Mental Element for Accessories" in P. Smith (ed.), *Criminal Law: Essays in Honour of J.C. Smith* (London: Butterworths, 1987) 40.
Department of Health, *Protecting Children, Supporting Parents: A Consultation Document on the Physical Punishment of Children* (London: Department of Health, 2000).
Department of Transport, *mv Herald of Free Enterprise: Report of Court No. 8074* (London: HMSO, 1987).
Devlin, P., "Law, Democracy and Morality" (1962) 110 *Pennsylvania LR* 635, 648.
——, "Mental Abnormality and the Criminal Law" in R.St.J. Macdonald (ed.), *Changing Legal Objectives* (Toronto: Toronto University Press, 1963) 71.
——, *Samples of Lawmaking* (London: Oxford University Press, 1962).
——, *The Enforcement of Morals* (Oxford: Oxford University Press, 1965).
Dickens, B., "Death" in I. Kennedy and A. Grubb (eds.), *Principles of Medical Law* (Oxford: Oxford University Press, 1998) 868.
Dillof, A.M., "Transferred Intent: An Enquiry into the Nature of Criminal Culpability" [1998] *Buffalo Criminal LR* 501.
Dingwall, G., *Alcohol and Crime* (London: Cavendish Publishing, 2005).
Dobson, A., "Shifting Sands: Multiple Counts in Prosecutions for Corporate Manslaughter" [2012] *Criminal LR* 200.
Donnelly-Lazarov, B., *A Philosophy of Criminal Attempts: The Subjective Approach* (Cambridge: Cambridge University Press, 2015).
Dougherty, T., "Sex, Lies and Consent" (2013) 123 *Ethics* 717.
——, "Yes Means Yes: Consent as Communication" (2015) 43 *Philosophy and Public Affairs* 224.
——, *The Scope of Consent* (Oxford: Oxford University Press, 2021).
Dressler, J., "Battered Women Who Kill Their Sleeping Tormenters: Reflections on Maintaining Respect for Human Life while Killing Moral Monsters" in S. Shute and A.P. Simester (eds.), *Criminal Law Theory: Doctrines of the General Part* (Oxford: Oxford University Press, 2002) 259.
——, "New Thoughts about the Concept of Justification in the Criminal Law: A Critique of Fletcher's Thinking and Rethinking" (1984) 32 *UCLA LR* 61.
——, "Provocation: Partial Justification or Partial Excuse" (1988) 51 *Modern LR* 467.
——, "Reassessing the Theoretical Underpinnings of Accomplice Liability: New Solutions to an Old Problem" (1985) 37 *Hastings LJ* 91.
——, "Reflections on *Dudley and Stephens* and Killing the Innocent: Taking the Wrong Conceptual Path" in D. Baker and J. Horder (eds.), *The Sanctity of Life and the Criminal Law: The Legacy of Glanville Williams* (Cambridge: Cambridge University Press, 2013) 126.
——, "Rethinking Heat of Passion: A Defence in Search of a Rationale" (1982) 73 *J Criminal Law and Criminology*.
Dripps, D., "For a Negative, Normative Model of Consent, with a Comment on Preference- skepticism" (1996) 2 *Legal Theory* 113.
Dsouza, M., "Criminally Ignorant—An Invitation for Broader Evaluation" (2021) 12 *Jurisprudence* 226.
——, "False Beliefs and Consent to Sex" (2022) 85 *Modern LR* 1191.
——, "Intoxication, Psychoses, and Self-defence: Evaluating *Taj*" [2018] 9 *Archbold Review* 6.
——, "Justifications and Rights-Displacements" (2024) 18 *Criminal Law and Philosophy* 519.
——, "The Corporate Agent in Criminal Law—An Argument for Comprehensive Identification" (2020) 79 *Cambridge LJ* 91.
——, "Undermining Prima Facie Consent in the Criminal Law" (2014) 33 *Law and Philosophy* 489.
——, "Understanding the 'House-holder Defence': Proportionality and Reasonableness in Defensive Force" [2016] *Cambridge LJ* 192.

——, "Why *Ivey* was a Mistake (aka Two Times I Flirted with Theft)"in A.P. Simester (ed.), *Modern Criminal Law* (Oxford: Hart Publishing, 2024) 71.

——, *Rationale-based Defences in Criminal Law* (London: Bloomsbury Publishing, 2018).

Dsouza, M. and Schmitt-Leonardy, C., "Old and New Tracks for Corporate Criminal Liability" in Ambos, K. *et al* (eds.), *Core Concepts in Criminal Law and Criminal Justice: Volume III* (Cambridge University Press, 2025) 179.

du Bois-Pedain, A., "*Novus Actus* and Beyond: Attributing Causal Responsibility in the Criminal Court" (2021) 80 *Cambridge LJ* (Supp) s61

Dubber, M., "The Possession Paradigm: The Special Part and the Police Power Model of the Criminal Process" in R.A. Duff and S. Green (eds.), *Defining Crimes: Essays on the Special Part of the Criminal Law* (Oxford: Oxford University Press, 2005) 91.

Duff, R.A., "Attempted Homicide" (1995) 1 *Legal Theory* 149.

——, "'Can I Help You?' Accessorial Liability and the Intention to Assist" (1990) 10 *Legal Studies* 165.

——, "Choice, Character and Criminal Liability" (1993) 12 *Law and Philosophy* 345.

——, "'De Minimis' and the Structure of the Criminal Trial" (2023) 42 *Law and Philosophy* 57.

——, "Fitness to Plead and Fair Trials" [1994] *Criminal LR* 419.

——, "Harms and Wrongs" (2001) 5 *Buffalo Criminal LR* 13.

——, "Incapacity and Insanity: Do We Need the Insanity Defence?" in B. Livings, A. Reed, and N. Wake (eds.), *Mental Condition Defences and the Criminal Justice System* (Newcastle upon Tyne: Cambridge Scholars Publishing, 2015) 159.

——, "Intention Revisited" in D. Baker and J. Horder (eds.), *The Sanctity of Life and the Criminal Law* (Cambridge: Cambridge University Press, 2013) 148.

——, "Intentionally Killing the Innocent" (1973) 34 *Analysis* 16.

——, "Intentions Legal and Philosophical" (1989) 9 *Oxford Journal of Legal Studies* 76.

——, "Professor Williams and Conditional Subjectivism" (1982) 41 *Cambridge LJ* 273.

——, "Subjectivism, Objectivism and Criminal Attempts" in A.P. Simester and A.T.H. Smith (eds.), *Harm and Culpability* (Oxford: Oxford University Press, 1996) 19.

——, "The Circumstances of an Attempt" (1991) 50 *Cambridge LJ* 100.

——, "The Obscure Intentions of the House of Lords" [1986] *Criminal LR* 771.

——, "Towards a Modest Legal Moralism" (2014) 8 *Criminal Law and Philosophy* 217.

——, "Two Models of Criminal Fault" (2019) 13 *Criminal Law and Philosophy* 643.

——, "Virtue, Vice, and Criminal Liability: Do We Want an Aristotelian Criminal Law?" (2002) 6 *Buffalo Criminal LR* 147.

——, "Who Must Presume Whom to Be Innocent of What?" (2013) 42 *Netherlands Journal of Legal Philosophy* 170.

——, "Whose Luck Is it Anyway?" in C.M.V. Clarkson and S.R. Cunningham (eds.), *Criminal Liability for Non-aggressive Death* (Aldershot: Ashgate, 2008) 61.

——, *Answering for Crime: Responsibility and Liability in the Criminal Law* (Oxford: Hart Publishing, 2007).

——, *Criminal Attempts* (Oxford: Oxford University Press, 1996).

——, *Intention, Agency and Criminal Liability* (Oxford: Blackwell, 1990).

——, *Punishment, Communication and Community* (Oxford: Oxford University Press, 2001).

——, *The Realm of Criminal Law* (Oxford: Oxford University Press, 2018).

Duff, R.A. and Garland, D. (eds.), *A Reader on Punishment* (Oxford: Oxford University Press, 1994).

Duff, R.A. and Hirsch, A. von, "Responsibility, Retribution and the 'Voluntary': A Response to Williams" (1997) 56 *Cambridge LJ* 103.

Duff, R.A. and Marshall, S.E., "'Remote Harms' and the Two Harm Principles" in A.P. Simester, A. du Bois-Pedain, and U. Neumann (eds.), *Liberal Criminal Theory: Essays for Andreas von Hirsch* (Oxford: Hart Publishing, 2014) 205.

——, "Crimes, Public Wrongs, and Civil Order" (2019) 13 *Criminal Law and Philosophy* 27.

Dworkin, G., "Paternalism" (1972) 56 *Monist* 65.
——, *The Theory and Practice of Autonomy* (Cambridge: Cambridge University Press, 1988).
Dworkin, R., "Hard Cases" in *Taking Rights Seriously* (London: Duckworth, 1977) 81.
——, *Law's Empire* (London: Fontana Press, 1986).
——, *Life's Dominion: An Argument About Abortion and Euthanasia* (London: HarperCollins, 1993).
Dyson, M., "Scrapping Khan" [2014] *Criminal LR* 445.
—— (ed.), *Unravelling Tort and Crime* (Cambridge: Cambridge University Press, 2014).
Edwards, J., "Duress and Aiding and Abetting" (1953) 69 *Law Quarterly Review* 226.
——, *Mens Rea in Statutory Offences* (London: MacMillan, 1955).
Edwards, J.R., "An Instrumental Legal Moralism" (2018) 3 *Oxford Studies in Philosophy of Law* 153.
——, "Coming Clean about the Criminal Law" (2011) 5 *Criminal Law and Philosophy* 315.
——, "Criminalization without Punishment" (2017) 23 *Legal Theory* 69.
——, "Harm Principles" (2014) 20 *Legal Theory* 253.
——, "Justification and Motivation" (2023) 18 *Criminal Law and Philosophy* 1.
Edwards, J.R. and Simester, A.P., "Crime, Blameworthiness, and Outcomes" (2019) 39 *Oxford Journal of Legal Studies* 50.
——, "Prevention with a Moral Voice" in A.P. Simester, A. du Bois-Pedain, and U. Neumann (eds.), *Liberal Criminal Theory: Essays for Andreas von Hirsch* (Oxford: Hart Publishing, 2014) 43.
——, "What's Public About Crime?" (2017) 37 *Oxford Journal of Legal Studies* 105.
Edwards, S., "Coercion and Compulsion: Re-imagining Crimes and Defences" [2016] *Criminal LR* 876.
——, "'Demasculinising' the Defences of Self Defence, the 'Householder Defence' and Duress" [2022] *Criminal LR* 111.
——, "The Strangulation of Female Partners" [2015] *Criminal LR* 949.
Eldar, S., "Human Dignity and the Innocent Agent" (2024) 18 *Criminal Law and Philosophy* 617.
——, "The Limits of Transferred Malice" (2012) 32 *Oxford Journal of Legal Studies* 633.
Elkington, A., "The Historical Development of Duress and the Unfounded Result of Denying Duress as a Defence to Murder" (2023) 87 *Journal of Criminal Law* 207.
Elliott, C. and de Than, C., "The Case for a Rational Reconstruction of Consent in the Criminal Law" (2007) 70 *Modern LR* 225.
Elliott, D.W., "Directors' Thefts and Dishonesty" [1991] *Criminal LR* 732.
——, "Dishonesty in Theft: A Dispensable Concept" [1982] *Criminal LR* 395.
——, "Dishonesty under the Theft Act" [1972] *Criminal LR* 625.
——, "Endangering Life by Destroying or Damaging Property" [1997] *Criminal LR* 382.
——, "Frightening a Person into Injuring Himself" [1974] *Criminal LR* 15.
——, "Mens Rea in Statutory Conspiracy" [1978] *Criminal LR* 202.
——, "Necessity, Duress and Self-defence" [1989] *Criminal LR* 611.
Elliott, I.D., "Responsibility for Involuntary Acts: *Ryan v. The Queen*" (1968) 41 *Australian LJ* 497.
Emmerson, B. and Ashworth, A., *Human Rights and Criminal Justice* (London: Sweet & Maxwell, 2001).
Emmerson, B., Ashworth, A., and Macdonald, A., *Human Rights and Criminal Justice* (London: Sweet & Maxwell, 2nd ed., 2007).
Engelhardt, H.T., "The Ontology of Abortion" (1973) 84 *Ethics* 217.
English, P., "What Did Section Three Do to the Law of Provocation?" [1970] *Criminal LR* 249.
Epstein, R., "Property as a Fundamental Civil Right" (1992) 29 *Cal West LR* 187.
Evans, J., *Statutory Interpretation* (Auckland: Oxford University Press, 1988).
Erens, B., McManus, S., Prescott, P., Field, J., Johnson, A., Wellings, K., Fenton, K., Mercer, C., Macdowall, W., Copas, A., and Nanchahal, K., *National Survey of Sexual Attitudes and Lifestyles II: Reference Tables and Summary Report* (London: National Centre for Social Research, 2003).
Fairclough, S., "Speaking Up for Injustice: Reconsidering the Provision of Special Measures through the Lens of Equality" [2018] *Criminal LR* 4.
Fallon, R.H., "Fact and Fiction about Facial Challenges" (2011) 99 *California LR* 915.

Farmer, L., *Making the Modern Criminal Law: Criminalization and Civil Order* (Oxford: Oxford University Press, 2016).
Farrier, M.D., "The Distinction between Murder and Manslaughter in its Procedural Context" (1976) 39 *Modern LR* 415.
Fauconnet, P., *La Responsabilité: Étude de Sociologie* (Paris: F. Alcan, 1920).
Feinberg, J., "Action and Responsibility" in M. Black (ed.), *Philosophy in America* (Ithaca: Cornell University Press, 1965) 134.
——, "Harm to Others: A Rejoinder" (1986) *Criminal Justice Ethics* 16.
——, *Harm to Others* (New York: Oxford University Press, 1984).
——, *Harm to Self* (New York: Oxford University Press, 1986).
——, *Harmless Wrongdoing* (New York: Oxford University Press, 1988).
——, *Offense to Others* (New York: Oxford University Press, 1985).
Feldman, D., *Civil Liberties and Human Rights* (Oxford: Oxford University Press, 1993).
Fenwick, H., *Automatism, Medicine and the Law* (Cambridge: Cambridge University Press, Psychological Medicine Monograph 17: 1990).
Ferzan, K.K., "Consent and Coercion" (2020) 50 *Arizona State LJ* 951.
——, "Consent, Culpability and Rape" (2016) 13 *Ohio State Journal of Criminal Law* 397.
——, "Opaque Recklessness" (2001) 91 *Journal of Criminal Law and Criminology* 597.
Finch, E., "Psychological Injury: Where's the Harm in it?" [2022] *Criminal LR* 358.
——, "The Elephant in the (Jury) Room: Exploring Mock Jurors' Understanding of Different Approaches to Dishonesty" [2021] *Criminal LR* 513.
——, "The Perfect Stalking Law: An Evaluation of the Efficacy of the Protection from Harassment Act 1997" [2002] *Criminal LR* 702.
——, *The Criminalisation of Stalking: Constructing the Problem and Evaluating the Solution* (London: Cavendish Publishing, 2001).
Finch, E. and Munro, V., "Breaking Boundaries? Sexual Consent in the Jury Room" (2006) 26 *Legal Studies* 303.
——, "Intoxicated Consent and the Boundaries of Drug Assisted Rape" [2003] *Criminal LR* 773.
——, "The Demon Drink and the Demonized Woman: Socio-sexual Stereotypes and Responsibility Attribution in Rape Trials Involving Intoxicants" (2007) 16 *Social & Legal Studies* 591.
Finkel, N. *et al.*, "Lay Perspectives on Legal Conundrums: Impossible and Mistaken Act Cases" (1995) 19 *Law and Human Behaviour* 593.
Finkelstein, F., "Involuntary Crimes, Voluntarily Committed" in S. Shute and A.P. Simester (eds.), *Criminal Law Theory: Doctrines of the General Part* (Oxford: Oxford University Press, 2000) 143.
Finn, J., "Culpable Non-intervention: Reconsidering the Basis for Party Liability by Omission" (1994) 18 *Criminal LJ* 90.
Finn, P., *Fiduciary Obligations* (Sydney: Law Book Company, 1977).
Finnis, J., "*Bland*: Crossing the Rubicon?" (1993) 109 *Law Quarterly Review* 329.
——, "Intention and Side-effects" in R.G. Frey and C.W. Morris (eds.), *Liability and Responsibility* (Cambridge: Cambridge University Press, 1991) 32.
——, "The Rights and Wrongs of Abortion: A Reply to Judith Jarvis Thomson" (1973) 2 *Philosophy and Public Affairs* 117.
Fisher, J., Milne, A., and Bewsey, J., *Arlidge and Parry on Fraud* (London: Sweet & Maxwell, 6th ed., 2020).
Fisse, B. and Braithwaite, J., "The Allocation of Responsibility for Corporate Crime: Individualism, Collectivism and Accountability" (1988) 11 *Sydney LR* 468.
——, *Corporations, Crime, and Accountability* (Cambridge: Cambridge University Press, 1993).
Fitzgerald, P.G. and Williams, G., "Carelessness, Indifference and Recklessness: Two Replies" (1962) 25 *Modern LR* 49.
Fleming, J., *The Law of Torts* (Sydney: Law Book Company, 7th ed., 1987; 8th ed., 1992).
Fletcher, G., "On the Moral Irrelevance of Bodily Movements" (1994) *U Pennsylvania LR* 1443.

——, "The Individualisation of Excusing Conditions" (1974) 47 *Southern California LR* 1269.
——, *Rethinking Criminal Law* (Boston: Little Brown, 1978).
Floud, J. and Young, W., *Dangerousness and Criminal Justice* (London: Heinemann, 1981).
Fortson, R., "The Modern Partial Defence of Diminished Responsibility" in A. Reed and M. Bohlander (eds.,), *Loss of Control and Diminished Responsibility* (Farnham: Ashgate, 2011) 21.
Freckelton, I., "When Plight Makes Right: The Forensic Abuse Syndrome" (1994) 18 *Criminal LJ* 29.
Freedland, M. *et al.* (eds.), *The Contract of Employment* (Oxford: Oxford University Press, 2016).
Freedman, D., "Restoring Order to the Reasonable Person Test in the Reference of Provocation" [1998] *King's College LJ* 26.
Freer, E., "'Causing or Allowing the Death of a Child': Challenges to Working Out 'Which of You Did It'" [2016] *Criminal LR* 618.
——, "We Need to Talk about Charlie: Putting the Brakes on Unlawful Act Manslaughter" [2018] *Criminal LR* 612.
French, P., "Fishing the Red Herrings out of a Sea of Moral Responsibility" in E. LePore and B.P. McLaughlin (eds.), *Actions and Events: Perspectives on the Philosophy of Donald Davidson* (Oxford: Blackwell, 1985) 73.
——, *Collective and Corporate Responsibility* (New York: Columbia University Press, 1984).
Friedman, N., "Corporations as Moral Agents: Trade-offs in Criminal Liability and Human Rights for Corporations" (2020) 83 *Modern LR* 255.
Furmston, M., *Cheshire, Fifoot and Furmston's Law of Contract* (London: Butterworths, 13th ed., 1996).
Galligan, D.J., "The Return to Retribution in Penal Theory" in C. Tapper (ed.), *Crime, Proof and Punishment* (London: Butterworths, 1981) 144.
——, "The Right to Silence Reconsidered" [1988] *Current Legal Problems* 69.
Gardner J., "Complicity and Causality" (2007) 1 *Criminal Law and Philosophy* 127.
——, "Justifications and Reasons" in A.P. Simester and A.T.H. Smith (eds.), *Harm and Culpability* (Oxford: Oxford University Press, 1996) 103.
——, "Rationality and the Rule of Law in Offences against the Person" (1994) 53 *Cambridge LJ* 502.
——, "The Gist of Excuses" (1998) 1 *Buffalo Criminal LR* 575.
——, "The Opposite of Rape" (2018) 38 *Oxford Journal of Legal Studies* 48.
——, "Wrongs and Faults" in A.P. Simester (ed.), *Appraising Strict Liability* (Oxford: Oxford University Press, 2005) 51.
——, *Offences and Defences: Selected Essays in the Philosophy of Criminal Law* (Oxford: Oxford University Press, 2007).
Gardner, J. and Macklem T., "Compassion without Respect? Nine Fallacies of *R* v *Smith*" [2001] *Criminal LR* 623.
——, "Provocation and Pluralism" (2001) 64 *Modern LR* 815.
Gardner, J. and Shute, S., "The Wrongness of Rape" in J. Horder (ed.), *Oxford Essays in Jurisprudence* (4th Series, Oxford: Oxford University Press, 2000) 193.
Gardner, S., "Appreciating *Olugboja*" (1996) 16 *Legal Studies* 275.
——, "Direct Action and the Defence of Necessity" [2005] *Criminal LR* 371.
——, "Is Theft a Rip-off?" (1990) 10 *Oxford Journal of Legal Studies* 441.
——, "Necessity's Newest Inventions" (1991) 11 *Oxford Journal of Legal Studies* 125.
——, "Property and Theft" [1998] *Criminal LR* 35.
——, "Reckless and Inconsiderate Rape" [1991] *Criminal LR* 172.
——, "Stalking" (1998) 114 *Law Quarterly Review* 33.
——, "The Domestic Criminal Legality of the RAF Drone Strike in Syria in August 2015" [2016] *Criminal LR* 35.
——, "The Importance of Majewski" (1994) 14 *Oxford Journal of Legal Studies* 279.
Gazzinaga, M., "On Determinism and Human Responsibility" in G. Caruso and O. Flanagan (eds.), *Neuroexistensialism: Meaning, Purpose and Morals in the Age of Neuroscience* (New York: Oxford University Press, 2018) 223.

Gearty, C.A., "Reconciling Parliamentary Democracy and Human Rights" (2002) 118 *Law Quarterly Review* 248.
Geddes, L., "On the Intrinsic Wrongness of Killing Innocent People" (1973) 33 *Analysis* 93.
Gentle, S., "The Corporate Offence" [2011] *Criminal LR* 101.
Gerry, F., Pagano, R., and Hodgetts. C., "Disorganised Crime: Legal and Evidential Challenges of Raising a Modern Slavery Act 2015 Defence" [2022] *Criminal LR* 961.
Gibson, M., "Deceptive Sexual Relations: A Theory of Criminal Liability" (2020) 40 *Oxford Journal of Legal Studies* 82.
—, "Diminished Responsibility in *Golds* and Beyond: Insights and Implications" [2017] *Criminal LR* 543.
—, "Intoxicants and Diminished Responsibility: The Impact of the Coroners and Justice Act 2009" [2011] *Criminal LR* 909.
—, "Three Justifications of Fair Labelling" (2024) 140 *Law Quarterly Review* 431.
Giesen, D., *International Medical Malpractice Law* (London: Nijhoff, 1988).
Gill, M., *Commercial Robbery: Offenders' Perspectives on Security and Crime Prevention* (London: Blackstone Press, 2000).
Gillen, M., "Sanctions Against Insider Trading: A Proposal for Reform" (1991) 70 *Canadian Bar Review* 215.
Giles, M., "Judicial Law-making in the Criminal Courts: The Case of Marital Rape" [1992] *Criminal LR* 907.
Giles, M. and Uglow, S., "Appropriation and Manifest Criminality in Theft" (1992) 56 *J Criminal Law* 179.
Giliker, P., *Vicarious Liability in Tort* (Cambridge: Cambridge University Press, 2013).
Gillies, P., "The Offence of Conspiracy to Defraud" (1977) 51 *Australian LJ* 247.
Glaze, C.L., "Combatting Prenatal Substance Abuse: Court Ordered Protective Custody of the Fetus" (1997) 80 *Marquette LR* 793.
Glazebrook, P.R., "A Better Way of Convicting Business of Avoidable Deaths and Injuries" (2002) 61 *Cambridge LJ* 405.
—, "Criminal Omissions: The Duty Requirement in Offences Against the Person" (1960) 76 *Law Quarterly Review* 386.
—, "How Old Did You Think She Was?" (2001) 60 *Cambridge LJ* 26.
—, "Revising the Theft Acts" (1993) 52 *Cambridge LJ* 191.
—, "Situational Liability" in Glazebrook (ed.), *Reshaping the Criminal Law* (London: Sweet & Maxwell, 1978) 108.
—, "Structuring the Criminal Code: Functional Approaches to Complicity, Incomplete Offences and General Defences" in A.P. Simester and A.T.H. Smith (eds.), *Harm and Culpability* (Oxford: Oxford University Press, 1996) 195.
—, "Thief or Swindler: Who Cares?" (1991) 50 *Cambridge LJ* 389.
—, (ed.), *Blackstone's Statutes on Criminal Law* (London: Blackstone Press, 9th ed., 1999).
—, (ed.), *Reshaping the Criminal Law: Essays in Honour of Glanville Williams* (London: Sweet & Maxwell, 1978).
Glover, J., *Causing Death and Saving Lives* (Harmondsworth: Penguin, 1977).
Glover, R., "Can Dishonesty be Salvaged? Theft and the Grounding of the *MSC Napoli*" (2010) 74 *Journal of Criminal Law* 53.
Gobert, J., "Corporate Criminality: New Crimes for the Times" [1994] *Criminal LR* 722.
Gobert, J. and Punch, M., *Rethinking Corporate Crime* (London: Butterworths, 2003).
Goff, R., "The Mental Element in the Crime of Murder" (1988) 104 *Law Quarterly Review* 30.
Goff, R. and Jones, G., *The Law of Restitution* (London: Sweet & Maxwell, 4th ed., 1993).
Goldberg, A. E. *et al.*, "Prior-Fault Blame in England and Wales, Germany and the Netherlands" (2021) 8 *Journal of International and Comparative Law* 53.
Goldberg, D. and Huxley, P., *Common Mental Disorders: A Biosocial Model* (London: Tavistock/ Routledge, 1992).

Goldberg, A.E. and Manguele, P. (eds.), *Criminal Law and Prior Fault* (Oxford: Hart Publishing, 2025).
Goldstein, A.S., *The Insanity Defence* (New Haven: Yale University Press, 1967).
Goode, R., "Ownership and Obligation in Commercial Transactions" (1987) 103 *Law Quarterly Review* 433.
——, "Property and Unjust Enrichment" in A. Burrows (ed.), *Essays on the Law of Restitution* (Oxford: Oxford University Press, 1991) 215.
——, "The Right to Trace and Its Impact in Commercial Transactions" (1976) 92 *Law Quarterly Review* 360 and 528.
Goodhart, A.L., "The *Shaw* Case: The Law and Public Morals" (1961) 77 *Law Quarterly Review* 560.
Gordon, G.H., *The Criminal Law of Scotland* (Edinburgh: Green, 1967).
Goudkamp, J. and Nolan, D., *Winfield and Jolowicz on Tort* (London: Sweet & Maxwell, 21st ed., 2025).
Gough, S., "Intoxication and Criminal Liability: The Law Commission's Proposed Reforms" (1996) 112 *Law Quarterly Review* 335.
——, "Surviving without *Majewski*?" [2002] *Criminal LR* 719.
Gray, O., "The Standard of Care for Children Revisited" (1980) 45 *Missouri LR* 597.
Greasley, K., "Sex, Reasons, Pro Tanto Wrongdoing, and the Structure of Rape Liability" (2021) 15 *Criminal Law and Philosophy* 159.
Greaves, C.S., *The Criminal Law Consolidation and Amendment Acts of the 24 & 25 Vict. with Notes, Observations, and Forms for Summary Proceedings* (London: V. & R. Stevens, 2nd ed., 1862).
Green, S.P., "Theft and Conversion" (2012) 128 *Law Quarterly Review* 564.
——, *13 Ways to Steal a Bicycle* (Boston, MA: Harvard University Press, 2012).
——, *Criminalizing Sex: A Unified Liberal Theory* (Oxford: Oxford University Press, 2020).
Greenawalt, K., "The Perplexing Borders of Justification and Excuse" (1984) 84 *Columbia LR* 1897.
Greenberg, A., "Awareness and the Recklessness/Negligence Distinction" (2024) 18 *Criminal Law and Philosophy* 351.
——, "Why Criminal Responsibility for Negligence Cannot Be Indirect" (2021) 80 *Cambridge LJ* 489.
Grevling, K., "Damaging Property" [2020] *Criminal LR* 497.
Griew, E., "Consistency, Communication and Codification—Reflections on Two Mens Rea Words" in P.R. Glazebrook (ed.), *Reshaping the Criminal Law* (London: Sweet & Maxwell, 1978) 57.
——, "Dishonesty: The Objections to Feely and Ghosh" [1985] *Criminal LR* 341.
——, "Reckless Damage and Reckless Driving: Living with *Caldwell* and *Lawrence*" [1981] *Criminal LR* 743.
——, "Stealing and Obtaining Bank Credits" [1986] *Criminal LR* 356.
Groning, L., "Has Norway Abandoned its Medical Model?" [2021] *Criminal LR* 191.
Groning, L. *et al.*, "Remodelling Criminal Insanity: Exploring Philosophical, Legal, and Medical Premises of the Medical Model used in Norwegian Law" (2022) 81 *International Journal of Law and Psychiatry* 1.
Gross, H., "Rape, Moralism and Human Rights" [2007] *Criminal LR* 220.
——, *A Theory of Criminal Justice* (New York: Oxford University Press, 1979).
Grubb, A., "Treatment Decisions: Keeping it in the Family" in A. Grubb (ed.), *Choices and Decisions in Health Care* (Chichester: Wiley, 1993) 37.
Grubin, D., "What Constitutes Fitness to Plead" [1998] *Criminal LR* 748.
Gunby C., et al, "Alcohol-related Rape Cases: Barristers Perspectives on the Sexual Offences Act 2003 and its Impact on Practice" (2010) 74 *Journal of Criminal Law* 579.
Gunn, M.J. and Ormerod, D., "The Legality of Boxing" (1995) 15 *Legal Studies* 181.
Hadden, T.B., "Conspiracy to Defraud" (1966) 25 *Cambridge LJ* 248.
——, "Fraud in the City: The Role of the Criminal Law" [1983] *Criminal LR* 500.
Hale, B.M., "Dishonesty" (2019) 48 *Common Law World Review* 000.
Hall, J., "Negligent Behaviour Should Be Excluded from Penal Liability" (1963) 63 *Columbia LR* 632.
——, *General Principles of Criminal Law* (Indianapolis: Bobbs-Merrill, 2nd ed., 1960).
——, *Theft, Law and Society* (Indianapolis: Bobbs-Merrill, 2nd ed., 1952).

Hall, L., "Strict or Liberal Construction of Penal Statutes" (1935) 48 *Harvard LR* 748.
Hall, L. and Seligman, S.J., "Mistake of Law and *Mens Rea*" (1941) 8 *U Chicago LR* 641.
Halpin, A., "The Appropriate Appropriation" [1991] *Criminal LR* 426.
——, "The Test for Dishonesty" [1996] *Criminal LR* 283.
——, *Definition in the Criminal Law* (Oxford: Hart Publishing, 2004).
Hamer, D.A., "The Presumption of Innocence and Reverse Burdens: A Balancing Act" (2007) 66 *Cambridge LJ* 142.
Hamer, D.A. and Crofts, T., "The Logic and Value of the Presumption of Doli Incapax (Failing That, an Incapacity Defence)" (2023) 43 *Oxford Journal of Legal Studies* 546.
Handler, P., Handler, "Criminal Intent in Nineteenth-Century England" (2024) 83 *Cambridge LJ* 334.
——, "Intoxication and Criminal Responsibility in England, 1819–1920" (2013) 33 *Oxford Journal of Legal Studies* 243.
Hanink, J.G., "Some Light on Double Effect" (1975) 35 *Analysis* 147.
Harris, D.J., O'Boyle, M., Bates, E., and Bockley, C., *Harris, O'Boyle, and Warbrick: Law of the European Convention on Human Rights* (Oxford: Oxford University Press, 5th ed., 2023).
Harris, D.R., "The Concept of Possession in English Law" in A. Guest (ed.), *Oxford Essays in Jurisprudence* (Oxford: Oxford University Press, 1961) 69.
Harris, J. and Grace, S., *A Question of Evidence? Investigating and Prosecuting Rape in the 1990's* Home Office Research Study No. 196 (London: Home Office, 1999).
Hart, H.L.A., "Definition and Theory in Jurisprudence" (1954) 70 *Law Quarterly Review* 37.
——, *Law, Liberty and Morality* (Oxford: Oxford University Press, 1963).
——, *Punishment and Responsibility* (Oxford: Oxford University Press, 1968); 2nd ed. edited by J. Gardner (Oxford: Oxford University Press, 2008).
Hart, H.L.A. and Honoré, A.M., *Causation in the Law* (Oxford: Oxford University Press, 2nd ed., 1985).
Hasnas, J., "Reflections on *Prince*, Public Welfare Offenses, *American Cyanamid*, and the Wisdom of the Common Law" (2018) 12 *Criminal Law and Philosophy* 427.
Hawkins, K., *Environment and Enforcement: Regulation and the Social Definition of Pollution* (Oxford: Oxford University Press, 1984).
——, *Law as Last Resort: Prosecution Decision-Making in a Regulating Agency* (Oxford: Oxford University Press, 2003).
Haynes, A. and Yeoh, P. (eds.), *Cryptocurrencies and Cryptoassets: Regulatory and Legal Issues* (Abingdon: Routledge, 2020).
Healy, P., "Legislative Revision of Extreme Intoxication Cases in Canada" [2022] *Criminal LR* 957.
Heaton, R., "Cheques and Balances" [2005] *Criminal LR* 747.
——, "Deceiving without Thieving" [2001] *Criminal LR* 712.
Hébert, J., Bittle, S., and Tombs, S., "Obscuring Corporate Violence: Corporate Manslaughter in Action" (2019) 58 *Howard Journal of Criminal Justice* 554.
Hecht, L., "Provocateurs and their Rights to Self-defence" (2019) 13 *Criminal Law and Philosophy* 165.
Herring, J., "Consent in the Criminal Law: The Importance of Relationality and Responsibility" in A. Reed and M. Bohlander (eds.), *General Defences in Criminal Law: Domestic and Comparative Perspectives* (Aldershot: Ashgate, 2014) 63.
——, "Familial Homicide, Failure to Protect and Domestic Violence—Who's the Victim?" [2007] *Criminal LR* 923.
——, "Human Rights and Rape: A Reply to Hyman Gross" [2007] *Criminal LR* 228.
——, "Mistaken Sex" [2005] *Criminal LR* 511.
——, Rape and the Definition of Consent" (2014) 26 *National Law School of India Review* 62.
——, "The Duty of Care in Gross Negligence Manslaughter" [2007] *Criminal LR* 24.
Heuston, R.F.V. and Buckley, R.A., *Salmond and Heuston on the Law of Torts* (London: Sweet & Maxwell, 20th ed., 1992).
Heydon, J.D., "The Corroboration of Accomplices" [1973] *Criminal LR* 264.

——, "The Problems of Entrapment" (1973) 32 *Cambridge LJ* 268.
Heywood, R., "Clarification on Assisted Suicide" (2010) 126 *Law Quarterly Review* 5.
Hill, D. J., McLeod, K. K, and Taniy, A., "The Concept of Entrapment" (2018) 12 *Criminal Law and Philosophy* 539.
Hirsch, A. von, "Extending the Harm Principle: 'Remote' Harms and Fair Imputation" in A.P. Simester and A.T.H. Smith (eds.), *Harm and Culpability* (Oxford: Oxford University Press, 1996) 259.
——, "The Offence Principle in Criminal Law: Affront to Sensibility or Wrongdoing?" (2000) 11 *King's College LJ* 78.
——, *Censure and Sanctions* (Oxford: Oxford University Press, 1993).
——, *Doing Justice: The Choice of Punishments* (New York: Hill and Wang, 1976).
Hirsch, A. von, Garland, D., and Wakefield, A. (eds.), *Ethical and Social Perspectives on Situational Crime Prevention* (Oxford: Hart Publishing, 2004).
Hirsch, A. von and Jareborg, N., "Gauging Criminal Harm: A Living-sStandard Analysis" (1991) 11 *Oxford Journal of Legal Studies*, 1.
Hirsch, A. von and Simester, A.P. (eds.), *Incivilities: Regulating Offensive Behaviour* (Oxford: Hart Publishing, 2006).
Hirsch, A. von *et al.*, *Criminal Deterrence and Sentencing Severity: An Analysis of Recent Research* (Oxford: Hart Publishing, 1999).
Hirst, M., "Assault, Battery and Indirect Violence" [1999] *Criminal LR* 577.
——, "Causing Death by Driving and Other Offences: A Question of Balance" [2008] *Criminal LR* 339.
——, "Guilty; But of What?" (2000) 4 *International Journal of Evidence and Proof* 31.
——, *Jurisdiction and the Ambit of the Criminal Law* (Oxford: Oxford University Press, 2003).
Hodge, J., "Alcohol and Violence" in P. Taylor (ed.), *Violence in Society* (London: Royal College of Physicians of London, 1993) 127.
Hodgetts, C. and MacPartholán, C., "An Evolution in Devolution? Welsh Criminal Justice and the Commission on Justice in Wales" [2021] *Criminal LR* 34.
Hogan, B., "The Criminal Attempts Act and Attempting the Impossible" [1984] *Criminal LR* 584.
——, "Modernising the Law of Sexual Offences" in P. Glazebrook (ed.), *Reshaping the Criminal Law* (London: Sweet & Maxwell, 1978) 174.
——, "The *Dadson* Principle" [1989] *Criminal LR* 679.
——, "Victims as Parties to Crime" [1962] *Criminal LR* 683.
Hogg, C., "The Insanity Defence: An Argument for Abolition" (2015) 79 *Journal of Criminal Law* 250.
Hogg, C. and Child, J.J., "Not Guilty by Reasons Other than Insanity" in A.P. Simester (ed.), *Modern Criminal Law* (Oxford: Hart Publishing, 2024) 155.
Hogg, P.W., *Constitutional Law of Canada* (Scarborough, Ontario: Carswell, 4th ed., 1997).
Home Office, *Consultation on the Possession of Non-photographic Visual Depictions of Child Sexual Abuse* (London: Home Office, 2007).
——, *Corporate Manslaughter: The Government's Draft Bill for Reform* Cmnd. 6497 (London: The Stationery Office, 2005).
——, *Criminal Statistics, England and Wales 1996* Cmnd. 3764 (London: Stationery Office, 1997).
——, *Fraud Law Reform: Consultation on Proposals for Legislation* (London: Home Office, 2004).
——, *Fraud Strategy 2026 to 2029: Disrupting Crime, Supporting Economic Resilience and Delivering Justice.* CP 1523 (London: Home Office, 2026).
——, *Managing Dangerous People with Severe Personality Disorder: Proposals for Policy Development* (London: Home Office, 1999).
——, *Protecting the Public-Strengthening Protection against Sex Offenders and Reforming the Law on Sexual Offences* Cmnd. 5668 (London: Home Office, 2002).
——, *Racial Violence and Harassment: A Consultation Document* (London: Home Office, 1997).
——, *Reforming the Law on Involuntary Manslaughter: The Government's Proposals* (London: Home Office, 2000).

——, *Report of the Committee on Homosexual Offences and Prostitution* (Wolfendon Report) Cmnd. 247 (London: Home Office, 1957).
——, *Setting the Boundaries—Reforming the Law on Sex Offenders* (London: Home Office, 2000).
——, *Stalking the Solutions: A Consultation Paper* (London: Home Office, 1996).
——, *Violence: Reforming the Offences against the Person Act 1861* (London: Home Office, 1998).
Home Office and Department of Health and Social Security, *Interdepartmental Working Group into Mentally Disturbed Offenders in the Prison System* (London: Home Office, 1987).
Honoré, A.M., "Necessary and Sufficient Conditions in Tort Law" in D. Owen (ed.), *Philosophical Foundations of Tort Law* (Oxford: Oxford University Press, 1995) 363.
——, "Responsibility and Luck: The Moral Basis of Strict Liability" (1988) 104 *Law Quarterly Review* 530.
Hooper, M., "The Impact of the Human Rights Act on Judicial Decision-making" [1998] *European Human Rights LR* 676.
Horder, J., "A Critique of the Correspondence Principle in Criminal Law" [1995] *Criminal LR* 759.
——, "Cognition, Emotion and Criminal Culpability" (1990) 106 *Law Quarterly Review* 469.
——, "Control Over Land and Criminal Pollution: Empress Car Reconsidered" [2024] *Criminal LR* 230.
——, "Corporate Criminal Liability under the Crime and Policing Bill 2025: A Critique of the 'Senior Manager' Regime" [2025] *Criminal LR* 452.
——, "Corporate Criminal Liability under the Economic Crime and Corporate Transparency Act 2023" (2025) 45 *Legal Studies* 13.
——, "Crimes of Ulterior Intent" in A.P. Simester and A.T.H. Smith (eds.), *Harm and Culpability* (Oxford: Oxford University Press, 1996) 153.
——, "Criminal Law at the Limit: Countering False Claims in Elections and Referendums" (2021) 84 *Modern LR* 429.
——, "Criminal Law: Between Determinism, Liberalism, and Criminal Justice" (1996) 49 *CLP* 159.
——, "Gross Negligence and Criminal Culpability" (1997) 47 *U Toronto LJ* 495.
——, "Harmless Wrongdoing and the Anticipatory Perspective on Criminalisation" in Sullivan and Dennis (eds.), *Seeking Security: Pre-empting the Commission of Criminal Harms* (2012) 79.
——, "How Culpability Can, and Cannot, Be Denied in Under-age Sex Crimes" [2001] *Criminal LR* 15.
——, "Occupying the Moral High Ground? The Law Commission on Duress" [1994] *Criminal LR* 343.
——, "On the Irrelevance of Motive in Criminal Law" in J. Horder (ed.), *Oxford Essays in Jurisprudence* (4th series, Oxford: Oxford University Press, 2000) 173.
——, "Pleading Involuntary Lack of Capacity" (1993) 52 *Cambridge LJ* 298.
——, "Questioning the Correspondence Principle—A Reply" [1999] *Criminal LR* 206.
——, "Reconsidering Psychic Assault" [1998] *Criminal LR* 392.
——, "Re-shaping the Subjective Element in the Provocation Defence" (2005) 25 *Oxford Journal of Legal Studies* 123.
——, "Rethinking Non-fatal Offences against the Person (1994) 14 *Oxford Journal of Legal Studies* 335.
——, "Sobering Up? The Law Commission on Criminal Intoxication" (1995) 58 *Modern LR* 534.
——, "Strict Liability, Statutory Construction, and the Spirit of Liberty" (2002) 118 *Law Quarterly Review* 458.
——, "The Courts' Development of the Criminal Law and the Role of Declarations" (2020) 40 *Legal Studies* 42.
——, "Transferred Malice and the Remoteness of Unexpected Outcomes from Intentions" [2006] *Criminal LR* 383.
——, "Two Histories and Four Hidden Principles of Mens Rea" (1997) 113 *Law Quarterly Review* 95.
——, "Whose Values Should Determine When Liability Is Strict?" in A.P. Simester (ed.), *Appraising Strict Liability* (Oxford: Oxford University Press, 2005) 105.
——, *Ashworth's Principles of Criminal Law* (Oxford: Oxford University Press, 10th ed., 2022).
——, *Excusing Crime* (Oxford: Oxford University Press, 2004).
——, *Provocation and Responsibility* (Oxford: Oxford University Press, 1992).

Horder, J. and McGowan, L., "Manslaughter by Causing Another's Suicide" [2006] *Criminal LR* 1035.
Horder, J. and Watts, G., "The Scope of Liability for Failure to Prevent Economic Crime" [2021] *Criminal LR* 851.
Hörnle, T., "Consensual Adult Incest: A Sex Offense?" (2014) 17 *New Criminal LR* 76.
——, "Hijacked Planes: May They Be Shot Down?" (2007) 10 *New Criminal LR* 582.
Hoskins, Z., "Collateral Restrictions" in C. Flanders and Z. Hoskins (eds.), *The New Philosophy of Criminal Law* (London, Rowman & Littlefield, 2016) 249.
——, "Ex-offender Restrictions" (2014) 31 *J Applied Philosophy* 33.
——, *Beyond Punishment?* (Oxford: Oxford University Press, 2019).
House of Commons Defence Committee, *Defence and Security in the UK: Sixth Report of Session 2001–02* HC 518 (London: TSO, 2002).
House of Lords, *Report of the Select Committee on Murder and Life Imprisonment* (Session 1988–89) HL Paper 78 (London: HMSO, 1989).
Howard, C., "Strict Responsibility in the High Court of Australia" (1960) 76 *Law Quarterly Review* 547.
——, *Strict Responsibility* (London: Sweet & Maxwell, 1963).
Howarth, W., "Handling Stolen Goods and Handling Salmon" [1987] *Criminal LR* 460.
Howes, S.K., Williams, K.S., and Wistrich, H., "Women Who Kill: Why Self-defence Rarely Works for Women Who Kill their Abuser" [2021] *Criminal LR* 945.
Hudson, A.H., "Abandonment" in N. Palmer and E. McKendrick (eds.), *Interests in Goods* (London: LLP, 1993) 423.
——, "Is Divesting Abandonment Possible at Common Law?" (1984) 100 *Law Quarterly Review* 110.
Hughes, G., "Criminal Omissions" (1958) 67 *Yale LJ* 590.
Hurd, H., "The Moral Magic of Consent" (1996) 2 *Legal Theory* 121, 165.
Hurd, H. and Moore, M., "Untying the Gordian Knot of Mens Rea Requirements for Accomplices" (2016) 32 *Social Philosophy and Policy* 161.
Husak, D.N., "Abetting a Crime" (2014) 33 *Law and Philosophy* 41.
——, "Conflicts of Justifications" (1999) 18 *Law and Philosophy* 41.
——, "*Malum Prohibitum* and Retributivism" in R.A. Duff and S. Green (eds.), *Defining Crimes: Essays on the Special Part of the Criminal Law* (Oxford: Oxford University Press, 2005) 65.
——, "Negligence, Belief, Blame and Criminal Liability: The Special Case of Forgetting" (2011) 5 *Criminal Law and Philosophy* 199.
——, "On the Supposed Priority of Justification to Excuse" (2005) 24 *Law and Philosophy* 557.
——, "Recreational Drugs and Paternalism" (1989) 8 *Law and Philosophy* 353.
——, "The Nature and Justifiability of Nonconsumate Offences" (1995) 37 *Arizona LR* 151.
——, "Transferred Intent" (1996) 10 *Notre Dame Journal of Legal Ethics and Public Policy* 65.
——, "Wrongs, Crimes and Criminalization" (2019) 13 *Criminal Law and Philosophy* 393.
——, *Ignorance of Law: A Philosophical Inquiry* (Oxford: Oxford University Press, 2016).
——, *Overcriminalization: The Limits of the Criminal Law* (New York: Oxford University Press, 2008).
——, *Philosophy of the Criminal Law* (New Jersey: Rowman and Littlefield, 1987).
Husak, D. and von Hirsch, A., "Culpability and Mistake of Law" in S. Shute, J. Gardner and J. Horder (eds.), *Action and Value in Criminal Law* (Oxford: Oxford University Press, 1993) 157.
Hutchinson, A.C., "Sault Ste. Marie, Mens Rea and the Halfway House: Public Welfare Offences Get a Home of Their Own" (1979) 17 *Osgoode Hall LJ* 415.
Hutter, B., *The Reasonable Arm of the Law Law? The Law Enforcement Procedures of Environmental Health Officers* (Oxford: Oxford University Press, 1988).
Huxtable, R., "Separation of the Conjoined Twin: Where Next for English Law?" [2002] *Criminal LR* 549.
Jackson, B.S., "*Storkwain*: A Case Study in Strict Liability and Self-regulation" [1991] *Criminal LR* 892.
Jackson, E. and Keown, J., *Debating Euthanasia* (Oxford: Hart Publishing, 2011).
Jackson, J., "Curtailing the Right to Silence: Lessons from Northern Ireland" [1991] *Criminal LR* 404.
James Jr, F., "The Qualities of the Reasonable Man in Negligence Cases" (1951) 16 *Missouri LR* 1.

Jareborg, N., "What Kind of Criminal Law Do We Want" in A. Snare (ed.), *Scandinavian Studies in Criminology* vol. 14 (Oslo: Pax Forlag A/S, 1995) 17.

Jarvis, P., "Conspiracy to Defraud: A Siren to Lure Unwary Prosecutors" [2014] *Criminal LR* 738.

——, "The Timing of Consent" [2019] *Criminal LR* 394.

Jarvis, P. and Bisgrove, M., "The Use and Abuse of Conspiracy' [2014] *Criminal LR* 261.

Jeffries, J.C., "Legality, Vagueness, and the Construction of Penal Statutes" (1985) 71 *Virginia LR* 189.

Jeffries, J.C. and Stephan, P.B., "Defences, Presumptions, and Burden of Proof in the Criminal Law" (1979) 88 *Yale LJ* 1325.

Johnson, R., "The Unnecessary Crime of Conspiracy" (1973) 61 *California LR* 1137.

Jones, G., "Unjust Enrichment and the Fiduciary's Duty of Loyalty" (1968) 84 *Law Quarterly Review* 472.

Jones, T.H., "Causation, Homicide and the Supply of Drugs" (2006) 26 *Legal Studies* 139.

——, "Insanity, Automatism and the Burden of Proof on the Accused" (1995) 111 *Law Quarterly Review* 475.

Jos, P.H., Marshall, M.F., and Perlmutter, M., "The Charleston Policy on Cocaine Use during Pregnancy: A Cautionary Tale" (1995) 23 *J Law, Medicine and Ethics* 120.

JUSTICE, *Breaking the Rules: The Problem of Crimes and Contraventions* (London: JUSTICE, 1980).

Kadish, S., "Some Observations on the Use of Criminal Sanctions in Enforcing Economic Regulations" (1963) 30 *U Chicago LR* 423.

——, *Blame and Punishment* (New York: MacMillan, 1987).

Kaiserman, A., "Against Accomplice Liability" (2021) 4 *Oxford Studies in Philosophy of Law* 124.

Kant, *Groundwork of the Metaphysics of Morals* (1785).

Katz, L.D., "On What Underlies Excuse" (2023) 18 *Criminal Law and Philosophy* 537.

Kaufman, R.M., "Legal Recognition of Independent Fetal Rights: The Trend towards Criminalizing Prenatal Maternal Conduct" (1997) 17 *Children's Legal Rights J* 20.

Kaveny, M.C., "Inferring Intention from Foresught" (2004) 120 *Law Quarterly Review* 81.

Kean, A.W.G., "The History of the Criminal Liability of Children" (1937) 53 *Law Quarterly Review* 364.

Keane, A. and McKeown, P., "Time to Abandon 'Beyond Reasonable Doubt' and 'Sure'" [2019] *Criminal LR* 505.

Keating, H., "How Should the Criminal Law Respond to the 'Special Status' of Children?" in J.J. Child and R.A. Duff (eds.), *Criminal Law Reform Now: Proposals and Critique* (London: Hart Publishing, 2019) 165.

——, "Protecting or Punishing Children: Physical Punishment, Human Rights and English Law Reform" (2006) 26 *Legal Studies* 394.

Keedy, E.R., "Ignorance and Mistake in the Criminal Law" (1908) 22 *Harvard LR* 75.

Kell, D., "Social Disutility and the Law of Consent" (1994) 14 *Oxford Journal of Legal Studies* 121.

Kelly, R. and Ormerod, D., "Non-fatal Strangulation and Suffocation" [2021] *Criminal LR* 532.

Kelman, M., "Interpretative Contraction in the Substantive Criminal Law" (1981) 33 *Stanford LR* 591.

Kennedy, C., "Criminalising Deceptive Sex: Sex, Identity and Recognition" (2021) 41 *Legal Studies* 91.

——, "Declaring Crimes" (2017) 37 *Oxford Journal of Legal Studies* 741.

——, *Inducing Intimacy* (Cambridge: Cambridge University Press, 2024).

Kennedy, I.M., "Switching Off Life Support Machines: The Legal Implications" [1977] *Criminal LR* 443.

Kennefick, L., *The Boundaries of Blame: Towards a Universal Partial Defence for the Criminal Law* (Cambridge: Cambridge University Press, 2025).

Kenny, A., "Intention and Purpose in Law" in R.S. Summers (ed.), *Essays in Legal Philosophy* (London: Blackwells, 1968) 146.

Kenny, C.S., *Outlines of the Criminal Law* (Cambridge: Cambridge University Press, 1902; 2nd ed., 1904; 14th ed., 1932).

Kentridge, S., "The Incorporation of the European Convention on Human Rights" in Cambridge Centre for Public Law, *Constitutional Reform in the United Kingdom: Practice and Principles* (Oxford: Hart Publishing, 1998) 69.

Keown, J., "Restoring Moral and Intellectual Shape to the Law after *Bland*" (1997) 113 *Law Quarterly Review* 481.
Kim, H., "Entrapment, Culpability, and Legitimacy" (2020) 39 *Law and Philosophy* 67.
King, A., Munro, V. and Young Andrade, L., *Operation Soteria: Improving CPS Responses to Rape Complaints and Complainants* (Final Findings Report, University of Warwick, 2023).
King, C. and Lord, N., "Deferred Prosecution Agreements in England and Wales: Castles Built on Sand?" [2020] *Public Law* 307.
King, M., "Against Personifying the Reasonable Person" (2017) 11 *Criminal Law and Philosophy* 725.
Kleinig, J., "Crime and the Concept of Harm" (1978) *American Philosophical Quarterly* 27.
——, *Paternalism* (Manchester: Manchester University Press, 1983).
Klockars, C.B., *The Professional Fence* (New York: Free Press, 1974).
Koffman, L., "The Nature of Appropriation" [1982] *Criminal LR* 331.
——, "The Rise and Fall of Proportionality: The Failure of the Criminal Justice Act 1991" [2006] *Criminal LR* 281.
Krebs, B., "Joint Criminal Enterprise" [2010] 73 *Modern LR* 578.
——, "Joint Enterprise Murder Is Dead—Long Live Joint Enterprise Manslaughter?" in B. Krebs (ed.), *Accessorial Liability after Jogee* (Oxford: Hart Publishing, 2020) 107.
——, "Withdrawal from Attempts" in A.P. Simester (ed.), *Modern Criminal Law* (Oxford: Hart Publishing, 2024) 177.
Kremnitzer, M., "Interpretation in Criminal Law" [1986] 21 *Israel LR* 358.
Kugler, I., "Conditional Oblique Intention" [2004] *Crim LR* 284.
——, *Direct and Oblique Intention in the Criminal Law: An Inquiry into Degrees of Blameworthiness* (Aldershot: Ashgate, 2002).
Lacey, N., "Beset by Boundaries: The Home Office Review of Sex Offenders" [2001] *Criminal LR* 3.
Laing, J. and McHale, J.V. (eds.), *Principles of Medical Law* (Oxford: Oxford University Press, 5th ed., 2025).
Laird, K., "Evaluating the Relationship between Section 45 of the Modern Slavery Act 2015 and the Defence of Duress: An Opportunity Missed?" [2016] *Criminal LR* 295.
——, "Rapist or Rogue? Deception, Consent and the Sexual Offences Act 2003" [2014] *Criminal LR* 492.
Lamond, G., "Coercion, Threats, and the Puzzle of Blackmail" in A.P. Simester and A.T.H. Smith (eds.), *Harm and Culpability* (Oxford: Oxford University Press, 1996) 215.
——, "Precedent in English Criminal Law" in A.P. Simester (ed.), *Modern Criminal Law* (Oxford: Hart, 2024) 287.
——, "What Is a Crime?" (2007) 27 *Oxford Journal of Legal Studies* 609.
Lanham, D.J., "Accomplices and Withdrawal" (1981) 97 *Law Quarterly Review* 575.
——, "Complicity, Concert and Conspiracy" (1980) 4 *Criminal LJ* 276.
——, "Drivers, Control, and Accomplices" [1982] *Criminal LR* 419.
——, "Duress and Void Contracts" (1966) 29 *Modern LR* 615.
——, "Larsonneur Revisited" [1976] *Criminal LR* 276.
——, "Primary and Derivative Criminal Liability: An Australian Perspective" [2000] *Criminal LR* 707.
——, "Wilful Blindness and the Criminal Law" (1985) 9 *Criminal LJ* 261.
Larcombe, W., Fileborn, B., Powell, A., Hanley, N., and Henry, N., "'I Think It's Rape and I Think He Would Be Found Not Guilty': Focus Group Perceptions of (Unreasonable) Belief in Consent in Rape Law" (2016) 25 *Social & Legal Studies* 611.
Lavoie, J., "Ownership of Human Tissue: Life after *Moore* v. *Regents of the University of California*" [1989] 75 *Virginia LR* 1363.
Lavrysen, L. and Mavronicola, N. (eds.), *Coercive Human Rights: Positive Duties to Mobilise the Criminal Law under the ECHR* (Oxford: Hart, 2020).
Law Commission, No. 177, *A Criminal Code for England and Wales* (London: HMSO, 1989).
——, Consultation Paper No. 177, *A New Homicide Act for England and Wales?* (London: HMSO, 2006).

——, Consultation Paper No. 131, *Assisting and Encouraging Crime* (London: HMSO, 1993).
——, No. 102, *Attempt and Impossibility in Relation to Attempt, Conspiracy and Incitement* (London: HMSO, 1980).
——, No. 143, *Codification of the Criminal Law* (London: HMSO, 1985).
——, Consultation Paper No. 139, *Consent in the Criminal Law* (London: HMSO, 1995).
——, Consultation Paper No. 183, *Conspiracy and Attempts* (London: HMSO, 2007).
——, No. 318, *Conspiracy and Attempts* (London: HMSO, 2009).
——, No. 76, *Conspiracy and Criminal Law Reform* (London: HMSO, 1976).
——, *Corporate Criminal Liability: A Discussion Paper* (London: HMSO, 2021).
——, *Corporate Criminal Liability: An Options Paper* (London: HMSO, 2022).
——, Consultation Paper No. 195, *Criminal Liability in Regulatory Contexts* (London: HMSO, 2010).
——, *Criminal Liability: Insanity and Automatism. A Discussion Paper* (London: HMSO, 2013).
——, No. 83, *Defences of General Application* (London: HMSO, 1977).
——, No. 412. *Digital Assets: Final Report* (London: HMSO, 2023).
——, No. 416, *Digital Assets as Personal Property. Supplemental Report and Draft Bill* (London: HMSO, 2024).
——, No. 89, *Draft Criminal Liability (Mental Element) Bill* (London: HMSO, 1978).
——, No. 420, *Evidence in Sexual Offences Prosecutions* (London: HMSO, 2025).
——, No. 273, *Evidence of Bad Character in Criminal Proceedings* (London: HMSO, 2001).
——, No. 276, *Fraud* (London: HMSO, 2002).
——, Consultation Paper No. 155, *Fraud and Deception* (London: HMSO, 1999).
——, No. 402, *Hate Crime: Final Report* (London: HMSO, 2021).
——, No. 348, *Hate Crime: Should the Current Offences be Extended?* (London: HMSO, 2014).
——, No. 10, *Imported Criminal Intent (Director of Public Prosecutions v. Smith)* (London: HMSO, 1967).
——, No. 300, *Inchoate Liability for Assisting and Encouraging Crime* (London: HMSO, 2006).
——, *Insanity and Automatism: A Discussion Paper* (London: HMSO, 2013).
——, *Insanity and Automatism: A Scoping Paper* (London: HMSO, 2012).
——, No. 314, *Intoxication and Criminal Liability* (London: HMSO, 2009).
——, No. 180, *Jurisdiction over Offences of Fraud and Dishonesty with a Foreign Element* (London: HMSO, 1989).
——, Consultation Paper No. 155, *Legislating the Criminal Code: Fraud and Deception* (London: HMSO, 1999).
——, No. 237, *Legislating the Criminal Code: Involuntary Manslaughter* (London: HMSO, 1996).
——, Consultation Paper No. 122, *Legislating the Criminal Code: Offences against the Person and General Principles* (London: HMSO, 1992).
——, No. 218, *Legislating the Criminal Code: Offences against the Person and General Principles* (London: HMSO, 1993).
——, Working Paper No. 23, "Malicious Damage" (London: HMSO, 1969).
——, No. 304, *Murder, Manslaughter and Infanticide* (London: HMSO, 2006).
——, No. 290, *Partial Defences to Murder* (London: HMSO, 2004).
——, No. 305, *Participation in Crime* (London: HMSO, 2007).
——, No. 302, *Post-legislative Scrutiny* Law Com. (London: HMSO, 2006).
——, No. 316, *Reform of Offences against the Person* (London: HMSO, 2015).
——, No. 55, *Report on Forgery and Counterfeit Currency* (London: HMSO, 1973).
——, No. 29, *Report on Offences of Damage to Property* (London: HMSO, 1970).
——, No. 364, *Unfitness to Plead* (London: HMSO, 2016).
——, Consultation Paper No. 197, *Unfitness to Plead* (London: HMSO, 2010).
Lazarus, L., "Positive Obligations and Criminal Justice: Duties to Protect or Coerce?" in L. Zedner and J. Roberts (eds.), *Principles and Values in Criminal Law and Criminal Justice: Essays in Honour of Andrew Ashworth* (Oxford: Oxford University Press, 2012) 135.

Leavens, A., "A Causative Approach to Omissions" (1988) 76 *California LR* 547.
Lederman, E., "Models for Imposing Corporate Criminal Liability: From Adaptation and Imitation Toward Aggregation and the Search for Self-identity" (2001) 4 *Buffalo Criminal LR* 642.
Leigh, L.H., "Sado-masochism, Consent and the Reform of the Criminal Law" (1976) 39 *Modern LR* 130.
——, "Some Remarks on Appropriation in the Law of Theft after *Morris*" (1985) 48 *Modern LR* 167.
——, *Strict and Vicarious Liability: A Study in Administrative Criminal Law* (London: Sweet & Maxwell, 1982).
Leipold, A., "A Case for Criminal Negligence" (2010) 29 *Law and Philosophy* 455.
Lenckner, T., "The Principle of Interest Balancing as a General Basis of Justification" in A. Eser and G. Fletcher (eds.), *Justification and Excuse: Comparative Perspectives* (Freiburg: Max Planck Institut, 1987) vol. 1, 493.
Lerner, C.S. and Yahya, M.A., "'Left Behind' after Sarbanes-Oxley" (2007) 44 *American Criminal LR* 1383.
Leverick, F., "Is English Self-defence Law Incompatible with Article 2 of the ECHR?" [2002] *Criminal LR* 347.
——, "The Use of Force in Public and Private Defence and Article 2: A Reply to Professor Smith" [2002] *Criminal LR* 963.
——, "What Do We Know About Rape Myths and Jury Decision Making?" (2020) 24 *International Journal of Evidence and Proof* 255.
——, *Killing in Self-defence* (Oxford: Oxford University Press, 2006).
Leveson, B., *Independent Review of the Criminal Courts: Part 1* (London: Ministry of Justice, 2025).
Levi, M., "Fraud Trials in Perspective" [1984] *Criminal LR* 384.
——, *Regulating Fraud: White-collar Crime and the Criminal Process* (London: Tavistock, 1987) 15.
Levi, N., *Consciousness and Moral Responsibility* (Oxford: Oxford University Press, 2014).
Lewis, D., "The Punishment that Leaves Something to Chance" (1989) 18 *Philosophy and Public Affairs* 53.
Lipscombe, S., *Householders and the Criminal Law of Self-defence* House of Commons Library Standard Note SN/HA/2959 (London, 2013).
List, C. and Pettit, P., *Group Agency: The Possibility, Design and Status of Corporate Agents* (Oxford: Oxford University Press, 2011).
Livermore, J.M. and Meehl, P.E., "The Virtues of M'Naghten" (1967) 51 *Minnesota LR* 789.
Lööf, R., "The Law Commission Options Paper: Doubtful Progress on Reforming Corporate Criminal Liability" [2022] *Criminal LR* 814.
Loughnan, A., "Between Fairness and 'Dangerousness': Reforming the Law on Unfitness to Plead" [2016] *Criminal LR* 451.
——, "The 'Strange' Case of the Infanticide Doctrine (2012) 32 *Oxford Journal of Legal Studies* 685.
——, *Manifest Madness: Mental Incapacity in the Criminal Law* (Oxford: Oxford University Press, 2012).
Loughnan, A. and Wake, N., "Of Blurred Boundaries and Prior Fault: Insanity, Automatism and Intoxication" in A. Reed and M. Bohlander (eds.), *General Defences in Criminal Law: Domestic and Comparative Perspectives* (London: Routledge, 2014) 113.
Loveless, J., "Domestic Violence, Coercion and Duress" [2010] *Criminal LR* 93.
——, "*R v GAC*: Battered Woman 'Syndromization'" [2014] *Criminal LR* 655.
Lowry, D.R., "The Blind and the Law of Tort" (1972) 20 *Chittys LJ* 253.
Lucas, J.R., "The Philosophy of the Reasonable Man" (1963) 13 *Philosophical Quarterly* 97.
Lucraft, M., *Archbold: Criminal Pleading, Evidence and Practice* (London: Sweet and Maxwell, 2019).
Lucraft, M., Payne, T., and Rawlings, D., "The Dunlop Three: The Cartel Offence Makes its Debut" [2006] 1 *Archbold News* 7.
Lynch, A.C.E., "The Mental Element in the Actus Reus" (1982) 98 *Law Quarterly Review* 109.
Macaulan, E. and Gil Gil, A., "The Rationale and Purposes of Criminal Law and Punishment in Transitional Contexts" (2020) 40 *Oxford Journal of Legal Studies* 132.

McBain, G., "Abolishing Obsolete Legislation on Crimes and Criminal Procedure" (2011) 31 *Legal Studies* 96.

McColgan, A., "In Defence of Battered Women Who Kill" (1993) 130 *J Law and Society* 508.

MacCormick, D.N. and Summers, R.S. (eds.), *Interpreting Statutes: A Comparative Study* (Aldershot: Dartmouth, 1991).

Macdonald, S., "A Suicidal Woman, Roaming Pigs and a Noisy Trampolinist: Refining the ASBO's Definition of 'Anti-social Behaviour'" (2006) 69 *Modern LR* 183.

MacEwan, N., "The New Stalking Offences in English Law: Will they Provide Effective Protection from Cyberstalking?" [2012] *Criminal LR* 767.

Macrory, R., *Regulatory Justice: Sanctioning in a Post-Hampton World* (London: Cabinet Office, 2006).

McGee, A., "Finding a Way through the Ethical and Legal Maze: Withdrawal of Medical Treatment and Euthanasia" [2005] *Medical LR* 357.

MacKay, R.D., "Intoxication as a Factor in Automatism" [1982] *Criminal LR* 146.

——, "Nature', 'Quality' and Mens Rea—Some Observations on 'Defect of Reason' and the First Limb of the M'Naghten Rules" [2020] *Criminal LR* 588.

——, "On Being Insane in Jersey Part Two: The Appeal in *Jason Prior v Attorney General*" [2002] *Criminal LR* 728.

——, "On Being Insane in Jersey Part Three: The Case of the *Attorney General v O'Driscoll*" [2004] *Criminal LR* 219.

——, "Pleading Provocation and Diminished Responsibility Together" [1988] *Criminal LR* 411.

——, "Post-Hinkley Insanity in the USA" [1988] *Criminal LR* 88.

——, "Righting the Wrong?—Some Observations on the Second Limb of the M'Naghten Rules" [2009] *Criminal LR* 80.

——, "Sleepwalking, Automatism and Insanity" [2006] *Criminal LR* 901.

——, "Ten More Years of the Insanity Defence" [2012] *Criminal LR* 946.

——, "The Abnormality of Mind Factor in Diminished Responsibility" [1999] *Criminal LR* 117.

——, "The Consequences of Killing Very Young Children" [1993] *Criminal LR* 21.

——, "The Development of Fitness to Plead in English Law" in R.D. Mackay and W.J. Brookbanks (eds.), *Fitness to Plead: International and Comparative Perspectives* (Oxford: Oxford University Press, 2018).

——, "The Impairment Factors in the New Diminished Responsibility Plea" [2018] *Criminal LR* 462.

——, "The *M'Naghten* Rules—A Brief Historical Note" [2019] *Criminal LR* 966.

——, "The New Diminished Responsibility Plea" [2010] *Criminal LR* 290.

——, "The New Diminished Responsibility Plea: More than Mere Modernisation? in A. Reed and M. Bohlander (eds.,), *Loss of Control and Diminished Responsibility* (Farnham: Ashgate, 2011) 9.

——, "The Trial of the Facts and Unfitness to Plead" [1997] *Criminal LR* 644.

——, *Mental Condition Defences in the Criminal Law* (Oxford: Oxford University Press, 1995).

Mackay, R.D. and Brookbanks, W. (eds.), *The Insanity Defence: International and Comparative Perspectives* (Oxford: Oxford University Press, 2022).

Mackay, R.D. and Gearty, C., "On Being Insane in Jersey: The Case of *Attorney General v Jason Prior*" [2001] *Criminal LR* 560.

Mackay, R.D. and Hughes, D., "Explaining the 'Explanation' Requirement in the New Diminished Responsibility Plea" [2021] *Criminal LR* 461.

——, "Insanity and Blaming the Mentally Ill: A Critique of the Prior Fault Principle in the Law Commission's Discussion Paper" [2022] *Criminal LR* 21.

Mackay, R.D. and Kearns, G., "More Fact(s) about the Insanity Defence" [1999] *Criminal LR* 714.

——, "The Continued Underuse of Unfitness to Plead and the Insanity Defence" [1994] *Criminal LR* 576.

Mackay, R.D. and Mitchell, B.J., "But Is this Provocation? Some Thoughts on the Law Commission's Report on Partial Defences to Murder" [2005] *Criminal LR* 44.

Mackie, J.L., "Causes and Conditions" in E. Sosa (ed.), *Causation and Conditionals* (London: Oxford University Press, 1975) 15.

Maclean, A.R., "Resurrection of the Body Snatchers" (2000) 150 *NLJ* 174.
Macklem, T. and Gardner J., "Provocation and Pluralism" (2001) 64 *Modern LR* 815.
Madhloom, O., "Deception, Mistake and Non-disclosure: Challenging the Current Approach to Protecting Sexual Autonomy" (2019) 20 *Northern Ireland Law Quarterly* 000.
Maier-Katkin, D. and Ogle, R., "A Rationale for Infanticide Laws" [1993] *Criminal LR* 903.
Manchester, C., "Knowledge, Due Diligence and Strict Liability in Regulatory Offences" [2006] *Criminal LR* 213.
Mandil, D.M., "Chance, Freedom and Criminal Liability" (1987) 87 *California LR* 125.
Mann, K., "Punitive Civil Sanctions: The Middle Ground between Criminal and Civil Law" (1992) 101 *Yale LJ* 1795.
Mannheim, H., "Mens Rea in German and English Criminal Law" (1935) 17 *J Comparative Legislation* 82, 236, and (1936) 18 *J Comparative Legislation* 78.
Manson, N.C., "How Not to Think About the Ethics of Deceiving into Sex" (2017) 127 *Ethics* 717.
Manwaring, J., "*Windle* Revisited" [2018] *Criminal LR* 987.
Marcus, P., "Criminal Conspiracy Law: Time to Turn Back from an Ever Expanding, Ever More Troubling Area" (1992) 1 *William and Mary Bill of Rights J* 1.
——, "The Criminal Agreement in Theory and in Practice (1977) 65 *Georgetown LJ* 925.
Mares, H., "Emergencies, Necessity and the Prevention of Crime" in A.P. Simester (ed.), *Modern Criminal Law* (Oxford: Hart Publishing, 2024) 201.
——, "*Shaw v DPP* (1961)" in P. Handler, H. Mares, and I. Williams (eds.), *Landmark Cases in Criminal Law* (Oxford: Hart Publishing, 2017) 213.
Marshall, A., *Principles of Economics* (New York: Macmillan, 8th ed., 1947).
Marshall, B., Webb, B., and Tilley, N., *Rationalisation of Current Research on Guns, Gangs and Other Weapons: Phase 1* (London: University College, 2005).
Marston, G., "Contemporaneity of Act and Intention in Crimes" [1970] 86 *Law Quarterly Review* 208.
Martin, R., "Convicting Peaceful Protesters: Proportionality's Proper Place at Criminal Trial" (2024) 44 *Oxford Journal of Legal Studies* 342.
Mason, J., "The Willed Trance: Volition, Voluntariness and Hypnotised Defendants" (2021) 85 *J Criminal Law* 26.
Mason, J.K., *Forensic Medicine for Lawyers* (London: Butterworths, 3rd ed., 1995).
Mason, J.K. and Laurie, G.T., *Mason and McCall Smith's Law and Medical Ethics* (Oxford: Oxford University Press, 8th ed., 2010).
Matthews, P., "Whose Body? People and Property" (1983) 36 *Current Legal Problems* 193.
Mavronicola, N., "Taking Life and Liberty Seriously: Reconsidering Criminal Liability under Article 2 of the ECHR" (2017) 80 *Modern LR* 1026.
McAuley, F., "Anticipating the Past: The Defence of Provocation in Irish Law" (1987) 50 *Modern LR* 133.
McBarnet, D. and Whelan, C., "The Elusive Spirit of the Law: Formalism and the Struggle for Legal Control" (1991) 54 *Modern LR* 848.
McCartney, C. and Wortley, N., "Under the Covers: Covert Policing and Intimate Relationships" [2018] *Criminal LR* 137.
McColgan, A., "Common Law and the Relevance of Sexual History Evidence" (1996) 15 *Oxford Journal of Legal Studies* 275.
——, "In Defence of Battered Women Who Kill" (1993) 130 *J Law and Soc* 508.
McCormack, S. and Herring, J., "The Duties of the Penetrator and the Limits of Consent" [2024] *Criminal LR* 94.
McEwan, J., "'I Thought She Consented': Defeat of the Rape Shield or the Defence that Shall Not Run?" [2006] *Criminal LR* 969.
——, "Murder by Design: The Feel-good Factor and the Criminal Law" [2001] *Medical LR* 246.
McEwan, J. and Robilliard, St.J., "Recklessness: The House of Lords and the Criminal Law" (1981) 1 *Legal Studies* 267.

McHarg, A., "Reconciling Human Rights and the Public Interest: Conceptual Problems and Doctrinal Uncertainty in the Jurisprudence of the European Court of Human Rights" (1999) 62 *Modern LR* 671.
McKeever, N., "Can a Woman Rape a Man and Does it Matter?" (2019) 13 *Criminal Law and Philosophy* 599.
McKenna, B., "The Undefined Adverb in Criminal Statutes" [1966] *Criminal LR* 548.
McKeown, P., "The Crown Court Compendium and the Criminal Standard of Proof: Suggestions to Aid Juror Comprehension and Help Judges" [2022] *Criminal LR* 893.
McKeown, P., Keane, A. and Stares, S., "Comprehension of 'Sure' as the Description of the Criminal Standard of Proof – An Empirical Study" [2025] *Criminal LR* 518.
McPherson, R., "The Problem of Complex Defence Strategies" [2025] *Criminal LR* 264.
Melissaris, E., "The Concept of Appropriation and the Offence of Theft" (2007) 70 *Modern LR* 581.
Mencken, H.L., *A New Dictionary of Quotations on Historical Principles from Ancient and Modern Sources* (New York: Alfred A. Knopf, 1942).
Mercer, C.H., et al, "Changes in Sexual Attitudes and Lifestyles in Britain through the Life Course and Over Time" (2013) 382 *The Lancet* 1781.
Merry, A. and McCall-Smith, A., *Errors, Medicine and the Law* (Cambridge: Cambridge University Press, 2nd ed., 2017).
Michalowski, S., "Sanctity of Life: Are Some Lives More Sacred Than Others?" (2002) 22 *Legal Studies* 377.
Mill, J.S., *On Liberty* (1859).
Milsom, S.F.C., *Historical Foundations of the Common Law* (London: Butterworths, 1969; 2nd ed., 1981).
Ministry of Justice, CP 588, *Human Rights Act Reform: A Modern Bill of Rights––A Consultation to Reform the Human Rights Act 1998* (London: Ministry of Justice, 2021).
——, CP(R)19/08, *Murder, Manslaughter and Infanticide: Proposals for Reform of the Law. Summary of Responses and Government Position* Response to Consultation (London: Ministry of Justice, 2009).
——, CP437, *The End-to-End Rape Review Report on Findings and Actions* (London: Ministry of Justice, 2021).
——, CP 586, *The Independent Human Rights Act Review* (London: Ministry of Justice, 2021).
Mirfield, P., "Intention and Criminal Attempts" [2015] *Criminal LR* 142.
Minkowitz, T., "Rethinking Criminal Responsibility from a Critical Disability Perspective: The Abolition of Insanity/Incapacity Acquittals and Unfitness to Plead, and Beyond" (2014) 23 *Griffith LR* 434.
Mitchell, B., "In Defence of a Principle of Correspondence" [1999] *Criminal LR* 195.
——, "Multiple Wrongdoing and Offence Structure: A Plea for Consistency and Fair Labelling" (2001) 64 *Modern LR* 395.
Mitsilegas, V., *EU Criminal Law* (Oxford: Hart Publishing, 2009).
Moiseienko, A., "The Limitations of Unexplained Wealth Orders" [2022] *Criminal LR* 230.
Moore, M.S., "Choice, Character, and Excuse" in E.F. Paul, F.D. Miller, and J. Paul (eds.), *Crime, Culpability and Remedy* (Oxford: Blackwell, 1990) 29.
——, "Intention as a Marker of Moral Culpability and Legal Punishability" in R.A. Duff and S. Green (eds.), *Philosophical Foundations of Criminal Law* (Oxford: Oxford University Press, 2011) 179.
——, "Responsible Choices, Desert-Based Legal Institutions and the Challenges of Contemporary Neuroscience" (2012) 29 *Social Philosophy and Policy* 233.
——, "Stephen Morse on the Fundamental Psycho-Legal Error" (2016) 10 *Criminal Law and Philosophy* 45.
——, "The Quest for a Responsible Responsibility Test: Norwegian Insanity Law After Breivik" (2015) 9 *Criminal Law and Philosophy* 645.
——, "The Strictness of Strict Liability" (2018) 12 *Criminal Law and Philosophy* 513.
——, *Act and Crime* (Oxford: Oxford University Press, 1993).
——, *Causation and Responsibility: An Essay in Law, Morals and Metaphysics* (Oxford: Oxford University Press, 2009).

——, *Law and Psychiatry: Rethinking the Relationship* (Cambridge: Cambridge University Press, 1984).
——, *Mechanical Choices: The Responsibility of the Human Machine* (New York: Oxford University Press, 2020).——, *Placing Blame: A Theory of Criminal Law* (Oxford: Clarendon Press, 1997).
Moore, M.S. and Hurd, H., "Punishing the Awkward, the Stupid, the Weak, and the Selfish: The Culpability of Negligence" (2011) 5 *Criminal Law and Philosophy* 147.
Moran, M., *Rethinking the Reasonable Person: An Egalitarian Reconstruction of the Objective Standard* (Oxford: Oxford University Press, 2003).
Morgan, P., "Vicarious Liability on the Move" (2013) 129 *Law Quarterly Review* 139.
Morgan, R., "What Makes an Attack Sexual?" (2021) 38 *Journal of Applied Philosophy* 518.
Morris, N., "The Criminal Responsibility of the Mentally Ill" (1982) 33 *Syracuse LR* 477.
——, *Madness and the Criminal Law* (Chicago: University of Chicago Press, 1982).
Morrison, S.M., "Should there be a Domestic Violence Defence to the Offence of Familial Homicide?" [2013] *Criminal LR* 826.
Morse, S., "Excusing the Crazy: The Insanity Defence Reconsidered" (1985) 58 *Southern California LR* 777.
——, "The Neuroscientific Non-Challenge to Meaning, Morals and Purpose" in G. Caruso and O. Flanagan (eds.), *Neuroexistensialism: Meaning, Purpose and Morals in the Age of Neuroscience* (New York: Oxford University Press, 2018) 333.
Moxon, D., *Sentencing Practice in the Crown Court*, Home Office Research Study No. 103 (London, HMSO: 1988).
Munday, R.J., "Handling the Evidential Exception" [1988] *Criminal LR* 345.
Munro, V. and Aitken, R., "Adding Insult to Injury? The Criminal Law's Response to Domestic Abuse-Related Suicide in England and Wales" [2018] *Criminal LR* 732.
Muraszkiewicz, J., "Protecting Victims of Human Trafficking from Liability: An Evaluation of Section 45 of the *Modern Slavery Act*" (2019) 83 *Journal of Criminal Law* 394.
Murphy, J.G. and Hampton, J., *Forgiveness and Mercy* (Cambridge: Cambridge University Press, 1998).
Murray, C., *The Emerging British Underclass* (London: IEA Health and Welfare Unit, 1990).
——, *Underclass: The Crisis Deepens* (London: IEA Health and Welfare Unit, 1994).
Murray, K.L. and Beattie, T., "Conditional Consent and Sexual Offences: Revisiting the Sexual Offences Act 2003 after *Lawrance*" [2021] *Criminal LR* 556.
Nagel, T., *Mortal Questions* (Cambridge: Cambridge University Press, 1979).
Nicholson, D., "Telling Tales: Gender Discrimination Gender Construction and Battered Women Who Kill" (1995) 3 *Feminist Leg Stud* 185.
——, "The Citizen's Duty to Assist the Police" [1992] *Criminal LR* 611.
Nicholson, D. and Sanghvi, R., "Battered Women and Provocation: The Implications of *R v. Ahluwalia*" [1993] *Criminal LR* 728.
Nobles, R. and Schiff, D., "Criminal Justice Unhinged: The Challenge of Guilty Pleas" (2019) 39 *Oxford Journal of Legal Studies* 100.
Norrie, A., "A Critique of Criminal Causation" (1991) 54 *Modern LR* 685.
——, "After *Woollin*" [1999] *Criminal LR* 532.
——, "Between Orthodox Subjectivism and Moral Contextualism: Intention and the Consultation Paper" [2006] *Criminal LR* 486.
——, "From Criminal Law to Legal Theory: The Mysterious Case of the Reasonable Glue Sniffer" (2002) 65 *Modern LR* 38.
——, "'Simulacra of Morality?' Beyond the Ideal/Actual Antinomies of Criminal Justice" in Duff (ed.), *Philosophy and the Criminal Law* (Cambridge: Cambridge University Press, 1998) 101.
——, "The Coroners and Justice Act 2009—Partial Defences to Murder (1) Loss of Control" [2010] *Criminal LR* 275.
——, *Crime, Reason and History* (Cambridge: Cambridge University Press, 3rd ed., 2014).
——, *Punishment, Responsibility and Justice* (Oxford: Oxford University Press, 2000).

Note, "A Rationale of the Law of Aggravated Theft" (1954) 54 *Columbia LR* 84.

Note, "A Rationale of the Law of Burglary" (1951) 51 *Columbia LR* 1009.

Nott, E. and J. Simmons, "Crossing the Rubicon: Implications of s. 75A of the Serious Crime Act 2015 for Consent and Reasonable Belief in Consent in Sexual Offences Act 2003 Offences" [2023] *Criminal LR* 512.

Nourse, V., "Passion's Progress; Modern Law Reform and the Provocation Defence" (1997) 106 *Yale LJ* 1331.

O'Connor, D. and Fairall, P.A., *Criminal Defences* (Sydney: Butterworths, 2nd ed., 1988).

O'Donnell, I. and Morrison, S., "Armed and Dangerous? The Use of Firearms in Robbery" (1997) 36 *Howard J Criminal Justice* 305.

O'Donovan, K., "Defences for Battered Women Who Kill" (1991) 18 *J Law and Society* 219.

Oakley, A., *Constructive Trusts* (London: Sweet & Maxwell, 3rd ed., 1997).

Oberdiek, J., *Imposing Risk: A Normative Framework* (Oxford: Oxford University Press, 2017).

Office for National Statistics, *Homicide in England and Wales: Year Ending March 2025* (2026).

Orchard, G., "'Agreement' in Criminal Conspiracy" [1974] *Criminal LR* 297 and 335.

——, "The Defence of Absence of Fault in Australasia and Canada" in P.F. Smith (ed.), *Criminal Law: Essays in Honour of J.C. Smith* (London: Butterworths, 1987) 114.

——, "Provocation—Recharacterisation of 'Characteristics'" (1996) 6 *Canterbury LR* 202.

——, "Surviving without Majewski—A View from Down Under" [1993] *Criminal LR* 426.

——, "The Golden Thread—Somewhat Frayed" (1988) 6 *Otago LR* 615.

——, "The Judicial Categorisation of Offences" (1983) 2 *Canterbury LR* 81.

Ormerod, D., "Cheating the Public Revenue" [1998] *Criminal LR* 627.

——, "The Domestic Abuse Bill 2021" [2021] *Criminal LR* 423.

Ormerod, D. and Fortson, R., "Drug Suppliers as Manslaughterers (Again)" [2005] *Criminal LR* 819.

——, "Making Sense of Mens Rea in Statutory Conspiracies" (2006) 59 *Current Legal Problems* 185.

——, "Serious Crime Act 2007: The Part 2 Offences" [2009] *Criminal LR* 389.

Ormerod, D. and Laird, K., "*Jogee*: Not the End of a Legal Saga but the Start of One?" [2016] *Criminal LR* 539.

Ormerod, D. and Taylor, R., "The Corporate Manslaughter and Corporate Homicide Act 2007" [2008] *Criminal LR* 589.

Ormerod, D. and Williams, D., *Smith: The Law of Theft* (Oxford: Oxford University Press, 9th ed., 2007).

d'Orban, P.T., "Women Who Kill their Children" (1979) 134 *British Journal of Psychiatry* 560.

Ost, S., "Criminalising Fabricated Images of Child Pornography: A Matter of Harm or Morality?" (2010) 30 *Legal Studies* 230.

O'Sullivan, J. and Hilliard, J., *The Law of Contract* (Oxford: Oxford University Press, 4th ed., 2010).

Ouyang, G. and Shiner, R.A., "Organisations and Agency" (1995) 1 *Legal Theory* 283.

Owusu-Bempah, A., "Silence in Suspicious Circumstances" [2014] *Criminal LR* 126.

——, *Defendant Participation in the Criminal Process* (London: Routledge, 2017).

Owusu-Bempah, A. and Walters, M., "Racially Aggravated Offences: When does Section 145 of the Criminal Justice Act 2003 apply?" [2016] *Criminal LR* 116.

Owusu-Bempah, A., Walters, M.A., and Wiedlitzka, S., "Racially and Religiously Aggravated Offences: 'God's Gift to Defence'?" [2019] *Criminal LR* 463.

Pace, P.J., "Burglarious Trespass" [1985] *Criminal LR* 716.

——, "Delegation: A Doctrine in Search of a Definition" [1982] *Criminal LR* 627.

Paciocco, D.W., "The Remedial Constructive Trust: A Principled Basis for Priorities over Creditors" (1989) 68 *Canadian Bar Review* 315.

Packer, H.L., *The Limits of the Criminal Sanction* (Stanford: Stanford University Press, 1968).

Padfield, N., "The High Price of Participation in Criminal Activities" (1993) 52 *Cambridge LJ* 373.

Palmer, M.J., Clarke, L., Ploubidis, G. and Wellings, K., "Prevalence and Correlates of 'Sexual Competence' at First Heterosexual Intercourse among Young People in Britain" (2019) 45 *British Medical Journal Sexual and Reproductive Health* 127.

Palmer, T., "Distinguishing Sex from Sexual Violation: Consent, Negotiation and Freedom to Negotiate" in A. Reed and M. Bohlander (eds.) *Consent: Domestic and Comparative Perspectives* (London: Routledge, 2017) 9.

Palmstierna, T., "One in Thirty Predictions of Assault by Discharged Psychiatric Patients Will Be Correct" [1999] *British Medical J* 1270.

Parry, D.L., "Judicial Approaches to Due Diligence" [1995] *Criminal LR* 695.

Patient, I., "Some Remarks about the Element of Voluntariness in Offences of Absolute Liability" [1968] *Criminal LR* 23.

Pearce, A.R., "Theft by False Promises" (1953) 101 *U Pennsylvania LR* 967.

Peay, J., "Insanity and Automatism: Questions From and About the Law Commission Scoping Paper" [2012] *Criminal LR* 927.

——, "Responsibility, Culpability and the Sentencing of Mentally Disordered Offenders: Objectives in Conflict" [2016] *Criminal LR* 152.

Pedain, A., "Intention and the Terrorist Example" [2004] *Criminal LR* 284.

Peers, S., *EU Justice and Home Affairs Law* (Oxford: Oxford University Press, 2nd ed., 2006).

Pegg, S., "Not So Clear Cut: The Lawfulness of Body Modifications" [2019] *Criminal LR* 579.

Penner, J., *Property Rights: A Re-examination* (Oxford: Oxford University Press, 2020).

Perkins, R.M., "Parties to Crime" (1941) 89 *U Pennsylvania LR* 581.

——, "The Law of Homicide" (1946) 36 *J Criminal Law and Criminology* 391.

Perkins, R.M. and Boyle, R.N., *Criminal Law* (Mineola, N.Y.: Foundation Press, 3rd ed., 1982).

Perlin, M. L., "God Said to Abraham/Kill Me a Son: Why the Insanity Defense and the Incompetency Status Are Compatible with and Required by the Convention on the Rights of Persons with Disabilities and Basic Principles of Therapeutic Jurisprudence" (2017) 54 *American Criminal LR* 477.

Perry, S., "Corrective Justice v. Distributive Justice" in J. Horder (ed.), *Oxford Essays in Jurisprudence* (4th Series, Oxford: Oxford University Press, 2000) 237.

Phillipson, G., "The Human Rights Act, 'Horizontal Effect' and the Common Law: A Bang or a Whimper" (1999) 62 *Modern LR* 824.

——, "(Mis)-Reading Section 3 of the Human Rights Act" (2003) 119 *Law Quarterly Review* 183.

Picinali, F., "The Presumption of Innocence: A Deflationary Account" (2021) 84 *Modern LR* 708.

——, "The Threshold Lies in the Method: Instructing Jurors about Reasoning Beyond Reasonable Doubt" (2015) 19 *Evidence and Proof* 139.

Pickard, T., "Culpable Mistakes and Rape: Relating Mens Rea to the Crime" (1980) 30 *U Toronto LJ* 75.

Picton, M. et al. (eds.), *The Crown Court Compendium* (London: Judicial College, 2021).

Pieth, M. and Ivory, R. (eds.), *Corporate Criminal Liability: Emergence, Convergence and Risk* (Dordrecht: Springer, 2011).

Plaxton, M., "Nussbaum on Sexual Instrumentalization" (2016) 10 *Criminal Law and Philosophy* 1.

Plomin, R., *Blueprint: How DNA Makes Us Who We Are* (London: Allen Lane, 2018).

Popper, K., *The Poverty of Historicism* (London: Routledge and Kegan Paul, 1957).

Posner, R., *An Economic Theory of the Criminal Law* (1985) 85 *Columbia LR* 1193.

Pound, R., "Common Law and Legislation" (1907) 21 *Harvard LR* 383.

Power, H., "Pitcairn Island: Sexual Offending, Cultural Difference, and Ignorance of the Law" [2007] *Criminal LR* 609.

——, "Provocation and Culture" [2006] *Criminal LR* 871.

Price, D.P.T., "Assisted Suicide and Refusing Medical Treatment: Linguistics, Morals and Legal Contentions" (1996) 4 *Medical LR* 270.

Pundik, A., "Coercion and Deception in Sexual Relations" (2015) 28 *Canadian Journal of Law and Jurisprudence* 97.

Purshouse, J., "'Paedophile Hunters', Criminal Procedure, and Fundamental Human Rights" (2020) 47 *Journal of Law and Society* 384.

Quick, O. and Wells, C. "Getting Tough with Defences" [2006] *Criminal LR* 514.

Quirk, H., "Abortion and the Process and Politics of (de-)Criminalisation" [2023] *Criminal LR* 489.

——, *The Rise and Fall of the Right to Silence* (Abingdon: Routledge, 2017).Quigley, M., "Property: The Future of Human Tissue?" (2009) 17 *Medical LR* 457.

Ramsay, P., "The Theory of Vulnerable Autonomy and the Legitimacy of Civil Preventative Orders" in B. McSherry, A. Norrie and S. Bronitt (eds.), *Regulating Deviance: The Redirection of Criminalisation and the Futures of Criminal Law* (2009) 109.

——, *The Insecurity State: Vulnerable Autonomy and the Right to Security in the Criminal Law* (Oxford: Oxford University Press, 2012).

Rawls, J., "The Idea of an Overlapping Consensus" (1987) 7 *Oxford Journal of Legal Studies* 1.

——, *A Theory of Justice* (Cambridge, Mass.: Harvard University Press, 1971; revised ed., 1999).

Raz, J., "Autonomy, Toleration, and the Harm Principle" in R. Gavison (ed.), *Issues in Contemporary Legal Philosophy* (Oxford: Clarendon Press, 1987; 2nd ed., 2009) 313.

——, *The Authority of Law* (Oxford: Oxford University Press, 1979).

——, *The Morality of Freedom* (Oxford: Oxford University Press, 1986).

Reed, A. and Bohlander, M., *Consent: Domestic and Comparative Perspectives* (London: Routledge, 2017).

Reed, A. and Wake, N., "Sexual Infidelity Killings" in A. Reed and M. Bohlander (eds.), *Loss of Control and Diminished Responsibility: Domestic, Comparative and International Perspectives* (Aldershot: Ashgate, 2011) 117.

Reid, K., "Strict Liability: Some Principles for Parliament" (2008) 29 *Statute LR* 173.

Reiman, J. and van den Haag, E., "On the Common Saying that It Is Better that Ten Guilty Persons Escape than that One Innocent Suffer: *Pro* and *Con*" in E.F. Paul, F.D. Miller, and J. Paul (eds.), *Crime, Culpability and Remedy* (Oxford: Blackwell, 1990) 226.

Reid, K., "Strict Liability: Some Principles for Parliament" (2008) 29 *Statute LR* 173.

Reisman, D., "Possession and the Law of Finders" (1939) 52 *Harvard LR* 1105.

Reiss, A., "Selecting Strategies of Social Control over Organizational Life" in K. Hawkins and J.M. Thomas (eds.), *Enforcing Regulation* (Boston: Kluwer-Nijhoff, 1984) 25.

Richardson, G., "Strict Liability for Regulatory Crime: The Empirical Research" [1987] *Criminal LR* 295.

Richardson, G., Ogus, A., and Burrows, P., *Policing Pollution: A Study of Regulation and Enforcement* (Oxford: Oxford University Press, 1982).

Ripstein, A., "Beyond the Harm Principle" (2006) 34 *Philosophy and Public Affairs* 216.

Robbins, I.P., "Double Inchoate Crimes" (1989) 26 *Harvard J Legislation* 1.

Roberts, J. and Saunders, Sir J., "Sentencing for Murder: The Adverse and Unintended Effects of Schedule 21 to the Criminal Justice Act 2003" [2020] *Criminal LR* 900.

Roberts, P., "Strict Liability and the Presumption of Innocence" in A.P. Simester (ed.), *Appraising Strict Liability* (Oxford: Oxford University Press, 2005) 151.

——, "Taking the Burden of Proof Seriously" [1995] *Criminal LR* 783.

——, "The Philosophical Foundations of Consent in the Criminal Law" (1997) 17 *Oxford Journal of Legal Studies* 389.

——, "The Presumption of Innocence Brought Home" (2002) 118 *Law Quarterly Review* 41.

Roberts, S., "More Lost Than Found" (1982) 45 *Modern LR* 683.

Robinson, P.H., "A Brief Summary and Critique of Criminal Liability Rules for Intoxicated Conduct" (2018) 82 *Journal of Criminal Law* 381.

——, "Causing the Conditions of One's Own Defence: A Study in the Limits of Theory in Criminal Law Doctrine" (1985) 71 *Virginia LR* 1.

——, "Competing Theories of Justification: Deeds v. Reasons" in A.P. Simester and A.T.H. Smith (eds.), *Harm and Culpability* (Oxford: Oxford University Press, 1996) 45.

——, "Criminal Law Defenses: A Systematic Analysis" (1982) 82 *Columbia LR* 199.

——, "Strict Liability's Criminogenic Effect" (2018) 12 *Criminal Law and Philosophy* 411.

——, "The Criminal–Civil Distinction and the Utility of Desert" (1996) 76 *Boston ULR* 201.

——, *Criminal Law* (New York: Aspen Law and Business, 1997).

——, *Fundamentals of Criminal Law* (Boston: Little Brown, 1988).

Robinson, P.H. and Darley, J.M., "Objectivist versus Subjectivist View of Criminality: A Study in the Role of Social Science in Criminal Law Theory" (1998) 18 *Oxford Journal of Legal Studies* 409.
——, *Justice, Liability and Blame: Community Views and the Criminal Law* (1995).
Rock, P., *After Homicide: Practical and Political Responses to Bereavement* (Oxford: Clarendon Press, 1998).
Rodwell, D.A.H., "Problems with the Sexual Offences Act 2003" [2005] *Criminal LR* 290.
Roffee, J.A., "No Consensus on Incest? Criminalisation and Compatibility with the European Convention on Human Rights" (2014) 14 *Human Rights LR* 541.
——, "The Synthetic Necessary Truth behind New Labour's Criminalisation of Incest" (2014) 23 *Social & Legal Studies* 113.
Rogers, J., " A Criminal Lawyer's Response to Chastisement in the European Court of Human Rights" [2002] *Criminal LR* 98.
——, "Applying the Doctrine of Positive Obligations in the European Convention on Human Rights to Domestic Substantive Criminal Law in Domestic Proceedings" [2003] *Criminal LR* 690.
——, "Chastisement" [2002] *Criminal LR* 98.
——, "Prosecutorial Policies, Prosecutorial Systems, and the Purdy Litigation" [2010] *Criminal LR* 543.
——, "Reclaiming the Essence of 'Second Limb' Abuse of Process" [2022] *Criminal LR* 665.
——, "Sexual Offences: Consent; 'Purpose' of Defendant" (2008) 72 *Journal of Criminal Law* 280.
——, "The Codification of Attempts and the Case for 'Preparation'" [2008] *Criminal LR* 937.
Rook, P. and Ward, R., *Sexual Offences: Law and Practice* (London: Sweet & Maxwell, 7th ed., 2025).
Roper, V., "The Corporate Manslaughter and Corporate Homicide Act 2007: A Re-evaluation 10 Years on from the First Case" [2022] *Criminal LR* 290.
Rowe, P., "The Criminal Liability of a British Soldier Merely for Participating in the Iraq War 2003: A Response to Chilcot Evidence" [2010] *Criminal LR* 752.
Royal College of Physicians Working Group, "Criteria for the Diagnosis of Brain Stem Death" (1995) 29 *J Royal College of Physicians* 381.
Royal Commission on Capital Punishment, *Report of the Royal Commission on Capital Punishment, 1949–1953* Cmnd. 8932 (London: HMSO, 1953).
Rubenfeld J., "The Riddle of Rape-by-Deception and the Myth of Sexual Autonomy" (2013) 122 *Yale LJ* 1372.
Rumbold, J. and Wasik, M., "Diabetic Drivers, Hypoglycaemic Unawareness, and Automatism" [2011] *Criminal LR* 863.
Rumney, P., "Review of Sex Offenders and Rape and Law Reform: Another False Dawn?" [2001] 64 *Modern LR* 801.
Rumney, P. and Fenton, R.A., "Intoxicated Consent in Rape: *Bree and* Juror Decision-Making" (2008) 71 *Modern LR* 279.
Rumney, P. and McPhee, D., "The Evidential Value of Electronic Communications Data in Rape and Sexual Offences Cases" [2021] *Criminal LR* 20.
Ryan, A., *Property and Political Theory* (Oxford: Blackwell, 1984).
Ryan, S., "'Active Deception' v Non-Disclosure: HIV Transmission, Non-fatal Offences and Criminal Responsibility" [2019] *Criminal LR* 4.
——, "Reckless Transmission of HIV: Knowledge and Culpability" [2006] *Criminal LR* 981.
Ryberg, J. (ed.), The Oxford Handbook on the Philosophy of Punishment (Oxford: Oxford University Press, 2024).
Sanders, A., "The CPS, Policy-Making and Assisted Dying: Towards a 'Freedom' Approach" in J.J. Child and R.A. Duff (eds.), *Criminal Law Reform Now: Proposals and Critique* (Oxford: Hart Publishing, 2019) 133.
Sapolsky, R., *Behave: The Biology of Humans at Our Best and Worst* (London: Penguin Random House, 2017).
Sarch, A., "Collective Knowledge and the Limits of the Expanded Identification Doctrine" (2024) 44 *Oxford Journal of Legal Studies* 920.

——, *Criminally Ignorant: Why the Law Pretends We Know What We Don't* (Oxford: Oxford University Press, 2019).
——, "Too Objective for Culpability?" (2024) 18 *Criminal Law and Philosophy* 19.
Saunders, C., "Myths and Realities: An Empirical Challenge to False Beliefs about Courtroom Practice in Rape and Serious Sexual Offence Cases" [2025] *Criminal LR* 396.
Saunders, J.B., *Mozley & Whiteley's Law Dictionary* (London: Butterworths, 9th ed., 1977).
Sayre, F.B., "Criminal Responsibility for the Acts of Another" (1930) 43 *Harvard LR* 678.
——, "*Mens Rea*" (1932) 45 *Harvard LR* 974.
——, "Public Welfare Offences" (1933) 33 *Columbia LR* 55.
——, "The Present Significance of *Mens Rea* in the Criminal Law" in R. Pound (ed.), *Harvard Legal Essays Written in Honor of Joseph Henry Beale and Samuel Williston* (Harvard: Harvard University Press, 1934) 399.
Schauer, F. and Zeckhauser, R., "Regulation by Generalization" Working Paper No 05–16 (Washington D.C.: AEI-Brookings Joint Centre for Regulatory Studies, 2005).
Schopp, R.F., *Justification Defences and Just Convictions* (Cambridge: Cambridge University Press, 1998).
Schott, L., "Fetal Protection—An Overview of Recent State Legislative Responses" (1991) 22 *Memphis State University LR* 119.
Schulhofer, S.J., "Harm and Punishment: A Critique of Emphasis on the Results of Conduct in the Criminal Law" (1974) 122 *U Pennsylvania LR* 1497.
Searle, J.R., *The Construction of Social Reality* (London: Allen Lane, 1995).
Seavey, W., "Negligence—Subjective or Objective?" (1927) 41 *Harvard LR* 1.
Serious Fraud Office and Crown Prosecution Service, *Deferred Prosecution Agreements Code of Practice* (2014), available at https://www.sfo.gov.uk/?wpdmdl=1447.
Sharpe, A., "Criminalising Sexual Intimacy: Transgender defendants and the legal construction of non-consent" [2014] *Criminal LR* 207.
——, "'Deception as to Gender': A Review of Proposed Revisions to CPS Legal Guidance on Rape and Serious Offences" (2025) 89 *Journal of Criminal Law* 29.
——, "Deceptive Sex: Rethinking Consent from the Gender Margins" (2025) 88 *Modern LR* 689.
——, "Expanding Liability for Sexual Fraud Through the Concept of 'Active Deception': A Flawed Approach" (2016) 80 *Journal of Criminal Law* 28.
——, "Queering Judgment: The Case of Gender Identity Fraud" (2017) 81 *Journal of Criminal Law* 417.
——, *Sexual Intimacy and Gender "Fraud": Reframing the Legal and Ethical Debate* (Abingdon: Routledge, 2018).
Shepherd, J.C., "Towards a Unified Concept of Fiduciary Relationships" (1981) 97 *Law Quarterly Review* 51.
Sher, G., *Who Knew? Responsibility without Awareness* (Oxford: Oxford University Press, 2009).
Sherwin, E., "Constructive Trusts in Bankruptcy" (1989) *U Illinois LR* 297.
Shiffrin, S., "The Moral Neglect of Negligence" (2017) 3 *Oxford Studies in Political Philosophy* 197.
Shulman, H., "The Standard of Care Required of Children" (1928) 37 *Yale LJ* 618.
Shute, S., "Appropriation and the Law of Theft" [2002] *Criminal LR* 445.
——, "Knowledge and Belief in the Criminal Law" in S. Shute and A.P. Simester (eds.), *Criminal Law Theory: Doctrines of the General Part* (2002) 184.
——, "Something Old, Something New, Something Borrowed: Three Aspects of the Project" [1996] *Criminal LR* 684.
Shute, S. and Horder, J., "Thieving and Deceiving—What Is the Difference?" (1993) 56 *Modern LR* 548.
Shyllon, F.O., "The Corruption of 'Corruptly'" [1969] *Criminal LR* 250.
Silver, K., "When Should the Master Answer? Respondeat Superior and the Criminal Law" (2024) 18 *Criminal Law and Philosophy* 89.
Simester, A.P., "A Disintegrated Theory of Culpability" in D. Baker and J. Horder (eds.), *The Sanctity of Life and the Criminal Law: The Legacy of Glanville Williams* (Cambridge: Cambridge University Press, 2013) 178.

——, "Accessory Liability and Common Unlawful Purposes" (2017) 133 *Law Quarterly Review* 73.
——, "Free, Deliberate and Informed?" in A.P. Simester (ed.), *Modern Criminal Law: Essays in Honour of GR Sullivan* (Oxford: Hart Publishing, 2024) 3.
——, "Intoxication Is Never a Defence" [2009] *Criminal LR* 3.
——, "Is Strict Liability Always Wrong?" in A.P. Simester (ed.), *Appraising Strict Liability* (Oxford: Oxford University Press, 2005) 21.
——, "Mistakes in Defence" (1992) 12 *Oxford Journal of Legal Studies* 295.
——, "Moral Certainty and the Boundaries of Intention" (1996) 16 *Oxford Journal of Legal Studies* 445.
——, "Murder, Mens Rea and the House of Lords—Again" (1999) 115 *Law Quarterly Review* 17.
——, "Necessity, Torture and the Rule of Law" in V. Ramraj (ed.), *Emergencies and the Limits of Legality* (Cambridge, Cambridge University Press: 2008) 289.
——, "On Justifications and Excuses" in L. Zedner and J. Roberts (eds.), *Principled Approaches to Criminal Law and Criminal Justice: Essays in Honour of Andrew Ashworth* (Oxford: Oxford University Press, 2012) 95.
——, "Prophylactic Crimes" in G.R. Sullivan and I. Dennis (eds.), *Seeking Security: Pre-empting the Commission of Criminal Harms* (Oxford: Hart Publishing, 2012) 60.
—— (ed.), *Appraising Strict Liability* (Oxford: Oxford University Press, 2005).
——, *Fundamentals of Criminal Law: Responsibility, Culpability, and Wrongdoing* (Oxford: Oxford University Press, 2021).
—— (ed.), *Modern Criminal Law: Essays in Honour of GR Sullivan* (Oxford: Hart Publishing, 2024).
Simester, A.P. and Chan, W., "Intention Thus Far" [1997] *Criminal LR* 704.
Simester, A.P. and Hirsch, A. von, "Regulating Offensive Conduct through Two-step Prohibitions" in A. von Hirsch and A.P. Simester (eds.), *Incivilities: Regulating Offensive Behaviour* (Oxford: Hart Publishing, 2006) 173.
——, "Rethinking the Offense Principle" (2002) 8 *Legal Theory* 269.
——, *Crimes, Harms, and Wrongs: On the Principles of Criminalisation* (Oxford: Hart Publishing, 2011).
Simester, A.P. and Roberts, P., "Strict Liability in UK Regulation" in R. Macrory, *Regulatory Justice: Sanctioning in a Post-Hampton World* Consultation Document (London: Cabinet Office, 2006) Annex E.
Simester, A.P. and Smith, A.T.H. (eds.), *Harm and Culpability* (Oxford: Oxford University Press, 1996).
Simester, A.P. and Stark, F.G., "Overwhelming Supervening Acts: A Corrective" (2025) 84 *Cambridge Law Journal* 345.
Simester, A.P. and Sullivan, G.R., "On the Nature and Rationale of Property Offences" in R.A. Duff and S.P. Green (eds.), *Defining Crimes: Essays on the Criminal Law's Special Part* (Oxford: Oxford University Press, 2005) 168.
Simons, K., "Is Strict Criminal Liability in the Grading of Offences Consistent with Retributive Desert?" (2012) 32 *Oxford Jounral of Legal Studies* 445.
Simpson, A.W.B., "The Common Law and Legal Theory" in W. Twining (ed.), *Legal Theory and Common Law* (Oxford: Basil Blackwell, 1986) 8.
——, *Cannibalism and the Common Law* (Chicago: University of Chicago Press, 1984).
Singer, P., *Rethinking Life and Death: The Collapse of Our Traditional Ethics* (Oxford: Oxford University Press, 1995).
Singer, R., "The Resurgence of Mens Rea: III—The Rise and Fall of Strict Criminal Liability" (1989) 30 *Boston College LR* 337.
Singh, A.C., "The Body as Me and Mine: The Case for Property Rights in (Attached) Body Parts" (2021) 66 *McGill LJ* 565.
Size, R., "R v Bashir? The Case for Charging Martin Bashir with Fraud" [2021] *Criminal LR* 774.
Sjolin, C., "Ten Years On: Consent under the Sexual Offences Act 2003" (2015) 79 *Journal of Criminal Law* 20.
Skegg, P., "Consent to Medical Procedures on Minors" (1973) 36 *Modern LR* 370.

——, "Medical Procedures and the Crime of Battery" [1974] *Criminal LR* 693.
——, *Law, Ethics and Medicine: Studies in Medical Law* (Oxford: Oxford University Press, 1984).
Slocum, B.G., *Ordinary Meaning: A Theory of the Most Fundamental Principle of Legal Interpretation* (Chicago: University of Chicago Press, 2015).
Slobogin, C., "An End to Insanity" (2000) 86 *Virginia LR* 1199.
Smart, A., "Criminal Responsibility for Failing to Do the Impossible" (1987) 103 *Law Quarterly Review* 532.
Smith, A.T.H., "Constructive Trusts in the Law of Theft" [1977] *Criminal LR* 395.
——, "Error and Mistake of Law in Anglo-American Criminal Law" (1984) 14 *Anglo-American LR* 3.
——, "Judicial Law Making in the Criminal Law" (1984) 100 *Law Quarterly Review* 46.
——, "On Actus Reus and Mens Rea" in P. Glazebrook (ed.), *Reshaping the Criminal Law* (London: Sweet & Maxwell, 1978) 95.
——, "Stealing the Body and its Parts" [1976] *Criminal LR* 622.
——, "The Human Rights Act and the Criminal Lawyer: The Constitutional Context" [1999] *Criminal LR* 251.
——, "The Idea of Deception" [1982] *Criminal LR* 721.
——, "The Use of Force in Public or Private Defence and Article 2" [2002] *Criminal LR* 958.
——, "Theft by Persons Required to Account" [1980] 1 *Canterbury LR* 15.
——, *Property Offences* (London: Sweet & Maxwell, 1994).
Smith, H., "Culpable Ignorance" (1983) 92 *The Philosophical Review* 543.
Smith, J., *The Nature of Personal Robbery* Home Office Research Study 254 (London: Home Office, 2003).
Smith, J.C., "A Note on 'Intention'" [1990] *Criminal LR* 85.
——, "Aid, Abet, Counsel, or Procure" in P. Glazebrook (ed.), *Reshaping the Criminal Law* (London: Sweet & Maxwell, 1978) 120.
——, "Burglary under the Theft Bill" [1968] *Criminal LR* 367.
——, "Civil Law Concepts in the Criminal Law" [1972B] *Cambridge LJ* 197.
——, "Codification of the Criminal Law" (1987) 2 *Denning LJ* 134.
——, "Conspiracy to Defraud: Some Comments on the Law Commission's Report" [1995] *Criminal LR* 209.
——, "Conspiracy under the Criminal Law Act 1977" [1977] *Criminal LR* 598 and 638.
——, "Criminal Liability of Accessories: Law and Law Reform" (1997) 113 *Law Quarterly Review* 453.
——, "Embezzlement and the Disobedient Servant" (1956) 19 *Modern LR* 39.
——, "'Intent': A Reply" [1978] *Criminal LR* 14.
——, "Intention in Criminal Law" (1974) 27 *Current Legal Problems* 93.
——, "Intoxication and the Mental Element in Crime" in P. Wallington and R. Merkin (eds.), *Essays in Memory of Professor F.H. Lawson* (London: Butterworths, 1986) 119.
——, "*Lister* v. *Stubbs* and the Criminal Law" (1994) 110 *Law Quarterly Review* 180.
——, "Mens Rea in Statutory Conspiracy: (3) Some Answers" [1978] *Criminal LR* 210.
——, "Obtaining Cheques by Deception or Theft" [1997] *Criminal LR* 396.
——, "Offences against the Person: The Home Office Consultation Paper" [1998] *Criminal LR* 317.
——, "Secondary Participation and Inchoate Offences" in C. Tapper (ed.), *Crime, Proof and Punishment* (London: Butterworths, 1981) 21.
——, "Secondary Participation in Crime—Can We Do Without It?" (1994) 144 *New LJ* 679.
——, "Stealing Tickets" [1998] *Criminal LR* 723.
——, "The Element of Chance in Criminal Liability" [1971] *Criminal LR* 63.
——, "The Presumption of Innocence" (1987) 38 *Northern Ireland Law Quarterly* 223.
——, "The Right to Life and the Right to Kill in Law Enforcement" (1994) 144 *New LJ* 354.
——, "The Sad Fate of the Theft Act 1968" in W. Swadling and G. Jones (eds.), *The Search for Principle: Essays in Honour of Lord Goff of Chievely* (Oxford: Oxford University Press, 1999) 97.

——, "The Scope of Fraudulent Conversion" [1961] *Criminal LR* 741 and 797.
——, "The Use of Force in Public or Private Defence and Article 2" [2002] *Criminal LR* 958.
——, "Theft and/or Handling" [1977] *Criminal LR* 517.
——, *Justification and Excuse in the Criminal Law* (London: Sweet & Maxwell, 1989).
Smith, J.C. and Hogan, B., *Criminal Law* (London: Butterworths, 1st ed., 1965).
Smith, K., Osborne, S., Lau, I., and Britton, A., *Homicides, Firearm Offences and Intimate Partner Violence 2010/2011: Supplementary Volume 2 to Crime in England and Wales* (London: Home Office, 2012).
Smith, K.J.M., "Duress and Steadfastness: In Pursuit of the Unintelligible" [1999] *Criminal LR* 363.
——, "Proximity in Attempt: Lord Lane's Midway Course" [1991] *Criminal LR* 576.
——, "Withdrawal in Complicity: A Restatement of Principles" [2001] *Criminal LR* 769.
——, *A Modern Treatise on the Law of Criminal Complicity* (Oxford: Oxford University Press, 1991).
Snelling, H.A., "The Alternative Verdict of Manslaughter" (1958) 32 *Australian LJ* 137.
Sparks, R.F., "Diminished Responsibility in Theory and Practice" (1964) 27 *Modern LR* 9.
Spencer, J.R., "Blagging and the Criminal Law" [2018] 3 *Archbold Review* 4.
——, "Child and Family Offences" [2004] *Criminal LR* 347.
——, "Controlling the Discretion to Prosecute" (2012) 71 *Cambridge LJ* 27.
——, "Criminal Liability for Accidental Death: Back to the Middle Ages?" (2009) 68 *Cambridge LJ* 263.
——, "Criminal Liability for the Desecration of a Corpse" [2004] *Archbold News*, Issue 6, 7.
——, "EU Criminal Law" in C. Barnard and S. Peers (eds.), *European Union Law* (Oxford: Oxford University Press, 2014) 751.
——, "EU Criminal Law—The Present and the Future?" in A. Arnull, C. Barnard, M. Dougan and E. Spaventa (eds.), *A Constitutional Order of States? Essays in EU Law in Honour of Alan Dashwood* (Oxford: Hart Publishing, 2011) 341.
——, "Handling and Taking Risks—A Reply to Professor Williams" [1985] *Criminal LR* 440.
——, "Handling, Theft and the *Mala Fide* Purchaser" [1985] *Criminal LR* 92.
——, "Incest and Article 8 of the European Convention on Human Rights" (2013) 72 *Cambridge LJ* 5.
——, "International Law, People Trafficking and the Power to Stay Proceedings for Abuse of Process" (2014) 73 *Cambridge LJ* 11.
——, "People-trafficking: Some Reflections in the EU Legislation, and its Implementation in the UK" (2009) 11 *Cambridge Yearbook of European Legal Studies* 000.
——, "Sex by Deception" [2013] 9 *Archbold Review* 6.
——, "The Criminal Liability of Directors Whose Companies Collapse" [2016] 10 *Archbold Review* 5.
——, "The European Arrest Warrant" (2003–4) 6 *Cambridge Yearbook of European Legal Studies* 201.
——, "The Metamorphosis of Section 6 of the Theft Act" [1977] *Criminal LR* 653.
——, "The Mishandling of Handling" [1981] *Criminal LR* 682.
——, "The Theft Act 1978" [1979] *Criminal LR* 24.
——, "Trying to Help another Person Commit a Crime" in P. Smith (ed.), *Criminal Law: Essays in Honour of J.C. Smith* (London: Butterworths, 1987) 148.
——, *Evidence of Bad Character* (Oxford: Hart Publishing, 3rd ed., 2016).
Spencer, J.R. and Brajeux, A.-M., "Criminal Liability for Negligence—A Lesson from Across the Channel?" (2010) 59 *International and Comparative Law Quarterly* 1.
Spencer, J.R. and Pedain, A., "Approaches to Strict and Constructive Liability in Continental Criminal Law" in Simester (ed.), *Appraising Strict Liability* (2005) 237.
Spencer, J.R. and Virgo, G., "Encouraging and Assisting Crime: Legislate in Haste, Repent at Leisure" [2008] 9 *Archbold News* 7.
Spencer, S., "Assault with Intent to Rape—Dead or Alive?" [1986] *Criminal LR* 110.
Squires, D., "The Problem with Entrapment" (2006) 26 *Oxford Journal of Legal Studies* 351.
Stannard, J.E., "Making up for the Missing Element: A Sideways Look at Attempts" (1987) 7 *Legal Studies* 194.

Stanton-Ife, J., "Horrific Crime" in R.A. Duff, L. Farmer, S.E. Marshall, M. Renzo, and V. Tadros (eds.), *The Boundaries of the Criminal Law* (Oxford: Oxford University Press, 2011) 138.

——, "Where is the Harm in Theft?" in A.P. Simester (ed), *Modern Criminal Law* (Oxford: Hart Publishing, 2024) 123.

Stark, F., "'A Most Difficult Case': on the Ratio of Gnango" (2013) 3 *The UK Supreme Court Yearbook* 55.

——, "Against Knowledge (in the Criminal Law)" in A.P. Simester (ed.), *Modern Criminal Law: Essays in Honour of GR Sullivan* (Oxford: Hart Publishing, 2024) 25.

——, "Deconstructing Constructive Liability" [2023] *Criminal LR* 118.

——, "Encouraging or Assisting Clarity?" (2013) 72 *Cambridge LJ* 497.

——, "In Praise of *Rose*" [2019] 8 *Archbold Review* 7.

——, "'It's Only Words': On Meaning and *Mens Rea*" (2013) 72 *Cambridge LJ* 155.

——, "*Jogee* and the Mechanics of Criminal Law Development" in L. Russell and J. Graham (eds.), *Public Law and the UK Supreme Court: Key Cases and Decisions* (Abingdon: Routledge, 2026).

——, "Judicial Development of the Criminal Law by the Supreme Court" (2021) 41 *Oxford Journal of Legal Studies* 1.

——, "Necessity and *Nicklinson*" [2013] *Criminal LR* 949.

——, "Omissions, Non-Interventions and Causation: Andrew Simester's Account" [2025] *Singapore Journal of Legal Studies* 108.

——, "*R v Howe* (1987)" in P. Handler, H. Mares, and I. Williams (eds.), *Landmark Cases in Criminal Law* (Oxford: Hart Publishing, 2017) 309.

——, "Reckless Manslaughter" [2017] *Criminal LR* 763.

——, "Recycled Malice" (2023) 82 *Cambridge LJ* 509.——, "Re-reading *Andrews v DPP*" [2024] *Criminal LR* 831.

——, "The Demise of 'Parasitic Accessorial Liability': Substantive Judicial Law Reform, Not Common Law Housekeeping" (2016) 75 *Cambridge LJ* 550.

——, "The Mens Rea of a Criminal Attempt" [2014] 3 *Archbold Review* 7.

——, "Tort Law, Expression and Duplicative Wrongs" in J. Oberdiek and P. Miller (eds.), *Civil Wrongs and Justice in Private Law* (Oxford: Oxford University Press, 2020) 441.

——, *Culpable Carelessness: Recklessness and Negligence in the Criminal Law* (Cambridge: Cambridge University Press, 2016).

Stark, F. and Bock, S., "Preparatory Offences" in K. Ambos, R.A. Duff, J. Roberts, T. Weigend, and A. Heinze (eds.), *Core Concepts in Criminal Law and Justice* (Cambridge: Cambridge University Press, 2020) 54.

Stark, S.W., "Facing Facts: Judicial Approaches to Section 4 of the Human Rights Act 1998" (2017) 133 *Law Quarterly Review* 631.

Steel, A., "Describing Dishonest Means: The Implications of Seeing Dishonesty as a Course of Conduct or Mental Element and the Parallels with Indecency" (2010) 31 *Adelaide LR* 7.

——, "Problematic and Unnecessary? Issues with the Use of the Theft Offence to Protect Intangible Property" (2008) 30 *Sydney LR* 575.

——, "Taking Possession: The Defining Element of Theft?" (2008) 32 *Melbourne University LR* 1030.

——, "The Harms and Wrongs of Stealing: The Harm Principle and Dishonesty in Theft" (2008) 31 *University of New South Wales LJ* 712.

Stephen, J.F., *A History of the Criminal Law of England* (1883).

——, *Digest of the Criminal Law* (4th ed., 1887).

Stoop, D.F. de, "The Law in Australia Relating to the Transplantation of Organs from Cadavers" (1974) 48 *Australian LJ* 21.

Strawson, P., "Freedom and Resentment" in *Freedom and Resentment* (London: Methuen, 1974) 1.

Stuart, D., "The *Actus Reus* in Attempts" [1970] *Criminal LR* 505.

Stuckey, J.E., "The Equitable Action for Breach of Confidence: Is Information Ever Property?" (1981) 9 *Sydney LR* 402.

Sullivan, G.R., "Accessories and Principals after *Gnango*" in A. Reed and M. Bohlander (eds.), *Participation in Crime: Domestic and Comparative Perspectives* (Farnham: Ashgate, 2013) 37.
——, "Anger and Excuse: Reassessing Provocation" (1992) 12 *Oxford Journal of Legal Studies* 380.
——, "Avoiding Criminal Liability and Excessive Punishment for Persons Who Lack Culpability" in A. Reed and M. Bohlander (eds.), *General Defences in Criminal Law: Domestic and Comparative Perspectives* (Aldershot: Ashgate, 2014) 25.
——, "Bad Thoughts and Bad Acts" [1990] *Criminal LR* 559.
——, "Cause and the Contemporaneity of *Actus Reus* and *Mens Rea*" (1993) 52 *Cambridge LJ* 487.
——, "Conduct and Complicity: Liability based on Omission and Risk" (2008) 39 *Cambrian LR* 687.
——, "Contemporaneity of Actus Reus and Mens Rea" (1993) 52 *Cambridge LJ* 487.
——, "Corporate Killing—Some Government Proposals" (2001) 60 *Cambridge LJ* 31.
——, "Crossing the Rubicon in Miami" (1978) 41 *Modern LR* 215.
——, "Doing Without Complicity" [2012] *Journal of Commonwealth Criminal Law* 199.
——, "Expressing Corporate Guilt" (1995) 15 *Oxford Journal of Legal Studies* 281.
——, "Fault Elements and Joint Enterprise" [1994] *Criminal LR* 252.
——, "First Degree Murder and Complicity" (2007) 1 *Criminal Law and Philosophy* 271.
——, "Fraud and the Efficacy of the Criminal Law: A Proposal for a Wide Residual Offence" [1985] *Criminal LR* 616.
——, "Fraud: The Latest Law Commission Proposals" (2003) 52 *Journal of Criminal Law* 139.
——, "Inchoate Liability for Assisting and Encouraging Crime—The Law Commission Report" [2006] *Criminal LR* 1047.
——, "Intent, Purpose and Complicity" [1988] *Criminal LR* 641.
——, "Intent, Subjective Recklessness and Culpability" (1992) 12 *Oxford Journal of Legal Studies* 380.
——, "Intoxicants and Diminished Responsibility" [1994] *Criminal LR* 156.
——, "Involuntary Intoxication and Beyond" [1994] *Criminal LR* 272.
——, "Is Criminal Law Possible?" (2001) 22 *Oxford Journal of Legal Studies* 424.
——, "Knowledge, Belief and Culpability" in S. Shute and A.P. Simester (eds.), *Criminal Law Theory: Doctrines of the General Part* (Oxford: Oxford University Press, 2002) 207.
——, "Law Reform and the Supreme Court: The Abolition of Joint Enterprise Liability?" in B. Krebs (ed.), *Accessorial Liability after Jogee* (Oxford: Hart Publishing, 2020) 7.
——, "Liberalism and Constraining Choice: The Cases of Death and Serious Bodily Harm" in S. Smith and R. Deazley (eds.), *The Legal, Medical and Cultural Regulation of the Body: Transformation and Transgression* (Aldershot: Ashgate, 2009) 205.
——, "Making Excuses" in A.P. Simester and A.T.H. Smith (eds.), *Harm and Culpability* (Oxford: Oxford University Press, 1996) 131.
——, "Parents and Their Truanting Children: An English Lesson in Liability without Responsibility" (2010) 12 *Otago LR* 285.
——, "Strict Liability for Criminal Offences in England and Wales Following Incorporation into English Law of the ECHR" in A.P. Simester (ed.), *Appraising Strict Liability* (Oxford: Oxford University Press, 2005) 195.
——, "The Attribution of Culpability to Limited Companies" (1996) 55 *Cambridge LJ* 515.
——, "The Bribery Act 2010: An Overview" [2011] *Criminal LR* 87.
——, "The Hard Treatment of Innocent Persons in State Responses to the Threat of Large Scale and Imminent Terrorist Violence: Examining the Legal Constraints" in G.R. Sullivan and I. Dennis (eds.), *Seeking Security: Pre-empting Criminal Harms* (2012) 293.
——, "The Law Commission Consultation Paper on Complicity: Fault Elements and Joint Enterprise" [1994] *Criminal LR* 252.
——, "The Need for a Crime of Sexual Assault" [1989] *Criminal LR* 331.
——, "The Particularity of Serious Fraud" in P. Birks (ed.), *Pressing Problems in the Law. Vol. 1: Criminal Justice and Human Rights* (Oxford: Oxford University Press, 1995) 99.

——, "Violent Self-help" (1983) 46 *Modern LR* 78.

Sullivan, G.R., Crombag, H., and Child, J., "Loss of Control in the Appeal Courts" (2021) 72 *Northern Ireland Legal Quarterly* 200.

Sullivan, G.R. and Dennis, I. (eds.), *Seeking Security: Pre-empting Criminal Harms* (Oxford: Hart Publishing, 2012).

Sullivan, G.R. and Simester, A.P., "Causation without Limits: Causing Death while Driving without a Licence, while Disqualified, or without Insurance" [2012] *Criminal LR* 753.

Sullivan, G.R. and Warbrick, C., "Territoriality, Theft and *Atakpu*" [1994] *Criminal LR* 650.

Sutherland, P. and Gearty, C., "Insanity and the European Court of Human Rights" [1992] *Criminal LR* 418.

Sutton, M., Schneider, J. and Hetherington, S., *Tackling Theft with the Market Reduction Approach* Home Office Crime Reduction Research Series Paper 8 (London: Home Office, 2001).

Syrota, G., "A Radical Change in the Law of Recklessness?" [1982] *Criminal LR* 97.

Szasz, T., *The Manufacture of Madness: A Comparative Study of the Inquisition and the Mental Health Movement* (New York: Harper & Row, 1970).

——, *The Myth of Mental Illness* (New York: Harper & Row, 1961; 2nd ed., 1976).

Tadros, V., "A Human Right to a Fair Criminal Law" in J. Chalmers, F. Leverick, and L. Farmer (eds.), *Essays in Criminal Law in Honour of Sir Gerald Gordon* (Edinburgh: Edinburgh University Press, 2010) 103.

——, "Fair Labelling and Social Solidarity" in L. Zedner and J. Roberts (eds.), *Principles and Values in Criminal Law and Criminal Justice: Essays in Honour of Andrew Ashworth* (Oxford: Oxford University Press, 2012) 67.

——, "Poverty and Criminal Responsibility" (2009) 43 *Journal of Value Inquiry* 391.

——, "Rape without consent" (2006) 26 *Oxford Journal of Legal Studies* 515.

——, "The Homicide Ladder" (2006) 69 *Modern LR* 601.

——, "The Ideal of the Presumption of Innocence" (2014) 8 *Criminal Law and Philosophy* 449.

——, *Criminal Responsibility* (Oxford: Oxford University Press, 2005).

——, *Wrongs and Crimes* (Oxford: Oxford University Press, 2016).

Tadros, V. and Tierney, S., "The Presumption of Innocence and the Human Rights Act" (2004) 67 *Modern LR* 402.

Taggart, J., "Duress of Circumstances and Voluntary Association" (2023) 74 *Northern Ireland Legal Quarterly* 388.

Tamblyn, N., "Reforming Theft: Taking without Consent" [2020] *Criminal LR* 597.

Tay, A., "Problems in the Law of Finding" (1964) 37 *Australian LJ* 350.

Taylor, R.D., "Complicity and Excuses" [1983] *Criminal LR* 656.

Taylor, R., "The Contours of Involuntary Manslaughter. A Place for Unlawful Act by Omission" [2019] *Criminal LR* 205.

——, "The Nature of 'Partial Defences' and the Coherence of Second Degree Murder" [2007] *Criminal LR* 345.

Teff, H., *Reasonable Care: Legal Perspectives on the Doctor–Patient Relationship* (Oxford: Oxford University Press, 1994).

Temkin, J., "Do We Need a Crime of Incest?" (1991) 44 *Current Legal Problems* 185.

——, "Pre-natal Injury, Homicide and the Draft Criminal Code" (1986) 45 *Cambridge LJ* 414.

——, "Sexual History Evidence—The Ravishment of Section 2" [1993] *Criminal LR* 3.

Temkin, J. and Ashworth, A., "The Sexual Offences Act 2003: Rape, Sexual Assaults and the Problems of Consent" [2004] *Criminal LR* 328.

Thomas, C., "Juries, Rape and Sexual Offences in the Crown Court 2007-2021" [2023] *Criminal LR* 200.

——, "The 21st Century Jury: Contempt, Bias and the Impact of Jury Service" [2020] *Criminal LR* 987.

Thorburn, M., "Justifications, Powers and Authority" (2008) 117 *Yale LJ* 1070.

Tolley, R.C., "Harmfulness and Wrongfulness in Sex-by-Deception" (2025) 19 *Criminal Law and Philosophy* 137.

Tomlin, P., "Extending the Golden Thread? Criminalisation and the Presumption of Innocence" (2013) 21 *Journal of Political Philosophy* 44.
Travis, M. and Hunt, K., "The Road to *R v R*: How Feminist Campaigners Abolished the Marital Rape Exemption" [2024] *Criminal LR* 154.
Tromans, S., "Environmental Crime at Ambridge" [2019] 6 *Archbold Review* 4.
Tse, P.U., *The Neural Basis of Free Will: Criterial Causation* (Cambridge, MA: MIT Press, 2013).
Tur, R., "Dishonesty and the Jury: A Case Study in the Moral Content of Law" (1984) 18 *Royal Institute of Philosophy Supplements* 75.
——, "Legislative Technique and Human Rights: The Sad Case of Assisted Suicide" [2003] *Criminal LR* 3.
——, "Subjectivism and Objectivism: Towards Synthesis" in S. Shute, J. Gardner, and J. Horder (eds.), *Action and Value in Criminal Law* (Oxford: Oxford University Press, 1993) 213.
Turner, J.W.C., "Larceny and Lucrum" (1941) 4 *Toronto LJ* 296.
——, "The Mental Element in Crimes at Common Law" in L. Radzinowicz and J.W.C. Turner (eds.), *The Modern Approach to Criminal Law* (London: Macmillan, 1948) 195.
——, "Two Cases of Larceny" in L. Radzinowicz and J.W.C. Turner (eds.), *The Modern Approach to Criminal Law* (London: Macmillan, 1948) 356.
——, *Kenny's Outlines of Criminal Law* (Cambridge: Cambridge University Press, 16th ed., 1952; 17th ed., 1958; 19th ed., 1965).
——, *Russell on Crime* (London: Stevens, 12th ed., 1964).
Ulph, J., "Confiscation Orders, Human Rights, and Penal Measures" (2010) 126 *Law Quarterly Review* 251.
Uniacke, S., "Was Mary's Death Murder?" (2001) 9 *Medical LR* 9.
——, *Permissible Killing—The Self-defence Justification of Homicide* (Cambridge: Cambridge University Press, 1994).
Virgo, G.J., "Criminal Attempts—The Law of Unintended Circumstances" (2014) 73 *Cambridge LJ* 244.
——, "Encouraging or Assisting More than One Offence" (2012) 2 *Archbold Review* 6.
——, "Joint Enterprise Is Dead: Long Live Accessorial Liability" [2012] *Criminal LR* 850.
——, "Making Sense of Section 46 of the Serious Crime Act 2007" (2013) 7 *Archbold Review* 4.
——, "Part 2 of the Serious Crime Act 2007—Enough is Enough" (2013) 3 *Archbold Review* 7.
——, "'We Do This in the Criminal Law and That in the Law of Tort': A New Fusion Debate" in S. Pitel, J. Neyers and E. Chamberlain (eds.), *Tort Law: Challenging Orthodoxy* (Oxford: Hart Publishing, 2013) 95.
——, *Principles of Equity and Trusts* (Oxford: Oxford University Press, 5th ed., 2023).
——, *The Principles of the Law of Restitution* (2nd ed., Oxford: Oxford University Press, 2006).
Vuoso, G., "Background Responsibility and Excuse" (1987) 96 *Yale LJ* 1661.
Wade, H.W.R., "The United Kingdom's Bill of Rights" in Cambridge Centre for Public Law, *Constitutional Reform in the United Kingdom: Practice and Principles* (Oxford: Hart Publishing, 1998) 59.
Waiton, S., "What Do We Know About 'Rape Myth' Research and the Claim That There is 'Overwhelming' Evidence that Juries are Prejudiced in Rape Trials?" (2024) 28 *Evidence and Proof* 154.
Walker, N., "The End of an Old Song" (1999) 149 *New LJ* 64.
——, *Crime and Insanity in England* (Edinburgh: Edinburgh University Press, 1968).
Wall, J., "Justifying and Excusing Sex" (2019) 13 *Criminal Law and Philosophy* 283.
——, "Sexual Offences and General Reasons Not to Have Sex" (2015) 35 *Oxford Journal of Legal Studies* 777.
——, "The Legal Status of Body Parts: A Framework" (2011) 31 *Oxford Journal of Legal Studies* 783.
Wallerstein, S., "'A Drunken Consent Is Still Consent'—Or Is It? A Critical Analysis of a Drunken Consent Following *Bree*" (2009) 73 *Journal of Criminal Law* 318.
Walsh, E., *et al.*, "Violence and Schizophrenia: Examining the Evidence" (2002) 180 *British Journal of Psychiatry* 490.
Walters, M.A., "Conceptualizing Hostility for Hate Crime Law: Minding 'the Minutiae' when Interpreting Section 28(1)(a) of the Crime and Disorder Act 1998" (2014) 34 *Oxford Journal of Legal Studies* 47.

Walters, M.A., Owusu-Bempah, A., and Wiedlitzka, S., "Hate Crime and the Justice Gap: The Case for Law Reform" [2018] *Criminal LR* 961.

Walters, V., "Prosecuting Money Launderers: Do the Prosecution Have to Prove the Predicate Offence?" [2009] *Criminal LR* 571.

Wanderer, N.A. and Connors, C.R., "Culture and Crime: *Kargar* and the Existing Framework for a Cultural Defense" (1999) 47 *Buffalo LR* 829.

Warbrick, C. and Sullivan, G.R., "Ship Routeing Schemes and the Criminal Liability of the Master" [1984] *Lloyds Maritime and Commercial Law Quarterly* 23.

Ward, A.R., "Making Sense of Self-induced Intoxication" (1986) 45 *Cambridge LJ* 247.

Ward, T., "Magistrates, Insanity and the Common Law" [1997] *Criminal LR* 796.

Wasik, M., "A Learner's Careless Driving" [1982] *Criminal LR* 411.

——, "Abandoning Criminal Intent" [1980] *Criminal LR* 785.

——, "Mens Rea, Motive and the Problem of 'Dishonesty' in the Law of Theft" [1977] *Criminal LR* 543.

——, "Partial Excuses in the Criminal Law" (1982) 45 *Modern LR* 516.

——, "Reflections on the Manslaughter Sentencing Guidelines" [2019] *Criminal LR* 315.

Wasik, M. and Thompson, M.P., "Turning a Blind Eye as Constituting Mens Rea" (1981) 32 *Northern Ireland Law Quarterly* 328.

Waters, D., "Banks, Fiduciary Obligations and Unconscionable Transactions" (1986) 65 *Canadian Bar Review* 37.

Watkins, J.W.N., "Historical Explanation in the Social Sciences" (1957) 8 *British Journal for the Philosophy of Science* 104.

Weait, M., "Knowledge, Autonomy and Consent: *R v Konzani*" [2005] *Criminal LR* 763.

——, "Taking the Blame: Criminal Law, Social Responsibility and the Sexual Transmission of HIV" (2001) 23 *Journal of Social Welfare and Family Law* 441.

——, *Intimacy and Responsibility: The Criminalisation of HIV Transmission* (Abingdon: Routledge-Cavendish, 2007).

Weare, S., "'Oh You're a Guy, How Could You be Raped by a Woman, That Makes No Sense': Towards a Case for Legally Recognising and Labelling 'Forced to Penetrate' Cases as Rape" (2018) 14 *International Journal of Law in Context* 110.

——, "The Penetrative Offence in Section 4 of the Sexual Offences Act 2003" (2020) 60 *British Journal of Criminology* 930.

Weisiger, G.B., "Negligence of the Physically Infirm" (1946) 24 *North Carolina LR* 187.

Wellings, K., Field, J., Johnson, A., Wadsworth, J., and Bradshaw, S., *Sexual Behaviour in Britain: The National Survey of Sexual Attitudes and Lifestyles* (London: Penguin Books, 1994).

Wells, C., "Battered Women Syndrome and Defences to Homicide: Where Now?" (1994) 14 *Legal Studies* 266.

——, "Corporate Criminal Liability: A Ten Year Review" [2014] *Criminal LR* 849.

——, "Corporate Failure to Prevent Economic Crime: A Proposal" [2017] *Criminal LR* 426.

——, "Stalking: The Criminal Law Response" [1997] *Criminal LR* 463.

——, *Corporations and Criminal Responsibility* (Oxford: Oxford University Press, 1993; 2nd ed 2001).

Wertheimer, A., *Coercion* (Princeton: Princeton University Press, 1987).

West, D.J. and Walk, A. (eds.), *Daniel McNaughton: His Trial and the Aftermath* (Ashford: Headley, 1977).

West, R., "A Comment on Consent, Sex, and Rape" (1996) 2 *Legal Theory* 233.

Westen, P., "Getting the Fly out of the Bottle: The False Problem of Free Will and Determinism" (2005) 8 *Buffalo Criminal LR* 101.

——, "Individualizing the Reasonable Person in Criminal Law" (2008) 2 *Criminal Law and Philosophy* 137.

Wheat, K., "The Law's Treatment of the Suicidal" [2000] *Medical LR* 182.

White, A.R., "Intention, Purpose, Foresight and Desire" (1976) 92 *Law Quarterly Review* 569.

——, "The Identity and Time of the Actus Reus" [1977] *Criminal LR* 148.

——, "Trade Descriptions About the Future" (1974) 90 *Law Quarterly Review* 15.
White, R., "Civil Penalties: Oxymoron, Chimera and Stealth Sanction" (2010) 126 *Law Quarterly Review* 593.
White, S., "Continuing Representations in Criminal Law" (1986) 37 *Northern Ireland Law Quarterly* 255.
Williams, B., "Moral Luck" in *Moral Luck* (Cambridge: Cambridge University Press, 1981) 20.
——, "Moral Responsibility and Political Freedom" (1997) 56 *Cambridge LJ* 96.
——, "The Actus Reus of Dr Caligari" (1994) 142 *U Pennsylvania LR* 1661.
——, *Ethics and the Limits of Philosophy* (London: Fontana, 1985).
Williams, Glanville, "Absolute Liability in Traffic Offences" [1967] *Criminal LR* 142 and 194.
——, "Appropriation: A Single or Continuous Act?" [1978] *Criminal LR* 69.
——, "Causation in Homicide" [1957] *Criminal LR* 429.
——, "Complicity, Purpose and the Draft Code" [1990] *Criminal LR* 4.
——, "Consent and Public Policy" [1962] *Criminal LR* 74.
——, "Convictions and Fair Labelling" (1983) 42 *Cambridge LJ* 85.
——, "Criminal Omissions—The Conventional View" (1991) 107 *Law Quarterly Review* 86.
——, "Evading Justice" [1975] *Criminal LR* 430.
——, "*Finis* for *Novus Actus*?" (1989) 48 *Cambridge LJ* 391.
——, "Handling, Theft and the Purchaser Who Takes a Chance" [1985] *Criminal LR* 432.
——, "Homicide and the Supernatural" (1949) 65 *Law Quarterly Review* 491.
——, "Innocent Agency and Causation" (1992) 3 *Criminal Law Forum* 289.
——, "Mistake as to Party in the Law of Contract" (1945) 23 *Canadian Bar Review* 271.
——, "Mistake in the Law of Theft" (1977) 36 *Cambridge LJ* 62.
——, "Obedience to Law as a Crime" (1990) 53 *Modern LR* 445.
——, "Oblique Intention" (1987) 46 *Cambridge LJ* 417.
——, "Offences and Defences" (1982) 2 *Legal Studies* 233.
——, "Recklessness Redefined" (1981) 40 *Cambridge LJ* 252.
——, "Temporary Appropriation Should Be Theft" [1981] *Criminal LR* 129.
——, "The Definition of Crime" (1955) 8 *Current Legal Problems* 107.
——, "The Logic of 'Exceptions'" (1988) 47 *Cambridge LJ* 261.
——, "The Mens Rea for Murder: Leave it Alone" (1989) 105 *Law Quarterly Review* 387.
——, "The Theory of Excuses [1982] *Criminal LR* 732.
——, "The Unresolved Problem of Recklessness" (1988) 8 *Legal Studies* 74.
——, "Theft, Consent and Illegality" [1977] *Criminal LR* 127.
——, "Three Rogues' Charters" [1980] *Criminal LR* 263.
——, "Venue and Ambit in the Criminal Law" (1961) 81 *Law Quarterly Review* 276, 395, 518.
——, "Victims and Other Exempt Parties in Crime" (1990) 10 *Legal Studies* 245.
——, "Victims as Parties to Crimes—A Further Comment" [1964] *Criminal LR* 686.
——, "What Should the Code Do about Omissions?" (1987) 7 *Legal Studies* 92.
——, *Criminal Law: The General Part* (London: Stevens, 2nd ed., 1961).
——, *Textbook of Criminal Law* (London: Stevens, 2nd ed., 1983).
——, *The Mental Element in Crime* (Jerusalem: Magnes Press, 1965).
——, *The Proof of Guilt: A Study of the English Criminal Trial* (London: Stevens, 2nd ed., 1958).
Williams, Glenys, "Duress and Loss of Control: Fear and Anger in Excusatory Defences" (2020) 71 *Northern Ireland Legal Quarterly* 401.
——, "Gross Negligence Manslaughter and Duty of Care in 'Drugs' Cases: R. v Evans" [2009] *Criminal LR* 631.
Williams, R., "A Further Case on Obtaining Sex by Deception" (2021) 137 *Law Quarterly Review* 183.
——, "Body Modification and the Limits of Consent to Injury" (2019) 135 *Law Quarterly Review* 17.
——, "Deception, Mistake and Vitiation of the Victim's Consent" (2008) 124 *Law Quarterly Review* 132.
——, "*R v Flattery* (1877)" in P. Handler, H. Mares, and I. Williams (eds.), *Landmark Cases in Criminal Law* (Oxford: Hart Publishing, 2017) 147.

——, "Voluntary Intoxication—A Lost Cause?" (2013) 129 *Law Quarterly Review* 264.
Wilson, W., "A Plea for Rationality in the Law of Murder" (1990) 10 *Legal Studies* 307.
——, "The Structure of Criminal Homicide" [2006] *Criminal LR* 471.
Wilson, W. *et al.*, "Violence, Sleepwalking and the Criminal Law" [2005] *Criminal LR* 624.
Winfield, P.H., "Death as Affecting Liability in Tort" (1929) 29 *Columbia LR* 239.
——, "Quasi-contract Arising from Compulsion" (1944) 60 *Law Quarterly Review* 341.
Winslade, W.J., "Brady on Recklessness" (1972) 33 *Analysis* 31.
Withey, C., "Loss of Control: Loss of Opportunity?" [2011] *Criminal LR* 263.
Wolf, L.K., Bazargani, N., Kilford, E.J., Dumontheil, I., and Blakemore, S.J., "The Audience Effect in Adolescence Depends on Who's Looking Over Your Shoulder" (2015) 43 *Journal of Adolescence* 5.
Wolf, S., "The Legal and Moral Responsibility of Organisations" in J.R. Pennock and J.W. Chapman (eds.), *Criminal Justice* (New York: New York University Press, 1985).
Wolfram, S., "Eugenics and the Punishment of Incest Act 1908" [1983] *Criminal LR* 308.
Wondemaghen, M., "Evaluating Predominant Causes of Insanity in Cases of Drug-induced Psychoses" [2015] 14 *International Journal of Forensic Mental Health* 76.
Wootton, B., "Diminished Responsibility: A Layman's View" (1960) 76 *Law Quarterly Review* 224.
——, *Crime and the Criminal Law: Reflections of a Magistrate and a Social Scientist* (London: Sweet & Maxwell, 2nd ed., 1981).
World Health Organisation, *Diagnostic and Management Guidelines for Mental Disorders* (Geneva: World Health Organization, 1996).
——, *International Statistical Classification of Diseases and Related Health Problems* ICD 10 (Geneva: World Health Organisation, 2010).
Wright, R.S., *Law of Criminal Conspiracies and Agreements* (London: Butterworths, 1873).
Yaffe, G., "The Child's 'Special Status' and Disenfranchisement" in J.J. Child and R.A. Duff (eds.), *Law Reform Now: Proposals and Critique* (London: Hart Publishing, 2019) 184.
——, "In Defense of Criminal Possession" (2016) 10 *Criminal Law and Philosophy* 441.
——, "The Point of Mens Rea: The Case of Willful Ignorance" (2018) 12 *Criminal Law and Philosophy* 19.
——, *Attempts: In the Philosophy of Action and the Criminal Law* (Oxford: Oxford University Press, 2010).
——, *The Age of Culpability: Children and the Nature of Criminal Responsibility* (Oxford: Oxford University Press, 2018).
Yale, D.E.C., "A Year and a Day in Homicide" (1989) 48 *Cambridge LJ* 202.
Yang, D., "Recklessness and Circumstances in Criminal Attempts" (2022) *Criminal Law and Philosophy* 359.
Yeo, S., "Sex, Ethnicity, Power of Self-control and Provocation Revisited" (1996) 18 *Sydney LR* 304.
Youdan, T.G. (ed.), *Equity, Fiduciaries and Trusts* (Toronto: Carswell, 1989).
Yu, F., "Putting the Presumption back in the Presumption of Innocence" (2023) 26 *Evidence and Proof* 342.
Zedner, L. and Roberts, J. (eds.), *Principles and Values in Criminal Law and Criminal Justice: Essays in Honour of Andrew Ashworth* (Oxford: Oxford University Press, 2012).

# INDEX